W9-BGT-518

Christopher Isherwood

DIARIES

Volume One: 1939–1960

Books by Christopher Isherwood

NOVELS
All the Conspirators
The Memorial
The Last of Mr. Norris
(*English title*: Mr. Norris Changes Trains)
Goodbye to Berlin
Prater Violet
The World in the Evening
Down There on a Visit
A Single Man
A Meeting by the River

AUTOBIOGRAPHY
Lions and Shadows
Kathleen and Frank
Christopher and His Kind
My Guru and His Disciple
October (*with Don Bachardy*)

BIOGRAPHY
Ramakrishna and His Disciples

PLAYS (*with W. H. Auden*)
The Dog Beneath the Skin
The Ascent of F6
On the Frontier

TRAVEL
Journey to a War (*with W. H. Auden*)
The Condor and the Cows

COLLECTIONS
Exhumations
Where Joy Resides

Christopher Isherwood

DIARIES

Volume One: 1939–1960

Edited and introduced by Katherine Bucknell

Michael di Capua Books
HarperFlamingo

First published in Great Britain in 1996
by Methuen London
Copyright © 1996 Don Bachardy
Introduction copyright © 1996 Katherine Bucknell
All rights reserved
Library of Congress catalog card number: 97–05501
First American edition, 1997
First American paperback edition, 1998

Contents

Introduction

Christopher Isherwood wrote in his diary several times a week almost continuously for about sixty years—from the early 1920s until July 1983, a month before his seventy-ninth birthday. This volume contains all the diary entries that he preserved from January 19, 1939, the day he left England for America with W. H. Auden, until August 26, 1960, the day he celebrated his fifty-sixth birthday in Santa Monica, California, with Don Bachardy. Most of Isherwood's pre-1939 diaries have not survived; the later ones will be published in a second volume.

Isherwood learned about diary keeping from his mother. Around the time of his christening in 1904, Kathleen Isherwood began a special record of his infant achievements, "The Baby's Progress," which stretched on into boyhood and was only brought to a close with her note of the publication of Isherwood's first novel in 1928, when he was twenty-four years old. By the time Isherwood was six, she had involved him in writing about his own life in "The History of My Friends," a tiny book they made together, she writing, he evidently dictating. The opening lines are predictably cute, but characteristically for both authors, they are precisely worded and emphatically unfanciful:

> I first met Arthur Forbes in December 1909 when we returned from Frimley to Marple. He was just going to be four. He made up all sorts of wonderful things that he meant to do when he was five, just as if five was when you were grown up.[1]

Kathleen Isherwood had first begun keeping her own diary at the start of 1883, one hundred years before Isherwood was to write in his diary for the last time. She was just fourteen years old, and by the end

---

[1] The little book is now lost, but this passage appears in *Kathleen and Frank* (New York, 1971), p. 348; (London, 1972), pp. 250–251.

of the year, her efforts petered away to nothing. Seven years later, at twenty-two, she began again, and thereafter she went on recording her life for nearly seventy years. Isherwood repeated the pattern, but slightly more precociously. On January 1, 1917, the year he would turn thirteen, he began keeping his first diary in a little page-a-day book similar to the ones his mother used; possibly she gave him the diary. His brief entries continue through the year, and then he began another diary on January 1, 1918.[1] This he carried on until September, not long after his fourteenth birthday, when the entries dwindle and stop. The same summer, for a school project, he also made a holiday journal describing visits with his mother to places of cultural interest such as Bath and illustrated with postcards; the holiday journal won a prize during Isherwood's last term at his prep school, St. Edmund's. After that it seems, he recorded nothing for six or seven years—at least nothing survives—until after his arrival at university.

Some time during his first two terms at Cambridge, late in 1923 or early in 1924, Isherwood again began to keep a diary. Initially this was part of the playful, excited fantasy life that he shared with his school and university friend Edward Upward. Having read Barbellion's *Journal of a Disappointed Man*, the pair began "keeping a journal of our imaginary lives called *The Diary of Two Shapes*."[2] But while their impulse toward fantasy led them to make up an entire town, Mortmere, about which they wrote juvenile, surrealist stories for one another, their commitment to reality quickly began to produce a record of their actual experience. Each adopted the diary-keeping habit and sustained it, more or less, for the rest of his life.

Diary keeping attests both to Isherwood's obsession with the passage of time and to his puritanical need to account for himself. On June 5, 1958, he wrote in his diary: "Who are you—who writes all this? Why do you write? Is it compulsion? Or an alibi—to disprove the charge of what crime?" In a sense, Isherwood wrote in his diary to provide evidence, week by week, that he was neither wasting his life nor spending it in the wrong way: that he was paying attention, that he was doing something of value, that he was keeping a record. Despite the gentrified atmosphere associated with his birth and lineage as the grandson of the squire of Marple Hall in Cheshire,

---

[1] The 1917 diary is at the Harry Ransom Humanities Research Center at the University of Texas in Austin, and the 1918 diary is at The McFarlin Library at the University of Tulsa, Oklahoma.
[2] *Lions and Shadows: An Education in the Twenties* (London, 1938), p. 73. Upward records the influence of Barbellion in *No Home But the Struggle*, the third volume of his autobiographical novel, *The Spiral Ascent* (London, 1977), p. 681. He also implies that he and Isherwood might have begun keeping the diaries in early 1925, a year later than Isherwood says in *Lions and Shadows*.

Isherwood was heir to a Puritan work ethic. His father's family traced their descent from John Bradshaw, the judge who sentenced Charles I to death; Isherwood's father was a second son, obliged to earn a living reluctantly in the army. Isherwood's duty-ridden mother was the daughter of a middle-class Victorian wine merchant whose business was just successful enough to afford him the life of a gentleman of leisure. The moderate wealth and class privilege to which Isherwood was born were nonetheless accompanied by high expectations of achievement, perhaps most of all on the part of his mother and, later, himself.

Isherwood used his diary to discipline himself in periods of laziness or dissipation, to clarify his thoughts, and to right himself in moments of spiritual uncertainty. Lapses in his diary keeping are revealing in this respect. During the late 1940s, he lived wildly for a time—he drank, kept late hours, was extremely promiscuous—and a gaping hole opened in his chronicle. Perhaps he simply felt too ashamed to record this period of his life, but certainly without setting down events in his diary he seemed unable to reflect upon and to master his behavior. Those years led him into a despair from which he only emerged simultaneously with a return to writing regularly in his diary. Don Bachardy recalled in 1994 that over the many years of nights which they spent sleeping very close beside one another, Isherwood would sometimes cry out in his sleep, a yelping animal cry, not human. At these moments, Bachardy sensed that, in his sleep, Isherwood was in a place of horror, and he would wake Isherwood, who would always express his relief. But Isherwood never could say where he had been; he could never precisely articulate the dream nor, it seems, could he rid himself of it. In his diaries, though, language rules over inchoate fears, over the chaos of experience, over the passage of time. Page upon page reflect the clarity of his mind, his absolute mastery of syntax, his easily ranging, precise diction, his effortless power of description, his gaiety, his delight in the ridiculous. As his curling line of ink stretches from inches into yards and, probably, miles, over a million words pile up, but only a few words are ever altered. There are hardly any mistakes of any kind. The diaries are an endless transcript of life—without blot, without error, without misstatement, without verbal crime. The recordkeeper is perfectly trained, alert, even fastidious.

But Isherwood goes well beyond simply recording what happens. He tries persistently to understand what his record means. A process of continual examination—the Socratic prerequisite for a worthy life—was applied not only to himself but also to his impressions of the society in which he was living, and this process of examination and reflection was the central task of his fiction, for which the diaries served as his raw material. He analyzed and dissected his observations, lifting out an episode here, a character there, and combining them with others, perhaps originally unrelated; then he invented whatever additional circumstances and atmosphere were necessary to convey certain essential qualities of his experience and of the fabric of society around him. Like Auden, Isherwood was fundamentally anti-Romantic in his determination to demystify the work of the artistic imagination, and thus he described in *Christopher and His Kind*—his autobiographical account of his life and his writing in the 1930s—the method whereby his real life friends and acquaintances in Berlin, Gerald Hamilton and Jean Ross, for instance, came to be represented in his novels of the 1930s, as "Mr. Norris" in *Mr. Norris Changes Trains*[1] and "Sally Bowles" in *Goodbye to Berlin*. In this way, *Christopher and His Kind* opens the workshop door and shows the reader precisely how Isherwood, as a writer, created art from experience. Readers of Isherwood's post-1939 diaries can observe the process even more closely. In particular Isherwood drew on the diaries contained in this volume (1939–1960) for his novels *The World in the Evening, Down There on a Visit*, and *A Single Man*, as well as for his much later autobiographical book *My Guru and His Disciple*.

Still, however much Isherwood's style and technique suggest that his novels are works of observation, the diaries, with their wealth of recorded facts, make clear precisely the degree to which he departed from actual experience in his fiction. Because his style tends to be heavily understated—a technique learned from E. M. Forster—Isherwood could achieve, with the slightest coloration of tone, entirely various literary effects, even when drawing closely on real events. And like the Modernist forebears he admired—Forster, Henry James, Virginia Woolf, Katherine Mansfield and others—his fiction makes its point objectively, by showing rather than telling. Certainly Isherwood was a master of compression and of the select detail; moreover, he constrained his imagination, so that in his best fiction he never invented more than was necessary. Thus, his novels are works of the imagination, but they are not works of fantasy. In this respect, Isherwood's work shares a common historical impulse with Edward Upward's mature social-realist fiction. Upward became a doctrinaire Marxist during the early 1930s, and in his 1937 essay "A Marxist Interpretation of Literature" Upward rejected fantasy, arguing that imaginative writing reflects the material world, and must, in order to be valuable, accurately represent not only the existing and past conditions of the society in which it is written but

---

[1] Published in the U.S. as *The Last of Mr. Norris*.

also the forces beneath the surface of material reality which will shape the future of society. Both Isherwood and Upward were trained as historians: both were top history students at their public school, Repton, and both went up to Corpus Christi College at Cambridge with prestigious financial awards in history. (In fact, Isherwood won two awards, because he sat the scholarship exam with Upward, a year older, before he was ready to leave Repton, and won an exhibition; the following year, Isherwood won a scholarship, worth even more.) Both Upward and Isherwood found they could not bear the way history was taught at Cambridge. Upward changed subjects to English, but Isherwood was refused permission to do the same. He soon found himself defiantly spoofing the questions in his second year tripos exams and being asked to leave. And yet he went on in his fiction to write what might best be regarded as a new kind of history: subjective, intuitive, vivid, widely accessible, and, as one would expect of an intimate of Auden, informed by the new psychological understanding associated with the influence of Freud. Even when they do not record actual historical events, his novels offer a moral history of the culture and psyche of their time. At its most autobiographical, Isherwood's history writing was, paradoxically, also highly stylized, so that it tipped over from history into mythology.

In their richness of detail, in the range of personalities they introduce, in the span of years they cover, Isherwood's diaries are a historical record of enormous significance, and they now have the extraordinary effect of opening Isherwood's carefully composed fictions and myths back out into the culture he was attempting to portray, recapturing in all its complex tragedy the wartime period already lost to us and afterwards the rebuilding years which have shaped our own times.

Christopher and His Kind leaves Isherwood at the rail of the *Champlain* arriving in New York Harbor with Auden in January 1939. With a few days of overlap, the diaries contained in this volume take up from there. At thirty-four years of age, Isherwood was already the celebrated author of five works of semi-autobiographical fiction (the fifth, *Goodbye to Berlin*, just about to be published) and, with Auden, of three successfully, if unconventionally, produced plays. He had worked as a writer on two film scripts, and during the past year he had been writing his first travel book with Auden, *Journey to a War*, about their trip to China to observe the Sino-Japanese conflict. Isherwood had already visited America briefly on the way home from China, and, having spent most of the preceding decade away from England, in various countries in Europe and around the Mediterranean, he planned to stay in America for good.

But the transition proved far from easy. Settled in Manhattan with an American boyfriend and with Auden—who achieved startling success and celebrity almost instantly in his new surroundings—Isherwood found he could not work. He feared he had reached the end of his talent as a writer, and he became increasingly obsessed by anxiety about the possibility of a coming war and what his role in it should be. With his boyfriend (whom Isherwood called "Vernon" in *Christopher and His Kind* and who in these diaries appears as "Vernon Old"), Isherwood set out for California in May 1939, hoping for guidance from his pacifist friend Gerald Heard and from Aldous Huxley, both already settled there. Since boyhood Isherwood had been in love with the movies, and after working in London with the Viennese writer and director of stage and film Berthold Viertel, he had every reason to believe he might be able to find work in the Hollywood studios.

As he explains in the opening passages of his 1939 diary, Isherwood realized while crossing the Atlantic that he had always been a pacifist. His father's profession of soldiering and, above all, his father's death in the First World War had wreaked havoc upon Isherwood's childhood and early years at school, and, before he died, his father himself had made fun of the fighting man's way of life and so-called virtues. After China, Isherwood no longer found war overwhelmingly frightening, as he openly acknowledged he had found it throughout childhood and adolescence; it was not cowardice which made him refuse to fight, but conviction. He was utterly unwilling to raise his hand against the army which numbered among its force the boy he had loved and lived with through much of the past decade, Heinz Neddermeyer. On June 17, 1942 Isherwood wrote in his diary: "Heinz is in the Nazi army. I wouldn't kill Heinz. Therefore I have no right to kill anybody." Isherwood was publicly criticized for failing to return to England during the war, and he was accused of cowardice, among other things. But when in 1940 he wrote to the British Embassy in Washington offering to return home, he was told, in a letter of July 12, 1940, that his position in America was "understood."[1] In any case, his future lay in America, regardless of the war.

In order to be able to work in Hollywood, Isherwood had applied for a quota visa, and on June 9, 1939—three months before the war started—he had already been readmitted to the United States from Mexico as a legal immigrant, no longer a visitor. A month later, he

[1] See p. 56 in this volume.

began the lengthy procedure to obtain U.S. citizenship. Six months after that, on January 20, 1940, almost exactly a year after leaving England, he wrote in his diary about his reluctance to return:

> Am I afraid of being bombed? Of course. Everybody is. But within reason. I know I certainly wouldn't leave Los Angeles if the Japanese were to attack it tomorrow. No it isn't that . . . If I fear anything, I fear the atmosphere of the war, the power which it gives to all the things I hate—the newspapers, the politicians, the puritans, the scoutmasters, the middle-aged merciless spinsters. I fear the way I might behave if I were exposed to this atmosphere. I shrink from the duty of opposition. I am afraid I should be reduced to a chattering enraged monkey, screaming back hate at their hate.

Throughout his youth, Isherwood had felt manipulated and coerced by "the newspapers, the politicians, the puritans, the scoutmasters, the middle-aged merciless spinsters," and he had fiercely rebelled against these purveyors of conventional values by deliberately failing his exams at Cambridge, by going abroad, by wandering from home to home, by his writing. Now it seems, Isherwood was finished with rebellion, the posture of his youth. He shrank from "the duty of opposition." In America, he had begun to turn his energies inward, to try to find out who he was and to wrestle, if need be, with himself. He wanted to remain in America so he could finish growing up.

Thus when Gerald Heard introduced Isherwood to Swami Prabhavananda in the summer of 1939, Isherwood was not only seeking direction, but he was prepared and evidently ready to offer up all the devotion and obedience that he had until then refused to yield to any figure of authority. In his youth, Prabhavananda had been involved in the Indian independence movement, and Isherwood, perhaps somewhat romanticizing the ferocity of these early terrorist activities, seems to have recognized in the Swami the same spirit of rebellion that had instantaneously attracted him, as a schoolboy, to Edward Upward. The Swami, too, had once been coerced and manipulated by the British Empire, he too had revolted, and he too had now outgrown such struggles. Perhaps more important, the Swami seemed almost entirely free from the puritanism that had so constrained Isherwood among the English middle classes. In his presence, Isherwood felt continually aware of the Swami's gaiety, his playfulness, his joy, his seemingly boundless love—in all the years of their friendship, Isherwood never records an instance of the Swami's expressing disapproval toward him. Swami did not regard Isherwood's homosexuality as a sin, and Hinduism, in contrast to Christianity, does not include the Judeo-Christian emphasis upon the problem of guilt. Swami simply regarded all forms of lust as obstacles to spiritual progress.

Isherwood loved Swami Prabhavananda almost from the instant of meeting him. He believed in the Swami's personal sanctity and above all in the Swami's belief in God. He was to believe in this more and more as the years went by. Isherwood was a natural and persistent sceptic. In his diaries he repeatedly questions his religious convictions, but these convictions were continually and irresistibly reaffirmed through the actual person of the Swami. On September 29, 1957 Isherwood wrote in his diary:

> I believe that there is something called (for convenience) God, and that this something can be experienced (don't ask me how), and that a man I know (Swami) has had this experience, partially, at any rate. All this I believe because my instinct, as a novelist and a connoisseur of people, assures me, after long, long observation, that it is true in Swami's case.

The guru-disciple relationship of Vedanta was eminently attractive to Isherwood's intellectual and psychological makeup. Before meeting the Swami, Isherwood had already developed by means of a series of other quasi guru-disciple relationships, perhaps beginning with his history master, G. B. Smith, at Repton, and including, for instance, John Layard, Gerald Heard, and Berthold Viertel. The particular example of the friendship with Viertel, as Isherwood represents it in his novel *Prater Violet*, suggests the way in which each of these mentors was, in some sense, a father figure, partly a replacement for the real father Isherwood had lost at the vulnerable age of ten. Their very unconventionality was part of their appeal to him, for they stood well outside, and even in opposition to, the parameters of institutional authority that Isherwood had found so straitening and so diminishing. The Swami offered, in addition to his subtle personal attributes, the ultimate dimension in any father figure—a relationship with God. And Isherwood indeed relied on the Swami to make God comprehensible. In his diary for April 28, 1958 he wrote, "Lately, I have arrived at this formulation: religion—as I understand it—means a relationship. Either directly with God, or with someone who has a relationship with God: belief in another's belief—as I have with Swami."

Swami Prabhavananda instructed Isherwood in meditation and in Hindu ritual and belief. Just as Isherwood had possessed sufficient intellectual flexibility and openness to enter into the imaginative intimacy and intensity of the Mortmere game with Edward Upward, and just as he had been able to immerse himself in German culture while living in Berlin, so he took wholeheartedly and seriously to the

Swami's teachings. Over the years they talked, worshipped, prayed, and meditated together, and they worked closely on translations of Hindu religious and philosophical texts. For Isherwood, Vedanta was most simply a process of gradually overcoming worldly attachments and habits of thought and behavior in order to free the spirit so that it could recognize and achieve oneness with God. The practice of Vedanta was a discipline in which he undertook to refine his mind and spirit to higher and higher levels of awareness, to purer and purer forms of love. In a sense, Vedanta proved to be a natural elaboration upon the training he had already begun by himself as an observer and recorder of his fellow man. On July 14, 1940, Isherwood set down in his diary a "prayer for writers," which, despite a tone of self-mocking bathos towards the end, makes clear that his religion and his art were, in his own mind, part of a single endeavor, and that he wanted the same power of love to inform the practice of both:

> Oh, source of my inspiration, teach me to extend toward all living beings that fascinated, unsentimental, loving and all-pardoning interest which I feel for the characters I create. May I become identified with all humanity, as I identify myself with these imaginary persons. May my art become my life, and my life my art. Deliver me from snootiness, and from the Pulitzer Prize. Teach me to practice true anonymity. Help me to forgive my agents and publishers. Make me attentive to my critics and patient with my fans. For yours is the conception and the execution. Amen.

In the summer of 1939, newly arrived in Los Angeles, Isherwood managed to eke out a book review and a detective-style short story, "I Am Waiting," about his anxiety to know what the future would bring. His first work as a writer in Hollywood was collaborating with his old boss Berthold Viertel on a film script about Hitler, *The Mad Dog of Europe*, but by November Isherwood got his first brief studio job. Then in January 1940, through Viertel's wife, Salka, he was hired by Gottfried Reinhardt to work at MGM on *Rage in Heaven*. The following summer, Isherwood's childless uncle—Henry Bradshaw-Isherwood-Bagshawe—died, and Isherwood inherited the Marple estate. Remarkably, he passed on the entire inheritance, both money and property, directly to his younger brother. This serves to emphasize how entirely committed he was to his new life in America; he was not interested in the past, in the family, or in owning property in England. His reflections about this in his diary on July 12, 1940, when he received the news of his uncle's death, once again make clear that England seemed to him to require that he return to a juvenile, or at least an adolescent, state of mind. The sole fascination of the Marple estate would have been the chance to turn all its formalities upside down, and he had outgrown the need to do that:

> It is too late now—not merely because of the war, but because the absurd boyhood dream of riches is over forever. It is too late to invite my friends to a banquet, to burn the Flemish tapestry and the Elizabethan beds, to turn the house into a brothel. I no longer want to be revenged on the past. Several weeks ago, I wrote to M[ummy] that Richard is to have everything, house and money. It's his, not mine, by right, because he loves the place and is prepared to live there. I confirmed this by cable today.

Although he was living far away from the central action of the war, Isherwood's life during this period, like the lives of so many others, hung upon its progress. Introspective as he may have aspired to be in his new Hinduism, he listened continually to the radio during periods of crisis and followed events in the newspapers. To a degree, his spiritual progress reflected his ongoing response to the events of the war. Soon after the worst bombing in the Battle of Britain, July to October, 1940, Isherwood was formally initiated by Swami Prabhavananda on November 8, 1940, the birthday of Ramakrishna's wife, Sarada Devi, worshipped as Holy Mother. In February 1941, he ended his domestic relationship with Vernon Old and, after living alone for a brief period, moved in with a new friend, Denny Fouts, who was then also taking up Vedanta. Isherwood was already thirty-six, too old for the newly established draft (having declared his intention to become a U.S. citizen, he was subject to the same military duties as a citizen), but during that spring he intended to volunteer as a conscientious objector at a Civilian Public Service Camp; Denny Fouts had registered as a conscientious objector and was waiting to be called up for the same type of service. Meanwhile, they undertook a monastic life together: chaste, spare and with frequent periods of meditation. This existence—the basis for the section called "Paul" in *Down There on a Visit*—lasted into the summer, when Fouts was indeed drafted to CPS camp and Isherwood learned that volunteers were not wanted. Instead, he made plans to go East to Haverford, Pennsylvania, where in the autumn of 1940 he began work in a Quaker refugee hostel (called the Cooperative College Workshop), helping to receive and resettle uprooted Europeans, mostly German Jews. In many ways, this time spent living and working among the diaspora of the culture by which he had been so fascinated during the early 1930s in Germany was Isherwood's most direct contact with the war. It spawned the idea for a new novel, *The School of Tragedy*—a novel which, in the end, Isherwood never wrote, and for which much of the raw material lies abandoned in his wartime diaries.

Isherwood was in Haverford when Pearl Harbor was bombed and the U.S. entered the war. The draft age was raised to forty-four, but still he was not called up, and he continued working at the hostel. He did very little writing, except in his diary. The following summer, 1942, he wrote another short story, "Take It or Leave It," which portrays the breakdown of a marriage over the inability of the highly conventional husband and wife to communicate with one another except through their private diaries. When the mixed passions expressed in the diaries at last come into the open, the marriage is not fulfilled but finally destroyed; neither can face the other. Some of the characters and names in the tale are drawn from the American friends and acquaintances among whom Isherwood lived in Haverford, and the theme reflects Isherwood's sense of isolation and unreality among the staid and marriage-oriented Quakers, whose wholesome virtue sometimes felt to him as oppressive as the genteel middle-class attitudes he had left behind in England with his mother. He rebelled against the Quakers only in small, essentially comic ways but clearly they aroused in him relics of guilt and anger stronger than any he had felt yet in America. He was, for the first time in a long while, concealing his homosexuality from the people among whom he was living, and he did this so successfully that one woman refugee he befriended fell seriously in love with him without recognizing that he was homosexual. In Haverford, his diary must have felt to him like the only place where he could express himself forthrightly, yet the short story "Take It or Leave It" (perhaps what he might have liked to say to the Quakers about his true self) seems to question whether a diary record is in fact any more genuine than the public persona offered to the world on a day-to-day basis. Isherwood introduces the story with a literary device—the narrator explains that although the story has occurred to *him*, it really ought to be told by someone else, a different kind of writer. This serves to emphasize Isherwood's discomfort with his identity in Haverford, and it is the first ominous sign of the alienation from his true narrative voice which was to overtake him when he later tried to write a novel about the time he spent there.

In July 1942, when the refugee hostel closed down, Isherwood returned to California. The Battle of the Pacific was at its height, and the war in Europe at its blackest; the Germans reached Stalingrad in September. He seemed unable to settle into any home of his own during this period, but lived alternately with various friends, Chris

Wood in Laguna and Peggy Rodakiewicz in Beverly Hills. In roughly October, he began working with Swami Prabhavananda on a translation of the central religious text of Hinduism, the Bhagavad Gita, or The Song of God. In November 1942 he went back to work at the movie studios, this time at Paramount, as an expert on the conscientious-objector position for Somerset Maugham's *The Hour Before Dawn*. And at the end of the year, for the Vedanta Society magazine, he wrote an attractive fable in the childlike style of Katherine Mansfield, "The Wishing Tree," which evokes what he had come to understand as the true religious attitude, that asks nothing of God but simply recognizes and is awed by God's existence.

As the Germans began to retreat from Stalingrad at the beginning of 1943, Isherwood finished working at Paramount and, after much consideration, moved into the Vedanta Center on Ivar Avenue in Hollywood. He was now seriously attempting to become a Hindu monk. He suffered gravely over the loss of his privacy and freedom, but he found he was able to work in the monastery. He continued with the translation of the Bhagavad Gita, and by May he was at last able to begin writing his next novel, *Prater Violet*. Like *Mr. Norris Changes Trains*, it begins as social comedy and ends by obliquely depicting the dark tragedy of Europe on the brink of the Second World War. "Friedrich Bergmann" is not merely a portrait of Isherwood's mentor Berthold Viertel. The narrator, "Christopher Isherwood," recognizes Bergmann's face on meeting as "the face of a political situation, an epoch. The face of Central Europe."[1] Bergmann's genius as an artist and a film director epitomizes the highest aspirations of European culture, but—as if by some Nietzschean principle—his neurotic artistic perfectionism and appealing sensuality—at once subtle and childishly melodramatic—make him the willing lackey of the British studio bosses:

> The face was the face of an emperor, but the eyes were the dark, mocking eyes of his slave—the slave who ironically obeyed, watched, humored and judged the master who could never understand him; the slave upon whom the master depended utterly—for his amusement, for his instruction, for the sanction of his power; the slave who wrote the fables of beasts and men.[2]

In the novel's denouement, Bergmann is easily manipulated by his British employers, and his attempt to impress upon them the importance of the socialist uprising in Austria in February 1934, along with his insistent prophecy of the coming war, are as quickly

[1] *Prater Violet* (*PV*) (New York, 1945), p.17; (London, 1946), p. 12.
[2] *PV*, U.S., p. 18; U.K., p. 13.

suppressed as the socialists were themselves by Dollfuss. The dilemma of the film hero Rudolf, which Bergmann sketches for Isherwood as potentially symbolizing "the dilemma of the would-be revolutionary writer or artist, all over Europe,"[1] paralyzes both the Isherwood character and Bergmann. Each becomes absorbed entirely in completing the film, despite doubting its artistic value, and in pursuing bourgeois success and comfort; neither remains committed to the cause of the workers. When Bergmann says to Isherwood during the uprising, "I am bitterly ashamed that I am here, in safety,"[2] he seems to refer not only to his wife and child in Vienna, but also to those fighting there for what he himself purports to believe in. And the remark reverberates, as indeed does the whole novel, within the circumstances of the Second World War during which Isherwood was writing it. Berthold Viertel's own wife and three sons had been safely in Santa Monica since 1928. But in his diaries, Isherwood describes a number of other refugees, both in Hollywood and in Haverford, who arrived in America while their wives and children or other members of their family were left behind in Europe, sometimes in grave danger; one, Ernst Jurkat, received news in Haverford that his wife, a Jew, had died in a concentration camp in Austria. And the sense of guilt expressed by some of these individuals, and recorded by Isherwood, unavoidably suggests the guilt borne silently by all those who were safe during the war, and in particular by the figure of the artist and intellectual upon whom Isherwood so ruthlessly and self-accusingly focuses in *Prater Violet*.

In the summer of 1943, the U.S. began retaking islands in the Pacific, and in July the Allies invaded Sicily in heavy fighting. In August 1943, after Isherwood had been celibate for six months, Denny Fouts introduced him to a young man called Bill Harris, toward whom Isherwood felt an almost overwhelming sexual response; in his diaries he at first could bring himself to refer to Harris only as "X." Lust preoccupied Isherwood increasingly, and he began to leave Ivar Avenue from time to time for spells of ordinary life, usually staying with friends and sometimes having small sexual adventures. He was still determined to become a monk, and his various projects of work were going well. In November he suddenly realized that a passage in the Bhagavad Gita he was working on could be brought to life if it were written in the Audenesque style of Old English verse, and he rapidly revised all the rest of the translation so that the various tones and moods of the Gita were rendered in appropriate English styles, alternating between prose and verse. In

[1] *PV*, U.S., p. 49; U.K., p. 39.
[2] *PV*, U.S., p. 96; U.K., p. 77.

early 1944 he worked on a film idea with Aldous Huxley, *Jacob's Hands*, and he completed the rough draft of *Prater Violet* by July. But meanwhile, in March 1944, he felt that he had fallen in love with Bill Harris, and by April he decided that he could never become a monk.

Isherwood resolved to remain in the monastery at Ivar Avenue until he felt certain what he should do next, but in fact having made this resolution, he moved restlessly from one place to another for most of the following year, living for a time at the Vedanta Center in Santa Barbara, intermittently at Chris Wood's in Laguna, and returning to Ivar Avenue for long spells, during which his moods fluctuated between calm stability, when he could meditate, pray, and work, and anxious claustrophobia, when he became almost hysterical with pent-up nerves and self-criticism. His inability to settle down is reflected in the conclusion to *Prater Violet*, where he describes the narrator as "A traveller, a wanderer."[1] In *Prater Violet* Isherwood lingers over the suggestion that this spiritual vagrancy derives from a deep ambivalence toward death. War and death work as one complex of images, in the novel, of inevitable darkness, both feared and desired, and the narrator meditates upon these images as he walks along the King's Road in the company and companionship of Friedrich Bergmann, the man whom he looks upon as a father and whom he loves as a father—thus once again referring to the enormous impact upon Isherwood of losing his own real father during the First World War:

> Death, the desired, the feared. The longed-for sleep. The terror of the coming of sleep. Death. War. The vast sleeping city, doomed for the bombs. The roar of oncoming engines. The gunfire. The screams. The houses shattered. Death universal. My own death. Death of the seen and known and tasted and tangible world. Death with its army of fears. . . .
>
> It can never be escaped—never, never. Not if you run away to the ends of the earth (we had turned into Sloane Street), not if you yell for Mummy, or keep a stiff upper lip, or take to drink or to dope. That fear sits throned in my heart. I carry it about with me, always.

For a time, Isherwood evidently felt that life in the monastery offered him safety from fear, but in the end, as he implies in *Prater Violet*, the annihilation of self that the monastic vows seemed to him to require was worse than fear:

> And, at this moment, but how infinitely faint, how distant, like the

[1] *PV*, U.S., pp. 122; U.K., p. 98.

high far glimpse of a goat-track through the mountains between clouds, I see something else: the way that leads to safety. To where there is no fear, no loneliness, no need of J., K., L., or M. For a second, I glimpse it. For an instant, it is even quite clear. Then the clouds shut down, and a breath of the glacier, icy with the inhuman coldness of the peaks, touches my cheek. "No," I think, "I could never do it. Rather the fear I know, the loneliness I know . . . For to take that other way would mean that I should lose myself. I should no longer be a person. I should no longer be Christopher Isherwood. No, no. That's more terrible than the bombs. More terrible than having no lover. That I can never face."[1]

Isherwood uses a slight, evanescent image for the spiritual life—the narrow goat-track disappearing through the clouds. It evokes the heights of the Himalayas and the solitude and harshness of a difficult journey, a path as difficult to tread as the razor's edge, and one from which Isherwood now veered away, determined that he could never entirely relinquish his identity, his ego, however committed he continued to be to Ramakrishna and to Swami Prabhavananda.

During the summer of 1944 the war turned decisively in favor of the Allies. The D-Day landings in Normandy went ahead on June 6; in Italy the Allies took Rome and then, in mid-August, invaded southern France. On August 24, the French underground rose in Paris and de Gaulle soon took charge of a provisional French government. Meanwhile in California, Isherwood turned forty on August 26, and during the same month the translation he had made with Swami Prabhavananda of the Hindu gospel, the Bhagavad Gita, was published. Isherwood finished *Prater Violet*, his first novel written in America, on October 15 and polished it until late November, while also preparing an introduction to *Vedanta for the Western World*, a collection of writings from the magazine of the Vedanta Society written mostly by monks and devotees, including Prabhavananda, Heard, Huxley, Isherwood himself, and many others.

In this period of energy and optimism, both in the war and in his personal life, Isherwood brought his first group of American diaries to a close on New Year's Eve 1944. Yet neither the war nor his future were settled. He seemed to be certain that the first phase of his commitment to Vedanta had come to an end, for he knew that he could never become a monk: he had come to recognize that he was a social and a sexual creature, and that he both wanted and needed to live in the world. He was poised and ready to leave the monastery, but his feelings for Bill Harris were not sufficient to move him. His

[1] *PV*, U.S., pp. 125–6; U.K., pp. 100–101.

relationship with Swami was untarnished, but he felt unsuited to the institutional life which was becoming increasingly suffocating as Prabhavananda's followers grew in number. Often in his diary Isherwood makes remarks to the effect that he felt himself to be a devotee of Swami Prabhavananda, but not of the Ramakrishna Order. Before entering the monastery, he had required special reassurance from Swami that while becoming a monk meant taking vows of poverty and chastity, it did not necessarily mean having to conduct lecture courses, officiate at rituals, or attend social lunches with uncloistered lady devotees—all things to which the Swami himself devoted a great deal of time. The Swami seemed never to forget how antipathetic organized religious life was to Isherwood's nature, and he happily permitted Isherwood to live remarkably freely.

Isherwood clearly recognized that his involvement with Bill Harris was essentially a sexual infatuation, for although the relationship undermined his resolve to remain celibate, he did not leave the monastery for Harris. By February 1945 the affair was over. But in the summer, Isherwood fell in love again, far more deeply and seriously, with a young man recently discharged from the navy, Bill Caskey. They met in the late spring, and by August they were seriously involved. Isherwood was working in the film studios again, on various projects, and the war was at last drawing to a close. Hitler killed himself in April; Germany surrendered in May. Japan surrendered on August 14, and nine days later, on August 23, Isherwood left Ivar Avenue for good. He moved into his own tiny apartment attached to the house of his friends, Dodie Smith and her husband, Alec Beesley, and Caskey at once began to come and stay with him there.

At the end of the war in the victorious countries, the sense of release, of joy, of abandon, must have been almost immeasurable in every quarter, and for Isherwood, to be in love, to be free of the difficulties of institutional life, of the commitment to long hours of prayer and meditation, of continual self-questioning, and to be certain at last that, whatever his life was for, it was not for adhering to monastic vows— all this was evidently intoxicating. The discipline and effort of the previous five years seemed suddenly unnecessary. He recorded nothing at all in his diary during this period, and indeed he hardly made any entries for the remainder of the 1940s. Thus some of the events of the missing years are described in a bridging narrative which introduces the second part of this volume. During the next five years, from 1945 to 1950, the excitement and enthusiasm which came with peacetime gradually turned for Isherwood to dissipation and chaos and eventually to despair. The years missing from his diary, while he was living with Bill Caskey, are years during which things went gradually, pervasively wrong with Isherwood's life, and during which his career as a writer briefly but quite genuinely foundered. The years with Caskey were certainly not wasted years, but they were, in more than one sense, lost years.

On leaving the monastery in 1945, Isherwood at first continued happy and productive. He began another translation with Swami Prabhavananda, the *Crest Jewel of Discrimination*, Shankara's eighth-century philosophical poem about the path to God through knowledge of how to distinguish what is real (God) from what is not real (the universe). *Prater Violet* appeared in *Harper's Bazaar* during the summer and was published as a book in November. But Isherwood was devoting a great deal of attention to Caskey, to domestic arrangements, to travel, to earning money at the studios to pay for their life together; less and less time was spent writing fiction. Caskey was handsome and possessed a forthright Kentucky-Irish eloquence that Isherwood found captivating; moreover, he was adventurous and independent, and he had the sort of rebellious nature to which Isherwood throughout his life was instantly attracted—as with Edward Upward and Swami Prabhavananda. But, more than being rebellious, Caskey was fundamentally belligerent; problems arose right from the start over his need for conflict, although initially his fights were not with Isherwood. In September 1945 Denny Fouts loaned his Santa Monica apartment to Isherwood and Caskey while he was out of town for a number of months; when Fouts returned in the spring, the three were to live together. But Caskey picked a jealous fight with Fouts which became so ferocious that Caskey and Isherwood were forced to move out of the apartment, and the friendship between Fouts and Isherwood was never the same afterwards. Other quarrels are recorded later on in Isherwood's diaries, and it seems clear that even in the most ordinary social conversation, Caskey's wit was bitterly caustic and his temper easily fired.

Caskey and Isherwood next settled in Salka Viertel's garage apartment, in April 1946. There they had probably their happiest and most productive months together. That summer and autumn, Caskey studied photography with the intention of making it his career. Isherwood had begun working early in the spring on a piece of fiction based on his experiences with the refugees in Haverford, and he was also planning a short novel about the time he and Heinz Neddermeyer had spent with Francis Turville-Petre in Greece. The second project was put off for a few years, while his plan for the first was quickly taking on epic proportions. Perhaps as a kind of preparation for writing about Haverford in precisely the way that he wanted to, that summer and autumn Isherwood revised his wartime diaries, producing the relatively polished version which makes up the first part of this volume. But he didn't get far with the projected novel.

On November 8, 1946, six years to the day since he had been initiated by Swami Prabhavananda (Isherwood, with his love of numinous dates, perhaps was able to influence the exact day), he formally became a U.S. citizen. And just after the start of the new year, 1947, he finished working with Lesser Samuels on an original treatment for a film, *Judgement Day in Pittsburgh*, about an art student drawn into scandal when she paints a picture of her beloved's face attached to a mostly nude body copied from Michelangelo. Thus, when Isherwood made his first trip back to England after the war (choosing to travel on another magic date, January 19, on which he and Auden had sailed for China in 1938 and for the U.S. in 1939), he was an American citizen and he was, at least soon after he arrived, as rich as a writer returning home from the dream of Hollywood ought to be. For while he was staying with his mother and brother at Wyberslegh, their home on the Marple estate, Isherwood received a dramatic telegram from Samuels saying that they had been paid $50,000 for their film treatment. (The script based on their treatment was later written by someone else, and the film was released by RKO in 1949 as *Adventure in Baltimore*.)

Because Caskey wanted to, Isherwood and Caskey lived in New York throughout the spring and summer of 1947, after Isherwood returned from England in April. Isherwood was struggling with his novel about the Quakers and the refugees, which by now he was calling *The School of Tragedy*, but he accomplished almost nothing amid the busy social life that he and Caskey were leading. Then, on September 19, the two of them set sail from New York for South America on a seven-month journey which Isherwood described in his second travel book, *The Condor and the Cows*. This was the last really fruitful time they spent together. Caskey took the haunting photographs for *The Condor and the Cows*, which make clear he had more than a slender talent. And the necessity of recording their journey for the travel book triggered in Isherwood his old diary-keeping impulse: in April 1948, at the end of their South American tour when he and Caskey were on board ship bound for Africa and Europe, he made the first proper entries in his diary since the war. Still, the habit of keeping the diary regularly was to take some years to reestablish itself entirely.

Their trip ended with another stay in England, and by the time Isherwood returned to California in the summer of 1948, to take a job writing a script based on Dostoevsky's *The Gambler* for Gottfried Reinhardt, he had been gone a year and a half, much of the time travelling. Caskey lingered in New York, and Isherwood arrived in California alone. Their relationship was by now far from monogamous, and Isherwood established several other romantic friendships during this period; sometimes he was promiscuous in a casual and energetic way. But Caskey soon joined him in California and they settled down together again in October 1948. Throughout this period, and despite his travels, Isherwood's faith in Swami Prabhavananda continued quietly to ballast him. Their Shankara book had been published in 1947 while Isherwood was away, and during the autumn of 1948, guru and disciple began yet another time-consuming translation, the yoga aphorisms of Patanjali. This exposition of Hindu spiritual disciplines and meditation techniques, formulated some time between the fourth century B.C. and the fourth century A.D. by the obscure Patanjali, eventually appeared in 1953, with Prabhavananda and Isherwood's modern English commentary, as *How to Know God: The Yoga Aphorisms of Patanjali*.

In October Isherwood finished working on the Dostoevsky film, *The Great Sinner*, and he soon got more film work in early 1949. In April 1949 he finished writing *The Condor and the Cows*, but he was floundering with his novel, *The School of Tragedy*. He worked on another script idea with Lesser Samuels, *The Easiest Thing in the World*—although they never repeated the bonanza they had achieved with *Judgement Day in Pittsburgh*—and he and Samuels also worked with Aldous Huxley on another film project, *Below the Equator*. Then in November 1949, Caskey left to go to the East Coast for a number of months.

Isherwood had affairs with various other men while Caskey was gone, and produced little serious work, although at the last of the year he squeezed out a memorial about his friend Klaus Mann, who had committed suicide in May. In fact, Isherwood seemed to be laboring against a genuine writer's block. And this was combined with actual physical impotence. On December 14, 1949, he wrote in his diary:

> Then there is this constant sexual itch, which never seems to be satisfied—or very seldom—because it is accompanied by a certain degree of impotence. And there is a hyper-tension, worse, I think, than I have ever experienced.
>
> And so I fail to write. I put it off and put it off, and I do nothing about getting a job, and I drift toward complete pauperism with nothing in sight. I am lazy and dreamy and lecherous. I hate being

alone. I don't exactly want Billy back—at least, I certainly don't want him the way he was when he left. And I am fundamentally unserious in my approach to other people. I don't believe in myself or my future, and all my "reputation" is just a delayed-action mechanism which only impresses the very young.

In 1946, Isherwood had undergone an operation on his urethra, inside the bladder, during which the doctor had tied off the sperm tubes, making Isherwood sterile and, in Isherwood's view, limiting his production of semen. Isherwood maintained that this did not adversely affect his sexual performance, and physiologically this should have been correct; but physiologically there is also no reason why such an operation should have affected his production of semen. Isherwood's self-acknowledged and immensely subtle propensity for symbolic psychosomatic symptoms seems a more likely cause for the reduced semen production, and it seems equally likely that the psychological effects of the operation may have contributed over the longer term to the impotence that he sometimes suffered. His imaginative paralysis during this period was worse than what he had experienced when he first lived in New York with Auden and with Vernon Old because then the entire culture was preparing to undergo a massive convulsion and his anxieties were, in a sense, widely shared, even emblematic. Now his crisis was private and entirely personal. Indeed it reveals the way in which the war had perhaps only delayed Isherwood in coming to terms with himself.

In 1950, Isherwood and Lesser Samuels tried out yet another script idea, a ghost story which they called *The Vacant Room*. Caskey came back to California in April, and then in June war broke out in Korea, reanimating Isherwood's old war fears, and making it even more difficult for him to work. Though the Korean war seemed more remote than the previous war, and though it presented itself with less urgency and magnitude in the society as a whole, it seems to have contributed to Isherwood's rising sense of panic about what he was doing with his life. Also, he feared that Caskey, despite having already served in the navy and being given a neutral discharge after becoming involved in a homosexual scandal, might be drafted. During the summer of 1950 Isherwood began reviewing for a literature and arts magazine, *Tomorrow*, evidently so that he would be regularly engaged in serious reading and thinking. Towards the end of the year, he and Caskey made an attempt at a fresh start in their relationship: they moved together to South Laguna, down the coast from Los Angeles, in December.

On December 11, 1950 Isherwood wrote in his diary:

Calm, meditation, work, regular habits, study, discipline, proper exercise; the absolute necessary regime for middle age. The past two years have been so incredibly wasteful. I've been like an engine with the belt slipping. And yet I know quite well how to employ the proper technique. (I certainly *ought* to, after impressing everybody with the clarity of my comments on Patanjali! What an old hypocrite, if I don't follow them!) The whole art of intentional living is in variety. You don't want to write your novel? Very well, do some other work, answer letters, get on with translating, read something instructive, take exercise, fix something in the garden, and fill every crack, every odd moment, with japam.

The phrase "intentional living," learned from Gerald Heard during the early 1940s (Isherwood first mentions it January 9, 1940), encapsulates Isherwood's apparent wish to lead his life on purpose and with a purpose, rather than allowing things to go on happening at random. And the word "art" implies his aim to make all parts of his life harmonious and lucid, even beautiful, as he had once done with his novels. He looked to the routine of domestic chores and *japam* (repeating and meditating upon the mantra given him by Swami) practiced in his monastic life during the war to help reestablish a measure of self-mastery. But his life with Caskey was too far out of control, and they now hit what was for Isherwood an all-time low of dissipation, with ceaseless spontaneous parties running late into the night, excessive promiscuity, and jealous, angry conflict. Isherwood longed for domestic tranquillity, a predictable routine, the possibility of getting his work done; and yet he was entirely unable to communicate this constructively to Caskey who refused to take a job and who continually drank too much. Isherwood knew by now that the more he pressed and tried to persuade Caskey, the more defiant Caskey, became, and he seems to have recognized in Caskey the embattled posture of his own youth. He cherished Caskey's flamboyantly antagonistic way with others, and he also blamed himself for trying to control in Caskey the self-destructive willfulness that, during this period, he was unable to control in himself. On April 27, 1951 Isherwood wrote in his diary:

What I really am trying to run away from is myself.

What I am trying to impose—under the disguise of "reasonableness"—is my own will. "Nothing burns in hell except the self," and I am miserable because the self is burning.

In the simplest, most terrible manner I am being taught that no other kind of life is possible for me. The monastery is *here*, is wherever I am. When Swami said: "Ramakrishna will hound you," he wasn't kidding.

For the first time, Isherwood recalled longingly his circumstances at his mother's house in Pembroke Gardens before he left London, where all his domestic requirements had been met, but where he had been able to come and go exactly as he pleased. On May 6, 1951, he wrote, "I must confess, I want to be looked after. I want the background of a home."

Yet Isherwood hardly devoted himself to Caskey's welfare or need for security. Later that month, after a dramatic scene during a party, at which Isherwood had evidently too openly expressed his attraction to several other men, he finally left Caskey and Laguna and fled to the Huntington Hartford Foundation, a retreat for artists and writers in Pacific Palisades on the northern outskirts of Los Angeles, with which he had already been involved through several friends. The Huntington Hartford Foundation was a secular equivalent to the Vedanta monastery at Ivar Avenue: a sheltered community where Isherwood's daily domestic needs would be met by institutional life. And at first, the foundation seemed to ask little of Isherwood in return. (Much later, Isherwood came to feel that the principles on which the foundation was run were hypocritical and manipulative, and he severed his ties with it.) The Swami continually encouraged Isherwood to come back, in one capacity or another, to the monastery, and even though Isherwood believed throughout this dark, confused time that Ramakrishna was somehow protecting him, he also felt certain that he needed to find his own individual solution to the problem of how he should live.

During the rest of the summer and fall of 1951, he shot back and forth from Laguna to the Huntington Hartford Foundation just as restlessly as he had moved from place to place in other, earlier periods of personal crisis. He first went to the foundation in May, then back to Laguna in August, then back to the foundation in September for three months. In September he decided once and for all that he could not go on living with Caskey. He was writing in his diary more often, but still only fitfully, and he tried with grave endeavor to get back to work on his novel. In the end, the years with Caskey were to produce Isherwood's least impressive literary achievement, *The World in the Evening*, begun in 1946, completed in the autumn of 1953, and published in June 1954. Its weaknesses are in many ways the culmination of artistic difficulties with which he had already been struggling long before he met Caskey, and the book reveals an enormous amount about Isherwood's career.

As a writer, Isherwood always aspired to work on an epic canvas, but he usually produced individual portraits or small groups of interrelated figures. During the 1930s, he worked on a novel about Berlin called *The Lost*. As he explains in *Christopher and His Kind*, the title was intended to describe the generation of Germans that was being "herded blindly into the future by their Nazi shepherds,"[1] as well as those who would be Hitler's victims (Bernhard Landauer), and also the moral outcasts who seemed to have no place in society at all (Sally Bowles, Otto Nowak, Mr. Norris). The characters were to be bound together by their awareness "of the mental, economic, and ideological bankruptcy of the world in which they live."[2] In other words, the novel was to represent the depleted atmosphere of a whole epoch. But Isherwood found he could not manage the massive book. *The Lost* was too big and unwieldy. Eventually he carved out the story of Mr. Norris from the epic canvas on which he had wished to work, observing in *Christopher and His Kind*, "It has been my experience that the embryos of novels tend to start their growth as interlocked Siamese twins or triplets, which can only be separated by the most delicate surgery."[3] This repeatedly proved true in his work.

Further on in *Christopher and His Kind*, Isherwood explains that he decided to publish the rest of his stories about Berlin as disconnected fragments only because John Lehmann needed short pieces of material for his magazine, *New Writing*. This freed him from conventional obligations of plot and produced the impressionistic, open-ended form of *Goodbye to Berlin*, which so successfully suggests that each of the stories and characters contained within the book is part of and even stands for the many similar and not-so similar people living outside the book, in real life. Thus the book has the desired effect of portraying a whole cultural milieu at a particular and, as it proved, immmensely significant moment in history. But this hap-pened, according to Isherwood, by accident. Once "Otto Nowak" had appeared in *New Writing* and *Sally Bowles* had been produced as a slim individual volume by the Hogarth Press, the many neglected characters of *The Lost* began crowding in upon him again. In May 1936, Isherwood recalls, he was working on a book of autobiographical reminscences which he thought he might call *Scenes from an Education*; he planned to include in it most of what he eventually published as three entirely separate books, *Lions and Shadows*, *Goodbye to Berlin*, and his next novel, *Prater Violet*. As he

[1] *Christopher and His Kind (C&HK)* (New York, 1976), p. 175; (London, 1977), p. 134.
[2] *C&HK*, U.S., p. 177; U.K., p. 134.
[3] *C&HK*, U.S., p. 178; U.K., p. 136.

observes of himself in *Christopher and His Kind*, "He probably didn't realize how huge this book would have been."[1]

One of the main ways Isherwood organized and compressed material in his fiction was to focus on his own relation to a single character: himself and Mr. Norris, himself and Sally Bowles, himself and Otto Nowak, himself and Berthold Viertel, and even in *Lions and Shadows*, which includes many friends, himself and one friend or mentor at a time, chapter by chapter. This practice corresponds to the way he seems often to have handled real-life relationships, and culminates in *My Guru and His Disciple*, which describes his relationship with the Swami. Isherwood's narrative persona in these works tended in the early years to be a bit like the narrator in a Henry James short story: bland, obtuse, without sexual identity, and intensely focused on the other figure in the tale—as if the quest to discover the true character of the other figure were as important as the quest to discover the holy grail. As Isherwood matured as an artist, his narrative persona became more vivid, more complicated, more dynamic, and in most respects truer to Isherwood's actual personality; in *A Single Man*—a small but undoubted masterpiece—the persona emerged as a character in its own right. But this was only in 1964, and as Isherwood points out in *Christopher and His Kind*, earlier in his career, it was not possible for him to write forthrightly about a homosexual character, and particularly not about himself as a homosexual. When he was writing *Mr. Norris Changes Trains* he "wasn't prepared to admit that the Narrator was homosexual,"[2] first because he feared to create a scandal, and second, because he did not want to shift the reader's attention away from Mr. Norris. The reader, he argued, would have been distracted if the narrator had been "an avowed homosexual, with a homosexual's fantasies, preferences and prejudices." Indeed, he explained, "The Narrator would have become so odd, perhaps so interesting, that his presence would have thrown the novel out of perspective." Thus, he left the narrator without explicit sexuality because he "dared not make the Narrator homosexual. But he scorned to make him heterosexual."[3]

The problem of the narrator didn't go away with *Mr. Norris*; Isherwood continued to be plagued by the difficulty that he could not without scandal and without possible legal difficulties write about homosexuality in the way that he might have liked to. In *Prater Violet*, the Isherwood character has a sex life, but his lover, referred to as "J.," is a genderless cypher without emotional importance: "After J., there

[1] *C&HK*, U.S., p. 244; U.K., p. 182.
[2] *C&HK*, U.S., p. 185; U.K., p. 141.
[3] *C&HK*, U.S., p. 186; U.K., p. 142.

would be K. and L. and M., right down the alphabet."[1] When Isherwood introduced two explicitly homosexual episodes into *The World in the Evening*, written during the early 1950s, his publishers in both London and New York asked for changes. In fact, Isherwood had foreseen such a request, and he had deliberately drafted these sex scenes rather strongly in order to be able to agree to alterations and still retain the minimum of detail that he felt was essential for his artistic purposes. In her 1929 essay, *A Room of One's Own*, Virginia Woolf argued that most nineteenth-century women novelists couldn't really write what they wanted to because there existed only a patriarchal tradition in which to write and because they were continually preoccupied as artists by having to apologize for or cover up their imaginative differences as women:

> The whole structure, therefore, of the early nineteenth-century novel was raised, if one was a woman, by a mind which was slightly pulled from the straight, and made to alter its clear vision in deference to external authority. One has only to skim those old forgotten novels and listen to the tone of voice in which they are written to divine that the writer was meeting criticism; she was saying this by way of aggression, or that by way of conciliation . . . she was thinking of something other than the thing itself.[2]

It seems clear that *The World in the Evening* is marred in a similar way both by repressed anger and by syrupy attempts at conciliation and apology, and it is no accident that the far more successful *A Single Man* is modelled on Virginia Woolf's *Mrs. Dalloway* (which Isherwood reread as he was preparing to write his own book). Instead of a day in the life of a Mayfair hostess, he offers a day in the life of a homosexual Englishman who is a literature professor in California. *A Single Man* is a boldly political book and offers none of the deference to conventional mores found in Isherwood's earlier novels.

Isherwood's diaries just as freely ignore contemporary literary decorums (he never had formal plans to publish them), but *The World in the Evening* shows the strain of Isherwood's not being able to deal directly with the emotional truths that were his real subject. The hysterical guilt of the main character, Stephen Monk, over the relatively minor sexual "sins" of his past life is pitched melodramatically high precisely because Isherwood cannot allow Monk to confess in detail the actual nature of those "sins" as Isherwood himself might have understood them. And the puritanism of the Quakers amongst whom Monk is temporarily living had to be

[1] *PV*, U.S., p. 125; U.K., p. 100.
[2] *A Room of One's Own* (London, 1929), p. 111.

exaggerated in order to justify Monk's extreme emotion. Isherwood thus substitutes contrived emotional intensity for psychological truth, and his perhaps unconscious anger that this should be necessary seems to mingle with the guilt and frustration he himself experienced while living among the Quakers. Isherwood imagines Monk as a bisexual, but the homosexual affair that Monk has is marked on Monk's side by coy reluctance and on his lover's side by a sulkiness so embittered as to suggest the lover deserves to be essentially unrequited. This is hardly rectified by the introduction of the two "good" homosexual characters—the hardworking doctor, Charles Kennedy, and his friend, Bob Wood—who are presented as being both settled in a long-term relationship and obviously contributing to society (Bob Wood volunteers for the army when the Second World War begins).

The sexuality of the women with whom Monk is involved is equally oversimplified and unconvincing—Isherwood is noticeably inventing for the sake of his plot rather than drawing on observation of real-life. Monk's second wife is a destructive nymphomaniac. His deceased first wife, Elizabeth Rydal, is an ethereal anthology figure, compiled from a variety of refined, high-minded and mortally ill women Isherwood admired—Katherine Mansfield, Virginia Woolf, and probably Helen Kennedy, a beautiful Vedanta nun he was half in love with when he lived in the monastery. Rydal is disqualified from motherhood by a near fatal miscarriage and consequently disqualified from sex by the threat to her already weak heart. A sexual encounter between Monk and the healthily attractive refugee, Gerda Mannheim, was revised out of the story in Isherwood's final draft. And Monk's foster mother, Sarah Pennington, is middle-aged; Isherwood permits her no sexuality at all. These characters together reflect above all Isherwood's passionate uneasiness about mature female sexuality, an uneasiness he reveals unselfconsciously in his diaries in describing his friendships with various real women. The sex life of a Sally Bowles figure was undaunting to him, because, after all, she might almost have been portrayed as a young boy, but Isherwood invariably flinched at any direct expression in a more adult woman of sexual appetite. Possibly this uneasiness was exacerbated by the great effort he made to be celibate during the war, but the seeds for it may be detected in his mother's sudden widowhood during his childhood and in his own sense of guilt in refusing to submit to her obsessive involvement with her lost marriage. He evokes such emotions in *The World in the Evening* when Elizabeth Rydal describes a scene from *Macbeth* in which the recently widowed Lady Macduff, "so utterly, angrily alone with her tragedy," watches her young son and "longs to break down the barrier between them, to get through to him and make him share what she feels, somehow, even if she has to hurt him."[1] The mutual destructiveness of the mother–son relationship had been a central theme of Isherwood's earlier novels, *All the Conspirators* and *The Memorial*, where the antagonism is presented in the context of the First World War and its effect upon Isherwood's whole generation. A revealing diary notation made in Haverford points to the sexual dimension (reiterated elsewhere) of the standoff between mother and son. In his entry for April 28, 1942, Isherwood describes how Caroline Norment, his boss at the Quaker refugee hostel in Haverford, has become jealous of another woman about to be married and flirts with one of the male refugees over lunch, openly enjoying his flattery: "I couldn't be more ashamed if it were my own mother," he concludes. Caroline Norment is the real-life original for Sarah Pennington in *The World in the Evening*, but in the novel Isherwood removed all signs of her sexual appetite as if to make her an entirely "good" character and an acceptable, refined mother figure. Indeed, he attributes to her some of the saintly qualities he had observed in Swami Prabhavananda, who had long been celibate. How much more poignant she might have been if she were, as in his diary impression of her, hungry for men.

Closely connected to the longstanding artistic problem of the inadmissible homosexual narrator was the problem, for Isherwood, of writing about pacifism so soon after the war. In his own particular case, his pacifism was inextricably bound up with his homosexuality, and he could not fully account for one without bringing in the other. In *The World in the Evening*, Bob Wood voices sentiments that perhaps reflect Isherwood's own, but which Isherwood's need to conceal his homosexual identity prevented him from expressing openly: "Compared with this business of being queer, and the laws against us, and the way we're pushed around even in peacetime—this war hardly seems to concern me at all."[2] When Wood joins the army he explains to Monk, "I can't be a C.O. because, if they declared war on the queers—tried to round us up and liquidate us, or something— I'd fight. I'd fight till I dropped. I know that. I'd be so mad, I wouldn't even feel scared. . . . So how can I say I'm a pacifist?"[3] Wood's outspoken rage looks forward to Isherwood's novel of the early 1960s, *A Single Man*, for which some parts of *The World in the Evening* seem to be a very dry run.

At the time that Isherwood wrote *The World in the Evening*, it seems he still felt sensitive and uncertain about how to present what his own

[1] *The World in the Evening* (*WIE*) (New York, 1954), p. 66; (London, 1954), p. 79.
[2] *WIE*, U.S., p. 281; U.K., p. 311.
[3] *WIE*, U.S., p. 281; U.K., p. 310.

role had been in the war, and this perhaps explains one decision about the novel which in a way changed the direction of his career. While he was struggling to write what he was then still calling *The School of Tragedy*, Isherwood turned to friends for advice, discussing the work endlessly with Dodie Smith in particular. Another friend, Speed Lamkin, advised him on May 29, 1951, "The refugees are a bore." So Isherwood took almost all of the refugees out of the book and set them aside for a later project. He found himself able at last to get on faster with the writing, but he had in fact jettisoned the only material that provided him with any direct point of contact with the war, and he had cut himself off from the relation to German culture which had nourished his fiction throughout the 1930s. The detailed observations which do survive in his wartime diaries—of the relatively ordinary refugees who arrived almost unnoticed in Haverford and seemed to evaporate into the atmosphere of America—offer a provocative contrast to his chronicles of the more glamorous and sometimes exceptionally gifted refugees Isherwood knew in Hollywood, in particular because the latter were obviously shaping American culture just as much as they were being shaped by it. But in *The World in the Evening*, the war is only background, a remote conflagration in which others are suffering and in which the main character, Stephen Monk, feels he ought to be more involved; it operates almost solely as an engine of guilt and the book has only a weak sense of connection to the historical period in which it is set. During the period that he was writing the novel, Isherwood repeatedly says of himself in his diaries that he is running away from something that he cannot identify. Likewise, Stephen Monk says of himself near the beginning of *The World in the Evening*, "What am I doing here? What's going to happen to me? What is it that I'm afraid of?"[1] For a long time Isherwood, it seems, simply did not want to understand himself, nor to examine his own psychology and motivations too closely. As his relationship with Caskey was nearing its end, he tried to substitute the strict discipline of monastic life for the self-analysis and self-understanding which he had always achieved through writing and which was necessary in order for him to grow. Isherwood needed discipline, and what he had learned by living in the monastery was useful to him throughout the remainder of his life, but he knew that he must not rely on the Swami's way of life too much—it was too easy a solution. On August 29, 1951, he wrote in his diary:

> What I now dimly begin to see is that there must be no more categorical relationships. I believe that's what went wrong with

[1] *WIE*, U.S., p. 42; U.K., p. 51.

Bill and me, and Ivar Avenue and me. Trying to fix a situation and ensure security by involving yourself, is no good. No good saying: "Now I'm married" or "Now I'm a monk"—and *therefore* I'm committed. It is simply weakness to talk that way.

Above all, Isherwood needed to write, for this was the only way he could rigorously examine and try to understand his experience. Once he began to make progress with *The World in the Evening*, however artistically unsatisfactory the final result, and once he began to make more frequent entries in his diary, then at last his life began to improve.

Meanwhile, at the beginning of the 1950s, some of Isherwood's friends were trying to solve his more practical problems for him. They felt what he needed was money. Dodie Smith and Alec Beesley conspired to challenge John van Druten to adapt some of Isherwood's Berlin stories for the stage. Van Druten was easily tempted, mostly because he loved money himself, and he recognized the potential of Isherwood's work. *I Am a Camera* began its pre-New York run in Hartford, Connecticut on November 8, 1951. Characteristically, Isherwood placed importance on the date, eleven years to the day after he was initiated by Swami Prabhavananda and six years after he became a U.S. citizen. This event, too, was to change Isherwood's life. When the play transferred to New York at the end of November, it became a hit and Isherwood became famous, both as the author of the original story and as the stage character, Christopher Isherwood, who was in fact so unlike himself. He had a share of the earnings—though a modest one—from the play, the subsequent films, and from the musical *Cabaret*. Yet as Isherwood himself said of *I Am a Camera* in his diary entry for November 8, 1951, "This isn't my own child." It gave him finances and reputation, but it did not solve his artistic or personal problems. At the end of 1951, he sailed for England for his third visit since the war. He planned to spend Christmas with his mother and brother, but he was alone—really alone—for the first time in years. Caskey joined the merchant marine and shipped out from the West Coast in the opposite direction.

In February 1952 Isherwood went back to Berlin and saw Heinz Neddermeyer for the first time since their dramatic parting in Luxembourg in 1937. Afterwards, he returned to California from England via New York. He felt greatly restored by seeing some of his oldest friends—Auden, Spender, Forster, Plomer, and others. He was determined to keep his diary more regularly, and he planned to spend more time with Swami as soon as he got back to California. Although he began another affair in New York, it proved unimportant. By early April he was home in Los Angeles, where he began in earnest the project of trying to live on his own. First he went to Trabuco, the Ramakrishna monastery south of Los Angeles, where he finished his share of work on the Patanjali translation and completed a draft of the first section of what he was still calling *The School of Tragedy*. From there he moved into a small apartment while he began fixing up a more permanent home in Santa Monica—the garden house belonging to his friend Evelyn Hooker and her husband. He was able to move into the garden house in the late summer of 1952, around the time of his forty-eighth birthday. That November he took a car trip to Mexico with Caskey, but their relationship was over. Caskey shipped out again early in 1953 and Isherwood spent most of January at Trabuco, where he was able at last to finish a rough draft of the novel he now finally titled *The World in the Evening*.

As soon as Isherwood had established himself for the first time as a single man with a real home, his life was about to change again. In February 1953, he became involved with an eighteen-year-old college student, Don Bachardy, and it rapidly became clear that Bachardy was to be the most important person in Isherwood's life, "the ideal companion to whom you can reveal yourself totally and yet be loved for what you are."[1] That month, Bachardy's elder brother, Ted, whom Isherwood had known already for several years, had a nervous breakdown—one of many—and Isherwood was drawn into the family circle when he tried to intercede with Ted and prevent him from becoming violent. Isherwood failed with Ted, who had to be hospitalized for several months, and so found himself sympathizing with Don, who was both frightened and saddened by his brother's condition. From the outset, Isherwood's feelings towards Don were fatherly as well as romantic; he wrote in his diary on March 6, 1953:

> I feel a special kind of love for Don. I suppose I'm just another frustrated father. But this feeling exists at a very deep level, beneath names for things or their appearances. We're just back from a trip to Palm Springs together, which was one of those rare experiences of nearly pure joy. There's a brilliant wide-openness about his mouse face, with its brown eyes and tooth gap and bristling crew cut, which affects everybody who sees him. If one could still be like that at forty, one would be a saint.

By April Bachardy moved out of his mother's apartment into a furnished room of his own so that he could spend more time with Isherwood, and then in May he moved into a friend's apartment

---

[1] *C&HK*, U.S., p. 339; U.K., p. 252.

partly as a disguise, because the relationship was evidently attracting disapproving attention from Bachardy's landlady and from some of Isherwood's friends. Isherwood finished *The World in the Evening* in August 1953, and then trouble arose. In September, Evelyn Hooker insisted that Isherwood move out of her garden house because her husband feared the relationship with Bachardy, who looked far younger than his nineteen years, would cause a scandal. Already Bachardy was far more "home" to Isherwood than the carefully prepared domestic arrangements in the garden house, so Isherwood kept the garden house for a time as a study, and the pair soon found their own small apartment. Isherwood then settled down to revise *The World in the Evening* during the autumn and at Christmas he took Bachardy on his first trip to New York.

Throughout his life, Isherwood was greatly influenced by his friends—the people he cared about and admired. In his domestic life, this characteristic had intensified significance. He had sought persistently for a long-term companion, and it still seemed that his greatest chance of happiness was neither in a monastery nor alone travelling the world, but settled in a home with the right person. It had become clear by the start of the 1950s that Isherwood was not the Yeatsian artist "forced to choose / Perfection of the life, or of the work";[1] on the contrary, everything about him as an artist and a man suggests an entirely different exemplum. For Isherwood, perfection of the work was impossible without perfection of the life; each depended upon and derived from the other. In *The World in the Evening*, Elizabeth Rydal, preparing for her death, expresses the wish to have struck a different balance between life and art:

> One just lets one's self be pushed this way and that. I'd like to have made my life so much more, well, intentional.
> . . . I feel as if I'd put all my will into deciding what to call a character, or whether to use a semi-colon instead of a comma. In life itself, I've drifted.[2]

Such a recognition had not come too late to Isherwood. Falling in love with Bachardy triggered such a powerful sensation in him of the numinous richness of life that Isherwood was at first overawed by his own emotions. A passage in his diary, written April 20, 1953, suggests the way in which this overwhelming experience of love was to move him, over the longer term, away from fiction toward a new, much closer connection between his work and real life:

[1] "The Choice," ll. 1–2.
[2] *WIE*, U.S., p. 246; U.K., p. 271.

Coming back at 10:45 from supper at Jo and Ben [Masselink]'s, with talk about the war, *This Is My Beloved*, and Jay [de Laval] and the old Canyon—the nice smell of redwood as I lifted the garage door. And the feeling of impotence—or, what it really amounts to, lack of inclination to cope with a constructed, invented plot—the feeling, why not write what one experiences, from day to day? And then, as I slid my door back, this sinking-sick feeling of love for Don—somehow connected with the torn shorts—and the reality of that—so far more than all this tiresome fiction. Why invent—when Life is so prodigious?

Perhaps I'll never write another novel, or anything invented—except, of course for money.

Excess of invention—partly forced upon him by the impossibility of writing openly as a homosexual, and partly the result of his own guilty uncertainty about who he was and how he should live—had fatally skewed the impulse of *The World in the Evening*; but his love for Bachardy, in which Isherwood felt utterly justified and convinced, was to bring about a renewed sense of involvement with life and restore his instinctive confidence in his own narrative voice. Isherwood evidently wished to make of his life a work of art, and to offer it up in complete detail as his subject matter. In part this was an impulse of self-preservation, even self-salvation, both for himself and for his talent, in the sense that writing, especially writing in his diary, preserved him from the dissipation and laziness to which he was susceptible and created order out of the chaos of his life. Moreover, in his diary Isherwood did not need to exert his will to decide what to call a character or even consider for long whether to use a comma or a semi-colon; instead, he applied his powers of analysis directly to his life. More and more as his career advanced, all his other writing would do the same thing. On January 12, 1954, mulling over his plans for the New Year, Isherwood once again expressed his determination to lead, as Elizabeth Rydal wished she had done, "a more intentional life." Now this life was to include Don Bachardy, and in many ways to organize itself around him.

Bachardy was young and still only half-educated when he and Isherwood met, so that Isherwood could and did enormously shape Bachardy's mature character. Bachardy was impressionable and eager to learn, and indeed he willingly modelled himself on Isherwood to such a degree that he even acquired Isherwood's half-British and half-American accent when speaking. In the early years of their relationship Bachardy followed Isherwood's intellectual guidance and acquired his taste and his very high standards. But Bachardy was also fiercely independent and rebellious—traits always attractive to

Isherwood—and he was highly intelligent, sensitive to a fault, and extremely tenacious. On February 14, 1960, Isherwood mused in his diary:

> What shall I write about Don, after seven years? Only this—and I've written it often before—he has mattered and does matter more than any of the others. Because he imposes himself more, demands more, cares more—about everything he does and encounters. He is so desperately alive.

These qualities of intense engagement and commitment were more important to Isherwood than any others. His existence and Bachardy's existence became thoroughly intertwined, and they shared one another's projects and concerns so intimately, and with such a strong emphasis upon self-reflection and self-examination, that the project of living and working together became in itself a kind of artistic undertaking. It was not long before Bachardy, too, began to keep a diary. Sometimes when they travelled, he kept Isherwood's pocket datebook for him (in which Isherwood made brief notations of appointments and events and listed people he met), and he was able to imitate Isherwood so skillfully that he seemed to be writing in Isherwood's own hand and style. Later, as a portrait painter, Bachardy recorded experience in a different medium, but his portraits, too—always completed in one sitting—are a kind of diary of his personal encounters with others. Their shared life, as Isherwood describes it in his diaries, clearly has iconic significance as a model of homosexual love and companionship, and it is also perhaps one of the most replete and persuasive accounts extant of the beauty and difficulty of sustaining a long-term bond between two people.

By 1954, Isherwood's ability to work seemed rejuvenated. January saw the beginning of a major movie-writing job, MGM's *Diane*, starring Lana Turner. This provided plenty of money to establish a home with Bachardy, and in February they moved into a little house together. Meanwhile, Isherwood had begun planning several writing projects of his own. On January 12 he first noted in his diary his intention to write a book about Ramakrishna, and he began to plan an anthology, *Great English Short Stories*. More importantly, he mentioned again the stories about Basil Fry and Francis Turville-Petre that he had been considering since the 1930s, and which he would during the next few years at last begin to write in earnest for *Down There on a Visit*. *The World in the Evening* was published in June 1954 and flopped with the critics; Isherwood was hardly surprised. Nonetheless, when in August he turned fifty, his sense of confidence in himself as a writer was perhaps somewhat damaged, even though he had many ideas already clearly established for new work.

I Am a Camera had closed in 1952, but now plans went ahead for a film, and because he took so much pleasure in showing the world to Bachardy and Bachardy to the world, Isherwood seems to have had renewed enthusiasm for travel and socializing. The two spent much of November in Key West watching the filming of Tennessee Williams's *The Rose Tattoo*, and then in December they drove to Mexico with close friends, Ben and Jo Masselink. Once again, travel seems to have been a relief and a release to Isherwood. In Mexico, he made a point, as on other trips, of writing more regularly in his diary. He also had an important inspiration about his future work. On December 16, he recorded:

> Very faintly, since yesterday or the day before—yes, it was at Álamos—I glimpsed an idea for a novel. Something quite unlike me—Kafkaesque—about a journey. A journey which is meticulously described and yet unreal: the reality being the relationships between the characters. Maybe they are all dead—as, in a sense, the characters are in Hemingway's *The Sun Also Rises*. Also, I see elements in it of *The Day's Journey*, my projected film.

The Kafkaesque journey proved to be far more in keeping with Isherwood's personality as a writer than he himself seemed to recognize, and it became the governing conception for *Down There on a Visit*, for which Isherwood had already gathered most of the material in his diaries and on which his thoughts now began to evolve fairly rapidly. The projected film, *The Day's Journey*—mentioned here for the first time—was to metamorphose into the later book, *A Single Man*. It is highly significant that Isherwood first thought of *A Single Man* as a film, for the novel reads somewhat like a screenplay— especially in the dialogue—and it is almost exactly the right length to be one. If *The World in the Evening* seemed to have absorbed the cheap melodramatic side of film writing to which Isherwood had exposed himself in Hollywood—and some of his old friends implied that writing for the studios had spoiled his style—*A Single Man* offers evidence that his writing was not ruined by studio work, but greatly enhanced. The writing in *A Single Man* is worthy of comparison with the lyrical prose of Woolf's *Mrs. Dalloway*, yet the book synthesizes the style of English literary Modernism with the most important genre of contemporary American culture—the film script.

Isherwood's job on *Diane* carried over into 1955, and he also began a new MGM script for a film about Buddha called *The Wayfarer*, which he finished that September. In March 1955 Ted Bachardy had another nervous breakdown, which once again deeply shook Don Bachardy. Isherwood felt a growing responsibility for Don, which he held as solemn as his commitment to his spiritual life, to his art, to the project of living in the right way. All were now bound up together in a unity as inevitable as his own eventual death. On August 8, 1955, Isherwood wrote in his diary:

> In the night, quite often now, I wake—not with the horrors, but calmly and lucidly. Then I know certain things clearly—it's almost as if they belonged to another order of reality: that I shall die one day—that much of my life has been wasted—that the life of the spirit is the only valid occupation—that I really care for Don and that I have, as it were, adopted him, much as I adopted Heinz, but more completely. In the daytime, these facts are obscured, by studio noise and as-if behavior, and insane resentments and mental and physical slumping. Also I know that all occupations, even Art, are symbolic, and all are valid, so long as they represent right-livelihood.

Bachardy had turned twenty-one that May, and Isherwood took him abroad for the first time. They left California—and Bachardy's place in college—at the end of the year for a sort of grand tour through Africa, Europe, and England. In Tangier Paul Bowles gave them hashish, an experience they found terrifying. Bachardy, haunted by his brother's schizophrenia, feared he had gone insane. Nonetheless, a few months later in London, on February 24, 1956, Isherwood tried mescaline for the first time. He approached the undertaking with ritualistic gravity, for he had been told by Gerald Heard and Aldous Huxley that mescaline could induce mystical experiences. Moreover, he had felt teasingly challenged by their refusal to give him any of the drug on the grounds that he wasn't strong enough to cope with its powers over the long term. Swami had always derided using drugs to achieve mystical insights, admonishing that drugs could only alienate the spiritual aspirant from God. Not surprisingly, Isherwood ended nearer the Swami's view than Heard's or Huxley's, though his diary account of his first experiment with mescaline suggests how closely he modelled his approach on Heard's and Huxley's. Like Huxley in *The Doors of Perception*, Isherwood pseudo-scientifically records times of day, and food and drink taken, and he tests the degree of change in his perceptual capacities by looking at reproductions of paintings in books, just as Huxley tells he did.

Although Isherwood was occasionally to try mescaline again, he found it essentially unimportant. It had no spiritual effect whatsoever, and it was of no use in his writing. In contrast to Huxley's rather dry, cerebral, scientific sensibility, Isherwood had a vivid and weird imagination. This is apparent right from childhood, when, for instance, he twice thought he saw ghosts in Marple Hall, and from the days of his friendship with Edward Upward, when together they invented the macabre world of Mortmere. On his recent trip to Mexico, this vein of Isherwood's imagination had opened again quite easily as he began to plan what he called the Kafkaesque story about a trip to a place that was, and was not, quite normal. He had no need of the drug-induced vision of mescaline or even hashish; he had enough imagination of his own. He recognized this himself when, after completing the novel, he actually removed an episode based on his hashish experience in Tangier; this episode wasn't central to the book, and he only published it much later in *Exhumations* as a separate short story, "A Visit to Anselm Oakes."

In February 1956, in England with Don Bachardy, Isherwood decided to call his Kafkaesque Mexican novel *The Lost*. Thus, both in conception and content, it was to be closely linked to his work of the 1930s. Indeed, the theme reached back even further than the 1930s, to Isherwood's adolescent friendship with Edward Upward and their Mortmereish obsession with doom. In *The Spiral Ascent* Upward recalls how one evening at a dance the pair of friends suddenly recognized that what gripped them about the dancers they were watching, and indeed about all the eccentric characters that had aroused their interest during their holiday in the Isle of Wight, was the fact that they were doomed. At this, Richard Marple, the Isherwood character in Upward's novel, exclaims: "Our duty is to live among the doomed and in our poetry we must record and celebrate what they are."[1] This, it seems, was the birth of Isherwood's epic ambition to portray a bankrupt epoch.

For his new version of *The Lost* (eventually published as *Down There on a Visit*), he drew inspiration not only from Kafka, but also from Dante's *Inferno*, comparing his "lost" characters to the damned. At first he planned to describe a group of expatriate Americans, marginalized from the mainstream of their culture and living outside or, as the map shows, physically underneath it, down south in Mexico. Gradually he moved closer to his own experiences of the 1930s and 1940s, drawing material from his diaries rather than inventing it, just as he had first begun to recognize he should do during the early months of his relationship with Don Bachardy. Yet while he was inventing less, his technique became more subtle and more directed. And his ambition for the book stretched out through a

[1] *The Spiral Ascent*, p. 18.

longer period of history, so that it would record the moral condition not merely of one group of people at a given moment in time, but of several people and groups of people in Europe and America during the first half of the century. He decided to tell the story through a revised version of the narrative persona that had served him so well during the 1930s and early 1940s, rather than trying, as he had in *The World in the Evening*, to invent a convincing character who could both embody the psychology necessary to convey the emotional truths in which Isherwood was interested, and also conform, at least superficially, to external heterosexual literary convention. Thus, he was once again free to concentrate on his true subject matter, and he pared this down until he produced four emblematic vignettes based on four episodes in his life and held together by his original conception of the narrator's journey among the lost, whose condition he shares in and examines without ever giving himself over to their fate.

While he was in England that winter, 1956, Isherwood stayed with his mother and brother at Wyberslegh again and visited Marple—now fallen, through neglect, into irretrievable ruin. In mid-March, before returning to California, he, somewhat symbolically, made a start on writing the novel which would eventually become *Down There on a Visit*. Then, back at home, he and Bachardy bought a house of their own for the first time, as if seeing the last of Marple had somehow prepared Isherwood to become a property owner elsewhere. Just as they were moving into their new house on Sycamore Road in May, all of Isherwood's ambitions and plans were heavily waylaid as first Bachardy and then he himself came down with hepatitis. This marked the beginning, for Isherwood, of a long period of chronic ill health, tiredness, and depression. Nevertheless, he began work in earnest on his biography of Ramakrishna, in which he tells the story of the mystical genius from his own point of view, as a sceptic who questions the possibility of visionary and supernatural experience. He freighted the book heavily with quotidian detail, attempting, characteristically, to approach as near as possible to the borderline between ordinary reality and the transcendent. The power and intensity of love that emanated from the disciples who gathered around Ramakrishna in his lifetime clearly fascinated Isherwood, and he focused in the book on describing the individual relationships between Ramakrishna and each of his main followers in order to establish how Ramakrishna's own charisma passed through a series of, for Isherwood, comprehensible and verifiable human relationships out into the world—from guru to disciple, guru to disciple. The analogies to the historical Jesus are made clear in the book in a variety of ways, not least of which is Isherwood's decision to tell the story in the style of the King James version of the Bible. This major biography was to take nearly a decade, interspersed with many other pieces of work, and although Isherwood often found it tedious, it is clear it was important to him. Isherwood's belief in Ramakrishna's status as an avatar does not stand or fall on the strength of whether the apparently miraculous events of Ramakrishna's life are literally true, but on the strength of the individual convictions of those who believed before Isherwood, and who established their belief on the basis of a personal relationship, just as Isherwood had done in his own familiar and credible relationship with Swami.

That summer, Bachardy made a step toward recognizing and beginning to cultivate his talent as a draughtsman when he enrolled in art school. Not long afterwards, despite his own and his critics' mixed feelings about *Diane* (released earlier that year), Isherwood undertook another major film script during September 1956, *Jean-Christophe*, also set in France. *Jean-Christophe*—written for Twentieth Century-Fox—was never made, possibly because it promised to be too expensive; still, Isherwood was well paid for his work, which lasted until the following June, 1957. During this same period, he had more problems with his health. He discovered a tumor on the side of his belly in February 1957, and although it was removed almost instantly and proved benign, it brought him abruptly up against the fact that he would die, and that he could die soon. He became even more determined to press on quickly with his work, but his anxiety and depression persisted, and it seemed that he had never really recovered from the hepatitis. The impotence which he had first mentioned in his diary in 1949 became more persistent. He refers to it several times during 1956 and 1957, and it made him anxious about his relationship with Bachardy, even though the little he records in his diary suggests that Bachardy was far less worried by the impotence than Isherwood. Isherwood tended to put the difficulty down to middle age, tiredness, and loss of libido partly resulting from the hepatitis; he consulted an endocrinologist and seemed satisfied that her vitamin and hormone treatments helped him.

From October 1957 to January 1958, Isherwood and Bachardy went on another long trip, this time right around the world, visiting Japan and southeast Asia and then travelling to India, where they stayed at the Ramakrishna Math and Mission and visited several other places in Calcutta and the surrounding area. Isherwood was gathering impressions and information for his biography of Ramakrishna, but he recorded nothing about this trip in his diary. Possibly he used all his observations in the biography itself—as he had done in his travel book, *The Condor and the Cows*, about his trip to South America—but the absence of any excited response during this pilgrimage to the scene of Ramakrishna's life is entirely in keeping with the fact that the essence of Vedanta, for Isherwood, lay in his own devotion to Swami. In fact, Isherwood's lack of affinity for Indian culture meant that such a trip probably made him feel distanced from Ramakrishna, rather than drawing him closer.

When he returned to California in 1958, Isherwood became involved in a number of projects that took him away from the real work of writing fiction, but to which he was attracted by the lure of earning large sums of money and by the pleasure of collaborating with others. In March, David Selznick hired him to develop a screenplay about Mary Magdalene; then, after several months of long, intimate conversations with Isherwood at high wages, Selznick moved on to another writer and later abandoned the project. From October 1958 to January 1959, Isherwood and Bachardy together wrote a play which they titled *The Monsters*. Ultimately, despite the riveting energy created between them while they worked on it, they decided it was an embarrassing failure. Around the same time, Isherwood also began a writing relationship with Gavin Lambert, and over the next few years the two worked on a film and on a television idea together—much as Isherwood had once done with Lesser Samuels— but they had no real success with either of their projects. Later, in April 1959, Isherwood went to New York to discuss collaborating with Auden on a musical version of *I Am a Camera*, but this, too, came to nothing.

During this period, Isherwood had yet another admonishing physical setback: he fell asleep at the wheel of his car in November 1958 and had a fairly bad accident. Nobody else was injured, but Isherwood broke his nose and some ribs, tore his pleura (which was very painful), and was badly cut and bruised. Thus it was not until March 1959 that he made much progress with *Down There on a Visit*. Once he got going with the first section, "Mr. Lancaster," he wrote steadily and constructively for many months. By June he was well on with the second section, "Ambrose," and he also produced what he called a "queer" story, "Afterwards." In the middle of this wonderfully productive time, the long years of vagrancy and wandering from home to home, which had characterized Isherwood's life from the end of the 1920s until he met Don Bachardy, were brought to a final close. In June 1959 Isherwood and Bachardy bought 145 Adelaide Drive, a slight and airy run of rooms perched on the side of the steep canyon wall overlooking the ocean at Santa Monica. They were to live there together for the rest of Isherwood's life. After a late summer trip to Europe, they moved in on September 30.

Isherwood made another important commitment during this water-shed year, 1959. He took up teaching at Los Angeles State College. For the man who had deliberately ruined his promising career at Cambridge in order to free himself from his mother's ambition that he become a university don, this was a remarkable development. And it marks, perhaps more than anything else, the final conclusion to his rebellious youth and the end of his need to run away from himself. He was now prepared to accept a place among the figures of the Establishment, and to undertake a relationship to the young that was entirely different from the romantic and fatherly bond he had shared outside society and in defiance of society with the many boys who had, in a sense, led up to and culminated in Don Bachardy. As a teacher, Isherwood adopted a formal, institutionalized role which required that he address youth as a group and within a thoroughly conventional framework.

All this presumed he had something he could teach the young, and anxieties attended his new stature. These were different from, but closely associated with his anxieties about being responsible for Bachardy. Around the time that he took up his first teaching post, Isherwood recorded in his diaries a number of dreams that reflect his fear of failing to come up to his public reputation. The dreams mingle his feelings about himself in several related roles—as traveller, writer, collaborator with the increasingly celebrated genius, Auden, and also as companion to Bachardy. On November 26, 1959, he wrote:

> A dream last night.
>
> Don and I were leaving on a journey. Our hosts (presumably) were seeing us off. I said to them, "One of my mottoes in life is: Always visit the outlying islands. It's amazing the people you find living there. And the others always try to discourage you from going. They say: There's nothing on it but sheep."
>
> The feel of this dream wasn't good. I was too pleased with myself. I was showing off. Because the truth was, I knew that I *hadn't* visited the outlying islands. Or only very seldom.

This dream seems to refer in particular to the "Ambrose" episode which Isherwood was writing at the time for *Down There on a Visit*; "Ambrose" takes place on a Greek island, and Isherwood both as author and in the persona of narrator was laying claim to a special knowledge of the rather exotic personalities in the tale, notably Ambrose himself. In a way, the ironically self-deprecating title he eventually chose for the book, *Down There on a Visit*, successfully responds to the anxieties expressed in his dream by making fun of his status as a mere tourist.

On January 13, just after the end of his first semester (with his characteristically revealing psychosomatic propensity, he had lost his voice during the final class), he recorded another dream:

> A dream, the night before last: Auden and I were talking—apparently after a lecture. (Don was present, too, but played no part.) Wystan and I were in great spirits, laughing. I said, "When you talked about the future, I thought you'd give the whole show away." "No—" said Wystan, "they didn't notice anything. I knew they wouldn't—" (Obviously he was referring to the audience.) Then I laughed some more, and kicked at a long electric light cord that lay on the floor. (In my workroom, here?) "My god," I said, "why don't we drop this whole farce?"
>
> Now the amazing thing about this dream is this: I am sure that in the dream, Wystan and I were dead—but no one knew it.

All those years ago, when he had first arrived in New York, Isherwood had disbelieved in himself as a public personality, and so, from his own point of view, he had felt he failed while Auden succeeded. But now those famed young writers of the 1930s—who did frequently lecture together—were indeed long dead, and a new Christopher Isherwood had come into being. The new Christopher Isherwood is keenly aware, as Isherwood in his diaries always emphasized he was aware, of a disparity between his public reputation and his private doubts about his talent and achievements; moreover, the material of the dream implies Isherwood's suspicion that being in the company of Auden had partly sustained his own reputation and might always continue to do so. The light cord on the floor, which he so unconcernedly kicks, seems to represent the possibility that the dreamer could, in the punning symbolism of dreams, pull the plug and expose the "truth" about their friendship and respective achievements. And the fact that the cord might be in his own workroom seems to refer to the way in which Isherwood's work, his novels, are the means by which he might do this. (He had already told the story of his friendship with Auden and others in *Lions and Shadows*, but forty years later he was to expose this version as not really true to life when he wrote his next, "truer" piece of autobiography, *Christopher and His Kind*, in which he was able to describe the homosexual dimension of his friendship with Auden and others and also to describe the uncertainties and difficulties which persistently circumscribed his writing.) But perhaps the most important thing about the dream is that both Isherwood and Auden were laughing. After a semester's worth of teaching, Isherwood had begun to feel lighthearted about these old insecurities. They were becoming objectified and emerging from a place of repression in the form of dreams because he was in fact discarding them. He had outgrown them at last.

Isherwood was a success as a teacher, and other teaching jobs were to follow over the coming years. Although he still found aspects of institutional life tedious and frustrating, he found acceptance and formal recognition gratifying. On February 17, 1960 he wrote in his diary:

> The people at the L.A. State College library, without saying a word to me in advance, have made an exhibit: "Christopher Isherwood—Man of Letters," with the foreign translations of my books which I gave them, plus newspaper articles, etc. etc. I was really touched and pleased and surprised.

And then on May 30, 1960 he wrote something even more important:

> On the 24th they had a "reception" for me at State College. . . . The president shook my hand and told me, "You're the kind of person we want here." How often I have been told the opposite! He gave me a printed testimonial and we were photographed as it changed hands.

Teaching provided Isherwood with a source of steady income that, unlike film work, did not interfere with his writing. But, more importantly, the persona of himself as a teacher is the one that he eventually found he could write about. Just as the community of his colleagues found him entirely acceptable, he also found himself entirely acceptable. In his next novel, *A Single Man*, written in 1963, he was to bring long-hidden aspects of his own character and personality out into the open—including his homosexuality—in the figure of George, the middle-aged Englishman and professor of literature. This role offered Isherwood respectability and accountability and required no further justification of himself to society. By the time he wrote the book, Isherwood seems to have been remarkably at ease with the idea of himself as a professor.

Meanwhile, in 1960, Charles Laughton asked Isherwood to help him write a play about Socrates in which Laughton could star, and this began another collaborative friendship, which lasted until Laughton's death in 1962, when Isherwood finally abandoned the project. Isherwood steamed onward with *Down There on a Visit*, now writing the "Waldemar" section, about the Munich crisis and based on his relationship with Heinz Neddermeyer and with other friends he knew in Berlin and London during the 1930s. He still toyed with titles, calling the novel *The Others* from about February 1960 and then by June reverting once again to *The Lost*. In May he accepted a new teaching post, at the University of California at Santa Barbara, reaffirming his commitment to his new role. In June his mother died. He was deeply affected by this, sadder than might have been expected from someone who had so outspokenly rebelled against and criticized his mother from so young an age. Still, he pressed on with his book, finishing the last section, "Paul," about his friendship during the war with Denny Fouts. By August 1960, he was drafting a frame for the novel. That same year saw the publication of his anthology, *Great English Short Stories*. *Down There on a Visit* eventually appeared in 1962.

Don Bachardy was also growing up. He had completed his education at UCLA and at the Chouinard Art Institute, and he was now intermittently obtaining professional drawing assignments. The years to come would bring profound conflict in Isherwood's relationship with him, as Bachardy struggled to establish his own independent identity, as an artist and as a man. Ultimately the conflict would be resolved, but not without great pain and difficulty and a tremendous effort of love, something of which Isherwood was at last genuinely capable. There would be more books, more plays and screenplays, more trips with Bachardy, and also more operations and ill health as Isherwood grew older. Isherwood's next novel, *A Single Man*, draws obviously and significantly on experiences described in the diaries up to 1960, but also upon Isherwood's life after that date and upon the process of aging and the challenge of continuing in his mature identity—no longer a renegade English writer, but now a permanent member of a community in which he wished openly to co-exist with others like and unlike himself. Christopher Isherwood the narrator figure quietly reporting from the edge of the picture was no more; the new Isherwood was to make increasingly clear to his readers who and what he really was. The work of the remainder of Isherwood's career was not to be about the doomed, the marginalized, and the lost; it was, in general, to be about the discovered, the invited, the admitted, the found.

Textual Note

In editing these diaries, I have used American style throughout because this was the style that Isherwood himself gradually began to adopt as soon as he arrived in America. English spellings largely disappeared from his diaries by the end of his first decade in California, and I have altered anomalies in accordance with this general trend. However, I have retained idiosyncrasies of phrasing, even some which are notably English, so that Isherwood's characteristic voice might resound in his work. A few English idioms which might read as typos to Americans are altered using square brackets. Otherwise, square brackets are generally reserved for information that I have added to the text, such as surnames or parts of titles abbreviated by Isherwood and for alterations and deletions made to preserve the privacy of individuals still living. In the remarkably small number of instances where Isherwood made what appear to be errors or omissions, I have made minor corrections for the sake of clarity. I have also spelled out a great many names and other abbreviations which I believe he himself would have spelled out for publication. Only occasionally have I marked a correction with square brackets or a footnote, and these instances should explain themselves. In the 1939–1944 diaries, and in the 1945–1949 outline, a slight indent marks material Isherwood wrote and added later than the dates of the diary entries themselves.

Readers will find supplemental information provided in several ways. Footnotes explain passing historical references, identify people who appear only once or possibly twice in the diaries, offer translations of foreign passages, gloss slang, explain allusions to Isherwood's or other people's work in progress, give references to books of significant interest to Isherwood, occasionally provide information essential for making sense of jokes or witticisms, and so forth. For people, events, terms, organizations and other things which appear more than once or twice, or which were of long-term importance to Isherwood, and for explanations too long to fit conveniently into a footnote, I have provided a glossary at the end of this volume. The glossary gives general biographical information about many of Isherwood's friends and acquaintances and also offers details of particular relevance to Isherwood and to what he recorded in his diaries. A few very famous people—Greta Garbo, Charlie Chaplin—do not appear in the glossary because although Isherwood knew them quite well, he knew them essentially in their capacity as celebrities. There are any number of other famous or highly accomplished people whom he knew as intimate friends, and readers who already know, for example, Igor Stravinsky's work or Aldous Huxley's, may find some quite familiar material in the relevant glossary entries, but they also will probably find some lesser known facts and observations which pertain to or explain particular passages in the diaries and whose importance will become clear at different points in Isherwood's text. (The direction "see Glossary," which sometimes appears in a footnote, occurs only if the footnote itself gives enough information to prevent readers from recognizing that there is still more information at the back of the book. Readers who do not find what they want to know in a footnote must generally seek out the glossary on their own.) Isherwood has audiences of widely varied ages, interests and backgrounds all over the world, and ideally his diaries should be equally accessible to every one of them, including those who may now be reading his work for the first time. Wherever Isherwood himself fully explains in the text the appearance of a new friend, acquaintance or colleague, I have not included such a person in the glossary unless he or she reappears sufficiently further on in time that readers may then wish to be reminded who the person is. In such cases, some of the material in the glossary is in fact derived from Isherwood's text and serves as a kind of cross-reference to it. Since Isherwood himself revised and polished the first part of these diaries, 1939–1944, and even added passages of explanatory narrative to his diary entries, there are a number of significant personalities from these early years who are not included in the glossary because Isherwood introduced them adequately himself. In the later parts of the book it is more usual for people to appear unannounced, as it were, and readers may wish to refer more frequently to both footnotes and glossary. A few names have been changed, again to preserve the privacy of the living, and these are indicated either in the glossary or in a footnote.

All the Hindu terms mentioned in the text are explained in the glossary in accordance with the way these terms are understood and used in Vedanta. Readers will also find in the glossary brief explanations of a few international political events to which Isherwood refers. The events of World War II, though, are generally not included in the glossary partly because they are more widely familiar and partly because it would have been practically impossible to do this. Instead, many of the main events of the war—particularly those Isherwood wrote about in his fiction as well as in his diaries—are mentioned in the chronology, which appears just before the glossary at the back of the book. The chronology gives a skeleton outline of Isherwood's whole life, but concentrates especially on the years leading up to and described in his diaries for 1939–1960.

The material in this book was written over a period of more than twenty years, and naturally Isherwood's life, interests and friends changed a great deal during this time. Many readers will probably notice and enjoy the changing texture and discontinuities of the diaries; apart from settling on American style, I have done little to minimize these characteristics. I have aimed to enable readers to approach the text on its own terms by supplying them with information readily in the minds of Isherwood or his friends at the time that Isherwood was writing the diary entries. In any book of this size there are many details which do not fit systematically into even the most flexible of structures, but I hope that my arrangement of the supplemental materials will be consistent enough that readers can find help when they want or require it.

Acknowledgements

The list of people who have helped me prepare this book is staggeringly long, and the debt I owe to some of them is immense. At the top of the list is Don Bachardy, who asked me to edit the diaries and then helped me with such patience and care that I wondered how and why he had not done the job himself. Obviously his knowledge of Isherwood's life is unrivalled, but his knowledge of the movies is nearly as complete; I benefitted from both areas of expertise again and again, and have felt it a continual privilege to work with him. Numerous people who appear in the diaries have answered questions about themselves and others for Don Bachardy and for me; I would like to thank Alice and Peter Gowland, Evelyn Hooker, Gavin Lambert, Dan Luckenbill, Ben Masselink, Ivan Moffat, the late Stephen Spender, Edward Upward, Peter Viertel, and especially Swami Vidyatmananda who has generously read and commented on most of the material in this book.

For help with individual queries relating to their particular areas of interest, knowledge or expertise, I would like to thank Monique Beudert; The Viscount Boyd; David Bradshaw; Helen Brunner-Spira; Elizabeth Carmichael, Curator of the Latin American Collection at the Museum of Mankind; Colin Clark; John V. Cody; Alison Falby; Flora Fraser; Philip Hurst; Dr. Abbas Kelidas; Mr. Roger Marwood; Harold E. Masback III; Ian Patterson; Emeritus Professor John Postgate FRS; Andreas Reyneke; Dr. Jonathan E. Rhoads; Ian Rod; James Taylor of the Imperial War Museum; Margaret Bradham Thornton; and Joan Weeks, Public Affairs Specialist at the Library of Congress, Washington, D.C. Sally Brown, Curator of Modern Literary Manuscripts at the British Library, gave me special assistance with Isherwood's manuscripts and typescripts, and also at the British Library many members of the Reading Room staff repeatedly furthered my research.

Some friends can always be relied on for help, and I am once again grateful to John Fuller, Nicholas Jenkins, Richard Davenport-Hines, and, in particular, Christopher Phipps for tracking down information for me. I am especially grateful to Edward Mendelson for engaging in so many discussions with me and also for reading several parts of this book in typescript and offering his usual demanding observations. Peter Parker, Isherwood's biographer, has been generous and forbearing, not only in the tact with which he has awaited the completion of this volume but also in the tact with which he has commented on nearly everything I have done in it with Isherwood's text; he has also shared his chronology with me. Christopher Potter has also worked particularly hard to make a contribution to this book. A number of friends and acquaintances gave valuable time translating and identifying texts: Francis Lamport, David Luke, Axel Neubohn, and above all Thomas Braun of Merton College, Oxford.

Somehow or other, various members of my own family knew things I have never known, and they have at last shared them with me so that I could use them in this book. I would like to thank Lucy Bucknell, Dr. Edward Carter, Louise Carter, George E. B. Maguire, J. Robert Maguire, Dr. Pauline T. Maguire, and Dr. Frank Reilly. I would also like to thank, from the bottom of my heart, my husband, J. Robert Maguire, Jr., my children Bobby and Lucy Maguire, and Sally Whitaker and Alison Lovegrove.

I have had very strong support throughout this project from Caroline Dawnay, and I would like to thank a number of hardworking editors who became more and more involved in this book as it neared completion, Mary Chamberlain, Michael Earley, and Douglas Matthews. I would also like to thank Helena Beynon, Harvey Starte, Jim Fox, Michael di Capua, and above all, Geoffrey Strachan, who seems to have understood and cared deeply about every nuance in this volume and many nuances that are not in it.

The Emigration
1939–1944

January 19, 1939–December 31, 1944

The first part of this book is based upon a series of diaries which I kept, rather irregularly, during the years 1939–1944. In the summer and fall of 1946 I worked right through them, often revising or expanding the entries and writing bridge passages of narrative to fill in the gaps. A row of dots after an entry usually indicates where the diary leaves off and a bit of explanatory narrative begins. [Sometimes short passages of explanatory narrative appear in parentheses.]

On January 19, 1939, Auden and I sailed from Southampton in the French liner *Champlain*, bound for New York. It was the first anniversary of our trip to China. I am always on the lookout for coincidences in dates, and I remember that this one flattered my vaguely optimistic belief that my life was somehow running to schedule.

Certainly, at that time, I had every reason to believe in the favorable aspect of my star. This post-Munich winter was the height of my little London success. I lectured, I broadcast, I was welcome at parties. I had plenty of pocket money. The Chinese travel book[1] was finished. I was running an agreeable love affair in which the other partner was more deeply involved than myself, and I kept a second, third and fourth choice waiting on the sidelines in case I got bored. In public, I was carefully modest about all this. In private, to my intimate friends, I boasted, with a vulgarity that still makes me squirm as I write these lines. Auden, particularly, disliked my attitude; it hurt him because he was really fond of me. But I suppose it somehow intrigued him, too—because he once told me, almost admiringly, that I was the cruellest and most unscrupulous person he had ever met. Edward Upward, now only

[1] *Journey to a War*, with Auden.

an occasional visitor, didn't say much. Something was broken between us. I couldn't meet his faintly ironical eye. When we were together, I covered my embarrassment with an awkward heartiness.

I think we all sensed that this was a long goodbye. M.[1] cried when I left, I cried, Jacky [Hewit] cried in the taxi to the station and gave me a keepsake, his first champagne cork. Forster, who had come to see us off, asked me: "Shall I join the communist party?" I forget what I answered. I think it was "No." At any rate, the question was oracular. The departing and the dying are credited with a kind of psychic wisdom.

As the train pulled out, there was a nasty sharp wrench, and then, as always when I am the traveler, a quick upsurge of guilty relief. Auden and I exchanged grins—grins which took us back, in an instant, to the earliest days of our friendship. Suddenly, we were twelve and nine years old. "Well," I said, "we're off again." "Goody," said Auden.

Why were we going to America? I suppose, for myself, the chief reason was that I couldn't stop travelling. The mechanism had been set going during those years of wandering around Europe with Heinz [Neddermeyer]. I was also running away from myself: that was why I never stayed anywhere long. I could remain in Portugal, for example, as long as I could believe in an objective Portugal. But, sooner or later, Portugal would dissolve and reveal itself as the all-too-familiar, subjective "Isherwood Portugal." Then I fled in disgust.

America was obviously the next place on the list. I'd had a brief, false, hysterical glimpse of New York the previous summer, under the guidance of George Davis, who has a genius for melodramatic showmanship. We shot up and down skyscrapers, in and out of parties and brothels, saw a fight in a Bowery dive, heard Maxine Sullivan sing in Harlem,[2] went to Coney Island on July the Fourth, met Maxwell Anderson,[3] Muriel Draper[4] and Orson Welles, drank all day long and took Seconal every night to make us sleep. I came back to England raving about Manhattan, and convinced, like every tourist, that New York is the United States.

Looking forward to our life there, I imagined a milieu in which my London "personality" would function more freely, more cynically, more successfully than ever. I saw myself as a natural

[1] Mummy; see Glossary under M. and under Isherwood, Kathleen Bradshaw.
[2] Black jazz singer, appearing at the Onyx Club.
[3] American playwright and journalist.
[4] Writer on dance and literary hostess.

citizen of the go-getters' homeland. Oh, I'd talk faster and louder than any of them, I'd learn the slang and the accent, I'd adapt like an Arctic fox. Before long, I'd be writing the great American novel. I was very sure of myself.

The possibility of war, that familiar, six-year-old shadow in the background, had less to do with my emigration than any of my critics will ever believe. At the beginning of 1939, I had honestly begun to think that the crisis had passed over, or had, at any rate, been indefinitely postponed. Even Dr. Katz, that Cassandra of the thirties, had predicted, for the first time, that there would be no war this year. It wasn't until March that the situation began to look really hopeless.

If I were writing a novel—trying, that is to say, to persuade a reader that I was telling him something psychologically plausible—I should have great difficulty at this point. Because now I have to describe a state of mind which introduces a new period in my life.

To put it as simply as possible, for the sake of making a start: while I was on board the *Champlain*, I realized that I was a pacifist.

Maybe it would be more exact to say: I realized that I had always been a pacifist. At any rate, in the negative sense. How could I have ever imagined I was anything else? My earliest remembered feelings of rebellion were against the British army, of which my mother and myself were camp followers, and against the staff of St. Edmund's School, who tried to make me believe in a falsified and sentimentalized view of the 1914 war. My father taught me, by his life and death, to hate the profession of soldiering. I remember his telling me, before he left for France, that an officer's sword is useless except for toasting bread, and that he never fired his revolver because he couldn't hit anything with it, and hated the bang. I came to adore my father's memory, dwelling always upon his civilian virtues, his gentleness, his humor, his musical and artistic talent. Growing up in the postwar world, I learnt—from my history master, from Noël Coward, from Wilfred Owen and Siegfried Sassoon—to loathe the old men who had made the war. Flags, memorials and uniforms made me tremble with rage, because they filled me with terror. I was horribly scared by "war," and therefore secretly attracted to it. I've been into all this at great length in *Lions and Shadows*. No need to repeat it here.

However, these neurotic fears were greatly reduced by our trip to China. True, it wasn't really very dangerous; I think there were only three or four occasions on which we were likely to have been killed by bombs or bullets. But a very little danger will go a long way psychologically. Several times I had been afraid, but healthily afraid. I no longer dreaded the unknown, or feared that I should behave worse than other people. When we were back in England and the Munich crisis began, I was frightened, of course, but I didn't get frantic. I even stayed on in London out of curiosity; I didn't want to miss the first air raid.

Before China, my pacifism was so entangled with cowardice that I could never examine it at all. After China, it was only a matter of time before I should stop repeating slogans and borrowed opinions and start to think for myself. Thinking was impossible as long as I was playing the returned hero, and exploiting it sexually. Thinking was impossible as long as I was lecturing on the Sino-Japanese war and appealing for aid to Chiang Kai-shek. Thinking was impossible during Munich. But the post-Munich hangover brought on the cold, meditative fit, and this boat trip provided the opportunity. A voyage, in this respect, resembles an illness. Time ceases to itch and distract us. We can pause and take stock of our position.

One morning on deck, it seems to me, I turned to Auden and said: "You know, I just don't believe in any of it any more—the united front, the party line, the antifascist struggle. I suppose they're okay, but something's wrong with me. I simply can't swallow another mouthful." And Auden answered: "No, neither can I."

Those were not our words, but psychologically it was as simple as that. It sounds incredible, but Auden's agreement took me completely by surprise. It appears that, since China, we had been living in such a rush that we had never been able to get in five minutes' quiet, sincere conversation—even when alone together. We had merely shouted to each other from two parallel, racing express trains. Auden is always cagey, anyway. Sometimes, when I'm talking, that furrow appears between his eyes, his mouth begins to twitch, and I know he's bothered about something; but he'll only disagree with me in public when the subject we're discussing isn't important to him at all.

Now, in a few sentences, with exquisite relief, we confessed our mutual disgust at the parts we had been playing and resolved to abandon them, then and there. We had forgotten our real vocation. We would be artists again, with our own values, our own integrity, and not amateur socialist agitators, parlor reds.

That was about as far as we went, for the present. Auden, however, had his Anglo-Catholicism to fall back on. Unwillingly, he had denied it, all these years. Now he could admit to it again. I had nothing of this kind, and I didn't yet clearly realize how much

I was going to need it. For myself, the positive part of the change consisted in putting my emotions back from a political onto a personal basis. Edward had always said, quite rightly, that my mind was unfitted for abstract ideas; it could only grasp concrete examples, special instances. Anti-Nazism had been possible for me as long as Nazism meant Hitler, Goering and Goebbels, the Gestapo, and the consuls and spies who potentially menaced Heinz on his travels. But now Heinz was caught. He had become, however unwillingly, a part of the Nazi machine, at work in a Berlin factory. Now Werner was helping to build the Siegfried line,[1] and dozens of boys I had known were in the German army.

Suppose I have in my power an army of six million men. I can destroy it by pressing an electric button. The six millionth man is Heinz. Will I press the button? Of course not—even if the 5,999,999 others are hundred per cent Jew-baiting blood-mad fiends (which is absurd). This attitude, which might be called the extreme Sodom and Gomorrha position, where only one Lot is required to save the Cities of the Plain, may be contrasted with the equally violent radicalism of some good democrats of the period, who declared that Hitler was responsible for every crime and that the German people were innocent lambs, and were nevertheless ready to burn down the Just City for the horrible sake of one little sodomite.

Both Auden and I felt it was our duty to tell our friends what had happened. We wrote to most of them, soon after our arrival in New York. M. accepted the change, and I think it pleased her—though she could never quite agree. John Lehmann wrote that he was "puzzled," but this didn't make him hostile, and he has been a faithful friend ever since. Edward, a good while later, sent me two letters, the first disgusted, the second a model of charity towards an attitude one can't understand. Olive [Mangeot], after much bewilderment, remembered only that we cared for each other— like the marvellous woman she is. Forster was greatly interested, and perhaps somewhat influenced. Stephen [Spender] made a typically subtle comment: "I rather envy you."

The voyage was stormy. The *Champlain* seemed very small, slithering down the long grey Atlantic slopes, under a heavy sky. One night I was sick—breaking my round-the-world record. Wrapped in rugs, like invalids, we sipped bouillon, or watched movies in the saloon, where French tapestries flapped out from the creaking, straining walls. We were bored, and amused ourselves by helping with the puppet show in the children's playroom,

[1] Possibly Werner von Alvensleben; see Glossary.

improvising Franco-English dialogue full of private jokes and double entendres. Off the coast of Newfoundland, we ran into a blizzard. The ship entered New York harbor looking like a wedding cake.

Erika and Klaus Mann were the first to welcome us. They had come out to the ship on the quarantine launch, posing as journalists who wanted our interview. Erika was nervous and ill. She kept coughing. Klaus was full of gaiety and gossip. As we came ashore, I looked around for Vernon [Old], whom I'd radioed from the *Champlain* to meet me. At first, I didn't recognize him among the crowd, his face was so pinched and scarlet with the cold. He had been waiting there for hours.

Somebody had recommended the George Washington Hotel as a place where we should feel "at home." And, indeed, our reception by Donald Neville-Willing was like arriving at the house of a maiden aunt. A short, stout, grey-haired figure, with a beaky nose, jingling keys and a roving eye, Donald ran the hotel, which specialized in Elks and women's clubs conventions, as though he were the Victorian housekeeper of an English ancestral mansion. He was proud of his double-barrelled name, and fervently patriotic. Although he had lived ten years in the United States, he still refused to take out his first papers. In his bedroom, he had signed pictures of the King and Queen, and a framed telegram from an equerry, thanking him for his loyal good wishes on some royal anniversary.

The discovery of some mutual "county" friends in Cheshire meant more to Donald than our dubious literary notoriety. We were respectable, and he couldn't do enough for us. Glasses of hot punch were sent up, free, to our rooms at night. Special prices were quoted on our weekly bills. The telephone frequently rang to summon us down to teas and evening parties in Donald's private sitting room. Donald had many theatrical connections. He introduced us to the English members of the cast of the Stokes Brothers' play *Oscar Wilde*, then running with great success at one of the Manhattan theaters. These actors were all staying at the hotel. One of them, a strikingly handsome boy who played Charlie Parker, tried, unsuccessfully, the effect of water waves in my hair. He was thirty, but looked eighteen, because Marie Tempest[1] had taught him the secret of perpetual youth—to go to bed every afternoon, except matinees, from two to four. I think his name was John Carroll, and I believe he was killed in the war.[2]

Donald not only accepted us, he accepted Vernon, also. It was at

[1] English actress and singer (1864–1942).
[2] Carroll was not killed in the war, but eventually gave up the stage because of a lung problem.

his suggestion that Vernon moved over to the hotel from a nearby rooming house. Donald tried to get Vernon a walking-on part in *The American Way*,[1] and, later, a job in Billy Rose's Aquacade. Vernon bought a pair of swimming trunks and practiced diving with a boy at the YMCA, but he wasn't good enough to pass the final test.

Vernon, at this time, was growing up very fast. His various interests, which I indulged as schoolboy crazes, were symptoms of a drive towards self-education. In the next five years, they produced extraordinary results. Auden and I laughed at his barbell exercises, but we offered nothing in their place. As for his drawing, it was a year before I took it seriously, and, by that time, he bitterly resented my lack of interest. It was like my mother's attitude to my writing, all over again. Even now, when we talk about his work, he often seems slightly on the defensive.

At that time, in any case—as the following extract from my diary will show—I was a most unsuitable companion for an eighteen-year-old boy. My conquering, confident mood had abruptly dissolved. I found I couldn't write a line. The European news, and the high costs of our living scared me. Day after day, I moped, a jelly of cowardice, indecision, defeat. We got plenty of invitations, of course; but it seemed to me that all these lunches, suppers and cocktail parties were being offered under false pretences, as far as I was concerned. They wanted to meet Christopher Isherwood. And who was I? A sham, a mirror image, nobody. To M. I wrote: "I believe I have come to the end of my talent." All this was very natural, of course, if I could only have realized it. I was merely going through a "change of life," and change is always uncomfortable.

March 18. Two months since we left England. Here we are—still at the George Washington. What has happened?

This time in New York has been a bad, sterile period for me. I've done practically nothing. Every day, I think: now I must get busy, now I must start work. But at what? My money—including the advance I got from [Bennett] Cerf—is rapidly running out. Wystan still has several hundred dollars, and the prospect of a teaching job, later on. I have no prospects. I don't even know what kind of job I want. My whole instinct is against teaching, or lecturing, or exploiting my reputation in any way. I would like some sort of regular, humble occupation. I got to know Berlin because I was doing something functional—the natural occupation for a poor foreigner—

[1] Kaufman and Hart's play.

teaching his own language. If I can't do something of the same kind here, I shall never get to know America. I shall never become a part of this city.

Meanwhile, as so often before, I am hypnotized by my own fears. Reading of Hitler's Czechoslovakian coup and his plans against Romania, I feel: After all, what's the use? In a week, or a month, I shall be for it. Wystan is determined to go back to England if war breaks out—and I shall go with him, I suppose. If I were alone, I mightn't. Quite aside from being scared, I am entirely disillusioned about the kind of war this is going to be. Just another struggle for world trade. But they are all over there—all my friends—and the impulse to join them is very strong.

Wystan himself is going through a curious phase. He's as energetic as I'm idle. He takes Benzedrine regularly, in small doses, followed by Seconal at night. He says that "the chemical life" solves all his problems. He writes a great deal—poems and articles and reviews—makes speeches, goes to tea parties and dinners, is quite brilliantly talkative. It's a little as if he and I had changed places. Wystan says, however, that he hates all this. But he's unwilling to return to England, because, there, he's the center of an even more intensive publicity.

There is much that is majestic but nothing that is gracious in this city—this huge, raw, functional skeleton, this fortress of capital, this jungle of absolutely free competition. Every street is partly a slum. Where the banks and the brownstone houses end, the slum tenements begin, with their rusty fire escapes and crowds of baseball-playing Dead End Kids.[1] Beyond, on the mainland, is a wilderness of scrapyards and shacks. This country is insanely untidy.

The Bronx is built almost entirely of billboards and monster advertisements, imploring you to relax. (As if anybody *could*—when every doorknob gives you an electric shock!) Take the advertisements away, and there would be nothing left; no town at all. At the lower end of the island, and uptown in Harlem, huge tribes of Italians, Negroes and Jews have pitched their foul, lively camps—at the feet of the skyscrapers which dominate their heaven like totem poles. Wystan and I call the skyscrapers "the fallen angels." You imagine them crashing down out of the sky, white-hot as meteors, to bury themselves deep in the Manhattan bedrock and slowly cool, through the ages. But the fallen angels are still angels. They are blasphemously insolvent, and utterly without pity. The young, ambitious man tries to climb them—having been told of a heaven at the top, called The

[1] Stars of the films of slum life—*Dead End* (1937, based on Sidney Kingsley's Broadway play), *Crime School* (1938), *Angels with Dirty Faces* (1938), and others.

Rainbow Room—and when he falls a little crowd collects, and stares. Nobody tries to help—or he might get into trouble with the insurance company. Then, down the street, come the screams of the police car and the clanging of the ambulance bell.

Vernon has been typing a poem of Wystan's with obstinate care, letter by letter. In the middle, he paused to ask me, very seriously, why people like Dickens.

Bennett Cerf, our publisher, and his uncle, who was an intimate friend of Hart Crane, took us to see *Hellzapoppin*.[1] They were rather shocked because we praised it so extravagantly—which shows how little they understand what made us write our plays.

A PEN Club dinner at the Algonquin Hotel. Dorothy Thompson presided,[2] in crimson velvet. I made a facetious speech, with jokes out of the *Reader's Digest*. When I sat down, Thompson said icily: "Delightful." Realized, too late, that we were being deadly serious. Wystan recited his poem on the death of Yeats.[3] A Polish poet recited a Polish poem on Abraham Lincoln. Nobody understood a word— until the last line:

"LINKOLL-NY! Linkoll-ny! *Leen-kool-ny!*" (Wild applause.)

First meeting with Lincoln Kirstein. I had taken one of Wystan's Benzedrine tablets, and the afternoon passed with an effect of terrific, smooth, effortless speed. Neither Lincoln nor I stopped talking for a single moment. We were intimates at once. Almost as soon as we had shaken hands, he began telling us about the American Civil War. He was breathless with it—as though Gettysburg had been fought yesterday.

George Platt Lynes, prematurely grey haired, with the arrogant profile of a late Roman coin, has photographed me peering out from behind a wooden property-pillar. Lincoln calls this picture "The rat with the nervous breakdown."

March 20. Last night, I had dinner with Lincoln, that somber, electric creature. In his blue pea jacket, he looks like a mad clipper captain out of Melville. His hair is cropped like a convict's, and his eyes, behind austere tin spectacles, seem to be examining you through a microscope. I call him Jean Valjean.[4]

We talked about war. Lincoln said he was certain he wouldn't be

[1] Olsen and Johnson's stage revue.
[2] American political journalist; the PEN (Poets, Essayists and Novelists) Club is for published authors.
[3] "In Memory of W. B. Yeats."
[4] The convict in Victor Hugo's *Les Misérables*.

killed. He thinks of himself as the average man. He'll always have the statistically usual number of accidents, illnesses, etc.

Later, his friend, Peter Martinez, came in, like the rare bird that nests for a moment in a tree in the garden, before flying away to the south. When it was time for Lincoln to drive me home, he asked Pete: "Shall you be here when I get back?" Pete looked up at him, almost sadly: "I *hope* so," he said, with his faint Mexican accent. Obviously, the matter was entirely beyond his control. He sometimes disappears for days.

Lincoln is so big that he has the air of protecting everybody, of holding up the world. He is like Gulliver among the Lilliputians. We seem to fascinate him. Lincoln regards Pete with painful, jealously affectionate intensity—like a savage who finds a tiny, brilliant bird in a wood, and stands holding it in his hand, uncertain what to do with it. Shall he eat it? Shall he worship it? Shall he simply let it fly away?

Pete alternates between a birdlike gaiety and a strange Mexican mournfulness. When he is sad, he seems to move far, far away from us, to sit huddled in his own private blanket, under an Aztec pyramid. Partly Spanish, partly Indian, he has very beautiful *old* manners. He moves with the compactness of a dancer; this makes him seem even smaller than he is. He has extraordinarily expressive eyelashes. All his gestures are graceful and comic. He is a walking parody of the ballet.

April 2. The day before yesterday, Wystan, Vernon and I moved into an apartment on East Eighty-first Street. Chamberlain announced England's support of the Poles. Yesterday, to forget it all, I went with Lincoln and Pete to Philadelphia, to see Orson Welles's *Five Kings*. At lunch, we got wonderfully drunk. We went to the Camac Turkish Baths, to sober up. The masseur slapped my face, as hard as he could, Pete says, but I only grinned. Then he threw me into the ice-cold plunge, where I sank like a stone and had to be fished out. We arrived late for the peformance, which was no loss. The stage revolved faster and faster, with the characters scrambling over it, in frantic pursuit of the play. They never caught up. The only really enjoyable day I've spent in America, so far. . . .

Eighty-first Street is on the edge of Yorkville, which, in those days, was a predominantly Nazi quarter. There were Nazi Bierkeller, Nazi bookshops, and Nazi films showing in several of the theaters. Our apartment was on the top floor of a made-over slum house. A lady named Mrs. Lowndes had furnished it with valuable knickknacks which I felt sure we should break. There was a hall with a marble-topped table, at which we ate, a big living room, a bedroom for Auden, a bedroom for Vernon and myself, and a little room which Auden used as a study, and which was soon ankle-deep in crumpled manuscripts and letters. In order to ignore her squalid neighbors, Mrs. Lowndes had covered the living room windows with heavy drapes and shades which wouldn't pull up—so that the electric light had to be kept burning all day—an arrangement thoroughly agreeable to Auden, with his womb fixation, and hateful to me. If you did look out, it was into backyards, planted with giant poles as high as masts, supporting innumerable clothes lines. On laundry days, it was really beautiful—like a harbor full of sailing ships.

Auden loved the apartment—partly because it had an English fireplace on which you could burn coal and logs; partly because we now had a colored cook of our own and could enjoy what he called "civilized meals." The cook's name was Elizabeth. She was enormous and cheerful, and her specialty was fried chicken.

We hadn't been in the place very long before we discovered that it was haunted. I forget which of us noticed it first, but we all had to agree—the footsteps were as loud as life. I'd be in the living room or my bedroom—it might be at night or in the middle of the day—and hear them distinctly, climbing the stairs, reaching the door of the apartment, passing into the hall, pausing, as if to look for mail, then going into one of the other rooms. They fooled me every time. "Vernon? Wystan?" I'd call. No answer. Then I'd look around and find the apartment empty.

We decided not to tell Elizabeth, fearing that she'd get scared and walk out on us. But she found out, somehow. One day, when I went into the kitchen, she told me grinning: "Ah'm jest sittin' aroun' waitin' fer that ole ghos'." About a week later, she claimed that "something" had actually passed through the room, behind her chair: "But ah didn' turn 'roun', because ah thought ah mightn' like what ah saw."

A small group of actors produced *The Ascent of F6* [1] in a studio in the Village. Their director was a boy named Forrest Thayr. No scenery was used. The mountain climbing was done on a staircase which led to a gallery at the back of the room—most of it in darkness, with electric flash-lamps. Thayr used one very clever trick. Lamp, offstage, is in danger of being trapped by an avalanche. The other players, watching him, shout futile warnings, louder and louder, more and more desperately. Then, suddenly, a door slams, with terrific force. Dead silence. You had the impression of final, irrevocable disaster.

[1] Auden and Isherwood's 1936 play.

Burgess Meredith[1] was interested in the play, and might have done it in summer stock, if it hadn't been for the war. He was a nice man, with a blotchy red face, always friendly and usually drunk.

The European crisis hung over us, all that spring, like a thunderstorm which won't burst. I alternated between manic flares of excitement—usually when drunk at Lincoln's—and fits of almost insane depression, in which I refused even to answer the telephone. One Sunday afternoon, a newsboy came down our street yelling, "War! War! War!" We raced downstairs for the paper. It was merely an interview with some American general who had said that there *might* be war within forty-eight hours.

Meanwhile, Vernon and I were planning a trip to California. For a long time, I'd wanted to get away from New York and into the "real" America. The real America, for me, was the Far West. All my daydreams were based on D. H. Lawrence's *St. Mawr*. But I knew that I should only be able to see America through the eyes of an American, and Vernon was the only portable American within reach. Vernon had run away from home at the age of fourteen and hitchhiked to Texas; this made him seem a specially suitable traveling companion. At first, we thought we'd hitchhike this time, too; but someone persuaded us that America is best seen from a bus.

Also, I wanted to talk to Gerald Heard. Gerald, Chris Wood and the Huxleys had gone to California some years previously and settled there. We often joked about them, and the mysterious practices which we vaguely described as yoga. We pictured Gerald levitating in a turban and floating out over the desert, at a great altitude. Nevertheless, I still took him seriously—at any rate as a pacifist. We exchanged letters. Gerald wrote that every pacifist should acquire medical knowledge. Order and creative accuracy must be opposed to disorder and destruction. We must create a doctorate of psychologically sound, well-equipped healers. This sounded authoritative and exciting—if rather vague. I had to know more about it. Certainly, my own life badly needed some kind of discipline. I was still suspicious of the occult, however, and hated anything which sounded like "religion."

Pacifism was also the basis of my newly formed friendship with John van Druten. I met him, for the first time, at the Gotham Hotel, where he was recovering from an operation on his arm. He was easy and funny and charming, very much in his theatrical element. Ruth Chatterton, the actress, came in. John told her he had started on the new play (*Leave Her to Heaven*) in which she was

---

[1] American actor and director; "Prince Hal" in Welles's *Five Kings*.

to star. I have never seen anyone put on such an act. "*Johnny*—!"
she tearfully, joyfully gasped, "Oh—Johnny, *darling*! Oh—I'm so
glad!" John handled her perfectly—he was cool and pleasant,
submitting to her kisses without a sign of disgust. I admired him as
one admires an expert animal trainer.

After some discussion, John and I formulated the following
questions, and John sent them to Rudolf Messel, Runham Brown
(secretary of the War Resisters' International) and George Lansbury.[1] They were:

1. What is a pacifist to do in wartime (apart from merely
   refusing to fight) and what activities are permissible to him,
   by way of defence or otherwise, if he is (a) in England, or (b)
   in a noncombatant country?
2. What permissible alternative is there to war in opposing an
   aggressor whose pledge cannot be relied upon?
3. If none, does one open all doors to the aggressor and let him
   take everything he wants?

Brown began his reply by saying that a pacifist should at all times
try to be a useful member of society, doing his job as well as he can.
In wartime, he should work harder than ever. He should do relief
work, but not under governmental auspices, and not as an
alternative to military service. He should practice civil disobedi-
ence to the aggressor, no matter what the consequences.

Messel was rather more militant. He wanted the pacifist to
sabotage the war machine. He felt that one probably shouldn't take
part in ambulance drill—in order that people might ask you why
you weren't doing so, and thus give you a chance to answer. He
thought it was important for the pacifist to be in England when war
broke out, to be able to demonstrate with the maximum effect. He
wanted total disarmament—unilateral, if necessary. He hoped the
war would turn into a revolution—"I just couldn't miss that." He
thought we should let the aggressor into the country, because a
bloodless victory wouldn't be an advertisement for fascism,
anyway. The pacifist, he concluded, should take no part in defence
schemes, since defence is impossible anyway. If people realize that
it is hopeless, they won't start a war in the first place.

Lansbury wrote that he agreed with Brown's replies. He added:

When the sun is shining the world is fairly easy to live in; when
the clouds are very heavy and thick, we always find it difficult to
think as brightly and clearly as in the other days. So you, like

---

[1] Prominent British pacifists; see Glossary.

many others, find it extremely difficult to realise your idealism in the midst of the kind of world in which we are living. All the same, comrade, whatever was true yesterday, is true today. Conditions may alter tactics, but they can never alter facts, and the fact is that war never has, never can and never will settle anything. If you and millions of other young men of all nationalities are once more thrown into this hell of war, nothing will come out of it but more and more confusion. Even though you, or I, or anyone else can show you an immediate way out, the fact that I have already stated still remains true. But this other thing is true, our way of passive resistance has never yet been tried out, but war has been tried through all the centuries and has absolutely failed.

Both John and I were more or less satisfied with these replies. Later, John changed his attitude, as Auden did, and provisionally supported the war. More about that, later.

Vernon and I were now ready to leave. We had very little money. Even if I got the offer of a movie job in Hollywood, I shouldn't be able to take it until I had a quota visa and became a permanent resident.[1] There would be all sorts of formalities to go through, first. In fact, the future seemed to be so full of difficulties that I preferred not to think about it, and just hope for the best.

May 6. Vernon and I left New York by Greyhound bus at 7:45 in the morning. The buses are built like streamlined Martian projectiles; they seem designed to destroy everything else on the road. When a new driver comes on board, he brings his nameplate with him, and hangs it up in view of the passengers. "N. Strauser. Safe. Reliable. Courteous."

Out through the Holland Tunnel, Jersey City, Newark. The Pulaski Skyway lifts you across the flat brown marshes and drops you into a country of factories, pylons, transformers, gas stations, hot-dog stands, tourist cabins (seventy-five cents to a dollar), used tire dumps, milk bars, cemeteries for automobiles or men. The stream of traffic is so swift that it is dangerous to swerve or stop. The road has eaten the landscape. Travel has defeated itself. You can drive at eighty miles an hour and never get anywhere. Any part of the road is like all other parts.

"Folks," says the driver, "the next comfort stop is Wilmington. You'll have fifteen minutes." Everybody must get out while we take

---

[1] A large number of immigrants were permitted annually from the U.K.; see Glossary under quota visa.

in gas. The first rush is to the toilets, where an old man tells us indignantly that the rear seats are hard on the kidneys. Then we line the counter for hot dogs, milk, Coca-Cola.

We cross the Maryland state line. The country begins to come alive. A little town with a leafy street of frame houses. The minister sitting on his porch under a sign which says "Marriage Licences," waiting, like the other tradesmen, for business. The war memorial has two separate columns of names—the white and the colored dead.

We got to Washington at 4:30. We shall stay here several days.

May 9. There is something charming, and even touching, about this city. For the size of the country it represents, it is absurdly small. The capital of a nation of shrewd, conservative farmers. Everything has to be made of solid marble. The public buildings are covered with quotations from the family bible—some of them, apparently, chosen quite at random. "The desert shall blossom like a rose" is engraved above the portal of the Union Station. The town is terribly conscious of its dignity.

The Potomac River curves around the city, through the moist, nostalgic woods of Virginia. Mount Vernon overlooks it—a grave white wooden house with frugal pillars and severe four-poster beds, in a formal garden; it suggests a furtive homesickness for tyrannical England. It must have been strange, in the eighteenth century, to sit among the English teacups and look out of these windows, feeling, at your back, the immense, savage, unexplored continent. Lee's home at Arlington is grander and more self-assured. The columns of its portico are thicker—as though civilization had now taken a firmer root.

Vernon has gone on an all-milk diet for the remainder of the trip. This seems to give him the energy of a demon. He loves the heat, which is humid and overpowering, and never tires of sightseeing— the White House, the Capitol, the Lincoln Memorial, the Washington Monument, the Supreme Court, the Smithsonian Institute, the Catholic Monastery, the Library of Congress (with that incredible series of frescoes called *The Poets' Boys*[1]). At the Bureau of Engraving and Printing we bought (for Lincoln Kirstein) a head of Abraham Lincoln made of old dollar bills.

We had a letter of introduction to Senator Frederick Hale, of Maine. A dried-up little reactionary, violently anti-Roosevelt. He has been a senator for twenty years and boasts that he has never

---

[1] H. O. Walker's depiction, in the Great Hall, of Shakespeare's Adonis, Milton's Comus, Wordworth's Boy of Winander, Tennyson's Ganymede, Keats's Endymion and Emerson's Uriel.

changed his opinions. He gave us a bunch of folders, like a travel agent. He took us to lunch at the Senate with an ex-congressman named Stetson, and introduced us to Garner[1] and Vandenberg.[2] Garner is an old Texan crab, with the thickest eyebrows I have ever seen. Vernon disliked him, because he shook hands sideways, not up and down.

The Senate seemed very informal. The senators wear light summer suits. They lounge and chat, hardly pretending to listen to the speakers. Around the president's chair[3] sit a bunch of messenger boys, in black knickerbockers, who giggle and whisper.

May 10. We left Washington yesterday evening, at 11:30. Bus travel by night isn't at all uncomfortable. The seats tilt far back, and you can doze without slobbering. We ran through hilly, wooded Virginia, getting deeper and deeper inland. Villages of shacks. The store porch, on which the inhabitants lounge all day, their eyes alive with malign curiosity in impassive sunburnt faces. Special waiting rooms and toilets for Negroes at the bus stops. Tennessee is more thickly wooded, and the hills are steeper. Knoxville, and the Great Smoky Mountains. Nashville. These towns still seem like settlements, isolated. Memphis, beside the broad, muddy river. They were holding the festival of King Cotton. All the cafés were decorated with dirty, fluffy festoons of it. We had hoped to travel down the Mississippi by boat, but the steamers don't run any more. We took the bus on to New Orleans, at midday.

The state of Mississippi seems terribly poor, flat, featureless. The earth is blowing away into dusty desert land, and nobody can afford to stop it. Negroes everywhere. Wretched, unpainted shacks. The poor little towns try to lure tourist custom, like elderly whores. The dirt and meanness of the South. We reached New Orleans at 11:30 in the evening.

May 15. Nothing much to say about this city. At first sight, it is too quaint, too consciously like Marseille. One would have to stay here much longer to get to know it. Vernon wanted to go on an alligator hunt, but we couldn't arrange it. There is a charming restaurant called The Court of the Three Sisters, where you eat by candlelight, out of doors.

We leave this evening, for a two-night stretch on the bus, to New Mexico.

[1] John Nance Garner, then Roosevelt's vice-president.
[2] Arthur Vandenberg, journalist and politician.
[3] The president of the Senate, usually the vice-president of the U.S.

May 16. The country toward Lake Charles is swamp landscape. The trees are bearded with moss, evil looking, very old and withered. Bluebonnets grow along the roadside. Beyond Baldwin, I saw my first oil field—the flame fluttering from pipes in the gathering darkness. The monster advertisements still follow us—"Coca-Cola: thirst ends here." The girl saying: "He's tall . . . dark . . . and owns a Ford V8." The pillow sellers: "C'mon, folks. It costs no more than a packet of cigarettes." Or "Pillows—all sizes, milk fed, Dominciker hen feathers, natural curls . . ." Someone remarks: "He's so black, you can't see him." Negro passengers have to wait until all the whites are on board. They sit at the back of the bus. But the driver treats them quite civilly.

Houston soon after daybreak. We turned north. Texas is dull and flat. Torrents of rain. Rain is headline news in *The Fort Worth Telegram.* A newspaper vendor, at Marlin: "I'd be glad to sell someone *The Houston Chronicle.* If you want one, come right down and get it."

Fort Worth is just another of these ugly, unplanned American cities. A few skyscrapers, too big, completely out of proportion, and without any functional necessity, since this is not an island. The rest is flat-topped garage architecture, cheeky and shiny when new, but ageing quickly into drab dumps.

Then cattle country, undulating, deserted. The cowboys in overalls, and half-boots with queerly sinister crooked heels. As it grew dark, lightning flickered along the horizon. A boy and a girl got on the bus—both deeply sunburnt and about fifteen years old, going through to California. The boy seemed utterly exhausted and rather lost, but his sister was lively. She flirted precociously with an unpleasant man in a straw hat. There was also a baby, apparently travelling alone. Everybody wanted to take charge of it. In a curious way, the atmosphere of the covered wagon survives. We were all pioneers, on this adventure together.

May 17. When I woke, the country had changed. We were in the badlands. Ahead of us, the bare hills were purple and mauve in the sunrise. The plain was deserted, but not empty; it was crowded with mesquite bushes, each a little individual presence, aloof from its neighbors, not forming a landscape. The hotel at Van Horn had Indian pots and blankets, and painted gourds for sale in the lobby— the gaudy, sterile art-fruits of the desert.

El Paso. Then northward, up the Rio Grande. The hills of Mexico, colorless in the glare. We got to Albuquerque late this afternoon. . . .

Next day, we went on to Flagstaff, where we spent the night and visited the Grand Canyon. I would have liked to stay there, but

Vernon was in a hurry to finish our trip. We had a quarrel, because I wouldn't let him climb out on a dangerous pinnacle to be photographed. He is absolutely without physical fear.

When we reached Needles, a patriotic lady passenger began to sing: "California, here I come!" It seemed little enough to arrive at, after such a journey—the furnace-hot, quivering, untidy desert, and then the gigantic truck-garden. Every orange and onion seemed already stamped with the exporter's trademark. I think one's disappointment, on first coming to the West, is really due to its size. The European mind cannot grasp such distances, such prodigality, such barrenness, such riches. It grows weary and bored. The eye refuses to look and the ear to listen.

Toward evening, we came into downtown Los Angeles— perhaps the ugliest city on earth. It was a Saturday night, and the streets were swarming with drunks. We saw three sailors carrying a girl into a house, as though they were going to eat her alive. From the hotel, we telephoned Chris Wood. "How wonderful," he said, "to hear an effeminate British voice!"

Next day, we took a taxi into Hollywood. I was amazed at the size of the city, and at its lack of shape. There seemed no reason why it should ever stop. Miles and miles of little houses, wooden or stucco, under a technicolor sky. Miles of little gardens crowded with blossoms and flowering bushes; the architecture is dominated by the vegetation. A city without privacy, where neighbors share each other's lawns and look into each other's bedrooms. The whole place like a world's fair, quite new and already partly in ruins. The only permanent buildings are the schools and the churches. On the hill, giant letters spell "Hollywoodland," but this is only another advertisement. It is silly to say that Hollywood, or any other city, is "unreal." But what the arriving traveller first sees are merely advertisements for a city which doesn't exist.

We had arranged to meet Chris Wood at three o'clock, outside the Owl Drugstore, at the corner of Hollywood and Highland. (I mention the rendezvous because it seemed, at the time, as bizarre as Stanley's meeting with Livingstone, or a date made with one's maiden aunt outside the Potala in Lhasa.[1]) We had an hour to spare, and we spent it finding an apartment.

We chose an apartment house called the Rose Garden, at the bottom of the steep hill on Franklin Avenue, between Cahuenga and Vine. It was a Spanish style building, with a courtyard full of trees and flowers. We had a big living room with a pull-down wall bed, a bathroom, a tiny dressing alcove and a kitchen—all

[1]Chief residence in Tibet of the Dalai Lama.

furnished, for thirty-five dollars a month, with gas and light extra. Most of the tenants were small-time movie actors and ex-actors (if there is such a creature as a *live* ex-actor). The place was run by a family named Lundgren, who kept the radio on all day, shouting reports from the various racetracks. Its atmosphere was quite familiar to me: I'd seen a house exactly like it, in a movie about a girl from the Middle West who sets out to conquer Hollywood. It seemed just the right starting point for our adventures in this city.

Chris Wood didn't look a day older—although he was now a Hollywood Chris, in blue linen shorts, with a walnut tan face, lean and lined, and streaky blond hair. His eyes were the same as ever—extraordinarily brilliant, intimate, mockingly amused. It was wonderful to see him. Instantly, I felt safe. The old world still existed. Everything was going to be all right. Chris took charge of us, as a matter of course. We'd dine together that evening. Tomorrow, we'd go swimming, and visit Hellmut [Roder] and Fritz [Mosel].

I forget whether we saw Gerald Heard, that day. The strange thing is, I can't remember our first meeting at all. I only know that Chris prepared me for the shock of seeing Gerald in a beard. He had grown it a few months previously, while he was lying in bed with a broken collarbone—he had fallen down some icy steps, somewhere in the Middle West, during a lecture tour.

But, even aside from the beard, I found Gerald strikingly changed. The Gerald Heard of the London days had been, as it were, exaggeratedly clean-shaven—barbered and tailored with a sort of fastidious understatement—carefully unemphatic, witty, catty, chatty, sly. William Plomer, in a letter to me, had once described the two of them perfectly: "Met Gerald and Chris in Regent Street yesterday. I like their dry eyes and voices." That was the point. One had thought of them, in those days, very much as a pair of brothers, this Anglo-Irish couple. Chris was the spoilt, wayward younger son, with his airplane, his musical boxes, his superbicycle, and all his other dangerous or expensive amusements and toys. Gerald was the elder brother, the guardian presence who lurked somewhere in the background of their London flat. Now and then, he would pop his head startlingly around the door, take in the appearance of Chris's latest visitor with a sly gleam in his eye, murmur something polite and disappear. The Gerald of those days had been essentially an agnostic, a liberal, a cautious investigator. He was much interested in psychical research. Some of the experiments impressed him, but he wouldn't go so far as to say that he was sure. He wrote books about evolution and prehistory, and broadcast once a week on popular science.

And now here was Chris, who hadn't changed in the least—he was just recovering from an accident to his latest plaything, an autoglide,[1] and kept picking, like a fidgety little boy, at a scab on his ankle. And here was a new Gerald—disconcertingly, almost theatrically Christlike, with his beautiful little pointed beard which tilted the whole face to an upward, heaven-seeking thrust; artistically, even dramatically shabby, in a sort of blue painter's smock, washed-out blue jean pants and sneakers. Sitting forward, alert as a bird, on the edge of his chair, his exquisitely formed hands folded in his lap, he was like someone who listens intently to sounds which are nearly inaudible. One could imagine him as a radio operator, with headphones on his ears. When he spoke, you often got the same impression: he was repeating a message which he had just received. (This was probably because Gerald was in the middle of writing a book, and he naturally tended to quote passages from it, trying them out on his various listeners.) His eyes, of an intense pale blue, had a trick, in thoughtful moments, of seeming to lose focus, and go blind. His dyspeptically red nose, with the beard and the high temples, gave him a slight resemblance to Bernard Shaw.

Chris and Gerald lived at 8766 Arlene Terrace, a curving lane high up the hillside of a branch valley, above Laurel Canyon. It was part of a building project which had petered out. Beyond the last houses, the pavement ended, but you could follow the road right up to the top of the ridge, where a gate led to a firebreak dirt track, which skirted the whole range of hills between Hollywood and the San Fernando Valley. This was Gerald's favorite walk. In the evening, the scenery reminded me of Hong Kong Island. Weird feelers and tendrils of fog twisted around the summits and coiled down the deep abrupt canyons, which were choked with chaparral, poison oak and yuccas. Far below, vast constellations of lights spread over the plain. Although these hills were in the midst of an enormous city, they were still quite wild; walking on the firebreak, you often saw coyotes, and rabbits, and deer, or a fat, sleepy rattlesnake, enjoying the warmth of the ground after sunset.

Gerald didn't actually live in Chris's house, but in an annex which he had built on to the back of it—a small bedroom and a tiny shower and toilet. There was no communicating door between the two establishments. To go from one to the other, you had to pass through the garden: an inconvenience in wet weather and at night. But both Chris and Gerald seemed to prefer it that way. They respected each other's privacy like cats.

When I came to know Gerald's habits and ways of life,

[1] Evidently a motor scooter.

I suspected that they formed a deliberate, or subconsciously intended picture of himself as a mendicant, an Irish "poor relation." For example, if Gerald invited you to dinner, he took the most exaggerated precautions not to disturb Chris. You couldn't go into the kitchen until Chris had driven down the hill for his evening meal in Hollywood. As the sound of the car died away, Gerald would stage-whisper, "Himself has gone away now. The coast is clear." Then we would tiptoe into the house, after a short bout of bowing in the doorway, which Gerald invariably won. The kitchen, according to Gerald, had more taboos and forbidden places than the most superstitious South Sea island. You soon learnt which shelves were sacred to Chris's bread, and Chris's imported English marmalade, and which dish in the icebox contained Chris's butter, which must never, never be touched, even if you were starving. Chris certainly had his fads and quirks of possessiveness—but Gerald's exaggeration of them must have made him seem, to strangers, like an ogre.

As soon as you were inside the kitchen, Gerald—talking very rapidly to distract your attention—would try to maneuver you into sitting down and doing nothing while he prepared the meal. It was like a game. If he didn't succeed, his next endeavor was to get you to eat "something solid"—eggs or canned soup—while he supped messily on scraps. His part of the cupboard was full of stale oddments—bits of old cake, very dry sandwiches, morsels of dusty cheese, rotten fruits, moldy cookies—which he had somehow acquired; usually they were the remains of some picnic with his friends, the Huxleys or the Hunters. "I'm a scavenger, by nature," he would tell me. If, as often happened, he had been given a specially made cake or pie, or a pat of home-churned butter, he would take what seemed a malicious pleasure in feeding it to a guest. In this way, he resisted Maria Huxley's attempts to "feed him up," while, at the same time, he kept alarming her by confessing to night sweats and otherwise hinting at TB. When you had finished the main course, Gerald would press you to raisins ("Why doesn't everybody prefer them to chewing gum?") and to raw carrots which are a corrective, as he invariably explained, to night blindness. The meal always ended with tea ("perhaps the only permissible stimulant"). Tea certainly stimulated Gerald. His most brilliant flights of conversation followed the fourth or fifth cup.

When I knew Gerald well enough, I ventured to lecture him on what I dared to call the pretentiousness of wearing jackets with ragged sleeves and going around with holes in the knees of his pants. (Sometimes he even wore them in the style of Robinson

Crusoe, chopped short with scissors just below the knee—because, as he explained, the cuffs had become so badly frayed.) Gerald wasn't very pleased at my rebuke—although he tried to defend himself by saying that he couldn't bear to see anything wasted—and he got back at me on later occasions by ostentatiously changing his jacket whenever I came to visit him. Gerald was not only a puritan but an inverted dandy. Some devotee once prepared a "list of Mr. Heard's works, in the order of their relevance to the spiritual life." At the very bottom was *Narcissus: An Anatomy of Clothes*.

Gerald's chief trial was the ordeal by noise. His six hours of daily meditation were done in his bedroom, and there he was exposed, from seven-thirty onwards, to the neighbors' quarrels and the neighbors' radio, which continued separately or together throughout the day. To this was added Chris's piano playing, morning and afternoon.

Chris, too, had his routine. He breakfasted at ten-thirty, and left around eleven for the beach—or rather for Hanns Ohrt's cycle shop in Beverly Hills, where he kept his bicycle. (Hanns Ohrt was a famous Hollywood character, a great apostle of the Wheel, a teacher of movie stars, whose shop was painted with inscriptions: "The bicycle is the safest, cheapest and healthiest mode of travel," "Cycle now and retain the health and youth which you will not be able to regain ten years hence.") From Beverly Hills, he cycled to the beach and back, making remarkably good time, for long practice had keyed him almost to champion pitch. Chris always went to the Solarium, a sunbathing court with an unpleasant smell, where elderly men, prima donnas of suntan, lay for hours, frying slowly in their own grease. He didn't stay there long, however. He pedalled hurriedly home, as if for an appointment. At one-fifteen, he would explain, there was a radio program he had to listen to. Did he, literally, listen? It's hard to say. If I happened to come in while the radio was on, Chris would be wandering about, ceaselessly restless, from room to room, picking up scraps, from the carpet, fiddling with something in the kitchen, changing his clothes. He ate no midday meal. After the program, he would sit down at the piano and practice till teatime. Practice for what? He seldom played for his friends, and would never have dreamed of giving a concert—although he was a very fine performer. After tea, which he made himself, there would be more radio, more piano playing. And then the evening in Hollywood.

Chris was very kind to us, those first days. He took us to all the best restaurants—Chasen's, Musso Frank's,[1] the Vine Street Brown

---

[1] Isherwood's habitual misnomer for Musso and Frank's.

Derby (where we saw Charles Boyer without his wig) and the Beachcomber where we drank Zombies amd Missionary's Downfalls in semidarkness, while the artificial rain drummed on the roof and streamed down the windows. He also interrupted his routine to take us to see Hellmut Roder and Fritz Mosel, who had landed up here after wanderings through France, Spain and Mexico. They had opened a restaurant on the Sunset Strip, with Chris's financial backing, but it had flopped. Now they were just lying around in the sun, and Hellmut was always sick. (I remembered Stephen's classic remark: "Du solltest nicht *Hell*mut sondern *Dunkel*mut heissen."[1]) He dragged himself about the house, reproaching us mutely with his patience. Now and then, he retired to a clinic, for treatment or a minor operation—and Chris paid and paid.

Chris seemed to be paying for everybody and everything. I suppose I had known perfectly well that he would pay for me, too—although, when the moment came, I put up a decent show of protest. But the logic of the case was unanswerable. How was I going to eat? By working in the movies. And how was I going to work in the movies before I had a labor permit? Obviously, I would have to get on the quota. Obviously, we would have to have some sort of car; our friends couldn't ferry us around indefinitely. I ended by borrowing two thousand dollars. (Chris, who was extremely generous in large matters, never reminded me of the debt and seemed genuinely suprised when, eventually, I paid it back.)

But to get back to my first meeting with Gerald. As I have said already, I can't remember a word of our conversation. But the sense of it was like this:

"Well, Gerald—so you're really doing all those things we heard about—meditating, and studying yoga, and so on?"

"Yes, Christopher, I really am."

"And you believe in it? You think it's worthwhile?"

"For me, it's the only thing that matters in the world."

Yes, he really believed. I could see that. Other people believed in mystical religion—but I had always been able to dismiss them as cranks, simpletons or sex maniacs, creatures of another breed. Gerald was different. He was one of us. He spoke the same language. He accepted the same values. He might be theatrical, affected, vain, eccentric, but he certainly wasn't crazy.

But if—and this was a terribly disturbing thought—if Gerald *was* sane, then I couldn't afford to ignore his ideas. I should have to study them—perhaps act upon them. Gerald, I could see at once,

[1] Roughly, "You should not be called *Bright*mood but *Dark*mood."

was expecting that I should. He had the air of having waited for my arrival. Very few people, he hinted—he hadn't forgotten how to flatter—could come to "this thing." (His favorite way of referring to the subject.) Only one man in ten thousand takes an interest. And of ten thousand who take an interest, only one does anything about it. "It's only when the sheer *beastliness* of the world begins to hurt you—like crushing your finger in a door," (Gerald's face contracted with pain as he spoke, for he always mimed out his remarks), "it's only then that you'll be ready to take this step."

And was I ready? Well, I had certainly been miserable enough, lately. My bridges were broken. I saw no way out. But still I couldn't honestly say that I'd reached the despair line. My ultimate remedy for everything was sleep, unconsciousness—produced no matter how—by Seconal, alcohol, a movie, a crime story, or sex. And now here was Gerald urging me in the opposite direction—towards greater wakefulness, consciousness, awareness. All my laziness hung back.

Nevertheless, what he now put before me was the most exciting proposition I had ever heard. He told me what Life is for. "And why was I never told this before?" I kept asking myself, almost indignantly. It was an absurd question. I had been told "this" many times. Every moment of my conscious existence had contained within itself this riddle, and its answer. Every event, every encounter, every person and object had restated it in some new way. Only—I hadn't been ready to listen.

Life, said Gerald, is for awareness. Awareness of our real nature and our actual situation. The day-to-day, space-time "reality" is, in fact, no reality at all, but a cunning and deadly illusion. Space-time is evil. The process of meditation consists in excluding, as far as possible, our consciousness of the illusory world and turning the mind inward, in search of the knowledge which is locked within itself—the knowledge of its real nature. Our real nature is to be one with life, with consciousness, with everything else in the universe. This fact of oneness is the actual situation, the only absolute reality. Supposed knowledge of individuality, separateness and division is nothing but illusion and ignorance. Awareness is increased through love (or, as Gerald preferred to call it, "interest-affection") and weakened by hatred. Hence, all positive feeling and action toward other people is in one's deepest interests, and all negative feeling and action finally harms oneself. Free will does not operate, as we like to imagine, in the sphere of events—averting this danger, choosing that advantage. No—there we are tied hand and foot, though we do not know it. "At the moment of action no man is free"—because our present problems are created by our past deeds and thoughts. Free will consists simply in this: that we can, at any moment, turn toward or away from the search for our real nature.

Gerald accepted the Buddhist and Hindu hypothesis of many worlds and states of existence, all bound to causality and all within time. The peculiar advantage of this world and life is that the opportunities offered for "leverage" are very great. Earthly events are of such a nature as to give you the possibility of working yourself a long way up, or down, by the way you handle them. Gerald—employing, as usual, the scientific imagery which made his conversation so exciting—compared the body to the lead shield used by Roentgen workers to protect themselves from the invisible rays. In other, disembodied states, such proximity to the vital radiation might be intolerable, unless one were accustomed to it. Our task, therefore, during our life in this body, was to expose ourselves repeatedly to the screened rays—so that, when the screen was removed altogether, at the instant of death, we should not be burned and blinded.

(This idea, though I didn't know it at the time, was taken from the Bardo Thodol, the Tibetan Book of the Dead. The soul, at death, is supposed to get a glimpse of the reality. If it is prepared for this glimpse, it turns naturally toward the reality and becomes a part of it. If it is unprepared, it feels terror and pain, escapes from the "Clear Light of the Void" into fresh illusions of separateness and individuality, and is consequently reborn.[1])

Gerald's highly pictorial methods of teaching are, of course, open to criticism. They arrested his hearers' interest, and thus obtained remarkable short-term results with beginners. In the long run, they were apt to produce mental habits which were slovenly and dangerous. A parable or a simile is only, at best, a mirror image of the truth. It has no substance. Whenever Gerald produced some dramatic illustration, like that of the Roentgen rays, he was fond of adding, "This isn't just an analogy. I believe it may actually be an homology." This sounded very exciting, but it meant very little. Also, most unfortunately—as I was to find out later—some of the facts upon which Gerald based his "homologies" were scientifically inaccurate. His followers would find this out, from time to time, and feel unreasonably dismayed—because Gerald had taught them to identify the parable with the truth it illustrated. Just as many Christians would lose their faith in Christ's teaching if it could be proved that Christ didn't exist, so many ardent Heardians lost their faith in Heard when they discovered that man is *not*

[1] See Glossary under Bardo Thodol.

descended from a small tree-shrew, and that his [Gerald's] knowledge of evolution was dubious. A little knowledge is a dangerous thing; and a lot of knowledge is even more dangerous. Gerald knew something about almost every conceivable subject, but he wasn't the *Encyclopaedia Britannica*. He relied far too much on his wonderful memory. Sometimes it let him down badly. However, I'm anticipating—

Gerald regarded the search for reality as an ordered process, with definite stages. In this, he was following the Christian mystics. You can find the whole system worked out in Poulain's big book on prayer.[1] The first stage is Purgation. The mind has to be polished, as it were, like a lens—through constant practice of meditation and renunciation. The ego, in Gerald's words, has to be "reduced" from its "strangulated" condition, and systematically freed from— Gerald used to tick them off on his long fingers—addictions, possessions and pretensions. Addictions (which included also aversions—anything from chain-smoking to anti-Semitism) were, according to him, the least harmful of the three. Pretensions were the worst, because, when you are free of all sensual attachments and all your household belongings, when you have forgiven all your enemies and said goodbye to all your lovers, when you have resigned from all your positions of honor and ceased to use your titles of nobility—then, and only then, you may fall victim to the spiritual pride which will destroy you. After Purgation comes Liberation—a condition of near-sainthood, in which the mind is free to continue its search dispassionately, without the obstacles of fear or desire. And Liberation ends with the accomplishment of this search, in Union with absolute reality.

At that time, Gerald was passing through an anti-Christian phase. He read Meister Eckhart and St. John of the Cross, but preferred Vedanta philosophy. Several times, he told me that he could never become a Christian, as long as the Church claimed for itself a monopoly of divine inspiration—which Hindus and Buddhists don't—and as long as the crucifixion was presented as the inevitable and crowning triumph of Christ's life. A few months previous to our arrival in Hollywood, he had found a Vedantist teacher. This was Swami Prabhavananda, the resident monk of the Ramakrishna Mission in Hollywood. Gerald went to see the Swami regularly at that time, and also lectured at his temple—a miniature plaster "Taj" at the top of Ivar Avenue. He was also

[1] Augustin Poulain, *The Graces of Interior Prayer: A Treatise on Mystical Theology* (1910), translated from French by Leonora L. Yorke Smith.

editing a magazine called *The Voice of India*, which was published by the mission.

If Gerald hadn't been so interested in yoga and opposed to Christianity, he would never have been able to influence me the way he did. My prejudices were largely semantic. I could only approach the subject of mystical religion with the aid of a brand-new vocabulary. Sanskrit supplied it. Here were a lot of new words, exact, antiseptic, uncontaminated by association with bishops' sermons, schoolmasters' lectures, politicians' speeches. To have gone back along the old tracks, to have picked up the old phrases and scraped them clean of their dirty associations—that job would have been too disgusting for a beginner. But now it wasn't necessary. Every idea could be made over, restated in the new language. And restatement was what I most needed—as a mental discipline, and even as an alibi, since it was embarrassing to admit to myself that I had been so intolerant.

I had always regarded Vedanta philosophy, or yoga, as the ultimate in mystery-mongering nonsense. (Like the vast majority of outside critics, I identified yoga with hatha yoga, and imagined that it consisted entirely of trick postures and breathing exercises.) Now it was suddenly revealed as a precise, practical, clearly stated philosophical system—the only one I had ever been able to understand. Here was a sort of metaphysical algebra, in terms of which every type of religious experience, from that of St. Francis to that of Charles Kingsley, could be tersely and adequately expressed.

In our Cambridge days, and after, Edward and I had had two slogans, "Religion is bad art," and, "Religion is nothing but sex." How silly they sounded now! Or rather, how entirely beside the point. By "religion is bad art" we had meant, simply, that it is illegitimate to substitute traditional religious values for aesthetic values—which is obvious, as far as it goes. A bad novel about Christ is easier to get away with than a bad novel about Mr. Jones; because the reader already knows Christ and is awed by the associations which surround him. The mere mention of Christ causes the reader to suspend his aesthetic judgment and make allowances for the writer's shortcomings. If the reader is an atheist, this process works in reverse, and he condemns the book out of hand. Mr. Jones's character is unknown to the reader. It is not surrounded by traditional values. Therefore, a novel about him will be judged on its own aesthetic merits.

But all this presupposes that "religion" means tradition, dogma, sentimentality about dubious historical facts, unquestioning acceptance of traditional values. And it doesn't. Religion, as Gerald had shown me, is not the opium but the adrenalin of the people. Religion is the struggle for greater awareness of reality, deeper understanding of the nature of life. Art, also, struggles for awareness and understanding. The goal is identical. Art, rightly practiced, is a way of religion. The better the art, the more religious its character. Conventionally minded "good" people can never see this, because they confuse religion with ethics (whereas ethics are only a necessary means to a nonethical end). They are told that a certain novel is "great" (i.e. that it heightens the reader's awareness and understanding) and then discover that the novel is about a prostitute and are shocked—because prostitution, and therefore the mention of prostitution, are automatically wicked.

As for "religion is nothing but sex"—that was typical puritan nonsense. Whether you accept Freud or not, the fact remains that the mind–body has only one life force. This force expresses itself in different ways at different levels of consciousness. In a department store, the same elevator takes you to the women's hats, the sports department, the furniture and the restaurant on the roof. The same force impels a man to paint a picture, run the quarter mile, have sexual intercourse, say his prayers. Most Europeans and Americans, religious or not, find this fact shocking, because they secretly think sex is dirty, and because they think that the life force is nothing else but sex. Hindus do not make either of these mistakes. Their theory of the kundalini corresponds to my simile of the elevator. Their legend of Krishna and the gopis never fails to shock westerners.[1] It even shocked Huxley and Gerald himself.

In writing all this, I have had to go far ahead of my narrative. The process of accepting Gerald's ideas was a long one, with many hesitations and revulsions of feeling. It covered many months. I suppose I shall never again in my life have moments of such intense excitement and revelation as I had then.

Actually, during that first month at the Rose Garden, I was too busy to think much about such things. We were in a whirl of minor occupations. First, there was the quota visa to take care of. Hellmut and Fritz had put us in touch with an immigration counsellor named Miss Dicky Bonaparte, who had helped them both to get into the country. Miss Bonaparte had a big clientele among Hollywood's alien actors and actresses. She would take your papers down to the American Consul at Ensenada, get everything ready in advance, and then run you down herself in her car. Vernon came along too. Miss Bonaparte was attractive, black eyed and obviously

[1]For kundalini, Krishna and the gopis, and for all Hindu names and terms, see Glossary.

full of temperament; we both had an uneasy feeling that something more than the fee was expected of us. We stopped a few hours at Tijuana, a dirty unpicturesque town of chickens and whores, miniature burros and sandals which reeked of urine, and then drove on down the wild empty coast of lower California. We spent the night at an auto-camp just outside Ensenada and saw the consul next morning. It was the merest formality. But at San Ysidro, on the American side of the frontier gate, I was interviewed again, by an immigrant-inspector named Leonard Kinstler. Mr. Kinstler had a strong sense of drama. "When I sign this form," he told me solemnly, "you will be legally admitted as a permanent resident to the United States." He took up the pen, formed the first letters of his name, hesitated, examined the nib, coughed. A terrible suspicion seemed to occur to him. He thumbed hurriedly through my dossier, found nothing, paused, sighed, glanced quickly up to see if I was watching the performance, grinned, flourished his pen and signed. As dusk was falling, we drove triumphantly home to Los Angeles, through dense, sour-smelling groves of oil derricks. This was on June 9. About a month later, following Miss Bonaparte's advice, I applied for my first citizenship papers.

Now I could take a job, if anybody would give me one. My first step was to visit a Mrs. Baker(?), at the office of the Sam Jaffe Agency on the Sunset Strip. Mrs. Baker was young, attractive and dressed in the height of chic. She told me at once that there was practically no hope of getting a movie assignment; business was very slack, now. Had I written anything? Had it ever been published? Yes? Well, she'd read it sometime if I sent her a copy, but— Plainly, she wasn't interested. I never heard from her again.

Still, I wasn't much discouraged. Work would probably turn up, sooner or later. I had my visa, and there was still money in the bank. Vernon offered to get a job in a drugstore or a fruit market, but we both agreed to wait till things got desperate. Neither of us seriously intended to live on eighteen dollars a week. I would sooner have borrowed more money. Vernon wanted to go to art school, and that, I argued, was a much better long-term investment than a dozen little jobs. So, instead of tightening our belts, we bought a car and moved into a house.

The car was an old T-model Ford. We got it from a couple of Englishmen who lived opposite Chris Wood, on Green Valley Road, in an apartment which I was to share with Denny Fouts, two years later. The car made a tremendous noise, but it went all right, at first. I got my California licence, after three attempts. The police tester, though pleasant, seemed determined to prove to me that Englishmen can't drive.

House hunting brought us into direct contact with the splendors and miseries of Hollywood architecture. Hollywood houses, especially those on the outskirts of the city, have an uncanny kind of artificiality, like movie sets. No matter whether they are Spanish, Mexican, Colonial, Tudor English, French Chateau or Cubist, they all look as if a gang of stage carpenters had put them up during the night and would take them apart again tomorrow. And, in amongst the merely artificial structures, there are some rather nightmarish freaks—a witch's cottage, with false dormer windows and gables almost touching the ground, a miniature medieval castle, with cannon on the battlements, a monastery with a totem pole in its cloisters, an Egyptian temple or tomb. Up Laurel Canyon, nearly buried in undergrowth, we found a Japanese bungalow, which appeared to have been fortified. The doors and shutters were several inches thick and studded with huge marine bolts. The furniture was made of heavy beams of wood, screwed together with enormous screws. The table could hardly have been lifted by four men. The bed looked like an instrument of torture: lying on it, you were enclosed as if within an open coffin. The house agent had to admit that the gentleman who designed it had been "peculiar." He had kept his stockade shutters closed all day.

It is not only the houses of Hollywood that have this theatrical, temporary air; the entire landscape is provisional. This was one of Gerald's favorite themes. Walking with us along the firebreak road, he loved to point out how recently this country had been desert, and how quickly it would lapse back into desert again, if the Japanese gardeners were to stop drenching it every evening with water. The houses are built, the pipes are connected up, the hoses start to spray—and, within six months, the devil grass is growing, the porch is heavy under vines, the big garish flowers burst from their buds, the eucalyptus sapling begins to shoot up into a great shade-giving tree. "These hills won't last long, either," said Gerald gleefully, picking up a handful of what looked like rock and crumbling it in his fingers, "decomposed granite. In five hundred years, most of it'll have washed down into Culver City." At different points along the ridge, there were building sites, flattened out by the bulldozer. We watched a steam shovel cut slices from the soft hillside, like cake, unearthing several rattlesnakes, which the men killed and threw into a bucket. Every winter, the rains would wash a few dollars' worth of your property down into the valley. But the course of nature wasn't quick enough for Gerald.

He enjoyed kicking big chunks out of the shoulder of the road, giggling wildly. It disconcerted me, to see him in this mood. He seemed quite fiendish. But it was funny, too, and I laughed and forgot it.

It is time for me to mention Peggy and Henwar Rodakiewicz. The firebreak reminds me of them, because, if you walked along it for twenty minutes or so, you came down into the valley where they lived. Peggy and Gerald were old friends; they had known each other in England. Gerald and Chris used to visit her every Sunday, or oftener. Indeed, it was part of Chris's Sunday routine to have lunch there, and afterwards to accompany Peggy on the piano while she sang. She had a beautiful voice and might have become a professional, if she hadn't married and had a family instead.

Peggy was an extraordinarily pretty woman, although her hair was turning grey and her features were sharpening a little. She had the figure of a college girl. She belonged to a Philadelphia family named Plummer, and she had married twice. Her first husband was Curtis Bok, son of Edward Bok who wrote *The Americanization.*[1] They had three children, Welmoet (usually called "Tis"), Ben, and Derek. (Welmoet, the eldest, was around fourteen, at this time.) When Peggy and Curtis got divorced, Curtis remarried and became a judge. Peggy married Henwar, who was small, square, jolly and very Polish, although he'd lived most of his life in America. He made documentary films.

It is very hard for me to write about Peggy, because I know her intimately—so intimately that I think of her with the kind of love-hate I'd feel for a sister. In some ways, we are deeply alike. I think the most dominant of her characteristics is her bad conscience. When she married Curtis Bok, she found herself very wealthy. She also began to realize that she was very attractive. She had to take an important place in Philadelphia society. She met all kinds of distinguished people. And she thought—"How terrible! How can I ever pay this back?"

That was how she began to manage things, to arrange people's lives for them, to load them with gifts. She wanted to be Florence Nightingale on a nationwide scale. One can't blame her. She was very young and she made some fearful mistakes. A lot of her interference was love of power; that goes without saying. She was terrifically tense and eager—always on her toes. She was ruthless with herself and everybody else. They all had to conform to what she hoped and expected of them. Sometimes she acted like a shrew and a schoolmarm; sometimes like an utter little bitch. She had a

[1] *The Americanization of Edward Bok* (1921); see Glossary under Bok, W. Curtis.

quick temper and a tongue like an adder. She cooed poison. Afterward, she had terrible revulsions, accused herself bitterly, punished herself without mercy. She was big enough to go straight to people and ask their pardon. Then you loved her.

If you were really sick, really in debt, really in bad trouble with the police, Peggy rose to her greatest heights. She was absolutely generous and fearless. She'd take charge of any problem and solve it efficiently. In return, she expected results. You must recover, promptly and completely, without laziness or malingering. When your debts were paid, you must turn over a new leaf. When you got out of prison, you must make a fresh start. If you didn't, woe betide you. How well I know that look in Peggy's grey eyes—a sharp glance of suspicion, then disappointment, cold disapproval. So you failed to make the grade. She sighs, she turns away. But not for long. No sooner do you get into another mess than she's back again. Perhaps, this time, it's going to be all right. She rushes to the attack with the same energy, the same optimism. Bless her heart.

She is so terribly unsure of herself. Meeting a new person, she can't keep still, she can't wait. She has to try for the right note. First it's sharp, then it's flat. Now she's hit it—or has she? Her laughter falters and sounds tinny. Her conversation bubbles over—it's nothing but froth. She gets absolutely desperate. She strains and strains. And then, suddenly, it's all right. She calms down, and is charming, human, sincere.

The Huxleys often compared her to Olenka in Chekhov's story "The Darling." Like Olenka, Peggy was always adapting herself. Her friends' interests were her interests. She read the books they advised, and repeated their remarks as gospel truths. She was far too enthusiastic. Then, when the friends had been revealed as mere fallible mortals, she was badly disappointed and inclined to be resentful.

At the time when I met her, Peggy was entirely under the spell of Gerald. Later, his influence waned, and she turned bitterly against him. And yet she always remained one of his best—or perhaps I should say his truest—friends. Henwar, too, she had to believe in—all the more passionately because he was, actually, a very poor filmmaker, a bit of a dilettante, and extremely lazy. When Henwar's movies were shown, none of us dared to tell Peggy what we really thought of them.

The house they lived in (9121 Alto Cedro Drive) was another product of Henwar's dubious artiness, and therefore an article of Peggy's faith. She never tired of its praises. It was strikingly beautiful, certainly: a dramatically modern building, with glass window-walls overlooking the valley and a distant glimpse of the ocean. But many of its details were badly and stupidly planned. It was too hot in summer, too cold in winter. The built-in beds in the library were awkward to make. The staircase was slippery and dangerous. The shower drenched the floor. The dressing tables which contained the washbasins showed the slightest mark of damp. And there were all sorts of queer niches and useless spaces which collected dust.

I think Peggy was attracted to Henwar because he was so unlike the other men she knew—the thin thinkers and the middle-aged college boys. She once told me, years later, that he reminded her of a character in a D. H. Lawrence novel. He was earthy and solid and Slav. He could do things with his hands. He was a sort of art peasant. Also, I am sure, he attracted her very much, sexually. Once, when we were in the garden together and Henwar was working, stripped to the waist, she exclaimed, with involuntary excitement: "Hasn't he got the most beautiful back you ever saw!"

The house which Vernon and I finally chose was 7136 Sycamore Trail. It stood high above the Cahuenga Pass. Sycamore Trail is a dirt road running up from Woodrow Wilson Drive. You had to climb several flights of steps to reach the house itself. The nicest thing about it was its terrace, shaded by a big pepper tree and overlooking the San Fernando Valley. There was a large living room, too high for its size, a breakfast alcove, a bathroom, a bedroom and a kitchen. Beneath the living room, on a lower level, there was a smaller bedroom and bath, very badly ventilated. The house had no back view, because the hillside rose sheer up behind it, to a height of about ten feet above the roof. Next [to] it were two vacant lots, crowded with dirty pine trees, which the agent urged us to buy as soon as possible, to guard our privacy.

I never really liked the place, from the beginning. It was curiously sinister. Perhaps there are more haunted houses in Los Angeles than in any other city in the world. They are haunted by the fears of their former owners. They smell of divorce, broken contracts, studio politics, bad debts, false friendship, adultery, extravagance, whisky and lies. Every closet hides the poor little ghost of a stillborn reputation. "Go away," it whispers, "go back where you came from. There is no home here. I was vain and greedy. They flattered me. I failed. You will fail. Go away."

With a heavy heart I joined in the planning and spending. Hellmut and Fritz were extraordinarily kind and helpful. One or other of them came every day and took us to secondhand furniture dealers on Santa Monica Boulevard, where we bargained for tables, chairs and beds. The Five & Ten supplied most of the kitchen utensils. And Peggy Rodakiewicz would drop in, with her car full of useful gifts.

I felt like a Christmas tree. Twice in my life I have experienced this peculiar misery—the guilt of possession mixed with the dread of imminent war. The other time was in Copenhagen, in the winter of 1934, just after King Alexander's assassination,[1] when the newspapers screamed "Krig! Krig! Krig!" and Heinz and I were buying things for the Classensgade flat. But that was only for six months, at the most. This time, our stay was to be indefinite. We had an arrangement whereby our monthly rental payments were also installments of the purchase price of the house—I think it was seven or eight thousand dollars. Maybe I was to be tied down at last.

Still, Vernon was delighted, and I couldn't help sharing his happiness—at any rate, at moments. There were so many ways of playing with the new toy. Vernon decided to build a wall, to keep back the next winter's landslide. He left it half-finished and began to plant flowers. Then he bought a parrot, which followed us from room to room, perched on our shoulders, pecked our ears and scattered its seeds everywhere. He decided that one should eat only steamed vegetables. He got a steam cooker and steamed them, several evenings, until I protested and we began going out for our meals again.

We moved into the house at the end of June or the beginning of July. Soon after this, Vernon started going to art school, and I was left at home, stranded without a car, several days a week. There was nothing to do. I wandered from room to room, or sat out over the valley, or listened to the radio, whose news bulletins chronicled the steady reduction of the chances of peace. The mornings were always the same, brilliant blue. The far mountains paled to silhouettes in the midday glare. Then the shadows moved sideways, shifting the sunshine inch by inch from the terrace, and the lizards disappeared, and the valley deepened and darkened back into color, and the hills cooled and hardened into scarred contours of ocher and crimson, and it was evening—another day which Chamberlain and I had wasted.

How awful that period really was! I was in a constant state of apprehensive tension and guilty paralysis of the will. What Gerald was telling me (just then I was reading the proofs of his *Pain, Sex and Time*) only increased my sense of insecurity. I knew I must do

---

[1] Alexander of Yugoslavia, assassinated in Marseille by a Croat subject, October 10, 1934.

something, but I didn't know what, or how. My only instinct was destructive. I wanted to throw all the ballast overboard—this house, this furniture, even Vernon himself. Perhaps it would have been better if I had let him go back to New York. I had nothing to offer him but my fears. And yet, more than ever, I dreaded being alone.

I forced myself to write—a review of *The Grapes of Wrath* and a story called "I Am Waiting"[1]—but there was no satisfaction in it. I was only imitating myself. All that interested me was the present moment, which I couldn't analyze, because I couldn't regard it objectively.

It must have been at this time that I made my first attempts at meditation. I had very little idea what one was supposed to do when one meditated, but Gerald had given me some valuable advice. I wasn't to set myself any program. I wasn't to *try* to pray or think, at all. I was merely to sit quiet, for ten to fifteen minutes twice a day, morning and evening. I was to remind myself of "this thing," what it was, and why I wanted it. This I said I would do.

I remember that the mere idea of actually meditating filled me with an extraordinary excitement. I don't know exactly what I expected from the experience. I was like the boy who says to himself, "Tomorrow I'll climb the highest tree in the garden." Or the young man who decides that, next week, he'll start learning Russian.

Gerald had also warned me that the decision would set up a violent resistance inside myself—and he was right. No sooner had I made up my mind that I would meditate *some time*, than the question arose, well, why not *now, this minute*? Immediately, a dozen voices were raised in postponement and excuse. Tomorrow would be better. Or next Monday. Or even next month. Then would come the doubts: "Isn't all this rather abnormal? What would Edward say? What kind of a joke would Stephen make?" To which the advocates of meditation (prompted by Gerald) would boldly answer: "Since when have you been afraid of abnormality? I always thought you were rather too proud of it, if anything. . . . Yes, of course it's dangerous. All exploration is dangerous. You might even, quite conceivably, go crazy. So what? You'll more than probably go crazy if you stay the way you are. . . . Edward would say, this isn't my cup of tea, but go ahead if you believe in it. . . . Stephen's joke? It's sure to be very funny." So the argument

[1] The Steinbeck piece was published that autumn in *The Kenyon Review* and the short story appeared in *The New Yorker*; both were reprinted in *Exhumations*.

went, backward and forward. Never before had I been so aware that our will is divided; we are not one but many.

The first obstacle is self-consciousness. Gerald himself usually meditated sitting in a chair. My own preference was for something more exotic: I wanted to be as oriental as possible. So I squatted cross-legged in a corner of the room. The advantage of this position was that it was an entirely new one: you saw everything—the furniture, the ceiling, the view through the window—from a different angle, and this in itself was a reminder of what you were doing. But it was also very embarrassing, even when you were alone. Suppose someone should walk in! I told Vernon, of course, what I was doing. I wanted him to get used to the idea and not find it mysterious or funny.

As soon as I was settled into position, the Ego began, as it were, to dance around the room, screaming: "Look at me! Look at me! Isn't it funny? Don't *you* think it's funny? Aren't I extraordinary? What do you think I'll do next? I bet you can't guess! Matter of fact, I don't know, myself. I say—look, look—aren't I a scream?"

Gradually, the prancing and the antics subsided. They were followed by the fidgets. "What's that bird outside? Why does it make that noise? Who can that be in the next garden? I can hear the neighbor's radio. Damn him—what selfishness, making such a racket! How loud the traffic is! That bird. And now there's a fly buzzing. It's too much—" Very often, at this point, I'd break off the attempt and get up. But, if the fidgets passed away, the next trouble would be sex. I sat and throbbed dully with lust. Bed. Darkness. Flesh. Arms. Legs. Lips. Sweat. Grunts and groans. Heaving, straining, jerking. Me. You. Yes. Now— If I waited long enough, however, the throbbing would subside, also. It was just a matter of time.

And then, on another level, the wheel would begin to spin—the roulette wheel of worries, fantasies, plans and plots, vanities and resentments, mixed in with scraps of nonsense, lines from poems, all the odds and ends of the mind's ragbag. Usually, the wheel whizzed on and on, long past the quarter hour I had set myself, and I would rise from it feeling merely dizzy. Very occasionally, while I still watched it, it slowed and almost stopped. Then I knew something approaching concentration.

I talk as if meditation (if you can call what I have just described by so grand a name) had become my regular practice. It hadn't. As a matter of fact, these first attempts were very irregular, and I soon gave them up altogether. The strangest thing about them was that they actually produced some kind of beneficial effect on my behavior. Vernon noticed it at once. One day, when I had said something unpleasant, he remarked priggishly: "I think Christopher, it's time you went and meditated again." This effectively stopped me from doing my "sits" for some time.

Vernon's attitude towards meditation was complicated by his relation to Gerald and myself. Gerald had taken Vernon up in a big way. They went for long walks together—from which Vernon returned soundly flattered and inclined to be superior. Probably, they discussed me, and decided that I hadn't much chance of "mutating" (a favorite Heard term). I was too old. Too corrupt. Too set in my ways. Whereas Vernon was young: he had the whole future before him. Perhaps I'm being unfair. At any rate, I was jealous—of both of them. I probably even set to work, subconsciously, to maneuver Vernon out of Gerald's favor. But it is absolutely no use my discussing all this. I can't write objectively about it, even yet—and self-accusation would be as pointless as fault finding.

Soon after our move to Sycamore Trail, we committed one final extravagance. We traded in our T-model for a new Ford de luxe convertible, to be paid for on the never-never plan. But it wasn't only the looks of the new car and the salesman's smooth line of talk that persuaded us; the Model T had become too expensive to be kept. Nearly every day, something would go wrong—the steering, the ignition, the transmission or the lights. At that time, the Cahuenga Pass road hadn't been reconstructed. To enter Woodrow Wilson, coming up from Hollywood, you had to make a left turn without a traffic light, right across the downstream of the traffic. This, during the rush hours, in a car which might stall at any moment, was really dangerous.

Sometime during July, Berthold Viertel returned from New York to his home in Santa Monica Canyon, full of schemes. He had a movie story which he wanted us to write together. The story was called *The Mad Dog of Europe*, and it was the usual anti-Nazi stuff. But Berthold planned to reconstruct it entirely; to make it a fair and objective account of how a young German army officer is slowly won over to the Nazi party after the last war, of what happens to him as a party member, and of his final reaction and change of heart. The subject, as Berthold described it, sounded wonderfully interesting (what subject didn't?) and it would be marvellous to work with him again. I agreed, of course.

So now, every morning, Vernon drove me down to 165 Mabery Road—that address which had become so familiar to me, years before, in London, when we were working together on *Little*

Friend. Every morning was like every other morning. The barking of the two frisky Irish setters and the old Alsatian at the gate. The German cook opening the front door, admitting me to the big, pleasant living room, with the piano and the books and the blue Picasso boy over the fireplace. "Herr Doktor Viertel kommt gleich."[1] And here he was, in his dressing gown and slippers, snorting through his nose, drawing grim-lipped on his first cigarette, shaking my hand: "Servus."[2] At this hour of the morning, he was always preoccupied, moody, stern, like a general before a battle. We would sit down on the porch to our coffee, and Berthold would scowl his way across the newspaper headlines. Our first talk was always about Europe. I forget what his particular predictions were, at that time. They were always startling and occasionally accurate. Anyhow, the future was double dyed in gloom. We shook our heads over it, almost suicidally. But, beyond the porch, the sunshine poured down through the leaves of the fig tree, the little garden was full of roses, the new morning, brilliant with possibility, opened over a sky-blue, milk-edged ocean, without hope and without despair. Our mood brightened, a little. We rose. We started to pace the lawn. Berthold plucked figs and gave me some. He lit another cigarette. He snorted. Slowly, subtly, inimitably, he began to develop an idea.

At twelve o'clock, we put on our swimming suits and went down to the beach. As we walked past the gardens of the little houses, Berthold was fond of saying: "One does not wander without punishment under palms." This was how he expressed his feeling of guilt at being here, in this improbably remote paradise, while in England the people he loved were threatened by the oncoming war. Together, we strolled along the beach. Berthold, his hands folded behind his back, wore his bathrobe as though it were a toga, with a sort of Roman majesty. Two aliens from doomed Europe, we carried our twisted, pain-ridden psyches amongst the statuesque, unselfconscious bodies of California, basking in the frank sunshine. Where would these bronzed and muscular boys be, five years from now? For what had they been born? For what would they die? Yes, Gerald's way of thinking was the only one that didn't point to utter nihilism and despair. I tried to explain it to Berthold, and he was interested, even excited—but only up to a certain point. His wit, his subtlety, his fearless frankness, his warmth and wealth of emotional reaction—all the qualities which made me love him so dearly—were, in fact, the

[1] ". . . is coming at once."
[2] "Hello."

virtues of his limitations. He had fossilized, long ago, into a "character." He was still capable, like a volcano, of superb fireworks, earth-shaking noises, devastating explosions—but he always remained stationary, a gigantic landmark, occupying a fixed position on the map. Gerald's asceticism repelled him. Pacifism he found cowardly: there were days when he became very violent about this—violent but never personal, because all his arguments were, so plainly, between the two halves of himself. Poor old Berthold—how prophetically I saw my future self, ten years from now, in him—worrying about money and my waistline, resenting imagined insults, a prey to sexual fantasies, pitifully quick tempered, fiercely ready to justify my most casual and ill-considered remarks on any occasion yet thrown into torments of doubt by the slightest word of criticism—that was the way I should be, unless I could do something to change myself before it was too late. And yet—was Berthold really pitiable? In spite of everything, he was a great man, a great human being who had struggled and suffered, failed and succeeded. His talent had never been stronger. All this time, he was producing poems, stories, articles. He fairly bubbled with creativeness. If Berthold was to be pitied, what about Bodo Uhse?

Bodo Uhse had been called in by Berthold to help us with our story, because he had once actually belonged to the Nazi party. Later, Uhse became a communist, and fought in Spain. His whole life had been involved in violence. As an officer's son in a garrison town during the 1914 war, he had joined an organization formed by other officers' sons in their teens—a kind of Junior Junkers' League. One of their members, a boy of fifteen, stole a bicycle. The group court-martialled him. They told the boy that he had disgraced them, disgraced his own father (who was at the front) and the entire German army. There was only one honorable way of atonement. The culprit agreed. They got him a revolver. That night, he shot himself.

Bodo was about thirty-eight years old, small and white and skinny. When he went in swimming, he looked like a shrivelled schoolboy, with his short untidy hair and big, sensitive grey eyes. His mouth was lined and compressed. He seemed always half dead with cold. Berthold said of him: "He's one of nature's orphans. He's so poor—so terribly poor—one can't imagine that he ever had anything—any warmth, any joy—" One day, I asked him: "Bodo, what was the happiest time of your life?" Bodo considered; then his eyes lighted up: "It was in Schleswig-Holstein, just after the war. I was living among the peasants. There was a rising. We made our own bombs. We went into town in a truck, and threw them at the Rathaus."[1]

I'm afraid Bodo didn't get much for his work with us—perhaps twenty or thirty dollars. I doubt if I got more than a hundred and fifty, altogether. Berthold, who privately considered himself a shrewd business man, had, as usual, displayed the innocence and trust of a ten-year-old child. In New York, he had met a producer named Al Rosen, who had offered him this job. Berthold was to get so much for writing the picture, and a further sum for directing it when written. There was a legal contract to this effect, but unfortunately this contract was already invalid—both parties had delayed their negotiations so long that the deadline date for delivery of the script was already passed. Correspondence began, to fix a new date; but, in the meanwhile, Berthold heard, from a private source, that Rosen hadn't yet raised the money for the production, although he had declared, months before, that it was already in the bank. He seems to have been one of those shoestring producers who build up a production on promises and sales talk, hoping that some writer will do them a script on which they can actually raise money, or that some backer will provide money with which they can buy a script. This method may be dishonest, but it often works. Ellis St. Joseph (of whom more later) got involved in a similar deal with his play *Passenger to Bali*; but the play was finally produced, and paid off.

However, Berthold was furious. He embarked on a whole series of letters, accusing, threatening, demanding. Rosen answered, counter-accusing. The letter writing took up a great deal of time (I had to translate them into English, with much search for the mot juste). Berthold really enjoyed this correspondence far more than doing the script itself. There was much barking and little biting. (The biting came two years later when, appealed to desperately by Berthold, I had suddenly to settle with Rosen out of court, for nondelivery of the script. This cost me several hundred dollars— but, at that time, I could well afford them.)

About this time, I gave a radio talk at the Beverly Hills "Station of the Stars," KMPC. It was an interview, in a series called "Meet the Author." "The Author," in each case, had to prepare his own script—and, reading through my colleagues' efforts, I had to admit that few of them suffered from inferiority complexes. "Mr. X., how do you explain the secret of your success with the public?" "Mr. Y., how did you get that marvellous idea for your novel?"

[1] Townhall.

etc. etc. However, I was able to avoid this kind of thing. I simply talked about our journey to China.

The talk got me two fans. The Viertels' Japanese maid, who listened in, was delighted because I said that the people of Japan certainly didn't want the war. And there was a very attractive dark girl, whorishly dressed in black silk and reeking of perfume, who waylaid me as I left the broadcasting studio. Could she speak to me alone? Not here. Wouldn't I come to her apartment? I made some excuse. Well then—would I answer just one question? "Certainly—" I began to get nervous, "That is, if I can—" The girl was now so close that I was practically holding her in my arms. She had me pinned against the wall. The station attendants were grinning in the background. She raised her face to mine, as though for a kiss. "Tell me, Mr. Isherwood," she murmured voluptuously, "*is* communism the *only* way out?"

At the beginning of August, Auden came out to the Coast, with Chester Kallman. They were going to stay in Laguna Beach, so we didn't see much of them. They had been in Taos, where they met Frieda Lawrence and Mabel Dodge Luhan. Both of them were very untidy, dirty and in the highest spirits: they looked curiously alike.

Auden went up to see Gerald. They had a long but rather unsatisfactory talk. Gerald commented later on Auden's jittery behavior and chain-smoking, and predicted that he would end up as a Catholic. Auden accused Gerald, as always, of being a Manichaean, a life hater. They were fond of each other, and respected each other sincerely. Their opposition wasn't really philosophical but temperamental. Auden had an excellent digestion and loved his dinner. Quite simply and frankly, he enjoyed comfort, wine and sex. Gerald was a dyspeptic who had passed the change of life. That was all. It would have been better to admit it, instead of defending their tastes with dialectics.

Gerald had already introduced me to Swami Prabhavananda. The following entry from my diary describes our second meeting, by appointment, alone.

August 4. The Swami was in his study when I arrived. He is smaller than I remembered—charming and boyish, although he is in his middle forties and has a bald patch at the back of his head. He looks slightly Mongolian, with long, straight eyebrows and wide-set dark eyes. He talks gently and persuasively. His smile is extraordinary. It is somehow so touching, so open, so brilliant with joy that it makes me want to cry.

I felt terribly awkward—like a rich, overdressed woman, in the plumes and bracelets of my vanity. Everything I said sounded artificial and false. I started acting a little scene, trying to appear sympathetic. I told him I wasn't sure I could do these meditations and lead the life I am leading. He answered: "You must be like the lotus on the pond. The lotus leaf is never wet."

I said I was afraid of attempting to do too much, because, if I failed, I should be discouraged. He said: "There is no failure in the search for God. Every step you take is a positive advance."

I said I hated the word "God." He agreed that you can just as well say "The Self" or "Nature."

He talked about the difference between yoga, meditation and autohypnosis. Autohypnosis or autosuggestion makes you see what you want to see. Meditation makes you see something you don't expect to see. Autosuggestion produces different results in each individual. Meditation produces the same result in all individuals.

This is what he told me to do:

1. To try to feel the presence of an all-pervading Existence.
2. Send thoughts of peace and goodwill toward all beings—north, south, east and west.
3. Think of the body as a temple, containing the Reality.
4. Meditate on the Real Self.
   The Self in you is the Self in all beings. I am infinite Existence, infinite Knowledge, infinite Bliss.

I explained how I had always thought of yoga as silly, superstitious nonsense. The Swami laughed: "And now you have fallen into the trap?"

August 5. I find number one the easiest—especially at night. It would be quite easy in the desert. Here, you keep hearing cars, steam hammers, distant radio, the clock, the icebox motor—and have to remind yourself that the Existence is also within these mechanisms. Number two is easy as long as I think of typical people in each country. For some reason, it is most difficult to send goodwill toward the South Americans. The points of the compass bother me, too. Where *is* everybody? This would be easiest on top of a mountain or a skyscraper. Number three very difficult. Much involved with thoughts of sex. Number four: relatively easy. When I think in terms of writing, I can easily see that the writer taps a great store of universal knowledge. The more daring, the more persistent he is, the more he finds out. "Infinite Bliss"—infinite possibility of bliss inside each of us. Why do I make myself miserable? Fear and desire are simply a blockage in the pipe. Get them out and the water will run. It's there, all the time. I am always trying to reassure myself that there is nothing and nobody in the universe I really want. Hence, my sexual adventures. To be able to say, "Oh, I've *had* X." So X. is taped, X. is eliminated. Then jealousy—because X. won't stay taped.

This evening, on bedroom floor, in the dark. Unsatisfactory. Stuck at number one, because I couldn't get over the feeling that everyone was asleep and therefore no longer part of "Consciousness." Posture is difficult. My back hurts. But I feel somehow refreshed.

August 6. Last night, a peculiarly horrible dream.

I was walking through what must have been a fairground, although, actually, the scene resembled a parking lot: a blank, grimy brick wall in the background, with trampled earth under foot. I saw a boy, about sixteen years old, stark naked, pale, unhealthy looking, with sloping shoulders and stocky, clumsy legs: there was a certain stolid, ungraceful toughness about his whole body. I knew that he was a fairground boxer. He had to fight all comers, for ten cents. He had a father who was very cruel to him whenever he lost.

At that moment, he was fighting a much larger boy, coarse looking and ugly, his face covered with pimples. This boy was also naked. They fought with their bare fists.

Then I noticed that the smaller boy was wearing a repulsive kind of truss or girdle, with an electric light switch projecting from his thigh. He was crippled, in some way. He was getting the worst of the fight. The larger boy hit him, drawing blood. The boy snorted up the blood through his nostrils and spat it out into a glass jar. The absolute stolidity with which he accepted his injury was what filled me with horror. I knew that his whole life would be like this—one cruel, stupid, savage fight after another—until he died.

Woke, sweating. I know this dream was somehow about a European war. . . .

And now, throughout August, we dropped rapidly toward disaster. There is little one wants to say about such a time. The radio broadcasts claimed large portions of each day. Liesl Frank (wife of Bruno, the writer) carried a portable set about with her, like a sick baby. She nursed it in her arms, bent over it as it muttered its advertisements, tuned it up loud for each new bulletin. But most of the Emigration didn't really expect war. They were sure England would "betray" them, as at Munich. Salka, Berthold's wife, was away in France, at Metro's expense, getting material for *Madame Curie*, on which Aldous Huxley had been working for Garbo. The Russo-Nazi pact was announced, and Berthold went into one of his biggest tailspins. He declared that he was through with politics. "You were right. Huxley was right. Even Heard was right." This mood lasted about twenty-four hours—at the end of which Berthold was right back on his feet again, defending Soviet policy like a wildcat.

October 1. Exactly one month since England's declaration of war.

The unimaginable has happened—and, of course, it's utterly different from anything we had pictured. One looks ahead to a war and imagines it as a single, final, absolute event. It is nothing of the kind. War is a condition, like peace, with good days and bad days, moods of optimism and despair. The crisis of August was actually, for us in Santa Monica, worse than this month which has followed the outbreak. I see Frau Frank's face, contorted with hate. I hear Gottfried Reinhardt yelling, Klaus Mann chattering like an enraged monkey, Berthold snorting like a war-horse. The night war was declared, Vernon and I sat listening to our radio at home. It was as though neither of us were really present. The living room seemed absolutely empty—with nothing in it but the announcer's voice. No fear, no despair, no sensation at all. Just hollowness.

A week or two later, we moved to these two rooms in a house above Santa Monica Canyon—303 South Amalfi Drive. They are airy and pleasant, with a view of the ocean. Our landlady's name is Mrs. Bayley. She lives with her mother, and her younger son, a schoolboy named Happy. Happy is very happy indeed, although he has diabetes. The Huxleys live on Amalfi, too; but their house is a mile further up the hill.

Whatever happens now, I am so glad to be out of that dreary Sycamore Trail house. We sold all our furniture at a seventy-five percent loss. I am tons lighter in consequence. Before we left, I buried Jacky's champagne cork in the hillside, behind the back door.

Vernon has caught my depression at last. He is very sick with it— like a South Sea islander who nearly dies of a common cold imported by a trader. He can't eat, can't work, can't enjoy anything. He drives our already battered new car into Hollywood, to visit his various friends. I spend my whole day at the Viertels', in a coma of nicotine poisoning, planning the film—which still hasn't started. Berthold, grimly pugnacious, flares up at the least imagined insult from any member of the family. He imagines a huge conspiracy against himself. He says he will take a room, out. Poor Hans, the eldest son, bears the brunt, because of his irritating deafness. Frau Steuermann gets quietly drunk. She is afraid to go into the kitchen, because the cook is her arch enemy.

Of course we are all as mad as hatters. What else can you expect? The radio works day and night to undermine the foundations of sanity. We all know by heart the advertisements for Packard cars, Borden's milk, Bulova watches, which precede the news. The European correspondents, trained in the literary school of Sheean and Farson,[1] broadcast local color: "The Paris sky is blue. The leaves in the Bois are turning yellow. A lark is singing over Montmartre." I hate them more than anybody else in this whole business. I swear that, if peace ever returns, if I am ever again freed from their clutches, I will never open another newspaper, never listen to another radio program. I feel about them the way some bums must feel about the Salvation Army worker who forces you to take hymns with your soup.

The madness of this war infects us all. But the war itself and its sufferers are utterly unreal. Morgan Forster, Heinz, Stephen, M. and all the others are inhabiting a different world. It isn't that I daren't think about them; I can't. Shall I go back to England? I don't know. Wystan is still in New York and wants to remain there. Unless America comes in, no decision is forced on me. I must make my own choice. Very few English residents have left California yet.

Meanwhile, the weather is heartlessly beautiful—after the flood which nearly washed the half-completed WPA[2] canal project into the sea. The great heavy pelicans skim over the waves, and dive into the water with a huge splash. The wind thrashes the eucalyptus trees. The drugstore is kept by an ex-actor called Doc Law, with a Napoleon III beard, who was an intimate friend of Will Rogers. Chris goes every morning to the beach, renewing his tan. Gerald's eye is a little wilder, his nose a shade redder. Vernon has just done a drawing and thrown it into the waste basket. Now he is reading to me from the two-volume *Oxford Dictionary*.

Courage, calm. I must restart my meditations.

October 16. Another heatwave just ending. Russia threatens Finland. I have just returned from seeing Gerald—to our empty rooms. Vernon has started working with his friend George Arnold at his pottery business. Sometimes he stays away for two or three days. I hardly see him, except when he is dead tired, late at night, or sleepy at breakfast.

I can't remember any time in my life when I seriously believed in God. At Repton, when I got confirmed—before I met Edward—

---

[1] Vincent Sheean and Negley Farson, American correspondents working respectively from Paris and London during the war, both novelists.
[2] Works Progress Administration, created by Roosevelt in 1935 to provide useful public employment during the Depression.

I was a cautious, diplomatic hypocrite. While I was constantly with Edward at Cambridge, I achieved a more or less continuous state of awareness which was religious in character, although we expressed it in terms of Art. But it was mostly at second hand, through books. Then came Wystan, preaching Homer Lane. I made more contact with the outside world. And when my books were published, I really felt I was doing what Life made me for. In actual fact, I was only giving a performance of the Ego as Artist. "To create, to love, to suffer." The "love" part of it was pretty phony. But still, all those legs and arms and bodies were parts of people. The people, when I got to Berlin, belonged to a certain class—poorer than mine. I had to spend money on them, and therefore doubted the love. So I became political. Marxism said, "I'll remove the barriers." Okay.

Marxism also said, "I'll kill the Ego"—but it didn't—even in the noblest of my revolutionary friends. So I despaired, and started to pretend that the Ego didn't exist. But the Ego did exist, and became stronger than ever. It ate up all the "love," and even began to paralyze the creative powers. It grew weary of itself, loathing its own tricks— so weary that, when I finally did get loved, really loved, the Ego was so nauseated by its own flattering, distorted mirror image, that it had to turn away. It was afraid of being found out.

That's my position now. And, however I may boast to Gerald, nothing has changed—except that the way out has become dimly visible. But *what* a way out! The Ego shivers. It smells the wind of its destruction.

"I love you," says the Ego, doggedly. How well I know that tone! It means, "I hate you and mean to torture you."

November 5. Still this wonderful weather. The beach is nearly empty now. Only the surf-riders linger, with their paddleboards. They are like a different race of beings, beautiful and golden, with their graceful, relaxed attitudes, as they balance on the brilliant crest of the wave. The other evening, I was walking along the shore at dusk, and one of them came sliding in through the foam—right to my feet. For a moment, we looked at each other, without speaking or smiling. He was so wet—his almost black skin saturated with water—that it was like meeting some marine animal, not a man. Then, without a word, he turned and paddled back into his element, until he was lost in the gathering darkness. . . .

John van Druten was in Los Angeles for a while, this autumn. Before he went back to the East, he introduced me to his friend Carter Lodge. Carter had an apartment in Westwood Village. We saw a good deal of each other. Being with him was easy, gay and pleasant—because he insisted on my being cheerful. Carter liked cheerful people. He didn't want to hear any complaints. Underneath, he was quite tough and efficient. And he knew exactly what he wanted, without any nonsense. His only sentimentality was about success, so he had taken up astrology—rather in the same spirit as a sailor studies navigation. He was determined to take care of all the angles.

I always remember a weekend when Carter and I visited Palm Springs. We drove out to the Salton Sea by moonlight and sat on the beach. A big Alsatian dog followed us. It belonged to the motel proprietor. After we had sat in silence for some minutes, the dog came circling and sniffing around, and finally lay down beside us. It was one of those moments that seem printed in our memory for no apparent reason, uncannily distinct. The tiny lake waves licking hurriedly at the white sand, lick, lick, lick, lick, lick. The black and silver-splashed levels of the water. The dry desert scrub behind us, and the reaches of the desert—a submarine garden, abandoned by the sea. The mountains all around—felt rather than seen, like furniture in a darkened room. And overhead the brilliant, uninhabited moon.

The biggest social event of that fall was an all-star picnic organized by the Huxleys at Tujunga Canyon. There were about thirty guests—Aldous, Maria, their doctor and his family, Bertrand Russell, his wife Peter and two or three stepchildren, Krishnamurti, Rajagopal and his wife Rosalind,[1] Anita Loos, with friends, Salka Viertel and Berthold and Garbo.

I had seen Garbo already, at the Viertels', but we had only been together for a few minutes at a time. She was always full of secrets to be discussed in private with Salka, her closest confidante. She wore the famous straw gardening hat, with slacks, and a tiny patch of plaster between her eyebrows, to prevent wrinkles from forming. She was kittenish, in a rather embarrassing way; and her lack of makeup and general untidiness were obviously calculated. Just the same, I liked her and felt quite at ease in her company. She climbed the figtree in the Viertels' garden to get me some specially ripe figs. I remember how she referred to some business dealings with the studio, and said that one must always pretend to be a child when talking to the front office. She had her own kind of little-girl slyness.

Garbo had been lured to the picnic under false pretences. They had told her it would be a very quiet affair—just the Huxleys and

[1] Desikacharya Rajagopalacharya, Krishnamurti's advisor and financial manager, and Rosalind Williams Rajagopal.

Krishnamurti. Garbo was anxious to meet Krishnamurti. She was naturally drawn to prophets—genuine and otherwise. Salka said that she was very unhappy, restless and frightened. She wanted to be told the secret of eternal youth, the meaning of life—but quickly, in one lesson, before her butterfly attention wandered away again. Hence Stokowski, and Dr. Hauser's salads.[1]

We picnicked on the stony riverbed, high up the canyon, where the road ends. It was a beautiful place, with forest precipices towering above us, not unlike a scene in the lower Alps. Garbo, of course, had her special diet with her in a basket. She and Krishnamurti were put next to each other, but they didn't speak much. I think they were both scared.

Krishnamurti was a slight, sallow little man with a scrubby chin and rather bloodshot eyes, whose face bore only faint traces of the extraordinary beauty he must have had as a boy. He was very quiet and modest, and never talked in ordinary company about philosophy or religion. He seemed fondest of animals and most at ease with children. Gerald complained that he got violently upset about trifles—like catching a train—and showed little sign of inward calm. Certainly, he didn't impress me as Prabhavananda did; but he had a kind of simple dignity which was very touching. And—there was no getting away from it—he had done what no other man alive today has done: he had refused to become a god.

After lunch, most of our party wandered a little further up the canyon, to a place where the forest rangers had built a high wire fence, right across the riverbed, with notices warning against trespass. (I think this was because a dam was under construction, to control the annual floods of the Los Angeles River.) Somebody said it looked like a barricade around a concentration camp. Anita Loos suggested that we should burrow under it, like escaping refugees. It was a rather sinister joke, and the laughter was a bit forced, as several people began to dig, with their hands or pieces of rock. I remember Bertrand Russell holding forth to Aldous on some philosophical topic and digging as he talked, with the air of a father joining in a game to amuse the children. Only, in this case, he was both parent and child.

Inside a few minutes, there was quite a large, shallow pit. Most of us got into it and wriggled under the wire. It was funny to watch how, having done this, people became grown-ups again and strolled off in twos and threes, talking about the war. I don't know why they had taken all this trouble, for they paid no attention to the

[1] The conductor Leopold Stokowski and Garbo's diet guru, Gayelord Hauser, with whom she had much-discussed relationships.

scenery. Berthold especially—that born city dweller—might just as well have been walking down Fifth Avenue.

I held back to the end of the procession, because I wanted to walk with Garbo. I had drunk a lot of beer at lunch, and knew no shame. I only wished my friends could see me. As we started out, Garbo said: "As long as we're on this side of the fence, let's pretend we're two other people—quite, quite different." "You know," I announced solemnly, "I really wish you *weren't* Garbo. I like you. I think we could have been great friends." At this, Garbo let out a mocking, Mata Hari laugh: "But we *are* friends! You are my dear little brother. All of you are my dear little brothers." "Oh, shut up!" I exclaimed, enormously flattered.

I suppose everybody who meets Garbo dreams of saving her—either from herself, or from Metro-Goldwyn-Mayer, or from some friend or lover. And she always eludes them by going into an act. This is what has made her a universal figure. She is the woman whose life everyone wants to interfere with.

Just as we had finished our stroll and were returning to the wire fence by another path, we met a forest ranger who was cutting some wood. I could hardly believe my luck. What a situation! Of course, he would recognize her at once. Garbo evidently thought so, too, for she pulled down her wide hat brim. I fairly swelled with gallantry. When he asked us what the hell we were doing and took our names, I'd get in front of her and swear she was Miss Smith from Ocean Park, or maybe Mrs. Isherwood—and I'd give him my own address to let me know the amount of the fine. This, I thought, will really impress her.

The ranger looked us both over, quite pleasantly. Then he said: "Do you know what I'm doing here?"

"No," I answered. (This sounded like the build-up for some heavy sarcasm about our trespassing.)

"I'm killing two birds with one stone. This ground has to be cleared; so I'm cutting me some firewood for my cabin."

We passed on. Berthold, who had no straw hat and was nobody's dear little brother, met a different ranger and got his name taken, with severe rebukes for smoking cigarettes in a fire area. Later, he was fined.

Throughout September and October, Berthold and I continued our collaboration. That is to say, we saw each other nearly every day, tinkered with the story (agreeing that the war had made it necessary to reconsider the whole idea on a different basis), drank coffee, smoked, joked, gossiped, swam. We even played with ideas for other stories. Berthold could hatch them out by the dozen.

About the beginning of November, to our utter amazement, I got a job. It was a spy story for Goldwyn. The story itself was so idiotic that there seemed nothing whatever to be done with it—but Berthold had the idea of scrapping it altogether and substituting one of our own, built around my character, Mr. Norris.

I went to see Eddie Knopf, of Goldwyn's story department, with this idea and got it accepted at once. Knopf was one of those shrewd, rude, man-to-man Jews who exude hairy virility. In telling our story, I ad-libbed the line: "I'd sooner cut off my hand than do that!" It must have been one of those dreadful subconscious "errors." I suppose I had already been told about Knopf's amputation, and forgotten. At the word "hand," his arm twitched, and I saw the stump jerk forward from his sleeve. It nearly stopped me dead.

(The story is that in Germany, after the 1914 war, Knopf went into a toy shop and saw a child buying what was supposed to be a toy hand grenade. Knopf saw at once that it was actually a live bomb—how it got there isn't explained—and that the child had already pulled out the safety pin. He grabbed the grenade and ran out into the street, where it exploded.)

Knopf was smart. He was working for a cunning old miser with plenty of taste, who posed as a roughneck illiterate boor for the same reason as Garbo posed as a child. Goldwyn would shout and stamp. Knopf would take the victim out to lunch and calm him down, without neglecting to cash in on his shattered morale. In this case, the object of their bullying was to get me to surrender the rights of *Mr. Norris Changes Trains* without paying me for them or guaranteeing more than a few weeks' work. Knopf soon discovered that I was down to my last fifteen dollars. Then he got tough. Against my better judgment, for Berthold's sake and for Vernon's, I gave way.

I continued to work with Berthold, on a fifty-fifty basis. Berthold was very fatherly during this period. He bewildered me with instructions. It was always assumed that the boot was on the wrong foot—that it was he who ought to be handling the interviews while I stayed at home. Actually, Knopf and Berthold would have gotten to death grips at once, and Berthold knew this. He was quite content to leave things the way they were, and poke fatherly fun at my maiden struggles with the Hollywood film world.

The Goldwyn Studios, at this time, were like a ghost town. The offices were emptying, the stages were standing idle, the employees were being laid off. Goldwyn was going into one of his hibernation periods; perhaps he was waiting to see how the war would develop. Soon, I was almost the only writer on the lot—except for a legendary lady named Jan Fortune, who, it was said, never got fired because nobody could find her. She dodged along the corridors from office to office, and always slept in the building. She was supposed to have parties there, at night.

I saw Goldwyn himself three or four times. The first time, he was friendly and flattering. The second, at his house in Beverly Hills, he was rude and unmanageable. "It's all nonsense!" he shouted. "It's stupid. The boy's a damn fool. I want something clever." I drank a big glass of whisky and felt superior—for by this time I knew that I had a job at MGM waiting for me after the New Year. Our last interview was a very curious one, because I had apparently succeeded in hurting his feelings, with a mock-polite letter I had written to the story department, outlining the various stages of our plot development, and Goldwyn's contradictory suggestions and objections. I had tried to make this letter sound as much as possible like a clinical report, merely substituting "Mr. Goldwyn" for "the patient."

Goldwyn sent for me in his office and put on an extraordinary act, in front of several subordinates. He asked, did I think him a stupid, obstinate hick who knew nothing about writers and couldn't appreciate their work? If so, it was just too bad, because, although he was only a plain business man, he knew a good thing when he saw it—he knew I was a swell writer and a swell person, and he thought of me as a friend, etc. etc. I saw through him a yard, but just the same I was embarrassed. I grinned and mumbled protests. When we were through with the playacting, I told him about the Metro job. This didn't please him at all. Automatically, he began a line about loyalty and checked himself: he knew that I knew he was going out of business. We said goodbye—one of those wordy Hollywood farewells which have no warmth but much superstition. Film people usually fear an unkind parting. It may bring you bad luck—especially if the other guy makes good, later.

Some months after this, I had a frank talk with Knopf, who had also left the Goldwyn Studio. "You touched Sam on his sore spot," he told me. "Call him a son of a bitch and he'll sock you on the jaw. Tell him he hasn't acted like a gentleman, and he'll crawl."

It was only much later, discussing Goldwyn with John van Druten, that I realized how cleverly Berthold and I had been handled, right from the beginning. The insult technique is designed to put a writer on his mettle, and make him produce the maximum number of story ideas in a very short period. Then, when the writer has been well milked, he's fired, and another writer is called in. Berthold had actually been tricked into presenting Goldwyn with three completely different stories.

Knopf told me of a talk he'd had with Goldwyn, the day I was hired.

> Goldwyn: If we've got to use his characters, we must take care he doesn't use any of ours. Nothing that's in the original script— (*looking through the outline of our story*) What's this about the Gestapo? He can't use the Gestapo.
> Knopf: But, Sam, the Gestapo isn't our property.
> Goldwyn (*after deep thought, sadly*): No—I guess you're right, Eddie. It isn't.

December 6. The war gets crazier every day. Italy denounces Russia, sends bombers against them to help the Finns—apparently with Hitler's sanction. Russia reported demanding Bessarabia. No fighting on the western front. No air raids on London. No peace. "Very soon," I told Berthold, "Britain and Germany will sign a mutual aggression pact—to keep at least five divisions facing each other on the Maginot line for the next ten years—while they both attack Russia." As poor Toller predicted, "Nie wieder Frieden" is the new slogan.[1]

It is silly, old-fashioned, nowadays to write: "I wish I were dead." I wish I were alive.

December 16. This evening, Gerald showed me a letter from Raymond Mortimer. He, and nearly every member of the Bloomsbury circle, seems to be pro-war. This war is not against men, against Germans—but against "a sort of cholera epidemic." The Americans are criticized, for wanting the English to fight their battles—but the Americans are not to get into the war, for fear they should insist on a stupid, liberalistic peace. The peace should be dictated by France—partition and both banks of the Rhine.

A. A. Milne has repudiated his own book[2]—because, "This is really a civil war." Harold Nicolson goes even further. He says it's holy.

December 22. A stupid, ill-considered letter I wrote to Gerald Hamilton has been quoted by William Hickey's gossip column in the London *Daily Express*. (Gerald, apparently, thought he was doing me

---

[1] "No More Peace"; see Glossary under Toller.
[2] *Peace with Honour* (1933); see Glossary under Milne.

a favor and getting me a little free publicity!) "The refugees here are very militant and already squabbling over the future German government. God help Germany if some of them ever get into power! Others are interested, apparently, in reconquering the Romanisches Café, and would gladly sacrifice the whole British army to make Berlin safe for night life . . ."

Berthold, who had this clipping sent him by an angry refugee colleague from London, wants me to publish some kind of explanation, or apology. I tried, but I shan't send it. There is a disgusting mock-humility in eating your own words. After all, I meant what I said. I *am* opposed to Prince Löwenstein's antics, Erika Mann's hate lectures.[1] My real offence is that I expressed myself badly. Berthold warns me that I have been very unwise, because my possibility of earning money here depends largely upon German refugees and their German-American-Jewish friends.

The alternative (which Berthold advises) is to use this occasion to make a statement about the war, my position, etc. etc. But the whole essence of my "position" is not to make statements. I am the only silent member of a community of all-too-noisy prophets. My motto: *Nescio, Nescio.*[2]

(I'm not sure, but I think that, by this time, Harold Nicolson had already published a mock-friendly article attacking Aldous, Gerald, Wystan and myself for not returning to England and taking part in the war effort.[3] A London newspaper, maybe the *Daily Express* or the *News Chronicle*, cabled each of us, asking for our comment. I don't know what Wystan said. Gerald didn't answer. I believe Aldous wrote a letter. I answered that I agreed with Heard and Huxley "one hundred percent," which was defiant rather than illuminating.

The publication of my letter to Gerald Hamilton seems to have touched off a whole press campaign against us, which lasted well into 1940. Questions were even asked in Parliament. I hardly refer to this at all in my diary, because, at the time, it made me feel so guilty—guilty, and, at the same time, defiant. There is a strange exhilaration in being attacked. Part of me wanted to turn and snarl back, like an animal trapped by hounds. I am glad now that I didn't.

However, on Auden's advice, I wrote to the British Embassy in

[1] See Glossary under Löwenstein and Mann, Erika.
[2] I do not know, I do not know.
[3] The William Hickey column (written at that time by Tom Driberg) appeared November 27, 1939; Nicolson's article didn't appear until April 19, 1940. See Glossary under Nicolson.

Washington asking if these attacks represented the official British attitude and offering, if necessary, to return to England and serve in a noncombatant capacity. A secretary named Hoyer Millar[1] answered, in a letter dated July 12, 1940: "I wish to assure you that your position in the United States, like Mr. Auden's, is understood and that the offer of your services is much appreciated. If you have not already done so, I would suggest that you keep in touch with the British Consul at Los Angeles who will be able to give you the best advice from time to time."

That was my first and last attempt to put myself in the right with the authorities. Much later, the consulate did appeal to all British residents to return to England—but only on condition that you signed a paper agreeing to accept *any* kind of service you were assigned to. This ruled out conscientious objectors. And, in any case, my attitude had somewhat altered. More of that in due course.)

Faced by Salka's lost job at MGM, the Viertels are displaying a fatalistic extravagance. Sheaves of cables to Europe. Shopfuls of gifts from an expedition to Tijuana. They are a real Chekhov family. Berthold writing his journal, poems, letters to England, upstairs in the room overlooking the ocean—the lair into which he has carried like an animal all the books he can buy, borrow or steal. He reads everything—from modern American poetry to Hindu mysticism, from astronomy to Aeschylus—with a frantic, greedy haste. A kind of Faust.

And Salka, around whom still floats the melancholy, nostalgic glamor of the theater—the glamor of extravagance, hopeless debts, disillusioned love. "Children," she exclaims, "I am *absolutely* exhausted!" She sinks sensually into a chair, like a big mother cat.

And Hans—the pale, unshaven "eternal student"—coming home at 4 a.m. from the Reinhardt School—stalking about the house in his bathrobe at noon—nervy, irritable, deaf; a horror to Berthold, who sees in him a slipshod caricature of his own youth, and loads him with reproaches, bitter, anxious, loving. Everybody bosses Hans, especially the women.

Etta [Hardt], the housekeeper, bosses everybody—Peter, when he is at home; dreamy, good-humored Tommy, with his untidy red hair, glasses and lisp; Mausi [Steuermann], Salka's niece, always half-

---

[1] Frederick Robert Hoyer Millar (1900–1989), British diplomat, First Secretary in Washington, D. C. from 1939, Minister from 1948; created Lord Inchyra in 1962.

smiling with the secret superiority of a future great actress; cantankerous Lena,[1] the cook; old rheumatic Buddy and the noisy younger
dogs. Erect in her blazer and flannel trousers, she works from
morning to night, like an undaunted pioneer, to prevent the home
from relapsing into virgin Jewish jungle—hacking tirelessly at the
ever-growing tangle of Berthold's untidiness, Salka's extravagance,
Hans's bad habits, his secret smoking and his late hours.

December 23. I have decided to write this diary only during the periods
when I am waiting for one or other of my friends to get ready. Nearly
everybody I know habitually keeps me waiting. Today it was
Berthold—for nearly two hours. I said to Frankie, the Filipino
houseboy, "The only thing we learn in this life in waiting." "Yes, Mr.
Isherwood," he answered, "we are all waiting for the last commencement."

Last night, Vernon and I went with Chris Wood to a big party at
the Huxleys'. Their place is like a house in one of the Sherlock
Holmes stories, where a murder will be committed. It stands back
from the road, completely hidden—a large bungalow built and
furnished in baroque-log-cabin style. It used to belong to a rich
doctor, one of the founders of the Uplifters' Club, who gave huge
parties here during the prohibition epoch. (The Uplifters' Club seems
to have started as a sort of retreat for unfaithful, married business men.
Now it is a mildly artistic, respectable colony—down in the canyon
below the Huxleys' home.)

The walls are hung with semierotic, fetishist pictures of "cruel"
ladies in boots, and with romantic photographs of nudes. The lighting
is dim and sexually inviting—like an old-fashioned Berlin night spot.
In fact, the living room was so dark that a lady—the first person I
spoke to—said: "Will you please light my cigarette, so I can see your
face?" This was Benita Hume, the actress, rather drunk. I liked her.
She was hunting everywhere for Ronald Colman, her husband. He
proved to be standing just behind her—the perfect tailor's dummy of
a "man of a certain age," with gracefully grey temples, bright
handsome dark eyes, an exquisitely discreet little moustache. He
seemed modest, gentle and kind—but now Aldous swam forward out
of the warm gloom, like a great, blind deep-sea fish, to introduce me
to his brother Julian, just arrived from England for a lecture tour.
Julian disappointed me. I had expected him to be more human than
Aldous, warmer, less pedantic. Actually, he seemed prim, severe and
schoolmasterish, and Aldous, by contrast, appeared much more

---

[1] Possibly Lena Frank, ex-wife of novelist Leonard Frank; she joined the Viertels
as a refugee with her teenage son.

sympathetic. Julian was very much the official representative of England at war. Behind his sternness, I thought I could detect a certain puritanical sadism—a satisfaction that the lax peace-days were over, and that we'd all got to suffer. Perhaps I am being unjust to him. Perhaps he was only unhappy and tired. But I didn't like the triumphant ring in his voice as he declared that "everybody was agreed" that the Hitler menace had to be removed for ever—it suggested a pleasure in totalitarianism for its own sake, and woe to the dissenters. Somebody asked him if he had come to make propaganda for aid to Britain. No—he was absolutely opposed to propaganda: "We are opposed to it" (meaning the British Foreign Office). "We" actually hoped America wouldn't come into the war; because America's function was to help with economic reconstruction, afterwards. "One's got to make that clear to the people here."

Just to hear what he would reply, I asked him if he thought I should return home. No. If you had a job in the USA, and were earning American money, it was your duty to stay. Not for propaganda, but to represent "the British point of view." Nevertheless, Julian added, it would be a good thing to get into touch with the British in New York. They liked to have reports on the state of opinion in different parts of the country.

The British and French, he assured us, had no intention of attacking on the western front. If the Germans attacked, so much the better. He added that the war would produce an economic revolution in England. The small rentier class would disappear entirely. (Again the grim gleam of satisfaction.)

I turned from him in relief to George Cukor, who was gaily boasting that he had lost sixty pounds by dieting. Then Matthew Huxley took us out to drink champagne secretly in the kitchen. Maria is an absurdly bad hostess—she was so busy with her particular friends, Salka and Anita Loos, that she forgot to make introductions or produce the drinks. When it was finally time for us to leave, she was nowhere to be found.

Berthold, meanwhile, was going after Bertrand Russell, who had adopted Julian's phraseology: "I hear we sank a German submarine yesterday." Berthold's eye gleamed. "I am surprised," he said, with deadly courteousness, "to hear you say '*we*,' Lord Russell. In the last war, your '*I*' made history."

Then old Bob Flaherty, whom I haven't seen since London in 1934, wandered into the house by the wrong door, carrying his big stomach uneasily under his clothes, like something he had stolen. He is working on a U.S. Government film about land erosion. He talked to Julian, who at once became nicer, discussing the habits of gannets and basking sharks.

Vernon was enjoying himself, getting drunk and lecturing a fat, stupid man about art. "He was so dumb," Vernon kept repeating to me, later, "I had to tell him everything." Vernon had violent stage fright before this party, and was so relieved to find someone he could talk down to. I am usually listening to him with half an ear, when we go out together, to hear how he is making out. When he gets on to familiar ground, and is able to hold forth familiarly on Suetonius, or Leonardo, or Picasso, I feel pleased and proud, like an uncle.

Heavy rain this morning. At last, the summer-autumn seems definitely over. Wild wet ocean, sands, mountains and sky. Even the hardiest of the sun-pickled veteran swimmers have deserted the sodden beach.

Talk with Berthold, about last night. He was very pleased with his retort to Russell. Actually, I feel sorry for Russell. He is a very honest man, and it can't be easy for him to abandon his pacifism—especially now that he is laid open to the usual sneer, that it is easy enough to support a war when you are in a neutral country and over military age.

We read Wickham Steed's article on the war aims.[1] Germany, he says, must be forced to recognize "the rule of law." But isn't British imperialism "the rule of law," according to Steed? If you carry his arguments to their logical conclusion, Prussianism's only fault is that it has so far failed. If it had succeeded, it would be respectable, like the Empire. The Steed mentality builds a world in which the ultimate law is "nothing succeeds like success." A nasty new upstart government has the bad taste to recognize this law and state it openly, without diplomatic trimmings. So it becomes "the enemy of civilization."

Steed apparently says: "Carry through this war with all the ruthlessness necessary to its success. Then, at the peace conference, suddenly start behaving like Jesus Christ."

The Finns claim that the Russians are retreating in the far north. Finland is now America's Public Sweetheart Number One.

Had Bud Mong to dinner. His brain tinkles with radio tunes. His lazy, half-joking ambitions to earn fifteen hundred dollars a week, and then go back to his home town and make the Girl Who Didn't Care eat out of his hand. Although he is chronically short of money, and sometimes doesn't have enough to eat, he won't give up his beautiful

[1] Henry Wickham Steed (1871–1956), British journalist and broadcaster, former editor of *The Times* and the *Review of Reviews*, also published one of the first books about the war, *Our War Aims* (1939).

Buick convertible, because, he says, it gives him "background."
Again and again, one meets this figure—the gay, pathetic little hero of
An American Tragedy.

Only the true sage, the advanced yogi, really knows what things are
for, and never forgets it. He can own a car and not be hypnotized by
the idea "car." He never forgets that a car is simply a convenient piece
of mechanism which will take him from one place to another. The
Tragic American, on the other hand, sees his car as a symbol.
Different makes of automobile, in ascending order of luxury, are the
punctuation marks in his success story.

"House," "Bank balance," "Swimming pool," "Beautiful wife,"
"European cruise," "Son who rows for Yale"—these are like bank
notes in a hopelessly inflated currency. They are only unreal
counterparts of the things and people they represent. They are no
longer important, primarily, in themselves—but only as symbols in a
scale of imaginary social, erotic, autohypnotic values. This state of
autohypnosis—in which my possessions have value as possessions, not
as intrinsically serviceable objects—is called "Real Life." One may
recognize this absurdity—but it is all too fatally easy to slip back into
the autohypnotic condition. Every advertisement, every radio
commercial, every popular movie or magazine story potentially
resembles the small bright object which the hypnotist uses to focus his
patient's attention. The rest—granted the patient's passivity—is very
simple.

During the past weeks, I have found myself repeatedly slipping into
the "Real Life" trance. This was because I was earning a lot of money
in a ridiculously easy way—for work which I knew to be third-rate.
The process was all the more effective because the hypnotic object
was unfamiliar—I am not accustomed to having five hundred dollars
a week. I even spent a great deal of this money for autohypnotic
reasons. Very symptomatic was the trip Vernon and I recently made
to Palm Springs. Because "Palm Springs" isn't just a place; it's a
symbol. It's the movie world's *idea* of a chic winter weekend.
However, we accidentally woke ourselves up in the middle of the
"Palm Springs" trance—acting on a sudden impulse, we got out of
the car and wandered on foot up a narrow canyon blocked with
bushes and rocks. This hot, tiring scramble, without any "object," in
a place not registered as a "beauty spot," did not belong to the *idea*
"Palm Springs"—and so it recalled us for a little while from our
trance. For this very reason, it was the only part of the trip either of us
really enjoyed.

The most advertised, and the most fantastically inflated and
distorted values in "Real Life" are "Sex" and "Love." D. H.

Lawrence knew this, and warned his readers, over and over again, not to "use" sex. How many men, for example, could go to bed with Lana Turner and honestly say that they'd enjoyed it *only* because she is an attractive girl? And the extraordinary importance which the autohypnotist attaches to the orgasm—like cutting your name on a rock at the top of a mountain. By autohypnotic love-rules, unless both names are carved on the rock you don't count as having climbed the mountain at all.

Day in the life of an autohypnotist: "Got my paycheck, got a Renoir, did the sights, did a matinee, had supper, had my wife."

December 24. At half-past three, last night, Vernon came home with a baby duck which he'd bought in a drugstore. The duck was wearing a kind of harness of brightly colored ribbon, and a little hat.

This morning, I went into the ocean—autohypnotically, in order to be able to say, "I swam on Christmas Eve." The water was cold, but the sun was still quite warm.

Lunch with the Bayleys—including Bud, the elder son, who works with his father, Mrs. Bayley's divorced husband, at Carmel, and is staying with us for the Christmas holidays.

(Mr. Bayley left Mrs. B. for her best girlfriend, married the girlfriend, divorced her, wanted to remarry Mrs. B., was turned down, and finally married the girlfriend for the second time.)

Mrs. Bayley's mother, Mrs. MacCabe, in her invalid chair—she has sprained her foot—talked about her late husband, an Englishman from Crewe. Happy was persuaded to play "Silent Night" on the piano. Mrs. Bayley brought in hot cups of Tom and Jerry;[1] Mrs. MacCabe faintly disapproving. Bud was kidded by his mother for "going with" a lady of thirty-five.

Stories of Happy's wisecracks. The teacher once asked him, "Happy, what's the matter with you? Are you hoarse?" Happy: "I'm so hoarse I could saddle me and ride home." Bud, getting a bit high, described a drunken woman farting at a party: "She let go with all she'd got." Mrs. MacCabe was shocked but indulgent: she adores her grandchildren. Mrs. Bayley and Bud discussed the behavior of a mutual friend, who had caused a scandal at somebody's house: "She'd just lost her husband, but I guess the champagne sneaked up on her."

After the turkey came the presents. Vernon and I got handkerchiefs; Happy a windbreaker, sweaters, ski boots, a key chain; Bud a bathrobe; Mrs. MacCabe framed photographs of her father and mother, over which she shed a few tears, somewhat dampening our

---

[1] A sweet, spiced rum drink using the yolk and white of an egg beaten separately, and topped with nutmeg.

spirits. The duck, which we'd put on the balcony, fell down the drainpipe, and ran around the garden, quite unhurt.

Evening party at the Viertels'. We sang "Stille Nacht" and "Tannenbaum," before the lighted tree. Etta, as usual, had to organize everything—building up the ceremony to the great moment when Salka's presents were opened. Bodo Uhse lit the candles himself, at his own request, because, "I like to set fire to things." Mausi played the piano, beautifully. Peter gave Berthold and Salka the bound manuscript of his novel *The Canyon*. Salka embraced him and wept.

If only Salka wouldn't invite so many people, all so ill-assorted, her parties might be more of a success. But no one I know here has the first notion of how to entertain. When I think of the fun we used to have at the Mangeots', in the old days! Where shall I find another Olive, another Bill Lichtenberg? It's not merely that the times have changed. I don't feel that the kind of men and women I meet at Salka's *ever* knew how to be really gay. They are too mental. Their wit is all spikes and sharp edges. And so competitive: each one wants to hold the floor. There is a lot of embracing and sentimental fuss, but so little genuine warmth. That cosy feeling, "I am among friends"—how seldom I get it, nowadays!

December 25. Christmas Day lunch at the Rodakiewiczs'. Chris and Gerald were there. Ben and Derek did conjuring tricks. Chris, with his specially English brand of rudeness, complained that the room was too hot and left abruptly on his bicycle in the middle of the performance. When he is like this—just a spoilt little boy—one wants to smack him. But Peggy laughs it off; and Henwar, after a good lunch, is too placid and porcine to care. As usual, I felt very fond of them both.

Later in the afternoon, I made rather a fool of myself, attacking Huxley's novels. Why do I always do this? It isn't mere jealousy. I think he represents the English academic tradition—or my idea of the English academic tradition—which I still violently hate.

Peggy had a new game—finger painting. Like all her games, it is really an intelligence test; you emerge from it higher or lower in her estimation. Gerald did the sign of kundalini. Vernon produced a very fine design of spirals. I tried to use all the colors at once, and created only dark grey mud. Peggy says it is of great psychological interest to notice if people use only their index finger, all their fingers, or the whole palm of the hand. She laughed at Gerald's ladylike delicacy—not wanting to get dirtier than was absolutely necessary. "Yes," Gerald agreed, shaking his head sadly, "I'm afraid it's an Aversion."

He then began to talk to us about a woman he knows, a passionate liberal humanitarian, who has devoted her life to working in the Far East. She is doing everything possible to mobilize public opinion against the renewal of the U.S. trade agreement with Japan. Another friend of Gerald's—equally passionate, liberal and humanitarian—is doing everything possible to support the renewal. "What I want to know," said Gerald, "is: can one lead the political life at all, and hope to keep one's integrity?"

Having done his day's quiet little deed of sabotage, he turned on his rubber soles and vanished into the darkness, silently and rapidly ascending the steep hill behind the house. "And it came to pass, while he blessed them, he was parted from them . . ." The timing was perfect. I thought of him walking home along the firebreak road, to his lonely room, his meditations, his single bed. Even the mildest kind of austerity affects me, sometimes, like a cold breath from the grave.

Henwar and Peggy remind me of the humble peasant and his wife who acquire merit by entertaining the holy man on the road. Chris doubles the parts of Judas and the Young Man with Great Possessions. Vernon for a while was starred as St. John, but couldn't hold the job down. I am any of the more cowardly disciples. Berthold is perhaps developing into St. Paul. He has started to read *Pain, Sex and Time* with enormous enthusiasm.

Christmas shopping in Hollywood has been on a mammoth scale, this year. Norma Shearer[1] is said to have spent a thousand dollars on handkerchiefs alone—as presents for the entire studio staff.

December 26. A morning of pathological sloth. What brings on this disgraceful, paralytic laziness? It is always dangerous, of course, not to dress before breakfast. I spent nearly two and a half hours reading *Life* magazine. Then I got shaved, collapsed again into a chair. Then I washed. Another relapse. Then, at last, I dressed. It was now two o'clock. The beautiful, intact morning, which might have been used for all kinds of valuable purposes, was wasted—as vulgarly, as meaninglessly as a millionaire wastes ten dollars on a flower which he will immediately throw away.

The duck has been given to one of Happy's friends.

Walk with Wiggs, the Bayleys' spaniel, along the shore. The gulls stood among the foam-suds, in crowds. Cormorants swam out and dived under the waves. Brown sandpipers, with tall legs and long beaks like chopsticks. And the tiny birds (called knots?) which look like white mice. They dart in as the water ebbs, peck rapidly at the wet sand, then turn and scurry uphill before the next wave, so fast that

[1] Canadian-born American film star (1900–1983).

you can hardly see their legs. They move as if by clockwork. You can imagine them whirring.

Berthold and I went to dinner with Cedric Belfrage and his wife. They have a nice house they built themselves, just off Mulholland, at the top of Laurel Canyon. Flaherty was there, and Theodore Dreiser. We both liked Dreiser, with his buck teeth, and heavy head and hands and humor. But Flaherty did most of the talking. He talked about the Russ cotton-picking machine, the smuggling of Mexicans over the border to work—they are called "wet Mexicans," because they have to swim the Rio Grande—and about a super-cheap automobile driven by a spring, which the Japanese are trying to introduce into India.

Belfrage has changed very much since I knew him at Cambridge. He is no longer the adroit social circumnavigator, the man-about-Europe, the born columnist. He is now a cut-and-dried Stalinist, conventionally cynical, a little sour. He has just finished a book about the South—showing how Negro evangelism has become a symbolic revolutionary language. According to Belfrage, when the colored preacher says "revelation" his congregation understands that he means "revolution." Not of course that this has much political significance, as yet; but it is preparing a state of mind.

Belfrage also told us about the novel he is starting, about the undertaking business, here in Los Angeles. At one time, rabid anti-New Dealers all began buying cemetery space—because money spent in this way isn't liable to taxation, and they grudged the administration every cent. Flaherty, who has to cap every story, described how, when one of the big U.S. airships was carried away in a storm, the rival morticians rushed about New Jersey following its course in their cars, and arguing about prices as they waited for it to crash.

December 27. Decided to give up smoking—at any rate for the day. But giving up smoking is a whole-time occupation in itself. I spent the entire morning sitting in a chair, jittering with disintoxication. At 11:25 there was a slight earthquake.

December 28. Second morning of disintoxication. Not so severe as yesterday, but very insidious. Desire to smoke came in sudden, strong puffs—like treacherous wind-gusts when you are sailing, taking you unawares. I felt I had to eat a Good Humor, and walked up to the top of the Palisades, looking for the ice-cream car. A glorious morning. The seashore almost deserted. The bland winter sunshine makes itself felt much more consciously than the full blaze of summer. During the summer days, you are plunged deep in the element itself. You are part of the weather. Now, you stand aside from it. These autumn-spring mornings have an extraordinary purity and pathos—like poetry in the great classical tradition.

It is as if you had been tossing in a delirium of newspaper headlines, film plots, philosophical riddles, metaphysical doubts, wish-dreams, recurring nightmares. Suddenly, you are conscious of the flowers, the gardens, the dry rustle of the palms, the mild, healing vastness of the light and air washing softly upon all your senses, as the ocean washes the sand. Just as a patient, drowsing and muttering in high fever, suddenly becomes aware of a figure standing beside his bed. A stranger? No—he recognizes her: it is his kind, beloved, familiar nurse. But where has she been—he reproachfully asks—why did she desert him? And the nurse smiles—her smile is the sunshine—and answers: "Silly—I've been here. I've been with you all the time."

Yes—she has been with me. But, lately, I've been aware of her so seldom. "I must have been very ill, haven't I, nurse?" "Yes. Very ill indeed." She smiles—but her smile isn't in the least reassuring. "Nurse—" I begin to get seriously alarmed, "am I going to die?" She nods: "Yes, you are going to die. Like everyone else. I have never saved a patient." She draws the warm blanket of the air around my limbs: "And now, *do* try to relax. Try to get some rest—even if it's only for a moment. You're only making things harder for yourself. Don't you know that?"

From the top of the Palisade cliffs you can look down into the courtyards of the luxury villas which stand along the shore. Many of their secrets, invisible from the street below, are revealed. One yard, for instance, contains a little swimming pool within its walls. And, on the surface of this pool, a boy was floating in a tiny rubber boat—only a few yards from the ocean itself. A perfect symbol of the private, artificially staged childhood of the very rich.

Lunch with Berthold and Uhse. Uhse is going to Mexico soon. And Berthold talks of leaving for New York. Uhse says that most of the Washington news experts are convinced that America will enter the war in another three months.

An earthquake in neutral Turkey has caused, so far, the biggest loss of life anywhere since the war began. Russia is said to be preparing a big new offensive against Finland. Washington experts announce that they can find no conclusive proof that the *Athenia* was torpedoed. [Edward] Murrow, speaking from London, tells us that a club has been founded to discuss peace aims on the basis of federal union. But the majority are doubtful of the value of any such "high-sounding ideals." France has "the right to demand" that Germany shall be kept in her place. This kind of talk makes me tremble with rage. Murrow succeeded very well in conveying what he thought of it, himself.

December 29. Ellis St. Joseph has arrived here, to see Walter Huston, who is going to play the leading part in *Passenger to Bali*. The play is being produced in New York very soon.

It is difficult to find anything charitable to say about Ellis—he is a mystery-monger with a bogus English accent, a Proustian conscience and a magazine-story style of conversation—yet I don't dislike him. Perhaps merely because he likes me—or, at any rate, is sincerely jealous of my writing. If only he would stop being so intimate, so brilliantly clairvoyant! He says he knows everything about a person after he has been with him for five minutes—and I dare say he does. So what? We drove down to Santa Monica together, and he analyzed, with masochistic Proustian acumen, his relationships with various friends. While he is talking, he watches your face so closely for a reaction that you soon feel as exhausted as if you had been playing poker.

December 31. A grey, cloudy, lifeless day. Lunch at the Viertels'—that non-stop debating society. Today, the chief subjects discussed were: "Is Pirandello a great dramatist?" "The significance of *Peer Gynt*." "*Gone with the Wind*." "What contribution has China to make to a future world-culture?"

Salka takes the "plus ça change . . ." line. According to her, there will be no progress, no new world-order. "All these words are simply *shit*!" Berthold explained to me later that Salka's cynicism comes from Gottfried Reinhardt. Gottfried, says Berthold, is cynical because his life is a vacuum. He is negative.

Berthold himself is now in a state of the greatest confusion. He has heard from New York that Erika and Klaus Mann want to conduct some kind of purge of the German refugee organization. All those in opposition to the war must go. Berthold feels that, if this rumor is true, he had perhaps better not travel East. Once he is there, he will never be able to keep his mouth shut—and there will be a battle royal. Meanwhile, he looks around feverishly for moral support. How far will he be able to go with Heard, or with Auden? Where can he find something positive, something constructive? I listen to all this without expressing an opinion—because I know that Berthold will never accept Gerald's ideas unless he discovers and edits and annotates them for himself.

1940

January 1. Last night, I went to a New Year's party at the Viertels', where I got full of punch, whisky and vodka. Peter had to bring me home and put me to bed. Today, the worst hangover I've had in years.

Went to tea with Berthold and Salka, who told me that my behavior had caused a sensation. I made violent love to that Russian girl whom Wystan and I first met in New York last spring, at Christiane Toller's apartment. Uhse, equally drunk, tried to stop me—because, he said, he was sure she didn't really care for me and was only leading me on; and he wouldn't see a dear comrade of his ruined by any woman. He then glared severely at the girl and muttered: "German Youth Movement. Typical." Later, on the way home, he jumped out of a moving car—apparently as a protest against the conversation of the other passengers. He wasn't hurt.

Salka got drunk quite early in the evening, as she was mixing the punch. She called me over to her. "Christopher—come here, darling. I want to drink blood brotherhood with you." We crossed arms, drank and embraced. "And now, darling," said Salka, "I am going to tell you a very important secret. If a man wants a woman enough, he can have her. Absolutely. It's only a question of time and place." Carl Zuckmayer[1] overheard her. He came up to us, sweating and snorting like a little bull. "You really mean that Salka? You mean that for yourself, too?" Salka laughed recklessly: "Certainly I do! *Any* man. Any man on *earth!*" She paused, considered for a moment: "Except Louis B. Mayer."

Berthold tells me that I was very much upset because I have to collaborate with Robert Thoeren on this picture for Gottfried Reinhardt at MGM. I met Thoeren for the first time, last night, and wandered around for the rest of the evening muttering: "Der Mann ist ein gemeiner Schauspieler!"[2] Toward the end of the party I also told Berthold: "I'm so tired I can't stop smiling."

Garbo was at tea with us today. I think Peter is right when he says she's "a dumb cluck." She actually didn't know who Daladier was.[3] If you watch her for a quarter of an hour, you see every one of her famous expressions. She repeats them, quite irrelevantly. There is the iron sternness of Ninotchka, the languorous open-lipped surrender of Camille, Mata Hari's wicked laugh, Christina's boyish toss of the

---

[1] German playwright, essayist, and screenwriter.
[2] The man is an ordinary actor!
[3] Then prime minister of France for the third time.

head, Anna Christie's grimace of disgust. She is so amazingly beautiful, so noble, so naturally compelling and commanding, that her ridiculous artificiality, her downright silliness can't spoil the effect.

After tea, Garbo, Salka and Mercedes de Acosta[1] (dressed in a kind of leather uniform) went out for a walk. I went with them as far as our house. They were going to the Uplifters', and I knew they'd have to return along Mesa Road. I kept a lookout, because I wanted Vernon to meet Garbo. When they finally appeared, I ran down the hill, explaining, quite unnecessarily, that I'd "happened" to see them go past. This didn't fool Garbo for a minute. She laughed, and said, with slightly sadistic amusement, "You were waiting for me, weren't you?" But she came back with me. Vernon, out of shyness, was very grand. When Garbo suggested we all three go on the beach, he declined, saying he was too busy.

Today, Garbo was playing the wayward little girl even more energetically than usual. Her dread of being recognized is coupled with a perverse desire to draw attention to herself. She stood on the fence, at the corner of Mabery Road, high above the shore, and theatrically extended her arms toward the sea. She waved at a goodlooking boy who was passing. She threw her arms around my neck. She skipped along the beach, darting at the waves to gather foam in her hands. Several people recognized her—and soon our path was continually being crossed by casually strolling groups. But nobody tried to speak to her, and she didn't seem to care.

Specimens of conversation with Garbo:

> She (*taking my hand, and letting go of it again immediately*): We must not do that. This is New Year's Day. It might become a habit.
> Me (*politely*): Well, it would be a very good habit—as far as I'm concerned.
> She (*in her Hedda Gabler voice*): How can you say that? You do not know me at all. I do not know you. We might make a terrible mistake.
> Me (*gallant*): I'm willing to risk that.
> She (*raising tragic-ironic eyebrows*): Ah! You are a very *brave* young man!

As we were walking along the beach, she asked me how I had met Vernon. I told her.

> She: And when you came back to New York he was waiting for you? How *wonderful*! Nobody *ever* waited for *me*!
> Me (*not knowing the answer to this one*): Look at that bird diving under the wave. What kind is it?

---

[1] Argentinian poet, novelist and translator, known for her relationships with Garbo, Marlene Dietrich and Isadora Duncan.

She (*the whimsical little girl*): A duck.

Me: And those big birds flying over there?

She: *Big* ducks.

Me: They're pelicans.

She: *No!* They are all ducks. And the people who live in that beautiful house—they, too, are ducks . . . You know, I am not surprised that people wait for you. You have a funny face.

Me: Thank you.

She: Tell me, are you never sad? Never melancholic?

Me: I used to be sad, but I've given it up. (*etc. etc.*)

January 2. From *The Los Angeles Times*'s account of the Rose Bowl game at Pasadena yesterday: "Like so many white-shirted specters, Southern California's powerful gridsters slashed their way through the gloom-glutted Rose Bowl yesterday and, before the dusk of this dark afternoon had blotted out the playing field entirely, the South's mighty Tennessee had been trampled under foot, 14 to 0."

Went to the studio, to watch Chaplin acting in his new Dictator picture. Meltzer had arranged it.

(Meltzer was a young man I'd met at the Book of the Day—a bookstore on La Brea which was, at that time, a meeting place for pink intellectuals, particularly left-wing movie writers. They stayed open late, for evening lectures and discussions. I once gave a talk there myself, on Auden, Spender and the others.

The manager, whose name was Larry Edmunds, later opened another store, on Cahuenga. Just before he was due to be inducted into the army, he killed himself. Meltzer, also, got killed in the war. But, in those days, an aggressive isolationism was the watchword, and the Book of the Day posted its door with the slogan: "The Yanks are *not* coming."

Chaplin had met Meltzer at some holiday resort, I believe; taken a fancy to him and asked him to collaborate on the script of his new picture. Meltzer had had very little experience, but that didn't bother Chaplin, who always knows exactly what he wants, and merely demands an appreciative audience.)

Today, the set was a banqueting chamber—a table covered with a black velvet cloth and set with immense silver goblets and dishes. The meal is over. Chaplin, as Hitler, makes a speech to the guests in the nonsense language he has invented (actually, it sounds much more like Danish than German), hunts through a box of medals, and pins one of them on "Herring's" breast. "Herring" is so much moved that he bursts into tears.

Chaplin's technique is amazing. His timing is so perfect that even the corniest gags—such as spitting in Herring's eye, or pricking him with the medal pin, seem startlingly brilliant and funny. His fluency in the nonsense language is unbelievable.

Making this picture, says Meltzer, is a tremendous strain on Chaplin. He is no longer young, and he has to do everything: he is star, director, writer and producer. If Chaplin relaxes for a moment, the whole machine comes to a stop, for there is very little discipline. He is not the sort of man who inspires awe. He is wooing everybody; we are all his public. Even between shots, he feels that he must keep us amused. He sings snatches of imaginary Russian and Italian songs, imitates famous actors. While his voice is being played back, he strolls around, watching our faces. He is his own most anxious critic.

Meltzer told me that Chaplin bought some land in the valley, to shoot exteriors for the picture. But the permission of the neighbors had first to be obtained, and a bundist of German descent organized an opposition. Permission was refused. Chaplin, in revenge, threatens to present the land to the Okie migrant workers.

When the picture went into production, he got a lot of threatening letters, and became so morbid about them that he would even stop shooting when a plane flew overhead, imagining sabotage. Paulette Goddard gives him a lot of trouble, too. There are violent fights— during which everybody else has to leave the stage.

Chaplin came over to talk to us—strutting with his funny little cock-of-the-dunghill air, very erect in his stiff tight-collared uniform. His hair is dyed brown for the part, and this makes him still look almost boyish. Henry Daniell, who plays "Garbage," joined us. We talked about the newly announced British draft—up to twenty-seven. Daniell said that no British actor in Hollywood wanted to go home, despite all the patriotism of the British colony before war was declared. Poor David Niven had been unwillingly propelled back to England by the momentum of his own publicity. "Thank God I'm fifty," said Chaplin: "I'm prepared to sacrifice my last relative that democracy shall not die." He laughed heartily, as he always does at his own jokes. This I find very sympathetic. Only the self-conscious humorist, the carefully built-up bogus personality, doesn't laugh. Chaplin inhabits the element of humor. He is enjoying himself, not just being funny for a living. He is constantly experimenting. He burns with a kind of amateur eagerness. He is an amateur, in the best sense of the word.

It is odd how English Chaplin has remained, after all these years of Hollywood. Not merely that his accent is British. His gaiety and enthusiasm are of an English kind. It isn't the gaiety of the British ruling class. He is still the cheeky, cocky East End boy.

January 3. This morning I woke up feeling terrible, after a night of violent dreams. Burning pains when I urinated and a slight discharge. I felt sure I'd got gonorrhea again, though I couldn't imagine how. Or maybe it never was properly cured, last time.

I called Gerald, who advised me to go to his friend, Dr. Kolisch— also a pupil of the Swami. Dr. Kolisch is from Vienna. He has a bald, egg-shaped, agnostic head, with aggressively bushy eyebrows. His diagnosis is of the clairvoyant type: "Mm, yes . . . thirty-five years old. You have a lot of gas, don't you? It wakes you up in the night—about two-thirty? And your memory's not so good as it was? I thought so . . . You have pains in your left arm and around the shoulders—just here? No? They'll come later. Acute fits of melancholy, of course? Yes . . ."

However, there was no trace of gonorrhea, chronic or otherwise. And Kolisch is very doubtful if I ever had it at all. He explained to me, in a nearly incomprehensible mixture of medical jargon, broken English and Viennese German, that some part of my nervous system is liable to "simulate" all kinds of symptoms—this being a peculiarity of my general condition. To hear him talk, you would think I was Oswald in [Ibsen's] *Ghosts*; the ruined victim of debauched and degenerate ancestors. I couldn't help smiling when I thought how this would infuriate M.

Kolisch examined me all over—heart, lungs, blood pressure, reflexes, eyes, teeth. "It amuses me," he said: "I like to know my patients." He despises specialists, who "know more and more about less and less." I am to come again the day after tomorrow.

January 4. Lectured to an English class at the Beverly Hills High, on expressionist drama. The teachers were rather depressing—hanging on to Culture by their eyelids. The pupils, in their casual, friendly way, were quite responsive. You could catch their attention for about a quarter of a minute at a time. The girls are powdered and painted, elaborately dolled up. The boys dress like tramps—in a gaudy, ragbag assortment of sweatshirts, lumberjackets, jeans and cords. There is no discipline whatsoever, in the European sense. The lecturer is merely allowed, by courtesy, to speak a little louder than the class. But— having seen the beautifully planned classrooms, the wonderfully equipped theater, the swimming baths, the gymnasium and the library—one can't help wondering; how long will this strange homage to education continue at all? The barbarian students are so much more vital than the culture they are supposed to be acquiring. This place is simply a temple to a dead religion. Study has become a cult, fossilized in ritual. Most of the questions they asked me were basically economic in interest. For example: "Can the theater *compete* with the movies?" When the bell rang, they stopped me instantly, by clapping.

Drove up to see Gerald, who had prepared the usual lunch of eggs, raisins and tea. We talked about Kolisch. Gerald says his energy and powers of concentration are amazing. He drives a big car at terrific speed—dashing up from his office to spend an hour with the Swami, then tearing back to his patients. By nature, he is intolerant, intellectually arrogant. But with Swami he is gentle as a lamb.

We discussed my film career and life in general. I can see that Gerald, in his sly, prim way, expects it to end in disaster. But "of course, you *may* be able to do it," he says: "Theoretically, it *is* possible to live in both worlds, and recognize that one of them is unreal. I shouldn't dare to try it myself. I shouldn't venture to poke that long red nose of mine outside. The danger is, of course, that one simply disintegrates—one might even become insane." He remarked that Aldous is getting more and more involved with MGM—making the excuse that it is "very interesting."

Then we talked about reincarnation. Gerald spoke so dogmatically that I protested. I simply can't swallow it, yet. Gerald agreed that one shouldn't lay down the law about these things. He himself was convinced—but only because he believed in the truthfulness of those who claim to have had actual mystical experience.

Gerald has thought a great deal about the problems of the sincere social worker—he did a lot of slum work and prison visiting in England, himself, years ago. "What we have to realize is that none of us can hope to do good to anybody. We can only avoid doing harm." But he doesn't dare say this in public.

If Gerald is right, life is evil. But the last person to be able to realize this is a member of an oppressed or underprivileged group. An Okie migrant or a Chinese coolie naturally believes that everything would be all right if only he had enough money. As for those who do have enough, and who enjoy all the autohypnotic "pleasures," they often realize in the end that they have been cheated, but only when it is too late. Their strength is gone. They have no energy left for the evolutionary advance. "And it is incredible," said Gerald, "how much energy you need to enlarge consciousness even the least little bit."

Gerald gives me to understand that he is making some progress. How much, and of what kind, he won't or can't say. Probably it is impossible to describe to anyone who hasn't had similar experiences. He admits that the effort involved is intense and sometimes agonizing. He has periods of discouragement, even of despair, but there is no question of turning back.

And now it is for me to decide: am I going to follow him? I am very lucky to have met him and been shown the way. And I am under no illusions. I know the alternative. If I don't go on, I shall have nothing but my own weakness to blame.

Today, the Nazis are showing definitely that they may back the Soviets in the Russo–Finnish war.

January 5. Two visits to Dr. Kolisch. He keeps his patients waiting for hours. I was reduced to reading *Fortune*, the most depressing magazine in the world. After taking the powders he gave me, all symptoms of gonorrhea have completely disappeared. I feel better altogether.

Supper at the Viertels'. The Huxleys were there. Aldous held forth against the appallingly low standards of western American universities; in the East, he admits, they are far better. This was the typical stage setting of an "intellectual" party. The men stood a little apart, scowling at their shoes, in prophetic condemnation of existing society. The ladies, seated, talked scandal and dirt. Maria Huxley's charming Belgian schoolgirl niece Sophie [Moulaert] sat on the arm of Maria's chair, plainly and becomingly dressed, with a small gold cross around her neck. Maria held her hand, as if to protect her from the dangers of the conversation.

I like all of them, and I am deeply fond of Berthold, Salka and Peter—but why the hell we met this evening is more than I can say. I suppose that people of Salka's temperament actually prefer to talk to their intimate friends when they are surrounded by a chattering crowd. She creates huge, expensively fed gatherings of bores as a background to her meetings with Gottfried.

January 6. Lunch with Ellis St. Joseph in his hotel bedroom. Ellis, very pale and unwholesome looking, in his brown velvet bathrobe and teddy bear bedroom slippers, wanted to consult me about his play. That is to say, he wanted to think aloud to someone who had a sympathetic wavelength. I know myself how helpful this is. Sure enough, we soon arrived at a solution of the difficulty that was bothering him.

After all, perhaps I have been rather hard on Ellis. I think he's genuinely well disposed. I hope his play will be a success, because I believe success will be good for him.

Not having read the whole play, I can't possibly judge how it will be on the stage. There is no characterization. All the characters are baldly symbolic; but a lot of the action is theatrically effective, I should think. (The stupidity of this paragraph is due to Happy Bayley, who has started to practice on the piano upstairs.)

This evening, I read *After Many a Summer*. The *idea* of the plot is magnificent. If only Aldous, with all his talents, were a real novelist! Here is one of the few people who write about something genuinely interesting, and he simply hasn't the gift—which scores of the dreariest little hacks possess—of "making his characters live." And so, instead of a great novel, we get a prim, chilly morality play, interrupted by philosophical conversations. Because Aldous isn't a novelist, the conversations are very poorly contrived. But if you read them simply as lectures, ignoring Aldous's clumsy attempts to dramatize them, they are brilliant.

January 7. In the early morning, as I lie in bed, too lazy to get up, the demons start whispering in my ear:

"You're trying something impossible. Even Gerald admitted he couldn't do it. You'll just slither back on to your old tracks. Why not give up? Get sick. Stay in bed. Develop paralysis or TB. Wait a minute—isn't that a pain in your lung, right now? Your heart isn't strong. You've had rheumatic fever, remember. It wouldn't surprise me if you collapsed altogether—considering the strain you've been under. Well, what if you do? It'd serve everybody right. They'd have to look after you. You're sick. You're very sick. Come on—let's have breakfast in bed for a start. . . ."

"Oh dear, oh dear. I'm so worried. So many responsibilities. So many debts. Can I hold that job down at Metro? When does the car insurance fall due? How shall I ever pay for everything? Aren't we being too extravagant? Oughtn't we to economize? Oh dear, oh dear. . . ."

"Ssh! Rockabye baby. Don't listen to that guy. Take it easy. Sure, you shall have your yoga. Sure, you shall have your job at MGM. And dough—lots of it. Buy that nice typewriter. Get yourself a new suit. Meet the stars. Forget the war. Have yourself a swell time. Confidentially, I think you're pretty smart. You get around. You know how to make the best of all the worlds. Your stars are set right. You'll always succeed. Sure, we'll take the kid along with us for a while. Always ditch him later. Always deal with yoga later. Always have time for everything. Lots of friends, lots of dough, lots of fun, lots of enlightenment. Just leave me to fix everything. You and me is going places."

"It isn't fair, I tell you—it isn't fair! You're too kindhearted. Too much of a sucker. Everybody takes advantage of you. Everybody. Don't let them! They don't understand you. They don't know your problems. If they had to spend one day in your shoes, they'd collapse altogether. What right have they to criticize? How DARE they? How DARE Gerald sneer at you for taking a movie job? How DARE the Viertels treat you as a child? How DARE Vernon go to art school, when you're slaving, killing yourself, giving up your work, sacrificing everything to support him? He ought to be slaving for *you*, waiting on you hand and foot! It'd be an *honor* to do it. You're a genius. You've more talent in your little finger than this whole crowd put together. Don't stand for it. Throw everybody out. Tell them to go to hell. Shoot them down, to the last man. Nobody exists but you. Nobody has any rights, but you. Nothing matters but your comfort, your will, your slightest whim. It isn't fair! It isn't fair! It isn't fair!"

At length I have to jump out of bed and escape from them into the bathroom. And so the day begins.

Lunch at the Viertels'. Berthold in a very nervous, difficult mood. Salka has been coaching Mausi in Gretchen's prison scene from *Faust*, which she is to recite at her school next week. Mausi was proud because she'd made the lady next door cry. "And did *you* cry?" Salka asked. "No," said Mausi: "At the beginning I felt bored, and towards the end I got goose pimples."

It is appalling how near some of the refugees live to the starvation line. There's Stern, the poet. His girlfriend acted in a play the other night for ten dollars, and was glad to get it. Little Guttchen, whose kidneys were injured in a Nazi concentration camp, asked Berthold for a job. Berthold did nothing for three weeks. Then he wrote to Guttchen, who got the letter on the very day he'd decided to commit suicide. He had only seven dollars left in the world. Berthold forced him to borrow twenty. But where is he to find work?

Mrs. Bayley, who works in the old-age pension department of the state office in Los Angeles, tells me that old-age relief here is higher than anywhere else in the world. Thirty-five dollars a month. You can find houses which board and lodge roomers for seven dollars a week—nine for a room of your own. Living is much cheaper here than in the East. But, aside from the movies and oil, there's less chance of earning big money. Marion Davies's Great Danes, which are kept at her house on the beach, get sixteen dollars' worth of meat a day.

January 8. Heavy torrents of rain yesterday. Rain again today. Started work at Metro—that is to say, I was installed in an air-conditioned office where I wrote letters. Gottfried Reinhardt is still away and not likely to return for three weeks.

Lunched with Frau Bach, Gottfried's flirtatious secretary. She tried to explain to me how Metro's organization works. But, to understand it, one would have to have the mind of an Einstein. How, except in the language of relativity, is one to define the importance of Mannix in terms of Lichtman, or Hyman in terms of Katz? Even L. B. Mayer himself is not an absolute. He can only be stated as an equation: Mannix times Lichtman to the power of Katz equals Mayer over X. (X. being Wall Street somehow related to a number of individuals named Schenck who appear to be presided over or owned by a mathematical abstraction called Loew's Incorporated.)

(I find I haven't yet referred to my agents, Leonardson and Schley. I switched to them on the advice of John van Druten. They were his agents, too. Edna Schley was short and dumpy, with white hair cut very close—almost an Eton Crop—a red face, and thick little legs. Dan Leonardson, her husband, was also tubby and small. There was something rather endearing about him: he was like an underground animal whose whiskers were always a bit grubby from digging: one imagined him burrowing down under the city and emerging, very dirty and breathless, with a torn dollar bill in his paws. He had been a doctor. Then he had gone into aviation, and later into the show business.

Edna had once been a movie writer and director. She was always talking about her connections around the studios. "Why, I've known Jack ever since he was in the prop department!" Whenever she and Dan came to visit me at work, she would ask anxiously: "How yer feelin', Chris?" as though I were a boxer before a fight. As long as we had dealings together, she never actually got me a job—that I did myself, through friends—but she was full of activity, especially after the contract with Metro was safely landed. And when some footling little adjustment had to be made, she would become very politic, gravely weighing tactical considerations. "I've been thinking it over, Chris. Maybe we'll let it ride another week. I have an idea . . . I think I'll say a word to Ken this morning—but nothing definite, y'understand." She yessed me unblushingly: "That's right Chris. That's what I've always said—" even when she'd been saying the exact opposite. "I'm working on it," she would tell me, when, obviously, she had done nothing: "I'm going right ahead now. Firing on all six cylinders."

Edna and Dan seemed constitutionally incapable of speaking the truth, especially in minor matters. Both van Druten and I found this very embarrassing. For example, Dan would tell one of the studios that Johnny was in New York, when actually he was in Hollywood and everybody knew it. He never did report his lies to us, and so we always appeared to be a party to them when they were found out. If you argued with Dan, he merely grinned and said: "I didn't want them bothering you, see?"

Edna and Dan had married fairly late in life—both, I believe, for the second time. They were deeply attached to each other. Johnny told me that he had once seen her inscription on a Christmas present—"Santa loves Danny, but not as much as Edna does."

These two "handled" me, as the trade expression goes. Sometimes I needed quite a lot of handling. I used to get mad at them and bully them unkindly, but they accepted it without rancor, as a matter of course. Probably nearly every writer gets mad, from time to time, at his particular bunch of parasites—but it's useless and stupid to do so. They have to be what they are. The system makes them that way.)

A bundle of letters from England—from M., Stephen, and Tony Hyndman—and a copy of *Horizon*, the new magazine which Cyril Connolly and Stephen are editing. *Horizon* makes me feel homesick for what is, after all, my only real home, "the gang." There they are, gaily and boldly standing up for their opinions—as long as they are allowed to. Stephen writes that he has planned all his work till October—a journal, a long novel, a play, a book of poems—"and then they can shoot me or do what they like, I will have had my little say." Tony's letter is equally sweet and touching. No word of reproach for those who are lucky enough to have escaped in time; only a rather wistful envy. Absolute fatalism toward the war. Utter disbelief in its "ideals" and "aims." Belief only in affection, friendship, art. A growing disgust with "politics" and a feeling that some kind of spiritual readjustment is absolutely necessary. But Heard and Huxley are still regarded with suspicion. And the real nature of yoga is, as you might expect, completely misunderstood.

January 9. Rain, on and off, all day. Sat in my office at Metro, writing letters and at last, out of sheer boredom, beginning to read James Hilton's novel *Rage in Heaven* on which the picture is to be based.

Lunch with Huxley. How kind, how shy he is—searching painfully through the darkness of this world's ignorance with his blind, mild, deep-sea eye. He has a pained, bewildered smile of despair at all human activity. "It's inconceivable," he repeatedly begins, "how *anyone* in their senses could *possibly* imagine—" But they *do* imagine—and Aldous is very, very sorry.

He told me of two new novels he is planning—a "brave new

world" which really *is* a utopia, based on Gerald's program of decentralization and "intentional living." And a novel which explores the problem of the meaning of words and the utter inadequacy of all existing language. He mentioned, for example, how schizophrenes are sometimes cured of their fear of dogs when it is explained to them that the dog which bit them in childhood isn't identical with the general concept 'dog'. That *all* dogs do not bite, in other words. But, unfortunately, there *are* no other words: just *dog*.

I talked about my early morning demons, and Aldous admitted that he has them too. Particularly a demon which suggests brilliant remarks for him to make on future occasions. He is still very much the prize-winning undergraduate, the nervous, fastidious, superintellectual boy. Stupidity afflicts him like a nasty smell—and how eagerly he sucks at the dry teats of books! I see how utterly he must depend on Maria, how blessed must be the relaxation in her thin Belgian arms—and I like them both, much better than before. I think Aldous knows that I like him. This is our only bond. We talk such different languages. Every time I open my mouth he is obscurely pained and distressed. I am such a hopeless ignoramus, such a barbarian. "And yet," I can imagine Aldous saying, "one *supposes* there is *something*. . . . These young men who *imagined* they understood socialism, when, all the time, of course, one saw *perfectly clearly*—"

This afternoon, I went to Kolisch. He has finished the treatment, but now he wants to start in and clean me up properly.

January 10. Heavy rain. Sat all day in Gottfried's office. I am to be given a new one tomorrow, without air-conditioning. Wrote letters. Frau Bach popped gaily in and out, flirting and snooping. We did a crossword puzzle together. She asked me about China, communism, etc., buttering every question with coquettish flattery. She is very happy at present, because of a mild conspiracy—Gottfried left secret instructions that I was not to work with Thoeren on the story until he came back. He doesn't want Thoeren to influence me. But Thoeren mustn't be told this, so I have to stall and make excuses.

The roads are all beginning to flood: the entire town seems to drain down into Culver City. Early listless supper with Vernon at the smelly Red Door restaurant, where the phonograph plays endless Strauss. Whiffs of expatriate Berlin. From the kitchen comes the tired gossip of exiles. A Wiener schnitzel which seems specially designed to convince you that meat eating is wicked.

January 11. Still raining, but not continuously.

My new office is on the ground floor, with a big window that opens. In the late afternoon, I had to go in and see Bernie Hyman, who is a nice, worried-looking little man. He has a round, gentle face which somehow appears damaged, although there are no visible scars on it. The face of a man who has been sent to prison for life.

Hyman wanted to know my "reactions" to the story. I bluffed, not having read the treatment—until I realized that Hyman hadn't read it, either. We regarded each other with gentle reproach, across an enormous writing table, on which stood a bronze statuette of three horses. On the wall, a big colored reproduction of a Renoir little girl. A grand piano in the corner.

Dinner with Chris Wood and a boy named Peter Finley, who is studying at Ouspenskaya's school of acting[1]—which develops the "five-sense response." Finley talked eagerly about his work. Chris hummed and yawned, interposing occasional bored provocative remarks. If you contradict Chris, he only grins. He can't be bothered to argue.

January 12. The weather is clearing. Blue sky at last, with immense clouds. Spent the day discussing the story with Thoeren; I couldn't put him off any longer. He is a big tomcat of an ex-leading man, who talks endlessly about his love affairs, with a kind of sadistic vulgarity. His attitude of cynical self-abasement amounts to saying: "I'm dirt myself. Therefore anyone who sleeps with me is less than dirt." He is a [bit of a] liar, but intelligent. We shall probably get along quite well together.

January 13. Thoeren and I had another interview with Hyman. We were talking about our hero's inferiority complex. Suddenly, Hyman started to tell us a story.

When he was a schoolboy, his best friend had a girl, and this girl had a sister. The first time Hyman saw her, he fell for her. "She was a perfect assembly of womanhood." Soon he was so much in love that he gave up making dates with her; he felt it was quite hopeless—there were so many rich, goodlooking boys around. Then, to his amazement, she sent for him and asked why he was staying away from the house. He told her the truth. She said: "I'm glad—because I've been in love with you for a long time."

In the same town there lived a very rich man, twenty years older than Hyman, who, for twelve years, had been unhappily married to an invalid wife. The wife died. The rich man met Hyman's girl at a

---

[1] The School of Dramatic Arts founded by Maria Ouspenskaya (1876–1949), a Russian actress who first arrived in Hollywood with the Stanislavsky troupe in 1923.

party and fell passionately in love with her. He came to Hyman and appealed to him, humiliating himself before the schoolboy: "If you really care for her happiness, give her to me. Think of all the things I can offer her." The widower's relatives and friends joined in the campaign; they carried the girl off to spend a weekend with them. The girl telephoned Hyman: "If you still care for me at all, come and take me away." But Hyman did nothing. The rich man's arguments had convinced him. He never saw her again.

A year later, the widower and the girl got married. They have been happy. The girl now has grown-up sons. Her elderly husband has lost most of his money. Hyman is earning two hundred and fifty thousand dollars a year.

Once, quite recently, he spoke to her, on the phone. She was very gay and "said all the wrong things." She also had a long conversation with Hyman's wife. Bernie told all this so modestly and simply that, for the moment, he seemed quite charming. The question is: how often does he tell this story, and to whom?

(Much later, after Hyman's death, I discovered that he used to tell it to nearly every writer who ever worked for him.)

All day I have been happy. Chiefly because this morning, driving through the cold sunshine in our open car to the studio, I saw, far behind Hollywood, for the first time, the snow-covered mountains. "Look at them!" I kept repeating excitedly, to a hitchhiker I'd picked up. He agreed politely that they were pretty.

Mrs. MacCabe treated us to a turkey dinner. Happy chattered all through the meal—about aviation, sailing, automobiles, and the good times he'd had with his friends. "Boy, I had more fun—!" He has to have several shots a day for his diabetes, but he is exactly like any ordinary, healthy boy. It never occurs to him to feel sorry for himself. (It never occurs to me not to.)

January 15. Lunch with Huxley. Now that he is getting over his shyness, he is charming. We talked about the Bardo Thodol, which he has been reading lately. An old lady sold us bunches of artificial violets. I gave mine to Frau Bach, who said: "You're fortunate that I don't reward you with a kiss!"

January 16. A man named Crane burst into my office this morning and sold me a subscription to the trade paper *Box Office*. He knew everybody, he assured me, and they all subscribed. Sure, he knew Huxley. Very well. Huxley had given him a copy of *After Many a Summer*. "I got a big kick out of it, because, to be very frank with you, he uses very very highbrow language." Mr. Crane was born in England, and came to the States as a young man, via South Africa. He has two American-born sons, very patriotic Americans. They asked him: "If there was a war between England and America, which side would you be on?" Crane said: "America." The sons were shocked. They found this unnatural.

Lunch in the commissary, at our usual table. It would be difficult, if you saw the people sitting there, to guess what their profession was. Car salesmen, possibly. Stephani, the producer, was an organizer of the Rhineland separatist movement, after the last war; he was lucky to escape lynching. Parsonnet, the writer, was a circus acrobat; he spends all his money on horses. Waxman, the composer, looks like a repulsive insect; his dark eyes immensely magnified by his rimless glasses. The talk is mostly movies, racing and sex. But today there was a lively discussion about the dismissal of Hore-Belisha.[1] They are all very friendly and polite to me, as a newcomer. The Americans are lazy, sentimental, good humored. The Jews satirical and sour. Thoeren, particularly, is always bringing up the Semitic question—which means the anti-Semitic question—to the slight embarrassment of the gentiles. They try to pass it off by laughing at his English. "The trouble with all you foreigners—" one of them began. "Why can't you say: 'All you Jews'?" Thoeren interrupted.

In the evening, I went with Berthold to a showing of the French film *J'Accuse*, under the auspices of the Hollywood Antiwar League. Dalton Trumbo and Dudley Nichols spoke.[2] Trumbo was quite good, but dull. Pacifism of this kind is really an indefensible position. It involves so many dishonest arguments, tu quoques, frank appeals to self-interest. We shouldn't help Finland because we didn't help Spain. We shouldn't fight on the side of England, because look what England did in India. How all these people fear the plain moral stand against killing! Anyone in the audience could have silenced them immediately by shouting "coward!" Nichols, who was obviously conscious of this, hastened to assure us that he was a "militant pacifist" and quite ready to get into a fistfight with anybody who said that America should go to war!

The film itself was boring and hammy to the last degree. Victor Francen exhibited all his most agonized grimaces. Later, we had coffee with Belfrage and half a dozen others. Belfrage is as conscious

---

[1] Isaac Leslie Hore-Belisha, a Jew, fell out with General Gort and resigned from Chamberlain's war cabinet January 5, 1940 amid talk that Hitler's propaganda had made the British reluctant to have a Jewish war minister.

[2] Both screenwriters; Trumbo wrote a novel about WWI, *Johnny Got His Gun* (1939).

of being English as Thoeren is of being a Jew. His Anglophobia is horribly embarrassing. He can't drop it for an instant. Why do we all feel so painfully responsible for our little social and racial groups? Why do Negroes talk of "niggers" and homosexuals of "faggots"? Always these aggressive apologies, this yearning love–hate.

Peter [Viertel], who had come with us, got into a long argument with Berthold on the way home. Peter thinks the U.S. should get into the war in order to stop it. Berthold took up a position which would have outraged him, six months ago. But this whole antiwar agitation here will achieve very little, either way, I believe, because it isn't based on a genuine condemnation of violence. And you can't only condemn *some* violence.

January 17. After lunch, Thoeren and I drove downtown to look at secondhand bookstores. He likes stories about pirates. When we got back to the studio, Thoeren pretended to Frau Bach we'd been to a brothel. There was a little Chinese girl there who earned a lot of money, just as a curiosity, for doing nothing. His details were so convincing that Frau Bach very nearly believed him.

At present, I'm obsessed by a mania for debt paying. I want to save every penny. For example, I've found that, if we're very careful, we can pay off the whole cost of the car in three weeks. I spend a lot of time doing calculations about this on my scribbling pad in the office.

The days go by, and I don't see the Swami, don't start meditating. This isn't mere laziness. The opposition is enormously strong. Incredible as it seems, part of me actually *wants* to wallow in black, lazy misery, like a pig in filth.

I think perpetually of Wystan's great lines on the 1914 war:

> While the disciplined love which alone could have employed
>   these engines
> Seemed far too difficult and dull, and when hatred promised
> An immediate dividend, all of us hated.[1]

For myself there is less excuse than for most people, because I know already that "the disciplined love" *isn't* dull: it's the most absorbing thing in life. And Gerald and Swami are there all the time, always available and ready to help me through the difficulties.

January 18. To [Max] Reinhardt's production of Maugham's *Home and Beauty*, adapted as a musical comedy. It's all very well to blame this fiasco on the unlucky Californian amateurs who had to struggle

---

[1] From "Here on the cropped grass of the narrow ridge I stand," in *Look, Stranger!* (1936).

through it. Actually the original show in Berlin must have been equally silly. Germans should never try this kind of thing. The pink boudoir curtains are trampled under their ten-ton boots.

Afterwards to the Vine Street Brown Derby, where Salka, Berthold and the boys ate raw chopped meat. Salka posed as a passionate Polish barbarian, thrilling and shocking a wide-eyed young dramatic student, who had her hair fixed like a Zola whore, and whose mental age was six. Felt lonely, sleepy and bored.

January 19. The lady dentist at MGM hacked my gums into mincemeat while cleaning my teeth. Toothache throughout the day. Guttchen came to lunch with me, in the commissary. His Chinese smile, politely masking the pain from his damaged kidneys. He was so happy, just to be among people. I kept thinking how marvellously interesting he would be, if I could only ask the right questions. But I couldn't ask them. This was all the worse because I knew he was thinking, "Isherwood only invited me here out of charity, because Viertel told him to."

Nevertheless, he chatted away brightly—describing the great Chinese scholar, his uncle, who forced him to start studying oriental art and literature at the age of eleven. He told me about his wife and child in Switzerland. About communism in China. About Chinese poetical conventions. It was maddening to get so much fascinating information at a moment when I couldn't even listen to it. I sat in a stupor of pain, longing to get rid of him.

January 20. A letter from William Hickey. Would I mind if he quoted the following verse—which is now, he says, going around London:

> The literary erstwhile Left-wellwisher would
> Seek vainly now for Auden or for Isherwood:
> The dog beneath the skin has had the brains
> To save it, Norris-like, by changing trains.

Why does this sting me so? Simply because it is really clever. It succeeds in making me look ridiculous—in a way that mere abuse can't. My vanity is hurt. Yes, I had better admit it. I am not in the least ashamed of myself, but I feel foolish.

I'll try to be absolutely honest about this. Am I a coward, a deserter? Not according to my standards. If I were told that somebody else had "run away from England," I should ask, "What did 'England' mean to him?" "England" to me meant a place that I stayed away from as much as possible during the past ten years. From a strictly patriotic standpoint, you can be "disloyal" in peace as well as in war. Yet no one blamed me then. And I certainly didn't blame myself.

Am I afraid of being bombed? Of course. Everybody is. But within reason. I know I certainly wouldn't leave Los Angeles if the Japanese were to attack it tomorrow. No, it isn't that. . . . If I fear anything, I fear the atmosphere of the war, the power which it gives to all the things I hate—the newspapers, the politicians, the puritans, the scoutmasters, the middle-aged merciless spinsters. I fear the way I might behave, if I were exposed to this atmosphere. I shrink from the duty of opposition. I am afraid I should be reduced to a chattering, enraged monkey, screaming back hate at their hate.

Am I being disloyal to my friends? My friends don't seem to think so. But perhaps I am. Maybe my place is with them, over there. Maybe my attitude would only pain them. Maybe I should become their enemy.

Oh, it's not the smallest use trying to work this out, logically. And it's certainly no use running home to protect my vanity. If I really have to go, I shall know when the time comes. Life will give me some signal. I must just wait for it.

January 23. A tremendous downpour of rain. Lunch at the Victor Hugo, with Knopf. The place is decorated like a theatrical Italian garden—concealed music, a rose-lit statue in a niche. The waiters served us with the flattering attention reserved for big movie men: Knopf is a regular customer. I like his bald, worried, man-to-man air, and the abrupt, fantastic gestures he makes with his stump. Sometimes he flaps it desperately, like the flipper of a suffocating fish; sometimes he nurses it like a newly born child.

Knopf doesn't believe America will go to war. He still suspects the British government of working for an anti-Russian line-up. He thinks great harm is being done to British prestige here by the seizure of U.S. shipping at Gibraltar.

He still refers to Goldwyn as "Mr G."—with a certain deference.

Yesterday, Vernon went to the barber's and had his hair crew cut, so that it all stands on end. All the careful culture of months is destroyed; in future, he has decided to be ugly, like van Gogh. I laughed, but it is really rather touching. Vernon wants to be taken seriously, as a grown-up painter. He is disgusted with his own boyish prettiness and the effect it produces on people. I remember how I once switched from horn to steel-rimmed spectacles, because I thought steel was less becoming.

January 24. At lunch in the studio today I got into conversation with Waldo Salt, one of the youngest of the writers. He is a nice little leftist, with a broad grinning face and flap ears. He told me how he had set off to Europe with his wife, a few years ago, to make a picture of "fascist tendencies in the democratic countries." Needless to say, this quixotic project had to be abandoned at the first customshouse. All they got were some shots of refugee camps.

Salt is naive and intelligent in disconcerting spots. I quite see why Huxley deplores the lack of intelligence in all these people. So much of their talk is in slogans. Take them one yard off their beaten party-track and they are bewildered. On the subject of violence, they are like kids playing at gangsters. Their morals are hopelessly muddled; they cover their dishonesty with a shamefaced impudent schoolboy grin. But at least Salt doesn't make the English left-wing mistake of disregarding domestic problems in favor of foreign politics. He knows all about the Okies and has promised to take me to see them.

Drove up to supper with Gerald. Chris, when I arrived, was banging out [Stravinsky's] *Petrushka*. He always plays specially loud when Gerald is meditating. He left almost at once, warning us that he would be back early with a guest, and we must be ready to leave the sitting room.

I asked Gerald about the survival of personality. He replied with a lot of metaphysics I couldn't follow. To him, the question doesn't seem to be very important. All he knows is that he must get on with his ego smashing. And of course he's right.

January 25. In the afternoon, I went to Chaplin's studio. Chaplin was in a talkative mood. He repeats himself, amplifies, contradicts. (Meltzer later imitated him saying: "The only thing I can say for myself is—I've never been melancholy. Never. Of course, everybody is melancholy around the age of twenty. When I was twenty-one, I was terribly melancholy. I was melancholy until I was thirty. Well, no—not exactly what you could call melancholy. I'm never melancholy, really . . . etc. etc.")

Today, he talked about the portrait painted of him by George Bergen, and its mysterious disappearance from the artist's studio, a few years ago. "Oh, it was a wonderful portrait. He painted me against a white wall, in a white silk jacket—a sort of a pyjama jacket. It was just a good straight portrait—none of that Van Dyck stuff—light and shadow." A day or two after it was finished, someone ripped it right out of its frame. The police searched everywhere, but they never found it.

Chaplin then got on to the subject of the Duke of Windsor, whom he met several times during a trip to Europe. Windsor was then the Prince of Wales. His first question was, "How old are you?" He wanted to know what Chaplin had done in the 1914 war—and when

Chaplin told him, "Nothing," there was a frosty silence. Then Chaplin asked him how many uniforms he owned and how he knew which one to wear on any given occasion: did someone tell him? "No one," Windsor replied coldly, "ever tells me to do anything."

Nevertheless, he seems to have taken a great fancy to Chaplin and often asked him down to Fort Belvedere. Chaplin nearly committed a serious breach of etiquette by going into the lavatory when Windsor was already there. This is strictly against the rules.

Although Windsor had at once begun calling Chaplin "Charlie," Chaplin had stuck rigidly to the formal "Sir." He imitated himself saying demurely: "Oh, *no*, Sir! Oh, *yes*, Sir!" Behind all these anecdotes, there was the sparkle of guttersnipe impudence. One sees him in his classic role of debunker of official pomposity, always, everywhere. "How can they possibly go on with all that nonsense," he kept repeating.

Today, they were doing a scene outside on the lot. Hitler and Mussolini (Jack Oakie) are leaving the railway station. The crowd breaks through the police cordon. Madame Mussolini is pushed into it, and the dictators' car drives off without her. Meltzer says that the Hollywood extras are the most miserable, stupid, gutless crowd of people you could find anywhere in the world. The girls were all copies of famous filmstars—literal copies, made without the least imagination or individuality. The men were sullen, round shoul-dered, down-at-heel gum chewers. They showed not the slightest interest in Chaplin's instructions—but, when the shooting began, they put up a surprisingly convincing performance.

January 26. Dapper little George O'Neil—who is also working for Gottfried, on the script of *Girl with a Cello*—told me some more about the theft of the Bergen picture. When the picture disappeared, the police suspected everybody—including Constance Collier,[1] Bergen, an old lady who collected Chapliniana, a laundryman, Chaplin's Japanese valet, the half-witted son of the studio caretaker, and even Chaplin himself. As the picture had been commissioned by the Tate Gallery, none of these people could possibly hope to get possession of it by lawful means—so the motive of the theft applied to all of them.

This evening, O'Neil arranged that I should be invited to dinner by a man named Durant—a tall, lean, horseman-playboy. His house has a heated swimming pool, filled with salt water. It steamed, exotically green, in the electric light under the orange trees. The other guests were Gladys Cooper, Flora Robson and Barbara O'Neil,

[1] British stage and, later, film actress (1878–1955).

who is George O'Neil's cousin. We drank champagne out of small Coca-Cola glasses. Slices of pie were served simultaneously with big drugstore cups of coffee. That's so typically Hollywood—super-swagger surroundings, and then something that reminds you of a Baptist mission station in the wilds of China. I find it rather sympathetic.

All the women were nice—three typical actresses in the three stages of the theatrical career: arriving, on top, coming back. O'Neil seemed the most human, because she is at the beginning.[1] We talked about the war. Robson and Cooper said the conventional things, steering discreetly between patriotism and pacifism. No actor can afford to be openly pacifist: it's bad for the box office. One saw that they really knew nothing and cared for nothing outside the theater. They were ignorant, good-natured and charming. I flattered Cooper and Robson—as one always can—by telling them how badly their colleagues had handled roles in which they themselves had appeared.

January 27. This morning, Thoeren and I had our first interview with Gottfried Reinhardt, who has just returned from New York. He is fatter and more piglike than ever, puffing at his cigar, wisecracking, exuding good humor, gossip and malice. In certain moods, I find this Viennese style of behavior very charming, but today I was impatient and critical. And I noticed that Gottfried used the word "success" several dozen times in the course of twenty minutes. Everybody in his world seems to be either "going up" or "going down." Gottfried himself is going up. In some mysterious way, his trip to New York—where he got drunk while Behrman[2] wrote dialogue for *Waterloo Bridge*—has greatly increased his prestige with the Metro front office.

January 28. The sunshine was wonderfully hot. Huge waves rolled in, almost to the steps of the houses. I lay on the beach and felt happy.

Lunch with Berthold. We talked about Guttchen. Guttchen is now making a precarious living by his knowledge of Chinese gambling. He goes to a gambling club in Chinatown and wins money. The proprietors dislike this, of course; so they want him to come in with them on a racket. Berthold is trying to talk him out of it: it would be very dangerous, and might lead to his arrest and expulsion from the U.S. Gutchen's attitude is fatalistic. "I'll have to do it—unless, of course, you find me something better." He knows that

---

[1] She was then about thirty years old, and Robson nearly forty; Cooper, past fifty, had previously made only a few films but made *Rebecca* that year and then many more.
[2] S. N. Behrman (1893–1973), playwright and screenwriter (often for Garbo).

Berthold won't drop him: he is a moral liability. "People like Guttchen and Uhse," says Berthold, "are our own bad conscience. While we talked, they acted."

Berthold's relations with Guttchen are extraordinary and hysterical. The other day, while they were driving together, Guttchen said something insulting about the Viertel dogs—which become more violent and unruly every day. Berthold flew into a terrific rage, and roundly abused him. He excused himself, in telling this to me, by saying that he was merely trying to rouse Guttchen from his apathy, to make him defend himself.

In the evening, Peter and I went to dinner with the Lewtons. Val Lewton is Selznick's story editor, a fat apologetic man, courteous and shy. His father, who was a Russian chemist, "discovered" Yalta, and helped develop it from a tiny fishing village into a fashionable resort.

Peter was rather uneasy, because, this afternoon, he'd had an outburst in my presence against two English boys who came over here after the war started and were shamelessly glad to have escaped. He hastened to assure me that my case was quite different. But he criticizes me in his heart, because he's feeling a bit guilty himself. Half of him would like to go to Canada and enlist; half of him wants to stay here in Hollywood and make money. During the first months of the war, he secretly took flying lessons. Then he got rather scared, and dropped them when the pilot who was teaching him went out of business.

We all went to the leftist revue, *Meet the People*. It has been a tremendous success—because, as Peter says, the film colony always enjoys anything amateur. There are some excellent numbers. Especially the Roosevelt impersonator who drawls: "The American people *hate war*. And *I hate* the American people." But the general intention is muddled. The authors are isolationist pacifists—but they daren't say so absolutely. They hide behind the Popular Will.

> We're not the kind the newspapers extol
> But we're a power in the Gallup Poll.

Suppose "the people" suddenly turn around and vote for war? Then, presumably, war's all right. The authors' bluff will have been called.

January 29. Lunch with Aldous. We get along best when gossiping—about Salka, about Gerald, about our salaries. Aldous is stuck fast in the script of *Pride and Prejudice*, which is to start shooting almost at once. He said how difficult it was for him to invent plots. We discussed the possibility of constructing them by some mathematical formula. Aldous, the ever-informative, knew of a Russian composer who has invented a machine for writing fugues.

Walked over to inspect the little bookstore opposite the studio buildings. It is kept by a very deaf, tiny Englishwoman. At the end of this week, she is having a clearance sale. "I've stared at that wall opposite for ten years, and now I'm going to get out." She will take a shop in Venice, near the oilfields. Her greatest helper and friend has been Noel Langley, the writer.[1] He has saved her from bankruptcy. Bought a copy of Plomer's *Paper Houses*.

In the afternoon, Gottfried went down to the court to become an American citizen. While he was away, some of the writers draped his desk with a huge American flag, on which they placed a plaster eagle, borrowed from the property department.

January 30. Conference with Gottfried. He is really very nice to work with—charming, easygoing, polite. I told him he'd get the best results out of me if he flattered me a bit and was careful never to snub me. He laughed. We start the script today.

During the past week, without any particular notice in the press, a faint whispering crescendo of war rumors has begun. They say the government is preparing to take over the studios. Employees are being discreetly investigated. Meanwhile, Finns kill Russians, Nazis sink shipping, the Balkans simmer, and nothing definite materializes.

January 31. Worked hard all day on the script. It is quite an amusing job and I am doing it as well as I possibly can. Gottfried seems fairly pleased. Thoeren is a model collaborator. He is brilliantly inventive and actually does most of the work. But he always supports me. I am beginning to like him very much.

Supper with Gerald. We talked about psychical research and its findings. They seem, on the whole, to fit in with Vedanta philosophy. Gerald thinks that people rediscover each other through a whole series of lives. But what if one develops spiritually and doesn't have to be reborn? Gerald admits that this idea torments him—because of Chris. Chris marched in upon our speculations. He was cross because we hadn't finished our meal. So we washed up in a hurry, while Gerald made delicately malicious remarks.

Gerald is anxious to get me away from MGM. He wants me to work with Henwar Rodakiewicz, who is just forming a unit to produce films on significant subjects, partly documentary. I said I thought Wystan would be much more suitable, because of his experience in Post Office films.

[1] South African playwright and screenwriter (1911–1980).

February 1. Rain and thunder in the night. When I drove to work, the Venice-Sepulveda intersection was several feet deep in water. Had to make a detour. I went out to the bookstore and bought several books. I had to insist on paying for them; the old lady wanted to give them away. While we were talking, Noel Langley walked in. A tall young man with a little "artist's" beard. He was aggressive and arrogant, beneath a mask of humility and admiration. What was I—the author of *The Dog Beneath the Skin*—doing in the movie studios? I ought to be ashamed of myself. It was different for him; he was a hack. I asked him to have lunch with me, and he developed a sour-grape line of talk which he called "the philosophy of self-respect." He believes that happiness is achieved by leaving "great works" behind you. But these "great works" that people like Langley are so fond of talking about are really the merest little discarded droppings. "The death shapes" of the mind, as W. J. Turner[1] calls them. A man has to be a hundred times as great as the things he produces. There is so much leakage of power between conception and accomplishment. We treasure the Ninth Symphony and *Hamlet* as one treasures the photographs of the dead: but how much do they actually represent of the genius of Beethoven and Shakespeare? We may admire them. They are all we have left. But, for their creators, they can only have been distorted images, imperfect tokens of an infinitely larger awareness.

February 2. A long, pleasant day of work with Gottfried and Thoeren. Frau Bach interrupts, coquets, contradicts, pouts, complains. She arouses the sadistic instincts of every man she meets, and she loves it. She is a masochistic flirt. Gottfried really enjoys himself. He isn't the slave of his work. *Rage in Heaven* is simply the chief topic of our conversation; but he is always drifting away from it into anecdotes and discussions. He keeps us at the story without ever seeming impatient or in a hurry.

Dinner at the Viertels'. Berthold, Hans and I went into town to see Valeska Gert[2] dance. A little sprinkling of the faithful in an almost empty hall. It was a heartbreaking flop. Gert had only a couple of good moments, and one of these was ruined by the "poet Stern"— she was doing a parody of a temperamental Spanish dancer, during which she recklessly kicks off a shoe: Stern, ever-helpful, dashed forward like a retriever and triumphantly caught it in mid-air!

Gert has quite lost that quality which thrilled Berlin in the twenties:

[1] Australian-born London music and theater critic, poet, and biographer (1889–1946).
[2] German character dancer admired by Brecht; she had her own cabaret in Berlin, the *Kohlkopp*, and later, in New York, The Beggar's Bar.

she is no longer even disgusting. A few young Americans looked on with bewildered dismay at these old-fashioned, unshocking perversities. Berthold came away deeply depressed—seeing in Gert the typical failure of the Emigration to make good in the New World. I cheered him up a little by citing Basserman, who has just had a sensational success in a small character part in *Dr. Ehrlich*.[1]

Berthold tells me that Guttchen went to Dr. Kolisch, who examined him free of charge and was very kind. But Guttchen won't promise not to frequent the Chinese gambling club, so they've parted. Berthold is very angry: he calls Guttchen a decadent poseur.

February 3. This morning, lying in bed, half-awake, I had a very strange experience. I remembered—or rather, relived, with extraordinary vividness—an instant of a certain morning, four years ago. I was sitting in a small park in Amsterdam, with Gerald Hamilton, and looking through the overhanging branches of a willow at a patch of brightly sunlit water, in which some ducks were swimming. Not only did I relive this instant (which was, I am sure, absolutely authentic) but, for a couple of seconds, I actually *was* the Christopher of 1936. I was—and yet I wasn't; because, standing aside from the experience, I was also aware of the present-day Christopher. I can't, of course, in the least describe the difference between the two personalities—that of 1936 and that of 1940—but, as I gazed at that strip of water, I was intensely conscious of it. I could hold the two selves separate, comparing them—and, in doing so, I caught the faintest glimpse of something else—that part of my consciousness which has not changed, which never will change, because it is a part of Reality.

Now, for the first time, I feel I have some inkling of what Gerald is really talking about. But it won't stay with me. Imagination, vanity and doubt are already at work. My mind suggests all kinds of literary touches, to improve the picture. My egotism preens itself—delighted to have had a "mystical experience." My scepticism—disgusted by their antics—urges me to discredit the whole thing. "After all," it tells me, "this was only a dream."

February 5. Today I went to see Kolisch and told him I want to begin the treatment he suggests. No meat, no fish, no milk, no butter, no candy, no alcohol, no bread except pumpernickel—nothing except vegetables and fruit. Herbal tea night and morning. Codliver oil. Red capsules before meals; green capsules after. Visits three times a week—for blood tests, shots, weighing, pulse taking, quartz-lamp baths. Price: one hundred dollars a month. Well, I asked for it.

---

[1] Albert Basserman, German stage actor, in *Dr. Ehrlich's Magic Bullet*.

February 6. Tonight, a party at the Viertels'. The Huxleys, Anita Loos and Gottfried were invited. The real object of our presence was to convince a producer, who has bought *They Walk Alone*, that Beatrix Lehmann should be brought over from England to play the chief part. Unfortunately, the Huxleys had never even heard of Beatrix, so our propaganda fell rather flat.

Berthold was in a tense, jumpy state—like a cannon, loaded and longing to be fired. He and Salka started a political argument, in Gottfried's presence, about the Russian policy. Berthold snapped: "I am absolutely for the extermination of Poland!"

Aldous informed us that female rabbits can now be impregnated from the ova of other female rabbits, but they can only produce females. In the same way, a future manless age of matriarchs might be created; a lesbian tyranny. Salka and Aldous began picturing the Hollywood of the future—Warner Sisters, Louisa B. Mayer, United Artistes, Twentieth Century Vixen, etc.

After dinner, Aldous and I got in a corner. He was a little drunk, and started on a favorite topic: the poorness of all literature. Homer was terribly overrated, Dante was hopelessly limited, Shakespeare was such a stupid man, Goethe was such a bore, Tolstoy was silly, etc. etc. We had disposed of nearly everybody, and Aldous was really enjoying himself—until a nasty doubt struck him: "What about Lope de Vega? I've never read him. Is he any good?" "Lope de Vega," I told him airily, "no—he's not up to much." "He *isn't*?" Aldous was immensely relieved: "Oh, I *am* glad to hear you say that!"

Later there was a violent row between Gottfried and Berthold, about the Russo-Finnish war. Gottfried, who is pro-Finn, was delighted because the Russian troops are said to be suffering terribly from the arctic weather. "God makes it colder for them," he said, gloatingly. Berthold left the room. Although he isn't jealous in the ordinary, sexual sense, there's no doubt that the friendship between Salka and Gottfried has a lot to do with these fights.

March 6. A month since I last wrote in this book—and where are we? A little nearer the advertised blitzkrieg outbreak, and perhaps the entry of the U.S. into the war. The Russians still haven't got Viipuri, the Turks haven't attacked Odessa, the President hasn't declared himself for a third term.

George O'Neil died of heart failure, one evening in Pershing Square, while listening to a political speech.

I am still at Metro—with, perhaps, another three weeks before the picture and my job are finished. I am still being treated by Kolisch, and still feeling much the same. Gas, fits of depression, nervous headaches. He has now given me *six* different sorts of medicine—but what use are they if I can't relax? My stomach is cramped in a tight knot of hate and fear.

I've seen the Swami. He says, if I'm too busy to meditate, I should think about the word *Om*, which is God. But I can only become aware of God by thinking all around him. Om says nothing. It's just a comic noise. I'm afraid the Swami is altogether too Indian for me, with his mantras and his parables. I must talk to Gerald again.

Vernon has been away since Saturday. I miss him when he isn't here, but when he is we quarrel. I'm absolutely unfit for any but the most casual human contacts. The split in my personality is now several yards wide; it's a marvel how I hold together. However much I may dislike the prospect, I know it's absolutely necessary for me to spend large periods of time alone. Independently alone—not sniffing like a spaniel around other people's comforting smell and warmth. Poor Wiggs is in agony just now, because a bitch down the road is on heat and he wants to get at her. He howls all night.

The studio doors are now guarded more strictly than ever—because, we are told, of a recent attack on Louis B. Mayer. The cops keep asking you for your pass—especially if you are going up to the sacred third floor, where the big shots have their offices. Never was back-slapping harder, cordiality louder, mistrust greater. Rumor travels the corridors on roller skates.

The morning etiquette of super-optimism. "Hi, Chris." "Hi, Jack." "How's the boy?" "Swell. How's everything?" "Fine. Just fine."

Of certain sinecure holders on the lot, it is said: "Oh, they'll never fire *him*. He knows where the body is buried."

An anecdote someone told me of the early movie days. Two tycoons were battling for control of a studio. One of them had the other attacked and shot up by hired gunmen. He was in hospital for several weeks. When he recovered and returned to the studio, the doorkeeper wouldn't let him inside. His rival had bought the place over his head.

March 31. Sunday morning. Dull warm cloudy weather. John Barbirolli, conducting Beethoven's Eighth over the radio from New York, competes with Happy's stolid thumping on the piano upstairs. Vernon is in his studio, in the house down the hill, doing a still life. Am sad and bored, with the boredom of a wage earner on Sunday, who has nothing to do, and finds himself furtively longing for the office.

Rage in Heaven is practically finished. It isn't nearly such a disgrace as I'd feared. Now Victor Saville wants me to do a picture about Chopin—not the real Chopin, but a fiery young revolutionary, whose every note is composed for Poland. George Sand is the heavy who lures him from the arms of his country and a simple Warsaw maiden. Can I really handle such filth?

On Easter, a week ago, we drove out to Victorville and stopped the night at a dude ranch, the Yucca Loma. It lies right in the middle of a desert valley, looking toward high snow-covered mountains—a little colony of luxury dwellings, in ranchero-Mexican style, complete with stables, swimming pool and tennis court. The place is run by a Mrs. Behr, one of those art-corsairs of the desert, in bold gaudy clothes, who speak of their guests as "my little family." The guests were third-rate film notables, some nice college kids, with sound teeth, clear empty eyes and consciences, and a young man dying of TB who publishes a weekly newspaper supposed to be written by his dogs.

A terrible, shameful, almost insane attack of self-pity and despair. "I hate this place," I told Vernon, "I hate all Americans. I don't belong here. I shall have to go back to Europe." Poor Vernon was much distressed. And of course, I didn't mean what I said about the Americans or the ranch. I meant: I hate myself.

Actually, in my sane moments, I love this country. I love it just because I *don't* belong. Because I'm not involved in its traditions, not born under the curse of its history. I feel free here. I'm on my own. My life will be what I make of it.

I love the ocean, and the orange groves, and the desert, and the big mountains around Arrowhead, where the snow comes down to the shores of the lake and you see the eagles circling above. Nature is unfriendly, dangerous, utterly aloof. However hard I may try, I can't turn her into a stage set for my private drama. Thank God I can't. She refuses to become a part of my neurosis.

April 1. Dinner with Frieda Lawrence and Angelino [Ravagli], her Italian ex-cavalry-officer lover. I had expected to find Frieda intense and domineering. Actually, she is already an old woman, with a croaking, witchlike laugh. She is very lively, interested in everybody and everything. Her figure is a lump. Her grizzled blonde hair is cropped very short. She and Angelino are a charming couple—living, apparently, in a state of continual unmalicious bickering, like children.

She wanted me to help her with an outline of *The Plumed Serpent* which Dieterle[1] has requested for a possible film. Obviously, the material is hopelessly undramatic, in its present form. Frieda wandered through the story, stopping at intervals to squabble with Angelino, who kept throwing cold water on the whole scheme. Finally, I suggested that Berthold was just the man to help them, and thus slipped gracefully out of the noose.

April 9. German troops landing in Denmark and Norway. All day long, the radio and the special editions were full of sinking ships, occupied towns, air raids, scares, rumors and lies. Felt too depressed to write the new scene for *Rage in Heaven.* Appropriately enough, it plays in a deathhouse cell.

Vernon left, this morning, for New York to visit his mother. Berthold also left for New York, two days ago. He has been asked to produce a play, called *Thumbs*—a thriller, starring Oscar Homolka.

I'm about to sign a contract which will tie me to Metro for a year. It's a long prospect of drudgery, with the Chopin film as a beginning.

Saw Gerald in the evening. We talked about the enlargement of consciousness. Three stages: first, you see something—some single object—as it really is, "in its own right"; then you see that the object is part of a plan—its position in time and space is inevitable—it isn't there by accident; then, in the highest state of illumination, you see beyond objects altogether—you trace, as it were, the line which connects them all with a single focal point, the absolute Reality.

Experience of the first stage is quite common to artists and other observant people. I have often had it myself. It may be achieved, for example, by an accident of light, or a disturbance in the normal laws of perspective. The door of Chris's bedroom is set at an angle to the wall, and this gives it—at moments when you happen to notice it—a most disturbing air of being, somehow, "outside the picture frame." Gerald told me how, the other day, he was looking into the bowl of the toilet: a green light fell on the porcelain, through the leaves outside the window, and it appeared to him "as it really was." "Nothing else mattered to me at that moment. I could have gone on looking at it for ever."

June 1. Throughout last month, this stunning avalanche of disasters—while I sat at Metro, studying the letters of Chopin and Sand. Victor Saville getting more and more desperate, day after day—then suddenly brightening into childlike faith, because [Hans] Rameau, the Metro writer who dabbles in astrology, has told him England

[1] William Dieterle (1893–1972), German director and former actor long in Hollywood.

won't be conquered. In the daytime, I'm blinded by anxiety and see nothing—although I now "sit" regularly. Ten minutes of comparative sanity—and how you have to plot to get them! Berthold writes frantically from New York, urging me to record everything. I know it is my duty; Horatio's duty.[1] But I can only keep this diary if I discard all fear. Every day must be described quite objectively, not as a history of moods. Leave literature to the war correspondents. Record. Record.

The other morning, an intensely clear waking vision of the futility of all literature—somehow epitomized by the title of James Branch Cabell's book, *The Cream of the Jest*, which I have never read.

July 5. For several days now, the coast has been muffled in thick fog; a mile inland there is brilliant sunshine. All yesterday, the firecrackers detonated invisibly. It seemed wicked, heartless to be making these harmless explosions while people are being blown to bits in western Europe. My right buttock still aches from Kolisch's latest shot—a kind of artificial cramp, which clenches the muscle into a hard, painfully sensitive lump. The Chopin film has been abandoned—it is too expensive a project for these times—and Metro has laid me off; I mayn't be working again for several weeks. Finished the Goncourt journals. Here, gossip achieves the epigrammatic significance of poetry. To keep such a diary is to render a real service to the future.

With Vernon to dinner at the Huxleys'. Aldous was in bed. Kolisch has given him a fever. Just now, we have our ailments in common. We compare notes on the symptoms produced by Kolisch's treatment—those intensely unpleasant sensations of restlessness and fatigue which make one feel, as Aldous says, "like an aviary." A kind of nervous deconstellation, with the frantic aimless activity you experience in a nightmare.

Maria had arranged a "children's party" of sandwiches, cold meat, hard-boiled eggs and flat champagne. Matthew was there, and Sophie (who has just joined the Reinhardt drama school) and Matthew's friend Sid. Afterwards, we went down to the swimming pool on the Uplifters' estate. There were fireworks. The rockets were beautiful in the thick fog—like drops of vividly colored liquid melting into water. A tenor sang "God Bless America," while a searchlight pointed at nothing in particular and someone rang a model of the Liberty Bell.

News of the battle between British and French warships at Oran. U.S. newspapers support the British action. This is the sort of thing statesmen describe approvingly as "realistic" and "in accordance with the logic of events."

---

[1] I.e. to tell the story (*Hamlet*, V: ii).

A couple of days ago, on Sunset Boulevard, I picked up two youths who were thumbing a ride. One of them carried a radio. As soon as they were in the car, he asked me: "Say—when you stopped to pick us up, what did you think this was?" "I don't know," I said, "I didn't notice it particularly." "You didn't think it was a suitcase?" "Well—yes, I probably did. Why?" "You see?" The boy turned to his friend and grinned: evidently this decided some argument they had been having. "It's like this," the other boy explained to me: "If some folks notice you've got a suitcase with you, they won't stop—because they think maybe you might be carrying a gun in it." I pointed out that he might just as easily be carrying a gun in the pocket of his pants. The boy thought this over for a moment, quite seriously. "Yes," he said at last, "I guess you're right."

Extract from a letter in today's issue of *Time* magazine, signed Ethel H. Barrow, Brooklyn, N.Y.: "Recently I spent a long vacation in one of America's most advertised resorts. There I got a concentrated picture of America's new generation and their attitude towards life. They have no respect for women; they have a shockingly immoral attitude towards them, and while defending America and a moral attitude towards women may not seem analogous, basically they are the same. . . . I firmly believe that wars are nature's way of getting rid of bad people, and as far as I can see the young men of America deserve to be shot."

Lunch with Hugh Chisholm, who has arrived here with his wife Bridget to organize war relief. He is working at the Goldwyn studios—where Sam, with no pictures to make, is devoting all his terrific and obstructive energies to the job. He vetoes every suggestion, argues, curses, makes scenes; then gives way and apologizes. Hours and hours are wasted in futile conferences. Goldwyn, in order to keep control of the project, has thrown open his empty offices and dressing rooms to the committee. And the film stars, Hugh says, are equally tiresome. Each one thinks only of his or her own publicity. Cooperation is made impossible by local private feuds.

Hugh looked plumper, whiter, older. His little cat's nose screwed up into a tiny point of scorn as he poured out his woes. He has all the airs of a harassed committee woman, breathless with indignation and greatly enjoying himself. He writes letters to the President. He knows just what is going on in Washington. During his flying trip to Italy, he talked daily to Count Ciano[1]—"Until I saw it was hopeless. Nothing we could do would keep them out of the war."

He predicts the destruction of England, followed by a monster fifth

---

[1] Foreign minister and Mussolini's son-in-law.

column offensive in the U.S. He is sure that all the key cities will easily pass into the hands of the bundists. America will become fascist during the winter, under Wendell Willkie.

But he doesn't really believe a word of this. For, with the next breath, he plans to take a little house in Washington and settle down. Bridget is going to have a baby next winter. When Hugh heard that I am earning six hundred dollars a week, he threw his arm around my neck with a little scream of joy—as though he were actually embracing a sack of treasury bills.

July 6. "We have got to take them by the back of the neck and kick them into it if they won't do it willingly. If they won't fight we can make them dig trenches. We send a gangster to the electric chair, but we do not treat these pacifists as traitors." Rupert Hughes,[1] speaking last night before the Rotary Club, in the ballroom of the Biltmore.

R. E. Smith, twenty-one, of Baldwin Park, staged a sit-down "love strike" outside Deanna Durbin's home. After being refused admittance, he sat down in her automobile. He told the police officers: "I feel as if I were glued here, I love her so."

Dinner with Hugh and Bridget Chisholm. John van Druten and Carter Lodge came in afterwards. Johnny has just received, from England, a copy of a poem attacking the "traitor," Leopold of Belgium. It's called "The Changeling." Lord Dunsany is supposed to have written it—but Johnny thinks it may be a fake or a joke; it's so incredible.

> If fairies, jealous of King Albert's fame,
> Once, in the cradle, changed his eldest son,
> Surely in Elfland with a fairy name
> There fights some hero till his war is won.[2]

Hugh was full of his scheme to organize a series of weekly broadcasts by the best talents of America to the English people—to cheer them up, asssure them of American sympathy and promote international friendship. He has already drafted an appeal letter, calling on prominent Americans to assist—in glowing journalese. Johnny tactfully tried to tone it down, a little. Carter, who was drunk and aggressive, untactfully declared that Americans loathed the

[1] American writer and film director formerly in the military.
[2] Albert I of Belgium resisted German aggression throughout WWI, but in May 1940 his son, Leopold III, cut off from the French army, surrendered; some Belgians fought on with the French and English until the Dunkirk evacuation in June. Lord Dunsany (E. J. M. Plunkett) was a soldier and a literary author.

English and always would. A quarrel might have started, but everyone was too sleepy.

July 7. Vernon and I drove to Laguna Beach with Tony Bower. Why does one make these excursions? Tony had to visit some friends, and we found ourselves with nothing to do. We went to a movie. Tony, meanwhile, was playing bridge in a room full of youngish men who had nothing in common but their tan and their immense boredom. Their too-communicative eyes light up hungrily at the entrance of a stranger. They are all waiting for something to happen. Gin is drunk, cigarettes are smoked, and they sit and sit and sit.

Sunday—that aimless trek of ten thousand cars along the wide black well-marked roads. Fifty miles out, lunch, supper, fifty miles home. The only incidents—the unexpected size of the bill, or a minor collision, or a police ticket. Grumbling, the sententious repetition of opinions from newspaper articles, dyspeptic nostalgia awakened by a glimpse of lithe figures running on the beach. The reliable image of the ocean. The men are nervous and irritable; the women placid. They have their eternal themes: clothes, illnesses, the neighbors' habits. Ritual behavior surviving an extinct art—the art of enjoyment. What we have left are the habits, and the machinery which serves the habits.

Few of us any longer know how to enjoy anything—a game, a glass of wine, even a swim in the ocean. Gerald speaks of the "boy-meets-girl" group as though these people were happy, at least on their own level. But they seldom are. Because boy no longer knows how to meet girl.

July 8. This morning, the embassy called on all British actors between eighteen and thirty-one to return to England.

Lunch with the Manns, at the new house they've leased for the summer on Rockingham. A big, half-empty place with an Italian garden and swimming pool. Klaus and I immediately got into an argument about the war. It seems that Wystan is being very cagey in New York—not telling anyone what he really thinks. I tried to explain my position and asked Klaus what he thought I should do. He said that I should "make a definite statement" in support of the Allies—since my silence is being misrepresented. Just a little statement; once or twice would be enough. I answered that, even if I believed this, I would hesitate to make propaganda, at a safe distance of six thousand miles, encouraging other people to get killed in my place. Klaus said I was being too "objective."

Of course, he added, he himself was a pacifist: he couldn't possibly kill anyone personally. But pacifism couldn't possibly be applied to every case: if you let the Nazis kill everyone, you allowed civilization to be destroyed. I quoted Aldous's argument, that civilization dies anyhow of blood poisoning the moment it takes up its enemies' weapons and exchanges crime for crime. Klaus replied that this view—that no war is always better than any war—seemed to him "merely cynical."

So we argued, each contradicting himself and slipping, as one always does, from one language to another—from the language of ethics to the language of politics, and back again. Klaus said that pacifism nowadays merely assists the work of the fifth column and the Nazis. That, I answered, is why I prefer to keep my mouth shut. Our talk was quite friendly, and I was glad, at any rate, to have had it out in the open.

At lunch were Thomas and Frau Mann. Despite their terrible anxiety over Heinrich and Golo (who were interned in France and may have been handed over to the Nazis) Thomas was urbane as ever. If the English saved democracy, he said, he would gladly tolerate all their faults, even the Oxford accent. He remembered how kind Galsworthy had been—lending the Manns his car while they were in London, and himself travelling by bus. Thomas told me how a sanatorium for consumptives in Colorado had invited him to visit them, adding as an inducement: "We have tried to make everything as much like *The Magic Mountain* as possible."

He looks wonderfully young for his age—perhaps because, as a boy, he was elderly and staid. With careful, deliberate gestures, he chooses a cigar, examines a cognac bottle, opens a furniture catalogue—giving each object his full, serious attention. Yet he isn't in the least pompous. He has great natural dignity. He is a true scholar, a gentlemanly householder, a gracefully ironic pillar of society—solid right through. He would be magnificent at his own trial. Indeed, he has been making his speech for the defence ever since he left Germany.

Klaus looks very tired. He is paler, fatter and has a bald patch like a tonsure on the crown of his head. He chain-smokes nervously. But, as always, there is something very attractive and even stimulating about him. He isn't a despairing loafer, like so many of the others. He's always on the alert, always working. He has energy and courage. He says he has started writing in English. He speaks very fluently nowadays.

July 9. To the Solarium, with Tony Bower and Chris—that dreary little sanded prison yard where the naked slaves of the sun lie all day long, in the crucified attitudes of the Inferno. Tony is much upset by the possibility of my return to England. As long as Wystan and I are here, taking the blame, the smaller escapists are safe from notice.

We walked along the beach and met a boy named Leslie Swaddling, an actor. Was he going back to England, I asked. No, of course not. He was an Australian. And, anyhow, nothing would induce him to risk his skin. "That swine Pétain," he continued peevishly—with the little flare-up of spite I know so well, "he betrayed us. He ought to be shot without trial. This is no time for mercy."

This is no time for mercy. We are all terrified, and so we twist about, striking at each other, wounding, killing. I am suffering—so everybody else shall suffer. Thus the poison spreads.

Overheard at the Solarium. Three men are discussing an actress. "At least," says one, "you'll admit she knew how to walk. She walked beautifully—like a swan."

July 10. To have lunch with Gerald, who has just returned from a lecture tour. For weeks he has been suffering from diarrhea, caused by his worry and misery about the war. "The Buddhists," he joked, "call it The Lower Form of Compassion."

While Gerald was travelling, he met a man named Starr Daily, an ex-gangster and convict who has written a book about his mystical experiences called *Love Can Open Prison Doors*. Daily had trained himself to hate everybody and to use hatred as a kind of stoicism whenever he was getting hurt. It made him able to bear great physical pain. Then, while he was in solitary confinement, he had some sort of glimpse of the Reality. Another time, when ten detectives were giving him the third degree, he suddenly stopped holding himself together by hatred and began to feel sorry for them. Immediately, the detectives stopped beating him.

The book is terribly sentimental, and far too breezily written. It recommends "Love" as the universal cure-all—without ever properly explaining what "Love" is. But there are some very remarkable passages dealing with what Daily calls "passive violence"—the ingrowing, impotent hatred which consumes the hearts of cowards and ultimately destroys them. Leslie Swaddling's remark yesterday was a good example of passive violence. And God knows I am devoured by it myself. As Gerald says, hate and fear are two halves of the same thing. And fear is the worse half.

Gerald sees, in this epoch, the steadily increasing destruction of "the ultra-clay of consent" which binds society together. Now there is hardly any more left. The Anglo-French battle at Oran destroys forty years of work on the Entente Cordiale.[1] As technical efficiency increases, consent diminishes, and the structure falls apart. The day of Germany is perhaps already nearly over. France is already disintegrated. Now it is Russia's turn. This will be the theme of his new book.

The problem of the future—to create new "ultra-clay," new force. Because, when this war period is over, people will have lost all faith in an earthly utopia. The question is, how shall the new force be organized—by setting up self-supporting communities on a monastic plan, or by working through existing institutions, such as Baptist seminaries, which are at present bankrupt of ideas? This will be discussed next Sunday, by Gerald, Allan Hunter, Huxley, Daily and others. Gerald asked me to come and listen to them.

War, says Gerald, seems to have begun as a form of dance. The Chinese character for "war" is the character for "dance" with one radical added. Perhaps the "warlike instinct" can be developed backwards again to its harmless, embryonic form, through competition in sports.

All evil is in time. Like animals, we cannot see a thing when it is moving slowly. We can't experience horror at evil until its movement is speeded up. If ten people die within six months, each in a different manner and in a different place, we don't care much. If ten people die within six seconds, all together in an automobile accident, we are shocked.

I came away from him feeling so calm and happy, as I usually do. I wish I could live in a temple where he was a monk, and just sweep the floor and listen.

A party at Salka's. Vernon came under protest and got drunk. Later, he poured out his resentments and fears. I don't treat him as a grown-up person, an artist—he says. I lost my temper, argued, talked of "affection" in a voice cold with dislike. What a mess it all is! I am simply being confronted by myself at the age of nineteen. There is so much in Vernon to admire and respect, and he is struggling so hard. How often I forget this! What if he is priggish and humorless sometimes? Can't I supply enough humor and understanding for both of us? If I can't, what is the use of having been through all those quarrels with M.?

---

[1] After the British navy sank the French fleet at Mers-el-Kébir near Oran, Algeria, on July 3, the Vichy government severed relations and bombed Gibraltar in retaliation.

July 11. A postcard arrived for Happy Bayley this morning: "Men of Tomorrow. Business meeting and beans. At Dr. Brown's. 777 Fiske Street. Please show up. Chuck."

Lunch with Robert Stevenson,[1] at RKO. He wants me to write an episode for the film they're doing in aid of the British War Relief fund.[2]

July 12. A cable from M. to say Uncle Henry was buried yesterday. I often used to wonder just when this would happen—and I always half knew that when it did, when Marple and all the money became mine, it would be too late. It is too late now—not merely because of the war, but because the absurd boyhood dream of riches is over forever. It is too late to invite my friends to a banquet, to burn the Flemish tapestry and the Elizabethan beds, to turn the house into a brothel. I no longer want to be revenged on the past. Several weeks ago, I wrote to M. that Richard [Isherwood] is to have everything, house and money. It's his, not mine, by right, because he loves the place and is prepared to live there. I confirmed this by cable today.

Poor Henry—he must be glad to get free of all this mess, at last. I'm glad he died in comparative comfort, with his housekeeper and valet at his elbow. I was fond of him, and he of me, in our different ways. No doubt he always thought of me as being after his money—as indeed I was. But this seemed to him perfectly natural and proper. He had the eighteenth-century conception of the relation between uncle and heir.

He had nothing whatever to do with 1940. He spoke another language, which has long since become obsolete. He thought in terms of "places" and family relationships, entails and mortgages. He would say contemptuously that a man wasn't "worth a penny piece," meaning that he had no unearned income. He belonged to a ninetyish world of smart Catholicism—in which scandal was sniggered over at the end of dinner, and one's confessor was like a rich man's lawyer— paid to get you out of awkward spiritual jams. He said that "certain kinds of sin can be very beautiful." He burnt incense in the drawing room, preferred memoirs to fiction but was a great expert on Dickens, whom he called "delicious." Sex, in his late middle age, he found "extwornrally soothin'." Italy was his spiritual home: he spent every winter in Rome and always approved of Mussolini, who had made the trains run on time. Once, when he was young, he entered a monastery, intending to give up the world—but, after a year, he got

[1] British film director in Hollywood from 1939.
[2] *Forever and a Day* (1943), about an English house over many years; roughly eighty stars participated.

rheumatic fever and left. The rest of the family always sneered at him for this.

July 13. Vernon has a terrible cold. He copied a Renoir head of a little girl, and produced the face of a murderess, with bulging corpse-cheeks and a stolid pout of hatred, all in a deep, luminous mucus green. When he had finished it, we both laughed a great deal.

July 14. This morning, Aldous, Maria, Matthew and three of his college friends came with us to Allan Hunter's church, to hear Starr Daily speak. To my dismay, it was quite a function. I hadn't expected so many people in disturbing, flowery hats. Evans Carlson (whom I haven't met since China) was there. And Glen Clark—the track coach who uses psycho-spiritual methods to train his runners. Also, of course, Gerald.

One's beliefs lead one into some funny places! I wonder what M. would think—seeing me sitting in the front pew of a Congregationalist church? Parts of the service moved me, because they were so informal. Allan behaved much more like the chairman of a meeting than like a minister. Daily still has a prison grimness about him which is very impressive; but he's got too much of the professional pulpit manner. He talks too glibly about "Lerv." Glenn Clark is stout and funny. Only Gerald, Aldous and Carlson seemed entirely above suspicion.

Nevertheless, this service, and the picnic meal afterward, and the discussion in the crypt, and the fundamentalist jargon of Mrs. Daily, and the quotations from the prophets were all very good for me. The dainty little Ego shrinks back, oh so fastidiously, from all this middle-class "togetherness." It wants its religion to be socially and intellectually chic. It would much prefer to talk about God at a smart cocktail party.

Carlson was very sympathetic—like a strange, weatherbeaten, prophetic buzzard. He described how he first discovered, while working in Nicaragua, that you could handle the native police by nonviolent methods. Two former police chiefs had been shot by their own men, in the back. So he made a point of always walking in front of them to show his confidence. He never used an interpreter, lest he should lose personal contact with the prisoners he was trying: if he couldn't understand or make himself understood, he laboriously looked up the words in the dictionary. He never condemned anyone until the prisoner had first confessed his guilt.

Aldous's speech was much the best. He pointed out that power comes into the organism from above and from below—up through the animal level and down through the spiritual level. But it can't circulate, because it is checked by the Ego—the level of self-consciousness which is in the middle. "Animal grace" is the functioning of the organism in accordance with the laws of its physical being: the lilies taking no thought for the morrow. "Spiritual grace" is the functioning of the organism in accordance with the laws of its spiritual being: we are all a part of absolute Reality. "Human grace" is pseudo-grace. It is only a projection of the Ego—into patriotic nationalism, for example. It may seem selfless, but it never really is. The whole problem of spiritual life is to keep the self-conscious Ego quiet. To stop it from interfering on the two other levels and allow them to function naturally.

The Ego wants to interfere. It commits original sin—the setting up of its own self-conscious power against the natural powers of body and soul. On the animal level, this interference produces physical disease; on the spiritual level, spiritual disease. So you have, on the one hand, the so-called psychologically induced diseases—TB, duodenal ulcer, etc.; and, on the other hand, the spiritual diseases—such as Pride. If you can only quiet the Ego, soul and body begin to function of themselves, in spiritual and physical health, and the aim of yoga is achieved. The Ego is the eternal wise guy, the Mr. Fix-It. It dances about in its impatience at the slowness of Nature—and yet, with its fussing, it holds up everything.

Beware, says Aldous, of confusing Spirit and Public Spirit. The most diabolical people are often the most public-spirited—e.g. Hitler.

Carlson is returning to China within a week or two. He wants to get back to the Northwest and spend more time in the communist communities—where, he says, communism is really working, without egotism and without the establishment of a power-aristocracy. How I envy him! One should live one's life as near as possible to the fountainheads of the New Force. This force is always striking up fresh wells—now in one country, now in another. There was a well in Spain, but it dried up. Perhaps there is a little spring here, but it's very small, as yet. Maybe, today, it grew a little larger—despite the cakes and the hats, which so disturbed Vernon and the boys that they left early. As Gerald says, a spring is always muddy around its source.

Goodness, this thing is difficult! New snares at every step. Daily went through the most ghastly experiences—the aperture of his consciousness was literally blasted open—and now he's exposed to all kinds of new risks. You become a teacher, a healer, and woe betide you—unless, every day, you can prostrate yourself in utter humility. The Ego, like a lazy collaborator, steps in when it's time to claim the credit. Throwing his arm around the shoulder of the Holy Ghost, he beams: "Well, old boy, between us we did a pretty nice job, didn't we?"

Prayer for writers: "Oh source of my inspiration, teach me to extend toward all living beings that fascinated, unsentimental, loving and all-pardoning interest which I feel for the characters I create. May I become identified with all humanity, as I identify myself with these imaginary persons. May my art become my life, and my life my art. Deliver me from snootiness, and from the Pulitzer Prize. Teach me to practice true anonymity. Help me to forgive my agents and publishers. Make me attentive to my critics and patient with my fans. For yours is the conception and the execution. Amen."

Stop trying to use the conscious will. Free the Ego from its attachments with expert gentleness, like a surgeon. Remember that the strangulated Ego is everything you hate in others—so how can you hate anybody? You are only hating yourself. The surgeon doesn't hate the hernia: he simply reduces it. This is what Homer Lane meant when he said: "You must love yourself." But I thought he meant "You must be complacent with your present condition." Forgive yourself, absolutely: then operate.

July 15. This morning, I picked up two hitchhikers, who had been waiting a long time on the road, thumbing without success. When I stopped, one of them exclaimed: "Hot dog! A gentleman at last!" And the other added: "A gentleman and a scholar, unless I'm mistaken."

We were summoned to a mass meeting at Metro, in aid of the American Red Cross. Stage Thirty—draped with flags and crammed with four thousand employees; actors in makeup, writers, stenographers, electricians, propmen, cameramen, carpenters—looked like Democracy's Nuremberg Rally. Miss Jeanette MacDonald, in pink frills, wearing a little girl's bow in her hair, sang "The Star Spangled Banner" with piercing sweetness. Robert Montgomery, just arrived from France, spoke out from the shoulder, in the clipped boyish tones of terse hysteria popularized by the war correspondents. Louis B. Mayer made a rambling, sentimental speech which Salka described as "Capitalism licking Labor's ass." God forbid, said Mayer, that we should fear him. He pleaded with us to believe that he was a nice guy. Even if he did have a lot of money, he gave most of it away in taxes. And if he gave a lot to the Red Cross he was only giving the government's money. So we should all give, too. No man would be forced to give, but Mayer pitied anyone who didn't because his conscience would hurt. And wasn't it better to be on the giving end than on the receiving end? Didn't it feel better? Especially when the receiving end was being bombed. He finished by saying that he hoped we'd often get together like this in the future and "talk things over."

Lying by Mrs. Dietz's sky blue swimming pool, Hugh Chisholm held forth on the war. *Of course*, he was opposed to rescuing German children. He only wanted to win. Humanitarianism was very nice, but not for him. And he coquettishly stretched his legs in their pink Hawaiian swimming trunks. But Bridget disagreed. She has a baby inside her.

July 16. To invent a new kind of grammar for writing about the Ego: "During the spring of 1940, I worked at the MGM studios. It left the house every morning in its car, at 9:30. People who knew me at this time noticed that, on Mondays, Wednesdays and Fridays, it returned home early . . . etc."

All this while, the Nazi attack on England has threatened but not begun. Today, the papers are full of rumors that Hitler will make another peace offer.

Vernon urges me to get a house. He is going through a violent reaction from his social life. He wants to stay home more, and study and work. I must say, I simply couldn't imagine living with anyone else at this time. Vernon does at least understand what I'm driving at. He is serious and honest—not a cocktail sipper.

July 17. John van Druten and I are working together on an episode for the British War Relief film. Murder of an old lady by her housekeepers, with slow poison, in the Dickens style. It is all Johnny's idea, and I can hardly contribute anything to it. Johnny is so inventive, anyway. He's always three jumps ahead of me. His mind is agile and graceful, like a nimble monkey. It takes naturally to parody and pastiche. Johnny really loves to write: there seems to be absolutely no struggle, no effort involved. It is all play, and he approaches it without inhibitions, like a child. Yet, at the same time, he is the shrewd, experienced professional, deliberately creating theatrical effects and very conscious of how his audience will react to them. He is charming and polite to me, but I don't feel that I'm being of the slightest use to him.

July 18. With Gerald and Vernon to the Swami's weekly lecture on the Upanishads. As at Allan Hunter's, the flowery hats were predominant. The Swami was dressed in his beautiful golden yellow monk's robe, which he only wears in the temple. Seated on a cushion, he smilingly exposed the ignorance of his class. He is gentle, persuasive and humorous. He speaks quietly, with an absolute, matter-of-fact authority. To him, spiritual truths are unanswerable facts, like the facts of geography. You don't have to get excited about them, or argue, or defend. You just state them.

I notice that he has a taste for very elegant, pointed shoes.

Western philosophy always views the Self as a subject. Berkleyism: the world exists in my own brain. The Upanishads say that the Self is neither subject nor object. The apparent paradox: that mind can be transcended with the help of mind—like a ladder, which helps you to "transcend" it and climb through a window.

On the way home, Gerald remarked that, since the whole of our physical world is an electric pattern, there can equally well be other worlds on other wavelengths, just as "real" to their inhabitants, and occupying exactly the same position in space and time as ours does. Where I am sitting, a man may be drowning in an ocean—unaware of me and my surroundings as I am of him and his. Hence the possibility of a "scientific" explanation of so-called psychic phenomena. Perhaps there are beings all around us who are too "unsubstantial" or too "solid" for us to perceive them. Except at rare moments when the other "wavelength" starts, for some unexplained reason, to "come through," like another program on the radio.

July 19. Vernon and I had lunch with the Manns. Klaus and Erika are much alarmed lest Hitler's peace speech should find a response in England. Later, an agreeably pedantic lecture by Thomas on the use of the German prefix *er.* Klaus is planning a magazine. It is to be called *Zero Hour*, a symposium of European and American culture.

Dinner with Chris, who was much excited by a visit from [Starr] Daily. When Daily was a boy, he met a tramp who taught him the whole art of begging—always insisting that the only effective force in the world is hatred. You have to hate in order to be tough; and you have to be tough because everyone in the world is against you. They stayed together until Daily was eighteen. The other day, in downtown Los Angeles, Daily met the tramp again, with another boy. The tramp asked what Daily had been doing, all these years, and Daily told him the whole story, including his conversion. "Well," he concluded, "it was a long road." And the tramp, with a very strange smile answered: "Yes—but you got there in the end." The suggestion is, of course, that the tramp was really a kind of Zen Buddhist saint, who taught love by insisting on its opposite.

I suppose I believe this story. I don't know. There's something about Daily, despite his impressiveness, which I don't altogether trust.

July 20. Worked all day with Johnny on the story.

As we were having supper, Vernon said he believed the time was coming when we should both be very happy. "I hope you're right," I said, "but first I've got to overcome fear." This is true, but how ridiculous it sounds! Like saying: "First I've got to build a range of mountains." To redirect, to concentrate all that waste energy—what engineering project could be vaster? It's much easier to turn hate into love than to turn fear into love, because fear is more diffuse. It saps one's strength in so many different places. You must search out your fear in its most secret corners. It has a genius for disguise.

The radio: "If you ever become an expert bowler—well, you can tell people you've *lived*; because it's just about the greatest thing in the world."

July 21. Vernon and I dined at the Huxleys'. Maria served cold supper to a crowd of boys and girls—Matthew's friends. Aldous and I talked in a corner about Lengyel's[1] dramatization of *Lady Chatterley's Lover*. He wants us to help him with it. The boys gaily bullied Vernon for liking Picasso. For some mysterious reason, the party was a success: the psychic currents were flowing harmoniously.

July 22. Thoeren wants to do a film about China: the migration of a university into the interior, to escape the Japs. Went up to his house to discuss it with him. Beautiful Mrs. Thoeren lurked in the background, embarrassed because she is so pregnant. She has an affected baby voice. Thoeren in shorts, hairy and fat. The patio of their house is lovely, with mimosa and great fruity cactus. But the brown hills all around, unwatered, awaiting the realtors, are ugly and dull. Below is the vast sprawling city—so dreary by day, so exciting and sparkling by night. Thoeren and I walked a little way along the ridge. Under a bush lay a pair of blue silk panties, stained and looking very forlorn. "A complete short story," said Robert. On the way back, we found a colony of red ants. One of them stung me, very painfully, raising a lump on my thigh.

I mentioned the red ant to Miss Whelan, the ladylike nurse at Dr. Kolisch's, adding that I should have whipped off my trousers immediately, if Mrs. Thoeren hadn't been present, and drawing the moral that the conventions are stronger than our fear of being poisoned. "As far as I'm concerned," said Miss Whelan primly, "I never notice if someone has his pants on or not."

[1] Hungarian playwright Menyhért Melchior Lengyel (1880–1974), in the U.S. for many years from 1937, wrote several screenplays (including *Ninotchka* for Garbo).

Hugh Chisholm took me to dinner at the Dietz house. Constance Bennett was there. She is the old-fashioned sort of film star—languid, overdressed, foulmouthed, "a good sort" — if you keep on the right side of her. The thin, anxious hands so much older than the pouting, blue-eyed baby face. "Well, I'll be Goddamned," she kept repeating.

But she was very amusing, telling stories about Mrs. Patrick Campbell, who came out to Hollywood at the very end of her career, when she was old and forgotten, and fought everybody who tried to help her: " 'The Fighting *Téméraire*' firing on her rescuers."[1] At the end of a dull party, she wrote in the visitors' book: "Quoth the raven—" On hearing that a friend had been buried in a casket which cost five thousand dollars, she said: "From what I know of B—, he'd much rather have been given the five thousand and been buried in a brown paper bag."

July 23. Lunch with Gerald. He told me how eager he is for death. His greatest temptation is suicide. He gets so weary of the Ego, perpetually teasing him with questions when he is meditating, like Baby Snooks:[2] "Look at that fly on the ceiling. Shall we kill it? There's Chris [Wood]—playing that tune again. Chris has a new car. He hasn't asked us to ride in it yet. Why hasn't he asked us to ride in it?" and so on. When Gerald is doing these imitations, his face is quite indescribable. He seems actually to become a tiresome, inquisitive little subhuman being, poking out his nose, screwing up one eye, twisting sideways in his chair. We talked about Chris, Daily and the Swami. Gerald says that Daily appeals to Chris's childhood fantasies of being a criminal. He doesn't think that Chris will remain impressed by Daily for long, however, because Chris demands a faultless hero. As soon as he meets anybody he respects, he begins looking for the weak spot. I am glad to say that this isn't one of my own difficulties. In fact, the process works the other way around: it is only when I have laid my finger on the weak spot that I can really admire anybody. Gerald is, as far as I'm concerned, simply a means to knowledge; and I love him because he's imperfect, because he's still struggling with quite glaring faults. I've even felt much more at ease with the Swami since I noticed his flashy shoes.

Dined with the Huxleys at Anita Loos's house on the beach—to discuss *Lady Chatterley*. We didn't get very far; but it's clear that

---

[1] Alluding to Turner's painting of the ship which had supported Nelson at Trafalgar, "The Fighting *Téméraire* tugged to her last berth to be broken up, 1838."

[2] Child scamp played by Fanny Brice in the Ziegfeld Follies and in the radio skit of the 1930s and 1940s.

Clifford and Mellors must somehow be given symbolic stature, they must clearly represent different points of view—as they do in the Lawrence novel—otherwise it's just a dirty little intrigue.

Anita had knitted a "peter heater" to send to Adele Astaire[1] in England, to cheer her up. It is a kind of woollen glove for the sex organs, suitably tipped with red. With it, go instructions: "The Peter Heater, knitted by an old maid—from memory. Before having a party, remove the heater, or you might become the father of a rag doll. Do not starch the heater—as you will only be fooling yourself."

Ray Goetz[2] was there. He is immensely fat, and very sympathetic, because he loves Anita so dearly. He had bought her and Maria little pots of syrup, in which were fish and water plants cut out of orange peel and cinnamon. On leaving, he asked wistfully: "Are you tired, dear?" Anita said she was. He kissed her on the cheek, and she submitted like a little girl being kissed by her uncle. She wore a startling red dress, with a white draped shawl and a clasp on the shoulder inscribed, "Liberté, Egalité, Fraternité."

July 24. Down to RKO to see Stevenson, that smiling young renaissance cardinal, and Lipscomb,[3] the actor-cricketer. We discussed the final details of the horror story for the British Relief picture.

In the afternoon, I lay on the beach among the crowd. The old lady telling her sister what the rabbi said about her talented grandson; the youths bribing their kid brother with a candy bar to ask an attractive girl the time; the boys turning somersaults with an inner tube as a springboard, watched admiringly by an elderly man and his wife; the handball players, jostling and cursing; the lifeguard's Newfoundland dog; the Japanese brothers wrestling, with vague, oriental smiles; Nellie, who keeps the hot-dog stand and was born in Sheffield; the kids with their tough talk: "Aw—what the heck. Park the junk here." No one is excluded. We are all welcome to the sunshine, and the dirty ocean with its dazzling surf, full of seaweed and last night's discarded rubbers.

Dinner with van Druten. Johnny says he feels that he will soon come to the end of his writing. He would like to do something about the spiritual life, but is held back by financial responsibilities, to Carter

---

[1] Fred Astaire's sister and his dancing partner until her 1932 marriage to an English aristocrat.

[2] Lyricist and Broadway impresario, producer of Cole Porter's early musicals; he proposed to Loos in 1934.

[3] W. P. Lipscomb (1887–1958), British screenwriter in Hollywood from 1935 through the war, who also worked on *Forever and a Day*.

and Auriol Lee. He will find it very difficult, I think. His Christian Science has reduced him to a state of the most dangerous, woolly optimism. Carter's astrology hasn't helped, either. And the theatrical world keeps wooing him back with deadly, flattering smiles. It is easier for a hardened criminal than for a thoroughly nice, harmless, well-meaning man to enter the kingdom of God. Like me, Johnny is soft.

July 25. Worked all day writing an outline of our murder story for Stevenson.

To the Swami's class in the evening, by myself. One very smartly dressed lady, who looked as if she'd arrived to attend a charity garden party, came in and began whispering to her neighbor with an English accent. Suddenly becoming aware of disapproving glances, she exclaimed: "Oh dear—is this a moment of meditation?"

The Swami began by defining immortality. It does not mean mere continued existence. That we shall have anyway, pleasantly or unpleasantly, according to our life on earth. Immortality means getting beyond time and causation. The Ego is an effect of the Self working on the *chitta* (the mind-stuff). When the Ego is dissolved, the Self is freed from the chitta. If this happens during mortal life, then the body returns to its elements at death and the Self is free. But, if freedom is not attained, the Self has to carry its bundle of desires and fears into other lives and other worlds. The free Self is finally absorbed into the Universal Self, beyond time. Certain great souls decide not to become absorbed. They return to the earth as teachers. Ramakrishna once asked Vivekananda what he wanted most. Vivekananda replied that he wanted to attain the higher samadhi and become one with God. Ramakrishna exclaimed: "Shame on you! I thought you were greater than that!" And he told Vivekananda that he would "lock the door and keep the key." By this he meant that Vivekananda should return to the world and teach. In order to teach, you must have a measure of ignorance. Otherwise—seeing God in every human being and in yourself—you would be unable either to teach or to learn.

Someone mentioned the Holy Ghost. The Swami was asked to explain It, and said that he couldn't, he wasn't a Christian. So everybody present had a try, and the difference in our definitions was a sufficient comment on the muddle of Christian theology. To every suggestion, the Swami replied: "No—that is too far-fetch-ed." At last he sent one of the girls out for *Webster's Dictionary*. Some of the class were quite scandalized. "You won't find it there," they told him. But the Swami was quite confident. "*Webster's Dictionary* can tell you everything." He was wrong, however. Webster said only: "Comforter, Paraclete." The Swami promised to "ask Mr. Hard." He seems to have great confidence in Gerald.

July 28. This morning, Gerald told me a story, about a Quaker. He was visited by a prominent English government official who was rapidly becoming a confirmed drunkard and wanted to be cured. The Quaker said: "I won't ask you to stop drinking, but you must promise to come and tell me each time you do it." For a while, the drunkard drank and confessed, getting more and more discouraged. At last, he came to the Quaker and asked to be released from his promise. The Quaker refused. The drunkard went away in a desperate state and didn't show up again for a year. When the Quaker saw him next, he was completely cured. The promise had done it.

Gerald had come down with me to the Hunters' church, to hear Dr. Fritz Kunkel[1] preach. A plump little man, with a German accent and only one arm. His lavish gestures and mixed metaphors reminded me of Berthold. He compared the young, inexperienced, "classic" type of human being to a giant sequoia. When life begins to educate the human being by suffering, the sequoia is inverted through the lens of experience and becomes "gothic." In order to have the true perspective, you must see both images—gothic and classic. I suppose this meant something very profound—Kunkel is obviously intelligent and sincere—but listening to him made me feel that I mustn't listen to too many lectures. If I sit at the feet of a lot of different masters, I shall be aware only of their mannerisms, and waste my time in an Athenian craze for novelty. I had better stick to yoga and the Swami, and not attempt too big a synthesis.

Drove Gerald to lunch with the Rodakiewiczs. Chris was there and Vernon came in later. I always feel happy in their house. Derek was jumping about screaming for recognition—he had cut his lip boxing with Ben and now wouldn't be able to eat salad dressing, which he hates. Welmoet, as usual, was sisterly and possessive with Vernon, bossing him around. The boys say that she has fallen for a waiter at the Colonial Drive-In on the Sunset Strip. When Vernon and I played badminton, the family backed me, because Vernon is regarded as one of themselves.

Am reading *Lawrence and Brett.*[2] What a horrifying book! The sudden screaming quarrels, the hate, the sulks. No wonder they all suffered from poisoning and feverish colds. Lawrence becoming

[1] Los Angeles psychiatrist.
[2] By Dorothy Brett.

religiously ecstatic over a hummingbird one minute, chopping off the head of a hen (because it wouldn't stop brooding) the next.

July 29. Terrific Nazi air raids on Dover.

Went to see the Swami. He told me to meditate on the real Self. "Imagine that there is a cavity within you. In the middle of this cavity there is a throne, in the form of a red lotus. In the middle of the lotus, a golden light is burning. Approach this light and say, 'Oh Self, reveal Yourself to me.'"

My imagination revolts from this: it sounds like a stage scene at the Radio City Music Hall. But I shall try to do it. I have put myself into the Swami's hands and I must follow his instructions, just as I follow Dr. Kolisch's. We always want to choose our own medicine. A rose, for example, wouldn't seem nearly so silly to me. But perhaps the lotus is better, just because I *don't* like it. A very subtle aversion is mixed up with this question. Maybe, even, a certain racial snobbery, against anything Indian. For me, one of the most significant things in the Old Testament is the story of Elisha and Naaman. "Are not Abana and Pharpar, rivers of Damascus, better than all the waters of Israel? May I not wash in *them* and be clean?"[1]

July 31. Lunch at the Huxleys'. Aldous told me he is stuck in his novel. Advised him to start a journal. He said he thought he would. He joked about the Mann family—he'd been dining there. The German cult of the "Poet-Prince," coupled with a terrific appetite for food.

He also talked about meditation, said he couldn't see the use of Ramakrishna's painstaking efforts to conjure up the various gods and divine incarnations. Krishnamurti (whose teaching is much more to Aldous's taste) never meditates on objects. He even believes that it may lead to insanity. Aldous seems to think Ramakrishna himself was a borderline case. He is particularly shocked by the story of how Ramakrishna dressed up as a woman, because he thought of his attitude to God as that of a loving wife. This conversation disturbed me very much. Suppose Gerald *is* barking up the wrong tree? But I'm also well aware that these doubts are not quite candid; they are being promoted by the Ego as part of its sabotage effort.

With Vernon to dinner at the Chisholms'. Bridget and Vernon began talking New York scandal, and listing "the nastiest people in the world." This kind of chatter degrades everybody who touches it. I felt deeply ashamed for both of them, and ashamed of myself, because I've so often talked in exactly the same way. How hard and

[1] 2 Kings 5.12.

vulgar their voices sounded; and yet Bridget is really sweet tempered and gentle. Left as soon as possible.

August 1. Woke in a muddled state, with cramps in the back. A feeling of complete bewilderment, as though I had lost the thread of life. I could no longer remember even the intellectual reasons why one should believe God exists, or try to be good. Meditation seemed longer than ever before.

Drove out to the airport to meet Wystan, who is paying us a flying visit. His plane was delayed and didn't arrive till the early evening. Wystan began questioning me at once about Kolisch. The idea of a diet shocks him profoundly. He would rather see me take to dope than become a vegetarian.

Returned home to find Metro rang up. I'm to go back to work tomorrow. I feel very disgusted.

August 2. To Metro, to report. I'm to start right away on a picture for Victor Saville. A remake of a Swedish film called *A Woman's Face.* Ingrid Bergman played it originally. This is for Joan Crawford. They want it in three weeks. Lesser Samuels, a fat, unhappy-looking man, is writing the screenplay already, and has nearly finished. I'm just to polish the dialogue.

Lunch with Salka. She told me that Garbo is terrified of cancer. Her sister died of it.

A row in the afternoon between Saville and Samuels: two fat men shouting at each other without the least intention of physical violence. Later, Saville was apologetic. He said: "I'm a man of quick decisions."

Wystan, Vernon and I dined at the Huxleys'. Far too many people, as usual. Maria added our handprints to her remarkable collection. The crazy hand of Robert Nichols[1]—like the bed of a dried-up salt lake, cracked in every direction.

August 3. At the Broox Randall office, when I went to pay the car insurance, they told me that more people have taken out earthquake policies during the past week than normally during an entire year. Someone has predicted a big earthquake for tomorrow, either here or in Japan.

Drove Wystan up to Palos Verdes for tea. "No one can be a pacifist," he said, "who isn't trying to live Gerald's life. The truth is, I *want* to kill people." If the U.S. gets into war, he'll let himself be

---

[1] English poet.

drafted. As for going to England, he'll leave that to the authorities. If he's called, he'll go. But, like me, he's taken out his citizenship papers.

Wystan is suspicious of Gerald's ideas, because Gerald thinks Time is evil. Wystan likes Time, and the material world—at any rate, his corner of it. "I'm not going to go about pretending I'm unhappy here. I'm very happy indeed." But I noticed that he said this rather aggressively, as if to reassure himself. I am quite sure that he is very homesick for England.

He has a whole new lingo of Christian theology, very abstruse. He said how much he disliked Sanskrit words. I told him I feel just the opposite. Wystan says that some basis of belief is particularly necessary in America, where no one has any roots.

August 7. Wystan left today. It has been an unsatisfactory visit: we've had hardly any time for a proper talk. In any case, we are both too much disturbed to be able to talk properly. We have agreed to do nothing about going to England without consulting each other first.

Toiled all day long at the script. Then to Kolisch's, and dinner at Perino's—simply because it is near his office, we often eat there: a stupidly expensive meal, which might as well be at a drugstore as far as I'm concerned. Kolisch has made it impossible for me to enjoy my food. Vernon is as miserable as I am, but he imagines all will be well if we own a house, bees, a violin, a phonograph, a python, two dogs and two bathrooms.

August 8. Saw [Hans] Rameau at the studio today. He is having an affair with Marlene Dietrich. Nothing could be more autohypnotic. He bulges with pride. The slogan is "Garbo next."

August 9. To see the Swami. Sat in the temple while he and several of the "holy women" who live there finished their evening rites. The bottoms of the women were enormous, as they bowed down to adore. Could concentrate on nothing else.

The Swami called me into his study afterwards. He gave me new and much more elaborate instructions:

First, I am to think of people all over the world—all kinds of people, at all kinds of occupations. In each one of them, and in all matter, is this Reality, this Atman, which is also inside myself. And what is "myself"? Am I my body? Am I my mind? Am I my thoughts? What can I find inside myself which is eternal? Let me examine my thoughts and see how they reflect this Reality—for I can only know it by its reflection. And now let me think of this Reality as seated in the top of my head, throned in a white lotus. I am infinite existence, infinite knowledge, infinite happiness. Finally, I approach the red lotus, in the heart. I look into this chamber, in which the light is burning. I say: "Reveal yourself to me."

Dinner with Gerald. He is rather worried about Wystan's new activities. "I've no use for theology," he said, "if it can't produce saints."

August 10. Took Bud Bayley out to dinner at Chasen's. It was supposed to be a tremendous treat for him. Mrs. Bayley has been building it up for days: she supervised his dressing this evening as if he were going to meet the president. I'm afraid he was badly disappointed. We ate snails. Bud told me his great ambition—to start a phonograph shop, where people can gather and form a little nucleus of culture. He was very enthusiastic and touching, and kept apologizing for using the wrong words. I wanted so much to give him something—some little gift out of my experience; but there was nothing I could find to say. And Bud waited devoutly all evening for the Word that wasn't spoken. I felt such a horrible old fake.

August 11. To Peggy's, for tea and dinner. They are going away soon. We shall miss them terribly. Gerald was there when we arrived, walking about the garden, looking at the flowers. "It's so odd about beauty," he said. "One can't quite see where it fits in." Meanwhile, Derek dashed up, fighting Vernon and Ben and screaming, "I challenge the winner!" He chatters to himself all the time, like a radio commentator: "He's down! No—he's up! Leading with his right. He's down again! Local boy makes bad! Ladies and gentlemen, the winner is—!" When he goes off to bed, he is still talking. All night long, he mutters in his sleep. The other night, Ben went into his room and tried to start a conversation with him, in the nonsense language he babbles. "Woozle woggle?" Ben suggested, by way of an opening. But Derek, still sound asleep, answered firmly: "No. Fuvvel."

August 12. I have noticed several times lately that if I go to bed right after meditating I get very unpleasant, confused, noisy dreams—like static on the radio. It is best to wait at least half an hour.

Meditation night and morning. It is much easier now, since Swami's new instructions, because I can begin with the external world and work inward. I start by thinking of the British and Nazi airmen fighting over the Channel. Then Hitler, Churchill. Then Teddy, our dog in Portugal. T. Y. Liu. Admiral Byrd. The ocean with all its fish, etc.

Miss Reeves, my new secretary at Metro, startled me by quoting

Traherne. We spent the whole afternoon talking seventeenth-century poetry.

August 13. Huge German air attacks on England. Invasion is expected hourly. I feel terribly depressed—as everybody does these days, who cares at all—but not frantic. It is amazing how much my "sits" help, however badly and unwillingly I do them. They clear the mind of that surplus of misery which is entirely subjective and unnecessary, and helps no one. Which, in fact, merely poisons the lives of everybody around you, and makes their own troubles harder to bear. Too much unhappiness over external tragedies is as bad as too little. Hardening and softening of the heart are both vicious. I begin to understand what T. S. Eliot means in "Ash Wednesday": "Teach us to care and not to care."

Lunch with Tony Bower, Jean Connolly (Cyril's wife) and Denham Fouts. Jean and Denny have just arrived here from the East. Jean is much thinner and really beautiful, with her big gentle cow-eyes. She has a way of suddenly looking up at you, smiling in a wistful, shame-faced way, and exclaiming hoarsely, "Hi-de-ho!" The effect is positively spectral: the voice of the ghost of a prohibition party. Both she and Denny had hangovers, which they nursed with the greatest satisfaction; while steadily tanking up for the next blind.

We ate at the Beverly Brown Derby, with its atmosphere of overstuffed dullness and melancholy midday rum. They were much amused at my collection of Kolisch pills, and very gay, because I was paying for lunch and smelt agreeably of Metro and dollars. The terrible, almost insoluble problem of choosing what to eat. The frowns over the menu. The waiter's smiling patience.

(If I try to remember how Denny struck me when he first came to California, I think of the lean, hungry, tanned face; the eyes which seemed to be set on different levels, slightly overlapping, as in a late Picasso painting; the bitter little rosebud mouth; the strangely erect walk, almost paralytic with tension. He had rather sinister clothes—wash-leather jerkins, bell-bottomed sailor's trousers, boxer's sweaters. They were sinister because they were intended for laughing, harmless boys, not as a disguise for this tormented addict, this wolflike inverted monk, this martyr to pleasure. His goodlooking profile was bitterly sharp, like a knife edge; his Floridian drawl seemed a sinister affectation. Goodness, he was sour! For a while, his sourness was stimulating: then you began to feel as if you were suffering from quinine poisoning.)

August 14. Lunch with Salka. She is very unhappy: weary of her job at Metro, her friendship with Gottfried, Berthold's endless jitters. She is enormously strong, but the strength is leaking out of her and being lost in the ground. She is warm and generous, primitive and superstitious, emotional and intuitive. Her men have all been intellectuals. They have tried to make her into something she isn't and never could be.

She says she wishes she could go into a convent. She wants to know about yoga. Promised to introduce her to the Swami.

August 18. Today, I finished an almost unbroken week of "sits." My chief effort is to stand outside the Ego, to try to catch a glimpse of the world with a non-attached eye. But the Ego, with its gross body and great swollen, sullen pumpkin head, is like a man who *will* stand right in front of you at a horse race: you can only catch glimpses of the race by peeping under his arms or between his legs. It is terribly difficult, but the mere discipline of trying brings its own rewards—cheerfulness, long periods of calm, freedom from self-pity. Vernon is the invaluable barometer of my failure or success. Yesterday afternoon, when we were laughing together, he suddenly said: "If only it could always be like this!"

Guard against feelings of self-congratulation, or holiness. Self-congratulation is of the Ego. The real self can't boast of its advance toward wisdom: it *is* wisdom. Real progress can never be attended by self-congratulation, because it is against the Ego's deepest interests. As Gerald says: "Love God without fear and without hope."

We are to have a house: 8826 Harratt Street, just below the Sunset Strip, behind the "English Village." Vernon found it, and has arranged everything. It will be his toy. We move in next week.

Furious scenes at the studio between Saville and Samuels. Saville turning purple and yelling: "You sonofabitch! I give the orders here!" Samuels wounded in his "dignity as a writer."

Willkie has plumped for conscription in his acceptance speech; so conscription we shall have. Chris Wood has gone to San Francisco, with Tony, Denny and Jean. Gerald described, last night, how sometimes in meditation he sheds tears of relief when he realizes that, "This thing *is* true, after all."

August 24. We've moved into the house, which is actually a little wooden shack, daintily camouflaged with pots of ivy, white fur rugs, painted furniture and frilly curtains, like ballerinas' petticoats. Vernon's bedroom (which used to belong to a Mrs. Blumenthal, wife of a movie writer) is a little bower of muslin and silk. We have a gardener and a colored maid. Once again, I feel the dreadful guilt of ownership. But Vernon is delighted. He runs around from morning till night, unpacking, paying bills. The noise of the neighbors' children makes meditation very difficult. Oh, the fuss and worry of it all! If I could join Gerald's future monastery, I think I'd regret the world less than at any other time in my life. But I have my problems right here, and it's no good running away from them.

Always, behind everything, the dull ache of this war. The deadly pessimism of the refugee writers: "America will be in it before the elections. Then they'll reintroduce slavery for Jews and Negroes." The endless beastliness of the air raids; and the amazing cheerfulness of a man like Samuels, who believes in "hedonism" and pinches typists' fannies. How can there be any happiness, nowadays, except in God? But, of course, all real happiness *is* in God.

(It must have been around this time that Vernon and I flew to San Francisco for the weekend. We saw the World's Fair, which had a very fine exhibition of paintings, and most of the other sights. But what I chiefly remember was a visit to the aquarium, because of an experience I had there. It is very hard to describe. I was looking at a small tank of damselfish—tiny, vivid specks of brilliant blue. All at once, I saw them, as it were, within a universe of their own: embraced, sustained by an intensely living "presence." And I said to myself: "He cares for *them*, too." This wasn't just a charming, romantic notion—otherwise it wouldn't remain with me as I write this, six years later. It was a realization of a fact. At the moment, I was so much moved that I almost burst into tears.

The awful, stony isolation of Alcatraz, out there in the bay, viewed by the wealthy terraces of the city, the cocktail lounge of the Mark Hopkins.[1] Society's ultimate, public confession of failure. We talk idly about cooperation, brotherhood. For these men, we can do nothing. They are excluded for ever.)

September 7. London had its biggest bombardment since the war began.

Rush work on *A Woman's Face*. Samuels's hypochondria. This morning, a mysterious rash spread suddenly over his cheek and forehead. He was pleased when I urged him to go to the doctor at once. We continued our script conference in the car—Samuels preoccupied and anxious about his symptoms. By the time we reached the doctor's, the rash had practically disappeared.

He calls Harriet, his secretary, "la Dog." Painfully raising his corpulent body from the chair, he tells me sadly: "I carry a great deal

---

[1] A grand San Francisco hotel.

of insurance." Saville, acting the he-man, laughs at Samuels's ailments, and tells Samuels he's too much tied to his family—he should call them once in a while and say he's not coming home to dinner; he should take the plane to Mexico City or New York and have himself a bloody good time.

Saville's malapropisms: "You see, in this scene, the crooks are trying to circumnavigate Anna."

On Saville's desk, a list of actors and actresses who have had filmtests, with comments by the assistant director. Of one girl: "All she had to recommend was a couple of Adohrs[1]—nothing else."

Driving home through the evening traffic along Sunset Boulevard, I was attacked by one of those spasms of cramp which often follow a Kolisch injection. It was so violent, and so unexpected, that I exclaimed "Oh God!" aloud. And now something extraordinary happened. The word, which I have misused ten million times, produced a kind of echo in my consciousness. Like the vibration after a bell has been struck. It seemed to vibrate down, down into the depths of me. It was so strange, so awe-inspiring, that I longed for the cramp to return. I thought: "I have called upon God." After a moment, I had another spasm, but this time there was no echo. The word was just another word.

This was quite different from the experience I had in San Francisco. It was briefer, but much more intimate. I seemed to open a crack of consciousness within myself. Whereas, looking at the damselfish, I was simply an observer. I saw the unique, absolute importance of each single fish as an entity and as a part of total Consciousness; but this realization, vivid as it was, only seemed to apply to myself at second hand. "Not one sparrow falls to the ground without my Father," was my feeling. Only I should have said, "their Father," and added, "he's mine, too," as an afterthought.

The Swami now says I must sit for an hour every morning, half an hour every night. And in contemplating the white light at the top of the head, I must meditate also on the sound, "Om." It's hard to do this, but a little easier after my experience today. Because I got an inkling of what is meant by "the power of the Word."

Looking in through the glass door of the sitting room at Ivar Avenue, I saw the Swami, sitting alone. He must have been meditating: his face was utterly transformed. It was very still, and almost frighteningly attentive—like a lion watching its prey before it jumps. Then he became aware of my presence and rose to greet me, his usual, gay, polite, Bengali self.

[1] Breasts; Adohr was a local dairy (named for the owner's daughter, Rhoda, with the letters of her name reversed).

October 26. Well, I've finished two months of more or less continuous work on the meditations; missing pretty often, but doing *something* practically every day. This week, because I haven't been needed at Metro, I've been able to go to the temple most afternoons. Concentration there is a lot easier. The atmosphere is extraordinarily calming, and yet alive, not sleepy. Elizabeth Hunter says it's like being "in a wood." This is a very good description. Just as, in a wood, you feel the trees alive all around you, so in the shrine the air seems curiously alert. Sometimes it is as if the whole shrine room becomes your brain and is filled with thought. Of course, the smell of the sandalwood also helps. It induces a special mood, by association—just as the smell of ether induces the pathic mood of the hospital patient.

The Swami has been away this last fortnight and isn't expected back for another week. Kolisch gallantly takes the Thursday evening class, tying himself into knots and bewildering us with his vagueness and bad English. Gerald speaks on Sundays. He always has a big audience. Much bigger than the Swami himself.

Despite all my failures, I'm surprised to find what a long way I've come already. There is no longer any question, now, that "this thing" works, as far as I'm concerned. Whatever happens, I don't think I shall ever quite lose this knowledge.

I am trying now to concentrate on the personality of Ramakrishna. He is "my friend." I try to feel him always beside me. This is not just a sentimental fancy, if you do it properly. What you have to realize is that a part of yourself *is* Ramakrishna (or Christ, or Buddha, for that matter). Just as a part of yourself is Himmler. The cult of a great teacher and saint only *seems* to be dualistic. The dualistic approach is just a convenient way to realization of oneness, identity. That's why it doesn't matter in the least if the real historical Christ never existed. He'll exist in you, if you want him to.

No use fussing about my life with Vernon or my job, and complaining that I can never do anything as long as I am "in the world." Keep your mind on God, and the world will fall away of its own accord. Poor old Ego, stop moaning over your wrongs. Lie down and go to sleep. You're not as indispensable as you imagine.

Lunch with Denny, who is anxious to start a new life as soon as the Swami gets back. He means to take a big plunge—get a shack in the hills, a menial job (as somebody's servant) and immediately renounce everything: sex, drink and the Gang. He's very nervous and much worried about his motives—is he wishing to do this for the right reasons? But surely, at the start, the reasons don't matter? If you are doing this for the wrong reasons, I told him, you'll very soon find out.

Meanwhile, Denny still goes to parties and gets drunk and talks nothing but religion, to the great amusement of Tony Bower and Jean Connolly, who call him "the drunken yogi."

Today, I took him to the temple, where we sat for some time in the shrine (or "the box," as Gerald calls it). I couldn't concentrate—I was thinking all the time of Denny—trying to "introduce" him to Ramakrishna, and hoping he wouldn't be put off by the photographs on the shrine, and the flowers, and the ivory and brass figures of Krishna, Buddha and Shiva. It *does* look rather like the mantelpiece in an old-fashioned boudoir. Actually, Denny liked it all very much, but was dismayed because he had thought what a wonderful place it would be to have sex in.

(Some days after this, the Swami returned, and Denny went to see him. I wasn't present at the interview, so I don't altogether know why it was such a disastrous failure. No doubt Denny's manner was aggressive and "wrong"—it usually was, with strangers. In any case, Swami rather discouraged him from attempting any drastic change in his life, and told him that what he needed was not meditation but hard work. He'd better go out and get himself a job.

Denny was terribly disappointed and hurt. As soon as we got back to his room—he was staying at the Highland Hotel—he threw himself down on the bed and burst into tears, sobbing that he was rotten, everybody despised him, and he'd better kill himself with heroin as soon as possible.

I protested, of course—as anybody would. In fact, I said far more than I meant. I told him that *I* didn't despise him, that I admired him and liked him and wanted to be his friend.

This episode had very far-reaching consequences, as will appear later in this story. It not only involved me with Denny—so that, in a little while, I really did become very fond of him—but it also threw Denny into the arms of Gerald. I took Denny up to see him, and told him the whole affair; and Gerald, all too humanly flattered and pleased at being able to demonstrate his superior charity, immediately accepted Denny as his protégé and disciple. What followed was all most unfortunate and quite inevitable—the break between the Swami and Gerald, the break between Denny and Gerald, and the lasting antagonism which made Denny oppose the Swami's influence over me on every possible occasion.

Looking back over it all, I'm inclined to think that the Swami showed very sound psychological judgment; although he might have been more tactful. Like most good spiritual directors, he is opposed to shock tactics in the religious life. He mistrusts hysterical "conversions" in nearly every instance, and has repeatedly told me that, if you try to do too much in too great a hurry, you are sure to have a reaction.)

November 7. Well, the elections are over, Roosevelt is in, and we settle down to the campaign for "national unity." I am still on a layoff from Metro, possibly for five weeks. But Edna Schley may get me a job at RKO.

Tomorrow morning, I'm going down to the temple, to be initiated by the Swami. I know he is only doing this to encourage me (because, he told Gerald, I am "arnest") but I feel terribly inadequate. Lately, I've been getting up too late and missing my morning hour.

The Swami has given me a breathing exercise: in through the left nostril, out through the right, in through the right, out through the left, and so on. As you inhale, you are to think that you are drawing in the Spirit through the nostril and down the left side of the spine; as you exhale, you are expelling all impurities up the right side of the spine and out through the nostril—and then vice versa. This is very useful for calming the mind before meditation. I am supposed to do it *after* sending thoughts of goodwill around the world. "We must think of others, fusht," the Swami explains.

Vernon has been sick, with a bad throat. He has moods of depression, little ailments, fits of rudeness. Underneath them all, he's sweet natured, generous, affectionate, and utterly unsure of himself. He is in the mess of being nineteen, and I can't help him out of it. Sooner or later, all his problems will be brutally solved from the outside: he'll be shoved into the army or some social service camp and have to make the best of it. If this happens, I believe he will actually be much happier: he has plenty of guts. But it's tragic—that we always have to find our solutions the hard way.

How much unhappiness there is in the world! No need to search for it across the ocean, in bombed London, or China, or Greece. The other evening, outside my window, a little boy cried to his mother: "You don't want *anyone* to play with me!" Even the most trivial unkindness is heartbreaking, if one weren't so deaf and blind. Every sigh, every tear, every cross word is really the last straw which breaks humanity's back. If we could be conscious, every minute, of the dreadful predicament of life, we should handle each other with the greatest gentleness.

Very occasionally, I'm aware of this; and it's almost more than I can bear. The other night (it sounds absurd when I write it) I ran the car over a tin can on our parking lot, and felt almost as bad as if I'd killed a cat. "Oh God," I said to myself, "must we *always* keep smashing things?"

Lunch with Denny. He's been looking for a shack to live in. He wants to get somewhere alone by himself and start meditating: his interview with the Swami hasn't dismayed him. He has extraordinary reserves of willpower, backed up against a huge black rock of despair, like a creature at bay. His despair isn't noisy. It's quiet and well mannered: the dynamic despair which makes dangerous criminals and, very occasionally, saints. Gerald says that he sees Denny as a figure "with something standing behind it"—an embodiment, perhaps, of certain acts, with a being of its own. Gerald says that Chris—during the violent neurotic quarrels of his earlier life—gave you this same impression. The terrible scene was actually being made by someone outside himself—and Chris's own face, at the moment of crisis, was curiously peaceful, almost disinterested.

November 8. Picked up Gerald in the car and was down at the temple by seven-thirty. When I went into the shrine, the Swami was already seated. I took my place on his left, holding a little tray with the flowers I had been given, by one of the women, to offer: two red roses, a white rose, and a big white daisy. First the Swami told me to meditate as usual. Then I had to offer the flowers—the red roses to the photographs of Ramakrishna and his wife, "Holy Mother," the daisy to the icon of Christ, the white rose to Swami himself, as my guru, my teacher. Next, he told me to meditate on Ramakrishna in the central cavity of the heart. Then he taught me my Sanskrit mantram (which I must never repeat to anybody) and gave me a rosary, showing me how to use it, repeating the mantram and meditating on Ramakrishna's body—"a thousand times more brilliant than the sun, but mellow"—the feet, the navel, the heart, the head. I worked on this for a time. Then I went into the house and had coffee and toast. About nine o'clock, we settled down to the festival of Holy Mother—this is her birthday. The Swami offered flowers, incense, water for washing. He made spots of red on the foreheads of Ramakrishna and Mother with sandalwood paste. Food was brought in, a complete meal: soup, curry and chocolate cake with whipped cream. The Swami's nephew Asit [Ghosh] acted as prompter, reading the ritual directions in Sanskrit. At the end of the ceremony, we each offered a flower. After this, we went into the Swami's study, where there is a grate, for the fire ceremony. All our actions, good and bad, were symbolically offered up and purified in the fire. The Swami made a sign on our foreheads with the ash, to symbolize the opening of the third eye, the eye of the spirit.

Then lunch, very gay, with all the "holy women." The food

offered in the temple is mixed in with what we eat, so that lunch is really a kind of communion service. They do this every day.

The Swami admitted that he oversmokes. "You must listen to me," he giggled, "not follow me." He told us that, during his first ten years here, he made no converts at all. Now he has about twenty-four.

Drove Gerald home. We agreed that this sort of thing could never be transplanted to the West. Ritual is valuable, certainly—but perhaps only for the person who actually celebrates it. The holy women seemed more concerned today with the mere domestic bustle of preparing and serving food. At least, that was the impression I got as an outsider.

Nevertheless, all this Hindu domesticity doesn't repel me. Precisely because it *is* so domestic. Ramakrishna really does seem to be established in that household. They fuss over him like a guest of honor. There is no dividing line between the activities of the temple and their daily lives. And, after all, if you admire the man at all, why not make him feel at home? Why not reproduce, as far as possible, the ceremonies he used to practice? It's really a matter of common politeness—like eating Chinese food when the Chinese ambassador comes to dinner.

November 12. Headache this evening, and rheumatism in my hip. So I did my meditation sitting upright in a chair in my room. Perhaps because of the headache, concentration was much easier than usual. My mind soon became calm. Sitting with closed eyes in the darkness, I suddenly "saw" a strip of carpet, illuminated by an orange light. The carpet was covered with a black pattern, quite unlike anything we have in the house. But I could also "see" my bed, standing exactly as it really stands. My field of vision wasn't in any way distorted.

As I watched, I "saw," in the middle of the carpet, a small dirty-white bird, something like a parrot. After a moment, it began to move, with its quick stiff walk, and went under the bed. This wasn't a dream. I was normally conscious, aware of what I "saw" and anxious to miss no detail of it. As I sat there, I felt all around me a curiously intense silence, like the silence of deep snow. The only sinister thing about the bird was its air of utter aloofness and *intention*. I had caught it going about its business—very definite business—as one glimpses a mouse disappearing into its hole.

November 13. I told Swami about the parrot, this evening. He said it was a "symbolic vision," not an hallucination. On the whole, he seemed pleased. He thought it a sign that something is happening to my consciousness. Probably, he said, there will be other visions. I must take no particular notice of them, and not regard them as a matter for self-congratulation. They have no special significance. The psychic world is all around us, full of sub-creatures, earthbound spirits, squalid little embodiments of desire and fear. To be able to see them is just a knack, a minor talent, like clairvoyance. Dogs see spooks, all the time. It is dangerous to let them interest you too much. At best, they are a distraction from the real objectives of the spiritual life. At worst, they may gain power over you and do you harm.

I also asked the Swami about sex. He said that all sex—no matter what the relationship—is a form of attachment, and must ultimately be given up. This will happen naturally as you make progress in the spiritual life. "The more you travel toward the North, the farther you are from the South." But he added that force is no good. A man came to Brahmananda (the Swami's teacher) and asked to become a monk: he had castrated himself to be free from sex. Brahmananda wouldn't receive him. When the Swami was a young monk, he once asked Brahmananda to release him from sexual desire. (Brahmananda had the power to do this.) But Brahmananda smiled and answered: "My son, if I did that you would miss all the fun in life."

To encourage me, the Swami quoted a saying of Ramakrishna's: " 'He who has been bitten by the cobra is sure to die.' The cobra has bitten you, Mr. Isherwood," he giggled, "you won't live long!"

Some notes from the Swami's lectures:

We make the mistake of seeking perfection outside ourselves. We want to achieve completeness by creating something, or by accumulating possessions, or by reorganizing a part of the external work. But completeness is within us.

The aim of life is to be reborn in spirit as we were born in flesh. To be born in spirit is to attain *samadhi*, transcendental consciousness.

It's no good just saying, "I have faith," and leaving it at that. Faith in someone else's revelation is not enough. It will get you nowhere. This is the characteristic mistake of the West. But India has never relied on this secondhand faith. Indians ask, "What is *your* experience? Do *you* see any light?" Experience, empirical knowledge, are what really matter in religion.

The universe, according to Vedanta philosophy:

1. The ultimate Reality. This, for convenience, has two names: *Brahman* (God transcendent, all around you) and the *Atman* (God immanent, within you).

2. *Ishwara*: the Reality united with its power, to create, preserve, and destroy the universe. This does not imply a philosophical dualism, because the Reality and its power are inseparable, like fire and its heat.

Brahman, the Reality, has, by definition, no attributes. *Ishwara* has attributes: it is "the personal God." The Hindus personify its powers as Brahma (the creator), Vishnu (the preserver) and Shiva (the dissolver). Jehova is also a personification of Ishwara.

3. *Prakriti*, or *maya*: the effect of Brahman's power, the basis of all mind and matter. Modern physics recognize the principle of *prakriti* in saying that the universe is composed of different arrangements of identical units. *Prakriti* can be roughly translated as "nature," "illusion."

4. The *gunas* (meaning, literally, "rope that binds"). Prakriti is said to be composed of three *gunas*, three forces.

(a) *Sattva*: the quality of fineness, beauty, purity, calm: the power of self-revelation in any object.

(b) *Rajas*: the quality of action, reaction, repulsion: the power which holds an object together.

(c) *Tamas*: obstruction: the power which veils and obscures an object's identity.

Psychologically, sattva creates the mood of peaceful, clear understanding. Rajas brings restlessness, hate, rage, aggression, and desire to enjoy. Tamas brings laziness, dullness, obstinacy.

All three gunas are present in everything, in different combinations, one or the other predominating. To see the Reality, we must go beyond the gunas, even sattva. But pantheistic nature poets who say they have seen God usually mean only that they have become aware of sattva.

The mistake of the West is the mass-application of all its standards. "If a thing is good for me, it's good for everybody." Indian thought does not agree. It discriminates between different types of people and the different approaches which are helpful for each. You cannot approach a sattvic man as you would approach a rajasic man. This does not imply any contempt for lower types; only a recognition that the guna classifications really do hold good in nature. This was the origin of the Indian caste system.

November 30. About two weeks ago, I had another vision. The same orange light, but redder, this time, like firelight. I thought, "It's happening again." A face began to form. It was my own face. I looked at it, quite consciously, for several seconds before it disappeared.

When I started to tell the Swami about this, he looked dismayed and exclaimed in alarm: "Not that parrot?" (Because, says Gerald, the parrot might eventually have "come through" and been visible to other people. Most embarrassing. And then the Swami would have had to exorcise it. We'd have a three-day sit at the temple, and, goodness, how much Ramakrishna would eat!)

However, when I explained, he was pleased and told me I'd seen my own "subtle body." He asked me if the face wasn't much handsomer than my own physical face. As a matter of fact, it was: very distinguished, rather like a Red Indian, with light blue eyes.

Since then, my sits have been most unsatisfactory. I seem to be stuck in the apparent world, like a fly in glue. Terrible attacks, storms of rajasic fury, sweep over me, until I begin to wonder how long I shall stay even outwardly sane. Back at the studio, since last week. I miss seeing Gerald. Denny is living up there, now, till Chris returns. We are putting a new beginning on to *Rage in Heaven*, which may go into production next week. Vernon now sits regularly. I can't say it's improved our home life. We still squabble and sulk. Mostly it's my fault.

(Sometime in December, Denny left for the East. Gerald had arranged for him to work on a farm in Pennsylvania, beginning after Christmas. The farm was run by a man named Pfeiffer, whose "bio-dynamic" system interested Gerald. He thought he could use it at the monastic community he was then planning.

We talked a great deal about the community at that time. Gerald had provisionally christened it "Focus." He only wanted quite a small place—just ourselves, Denny, and maybe a friend named Sandy Parness from England. There was a good deal of discussion as to whether my cousin Felix Greene would be suitable. Gerald thought not. He was too "unstable," and, to use another of Gerald's favorite condemnatory phrases, "under very great strain." As for Sandy Parness, the problem was to get him without his friend Nik Alderson. "If Sandy wants to bring him over," he told me, "you'll see the hard side of your Gerald." We never did. Nik was killed in Libya, serving with the Friends Ambulance Unit, on February 14, 1942.)

December 9. Rage in Heaven is now supposed to start shooting in four days. Yesterday, we had a conference at Gottfried's house, with Thoeren and [Robert] Sinclair, the director. Sinclair has a great deal of charm. He is very much one of the Lost Generation; boyishly irresponsible, a prey to whisky and sexual despair. His wife has just left him, and he sits alone in a big rented house on the hill above the Sunset Strip, contemplating a bookcase full of beautifully bound editions—Boswell, Thackeray, Gibbon—and thinking about—what? I daren't even try to imagine. The lives of so many of these studio people, when you get to know them, are terrifying in their emptiness. When their big, noisy parties break up, and they are left to themselves, what happens? Don't they simply disappear? Al Mannheimer, the writer, is another, with his red, curiously swollen face, which looks as if he'd just been beaten up. His gnawing worry about the draft. His blinding headaches. They all take refuge in marriage, in a series of marriages; they are bound to their jobs by chains of alimony.

Then there's Bill Lipman, a writer whose specialty is Westerns: a cowboy spirit imprisoned in a pudding of sullen grey hairy fat. He is on a diet: all week, he drinks orange juice and black coffee, eats nothing. It doesn't help. In his house are thousands of dollars' worth of electrical reducing apparatus which he is too lazy to use. His father invented crepes suzette. He knows more about food than anyone in Hollywood. Is in favor of sending over a U.S. expeditionary force.

I am fondest of Chuck Reisner, with his great flat ex-bruiser's face. His son made him the hero of a story, "The Champ," which later was turned into a movie with Wallace Beery and Jackie Cooper. Chuck says that picture writing is pure mathematics. In every story, you must ask yourself, "What's the main pursuit?" At present, he's directing *The Big Store* for the Marx Brothers. Groucho, Chico and Harpo eat at our table in the commissary nearly every day: being intellectuals, they prefer the writers to the other actors. Groucho is very funny, but aggressive and malicious. He's always picking on somebody and getting a laugh against them. His great enthusiasm is Gilbert and Sullivan.

Chuck Reisner worked on most of the early Chaplin pictures. He told me all about Chaplin's disastrous marriage to Lita Grey. According to Chuck, the Grey family set out deliberately to catch Chaplin: they arranged for Charlie and Lita, who was a juvenile whore of great talent, to be left alone together all one rainy day. Charlie, stronger minded than usual, held out until the evening. "He showed her his pictures and his books, and he played for her on his organ, and they played cards and dominoes and checkers, and by six o'clock, there wasn't a thing left to do—so Charlie laid her." Immediately, Lita's mother appeared with her lawyers, and Charlie was in the trap. Lita was so young, they had to marry in Mexico. When Mrs. Grey Senior got down to the border (she was travelling separately from the others) there was a cholera epidemic, and the Mexican authorities insisted on special sanitary precautions. They took Mrs. Grey, an imposing lady dressed in all her finery, and put her into a box in the middle of the street in Tijuana, among the chickens and goats. Then they burnt herbs under her to fumigate her. So poor Charlie was indirectly revenged.

Chuck also specialized in farces featuring chimpanzees and lions. He had one chimpanzee which was particularly intelligent. They were making a picture with the chimp and Sid Chaplin, Charlie's brother. The chimp had to put on a mock fight with Sid. It got rather rough, and Sid received a bad cut on the forehead. Someone yelled, "Keep the chimp away! If he smells blood, he'll go crazy!" But the chimp, instead of attacking Sid, ran across the studio, fetched the first-aid kit, opened it and tried to dress the wound.

Chuck believes firmly in psychology. The whole technique of living, he says, is to relax and smile. A smile in the morning on the face of a director will go right around the studio. It creates confidence. People tell their wives about it at night: "The boss smiled at me today."

He decided to live in Laguna Beach, because he wanted to get right away from Hollywood every evening. By taking short cuts, he found he could drive down there in an hour and ten minutes. He went into training for this drive. People were amazed. It became famous.

Chuck has tried various religions. At present, he is enthusiastic about Unity. Every evening, he prays for the heads of the studio: "God bless Louis B. Mayer. God bless Louis B. Mayer. God bless Louis B. Mayer . . . Louis B. Mayer is God's perfect child —" And so on, down the list.

The other day, he was counting the steps from Hollywood Boulevard to his apartment. He got so excited that he arrived out of breath. In the elevator was a pretty girl. Chuck didn't want her to think him short-winded and middle-aged, so he held his breath, way up to the eighth floor. When he got into his apartment, he collapsed and had to lie down, gasping, on the bed.

December 30. Thoeren had a dream. He saw a copy of *Box Office*, with a list of the year's worst pictures—and against each title a brief sentence of comment. Looking down the column, he read: "*Rage in Heaven*. . . . Must vanish."

In Paris, the film company gave Thoeren a collaborator he didn't want. For six weeks, the man sat in Thoeren's apartment, making no suggestions, not saying a word. At length, Thoeren got exasperated: "Look here," he exclaimed, "can't you help me? I'm stuck. What does the girl do now?" The collaborator thought for a moment. Then he jumped energetically to his feet, and started to stride across the room. "The girl—" he began. "You see, the girl—" He reached the door, opened it, went into the corridor: "It's like this—the girl—" Then the door closed. Thoeren never saw him again.

1941

January 1. I must really try to keep this journal more regularly. It will
be invaluable to me if I do. Because this year is going to be one of the
most decisive periods of the twentieth century—and even the doings
and thoughts of the most remote and obscure people will reflect the
image of its events.

That's a hell of a paragraph to start off with. Why are we all so
pompous on New Year's Day? Come off it—you're not Hitler or
Churchill. Nobody called on you to make a statement. As a matter of
fact, what did you actually do?

Last night, you went up to see Tony Bower and Chris Wood and
Dwight Ripley.[1] They were rather drunk. Dwight and Tony were
preparing for a bar crawl. You talked to Tony's half sister, Jean, about
Al Mannheimer, whom she likes, but who fails to kiss her, although
he often stays till four a.m. Then you went on to the temple, where
the Swami, wrapped in a blanket, read aloud from the sayings of
Ramakrishna, the Vedas and the Bible, until a quarter past midnight.
Then you came home and couldn't sleep, so you reread most of
Wells's *First Men in the Moon.* In the morning you meditated for an
hour, not very successfully, then had breakfast, wrote to your mother
and balanced your accounts. Vernon slept till one. He had been out all
night. You discovered that a big tooth had split in half and would have
to be extracted. In the afternoon, you drove with Vernon up to
Mount Wilson. There were crowds of cars on the roads, and you
squabbled most of the way, and it was cold, and the telescopes weren't
on view. You came back and had early supper at A Bit of Sweden, and
Vernon played the violin, and you read a translation of Rilke's *Malte
Laurids Brigge,* and then you went to bed without doing an evening sit.

Nearly everybody is now convinced that we shall be "in it" very
soon. Being "in it" is envisaged as sending munitions, planes (with or
without fliers) and warships (with or without crews). But the
government still insists that, "Not one American boy shall ever—
etc." Just exactly how the war is to be won is a question they leave
carefully vague. Is it still seriously supposed that the Germans will
revolt? Tom Treanor (whom I trust merely because I like his face, and
because he's not a professional war correspondent) writes from
Belgrade that even non-Nazis are behind the regime. They feel they
must support Hitler, despite the defects in his system and despite his
own political record. Many Englishmen feel the same way about
Churchill. In a war, there are two sides. On each, the mass of average
decent people deplore the bad characteristics of their regime, and

[1] Wealthy English versifier, painter and botanist.

decide, nevertheless, to cooperate with it, because of the worse characteristics of the opposing regime. Aerial bombardment cements this cooperation.

War is only possible because people lack imagination and charity, and are so morally lazy that they prefer compromise with the lesser evil to the absolutes of right and wrong dictated by their own consciences. If one country is overthrown by force or overrun without resistance, it then becomes a question which way of life is spiritually stronger—that of the conquerors, or that of the conquered. People, on the whole, are ready to sacrifice their bodies in war, but most of them lack the other kind of courage—the courage by which the spirit survives—because they haven't been trained to it. Here, yoga comes in. It offers a technique of spiritual training. Pacifist propaganda is useless in itself, a mere political gesture, and an ineffective one. You can't make propaganda for the spiritual values. You can only demonstrate them by *being*. And you can only make such a demonstration after you have been properly trained. No use rushing unarmed into the struggle and trusting to luck. Gerald and the Swami are so right about this. "At the moment of action, no man is free." Why do we fool ourselves that we can suddenly behave like heroes and saints after a lifetime of cowardly thinking, daydreaming and hate? The acts of 1941 will be the thoughts of the past ten years.

January 2. The day went pretty well at the studio. Managed to read some of Vivekananda's book on *jnana yoga*, the discipline of discrimination. "The Real Nature of Man" is one of his best lectures. Even to read it gives you something personal, a contact.

We are now working on the last scenes of the picture. Van Dyke goes back to his marines at the weekend, and Gottfried will have to find another director.

(Gottfried had a tough time with *Rage in Heaven*. Sinclair started to direct it but had to be taken off. He was weak and undecided, and utterly unable to handle Robert Montgomery. Montgomery sulked from the beginning. He disliked the script—chiefly, I think, because Gottfried hadn't invited him to sit in on our story conferences. This was a pity, anyway, quite aside from tactical considerations: Lesser Samuels told me that Montgomery had a lot of helpful ideas when they were working on *The Earl of Chicago*. I urged Gottfried to consult him, but for some reason he wouldn't.

When the front office ordered Montgomery to play in the picture, on pain of suspension, he became sullen, snooty and obstructive. He did all his scenes deadpan, speaking in a dull, weary voice. When Sinclair tried to remonstrate with him, he snapped back: "What do you expect me to do? Chew up the scenery?" Finally, Arnold, the president of the Actors' Guild, was called in to see the rushes. His verdict was, "Sure, that son of a bitch is sabotaging you, but you'd have a hard job pinning it on him legally." Gottfried wanted to release Montgomery from his role, but the front office was mad by this time and insisted that he stay, even if the picture could never be shown.

Meanwhile, "Woody" Van Dyke was called in. Van Dyke was one of those hard-drinking, melodramatic Hollywood "characters." He had been down in San Diego, having just rejoined the marines, in which he was a reserve officer. He returned to us on leave, with all the glamor and authority of the military machine behind him. We all felt relieved. It was as though a dictatorship had been declared. We were certain Van Dyke would be able to handle Montgomery, but, actually, he didn't do much better than Sinclair. He directed about half of the picture, at top speed, as though it were farce, and then returned to his barracks.

So we switched to a third director, Dick Thorpe. Thorpe was very relaxed, slow-spoken and easygoing: he always worked with his hat on. He had directed *Night Must Fall*, and Montgomery liked him: he even used to come and sit on Thorpe's lap. However, his performance didn't improve. After the sneak preview, we had to have a lot of retakes. Thoeren and I had the idea of writing in a scene in which the psychiatrist, describing Montgomery, says: "At first, you might think he is quite normal, quite sane. But, if you watch him carefully, you'll notice things—a curious lack of expression in the face, a tonelessness in the voice, an air of listless fatigue—" This speech served a double purpose. It explained away Montgomery's bad performance and made it seem deliberate. (So effectively that many people told me they thought his underacting was simply brilliant.) And it was our private message to Montgomery himself. It told him exactly what we thought of him. The picture was actually quite a fair success. As Gottfried put it, "We escaped with a black eye."

The psychiatrist was played by Oscar Homolka. It was a small part, but he developed it into a one-man circus. He is the most outrageous of all hams. In one scene, with Ingrid Bergman, he had an umbrella. He handled it in such a way that it filled the entire set. Whenever Bergman had a speech, Homolka would contrive to get the umbrella between her and the camera. Once, he opened it and drove her right off the stage.

But Bergman could take care of herself. She was good-humored throughout, but severely professional. She studied her lines comma by comma, with unsmiling Swedish thoroughness, and always demanded some little change. I used to look into her dressing room every day and ask, "Any complaints, Miss Bergman?" She had an elocution teacher, with whom she worked whenever she wasn't actually on the set. The moment a scene was finished, she walked away into a corner, murmuring "oo, ee, *ah*, ay, *eu*."

She wasn't beautiful like Garbo, but she was radiantly appetizing. When she appeared, everybody brightened. Her presence was like breakfast on a sunny morning—a clean tablecloth, freshly made coffee, rich cream, deliciously crisp toast. I was absolutely fascinated by her. I hung around her like a high-school boy, gaping. The fat, thick-necked movie men came into her dressing room and tried to treat her like any other young actress. They called her "baby" and pinched her fanny. She laughed—but it was like pinching the Venus de Milo. They merely looked silly.

George Sanders was the most human of the cast. He asked riddles, made foolish jokes, and read a German book on sexual science in his dressing room. At Christmastime, he told us, he had been much perplexed, "wondering what to give my three mistresses."

I had a secretary named Joan Keating—a homely sunburnt girl of whom I'd become quite fond. We used to hang out of the window of my office, discussing the boys who went past and arguing as to which of them was the most attractive. (Later, Joan got herself a very nice and extremely goodlooking husband.) At this time, she fell violently in love with George Sanders. So Thoeren and I promised to get her his autograph. She was very embarrassed, and made us promise not to tell Sanders who had asked for it. Thoeren had an idea. Just before a scene was to be shot, he said to Sanders, "George—I've got a new game. I'm going to tell your fortune. All you have to do is to sign your name . . . Miss Keating, will you please lend us your script?" Rather mystified, Sanders signed, and, before he could ask what it was all about, Thorpe called him onto the set. By the time the scene was finished, Sanders had forgotten all about "the game." Joan tore out the signed page of the script and framed it. Later, when we told Sanders the story, he gave her a signed photograph as well—but the trick was typical of Thoeren's love of mystery. By now, he and I had become firm friends.

The weeks we spent on the stage, shooting the picture, were the happiest of my time at Metro. In a minor capacity, I was able to indulge my frustrated desire to be a movie director. I would far rather direct films than write them—and I shall always secretly believe that I could. On one occasion, I actually saved the studio a good deal of money. Snooping around the next day's set, one evening, I discovered what nobody else had noticed—that it would be physically impossible to play the scene on it as written. The doors were all in the wrong places. I forget whether we altered the scene or the doors—but I felt very pleased with myself.)

M. just sent me a pamphlet by Forster, called *Nordic Twilight*. It makes me sad to see Morgan writing this kind of thing. Not that it isn't decent and frank and honorable. He begins, "This pamphlet is propaganda. I believe that if the Nazis won they would destroy our civilization. I want to say why I think this . . ." And he goes on to describe how Hitler suppressed "decadent art," burned the books and is now ruthlessly interfering with the cultural life of Czechoslovakia, Poland, Norway, etc.—which is all very true.

But what is this "civilization"? For Morgan, it means the right to freedom of self-expression. "To *feel* free is not enough. It may be enough for the mystic, who can function alone and can shut himself up and concentrate even in a concentration camp. The writer, the artist, needs something more: freedom to tell other people what he is feeling."

Morgan fully admits that this self-expression may take political forms; yet he seems amazed that it should be countered by political means, i.e., violence. Talking and writing, like any other acts, produce results in the external world. It is absurd to be surprised by this fact. You can't just plump for irresponsible, anarchic freedom of expression, and then sit back and say you are "civilized." The communists, at least, don't make this mistake. It is the classic fallacy of liberalism.

Certainly, life would be ten thousand times worse under the Nazis. Churchill, from his point of view, is absolutely right when he says this, and absolutely right to fight Hitler. But from Morgan, our philosopher, we expect something more. Somebody, in the midst of this turmoil, has got to keep his head, preserve his judgment, and see the war *as a whole*, as a tragedy for which we are all responsible.

There are plenty of people able and willing to sound the call to battle. To stand up for the half-truths and the relative values. To preach the doctrine of the Lesser Evil. That is not Forster's function. He may fire an anti-aircraft gun, if he likes, to protect his house and his old mother, but he has no business to "take sides" in the ordinary sense. He *must* see this war more disinterestedly, more completely. If he doesn't, if the few people like him don't, then "civilization" is lost, no matter what the outcome. A country is no better than its philosophers. Usually, it is far, far worse. But a philosopher has his duty. Most of all at a time when he is unlikely to be listened to.

Dear Morgan, how can you write, " 'Cracow' has become for me the symbol of Nazi bullying on the continent, and I can hardly see the name without trembling with rage?" I should like to read aloud to you the scene from *Howards End*, when the boy dies of heart failure and Miss Avery comes out of the house with the sword. It was you who taught us the futility of hate.

When "peace" returns, let me never again forget that suffering is always with us. This war is not unique. During the gayest periods of my life, people were being killed and starving and dying in agony. When you are personally involved, don't be provincial and exclaim, "*This* is the Big Thing!" That kind of talk is for journalists and businessmen, who rate the bombing of London above the bombing of Chungking because the real estate is more highly insured.

January 5. To the temple. The Swami lectured on the universality of religion, against sects and fanaticism. Today, he looked very young, and sounded vigorous and political. I could picture him in the days before he joined the monastery, as a young student agitator and terrorist, fighting for a free India. He kept thumping his fist on the pulpit. As usual, he worked in a little nationalism—the Hindus were tolerant, the Christians and Mohammedans were not.

Lunch with the Chisholms. Bridget looked beautiful, pale and slim again, and somehow mysterious, like Mother Earth. We went in to see the baby. It was screaming desperately, in spasms, and plucking frantically at its mouth, as if fighting to express something—and it couldn't, it couldn't. The effort was almost as painful to watch as a death agony. Such a bitter struggle at the beginning of life. Such a superhuman effort: one can't believe that this little wrinkled crimson creature will survive it. But it forces its way, on and on, grimly, into time-consciousness—fighting and resting and fighting again. We stood awed and silent at the foot of the bed, unable to help—till the lady nurse bustled in, exclaiming, "Isn't he cute? Isn't he? And doesn't he want his milk? I'll say he does!"

Then Hugh entered, fresh and dapper from his bath. He looked so ridiculous—the absurd little rooster who had graciously donated his valuable semen for this creative act. Bridget said she'd been told that male sperm and female ovaries can now be introduced into the body of another woman, who will then be able to bear the child. Under these circumstances, the child still inherits everything from its parents, not the foster mother. We imagined a society lady introducing "Miss Jones—our carrier." And Miss Jones would refer casually to her clientele: "Last spring, when I was carrying for the Duchess of Devonshire . . ."

To Gottfried's in the afternoon. He wanted to finish off a scene. Salka came in, in tears. Peter has just given her a note—to avoid discussion—saying that he has absolutely made up his mind to leave for Canada in five days and enlist in the anti-aircraft ambulance unit. Salka is determined to stop him—if necessary, by informing the border police that Peter is still a minor, and goes without her consent. Gottfried tried to persuade her to be more cunning—to appeal to sentiment, to point out that he is the future breadwinner of the family, etc. etc. But Salka's Polish blood is up. She is going to make a big row.

Poor Peter is the hero-victim of the refugees here. For their hate, he must risk his life. Bruno Frank will approve—and all the other old war-horses who fight Hitler from Beverly Hills. Of course, it'll probably all end happily—Peter will have some exciting adventures in the best Hemingway manner, and come home to be our best postwar novelist. But that doesn't make the others less guilty.

Again I ask myself: should I go, too? The answer, after these last months, is much more decidedly, No. I've chosen to solve my problems here. And here I must stay. I wish I could get into that C.O. camp at once. Then everything would be simple and clear.

(The C.O. camp was the Civilian Public Service camp at Tanbark Flats—usually called the San Dimas camp. It had belonged to the Forestry Service and was used by the C.C.C.[1] boys. Then, when the draft started, they moved conscientious objectors into it, under the supervision of the Forest Rangers. Their job was to fight fires and work on various forestry projects. I made up my mind to go there as a volunteer, as soon as it opened. Why? Chiefly because I wanted to commit myself to the C.O. position, on which I had now definitely decided. Although I was over draft age, I felt pretty sure I'd be called in the event of war. If you can volunteer for the armed forces, I argued, then why not for civilian public service?

But I had another motive, also. I wanted to put an end to the life I was leading. I knew that Vernon and I had to separate; but I could only imagine myself doing this if I forced my own hand.)

January 6. Sometimes I feel that my whole day depends on the first ten minutes after I wake up. Which kinds of waves will first break the surface of undifferentiated consciousness? The war, resentment

[1] Civilian Conservation Corps; see Glossary under CPS camp and under Selective Service.

against Vernon, my health, the studio, the weather—anxiety, resentment, depression—they wait just outside the illuminated field of thought, ready to move in and impose their ugly, vulgar little pattern, the pattern of the day. But suppose one puts some other arrangement of one's own, consciously, in the middle of the field? Then they cannot combine.

Mina Curtiss (Lincoln Kirstein's sister) came to dinner, on her way from San Francisco to New Mexico. She talked about her friendship with Hans Otto Storm, the writer. And about Anne Lindbergh,[1] who had said that all women are mothers and all men are brothers—hence the difficulty of making a successful marriage. Mina is a bit cursed with Lincoln's intellectualism, and she hangs on to "Love" with grappling irons. She's a fine creature, very strong, but she ought to stop evaluating people so intensely. She needs religion, of course. And all she has in its place are Art and Leftism—as mental states. Nothing is any good unless you practice it: so many of us get a bug in our brains and just waste our lives cerebrating. That's why Mina was so impressed by Storm: he doesn't just talk about writing, he writes. But all she could do about it was to go to bed with him, and make both of them unhappy.

January 7. Gottfried tells me that he spent last night arguing with Peter about going to Canada. Gottfried had taken the hard-boiled Jewish line (as opposed to the crusading Zionist line): "What the hell—war isn't romantic, any more. That's nineteenth-century stuff. I'll tell you what war is—it's a bore. Sure, there's a lot of heroism. There's a lot of heroism in an earthquake, too. Everybody's a hero, when he has to be. Cowards are only the exceptions. Hell, I dread going to the dentist, but I go just the same, don't I? If the war comes here, I won't try to dodge. But why should I run after it over there? People talk about the Jews. The Jews! The Jews! The Jews have to fight Hitler! I tell you, the Jews have done enough against Hitler already. Let the others do something. Don't be such a sucker!"

Poor Peter! Gottfried's attack must have gotten him all confused. For he's so determined to be the hard-boiled guy at any price. I can picture him wondering if there wasn't, perhaps, something even tougher than war. How awful if one weren't cynical enough, after all! "Don't get me wrong," he is supposed to have replied: "If I'm sent over there, I'll pick a soft spot. I'm not sticking my neck out." And later: "Of course, if I'm offered a job at two thousand a week, I'll stay here." There you have the tragedy of a generation which is without belief; the generation which my generation taught and betrayed.

[1] Anne Morrow Lindbergh, writer, wife of the flying hero Charles Lindbergh.

January 8. A long telephone call from Mrs. McCullagh, the landlady of Joe Valentine,[1] Denny's protégé. (Denny picked Joe up on the road one day, in his car. Joe had run away from his home in Pennsylvania—an overcrowded shack in a mining town—and taken to the road. Denny felt sure he would grow up to be a gangster, if he wasn't taken care of; so he'd found him a room, paid several months' rent in advance, and asked me to keep an eye on him till he got a job.)

Mrs. McCullagh is getting more and more alarmed about Joe, whose "job" is very mysterious, if not actually sinister. She says his room is always full of men. "I don't know what they're doing," she told me, "but I'm going to find out." She has already informed the police, and the men are being watched.

January 9. To see Gerald in the evening. He plans a seminar of some kind for this summer, at which various problems of the religious life will be discussed. I may be able to come to it, if I can get leave from the San Dimas camp. Many of the most important Quakers are cooperating, and it seems possible that this work will be somehow integrated with the activities of the Friends Service Committee. The Quakers, says Gerald, are beginning to realize that they have laid too much emphasis on social service and too little on mysticism. The balance is upset, and their motive power is weakened in consequence.

January 10. Out with Tony Bower in the evening. We drove down to Thelma Todd's[2] and drank coffee. Tony, as usual, was very eager to talk about yoga. He sniffs all around the subject with jealous curiosity—surely there must be a hole in it somewhere? He's hoping it's all true, and yet he's hoping like hell that it's a fake, and that I shall come to my senses finally and have to admit this. He's hoping also, particularly, that Denny will have a relapse and return to his old ways. Denny causes more resentment than any of us, because he is a traitor to the gang, and because everybody had him so neatly taped as a drunken, doping sex maniac. Denny's desertion is very disturbing. Poor Tony—he feels the foundations giving way under him. And religion is so dreary, so madly ungay. It makes him shudder. Psychoanalysis, now—that's something else again. That's scientific. So he's going to be analyzed as soon as possible.

January 11. I'm through with the picture at last. Now I have a few days' vacation. The Swami is in bed, with a slight heart attack. Gerald had to speak, this Sunday, at Allan Hunter's church, so I pinch-hit at the temple. Read poems aloud—by Herbert, Vaughan, Emily

---

[1] Not his real name.
[2] A restaurant; see Glossary under Todd.

Brontë, Tennyson, Swinburne; and the duel scene from *The Brothers Karamazov*. Then down to lunch at the Hunters'. As Allan and I were walking out to the car afterwards, we met a small red-faced man carrying a little parcel which nevertheless seemed too heavy for him. "Are you tired?" Allan asked. "No," said the man, in a very matter-of-fact voice, "I'm drunk." We drove him to his house. He was a barber, who'd been working overtime to pay his debts: yesterday, he'd worked sixteen hours. So he took a few drinks to keep him going.

January 13. Went round to see the McCullaghs. Joe was out. He'd got a new job, working all night at a hot-dog stand. Mrs. McCullagh showed me his closet, which was full of brand-new suits. Where did they come from, she wanted to know? She is fond of Joe—"He's just a big open-faced boy trying to buck the world"—but she's very suspicious of the life he's leading. Mr. McCullagh, who has only one eye, was much more charitable. "We don't know that, dear," he kept interrupting, "we haven't any right to say that." However, they both promised that they won't throw him out without warning me, first.

(A few days later, Mrs. McCullagh called me on the phone. "Mr. Isherwood," she told me dramatically, "at last I've found out what Joe does with all those men. It's terrible—" She lowered her voice: "He *gambles*." She was disappointed and slightly shocked when I burst out laughing.

As far as I remember, we lost sight of Joe shortly after this. He left the McCullaghs of his own accord, without giving them any notice, and disappeared. Neither Denny nor I saw him again until the summer of 1942.)

January 14. Lunch with David Kirk, who is probably going to the San Dimas camp. The draft board first passed him as a C.O. and then changed its decision. He has appealed. The law still seems very vague on these points. He is in a specially difficult position, because he is a refugee. So everybody expects him to want to fight Hitler.

David is very intelligent, and not without charming qualities; but he's so terribly conscious of being a Jew. He is pedantic, fastidious in his choice of words. He seems to suffer from a kind of nervous exhaustion. He told me how—when he was studying at Owen's College, Manchester—he made a pact with the Devil, in order to pass his maths exam. And he did pass—although he was perfectly certain he must have failed. Even when he made the pact, he says, he intended to wriggle out of it; and he knew he could do this if he stopped masturbating. Now he's gotten engaged to a gentile girl in

Kansas City, and he's haunted by the fear that the Devil will revenge himself by making her marry someone else. David was perfectly serious when he told me this. In a kind of way, he believes it.

Gerald lectured to the class at the temple, on the difference between contemplation and meditation. Meditation is the stage of effort—in which we struggle to fix our mind on the Object by means of images, similes and metaphors. Contemplation is effortless. When we achieve it, we are unaware of the passage of time; our mind has become one-pointed. The need for images stops. We pass beyond the stage of logical analysis. We cease to infer. We know.

On the way home, we talked about the Devil—or rather, that part of our Ego which represents the Devil. Gerald said that lately he's been very conscious of his presence; not as someone terrifying, but as an unwearying Watcher—a presence which is always waiting its chance, bold and impudent and brutally cynical. . . .

By this time, Willie Maugham and his friend Gerald Haxton had turned up in Hollywood. They had taken a house with a huge swimming pool on Beverly Glen Boulevard, and Willie was rumored to be working with or for Selznick. (I believe he was actually writing his potboiler *The Hour Before Dawn*.) I was so pleased to see Willie again—that old, old parrot, with his flat black eyes, blinking and attentive, his courtly politeness and his hypnotic stammer. He is my ideal uncle.

At Gottfried's suggestion, I invited him to the studio. On that particular day, we were remaking the steel-mill scene, and the gas flames of the fake furnace nearly singed off Willie's moustache. There were two unforgettable encounters—the first with the Marx Brothers, who rushed out upon him screaming like devils, and climbed all over him, hugging and kissing him, as Willie submitted to their embraces with shy pleased smiles; the second with Joan Crawford, who greeted him with extreme aristocratic languor, on the set of *A Woman's Face*—like a reformed and ladylike Sadie Thompson meeting the doctor in Australia, ten years after the "Rain" episode.[1] The young studio messenger who showed us around was quite overcome, at the end of it all, by Willie's chattiness and his five-dollar tip. "He's a wonderful man," he kept repeating, "a wonderful man."

Willie also came up to see Gerald, and spoke simply and touchingly about himself. "I'm getting an old man," he said. All he wanted now was to go back to India and write a last serious book

---

[1] Crawford played Sadie Thompson, the American prostitute, in the 1932 film of Maugham's story about Western Samoa, "Rain".

about Shankara, spending his last days in a monastery. I was much moved on hearing this—until the news reached us, through van Druten and others, that Willie had made fun of Gerald, albeit quite affectionately, at a cocktail party next day, and had deplored my wasting my time with mysticism when I ought to be writing novels. But then he's like that: a mass of guilt and contradictions. I doubt if anybody really understands him.

I don't know if it was in January, or a bit earlier or later, that Gerald suddenly decided to break with the Swami. He arrived at this decision after a good deal of consultation with Allan Hunter and others, including myself. (Gerald's arguments convinced me at the time—partly because I really knew very little about the Swami's household, partly because they appealed to my innate puritanism. Did a love of mischief making also have something to do with it? I don't know. Perhaps. At any rate, I hadn't the least intention of following Gerald's example. I continued to see the Swami regularly, and even made repeated efforts to bring the two of them together again.)

Gerald felt that he couldn't any longer be publicly associated with the temple and the Swami's household: "the holy women" were too much for him, and the little tea parties, the automobile and the other minor luxuries which the Swami permitted himself—especially his cigarette smoking. So he wrote the Swami a letter in which he said he must stop lecturing at the temple and writing for the magazine.

Gerald said that this protest didn't make any difference to his feelings for the Swami; but, after this, they seldom saw each other. He used to declare, later, that he had been moved to take this action because some of his "ex-left-wing friends" (not named) had objected to the Swami's comfortable way of life and to the ministrations of the "holy women," which might easily be misconstrued. Gerald's critics retorted, needless to say, that Gerald's friendship with Chris might also be misconstrued, and with far more reason—and that it was all very well for Gerald to live in rags on four hundred dollars a year, when his transportation, much of his food and most of his books were provided by friends. To which Gerald would reply that the two cases were quite different, because Swami deliberately set himself up as a monk, a holy man, an official teacher. To which Gerald's critics would answer that Gerald had set himself up as a teacher, too, in a much bigger way than the Swami, by writing his books. And so on, and so forth.

The Swami was, as a matter of fact, greatly hurt by Gerald's criticism, and even answered it indirectly by an article in the magazine, in which he pointed out that true renunciation is of the heart, not the purse: a beggar may be attached to his few possessions while a king may be nonattached to his riches. In private, he gave way to indignant outbursts: "Mr. Hard had the cheek to talk to me like that!" In the end, I just felt embarrassed, whichever one of them spoke about it. Aldous best summed up the whole business by saying that it was a disastrous pity—considering the scarcity of sincere followers of the spiritual life—that two of them should have fallen out. "Judge not," he quoted, "that you be not judged."

During this period, Gerald and Denny were exchanging daily letters. Denny was trying to live entirely without sex, and his lurid accounts of his temptations and struggles made Gerald exclaim repeatedly, "My word, what a tough!" Denny was certainly the white-haired boy of our little circle. We all went around discussing him, raving about him, and dwelling with frissons of excitement on the awful life of sin he had lived before his "change." We were pretty ridiculous, no doubt—like church spinsters cooing over a converted burglar. And it wasn't very fair to Denny, who had later to try, and fail, to live up to this impossible ideal.

Was it at this time that Hollywood rang with the Paulette Goddard scandal? She was said to have misbehaved in public with a drunken movie director in a nightclub on the Strip. There were many versions of the story. There was even a joke: "Dial Crestview 7000 and you'll hear what Paulette said." The combination CR7 happens to be nonexistent in the Hollywood telephone system, and if you dial it, or any other such number, the instrument sets up a modulated yowling noise, suggesting the scream of a raped cat.

However funny this may have seemed to most of the population, it didn't amuse Chaplin. The Huxleys told us he was suffering a great deal; and one evening Maria suggested that we should all go out together, to cheer Charlie up. So Charlie, the Huxleys, Vernon and I went down to the fish restaurant on Santa Monica Pier. Charlie was quite gay during dinner. He and Aldous sang old London music-hall songs. Later we went over to the booth of a "reader" of handwriting—a stout, strangely charming, well-dressed lady, who told us that she suffered from asthma and worked here for the sake of the sea air. We were careful not to let her see Chaplin's face. It was dark by this time, and he stood back in the shadows behind us while we showed her a piece of paper on which he had written "Charles Spencer." The lady became very much disturbed. She kept repeating that this was a most extraor-dinary hand. What was the gentleman's profession? "The theater business," she was told. Oh, no—that wasn't right, at all. The gentleman was a musician. He ought to concentrate on that. And he was deeply interested in oriental religion and mysticism. Also there was a woman, a long way off: she was very unhappy about him. (This, said Maria, was undoubtedly Chaplin's mother.) The "reader" urged Chaplin several times to come back and have a session with her in private—but I don't think he did. He seemed rather impressed and upset by what she had told him.

Like people who try to cure an unhappy marriage by having children, Vernon and I bought two Persian kittens—the most charming I have ever seen. It was at this time, also, that Vernon brought home a little scarlet snake. He always loved snakes; I am afraid of them, but I petted this one gingerly. He put it in a wire-covered cigar box in the garage. Vernon explained to me that it was a Coral King Snake (*Cemophora coccinea*), quite harmless but hardly to be distinguished from the poisonous Coral Snake. What exactly, I asked, was the difference between them? Vernon couldn't say, so we looked it up in Ditmars's big book on reptiles.[1] The harmless Coral King Snake, we read, has pairs of black half-rings inclosing a wider half-ring of yellow, while the poisonous Coral Snake has yellow rings bordering the black. . . . Vernon and I looked quickly at each other—struck by the same doubt. We rushed down to the garage and bent over the box. The snake had escaped. We never found it again. As there were a lot of children playing all around, we thought it best not to mention the loss of the snake to our neighbors.

The kittens frisked all over the house, scratching the furniture and making their little messes. But the mess of our own lives was bigger, and couldn't be mopped up. Nothing helped any more, even fights. We never laughed. The worst thing about resentment is that it is entirely humorless. We hated the very fact that we had become so dependent upon each other. On February 17, we parted. I must be grateful to Vernon that, at the last moment, when I would have patched things up for the hundredth time, he insisted on carrying through our decision. He moved to a little house on Gordon Street. I went to the Hotel Stanley, on North Wilcox, just above Hollywood Boulevard.

The Stanley was a small place, only recently opened. There was a plainness about its furniture and decoration which appealed to me. After the great burden of possessions at Harratt Street, I wanted to feel that I was travelling very light. I had brought nothing with me but my clothes and about a hundred of my books, which I had

---

[1] Probably *The Reptiles of North America*, revised edition (1936).

had trucked to the hotel in a bookcase, to give me some slight illusion of being at home.

Loneliness is as terrible and irrational as passion. You can't argue with it. You can only oppose it by a careful ordering of your life. It is always crouched ready to spring, waiting for the unguarded minute. I saw as much of Gerald as I could, kept much more strictly to my times of meditation, and tried, as far as possible, to fill my whole waking life with activity. The studio wasn't helpful in this respect, however: the work they were giving me could hardly be described as exacting.

For instance, there was an excellent British picture called *The Stars Look Down*. Somebody from Metro had bought it, in a lapse from bad taste, and now the front office was scared to release it—it was too left-wing. But, since the money had been paid, the left-wingishness would have to be "cured" somehow. So they'd told off Harry Rapf to get himself a writer and fix it.

Harry Rapf was quite an important figure at Metro. Maybe he, too, knew where the body was buried—although I doubt if he was capable of remembering. Or maybe he was simply a relative of Louis B. Mayer. They resembled each other a good deal. Both were rodent types, but Harry was distinguished by his enormous nose. There was an unkind story of a young man whom Rapf had discovered and groomed as a writer, believing ardently in his talent. One day, after many expectant months, the young man came to Rapf in triumph. He had an idea for a comedy, a really great idea. Rapf was delighted. At last his protégé was going to make good. He urged the young man to shoot without delay. "Well, see—" the boy began, "it's like this: there's a guy, and he has a big nose—no, not just a *big* nose—a super-colossal, amazing, sensational nose—" Here, his eye fixed on Rapf's nose, and glazed in horror. Apparently, he had never been aware of it before; or he had carefully censored it out of his consciousness. He faltered. His voice died away in his throat. He rushed from the room. Neither Rapf nor Metro ever saw him again.

Because of this perhaps, or similar experiences, poor Rapf had become very quiet and vague. He didn't want any kind of trouble, any decisions. He was stupid and he knew it. He explained to me that the film was to be "cured" by a prologue, explaining that the miners, whose lives are described in *The Stars Look Down*, are the same men who are suffering the dangers of wartime England. "Humanity," said Rapf, "that's the keynote. Humanity's the important thing, not politics. That's what we've got to put across. I don't want much, mind you. Just about eight hundred words."

So I went back to my office and started composing prologues. It was fun, at first, like writing prose poems; but the joke wore thin. By the end of the week, I had presented Rapf with half a dozen of them—none of which, I am happy to say, were used when the picture was finally released.

From Rapf, I went to Milton Berle. I took to Milton at once. He was youngish, well built and pleasant. As a high-school boy, he used to spend his summers at Catalina, working at the hotel cigar stand and aquaplaning in his free time with the local girls—among them, the future Carole Lombard. One year, the hotel was visited by Charlie Chaplin. Charlie, already a world-famous star, was at a loose end and bored. He conceived a kind of Proustian, romantic, collective passion for the "little band" of girls, and asked Berle to introduce him to them. Chaplin dazzled them all with his fame, his wealth, his jokes; he hired a motorboat for their aquaplaning, he gave parties for them, he loaded them with presents. By the end of the summer, he and Berle were like old friends. Charlie wanted to send him to college, and then to take him around the world as a sort of secretary-pimp. "Just because I was young," Berle told me, "he thought I could get acquainted with any girl I wanted to. The funny thing is, he's really scared of girls. He was awful shy." However, Berle had to refuse the offer, because of his family. A year later, when Chaplin was making a picture, Berle went around to the studio and gave his name to the doorman. Chaplin said he was "busy." Berle made several more attempts, but Chaplin wouldn't see him.

Berle told me all this without the least hint of resentment. To him it seemed perfectly natural. He was a true child of Hollywood, and accepted the violent ups and downs of movie life as a matter of course. As a young man, he had been very wealthy. Then he lost everything, and had to start again from the bottom. Now he had thirty thousand a year outside of his earnings, a beautiful wife, two or three children, a fine house and a biggish yacht. He was quite a tough little customer, probably capable of getting nasty when drunk, but fundamentally amiable and, like so many of his kind, as soft as putty in the presence of what he would describe as a "cultured" Englishman. It's our accent that does it. I've seen the broad a's work wonders in Hollywood. You might call the effect "His Butler's Voice." Berle said of himself: "I can get mad awful easy. You see, like most Americans, I come from a bad neighborhood."

Berle was very apologetic about the picture we were to work on together. It was called *Free and Easy*—a comedy of the late twenties or early thirties, written by Ivor Novello, and originally played by Robert Montgomery and Mady Christians. Bernie Hyman was determined to remake it—for sentimental reasons, Berle said: Bernie had fallen heavily for Mady while the original version was being shot. (Mady, as she appeared in the movie, was the usual fuzzy-haired, shapeless, continental frump of that period, with a makeup that suggested galloping consumption.) The dialogue, bad enough when it was written, now dated like a newspaper, but Bernie would hardly let us alter a line. He insisted, however, on calling us frequently into his office in order to give us a performance of the love scenes. "And now," he would drool, his eyes blinking with tears, "now she can't say any more . . . He's won her . . . She gives him her lips . . ."

So Berle and I exchanged glances of mutual pain and mentally loaded Bernie with the entire responsibility of whatever might follow. Actually, the picture *was* made, with a fairly good cast, including Robert Cummings and Ruth Hussey, and it stank: though not as strongly as I'd feared and hoped. As this was only a polishing job, my name wasn't on it. Once again, I had wasted hours of studio time. It seems uneconomical to hire a writer at six hundred dollars a week to dictate another man's script to a stenographer.

One day when I was up visiting Gerald, a lady named Mrs. Allen, who owned the house on the corner of Arlene Terrace and Green Valley Road, came out to tell me that her annex apartment—living room, bathroom and bedroom—had just fallen vacant. I'd once asked her to let me know if it ever should. The chance seemed heaven sent. I could be next-door neighbor to Gerald at the very time I needed him most. So, in the middle of March, I moved to 2407 Green Valley Road.

Mrs. Allen wasn't altogether an agreeable character. She was fond of whacking up the rent with extras, and no doubt she would have been merciless if her snoopy nature had revealed any irregularity in my sex life. But I had plenty of money, and, for the first time since the age of ten, nothing to hide: so we never actually fought. Mrs. Allen had a nephew named Jerry, with a big bucktoothed grin, who was in the air force. He was our chief topic of conversation. He was always passing, or failing to pass, some exam.

Gerald and I had supper together practically every day. On weekends, we took sandwiches up to the firebreak road for picnics and discussions. The Hunters usually came too. And there were three charming boys from Allan's congregation—Phil Basher and

Bob and Bill Forthman. Phil and Bob were in their early teens and Bill was even younger; but they seemed, in an almost intuitive way, to realize what Gerald was driving at. He never talked down to them. One day, when Gerald had finished one of his brilliant discourses, Bob suddenly blurted out: "But—if that's all true— why do we ever do anything else?" An unanswerable question, followed by silence.

At the Swami's suggestion, I did my first all–day sit at the temple. This sounds like an impressive austerity; but in practice it wasn't. You were supposed to keep silent and fast from dawn till dusk— but you were allowed to talk to the Swami himself, and you were allowed to drink as much water and fruit juice as you wanted. Also, you didn't have to stay entirely in the shrine room. You could read, in the Swami's study; or walk in the garden, or up and down the street. I read several of the essays in Sri Aurobindo's book on the Gita. While I walked in the street, the Swami told me to repeat my mantram and to try to give everybody who passed me a mental blessing—which wasn't hard, because this part of Ivar Avenue is very quiet. Sitting in the shrine was rather like a long railway journey. I felt curiously exhausted. The stale incense gave me a headache, and from time to time I dropped off to sleep.

By this time, I was getting to know some of the other occupants of 1946 Ivar Avenue, and had stopped vaguely lumping them together as "the holy women"—that phrase invented by Gerald, and so typical of his thinly veiled misogyny. First, there was Mrs. Wykoff, always addressed as "Sister"; a gentle-voiced, deaf, tough and extremely active old lady in her eighties, to whom the house belonged. Sister had met Vivekananda in 1899, during his second visit to America, and had been interested in Vedanta ever since. Her husband died, her son grew up, became an engineer and was killed in an accident near Palm Springs in the 1920s. Shortly afterward, she heard Prabhavananda lecture in San Francisco: he was then a young man, lately arrived in the United States and in charge of the Portland Vedanta Center. Sister invited him to come down and live at her house and form a center in Hollywood. He accepted. For a long time, they lived quietly, with a couple of other ladies. The Swami gave lectures in the living room on Sundays. Only a few people came. But the congregation slowly grew, and in 1938 they had sufficient funds to build the temple, in Mrs. Wykoff's garden. Sister loved gardening. The Swami laughingly complained that she would never let anything grow; she was always furtively transplanting her flowers from one corner of the yard to another. She also loved her ill-tempered old collie, Dhruva (named for a minor Indian saint who, according to Hindu mythology, was taken up to heaven by Vishnu and became the polar star). In her old age, she had become violently political. She read radical magazines and was a great champion of Indian nationalism.

When Sister and the Swami had been living together for a few years, they decided they must have a housekeeper. They engaged an Englishwoman named Mrs. Corbin, who had just arrived from England. The Swami renamed her Amiya: he was in the habit of giving Sanskrit names to all of his devotees, as part of their initiation. Amiya was a big blonde woman who must have been very pretty, but was now running to fat. A marvellous cook and a born manager, she was jealous and bossy. Like Peggy Rodakiewicz, she said bitter things which she immediately regretted. She adored the Swami and was terribly possessive: she hated anybody else to wait on him: she wanted to be undisputed mistress of the household. The Swami knew this and scolded her unmercifully, often humiliating her to tears in public. At first, this shocked me. Then I began to see how much Amiya needed it, how necessary it was for her to be forced to submit—even to occasional injustice. As a girl, she had been vain, silly, spoilt. She had separated from her husband (as she now admitted) for quite insufficient reasons, out of pique. Now she was achieving, painfully, a kind of greatness. She was warmhearted, passionately loyal, absolutely sincere, tactless, emotional, rude: the prototype of Martha in the Gospels. She overworked herself, unnecessarily, almost hysterically, and kept getting sick. Dr. Kolisch attended her. The two dictatorial natures clashed, and produced a permanent feud.

If Amiya was Martha, Sarada Folling was Mary. Sarada was a girl in her early twenties, of Norwegian descent. She had studied music and dancing. Often, when she thought nobody was looking, she would strike ballet postures, humming to herself. She was very beautiful, with the pale, serene face of a saint. She took naturally to the life of meditation, spending long hours in the shrine, doing the ritual. She had learnt quite a lot of Sanskrit. The Swami was specially fond of her, regarding her as his prize pupil. This of course made Amiya jealous. She loved Sarada dearly; but Sarada's vagueness about housekeeping drove her frantic. It was all very well for Sarada to pray, to grow more and more spiritual: somebody had to fix the dinner. Sarada understood how Amiya felt, and didn't resent it. She had an extraordinary, quite unsentimental sweetness about her. And she was gay, lively, full of jokes, quite a tomboy. Like all genuinely religious people, she wasn't a puritan, she didn't cut her life into compartments; she joked about Ramakrishna, the ritual and Vedanta in general in a way which would have shocked any member of the Swami's congregation to death. Blasphemy is only possible for those who don't really believe in God.

The atmosphere of Ivar Avenue and of Gerald's room on Arlene Terrace were, in fact, entirely opposed to each other. It was very instructive for me to be able to inhabit both. On the one side, apparent disorder, religious bohemianism, jokes, childish quarrels, dressing up in saris, curry, cigarettes, oriental laissez-faire; on the other, primness, plainness, neatness, austerity, discreet malice, carrots, patched blue jeans, wit and western severity. My puritan middle-class upbringing pulled me in one direction; my past life pulled me in the other. Forster, I felt, would feel much more at home with the Swami than with Gerald. The Swami, I felt, would better understand my nights in the Berlin underworld—a period which Gerald could ignore but never forgive, because it awakened some reminiscent insecurity in himself. Gerald offered me discipline, method, intellectual conviction. But the Swami offered me love.

However, I wasn't in the mood for love, just then. I didn't trust it. I didn't dare venture again outside my shell. I wanted discipline and austerity—the gloomier the better. I wanted to take some definite step toward "purgation," however small. It was the only way I could strengthen my shattered morale.

So I decided to give up smoking. This was to be the final test. If I couldn't succeed, then I was no good. I'd better retire to the Sunset Strip and relax—at any rate, that was what I told myself. My addiction to nicotine had grown, during the past year. I had to start smoking before I got out of bed in the morning; my fingers were permanently stained (I had always objected to this, in Wystan) and there were little burns all over my clothes.

The first two weeks of disintoxication were very unpleasant. I was quite unable to do any work, or concentrate at all. I trembled. My nerves were on edge throughout the day. I longed to strangle my secretary, who happened, by ill luck, to be a rather silly murderee girl with eyeglasses. However, by a minor miracle, I succeeded. I didn't smoke again for nearly two years.

My final job with Metro was a picture called *Crossroads*, a remake of a French movie about amnesia. The producer was Eddie Knopf. I'm afraid I disappointed him badly. What with my disintoxication, and my general preoccupation with my life outside the studio, I was much stupider than usual. My contract's first year expired early in May. I gave Metro notice (against great opposition, including my agents', I'd insisted on the right to do this when I signed) and told [Ken] MacKenna, head of the story department, that I intended to join the San Dimas camp. He was very nice and understanding, and even had the grace to pretend that Metro would have taken up my option, which I doubt.

My first weeks of freedom from Metro were spent with the Huxleys—on a motor trip through the desert. We drove out over the Tejon Pass, past Lebec (named for a young French trapper of the Hudson Bay Company who was killed there by a bear) and down the Grapevine Grade. The valley toward Bakersfield was still covered with lupines. As far as the eye could see, they stretched away into the dusty golden distance, like the blue, shadowed levels of a vast lake. Maria cried out and clapped her hands like a little girl. She would have liked to leave the car and wander off over the ranch. I warned her not to. Only a week before this, Gerald, Allan and I had come here and nearly trodden on a sleepy old rattler, coiled among the flowers. Gerald and Allan had had one of their serious philosophical discussions: should one kill it, or leave it as a danger to other picnickers? Nonviolence won the day, and we ended by driving it away—for no particular reason—by pelting it with handfuls of dirt.

We turned east along a side road which wound up into the mountains and over the Tehachapi Pass. The temperature on the valley floor was at least eighty: in the mountains it was snowing. Tehachapi, where the state prison for women is, looked like Wuthering Heights.

Down from Tehachapi and into the desert at Mojave, where we turned north along the truck-route road to Reno. We stopped the night in motel cabins at Olancha. It was very cold. Maria fussed around, seeing that Aldous was comfortable; and I suddenly felt excluded from their quietly affectionate domesticity. I lay awake a long time, listening to the roar of the great ruthless trucks, as they tore past along the black highway, swinging fans of light across my ceiling and rattling their chains. Now, at last, I said to myself, I am utterly alone.

Next morning, we drove down, through the jagged brown ranges, into Death Valley. It was surprisingly cool, although the hotel was already closed for the summer. From Dante's View, we looked out over the gigantic wilderness, from the long winding sparkle of dried salt on the valley bottom to the scarred canyon walls, streaked harshly with vermilion, green, gold, crimson, blue and orange—the Funeral Mountains and the Panamints—and, towering against the far sky, Mount Whitney, all in snow. I'd read of the pioneer clergyman shaking his impotent little fist at nature's appalling indifference and crying, "Goodbye for ever, Death Valley!" A desert is a great empty picture frame, and we can't resist using it for a portrait of our private disaster. To me, the scene was beautiful but horrible—like a vast geographical demonstration of Vernon's total absence.

After we had passed the ranger station, Maria triumphantly produced a little bush of silver desert holly: you are forbidden to remove plants from a national park. We drove on, through the empty plateaux of Nevada to Las Vegas, that little paradise of expensive dude ranches and cheap gambling, self-centered in its own circle of garish lights and noise, manufacturing the quick, rash marriages that Reno unmakes, and gaily unaware of the surrounding darkness and silence. After supper, we wandered through the little red light district. The girls laughed and joked with us from the open doorways of the cribs, and Maria chatted with them like a sister. I had never seen her so charming, so genuinely enjoying herself. All night, I kept waking to hear the deep-throated baying of locomotives in the yards in front of our hotel. I wrote Vernon a letter: "Whatever happens, we shall always be friends."

Next morning, we drove to Boulder City and visited the dam. Pylons like marching robots stride down into the black volcanic gorge: Maria called them "the Boulder men." Aldous said it looked like the entrance to hell. Down in the powerhouse, we saw the turbines, through which the water passes at a hundred miles an hour, with the faintest singing noise, like an insect's hum. Huge calm saints, receiving and transmitting power, impersonally, to do good to crops and men. The saints are like that, I thought: the power which would shatter an ordinary human being like an eggshell cannot harm them, because they do not want it for themselves, they are truly vehicles, without greed or pride. And I remembered the line from the Upanishads which Eliot quotes: "Give, Sympathize, Control."[1]

From Boulder Dam we drove to Barstow, where we spent the last night of our trip. Its inhabitants have made the desert hideous with enormous dumps of cans. Wherever we walked, we came upon them, all around the outskirts of the town.

Throughout our journey, Maria and Aldous were watching like hawks for rare desert flowers. I noticed that Aldous's sight was really remarkable for distant objects—far better than mine. Once, as we were travelling at full speed, Maria suddenly pulled up with a

[1] *The Waste Land*, ll. 402 ff and note to l. 402.

jerk which nearly pitched me through the windscreen, and the two of them jumped out of the car and rushed off over the desert. I thought they had gone crazy. Actually, they had spotted a group of mariposa lilies, at least a hundred yards away.

I came back to Green Valley Road to find that Denny had arrived, driving his car from the East. I'd invited him to share my apartment until he was drafted. He'd already filled in his form 47 and been classified 4-E as a conscientious objector.[1] He might expect to be sent to camp almost any time, but we hoped that, in any case, he would be allowed to spend some of his leave at the seminar which was then being planned.

Friction between Denny and Gerald began almost at once. It must always have existed. I seem to recall that Gerald told me of scenes between them even while they were actually living together, before Denny left for the East. They were bound to clash, sooner or later: Denny, sharp edged, raw, sour, uneducated, rude, chronically suspicious of other people's motives; Gerald with his old-maidish habits, his precise tricks of speech, his Irish blarney and his Irish evasiveness. Denny was prepared to worship, to throw all his weight on the arm of the Good Shepherd; he was incapable of discrimination, qualified admiration, of separating out the gold from the sand. Either Gerald had to be the new avatar, or an old phony. Gerald was neither.

Chris made things worse, by getting an attack of sulks. Gerald announced, two days after Denny's arrival, that we could no longer all have breakfast together in the Arlene Terrace kitchen: Chris had forbidden it—saying that the house was getting too full of people. Denny was very bitter about this. Chris, he said, was childish and spoilt, but he also accused Gerald of running halfway to meet Chris's whims, instead of telling him not to be a selfish fool.

Then there was the money problem. Some months before this, Gerald had acquired a very large sum—I believe around a hundred thousand dollars. I don't know who gave it him, but it was earmarked for the foundation of his center, "Focus," which I've mentioned already. Gerald felt, quite logically, that he could legitimately use some of it to help the future Focus members. He offered Denny ten thousand dollars, and Denny accepted them. This happened before Denny went to Pennsylvania, and I am sure that the money was given and received in perfect good faith on both sides. But, nevertheless, it constituted a kind of option or advance on royalties. As soon as Denny had taken it, he was obligated; as soon as he was obligated, he began to feel guilty. As

[1] See Glossary under Selective Service.

long as he continued to follow Gerald's way of life, and honestly intended to join the center, some day, the sense of guilt wasn't very strong. But, as Gerald and he drifted apart, it grew and grew, and turned into resentment and near hatred. I don't think the ten thousand dollars were ever mentioned between them again; but Denny often spoke of them to me. As long as a cent of the money remained—and it lasted nearly two years—Denny alternated between self-accusation and guilty extravagance. I think Gerald was largely to blame. After all, this was really a kind of bribe.

I am quite ready to admit that I also contributed my drop of poison to the brew. I wasn't altogether sorry to see a chilling of diplomatic relations between Arlene Terrace and Green Valley Road: I wanted to have Denny all to myself. I began to look at Gerald through Denny's jaundice-yellow spectacles. Gerald, who was extremely sensitive to the faintest hint of criticism, reacted to this: unsure of himself, he began to exaggerate his least agreeable mannerisms. He began to talk, more and more frequently, in his masochistic, life-hating vein. He saw nothing but evil and ugliness around him. He delighted in descriptions of disease and corruption. He found fault with everybody. He said he hoped he'd die soon. One day, while we were walking on the firebreak, he told us that the male sexual organ reminded him of a loose end of gut hanging out of the body. In my already critical mood, this so disgusted me that I got very angry. "Gerald," I exclaimed, "if you go on talking that kind of filth, I shall walk home alone." This was childish, and I later apologized; but Gerald was very much hurt. Denny, needless to say, was delighted.

Actually, those weeks of May and June were some of the happiest of my whole life. Real happiness is simply the absence of pain. After the tension of my life with Vernon and the period of loneliness which followed, I suddenly found myself quite contented, needing nothing. And this, in itself, was pure joy.

We woke early around six o'clock, and got out of our beds without a word—Denny going into the living room, I remaining in the bedroom—for our respective sits. They lasted an hour—after which I would read, lying on my bed, while Denny used the bathroom. Then, while I got washed, he prepared breakfast. Until it was ready, we didn't speak—even to say good morning. After breakfast, I washed up; and then we would read aloud to each other, usually from William James's *Varieties of Religious Experience*, a badly written book which we both criticized violently. At twelve, we began our midday hour; and then it was time for lunch.

In the afternoon, we had various occupations. If we drove

anywhere in the car, one of us would take the book along and continue the reading. At six, we always returned home for our evening sit. And, all day long, never a cross word, never a disagreement. We were perpetually busy and gay. Everything we did seemed interesting and amusing. The apartment acquired a kind of nursery atmosphere of innocence.

We had agreed, of course, to give up sex. And we did, for two months: but this little austerity was purely technical. We didn't give up thinking about sex, talking about sex, even boasting of our glamorous love lives. Sublimation is of the mind, not the deed, and we never seriously attempted it.

Through the Huxleys, I had met a lady named Claire Stuart, a teacher of hatha yoga. She was a pupil of the somewhat dubious Theos Bernard, who had just gotten himself mixed up in some kind of sex scandal in New York. There was nothing dubious about Miss Stuart, however. She was eminently respectable, and had many pupils who were being taught, on a merely athletic basis, to improve their health and their figures. Miss Stuart was herself, perhaps, a more complicated human being than these youth-and-beauty-seekers. Denny and I felt sure she was a lot older than she looked and we thought we could detect unhappiness and strain beneath the sleek disguise of her suppleness and charm. She had a really amazing body which she could twist and stretch in every direction with the utmost ease.

She taught us bastrika, hollow tank, air swallowing and many other exercises and postures. It took us about an hour and a half a day to work through them all. Even when we were all three lying nearly naked on the floor, Miss Stuart remained the perfect lady. She explained that the air which is passed through the body in the swallowing exercise should come out "quite odorless"—and she smiled with playful disapproval when one of us released an evil, noisy whiff of gas.

I must admit that the exercises, which we practiced daily for about three weeks, made me feel wonderful. My insides felt like a well-packed suitcase. But then Miss Stuart began to advocate the use of an enema—as a preparation for the yogi trick of washing out your intestines with water by muscular effort alone. I objected to this, feeling that I was getting out of my depth. In any case, I had never intended to continue the exercises for long. I did them chiefly because hatha yoga is such a misrepresented occupation, and I wanted to know something about it at first hand.

The Swami, when he heard of it, was highly disapproving. He told me that the breathing exercises produce hallucinations, and that he had seen people in India who retain a boyish physique up to the age of sixty, but are complete idiots in consequence. "What is the matter with you, Mr. Isherwood," he asked severely, "surely you do not want Etarnal Youth?" I was silent and hung my head—because, of course, I did.

I was working for the American Friends Service Committee on and off during the whole of this time. I used to drive to the Friends Center on Orange Grove, Pasadena, and pick up bundles of clothes to be delivered to the Okie camps in the valley around Bakersfield. These camps were certainly an improvement on the "Hoovervilles" described in *The Grapes of Wrath*, but they were miserable enough: long narrow corrugated iron huts, which became uninhabitable ovens in the midday heat. On these trips, I cooperated with the Chisholms, who were rapidly developing social consciences and convictions to suit them. (They now had a beautiful old Spanish crucifix, insted of an erotic surrealist "object," lying on the table beside their bed: the Bible and the works of Heard had replaced *Ulysses* and *Lady Chatterley* on their special shelf.) We had much consultation, before our first visit, as to what Bridget and Hugh should wear—lest the Okies' feelings should be hurt. Something "*very* plain" was agreed on. They finally showed up in brand-new denim pants and gaudy silk neckerchiefs, like guests at a dude ranch. But we needn't have been afraid of striking the wrong note. We scarcely saw the Okies at all. Quaker volunteer workers received our bundles, and our stay at the camps often didn't exceed ten minutes.

In addition to the Okie work, I took on a certain amount of visiting. There were a lot of refugees living around Hollywood and Beverly Hills who needed help of one kind or another. One man could get a job if he had an artificial leg. The Chisholms invited Barbara Hutton to dinner and told her the story. Next morning, she sent a check. Another needed a camera for professional work. Another canned goods. Another, a job as a gardener and the necessary tools. Actually, we were much more successful than most of the local workers at raising money, because the Chisholms had such influential friends. Our reputation at Pasadena was soon considerable. We even considered the idea of opening a regular office and acquiring a staff.

But my most interesting "case"—the only one that taught me anything at all—was a total failure. One day, I met Guttchen in the street. He was in the depths of poverty and despair—and aggressive, cunning, theatrical and cynical as ever. We began by arranging that he should live at the house of a Quaker named John

Waye. He didn't stay there long. He savagely tore their sweetly reasonable goodwill to shreds. He refused to have a doctor examine his kidneys: "That man knows nothing—he's just a shoe salesman." Bitterly he assailed our bourgeois, wishy-washy philanthropy. It was all a pose. "You call yourself a Friend," he railed at me, "all right, go ahead—do something. I'm not *your* friend. You're *mine*—or so you say." If I had any religion, any consolation, any spiritual strength—I was to give it to him. I said I was a believer. Very well, then—what did I believe? Or didn't I believe, really? "Of course I believe—" I protested weakly, my vanity smarting under his jabs. But when I tried to tell him, the words just wouldn't come. No—not with my Chevrolet standing outside. Not with Denny waiting at home to cook a tasty evening meal. So I gave him money. And Guttchen sneered, "You're bribing me to leave your conscience alone." It was true.

From Guttchen I learned some of the problems of social service. You can't only help people, like a Lady Bountiful, from ten to four. If you want to be of any real use, you must share your life with them. Otherwise, it's probably better to avoid them, and subscribe to charities. My experience with Guttchen had a good deal to do with my decision to go to Haverford, later in the year.

Denny sometimes came with me on these visits, and on the Okie trips. We also made two semi-pleasure trips—hunting real estate for Gerald's future center—one to the Sequoia Forest area, the other to the coastal country south of Laguna Beach, the mountains around Julian, and the Palm Springs and Mojave deserts. We found several more or less suitable ranches for sale—including one behind Oceanside, called the Blue Bird, which we particularly liked. Later, we drove Gerald down to see it, and Gerald turned it down. Denny took his refusal personally, and was very indignant. Actually, I doubt if Gerald would ever have bought any property at all—he was as undecided and full of excuses as Queen Elizabeth—if Felix Greene hadn't finally taken matters into his own hands, and bullied Gerald into the purchase of Trabuco. But that was many months later.

Another companion on my Okie trips was Vernon. We had gone on seeing each other, at intervals, ever since we parted. Vernon and Denny could never meet, because Vernon hated him—violently, unreasonably, with a mixture of jealousy and self-recognition: the two of them were really very much alike. Denny realized this too, but reacted in just the opposite way. He sympathized with Vernon and would have liked to help him and be his friend. He even blamed me for breaking with Vernon, and said he was sure the fault was mostly mine.

Vernon was living in wild untidiness and dirt in his little adobe house on Gordon Street—painting a little, drinking a great deal, and having promiscuous sex off the boulevard. One night I arrived to find him apparently dead drunk. Actually, he had swallowed half a bottleful of Seconal tablets. A friend who happened to be there helped me work on him for a long time, with cold water and black coffee. When Vernon came around, he professed to be very angry with me. He'd wanted to kill himself, he said; but I doubt it. After this, I persuaded him to see Allan Hunter. They had long talks which seemed to make Vernon feel better about things—rather to my surprise. Allan was unexpectedly good at dealing with such cases.

I longed to help Vernon somehow, but I really knew that I couldn't. We knew each other too well. However, we continued to meet. Sometimes it was so enjoyable that neither of us could believe, or remember why, we had ever quarrelled. Sometimes we only made each other miserable: one wrong word led to another, and we'd part angrily after a few minutes—jarred to the bone on each other's basic obstinacy.

Denny had trouble with his back, and Miss Stuart's exercises were continually putting him out of joint. So we went to see a Swedish osteopath named Dr. Inglemann, whose office was on Hollywood Boulevard. He, also, had been recommended to us by Maria Huxley, that connoisseur of doctors, clairvoyants and cranks. Inglemann twisted Denny this way and that: his most agonizing trick was the jerk with which he adjusted the first vertebra of the neck (he called it "th'Aatluss"). I went to him a few times, myself, but gave up after a horrible operation for draining the sinus: he stuck his little finger right up my nostril and seemingly far into the brain.

Dr. Inglemann was also a diet enthusiast, with a phobia against commercial chocolate—which he said was a deadly poison, containing arsenic. He regarded the chocolate makers as the real merchants of death, exploiters and enemies of mankind; far worse than any dictator or munition merchant. He was a vegetarian and an ardent disciple of Krishnamurti.

It now became apparent that I shouldn't be going to the San Dimas camp. Volunteers were not wanted: the draftees were already arriving in sufficient numbers. Edna Schley tried to get me an interim job at Metro, to last until the opening of the seminar in July. So, one day, I was sent for by a producer named Jack Chertok.

He had a movie story about a Nazi gas factory in Czechoslovakia and a Scarlet Pimpernel Englishman who destroys it. I read the script through and told him I was sorry—I couldn't conscientiously write a picture on such a subject. Chertok was very nice about this, and much interested in my description of the C.O. philosophy, which he had never heard before. I also told him about the work of the Friends Service Committee. "Come to me after the war's over," he said, "and I'll be glad to help you in any way I can."

At this time, I met Kagawa, who was touring America on a peace mission. He was an old friend of Allan Hunter's. Gerald, Denny and I drove down to an early morning service at Allan's church, at which he was present. He preached very badly, on a text from the Apocalypse, arguing with the most dreary kind of Christian fundamentalism. And afterwards there was a stupid breakfast party, at which Kagawa's secretary, Mr. Ogawa, talked fulsomely of their prison experiences—revealing, as an anticlimax, that they had only been in jail three weeks. But Kagawa himself was strangely impressive—very pale, in his heavy black frock coat, with thick glasses covering his weak, trachoma-inflamed eyes. Because of the trachoma, he wasn't allowed to shake hands: he offered each of us his forearm to grasp in greeting. There was about him an air of great gentleness, and of an infinite sadness and pain. He seemed to move in pain, as if within an element, softly, selflessly. A Japanese man of sorrows, burdened with all the soft, heavy, overpowering melancholy of his manic-depressive islands.

Allan Hunter brought other interesting visitors to see Gerald— [Frank Charles] Laubach, who wrote *Letters by a Modern Mystic*, and [John Allen] Boon, the author of *Letters to Strongheart*. I can remember nothing about Laubach except a general impression of benevolence. He had spent most of his life as a missionary in the Philippines. He seemed quite dazed with pleasure at finding other people who shared his concern with mystical religion. I felt embarrassed because he treated me as an equal, and assumed that I was as experienced as himself.

Boon, by contrast, seemed a bit phony. He was highly individualistic and Californian. He talked about Strongheart—the German Shepherd dog which Larry Trimble changed from a savage police-trained killer into a creature so intelligent that it literally died of its own attempt to become a human being. He also claimed that insects can be communicated with, just like animals. He had argued with a train of ants and persuaded them to stay out of his icebox. He had trained a fly to come and sit on his hand while he was writing, and even to run down inside his fist, such was its trust in his good intentions. One evening, he was having supper with Sid Grauman, owner of Grauman's Chinese Theater. Boon told Grauman about the fly, and Grauman became greatly excited and said he just had to see it at once. Boon warned him that, at that hour of the night, the fly would probably be asleep, but Grauman couldn't wait. So they drove down to Boon's place. For a long time they waited, and at last the fly appeared and settled on Boon's hand. "Get him to come to me," Grauman begged. "I'm afraid he won't do that, Sid," said Boon, "you see, you despise him. You think you're better than he is." "I *don't* despise him," Sid was nearly in tears, "honest, I don't. I don't think I'm one bit better. I swear to God I don't." "It's no use just saying that, Sid. He knows how you feel." "But I swear to God—" "It's no use, Sid. I'm sorry." Poor Grauman! His eyes were turned into his very soul. All his life, he'd despised flies and thought himself better than they were—and now, suddenly, he wanted to repent and be forgiven. But the laws of karma work otherwise. The fly wouldn't come.

The La Verne Seminar began on July 7. It had been organized—to misuse a verb—by the Friends Service Committee. The AFSC had, to be quite frank, given a display of incompetence which, if I didn't know the facts, I shouldn't believe possible. Their job was to choose, from a number of applicants, twenty-six men and women, and to assemble them in Southern California. The cost of this—including telephone calls, telegrams and travelling expenses for the AFSC executives—was *seven hundred dollars*. The railroad fares of the seminar members and the costs of the seminar itself were over and above this figure.

La Verne is a little town in the citrus belt, east of Los Angeles, between the San Gabriel Mountains and the ocean. It lies deep in the orange groves and is sleepy with heat all summer. Midday out of doors is almost unbearable. The population is largely Mexican. The railroad runs through the town, and there are four packing plants for shipping off the oranges, lemons and grapefruit. Toward evening, you can see the peak of Old Baldy, rising ten thousand feet above the valley, through the heat haze.

La Verne has a college, founded by the Dunkards.[1] We had rented their girls' dormitory to hold the seminar in. It was a dirty, old-fashioned building, badly supplied with showers and toilets; but it had a largish basement room which could be used for group meditation and a lounge-hall which would do for our discussions. Somebody tried to add significance to our choice of a site by pointing out that La Verne might well have been named for La

---

[1] A Baptist sect.

Verna, Italy, where St. Francis received the stigmata. I doubt if this theory is correct.

The seminar can be considered roughly as a conference between the Gerald Heard group and the Friends Service Committee group; its subject—the relative merits of the two ways of life, "active" and "contemplative." The rest of the seminar attenders were either undecided semineutrals who wanted a lead, or high-powered individualists who had come, albeit with the best intentions, to impose themselves, their problems and their message on the rest of us.

Gerald's group consisted of the Hunters, Eugene Exman, Lucille Nixon, Felix Greene, Denny and myself. I have already said a good deal about Allan [Hunter]. He was a lean sunburnt man with thin fair hair and a gaunt, deeply lined boyish face. He was vague to the point of idiocy sometimes, hardly ever finishing a sentence and changing the subject twice a minute. Christ was his personal leader—as real to him as Roosevelt. On this point, he and Gerald didn't see eye to eye; and Gerald had to be very tactful to avoid hurting Allan's feelings. Allan was a fearless pacifist and champion of racial minorities, and he often shocked his parishioners to the edge of revolt; but he was personally very popular with them, because he worked so hard and was so friendly and helpful. His home stood wide open to the world like a club room. He looked terribly tired, but I think he was a very happy man—loving his work, and dearly loving Elizabeth and his daughter and son. Denny found his boyish gaiety irritating, but it wasn't facile. Nature delighted him. He was a passionate naturalist. On a country walk, he seemed to see, hear, smell and experience ten times as much as the ordinary person: he was perpetually exclaiming at the beauty of some birdcall, flower or insect.

When Gerald held forth, Allan listened rapt and awestruck; at such moments, he looked about ten years old. Allan's utter humility before Gerald's knowledge was balanced by Gerald's admiration for Allan's innocence. (Gerald was fond of saying to me that we were like people who had been crippled: we could never hope to use our own mutilated limbs again; the best we could achieve in this life would be a fairly good technique with artificial legs, arms and hands.) Allan could never have enough of Gerald's talk. "A little more on that, Gerald, please—" he would say, as though asking for a second helping. His humility extended to everybody: it was genuine but tiresome and could land one in most embarrassing situations. Each of us had to be *the* expert on something. If you had spent a day off the boat at Yokohama, for example, Allan was apt to trick you into addressing a large meeting on the foreign policy of Japan.

Elizabeth Hunter, at first sight, might have seemed a common type of minister's wife—a large, grey-haired, sweet-faced woman with a quiet voice. But her eyes, when you looked into them, were disconcertingly mature, wise and sad. She drew deep experience from her prayer life: Gerald thought she was a natural contemplative. She spoke little unless questioned and her answers were well considered. Spiritually, she was the most adult member of the group, Gerald not excepted.

Eugene Exman was Gerald's publisher; the head of the religious department at Harper Brothers. He was a short, pale, fair-haired man whom one could easily imagine in a monk's robe with tonsure and rosary. His serious plumpish white face with the rimless glasses might, superficially, have appeared merely goody-goody—he had something of Disney's Three Little Pigs—but his eyes were mature and calmly alert, like Elizabeth's. Also, there was a suggestion of worldly-wise humor; he was, as they say, nobody's fool. In the course of his business life he had met and sized up plenty of cranks, lunatics and crooks; and his approval was worth having. He had always been devout. Devotion came easily to him, and this made him seem unctuous to those, like Denny, whose stomachs were sensitive. At La Verne, Eugene told us, he experienced, for the first time, "aridities" in his prayer. He was much distressed in consequence, but probably learnt a good deal.

Lucille Nixon had been a regular visitor to Arlene Terrace for some time. She was a schoolteacher in Palm Springs. She had the severe, clear-cut face of a nun, but her eyes were not serene, and her heavy muscular body showed much tension. She had spent some time in Germany, where she was psychoanalyzed. She seemed to have a strong will and great driving power: she was ruthless with herself and critical of others. However, she was marvellous with children. When she spoke of her pupils, you sensed her subtle intuition and extraordinary patience. She had probably made a mess of her adult relationships, and so children were, for her, a race apart: for them, her charity had no limits. She was successful in her profession, and had to keep refusing more important and responsible jobs, which would have interfered with her meditations. You felt the prayer faculty in her very strongly.

Felix Greene, my half-German cousin, was a very remarkable man, with a real genius for organization. The blue eyes in his tanned hawk-face blazed with rajasic power. Felix organized everything at La Verne—the sleeping accommodation, the work schedules, the menus, the activities of the hired cook—and he didn't merely give orders, he pitched in and fixed things himself: the plumbing, the electric light, the furniture. There was nothing he wouldn't tackle. He worked, as Gerald put it, with an energy "almost epileptic." Felix had had an important post with the BBC in New York. Then he joined Henwar Rodakiewicz in their film unit, Film Associates. He was now working at the Philadelphia office of the Friends Service Committee. He was a born executive, but erratic, both in public and private life. Again and again, according to Gerald, he had acted emotionally, hysterically, and left his partners or lovers in the lurch. (Years before, there had been something between him and Peggy; and she was now sharply critical and suspicious of his motives—especially since his break with Film Associates, which, I gather, was unpleasant, though I don't know the rights and wrongs of the story.) At that time, Felix was desperate to win Gerald's favor, and Gerald, that old coquette, was cruel but slowly relenting. It was unofficially understood that this seminar was to be the probation period. If Felix made good, he would be admitted to Gerald's circle and to Gerald's center, if and when it materialized. He did, and he was.

Such, with Denny and myself, was the inner ring around Gerald. Not a well-made ring: there was already a dangerous flaw in it. But at least we would all have subscribed to what might be called Gerald's minimum position: the postulation of prayer as the central, coordinating activity of human life. Gerald's maximum position, which he seldom stated openly to any large group, included the complete monastic vow: poverty, chastity, anonymity. Allan, of course, wouldn't have accepted the chastity: he believed firmly in marriage. Gerald made frequent, rather sharp-edged jokes about this. Eugene Exman was married, too—although, according to Gerald who knew all our secrets, he wasn't any longer having relations with his wife. The rest of us—Lucille, Denny, Felix and myself—had all more or less made a mess of our sex lives, and would, on the whole, have been glad to be rid of them, if it could be managed without too much difficulty. As for the anonymity, Gerald, Allan and I were all writers and meant to remain so. I suppose Gerald had some ingenious rationalization to cover this, but I've forgotten what it was. Poverty was the least of our worries: none of us happened to want a big house with a swimming pool. In any case, we all had friends who had them and would shoulder the guilt of ownership, if we ever wished to swim.

Gerald approached the seminar with one quite clear objective: he wanted to see how far he could go along with the Society of

Friends. In his books he had referred to the society as the one hope of spiritual regeneration within the Christian Church, but he had also criticized its complacency, its possessions, its puritanism, its lack of serious interest in the techniques of prayer, its general happy-go-lucky approach to the spiritual life. And Gerald was, of course, entirely opposed to the theory of social service as an end in itself. He would have agreed with Vivekananda in saying that social work is purely symbolic. It helps the doer, spiritually—but its material consequences cannot possibly be foreseen.

As for the Friends, they were interested in Gerald's books and life, if somewhat suspicious of his "oriental" tendency. They certainly wanted to welcome him—at any rate into the outer fold. (And Gerald did, as a matter of fact, join the Wider Quaker Fellowship at this time.) But they all, even the most liberal minded of them, regarded Gerald's monasticism with the liveliest alarm. The Society of Friends, as I was to discover later for myself, is an institution based firmly upon the family and marriage.

Harold Chance, the convener of the seminar, was a very good choice for the job. He officially represented the AFSC. He was small, stocky, muscular, alert, sparkling with American pep, intelligent, sincere. His teeth flashed, his eyeglasses were well polished; he kept his shoes shined and his hair combed. His boyishness had something of the nicer kind of scoutmaster: when you looked at him, you brightened. Nevertheless—and this made him interesting—beneath the brightness and bounce, he was a weary man. For years, he had crisscrossed the country, attending meetings, sitting on committees: he worked in the Peace Section of the Service Committee. And now, evidently, all this activity was beginning to seem stale and fruitless. Harold had come to La Verne in a bona fide mood of enquiry: he really wanted to know if Gerald had anything to offer which could help him. Harold had been raised in California as a boy, and he had spent much of his adolescence riding around the mountains on horseback; alone, sometimes, for weeks on end. He had evolved a kind of nature mysticism, he told us. In middle life, it seemed, this was reasserting itself.

Denver Lindley was a friend of Eugene Exman: he worked on *Collier's Magazine* as an assistant editor, dealing chiefly with popular scientific subjects. Everybody liked him. He was my idea of the classic type of New Englander—tall, handsome, grave, slow-spoken, careful of his words, sedately humorous.

Harold Stone Hull was a minister, a friend of the Hunters. Like

Allan, he was an active member of the Fellowship of Recon-ciliation.[1] He was a rather fussy little man; intellectually a bit under-privileged, but very witty on occasion; decent and sincere.

Rodney and his wife Marian Gale were schoolteachers. Rodney Gale had been a Christian Scientist and his approach to religion demanded carefully de-Christianized language. He was a big man with bad acne scars, very likeable. Marian was rather beautiful. Her face had repose. A younger version of Elizabeth Hunter.

Etta Mae Wallace was a journalist and poetaster from San Diego; a bit messy and arty-crafty, she varnished her fingernails, and used a good deal of makeup. Intense, and apt to sound off on the high notes, but seriously interested in the spiritual life. Denny and I once saw her, through an open window at night, dancing fantastically to the music of a phonograph, all alone. We were lucky to have only one such in our group, and a mild specimen at that.

Ted MacCrea had been a schoolmaster; now he was getting ready to become an Anglican priest. He must have been very attractive as a young man: he still had great physical charm. He was almost the only member of the group who believed primarily in the value of ritual. I went with him a couple of times to mass at a very "spiky" little church in the neighboring town of Ontario. I objected, I remember, because the priest gabbled through the words of the office, and Ted disagreed, saying that this was better and more sincere—if you put in too much "expression," mass was apt to degenerate into a theatrical performance. His point of view was always interesting on such matters, and he made a real contribution to the seminar.

Then we had a bunch of college students—George Little, Margaret Calbeck, Bill Rahill, Harry Farash, Donald Booz and David White. George was from Maine—lean and angular. He had studied European history and wanted to do something about it: he would probably get into politics, later. Margaret was the student-secretary type, very bright, with a dutch bob. Bill had worked on Wall Street, and was slightly suspect, a trifle too diplomatic. He was a nice looking boy with wavy hair and a good figure; somewhat of a male flirt. Harry was a muscular little Jew from the Lower East Side of New York, who exercised with barbells, admired Huxley and went after girls like a stoat. He had worked as a navvy. He took a strictly intellectual-agnostic position, and was bothered by but rather proud of some symbolic visions he'd had while meditating. (Like myself, he'd had a glimpse of the "subtle body.") Donald, the son of a rich father, was a big football player who had dabbled in

[1] The international Christian pacifist organization.

student left-wing politics and was looking for a leader: he might easily end up as a fascist. David White was probably Jewish, rather moist lipped and very nearsighted, unexpectedly athletic and an expert hitchhiker. He was one of the contemplatives, with highly developed spiritual intelligence. He wrote a report on the seminar which was later distributed.

To come next to the big-shot individualists—Pat Lloyd, Cora Belle Hunter, Rachel Davis DuBois. Perhaps this grouping is a little unfair to Pat, because he was on his very best behavior during his stay at La Verne. But he had a big reputation as a conference buster and spiritual prima donna. While in the trenches, during the last war, he had had a vision of Christ which decided him to refuse to kill. He told his commanding officer, who was perplexed: he didn't want to have Pat shot, as a deserter. Finally, they agreed that Pat should continue to take part in every attack, but with his rifle slung on his shoulder. Pat used actually to jump into the German trenches and shake hands with German soldiers. And there were many other stories of the success of his nonviolent tactics. He had once surprised a burglar and persuaded him to give up his gun. Allan Hunter had described all this in his recent book *Secretly Armed*.

Pat was still dark eyed and handsome, in his mincing way, despite his large middle-aged stomach. He moved with the assured, skipping freedom of an artless little girl. He sold books, giving all the proceeds to charity, and was a religious counselor at UCLA,[1] advising the students on their problems. His greatest problem, he told us, was with sex. One of his recent cases was a homosexual who had become a chronic masturbator. Pat told the boy, "Imagine yourself doing it with your best friend." This didn't work. The boy masturbated more frantically than ever. "Tonight," said Pat, "I want you to try something else. Try doing it with Jesus Christ." The boy nearly fainted with horror: "Jesus Christ?!" "Yes," Pat told him, "go ahead." Next day, the boy came back and reported: "Last night, I did—what you said. I fell asleep in His arms."

Pat was the kind of character who would send the average novelist into paroxysms of scorn and hate at this hypocritical, sublimated satyr, whose jaws dripped with honey. But if you were a little less queasy, and could dig down through layers of spiritual marshmallow, you would find someone very different—quite austere, genuinely kind, fearless and deeply understanding. Pat was probably one of the very few Quakers who really had spiritual

[1] University of California at Los Angeles.

discernment coupled with absolutely disinterested goodness. He was still capable of an entirely unselfish heroic act.

Cora Belle Hunter was a healer. She had some method of releasing tensions by taking the weight off different parts of the body, which she called, "Freeing the struggling Christ within you." She had an obscure, phony line of talk, and often, when she had made up her mind to speak, there was no stopping her under half an hour: but she obviously knew something, though she couldn't impart it. She was curiously beautiful, with a beauty that seems characteristic of the southern states—powder-grey hair, a charming slim figure and wide, over-innocent grey eyes.

Rachel Davis DuBois was a Hicksite Quaker: a nice dowdy woman, with frizzy black hair and luscious black eyes which suggested Negro blood. Her specialty was organizing folk festivals, at which members of as many nationalities as possible would assist—each contributing something: a dance, a song, a fairy story, a bit of ritual. Rachel, acting as chairman, would combine all these into a new, synthetic ritual, appropriate to the occasion. You might find yourself beating a tom-tom, dancing a Highland Reel and singing a Buddhist psalm, simultaneously. This helped, no doubt, to produce surface results and moments of warmth resembling the friendliness of drunks. But, as she told about her experiences, very amusingly, one couldn't help feeling how superficial it all was, and how silly. Rachel seemed to be attacking just those racial differences which are valuable and avoiding the actual areas of conflict altogether.

This accounts for everybody except the two who only stayed with us for a very short time—Harold Winchester and Edna Acheson. Harold was a pleasant fattish man who had some kind of a small factory. He was ill-informed but very earnest. He had to leave at the end of a week, for business reasons. No one could quite understand why he had ever been invited.

Edna Acheson was headmistress of a girls' school. She seemed a quiet, mousy academic female who would give no trouble—and she didn't until, about a week after the seminar opened, she went mad.

It was during supper, and I was reading aloud to the group from Vivekananda's *The Real Nature of Man*. Suddenly, Edna Acheson started to interrupt. She was tremendously excited. "Yes, that's it!" she exclaimed: "Don't you see? It's number seven! Don't you understand? It's all hypnotism!" At first, I tried to go on reading—hoping it would calm her; but she only got more and more frantic, and finally she was taken upstairs and induced to lie down in her room. She asked for me: "Christopher is laughter. Make him bring the laughter." I talked to her, but it didn't do any good. She also asked repeatedly for Gerald. She seemed to have him on her mind, and somehow to be frightened of him: he was connected with the "hypnotism." She said she had something very important to tell him. Gerald wouldn't see her. He said it would only excite her, but I think he was also a bit scared: he had met a lot of borderline cases who were "in love" with him and made terrible scenes. Some of the time, she was quite violent, biting and scratching: Denver Lindley and Donald Booz had to hold her down. Then she had lucid moments, and said quietly to those around her, "It's dementia praecox, isn't it? That's what we're fighting." She kept talking about numbers and hypnotism. It was obvious that she'd arrived at La Verne in a state of great distress and tension which, by a tremendous effort, she'd managed to repress until this moment. We all waited around—part of the time we held a silent prayer meeting—until near midnight, when a trained nurse and an ambulance arrived from the hospital to take her away.

Within a few months, Edna Acheson recovered completely. She went back to her job, and often wrote letters to members of the group, seemingly quite friendly and unembarrassed by what had happened. But a lot of us had an uneasy feeling that we'd somehow failed her.

The schedule of the seminar was as follows:

5:00. Get up.   5:30–6:30. Meditation.   7:00. Breakfast.
9:00–10:30. Discussion period.   11:30–12:00. Meditation.
12:30. Lunch.   4:00–5:30. Discussion.   6:00–7:00. Meditation.
7:30. Supper.

The weekends were free, and most people made expeditions to the mountains or the beach. Free, also, were the afternoons, from lunch till four o'clock, aside from our rotating duties as dishwashers, table setters, etc. A few of us often met, at that time, to discuss topics of more limited interest—such as diet, or the problems of the householder—in groups which Gerald, with his flair for official language, called subcommittees. These subcommittees were supposed, in due course, to make a report to the group as a whole, during one of the discussion periods.

The meditation periods were what I most looked forward to, throughout the day. Being in the group, filing into the darkened room, descending into the silence as if into a pool, fitting into your accustomed place in the circle—all this gave me an extraordinary feeling of safety, even of comfort. For the first time, I understood the basic appeal of a monastery. Actually, the degree of concentration possible wasn't as great as in solitary meditation—people coughed and sneezed and shifted—but the low-water mark, on the other hand, wasn't so low. The minimum effort of the group kept you partly afloat. We were all helping each other.

By starting earlier and finishing later, it was quite easy to increase the scheduled two and a half hours to three and a half or four. Gerald, as always, was doing his six. I used to meditate a good deal in my room, when I wanted to be alone.

Over and above the practice of meditation, I learnt, at La Verne, a little of what continuous vigilance ought to mean. To watch, every moment of the day, every word, every action, every thought. Never to loll and lounge. Never to be idle. Never to give way to gossip or anxiety. (All this while, the Nazi armies were pushing deeper and deeper into Russia, and one longed to sneak out to the drugstore and peep at the latest headlines.) To ask the Real Self, at the end of every task, "What do you want me to do next, Sir?" (There is always an answer; usually something distasteful.) To try to annihilate your ego, to let the Real Self walk about in you, using your legs and arms, your brain and your voice. It's fantastically difficult—and yet, what else is life for?

At breakfast and supper, one of us read aloud to the group; in this way we worked through or dipped into *The Practice of the Presence of God*,[1] Kelly's *Testament of Devotion*, Fénelon's *Letters to Women*, Waddell's *Desert Fathers*, Leen's *Progress Through Mental Prayer*, Laubach's *Letters by a Modern Mystic*, the *Theologia Germanica*,[2] and several others. Sometimes, after supper, I read poetry aloud to the group. Denny never came to listen to this. It was too shaming, he said. And it probably was: I used all the theatrical tricks.

Gerald was the unofficial chairman of our discussions, and he managed them wonderfully: I can't imagine anybody doing it as well or better. He was tact itself in checking the overtalkative and encouraging the shy to speak. Also, he was really brilliant at summing-up, in a couple of sentences, the meaning of some rambling speech which nobody else had been able to understand. His own orations were as spellbinding as ever; but Denny and I knew them practically by heart, and so we were hypercritical.

Denny was my great problem at La Verne, and I, no doubt, was

---

[1] *The Practice of the Presence of God: The Best Rule of a Holy Life* by Brother Lawrence (1611–1691), a French Carmelite monk.
[2] Then thought anonymous and attributed since 1955 to Heinrich von Bergen, a fourteenth-century German priest of the Teutonic Order; also see Glossary under Meister Eckhart.

his. Our influence upon each other was disastrous. I think the breakdown of our chastity resolutions had a lot to do with this. As soon as we were alone together, we would begin picking everybody to pieces, from Gerald downwards: Gerald, of course, was our special victim. We made jokes about his well–cared-for beard, parodied his favorite phrases, detected new dishonesties in everything he said. We were really venomous. Denny's attitude, then as later, was, "Well, if they aren't acting up to their principles" (and he always managed to prove to himself that they weren't) "then I needn't act up to mine." I was even more guilty, because I egged Denny on in order to be able to enjoy the contrast of someone even sourer than myself.

Nevertheless, this negative emotion didn't always persist. We had our better days. (The better days are recorded in the diary I shall quote from in a moment: the bad days aren't mentioned, because then I didn't feel like writing at all.) During my lucid intervals, I could look into the future and come to certain decisions. Chiefly, I felt that the contemplative life was not for me—at any rate, not yet. I must do some social work. I told Harold Chance this, and he agreed to give me introductions to the appropriate members of the AFSC in the East. Felix, as the result of his stay at La Verne, had decided to leave his job in Philadelphia and come to be with Gerald in the West. So the score stood at one all, in the Monks versus Quakes game.

Here's my diary, written at the time of the seminar itself. It begins with some "case histories." Quite early in the seminar, we each of us made a personal statement, explaining how we became interested in the problems of the spiritual life. I wish I had reported them more fully. All I have are these "headlines."

Gerald Heard: Educated to believe in humanism backed by machine guns. An efficiency cult. Then the 1914 war, and despair. Discovery of an essential religion in the Society of Friends, the Catholic Church, Buddhism, Vedanta. "He who is within my heart is within the sun." God, not the ego, must be central.

Allan Hunter: I'm the rat that refused to leave the sinking ship. Blind, pig–headed loyalty. In 1918, a revelation: that Christ's way is practicable.

Harold Winchester: Atheism. Social work which became futile, because the trouble was inside myself.

Ted MacCrea: Worked my way through college by preaching. I simply repeated what my father (a minister) had told me. Then teaching for nine years, with "cultural" interests and a feeling of despair. Anglo-Catholic priest recommended confession and a retreat.

Denver Lindley: I was a materialist, and I found myself surprised I wasn't leading a much worse life. The idea of religion came with tremendous impact. Am prejudiced against the Christian church, because I dislike the idea of a personal God.

Denham Fouts: Somebody said (about God), "I have no need of that hypothesis." I have desperate need of God as an hypothesis.

Cora Belle Hunter: Reality abides in that point of interaction between the Personal Mind and the Greater Mind. Relaxation, peace, healing, forgiveness are all one process.

Felix Greene: A wildly swinging pendulum: belief, disbelief, belief. Clubs for the unemployed. Met an old disillusioned philan-thropist who told me that he'd never created any kindness. Little by little, came the intellectual conviction.

Donald Booz: I'm a student in the worst sense of the word. Arrant intellectualism. "What gives us power is our God."

Harold Stone Hull: Like the bugs, I didn't like the light. Took refuge in building a new Jerusalem.

Elizabeth Hunter: The problem of being married to a man who believed in Christ. At first, I felt I was only working for an absentee landlord. Ten years ago, I heard Kagawa, but didn't see how to go on from there.

July 15. Almost every morning, lately, I've woken repeating some line of poetry. Today's was, ". . . . like rats that ravin down their proper bane, a thirsty evil, and when we drink we die."[1]

First watch, sixty-five minutes. Difficulty with worship. As before, I found it helpful to picture the group as skeletons, in X-ray anonymity. Again the feeling, what else should I be doing, if not this? "Whither should I go then from Thy Presence?"

Every instant must be intently observed: one can't be too alert. My annoyance when Felix used the downstair bath; my anxiety when he seemed about to ask to borrow my car. My aversion to Bill Rahill's mannerisms when reading aloud. My vanity displayed in talk with Allan and Eugene Exman, after breakfast, in the park.

Gerald spoke on compassion. The original sin of the animals. (Rodney Gale suggested that "previous sin" would be a better term.) They have sinned *more* than man, because they are living fossils—the bird sacrificed awareness in order to fly, the fish to swim. Awareness comes through the struggle to advance. After terrific efforts, the forebrain develops, the forefinger is opposed to the thumb, things can

[1] Shakespeare, *Measure for Measure*, I: ii.

be picked up, fashioned into tools and used. The failure of the huge and predatory animals; the survival of the small and adaptable. The Tao-te Ching teaches us to be flexible, like water; not unyielding like rock. The little monkey evolved into man. The mammoths didn't. Now, if we fail, no creature can take our place: we are the only unfossilized species. There is no excuse for anything that has life, if it fails. Because the deep will is present even in the protoplasm.

Walked across to the drugstore, ostensibly to buy something, actually to read the headlines. No special news, but I returned tense and restless.

Second watch, fifty-five minutes. Fairly good. Moments of awareness that this search is all that matters; nothing else has any interest. Strong sense of interchange with Denny, who sat next me.

This afternoon, Cora Belle Hunter lectured on her system. The period of the removal of tensions corresponds to purgation. Our bodies are the event in space-time which is the interaction of the cosmic and the individual will. Our tensions are our separateness, i.e. our sins.

Gossip and boastful sex talk with Denny this afternoon spoilt the third watch, thirty-five minutes, dull and scattered. More boasting, this evening, to Denver Lindley, about my knowledge of German. Pushful eagerness to speak when others are talking. Am reading the Tao-te Ching, and *Secretly Armed*.

July 16. Dreams: a movie job with Orson Welles—some kind of wartime film, connected with the Isle of Wight. A lumberyard (in Reykjavik, Iceland). Small boys in sweaters, fighting. One boy is knocked down and killed with a wooden rolling pin, his neck broken, his skull bashed in. A voice in my ear explains: "He's the Totem Seal." A feeling of horror at ritual murder, tied in with the war.

An indignation dream about being kept waiting by Mrs. Chisholm (Hugh's mother) first at Santa Monica, then at Cambridge, England. Vernon wants to stay to lunch, but I insist on leaving, as a protest, which makes him unhappy. A tremendously strong emotional realization that even the least unkindness is intolerable.

Woke repeating: "Follow the deer? follow the Christ, the King— Else, wherefore born?"[1]

First watch, seventy-five minutes, medium poor. Selfishness over window shade in meditation room. It was letting in light, so I shifted my place to avoid it, and somebody else had to sit there instead.

About the spiritual life: If you are learning Chinese, speak nothing but Chinese, even if you know only half a dozen words. The

[1] From Tennyson, *Idylls of the King*, "Gareth and Lynette" (ll. 116–118).

temptation to relapse into "English" (the daily gossip of envy, hatred and vanity) is terribly strong.

I shouldn't have told my dreams to Denny. Shouldn't have suggested I find another K.P. helper—thus calling attention to myself as a volunteer, instead of simply doing the job. Must stop wandering aimlessly about the passages: they lead to the drugstore and the headlines. Ate too much breakfast.

Got in half an hour's meditation this morning, alone. Disturbed at first—it's amazing what a flutter just walking upstairs and talking to people can produce—but good later. Was able to pray on my knees, which I like. Unfortunately someone came in and saw me: which was exactly what my ego had wanted.

Voted for individual statements at discussion, because I wanted to speak my piece. Raised my voice too loud in discussion with David White. Failed in courtesy toward other speakers, and didn't listen carefully enough to their views. Result: Second watch, thirty minutes, greatly disturbed and very poor. But I did get the conception clear which Gerald often speaks of—of looking over the Ego's shoulder while it's jumping about.

Useful to think of that part of my will which wants this way of life as a research worker, fallible but serious minded. The research worker has to share his study with Maggie, his lisping, cute little daughter, Grandfather Chips, his miserly, selfish old parent, and Libido, an immense gorilla who, when aroused, can be really dangerous, but who spends most of his time snarling, or bolting his food, or snoring, or nastily playing with himself. The research worker tries to concentrate, while Maggie dances about, prattling of her exploits, and Grandfather Chips fusses over his money and plans to get more. Sometimes he has to intervene to restrain the gorilla, who is apt to smash up all the furniture, and overturn the workbench with his apparatus. Sometimes, he gets rattled and gives up in despair. But, sooner or later, he must pull himself together and continue his work.

Remember: every word spoken to another human being is spoken in the presence of these four. They all hear it, and make a note of the information, privately planning to use it for their own purposes, when the opportunity offers. Maggie, Chips and Libido are the most ruthless black-mailers: they are entirely without shame or pity. "I'll never leave you," says a lover. "Good," thinks Maggie: "Now I've got him where I want him." A friend tells us he has just landed a well-paid job. "Aha," thinks Grandfather Chips, "in a week or two, I'll touch him for a loan."

Selfishness about swimming spoilt the whole afternoon. Also my rudeness to Bill Rahill, David White, Margaret Calbeck and the rest of the junior group on the subject of confidences. They were having a discussion of their sex problems. Gerald wanted me to take part in it, and be frank. I refused. I'm bored sick of confessions.

Talked too much during discussion period. Third watch, seventy-five minutes, very poor.

July 17. Dream: Returning to London. The houses were smashed, but only the top floors. Thought of John Lehmann, with his top-floor flat in Mecklenburgh Square. Looking from Piccadilly Circus in the direction of Leicester Square there were so many ruins you could see a hill in the distance. Went out to Pembroke Gardens on a bus. Described Los Angeles to the family with great enthusiasm. Tried to get a job through an agent. In the newspaper, an advertisement in fake Elizabethan language for seats in a fighter plane to take part in an air raid. Woke with enormous relief that I'm still here.

First watch, ninety minutes, very poor. Wandering thoughts. Second watch, thirty minutes, poor. Third watch, thirty minutes, at the waterfall on Baldy Camp road—poor, but would probably be good if repeated a few times.

July 18. Detective-story dream, bright and amusing, highly self-satisfied, with touches of sexual vanity.

First watch, ninety minutes, medium poor. Second watch, began well, poor later.

At breakfast, reading from Waddell's *Desert Fathers*. Very moving. But I had to put my oar in. Too much chatter while washing up. Ratlike preoccupation with my comfort. Slight cowardice while swimming at dam—scared of sliding down steep slope into water: covered this by pretending the place was uncomfortable.

Third watch, some moments of compassion, but competitive clock-watching toward the end.

July 19. Beginning of sex dream with B. But this turned into a parting, and I saw B. go off with someone else, without regret. Woke at 4:30. First watch, one hundred twenty minutes, medium poor.

Read headlines at drugstore. Usual pointless despair. Must concentrate every moment on interior life. Avoid daydreaming. This idiotic desire to run upstairs, see what's doing, and run down again, like a chicken without a head.

Weekend disturbance. Many of the others plan to get away and "relax." But the real relaxation would be to stay here and try to calm myself inside.

July 24. Dreams: Ted MacCrea, seen from a courtyard window, is late for mass and in a hurry. He begins to say mass as he runs. I kneel at the window and follow his example. Feelings of sympathy.

At Venice, California. Stormy sea. Going to visit a crippled boy. Then with Morgan Forster to see his mother, who was quite blind. Dr. Upward (Edward's father) also partially blind, came too. Morgan's mother turned into a man. He, too, was a doctor: he had cataract. Dr. Upward examined him and said, "I wish I could do something for you, old chap." This dream, also, had the right feeling.

July 29. Woke remembering the text, "learn ye from me; for I am meek and lowly of heart."[1]

Allan Hunter talked about the methods of his discussion group. During the period of silence, they try to think of each person as having come to seek the truth, not to debate social questions. They study techniques of personal behavior: for instance, how best to keep your temper. And simple applications of nonviolence: Phil Basher making friends with the police dog that scared him.

They turn out the lights and sit on the floor facing the fire, as a focus for the surface attention. No one is looking at my face. Silence. Then extempore prayer, aloud. At least once each day, each person in the group must think of every other in turn—as a fellow seeker working toward the same goal.

"There can never be a psychology of apes. There must be a psychology of each separate animal." [Wolfgang] Koehler.

How big should a group be? No more than five Japanese meet for tea. The Jewish service requires ten. The Buddha limited his group to eighteen. Limited groups for the agape in the early church. "A dinner party," said Samuel Rogers,[2] "must be more than the Graces and less than the Muses." Porters at the Gare du Nord divided into groups of twelve for work organization. Rachel DuBois commented that if you used a larger group you could still get a sense of oneness, provided you had a leader.

The problem of personal relationships. What is one to do with one's antipathies? "I do not like thee, Dr. Fell."[3] A frontal attack is no good. "I said I *will* love that man—and I did—desperately." (*The Gondoliers*.[4]) How to deal with spiritual vampires: the pupil who takes up all your time?

---

[1] Matthew 11. 29 reads, "learn of me; for I am meek and lowly in heart."
[2] English poet (1763–1855).
[3] Thomas Brown, after Martial, *Epigrams*, XXXII.
[4] The Gilbert and Sullivan operetta.

Today I had what has been my most vivid experience at La Verne, so far. I walked out, after lunch, into the little park in front of this building, feeling very much alert and aware. The park was empty in the midday heat, but it seemed crowded—every shrub and tree was an individual presence, a distinct, daring essay in self-expression. The big eucalyptus and the palm stood up like statements, apparently contradictory yet confirming each other. The flowering bush, which at first glance seemed motionless, had its own tiny oscillation in the scarcely perceptible current of rising air. (Allan has taught us to watch for these movements: every plant, he says, has its characteristic swayings and rustlings and agitations.)

And then I thought how, if this Force, which is behind all life, could ever become the consciously controlling factor in myself—if I could ever surrender myself to it completely and fearlessly—then my life would become the most amazing adventure, every moment would be incalculably strange and new, because then everything would be possible, there would be no limitations, no habit patterns—in fact, it wouldn't be my life any more. I should be an instrument, absolutely dedicated, absolutely safe in the worker's hand.

Holding this mood for a while, I jumped into my car and drove toward the mountains along the Camp Baldy road, high into the coolness of the upper timberline: the great pine forest, where the waterfall spills over the precipice. Swam in the pool at Snow Peak Camp. Came down feeling very happy. But the shutter had closed again.

We talked about meditation. Most people, except myself, agreed that they found group meditation more satisfactory than solitary. But Harry Farash thought the group should be smaller. Etta Mae Wallace said she wanted some images to help her comprehend the transcendence of God, his "outsideness." People suggested: an Alpine peak, with the wind driving over the summit, blowing up the snow; a waterfall, in its solitude; the vastness of the spiral nebulae. I told of a technique I've found useful when meditating alone in a room. Mentally remove yourself from the room. Then try to feel the aliveness, the intense awareness which is present in the room even when it is empty. Also, you can picture the deserts of the moon—the craters standing around—the meteorites plumping down noiselessly into the sand—and this Consciousness, the sole, total inhabitant.

Harold Stone Hull, to whose condition this word weaving didn't appeal, asked sarcastically: "When do we stop the motion pictures and start meditating?" Gerald explained the theory of discursive meditation. But, somebody objected, wasn't it all autohypnotism?

"Ah," Gerald retorted with a sly smile, "but whom do you mean by the 'auto'?"

"If you want to find God, go and look for him at the spot where you lost him." Eckhart.

July 30. Discussion on friendship. Allan said, "We're always pelting people with our thoughts." He quoted Boon's description of hearing a bird singing—"And then the bird flew away, without looking back to see if it had been heard." And this from Emerson: "What you are speaks so loudly I can't hear what you say."

July 31. Discussion on Grace. Denny said, "When you become aware of the pattern, that's Grace." Gerald quoted from Ruysbroeck:[1] "Grace is a synthesis of God's love and will, which pours like a mighty torrent through the universe."

August 1. Subcommittee, headed by Denver Lindley, reported on the question of diet. Meat should be omitted from diet because:

a. You can do quite well without it. There are adequate substitutes.
b. A degree of cruelty is involved in its preparation.
c. We should show reverence, as far as possible, to other forms of life.
d. There is some evidence that a nonmeat diet is better for meditation.
e. Without meat, the risks of intestinal infection are reduced.
f. All the saints support vegetarianism.

But, it is very important to find substitute values—milk, eggs and cheese. Milk, even when skimmed, has all the proteins and minerals. Take at least a quart a day, at least one egg a day, and some cheese. Fish might be included. It is lower down the life scale, and much less suffering is involved in killing it. Fats are not necessary. They must be balanced by at least double the quantity of carbohydrates (fruit or sugar). Brown sugar is better than white. There are not many carbohydrates in bread. For cereals, get any kind of grain and grind it in a handmill. Oatmeal has more calcium, for those who find it difficult to take milk. Soya and peanut are good sources of protein. If possible, get whole wheat bread enriched by vitamins. Carrots, onions, tomato, lettuce, beets and potato are the best vegetables. Bulk is very important.

[1] Jan van Ruysbroeck, medieval Flemish monk, theologian and mystic.

August 2. "And what do you get out of all this?" He answered: "A better order in all my living." (Jacopone da Todi.[1])

"Why do we go wrong in our relations with other human beings? Because of a basic inattention." (Royce.[2])

"Every time you destroy a species, you put out one of the eyes God gave you to see the universe." (?)

Felix Greene has a chart of the electromagnetic radiations, prepared by a commercial company. It is drawn to scale, and it is very suggestive because it shows the relatively tiny place occupied by the spectrum—the only wavelengths directly visible to our eyes. So how can we trust the evidence of the senses?

The arrangement is like this:

a. Electric waves.   e. Ultraviolet rays.
b. Radio waves.   f. X rays.
c. Infrared rays. (Heat.)   g. Gamma rays. (Radium.)
d. Visible spectrum.   h. Secondary cosmic rays.

The secondary cosmic rays are so "hard" that they go through us like an express train through fog. Felix quoted cases of X-ray vision occurring, for short periods, in human beings. Not understanding this phenomenon, they usually went crazy.

The electric waves, said Gerald, at the other end of the scale, get huger and slower—"until there is perhaps one vast wave that comprises all time and space." This chart, he added, shows us how consciousness and matter are one.

Other points in Gerald's talks:

Recollection in reputation: stop constantly asking the world for its approval. Resolve: I won't ask the approval of anyone in this matter who hasn't tested it out for himself.

Try to avoid negative emotion. Most newspaper reading, especially in wartime, is crying over spilt milk.

Exultation in the fact of God's existence. Use the collect: "Therefore with angels and archangels—" Begin to lead the rationed life: no more toys, only tools. There isn't any such thing as human nature: we can rise to anything because we can sink to anything. God is the only coordinator. We can judge nobody: life is sailed under a sealed handicap.

I must balance my acts of treason by acts of affirmation. Our ideal should be to accept unlimited liability for all the acts of all our fellow human beings. We are all members one with another. . . .

[1] Italian religious poet, monk and mystic (*c.* 1228–1306).
[2] Josiah Royce (1855–1916), American philosopher and author; he taught pyschology at Harvard in William James's absence.

On August 3, more than half of the group left La Verne for their homes. The ten of us who remained until August 7 decided to try a more intensive schedule, with four whole hours of meditation, including an hour from midnight to one. It is quite easy to take your sleep in two installments, and maybe more refreshing.

There is a lot more I might write about the seminar, but it all boils down to this—it's perpetually amazing to find what a long way even a very little goodwill and good intention will take you. The majority of the group remained, socially speaking, almost strangers to me throughout our stay at La Verne—and yet, when I later met some of them again, I felt a curiously strong bond with them. The only subject we could discuss, the only experience we had in common, was prayer; the most intimate of all.

The seminar left Gerald terribly tired. He hadn't slept much throughout the whole period. I suppose he worried a lot, and lay awake composing his talks. He even left La Verne two days before it was absolutely necessary.

Meanwhile, Denny had received his call to the San Dimas camp at last. We spent a melancholy two weeks buying his ugly trousseau, the stiff blue denim work clothes and the clumsy boots. He left on August 21. I drove him as far as Glendora, where the camp director's wife would come down to fetch him. As we approached the scene of parting, Denny began to talk nostalgically about Paris, and his former loves and triumphs at big society balls. Next morning, I left Los Angeles by strato-liner to visit Wystan in the East.

The flight was very beautiful. Falling asleep in the high cold air, at seventeen thousand feet. The blue of the morning sky, when you looked into it, seemed only a reflection of light upon millions of particles of ether, beyond which gaped the illimitable, bottomless vault of black.

Earl "for whom the belles toil" Carroll[1] was one of the passengers, an elegant death's-head. He rested his eyes with favor on a floppy-haired blonde, and at Albuquerque, where a storm delayed us for four hours, he and his bodyguard took the blonde around the night spots. Carroll left the plane at Chicago, and the blonde, very late out of her bunk, swept down the aisle in her wrap, with a defiant you'd-have-done-the-same-if-you-could expression on her face, and disappeared into what the air line calls "the Charm Room."

Wystan and Chester Kallman were staying near Jamestown,

[1] Producer of *The Earl Carroll Vanities*, a showgirl revue; he co-wrote a play, *Murder at the Vanities*, set in his Sunset Boulevard nightclub and later filmed.

Rhode Island, at the house of Caroline Newton, daughter of the late Edward Newton, the book collector. Caroline was a silly, snobbish, well-read woman with very little taste, often pathetic and always kindhearted. She was in love with Auden. The atmosphere was in the highest degree embarrassing. Wystan and Chester were in a state of great tension, and there were occasional explosions. We had no privacy, except that of our bedrooms. I had to keep going on walks, alternately, with the three others, to discuss the latest developments. Wystan was in a difficult, strained, provocative mood, and kept attacking Gerald and talking theology.

I was glad when we returned to spend the last few days in New York, at the Brooklyn house which Wystan shared with George Davis: an attractive, insanely untidy place where, owing to some freak of plumbing, the water in the toilet was nearly boiling. The weather was overpoweringly hot and sticky. I spent a day in Philadelphia, interviewing Caroline Norment, director of the Cooperative College Workshop, an AFSC hostel for refugees at Haverford: Harold Chance had suggested I might work there, later that fall. Caroline and I liked each other at sight, and I was accepted. In every other respect, my visit to the East had been a dismal failure, but poor Wystan cried when I left for Los Angeles, toward the end of September.

As our plane neared Chicago, one of the passengers noticed a strange glow in the sky ahead of us. She pointed it out to the stewardess, who looked slightly worried, I thought, as she answered reassuringly, "It's probably summer lightning." A few minutes later, however, she went forward to talk to the pilot, and returned with a message that these were the northern lights. The pilot, who had flown this route for ten years, had never seen them before. Soon, they were all around us—luminous, flickering curtains, gigantic and forbidding, hanging earthward in folds of icy green. The plane seemed to shrink, to become tiny and lonely, a droning insect lost in the arctic solitude. That night, the northern lights were seen as far south as Jacksonville, Florida.

In the short time I had to pack and say my goodbyes, I managed a last trip with Vernon. We stopped at a snake pit along the road to Palm Springs and talked to the proprietor. The rattlesnakes were crawling all around him and over his boots. He picked them up and held them in his arms like babies, weaving dumbly and sniffing blunt-nosed towards us across the low wooden barrier. When a snake had been in the pit for twenty-four hours and had gotten accustomed to him, he told us, it would no longer rattle at all. So he kept one in the dark, under a carton, for the benefit of visitors. "Now watch," he said, "I'll show you something." He lifted the carton. The snake began to rattle angrily. The man walked slowly backwards and forwards in front of it, getting nearer and nearer. The snake twisted and feinted with its head, until it had to lean over backwards to avoid the man's boots. "You see?" he said. "It hates to strike if it can avoid it." He told us that baby rattlers are the deadliest right after birth, before they have been fed: they can kill a man. He also declared that the Black Widow spider has only become dangerous since 1930. (This sounds fantastic, but Aldous told me later that the musk plant suddenly lost its perfume during the nineties, all over the world, and has never recovered it.)

That night we spent at a cabin on the Salton Sea and went rowing in the moonlight. Next day, we drove up to Idyllwild and stayed at another cabin, high in the forest on the slopes of San Jacinto. I read Vernon stories from *The Beast with Five Fingers*,[1] sitting before a roaring log fire. Next day we climbed in the mountains. The next, we returned to Hollywood.

I will never forget that trip. I knew that I loved this country more than any other since my boyhood in the Peak District. I didn't care if I never went back to Europe again, never crossed the Mississippi. I had become a Californian.

I also knew that I really cared for Vernon. The bond would always exist. No matter what either of us did, or where we went, we should be, in some way, responsible to each other for the rest of our lives.

On the evening of October 11, I left Los Angeles again, for Philadelphia and the hostel at Haverford. Vernon and the Huxleys came down with me to the Union Depot, but it was Aldous who actually saw me on to the train. "God bless you, Christopher," he said, patting my shoulder with a shy, near-sighted gesture. Coming from him, this so touched me that I nearly burst into tears.

My first impression, as the local electric train took me out of Broad Street Station, Philadelphia, down the Main Line to Haverford, on the morning of October 15, was that all the people in the coach belonged to one of three or four distinctly recognizable families. Maybe this was only the contrast between relatively homogeneous Pennsylvania and the ever-changing polyglot population of Los Angeles—but not altogether, because I noticed the same thing again and again during the months that followed. One of these "families" or physical types my imagination immediately identified as Quaker. The men were tall, bony, big

---

[1] By W. F. Harvey.

shouldered, fair haired and quite nice looking, but somehow fatally "pithed," as though the marrow had been drained from their bones. They had an air of quiet anxiety. They spoke slowly, prudently, selecting their words from a small, odd vocabulary. The women were bright and energetic. They used no makeup, and their white thick skin was dotted with freckles. They had sandy gold hair, dragged back and twisted into a knot. They wore flat heels, cheap sensible dresses, and, in summer, straw hats which obscurely resembled sunbonnets. Everybody was married, with plenty of children, and more to come.

The country through which we were passing couldn't possibly have been less "my sort": it was tame, suburban, pretty, a landscape without secrets, inhabited by people whose every word, thought and action would bear thorough investigation by the FBI. But my spirits didn't sink: they had already reached subzero. I had turned my back on California and my friends. I had made up my mind for anything. Nothing could touch me any more. Haverford Station, when it came, was actually a shade less depressing than Ardmore and Narberth. I telephoned the hostel, spoke to Caroline Norment, and was told that her secretary, Elizabeth Porter, would be down with the car to get me. She arrived five minutes later, a fair-haired girl with a slightly foolish shy smirk and a pale longish face which just missed being beautiful, in the Madonna style. We shook hands, but the clatter of a passing train drowned what we said. "All right," I told her, after it had gone by, "now let's do that over again as a talkie." I have felt ashamed of that Hollywoodish crack ever since.

I didn't get much out of Elizabeth as we drove up from the station. She seemed shy and quiet, but obviously full of submarine currents—the typical secretary of a Dominating Personality.

Caroline Norment strikingly resembled the actress Sara Allgood. She was Maryland Irish, sandy haired, dumpy, homely, with beautiful deep-searching brown eyes. Later she told me that, as a girl, she had been delicate and tubercular; now, it seemed, she had made one of those subsconscious "decisions" to be healthy, and her body had grown out of all shape: it was solid and vital as the trunk of a tree. She moved quickly and alertly, with great decision, and her eye, with its merest flick, detected all that was lacking.

Buck Lane really *was* a lane, with high hedgerows overarched by big trees. Down at the bottom end, it ran into a Negro district, where there were small charming ramshackle houses noisy with dogs and children and Saturday night drunks. Old Railroad Avenue—so-called because the tracks had once run along it—was the Mason-Dixon Line. Above this, the houses were large and grand: the homes of discreetly prosperous Quakers and other esteemed Philadelphian burghers. The Meeting House was there, too. Number 824 belonged to a Mr. Bigelow, one of the proprietors of *The Saturday Evening Post*. The shares in the *Post*, once worth a goldmine, had slumped—and now old Mr. Bigelow, somewhat weak in the head, lived in a little apartment in town with his son. His house, which the AFSC had rented for our hostel, was a biggish, undistinguished mansion, built around the beginning of the century. It still contained quite a lot of valuables—old cabinets and clocks, collector's pieces of china, first editions, etchings by Blampied, Pennell and Muirhead Bone. (Their safety was one of Caroline's most constant sources of anxiety.) Behind the house there was a big lawn separated by a thick hedge from the playground of the community center—and from the "common" which made Haverford look like an English village.

I was introduced to Rachel Garner, the fourth member of our staff, who cooked for the group. Rachel was a big soft girl with strong wholesome legs, who belonged to the Church of the Brethren, and had a raucous upstate Pennsylvania accent. She was older than Elizabeth but much more of a child. She cried for what she wanted and bossed her helpers around the kitchen, getting impatient if they didn't understand her "Dutch" brogue.

I was to sleep at the home of Mr. and Mrs. Yarnall, right around the corner, at 605 Railroad Avenue. Mr. William Yarnall was a little old gentleman, close on eighty, half crippled by arthritis, very pink and clean, with hair cut in a short fringe like a Japanese doll. He shuffled about the house, lowering himself into chairs with exquisite difficulty and skill. All his movements were in weirdly slow motion—reminding me of the growth of plants "speeded up" by the movie camera. For example, he would take a whole morning to hammer three nails into a chair, persisting, with an incredible patience, until they were well and truly driven in. He was amused by his own helplessness, and joked about it. He lived in placid, hourly expectation of death. As I left the house and said, "See you later," he would reply, significantly but without the least melodrama, "I hope so, Ishy."

Mrs. Yarnall was portly, with three chins, a figure like a small sofa, pretty white hair, lively satirical eyes behind pince-nez. I loved them both dearly. But there was little I could do for either of them, except bring them gossip. Sometimes I felt like the parent bird returning to the nest—I couldn't disappoint them; there simply *must* be a worm. "How I wish," I exclaimed one day, "I had some really *awful* piece of scandal to tell you!" They didn't know quite how to take this.

Mrs. Yarnall tended her husband all day long—washing him, dressing him, getting him downstairs, feeding him, getting him back up again. (There was a special lift for raising him out of a chair, without which he was practically immovable—you slipped your forearm under his and gripped him around the biceps.) During the night, he had to be helped out of bed to urinate. She seldom slept for long.

Also staying at the Yarnalls' were two of the group members. (824 Buck Lane hadn't enough rooms for everybody, and several refugees were guests of the neighbors.) Frederick Caro had been a judge in Berlin. He had a beautiful head, not unlike Goethe's, but without Goethe's heaviness and pomposity. His eyes were very light blue; the eyes of a mystic introvert. He spoke English well, carefully choosing his words, and expressing himself with a genuine, touching humility. He worried terribly about his wife and two little girls, who were in occupied Belgium. He seemed the perfect type of liberalistic public servant under the German Republic: a permanently saddened man, the victim of profound philosophical doubts. He told us, half jokingly, that he was supposed to be descended from the famous Rabbi Loew, who made the legendary Golem.[1]

Jacob Picard made a good companion for him. He was a lawyer by profession, a poet by vocation—really talented, I believe—from the region of Lake Constance: hollow cheeked, an aristocratic Jewish Dante. Unlike Caro, he was merciless toward the Nazis. He was skeleton thin, grey haired, spectrally elegant, startlingly funny when he put on a derby hat and clowned for the children. He suffered from a complication of nervous tics. Caroline said that he had once been a great ladies' man. He had a daughter, in England.

I had come to Haverford, I told myself, as a sort of invisible monk: my spiritual life was to be neither seen nor heard. As I had a room to myself, I should be able to meditate without difficulty, at any rate night and morning. There wasn't to be a moment's relaxation on the job. If I got exhausted, I merely had to lie down and go to sleep. Otherwise, constant alertness, every minute of the day. It sounded so simple.

On arrival, as a physical protest against the move from California, I'd developed a violent cold. I took a somewhat masochistic pleasure in ignoring it and going into Philadelphia to assist at a party for refugees organized by some Quaker ladies of the

[1] A human being made of clay and brought to life by the medieval Prague rabbi.

city. All evening long, a self-satisfied martyr, I played musical chairs—which most of the refugees hated as much as I did—handed coffee and cakes, and made polite conversation to several hundred people, most of whom no doubt, I infected.

On days when the refugees seemed particularly tiresome or repulsive, I would play a game with myself. Every one of them, I would say, is the Lord. Let me recognize Him beneath these preposterous disguises. He is Martin Gleisner, the bouncing ex-dancer and *Wandervogel*,[1] perpetually plucking at my sleeve to grab my attention away from the others; he is Mr. Haas, the botanist with the spectacles, the wiglike hair, the disgusting breath; he is rat-toothed Klaus Berger, who habitually tries to dodge his share of the housework. Each one of them has a word for me, a message to be decoded, an intelligence test presented in the form of a tiresome request. Don't let me be deceived. Let me detect significance in all they say and do. I am not teaching them, I am being taught. This isn't a dreary chore, it is a fascinating game.

Meeting on Sunday mornings, I found quite valuable, despite all the talking. And Rufus Jones—the uncrowned Quaker "pope"—was a really good speaker. Of course, his utterances were completely against the Friends' creed of inspiration: they were obviously prepared beforehand, beautifully composed and richly furnished with the biblical and poetic quotations which Rufus seemed able to unwind endlessly from the immense spool of his memory. Despite his great age, he was head and shoulders above anybody else at Meeting, both as an orator and a scholar. The Joneses were very kind to me while I was at Haverford—treating me like an old friend because of our meeting in 1938, on board the *Empress of Asia*, when Auden and I were crossing from Japan.

Before Meeting, from ten to eleven, we had an adult bible class, at which various people spoke. This class was organized by Wroe Alderson, who lived with his wife and three children further down Buck Lane. Wroe was an advertising and marketing expert who worked for the Curtis Publishing Company. He was a stocky broad-shouldered man with short vigorous grey hair, smiling grey eyes, a cauliflower ear (from wrestling at college), a lazy drawling voice and a good-natured mailbox mouth. He read Gerald's books and was the one person in Haverford with whom I could talk quite freely about mystical religion. He was a convinced Quaker—having joined the Society of Friends about five years before—and was therefore regarded with slight suspicion as a newcomer by

---

[1] Literally, "bird of passage"; a member of Heinrich Hoffman's youth group promoting outdoor life, especially hiking and folk culture.

ultraconservative Haverford. He talked a great deal in Meeting, not well.

On Monday evenings, Wroe and I formed the habit of driving over to Pendle Hill (the Quaker training center) to attend Dora Willson's gospel class. Dora Willson was a Swiss lady married to an American Friend. She spoke English with a faint, attractive lisp. She had a thin, grey-eyed, ascetic face and a somewhat angular figure. Sometimes she looked dowdy, sometimes quite beautiful. Wroe, who had a bit of a crush on her, called her jokingly "the Pendle Hill Madonna."

Dora Willson was a pupil of [H. B.] Sharman and used his technique in her classes—leading rather than teaching, referring every problem to the text, insisting that we try to imagine ourselves reading it for the first time, never speaking of "Christ," but always of "Jesus" or "this individual," and demanding our individual opinion, not something we'd read in a book. Bill Rahill, from La Verne, was one of the students, and I soon got to know others. I used to look forward to these Pendle Hill sessions extremely. It was like a weekly visit to the theater or the movies. And, for the first time, very dimly, I caught glimpses of an extraordinary figure moving behind the inaccuracies, contradictions and propaganda of the gospel story.

Meanwhile, the pattern of our daily life at the workshop stabilized itself. We breakfasted at 8:15, washed up the dishes, and had about twenty minutes' silent meeting, at 9:00 or a quarter after. Then some members of the group would go over to Haverford College (only three or four minutes' walk away) and sit in on lectures—most of them were planning to take teaching jobs later, themselves. They were pedagogues of the strict, mid-European kind, and they had much to learn about American teaching methods and American students. The informality shocked them a good deal, at first.

I was giving individual English lessons—five or six a day. I wasn't the only English teacher, but most of the others—volunteers from Bryn Mawr College, Haverford and the neighborhood—were very uncertain about keeping their teaching appointments; and the schedule had to be switched around all the time. The only other teacher who showed up regularly nearly every evening in the week—and this after a hard day of office work—was Leah Cadbury. Leah was a lively spinster in her fifties (about Caroline's age) who had a naughty-harmless way of flirting with her male pupils. At 5:00, the whole group went to the Meeting House, where they had lessons in phonetics under Mr.

Severinghaus, a relative of Henry *Time* and *Life* Luce, and one of the best language teachers I have ever met. This gave me an opportunity of doing my evening sit, before dinner, which was at 6:30.

It wasn't an unpleasant life. According to work hours, it wasn't even exacting—but I found myself curiously tired. The Pennsylvanian fall, which was coming to an end in unbelievable tints of flaring canary-yellow, gold, vermilion and crimson, seemed to sap my vitality. And the job, if conscientiously done, demanded a concentration which was unlike anything I'd ever atttempted before. The lessons were not really lessons, they were psychiatric sessions. You had to give all your time, confidence, faith, courage, to these badly rattled middle-aged people whose lifeline to the homeland had been brutally cut, and whose will to make a new start in the new country was very weak. The giving wasn't confined to lesson times. From the moment I entered the house in the morning until I left it at night, I was open to attack. "Excuse me for disturbing you, Mr. Isherwood." "That's what I'm here for, Herr Seidemann." And then came the problem. If I was lucky, it was just a request to clear up some grammatical point. More likely, however, it would be a discussion of Shakespeare's meaning in *Measure for Measure*; or a letter to be translated; or a legal document to be explained; or a whole short story to be criticized. And out of these conversations came life stories, confessions of fears and inhibitions and failures, and the endless demand for reassurance. (Nearly all the group were agnostics or freethinkers, and they were greatly curious about, and puzzled by, the Quaker philosophy.) To meet this demand consistently was a task worthy of someone infinitely more disciplined than myself. I failed, five days out of six.

These failures had a curiously close relation to the regularity, or otherwise, of my personal life. I was able to check this again and again. If I missed meditating, or telling my beads, I was just that much less efficient next day. Sometimes, I had really bad breaks, when I flew right off the handle and barked at the refugees like a drill sergeant, or said something really inexcusable. ("You put me at a disadvantage," I once told Mr. Berger, who had been dodging the dish washing, "I'm not a storm trooper and this isn't a concentration camp—unfortunately.") Most of the time, I was just in a bad, grumpy mood. Outbursts of temper, signs of impatience, a tendency to dogmatize—these were the symptoms of weakness which my pupils soon learnt to expect. They played up to them and on them with all the impudence and tact of their race.

I write as if I didn't like the refugees. In fact, I was extremely fond of them. And, even considered as a random collection of people, they were absorbingly interesting. I had my favorites, of course; and also my black sheep. The black sheep changed from time to time: a psychologist would have watched with curiosity this shifting focus of resentment in myself.

To begin with the favorites. There was the Amann family— Paul and Dorothy, and their children, Peter and Eva. They were Viennese. Mr. Amann was a little sandy-haired ferrety man with very bad breath, who had worked as a schoolteacher. He was a writer and translator. After Hitler's coming, he had taken his family to settle in France. His wife was a big dark untidy woman, very good-natured and soft. She worked as a dressmaker, and sang Tyrolean folk songs to the accompaniment of a lute. Some of the songs were dirty and very funny: I used to make her repeat them over and over again, until I ached with laughing. Both Peter and Eva were pretty children, although Peter, who was light blond, had a large nose. He was thirteen, Eva about ten.

Then there was the Duncker couple, non-Jews. Dr. Duncker was elderly. He had cataract. It had been operated once, but badly, and now there was nothing to be done for him. It was heartbreaking to see how he struggled to learn English while his eyesight lasted; and how he and his wife corrected each other's mistakes with ferocious, loving irritability. He had taught in the Marxist Workers' School in Berlin. He was a passionate Marxist, but his real hero was the anarchist, Prince Kropotkin.[1] Sometime in the previous year, the Dunckers' adored only son had come to Swarthmore College to take a research job: he was a brilliant scholar. And then, suddenly, without any apparent reason, he had committed suicide.

Hermann and Gretl Eberhart[2] weren't Jews, either. They were a youngish couple who had been in trouble with the Brandenburg Nazis right from their student days, before Hitler came to power, because they were communists. Hermann was very good-looking, in the German intellectual manner, with a high forehead, dark eyes, bad teeth and a very clear incisive voice. He was a trained speaker, with plenty of courage, ideas and drive, a good deal of egotism and vanity, and very theoretical. Gretl was blonde, fair skinned, plumpish, with a good figure. Sometimes she looked rather beautiful. She had lovely sparkling light blue-green eyes.

These two had been right through the war in France. Hermann had joined the British army; Gretl had gone into a concentration

[1] Moscow-born geographer and revolutionary (1842–1921); he renounced his title in 1871.
[2] Not their real names.

camp. When they were at liberty again and nearly penniless, they had lived for a while in Marseille. A Polish Jewess whom they knew had had a baby girl named Jeanette. The child was born crippled, suffering from Little's Disease; her legs were curled up under her body. When the mother discovered this, she went into hysterics and declared that Jeanette was no child of hers, it was impossible that she could have given birth to such a monster. She refused to see Jeanette or have her in the house. It was then that the Eberharts decided to adopt her. The French doctor who examined her assured them that there was no hope—but, as Hermann said, "We might easily have had a child like that, ourselves." They brought Jeanette over to America. A surgeon in New York had operated twice—once cutting through the abdomen to the spine, once cutting the tendons to release the feet. And now Jeanette could stagger along, supported under the armpits, and it was hoped she'd recover entirely. She was a very gay child, but mentally backward—like all children suffering from this disease. Gretl looked after her with enormous patience and a great deal of scientific skill. She had been trained as a teacher of backward children, and had worked with them many times before.

Carl Furtmueller and his wife arrived somewhat later than the others. Carl had been a school inspector in Vienna: in fact, he was Mr. Amann's boss. He was a big, heavy, slow-moving man, white haired already, but still full of vigor. His wife looked like an old woman. She had been terribly sick in a Spanish prison, where the two of them were interned. Caroline told me, soon after their arrival, that the doctor didn't expect Mrs. Furtmueller to live long. She had cancer of the lung. Furtmueller didn't know this.

Ernst Jurkat was another non-Jewish refugee. A pale, fair-haired, bespectacled little shrimp of a man with a big adam's apple, quite young. When you looked at him more closely, you saw that he was muscular and tough. He had bad teeth, no chin, a long nose and immense boyish charm. His grey eyes behind his glasses were courageous and serene. He was an expert on statistics, and had worked in Berlin at a government institute which dealt with trade and economics. When the Nazis took over, Ernst stayed at his job. But at night he went home and printed pamphlets, inciting the nation to revolt against Hitler. The penalty for this kind of illegal work was to be beheaded, facing up toward the axe. Ernst lasted quite a long time—until shortly before the outbreak of war. One day, while he was at his office, his wife called him on the phone and gave him the prearranged signal. The Gestapo were watching his home. Ernst always carried his passport in his pocket, so there was nothing to take with him but his hat. He got out of Berlin by tram, found his way down to the Swiss frontier and dodged over the line in the twilight, when the guards can't see so well to shoot and the searchlights don't help much. The Nazi consulate at Bern hadn't been advised of his escape, and he was able to walk boldly in and get money and permits to go to France. In Paris, he offered his services to the Second Bureau,[1] on condition that they smuggle his wife out of Germany to join him. This the French did. During the war, he had fought in the French army. He was now badly worried about his wife and child, who were still interned in France. The wife was Jewish.

Simon Kaplan was a thin smiling Russian with charming eyes and a shrewd wizened face. He had been assistant to a rabbi, and was an authority on Jewish religious law. Moritz Robinson, a pop-eyed man with a moustache, nervous as a rabbit, had been active in working-class education in Austria. His wife and daughter were in Sweden and were coming out to join him: he felt sure they'd be torpedoed on the way over. He always expected the worst and couldn't sleep without taking dope.

Otto Rosenberg was the best English-speaker in the group, but with the worst accent. He had been a great drinker, and liked to boast of this, which annoyed Caroline. His manners were formal to the verge of parody. I believe he had been a chartered accountant. He was proud of his humor. A specimen: Rosenberg was having an argument with a French Negro, about politics. The Negro told him, "You're the blackest pessimist I have ever met." "And you, my dear Sir," Rosenberg came back at him, "are the blackest optimist."

Betty Schloss had the largest behind in the world. She was a schoolteacher who had lost her husband in the last war. She adored children and animals, but was tactless, gauche and bossy with adults. She was quite a competent biologist. While she was passing through Spain on her way to Lisbon and the USA, someone had slammed the train door on her finger, crushing it to pulp. It had been twenty-four hours without medical attention and had had to be amputated.

Then there was Alfred Seidemann, the philosopher—an extraordinary-looking man, lopsided, with a great melon-head, huge teeth and the saddest eyes I have ever seen. He had been a pupil of Husserl.[2] He and Mr. Caro and I had a number of very interesting religious-philosophical discussions. Seidemann would

---

[1] French intelligence.
[2] Edmund Husserl (1859–1938), German founder of phenomenology.

expound Hegel to us. Certain categories were his special property. Evil, for instance. If anybody mentioned the word, Seidemann would make a gesture of the kind with which old theatergoers recall Sarah Berhardt. "Ah—Evil . . !" Or he would interrupt excitedly: "Excuse me—I have done a great deal of work on this subject. The Problem of Evil . . . Ah, yes . . ."

Josef Luitpold Stern was a poet. *The Poet*, one might say. What a wonderful little prima donna! What fine dark eyes, what coquetry, what Viennese charm! He was so childlike, so archly innocent. "Please? May I speak?" he would ask. He agreed to everything: "Oh, very fine!" He had organized chains of libraries in Vienna, and printed his own poems, distributing them himself, very cheap, in paper booklets, for the workers. He had considerable talent, as far as I could judge, for the Whitmanesque, free-verse style. He also played the violin, not very well, to Elizabeth Porter's piano accompaniment. Like Dr. Duncker, he had cataract, but it would be operable. He never referred to this; just as he refused absolutely to accept help from his son, who was in the U.S. and had a job. He had a great deal of pride.

Jacob Walcher had been active for years in the German Communist Party. He wasn't a Jew, but his "freundin,"[1] Hertha, was a Jewess: she'd been secretary to Rosa Luxemburg. They had lived together a long time, scorning marriage as "bourgeois," and Hertha had only become Mrs. Walcher for form's sake, a year or two ago, when they were getting ready to leave for the U.S. Jacob was a big burly man with dark, sparkling, merry eyes. On the Spanish frontier, the officials were turning back non-Jews into France and the hands of the Gestapo. Jacob, with his life in deadly danger, calmly gave his name, as Jacob *Israel* Walcher, and got let through. Hertha had been at a sanatorium with consumption. She'd been discharged, but had to be very careful and rest up a lot. Jacob waited on her devotedly.

That leaves one or two unmentioned, chiefly because I had less contact with them. Richard Goetz was another Viennese, very intelligent, with Mephistophelean eyebrows, who wrote and delivered lectures in an almost incredibly florid but correct English. He and Rosenberg were great friends, exchanging their bitter coffee-house jokes. John Hannek was sympathetic, but I saw him least of all the group. A tall, bony man, he had the rare reputation of loyalty to his Viennese friends and bravery in coming to their help, although he wasn't himself a Jew. Then there were the Sheldons (that wasn't their real name, but they had Americanized it), a

[1] Friend.

Czechoslovak couple, who had come to the U.S. from Europe, via Ecuador. Mrs. Sheldon was very sexy and attractive, and both Rosenberg and Goetz had hot pants for her. A bitchy ingenue. Karel, her husband, was fattish and stupid looking. They had more money than the others and had brought a lot of clothes with them which they kept changing and displaying with a stupid lack of tact. I often felt irritated by them and was glad when they left. Finally, there was a really neurotic middle-aged Viennese woman named Rita Willfort. She would, no doubt, have made a lot of mischief in the group with her sharp tongue—but, thank goodness, she got a job in Massachusetts and left after a couple of weeks.

Every morning—while I and my pupils ploughed through grammar, correcting exercises, reading aloud from the *Reader's Digest*, or drilling with verbs and consonants ("You're a Yank yourself, yelled Yetta")—Caroline would be sitting in her office with Elizabeth Porter. What did they do? Not very much, said Elizabeth. A few checks were signed, a few letters were dictated, but the main business of the day was gossip. Caroline was an artist at it. No one knew better than she how to make the most trivial interview (the ordering of the dinner, for instance, or a discussion with Caro about getting him some new shoes) into the occasion for solemn generalizations about the universe, sex, time and God, all illustrated by anecdotes of Caroline's life in Baltimore, her work at Antioch College as Dean of Women, or her relief work in Russia and Germany, during the famine and the civil war. She was such a ham, but you had to admire her—even at her most theatrical. The tears poured down her cheeks whenever she spoke of suffering or want. Needless to say, Caroline's act appealed strongly to the "little Maggie" part of me,[1] and I soon began playing up to it. I took to coming into her office and announcing solemnly, "Caroline— I have a concern." And it wasn't long before I was murdering grammar in the best Quaker style: "Caroline, is thee driving to Haverford this morning?" "Does thee know about Mr. Seidemann's extra blankets?" "Does thee mind if I telephone from thy room?"

What did Elizabeth think of her, and of me? Elizabeth was a bit of a marvel. She sat very erect at her desk, took the dictation, listened for the hundredth time to the anecdotes, tapped out the letters—and at five o'clock slipped upstairs to her tiny room and her private life. She collected miniature china figures of animals. She wrote letters. She had girlfriends, and a boyfriend no doubt, in

[1] See diary entry for July 16.

Ohio—where she and Caroline had first met. She giggled with Rachel: they had all sorts of intimate jokes.

Of course, I was quite the little rooster in this hens' barnyard. And that is what makes it so difficult for me to write fairly about Caroline. I get mad when I think how she treated those girls, and I get soft when I remember how extravagantly she flattered me—at any rate, to begin with. ("See if you can't do something with her," Rachel appealed to me once, at a moment of crisis, several months later, "you've got pants on.") But, when all is said, Caroline was a marvellous woman. She worked all day and half the night—chiefly, no doubt, because she wasted so much time—but, at least, she kept going till she dropped.

Like all hysterics, she was everlastingly appealing to the norm. "In a perfectly natural and normal way," "She's so wholesome," "Oh, they were a splendid pair of kids—so straight . . .": such were her favorite expressions. And in this she was a true Quaker. She believed passionately in marriage, that dogma and first article of faith among Friends. Caroline had had two great romances in her life. The first was with a young man to whom she actually got engaged: he died of TB. The second—while she was doing relief work in Germany—was with a fellow worker, the husband of a friend. She had nursed him through a bad illness, and one day, when he was convalescent again, he had come into her office and declared his love. "It wasn't strength," Caroline would tell you very solemnly, "that saved me from going over to him and taking him in my arms. But it was a very hot day, and I had undone some of my clothes. I couldn't move. . . ." It was ridiculous, of course, but it was also painful and disconcerting to hear her talk like this. After such a life of devotion, energy, real insight—was she, well over fifty, only another sex-starved spinster; the kind they make jokes about? Hadn't her career of self-dedication been somehow more its own reward? The refugees, watching Caroline, were not dismayed, however: to them, the spectacle was perfectly comprehensible: an old maid needs a lover. If she had one, she would calm down.

An almost daily caller at the house was Susan Dewees. Susan was a big sandy-haired gaunt woman with a grim Dutch face, who knew all the Haverford answers. She was secretary of the Meeting, but could just as well have been holding down some big executive job. If anybody wanted to know anything—from the time the next bus left for Chester to the name of the man Eliza Fry married—they would ask Susan. Susan took the workshop under her wing as a matter of course. And, as a matter of course, Caroline resented her interference—though, in practice, she relied on Susan a great deal.

Caroline, who was basically inefficient, hysterical, intuitive, was in the awkward position of being ground between the two most methodical, efficient and unemotional women in the district: the other was Hertha Kraus. Hertha was a German Jewess, a Quaker, with whom Caroline had worked on relief projects in Germany, twenty years before. She had come to the U.S. some time back and was now on the staff at Bryn Mawr College, teaching economics. If Susan Dewees could have run a big business corporation, Hertha could have run the United States—as a dictatorship. She was a whale of a girl, with breasts like an Alpine meadow, and a great pouchy purple face surrounded by nondescript hair like sofa stuffing, worn in a sawed-off bob. She talked wheezily and precisely, with a high-class British accent, out of the pit of her stomach, which was about ten thousand feet below. Hertha, as a sideline to her teaching, was placement director to the work-shop—which, being translated out of Quakerese, meant that she was supposed to find the refugees jobs. And she did; you had to admit that. However, her methods were certainly a bit high-handed. She was quite liable to make all arrangements behind Caroline's back—and the first we would hear of them would be when Mr. Schmidt walked into the office and announced he was leaving for Iowa that evening. And then Caroline would hit the ceiling, and the telephone wire between Bryn Mawr and the workshop would soon be glowing dull red, with occasional green flashes.

But Hertha was by no means the biggest thorn in Caroline's flesh. Hertha at least was efficient. The boys and girls at the Quaker headquarters in town, 20 South 12th Street, interfered just as much, and were the laziest, stupidest, most muddleheaded crew you could have feared to find. Two of them used to come out and visit us regularly—Rebecca Timbres and Katherine Hanstein. I quite liked Timbres, who was a trained nurse and had been in Russia with her husband on some project when he died of typhus. She was a big woman with eyeglasses who made herself look like an elephant by unwisely wearing light blue. Hanstein was rather pretty and rather a bitch. Mesdames Timbres and Hanstein used to interview the members of our group for hours on end, taking pocketbooks full of notes, to determine what kind of a job they were most suited for. Hertha didn't waste any time determining; she got the job and rammed the refugee into it, cutting off a foot here and a nose there, to make him fit. So Timbres and Hanstein were popular, while Hertha was disliked, admired and feared.

The objective of the Cooperative College Workshop—and I quote—was not only to improve its clients' knowledge of the English language and American educational technique, but also to help them adjust themselves to the American Way of Life. The A.W. of L. was our specialty, and it meant just exactly what Caroline happened to want it to mean at any given moment. I used to get mad at her about this—especially when the American Way clashed with the British; as for example, over the question of cutting up meat before you eat it—but the strange and disconcerting fact remained that most of our group had practically no table manners, either American, British, German or Chinese. The German-Jewish intellectual (and I'm generalizing from all my experience, not merely that of the workshop) has bad manners for two reasons: at home, he was waited on hand and foot by his womenfolk, while he and his friends discussed philosophy and politics; abroad, or in concentration camps, he learnt to grab whatever he could get. The result was that the people who came to Haverford had to be drilled in the most elementary consideration for each other. We had to make rules that the vegetable dishes must be passed around the table, not snatched back and forth, and that people mustn't make "long arms" for what they wanted. They had even to be told to keep their chins out of the soup.

Caroline made a tactful speech to them one day on the subject, suggesting that these customs were specifically "American," but this defeated its own object, because the refugees took her at her word, and accepted the intended rebuke as an interesting piece of anthropological information. They even wrote letters to their friends, describing the American table etiquette as though it were part of the mores of a South Sea island, complicated, fetishistic and quaint. And, this being their attitude, they naturally regarded it as unimportant. Were they thick skinned? Yes, they were. Also, they were pretty arrogant, down underneath, as every immigrant is. They thought America silly. They were Europeans, representatives of the senior culture. It was quite understandable. I think, too, that they didn't really grasp much of what Caroline told them. She spoke very fast, with an accent which became more and more southern as she warmed up. Oddly enough, after all these years, she hadn't mastered the art of speaking English to foreigners.

We made excursions to schools and colleges in the neighborhood, and were lectured and conducted around and given meals. And, on Sundays, there was "open house" for five o'clock tea. The neighbors came in and talked till we dropped, and the samovar (brought back by Caroline from Russia) had to be filled and refilled. Sunday was always the hardest day. I suffered a lot, personally, from the prevailing Philadelphian Anglophilia: my accent was considered just too cute for anything.

Then, on Friday evenings, there were lectures—on municipal government, civil liberties, and suchlike. The lectures were arranged by a very nice couple named Watson—both teachers at Haverford College—who had four sons, one of them a C.O., another just about to join the army. The lecturers had one thing in common; they didn't know how to lecture. Only the smallest percentage of our group understood one word they were saying. I sat there rigid with boredom and just offered it all up to the Lord. Or furtively wrote letters and offered them up instead.

I haven't yet mentioned Caroline's dog Pete. Pete was a Boston bull: elderly, lame and very scrappy. He had poked out one of his eyes when jumping out of a car into a bush, to attack another dog. Pete and Caroline had a really extraordinary and beautiful relationship. She claimed that he knew a hundred words of English. She spoke to him without gestures, very quietly, and he always seemed to understand. If she told him to, he would run upstairs, or into the office, or into the kitchen. He would climb on to a certain chair, or exchange it for another. When Caroline was talking to Pete, or to children, her whole manner changed. She was very gentle; humble, almost. One felt that she really regarded Pete as an old friend, with affection, and, oddly enough, without sentimentality. Pete's reaction to her treatment was all the more remarkable because, as I say, he was such a violent tempered, hysterical little dog, apt to snap at anybody when excited. Pete always came to the meeting we held after breakfast, and it seemed somehow right that he should be there, although he frequently sneezed and snorted and fidgeted throughout the silence. "He's such a funny little dog," Caroline used to say of him, apologetically.

When I first came to Haverford, I made up my mind to avoid as far as possible making contacts outside the circle of the workshop and the Meeting. My life was going to be quite difficult enough, anyhow, without the distraction of being reminded that I had other tastes and interests. However, Teddy le Boutilliere, who kept the Country Book Shop at Bryn Mawr, heard where I was and called me up; so I had to go and see him. He was an old friend of Fritz Prokosch, and had once entertained Auden after a lecture. He and his friend Jimmy Quail knew the Mortmere part of *Lions and Shadows* almost by heart, and had had private jokes based on it for years. This would have softened any author—and, anyhow, I grew very fond of Teddy, and of Una, his wife, a large, beak-nosed Englishwoman, who drawled, and was funny and kind. They had two small boys, and lived in a beautiful old farmhouse near Phoenixville. The army had established a listening post for planes in the backyard. I visited them often, but always somewhat against my better judgment, because they spent their time trying (successfully) to persuade me that this Quaker stuff didn't suit me at all, and that I should snap out of it and be my age and get drunk.

Here are the chief events of our life at the workshop, that fall:

Sometime in November, we got a Russian housekeeper named Tanya Korbett.[1] She was an art historian by profession, and not at all the right person for the job: she was scared of asking any of the group to do anything, and got into quite a lot of trouble in consequence. Caroline soon turned against her. She had a rather charming face, monkeyish, not pretty. She played the piano fluently, but with a heavy insensitive touch. I think she had spent too much time in German universities. That's never good for Russians. It takes the edge off their intuition, which is their chief asset. The thoroughness of true German scholarship they can never acquire. So they become dogmatic and obtuse—and, if you question their sources of information, annoyed.

Toward the end of November, Mrs. Furtmueller died. Dr. Tatnall, a gaunt red-haired young man who was related to Susan Dewees, had said she would have to be moved to hospital next day, and she was dreading this. That night, he gave her a big shot of morphia. Maybe it was a merciful overdose, and done deliberately. She passed out easily and quietly, sitting up in bed with a book in her lap. Carl found her dead. The shock was terrible, for he had only been told that afternoon that there was any danger. He came out of the room and met Caroline in the passage. She described the scene to me later. "He looked at me with those tragic eyes of his. Then he said, 'Caroline—ich habe solche Angst . . .'[2] I took him in my arms."

We were all very silent at breakfast next morning. Only Jeanette crowed and chuckled. Carl didn't come down. Leah Cadbury volunteered to take him out to lunch, for which we were grateful. Caroline had tidied up everything the night before, and we agreed that the room should be occupied again as soon as possible, before a death atmosphere had had time to form. The cremation was held next day, and a very moving Quaker meeting at which Rufus Jones

[1] Not her real name.
[2] —I am so afraid. . .

spoke, saying exactly the right things. Otto Leichter, Carl's greatest friend, came down for it. Otto's wife was in a concentration camp in Austria. He only got news of her indirectly; she was having a very bad time. He was a stocky little man, with a big head and hurt eyes like a dog's. Somehow, he had made peace with himself and gotten over his hatred. He was one of the best of them all.

At the beginning of December, I took a trip to New York, and saw Berthold Viertel. I got home just as war was declared with Japan. Of course, our group was wildly excited—which surprised me, in a way, because I had seen it coming so long, and anyway I could never relive the days of August and September 1939. Then came news that San Francisco had been bombed: a journalistic rumor. A stout belligerent woman in the Haverford drugstore opined, "Well—I guess we can take it."

Toward Christmas, Rachel Garner's cooking, never spectacular, got worse and worse. It was so bad that Mr. Rosenberg and sometimes Mr. Goetz took to going into Ardmore, to Horn and Hardart's restaurant, for a second lunch. My meals at the workshop were particularly dreary, anyway, because I was vegetarian all this time, and Rachel had no idea of preparing vegetables, much less fish.

Mr. Seidemann developed a stone in the bladder and had to go to hospital to have it removed. When Caroline and I visited him, he talked with the utmost gusto about his operation, and even wanted to show us his penis. His interest in his body as a phenomenon appeared to be entirely nonattached.

Hannek—whose only positive accomplishment was his skill as a chess player (he had once edited a chess magazine in Vienna)—got a Christmas job carrying boxes at the co-op. The Dunckers left, to live with an old lady in Media[, Pennsylvania]. Dr. Duncker resisted this move violently. He wanted to work, he said, and here he was being treated as an old man. It was horribly pathetic.

And then, to balance our tragedies, Mr. Robinson's wife and plump, sloe-eyed daughter Maria arrived from Sweden, perfectly safe. We all joined in the rejoicing. Caroline decided to approve of Mrs. Robinson, who was calm, smiling and efficient: she even described her as "beguiling." But little Robinson, that master pessimist, went right on pessimizing. The day after the family reunion, I found him standing in the hall, looking very glum. "Why, Herr Robinson—what's the matter? All your troubles are over now, surely?" "Ah—" Robinson shook his head, but I could see he was enjoying himself quite a lot, "Now the *real* troubles start."

The Christmas Eve celebrations were really charming. We sang German carols around the tree. Then Mr. Caro appeared at the door, dressed as the ghost of an early German settler, and made a speech, in verse, welcoming the new immigrants to Pennsylvania. It had been composed by Mr. Amann. Peter Amann dressed up as a girl and flirted cutely. And Otto Leichter's two sons, who were with us for the vacation, acted a very funny playlet, which they had written themselves.

Nevertheless, gloom wasn't lacking. Gretl Eberhart told me that Hermann wouldn't come downstairs, he was sick. She was obviously much upset, and finally admitted that, as a matter of fact, he was drunk. He was drunk because he had just discovered something unpleasant. What? Gretl didn't want to say.

Later that night, after the party, Gretl and I walked up and down the lanes in the dark, and it all came out. Hermann had gotten the offer of a job for Gretl and himself, looking after boys' clubs and an infant school at the college settlement on Christian Street, in Philadelphia's Negro district. When he had told her about it, she had begun to cry, and he had realized that she was so upset because she didn't want to leave the workshop: she was in love with someone here. "Someone in the group?" I asked. Gretl shook her head. Then she said, "Do you really mean you didn't know?"

For the moment I was embarrassed, flattered and alarmed; but we soon got used to the situation. This confession altered my relationship with Gretl entirely. I had always liked her, but now we became indecently frank with each other, and thicker than thieves. There was nothing we couldn't discuss. Not only did Gretl tell me all about her marriage with Hermann—it had already gone wrong, as far as she was concerned, in France, though she'd resolved not to show it and to continue living with him—but she took the lid right off the workshop. I was staggered to find how much had been going on right under my nose. Gretl told me that Tanya Korbett was having a very serious affair with Jurkat: they both had a bad conscience about his wife, but were resolved to get a divorce and marry as soon as she'd arrived safely in the U.S. Stern and Elizabeth Porter had been having a romance, and maybe an affair, for ages. Gretl said Caroline was worried about this, though she didn't know the half of it. Leah Cadbury and Carl Furtmueller were also getting very fond of each other: developments might be expected soon. And Gretl thought that Rachel Garner's bad cooking might be due to a love affair, too.

The final touch was put to this Quaker Decameron by Klaus

Berger who'd been away for Christmas and now wrote announcing his marriage to a schoolteacher, an American girl he had met last summer at one of the vacation seminars. She was quite presentable looking, too. Caroline was a bit indignant at not having been told before (I wondered what she'd do if she knew all I knew) but also amused and grudgingly admiring. You had to admit that the little runt had taken care of himself better than any of them. At one stroke, he got a wife, solved his citizenship problems and found someone to support him. He must be a hypnotist—with that face!

On Christmas Day, I got a message from Vernon, just arrived in New York. I took the train there to see him. We got very drunk. Vernon wanted me to live with him again: he seemed curiously unaware of everything that had happened in between. The evening ended in a quarrel. I felt rather disgusted with myself, and returned to Haverford next day.

The New Year's celebrations, also, were a success. They were organized by Carl Furtmueller—which was as much as to say that we needn't any of us be afraid to enjoy ourselves, if he set the example. We all admired him for this. The group was holding together well, now: Mrs. Furtmueller's death and the arrival of the Robinsons had provided the ultra-clay. This was our best period. We never quite achieved it again.

1942

January 1. Drove Hermann and Gretl Eberhart over to lunch at the Stonorovs'. He's an architect who lives in a super-modernistic house beyond Phoenixville, which is absurdly unsuited to its rustic surroundings. Had an argument with a young Quaker who has decided, like so many others, to join the army. His case against pacifism is simply that his parents are pacifists, and that he knows his parents are hypocrites. It makes a lot of sense.

Am embarrassed at being with Hermann and Gretl together. Not because Hermann is mad at me—quite the opposite. According to Gretl, he sentimentally protests that I'm far better than he is, no wonder she loves me, etc. etc. So far, he and I haven't discussed this business.

Tomorrow, partly because of my persuasion, they are going to live in Philadelphia and start work at the Christian Street Settlement.

January 2. Vernon came for the day, from New York. He was in his most negative mood. He'd arranged to stay the night, but later announced that he must be going home after tea, because Haverford was "too depressing." Actually, I think he was mad at me because he'd suggested settling in the village and painting—me to support him, of course—and I'd pointed out that this wouldn't work, unless he was ready to help out at the workshop and make himself generally agreeable. Vernon announced that he wouldn't be able to stand the refugees for twenty-four hours. He certainly didn't see them at their best. And Mr. Haas, who never misses anything for want of trying, asked Vernon to send him several different kinds of seaweed, if and when he returned to California. As Vernon was getting into the train, I said: "Please remember, every minute you spend sulking and groaning, you're adding to the sum of misery and hatred in the world and making life more horrible for everybody—yes, and even prolonging the war." Excellent advice. I must remember it myself.

January 3. With Teddy and Una le Boutilliere to have supper at the Bertrand Russells' farm. It is tucked away in one of the lonely valleys out beyond Paoli, which so much resemble the Derbyshire Peak District, especially in winter.

(Russell, at that time, was working for the eccentric millionaire [Alfred] Barnes, as a kind of tame philosopher. He had to waste his lectures on a small and pretty stupid group of Barnes's friends. Not long after this, they quarrelled, and the Russells went back to England.)

There seemed to be a lot of people living in the house. Bertie himself—that monkey-gland lobster in a woolly, toy-sheep wig; Peter Russell; a son of Bertie's by a former marriage, whose name I forget; one or more small children of Peter's; a daughter, also by a former marriage; a governess; and Julian Huxley, who is over here for a few weeks on some British propaganda mission. Julian looked very tired; quite an old man. He and Bertie were anxious to hear the latest news of Aldous—that was chiefly why I was invited. *Grey Eminence* had alarmed them both. "Did he—I mean—er, that is—do you mean to say he actually, er, really—*prays*?" "And why," asked Bertie, "does Aldous talk about Ultimate Reality? Surely one kind of reality isn't any more or less real than another?" I feebly tried to argue, and fell into a number of traps, while Peter protested that I shouldn't be heckled. We were talking different languages: they spoke theirs with the fluency of natives, I stumbled over mine. We couldn't communicate at all. Seeing this, they relented. "You mean"—Julian was helping me out, now—"that what Aldous is after is actually some kind of psychological adjustment?" "Well, yes," I said, "if you like to put it that way: everything's a psychological adjustment: marriage, for instance, or learning Spanish, or becoming a fascist." But they only nodded indulgently. "A psychological adjustment—" they murmured to each other, no longer giving me their full attention, "Well, in that case, of course, one quite sees—" The formula had been found. The affair was disposed of, pigeonholed. The slight alarm which had flickered in their eyes—the alarm of two weary, disillusioned men sensing a challenge to their way of life—a way which they know isn't very good but which seems infinitely preferable to any sort of change—died down; and they returned to the academic shop, the London gossip and the schoolboy dirty stories which they'd been exchanging throughout dinner.

But, just as some more guests were arriving and the evening was about to become purely social, Julian Huxley got me into a corner by the fireplace and asked abruptly, in a low voice, so as not to be overheard: "And you—you do this thing too?" "Yes," I said, "I do." "And you believe in it? It really helps you?" "I believe it's all that really matters," I told him, and felt ashamed that I had a glass of whisky in my hand. Julian scanned my face—I was touched and almost shocked to see how desperately eager he had become: "You know," he told me, "you look quite different from when I saw you last. It's an extraordinary change."

I like Peter Russell. So do Una and Teddy. No doubt she's terribly tactless and difficult. She hates America and says so. She likes to be called Lady Russell. She is curiously jealous of Bertie's fame, and is apt to interrupt and contradict whenever philosophy is discussed: she knows a lot about it, too. But underneath her disagreeable, aggressive mannerisms, she seems extraordinarily kind and decent. Peggy Rodakiewicz once told me how good she has been with Bertie's grown-up children. It can't be easy to be married to a man forty years or more older than yourself; even though Bertie is so incredibly vigorous, mentally and physically, for his age. And Peter is a very attractive, sexy woman. Teddy says he'd love to go to bed with her. They flirt a lot.

When we opened the door to go, it was like a theatrical transformation—the garden and the hills were deep, luminous blue-white in the darkness, and the night was full of falling snow. Teddy ditched the car a couple of miles down the lane in a drift, and we'd have been there till morning if a neighbor hadn't miraculously appeared, towed us out and helped us put the chains on our wheels. The marvellous beauty of the sharp ruby tail-light, surrounded by a pink halo in the whirling snowstorm. Slept at the le Boutillieres' house.

January 4. Peter and Bertie Russell and the son and daughter picked me up in their car after breakfast. They were driving into Philadelphia, where Bertie was to deliver a lecture, explaining why he supports the war. The son asked me if it was true that I intended to register as a conscientious objector. Peter intervened: "I'm sure you hate talking about it." I assured her that I don't. "Bertie does," she said. I felt very touched.

The red barns in the snow, around Valley Forge.

Mrs. Yarnall's mouth, when I told her I'd had supper with the Russells, contracted to the size of a small o. "I suppose," she said very primly, "that their chief topic of conversation is *companionate marriage?*"

Finished reading *A Winter's Tale*—for the first time in my life. Because Wystan sent me a postcard the other day saying it was "his best."

January 7. To Lael Kelly's house. (The widow of Tom Kelly, who wrote *The Testament of Devotion*.) A meeting of Tom Kelly's group: all Haverford College boys. They are growing up now, and about to leave. They have continued these meetings since his death. I often join them.

> (Tom Kelly was on the staff of Haverford College. Everybody regarded him as the white hope of Quakerdom, the future successor to Rufus Jones. One day, not so very long ago, he fell dead of heart failure while washing the dishes. He seems to have been very outspoken and tactless in his criticism of the orthodox Quakers. Gerald often used to talk about him—managing to insinuate that the Joneses had had him poisoned.)

The leader of the group is Phil MacClellan, a big husky footballer and wrestler. He has a perpetual half-smile, rather conceited. He and his friends are so very certain that Kelly gave them the exclusive lowdown on the spiritual life, and that Rufus Jones is an old dope. We bring books with us, sit silent for quite long spells, then read aloud, discuss a little. I quite enjoy it. Wroe Alderson comes too, sometimes. But he's going to be increasingly busy in Washington: a very important job under Henderson,[1] price fixing. He has a bad conscience about this, and keeps trying to reassure himself by telling us it's purely theoretical work. "That's all very fine," I kid him, "you supply the blueprints, and the horrid practical men put them into operation with tear gas and rubber hoses."

---

[1] Leon Henderson, head of the wartime Office of Price Administration.

January 9. Gretl came out from Philadelphia with Jeanette. Caroline
has arranged that they shall come to us every weekend, so Jeanette can
get the country air. Gretl is in despair over Christian Street. She says
their rooms are miserably small and dirty, no place for a child, and the
nearest park is half an hour's trolley ride away. Also Hermann is acting
up, making scenes, being theatrical and tiresome and tragic. He says
he doesn't understand Gretl. She is false, she's never loved him, etc.
Then he threatens to relieve his feelings in a whorehouse. Go ahead,
says Gretl. He tells her she's heartless.

Stern is living there, too. He manages the bank for the boys' clubs.
The boys' clubs have very fancy names: one of them is called "Golden
Nights." Their favorite game is "Murder": they simply switch out
the lights and have a free-for-all in the dark.

January 10. Much discussion of the new regulations for the
movements of so-called "enemy aliens." Our group violently resents
the title, and no wonder. Ernst Jurkat is particularly bitter. He got
mad at Karel Sheldon. That fat tactless fool had said, "What do *we*
care? We're Czechoslovaks." Ernst asked him what *he'd* ever done
against the Nazis. There was very nearly a fistfight. Many of the others
are lapsing into pessimism. "It's France all over again," they say: "The
next thing will be the concentration camps."

And, in fact, if the District Attorney's rulings are to be literally
applied, our German and Austrian members will be confined to a
ridiculously small area, in which there is no post office, no drugstore,
no movie theater—nothing except the college campus and a
residential district with a golf course. But Caroline is determined to
protest—if necessary to the D.A. in person. On occasions like this she
is at her best and most lovable. She made a speech to the group,
assuring them that there was no reason to get rattled, the regulations
were certain to be modified. "And if," she concluded, "we make
such a mess of bureaucracy in this country, it's because we're not used
to it." She suggested that we shall spend the next day or two exploring
the boundaries of our area. On Monday, she's going into Philadelphia
to explain to the D.A.'s office why we must have more room.

(Caroline was entirely successful. The people in the D.A.'s office
were charming and sympathetic, and immediately lifted nearly all
the restrictions. After this, our group could move freely anywhere
in the Philadelphia area. Only if one of them wanted to go to New
York, he had to get permission—and this was always granted.)

January 14. Rachel Davis DuBois, whom I haven't seen since La
Verne, lectured at the workshop yesterday. This evening she held a

"festival" at the Watsons'. Only three or four of our lot came, including Caro and Martin Gleisner: the rest weren't interested. There was a party from Pendle Hill and another from Sleighton Farms—including a French, a Spanish and a Japanese girl. And there was a very cute Chinese student from Haverford College. Rachel had her friend and assistant with her—a dancer, whose name I forget. We were all asked if we could remember bits of ritual or old customs connected with New Year's and Twelfth Night. Then the dancer mimed them. She was terribly arty. Several of the Jews present were offended because she introduced some of their religious ritual: they thought it blasphemous. Afterwards we danced the Virginia Reel, with Martin Gleisner bossing us around and shaking the floor with his stomping. Rebecca Timbres did a Russian peasant dance which was like one of Disney's comic elephants come to life. The party was quite a lot of fun, but I don't think it proved anything at all, from Rachel DuBois' point of view.

January 16. Philadelphia in mid-January and wartime is a kind of nightmare Manchester, drearier than the grave, and full of naval and military drunks. To Benjamin Britten's concert.[1] Benjy and his friend Peter Pears met me afterwards. They are leaving soon for England, where Benjy has decided to register as a C.O. We all got sadder and sadder and drunker and drunker. Cold drizzling thaw.

January 20. Mr. Kaplan left today, for a teaching job. In the evening we had a meeting of the workshop committee, which included several local Quaker ladies. They discussed Naomi Maiden. (She's the colored woman who does house cleaning for us: she has a twisted arm and naughty bulging eyes. The first time Caroline met her, she said, "*You're* no maiden," and Naomi agreed that she wasn't; she has five or six children.) One of the old Quaker hens piped up, "Is it true that Naomi—drinks?" I said: "Of course Naomi drinks. And from what I've seen of her, she carries her liquor very well—much better than most people." Minor sensation.

January 21. Went to see Teddy le Boutilliere at the bookstore. He told me he's volunteered to go to Libya with the American Field Service. He may be leaving quite soon. He wants me to come too. I'd like to, in a way; but you have to be a citizen.

January 22. With Caroline to the Foreign Service Meeting of the AFSC. Paul Harris spoke very dramatically about the Mennonite

---

[1] The first performance, by Paul Wittgenstein with the Philadelphia Orchestra, of Britten's *Diversions* for piano (left hand) and orchestra.

colonization project in South America. But John Rich (our next-door neighbor) says that the Mennonites are simply making a nuisance of themselves by settling in an area which is practically uninhabitable for white men, and then having to have special equipment rushed to them and airplanes to take their sick back to hospital.

Peter Amann was wrestling with a friend and got pushed through a window, badly cutting his arm. The other boy applied a tourniquet. If he hadn't, the doctor says, Peter would have bled to death in a few minutes.

January 28. We had a kind of commencement celebration at the Meeting House, with speeches by Furtmueller, Jurkat, Mrs. Sheldon, Hannek, Hermann Eberhart, Stern and Amann. Hermann's speech was much the best.

Hermann is still being melodramatic: I can't feel sorry for him because he's so sorry for himself. He's constructed a tragic triangle, in which everybody is in love with somebody else. All that is lacking, as Gretl pointed out, is that I should be in love with Hermann.

Caroline knows. She'd noticed something, after all; and the other day she asked Gretl right out, was it true? Gretl didn't deny it. The awful result is that Caroline has become super motherly with Gretl, and keeps getting her into the office at odd moments for weeping bees, varied with sly hints that, after all, Christopher is only human, and if Gretl really wants him—well, somehow, some day, it can be fixed.

Worse still, Caroline also knows about Carl Furtmueller and Leah Cadbury. They have been to Rufus Jones and told him they want to get married, and Rufus has given his blessing. Caroline is absolutely beside herself. She's horribly jealous—not so much of Leah because of Carl, but of Leah because she's caught a man. The form her jealousy takes is that she's turned herself into an unofficial watchdog over their reputation. The world mustn't know, because the world would misjudge them and be shocked. But the world will know very soon, because Caroline has told so many people, each time as a deadly secret. And then, of course, she'll start "defending" Leah and Carl—particularly Carl. I feel so humiliated for her. Thank God I'm getting away from it all for a while. It's a great pity the workshop can't come to an end with this semester, as originally planned. But we're to have a new lot in, and start again about the middle of February.

January 31. Drove into Philadelphia with several of the group, to see about travel permits. Mr. Amann has a study fellowship at Yale, Peter is going to some friends of Caroline's at Yellow Springs, Ohio, Mrs. Amann and Eva will get hospitality around here. Caro is to go to Pendle Hill for a term as a guest. Gleisner has a job in Philadelphia, teaching dancing: he'll adapt more easily than anybody, in this land of extroverts. Goetz has gone back to his wife in New York: she has a small job and can support him. Haas has been given work with the Philadelphia Museum. Jurkat will work with Wroe Alderson, doing research for a book on marketing which Wroe has to revise. He'll live with them, here. Tanya Korbett has a job somewhere in New England. Picard has been invited to stay on a farm, by a clergyman who likes taking in literary refugees. Mrs. Robinson has a domestic job in the neighborhood, and Mr. Robinson may live in the house with her: he's merely required to play pinochle with her employer. Mr. Rosenberg also goes back to his wife in New York: he has a teaching job waiting for him in the fall. Mrs. Schloss is staying with us: she'll study at Bryn Mawr. So is Mr. Seidemann. The Sheldons have a job at Columbia University. The Walchers are to go to Long Island, with the prospect of a job there.

February 1. Left for New York. Saw Berthold Viertel, who may be going to organize a series of broadcasts to Germany. He seemed well and vigorous; full of projects as ever.

February 2. To stay with Johnny Dickinson, Tony Bower's friend. He is in an apartment in the east sixties, near the park: Tony and he had barely rented it and moved in before Tony was drafted back into the army, because of Pearl Harbor. Johnny is feeling lonely and wanted company. He is a nice, friendly boy, very easy to get along with. His home's in Ontario, California, the little town near La Verne.

Eugene Exman, Denver Lindley and the rest of the New York ex-La Verne members hold a meeting every Monday with others who are interested, at the downtown Quaker Meeting House just off Gramercy Park. We switched off the lights and sat in the dark. In the next room, someone began to sing, in a giggly falsetto. Suddenly the door flew open and the singer frisked into the room. When he saw us, he uttered a scream of embarrassment and fled. It was Hugh Chisholm. I talked to him later. He is working with the Quakers on a projected alternative to compulsory civil defence, for the benefit of C.O.s who don't want to join anti-aircraft units etc.

February 4. Posed for Paul Cadmus, who's making a drawing of me. Although we've only met three or four times, I feel he's an intimate friend: we have so much in common—chiefly our love for Forster, whom Paul has never met. Perhaps Paul should have been a writer; he's far more sensitive and intelligent than his pictures. The sensual pleasure of being drawn or painted: this isn't a question of ordinary vanity: you command, as at no other time, somebody's total attention: every touch of his pencil on the paper is like an exquisite kind of massage. It is intensely intimate and yet impersonal: there are really three people present—the artist, yourself, and yourself as the model. And you find you can talk to the artist in a particularly frank, natural way. The ego doesn't interfere. It is far too busy posing.

February 8. Drove with Johnny Dickinson and Jean Connolly to Camp Upton on Long Island, to visit Tony Bower. A landscape of dwarf conifers and howling, wind-driven mist. It was so cold we had to sit in the cars with the engines running; there was nowhere else to go. We drank wine and whisky out of paper cups, and ate bits of greasy chicken which Jean had brought. Tony was heroically gay, but we could see how he loathes it all: the raw misery of the army, the awful crowded loneliness. Later I wandered off stupidly drunk into the miniature woods to vomit, and was nearly shot by a sentry. It was like a visit to purgatory. The poor windbitten boys, huddled in huge coats, with their red hands and ears.

February 9. With Lincoln Kirstein again to Camp Upton, to take Tony his typewriter. After hunting everywhere, we found him, by the merest chance, in a tent. He was almost shockingly grateful. Like a starving man.

On the way home, we talked about Pete Martinez. He volunteered for the navy and they wouldn't take him, apparently because he's Mexican. Now he has nothing to do until he's drafted. Lincoln wants him to come and work with us at Haverford for a while. Said I thought it was a marvellous idea. Lincoln calls the workshop "Humble Hall."

February 13. Back in Haverford since the tenth. Caroline returned two days ago. Today, Pete Martinez arrived. I'd prepared the staff for him as well as I could. I was very nervous what kind of an impression he'd make but I needn't have been. He charms everybody. Pete acted the perfect little gentleman during the introductions and supper. Later, we ran most of the way to Ardmore—to see Garbo in *Two-Faced Woman*—screaming hysterically with laughter and release from tension. It is wonderful, having him here.

February 14. New arrivals: Mr. and Mrs. Reisner, an elderly ex-lawyer with a shabby little wife who plays the piano beautifully; Mr. Ganzel, who looks rather like Lloyd George, with silver hair and moustache, a teacher and a member of the Wider Quaker Fellowship; Mr. Lippman, a big handsome middle-aged lawyer from Leipzig, who is one of Europe's leading Esperantists; Mr. Buchs, a fiery little Pole who was a schoolmaster at Grenoble and is Frencher than the French; Madame Alguadiche, a great beautiful huge big French-woman, who speaks no other language, and is like a lovely shy cow. They are all Jews, I think.

February 15. In the evening, the whole group went to one of Hertha Kraus's soirees. Pete was wonderful. He talked to everybody, saying exactly the right things, with exquisite politeness, and occasionally winked at me across the room. Life at the workshop, since he arrived, has turned into a kind of private game between us. It is like a parody of itself. Everything that happens seems startlingly funny. I keep fearing he'll leave on the next train, but it all seems to amuse him as much as it does me.

February 16. Pete has started teaching English to the two weakest members, Mrs. Reisner and Madame Alguadiche, whom he dearly loves. At five o'clock, I happened to meet him in the hall and asked him what kind of a day he'd had. "Darling," he exclaimed, for the benefit of several people who were listening, "if you don't kiss me I shall *scream*!" Pete is certainly an unusual figure for Haverford—with his fluttering black eyelashes, flashing white teeth, ballet gestures, and the scarf which he winds around his mouth like a yashmak—but Haverford takes him very well. The Yarnalls are devoted to him. Caroline is still watching him, however: she says guardedly that he's "a graceful kid." Pete doesn't like her. He says she hates him because she recognizes a rival actress.

February 17. Dorothy Bloch arrived: a pretty little Polish Jewess, an economist. She has neat little black velvet shoes and washed-out blonde hair. Speaks excellent English.

February 18. Mrs. Abel arrived: a bedraggled Russian psychoanalyst in the last stages of exhaustion. Caroline had to put her to bed at once.

February 23. The other day, I wrote to the Swami asking should I join the Quakers. When I first came to Haverford I had every intention of doing so. But today he replies and more or less advises me not to:

"You as a follower of Ramakrishna would have full sympathy with the Friends and all other religious orders who are seeking the truth of God. But the question is, will the Friends fully sympathize with you and accept you as a member of their order knowing full well that you belong to Ramakrishna and are an initiated disciple of a Hindu monk?"

This, I now realize, is what I wanted him to answer. I no longer feel I could become a Quaker. Not so much for his reasons as for purely social ones. I can't belong to a religious group which would be shocked by even many comparatively innocent features of my private life—by my novels, by the conversation of my friends, by my literary and artistic tastes. They are admirable but fundamentally stuffy, and a lot of their "plainness" is just provincialism, middle-class prejudice. Pete's being here has made this more obvious than ever. Instinctively, we spend our time trying to shock the Quakes, just because they are so shockable.

Pete now teaches Mrs. Abel, as well as Mesdames Reisner and Alguadiche. "Now girls," he tells them, "you *know* you can do better than that!" Mrs. Abel has disgustingly bad breath: Pete says she has swallowed a dead mouse. We have all kinds of jokes, and our behavior in front of Caroline and the others is getting worse and worse. At table, he will turn to me and say seriously, in a conversational voice: "Remember that time you played Carmen at Cedar Rapids?" "Do I remember!" I play up to him: "Why, wasn't that the night you fell through the big drum?" "Yes, dear," says Pete, "and I have a pretty good idea who it was that pushed me."

The other Sunday, as we were all coming out of the Meeting House, Pete said very loud, pointing to an engraving of Elizabeth Fry, "You know, Chris, I never did like that picture of you. It makes you look so *old*."

Then we have an insane game which began with singing, "Sailing, sailing—over the bounding main." We now have a rule that when either of us interrupts with the word "main" the other has to break off immediately in the middle of whatever he's saying, and change the subject. As soon as we leave the house after supper, we go completely mad. Pete dances down the lane, waving his arms and crying, "Oh, l'Amour, l'Amour!"

February 27. Lunch with Douglas Steere. He's on the staff of Haverford College, and one of Quakerdom's leading philosophers. He's off to California to see Gerald, and visit Trabuco, Gerald's newly established center. Steere's a bit of a wetleg, I think; there's something greasy about him. He acts so monklike, and all the time one knows he's having sex with his wife hard—but somehow not quite hard enough. He's writing an essay on immortality, but refuses to read the reports of the Society for Psychical Research, dismissing them as nonsense.

March 1. Yesterday evening, Pete and I went into Philadelphia and met Lincoln Kirstein, Paul Cadmus and Fidelma (Lincoln's wife, Paul's sister). We all got very drunk. The others went back by a late train to New York: Pete and I spent the night at our favorite haunt, the Camac Baths.

> (It has always seemed to me that there is in fact only one Turkish bath—an enormous subterranean world, a delicious purgatory, a naked democracy in which the only class distinctions are anatomical. And that this underworld merely has a number of different entrances and vestibules in all the cities of the earth. You could enter it in Sydney and emerge from it to find yourself in Jermyn Street.)

When it was time to go home, we found that Pete had lost our locker key, presumably in the pool. We had to leave our money and valuables behind and borrow just enough to ride home breakfastless. As we got out of the train at Haverford Station, dazed and wan, with hangovers to our ankles, we met the Robinsons, who were just getting into it. Mr. Robinson was delighted to see us, for he had some bad news. He shouted something about a "terrible disaster at the workshop," almost inaudibly, above the noise of a passing freight train. Before it had gone by, the Robinsons had had to board *their* train, and were carried away, leaving us bewildered on the platform.

The nightmare atmosphere was only heightened when we got back to the Yarnalls' house. Our latchkeys were in the locker at the Camac Baths, so we had to ring the bell; whereupon a completely strange man opened the door, exclaimed, "No, no—not at home!" in a thick German accent, and tried to slam it in our faces. We had to force our way in. To cap it all, Mr. Yarnall mysteriously told us that Caroline had left a note for me, and then telephoned Mrs. Yarnall not to let me read it—so Mrs. Yarnall had hidden it. We begged him to tell us what had happened, but he shook his head: "You'd better go round to the workshop. Caroline will want to tell you herself."

We ran down the lane to the workshop and found it empty: everybody was out at the Meeting House. But the nature of the "disaster" was sufficiently obvious. A great hole has been burnt in the roof. The Walchers' old room (which they left such a short while ago) has been destroyed almost entirely; there is a hole in Caroline's bedroom ceiling and many of her books have been spoilt by water and debris; the Reisners' room (where Mrs. Furtmueller died) has been slightly damaged; and the firemen have bored holes in the living room ceiling to prevent the weight of water breaking it down.

We hurried to the Meeting House and got there just as everybody was coming out. Caroline embraced me publicly and wept on my shoulder. I shan't even attempt to reproduce her account of the accident: it has only once been equalled in the theater—by Sara Allgood's "Sacred Heart of Jesus" speech.[1] And Caroline's lasted half an hour.

Very briefly—the fire (cause still unexplained) broke out late yesterday afternoon, while Caroline was away, and Elizabeth Porter was alone in the house with a refugee named Ruth Fales. They were both asleep—resting after housework—and might easily have been burnt alive. Some neighbors saw the smoke rising from the roof and called the firemen. The noise of their arrival woke Ruth and Elizabeth. Two rival fire departments answered the call (I think because Buck Lane forms some kind of local boundary line between areas) and a fight developed between them: one department accused the other of turning the hoses on them, and there were blows. This gave the fire additional time to spread.

When Caroline returned, and found we were out, she left me a note to await my return. Then, as it got late, she very considerately decided not to have me upset in the middle of the night, so she telephoned Mrs. Yarnall. I think also she wanted to be quite sure that nobody else should tell me the story and steal her thunder. As for the mysterious man at the Yarnalls', this was a professional violinist named Mr. Philip who has just joined the group. He is very selfish and hates talking English if he can avoid it; and so, as Mrs. Yarnall had gone to Meeting, he was anxious to get rid of us quickly without explanations. He didn't know we lived in the house.

Caroline didn't say anything outright, but there was an atmosphere of reproach because Pete and I were out all night—not on moral grounds, but simply because we didn't happen to be there when the crisis occurred. Actually, I think Caroline herself feels guilty—and for a very queer reason. This is her fifth fire. In two others—both unexplained—one in Russia and one in Yellow Springs—she lost nearly everything she had. She has an absolute obsession about fire, not unnaturally; and spends a lot of time every night emptying ash trays and dousing smouldering coals on the hearth. And, of course,

[1] As "Juno Boyle" in Sean O'Casey's *Juno and the Paycock*; see Glossary under Allgood.

one can't help wondering—does she, in some extraordinary way, *attract* them? Is she even perhaps a kind of schizophrenic pyromaniac?

(This sounds absurd; but the fact remains that, in the next two months, there were two more near fires at the workshop. On one occasion a big carton of wood shavings left by the carpenter was found already in flames; on the other, an electric iron, with the current switched on, was left on the ironing board, and the cloth was burnt and smouldering. Rachel and Elizabeth, who were inclined to share my theory, both swore that Caroline had been ironing, shortly before this happened.)

March 2. The Schindlers have arrived: a big ham actor who used to work with [Max] Reinhardt, and his rather charming but neurotic, spoilt, babyish wife. Also Mr. Oppenheim—a very sympathetic hysterical sissy, who begs everybody to stop him when he gets too excited.

Caroline abounds in emergency regulations to prevent another fire, or the possible collapse of ceilings, due to the damage. Her slogan is: Business hysterically as usual.

The workmen have put a tarpaulin over the hole in the roof. Tonight it broke loose in the wind. Later, rain began, heavily. So I had to sit up nearly all night, watching the buckets in Caroline's bedroom, and emptying them every few minutes. When we were alone together, around midnight, Caroline said suddenly, "I can't help it, Christopher . . . I *know* she just set herself to catch him!" This would have been the beginning of another diatribe against Leah Cadbury if I hadn't managed to persuade her to go off to bed, in one of the other rooms. Toward 3 a.m. the rain got so violent that I could no longer deal with the buckets. I had to wake Caroline, who called Bradford, the colored man who does odd jobs for us. We all mopped and emptied frantically for about an hour. It was like taking part in a very realistic performance of *The Flying Dutchman*:[1] the great sail flapping overhead in the storm, and the spray showering over us. Toward morning, the rain stopped.

March 16. There's no doubt about it: this group is altogether inferior to the last. These new people are just middle-aged, middle-class pension guests: they grumble, they gossip, they dodge their share of work, they are thoroughly selfish and dishonest. Mr. Philip is probably the worst of the lot—and yet I don't dislike him: he's so crafty he makes me laugh. He came here to be made comfortable, to

[1] Wagner's opera.

eat heartily, to take walks, to practice his fiddle. (He plays beautifully. Right now, he's working on the *Kreutzer* Sonata,[1] which gives me so much pleasure that I forgive him everything.) He has already told the Yarnalls that he won't join us at Sunday morning breakfast— obviously because our company bores him. He won't do anything that puts him out. When I suggest English lessons, he either says curtly that he's too busy, or insists on talking German to me throughout the hour. We are all a bit flabbergasted by his nerve, and consequently unable to deal with him.

Of my regular pupils, Mr. Lippman is rude and offhand. He receives me in his room, when I come to teach him, as though I were a client to whom he was doing a favor. He is a humorless prig. He writes immense letters to his teenage son about Zionism. Is opposed to intermarriage between Jews and gentiles, calling it "racial suicide." In his wandering journey from Germany to America he was helped in all sorts of ways by fellow Esperantists: apparently, they are like Masons. Caroline says Lippman is a Don Juan. He disappears into Philadelphia from time to time, rather mysteriously.

Mr. Buchs is very cocky, too. As a representative of Gallic wit, he scorns all Teutons. He pours out his contempt on the Anglo-Saxon hypocrisy of Haverford. According to him, every Quaker should have a mistress: then they wouldn't be so stuffy.

Pete, whose patience with his pupils is a real lesson to me, has found out a great deal about Mrs. Abel. She had a son, nineteen years old, extraordinarily handsome, who was a kind of communist saint. He joined a collective farm in Palestine: it was a terribly tough pioneer life. Then, one day, he was killed by a bomb the Arabs had planted. Mrs. Abel herself is a remarkable woman, and maybe a very good psychoanalyst: she knows a great deal more than the usual Jung stuff. She's a mystic. Has visions, but unfortunately insists on telling them to everybody.

The Reisners, like the Dunckers, had a son who committed suicide. Gretl says it was because he was homosexual. Mrs. Reisner and Mrs. Abel, like two faded flowers, are reopening in the sunshine of Pete's outrageous charm. Psychologically, Pete does more for the group than any of us, simply by being gay and kidding the dreary ones out of their depression and gloom.

March 21. Two days ago, Pete and I moved to the big bedroom upstairs at the Yarnalls', leaving my room for a new arrival today, Mr. Jacoby—a pudgy bibliophile who used to be a district attorney in Berlin. Yesterday I went to bed with a cold, and shall stay here till

[1] By Beethoven.

tomorrow at least. I have never enjoyed being sick so much in my life. Pete spends practically the whole day with me. He dresses up in blankets and clowns around, or he sings Mexican songs, or we tell each other stories. Caroline came up to see me, yesterday. She didn't know what to make of us—particularly of me, because my workshop personality had entirely disappeared. I was another person, whom she'd never met. I couldn't switch off the giggles. In a corner of the room, there is a little colored reproduction of Leonardo's *Last Supper*. Caroline, who is rather nearsighted, asked what it was. "Oh that—" I said: "It's just a little party I gave last New Year's, for a few business friends." Caroline went over to examine it. She was rather shocked, though she tried not to show it.

March 30. Mr. Jacoby is the oiliest man I've ever met. He washes his hands in the air all day long, and ties his legs in knots, sidestepping and bowing. If only these people could realize how *rude* their phony insincere politeness is!

Wroe Alderson lectured on "Competition, Conflict and Cooperation." Goodness, how boring! We moved the furniture out of the living room afterward, so the plasterers can fix the ceiling. Caroline in a tailspin of nerves.

April 1. The Levys arrived: a short fat Berlin physicist, with cropped hair, who suffers from acne; and his wife, a girlish little witch, who plays the violin and thinks she resembles Elisabeth Bergner.[1] Levy entered the United States with introductions from Einstein and Millikan:[2] he seems to be quite a big noise. During the last war, he invented a way of determining the position of an enemy battery by its sound. This is now used, in some form or other, by all the armies of the world.

April 4. Into Philadelphia with Pete. The usual program: lobster, whisky sours, the Camac Baths. (There is always a psychological moment at which I remove the AFSC button from my coat, so as not to be seen wearing it drunk on the streets.) I revolt against these outings more and more and am beastly to Pete in consequence, because I'm mad at myself. Pete is getting pretty sick of Haverford, too. The Quakes just distress his Mexican soul. I get greyer and more Calvinistic by contrast, and all our spontaneous gaiety is disappearing.

April 5. Talked to a group from the Chestnut Hill Meeting about La Verne and prayer. They would have had fits if they could have seen

[1] German actress and film star (1898–1986), settled in England from the 1930s.
[2] Robert Millikan (1868–1953), American Nobel physicist.

me last night, and yet I'm not exactly being hypocritical: as far as I am able, I try to tell the truth about myself and impart information without suggesting that I'm holy. The worst of it is, you can say you're lazy, vain, sensual, full of resentment and hate, and your audience doesn't turn a hair. But if you illustrated these statements by describing your actions, they'd die of horror. And yet the actions are merely symptoms: they're the least part of the trouble.

April 7. Drove over to West Town with Douglas Steere, returned from his trip to California. He is very anxious that Trabuco shan't be in any way a monastic institution. He wants lots of married people around—and children.

(When Steere suggested the children to Gerald, Gerald is supposed to have murmured wanly, "Later . . . later, perhaps . . ." On being asked, after Steere had left, what he'd meant, he explained: "After my death." My informant is Denny, in a letter.)

Steere is a good speaker, and awfully glib about Christ's love, passion, death, etc. But it just doesn't have any teeth in it. One looks at his wife and his job and his nice little house, and says, "Oh yeah?"

April 22. Pete left yesterday. He has gone to stay with his friend Wilson in Washington, as a thorough change of air. (Specimen of Wilson's conversation: "My dear—I was so humiliated I didn't know whether to shit or go blind.") Haverford seems very dull and empty. I miss Pete terribly, and yet I'm curiously relieved that he's gone. Now I can get back into the thick Quaker gloom which I hate but in which I feel strangely at home. I often detest the Quakes and the Jews for being so stuffy and cautious and safe; but I understand them because, at bottom, I'm stuffy and cautious, too. I'm a cautious old auntie who, in her heart of hearts, rather hates being jostled around and disarranged by her lively, rowdy nephews, such as Pete and Denny. That's the truth.

Lunch with Teddy le Boutilliere at his shop. He's getting terribly impatient because the call hasn't yet come for him to sail for Africa, and he's already said goodbye to everybody three times over. He relieves his feelings by violent outbursts against the Quakes and the C.O.s, and by reproaching me "as a writer" for trifling with this nonsense.

(Why do one's friends almost invariably object to whatever kind of life you happen to be leading, on the grounds that it's bad for you as a writer? As if any kind of life, considered as subject matter, could be either better or worse than any other. And as if, too, that strange shrewd little self that determines the pattern of our life didn't know its own business.)

Saw René Blanc-Roos later. He teaches French and Spanish at Haverford College and coaches the wrestling team. We are meeting more and more often. Like Denny, he is sour. It's a relief to suck his sourness like a lemon, after too much sweetness and light. He is small and muscular and quietly furious, with a perpetual frown between the eyebrows, bulging sulky light grey eyes and a French lisp. His mother is French. He injured his spine wrestling and has to wear a brace, which he loathes—along with the Quakes, Haverford, his students and everything "decent." He drinks whisky savagely when the pain in his back gets bad.

René has separated from his wife, Esther: they maintain a queer, teasing relationship. She comes down to visit him every now and then, and they make love violently, after which his back hurts more than ever and they quarrel. Esther is very attractive and intelligent and funny. I met her the other day.

René lives in an apartment at the top of a house built in what Pete calls "Early Frankenstein." It has queer Gothic dormer windows and black eaves like the wings of bats. In the daytime it merely looks shabby; at night it is terrifying, especially by moonlight.

René's attitude to myself is possessive, admiring, bullying. He doesn't make the mistake of supposing that life with the Quakes is necessarily bad for my "art," but he sternly demands that I write something. He fears I shall get out of condition, like one of his wrestlers. He takes an immense interest in everything I do or say, which slightly embarrasses me: I cover this by pretending to think he's unconsciously in love with me—which infuriates him.

We talk a great deal about French literature: especially [Céline's] *Voyage au bout de la nuit*, which René loves and I dislike, and Rimbaud, whom we both love. He reads French beautifully. Over and over again, I get him to recite: 'Si je désire une eau d'Europe, c'est la flache / Noire et froide. . . . etc."[1]

April 26. Walked on the college campus with Gretl. She tells me that, now Tanya Korbett has gone, Jurkat is having an affair, or at any rate a flirtation, with Miss Bloch. We met a white-haired lady and her twelve-year-old son busy destroying the nests of the tent caterpillars on the campus fruit trees. They look like very thick spiders' webs. All

---

[1] From Rimbaud's "Bateau ivre," the penultimate stanza: "If I want a water of Europe, it is the puddle black and cold . . ."

the fruit blossom is out, now. The dogwood and lilac are just beginning, the forsythia is nearly over.

I have swapped rooms with Mr. Philip. He grumbled a great deal about this, but Mr. Yarnall insisted, because if Mr. Philip is on the top floor his playing isn't so audible. Also, Mr. Yarnall wanted me to have the better room: he has taken a violent dislike to Philip and wants to spite him. Mr. Philip is certainly intolerable, noisy and rude, but I always end up finding him rather sympathetic and touching. He turns up the cuffs of his trousers to save them from getting frayed. He economizes with every cent, because his family is paying for him here (actually, we discover, his wife insisted on his leaving Pittsburgh for fear he'd make trouble and lose her her job), and yet he bought candy for Gretl and Elizabeth after a concert the other night, and showed them how to eat ice cream (he knows a "right way" of doing everything) because, as he said, he felt as if they were his daughters.

At our "at home" tea, we were visited by a boy named Bronson Clerk and his wife, both rather charming: they were students at Antioch College in Caroline's time. Bronson's attitude to the C.O. problem is hotheaded and quixotic. He feels it is vitally important that the Japs shouldn't have India, so he wants to go there and help Gandhi with his passive resistance. In this way, he hopes to learn techniques of nonviolence which he can apply in strikes and labor disputes in the U.S. later. Naturally, Bronson is quite well aware that the British, not to mention the State Department, will never give him a passport or a visa to enter India with such intentions. So he and his friends are planning to buy a fishing boat and set forth from some port in New England, sailing clear around the Cape of Good Hope! When I pointed out that this is wartime and they'll almost certainly be stopped by the Coast Guard, he replied gaily that they'll sneak past somehow. Why wouldn't I come with him, he asked accusingly. I said I thought they'd simply fail to leave the country. "And would you," said Bronson very severely, "call that a *failure*?" I think actually that he's bored stiff and dreads the prospect of a C.O. camp. His wife takes the whole idea very calmly. She has a shrewd idea that nothing much is going to happen.

To supper with the Briens. Donald Brien is a boot salesman and a collector of Henry James; his wife, who is comfortable and fat and cute, used to sing in the opera under the name of Louise Lerch. They have a four-year-old son who is terrifically husky and noisy. Mr. Brien told me that narrow-toed shoes are generally worn west of Harrisburg, because a lot of the inhabitants come from Central Europe. He says the shoe trade in general doesn't seem aware of the war; the retailers are still demanding competitive styles. One and a half million pairs of boots are being made for Russia.

Henry James's nephew, who was jailed for agitating at the time of the Sacco and Vanzetti case,[1] has been arrested again today for attacking the President and inciting to sedition. He is an isolationist. He wants to throw out Roosevelt and frame a new constitution on the banks of the Mississippi.

April 28. Caroline is getting worse and worse, as the spring advances and the date of the Cadbury-Furtmueller wedding draws near. She goes around with a look of agony on her face and keeps explaining to all of us that she is nearly distracted worrying what Carl and Leah are going to live on; neither of them has any money. Everybody in Haverford can see that this is nothing but raving sexual jealousy, and yet Caroline doesn't realize it, or won't admit it to herself. Meanwhile Leah, who has plenty of the bitch in her, has had her hair cut short and waved. She looks like hell, but it maddens Caroline, who has responded by announcing publicly that she is going to lose twenty pounds. She tells this at table to Mr. Jacoby, who replies with some gooey Prussian gallantry that had whiskers on it already in 1900. And Caroline smirks. I couldn't be more ashamed if it were my own mother.

Caroline's lectures on the "American Way of Life" have become more and more frequent: they are simply a means of venting her irritation against different members of the group. The prize, so far, is: "This water's so hot that only an American WOMAN could put her hands in it." (I stuck both my hands in at once, and stifled a yell: it was nearly boiling.)

A true story, from one of the other refugee hostels. An American social worker is approached by a German lady, who asks, "Please— where are the classes for Jews?" The American is puzzled, "But we don't have any classes for Jews, what do you mean?" "Oh, but you do! You had them yesterday." "Classes for Jews? You must be mistaken." "Oh, no, I am quite sure of it." "But, Mrs. Gold-schmidt—what an extraordinary idea! Why *should* we have classes for Jews? Surely—I mean—that isn't a thing you have to learn. You *are* Jews, already." Finally, it's explained that Mrs. Goldschmidt was trying to say "glasses for juice."

In heaven, the day after a pogrom. A big party of Jews are expected. St. Peter can't understand why they haven't arrived. They must have gotten lost. Angels are sent out to search. Just outside the

---

[1] The anarchists executed in 1927 for alleged murder in the course of armed robbery; the evidence was slight.

heavenly gates, they notice a door marked "Lectures on Heaven." All the Jews have gone in there, in preference to heaven itself. Our group loves this story. I've been told it a dozen times—which I think shows an admirable capacity for self-criticism! How dearly they love theorizing! I remember, last winter, I was watching a football game on the Haverford campus, with Mr. Caro and Mr. Seidemann. We got into a discussion of Shakespeare. I claimed that the English Shakespeare and the German Shakespeare are two entirely different writers. The German Shakespeare is a philosopher, the English one isn't. Caro and Seidemann protested energetically. We became so absorbed that, when a newcomer among the spectators asked us the score, we hadn't the slightest idea. He stared at us, thinking we must be crazy.

We have just heard that Otto Leichter's wife died in the Austrian concentration camp, two months ago. Caroline left for New York today, to see him and the boys.

April 29. Not far from here is a J.P. who sells marriage licences and calls his house "Wits' End."

Mr. Yarnall frequently sees hands and figures outlined by the folds of the curtains, the clothes hanging in the closet, the shadows cast by the streetlamp. This is really a functioning of his artistic capacity: he used to paint. He isn't exactly afraid of them, but he doesn't altogether like them, either. This evening he detected, amidst the sofa cushions, the face of a one-eyed Negress wearing a white hat and grinning at him. These fancies make Mrs. Yarnall humorously impatient, because she has to keep moving things to dispel them. Mr. Yarnall tells me about them with one eye warily on her, like a little boy naughtily alluding to a subject Nanny has forbidden.

April 30. The twenty-fifth anniversary of the founding of the AFSC. We all went over to Swarthmore, with box suppers. There were to have been movies of the AFSC work in Russia, but nobody had bothered to find out (a) whether the Meeting House could be sufficiently darkened, and (b) whether the projector was strong enough for a full-sized screen. The answer to both these questions was found to be in the negative, so the movies were cancelled. Rufus Jones spoke, and Clarence Pickett, and others. Everybody knew everybody. It was noisy and friendly, with lots to eat—like the poultry yard on a prosperous farm.

May 1. Leah Cadbury, reading Shakespeare with Mr. Schindler the other day, came on a word she wasn't sure how to pronounce, because she'd never heard it spoken. She *thought* it was something like "whurre." Today, however, she came back beaming to Mr. Schindler and announced: "I've made enquiries and I find I was wrong . . . It's 'whore.'"

Rachel Garner has announced definitely that she's going to be married at the beginning of June, to a young minister of her church. Caroline sheds more tears and is reproachful, because she feels Rachel is deserting her before the workshop closes. Caroline is always being "deserted." She now talks a great deal about Otto Leichter, and it's all too apparent what's going on in her mind. But Gretl (who came out today) tells me that Otto already has a girlfriend, quite young and attractive. Gretl also says that Stern and Elizabeth are seeing more and more of each other, and that Stern is beginning to talk about marriage.

May 2. With the group to Valley Forge, to view the notorious dogwood. Caroline gave us a nature lesson, pointing out the tulip poplar, which she says is called "the queen of the American forests," the hickory, the judas.

Edward Newton, the late bibliophile, in one of his books appeals to the reader to visit his grave at the chapel in Valley Forge and whisper the latest prices of rare editions into the ground. Mr. Jacoby announces that he actually did this, today. "But I didn't mention the price that was paid for his First Folio Shakespeare. Mr. Newton would have been so disappointed."

May 3. Carved in the wall of the Meeting House, near my usual seat, is a heart, with the initials R.D.B., J.L.R.

After Meeting, one of the neighbors, Dr. Wilson, introduced me to an elderly gentleman who has the job of inspecting any cargo of birds or animals which arrives at the port of Philadelphia. His last assignment was a thousand monkeys from South Africa. He is very proud of his new harbor permit, issued since the war began, with his photograph and fingerprints. An Ibsen character.

Elizabeth and Ruth, after dark, destroying the nests of tent caterpillars in the big apple tree with a kerosene flare at the end of a long bamboo pole.

May 6. The sweet gum tree in Mrs. Williams's garden. The azaleas in bloom, making a background for the American flag: the clash of reds gives you a strange, almost insane feeling; rajasic.

Caroline's use of the word "difficulty"—to denote sickness. "While in Cuba, she had some subtropical difficulty." Her expressions: "Hot as hinges" (i.e. the hinges of the gates of hell), "Trig" (tidy, shipshape, in order), "A double distilled duck fit" (state of hysterical collapse), "Serving Joseph John's" (serving extra good food which is left over from a big banquet or celebration: this because, when Joseph John Gurney, the brother of Elizabeth Fry, came to the U.S., he was entertained so lavishly that every Quaker household had enough left over to eat for weeks after his visit).

May 8. The neighbors are already "quilting" for Leah and Carl. Before a wedding, quilting parties are organized at the Meeting House, to make a quilt for the bride. Eight to ten ladies can work on a quilt simultaneously. They bring a box lunch and take turns. It is quite a social event.

Remark from a speech made at a ladies' luncheon, quoted by Mrs. Yarnall: "As for old women, you never can tell when they're going to die. They're like stewed owls—kind of tough."

Douglas Steere lectured to us on Quakerism, this evening. Talking about Quakerism and the arts: "Those old Philadelphia Quakers— most of them can't carry a tune in a bag." In 1880, they seriously considered putting Pliny Chase out of Meeting, because he had a piano in his house.

Quaker expressions: "I have a stop in my mind about this." "Friends, I am not easy for this to go forward."

He also spoke about the Quaker theory of meditation: contact with the Inner Light. "The Quakers," said Steere, "have only one dogma: God is available." Of course, the connection between this and Vedanta is obvious. To hear what he'd say, I asked him, "Does a Quaker necessarily have to be a Christian?" Steere looked very sly and mysterious: I think he realized what I was driving at. "Well," he answered, after a moment's hesitation, "perhaps not necessarily. No."

May 9. To stay with John Judkyn and Dallas Pratt at their home, Brandywine Farm, out beyond Paoli. Judkyn is English. His friend is an American doctor. Judkyn interests me because he has become a Quaker without giving up his urban chic, upper-middle-class tastes: he is still the kind of elegant, well-tailored youngish man you meet at New York cocktail parties. The Quakes are puzzled by him, no doubt, and by Pratt, but they accept them because Pratt is a doctor and Judkyn is very efficient at organizing relief work. Nevertheless they don't fit in at all. They are still really outsiders. Socially, Judkyn would only make sense as a Catholic.

Their dining room is decorated with early nineteenth-century French wallpaper, bought for a stiff price at a New York auction: John and Dallas have a standing argument, because Dallas insisted on papering the room with the pineapple frieze upside down. Their court cupboard. Their Crown Derby. Their pseudo-Chinese chairs from the Royal Pavilion at Brighton.

May 10. Went over to Caln, where a small group, mostly young married couples, have started holding meetings in the grounds of the deserted Meeting House: it hasn't been used in years. The place was littered with picnickers' whisky bottles, soiled handkerchiefs, girls' panties. We collected them before sitting down to our outdoor meeting, on rugs, and along the burying-ground wall. A member of the group had died, only a week or so before. One boy made a speech about him. It was very moving; with the atmosphere, somehow, of pioneer America.

May 15. The snowballs are in bloom. Tent caterpillars have stripped two small trees in our garden quite bare; now they are crawling all over the ground. The lane is littered with dry winged seeds, maple keys.

Christopher Sharman, an English Quaker on his way home from working with the Friends Ambulance Unit in China, lectured at the Meeting House. He has fair curly baa-lamb hair and a charming gay silly laugh: just my idea of a real hero. John Rich is organizing an American Friends Unit to go to China, also. I've volunteered.

(This fell through, because John Rich finally said they wanted only doctors or trained automobile mechanics. However, Bill Rahill got accepted, to my enormous disgust, by means of charm and string pulling.)

May 19. Went into Philadelphia with Caroline, to hear paunchy Arthur Dunham read his report on the refugee section of the AFSC. The workshop is to be discontinued; partly for financial reasons, partly because no more refugees will be coming over, partly because Caroline isn't in very good odor at 20 South 12th Street. She, I and the rest of the staff were all complimented off the stage with much flowery jargon. Hertha Kraus, who has made many enemies by her high-handed energy, is also being politely gotten rid of—to write a book. Gosh, they're demure and cunning—these Quakes. Specimen of Dunham social-work jargon: "There is an actual decrease in the migration case load."

When Mr. Seidemann is through drying the dishes after breakfast, he invariably exclaims, "Erledigt die Sache!" And "Das ist der Rest vom Schuetzenfest!"[1]

---

[1] "Case closed!" and "That's what's left of the shooting match!"

May 21. Lunched with Teddy le Boutilliere to say goodbye. He's off to Libya very soon, now.

The peonies are in bloom. We went over to Sleighton Farms for the May Festival. It's a reform school for girls, run on modern lines, without guards or bars, and only mildly dreary. The girls danced folk dances; the Durham Reel, Wind Mill, Fandango, the Hatter, Jarabe Tapatio. By this time, I know half Quakerdom, and am perpetually bowing and grinning and shaking hands, like any curate at a tea party, perspiring with goodwill. When Caroline and I go out together, we are exactly like an old respectable married couple: we never monopolize each other publicly, but now and then we meet in the crowd and exchange critical asides about the other guests. If I were fifteen years older, I should be in serious danger. As it is, I'm told by Rachel that Caroline vowed to see me married before the workshop closed, and is now becoming sadly disappointed.

May 24. Now that the warm weather has come, the ladies at the Meeting House use leaf-shaped fans of cardboard or basketwork. The lady who sits in front of me has a fan with a picture of Frances E. Willard, the nineteenth-century temperance crusader. I asked the Yarnalls about her, and Mrs. Yarnall, sensing my opposition, said very sweetly and almost apologetically, "You see, Chris, in those days the whisky in this country was very bad quality."

May 28. We all went over to Martin's Dam and swam and had lunch under the trees. Helene Wilson had arranged a really charming table decoration—all the paper cups and napkins in shades of green, to blend with the leaves and the shadows. When we were all seated, it was like living in a painting by Renoir.

Peter Amann came back last Monday. He has grown enormously, and turned from a child into a big husky youth, very strong for his age. The other day we were wrestling on the lawn. When I finally threw him, Mr. Jacoby exclaimed, "That's a good omen! England has beaten Austria!" How typical of their mentality that remark is!

May 30. Yesterday, I came up to New York for the night and stayed at the Kirsteins' apartment. Fidelma and Pete Martinez were there: Lincoln is away in South America on a cultural government mission, picture buying mixed with politics. Pete and I got very drunk and had a wonderful time.

Lunch with Vernon. He now plans to go into the Holy Cross Monastery, up the Hudson. Eugene Exman arranged it. I certainly hope he can make a go of it. The Holy Cross people are Anglicans.

They sound quite sensible. They have a psychologist to examine applicants and discourage cranks and freaks. Certainly, Vernon is very unhappy and unsettled in his present state. He could live with his mother, but doesn't get along with her new husband. Two or three times, he has tried to join the Merchant Marine, but there are difficulties—probably of his own making; he forgets to fill out some form, or oversleeps and misses the boat. He talks aggressively about art, and snubs people at parties, but he doesn't do much actual painting. As he says himself, he needs discipline.

June 1. John Rich's birthday party. He is such a timid-looking, pop-eyed little thing, but the rabbit has teeth. Though he's a pacifist, he gets wildly excited at any military success of the Allies, and he shoots and fishes "for sport."

We had a practice blackout. (A lot of people seem to believe that this part of Pennsylvania, with all its war plants, is in real danger of air attack.) I walked down the road. Mr. Severinghaus, who is chief air-raid warden, saw me and called out jocularly, "Don't lose your nerve, Isherwood! Don't stampede!" Then René Blanc-Roos came round for me in his car and we drove back to his apartment. Esther was there, and a man I didn't know. We were introduced to each other in the dark and sat talking for an hour before the blackout was over and the lights could be switched on. I kept trying to guess what he'd look like, from the tones of his voice, which sounded interesting. I was quite wrong. A good situation for a story.

June 11. Mrs. Rich had a long talk with me about her children. She feels she hasn't been a good mother to them. What should she do? Told her to be a good mother.

June 13. Day of the Furtmueller-Cadbury wedding. In the morning, sitting outside on the porch, I heard Caroline say to Mrs. Levy, "Mrs. Levy—that's a thing which it's absolutely impossible to say in America. It just *couldn't*, under any conceivable circumstances, be said." Later, I found that Caroline's dog Pete (whom we often refer to as "Peter Norment") had made a mess under the piano. Mrs. Levy had asked Caroline quite seriously if someone had put it there "to bring luck." This certainly gives you a glimpse of her background. It's a little bit frightening, because it reveals certain basic assumptions she must have about life: something primitive, witchlike. I've had this feeling about Mrs. Levy before. For instance, in her weird way she is an exhibitionist. She'll undress and change her clothes behind the thin screen door while I'm giving Mr. Levy a lesson on the balcony of their room. She must know perfectly well that I can see her. They are queerly dirty, furtive, greedy little animals, both of them. But I don't dislike them. Mr. Levy has a rather sympathetic habit of making very bad puns.

By lunchtime, the house was full of arrivals. Many of last year's group, and some members of an earlier group (before my time) including Mr. Adler, the man who shot the Austrian prime minister Stürgkh, during the last war:[1] he is shock-headed, gentle and serious—not unlike Einstein. Jeanette, as usual, dominated the party. Her walking is getting much better.

The latest bit of gossip among the Haverford ladies is that Leah has Jewish blood: this is supposed to explain her insanity in marrying an elderly penniless refugee.

The wedding was in the Meeting House, shortly after lunch. John Rich and I were the ushers. We had to bring Leah and Carl the little table on which lay the marriage certificate, with blotting paper and pen. Carl announced his intention very slowly and carefully; Leah was very decisive, perhaps a shade defiant. Afterwards, we all signed our names. I wore René's best jacket and white flannel pants.

Our reception at the workshop was planned for five o'clock. I had bought some bottles of wine, and these were smuggled up to the Amanns' room, as we couldn't have any drink downstairs. Chosen friends were asked to come up and partake. There wasn't enough— but Leah and Peter Amann both got high—Leah noticeably so. She danced about among the guests, laughingly wildly and kept sidling up to me and whispering, "Oh, Christopher—I feel so giddy!" However, nobody noticed, except perhaps Rufus Jones, who pardons all. Later, we drove the bridal pair down to Bryn Mawr station: they were to spend the first night in Philadelphia. (I didn't envy them, it was stifling hot.) We arrived very late, and there was much baggage to register through, but Leah was superbly calm. She asked the ticket collector to have the train wait—and it did, for nearly ten minutes. The passengers all hung out of the windows to see what was the matter, and our send-off couldn't have been more public.

June 17. Today, I sent off form 47 to the draft board, applying for 4-E classification as a conscientious objector. When you write these things down for official consumption, they sound horribly priggish and false—because you are presenting yourself as a strictly logical, rational human being with "principles," a "philosophy of life" etc. Whereas I, personally, am much more like a horse which suddenly stops and says, "No. That's going *too* far. From *that* pond I won't drink." I have

[1] Count Carl Stürgkh, assassinated October 21, 1916.

reasons, of course, and a philosophy. I can explain them—quite lucidly, if necessary. But how dry and cold they would be without the personal factor behind them: the simple equation which no draft board could ever understand. Heinz is in the Nazi army. I wouldn't kill Heinz. Therefore I have no right to kill anybody.

Everything else, as far as I'm concerned, is just talk. Perfectly sincere, as far as it goes, but theoretical. Of course, there are a dozen ways in which you can come to the pacifist decision. And I don't doubt that there are many people who honestly arrive at it on general principles: they simply know that it is wrong for them to kill. But I have never been able to grasp any idea except through a person. For me, Vedanta is primarily the Swami and Gerald. I once shocked a communist friend by admitting that I should only understand Marxism if I'd met Marx. Tolstoy really says the same thing in *A Confession*, when he describes the public execution he saw in Paris: "When I saw the head part from the body and how they thumped separately into the box, I understood, not with my mind but with my whole being, that no theory of the reasonableness of our present progress could justify this deed; and that though everybody from the creation of the world had held it to be necessary, on whatever theory, I knew it to be unnecessary and bad; and therefore the arbiter of what is good and evil is not what people say and do, nor is it progress, but it is my heart and I."[1]

June 19. Lunch with Teddy le Boutilliere, who's back here again. The boat in which he was sailing for Africa got torpedoed, and he was in a lifeboat for five days before they were picked up. His feet were badly sunburnt but they're getting better now. He'll sail again soon.

I asked him how he felt when the ship was hit. His only thought was God damn that bastard Stimson[2]—because Stimson made a speech only a day or two previously, declaring that the Atlantic was now free of Nazi U-boats.

The Briens gave a concert at the workshop—he accompanying her on the piano. What truly nice people they are! Brien sang a few songs, too: he later described this as "strange interlude."

June 23. The Levys left yesterday; Jacoby left today. It is amazing that these people, who have been chased from country to country, are still overburdened with baggage. Somebody else always has to carry it. Just as the train was starting, Jacoby's ninth bag burst open, covering

[1] Chapter 3.
[2] Henry L. Stimson (1867–1950), then U.S. Secretary of War.

us with talcum powder and showering the station steps with toilet articles. His flabbiness made me horribly sadistic.

June 24. The Schindlers left. They have been a great trial, recently— especially since their little son Andy arrived. Andy was girlish and affected, and he played upon his mother's hysteria—thoroughly enjoying himself. Whenever he was late for school, Schindler would bellow "An – dree – as! An – dree – as!" until one longed to hit him.

Schindler was a Catholic—he reminded you of this repeatedly (being a very obvious Jew)—and he used his Catholicism quite cynically to help himself to useful introductions. He liked to boast of his "escape" from Germany—when, actually, all that had happened was that he'd had the luck to meet a comparatively decent Nazi official, who'd helped him. He boasted also of having gotten himself the best room in an Italian concentration camp, by flattery and wire-pulling.

They left their room so untidy that Stern, who is helping us get the house tidy, remarked severely: "Such people are not fit for the school of tragedy."

June 25. Went down to the college settlement on Christian Street, for supper with Gretl and Hermann. It was sad and embarrassing, but Hermann wanted it, for some obscure masochistic reasons, and there was no way I could refuse. We drank a good deal, and Hermann got sick, and kept murmuring in a maudlin tone, "Ja, ja—who knows if we shall ever meet again . . ." I got away as early as I could.

June 28. Wystan is staying at Caroline Newton's house at Daylesford. Today he gave a poetry reading to a large party of rich women. Nobody understood a single word; but they were very impressed. Wystan's untidiness and brusqueness impress them. He is never untidier than when he is wearing his best suit. He read in a loud bored indistinct voice, repeatedly looking ahead to see how much further he had to go.

June 30. Medical examinations at the draft board. All these kids seem so utterly helpless, so unprotected. You feel, "Let me go, instead of them." Their nervous little jokes. The old-timer who scares them with his army tales. The boy who's afraid he'll faint when they take his blood. (He didn't.) The young Negro's beautiful body, perfectly dignified, stark naked; nearly everybody else wore undershorts.

I had to wait till last, because, for me as a C.O., this wasn't just a preliminary but the only examination I shall get. They didn't do much beyond establishing the fact that I was alive.

Am writing a potboiler story for *The New Yorker*, called "Take It or Leave It"[1]—chiefly because René demands that I produce *something* before leaving Haverford.

July 1. Drove Gretl and Jeanette over to Mrs. Johnson; the old lady with whom she's to live and work this summer. Hermann is going elsewhere. A parting which was all the more painful because I couldn't help feeling relieved. We could have been real friends if it hadn't been for this business. Perhaps we will be, one day, when she gets over it.

I see René every day, now. In the afternoons, he holds his wrestling class on a mat out on the lawn near the college library. I find him sitting there, sulkily regarding the naked, sweating boys, like a tyrant. "Come on," he growls at them, "for Christ's sake—haven't you any guts left? God, you're getting a belly on you. Stand up, man, for the love of Jesus. Now—now grab him: that's better—"

The college campus has great charm now, at the height of summer. At dusk the air is full of fireflies, circling up, up, to the very tops of the trees. They look so like stars between the branches that you get a shock when they move.

July 4. Vernon came down yesterday, left today. He's still set on the idea of Holy Cross monastery; and they've accepted him. The snag is that his stepfather has gone into the army, and so he may have to work for his mother. And meanwhile, of course, the draft may get him before he can plead exemption as a theological student.

July 6. Last day at Haverford. When it was time to leave the Yarnalls' we shed tears. Mr. Yarnall said, "I'm an old man, Ishy. You were kind to me." But Caroline was so busy packing and fussing that she hardly bothered to go into an act. Lately, there's been a coldness between us: we should have parted earlier. I left Elizabeth faced with the double problem of getting Caroline out of the house (they're driving together back to Ohio) and of saying goodbye to Stern. He went on hoping, I'm afraid, right to the last. But Elizabeth told me, in a curiously intimate conversation we suddenly had yesterday, that she doesn't care for him "in that way." She assured me she didn't realize how seriously he felt about her: but I don't think this was quite sincere.

---

[1] Published in *The New Yorker* in October 1942 and later reprinted in *Exhumations*.

René drove me to Daylesford to say goodbye to Wystan. Then I caught the train at 7:22 from Paoli. I'll be in Chicago in the morning. In spite of leaving behind so many people I'm fond of, I must admit that I'm wildly, indecently happy. My only thought is, I'm going back to the West. Hurrah. Hurrah. . . .

I arrived in Los Angeles four days later, on the morning of July 10. Peggy Rodakiewicz met me at the station: we had arranged that I should live at her house until I heard something definite from the draft board. Being back in Los Angeles dazed me with joy. Everthing seemed delightful: the hideous streets around the Union Depot, the heat, the shabby houses. I picked up my car, which I'd left in a garage on Sunset, and was immediately plunged into the dangerous football game of Los Angeles traffic (Angelenos are among the worst drivers in the world): even this seemed amusing. When we arrived at Peggy's home, up on Alto Cedro, I was nearly overpowered by the luxuriance of the flowers and bushes. Had California always been like this? It seemed ten times more beautiful than ever.

Peggy couldn't have been sweeter, or more thoughtful. She had planned everything in advance, to make me feel at home. I was to sleep in the library, a charming little room with a glass door opening on to the terrace which overlooked the ocean. As she darted about, fixing things, helping me unpack, she told me all the news, questioned me about Haverford, laughed and joked. I think we talked for the rest of the day without stopping for a moment.

The next three days I spent reestablishing contacts. I drove down to the beach and lay in the Solarium. Denny arrived on leave from the San Dimas camp. Tony Bower (now a sergeant, and transferred to a camp near San Diego) came up to visit us. We had lunch with the Huxleys, at the Farmer's Market.

On July 13, my draft board informed me that I'd been classified 4-E. This meant that I'd be sent to CPS camp soon—probably within the next six weeks. While still at Haverford, I'd applied for the Los Prietos camp near Santa Barbara: you were allowed to state your preference. I chose Los Prietos for two reasons. It was run by the Church of the Brethren, not, like San Dimas, by the Quakers; and I was then in a violently anti-Quake mood. Also, remembering La Verne, I wanted to keep away from Denny. Each of us would get along better alone. When I met Denny again, I felt very glad I'd already made the decision: otherwise, I'd certainly have surrendered to the charm of his company and joined him, against my better judgment.

On the whole, Denny seemed to be having a wonderful time at

San Dimas. He made the place sound like a madhouse, a zoo of freaks and cranks. But he liked several of the boys, and I think it reassured him to find he could get along in a group and be accepted and popular. He spent money wildly, on all kinds of luxury equipment—waterproof wristwatches, super-sleeping-bags, fur-lined jackets—for himself and as presents for his friends. His bad back excused him from most of the heavy work, and he got plenty of leave. He looked very well, and grumbled furiously.

Peggy and her daughter Tis left for New York on the 14th, to visit Henwar, who was busy on some documentary film. Next day, I went down to stay with Chris Wood, who had moved from Arlene Terrace to 1 Rockledge Road, Laguna Beach. (The house will be described presently, in an entry from my diary.) Gerald was there, too, and a friend of Chris's, named Paul Sorel.

As Paul Sorel's real name was Carl Dibble, it is hardly surprising that he'd changed it: yet his doing so was characteristic: he was a strange, bogus creature, verging dangerously on paranoia. Very thin, very blond, he had a long smooth face which sometimes looked quite handsome, sometimes hideously ugly. Vanity surrounded him like a perfume—a vanity so exaggerated that it seemed both sinister and ludicrous: a smile of total self-satisfaction seldom left his large, expressive lips. What was behind this smiling, absurd mask? A peeping demon of mischief—ruthless, nihilistic, cowardly, cruel. Yes, but also a desperately unhappy, frightened, sensitive little boy.

Paul was undoubtedly a borderline case. One day, he might easily go mad. Perhaps he was even capable of murder. On the surface, he was usually friendly, a bit patronizing, a chatterbox, rather a bore. Occasionally, he had bursts of utterly irresponsible rage, when he screamed and threatened. Then he would fast, for several days at a time; or pray and go to mass.

He was a genius, he told us. Actually, he had a considerable but undisciplined talent for painting and drawing, and a flair for writing verse. He also played the piano, not well. All these occupations were highly compulsionistic. He'd announce, for example, that he was going to paint a picture a day for fourteen days, working only two hours on each. And he'd do it.

Paul and Chris had a very curious relationship. They had known each other a long while, and Chris had somehow come to feel himself responsible for Paul. Chris gave him money—far too much—and let him go to New York and stay in expensive hotels, where he ran up bills which had to be paid by telegram. He was fond of Paul, but in a strangely impersonal way. He saw all Paul's weaknesses and could talk about them with the intelligence of a good psychologist. And yet, when Paul made his outrageous demands for money Chris would give way to them in a way which seemed feeble and cowardly. He depended enormously on Paul's companionship; and at the same time he loved him, quite disinterestedly, without illusions, like an elder brother. Paul also, I'm sure, was fond of Chris. Part of him was enormously grateful for Chris's affection. Part of him resented this gratitude, and was set to exploit and blackmail Chris's feelings to the utmost limit. He'd be as sweet as honey one minute; sneering and brutal the next. Chris suffered terribly, and covered it by making nervous jokes.

Peggy said that Chris's friendship with Paul was one of the most startling instances of karma she had ever known. For years, Chris had been charming but selfish—never really committing himself to anybody, always keeping a little wall around his privacy and his possessions. So now he had to meet someone like Paul who would break the wall down and ride roughshod over his life. This didn't prevent Peggy from disapproving violently of the whole relation-ship. She detested Paul, in her aristocratic way, for being middle-class, vulgarly ostentatious, essentially small and cheap. "It's such an *inferior* little tragedy," she'd say. Not long after this, Paul made their relations even worse by insulting Peggy personally: he went to see her and made a florid, half-mocking declaration of love. Most people would have found this behavior merely crazy; but Peggy was genuinely disgusted—you might have supposed he'd tried to rape her. She was outraged in her dignity as a woman. Really outraged—and quite cross when I laughed. Paul must have sensed this weakness in her. He had an amazing instinct, and always knew the right place to stick a pin in you. I'm sure he insulted Peggy deliberately—knowing she didn't like him and itched to interfere and influence Chris against him.

Gerald hated Paul also, but in his deeper, more subtle manner. He hated Paul because he was jealous of his influence over Chris, and because he was sure he would do Chris harm. However, at the time of which I'm writing, he was very careful to hide his feelings as much as possible, and I think he prayed hard to overcome his aversion. Paul, who was well aware of the situation, teased him in all sorts of malicious ways, and kept poking fun at Gerald's religion and spiritual exercises—but, for the present, he avoided any open quarrel.

It was during this visit that I first saw Trabuco. It was a big ranch lying about twenty miles inland, under the mountains. Its very name indicated its loneliness: nothing noteworthy had happened in that area since a day in the seventeenth century, when a Spanish soldier had lost an arquebus there—a "trabuco." There is something weird about the emptiness of these South California uplands. The foothills and creeks and woods look deceptively tame and inhabited. You could wander for miles, always expecting there'd be a ranch house around the next slope, just out of sight, with a little town beyond. But there are no towns, and very few houses, in the whole neighborhood. A local architect named Van Pelt (who was also the designer of the house Chris Wood had bought in Laguna) had evolved, with Felix Greene and Gerald, a long, straggling building: a series of cloisters which mounted, in flights of steps, the slope of a little hill. The total effect was beautiful. The buildings fitted perfectly into the landscape. Gerald said they reminded him of a small Franciscan monastery in the Apennines.

You entered a big courtyard which was also an orchard, planted with fruit trees. To your right were garages, toolsheds, and the pumping house; a long, low dormitory for married couples, and the circular meditation hall, which had no windows and was built on three levels, so as to hold the maximum number of people. You entered the cloisters through a pair of big wooden gates, with a bell turret above them. All along the cloisters were bedrooms and bathrooms, comfortable but very plain, with built-in closets, and a minimum of furniture. At the top of the cloisters were three big rooms, a library, a living and dining room, and a kitchen. When you were in the courtyard, your view was bounded by the irregular line of red tiled roofs against the sky. But when you opened the big gates and entered the cloister, you found yourself at the edge of a hill, looking away over the woods and hollows to the distant ocean.

When I first saw Trabuco, a great deal was still lacking, but the buildings were there and inhabitable—a miracle in itself, considering that this was wartime. Felix Greene had worked all winter, with his superhuman energy, collecting materials, bullying contractors, grabbing the last available supplies of wood and metal fixtures before the government froze them. Trabuco was three-quarters his creation, physically—ideologically also—for I soon began to realize that this place, this institution, was altogether in excess of anything Gerald's timid conservatism had ever planned or wished. The snug little anonymous retreat for four or five people, "Focus," had been swallowed up by "Trabuco College," which was capable of holding fifty. Already, Felix was talking of a printing press to issue pamphlets, and was planning next year's seminars. For the present, Gerald went along with all this, a little dazed, a little unwilling, but tremendously impressed and excited. It seemed to me that a new cult, Heardism, was being born, with Felix, a sunburnt and smiling Eminence, holding the real power behind the throne.

Such, however, was far from Gerald's intention. However much he might enjoy the limelight, the prestige of leader, I am sure that his intentions were sincerely democratic. He spoke repeatedly of Trabuco as a "club for mystics"—nonsectarian, nondogmatic, strictly experimental, a clearinghouse for individual religious experience and ideas. Its members were to be colleagues, not masters and disciples, superiors and inferiors. I suppose this was an impossible ideal—maybe even an undesirable one. The Quakers have maintained a large degree of democracy (though they do have elders or "weighty Friends") but only at the price of diverting their attention from really businesslike mysticism to social service: their standards of meditation are low and vague. The Swami, on the other hand, would have said, "Nonsense, of course they must have a teacher": he would only have questioned Gerald's suitability for the job. But, at Trabuco, it was Gerald or no one. And so, eventually, inevitably, it was Gerald.

Chris regarded Trabuco with a kind of wistful amusement. He was like a child who does and yet doesn't want to play with the others. His status was that of a sort of honorary outcast. He could go there whenever he liked—for the afternoon—but he wasn't really welcome: Felix was heartily polite to him. When the building fund ran out, Chris had contributed several thousand dollars, and this made things extra awkward. "Well, anyway," he'd say, with his twisted, little boy's grin, "their kitchen belongs to *me*." At that time, Gerald was commuting regularly between Trabuco and Rockledge Road—a fact which made for further embarrassment, since several members of the college knew and disapproved of Paul. Just how Gerald spoke of Chris and his affairs when he was up at Trabuco, I shall never know: but the general effect of his remarks must have been deplorable—for the Hunters and many of his other friends regarded Chris with horror, and sympathized with Gerald as one sympathizes with the victim of an unhappy and impossible marriage. Chris knew this, and took it very well and humorously, without the least humility or resentment. From this time onward, I began to like and respect him enormously. With all his babyish weaknesses, he was a living demonstration of the one cardinal virtue Gerald lacked—charity. Also, I began to realize that I had never once heard him tell a lie. The truth—however shameful or

embarrassing—seemed to blurt itself out of him, accompanied by a
nervous, apologetic laugh.

On July 20, I returned to Peggy's house in Beverly Hills: Peggy
was still in New York. Matthew, the Huxleys' son, came to stay
there, too. He was a pink-faced, jovial, loud-voiced boy with a
good deal of lingering British pomposity, extremely sweet-natured
and kind. Neither Aldous nor Maria knew quite what to make of
him: he wasn't, in their sense of the word, an intellectual at all—
that is to say, he was neither sensitive nor retiring: he was an
extrovert, a natural "mixer." At this time, he was greatly worried
by the problem of conscientious objection. As the son of his father,
he couldn't bring himself to fight, but he equally didn't want to
take 4-E and go to CPS camp. Finally, he got himself classified
1-A-O, and took noncombatant service in the Medical Corps.

Peter Viertel, too, was getting into the war—at last. He joined
the marines, and later served in the Pacific.

During this time, I saw a good deal of Tony Bower, Johnny
Dickinson, and Denny. Denny and I went down twice to the
county jail, to see Joe Valentine —the boy whose behavior had
given his landlady so many headaches in January 1941. Poor Joe—
he seemed to have gotten sillier and sillier: he'd been going around
town under the name of "Danny Malone"—an alias which
corresponded to his wish-dreams as closely as "Paul Sorel" did to
Carl Dibble's. And now here he was, on a charge of rape. The girl
was also a minor, and, as it later appeared, a whore with a
blackmailing mother. Joe had been framed: he boasted sky-high,
and no doubt they thought he had money. Joe told us all this
through the bars, as we stood in a row of visitors: you had to shout
to be heard above the din. "I wouldn't have done it if she hadn't
begged me to," Joe yelled. "The dirty old bag. I screwed her for
four hours, and she liked it fine. Then she starts yelling for her Ma."
His case was handled by the juvenile court. We weren't allowed to
be present but we sat in a waiting room, confronted by five
Mexican gangster youths who had knifed somebody to death and
had the faces of El Greco saints. Joe was finally released, on
condition that he either went back home to Pennsylvania or joined
the navy. He chose the navy.

(The navy didn't do much for Joe, I'm afraid. He was around
town for a while, very rowdy, pugnacious and drunk. On one
extraordinary occasion, he made a pass at Peggy, who had taken an
interest in his case and was driving him somewhere in her car.
Peggy was furious—as with Paul—and all the more so when
Denny tactlessly hinted that she ought to be rather flattered, at her

age. After that, Joe went overseas, and didn't show up again for a couple of years, when he'd become a minor black market racketeer.)

On August 11, Peggy returned from the East. I don't remember whether she told me at once, but I soon learnt that her marriage with Henwar was going to pieces. They were really quite unsuited to each other; there wasn't much beside the physical and romantic attraction; and Peggy couldn't go on indefinitely pretending to herself and others that Henwar was the kind of man she approved of. I think Henwar was sorry to break with her, in his lazy way, but not sorry enough to do anything about it. Also, there was another girl in the background.

And another man. Some time before this, Peggy had been a great deal worried about her elder son Ben, who had now turned into a large muscular youth with spots and the bushy eyebrows of a caveman. Ben was a bright, intelligent, athletic boy, but he had strange streaks of sullenness and violence in his character. Peggy had discovered, to her great alarm, that he would buy [. . .] revolvers and hide them in his room. Maybe she exaggerated the danger, maybe she didn't. She certainly inspired the most violent love-hate in [various people she was close to]; and it wasn't impossible to imagine [someone] killing her [. . .] with a gun or an axe. [Ben] wasn't a coward either, like Paul Sorel. And he was completely reckless.

In her distress, Peggy had consulted a doctor named Bill Kiskadden. I don't know exactly why—because Bill was a surgeon, one of the best plastic surgeons in the country. Probably they met socially and she found him sympathetic. He was a very tall man of fifty, with silver hair, chinless but extremely distinguished looking, with a most reassuring drawl: he inspired confidence, at a time when Peggy desperately needed it. And now, it seemed, the two of them were falling in love with each other. Bill was in the Medical Corps. He was stationed somewhere out in the desert, and could come in and see her sometimes.

On the afternoon of Peggy's arrival, we drove out to visit the Huxleys, in their new home in the Mojave Desert, at Llano. Llano now scarcely exists, but, at the beginning of the century, it was the scene of an experiment in cooperative living; quite a large party of people went out there, built houses and even started an orchestra, which played at night, under the stars. The experiment failed, however—chiefly because the community had no particular purpose, ideal or religious belief to hold it together. Its members failed to develop any self-supporting agriculture; all the vegetables had to be brought out from Los Angeles, and this was too expensive. Now only a few ruins remained, among the kerosene bushes and the dying walnut trees. The Huxleys had reconstructed an old house which used to be the post office, and had built a study for Aldous and a bedroom for Matthew, about a hundred yards from it. They had their own windmill well and their own self-starting electric light plant. The latter was half sunk in the earth, under a wooden door, on which stood a terra-cotta bust of Gerald made by Angelino, Frieda Lawrence's lover. Aldous called it, "Gerald's Tomb," and that was exactly what it looked like.

Peggy was more talkative than ever: she radiated energy, resentment, optimism and worry. She was energetic about my approaching departure for camp, bought me work clothes, darned my socks, sewed in name tabs. She was resentful against Henwar and against Gerald—the latter because he hadn't invited her down to Trabuco, and now she wouldn't go if she were asked. She was optimistic about the future—largely because of Bill Kiskadden, though she wouldn't yet admit this, or the possibility of their marriage. She was worried about Ben. She watched him anxiously, all the time—although, as far as I could see, he seemed normal enough. Her great fear was that he might do some harm to Derek, his younger brother. Ben adored Derek, but often lost his temper with him and hurt him more than he meant to. Derek was a bit of a murderee: he had reached that bumptious, bitchy stage of early adolescence when small boys would rather be hit than ignored.

In the middle of August, I spent another week at Laguna Beach, visiting Chris Wood. All this while, I was revising my old diaries—working at breakneck speed, like a dying man, because I expected the draft board's call to camp at any moment. I wanted to wind up my old life, as it were, before starting on a new one.

I returned to Peggy's house on August 22. Judge Curtis Bok, her first husband, was staying there: every summer, he either came West to see his children or had them to visit him in the East. He was a tall, handsome, athletic man, still very pink and collegiate despite his greying hair. He wasn't unintelligent, but he seemed somehow emotionally undeveloped, and, in a sense, young enough to be Peggy's son. I wondered if their marriage had failed simply because she had outgrown him. He made bad puns and told silly, funny stories which delighted the children. All three of them loved him dearly, without any of the neurotic love-hate they felt for Peggy. Two days later, he took them down with him to Balboa, where he had rented a house, to go sailing. Peggy supervised the move, providing bed linen and kitchen utensils, like a careful grand-mother.

Someone had bought Ben a beagle, named Cerberus. It had been sent to Larry Trimble, the trainer of Strongheart, to be housebroken. We went to visit it, at Trimble's farm in the Valley. Trimble's specialty was training unruly or "mean" dogs. He had worked, not very successfully, with some of Salka Viertel's. He was a biggish, middle-aged man, whose curiously quiet strength of character was only apparent when he was working with animals. He told me that Strongheart used to receive a lot of fan mail, which he had had to answer. One fan asked, "How can I train my dog to attack burglars?" Trimble had answered, "According to present statistics, a burglar will enter your home about once in a hundred years. Your friends come to see you every day. Wouldn't it be better to train your dog to welcome *them*?"

(Allan Hunter had described a visit to Trimble when he was training six large police dogs to jump over a table. One of the dogs failed to do so. Trimble put the other dogs out of the room and practiced with him until he could make the jump. "I had to send the others away," he told Allan, "otherwise this one would have been humiliated, and he'd never have learnt the trick.")

On my birthday, the Huxleys came up to supper. Denny showed up later, unexpectedly, with a boy from camp named Jim Pinney. Denny was in one of his bad moods, extraordinarily aggressive and sulky. Jim I'd met before, at Allan Hunter's church. He was a rather nice-looking, extremely sanctimonious boy—the "seeker" type—with elaborate middle-class manners: he was continually asking us to pardon him. A couple of days after he left, Peggy received this note:

Dear Friend,

Every now and then one comes, a stranger, into a home where the welcome is a rare combination of easy, unthinking simplicity and very evident elegance, and the wonder is increased on awakening there the next morning with an established sense of being at *home*. The mistress of such an eventful home is indeed an artist, and I find I must thank you again for permitting Denny to share your artistry with me. It was also a great joy so unexpectedly to meet your other guests.

In the Presence, Jim Pinney

This letter provided Peggy and myself with household gags for weeks. I used to call her "my artist-hostess," and wrote her notes signing myself "eventually yours," or "with evident elegance."

But the real payoff didn't come until nearly two years later, when an extremely frank and experienced girl I knew was discussing her lovers, and summed up as follows: "But I must say—the best boy I ever had—the only one who was really sensational in bed—was a Quaker. I don't suppose you ever met him—Jim Pinney?"

At the beginning of September, I drove back to Laguna, where I finished revising my diaries, and made the first entry since leaving Haverford:

September 16. Still nothing from the draft board. The Swami and Gerald have both suggested that I apply for reclassification as a theological student, 4-D. I'm certain it won't work, at this late date— but when I tell the Swami this, he just giggles and says, "Try." I think I shall. If the board *were* to reclassify me, I could work with the Swami on his translation of the Gita, and I could spend part of my time at Trabuco. But maybe I should at least spend some months in camp, first.

Paul, Gerald and I walked to Treasure Island rock, this afternoon. As we were picking our way over the rock, Gerald slipped and fell. Instead of getting immediately to his feet, he lay there, quite passive and peaceful—almost as if he hoped his back was broken, and was unwilling to be reassured to the contrary. Actually, he had nothing but some scratches on his hands, which bled a good deal. He held them up all the way home to stop the bleeding, and this made him look like a Christ crucified in blue jeans. In spite of these precautions, a good deal of blood got on to his pants, but he refuses to change them, saying that the effect is rather decorative.

September 23. Finally decided to write to the draft board today, asking for 4-D reclassification. There's no harm in trying. Actually, if I were working with the Swami—even if I continued to live up at Peggy's— I should be a theological student within the meaning of the act; because a boy at Swami Ashokananda's center in San Francisco has already been passed as 4-D by his draft board, thereby establishing the precedent.

Yesterday, the Swami drove down to visit us. The day passed off quite pleasantly, although there were some embarrassing silences. The Swami, as always, was very quiet and polite. We drove him up to Trabuco. "Iss smoking parmitted here?" he asked. It isn't. But he smoked.

How beautiful this house is! I feel as if I could never tire of being in it. It has a wonderful air of privacy—from the moment you enter the garden, with its high cypress hedges, bottlebrush trees and Cape honeysuckle. At first, you see only the tiled roof of the house, below you, on the very edge of the cliff. It comes gradually into view as you descend the steps, terrace by terrace, past the oleander bushes and the pomegranates and the orange and scarlet zinnias. On the balustrades of the garden stairs are two green Chinese dragons, and four elephants, two white and two green, with long crafty eyes. Gerald calls one pair of elephants "Apoplexy" and the other "Liver."

At the bottom of the steps is the patio, with a banana plant, a fish pool full of big goldfish and lotuses, an ugly blue and white Della Robbia plaque half-hidden by the ivy on the wall, and an outdoor fireplace with antique Spanish fire irons, within which a monster fern is growing. Behind the waxy white blossoms of a gardenia in a tub, a great glass screen shows you the terrace and the ocean: a blindingly illuminated picture which seems as unreal as back projection in a movie. The walls of the house are netted with quivering light. At the foot of the curving staircase to the balcony, there is a dwarf monkey puzzle in an Italian majolica pot, on which a sportsman is painted, out hunting with his gun and dogs. The balcony leads to Chris's and Gerald's bedrooms: there is an old ship's bell hanging above it, which is used to summon Gerald down to his meals. A corkscrew staircase, cut out of the rock, takes you from the patio to the bedroom in which I sleep. The steps are pitch-dark, even in the daytime: for some reason, they remind me of *Macbeth*. They would do as an air-raid shelter, if necessary. Chris keeps his musical boxes there.

The front of the house rises sheer above the cliff. The ocean is right at your feet, bubbling and creaming over huge lava reefs. The house stands on an outcrop of lava, which makes a firm foundation and enriches the soil of the vegetable garden. The air is so full of salt that very little can be gotten to grow on the terrace—only the cypress, and the aloes, like twisting green octopi with bloodstained tentacles, and an Australian tree with white blossoms and a flaky bark. The ironwork has rusted away to thin wires.

The day begins, usually, with thick fog—blowing up against the cliff face or standing out to sea in a dark wall. There are times when the ocean is clear, but grey and empty and unspeakably forlorn, with a single great gull flying across it—like the Spirit moving upon the face of the waters. Rarely, the sunshine comes early, lighting all the coast as far as Seal Rock, with fishing boats standing out white and far against the hard blue edge of the morning. The sun usually emerges around noon, and by teatime it has left the patio, and the seaward terrace is too hot to sit in. When the sun sets into a clear sea, with a low bar of cloud down along the horizon, its disk grows distorted, bulging and flattening into a glowing pyramid of red coal, without a top. Then, within half a minute, it slides away under the edge of the world, and suddenly the ocean seems enormous and cold, teeming with wrinkled waves, unutterably wet.

Tonight, the evening was grey, with sad steamy clouds and sharp gold gleams on the sea. The gulls winged past silently, just after sundown, northward. A small black dog ran out across the lawn of the villa on the headland with the striped garden umbrellas, and barked wildly, too late. Down below on the reef, on old grizzled gull was standing. He looked up at me, as I leaned over the terrace railing. "Don't trust that facile feeling of oneness," he warned me. "Oh yes— I know we're brothers—in a sense. But you wouldn't care for our life."

Gerald and I breakfast together every morning at 8:30, in the pink octagon dining room with the venetian blinds. Gerald very quiet, in deep blue, slyly trying to make me eat twice as much as he does. We talk about Vedanta, Trabuco, the difficulties of purgation, the failings of the Quakers and the Catholic doctrine of sin. At about 10:00 Chris in his dark blue silk bathrobe and Paul in his rainbow-colored robe come down; Chris looking bung-eyed with sleep, Paul sprightly and frisky. Swimming is at 11:15, lunch at 1:00—Gerald and myself inside the dining room, eating vegetables, served by Josephine, the ancient, skinny, talkative Irish cook; Chris and Paul outside on the terrace, taking their beer and sandwiches on two trays. Later, we drive up to Temple Hill and walk there, or we stay home, and Chris and Paul go cycling. Paul does water colors all day long—bringing them in for us to inspect. At present, he has made a rule to do six water colors a day for twenty-one days. Then he'll switch to oils. And, in October, he'll start a novel—writing five thousand words a day for a hundred days.

We have tea at 4:00. At 7:00, tomato juice is brought on to the terrace and we sit drinking it and watching the sun sink. Supper is at 7:30. Afterwards, we sit out of doors—in darkness, for we are not allowed to show any lights to seaward; or we go into the living room, and Chris plays the piano or the phonograph with the big horn. Sometimes Gerald or Chris reads a manuscript aloud. Gerald writes with incredible facility, sometimes finishing a full-length novel in a couple of weeks or less. He has already published two crime novels and several short stories: he says he gets the ideas while he is meditating, much against his will. Chris has started writing ghost stories again, as he used to in London: they are very good, but he won't publish them. Two or three times, I've written and acted one-minute monologues for Chris's recording machine, and I play them back to the others in the evening—a man in a telephone booth, desperately calling the police, as gangsters close in to murder him; a homicidal madman in an asylum, talking to a visitor; a husband raging at an unfaithful and sulky wife. The action must be noisy and simple.

Incidentally, Gerald has decided that this house is haunted. On the terrace stands a carved fifteenth-century Italian dower chest. Gerald says that he was sitting writing in the living room one afternoon; he happened to look up and saw the lid of the chest slowly rise and then close again. He thought some large animal, maybe a raccoon, had gotten into it, so he called the gardener. But when they opened the chest, it was empty.

The living room is rather beautiful. It is paneled in pine which has been scraped, leaving a surface like the woodwork of old sailing ships. The floor is darker, of Brazilian walnut. And, let into the paneling within baroque frames, are six paintings by Guardi (or a pupil) which the lady who built the house brought back from Italy: scenes of eighteenth-century Venice—colonnades, streets, bridges, picturesquely ruinous, with waving grasses growing from cracks in the plaster of archways. All of them are somehow furtive, sinister in feeling. The two cloaked gallants getting into a gondola at dusk to keep some dangerous assignation. The queer, mature little children, like dwarfs. The beggars lurking in the noonday shadow. The enigmatic figures who watch from windowsills, over which great colored cloths or bed linen are untidily draped. The pimp waylaying the young man. The gentleman in sky blue satin bowing to the lady in the three-cornered hat. In the background are tall cypresses, rising above the walls of graveyards, or white sails on the hidden lagoon, like scarecrows' shirts, ragged and uncanny in the Venetian sunshine.

The ceiling is greenish blue, with a suggestion, here and there, of small clouds.

I think Chris likes my being here and fears the day of my departure, because it will mark another milestone on his own progress toward a CPS camp: he also has registered as a C.O. It's really touching, how he clings to the least scrap of security. Today, seeing my writing materials and spectacles on the table, he exclaimed, "How nice that looks! It makes me feel as if there wasn't any war on, at all."

This afternoon, we walked from Emerald Bay to the Seal Rock, peering into the rock pools full of purple anemones and great bunches of seaweed, like heavy heads of gorgon hair, dragged back and forth by the pull of the tide. We talked about the Bloomsbury group, and intellectuals in general. Some brilliantly cultured people are like great cities; you promenade through their minds, awestruck, admiring the superb buildings of the central boulevards; but if you wander further you find yourself lost in suburbs which grow more and more squalid and repulsive until they cease in the darkness of a landscape of total and empty despair. However, there are other towns of the mind which are far less imposing but charming and healthy throughout—because even the narrowest alleys are full of light and air from the neighboring ocean, the universal consciousness.

It must have been on September 23 or 24 that I received the following letter, datelined the Payne Whitney Psychiatric Clinic, New York Hospital, September 21:

My dear sir,

This is going to be an exceedingly badly written letter, as it is being cooked up against time and George Edington is taking it to the post in the next fifteen minutes. I am writing to you at Mr. Exman's suggestion, because he feels that I am somewhat closer to recent events in the histories of Vernon and Hugh Latham. We came into the picture some months ago, when Vernon expressed a desire to become part of the Order of the Holy Cross, an Anglo-Catholic monastery. I had seen something of Vernon—precious little, but was interested—and Father Tiedemann, the Assistant Superior, consulted us somewhat. Since then, we have almost literally found it necessary to form a Society for the Friends of Vernon and Hugh. I have asked Auden to send you a note stating that I am not quite insane.

Very, very briefly, this is what has happened. Vernon left Holy Cross with Hugh to go into a retreat in the Catskills where they opened a little monastery with Hugh as Father Superior and Vernon as novice and repentant sinner. (The phrase is Edington's.) Over the weekend of Labor Day, both boys descended on me, asking me to help them put themselves in jail as conscientious objectors. I called Edington in to help me persuade them that jail was an uncomfortable place. Finally, both agreed to accept certification to the public authorities that their previous psychological handicaps were such as to render them unfit for military service, and they returned to the Catskills to their monastic establishment. George went up to visit them (I may say that Edington is a twenty-five-year-old boy, a Master of Arts from Columbia, who served here for a year as a student assistant—an extremely fine person for whom Auden has much praise), and found them obdurate in their idea that they would somehow find God in the mountains. The going, however, might be a bit rough. It is questionable whether Vernon could stand the severe winter, and Hugh has some idea that Vernon would do best in California.

It is to this that I address myself. Are you quite determined to go to a C.O. camp? If you decide to do otherwise, it is possible that you might be able to make some arrangement to carry Vernon through the winter if you were so minded. Mr. Exman thought it might be well for you to consider the possibilities of giving him houseroom and possibly taking on helping him come to a more realistic position with regard to his future. It seems extremely doubtful that he would adjust to the monastic life. It is equally doubtful that he would be successful in the venture in the Catskills, although time alone will tell here. . . .

    Yours very truly, Alfred A. Gross.

By the same mail, or shortly afterward, came letters from Wystan and from Eugene Exman—explaining that Hugh Latham was a young man who'd applied for admission to Holy Cross (Vernon had met him there) and been refused: he seemed, from all accounts, to be an irresponsible, romantic character. Gross's letter irritated me, with its grannyish fussiness. I replied courteously but briefly (which offended him, I later heard) pointing out that there was no question of my being "determined" to go to the C.O. camp; the Government was determined to send me there: and that I was surprised—if he knew anything about Vernon's past life—that he should suggest Vernon's returning to live with me, of all people. I felt annoyed with Gross for shielding Vernon just at the very moment when he'd at last taken an independent step. Vernon needed, above everything else, confidence in himself. If he'd decided to go to prison for his opinions, he should have been allowed to do so. Whatever the merits of the gesture, he would have felt good about it, later. He never lacked physical courage, and I couldn't see him as a tender flower. Yet Gross and Edington seemed determined to get him away from the Catskills—apparently because the roof of their shack leaked and Vernon might catch cold: Edington later wrote me a long and positively mawkish letter about this. I answered, protesting energetically. Vernon remained silent throughout. After a few weeks, and some difficulty with the FBI, they did finally leave, and Vernon drifted unhappily about New York for the next eighteen months. Thanks, largely, to Gross's interference. My opinion of psychologists sank lower than ever.

September 25. A letter from Roger Spencer, a boy at the Los Prietos camp whom I met at Trabuco some weeks ago, to say that I was expected at camp last Tuesday. This worries me: am I technically AWOL without knowing it? But I've had no induction notice from the draft board yet. There must be some mix-up. I've telegraphed to the director of the camp asking him what to do.

Aldous came down here yesterday. He, Gerald and I came up to Trabuco for a weekend seminar. There are about twenty-seven of us here—including some old La Vernites: Felix Greene, of course, and Lucille Nixon, the Hunters, Marian and Rodney Gale, Etta Mae Wallace and Harry Farash. Also Bob Forthman; a Quaker named Esther Rhodes who has worked in Japan and with the Japanese in the U.S. internment camps; Evan Thomas and his wife, both members of Allan's congregation; Herbert Douglas, a music teacher and veteran seminar attender, who also visits Krishnamurti and the Swami; and David Signer, a Jewish boy from New York, half-crippled by arthritis, who is a friend of Harry Farash—Harry met him in a park one day, it is said, and persuaded him not to commit suicide.

September 26. Morning discussion: What is prayer?

"Prayer is a way out of prison." Felix Greene.

"The only thing that does any good. Prayer dissolves away my self-will." Rodney Gale.

"Sometimes it's just a stubborn desire to hang on to a commitment—but it's all on different levels. To get everything permeated with a sense of meaning—everything related to an effort that the Kindom of God can come in. An effort to be honest about Evil, and the Good behind the Evil." Allan Hunter.

"I must put my hand in and pull out my will. I keep repeating the two questions, 'What is God?' and, 'What am I?' . . . I hope to merge the two questions." David Signer.

"What a little we see of the total realities—and yet what a mess we have made of that little!" (I forget who said this.)

"Prayer is the line of least resistance." Herbert Douglas.

"My spiritual exercises are designed to help me to withdraw from self-will and regard myself more detachedly: sometimes I have felt that detached feeling which I realize is love." Harry Farash.

"I pray to get out of the car which is bound to crash over the cliff sooner or later . . . to detach your soul from your body before it dies." Bob Forthman.

"I came to this thing in a rather curious way, as a reductio ad absurdum. I have mainly lived in the world of intellectual life and art. But the world of knowing-about-things is unsatisfactory. It's no good knowing about the taste of strawberries out of a book. The more I think of art, I realize that though artists do establish some contact with spiritual reality, they establish it unconsciously. Beauty is imprisoned, as it were, within the white spaces between the lines of a poem, between the notes of music, in the apertures between groups of sculpture. This function or talent is unconscious. They throw a net and catch something, though the net is trivial. But one wants to go further. One wants to have a conscious taste of these holes between the strings of the net. . . . Now, obviously, one could never possibly give it up." Aldous Huxley.

"Prayer is a mode of life which is a kind of training which will help us generate this charity." Marian Gale.

I quoted to the group a passage from Bishop Hedley which I found in Bede Frost's *The Art of Mental Prayer*: "It (mental prayer) is the hour in which the soul lives: that is, lives its true life and rehearses for that life of eternity, in which prayer, in its highest sense, will be its rapture."

That prayer is actually a *rehearsal*, I find extraordinarily suggestive. It seems to mean that our prayer is a kind of sample of what life after death, without a physical body, would be like. And this, in its turn, gives a hint of the nature of purgatory. To be set fast in one place, incapable of movement, confronted with the Godhead yet held apart from it by all our everyday distractions, greeds and fears—that, as Gerald says, *would* be "hell with a time limit." Boredom stepped up to the point of agony. (If fear is crystallized greed, boredom is crystallized selfishness.)

If I really desire God more than anything else, then I must desire my periods of prayer more than anything else. (I most certainly don't.) And if I believe that God is Reality, then I must regard my prayer periods as real, or approximately real, and the gaps between them as less real. The pattern of my day must be, not EVERYDAY LIFE with little patches of prayer in it, but PRAYER with huge patches of everyday life in it. Instead of thinking of my life as a journey and myself as a traveller, I should think of the real Self, the Atman, as essentially static, perpetually contemplative within the shrine, always in the presence of God. Never mind how much the body and the Ego run around in the intervals between prayer. In the course of a week you may travel thousands of miles, but your prayer will always be offered up in the same place. That's why it's so tremendously important to keep the prayer hours, even if only in token—never mind where you are.

The meditation hall has a dome like a planetarium: in the darkness, it seems to have no top. Its circular form makes it into a whispering gallery; seated against the wall, you hear the faintest sound. After twenty minutes or so, when your eyes grow accustomed to the darkness, a very faint light is apparent, through the ventilators, revealing the circles of seated forms muffled in blankets (the early mornings are chilly): they look mysterious and cosmic: they seem like the Fates or the Norns. The place smells very peculiar—a blend of glue, carpet and mice. One false step, and you tumble headlong into the central pit, where Gerald sits, in a strange deprecatory attitude, half Buddha, half beggar.

September 27. Gerald on prayer. (This is verbatim, as near as I could get it):

But there is no doubt, as an empirical fact, that man has these two sides to his mind. The one has risen to an acute state of illumination, (Gerald meant mankind's advance in technology) the other has sunk like Atlantis, carrying almost all human values with it. . . . The animals are much wiser than we: none of them trusts the five senses. It has "a law written in its heart." In many ways, man is the most unhappy of all animals. We may be superhuman, we may be mad, but we are certainly not animal. We have no healthy animalism left. Either you must go on or go back.

No form of rapid transition, no form of birth is pleasant. It is again, of course, what Plato said, that our feet point forward and our face points back. . . . The life of prayer *is* always your individual adventure. Everybody in that life is a creator. Something unique is coming into the time sequence that has not been there before. And then, of course, another very difficult thing with religion—each generation is unique. (Gerald meant that each generation has its own peculiar type of devotion, of religious consciousness. One generation can't simply take over from another.)

So those, I think, are the three assumptions we have to make . . . This thing is *never* comfortable. I remember it was, I think, Bernard Hart[1] once saying the only adaptation which is perfectly sane is the perfectly stabilized person. And that person is *no* use whatsoever.

I think that, before we have anything to give, we have to get quite clearly in our minds that this life is a birth. . . . Thales,[2] because he cornered the olive crop and got rich, was supposed to know what this life ought to be. Heraclitus was dismissed as a mystic. . . . Greed and fear are caused by some sort of strangulated hernia, jammed off from the main life. . . . The next thing people have to realize is that this hatching process will go through certain stages. I believe the analogy may almost be an homology.

I don't think there's any doubt that this development follows the familiar cocked-hat curve. . . . (Gerald meant that the chances of success in the spiritual life diminish very rapidly as one grows older.

[1] American producer, brother of playwright Moss Hart.
[2] Thales of Miletus, sixth-century B.C. Greek philosopher.

First-magnitude saints are child geniuses: they show signs of spirituality already in the first ten years—"the first call for lunch," as Gerald puts it. Most other saints begin in their teens. Very few afterward.) The saints don't waste much crocodile tears on those people who don't intend to try but who only want sympathy—not the infinite, but a second helping of the finite. The difference between hell and heaven is seeing Him prepared and seeing Him unprepared. The religious person is the only one who is awake. (Here Gerald quoted the Jack London story "To Light a Fire"—to illustrate how we have to take the greatest possible precautions, in order not to become spiritually frozen.) We're all out in a subzero temperature. . . . Hardly any religious person believes this to be true . . . I believe we've got to put every single element into a suspense account which doesn't make sense for us.

Low Prayer—I put the screws on the Infinite and He turned up trumps. But there is this other thing, Magic. I believe that most of the answers to prayer have nothing more to do with God than a fourteen-inch gun that blows a town to pieces. The most deadly thing these powers do is to make the Ego contented with itself. It may be no harm people starting with Low Prayer as long as they go on with it—because, by the mercy of God, it will always let them down.

What you do in spirituality is you loosen this passionate grip of greed and fear which says this moment is all. . . . God *isn't* "The Ancient of Days"—that unfortunate Jewish remark. *We* are the miserable seedy Ancients of Days. He alone is young, with that appalling instantaneity. . . . God gives Man everything, save Time. Of the Tree of Life you shall not eat—for the Tree of Life is Eternity. One fate I put upon you, you can only go in one direction. . . . Till we have forgiven, we are bound and tied. The whole process of Life is the process of getting rid of Time. Olier[1] said—that last great saint of the Oratorians—that no saint would be concerned with prophecy. They know God's intention—but they can't put it down in a way which would allow a stock-exchange man to make a fortune. The saints *do* take events as though they weren't surprised. There is no accident in the Inorganic: there is no accident in pure Consciousness. We're the sport of circumstances because we *want* to be. Every crisis is the code word for opportunity.

Middle Prayer—asking things for other people. You're doing, if you like, long-distance hypnosis. You're racked with the lower

[1] Jean-Jacques Olier (1608–1657), French mystic and founder of the seminary of Saint-Sulpice.

compassion. The last infirmity of noble minds *isn't* ambition—it's the wish to be of *use*. Middle Prayer is nearly always the struggle with God to ask for his kingdom to come on earth *now*.

As the saint passes to High Prayer, he wills nothing. That's what made Eckhart cry out, "Why, even if He willed my sins, then I will them too!"

Drove Aldous back to Laguna Beach. He wanted to catch the bus into Los Angeles. Hadn't been at Chris's house long before, over the light blue hills there came a noise of revellers, and it was Bacchus and his crew—Tony Bower, Johnny Dickinson, Martin Whiteman and Dick Kitchen, that nice English painter. Drinks were drunk, and Trabuco seemed pleasantly far away. Right now, I like both my worlds in small doses. If only one could keep commuting! But that way lies destruction.

September 28. A reassuring letter from the director of the Los Prietos camp. If I haven't received the induction notice, I needn't worry. I can't come to camp till I get it.

The advance copies of Gerald's *Murder by Reflection* arrived. I asked Gerald why he has to dash his books off so quickly, and urged him to take more trouble with the details—here is a really excellent idea, and he hasn't bothered to develop it. But Gerald insists that it has to be this way. Says he's "mediumistic" and must "pour this stuff out" while the spirit moves him. If he lets it get cold, he begins to strain and worry and his prayers are distracted in consequence.

Had a conversation with the Swami on the telephone. He wants to write a letter, backing up my appeal to the draft board for 4-D reclassification. But first, he wanted me to assure him that I really intend to become a monk. I said yes, of course—but later I was bothered by all kinds of doubts. Just what does the Swami mean by "monk"? One who takes vows of chastity and poverty? Or one who belongs, specifically, to the Ramakrishna Order, conducts lecture courses, officiates at the Tantric ritual and goes to lunch with Lady Bateman and other "devotees"? I've decided to drive to Hollywood tomorrow and ask him.

September 29. As I expected, the Swami waved my doubts aside. Of course—he said—I wouldn't be asked to do things I wasn't fitted for or wasn't inclined to do. "Why," he added, "I would accept even an atheist if he would take the vow of chastity." *If*!

Went to the barber's. Whenever I've been out of town for some time, Hollywood Boulevard affects me with the most violent kind of depression. The bottles of Wildroot Tonic and Oil seemed scarcely to have the heart to keep up their pathetic pretence a moment longer. "We know we're not the best tonic," they sadly admitted. "We know we can't really stop your hair from falling out. We know it doesn't really matter about being well-groomed, or attracting girls, or making the grade, or selling your personality. We know you'll grow old and die, and others will be born, and new tonics will supersede us, with new slogans and old lies on the label." They despaired, already. And the tiled barber's shop, with MOVIE-LAND picked out in gold lettering on the arch above the basins, was like a tragic museum of stale, twenty-year-old glamor. And the gallantly lecherous customer in his fifties with a neat military moustache, who told dirty jokes to the barber and flirted with the manicurist—he despaired, behind his alert, smirking smile. And the manicurist glanced at herself in the mirror without enthusiasm: she was no longer quite fresh. Her voice was weary as she told the customer about her dog. What age was he? "Oh, he's ten years. He's *old*." These people, and the crowds in the street, and the trash in the shop windows, and the movie placards, and the advertisements warning you to get wise, get smart, get relaxed, get well, get sunburnt, get thrilled, get rich—and the newspapers with Japs fleeing and Stalingrad still unfallen—all these, silently or aloud, were yelling their despair because the "life" of *Life* magazine is deader than death, and there is nothing—no hope, no comfort, no refuge anywhere—but in the unthinkable, bottomless, horrible immensity of God.

When I tried to tell Peggy all this, she understood at once. "It's those *pitiful* little shops," she said. I'm spending the night at Alto Cedro, and shall go back to Laguna Beach tomorrow. This is Ben's birthday. He has a snare drum and Derek a clarinet.

Ben's beagle Cerberus has all the airs of a lapdog. He's like a son-in-law of whom Peggy and the rest of the family don't altogether approve. Peggy looked out of the window the other morning and saw Cerberus in the garden wistfully confronting a rabbit, with a look which seemed to say, "Oh dear—*why* can't we be friends?" He didn't attempt to chase it, and this shocked Peggy. Even in a pacifist household, the women like a man to be a man.

October 1. All day long, the sun didn't shine. A slow grey swell on the ocean. Swam with Johnny Dickinson. The house next to the one the Dickinsons have rented used to belong to a paralytic. In order to get him down on to the beach, a kind of miniature tramway with a wooden car was built down the cliff. But now the tracks are rusted and grown over with tough green ice plant.

October 2. Throughout the night, the waves have been storming the rocks. This morning, the ocean has the wild grey face of a madman after hours of raving—all raddled with yellow foam. Around the reefs, the water is white like boiling milk, and the jag-edges of the lava stream with hissing niagaras. I sleep with my bedroom door open to the sea, in a tremendous, and strangely comforting chaos of noise.

I would like to remind myself by recording, once more, the absolute value of keeping the prayer hours, even when they have been as unrewarding as during the last few days. The discipline makes a track down which your life can run, with immensely decreased danger of a really bad swerve. But then I ask myself—*can* I decide, of my own volition, to pray or not to pray? Isn't the praying, in itself, just a symptom of a favorable mood? The part of my will of which I'm aware, is so rotten, so full of cracks and breaks badly spliced or half-grown-together that I feel I couldn't trust it to make me lick a postage stamp. So that leaves me back with the utter mystery of grace.

October 12. Back at Peggy's since October 5. Every day, I go down to the Good Samaritan Hospital, where Denny is recovering from an operation on the scar tissue of his old hernia. Most days, I see the Swami, and we work together on his translation of the Gita, turning it into more flexible English. This is a very valuable way of studying, because I have to make absolutely sure I understand what each verse means. Some of the Sanskrit words have meanings that sound very bizarre in English, and the Swami, who has long since learnt to paraphrase them, has practically to be psychoanalyzed before he'll admit to the literal translation.

No call from the draft board yet.

In the evenings, Ben plays his drums. He now has a big drum, a snare drum, a woodblock, a cowbell and a cymbal—all bought in a splurge of his birthday money. He plays this one-man orchestra in the baggage room under the living room, and the whole house shakes. It's fascinating to watch him. He starts quite gently, keeping time to some tune on the portable radio. Gradually, he speeds up, becomes more reckless, more decisive. His hands seem to take over from his brain, darting here and there over the instruments—trembling in a furious tattoo, lashing out vindictively at the cymbal, thundering on the big drum, hammering on the block like a woodpecker. His face changes. It is no longer attentive and alert; it relaxes into a curiously peaceful, mindless half-smile in the midst of the din. It's as if all the violence, all the frustration in Ben's nature had been externalized and resolved: it is around him, not within him; and he sits in the midst of it, refreshed and calm. I'm no judge, but it seems to me that Ben has real talent for drumming. Peggy dislikes it, however. With her own background of classical music, she hates jazz, and would much rather that Ben had learnt the piano or the violin. It isn't apparent to her—as it is to me as an outside observer—that Ben's preference for jazz was psychologically inevitable. He inherited a strong musical talent from Peggy, but his instinctive resistance to her domination forced him to find a kind of music which didn't "belong" to her: it had to be jazz or nothing.

The weather is quite cool today, and very clear. You can see the ocean, a hard grey line, beyond the gap in the hill. Sometimes, in the morning, there is thick uncanny fog, fuming up the canyon, choking the little valley, pressing in upon the huge aquarium-windows of this house, until you feel like a fish in a lighted glass tank, with the plants and bushes of the garden peering in at you like dimly outlined spectators. The tall papyrus, with tiny drops of moisture, diamond clear, on each point. The ginger lilies, whose withered heads must not be cut off, or they won't bloom next year. The white jasmine, breathless with perfume, all along the terrace wall, and the blue-eyed plumbago bushes. The crimson and white hibiscus flowers which Peggy cuts and lays singly on a table or shelf, like offerings. And the red-black light-absorbing dahlias which she puts in a vase on my desk, because she knows I like them. They're called "Bishop of Llandaff."

Peggy gardens and housecleans all day long, almost instinctively. Even while she's chattering away to you, her body darts this way and that, with anxious, birdlike abruptness—snipping off a flower head, flicking dust from a chair. Sometimes, she becomes aware of it, and murmurs, "Sorry, darling—I *must* just—" She pounces upon her task, performs it, returns smiling apologetically: "Yes? You were saying—" She runs everything—including my spiritual life. Ben and Dek have a small hut at the end of the garden which they used to play and sometimes sleep in. Peggy has commandeered it as my meditation room. I'm supposed to go off there, three times a day. Peggy sees that I do, too. If we're talking and it's around six o'clock, she'll say, "Darling—I don't want to hurry you—but—you see, supper's at seven-fifteen this evening—and I thought perhaps—" She wanted to stop Ben from drumming between six and seven, lest I should be disturbed, and I've had a hard time persuading her not to. In the morning, if I oversleep, she'll look at me reproachfully: "Darling—if you want to—I mean—do whatever you like—but I can easily keep breakfast till you're ready—" And out to the hut I have to go.

The Swami's stories of Brahmananda. How he received Vivekananda when he returned from America, and prostrated himself and offered a garland. Vivekananda refused it, and prostrated himself before Brahmananda and offered *him* the garland, saying, "The Son of the Guru is also the Guru." Brahmananda, not to be outdone, offered Vivekananda the garland for the second time, replying, "But the elder Brother is the same as the Father." Vivekananda didn't have any comeback, so he gave up and accepted the garland.

In 1923, when the Swami was planning to go to the Himalayas and practice meditation and austerities, he was told by his superiors that he was being sent to America, to the San Francisco center. "But *I* can't teach!" he protested, in dismay. "Nonsense," replied one of the elder monks, severely: "You have seen the son of God, and you *dare* to say you cannot teach?"

October 16. Denny introduced me to a friend of his from camp, Collins George. Collins is a Negro, but you couldn't tell it: he could easily "pass" anywhere for a South American. This, actually, makes his position all the more difficult, because he is extremely conscientious, as well as sensitive and intelligent. He can go into restaurants where Negroes aren't allowed, and yet at the same time he doesn't feel he ought to: he feels compelled to tell people what he is. And, as a conscientious objector, he has enough troubles of his own, anyway. He lost his job teaching French at a Negro college because the staff were against pacifists. Denny's attitude toward Collins is at once protective and sadistic—complicated, no doubt, by his own southern upbringing. Collins is fat, soft and sensitive, and Denny can't help saying cruel things to him, every so often; and yet he has put himself aggressively on Collins's side in camp (quite unnecessarily, because the Quakers lean over backwards to avoid even the slightest hint of race prejudice; and it would take a Denny to detect involuntary symptoms of it in their attitude). Through Collins, Denny has made friends with Hall Johnson, the leader of the Negro choir. When Denny and Collins are on leave together, they often go down to night spots, in the colored part of town, and Denny is proud of being accepted in places where whites are not welcome.

October 20. Denny is out of hospital and has gone to stay at the Beverly Hills Hotel. He has decided that he needs a little luxury to help his convalescence. I went down there today and swam in their pool. It is a USO[1] Center, and servicemen are allowed in at certain hours. There was one very drunk sailor-boy who told us all that he was on leave and going to see his folks in Alabama. He whistled like a steam

---

[1] United Services Organization, a mostly volunteer charity chartered February 1941 to provide welfare, recreation and live entertainment for U.S. armed forces at home and abroad.

engine, out of tune, and did running dives into the pool, splashing everybody from head to foot. He was under the impression that he had a date with a movie star named Ellen, or maybe Helen, he wasn't certain; so he asked each girl in turn: "Hey, beautiful—what's your name?" A snooty-looking brunette who must have been sultry in the 1920s regarded him with extreme pain: she was reading Vivekananda's book on raja yoga. Denny claimed that she was a character from a Scott Fitzgerald novel who'd passed out during a wild party and slept for twenty years. Now she'd just woken up and thought this was all a horrible dream. Finally, the Alabama boy, who'd so far been tolerated with indulgent smiles, scandalized everybody by shouting to an old lady, crippled by arthritis: "Hey, beautiful—come on in! The water's fine!"

Still no word from the draft board. It's very odd. Can they possibly be considering my appeal? I try to keep my mind prepared for a call at any moment. But inevitably, after all this delay, a voice begins to whisper, "Who knows? Maybe they've forgotten you. Maybe you won't have to go."

Very hot weather. At night, the cicadas make a tremendous racket. One of them, which is nearly colorless, is as loud and shrill as a police whistle. A big brushfire in the hills above Malibu. The sun set right behind a ridge that was burning—lighting up the great crimson-purple cloud of smoke hanging in the airless sky. It looked like a volcano in eruption.

October 21. Seen at the Beverly Hills Hotel: a man (probably the house dick) sitting under a palm tree with a magnifying glass and very carefully comparing the signatures on two checks.

Peggy on the phone (to Maria Huxley, probably): "Well—*you* know how it is—I'm sorry, darling—hold on just a minute—*that's* right—I thought the soup was boiling over, but it wasn't— Oh, no, no. You mustn't think that . . . The only thing *I* mind is, as soon as I've finished, I have to start all over again. Yes—I'm sure it's the most beautiful discipline in the world. . . . *Well! Golly!* That just *shows*, doesn't it? We've got the *rich* point of view, you and I! Isn't it *fun?* Mercy—my face is *red*! . . . My dear, when did *I* ever get away with that? *Oh no*—other people can, but not yours truly! I would just *know* I'd probably begin vomiting and have *all* the appearance of ulcers! . . . No—well, you see, it was like this—*she* wanted to have a party and she said now what would *you* think—and I said why, I think that's perfectly *splendid*—" (And so on, for at least half to three quarters of an hour.)

October 30. Here I am with Denny in Palm Springs, staying at the Estrella Villas—one of those luxurious bungalow courts with a swimming pool and a bright green lawn which looks as if it had been ordered from a Los Angeles furniture store and unrolled like a carpet. It is crossed by paths of colored crazy pavement. Each cottage has a rustic fireplace, tasselled ropes draped around the windows, Japanese prints, brass marine lamps, fluffy white rugs, cream upholstery with lemon cushions. We've already gotten into trouble with the landlord for bringing in puncture-weed thorns on the soles of our shoes: the ground is covered with them.

All around the village and the airfield with its winking light, spreads the untidy desert with its dry silvery bushes alive in the heat, as seaweed is alive in the sea. In the late afternoon, when Palm Springs is already in shadow, the mountain range across the valley turns mauve and violet in the setting sunshine. It shines in the distance like the landscape of another planet, unearthly, beautiful and dead. Actually—like the mountain behind us—it is nothing but a huge litter of ugly, smashed stones: nature's lighting effects supply all the glamor. Overhead, the P-38s whine and drone. Since the outbreak of war, the desert seems to belong naturally to the army. It is dotted with new airfields and camps, where troops are trained in warfare under North African conditions. The sterile activity of war drill finds here its ideal setting.

We go back to Los Angeles the day after tomorrow. Denny is restless and bored, but he really needed the change. While he was in hospital he got terribly thin, with long sinister birdlike legs. A change has come over him—not in the way Gerald hoped and expected, and yet somehow due to Gerald's influence. He wants to become a psychologist. But before he can even begin to study for his medical degree, he must first get his high-school diploma. He left school without graduating, and now he must start again where he left off all those years ago: one never really dodges anything. As soon as we're home, he'll go to UCLA and arrange to take a correspondence course. He can do this in his spare time at camp.

November 13. Went to Metro, to talk to Lesser Samuels about Maugham's *The Hour Before Dawn*, which Lesser may be going to write for Paramount. He wants me to help him—chiefly as a sort of technical adviser on the scenes for the conscientious objector.

A surprisingly large number of elevator boys and messengers were still at their jobs, despite the draft. There are now exits to air-raid shelters at the ends of the corridors. A writer told me how Victor Saville had reprimanded him for writing a scene in which a man runs in and takes his hat and coat from a bedroom chair. "My dear fellow," said Saville, "surely you know that the only place a man leaves his coat on the back of a chair is in a whorehouse?"

We discussed the almost pathological mania which nearly every Hollywood producer has for "virility." Dore Shary had told Samuels that a scene was "faggoty" merely because it showed an older man talking to some youths of college age.

Salka Viertel and I had tea with Saville. He was much excited by the favorable war news from Egypt. "Isn't it marvellous," he said to me, "to think you and I were sitting in this office at the fall of Dunkirk?" He wants to see Italy not only invaded but thoroughly bombed—"to soften 'em up." And he'd have Darlan shot as soon as the war is over: "that goddam turncoat sonofabitch."[1]

November 16. Peggy and I went down to the temple for a puja, from 10:00 till 2:00. A big lunch party afterwards, with curry and chatter—about some lady's hat, and about the beautiful character of the actor Robert Montgomery (I kept my mouth shut): one of the girls was convinced he *must* be spiritual—with those eyes. Through all this, the Swami sat smiling his Chessy-cat smile.[2] Peggy was elaborately bright, but I think the whole thing rather repelled her. She's very careful, however, not to hurt my feelings. Whenever the temple, or Vedanta, is mentioned, she puts on a specially "arranged" face, decorous and grave—like a little girl in church. Over and over again—rather too often—she says how wonderful the Swami is, and reads all kinds of significance into his slightest remarks. "Did you notice—when Amiya insisted on his taking some more rice—he just smiled very sweetly and said, 'Thank you'? I though that was *beautiful . . .*"

November 19. Peggy left today for Nevada with Derek, to get her divorce. They're going to stay at a ranch a few miles outside Reno. They won't be back till after Christmas. I'm to keep an eye on Ben and Tis—in my capacity of "Uncle": Peggy has carefully built me up in this role, assuring the children that they adore me, until I feel uneasily that they must hate my guts. However, I've already had a deliberately hard-boiled conversation with Ben, telling him that he and Tis can do whatever they like, as long as there is no scandal, no baby, no venereal disease, and provided I don't have to know about it officially.

[1] The French admiral and Vice-Premier collaborated with the Germans, then negotiated with Eisenhower once the Allies landed at Casablanca and Algiers in November 1942. He was assassinated soon after; see December 30 below.
[2] I.e., grinning like a Cheshire cat.

November 28. Last night, Ben and Tis and some friends took the family car and drove downtown. Around midnight, when I was already in bed, the telephone rang. "This is Sergeant Schaefer," said a man's voice, "are you a relative of Benjamin and Welmoet Bok? Well, you'd better come down to the jail. We're holding them here, on a traffic violation charge. No—they aren't hurt. But you'd better come down, or they'll have to spend the night in the cells." I was sleepy and cross. "I'm not coming down," I said. "If they've been fooling around with the car, it serves them right. A night in the cells won't hurt them. I'll take care of it in the morning." And I went back to bed.

Next morning, when I came up to breakfast, there sat Ben and Tis. "Well!" I said, feeling relieved and a little bit guilty because of my callousness, "so they let you out after all?" Ben and Tis gaped at me; they didn't understand what I was talking about. It seems that "Sergeant Schaefer" was a hoax. One of their friends must have done it. Ben says he can guess who it was, and he'll have his revenge— which rather alarms me. But the effect of my behavior has been highly salutary. I can see that Ben and Tis are shocked because I didn't rush downtown to save them, but they're also impressed: it makes them feel that they really *are* on their own and responsible for what they do. They may not like dear Uncle as much as they did, but at least they don't despise him.

I have bought one of Chris Wood's bicycles. Went down to Hanns Ohrt's today to pick it up. I plan to do a good deal of cycling— because it's healthy and I like it, and because, with gas rationing, my car isn't going to be much use anyhow. I may sell it later.

November 29. With John van Druten to have tea with the Beesleys— Dodie Smith the playwright and her husband Alec. They live in Beverly Hills, on Palm Drive. Johnny has often talked to me about them—they used to live up in Carmel and have only moved down here lately: Dodie, it seems, is wildly neurotic about ants and bathroom taps. She lies awake fearing that the ants will be killed or the taps left running. Also, she and Alec have two extremely nervous dalmatian dogs, who run the house and are waited on hand and foot.

Dodie reminds me a great deal of Forster. She has his nervous, touching eagerness to communicate with you, to be friendly, to understand what you mean. She isn't tense, like Peggy. And if she's a bit crazy, at least it's about something demonstrably silly, which is a great advantage. Craziness is only sinister when it's concerned with something apparently reasonable. Better ants than America, any day.

Alec is a very good-looking man with prematurely grey hair. It seems quite natural that he's a C.O. He has that peculiarly British kind of individualism which takes the unpopular side as a matter of course. He's no crank, either. He didn't talk much today, because Dodie and Johnny were chattering away about the theater: they both know every actor in the cast of every play since 1900.

November 30. Started work with Samuels at Paramount on *The Hour Before Dawn.* I've never had an easier job. Lesser does everything. I merely have to let myself be cross-examined on the C.O. position. But I see already how terribly hard this will be to dramatize. Because, when you're dealing with an actual character, you can't be content with reasons and argument, otherwise he's just a lifeless prig. Behind all that, there has to be the simple, human decision not to kill. And this decision must be dramatically explained. Bill Dozier, the pleasant but extremely dumb story editor, wants a prologue in which the hero accidentally shoots his pet dog and thereby gets a horror of firearms. Even Lesser can see how fatal this would be: it reduces the man to a pathological "case." But what's the alternative? We're not allowed, of course, to suggest that conscientious objection is "right"; and yet this guy is the hero of our story and his sincerity must be above question. I think we'll simply have to say he's a C.O. and go on from there.

(On December 6, I saw the Beesleys again, and from then on began to visit them often. It soon became clear that we'd be real friends. Dodie and Alec both made me feel perfectly at home with them. Dodie was extraordinarily sensitive and intelligent—though I saw her more as a novelist than a dramatist. The kind of plays she wrote apparently didn't make sufficient demands on her sensibility: much of her was left out of them. She had a tremendous nostalgia for England. She kept saying that she'd missed everything, because she wasn't in London during the blitz, and that she hated California. In fact, she was determined to hate it. She couldn't go back, however, because the British authorities discouraged the return of C.O.s. The dalmatians were also a problem: Dodie was sure that the wartime quarantine arrangements would be inadequate. The two of them, Buzzle and Folly, were very handsome animals, but their nervousness was extraordinarily irritating. You had to be careful to avoid sudden movements and extravagant gestures, or they'd leap from their places barking hysterically.

Alec was a most reassuring person. You couldn't imagine him flustered or bored. He always had something to do, some little chore, even if it was only writing a letter or fetching more hot water for the teapot. Some months after I met him, he became a kind of unofficial legal adviser to C.O.s on the technicalities of the draft law, and spent a good deal of time downtown, attending C.O. trials. Boys were always calling him on the phone, in utter desperation, expecting they'd be arrested at once; and Alec, in his clear, energetic voice with its very faint Cockney twang, would reassure them: "Oh, I wouldn't worry too much about that, if I were you. They can't do a thing to you, really. If they make any trouble, just tell 'em to look up paragraph 47, section 3. Got that? The trouble is, they don't know their own damned law . . ." Dodie greatly respected Alec's activities and joked about them continually. When the telephone rang, she'd say, "There's another of Alec's schizophrenes!")

December 9. Dinner with Huxley and van Druten at Romanoff's. The choice of restaurant was Johnny's idea. He wanted to meet Aldous again, and I suppose he felt that only the best was good enough: he admires Aldous enormously. Johnny seemed very young: an admiring boy in his teens. One of his nicest qualities is his entire humility in the presence of someone he considers his superior: he assumes, as a matter of course, that all his plays and his success are just so much junk in comparison with Aldous's least word, and yet he never once flattered him or said anything embarrassing. Actually, Aldous has a lot of respect for Johnny's kind of technical ability, and he set himself out to be as friendly as possible. He was very amusing about psychical research—imagining a society of ghosts endeavoring to prove the existence of human beings. The evening, despite our ritzy surroundings, was a great success.

December 12. Last night, Ben and Tis had a party up at the house, so I spent the night at Johnny's apartment in the Chateau Marmont. This wasn't just altruism. Ben's friends are apt to make a fearful noise, and it's nearly impossible to sleep. The party seems to have been a knockout. The boys got very drunk, and Tis had to retire up to Peggy's room with her girlfriends and lock the door to protect their honor. Ben's friend Douglas Rose stripped stark naked and ran all around the neighborhood, diving into people's pools. Doug is the Micky Rooney type; an erotic, herculean dwarf. When he necks with the gigantic Tis, which he does at the drop of a hat, it's like a man trying to climb a totem pole. Ben stayed in bed all day, with a terrible hangover.

December 21. Ben and Tis left for Nevada today to join Peggy and Dek. Two nights ago, I took them out to the Florentine Gardens. It was a flop. I made the fatal mistake of being absolutely sober and of not giving them a couple of drinks at home before we started out. Ben and Tis wanted sherry and I very stupidly ordered it, and of course the manager spotted them and came and asked their ages, and I looked foolish. We pretended very heartily to be having a good time.

We've finished the treatment on the picture, and now I won't have to work any more until, at any rate, after Christmas. Every day, I've been cycling to and from the studio, leaving my car at the Beverly Hills Hotel. Lesser regards this as an almost unheard-of athletic feat, and seems to expect I'll drop dead of heart failure any minute.

December 30. Well, Darlan got shot, even sooner than Saville wanted, as a Christmas present for the Fighting French. Here I am , writing in the patio of Chris Wood's Laguna villa, with the sun streaming down nearly as warm as summer, and the Pacific morning all one wide vague blue smile beyond the glass screen. I arrived here on the 27th. Gerald is upstairs. Chris is at the piano. Paul is washing his hair. The perfect maids are dreaming up a perfect lunch and supper. This place seems to be one of those favored nooks in the midst of the tempest which the Destroyer has been too busy or too merciful to shatter.

In the afternoons, I go cycling with Chris and Paul. As the result of all this exercise, I'm in marvellous health and have a huge appetite. This quite shocks Gerald. "I'd no idea," he said, looking at me yesterday with involuntary distaste, "that you had such a *grip* on life."

On February 6, Brahmananda's birthday, I'm scheduled to go and live at the Swami's and at length begin the monastic life. No word has ever come from the draft board about my application for reclassification. But now, since the age limit has been dropped to thirty-seven, I'm automatically let out of the liability of being sent to camp. It's very odd to glimpse—or fancy one glimpses—the workings of the karma mechanism. If the question of my going to CPS camp had never arisen, I would probably never have actually signed on with the Swami at all.

Not that I want to kid myself that going to live at the Swami's, or anywhere else, will do more than fifty percent toward keeping me on the tracks. But it *will* help. Allan Hunter asked me, a short while ago, why I was going up to live at Ivar Avenue, and I answered, "Because I'm so bored with not being innocent." That was a terrible phony-sounding reply: but what I meant was that I'm feeling, increasingly, the misery of not being all of a piece, of living my life in a number of compartments with connecting doors which are narrow and hard to open. Not that I have done anything hellishly wicked during the past two months, but my life has been a mess and a lie, a messy lie—everything I've said and seemed to represent has been tainted with disingenuousness. If you'd spoken to me as a stranger on a trolley car and asked, "What are you?" how could I have answered? "A would-be monk," "A writer at Paramount," "A celibate as from February 6," "A vegetarian, except on Christmas Day." That state of affairs has got to stop, finally, when I settle in at Ivar Avenue. I've got to belong to the Ramakrishna Order with as few reservations as I can manage. I know that that's the best way for me. The obstacles have been cleared from my path, one by one. Well—what am I waiting for, now?

December 31. Today, I wrote a story for the Swami's magazine, *Vedanta and the West.* It's called "The Wishing Tree." I read it aloud to Gerald, Chris and Paul this evening. Paul, with his usual flair for malice, commented that it was "very delicate." It sure is. You could blow it over with a Bronx cheer.

I'll be returning to Alto Cedro in two days' time, and Peggy will be getting home on January 5, or thereabouts. I'll have to go back to work at Paramount almost immediately.

Today a year from now, I wonder how I'll be feeling?

1943

January 29. Today I finished work at Paramount. I think that, between us (ninety percent Lesser) Samuels and I have done quite a decent job on the script. Susan Dewees—of all people—has helped us a good deal. I wrote her at Haverford to find out about British C.O. tribunals, and she was efficient as ever and sent us lots of material. The worst of it is, the Quakers are now on the watch for the picture, with high hopes that, at last, the C.O. position is going to be fairly presented.

Two scenes I quite like. The hero is waiting for his hearing before the tribunal, which is to take place in a small English market town. His father and his uncle, who deeply disapprove of his opinions, make a last effort to dissuade him. They take him into the local hospital, where the crew of a torpedoed minesweeper are being treated for various injuries. One boy of sixteen has been blinded: he is writhing in pain and crying out, and it's very horrible and distressing. When they have walked right through the ward in silence, the hero's father says to him, "Well—do you feel the same way now about refusing to fight? Don't you think you owe these boys something?" And the hero answers, "Yes, I do. . . . Don't you see, father? Now, more than ever—just *because* of those boys—I can't back down from what I think is right . . . *They* didn't." And then, at the tribunal, he is asked what he'd do if he came back home that afternoon and found the

Nazis there. He answers, "I'd try to remember that they were human beings." Nevertheless, he gets a big shock when he does return home, opens the front door, and there are two Nazi officers in the hall, drinking cocktails with his sister. The explanation is that his sister's an actress: they've been on location, shooting a movie, and she's brought two of the actors back with her, still in costume, for supper.

(Unfortunately, the front office didn't like our script. They got in another writer and changed it utterly, scene by scene, word by word. Sometime later, I saw the finished product, in the projection room at the studio, with a man who was Paramount's representative in England. It was ghastly. "What'll they think of it, over there?" I asked him. "Oh, they'll like it all right." "But how *can* they?" I protested, "it isn't like England at all." "That doesn't matter," he told me calmly, "they never expect that. Not since Mrs. Miniver.")

The opening of Brahmananda Cottage (as the Swami has rechristened the house where we're to live) is still fixed for the sixth of February. At the moment, this, and all that it implies, seems utterly remote and unreal. As I told the Swami some weeks ago, "I've been ten thousand miles away from you." And I have. These are the real journeys—the journeys of the mind. Stone-dull, frantically tense, I've lost all hint of the mood in which I made my entries of last September in this diary. That calm is as far from me as London is from Los Angeles.

What keeps me from my prayers? The poorest, most compulsionistic daydreams of a "last fling." Some part of me is secretly, irrationally convinced that somehow someone will show up to give me a glamorous final twenty-four hours in the best Elinor Glyn[1] style.

Then there are all sorts of tensions, resentments and fears in connection with Ivar Avenue itself. I'm scared that Peggy will somehow control my life at long range, by brightly passing hints to the Swami on the telephone, or getting him up here to lunch for a "good talk" about my case. I've already had a violent row with her on this subject. The other day, she and Swami were out together in Swami's car. It came on to rain very heavily. Swami was late and he couldn't drive her all the way back to Alto Cedro, so he put her down at a drugstore in Hollywood and very naturally suggested she should phone me to come down with my car and pick her up. However, when she phoned—instead of explaining all this—she cooed archly, "Swami's orders!" I was absolutely white with fury and wouldn't speak to her for the rest of the day.

[1] English author (1864–1943) of steamy romances.

Then I'm scared that Swami's nephew Asit, or maybe the other boys, will somehow disturb me—perhaps by playing the radio all night, or when I want to work. I'm scared that I may behave badly and possessively about my books—the last belongings I cling to. Oh, I know myself so well, with all my thousand weaknesses of vanity and self-indulgence and chatter, that I wonder, "How can I possibly *not* fail?" To which the answer is, as always, that all such weaknesses are nothing beside the strength that each of us can call upon when he chooses. I simply have to pray.

There is plenty to do, this coming week, in preparation. I'm lucky not to have to go to the studio. Above all, I'd like to get started on the first of the stories I've planned—the one about Berthold Viertel and Gaumont-British.[1] If I could write even a few pages, it would be such an encouragement.

February 3. The time is running short, and, despite what I wrote above, nothing has altered. I'm still in a dither, still banking on some wild, last-minute adventure, which, intuitively, I know won't take place, because things aren't lined up that way. However, I doubt if I'll be able to snap out of this state before I'm actually installed at Ivar Avenue.

McNutt[2] has just given notice that he may raise the draft age again, if it becomes necessary—and I still don't have that 4-D classification. So I'd better not flatter myself that I'm taking a final step.

This weekend, incidentally, promises to be quite eventful for several people. For Peggy—because Henwar may be arriving in Hollywood to take a job with Twentieth Century-Fox, and because Bill Kiskadden may get leave. (Bill has given Peggy an album of songs of the African veld; and one of them is tacitly accepted as his theme song—"Here am I, here am I, and I'll stay here till I die. I've come for you, I'll get you too.") For Matthew Huxley—because he is being drafted on the 8th, and Sophie is giving a party for him and all his ex-girls. For Felix Greene—because he is leaving for England on the 5th. He is to inspect the work of the English Friends, and return to report on the result to Philadelphia. The astonishing thing is that the British authorities have, apparently, granted him permission to come and go, despite the draft. I'm anxious to see him before he leaves, because I want him to visit M.

(Felix did visit my mother and Richard. The results were not satisfactory. He struck the wrong note. My mother was repelled, in

---

[1] *Prater Violet.*
[2] Paul V. McNutt (1891–1955), then Chairman of the War Manpower Commission, which ran Selective Service from December 1942 until December 1943.

spite of herself, and therefore alarmed—wondering what kind of a bunch I had gotten myself mixed up with.)

Lunch with Berthold Viertel at the Brown Derby. He is anxious about my move to Ivar Avenue. He disapproves of it with all the jealousy of his fatherly affection and his liberalistic Marxism. The Quakers he could understand, an ivory-tower literary retirement he could understand—but what am I doing with this old, unfashionable Indian stuff? What relation can it possibly have to America and 1943? Also, I think, he feels a deep, intuitive suspicion of Gerald, whom he naturally associates with Vedanta and the Swami. He asked, "Would you be doing this if you'd never met Heard?"—as though the question would be likely to throw me into confusion and rage. "Would I have written for the movies," I countered, "if I'd never met *you*?"

In the afternoon, Peggy and I read an article by park planner Moses[1] on postwar problems. Moses takes his stand on a patriotic, reactionary plea for "the middle of the road," and don't let's pan imperialism. In other words, he's completely pessimistic about the chances of implementing the Four Freedoms,[2] and pretty smug in his pessimism. And this is the man who transformed Manhattan Island in the teeth of capitalistic vested interest!

Peggy is very anxious that I shan't rely too much on the Vedanta Society as an institution—and of course she's right.

We talked to Denny on the phone—for the first time in weeks. He seems to be completely (even rather mysteriously) happy up at camp. He has been skiing. Is still busy with his correspondence courses. He showed no special desire to come down and visit us. That's all to the good, I think.

Supper with Chris Wood and his friend Karl Hoyt. We went to the Club Gala on the Strip. My farewell visit to the End of the Night. I haven't been to a place of this sort in ages, and it was so nostalgically reminiscent of all the other times—the baroque decorations and the cosy red velvet corners, the sharp-faced peroxide pianist with tender memories and a tongue like an adder, the grizzled tomcat tenor, the bitch with the heart of gold, the lame celebrity, the bar mimosa, the public lovers, the amazed millionaire tourist, the garlanded cow, the plumed serpent and the daydream sailor. . . . I have loved them all

---

[1] Robert Moses, New York City Park Commissioner from 1934 to 1960, built new highways, bridges, parks, and beaches; a power broker, he also ran for Governor of New York.

[2] Of speech and worship, from fear and want; first named by Roosevelt in his January 6, 1941 Congressional address proposing Lend-Lease.

very much and learnt something from each of them. I owe them many of my vividest moments of awareness. But enough is enough. And here we say goodbye.

Or do we? Isn't this entirely the wrong spirit in which to enter Ivar Avenue? I am not going there to forget such places, or any other part of life. No—if this training really succeeds, I shall be able to return to the Gala, or any other scene of the past, with the kind of understanding which sees what it is really all about.

February 4. Went down to Santa Monica in the morning and walked along the front. The cool winter sunshine. The big shabby hotels, now taken over by the navy. The reek of hamburgers, popcorn and pickles. The tumbledown bathhouses, smelling of old men, sweat and urine. "Muscle Beach," with the Mexican boys doing back flips. The great engines of amusement, standing idle. The pelicans and the human anglers. Goodbye. Goodbye. I shall see you often—but differently, I suppose.

Soldiers everywhere. The army will soon have absorbed all other types of life. Civilians will creep around the streets like clergymen, rare and queer.

February 5. Last day. Walked up the firebreak road with Peggy. The sun went down into the stormy blue sea of hills. Peggy said she saw shapes rising out of it as it set. I saw them too. It was the optical illusion produced by staring. She said, "They're lotuses." To me they looked like black derby hats. . . .

Before I go on quoting from my diary, I must write something about the general setup at "the Swamitage"—as Ben or Derek christened it.

Up to the end of 1942, the Vedanta Society had no other accommodation than the house at 1946 Ivar Avenue and one small room at the back of the temple, the twin to Swami's study. Now, however, the house next to the temple had been bought and refurnished: this was number 1942—henceforward named, but seldom called, "Brahmananda Cottage": we usually referred to it as "the monastery." It had two bathrooms, a washroom, a living room and four bedrooms, and was to be used exclusively by the men: Asit Ghosh, George Fitts, Webster Milam, Richard Thom and myself.

Asit, the Swami's nephew, was a slim, lively, attractive Bengali boy of about twenty-five. He had come to America on a visit, some years previously, and now he couldn't go back because of the war. He studied at the University of Southern California, where he had already graduated in cinematography. He wanted, eventually, to return to India and become a movie director. He was quite religious in his own way, but he hadn't the least intention of becoming a monk, and his presence in this more or less intentional household was certainly a trial—to himself and everybody else. He was gay, lazy and wildly untidy; a shameless flatterer and beggar. Americanized as he was, he still stuck to the good old Indian tradition that women should wait on men, and he got plenty of service out of the girls, who petted and cursed him by turns. He excited my fiercest sadism (as this diary will show) but one couldn't be angry with him for long: he was much too charming.

George Fitts was a man of about my own age, nearly bald, very much a New Englander, taciturn and rugged, with surprising stabs of catty humor. He had something very strange the matter with his neck. It seemed, somehow or other, to keep getting out of joint, and he would jerk it back into place with weird grunts and groans. They sounded agonizing, as though he were in great pain—but nobody could be sure of this. Nor were they entirely involuntary. Sometimes, when we were all in the shrine room and George was making his noises, Swami would whisper reprovingly, "*George!*"— and George would quieten down at once. The family accepted George's infirmity as a matter of course, and even sometimes joked about it, quite unmaliciously, to his face. It was generally understood that he had been this way since youth, as the result of unskillful treatment by various chiropractors.

George, in his own eccentric way, was very nearly a saint. He accepted Hinduism with fewer reservations than any of us. He was a natural devotee. He adored Swami and followed him about like a dog. If Swami went away and didn't take George along with him, he would become utterly miserable and even sometimes shed tears. He would write down Swami's most trivial remarks in a notebook—although Swami would try to stop him doing so. He had a recording machine and made records of Swami's Sunday lectures and Thursday night classes. During the week, he typed them out, religiously including all the sound effects—such as "er, er," or a cough, or the noise of a plane passing overhead. As he typed, he chanted at the top of his voice, or shouted "Jaya Sri Ramakrishna!" He could be heard all over the block, but the neighbors didn't seem to mind.

George's rooms formed a separate apartment, walled off from the rest of the house. He had paid for the reconstruction himself, being extremely jealous of his privacy. The place was like a museum. Every inch of wallspace, every table and chair was crowded with photographs—enlargements, in all sizes, of the few existing pictures of Ramakrishna, Holy Mother, Brahmananda and Vivekananda, together with dozens of snapshots of Swami, taken by George himself. There were also busts and statuettes and altar lights and sticks of smoldering incense. And glass jars full of withered flowers which George collected every evening from the shrine and treasured for months. They made his room smell terrible. In the midst of all this, George sat on the floor, with the typewriter before him and the recording instrument playing back Swami's voice at full blast—as happy as a child.

Webster Milam was a square, plump, muscular boy of about seventeen, prematurely going bald, very hairy and strong as an ox. He was deadly serious, very obstinate and very good-natured. He had a great aptitude for carpentering, building and fixing things. He was a champion at jujitsu. He had decided to become a monk at the age of fourteen: that was all there was to it. His mother was interested in Vedanta, so she didn't oppose him. It wouldn't have made any difference if she had.

Richard Thom was about Webster's age. He was a nice-looking boy, curly haired and brown eyed, but with a strangely crafty expression: he reminded me of a bear. He had a magnificent body, developed by barbell exercises. His father and mother, a bank manager and his wife from Portland, were pupils of Swami from way back, so Rich had come to Vedanta naturally. He had an undoubted vocation, which he violently resisted: we never knew from one day to the next if he would stay at Ivar Avenue. He didn't seem to know, himself. Webster loved Richard dearly, and used all his influence to keep him on the tracks. When Rich disappeared for hours into Hollywood, Webster would cover up for him, or go off and fetch him home. Actually, Rich was usually eating ice cream with his friends; but he was so secretive about it that he might just as well have been to a brothel. Both he and Webster were pupils at Hollywood High School—not the ideal place for would-be monks.

There was much going and coming at Ivar Avenue, and I can't remember exactly which of the girls were there when I arrived. I've described Sister, Amiya and Sarada already. There are only two others I need mention here: Yogini and Sudhira.

Yogini was a Mrs. Brown. She had come to stay with us provisionally, while her husband, Yogi, was in the army. She was about thirty years old and quite attractive, in spite of a long, comically shaped nose. She had a good figure and lots of frizzy hair. She was very lively and gay: it took me a long time to realize how serious and intelligent she was about religion, and how much it meant to her. I grew very fond of her indeed. We had a teasing, brother-and-sister relationship which improved throughout my stay.

Sudhira's name was Helen Kennedy. She was a trained nurse, who had worked for Dr. Kolisch, and she had first come to Ivar Avenue in a professional capacity, to nurse either Sister or Amiya—I forget which. She was an Irish Californian: one of the most beautiful women I have ever met—in the same class as Garbo and Virginia Woolf. Her beauty wasn't so much in her features or her figure as in her manner, her voice, the way she carried herself: she was physically aristocratic.

I won't write much about Sudhira now, because she is mentioned so often in the later parts of this diary. I suppose that, within the limitations of our respective neuroses, we were in love with each other. I had a kind of metaphysical feeling about her— especially after I had been sick a couple of times and she'd nursed me. To me, she was the universal, cosmic Nanny; the beautiful, mysterious figure whom we meet twice in our lives, at the entrance and the exit, the midwife and the hospital nurse, the life-giver and the bringer of death. Sudhira exercised what was really a most dangerous kind of fascination over me. In a way, she *was* death, and our relationship could only really exist as long as I was sick. She was addicted to death, as people are addicted to drugs— and, like every addict, she was always looking for a convert: the convert had to be somebody she loved. I tried to write a poem about her, but never got beyond the first line: "Is that the needle, Nanny, you are bringing?"

I know all this sounds like a purely literary, subjective fantasy; but it was more than that. Sudhira's death addiction had grown naturally out of the circumstances of her life. When she was a girl, she fell in love with a young flier. They got married, and three days later he was killed in an accident. Sudhira became obsessed by the fact of his death. She wanted to know what death is. She was already trained as a nurse, and now she made a point of getting assigned to hopeless cases. She wanted to watch people die. The only trouble was, she was so good at her job that she frequently saved them, and immediately lost interest. She had worked at the county hospital, downtown, where she had managed to catch most of the infectious diseases, as well as getting involved in a number of bad automobile accidents; but she survived them all. I think it was just this very death addiction that gave her abnormal powers of recovery. She loved to wander along the frontier, but she had no intention of crossing it.

In fact, she was Irish, in the best and worst sense of the word. Wonderful, amusing, soothing, funny, infuriating, unreliable, malicious, hysterical: a born liar, a ministering angel, a bitch. She caused more trouble at Ivar Avenue than everybody else put together, and the place would have been intolerable to me without her.

I'm pretty certain she must have been away, for some reason, when I moved in there on February 6: there is no reference to her in my diary for some time. But this may merely be because I was so obsessed by my own problems that I scarcely noticed anybody at first, except the people who actually inconvenienced my life.

The opening of Brahmananda Cottage was, of course, a big event. Most of the Swami's regular congregation attended the puja at which the house was dedicated. Peggy came, in her smartest clothes, like a mother to a prizegiving at her son's school. The homa fire was lighted in the living room fireplace. Everything was clean and new. Amiya had worked for forty-eight hours at a stretch—cleaning, scrubbing, dusting, fixing up curtains, laying carpets. It took us nearly a week to undo all her tidying.

Asit had the best room—the one I was to move into later. He had obtained it by alternative sulking, coaxing and bullying. Web and Rich were in the big bedroom. I had a dark little anteroom, with nothing but a door between me and Asit's radio, which he was apt to play all day and most of the night. This radio was the cause of endless friction between us: a friction which became a curious microcosm of Indo-British relations. Asit reacted quite differently toward me, just because I was British. He was altogether more resentful, more suspicious, more flattering, more deferential than with the Americans. He never lost any opportunity of making me responsible for the British policy in India. Sometimes this was a joke, sometimes it wasn't. Sometimes I was amused, sometimes I lost my temper. But I'd better get back to the diary. . . .

February 8. Well, now that we've slept two nights in Brahmananda Cottage, now that the mimosa is withering in the vases and the homa fire leaves no traces beyond a stain of clarified butter on the hearth—is there anything I can say about the monastic life?

No. Nothing. As a matter of fact, my subconscious hasn't even cocked an eyebrow or twitched an ear, yet. And, for the next two or three weeks it probably won't. Like a drunk who has been pitched into the lockup, it just lies there snoring, quite unaware that it can't get out. When it begins to wake up, I suppose the trouble will start.

Richard is the chief problem in our little world, at the moment. He's so like a bear, with his muscles and his slowness and his long, sleepy, crafty eyes. He trusts no one an inch. Today he came in and asked me if I'd ever heard of an American poet named Richard Brimstone. I racked my brains, consulted reference books. Then he told me he'd made up the name himself, for a story he has to write in his homework.

February 11. Two mornings ago, we were sitting in the shrine room in the half-light of dawn. Two kids delivering the newspaper peeped in through the temple window and saw us. "Gee—" said one of them in a loud whisper, "for a minute I thought they was real." There was a pause, then a gasp: "Gosh—they *are* real!"

Last night was bad. The first of many, no doubt. My nose was like a brick wall, with sinus trouble. Went into the living room and stood a long time looking at Vivekananda's photograph, with its wonderful glare of burning determination. This made me feel much better.

But, good or bad, this is the place for me. It will be tough here, but easier than anywhere else. Not because of Amiya, or George, or Sister, or Sarada (though they all help, in different ways, by their mere presence). Not even because of Swami. It's the shrine that really matters. The fact of its being there, always, right in the midst of our household. It's particularly wonderful at night. You feel so safe there. So strangely reassured. And there is such a sense of contact. Like sitting face to face with someone you know very well, and not having to speak.

February 26. In the next room, Asit and Richard are discussing Rich's future: I can hear every word through the door. "Well, go ahead," giggles Asit, "marry—get some keeds!" And Rich, who is thoroughly enjoying the conversation, answers, "But I don't want that. I want to be a vagabond."

He is always telling us this. His daydream figure is the Hobo—the wandering, drunken philosopher. Somehow or other, he found out about Rimbaud and pestered me until I lent him my copy of *A Season in Hell.* (It never occurred to me that some of my books might become liabilities in a place like this!) Now Rich keeps repeating, "The best thing is a good drunken sleep on a sandy beach."[1] If Swami hears him I shall have to do a lot of explaining.

---

[1] As in "Bad Blood" in *A Season in Hell.*

Sometimes, at home in Portland, he used to disappear for several days at a time and sleep in the woods.

He was suspended from school the day before yesterday—for doing handstands on the scaffolding of a sixty-foot smokestack in the Hollywood High playground. It was during the lunch hour, with a big crowd watching. Now, of course, he's the students' number-one hero. He says he wants to leave Ivar Avenue, get a job at Warner's Theater as an usher and enjoy the pleasures of "the world." I should be the last to laugh. If anybody can understand Rich, it ought to be myself.

And yet it's a disaster. Imagine discovering this place and this way of life at seventeen, and not being able to hold on to it! And then having to crawl back, inch by inch, at my age or maybe older. I'm still hanging on by the eyelids, myself, after nearly three weeks. I've got to convince myself practically that the shrine can give me strength to do what I could never do alone. If I stay here, I shall *know* that I've been helped by something outside the scope of my personal will. Swami insists that Brahmananda is actually present here, actually watching over us. I can accept this, in a way—but only as a kind of symbolic truth. If I were actually to see him, I'd be as amazed as the crassest materialist could ever be.

Last night, Swami said, "Meditate three times a day and pray to the Lord in between—and you will become a saint." I laughed and asked, "In how many lives?" Swami was quite indignant: "In how many lives? In *this* life! How can you say in how many lives? You are here, aren't you? That means Ramakrishna has chosen you."

The shrine is like a bank, in which we have put all our money and can never get it out again. But it pays interest—so the only thing to do is to invest more and more and more.

March 1. Richard finally decided to stay, after a last-minute interview with Swami in which they apparently went through every mood known to psychology. What an extraordinary character Rich is! Part of him is so sincere that it makes you want to cry; part of him is quite cynically cunning—as for instance, when he plays up to Swami and pretends to be under the influence of Swami's hypnotic power. The other day, while Swami was out, he sat in Swami's place on the living-room sofa and imitated him puffing at his cigarettes and curling up his toes. Sarada and Yogini and I pretended to be disciples and asked him questions. And Rich, catching Swami's tone perfectly, answered us. "Swami," said Sarada, very wide-eyed, "what shall I do? I don't have the time to meditate. I'm so involved in the cares of the world." "Aw wairl," replied Rich, absolutely dead-pan, "jarst try to think of God okkezzionelly . . ." When Swami heard about this, he was delighted.

The other night, Sarada found a prose poem which Rich had typed out and hidden in the shrine. It was headed "A Farewell to Vedanta." I can't quote all of it, but there was a bit about, "As I lifted my weights, may I lift the weight of my ignorance . . . As I climbed to heights unknown, so may I climb toward Thee."

"Heights unknown" referred, of course, to the smokestack. Swami and I went round to interview the principal of Hollywood High this morning and plead (unsuccessfully) to have Rich taken back. The principal was like a bank manager on the day of a crash: a desolate, shattered figure in the midst of utter confusion. One had the impression that he and his staff had long since lost control of the huge, hygienic, rowdy school and its gang of husky, sexy, tramplike students. Wearily, he pointed out to us that Rich has scarcely attended a single class in any subject: some of his teachers don't even know what he looks like. As for the principal himself, he is entirely resigned to rudeness, ignorance, inattention, rowdyism, venereal disease, illegitimate babies and sex in every form—but he still has one proud boast: no student has ever actually met a violent death on the premises. And no one shall, if he can help it. Here he is really obstinate. "Why," he exclaimed, "it would be in every newspaper in the country!" He seemed to take it as a matter of course that Mr. and Mrs. Thom would have sued the school, if Rich had fallen.

As we were driving away, we passed the celebrated smokestack. It looked horribly dangerous. The scaffolding seemed insecure, and the fall could only have been on to asphalt, or a spiked iron fence. Swami folded his hands, glanced upward for a moment, and murmured, "May *I* have that courage!"

So Rich is to stay home, and study Vedanta and try to be a real monk. For a month's trial.

Yesterday, I had lunch with Peggy, up at Alto Cedro. Bill Kiskadden was there, on leave from the Santa Barbara Hospital. He's bored and dissatisfied, as well he may be. He gave up his private practice to volunteer, but so far he's had no surgical cases whatsoever. They are all sent elsewhere. Most of the wounded who come home from the Pacific are suffering from nerves or shell shock.

Peggy, who has been hunting the city for a new cook, seemed as tense as ever. She makes every topic of conversation an excuse to let off steam. Today it was the movie *In Which We Serve.*[1] Peggy liked it: I didn't. So she analyzed my motives for disliking it—proving that

[1] Noël Coward's 1942 film about a British warship in WWII.

they stemmed from guilt feelings, snobbery and anti-British prejudice. All this, of course, in her sweetest, most "unbiased" tone of voice.

March 5. Yesterday and early this morning, we had the Shiva puja, or series of pujas, preceded by a twenty-four-hour fast. You are not even supposed to drink water. Fasting gave me a seasick headache. I couldn't work and sat in the living room in a daze, listening to an almost endless description of the New York production of *Our Town* by Bill Roerick. Roerick is a very nice, dark, extremely handsome young actor who is in the military cast of *This Is the Army*: right now, they're making it into a movie at "Camp Warner Brothers"—every player is required to spend at least one night under canvas, on the back lot, every week! John van Druten brought him up to a lecture ten days ago, and since then he has visited us twice. Sarada, that incurable monk- and nun-grabber, is already convinced that he's a candidate for the yellow robe. And everybody is charmed by his looks.

Shiva is represented by a little knob of clay (which I suspect of being, originally, a phallic symbol). After the puja and the huge 4 a.m. meal were over, one of the devotees had to drive down with it to Santa Monica and throw it into the ocean. It mustn't be kept.

March 9. Allan Hunter came over to see me this morning. A crisis has arisen up at camp, because of Denny's behavior. Not only is he a subversive influence, but he's accused of bringing in liquor and even marijuana for the others to smoke. I said I didn't believe this. Because I saw Denny the other day, and he would most certainly have told me about it. Allan then revealed the purpose of his visit, which was to have me sit in on a conference on Denny's case. We drove clear across town, to the house of Phil Wells, the camp doctor, a self-satisfied Quaker with a know-all smile. The camp director was there, and a couple of other senior C.O.s: dead-serious juvenile prigs. I could have smacked their earnest, good-looking faces. I could have smacked Denny's, too, for involving me in this mess. However, I confined myself to sarcastic politeness. The charges against Denny (and also his colored friend Collins George) proved to be pretty vague. The camp director had to admit that everybody liked Denny, that quite a number of the boys drank hard liquor, and that there was no clear evidence of the marijuana smoking—or, as he put it, "I can't say that I actually saw them—er—partake." In fact, the long and short of it is that Denny has simply been talking about his gay life in Paris and making them discontented. He will probably be gotten rid of. If the draft board medical examination for C.O.s hadn't been so superficial in those days, he would probably never have been inducted at all.

When it was all over, the most priggish of all the boys staggered me by telling me how much he had enjoyed *Mr. Norris Changes Trains*. What goes on in their minds? They are mysterious to me as the Chinese.

March 18. I'm down at Laguna Beach again, staying with Chris Wood. Gerald is here, and Aldous, and today we expect Karl Hoyt, who's being inducted into the army next week. I return to Ivar Avenue tomorrow.

Chris just got a telegram to say that Paul Sorel is returning to California from New York. He hates New York, although he's been staying at the Hotel Gotham on an allowance of eighty dollars a week. Chris is black and tense with worry over Paul. Also, a couple of days ago, he heard that his best friend, Mark Palmer, has died in England.

The atmosphere in this house is bad and squalid. Something is wrong with Gerald—partly, it's that he's upset because Paul is returning. He gives forth no light. His conversation with Aldous at breakfast this morning seemed particularly sterile, bookish and malicious. He described Queen Victoria's deathbed with almost fiendish relish: "At the end, she was broader than she was long, and quite blind." What's so unpleasant about Gerald's aversions is that he hasn't the guts to come out with them openly. He hasn't the guts to say, "I loathe that dreary old imperialistic bitch, and I hope she's frying in hell right at this minute." It's the same when he talks about Paul. Always cautious. Even Aldous seemed less of his kind, decent self than usual.

I shouldn't have come down here. Perhaps I shouldn't leave Ivar Avenue at all, just now. I feel shaken and insecure.

March 26. Woke murmuring a line from Yeats's translation of the chorus from *Oedipus at Colonus*: "Even from that delight memory treasures so . . ."[1] I am reading and thinking often of Yeats, just now: he represents a most elegant kind of sexual sublimation.

Felt a bit heavy after Sudhira's B_1 shot, last night. (She has decided that we all need pepping up, and goes around at bedtime with the hypodermic, visiting her "customers.")

Tried to think that the real Self was already sitting in meditation before the shrine, as I herded my sleepy but obedient body out to the washroom, emptied its bladder and sponged its face. Webster, who

---

[1] In "From *Oedipus at Colonus*," first published as an individual poem in *The Tower* (1928); the play is by Sophocles.

had called me, was in the boys' bedroom, finishing his homework by electric light. Thought: "Shall I point out that it's already daylight outside, if he'll lift the shades?" Decided not to be such an old fusspot. "But surely," I said to myself, "it's time he went into the temple?" And I answered, "That's his affair, not yours. Shut up." As usual, I raised the shades in the living room, thinking, with a kind of maudlin self-pity, how much I love the daylight. In this mood, I think of myself as a wistful prisoner—the type that watches the swallows and waters a flower with his tears. A grey morning. Noticed that the pittosporum outside my window has no more blossoms. But there are blossoms on the big acacia on the lawn in front of the house, and the Indian hawthorn is in bloom all round the temple steps. My nose, as so often, was stuffy. Tried to clear it, before going into the shrine room, with bastrika and alternate breathing. Not much good.

Arrived to find the shrine room empty. Tried to pray for my friends, but could feel absolutely no affection for anybody. The only thought which almost always seems valid is of the boys fighting each other all over the world: that gives me a sense of responsibility. Because of their suffering, even if for no other reason, I must contribute my tiny effort towards this other way of life. Then the usual bad feelings—vanity, because Swami came in late and saw that I was already in the shrine; self-accusations, because I'm not in England (these still sometimes recur—although I know perfectly well that, whatever my duty may have been in the past, it is now to stay here; and that I only wish to return because I still care what the world, the readers of *The Daily Mail* and *The Los Angeles Times*, thinks of me). Then satisfaction, because, technically, I'm still keeping all the rules. Then sex thoughts. Then resentful feelings toward Chris and Gerald and Peggy and Paul Sorel. A mental conversation with Chris, in which I told him that I resent Paul's association with him chiefly because I fear it may bust up the household at Rockledge Road and thus deprive me of a holiday home. I imputed similar motives to Gerald and felt angry with Peggy for trying to interfere, calling her a nosey bitch. We all, I thought, conspire to keep Chris a little boy with toys.

After worship, there was just time to drop my cushions and wrapper on my bed before the chimes rang for breakfast. A special delivery letter was brought by the mailman as I was going across to the other house, from Mr. Thom to Swami. I touched it in mock salutation to my head, before giving it to Swami, and immediately felt the joke was silly. Swami read the letter, which had an enclosure for Rich, while I watched him inquisitively and Sudhira brought in spoon bread and eggs and we ate our prunes. Swami passed me the letter to read. Mr. Thom wasn't sure if he should take Richard's decision to leave Ivar Avenue seriously, since Rich hadn't mentioned that he and Swami had discussed the matter. Rich didn't read his letter, but took it away with him from the table. Sister remarked that she'd have to hire a gardener, now that Rich is leaving. When we got up from breakfast, I urged Swami to get Rich away as soon as possible—chiefly because this interim period, with Rich smoking up the living room and listening to jitterbug music, is getting on my nerves. Also I know that he's planning some kind of sex excursion for tomorrow night—as why the hell shouldn't he? But it makes me feel so insecure.

Asit put me into a good temper by flattering remarks about my laugh and my new haircut. Returned to the other house, to burn trash in the incinerator—very little this morning, except faded flowers, which have been used in the worship and then laid in front of the photographs of Ramakrishna and the others in our bedrooms. I often feel mad at Asit when I'm burning the trash, because he's apt to leave razor blades among the paper, and once or twice I nearly cut my hand open. However, this morning, he hadn't, and when I met him and Rich I suddenly felt a warmth towards both of them, and asked, "Haven't you old smokers got a match?" The first decent feeling of the day. Lit the incinerator and threw the flowers on to the compost heap which Web has started.

Returned to the kitchen to help with the dishes—after starting a letter to Paul Cadmus and asking Asit, as politely as I could, to turn down his radio with the news. George's recording instrument was shouting away next door, accompanied by queer animal noises from George himself. Sudhira said she'd been having an argument with George about Richard. George thinks that Richard should be forced to stay here, no matter how, because the Lord is sure to work on him gradually if only he sticks around. Sudhira disagrees. She told about a marmoset she'd had as a pet. It bit, and the vet filed its teeth, and it got toothache and sat with its paw to its mouth and the tears running down its face. And Sudhira, who had hated it, began to feel sorry for it and got codeine for it from the hospital and it turned into a dope fiend, and died. She was so beautiful as she described this. I love her very much. I love Yogini too, with her air of a burlesque Ophelia: she always wears flowers in her hair. She came in, and I told them about the games Edward Upward and I used to play, years ago, pretending to be Professor Koehler's apes building towers of boxes to reach a banana. There was one picture captioned "Grande achieves a three-storey structure." So we all tried it and laughed a lot.

Dishwashing is always a pleasant part of the day. I make up verses to amuse the girls—particularly Sarada, who is very sensitive to words. The charm of this sort of humor is simply that it is so specialized—like the jokes of airmen or scientists. Nobody outside Ivar Avenue could appreciate it. Some specimens:

> With many a mudra and mantram, with mutterings and mouthings and moans,
> The rishi flew into a tantrum, and rattled the avatar's bones.

> After reams of ridiculous ritual, after offerings of ointment and eggs,
> The cripples were kissed by Rasputin, and recovered the use of their legs.

> So the Swami has put her in purdah, we may none of us speak to her now.
> Perhaps she's committed a murder, or even *insulted a cow*!

Or this—to the tune of "Deutschland über Alles":

> Never smoke before the Swami
> For he hates a bad cigar,
> Water pipes would be pretentious—
> They are for the avatar:
> Only saints may stoop to cigarettes,
> Only rishis dare to chew,
> Therefore, if you see the Swa-ami,
> Hide that Camel undernea-eath the pew.

Returned to my room, finished my letter to Cadmus, and went into the temple to watch Sarada doing the first part of the ritual. Swami wants me to learn it. I had the book of instructions open in front of me and followed. Then I went in to see Swami, who showed me the rest. He had been talking to Richard, who had said he wanted to be a military policeman and shoot someone in the belly. "He's an egomaniac," Swami said—but he couldn't help smiling: he loves Rich very much. In the middle of our conversation, Paul Sorel rang up, from Hollywood, very polite and elaborately friendly. I think he wants to get me on his side in the forthcoming battle with Gerald. He and Chris are leaving for Laguna at once.

March 30. Harold Ehrensperger (the editor of the magazine *Motive*[1]) writes this morning that he's coming out to the Coast in June and would like to meet me and have me meet George New, "a distinctly

---

[1] *Motive: The Magazine of the Methodist Student Movement*, published in Nashville, Tennessee.

worthwhile younger chap."[1] I quote this phrase because it's so typical of the fast young religious set in this country.

After that sour crack, you can guess that I'm not in the best of moods. I have a cold coming on—a throat infection apparently caught from Web, but actually my usual defense mechanism because Swami has given me too much work (on the magazine, etc.), because I feel fussed, because Rich is still messing around (he has the most uncanny knack of slipping off the premises whenever he's wanted) and because tomorrow I was to have done the worship for the first time, under Swami's supervision. Very bad sex tension, the past few days, and complete dryness.

April 4. Headline from *The Los Angeles Times*: "Uniform Veal Ceiling Near."

Lunch with Bill Roerick and two of his friends named Bruce and Tommy, both naval air gunners. Bruce is a thoughtful, gentle, rather charming boy, who used to be an architect; Tommy is small and square and lively and rowdy. They made friends the first day in boot camp and have been together ever since. Now they're in the same aircraft, and, as Tommy said, "At least, if we go we'll go together." He keeps telling Bruce, "I don't know what in the world you'd have done, if you hadn't had me to look after you." They love each other so much, and are so open about it, that it makes you want to shed tears. I had an awful feeling that they are both doomed; but I hope this is just romantic sentimentality.

The log cut from the walnut tree which used to stand by our back door has begun to sprout leaves. Sister said, "Somehow, it seems pathetic."

Have bought a Remington electric razor, on the excuse that a shortage of blades is expected; actually, as a toy.

Carter Lodge was up here yesterday. He offers me a job at the ranch, if the draft board refuses to classify me 4-D and wants to get me into CPS camp. That way, I'd have agricultural deferment. I think this would be about the worst alternative I could possibly choose—so maybe I'll find myself choosing it.

April 6. Talk with Sudhira this morning, while washing dishes. About Rich, who is still supposed to be leaving next Saturday, and about Web and his sister Jean—a fat, charming, slightly hysterical girl who often visits us and is in perpetual indecision whether to marry or sign on here as a nun. Rich is now spending most of his nights out—at all-

[1] An academic (b. 1915); studied at Northwestern and Columbia and later became Professor of Speech and Drama at Pratt Institute, Brooklyn.

night movies, or with friends. However, he keeps dropping hints that he'd like to stay on here. Swami says no, he'd better leave. Web, thinks Sudhira, is suffering on Rich's account much more than he shows. His throat is chronically inflamed. Jean, according to Sudhira, has said she doesn't believe he'll be here in three years' time. Jean herself shed tears on Saturday night, because there'd been so much talk at supper against marriage, and she's engaged to a boy named Jack, who's in the army.

I must say that none of this bothers me much. Let those who want to leave leave. I can't agonize over straying sheep. Whatever else the spiritual life is, it isn't tragic, because every effort and discomfort is purely voluntary: you can stop whenever you wish. And this talk about the world's pleasures being wretched and tasteless is just silly, as far as I'm concerned. Sure, you have to pay for them, but they're marvellous while they last. You can't wish them away, and groan, and say you never did like them, really. They have extraordinary beauty and significance, and woe to the wetleg who denies it. The world at its best isn't miserable, isn't hateful—it is mad. The pursuit of worldly pleasures as ends in themselves is madness. Worldly-mindedness is madness because it presupposes a purely imaginary situation, instead of acknowledging the real situation, which is the presence of God. To be sane is to be aware of the real situation. The desire, the homesickness for sanity, is the only valid reason for taking up a religious life.

If there's anything I'm sick of, it's personal relationships, on which I and the rest of my friends used to expend a positively horticultural energy. Ah, what a coldness there was, underneath those "darlings," those kisses, those hugs, those protestations! Here, I'm happy to say, all that seems meaningless. You plow your own furrow, and the most lovable is he or she who most unswervingly plows theirs. The only worthwhile thing we can do for each other is to set an example.

April 16. Richard did finally leave on the 10th, as arranged. Today, Yogi arrived. Also Donald Hayne.

(Yogi, as I've said already, was Yogini's husband. His real name was Walter Brown. At the time of this visit, I think he must still have been a technical sergeant in the army, stationed near San Diego. He was a grey-haired, good-looking man, with a tiny moustache and eyeglasses: a typical, careful office worker. He wouldn't be sent overseas, as he had some physical defect, and the army was about to discharge him. He had caused quite a sensation in camp by having a picture of Ramakrishna by his bed and burning incense in front of it every evening. He had also formed a small group for Vedanta study, much to the annoyance of the chaplain.

I had met Donald Hayne some time before this—the previous year, I think—at Chris's Laguna Beach house, where he had come to visit Gerald. He was a big man, good-looking in a heavy Roman way, but flabby. At that time he was a priest, who taught history at the University of Iowa.

One day, after I'd come to live at Ivar Avenue, I got a letter from Donald, saying that he had decided to give up his job, because he couldn't conscientiously continue to teach history according to Catholic dogmas. He was also seriously considering giving up the priesthood altogether. He wanted to come to California, talk to Swami and find a job. The trouble was, he had no money. So, with Swami's consent, I invited him to come and live at Ivar Avenue while he looked around.)

Hayne is to have my room. I'm moving in with Webster. The girls, particularly Sarada, are greatly excited by his arrival. They are sure he'll be converted to Vedanta—and what a scoop to get a real Catholic priest! Also they admire his looks. They think he resembles the actor, George Sanders. As a matter of fact, he does.

April 17. A long talk with Hayne, last night. Apparently, his doubts about his vocation had a great deal to do with a sudden wave of sex feeling. He must be a case of arrested development. Now, he wants to get married—never mind to whom. As a good Catholic, the idea of unmarried sex is impossible to him, he says. Told him I think he's crazy. He must try it out first. Otherwise, he can't really know if he wants it. And he'll make some girl miserable. When I told this to Swami later, he said he was so glad I'd said it. "Of course," Swami added, "*I* couldn't possibly tell him that." Swami's attitude is, once a monk always a monk: so far better let Hayne visit every brothel in town than tie himself up for life—especially since the Catholics don't permit divorce.

But there's something fantastic, and deeply disingenuous about Hayne's whole attitude—despite the fact that he's very friendly and can be quite charming. I don't know what to make of him. A rather mysterious girl named Miss Heinen keeps calling him on the phone. Hayne says that she was a pupil of his in Iowa, and hints that she's practically a mental case. He's been out to see her a couple of times, already.

(Here I'll insert two letters, written at this time. I happen to have kept carbon copies, which I very rarely do. They are worth putting in because they were written to be read, and therefore represent a "presentation" of my state of mind. To some extent, they are propaganda. I find them both horribly embarrassing, and it will be noticed that they contradict each other on some points.

The first letter is to a C.O. named Hoosag Gregory who was working on detached service as a male nurse in a lunatic asylum. As will be seen from my reply he had written me about an article which criticized Heard and Huxley. He wanted to know about Vedanta and Ivar Avenue. And he also asked me—as one sometimes asks perfect strangers—if he should get married. My reply is dated April 20th):

Dear Hoosag,

Many thanks for your letter. I'm glad your work continues to interest you. Don't despair because, as you say, the patients respond more to electricity and insulin than they do to love: that's only because very few of us can generate an amount of love equal to a powerful electric shock. You know that early poem of Stephen Spender's?

> I must have love enough to run a factory on,
> Or give a city power, or drive a train.[1]

Personally, I doubt if I could make even a toy train move one inch.

Yes, I saw Richard Chase's article in the *Partisan Review*.[2] It had been advertised, and I was looking out for it. It disappointed me, rather. I'd hoped for something bold and slashing; whereas this was just academic stuff making academic points, and reproving Heard and Huxley on purely academic grounds. This was just, no doubt, as far as it went, and interesting to some—but not to me, not to anybody who ever seriously wanted to know how to live their life, not to anybody whose reaction to any statement is: "How does this affect *me*, and what, if anything, ought I to do about it?" Ah, what poor, lifeless, barren talk this is—this tripping up of the experimenter by the theorist who hasn't the guts even to bet a dollar on a horse! I don't mean anything personal against Chase (about whom I know nothing) but it's the mentality of all that tribe. I have associated with it, before now, myself, and been guilty of just that archly snooty tone.

---

[1] "Acts passed beyond."
[2] "The Huxley-Heard Paradise," *Partisan Review*, 10.2 (March–April 1943), pp.143–58. Chase (1904–1988) was a freelance writer and part-time academic.

The talk about escapism and the life of action seems to me every day more meaningless. If God exists at all, there can be only one question: how can I get to see Him and know Him? For some, this may be through prolonged contemplation; for others, no doubt, through social service. But there is no basic difference between the two kinds of life, because the object of both is exactly the same. Whether you sit motionless all day in prayer before a shrine, or work your hands off in a hospital, you are helping nobody but yourself. Either you are moving nearer to God, or you are not. In either event, the material world, as it is pictured by the social reformers, is not being improved one particle. Yes, indeed, large quantities of filth are being shovelled up in one corner and carted away to another; but the amount of filth remains the same. Nobody going into a bowling alley supposes that some socially valuable object is served by knocking over the pins. We all know that the players are doing it for exercise. But our insane vanity and self-love blind us to the painful truth that this also applies to the whole of human activity. We can *do* nothing to help each other, nothing whatever. We help each other only by *being*, by setting an example, by giving forth the light of God inside ourselves. Nevertheless, the hospitals must be kept open, and the blueprints must be drawn—not to cure or house the patients, which is utterly immaterial and unimportant, but in order that, by offering all this activity to God, we may come nearer to Him—may "take exercise" in fact—and, in doing so, may attract others to His light within ourselves.

The only escapism which really means anything is the attempt to escape from this duty of offering our lives to God—and the form which this escape takes is always either a flight into exaggerated activity, or into the narcotics—exaggerated sexuality, drink, dope, etc. Of these, the flight to narcotics is less vicious and degrading, because society disapproves of it; therefore it is seldom coupled with the worst sort of self-love. Also, in the states produced by overstimulation of the nerve centers and glands, people get half-glimpses of reality. You seldom find a drunkard who is an atheist at heart. Whereas these other escapists—most of them engaged in activities which *Time* magazine would describe as admirable—they are much farther from the truth. They live in a mad world of vanity, in which they believe themselves to be indispensable, and directly responsible for all kinds of striking improvements in the material world around them. When they discover that this is not the case, they often commit suicide.

Oh yes, you say, very fine and high-class sentiments, provided you have shed the teardrop of faith, and can honestly say you believe in God. Well, then, why do I believe in God? Not for any reason which would sound well in a sermon. I have had no visions, or revelations, or direct experience—except of the most cloudy and untrustworthy kind. No, I believe in the belief of others—that's all, and yet it's more than enough. I don't mean the belief which the saints had—although that, in itself, is impressive; especially in the case of St. Francis, St. Philip Neri, Ramakrishna, Jesus. I mean that a man I have actually met—the Swami—believes in God so entirely, so simply, so calmly, so intelligently and so lovingly, that I am bound to say that, in all my quite large experience of human beings, disbelief has never produced a representative one quarter as convincing. Yes, I have known some very admirable stoics—loving, upright, gentle, courageous—but, somehow, just because of this failure to believe, they were curiously impotent, twisted, maimed. Fanatics don't impress me much, on either side of the fence. But the Swami is neither crazy, nor tense, nor stupid. I wish you could meet him—or, indeed, any monks of the order. I think they could help you.

About sex, just this. For God's sake, don't get married, until you are quite quite sure that you are not ready for the spiritual life until your next incarnation. If there is still a lot of curiosity, have sex, have lots of it (you'll pay later, but that can't be helped) but don't marry. Then—if you're bitten already with this other way of life—you will make a wretched husband, and some poor girl will be very unhappy; and you will have a ghastly time unlocking all the handcuffs again—especially if there are children. Don't let anyone, especially any Quaker, confuse you about this. There is lots of talk about the way to God through married life. That way exists. It is exactly twice as hard as the monastic way. Very few get to the end of it.

Well, I've certainly given you an earful! It's much too dogmatic and oracular, but it's how I feel at the moment, so excuse the tone . . .

(And here—after that icy douche of asceticism, in which I now detect a good deal of sadism and spite (maybe Gregory, in his letter, had seemed to approve of the Chase article?)—is a more moderate and somewhat more sincere reply I wrote to Caroline Norment, dated April 24th):

Dear Caroline,

Thank you so much for your letter, and for asking me such clear, answerable questions, unlike some of my other friends who either don't ask at all, out of a kind of shyness, or, if they do ask, make it only too painfully clear that they think I am—well, not crazy exactly, but temporarily touched.

Yes, the picture I sent at Christmas is a photograph of the temple at our Hollywood center. Its exterior is by far the most exotic thing about it. Inside, it is a very plainly decorated lecture hall, with a small inner room at one end which is used for meditation, and contains a shrine. We live in houses on either side of the main building, just ordinary Hollywood houses, one Spanish style, the other vaguely Japanese. I tell you all this because there is no need for you to picture us living in a sort of oriental-theosophical atmosphere, with robes and mysterious symbols and dim lights. There is ritual, of course, in the worship: ritual which has been practiced in India for tens of centuries; out of which, I imagine, the Catholic mass evolved. There are many points of resemblance.

"Does it bring strength in a positive way?" I don't have to hesitate before I answer yes to this. I think you know me well enough to know that I am not the sort of person to be interested in renunciation for renunciation's sake. If anything, I err in the other direction, because I am perpetually reacting from my puritan family background: I can never feel that the pleasures of the world are either sinful or tasteless, and I could never get much nourishment from a religion which said they were. This is, of course, just a temperamental matter: I happen to have had a particularly interesting, pleasant, successful, exciting life, so naturally I tend to be optimistic about life in general, despite all the evidence to the contrary.

At the same time, I have always felt the need, in life, for some sort of dedication and meaning—as who doesn't? At one time, when I was a very young man, I was able to think of the profession of writing as a kind of religious vocation, for the sake of which one made certain sacrifices and accepted certain disciplines. I still think this is true, or could be true—though there are probably very few artists or writers or musicians who really live up to the challenge of their profession as a way of religious self-dedication. If even Tolstoy can write about this the way he does in that wonderful passage in *A Confession*,[1] then what are the rest of us to say?

[1] See diary entry for June 17, 1942.

So, without in any way giving up writing, I had to look around for some more complete kind of dedication. That was why I came to Haverford. That was why I was at one period interested in socialism. That is why I have come here. To me, all these stages have been part of the same search. And, of course, the possibility of spiritual growth existed in each. I don't feel that the work we did at the college workshop is either better or worse, more escapist or less escapist, more "practical" or less "practical" than the work we are doing here. To people trying to lead the life of prayer and meditation in a monastery or retreat, the danger is, no doubt, that they may become insensitive or callous, and lose their sense of the world's suffering and need. But for the people who lead the life of social work and active relief in the world there is equally the danger, as you and I well know, that one may become so deeply involved, so eager to achieve certain results, that one loses altogether the sense of what it is all *for*, the sense of God, in fact. And so the two lives are complementary. Whether one stays in one, or the other, or switches back and forth, must be an individual matter, dictated by circumstance and what we can guess of God's will for us. Again and again, in Haverford, I felt the need of the kind of training I'm getting here: I could have helped Caro and Mr. Robinson ever so much more if I had had it. And often, here, I've wished I could spend a week working in a hospital, or back at the workshop, to keep the perspective. Of course, there is still, quite aside from all this, the question of vocation and ability. You, for instance, are obviously an organizer, a counselor, and you belong in the kind of work you are doing. I am only an amateur social worker, and whatever I do in that way would be more for the good of my soul than for any efficient result it produced. My real job is literary, and belongs much more to the monastery than to the hostel.

So I can't, you see, say how long I shall stay here. Nor can I say that this life is a preparation for work in the world (though in a sense it is) or that work in the world would be a preparation for this life (though in a sense it is). Certainly, there is no question of severing any friendships or making any breaks. We don't have the restraint here which seems to exist in most Catholic houses. I go out and visit people when I have time—though that isn't so often!—and all kinds of visitors are with us continually. About celibacy, yes, there is a vow—a conditional one, which can be terminated after three years; and a lifelong one, which is made after ten, when one becomes a full-fledged monk, and presumably takes up some kind of ministry. When I spoke of Friends disagreeing with monasticism and celibacy, I was quoting Douglas Steere, who expressed himself quite definitely on this point to Gerald and myself.

That is all there seems to be to say at the moment. I hope this letter will reassure you, if you need reassurance, that I haven't "turned my back" on anything you value or believe important. I am not bound, as yet, in any way whatsoever; and, as I have been here only ten weeks, these are very early days to be making statements.

I pray for the greatest possible success and enrichment of your work in New York. I shall be thinking of thee (after all, I slip back into saying thee as soon as I imagine myself talking to thee!) very very often. . . .

May 1. Shaky after two days in bed with flu. But I want to write down a few things.

While in bed, I read Waley's translation of the Chinese novel *Monkey*,[1] and *The Light of Asia*,[2] and several Buddhist writings from Lin Yutang's anthology.[3] And the result is that I feel, very strongly, we must not rave against the body. The body is *not* a lump of corrupt filth, it is *not* evil. It is our faithful, loyal servant, in sickness and in health: it really does its best. Of course, if you let it be the master, then it will display all its greed and stupidity and brutishness. If you put your dog on the dining room table, you mustn't be surprised if it gobbles everything up. We must be very firm with the body, and also very kind. Also, I do feel that we must be ready to accept sickness—*not* as a burden, but as a profoundly educational experience, neither less, *nor more*, educational than health.

Sudhira has been looking after me. She tells me stories of her work at the county hospital. The bellhop from the Beverly Wilshire Hotel who suddenly developed leprosy. They usually had two or three lepers at the hospital. During the first weeks you have to watch them, for fear of suicide. Later, they adjust themselves, and can be sent to the colony in Louisiana. While Sudhira was nursing in the children's ward, she caught meningitis and became delirious. Two beautiful white horses appeared in her room and told her that they'd come to take her away with them to Mount Shasta, but that first they must all three go into the chapel and say a prayer. Sudhira actually followed them into the hospital chapel, dressed only in a short nightgown. She

[1] By Cheng-en Wu.
[2] Edwin Arnold's long poem about Buddha.
[3] *The Wisdom of China and India* (1942).

was kneeling at the altar rail and laughing at the awkwardness of the horses, who couldn't kneel properly, when a doctor found her and led her back to bed. After this, she didn't see the horses any more. But, a few days later, she became convinced that an escaped convict was hiding in her room. Whenever the nurse came in, she made him get under the bed, and dragged the bedclothes down on one side to hide him. She gave the convict most of the food they brought her: the nurse could never understand why it was always spilled on the floor.

The woman from next door, calling to her husband: "Don't you go sweeping the path. I don't want you to get sweaty." "What are *you* doing?" the husband calls back. "I'm cleaning the bathroom." "Well, don't *you* get sweaty either." Their old voices, affectionately quarrelsome.

May 4. Got up this morning, but I'm back in bed again this evening, resting. Web hurries in and out, bringing me things, like a hospital orderly under Sudhira's command. He shows a kindness and gentleness which are almost feminine. He takes our monastic relationship absolutely literally. As far as he's concerned, we're brothers, and that's that.

I have no idea "where I am." Have I made progress during these three months, or haven't I? To a certain degree, I do feel yes, I have. Just being with Swami has given me a much clearer idea of what the spiritual life ought to mean. How infinitely difficult and yet how utterly simple it is! Want God? All right, go ahead and dig him out, like a terrier.

The worship is very helpful. I did it again today—for about the eighteenth time. Nearly always, I at least manage to get a great sense of *responsibility*. Here am I, with all my karma upon me, presenting myself before the unthinkable majesty of God's throne. "I'm sorry, Sir. I was the only one they could find to send." Offering the prayers and mudras, the flowers and lights and incense, I am the representative of everybody I have ever known, and of all my human brothers and sisters, and of the millions of the dead. I do this for Vernon's sake, for Heinz, for the girl who used to keep the kiosk at Freshwater Bay,[1] for my mother, for an old lady who once asked me the time in Amsterdam, for the Huxleys' toy pomeranian, for Letts, Siamese, Bantus, Swiss, Esquimoes, for all those imprisoned in all the hells.

George is making a quite new sort of hooting noise through the wall, which is extraordinarily disturbing. It reminds me that, some weeks ago, Web and I were wakened in the dead of night by a mysterious thudding. I had no doubt of what it was—distant anti-

---

[1] In the Isle of Wight.

aircraft fire; we've had a couple of alarms already. Web was excited but a little scared. I tried to reassure him. It could only be a nuisance raid, a few planes from a Jap carrier which had somehow sneaked past the patrols in a fog. The chances of our being hit were microscopic, etc. etc. And then—we both realized it was George's typewriter!

At the lecture, Swami dealt with the passage in Patanjali which describes the psychic powers and how to acquire them. As usual, he was very severe against clairvoyants.[1] But the mad fortune-teller, with her corpse-white skin and strange black bedraggled hair, didn't seem offended: she kept smiling in all directions at the gremlins and spirits which she sees floating around her.

Webster is busy, as usual, studying his bible—Kidder-Parker's manual on construction. The text for the day is chapter 21, article 7: "For workshops on cheap, level land, and especially for buildings in which the stock is heavy, one-story buildings have proved to be more economical than higher buildings, in cost of floor area, supervision, moving stock in process of manufacture and repairs to machinery, much of which can be run at greater speeds than when it is in high buildings."[2]

May 7. Drove down to visit the Huxleys at Llano, with Swami, George, Hayne, Sudhira and a woman named Mrs. Maury. Sudhira had a special interest in coming to Llano, because her father and mother were members of the original colony, and she herself spent some time here, as a child.

We all walked out to the little abandoned cemetery, where some of the colonists are buried. Aldous says that the Los Angeles morticians are actually agitating to force their descendants to pay for the removal and reburial of the remains in an official graveyard. Lulu, the toy pomeranian, came with us, plunging fearlessly through the undergrowth and continually disappearing. It is the perfect dog for Aldous. He cheers it on, waving his arms and crying, "Luloo! Luloo!" Maria is greatly worried, because of the plague of rattlesnakes this year: she's sure Aldous will nearsightedly tread on one of them.

The others drove home. I'm staying the night, returning by bus tomorrow. Maria has explained to me that I must use a candle if I want to read, because the power plant in "Gerald's Tomb" makes a

[1] Patanjali's yoga aphorisms, which Prabhavananda and Isherwood later translated as *How to Know God* (1953); the passage on clairvoyants, with Swami's commentary, begins in Part III, aphorism 16.
[2] Frank Kidder and Henry Parker, *Kidder-Parker Architects' and Builders' Handbook.*

noise like a motorcycle if it is switched on, and wakes both of them up.

May 13. Six years ago today since Heinz was arrested by the Gestapo. He's dead, probably. I imagine they forced him to join the army. I wonder if I shall ever know what became of him.

Yesterday, I had lunch with Tennessee Williams, the writer. He's a strange boy, small, plump and muscular, with a slight cast in one eye; full of amused malice. He has a job with Metro. He wanted to buy an autoglide to ride to work on. I tried to dissuade him, but he insisted. We went to a dealer's, and he selected a very junky old machine which is obviously going to give trouble.[1]

May 14. Drove down to Santa Monica for lunch with the Viertels, in Salka's car; she picked me up in Beverly Hills. She says she has always believed in God and prayed to Him. She can't even imagine what it would be like, not to have faith. "Do you really pray to God," she asked, "the way I do?" And she said, "Doubt is just fear—that's all it is."

She is going to England, possibly, in the near future, to write a movie version of Shaw's *St. Joan*, for Garbo. Berthold is working on a play, with an American writer. It was lovely, seeing them again.

After lunch, Garbo came in. She and Tommy Viertel and I walked along the shore, right to the pier. The sun was brilliant, with a strong wind—the palms waving all along the cliff, and the ocean dazzling with light and foam. The air was full of spray and falling light; it was beautiful beyond all words; the afternoon had an edge of extra keen, almost intolerable sensation on all its sights and sounds and smells. Seeing a human body in the far distance, you wanted to seize it in your arms and devour it—not for itself, but as a palpable fragment of the whole scene, of the wildness of the wind and foam, of the entire, unseizable mystery and delight of the moment. I glimpsed something, for an instant, of the reality behind sex. Something which we reach out towards, as we take the human body in our arms. It is what we really want, and it eludes us in the very act of possession.

Garbo chattered away. She was nice. I liked her better than ever before. She's much interested in Vedanta, and says she'll come and visit us. Later, she drove me back to Beverly Hills, shooting all the stop lights. But the afternoon was more memorable than she was.

May 15. The first lesson I have got to learn is submission. As Amiya says, it's the little things which are hard to take. No good making up

---

[1] Evidently this is the motor scooter Williams bought while in Santa Monica; he had at least one accident and returned it to the dealer.

all sorts of excellent and perfectly valid reasons why I should no longer be deprived of my room by Hayne, or annoyed by George's chanting, Web's alarm clock, Asit's radio, Aparna's beads. (Aparna was a schoolmistress who lived next door and came in fairly regularly. She had a trick of rattling her rosary very loud while she was telling it.) Stop cackling about rights and justice. Sure, you're entitled to them if you insist. But you're an idiot if you do insist. This is infinitely more important.

This morning, for the first time, I did the ritual through without looking at the book of instructions. Got through the newly learned part—the external worship—pretty well, although I forgot the bang mudra over the food; but a whole chunk of the purification ceremony slipped right out of my mind. I missed the prayer for the liberation of earthbound spirits and all the precautions against psychic obstacles. I've never forgotten them before.

After lunch, I finished reading *Leave Her to Heaven*, Johnny [van Druten]'s unsuccessful play, which I rather like. Most of the afternoon, I tried to get started with my novelette about Viertel and Gaumont-British, which I shall call *Prater Violet*: after three quite promising pages, I'm stuck. Web and I went down to Hollywood Boulevard to take the copies of the May-June issue of the magazine to the London and Hollywood Bookshops. Then Amiya made me a cup of tea and we let off steam together over the horrors of American food—mint jelly and mayonnaise on fruit salad. Yogini is the worst offender: her mixtures would shock the witches in *Macbeth*. Sarada came by, overheard us, and laughed.

In the evening, after supper, Swami described how Premananda hated business meetings and used to try to avoid them by going into the shrine. So one of the other swamis went in and picked him up as he sat meditating, and carried him down to the courtyard and threw him into the air. And then all the swamis suddenly began to dance, making a circle around Brahmananda, who sang, improvising the words, calling on all the people of the earth to come and share the joy of knowing God.

I asked, if Vivekananda had already experienced the highest samadhi, why did he have any more doubts. Swami explained that Ramakrishna wished him to have doubts. He deliberately "locked the door and kept the key," in order that Vivekananda should return to ignorance. Vivekananda had to doubt, for our sake. Otherwise we should say to ourselves, "It was all very well for *him* to believe: he was simply hypnotized by Ramakrishna's personality." But Vivekananda did our doubting for us. Like Thomas in the Christian gospel, Mr. Hayne added.

May 16. Peggy came down to the lecture and drove me up to lunch at Alto Cedro. Another crisis is on at Laguna. Paul Sorel threatens all kinds of scandal because his money is cut short: he's reckless enough to invent any lie—particularly about Trabuco—and stick to it. Chris has run away somewhere, hoping Paul will eventually get tired and leave. Hearing about this was probably what gave me a sore throat.

On to tea with the Beesleys. I go there a lot, sometimes on my bicycle. They are always restful, always kind, always pleased to see me. Their house is a haven of peace, after the tumults of monastic life.

Beautiful golden yellow Peruvian lilies on the steps of the shrine. Felt so exhausted that I went to bed immediately after vespers. Sudhira brought me bacon sandwiches and hot milk with pepper, and sprayed my throat. Slept well, after feelings of resentment against Asit, George and an unidentified radio because of the noise they were making.

May 17. Swami, Sister, Amiya, Sarada, Yogini, George, Web, Hayne and I drove up to Peggy's for tea. Peggy and Sister talked gardens. Web was interested in the heating system and the furnace. "They've stolen my idea!" he exclaimed. George took a group snapshot, which no doubt will be out of focus as usual. Yogini suggested that the front door should be painted Chinese red. She loves bright colors. Sarada wanted to see the hut where I used to meditate. She pretended that it was a famous shrine and place of pilgrimage, and took off her shoes before entering. We have a lot of jokes of this kind. Sometimes, when we're going in to a meal, Sarada and I will spend several minutes bowing to each other in the doorway with folded hands and murmuring, "Not worthy!"

May 19. The man came round today who exterminates vermin and termites; he calls regularly every few months, Swami being no Buddhist. Sarada had one of her missionary talks with him and excitedly reported that he was much interested in Vedanta. "I'm sure he's got the makings of a devotee," she said. George commented dryly: "From ratman to Atman."

Today and all night till 7 a.m. tomorrow morning, we have a twenty-four-hour vigil, taking it in turns to chant Ramakrishna's name in the shrine, an hour at a stretch—because it is the full moon of Buddha's birthday and because Swami thinks we are getting lazy.

Hayne is just returning with his girl, Miss Heinen: it's now pretty obvious that this is [a romance]. The sooner he clears out of here, the better.

George got a card from his draft board today, classifying him 1-A-H. He was a bit surly because I bossily offered to write a letter for him, appealing for 4-D—at Swami's suggestion.

Churchill, over here on one of his flying visits, promises England will help the U.S. reduce Japan to ashes.

Have just done my stint in the shrine room, chanting "Jaya Sri Ramakrishna!" The first ten or fifteen minutes are the worst, because they are a conscious effort. Then, as Sudhira puts it, "The thing begins to say itself." You find yourself changing gear, from one inflection to another: "JAYa Sri Ramakrishna!" becomes "Jaya SRI Ramakrisha!" and changes to "Jaya Sri RAMakrishna!"; then back again. Sometimes you begin to rock back and forth, keeping time to the chant. Sometimes you go up and down the scale, almost singing it. Sometimes, you get terrifically loud, and start shouting it. Sudhira, who loves anything emotional, says that it's best in the middle of the night. Once, she and Asit and Aparna got in the shrine together and made such a noise they could be heard all over the neighborhood. Another time, Madhabi (who isn't here now, but will return soon) actually stood up and started to dance. The shrine room "feels" quite different while the chanting is going on: the atmosphere seems to become tremendously charged with energy and excitement. It's something like a jive session.

May 22. Right now, I'm going through an ebb-tide phase—one of those recurring periods during which, ordinarily, I would over-smoke, lounge around doing nothing, go too often to the movies, run after sex, read crime stories, drink too much, wallow in the newspapers and feel depressed. The problem is not to lose everything I have gained. I must watch myself, or I shall be apt to grab some excuse for leaving Ivar Avenue altogether—such as an order from the draft board. Even CPS camp now presents itself in a furtively attractive aspect, because it would rationalize a return to sexuality. I now think of sex in entirely promiscuous terms: I've no desire whatever for any kind of relationship. I don't know if this is a good sign, or not.

Reading the life of Vivekananda[1]—especially the part about his austerities at the Baranagore Math—I ask myself, what were all those agonies and struggles *for*? There are times when I feel I have absolutely

---

[1] Probably *The Life of Swami Vivekananda* (1949) by his eastern and western disciples, although others had been published by Nivedita, Rama-Prasada K. Desai, and Romain Rolland.

no idea. But then I always think, well, can you tell me what Churchill's blood-toil-tears-and-sweat are *for*?[1] I don't know that, either; so the balance is restored. The spiritual life is, at worst, no more unreal than the political.

May 23. Lunch with the Beesleys. Afterwards, we drove up Topanga Canyon and down through the hills to Malibu. Whenever they drive around, there are amused and sympathetic smiles—partly because of their cars, partly because of the dogs. (Folly, after being given a medicine called "Pregnant Mare," has puppies coming.) Their 1938 Rolls Royce awakens the same nostalgic and slightly contemptuous sentiments in the average American as a covered wagon or a sedan chair. And the little Bantam always gets a laugh. A boy driving a jeep said to us, "And I used to think *this* was small!" When the three of us and the two dogs are in the Bantam, it looks like a trick—like a model sailing ship in a bottle: how on earth did we ever get inside? When we are in the Rolls, the car appears to belong to the dogs: they sit in the back, like prince and princess, with Dodie as lady-in-waiting, and Alec and myself in front, as chauffeur and footman.

May 24. Sister was very contrite this morning, because she'd disagreed with Swami yesterday when he denounced present-day patriotism. "Well," she sighed, "that's just one more hump I'll have to get over." Swami should be the last person to scold anyone for being patriotic: at heart he's still a flaming Indian nationalist, and gets very heated when British policy is discussed. But I'm never really shocked by his inconsistencies because, fundamentally, he's so truly humble. He lets the women devotees flatter him and gush about gurus, and he laughs. I am certain that he never thinks of himself as being anything but Brahmananda's most minor disciple and representative. He refers every problem back to the shrine. I'm even glad that he's sometimes silly about politics and vain about his youthful appearance. He's so entirely unimpressive in an immediate, theatrical sense: his great quality is that he never gets in the way of what he stands for, his figure doesn't block out the light.

Hayne left early, to escort Miss Heinen to her new job at a bookshop in Westwood Village. Developments are expected any day, now. Swami never fails to get in some nasty crack at marriage when he's present. This morning, celibacy took another knock. Roger Spencer called in to tell us that he's getting married to an

[1] Alluding to Churchill's "blood and toil" leadership speech in the House of Commons, May 13, 1940.

eighteen-year-old girl. Swami insists that he'll still end up as a monk, however.

May 25. Last night, I dreamt I was told by a doctor I had incurable cancer. Misery, horror and dismay—so vivid; a memory, surely, of some former experience? These are the chasms of the ocean of sleep. At such enormous depths, not one ray of light from the surface life can penetrate. Down there in the darkness, I knew no consolation, nothing about God or Ramakrishna, nothing but helpless fear. It's a long time since I've had one of these *deep* dreams. In them, I've experienced almost every emotion—especially fear, pity and rage—with an intensity quite unknown to my waking life. However fantastic the circumstances of the dream may be, the emotion itself is always absolutely valid. I bring it back to the surface consciousness and keep it with me, like an experience. It always teaches me something.

A ridiculous quarrel with Yogini, who said that Honolulu is larger in area than Los Angeles. We both got quite angry. She called the Bureau of Statistics, and proved she was right.

Asit has brought home some Indian records, and George plays them on his machine: the whole house and garden is full of their wailing. Very irritable and nervous in consequence. I *must* learn to take these things. Relax *towards* them. See them as an intelligence test: nothing happens by chance. And what little conditioning I'm being subjected to at present—our overcrowded quarters, Web's noisiness, etc.—is so very mild. Remember all those millions of boys in camps, in ships, on the battlefields. And *I* claim to have a vocation, a philosophy of life! Shame. I've got to do a hundred times better than this. Vivekananda's photograph, on my desk, is fixing me with its terrible, reproachful stare. "Run along and do the worship," it says. "Enough of this nonsense!" Okay, okay, I'm going.

May 28. Yesterday morning, I went down to the Red Cross center on Western Avenue to donate my pint of blood. An absurd mental fuss about this, simply because the operation took place in semisurgical surroundings. It was far less unpleasant then Sudhira's B$_1$ shots, which sting like a bee—not to mention Kolisch's injections, which were like assassinations; he used to come striding into the room and, without pausing to find a suitable spot, stab you with the hypodermic, which he gripped in his fist like a dagger. The blood donors are all treated like heroes—soothed, petted, supported from the operating room into an improvised lounge (furnished by Barker Brothers[1]) and

---

[1] A furniture store.

strengthened with coffee, orangeade and doughnuts. As they leave, they are given a donor's button, like a decoration for bravery. And, in fact, some of the tired, elderly women I saw there *were* being brave. For them it was really an ordeal: a few nearly fainted. As I lay on the bed, a lady doctor started to examine my feet. I couldn't think why, till she explained: "I'm just looking at your beautiful socks. Are they real wool?"

Doris, Sarada's "convert," now comes in every evening. She has brushed her hair back into a knot, in imitation of Sarada's, and now looks charming. She might be a younger sister of Heinz.

A blue jay, with a particularly harsh note, has gotten terribly on Swami's nerves. He throws stones at it, jumping into the air with a little hop and nearly overbalancing. Amiya and Sudhira like the bird, however, because he enrages Dhruva, whom they both dislike. Dhruva barks frantically at the jay, who perches just out of reach and screeches insults.

May 30. It's high time we had an inspection:

Well, boys—we've been in this place three months and three weeks. Any complaints?

Oh, *no*, Sir!

Nothing *at all*? Food all right?

It's *marvellous*.

Funny. . . . I thought I heard some talk yesterday evening. Those *parathas*[1] Asit cooked. Didn't someone say they tasted like cardboard boxes?

Oh well—that was just Asit—

I see. . . . Just Asit . . . How's the sleeping accommodation?

Well, Sir, we don't want to complain—

Seems to me you were complaining yesterday night, all right.

Well—after all, Sir—that's only temporary. It's not that we're fussy. It's just—well, we hate to see that great flabby Catholic priest taking advantage of Swami's hospitality to run around after that girl with her spindly legs, monopolizing *our* room and filling it with cigarette smoke—and then there's Web—well, of course, on weekdays, we wouldn't say a *word*—but on holidays it hardly seems quite fair that a high-school kid *young enough to be our son* should have the selfishness and stupidity to make that clock ring at five, when he doesn't even *intend* to get up—and what's more—

NOW LISTEN—why did you come to this place at all? Was it to be comfortable? Was it to have your feelings considered? Was it for the sake of your writing? Was it for the food? What makes you

---

[1] Fried unleavened bread.

suppose that, because you couldn't handle your relationship with Vernon, all your problems could be solved simply by not having a Vernon in your life? Do you see any future for yourselves in the way of life you used to lead? Can you think of anything really constructive you could be doing, except this?

No, Sir. We can't.

Well then, for God's sake pull yourselves together.

Yesterday, I cycled out to Beverly Hills. Denny met me there, to pick up the bicycle he's bought from Hans Ohrt. We rode around for a while, and then Denny suggested we should look in on Lena Horne, the colored singer. She has a little house just above the Sunset Strip. They have become great friends. Denny opened the door and shouted, "Lena darling, I've brought a friend in to take a shower." Lena seemed to find this perfectly natural. She is a very nice girl, not in the least grand or affected. She hadn't gotten out of bed, although this was the middle of the afternoon, and she didn't get coy about our seeing her with untidy hair and no makeup on.

This evening, I feel curiously exhausted. Swami, Web, Franz Dispecker and Mrs. Nixon are sitting outside on the steps, talking about reincarnation. Mrs. Nixon said dreamily, "But, eventually, they'd all be *merged*, wouldn't they?"

(Mrs. Nixon was a garish but rather sympathetic southern lady who was one of the most regular members of Swami's congregation. She specialized in weird hats, in strange rich garments, and in flower decorations, often very ingenious. She had travelled all over the world. Her daughter Phoebe, a very attractive dark girl, used to help us with the secretarial work from time to time.

Franz Dispecker and his wife came from Switzerland. He was a banker by profession and quite wealthy. At first he seemed like a typical fussy, bossy Prussian Jew, but he was serious about Vedanta and very good-natured, and the whole family gradually became very fond of him. He made horrible puns. His wife was much younger than he was, very chic and feminine and clinging, but nice too.)

A glorious evening—except for the army planes, which are becoming more and more of a nuisance, power-diving all around. Web claims to have driven the blue jay away for good, with a slingshot.

June 3. He was wrong. The jay is tormenting Dhruva again, swooping at him and pecking tufts of hair from his tail. Another bad night, on account of the alarm clock. I've screwed myself up to tell Web that it's not to ring until six on schooldays, and on holidays not at all. I haven't told him yet, however. Merely making the decision required several hundred rehearsals, and the rest of the nervous energy I had in reserve for the day. Now I won't be able to do any work at all. When I don't sleep, I'm simply not quite sane.

June 7. And now, only four days later, everything is changed: almost absurdly so. Swami has gone away. He left last night, with George, for the East, because Swami Akhilananda is seriously ill in Providence. He won't be back for at least six weeks. Meanwhile, I have moved into his room. I am very conscious of his presence here—practically apologizing to him each time I use the toilet. Hope I continue to feel that way. It will help me a great deal.

June 21. Two weeks whizzed by—probably because I'm feeling much better about everything, particularly sex. Hardly any trouble since I've been in Swami's room. Sarada left last Tuesday, to visit her father in New Mexico. Hayne left last Wednesday, to work in a box factory in Beverly Hills: Peggy decided to deal with him—it was largely my fault—and told him in no uncertain terms that it was up to him to clear out of here and support himself. Web and his sister Jean left today, to visit their family in Avondale, Arizona—such a wonderfully unsuitable name for the Far West! Roger Spencer is here, with Laurie Fallas, the girl he plans to marry. She's about fifteen years younger than he, a Quaker and [seems unintelligent]. Very snooty because we don't live poorly enough. They are out all day, discussing their relationship, which is to be without sex. No, I mustn't begin to sneer. What I can't sympathize with, I needn't notice. Who made me the judge?

Denny has been living for some time in a house in a bungalow colony on Descanso Drive, two-thirds of the way downtown. It's rather attractive: the buildings are on a flight of wide steps, with a big meadow at the top of the hill, overlooking the city. Collins George shares the place with him, and another colored boy named Al is there most of the time. Denny is half in and half out of the CPS camp; that is to say, his discharge hasn't been made official yet, but they're obviously letting him go. He spends nearly all of his time with Negroes, and his conversation is full of their slang. He seems to be having a lot of fun, and he still keeps up his studies—which is a wonder, for life at Descanso Drive is practically a nonstop party. Lots of C.O.s come down from camp and sleep on the floor, every weekend, and mix peacefully with sailors on leave who are stranded in the city without a bed.

Wrote to Morgan. Walked up the hill with Dhruva. Fleecy clouds, very warm: earthquake weather, people say. The hills look like my idea of Italy, with their white houses and terraced gardens. The ocean grey and sad in the distance. The oil fields like a crowd of calvarys, on the bare ugly heights behind Long Beach. Nothing anywhere but God, and not much of Him today. A sardonic-looking man, in one of the gardens, tossed a pebble at Dhruva and hit him: Dhruva scarcely noticed. "He don't scare easy, does he?" the man said to me.

June 23. Had supper at Chasen's, with Lesser Samuels, his wife and his daughter Helene. The Samuelses eat out nearly every night, at Chasen's or the Derby: Lesser is earning a thousand a week, and they can't get a cook. The atmosphere of pre-inflation is curious; nearly everybody has heaps of money, the restaurants are packed, and there is less and less to buy in the stores. Women stand in line for shoes. After dinner, Lesser and I talked about the Gaumont-British days. He told me a lot about Saville, and about picture making in general which will be very valuable for my story. I hope to restart it, now that the magazine has gone off to the printers.

June 24. Asit got a job yesterday, at a photographic studio downtown, earning $140 a month. He is really delighted. When there's nothing special to do, he's the laziest creature on earth, but when he has to work, he'll work like a horse. The girls tell me he was just the same when he was studying for his degree at USC.[1]

July 1. Who should saunter in this afternoon but Richard Thom, with the wire gone from around his teeth, and his hair cropped short? He wore a blue navy denim shirt, blue jean pants and a seaman's sweater. He was three weeks in the merchant marine, on Catalina Island, and then got himself derolled, because they taught him nothing except cleaning toilets. Now he has a job as usher at the Warner Theater. He plans to stay there two or three months, till he can join the Marine Corps. As soon as we look at each other we always begin to laugh, like two people who are bluffing each other at poker. Only, at the same time, I get the uneasy feeling that maybe Rich *isn't* bluffing. It's hard to explain just exactly what I mean by this. But Rich sometimes gives you a look which is disconcertingly mature, indulgent almost as though he were a grown-up playing with a child.

Here's a poem I just wrote. Heaven knows why. It came to me all in a lump, while I was in the shrine room.

---

[1] University of Southern California.

On His Queerness

When I was young and wanted to see the sights,
They told me: "Cast an eye over the Roman Camp
If you care to,
But plan to spend most of your day at the Aquarium—
Because, after all, the Aquarium—
Well, I mean to say, the Aquarium—
Till you've seen the Aquarium you ain't seen nothing."

So I cast an eye over
The Roman Camp—
And that old Roman Camp,
That old, old Roman Camp
Got me
Interested.

So that now, near closing time,
I find that I still know nothing—
And am not even sorry that I know nothing—
About fish.

July 3. Cycled down to the beach with Denny and his friend Johnny Goodwin. Johnny's handsome body has turned skinny, and his face is lined and ravaged, as if by intense hunger. His blond hair is all faded. His nose turns up as though sniffing a chronically nasty smell. He and Denny are like brothers. In many ways, Johnny is simply Denny with money. But he's quite talented and intelligent, if he weren't such a dilettante. Maybe Denny would be nicer with money and Johnny without it.

I left them in midafternoon and went around to the Viertels'. They are having another financial crisis. Salka has left Metro, and the projected trip with Garbo to England to make *St. Joan* probably won't be till next spring—if at all. Garbo was there today, in unbecoming shorts; much worried because they had a fruit stain on them. Berthold, working hard on his play, looked much older; rather like the late self-portraits of Rembrandt. He told me—as a fact—that Peggy is going to get married very soon; and added, rather nastily, that this is an excellent thing, because a beautiful woman who is still young shouldn't waste her life with religion. Berthold still bitterly resents my retirement to Ivar Avenue, and keeps hitting at it in all sorts of ways. I avoid answering him, as far as I can—or there'd be a row.

July 4. Up to lunch with Peggy, who is thinner but not looking as badly as I'd expected after her severe attack of flu. She says that Bill Kiskadden has announced that he's "coming to get her" in a couple of weeks—that she doesn't know what to do—she's incapable of any decision—the children will always come first—etc. etc. In other words, it's definitely settled. Peggy had told the Zinnemanns (who are neighbors of the Viertels on Mabery Road) and the Zinnemanns had told Berthold. Ben doesn't know yet. Neither does Henwar. I told Peggy I was thoroughly in favor of the idea; and I really am. Peggy's remarriage will make the children feel ever so much freer—especially now, when they are just growing up.

July 5. Supper with my agents, Edna and Dan Leonardson, at the Hollywood Hotel. We had met to settle up our accounts, and this led to a most impudent and ridiculous claim that I should pay half the amount it finally cost them to settle with another agent whom they tried to swindle on my account, back in 1939. However, I was in a good humor; so I agreed. (I think it cost me around eighty dollars.)

Strangely enough, after such a beginning, the evening was really enjoyable. Dan talked about Judaism, Sarah Bernhardt and the old days in Hollywood. The Hollywood Hotel used to be the only smart place in town; it looked across a big orange grove on the opposite side of the street, and there was a horse tram to take you into Los Angeles. Dan is really much more intelligent than Edna, and more sensitive. Edna's brother has invented some kind of television or radar apparatus, which is highly secret, and which interests the U.S. government. Dan helps him demonstrate it. The two of them are at the disposal of the army, at all times; cars arrive dramatically and whisk them away to airfields; some weeks ago, they were flown up to the Aleutians, to make a test. One day, they may become very rich, but government compensation is very slow in coming: Washington has only just finished paying for the inventions of the last war.

Dan predicts a new and much more elaborate machine age after the war: larger and lighter automobiles, television in every home, and a portable radio-telephone in every pocket. "It may sound funny for me to say this," he added, "but I wish we could scrap all these machines."

July 6. Chris Wood came around to see me. He looks terribly battered. Paul Sorel has retired to the Coast Inn in Laguna and Gerald has been staying at Rockledge Road—behaving, as Chris put it, "like the British after they'd run Rommel out of Africa." Apparently, Gerald grew quite skittish in his triumph, and even missed his meditation hours to come swimming with Chris: Chris described Gerald in the water, "like a young demoiselle, with his beard floating on the tops of the waves."

Chris wants me to come down and stay with him. I said sure, as long as I don't have to see Paul. This disappointed him, and I hate to be stuffy, but I know Paul would use my visit for propaganda purposes.

July 7. Out for a turn around the block before vespers, I met Rich. He looked a real bum, dirty, unshaven and slyer than ever. He has quit his job at the Warner Theater and is going around mowing lawns. He refused supper, because, as he said, he can't eat here without going into the shrine room first, and he won't go into the shrine room because he has broken with Ramakrishna. His scruples are the greatest part of his charm.

A talk with Amiya. We had quite a row last night, because she spoke against Kolisch, which always makes me mad. Today we made it up. Amiya told me that she was so happy when I kissed her goodbye at Glendale Station, when she was leaving for San Francisco. I must never forget this about her: her longing for affection, her loyalty, her struggle to create a family and a home.

July 8. Another day of concealed idling: that is to say, I was very busy doing everything but my duty. I copied verses from Angelus Silesius[1] into my notebook and mowed the front lawn. Cadmus sent me some photographs of his paintings, etc. One of them I shall have to destroy: it excites me rather.

Swami has wired that he's coming home on Friday of next week, with George, Madhabi and Swami Vishwananda of Chicago. I'm so afraid I'm going to loathe Madhabi: everything Sudhira tells me about her makes her sound such an utter bitch.

July 15. Fifteen minutes till vespers, but it's important that I don't let any more time go by without making a few notes. The whole family reassembled yesterday, plus Swami Vishwananda and Madhabi.

Vishwananda is fat, black, jolly, very Indian. He nearly chokes with laughter at his own jokes, and talks Bengali with Swami and Asit. Everything delights him here, especially the food: in Chicago, he can't get proper curry. His Indianness makes Swami seem Indian too—I realize now how little I usually regard him as an Oriental—and this is slightly disconcerting. Vishwananda is staying in our house, in Web's room, and Web has moved to the living room, thus producing a new crisis of overcrowding which fills me with jealous

[1] German mystic and religious poet Johann Scheffler (1624–1677), from Silesia; he took the name Johann Angelus when he converted to Roman Catholicism at eighteen.

possessive jitters: I'm afraid Asit will use "my" washroom and disturb me in the morning. Not that this really makes the least difference—as my fear of being wakened wakes me, in any case, at 5:30, when Asit's alarm clock is about to ring. I have a headache now because I haven't slept properly for the past three nights—or rather, because I have an obsession about insufficient sleep. However, this whole business has got to be settled, once and for all—just as it would have to be settled if I were in camp or in the army. (Isn't it, perhaps, just because I'm *not* in camp or the army that this problem arises at this particular time? Do we ever avoid anything?)

Saw a movie called *Stage Door Canteen*: the usual saccharine lie, but very moving, just the same, because it is about an actual situation— the loneliness of millions of homeless boys in uniform, and their pitiful gratitude to the hams who so patriotically spare a few minutes of their precious time and invest in some free publicity, in order to entertain them. I kept remembering Wilfred Owen's lines: "These men are worth / Your tears. You are not worth their merriment."[1] We see the same thing here in Hollywood. The other day, I was driving out to Beverly Hills in the family car and gave a service man a ride. He had a camera with him. I asked him where he wanted to be dropped off. "Oh, anywhere," he said. Then, lowering his voice with instinctive reverence, he added: "I'm just going to walk around and look at the *Homes*."

July 16. Overstimulated by two and a half cups of coffee, I've been running around since breakfast. I just had a talk to Swami, and, as nearly always, he gave me something. I feel such a deep relationship with him. "Love" is too possessive a word to describe it. It is really absence of demand, lack of strain, entire reassurance. I can't imagine being jealous, as the girls are, when he seems to favor one person; because it's so obvious that his attitude toward each one of us is special and inalienable. "To divide is not to take away."

He touched my cheek with his finger and giggled, because *The New Republic* had referred to me as a prominent young writer. I told him how free I've been from sexual thoughts and fantasies during the past weeks, and he said, "Yes, I saw that in your face yesterday. But don't get too confident. They will come back." I also told him that the worship has become so mechanical to me at present that, in future, I only want to do it twice a week. Swami said that freedom from sexual thoughts is more important, anyway, than conscious devotion. As the Catholic writers insist, one mustn't seek too much emotional satisfaction in prayer. Yes—I know all these things out of

[1] "Apologia pro Poemate Meo."

books; but until Swami himself points them out to me I never really believe them.

Swami Vishwananda came into "my" washroom this morning, spilled water on the floor and left a brownish gob of spittle in the basin. This is just the sort of thing I've got to take, and like.

Madhabi is a tiny middle-aged woman, with a sort of pinched, childlike prettiness. She affects dirndl clothes and is "dainty" and terribly middle-class, bristling with prejudices, and addicted to "gracious living." She used to be an actress. Her husband is an officer in the marines. We both realize, I think, that we have got to be careful with each other, so we're very polite. Madhabi made a good start by admiring the way I'd decorated the shrine, the day she arrived. I helped her fix her room. If we don't see too much of each other at first, it may be all right.

The other day, I was walking along the street, and several kids were firing at each other with toy pistols, capturing Sicily or Kiska.[1] In the midst of all the yells and banging, one of the boys turned to me and said, in a very grown-up, slightly apologetic tone: "It's a great game!"

Rich is in here this morning, sawing wood with Web. He has been around ever since Swami returned home, popping in and out, quite one of the family again. No one knows just what he plans to do.

Later. . . . Swami Vishwananda got hold of me and put me through a regular examination on the mudras we use in the worship; from these we went on to talk about my travels in China. I saw no escape, until Peggy created a diversion by coming out of the living room with Swami. She'd called to get a "dispensation" for her marriage with Bill, and of course she got it, and was let off with a caution not to do it again. Scarcely was I back from talking to Peggy, when Mrs. Herbold (one of Allan Hunter's parishioners) drove up with a woman from some government office which sends out literature to foreign countries about U.S. culture. She had gotten Wystan to broadcast in New York, and she wanted me to write something about the Vedanta Society—to show how wonderfully the U.S. tolerates all religions. (When I told this at lunch, Yogini said, "I think it's wonderful the way *we* tolerate the United States.") Refused politely, loaning her my copy of *On this Island*,[2] and prepared to go into the temple, but first I had to talk to Joan Keating, one of my Metro ex-secretaries, who called up out of the bluest blue to gossip. Rushed into the shrine room, prostrated, offered a flower, had lunch, slept till four, hurried down to the boulevard with Swami's watch to be repaired and a letter

[1] An island in the U.S. Aleutian chain, seized by the Japanese in June 1942 and recaptured in May 1943.

[2] Auden's 1936 volume published in the U.K. as *Look, Stranger!*

to Willie Maugham about the exact translation of a verse in the Katha Upanishad which he wants to use as a title for his new novel, *The Razor's Edge* or *The Edge of the Razor*, nearly lost Dhruva in the crowd, got home, sawed some wood, joined in a discussion as to whether or not Rich should forget about the Marine Corps and try to get classified as a C.O., had tea, translated a verse of the Gita, ate too many peppermint drops, and am now late for vespers. This is what they call an escape from the world!

July 19. This weekend has been stormy, unexpectedly so. We had a puja, and there's nothing like a good puja for stirring up lust. As we sat there in the shrine room, it came to me with the fullest force how much I should like to give up Vedanta, pacifism, everything. Yes, get into a uniform and be the same as everybody else. Join the navy. I really wouldn't care what happened to me, I thought, provided I could spend a few more rousing Saturday nights.

Suppose Swami's just kidding himself? Suppose there's no God, no afterlife? Well—suppose. Then death is best, at once. But if you don't want to die? Could you be satisfied with a life of cautious, rationed sensuality? I don't think you could. You've got to renounce or destroy yourself. So the minimum Buddhist position still stands— wrote he, taking another peppermint.

There is no point even in writing this down, however. In a stormy sea there's no point in doing anything but continuing to swim. Keep going through the motions—don't ask for anything—just go right on swimming. This will pass.

July 22. The storm is slowly blowing itself out, it seems.

What I didn't mention in my last entry is that a good deal of my state of tension was concerned with India: Swami Vishwananda, and the arrival of a copy of the rules and regulations of the Belur Math. (The central monastery of the Ramakrishna Order, in Calcutta.) My God, I thought, what is this gang I am joining? Is it to be curry and turbans unwinding uphill all the way, to the very end?[1] Swami was quite wonderful, because he answered my fears and doubts indirectly, telepathically almost, by asking me to write a letter to the Math for him, explaining that their rules could not possibly apply to western probationers. "If they refuse to change," he said, "I shall leave the order!" What a little rock of safety he is!

Then George, in his rigid New England way, refused to sign the admission application, because he said he couldn't agree to give up his money to the order.

[1] Cf. Christina Rossetti, "Up-Hill."

Yesterday, at supper, Swami told us how his brother monks, for a joke, gave him a drink prepared from hemp. He was terribly sick, after it, and had psychic visions, followed by a violent reaction: for six months, he lost his faith altogether. I asked him, didn't he consider leaving the monastery, during that time? "*No!*" he answered, "why should I do that? Because I had stopped believing in God, that did not mean that I believed in the world."

The day before yesterday, Peggy and Bill Kiskadden got married. She's bringing him to vespers; starting his training at once.

July 23. Just before vespers, I had a talk with Sudhira, who had announced she was going to leave this place permanently. Told her she's the one I like best here, and that I'd regard her going away as an act of desertion. Sudhira replied that, if she stays here, she'll become a mental case. Now that Madhabi is back, she can't resist ganging up with her against Amiya—and, rather than do this, she'll leave. However, when we were through talking, she told me: "You've succeeded in pricking my conscience, a little." That was yesterday. This morning she says she's not going.

I'm writing this before lunch—having gabbled through 500 of my daily 2,500 beads, while Vishwananda, like a curly-headed black elephant, puffingly offered flowers to the Lord. Sarada is sick, and yesterday and today he has done the worship. I went out of the temple early, to avoid being asked to clean up the shrine when he had finished.

I'm at what seems a new all-time low ebb. We are in the midst of a heat wave. I haven't said a real prayer in weeks, or meditated in months. I spend all the meditation hours rattling through my japam, so as not to be bothered with it at any other time. At present I have no feeling for the sacredness of the shrine and not the least reverence for Ramakrishna or anybody else. If you ask me what I want, I reply: Sex, followed by a long long sleep. If offered a painless drug which would kill me in my sleep, I would seriously consider taking it: and I've never played much with thoughts of suicide before.

I inhabit a world in which people are scarcely real. Real are my sex fantasies and memories. Real are the devices I think up for not being woken by Asit's alarm clock. Utterly, utterly unreal are Ramakrishna, religion, the war with all its casualties and suffering, and the problems of other people. I *long* to get away from this place. And yet, if I do manage to wriggle out somehow, I know that, in two or three months, I'll pine to get back in again.

July 26. This is the hottest day so far, with no letup in sight. But I don't really mind, because today has been relatively a good day. I got up early, went into the shrine at six, and cycled down to the printers' before breakfast, to take them the copy for the leaflet announcing Swami Vishwananda's lectures. This morning I roughed out another page of my novelette, did three verses of the Gita, and my 2,500 beads.

There is an old man who is rather on my conscience. He is little, skinny, white haired, crooked and alert, and has a German accent. He says he's a research chemist who took up Vedanta, renounced everything, invented a special diet, and went to India, where he stayed at several of the Ramakrishna monasteries. This much seems to be true, but Swami says he was a nuisance and got into a lot of trouble. However, he's now living in a room without washing facilities and has to wait until 8 a.m. before he can use the bathroom; so this morning he came here and used ours. He would like to live here and sleep on the floor; and we won't let him, because he'd be in the way. So I feel guilty, like a rich, fat old friar.

On Saturday, I cycled down to Santa Monica and lunched with the Viertels. The air was so fresh after sticky Hollywood, and the Viertels' political talk was refreshing, too—as a change. Hans was there, and Tommy, and a nice young Jewish boxer named Dick,[1] and Stefan Brecht—Bertolt Brecht's son. Stefan is a spotty boy with glasses, very sweet, gentle brown eyes and a small slim muscular body. He plans to return to Germany after Hitler and become a political journalist. He's a deadly serious Marxist, studies chemistry at UCLA, and plays chess with Eduard [Steuermann], Salka's brother. When introduced, he bows stiffly from the waist.

Everything in the household was just as usual. Berthold and Hans got into one of their heated arguments. It might easily have been 1939—except that Peter is in the Pacific war zone with the marines, and Tommy will shortly have to register for the draft. Salka came home around three o'clock, attended by collaborators, secretaries, etc. She is writing two stories at once—one about Iceland, for Garbo; the other about refugee domestic servants.

On the beach, I noticed a very handsome blond young man, lounging on the sand talking to some girls, in an attitude of such imperious elegance that it was downright funny. As I came up from the ocean after swimming, the girls were getting into a car and the boy was just rising to his feet. He braced one leg, brown and muscular, and stood up—and then I saw that the other leg hung useless, quite tiny, withered and crooked as a scythe. And now the

[1] Probably Dick LaPan.

boy's face looked entirely different. It was nicer, kinder and more mature, and there were lines of pain around the mouth.

July 27. Sudhira often brings me candy from the market. We call it "medical supplies." Today she left a whole box of it in my room, with a note, "I'm tired of being treated as an anticlimax." However much or little this meant, it seemed to require some reaction: after all, we are declared allies. So we went for a walk on the hills, looking down over the reservoir full of strange confused gleams from the overcast sky, and over the city lying dully beneath moist hot thundery clouds. I told Sudhira that I don't really like Indians as a race; Swami is an exception. Swami Vishwananda is sympathetic, but he's a murderee like nearly all of them, and I don't respect him.

July 28. Salka brought Garbo up to lunch at Ivar Avenue. The girls were all a-flutter, and Garbo didn't disappoint them. She played up outrageously, sighing about how wonderful it must be to be a nun, and flirting with Swami, telling him about his dark, mysterious, oriental eyes. Sarada, of course, was convinced that Garbo's soul is halfway saved already, and Swami says that now I have to bring him the Duke of Windsor—his other great object of admiration.

August 6. Terribly late for vespers, I must just write a few lines in recognition of this important date: six months at Ivar Avenue, six months of technical celibacy. Last year, that achievement would have seemed positively supernatural. Now I see it as the very first step, merely: less than the first. It has no value except as a reassurance that nothing is impossible.

Today, Swami Vishwananda started to teach us a chant: *Ram, Ram, Ram, Jaya, Ram.* It sounds so idiotic—just like the fake-Tibetan chant in *F6.*[1] And it is the perfect example of the kind of thing I've got to learn to take. If I am too dainty-stomached to swallow a little Sanskrit, how can I possibly prove to my friends that there is something more to Ivar Avenue than mere quaintness? I think how they would laugh at Vishwananda, and at moments I really hate them all—everybody outside this place—savagely: there they sit sneering and doing nothing to find out what it's all about. But I'm really hating myself for not being strong enough to convince them. To *live* this synthesis of East and West is the most valuable kind of pioneer work I can imagine—never mind who approves or disapproves. Last night, Swami told me: "One thing I can promise you. You will never regret having come here. Never."

[1] *The Ascent of F6,* act 2, scene 1.

Madhabi is back. Her sister in Riverside has been ill. When Madhabi went into the sickroom, she was wearing a prasad ring on her finger. (At pujas for Kali and Holy Mother, rings and ornaments are offered in the shrine and afterwards distributed among the girls as *prasad*—consecrated offerings.) Madhabi's sister was scarcely conscious, the room was darkened and, anyhow, she knew nothing about the ring's existence. But she asked at once, "May I have that ring you're wearing?" Madhabi gave it to her. When the sister got better, she returned the ring, saying, "Goodness knows why I asked you for it, or how I knew you'd got it—but it seemed awfully important at the time." She also told Madhabi how, one night while she was still very sick, a lady came in and sat by her bed. "I knew it wasn't the nurse. Perhaps it was the superintendent. She seemed very important." The remarkable thing about this story is that Madhabi's sister violently disapproves of Hinduism and Hindu ritual, which she regards as superstitious nonsense; and Madhabi is sure that she knows nothing whatever about the custom and theory of prasad, or the nature of this particular ring.

August 10. Last night, Madhabi read aloud her play about Ramakrishna. It's terrible. Poor thing, she was so embarrassed—and Vishwananda made things worse by shedding tears. I like her now, definitely.

Afterward, I went for a walk with Sudhira in the hills. She's such a strange mixture: half of her so matter-of-fact and scientific, half of her as superstitious as any old Irish nanny. Her whole attitude to the shrine is superstitious, and she has endless stories of minor miracles which have happened around the house—pictures moving, dark figures appearing, etc. etc. On one occasion, an invisible man jumped off the roof and ran away down the street, after somebody had pronounced the Holy Name.[1] I don't believe a word of it, but I enjoy these fairy stories very much.

Sudhira has hardly ever been out of California in her life, and has never studied anything except medicine; and yet she's very worldly-wise and has excellent natural taste in poetry and painting. She discovered D. H. Lawrence some years ago, and knows all his descriptions of the West.

Got up at 4:45 a.m. and went into the shrine for a long think—with the result that I nearly decided to tell Swami, "India is getting between me and God."

Read Novalis's diary. He's so sweet. "Den Morgen hatte ich die

[1] Probably "Om."

fatale, drückende, bängliche Empfindung des eintretenden Schnup-
fens."[1] "Früh weint ich sehr. Nach Tisch wieder."[2] Etc. etc.

August 13. Yesterday morning, while I was doing the worship, I
suddenly thought, "If they *do* take me away from this place, why
should I go to CPS camp?" Now that C.O.s have been guaranteed
automatic induction into the Medical Corps, my objections to 1-A-O
don't really hold water any longer. I'd refuse to do noncombatant
military duty, but medical work is something else again: I can't see
why wounded men should be left to die simply because they happen
to be soldiers. Or is this just a rationalization? I don't know. As long as
I'm here, I can't judge any of my motives because they're all colored
by my wish to escape.

I asked Sudhira what she thought about the idea, this afternoon, as
we drove out to the San Fernando Valley, to avoid rehearsing the
Ram chant with Swami Vishwananda and, incidentally, to buy some
chickens. Sudhira was all in favor. She'd join the Army Nursing
Corps at once, if they'd let her through the medical exam. Chiefly
because of restlessness, and also because she's "opposed to foreign
domination." She told me that Madhabi is secretly planning to leave
at the end of the month.

Sudhira didn't know just where the chicken ranch was, and so we
drove all over the valley, enjoying the ride anyhow, along old
winding dirt roads where the eucalyptus trees have grown gigantic,
and there are no new houses—nothing but a few tumbledown barns
and shacks, half-hidden in the dark, secret, dusty green of the orange
groves. It's like another country altogether, and year by year it is being
swallowed up into building estates and the slickness and self-
advertisement of the new California. At last we found the ranch, quite
near Universal Studios.

August 17. Yesterday, I spent the night at Alto Cedro with Peggy. Bill
has left again; his leave is over. Peggy told me a funny thing about
their marriage. Bill, who is very meticulous, had arranged everything.
They were to go downtown on July 20, get married, and then spend
the night at the Town House hotel, where Bill had booked a room
and registered them as Dr. and Mrs. Kiskadden. Every last detail,
apparently, had been taken care of—but at the last moment, Bill
discovered that he'd entirely forgotten to arrange for a blood test for
himself. (Peggy had gotten her certificate a few days earlier.) Frantic,

[1] "In the morning I had the fatal, depressing, frightening sensation of the onset of
my cold." (April 26, 1797.)
[2] "Early I wept much. After luncheon again." (May 1, 1797.)

he called all the doctors in town, and even tried to see if the authorities couldn't waive the rule and allow the test to be made next day. But it was no use. So he and Peggy had to go back to the Town House and spend the night in sin and under false pretences. They were actually married, *very* quietly, on July 21. Peggy hasn't told anybody else this story, because she says it would so humiliate Bill if it got around—not on account of the sin, but of the inefficiency.

Today I've moved down to Santa Monica Canyon for a few days' rest from Ivar Avenue. I've taken a room in a house on Mabery Road, number 206, opposite the Viertels. Eduard Steuermann, Salka's brother, is also in the house. The last occupant of the room was Liesl Neumann, a middle-aged character actress with whom Berthold is having an affair. She moved out today, having been unexpectedly called to New York for a part in a play about a Nazi boy who comes to an American household—*Tomorrow the World*. Liesl is a nice, kind, motherly woman, with strangely dirty habits. She left the bathtub with a huge ring of grime around it, and I've just had to burn some foul female garbage I found in the bathroom. The bedroom is pink, with a pseudo-Egyptian stencil of flowers. The whole house smells sour and shut-up. Eduard says this is due to years of bourgeois stuffiness and can't be cured—but I've opened all the downstair windows, and it's better already.

August 18. Strange—I've been looking forward to this outing for several weeks, and now that I'm here I find I'm bored. This is chiefly because of the Viertels. I'd blandly assumed that they would be delighted to see me, and that they'd devote all their time to keeping me amused. They *are* quite pleased to see me, but they're all working hard, or busy with their own problems. Berthold has his play, Salka her movie stories, Eduard his music, Mausi her sulks, Salka's mother her housework, Hans his sleep. Only Tommy is nearly always available.

Last night, because I was bored, I found myself doing what I would least have expected—hunting up Tennessee Williams. I located him, after some search, at a very squalid rooming house called The Palisades, at the other end of town—sitting typing a film story in a yatchting cap, amidst a litter of dirty coffee cups, crumpled bed linen and old newspapers. He seemed not in the least surprised to see me. In fact, his manner was that of the meditative sage to whose humble cabin the world-weary wanderer finally returns. He took it, with discreetly concealed amusement, as the most natural thing in the world that I should be having myself a holiday from the monastery. We had supper together on the pier and I drank quite a lot of beer and talked sex the entire evening. Tennessee is the most relaxed creature imaginable: he works till he's tired, eats when he feels like it, sleeps when he feels inclined. The autoglide has long since broken down, so Tennessee has stopped paying for it, and the dealer is suing him, and he doesn't give a damn. He also has a fight on with Metro. He probably won't stay here long.

August 20. Yesterday morning, I cycled to Malibu and back before breakfast: it was much further than I expected. In the evening Berthold took me to the Brechts'; [Hans] Eisler was there, too. I liked Brecht immediately. He has close-cropped hair, very deep-set eyes and a pale, scarred face: he dresses in loose grey clothes and felt slippers, like a convict prepared for electrocution. He's very lively, alert and nervous, with a high-pitched voice, not unlike Forster's. Frau Brecht,[1] who's a Jewess, looks very strange; beautiful, in a way, and almost Chinese. She probably knows this, because she has smoothed her black hair back and tied it into a knot, and she wears the clothes of a Chinese peasant woman: a short jacket with a high collar and dark blue trousers. Eisler, the Red composer, is a little moon-faced man with peg teeth, short fat legs and a flat-backed head, who talks very rapidly in a loud unharmonious voice, with whirring wittiness. Stefan retired early to bed, with a deep bow: he had a chemistry test in the morning.

Spent most of today down on the beach with Tommy Viertel. He asks questions all the time—about politics, Buddhism, literature, everything—with his laborious, impeded articulation, listening very carefully and earnestly to my replies. I enjoy this, partly out of vanity, but also because I always like trying to state any problem in the simplest possible terms, and my frustrated schoolmaster instinct hasn't been indulged for a long time.

This evening, Berthold has been reading me poetry—Hölderlin, Brentano, and some of his own. It was very enjoyable—this time, I was the student, and I got Berthold to explain to me the difficult lines in "Heidelberg" and the three marvellous versions of "Dichtermut."[2] We almost wept with excitement. It was like the old times—or as near as we can ever come to them now. For Berthold really does seem to be changed. He looks so much older, so furrowed and battered, and he is so desperately nervous. His preoccupation with the purely ephemeral aspect of this war—the opinions of commentators, the speeches of politicians, the exaggerations of journalists—sometimes seems just childish. I think he thinks of himself as a kind of prophet—

---

[1] Helene Weigel, the German actress.
[2] Hölderlin's poems.

it's the last pitiful bit of fancy dress in the depleted wardrobe of his egotism—and in this he is like most of his fellow refugees. They can't see how futile this role is. Even if they are right, occasionally—who cares? The war moves too fast. Prophecy is for peacetime. And they are seldom right: their judgment is shaken by their hope and their fear. They have nothing to contribute to the postwar world but the idea of mercy—they might be truly great in that, because they, as victims, have the right to forgive—but how many of them are capable of mercy? Berthold far more than most. But he's so unstable. A breath of emotion can set him raving.

August 23. Very late at night. This has been a long day. I spent most of it at Ivar Avenue, where we had a puja. Swami Vividishananda from Seattle was there—a little grey man with a quiet smile, who impresses me more than Vishwananda: he really has something. This evening, a big party at the Viertels'. Eisler attacked what he calls "religion" (he means clerical politics) and I had to defend "pacifism." They were all very apologetic about this—as though they'd been guilty of bad taste in even mentioning the subject—rather as though a Negro had been dragged into a discussion of race prejudice. It was silly and futile. I felt like a fake. . . .

On August 24, quite unexpectedly, irrelevantly and insanely, I had a sexual adventure. There is no point in describing it: it would only be interesting if I went into details, and these memoirs are not pornographic. Enough to say that it was funny and silly and not in the least enjoyable. Its only importance is in its effect on my subsequent life at Ivar Avenue, and there will be plenty about that in due course.

My immediate reaction was to return to Ivar Avenue at once—two days earlier than I'd intended.

August 31. My chief reason for opening this book today is my intense disinclination to write a single word. I feel just awful. High sea and no land in sight anywhere. Can I possibly stay on here? Can I possibly leave? I find myself longing for the navy, for the battlefront, as a positive haven of peace. Even cowardice loses its bearings in such a storm.

When I told Swami, vaguely, that I'd had trouble with sex, he smiled and patted my head. "It's a hard life," he said: "Just pray for strength. Pray to become pure."

So there we are. I've got to become pure.

I'm not the only one who's upset. Madhabi told me, this afternoon in the kitchen, that she doesn't know how long she can stick it out.

Her bags are packed right at this moment. She's revolted by Vishwananda's gluttony and bad table manners; says she can't understand why Brahmananda ever initiated him. And there's someone in the family she hates desperately; because of this she has already left Ivar Avenue four times. This must be Amiya.

Meanwhile, Sudhira is groggily scrambling on to her legs after a breakdown following insomnia and overdoses of Benzedrine. Last night we went for a walk and she told me what a hard time Sarada went through before she settled down—fainting fits and crying.

One's first reaction to all this is the world's reaction: mustn't there be something radically wrong with this place, if everybody is so hysterical? But that objection arises from the fallacy that the aim of religion is to make you happy in a worldly sense. It isn't. The death of the Ego was never supposed to be pleasant; and this misery may really mean that we are getting ahead with it. So let the squeezing process go on, as long as we can take it.

September 1. Roger Spencer, with the wen on the side of his face bulging unappetizingly under a patch of plaster, arrived here in the middle of the night—another source of aversion. Vishwananda, after making an appointment with me for ten o'clock to discuss translating a sonnet on Ramakrishna, has forgotten and gone out to get his hair cut. Master, thy will be done.

I have a gnawing desire to go and see Denny and cry on his shoulder. He's the only person I can discuss the situation with, quite frankly. But discussing it will only make it worse. What's done is done. Oh wretched little ego, are you mad? What do you hope for yourself from this self-torture?

How many times must I repeat it: at the moment of action, no one is free? What happened the other day could never have happened if I hadn't been lounging and slacking for days before. The whole time I was in Santa Monica, I scarcely meditated once, or told my beads, or kept up any discipline at all. The act itself was nothing. I only mind about it because it breaks a record and hurts my vanity. It was even a very good thing it happened—or rather, it will have been a good thing, if it jolts my complacency. It's amazing, how one blinds oneself. How, with closed eyes like a sleepwalker—or like one who is *pretending* to sleepwalk—one edges nearer and nearer to the table on which the candy stands.

And, as always, within this defeat lies the possibility of an enormous victory. If I can resume my life here and carry on as if nothing has happened, then that'll be much more reassuring than if I'd never slipped. Morale is the only thing that matters.

I wonder what is happening to Webster. We are like two men drowning in neighboring wells, completely isolated from each other. But I know that he's going through a tough time, because he is slacking so much in every way. He meditates very little, dodges housework, eats hugely and lets himself be mothered and practically hand-fed by Amiya, who is getting far too emotionally involved with him.

September 15. It's just 3:45 in the afternoon, perhaps three or four minutes earlier, because my watch—that same watch which has been with me round the world and known all my friends—is gaining a little. I have a slight cold, and have just taken an aspirin and gotten undressed and into bed. I've had lunch with Aldous, Maria, Peggy and Bill Kiskadden, at the Beverly Derby. Aldous has had to leave Llano and come to live in town because of one of his allergies. It seems that, last rainy season, the floods washed a lot of topsoil down from the hills, and Maria found a pretty little plant lying stranded outside the house. She felt sorry for it and planted it right under Aldous's study window, and it grew up into a huge ragweed, and gave Aldous a terrible rash. Bill, who is home on short leave, has already taken on the duties of head of the family and is mobilizing the boys to put in a pipe system for watering the garden. He and Peggy are obviously still in the honeymoon stage: she looks years younger.

Swami Vishwananda left this morning and Yogi arrived. After a few days' holiday with Yogini, he's to start living here as a monk. When Vishwananda left from Glendale Station, most of the family went with him and sang the *Ram* chant on the platform, to the awe and wonder of the other passengers.

This morning, I had a letter from René Blanc-Roos, confirming what Gretl Eberhart told me in a letter a few days ago (she'd seen it in a Philadelphia newspaper): his wife Kate—whom he married soon after I left Haverford—has committed suicide. Shot herself. René found her dead in the bedroom when he came home from town. She was very young. She was going to have a baby, and René thinks she thought he didn't want her to have it. He is in a terrible state, on the verge of complete collapse. He says it'll help if I write to him a lot. So I'll try to, every day.

A couple of days ago, I heard from Vernon. He's still in New York, working at a power press, and has been painting.

And now, lying in my little blue-walled room with the white flowered paper, the picture of Vivekananda, the sensible brown furniture, my books and practically all my worldly possessions around me—what statement can I make about the future? Only this: I really have *no* idea what will happen. I haven't a notion what degree of pressure I can stand, or what I'll do if I can't stand it. My only visible means of escape from this place would be into the Army Medical Corps (I've already written to the draft board about this) but it seems most unlikely that the older group will be drafted now, despite the news of heavy fighting and casualties in Italy. Do I *really* want to escape? No. But I do need some kind of shot in the arm. At present, I'm just coasting.

To be quite frank with myself, Denny's company is very disturbing to me, a lot of the time. Because his life is free, bohemian, agreeable and full of affairs. He has a very soft daytime caretaking job at a film manufacturing company on Santa Monica Boulevard, and he's able to study for his high-school diploma during work hours. He's practically through now. Being with Denny unsettles me, and yet I need him more than ever before, because he's the only person who can view my life as a whole, and therefore the only one who can give me any valuable advice. He isn't shocked by the squalid bits of it, and he isn't repelled or mystified by Vedanta. He's always getting in digs at Swami, whom he's never forgiven, but he doesn't suggest I shall leave. His attitude was summed up the other day when he said, "Either make up your mind to be a monk or a dirty old man." Sometimes, I find this kind of brutality bracing; sometimes it just annoys me, because I know, and Denny knows, that he has no right to talk to me like this, when he isn't faced with the same problem himself. If I were to leave Ivar Avenue, he'd be pleased in a way, because it would shock a lot of people he dislikes, and because he knows I could only turn to him and depend on him more than ever— most likely we'd live together again. But he'd also be a bit dismayed, I'm sure, because, in a strange way, he relies on me to do his praying for him; and he would love to be able to believe in my belief. Whatever happens, he can't lose. And I, it seems, can't win.

Sometimes, I feel that everything would be solved if I could get the right kind of person here. Somebody who had the same problems as myself. Somebody who spoke my language. Somebody I could talk to. But I know that this is only another attempt to wriggle away from the relationship I have to cultivate: the relationship to the shrine and what it stands for. Everything else is a substitute, and would end as all substitutes end.

Lately, I've been getting more and more depressed. It's as if I'd walked into a trap at last. After all my antics, all my different impersonations, I have picked up yet another funny mask and stuck my nose into it—and now, all of a sudden, it won't come off. Have I really got to spend the rest of my life with these people—or any people? How I long for the mere sensation of freedom again—"la chose enivrante"[1]—I don't even mean sex—it's far more trivial than that. Just to sit at the wheel of a car at a drive-in, eating pie and coffee, and to know that there's enough money in my pocket to go any place I want to—Seattle, San Diego, New Orleans, New York. . . . No! What utter nonsense I am writing! To say that I really *want* any of those things is as untrue as to say I want the vision of God. I don't know what I want. The very use of the word "I" immediately turns any statement into a silly noise. Do I want to die? My goodness no—for what? Do I want to live? My goodness no—for what? Maybe I would like to lose consciousness. To go into a coma for ever and ever. But, from all accounts, that's the one thing which isn't possible. To believe in total extinction sounds terribly like sentimental optimism. It would be an altogether unnatural mercy.

Meanwhile, my prayer is: "Oh Lord, make something turn up! Either bounce me out of this way of life, or bounce me deeper into it, but don't leave me stranded on the edge." He won't either. I know that. The mere movement of life will carry me somewhere. Meanwhile, I just have to keep my head above water.

How delightful religion used to be—in the days when I wasn't doing anything particular about it! What delicious emotions, what pleasantly sentimental yearnings! Now it's just a stupid, boring misery. I seem to get worse and worse. I know that I'm ten times more disagreeable than I have ever been before in my life. Oh, of course, I know the answer to that one, too. Swami says it's like cleaning out an inkwell which is screwed to the table: you keep pouring in water, and nothing comes out but dirty old ink.

Later. . . . Sudhira just came in, to give me a nightcap glass of lemon and rum for my cold. Her face, with its slap-happy, masochistic smile, looked moist, as if from crying. "Aren't you terribly lonely here?" I asked. "Yes, terribly." "So am I."

September 20. Down to Santa Monica. Lunch with the Viertels. Supper with the Brechts. We talked about the adaptation of *The Duchess of Malfi* which Brecht has made for Elizabeth Bergner. Aside from some very ingenious rearrangements and cuts, Brecht's object has been to give Ferdinand a stronger motive for his persecution of the Duchess. Brecht says he must have been in love with her. In order to point this up, he has written in about a dozen lines of verse, in

---

[1] "The intoxicating thing," from the duet and finale in act 2 of Bizet's *Carmen*, when Carmen and the gypsies urge Don José to come with them to the mountains.

German; and these he wants translated into Elizabethan English. So he switches on all his charm, to woo me as a possible collaborator.

Until Berthold arrived. Then, fatally, we got on to the subject of Vedanta, and Brecht fairly blew his top. To him, it's all fascism and superstitious nonsense. Frau Brecht joined in—like a Salvation Army lass—calling on me to repent and remember my duty as a revolutionary writer. Berthold took my side—or rather, he apologized for my deviation, and tried to suggest that it was only temporary; that, in fact, I might be regarded as a sort of spy in the enemy's camp. If only—after two or three years—I'd write a book "showing up" mysticism once and for all, then my retirement would have been well worth while. All this was fairly funny, until they left me and got on to Huxley. Brecht said he was "verkauft"—had sold out. I was so angry that I nearly got up and left the house at once. I *did* leave very shortly afterwards.

Brecht is obviously sincere, in his way. But, humanly, he's no more worthy to criticize Aldous than I am to criticize Swami. He's just as arrant an individualist as I am, and pretty much of an opportunist, too. I asked him what he'd do if a local soviet committee of peasants didn't like his writing, and he answered that he'd talk them into liking it. In other words, he accepts the will of the majority as long as it's his will. I think it was extremely smart and realistic of him to align himself with the communists: they'll probably win out in Germany, anyway, and then he'll be on top. What I object to is his claim to be more *honest* than a man like Aldous, and his conviction that everyone who disagrees with him is getting a paycheck from the capitalist bosses.

Stefan, the ever-polite, sensed my rage and discreetly accompanied me to the bus stop. He would order my execution without flicking an eyelash, but, in contrast to his father, he has beautiful manners. . . .

Next day, Berthold wrote me the following letter:

> . . . . You know, I'm not as radical as Brecht is, or in a different way—and we two know each other too long and too well to change our behavior towards each other. But the funny thing is that you've become dear to Brecht too, after so short an acquaintance. *Therefore* his bitter fight for your soul, his utter frankness (he is a *man*, and a good one!) even if he should lose an ideal translator, a helper for his work that is everything to him. It was so bitterly well meant that I couldn't stand behind—and my risk was a greater one: to lose one of the very very few friends I still am calling mine—perhaps the only one left who connects me with these ominous years since 1933. You know what I mean with that. It was a depressing, or, better said, a torturing

evening, yesterday, for me. There was the great struggle of our time being fought between *friends* in this room—and, as I felt, the battleground was your heart, your sensibility (and mine too). It couldn't be helped, and may it lead to something better! All of us will be able to judge this evening *definitely*—let's say, five years from now, if we still are alive. If not; everyone of us has certainly tried to find the "right way." What we called your "experiment" will have brought you experience: I do hope, the decisive experience of your life, if not the solution. Would I stop you if I could? I have to answer with "yes." You see, love does answer without hesitation, so does conviction. But I cannot stop you. I can only wish you the very best, fullheartedly. And, certainly, I'll never finish to be proud of your friendship, I have to thank you for so much: that can't end. My feeling for you is unchanged. And don't worry about me. I'm not bewildered, *not* confused. I am, may I say, clearer than I ever was. Work progresses, modestly but steadily. It's not easy. What will come to everyone of us—nobody knows . . .

To which I answered:

Your letter just arrived. Thank you for writing it—but your anxiety is not necessary—*nothing* you said to me could shake our friendship. We understand each other deeply, and love each other, and, as you put it, we cannot "change our behavior towards each other." I would not even wish it.

With Brecht it is another matter. Fine, if he likes me. I like him. He may genuinely feel that I am somehow a decent person, although misguided—but he himself said that this human quality is not what matters to him. There we differ, radically. With you, it is different.

Yes, you can warn your friend (you *must* warn him) if you think the girl he wants to marry is a whore. But there are ways of doing this. It is not necessary to trample on all his feeling for her with the crudest, dirtiest words you know. That's not frankness, it's brutality. When Brecht said that Huxley was "verkauft" I nearly walked out of the house. It is weakness and cowardice to sit and hear your friends insulted—and I only stayed because I felt that, at that moment, Brecht was simply not responsible for his words. He was so excited. When *you* say things like that, you have told me to take no notice, because it is due to your diabetes. Is Brecht sick, too? If so, I can, of course, understand everything. If he is not sick, well, then I can only go back to his house if he is prepared to treat me like a human being, whom he likes. Yes, we can discuss anything—but that was no discussion, it was denunciation. For once, it's okay. Now, he has told me my fiancée is a whore. He has warned me. If he goes on saying it, that's merely abuse. It is fruitless. It helps nobody. It bores me. And it makes me mad.

I am well aware that I will never be able to fit into the new world he desires. I will be killed quite soon, for being an individualist, and I will be *glad* to die. I could *never* breathe that air. But meanwhile I genuinely and truly like Brecht and his wife and Stefan (who is just as radical, but has much better *manners*! He should be an example to his father). I even find Brecht's violence sympathetic. But I will never submit to it—that's the difference between being a pacifist and being a slave.

You see, unfortunately perhaps, I feel that Brecht is absolutely right, in *his* way, and I also feel that *I* am right, in *mine*. So I can object to nothing—not even his intolerance—theoretically. Only, practically and humanly, I just won't stand for it!

You may show him this letter, if you like. In fact, I wish you would. But that is a matter for your judgment. In any case, tell him what I said. . . .

September 22. I'm just back from spending the entire night down-town, meeting Pete Martinez, who's here on leave to see his parents. They recently moved out to the Coast, from Houston, Texas, and now have a house in Long Beach.

Pete was supposed to get here around 10:30. He didn't arrive till 2:30 a.m., very small, very brown, with a terrible cold, staggering under a huge kit bag which he dropped, to give me an unmilitary, public hug. He had been on the train for days. He wears his uniform with the slightly apologetic, self-consciously comic air of someone in fancy dress. We drank coffee at a dreary, all-night place with marble-topped tables and then trudged around the bus stations, only to find that there was no way of getting out to Long Beach till 5:00 a.m. The hotel lobbies were littered with service men, sprawling asleep all over the floors and couches. So we retired to a cubicle in the Pershing Square turkish bath, where Pete, who was exhausted and had a bad headache, kept asking the attendant mournfully for a drink. He talked about his army life, not complaining at all, but darkly fatalistic, in his somber Mexican way. He begged me repeatedly not to tell Lincoln that this may be his last leave before going overseas.

Today is another scorcher: the temperature scarcely dropped, all night. The Santa Ana wind is thrashing the trees like a breath from a furnace.

September 24. Yesterday, Pete called and wanted me to go down to Long Beach last night. No other time, he said, would be possible; so I had to ask Swami if I could skip the class. This made me feel guilty. I sat with him for a few minutes, because I didn't want to seem eager to rush off. Suddenly, he turned to me and said, "You know, Chris—even if one gives up the spiritual life altogether for a while, he will come back to Ramakrishna before he dies. We know that, for a fact. We have witnessed it." As so often, the remark seemed telepathic. It gave me exactly the reassurance I needed.

I borrowed Denny's car and drove down to Long Beach—the dreary inland route along Manchester Avenue, where the city never stops. Pete's new home on East Fourth Street, was a dark little wooden house with a big porch, fly screens already rusted, and a Red Cross sign and service star in the window—just like ten thousand others. The whole family was there: the white-haired, handsome father who speaks scarcely a word of English, and who greeted me with a wave of his hand; the dark-eyed, rather tragic little mother, with her elder son dead already and now fearing for her younger; the three sisters, Dolores, Carmen and the youngest, with the cute little nose, whose name I forget. All three girls were charming, but they seemed homely beside their vivid little wonder-brother, with his flashing eyes and teeth, short-cropped vigorous hair, and powerful compact figure (he has put on a little more weight) in the clumsy uniform and G.I. boots. We ate tacos, and Pete got out a bottle of tequila which we drank under the mother's doubtful, not-quite-approving eyes. Not that anything Pete does in that family could ever be really disapproved of. His anecdotes of New York parties, his ballet photographs, his imitations of friends and enemies—all are accepted, gratefully, uncritically, like holy writ. Carmen (nicknamed "Butch") had received a proposal of marriage on a phonograph record from a strikingly handsome sergeant she had only met once. The sergeant had also sent a record to the parents, asking for her hand. We listened to them, amidst much giggling. Then Pete and his sisters sang Mexican songs, in gay heartbroken tones. And I was asked to read poetry out of a drugstore anthology—which I did—the tequila beginning to take effect—with reckless freedom of expression. The mother and father listened to Browning's "Youth and Art" with the greatest pleasure, not understanding a single word. It seemed perfectly natural that I should be drinking, and smoking one cigarette after another. (It is an extraordinary psychological fact, which I've tested several times, that an ex-smoker can smoke when drunk without reviving the nicotine addiction.) I felt like quite a different version of myself—Pete's Christopher—who hadn't been taken out of the closet in a long while, but had been there all the time, waiting to be called forth. The whole legend, the whole cult of Pete, which Lincoln has established, made the room into a sort of shrine, with Pete himself cross-legged in the middle of the floor, a minor but authentic deity.

September 27. Last night, I went down to the Union Station and saw Pete off. We had some drinks in a bar before he left. Pete said, "You'll always want to be different, Chris—whatever you do. You want to fight everybody. You want to take your soul out and look at it." He believes that he'll never dance again. He's thirty-one. All that life he loved is over. We said goodbye at the barrier and he disappeared— still cocky, still marvellous as ever—into the grey future, to become a tiny part of this dismal worldwide military mess.

September 30. This afternoon, I'm leaving for San Francisco—then on to Portland, to assist at the Durga puja and the dedication of Swami Devatmananda's new center.

I'm glad to be getting away from Ivar Avenue, which is verging on an eruption. Amiya is going to look after Ben and Derek while Peggy dashes East for another month with Bill—and this arrangement is most desirable, because Mrs. Milam has just written a really poisonous letter, accusing Amiya of more-than-motherly feelings toward Webster, and Amiya is so upset she got pains in her legs and retired to bed. Also, Yogi is suddenly aware that he's a probationer-monk, and can't sleep with Yogini any more; and Yogini says she'll stay here even if he quits. So he's getting a job and sticking around, sulking and grumbling.

There's also Kolisch, who's making a comeback here, despite terrific resistance from Sudhira and Amiya. Sudhira tells me that Kolisch has a theory that everybody in the world is suffering from syphilis—either as an hereditary or a primary infection. He used to tell his patients this, but they got so indignant that now he keeps his mouth shut and just treats them for it. (Hence his mysterious remarks, when I first went to him, about my family background.) Sudhira finds this theory amusing and even tentatively plausible, but she is outraged when Kolisch applies it to someone like Sarada, because it seems to reflect upon Sarada's purity. (Where Sarada is concerned, Sudhira ceases to be a nurse and becomes a sentimental Irish nanny—to such a degree that I used to suspect her, quite wrongly, of being a lesbian.) Web has a sore in his mouth—and of course, according to Kolisch, there's only one explanation of *that*. Last night, Roger Spencer went to Kolisch and told him he had shingles; and Kolisch gave Sudhira a significant glance. She dashed into the kitchen and told me in a stage whisper, "Roger's got it now!" We both went into hysterics.

The obvious conclusion is that Kolisch has syphilis himself.

October 1. Well, here I am, in the absurd 1905 Hindu fretwork building of the San Francisco Vedanta Center on Webster Street, with its balconies and galleries and greenhouses and sharp-pointed metal domes. Tinted photographs of the Holy Family cover the walls. Downstairs, in the lecture room, is a gigantic oil painting of Ramakrishna, which looks like King Kong emerging gibbering from the jungle.

If Swami Ashokananda were a Catholic, I think he'd be a Jesuit. He's quite a complex character—very intelligent, very ambitious probably, and underneath his politeness, quite scornful of western ways. His disciples, Adolph Gschwend and Al Clifton, are both nice, but somehow *crushed*. Adolph used to be an athlete; he sometimes swam the Golden Gate. Al has been to India, with Ashokananda. He is the only real monk in the whole of American Vedanta; that is to say, he's actually taken the first vow, of brahmacharya. There is also a tall boy named Fran, with crooked teeth, who works in the shipyards. And another man who carpenters, and believes the Catholics are to blame for everything. And an elderly Englishman named Mr. Brown, who started to be a monk under Swami Trigunatita, quit to get married, and is now back here again in his old age. The whole atmosphere of the house is frugal and depressing: a typical all-male ménage. I've just written to Sudhira, saying, "I never realized before how absolutely *necessary* women are."

Just to give an idea of my state of mind, I actually looked in the telephone book to see if I could find an address Paul Sorel once gave me, which he said would be "amusing." Thank God, it wasn't there.

Oh, Master, are you really here—in this weird museum of Victorian India? Come out from wherever you're hiding. I need someone to talk to.

October 2. Swami Ashokananda is a handsome grey-haired tomcat: quite the tyrant, underneath his tomcat charm. He was really rude and unkind to Mr. Brown, at a class he held this morning before breakfast on Shankara's philosophy. He drove me to see the temple at Berkeley: Gschwend chauffeured us, and wasn't spoken a word to, all the way. And the women call him "Swamiji" and practically salaam when they see him. The temple has a nice garden and isn't too bad, except for the fittings, and the altar which looks like a dressing table in a cheap hotel. The day was glorious. What a nostalgic city this is! It is preeminently the city of departure. The ships steal out into the fog and the shadowy Pacific, where the war is, across the cold water-hemisphere. And in the bars, the young soldiers sit waiting for their orders to leave and go into battle. You long to take wing from the tall terraces and fly, fly away to the uttermost islands. From the roof of the center, you can see the great spider-slung bridges, and Alcatraz, that other kind of monastery.

After lunch, I went out by myself into the town, vaguely intent upon adventure. But there was actually nothing I wanted to do, except get away in a corner by myself and burst into tears. I just wandered around, and thought of my visit here with Vernon—which was even more depressing—and felt as sad as hell. I'm thrown back, again and again, upon the terrible recognition that what I am now doing, however badly and unwillingly, is all I am fit for, at present. There is simply no alternative.

Hotel sign: "Hotel Cosmos: no vacancy."

October 9. I'm writing this on the improvised trestle-and-plank dining-room table, at the Vedanta Center in Portland, before starting on an expedition to the retreat, where the Swamis are going to lay the foundation stone of a future temple. Four of them are here—Ashokananda, Vividishananda, Devatmananda, and Vishwananda. Vishwananda spends all his time eating, chanting, or playing the harmonium: it is wonderful to see him at breakfast, clapping his hands as though he were in an oriental inn and shouting, "Bring eggs!" Ashokananda jokingly but rather maliciously finds fault with everything. Vividishananda smiles and smiles. Devatmananda is Hinduism's boy scout. He's younger than the others—almost boyish—and his motto, taken from Vivekananda, is "Face the brute!" He fixes everything himself—the other morning, he stood on a step-ladder tinkering with the electric light and wincing at innumerable electric shocks: he telephones, he hammers, he saws, he puts up pictures, he dashes in and out of the house on errands. And he drives his followers, mostly elderly women, to the point of exhaustion. They have only lately moved into this house, which used to be quite a grand mansion, but is now shabby and ramshackle, and there is much to be done. We are in the midst of a clammy heat wave. The street outside reminds me of Denmark: a wide old avenue of beech trees. But this town, like San Francisco, has the weird, all-pervading Pacific sadness.

We've just gotten through three days of severe puja, with aversion prevailing. An avalanche of flowers, fruit, sandal paste and six-armed sacred pictures has been pouring down between me and Rama-krishna. No—it's better not dwelt on.

Richard Thom, who leaves for the marines today, has been my only relief. He dodged all attempts to make him work, and threw a heavy breadknife around in the garden, as a preparation for "Jap hunting." On his last day at home, he smashed the Thoms' water pipe by backing the car into it, and leased his weights to a friend for five dollars. I sneaked off with him, the day before yesterday, to see *The Leopard Man*,[1] when I was supposed to be handing sandwiches at a party. Devatmananda didn't quite dare to reprimand me.

My journey up from San Francisco, on October 3–4, was the nicest part of the trip, so far. On the train, I read *Jane Eyre*, for the first time: she's one of my favorite characters in fiction. I *so* understand her when she says, "I never in my life have known any medium in my dealings with positive, hard characters, antagonistic to my own, between absolute submission and determined revolt."[2] I like to feel myself alone in a crowd and yet part of it, more than I ever did: it's the way a writer should live. Three sailors talked about a boy they knew who was exempted because he was in the dairy business. "He buys a new Buick every year." "Not this year, he won't." "The trouble is, he's had too many things." How nice they were! There was absolutely no malice in their voices. And I felt so happy to be with them, and accepted on face value: they hadn't the faintest idea that they were sitting with a freak. And yet, if they'd known what I was, where I was going, they'd have accepted that, too, with perfect good nature. They'd have accepted Vishwananda himself, and called him "Reverend," and fed him like a bear in a national park.

In my berth next morning I was wakened by the sun rising over the broken bridge of my nose, shining into my right eye. The hollow of my eye was still dark and crowded with black, lance-headed conifers; it was a prehistoric crater. Oregon, giant land where the forests swallow the sun. By breakfast time, we were passing through beech woods. "They changed the trees," I cracked, "someone must have complained." But I always throw these lines away. Nobody laughed. The M.P.[3] and the Shore Patrol yarning in the washroom: two pariahs, misunderstood. "I always try to give them a break," said the M.P., rather wistfully. And the Shore Patrol agreed, "Me too."

A sudden gust of aversion and fear that Swami will give me a Sanskrit name. Decided to write to him, "I am your disciple, not a member of the Ramakrishna Order." But I didn't, and I won't.

[1] A murder thriller.
[2] Chapter 34.
[3] Military Police.

Later. . . . Well, we drove out to the retreat, which is quite a large property, about ten miles outside the city: a birch forest, with a group of wooden houses, very Scandinavian. The Swamis gathered, in their yellow robes, at the spot where the foundation stone was to be laid. It started to drizzle. Ashokananda, with his malicious smile, told Vishwananda to go and pray for the rain to stop. Vishwananda waddled off by himself among the trees. The rain stopped. The ceremony began. The drizzle started again. "Go and pray some more," said Ashokananda. Vishwananda sighed: "The second time is more difficult." But he went off obediently, nevertheless—only to return, an instant later, gasping and trotting: he had disturbed a nest of wild bees. The rain continued, and we finished the ceremony under umbrellas. I left early with Mrs. Thom, who had to see Rich off at the station—because I wanted to avoid the mass picnic of devotees. Ate too much salmon loaf.

This evening, a member of Devatmananda's congregation drove us in his truck to visit his little home in the country. He raises begonias and tomatoes chemically, in a solution of Epsom salts. The house is built of firwood, with compressed sugarcane walls. A red brick dust path leads to a lily pond which leaks. Fairy lights are strung around in the trees. The awful squalor of small pinewoods: they are only fit for the burial of murdered corpses. Ashokananda earnestly recommended a certain kind of rhododendron: I've never seen him so passionate before.

The old lady at the puja who offered to pay for my training as a monk, because, "You boys are doing such splendid work."

Mrs. Soulé, the singer, from San Francisco. Her greatest experience was singing at Glacier Point, Yosemite. She had to pitch her voice right across the valley, and make it echo back from Half Dome rock.

October 15. I got back to Ivar Avenue yesterday, after spending a night as Swami Vividishananda's guest at the center in Seattle.

Vividishananda has a female disciple named Omala (I don't know here real name) who came down with him to stay in Portland. She is a silly, pudding-faced girl with an affected voice and a coarse white skin: a real murderee type. At Portland, Omala had to sleep upstairs, on the third floor, which is attics and little bedrooms, probably intended for servants. Before the place was taken over by the Vedanta Society, it was used as a rooming house, and two of the occupants had been allowed to go on living there, until they could find other quarters. One of them was an old woman—a nurse, I think—and her room was next to Omala's. She was perfectly harmless, but a little crazy, and she had a queer, witchlike appearance. Omala was terrified of her.

The night before we left for Seattle, Omala wakened me around 2 a.m. by banging on my door. She was whimpering with fright. She told me that the old woman was doing something "dreadful" in her room. She'd been tapping on Omala's wall, and seemed to be dragging chains around the floor. Omala had decided she must be some kind of supernatural being: a kind of werewolf or vampire. "I'm not sure she's—really—alive." She refused to go back to her room unless I'd come with her to find out what was the matter. I was sleepy and cross. "Don't you know this house has been dedicated to Ramakrishna?" I told her, "You ought to be ashamed of yourself. How can there be any spooks here?" Just the same, I felt slightly uncomfortable, going up the stairs in the dark: the old house is so creaky and creepy. But there wasn't a sound to be heard from the nurse's room, and Omala finally went back to bed. In the morning, Devatmananda confessed that he had tapped on Omala's wall himself to frighten her, because she was so silly. The old woman wasn't even at home at the time.

Ashokananda came up with us to Seattle. As soon as we crossed the state line, he started bullying Vividishananda, complaining and holding him responsible because there wasn't a dining car on the train. But Vividishananda merely smiled.

He lives in a smallish house, with a boy named Eli Morozzi, who is a musician, just gotten out of the army. Eli is deadly serious, attentive and loyal. He is exactly the right kind of disciple for Vividishananda. They are a real guru-chela[1] pair. Eli told me that they go for a walk every day, through the park. "But we shan't be able to do that when summer comes," he added, "because girls lie around in swimming suits."

Seattle smells of the North, which is the same all over. This might just as well be the north of Scotland. The clear, rainy light, the cold waterways and the little wooded islands. A city of small boats, like Copenhagen.

Oh God, I'm glad I don't live at any of the other centers! Actually, I couldn't. Vividishananda is the best. Life with him would be dry but nourishing, like a ship's biscuit. But I would hasten to get TB and wither away and die. I couldn't endure Devatmananda's boy-scout camp; his irritating bossiness. Ashokananda I would fight to the death: he's a tyrant with a spiteful tongue who despises his slaves. As for Vishwananda, I'd probably corrupt him utterly: I'm sure, with a little encouragement, he'd take to drink. Prabhavananda is the only one of

[1] Disciple.

them who's really civilized, really tolerant; the only one who really understands the West.

November 19. A lot of time gone by, but little news. My position is exactly the same. The shrine is always with us. As long as some contact is maintained, all is simple and possible. As soon as contact is broken, all is horrible, difficult, tense, confused. To be a monk and to be a writer are the same, there's no clash of purposes. Dedicate everything to Him. Don't strain. Don't loll. Don't bother about love: that will come of itself, when the obstacles are removed. Don't be indecently indiscreet about all this, either. Guard it for yourself, like bedroom secrets. Times will come for you to tell about it, to the right person, at the right moment, not boasting. You'll know when.

That small voice which sometimes says, so humbly and yet with such entire assurance: "Admit—isn't it much nicer when we're alone together, like this? Why not be honest? You know you like me best."

There's been a lot more trouble with sex. Two more incidents, even: which I must admit I thoroughly enjoyed. But I won't let this throw me, or indulge in orgies of confession and remorse. Keep to the positive acts. Fill your life with them. That's what really counts. The other day, Swami said to me: "Do you know what purity is, Chris? Purity is telling the truth."

The Beesleys have a new home, up above Benedict Canyon, with a big patio, a pool, and a wide view over the coast. I keep seeing them—on Sundays, mostly. I would rather be with them than anybody, right now, because there is absolutely no clash, no tension: we meet in a delightful, neutral area of talk about books and plays and England and Europe. I can even talk to them very frankly about Vedanta—though I'm careful not to say much about our domestic problems at Ivar Avenue. When I'm with them, I feel rather like a soldier on leave. And that's how they treat me. I'm entertained, well fed, encouraged, made comfortable—and never unduly cross-examined or reminded of my army life.

Two soldiers are passing the temple. One of them looks at it and exclaims "Boy! The guy who built that thing sure had a screwy wife!"

November 22. Peggy has been coming here a lot, helping us revise our translation of the Gita. Her criticism is enormously valuable, but she keeps getting in Swami's hair—pointing out, in her archly playful way, that the text is full of contradictions. This makes him very mad. Today, we had a really historic showdown. After much hesitation, Peggy confessed that she thinks our version really isn't much better than any of the others. It's dull and it's clumsy and it reeks of Sanskrit.

What's more, she's already talked to Aldous (who's seen some of it) and he agrees. It was an awful moment, because, once she'd said it, it was only too obvious. I felt a wave of depression sweep over me—and Swami, seeing how I felt, suddenly turned very small and grey and shrivelled, a bird on a winter bough. And then—it was really amazing—I saw, in a flash, what was wrong. I went to my room with the manuscript. Our version began:

> Oh changeless Krishna, drive my chariot between the two armies who are eager for battle, that I may see those whom I shall have to fight in this coming war. I wish to see the men who have assembled here, taking the side of the enemy in order to please the evil-minded son of Dhritarashtra.

In about half an hour, I had turned this into:

> Krishna the changeless,
> Halt my chariot
> There where the warriors,
> Bold for the battle,
> Face their foemen.
> Between the armies
> There let me see them,
> The men I must fight with,
> Gathered together
> Now at the bidding
> Of him their leader,
> Blind Dhritarashtra's
> Evil offspring:
> Such are my foes
> In the war that is coming. . . .

I brought this back and showed it to Swami and Peggy, and they were both very excited. I'm excited myself—because it opens up all sorts of possibilities. I now realize how horribly bored I was with the old translation. I don't see my way clearly, yet, but obviously this method can be applied throughout the book. There should be several kinds of verse, including, maybe, some hexameters; and I think I can vary the prose style too. We are going to Aldous this evening, to discuss the whole thing with him.

December 9. Since our decision, the revised Gita has been going ahead as if by magic. I've never worked so hard. The whole thing seems to be already in my head: it's as though I'd been secretly assembling it there, like an invading army, all these months. Unfortunately—perhaps due to the strain and excitement—I've started smoking again, more than ever. At first it made me sick to my stomach, but I kept right at it.

Just back from seeing Robert Medley downtown. He's visiting here for a few days on a mission. He's a major in the British army, stationed in Cairo. He did a lot of important camouflage work in the African campaign. We went to see a movie called *Sahara*, because Robert wanted to know if they'd gotten the details accurate. They hadn't. At one point, Bogart and his friends are cut off in a small village. They're lost, and there's no water, and no way out. "What utter rot!" exclaimed Robert, in his penetrating British voice: "I drove through there myself, only three months ago. There's an excellent motor road, and they have three wells." We left before the end—much to my relief. Several people, preferring Bogart to the truth, were getting bored with us.

On the whole, Robert has had a "good war": he feels justifiably pleased with himself and his achievements. I sensed a little criticism, at first, but, for some reason, he was entirely reassured when I told him that I'd actually registered as a conscientious objector. That apparently made all the difference. Nevertheless, there *was* a gulf between us, and I think it would have existed just as much if I'd been living over here for four years of peacetime. I realized, as I seldom do, how Americanized, in some ways, I've become. Robert's tone is already alien to me. Americans call it superior, but it's not exactly that. It's simply older and wearier: a kind of shadow falls. This weariness is extremely attractive, and also exasperating, because, without meaning to, it necessarily *implies* wisdom; and, of course, the British *aren't* wiser than the Americans or vice versa: their wisdom is merely of another kind. We parted very politely but with a certain relief. No doubt, if circumstances arose, we could be friends again, but on a different basis.

December 21. Amiya, talking of Christmas preparations, said, "Well— I shall just cook a little turkey and offer it to Christ, that's all." So now I've composed a Christmas hymn (to the tune of "John Brown's Body"):

> I cooked a little turkey and I offered it to Christ,
> The money that I paid for it was gladly sacrificed,
> I flavored it so nicely, it was beautifully spiced—
> But Christ had just had lunch.

> *Chorus*: He'd had lunch with Allan Hunter,
> He'd had lunch with Allan Hunter,
> He'd had lunch with Allan Hunter,
> Where they gave him soya beans.

Jesus wasn't hungry, but he bashfully confessed
That he liked a nice young turkey and he'd take a bit of breast.
Soon he'd got the legs off, and gobbled up the rest—
Although he'd just had lunch.

   Although he'd had lunch with Allan Hunter, etc. . . .
   Where they gave him gluten steak.

When Our Lord had finished, he wiped his lips and sighed
"For God's sake don't tell the Hunters, or they'll be horrified,
But a fellow gets an appetite when he's been crucified—
He needs a second lunch."

   Especially when he's lunched with Allan Hunter, etc. . . .
   Where they give you cashew nuts.

So listen, all you Christians, and follow my advice:
Let Buddha have the vegetables, let Krishna keep the rice,
But when Jesus comes to visit you, just fix him something nice,
And *perhaps* he'll stay for lunch.

   Even though he's had lunch with Allan Hunter,
   Even though he's had lunch with Allan Hunter,
   Even though he's had lunch with Allan Hunter,
   Because he HATES those SOYA BEANS!

1944

January 3. Swami, George, Sarada, Yogini, Doris, Franz and I went to see *The Song of Bernadette*.[1] On the whole, Swami approved of it. He liked the deathbed scene, and the vision of the Lady, because, he told us, visions usually appear in the *corner* of a room, and that's what happens here. Needless to say, he was convinced that the roses on the Lady's feet were really lotuses. He is extraordinarily obstinate on this point. As for me, I had a real good cry, from about reel two onwards, and greatly enjoyed myself.

I've just translated this, from Hölderlin:

> Where are you? Drunken, the spirit grows dark in me
> With all your delight. For, listening
> Lately, I heard in what golden harmonies
> The boy played, the enchanting sun god,

[1] Based on Franz Werfel's novel about the dying French girl, Bernadette Soubirous, who during the nineteenth century had visions of a Lady—presumed to be the Virgin Mary—in a grotto at Lourdes; afterwards the grotto waters wrought miraculous healings.

On heaven's harp his hymn to the evening,
Echoing back from the woods and the hills around.
Far from us now, to more faithful worshippers,
His pious peoples, he has departed.[1]

January 5. Madhabi went to hospital yesterday for an emergency appendicitis operation, taking Sudhira with her, as a private nurse. Sudhira in uniform is a different person, radiant with happiness. She smells the breeze of freedom. Had supper with Dick LaPan, the boxer. He's a nice, gentle, intelligent boy, but agonizingly unsure of himself. The mixed irritation and vanity of being treated as an oracle. Madhabi was operated today, quite successfully.

January 7. Aldous wanted someone to type the manuscript of his novel, *Time Must Have a Stop*. So I took him to Mrs. Herbold, who is excellent. As we approached the house, Aldous became slightly uneasy. "I don't quite know what she'll make of it," he said. "It's a curiously *trivial* story, told in great *detail*, with a certain amount of *squalor*." Mrs. Herbold was very businesslike. She insisted on reading out a passage in Aldous's handwriting, to see if she would be able to decipher it. Sure enough, she hit the "squalor" right at its worst. Mrs. Herbold didn't falter, though maybe she swallowed, very very quickly. I giggled. Aldous looked immensely nonattached; a dozen light years away from us, and it. On our way home, he remarked, "Oh well—I dare say she's quite a gay old thing, really."

January 10. Madhabi back from hospital. Peggy wants me to go up to Alto Cedro and look after the boys while she's away. Ben has been suddenly found to be suffering from some mild kind of arthritis. Nothing serious, but he must wear a brace on his back for six months.

January 13. Yesterday, Swami gave a lecture on Vedanta to a Young Methodists' club at UCLA. He was disgusted by the students' behavior: the girls sat on the boys' laps throughout.

With Denny to the Red Cross blood bank. The nurse called us sissies, because we wanted to lie side by side, in order to go on talking.

Sarada has become a *Song of Bernadette* addict. Whenever anybody wants to see it, she goes along with them.

January 14. With Swami out land shopping for the new center. A realtor showed us a marvellous property right up in the hills above Brentwood, with a view over Santa Monica Bay and away across the

---

[1] "Sonnenuntergang" ("Sunset").

city to Mount Wilson and Baldy. But it would cost hundreds of thousands to develop. No road, even.

Supper with the Huxleys. Matthew showed us his color photographs of the desert. They're very remarkable: some like Corots, others as beautiful as Japanese prints. Two awful pictures of me, taken while I was living at Peggy's, all head and no shoulders, with a pot belly. Maria said, "You know, Christopher, there's something we've wanted to tell you for two years—I think we know you well enough now—what do *you* think, Aldous? *Can* we tell him? We can—can't we? You see, Christopher, you have a *very* long neck—and you should *never* wear a shirt without a collar."

January 31. Sudhira has been up at Alto Cedro, minding the house while Peggy is away. (I didn't go myself, because I wanted to be in constant contact with Swami during the Gita revision. It'll be finished tomorrow.) Today, Sudhira called me to say that she's had a letter from Peggy. Peggy and Bill have shown the X rays of Ben's back to several specialists in the East, and it has now been decided that his arthritis is very serious indeed. It's a kind called Marie-Strümpell: three to five years of gradually increasing stiffness, with bouts of pain; and then you have a stiff back for life. X-ray treatment sometimes arrests it, but there's not very much hope.

Later in the day, Ben and Sudhira came down here, because Sudhira wanted to use Kolisch's quartz lamp on Ben's acne. Ben knows nothing, yet. I could scarcely bear to be with him, and laugh and talk as though nothing were the matter. It made me feel quite sick.

Sudhira tells me that she volunteered to go back to nursing, while she was at the hospital with Madhabi. But now she says she'll stay on here another year, if I'll promise to stay too.

February 7. Here I am down at Llano, staying with the Huxleys. I'll go back tomorrow.

On the 2nd, I took Amiya out to a restaurant for her birthday treat. She drank three Bacardis and got the giggles. On the 5th, Tommy Viertel was drafted into the army, and Peter Viertel, back in this country to go to officers' school, was married to a very attractive girl named Virginia, who used to be the wife of Budd (*What Makes Sammy Run?*) Schulberg.

Aldous is finishing the revision of his novel. The sun on the terrace is almost hotter than you can bear to sit in. The long view down the desert slope—the Joshua tree with its rigid gestures, and the cactus like a disconnected section of plumbing. The dark buttes, sterile and volcanic, rising out of the green desert floor. And, far, far beyond the horizon, the whole range of the High Sierras, snow covered and piled high with ominous clouds. It's the kind of spring day on which you feel that perhaps you will live forever. Everything seems eternally alive—the joyful blue sky, the fat sly thievish cats, the two big bounding dogs, the thorny locust tree infested with little birds. Maria is in the kitchen, cooking wildly, with everything boiling over. The blue-eyed Texan handyman, in his big hat and western belt slung low around his hips, moves easily around, attending to his chores, as though he had a hundred years to spare before supper. The cattle— Herefords and Holsteins and Shorthorns—are cropping in the bush. There is no sign of the war, except the olive-drab army trucks, moving almost invisibly through the landscape, along the road below the house.

I'm staying in Matthew's room. (He was invalided out of the army and is now about to get a job in the reading department at Warner Brothers.) The walls are covered with relief maps of Chile, Peru, Argentina and Brazil and a plan of the LZ–130.[1] There are white droppings on the desk, made by a bird that got down the chimney. Over the fireplace is a "family portrait": an eighteenth-century American primitive which the Huxleys picked up in a junk store. Matthew's books: the Smithsonian Scientific Series, Chandler's *Introduction to [Human] Parasitology*, Robin's *La Pensée grecque*,[2] Wolcott's *Animal Biology*, Bloch's *Le Marquis de Sade*, the *Encyclopaedia Britannica* (from which I learn today's piece of useless information—that Catamitus is the Latin name for Ganymede). In the closet are his uniforms. He has cut off the Medical Corps insignia and pinned them up on the door.

February 18. This evening, Swami asked me to read aloud a speech by Gandhi, which is reprinted in the *Vedanta Kesari*, the magazine of the Ramakrishna Mission published in Calcutta. There was also an article about Krishna, saying that he "gladdened the cows." Which reminds me of a story Kolisch told at supper. A man dies. The widow goes to a medium, who tells her, "I see your husband in a beautiful meadow— mountains all around—a blue sky." "Oh, darling—" says the widow, "I'm so glad you're happy!" And the husband's voice answers: "Happy? Hell! I'm a cow in Montana!"

The Thoms are here—just back from visiting Rich at the San

---

[1] Landing Zone, designated by number rather than location for security.
[2] *La Pensée grecque et les origines de l'esprit scientifique* (*Greek Thought and the Origins of the Scientific Spirit*).

Diego marine base. He'll go overseas soon. He is the camp eccentric; everybody knows and likes him.

Perhaps the only thing that would ever reconcile me entirely to this place would be having someone here I could talk to as I talk to Denny; someone who, at the same time, was convinced of the necessity for this way of life and absolutely determined to stay. But that's a daydream. And, meanwhile, I've simply got to strike my own roots. After all, what's the alternative? But the body doesn't reason. It wants to get out and break all the rules. For a weekend, for a single night, it would trade eternity—until next morning, when a hangover transforms it into the nastiest little puritan of them all. This is called "suffering human joys and sorrows." What filthy, sentimental, lying rubbish.

February 28. Swami has been sick. Now he's recovered. He sits on the sofa and we forget him. We play, unmindful like children, in the completely uninteresting certainty of their father's love. If we cut our fingers, we'll remember and run to him at once. It isn't a relationship, because there's no element of surprise, no possibility of change. He could not cease to care for us. Our demand on him is total and quite merciless. *Of course* he is and will be there—now, tomorrow, whenever we decide we want him.

Last night, I was walking home from the Marmont after seeing John van Druten, and it struck me so strongly how very misleading it is to think of *oneself* as getting better or worse. How can the ego improve? It can't. It can only wear thin, and let more of the light through. Then, again, I must remember that growth isn't continuous: there are certain to be violent ups and downs. Quite an ordinary person may have moments at which he thinks and feels and acts like a near saint. The sun shines occasionally, even in Iceland. And when it does, it's the same sun as one sees in Arabia always. It's only the weather that's individual.

When the sun shines—ah, what joy! Walking in the street, saying mentally to all the people: "Please help yourselves, dispose of me, take anything you want, just ask." Oh God, make me into a public convenience.

Roger Spencer came to me yesterday evening, and began, "I think one ought to be frank about these things—" (Oh, oh, I said to myself—here it comes. What have I done now?) "While I was meditating," he continued, "I realized how much I like you." Needless to say, I felt vain and pleased; although I know perfectly well—considering the way I've often behaved to him—that it was Roger's triumph, not mine.

March 11. A week ago, I went down with the Huxleys again, and Aldous and I worked out a story for the movies, based on a real character, an old man who lives in the Mojave Desert and has the power to heal animals. It seems quite good and we are going to try and sell it.

(We never succeeded. Nobody liked the story—least of all, James Geller, who'd been practically prepared to buy it sight unseen: he was the story editor at Warner's, and one of Aldous's warmest admirers. Either they thought it was goody-goody, or that it was superstitious, or both. Nevertheless, I still think it really had something.)

Denny has just taken an apartment down in Santa Monica Canyon, at 137 Entrada Drive. I cycled down to visit him yesterday, stayed the night and returned this morning. His landlady is a Mrs. Eamons, who is nearly blind and very old. They are fighting already. She wanders in and out of the apartment, complaining about the holes he is making in the walls and the damage he's done to her furniture. She has a son of forty who drinks. She beats him and he yells for mercy. Denny is now starting to study medicine at UCLA.

March 13. Cold, grey and sad, after last week's hot sunshine, with a few tears of rain. Today I first met Heinz, twelve years ago. I've just heard from Bill Roerick, who's now in England, that Bruce (see April 4, last year) is missing in action. I don't know why I mind so much. I mind for Tommy.

Where are you, Heinz? You are so near me, still. Even for your sake alone, without any other reason, I ought to be kinder, more understanding than I am. Perhaps Bruce is a prisoner, and you're guarding him. . . .

A few days after this entry, I started to fall in love, with someone whom I'll call X. There is a reason for this, other than mere discretion; because, as far as I was concerned, X. wasn't a human being at all but simply a state of mind. Unrequited love is valuable in literature, but in life it bores me—especially my own. And the X. situation (which persisted throughout the year) was particularly idiotic, because I never had any real intention of doing anything about it: even if X. had returned my feelings, I would never have left Ivar Avenue on that account. My "love" for X. was, in fact, nothing but sentimental obstinacy—quite cruel and calculating under the sugar coating. Such crazes hit most of us from time to time. They are like the common cold—incurable but temporary—and deserve no more consideration. The X. situation was a particularly violent craze, chiefly because I indulged it, and even gratified it, as they say, physically. The other person involved behaved, from first to last, with extraordinary decency and generosity, for which, now that the craze is over and we are friends, I hope I shall never stop being grateful. I shall have to refer to X. from time to time in this diary, but I do so unwillingly and without any masochistic pleasure.

March 27. Down for ten days at John van Druten's ranch, at Thermal, near Indio. I'm returning to Hollywood next Friday. Much too much sex talk since I've been here, but I expected that. In sane moments, I am very happy to be without sex—oh, much more than happy, utterly thankful. The way I am living is "the only way I can do anything now," and it includes writing. In fact, it makes writing possible, with a new sense of responsibility. I am slowly roughing out the first draft of *Prater Violet.* (Johnny is amazed because I sometimes don't work more than twenty minutes a day.) It's wrong—the way it is—but that doesn't matter. Gradually, gradually, the muscles of the invention become more flexible. I just have to keep on at it. It's my karma yoga.

London was badly bombed, yesterday. People are suffering, all over the world. Let me never forget them. Let me never harden my heart. Let me never sentimentalize, either. Hardness and sentimentality both hinder awareness. If I can't think of Ramakrishna, let me at least remember Bruce.

A glorious morning, with the breeze sending fluff from the cottonwood trees floating out high over the garden. The brown hills—enormous piles of volcanic refuse—pushing down into the flat, fertile valley of carrots, onions, grapefruit, dates, alfalfa and corn. Called the Coachella Valley, because the soil is full of tiny shells—this land used to be at the bottom of the sea. You can still see the stone fish traps made by the Indians, high up the slope of the mountain. The ducks on the reservoir. The drone of a high bomber. The three male date palms in the corner of the grove. (How to pollinate dates: The sour smelling male date blossom, within its fibrous, swordlike spathes, is shaken through a sieve to collect the pollen. Then the pollen is dabbed on bits of cotton, which are tied up inside the female date flowers. If you leave the process to nature, a certain amount of pollen will be carried around by the wind, but not enough for all the trees.) A car drives by, raising great clouds of sweet smelling dust, which for some reason reminds me of the dust of China, although it isn't blowing off the grave mounds. Mexican nationals are imported as ranch workers, owing to the labor shortage. They are known as "dry"

Mexicans and "wet" Mexicans. The "wet" ones—those who have entered the U.S. illegally—are so called because they are supposed to have swum the Rio Grande. The bumpy "washboard" back roads leading into the Indian reservation, where there are weird natural clearings, like lawns, in the mesquite and sage bushes. You seldom see a house there, and never an Indian.

Yesterday, we drove up into the mountains. Johnny has bought a cabin in the forest above Idyllwild, to come to in the hot weather. There was a big fire there, a few months ago. It travelled so quickly that the rodeo rider and his wife, who live next door, had to grab their child and run. But Johnny's cabin wasn't burnt, because it had stone foundations. All the trees, including the great sugar pine above the house, are scarred and blackened by the flames. The fire even got into the well, burnt the wooden supports and caused the windlass to fall down the shaft, making it useless. This little settlement of cabins is squalid as any slum, because of the dumps and the litter of building materials all around. I don't like the place at all. Even by daylight, it is spooky. There is a moment in the afternoon when the light changes and the woods become suddenly unfriendly. Something says, "We'd advise you to start home now. Visitors are not welcome here."

April 1. Got home last night, to find that (1) Swami has directed that we all do at least three hours in the shrine daily, and one day of individual vigil a month, (2) Sudhira has to have an operation for colonic ulcer, and (3) Johnny Latham crashed near San Franciso, at the start of a flight to the Pacific; his spine is hurt and he's still unconscious; Kolisch is attending him, and Shanta and Amiya are with him.

("Shanta"—Mrs. Latham—was a pudgy, rather drab elderly woman who came regularly to Ivar Avenue. She was a widow, and owned an apartment house, and lived off its rents. Her son Johnny was a grown-up man of around thirty, but she treated him as a little boy, talked about him continually, and had directed every movement of his life until he entered the army. He was a radio operator, and often flew back and forth between San Francisco and the various Pacific bases. A nice boy, large and dumb and friendly.)

It's so pleasant to be back, and feel that the family is pleased to see me. "We missed you, Chris," Sarada tells me, in a tone of naive surprise. And last night, as soon as vespers were over, Web went to the shrine, took a rose from it, and gave it to me. I was so touched, I didn't know what to do or say.

Lunch with the Huxleys, at the Farmer's Market: they love it there, despite the crowds, the jostling, the discomfort and the noise. I suppose, after the quietness of the desert, it seems gay and exciting. A perfect stranger admired my bicycle, but scolded me quite severely for scratching some of the varnish off against a metal post.

Brecht wants me to translate his version of *The Circle of Chalk*.[1] I'm in a dither; there seems so much to do, in all departments. The thought of sex hovers in the background, like potential panic amongst the audience in a theater where there is no fire escape. And yet—I wouldn't take John van Druten's life if you paid me the gross earnings of *The Voice of the Turtle*. The misery of owning that ranch, of having all those responsibilities, of being called long distance by Gertrude Lawrence! Not that I didn't enjoy being down there. As a matter of fact, Johnny and Carter, either separately or together, always put me entirely at my ease. The nicest thing they said to me was, "We can't imagine you ever putting on an act." If they only knew!

April 2. While we were at breakfast, Kolisch telephoned to say that Johnny Latham died yesterday. He never regained consciousness. If he had lived, his brain would have been permanently affected. (Or is that what they always say on such occasions?)

This evening, Shanta and Amiya returned. I avoided seeing them. Madhabi and some of the others made a great theatrical fuss, hovering around, as they came up the steps, and leading them into the temple, where the doors were already standing open and the candles lighted. It was disgusting but very natural: curiosity, largely. None of us are nearly so sorry for Shanta as we pretend, but only Sudhira dares admit this. Swami alone can rise to such occasions, because he is genuinely capable of love, without ulterior motives. To him it is quite simple— a mother has lost her son. His ego is not in any way involved.

Eight other boys were killed in that plane. At least one person must be suffering for each, as Shanta suffers. And the wreck wasn't a headline, barely a news item, the sort of thing which happens every day—a piece of carelessness. Utterly insignificant beside the advertised losses in Russia, Italy, the Pacific and the big air raids. Remember that.

April 3. Shanta, at breakfast, was rather wonderful. She made a real effort to put us all at our ease—and soon we were talking and laughing fairly naturally. But the worst time for her will come much later—

---

[1] Klabund's 1925 play, adapted from the Chinese; Brecht titled his version *The Caucasian Chalk Circle*.

when people imagine you've forgotten, and then are bored and a little indignant because they find you haven't.

Brecht came, and spent an hour trying to get me to say I'd do his play. He is an expert wheedler, and I nearly gave way; but I didn't like him so much when our interview was over. He is utterly ruthless, opportunistic and selfish. I don't believe he'd waste five moments on anyone who wasn't in a position to do him a favor. Also, he couldn't help showing his scorn and impatience of all my other non-Brecht obligations which came between him and my consent.

This evening after vespers, Sudhira, Amiya, Sarada and I went down to the funeral parlor, to look at Johnny Latham's corpse. It was lying in what looked like a cheap hotel sitting room, with a standard lamp, an ugly little couch and some crude framed paintings of flowers. Johnny, in his sergeant's uniform, was quite unrecognizable—no neck, great pads of flesh around the collar, the lips pouting in a slightly sarcastic smile; he looked fifteen years older. They'd rouged his cheeks and lips and covered a scar on his forehead with orange makeup. Amiya and Sudhira were furious. Sarada was afraid to touch Johnny's hand, but she finally did: it was soft and cold, like jelly. From the neighboring chapel, we heard a woman singing the Schubert *Ave Maria.* Johnny, who had seemed so near to us in the shrine room, obviously wasn't within miles of this lifelike dummy stranger. Sarada became more and more daring. She pretended to faint, and, when I accused her of showing off, actually threw herself on the carpet, to demonstrate how she could do a theatrical fall. At length, when Sudhira was about to yank Johnny clear out of the casket, the mortician came in, very pleasant and businesslike. There was nothing to be done, he told us. The embalming fluid often has this fattening effect after an autopsy—and anyhow, he politely insinuated, the local firm up north had made a poor job of it. With the aid of a husky young assistant, he lifted the heavy rigid body a little; but the jowls wouldn't fall back into place, they were as hard as wax. So we asked them to close the casket and screw it down before the service tomorrow: Shanta mustn't see him like this. We returned home in a slightly hysterical mood, full of private jokes about the incident, which puzzled the others at supper—they didn't know where we'd been.

April 4. Johnny's funeral, at the mortician's. The curtains of the chapel (it's really more like a theater) parted, to reveal the casket banked with flowers and Swami, looking incredibly beautiful, seated beside it in his yellow robe: he reminded me of Gauguin's *The Spirit of the Dead, Watching.* An army chaplain read two psalms, very badly, with a horrible drawl: he pronounced *womb* "wewmbe." Swami read well, but the Nivedita selections are so badly arranged.[1] The only thing that really moved me was the expression on the faces of the coffin bearers—Johnny's air force friends. They were thinking to themselves, "Who's next?"

April 6. This morning, Mrs. Sabato (the stout, beautiful wife of the Italian character-actor, Alfredo Sabato) arrived in tears, because there was a snake on the terrace steps, attacking a lizard. It wasn't that Mrs. Sabato was sorry for the lizard; she was simply frightened of the snake. I shooed the two of them into the jasmine, but Mrs. Sabato went right on crying for an hour. Merely to have *seen* the snake had ruined her day. Sudhira, who is equally neurotic about lizards, but not in the least frightened of snakes, said she'd like to give the snake a medal. She's leaving for her operation tomorrow.

April 8. Sudhira was operated this morning, at St. Vincent's Hospital. Alfredo Sabato drove Swami and me over to see her, this afternoon. She was moaning, only half conscious. She said miserably: "I know I'll find it was just a dream. You aren't here, really."

Did another little chore for Vedanta today: fixed up the most sentimental parts of the funeral prayers in Nivedita's book,[2] so they'll be less awful for a funeral Swami has to assist at next Tuesday—his fourth in the last two months.

April 9. High wind this morning. The upruffled leaves of the cottonwood, seen through the temple window, reminded me of poplars, I suppose—because suddenly, and so poignantly, I remembered springtime in Germany, the lilac, and the old farmhouses down by the Mohriner See, and Heinz in his magenta sweater, waiting for me at the station. "Gone with the wind," I kept repeating to myself, "gone with the wind." Until the phrase dissociated itself from David Selznick and seemed quite beautiful.

April 13. Down to Santa Monica yesterday, to see Denny. I missed the ten o'clock bus home, so slept on Denny's sofa, under the giant Picasso of the girl reading, which belongs to him and Peter Watson.[3] He has had it shipped out here from the Museum of Modern Art in New York. The girl has a violet face, two noses, hands like bird's wings and a crown of poisonous looking flowers. I think it was she

[1] "An Office for the Dead," mostly excerpted from *An Indian Study of Love and Death* (1905) by Sister Nivedita (Margaret Noble), an Irish disciple of Vivekananda.
[2] Isherwood's arrangement is sometimes still used.
[3] "Girl Reading" (1934); see Glossary under Fouts.

who gave me a nightmare—extraordinarily coherent and vivid—about Nazi Germany. (I needn't describe this here, because I used it, with only one tiny addition, in *Prater Violet*.)

Some Santa Monica notes: Early morning fog. The rocks of the breakwater, the pier, the dotted line of fishing boats in the harbor are very black and precise, but they only serve to heighten the immensity and mystery of the hazy ocean and sky. Like a statement about God.

Sign at Sam's hot-dog stand: "The California Bank does not serve food. Sam the Greek does not cash checks."

Early morning. A very black Negro driving a black truck at tremendous speed, like the last fragment of the night hurrying away before the rising sun.

I am reading a book about God in a coffee shop. The waitress thinks it's a crime story and asks, "Have you caught him yet?" I answer, "No—unfortunately."

The astonishing American talent for ignoring the radio. Denny has it. He turns it on full blast and then carries on a shouted conversation about some serious philosophical subject.

Some of our favorite catchphrases: "Famed in song and story." "All ghoul and a yard wide." "Quoi qu'il soit qu'il soit." (Dog French for "Be that as it may.") "As far as the eye can see." "Der sogenannte . . . . besteht aus zwei Teilen, und zwar, der Vorderteil und der Hinterteil."[1] (This was supposed to parody a German professor lecturing.) "Dans la plus grande manière." (Dog French for "In the biggest way.") And all kinds of expressions borrowed and sometimes inverted from Gerald Heard: "Some of us who care a little less for this thing." "Appalling instantaneity," etc. etc.

Notice in Doc Law's Friendship Bar in the Canyon: "Dine in a nautical atmosphere. Open during blackouts and all clear. In case of direct hit we close immediately. Latitude 34.1. North. Longitude 118.30. West. Course straight ahead."

There's an advertisement you see everywhere nowadays: "When you think of furs, think of Fink." So I composed this song, to the tune of Beethoven's Minuet:

> If you want a mink that doesn't stink,
> And will not shrink,
> Just think of Fink.
>
> We've a lovely coat that looks like seal,
> What it really is we won't reveal.

---

[1] "In treating the so-called . . . there are two sides to the question, namely the front side and the backside."

If you think *that's* polar bear,
What do we care? It's your affair.

And even if our ermine ties
Are made of mice—well, they're just as nice.

Back home on the bus. The rest of the day was bad. Sudhira came home from the hospital and I was rather horrid to her, because she'd allowed Alfredo to read one of my stories. The rationalization for this was that, a day or two ago, Swami said to Madhabi in my presence: "Why do you read novels? All books that do not give the word of God are just a trash." So I worked this up into a sulk, the usual kind— that I'm not "understood" here, that Swami hates art, and that this is what keeps all my friends away from Ivar Avenue, etc. Actually— don't I know it all too well?—I'm merely sulking because I want to run off and play around X. I worked off some spite at the committee meeting of the Vedanta Society by announcing that I'd resign from being president this year.

April 14. Swami, sitting on the temple steps this morning, asked me so sweetly why I'd resigned from the committee. I put it that I dislike taking any official position here because I want to feel free to walk out at a moment's notice. Swami accepted this as though it were the whole truth—and, as usual, his love and utter lack of egotism melted me completely. I suppose that's what Brahmananda did to you: you felt he was more on "your" side than you were yourself. "I'm thinking of nothing but your own good": only a saint can honestly say that.

Took Sudhira to the doctor. Told her about X. I had to talk about it to someone. The X. pains are bad, this evening. Every mental area has its sore spots. If I happen to think of Australia, or Santa Monica Pier, or the art school, or a certain kind of tweed, I involuntarily mutter, "Ouch." It's like stubbing a sore toe. And every bit of it is in my own mind! Oh Shankara—if I could only learn your lesson!

April 17. My day of silence. Eight hours in the shrine. Boredom. Blankness. Storms of resentment—against Asit, against India, against being given a Sanskrit name (extraordinary how violently I react against this—because I know Swami won't ever insist on it, if he sees that I really mind). "Decided" not to become a monk, and to tell Swami so tomorrow (doubt if I shall) but to stay here, at any rate, till Brahmananda's next birthday. Where would I go after that? I don't know. Just "out." Sex, of course. But it's much much more than that. I have to explore every corner of the cage, before I can assure myself that it's as big as the universe.

But now that the storm has died down, I feel a kind of cleanness and relief.

April 18. Talked to Swami after breakfast and told him about yesterday. I forget already just exactly what he said—it was the way he said it that matters. No, it didn't make any difference if I left this place: it would always be my home. God wasn't specially here. Acts aren't important in themselves. It's no good promising not to do things. "That's your Christian training," said Swami smiling; and he added, "can you imagine *me* as a Christian monk? I would *never* have been a monk if I hadn't met Brahmananda."

One things seems clear. I must stay here for the present. I must try at least to complete another year.

Al Clifton visited us, from the San Francisco Center. Poor boy, he looked so sick. His father has just died. Al brought with him an atmosphere of jnana yoga, fog and salad—the very smell of Webster Street. Sudhira sent a message that he should come in and say hello to her in bed. Al was quite shocked, and terribly shy of entering her bedroom. He seems to expect that the demons of lust would swoop down and devour him on the spot.

April 24. Am in bed. The day before yesterday, while seeing *For Whom the Bell Tolls* with Sudhira (who is up and about again) I developed a pile. I called Peggy and suggested that Bill Kiskadden should come down and cut it open for me—thinking, in the kindness of my heart, that this would be a nice treat for him, since he never gets any surgery to do in the army. So Bill came, with his little knife. It hurt like hell. I yelled clear around the block, and immediately knew I'd gotten a black mark for doing it. Bill is a spartan.

However, the pain—or rather, the discomfort: it's nothing more—is a great relief, because, for the moment, it takes the sting out of the X. situation. You can't be in love when you have a sore behind.

May 14. Last Monday, the 8th, we had a puja for Buddha's birthday. Afterwards, Sudhira called me to eat outside with her on the terrace, and she told me: "It seems this whole thing may be malignant. Bill Daniels called Mark Rabwin about it. They want to cut me open and look. I'm not going to let them. I'll just clear out and disappear."

At first, I didn't understand what she meant. And when she went on to explain, I just felt numb. It appears that Daniels, who operated on her, suspected that some of the tissue he removed might be cancerous. So he consulted with Rabwin, who is one of the best surgeons in town and a very old friend of Sudhira's: they used to be lovers. Rabwin and Daniels were being very cagey, but Sudhira said she could get the truth out of Rabwin eventually; he knows her too well to be able to lie to her. If it is cancer, Sudhira will go away some place where she isn't known and kill herself with an overdose of morphia. She has it by her all the time.

In the evening, I suddenly realized that this is all true, that it could really happen. To have to say goodbye—as I did to Heinz—but knowing for certain that I'd never see her again. I pictured her turning away and walking down the temple steps, in her grey coat and skirt . . . I'd rather face anything else—even to stand by her deathbed. I started to cry. And she said, "Darling, I'd no idea you'd take it like this . . . I'm so sorry."

Tuesday was awful. I kept bursting into tears, uncontrollably, at odd moments. I don't think anyone else noticed. I went into the shrine room and tried to say, "Master, let me have it instead of her"— but I couldn't. I was scared. I could only say, "Your will be done, and help us to accept it."

Then Sudhira talked to Mark Rabwin on the phone. It isn't certain. They're just suspicious. She's to have X-ray treatment. My fear jumps at any ray of hope. I daren't believe it till I must.

Oh Thursday, Aldous came up to town and we talked about our movie story. I went to the dentist, who pulled two big back teeth. My mouth has been in a mess ever since, and the tonsil swollen. On Friday, Aldous and I lunched with Wolfgang Reinhardt, and discussed *The Miracle*: maybe we shall work on it. Today I drove with the Huxleys to Ojai, to hear Krishnamurti speak in the famous oak grove. He is really very nice. Such a modest, slim, white-haired, boyish figure standing in the sunny shadows. He obviously hates lecturing: he seemed terribly nervous and embarrassed, and winced visibly when people interrupted with questions. An extraordinary assortment of people go to hear him—C.O. boys from work camps, schoolteachers, apparently normal businessmen, small children, rich ladies, movie actors, farmers. And there are a few Theosophists of the old guard—bearded, smocked and sandalled—who sit regarding Krishnamurti with a kind of reproachful curiosity, because they firmly believe that, one day, he will announce his return to the movement and make a great historic speech in favor of Mrs. Besant.

Afterwards, Maria, Aldous and I went to lunch with Iris Tree and her friend Allan Harkness. Iris must be well over forty, but she still wears a blonde pageboy bob, and the flowing blue clothes which combine a suggestion of cultism with the gypsy artiness of her Augustus John girlhood. She is very gay and sympathetic. The house is dirty and untidy beyond belief, and there is a beautiful white police dog which bites the neighbors. Gay and vague, Iris brewed us some coffee, which tasted of bitter aloes. Maria took a sip of it and her face contracted with horror, but she recovered immediately and exclaimed, with a girlish little cry of delight, "Aldous—remember! Naples! Doesn't it take one *back*?" She contrived to suggest that Iris had made the coffee taste Neapolitan deliberately, as a kind of charming nostalgic surprise. I think this was one of the most tactful performances I have ever witnessed in my life. But Aldous didn't play up very well. And Iris spoilt it altogether by agreeing, in her deep beautiful voice: "It's *horrible*, isn't it?" And laughing her giddy, delighted laugh.

Allan Harkness is Ojai's answer to Gerald Heard. In fact, he's not unlike Gerald, with his beard and his red nose and long mild goat-face. He's a devoted Heardian, with a little anthroposophy thrown in. He and Iris have a small group of actors here, and plan to perform the plays Iris will write. Several of them have been pupils of Michael Chekhov.[1]

Such lovely spring weather. The hills are streaked with patches of mustard weed. In the distance, it looks like sunshine.

Sudhira goes down to the hospital every afternoon, to nurse Helene Sabato, who has just had an operation. Sudhira herself will have more treatment later. Without anything particular having been said or discovered, the menace seems to have lifted a little. Perhaps it is simply that she herself is no longer so worried about it, now that she has something to do. The other day, while she was with Helene, a nurse came into the room and whispered that they were in a fix: a woman had been brought in dying, and there was no bed for her—they'd wheeled her into one of the waiting rooms and screened it off, and now the staff was so short-handed that there was no nurse to spare—would Sudhira go and be with her for a while, so she wouldn't have to die alone? Of course, Sudhira was delighted. She went and sat with the woman, who took about twenty minutes to die. No chaplain appeared, so Sudhira repeated her mantram all the time. "And just before she died," Sudhira added, "she opened her eyes and gave me such a funny look; as though the whole thing was a huge joke between us two."

June 7. First news coming in about the D-Day invasion of France. I keep wondering if Heinz is alive, and if he's fighting there; and what has happened to Pete Martinez, whom I last heard of over in England.

---

[1] Russian-born actor and film star (nephew of the playwright), he incorporated the insights of Eastern philosophy and of Rudolf Steiner's anthroposophy into his acting system.

Sudhira went down to stay with the Sabatos, when Helene left the hospital. Yesterday she [Sudhira] fainted, and now she's to be examined again. Everybody knows. Alfredo told Swami, who very secretively made it obvious to the whole family what is the matter. The funny thing is, he doesn't seem in the least worried. Can he possibly *know*? But I mustn't catch Sudhira's superstition.

I ache with loneliness. Looking out toward the ocean and the distant tower of the bank in Santa Monica, I think, "X. is there." I feel almost as if I had created X. myself, out of the blue sky and the water and the golden light. In a way, I suppose I have.

Vernon has now definitely suggested that he shall come West and live with or near me, and paint, and study with Swami—though he doesn't want to join up at Ivar Avenue, at any rate for the present. I need him badly—or someone like him; but a lot of the old suspicion remains. Can he really have changed as much as his letters suggest? Well—perhaps it's worth trying.

June 8. Grey, rainy weather. Terrible X. jitters, producing the most squalid, hard, insensitive state of egotism. I try to pray for all those boys fighting each other on the French beachheads, and I can't feel anything. I can't care. I can't even feel for Sudhira, at the moment. I just sit in the shrine room rehearsing speeches to X.

Just after writing the above, I went into the living room, and Swami said smiling, "You are worried about something, Chris." I mentioned Sudhira, Vernon, the invasion—but not X. However, as always, I began to feel calmer.

June 9. Ben's graduation day at Harvard Military Academy. The X-ray treatments seem to have arrested the arthritis, although it's too soon to say definitely yet. A little section of his spine is stiff, but not enough to make the slightest difference. In fact, thanks to the corrective exercises he has been doing, he can actually raise his legs much higher than most boys of his age.

Peggy, Judge Bok (here on a visit) and I attended the graduation exercises. Ben looked very slender and almost handsome in his uniform: thank God, he already has a 4-F from the draft board, and with any luck the war will be over before the doctor can be quite certain about his back. The usual inspirational speeches. While the boys were parading, a right turn was ordered, and one cadet made a left turn and marched proudly off by himself. Sure as hell, it was Derek. Peggy was terribly embarrassed and didn't talk about anything else as long as we were together; trying to cover her shame with little jokes.

Just to keep me in my place, she told me that Bill Kiskadden had said that his cutting open my pile "couldn't possibly have hurt much." So that makes me a neurotic sissy.

With Denny to see Sudhira in bed at the Sabatos'. She's obviously very sick. Denny and Sudhira made a terrific click. When he came into the room, he exclaimed, "Why—you're beautiful!" They'd never met before.

June 12. 11:00 a.m. Have just finished three hours in the shrine, had breakfast, read my mail. Putnam's won't publish our Gita translation, even as distributors. A letter from my brother Richard. I never can make out if they have been in any air raids or had any other unpleasant experiences. Both he and M. in their letters stick to gossip about the neighbors, and the war is mentioned as little as possible. Felix Greene did tell me that a bomb had once fallen somewhere in the neighborhood, but he didn't seem to know if it was near our home.

(Which reminds me how, quite early in the war, M. developed an absolute phobia about war secrecy. She even cut the word "war" out of her letters altogether. Once, when she and Richard were paying a brief visit to London, she wrote: "Last Sunday, we went to N.'s wedding, at —. *Owing to the political situation,* there was a large hole in the roof of the church . . .")

My sit was uneventful, lots of japam, avoided thinking much about X., or worrying, or feeling mad at anyone. I yawned a great deal, and the salt from the tears has dried under my eyes. A dull grey morning. Have just smoked a cigarette, which I didn't mean to.

2:00 p.m. Have just finished the worship. Found I'd forgotten most of the ritual, but muddled through somehow. It's very distasteful to me, just now. And I hate the thought of all pujas. With one exception: on the morning of Vivekananda's birthday puja, Sister personally serves him his coffee in the shrine room—two cups—and a cigarette, which she lights and leaves burning on an ashtray. Meanwhile, somebody reads the Katha Upanishad aloud; because it was his favorite. This little ceremony still seems to me charming and "right"—chiefly because it's based on a real relationship: Sister is commemorating her actual friendship with him while he was alive. If only all ritual could be like that; with a personal significance.

I feel bored, sullen, resentful. Envious of Denny, who told me the other night in a bar, "I've decided to hold on to the things I can see." Must I be the only one of my friends to follow this way of life? Well, that's where Vernon comes in. If it works out.

Sudhira came up here with Alfredo this morning. I didn't know, until I saw her leaving. Maybe she wanted just to see me. I'd have run down the steps and waved—but Swami was there. Somehow, that stopped me; because it's my day of silence, and he wouldn't understand.

Denny says he's sure I'll be out of here in six months.

Something is sore in my left eyelid. I'm getting old: my hips are fat.

3:30 p.m. Did half an hour in the shrine. Ate bread and honey, and peaches with sour cream. Outlook on life a little brighter, but still quite unconstructive. Swami is gay and excited, because they've found a big property on the Pacific Palisades which would do for the new center. It costs $35,000; but this amount can probably be raised by selling off the outer lots to various members of the congregation who want to build homes there.

5:15. Just spent an hour in the temple. This much I have doped out: I would never leave Ivar Avenue on X.'s account.

10:00 Finished vespers. Ate a sardine supper. Put in a final fifteen minutes, to make up seven hours. I feel a kind of stolid, forlorn satisfaction; nothing more. Terribly tired. I'm like a nursemaid who has been dragged around all day by a spoilt child, full of energy and whims and demands. The child is asleep at last; but he'll be awake at crack of dawn and rarin' to go. Oh God, I am so sick of him, and his complaints, and his damned love affair. He needs a sound whipping.

June 14. Got up at 4:15 and did three hours in the shrine. Merely in order to have it over with, and be able to run away and play in Santa Monica.

Before breakfast, in the living room, Swami said, "Take away God, and what is left? Ash cans!" Two other Prabhavananda sayings: "The shrimp is a kind of vegetable." "Krishnamurti is transhient, I am etarnal."

When I got down to Entrada Drive, there was nobody at home. Denny was out on the beach. This happens quite often. Whenever I haven't seen Denny for some time and find his apartment empty, I walk around it like a detective—alert for clues to his visitors and any new developments. Today, the place was very tidy: that must mean they had a big party and made such a mess that Denny couldn't bear it and had to clean house. In the kitchen, a dirty plate with broken crackers and a bit of stinking camembert: that must be the fat boy who works at the garage. No new snapshots over the desk or postcards stuck in the mirror. The frame of the Picasso is a bit more chipped. A fight? An unfamiliar pair of trunks on the shower curtain rail above the bath tub: Johnny Goodwin must be here. On the whole, I'm satisfied. The indications are not alarming.

June 15. At vespers, a sudden thought: a way of leaving this place without abandoning everything. Why couldn't Vernon and I live together, somewhere in the neighborhood, not too much involved with Ivar Avenue but keeping all the rules? I hate the present setup, because my chief motive for abstaining from sex is merely guilt; and this is hypocritical, even when my conscience is clear. I must have a stricter check on my life than Swami. I need someone like Vernon— someone who'd have a stake in my life; so that my failures would be his failures, and vice versa. This worked for a short time with Denny, in 1941: we really relied upon each other. But Denny is now going along a different road. His discipline is all built on his studying, which I can't share. Vernon is the only person who really needs me right now; and by the same token he's the only person I really need. I wonder if Swami would understand? He must. I'll make him, somehow.

We have just heard definitely that the Pacific Palisades property is already sold.

June 16. To see Sudhira at the Sabatos'. She is alarmingly sick, and the doctor doesn't seem to know what's the matter with her. She runs terrific temperatures and keeps lapsing into coma: her face turns quite blue. For a few minutes, I really thought she was going to die, right before my eyes. Then she recovered surprisingly, and talked quite logically for half an hour. Something is terribly wrong with her, but obviously it has nothing to do with the threatened cancer, and so, in a quite irrational way, I feel reassured.

June 20. Tomorrow will be the longest day, but it's still not real summer weather. There's a breeze, and a coolness under the heat— like cold water seeping into a very hot bath.

The page proofs of the Gita are corrected and it's practically ready to print. Marcel Rodd is going to take over the distribution, and publish the next edition. (He used to keep the London Bookshop on Hollywood Boulevard: Denny worked there for a while last year. He's a strange, pale, little shrimp of a man, with great dark eyes, full of a sort of sly, boyish impudence. He's English—with Levantine blood; a Jew, I think. He makes Swami become much more oriental than usual: they meet, as it were, at a halfway house in the Near East, and sit bargaining and giggling, understanding each other perfectly. Marcel is a slippery customer, with a taste for pornography, but I think we shall be able to get along with him because he is terribly anxious to become a respectable publisher, and the Gita, with Aldous's introduction, represents prestige.)

Two days ago, I finished my draft of the movie story I'm writing with Aldous. *Prater Violet* will be ready, in its first draft, after four or five more working days. There is the usual stack of letters. And then I have to start thinking about a book of selections from Vivekananda's writings. Calm. Don't strain. Go quietly ahead. Do each job as it comes to hand. These jitters, this gnawing anxiety—they get you nowhere. You know how to stop them. And yet you daydream, smoke and idle. You chatter and spill what should be secret. You long for Santa Monica. You are so restless—for what? You don't want X., really. I'm not sure you need Vernon, either. Only your weakness needs him. And the needs of weakness turn quickly into hatred. Grow like a tree, and let the birds come to you or stay away, as they feel inclined.

June 21. Woke at 2:15, with a scalding sore throat. Tried to go into the temple, but someone had locked it. Today I'm feeling lousy.

Now I feel *sure* I'm going to leave Ivar Avenue. The only question is—when? I feel sure I'm not going to be a member of the Ramakrishna Order, or any kind of monk, or anything outward. I've got to be C. Isherwood, and that's that. The spiritual life has to turn inward completely. A rationalization? Certainly. But that's the way things are going to be. Meanwhile watch and wait your chance.

June 22. I still have a temperature. This is one of the bad spots. Sudhira tried to escape from the Sabatos' this morning. She got her clothes on when no one was around, and slipped out of the house with a high fever. Alfredo caught her, and Swami saw her later and persuaded her to stay till she's better. She said she wanted to go to her mother.

A long talk with Kolisch. He believes that everybody who tries to lead the religious life is sure to get sick; it's part of the process of renunciation, "dying to the world." If you persist, you snap out of it again and your health improves. He may be a quack and a crank, but there's something wonderful about him; a kind of calm strength. He sat on the bed, smiling and holding my pulse, and I began to feel better immediately.

June 23. Denny and Johnny Goodwin visited me. They are planning to go to San Francisco—chiefly because of a very dreary intrigue involving one of Johnny's friends. Denny, of course, was thoroughly enjoying himself, and I found myself laughing too. But why? All lies, all cheating, all disagreements are against our deepest human interests. They hurt us all. What is there to gloat over? Of course, my own motives are simple: if Denny goes away, I can move down into his apartment for a few days, and be alone with X. For what? What do I hope will happen? But the Ego doesn't answer questions like that.

Sudhira has been moved to the Cedars of Lebanon Hospital. She fainted and fell, badly hurting her head. However, it seems that the possibility of cancer is definitely out. They're afraid something may be wrong with her kidneys.

June 30. I got back from Santa Monica yesterday, after spending four days.

Denny called early this morning, having flown down from San Francisco last night and been landed in Palmdale because of the fog. He had a black eye, and his ribs are hurt. He got into a terrific drunken fight with a sailor, who knocked him out. The sailor was about to steal Denny's billfold when he found the blood-donor's card, and immediately became very remorseful and sentimental, because he had a buddy in the Pacific whose life was saved by a blood transfusion. So, instead, he helped Denny to a doctor.

After breakfast, I went into Swami's study and told him everything—all about my relations with X. Swami rose to the occasion, as he always does. "Once you have come to Ramakrishna, you will be taken care of," he said: "I promise you that. Even if you eat mud, you will be all right."

I also told him about my plans for Vernon. I said we would want to live separately, maybe around the corner. Swami agreed to everything, but of course I can see he wants to get Vernon into the family, right from the start. He said, "I don't want you to leave here, Chris. I want you to stay with me as long as I'm alive. I think you'd be all right, even if you left here. But I want you . . . I think you have the makings of a saint."

I laughed. I was really staggered. "No," said Swami, "I mean it. You have devotion. You have the driving power. And you are sincere. What else is there?"

July 4. Have been in bed again, with a temperature; my usual reaction to being fussed. Peggy came to see me, and suggested her usual remedy—for me to go up there and stay. Swami didn't want this—so I didn't go—largely because I didn't specially want to, myself, and didn't think it worth making an issue of. Peggy was offended, of course. She has decided that Swami dislikes her because she criticized the Gita, which is fantastic. But the fact remains that Swami does disapprove of her influence over me; I don't quite know why—but maybe he's right. I really shouldn't run to these elder sisters, nannies and mummies. Dodie is different. I never cry on her shoulder and I never could. I think of her more as a colleague, another man, almost.

Today I'm still tired and empty, and feel dry and depressed but stronger, because I've done some work. Vernon plans to arrive at the beginning of August, and that, at present, simply makes me feel weary. I have nothing for him—no strength, no encouragement. But that's just a mood and will pass. It's actually far better not to be too enthusiastic in advance.

July 8. Sudhira has been here. She left this morning, to visit her mother. Last night she told me that, on the day she was moved to the Cedars of Lebanon, she took three cc's of typhoid vaccine—thirty times the maximum dose. She figured it would kill her and no one would know it was suicide—she can't understand why she didn't die. Rabwin knows she did it; no one else.

Later . . . I've just had a talk with Swami, alone. I told him that I feel so frustrated whenever there are any rules to follow. He said that there weren't any rules; you were just to do what you felt you had to. I said I felt bothered by pujas. He said, well then, don't come to them.

He told me how tired he sometimes gets, and how badly he feels when he seems to lose all control over people. The only way he can help them is by prayer, and sometimes it appears not to work. They go "hay-weird," as he calls it. He recommends japam, and talking about God, continually, to everybody—in whatever terms each one will accept. I do do this quite a lot, actually, with nearly all my friends, and it's surprisingly easy and natural. You can express the same basic idea in terms of art, or science, or politics, or even sex. In fact, one never need talk about anything else.

Denny, that sourest of all critics, refuses to be impressed when I tell him about Swami's tolerance and open-mindedness. According to Denny, Swami is bound to accept me on any terms, because I'm so useful to the Vedanta Society as an editor and translator. I get very angry with him when he talks like this, and I think it's utterly unjust to Swami. But the fact remains that he *is* much more lenient towards me than he is toward the others. I don't think this proves anything either way, except that I'm much more tiresome and demanding. Maybe, also, that Swami realizes what a lot of karmas I dragged into Ivar Avenue out of the past. With Sarada, who's young and has a real vocation, he can afford to be strict; and, in many ways, I think he's fonder of her than of any of us. It's really no compliment to be let off lightly: it merely means that I am too weak to be disciplined.

July 10. My day of silence. Asit and I had late breakfast together, after my first session in the shrine room. Yogini came in and asked me questions which I answered with signs and written sentences on a scribbling pad. As usual, it turned into a game. Asit said, "If you shek your haid so vylently, you will injoor it." I wrote, "That's one thing *you* need never be afraid of," and handed it to Yogini, who replied, "I take aspirin sometimes." I wrote, "Show-off!" I record this conversation because it's typical of the nicer aspect of my life in this house.

The proofs of the Gita arrived. In the afternoon, Marcel Rodd called, and Swami had to release me from my silence, to discuss business. Rodd was much amused. I could see him thinking that religious people are all alike: God is forgotten as soon as there's any money involved.

Here's a hymn to Ramakrishna—my latest effort to amuse the family. To the tune of "Bye, Bye, Blackbird."

> There was a man lived in Bengal,
> He had no ego, none at all—
> Ramakrishna.
> Never wore a derby hat,
> Taught his devotees, "Thou art that"—
> Krishna, jai, jai!
>
> For he'd prayed and prayed and prayed so hard, he
> Kept on going right into samadhi.
> You could yell in his ear and tickle his toe
> And pull his beard, but he'd never know—
> Krishna, jai, jai!
>
> G. C. Ghosh[1]—he was no monk—
> Showed up one evening stinking drunk,
> So Ramakrishna
> Said, "Why waste dough on liquor, you fool,
> When the Bliss of God's got a kick like a mule?"
> Krishna, jai, jai!
>
> In came Naren,[2] as fresh as paint,
> Said, "My! your old superstitions are quaint!"
> Then Ramakrishna
> Put his foot on his chest and began to press
> Till the kid didn't know his home address—
> Krishna, jai, jai!

[1] Girish Chandra Ghosh, Bengali playwright, actor and director, who gave up his worldly life to become a devotee of Ramakrishna.
[2] Boyhood name of Vivekananda.

Keshab[1] said, "I wish you'd been
With me in London when I met the Queen,"
But Ramakrishna
Said, "Listen, old boy, and don't get cross—
I don't have to meet her, 'cause I know her Boss—"
Krishna, jai, jai!

M.[2] wrote down his words for publication,
Now they're read throughout the Hindu nation,
And in fifty more years—we are such dopes—
We'll have built him a church, with priests and popes.
Krishna, jai, jai!

July 11. Drove out with Swami, Sister and Dr. Manchester for a land hunt on Palos Verdes. It was so beautiful there that I felt more depressed than ever. The dreadful hungry boredom of not being with the person you love. The name of a street, Hobart Avenue; and a phrase of Manchester's to the house agent, "Now I'll let Swami take over"—rang hollow with X.'s absence. The people we love illuminate whole territories by their presence: for them, the oleander has fragrance, the ocean shines. Without them, the sunlight is in vain. The house agent was very cagey: no, they had hardly anything— times were so uncertain—it would be too expensive, etc. etc. Then he took Manchester aside and murmured something, and Manchester shook his head violently. The house agent's manner changed at once: well—after all, there *were* some excellent lots, a real bargain, just what we wanted. . . . Later, Manchester explained to us that he'd thought Swami was a Negro. An East Indian, of course, is altogether different; almost a white man. We all agreed that we didn't want to have a center in a restricted area.

On the way home, I argued with Manchester (who is prissy and academic, and teaches English at Occidental College) and made stupid generalizations: "Whitman and Jefferson are the two greatest Americans" etc. etc.

If Vernon doesn't come, it will be necessary to invent him.

Master—if Vernon isn't to come, if our film story is not to be sold, if the X. situation is to continue—and I wouldn't put it past you— then please, please dream up something else.

---

[1] Keshab Chandra Sen, Indian reformer and spiritual leader, influenced by Christianity and personally by Ramakrishna, believed himself divinely appointed to teach a New Dispensation of God's law.
[2] Mahendranath Gupta, see Glossary under M.

July 27. Well, I finally finished the rough draft of *Prater Violet* three days ago. It's very confused, but I feel that a jinx is broken. Seventy-four pages of writing! That's a triumph in itself.

Vernon wired today that he hopes to start Monday or Tuesday. Before this, he'd proposed waiting six months and earning some more money, but I told him not to bother. Was this a mistake? I don't think so, but we shall see.

Dhruva got hit by an automobile, and now limps around, enjoying Sister's attentions. Today she told one of the girls, "Take Dhruva out into the garden, but be sure to bring him back in good time for the reading. He'd hate to miss that!"

A woman named Meta Evans, who often comes up and helps with the laundry, was talking to a colored girl whom she knows. The girl asked who Meta worked for, and Meta, not wanting to go into a lot of explanations about Swami, said, "A minister." How many children did he have, the girl asked. "Twelve," said Meta. The girl was shocked: "Twelve! And him a minister!"

July 30. Cycled to and from the Beesleys'. Alec tried to show me how to dive properly: I never straighten my legs. The charm of their garden, with the whole city spreading away into the hazy distance below. Talking literature and writing-shop to Dodie under the tree above the pool; the endless fun of playing with ideas. And Dodie, the ever-enthusiastic and encouraging, exclaiming, "Oh, *write* it, Chris!" More than anybody else, she has helped me struggle through *Prater Violet*. Every time we meet, she asks firmly, "How many pages?"

(To write a new kind of stream of consciousness. Like a fugue. Certain thought motifs recurring at regular intervals—England, Dentist, God, X., Money, War, Novel, England, Dentist, God, etc. etc. Over this pattern play the more conscious, fugitive thoughts—the thoughts connected with immediate external stimuli. Maybe the whole thing would have to be written down in bars, like music. I would like to show thought as feeling, and feeling as thought, for the two are inseparable. I feel a twinge in the joints, and think of England. England is the twinge, the twinge is the thought. The roughness of stucco on a wall is the pimples on one's face. The hardness of iron against your hand is the income tax. The bitterness of overcooked coffee is anxiety about money. Most of the time, people don't really impinge on my consciousness as complete entities, or even complete images. There are moments when a friend is only apprehended as a pair of bowlegs, or a lisp, or as something which is cooking the dinner. At other moments, the people and things of the external world come much more sharply into focus and claim one's whole attention. Characters, to be subjectively realistic, should emerge like this, and recede again. But how to do it?)

This evening, Swami said how important he thinks worship and japam are. He said that this was why Amiya and Sudhira had been ten years in Ivar Avenue and not made more progress: they had neglected worship. He insisted specially on japam, because it leads naturally to meditation. He told me how he longs to go back to Benares, Vrindaban and Puri: the atmosphere there is so wonderful for meditation.

August 3. It's quite hot. I'm sitting in the garden, before our five o'clock reading from The Gospel of Ramakrishna (always a trial, because Madhabi is allowed to do it—as a concession to her vanity as an ex-actress—and she reads so badly). The boy who sells silk socks, Gaston Cabaret, has been round again. He was shell-shocked by the explosion of an ammunition dump, somewhere in this country. He has a long French face and nose, bony and ugly, but with such touchingly sweet childlike grey eyes. He is getting better, he says, but his hand still shakes so much that he can scarcely write.

Today I lunched with Maria Rosa Oliver; Lincoln Kirstein's friend from the Argentine. Her hand shakes too, from cigarette smoking. She is pretty and plump and immensely "intelligent," and one can easily understand how she gets lovers, despite her paralyzed legs and wheelchair. I really admire and like her, and would like to become friends with her—but not at a thousand miles an hour, which is her speed. She's leaving for Mexico very soon; and I'm invited to stay with her in the Argentine. We lunched at Ivar House, under the trees, and talked about Love, Lorca, Lincoln, Courage, National Characteristics, Death and Modern Poetry. I got the chore of collecting a bunch of modern writers to be translated into Spanish for her magazine *Sur*. When we said goodbye, she beckoned me to bend over and kiss her cheek. It was like being given a medal by royalty.

The rocket bombs are very bad over England. Today came a letter from Gretl Eberhart, about the death of her friend Heinz Behrendt: after underground work in Germany, arrest, concentration camps, escape and endless adventures, he was drafted into the American army, and got killed in the Pacific. Such an utterly tragic life, from start to finish, and yet—what a triumph! What amazing courage, moral and physical!

What have I done today, to express my solidarity with such people? Nothing. Only one hour of meditation. And only an hour and a half yesterday. I ought to be ashamed of myself. Or rather, I ought to *do* something. Just being ashamed is worthless, is even bad, because negative. Aren't I reverting to the masochistic self-flagellation of my twenties? I'm so *bored* with myself in that role. The whole of this diary is becoming a bore. Let's snap out of it. Come on, St. Augustine— amuse us. A little less about your sins.

A very revealing dream. I was dishwashing. Asit had slipped out without helping (this is a standing grievance) through the window. I was so furious that I ran to the door of his room and banged on it—but my blows were feebler than the tapping of a moth. As I woke, I *knew* that this is what it is like when you're dead. Gusts of rage and desire sweep you around, but you are impotent to vent them on the living.

Just as the ocean has a different "feel" each day, so life has a different "feel." Right now, the "water" is absolutely "dead." Nothing succeeds. Even if I call someone on the phone, the number is usually busy. I know that, until this condition changes, Vernon won't come or even write me a letter, and that I won't be able to find a room for him, and that Aldous and I won't sell our story. And yet, hoping against intuitive certainty, I keep making efforts. It's very irritating, and a good exercise in nonattachment.

August 6. Vernon sent a wire that there are "tiresome complications" in New York and he hopes to arrive about Thursday. I'm full of anxieties; can it be trouble with the draft, or merely delays in getting a reservation? I blow hot and cold. Sometimes, I almost wish he wouldn't come. Then again I feel that I can't possibly get along without him: I need him for the rest of my life. But, underneath this feeling, I know that I mustn't need anybody. I have to turn always to the inward resource. There's no other safety. People are only props— if you try to "use" them; and props can be knocked from under you.

August 28. Well, I'm forty. How does it feel? Can't feel a thing. I suppose the machine is gradually running down, but, right at this moment, it appears to be ticking away as well as ever. Maybe I get tired more easily—that's all.

Vernon arrived more than two weeks ago, on August 12. We had rather a strange meeting, at the Union Station, because there was an old man who travelled with him and was coming to the Coast to visit his son who was very sick in a San Diego naval hospital. The old man had another son in Los Angeles who would drive him down there, so we gave him a ride to his son's address. I'd borrowed Yogi's car. Over the old man's head, our eyes kept meeting, and I was wondering if and how he'd changed. Certainly, he didn't look much older than before. There were a few new lines in his face, that was all. But he *seemed* older, more grown-up, more relaxed. When he smiled, it wasn't so self-conscious. We said goodbye to the old man and I asked, "What's wrong with your boy?" And he told us, "Leukemia."

And then Vernon and I were alone, and, after all, there wasn't much to say. All the speeches I'd rehearsed seemed unnecessary, and the long exchange of letters, with their hesitations and qualifications and cautions, were already out of date.

The first week, Vernon stayed at Ivar Avenue, in Web's room. Then he moved up the street, to a tiny apartment at 2050—which I'd taken for him with the idea of moving in there myself too, later. But meanwhile all plans have changed. Old Mr. Kellog has quite unexpectedly given the Vedanta Society a house and several acres of land, up above Montecito, near Santa Barbara. Swami has decided that this shall be the new center we've been looking for. For the present Amiya is to be in charge there, and other members of the family will take it in turns to stay. Swami will commute back and forth; and, after the war, the whole establishment will move up there and the society will build.

Swami has invited Vernon to live at Montecito. There's a studio he can have, apart from the main house. Mr. Kellog dabbles in painting. Vernon seems pleased with the idea, and wants to go as soon as possible. I don't know what to think. I didn't want him to plunge into the family so quickly—but then, I didn't altogether realize how sold he is on Vedanta. And, after all, why hesitate? We have to try it. I'll probably spend most of my time at Montecito, myself. It's very beautiful. We were up there on the 20th. The house, which Kellog has named Ananda Bhavan (no half-hearted Hindu, he), is right up the mountain slope, on the edge of the national forest land. You look over the bay, with its islands: a much finer view than any around Santa Monica. It's still quite wild country, with lots of deer and mountain lions and coyotes. We couldn't have found a better place. The other houses in the neighborhood are all quite large estates; and the neighborhood has a settled, out-of-the-way atmosphere. It's not expanding, like Los Angeles, and the war seems hardly to have touched it.

It's difficult to say if Vernon has really changed; only time will show that. But he certainly has a different attitude towards me, and he has certainly learnt a great deal. He is wonderful to talk to—really intelligent, not just repeating things out of books; and he speaks my language. He has exactly the right attitude towards Ivar Avenue; sees the funny side of it, and yet realizes the necessity of the funny side, and the significance behind it. I think he may be on the way to becoming a good painter. That I can't judge. I only know that his being here seems to lighten up the whole place and every minute of the time.

I no longer want to rush away to Santa Monica. And the X. situation has practically ceased to exist.

He still hates Denny. That shocks me, in a way: it seems ungenerous, when the reason for it has disappeared. But probably he'll get over it. The Beesleys seem to like him, and he's really popular with the family already. Swami says, "Who could help loving him?" Amiya coos over him. Sarada is quite romantic about his looks. He wrestles with Web and teases Asit. Sudhira hasn't met him yet. Peggy, I can see, is doubtful. Well she may be. She knows all our past history, and naturally she'll have to be convinced.

I spent part of my birthday up at Alto Cedro, without telling Peggy what day it was. But it slipped out, somehow, in the course of the conversation, and there was a dreadfully embarrassing scene—because Peggy was covered with shame, and dashed out to mobilize the boys, who brought in a half-eaten birthday cake with four candles, and some hastily improvised presents. All this took place under the sardonic blue eyes of Bill Kiskadden. He makes me feel about eighteen years old, and a crook at that.

Yesterday, Vernon and I went up to the Beesleys'. Chris Wood was there, because, as he explained, his cook Josephine is busy writing a novel, so he had to come to Hollywood. Dodie and Alec have taken a great fancy to him. He seems to get nicer and nicer, as the years go by. The other day, he came to Ivar Avenue; and when he left, Swami exclaimed, "What a *good* man!"

So now another attempt begins, to live this life the way it ought to be lived. There are, as usual, all sorts of obstacles in the way. The war in Europe may well end very soon, and I will have to go to England and see M. and Richard. But it's no use worrying about difficulties. I have Swami. I have Vernon. I have this place. I have some experience behind me, and some acquired confidence. I'm still not too old. If I fail, I will have no alibi whatsoever. In my position, with all my advantages, it would be disgraceful, criminal, to fail.

In fact I very much doubt if there is anybody in the whole world who, from my point of view, is luckier than I am right at this moment.

August 29. Last night, I had a date with Gottfried Reinhardt in the bar of the Vine Street Brown Derby. He is here now, still a sergeant in the army, making training films.

Gottfried, as I expected, was late. I kept looking into the bar for him, and going back to the Satyr Bookshop next door to pass the time. Around ten o'clock I was about to give up and go home, when I was grabbed by an attractive girl, rather drunk, who yelled, "Here he is!" She was Gottfried's wife. They've been married seven months. Nobody told me.

Earlier in the evening, Mrs. Reinhardt had gone into the bar alone, looking for me. There was only one civilian—a character of gloomy and consumptive appearance—sitting there among the service men. She went up to him: "Are you Christopher Isherwood?"

"Sure I am."

"Oh, I'm so glad. Gottfried has told me so much about you."

"The hell with Gottfried."

Mrs. Reinhardt thought this a bit strange, but decided I must be one of these brutal, eccentric geniuses. The man then began pawing her leg. She was still trying desperately to be polite and make conversation when Gottfried appeared and signalled to her that this wasn't Christopher at all. The man saw him, rose hastily, and disappeared into the toilet. Gottfried declared that he was still hiding there.

He also was drunk, but looked younger and less gross. He kept smiling the shy fatuous smile of a husband apologizing for being in love with his wife. "You haven't changed a bit," he kept repeating. We drove wildly all over town looking for a restaurant, and ended up at La Rue. We parked very close to the side of a wall, up against some bushes. Gottfried had difficulty opening the door of the car. "This is a forest," he said, "which can only be penetrated by half-Jews." He mentioned Jews and half-Jews frequently throughout the evening. The Jewish problem seemed to be specially on his mind.

I think his brother Wolfgang must have told him something about Ivar Avenue, because he kept skirting around the subject, half teasing, half embarrassed. "Tell me about Krishnamurti," he demanded. "Has he read Voltaire? I want to know how he answers Voltaire."

He told me that his flirtatious Metro secretary, Frau Bach, died quite suddenly, of leukemia.

It was nice, seeing him again. There is something very sweet and childlike and appealing about him. And he was so anxious that I should like his wife.

A stupefyingly hot day. I sat under the acacia, on the front lawn, correcting the magazine proofs. Vernon came out of the temple to tell me that he'd had the best meditation of his whole life. It makes me so wonderfully happy, having him here.

A great fire over in Canoga Park, this evening, fills the whole sky with purplish smoke. The sun is setting behind it, a dusky red ball. Ashes are falling out of the air, all over the leaves of the garden. I must go and do vespers.

After supper, Vernon, Roger Spencer and I went round to look at

Franz Dispecker's paintings. It seems strange to find a Goya, a Van Dyck, a Rubens and a Fabriano hanging on the walls of a furnished apartment in the midst of Hollywood. Vernon talked so intelligently about them, and knew such a lot, that I felt very proud of him.

August 31. At breakfast, Swami and Sister were discussing Ganna Walska,[1] whom they lunched with the other day in Montecito. (She lives quite near Ananda Bhavan.) The girls were being a bit catty. One of them said scornfully, "I dare say she's very attractive to *men*." And Sister retorted, so sweetly, "Well, *I* liked her. And the things which attract men don't usually attract an old lady."

An interview, at Columbia, with Doran and Blumenthal: Aldous and I had to see them about our story. Doran is a genial, slippery business ham—not unlike Bennett Cerf. He told us, "There's nothing more cowardly in the world than a million dollars." In other words, he won't risk buying us. Blumenthal, who is now a producer, is the same man who used to live in the house Vernon and I rented on Harratt Street. He lectured Aldous and myself sententiously on the world's need for faith. "Hollywood has been waiting ten years for a second *Miracle Man*." As we left the office, Aldous said, "He's almost *too* spiritual, don't you think?"

Later, we lunched at the Knickerbocker. Aldous talked very well about Christianity and Marxism. He said, "Whenever a movement has its objectives within time, it *always* resorts to violence." But he thinks that some of the latest Marxist philosophers leave a door open to mysticism when they say that, although they only believe in matter, the possibilities of matter are unlimited.

In the garden, this afternoon, Swami told me to beware of Sudhira's tongue: one mustn't confide in her. Apparently, she gossiped about me and X. to some of the girls, Amiya particularly, and even invented some fantastic lies. I don't mind for myself, but I do mind for Vernon: if he knew that this kind of thing goes on here, it would make him feel terribly insecure. Also, I must admit that it undermines some of my feeling for Sudhira. Because I can't help wondering if she deliberately played up the cancer scare in order to exploit my feelings. Swami is going to give her a good talking to when she returns.

September 5. Sudhira returned and was talked to. She and I haven't discussed it, and now maybe we won't. I can see that she's terribly ashamed of herself. We are on very good terms otherwise. And there is really nothing very much to be said.

[1] Polish–American opera singer retired in Santa Barbara.

September 9. The day before yesterday, Vernon had a visit from two of his old friends—Richard Nibley (who used to teach Vernon the violin) and his wife. He's in the army now. He brought records of some of his own compositions for violin and piano. He said of one of them, "This is kind of a moody deal." Vernon loves them both, and I can see why: they're so simple and friendly. Vernon says of himself, "I'm a sucker for gemütlichkeit.[1]" And he's had so little of it. That's one of the good things in his being here: he's able to be part of a family.

Yesterday evening, we had supper together in Beverly Hills, and he said how unbelievable all this is—in less than a month, we've built up an entirely new relationship, we're like two different people. "And yet," he added, "anyone who heard us talking might think we were just the same." That's true, too. We still squabble; and Vernon still sulks. As, for instance, while we were washing dishes after breakfast, this morning. But that doesn't make me angry any more: he will get over it, if I handle things the right way. At present, he needs so much reassurance, so much gentleness. But the gentleness must always have a hard surface—quite casual, friendly, unsticky, without strings attached. I am gradually learning the right tone of voice.

Vernon started to grow a beard. Swami told him to shave it off. "This is not Trabuco," he said.

Swami told me that when he joined the monastery all his friends were amazed: "They thought I was just a dandy boy. I parted my hair and wore rings and a gold chain. I liked to play practical jokes. I was known as the best-dressed boy in Calcutta."

He says that when I go up to Ananda Bhavan he wants me to make a great deal of japam. "When once you are established in that, you can go anywhere. It is all the same."

"Once thrown off its balance, the heart is no longer its own master"—this is from St. François de Sales's *Introduction to the Devout Life*. The word "balance" is very significant, as far as I'm concerned. Again and again, the image of the tightrope walker suggests itself to me. As long as you remain alert, every danger can be avoided easily, by the slightest kind of adjustment—a mere movement of the hands and arms, as it were. But once you lose your balance and begin to fall, there's nothing to be done but try to land on your feet, or roll over like a paratrooper, to avoid breaking something.

September 10. Vernon left for Santa Barbara today. In rather a dither, because there were sixteen people to lunch, including the Kolisches, and Swami gaily announced that he is going to have the boys live up on Kolisch's ranch near Idyllwild, after the war. Vernon's dream of

[1] Comfort.

privacy and security in the studio at Ananda Bhavan is threatened already. Lots of people have gone up there today—Swami, Sister, Web, Madhabi and the Kolisches. (Swami habitually invites twice as many guests as there are beds.) Poor Vernon's first night won't be spent in the studio at all, or at any rate not alone. If his privacy isn't respected, he's ready to leave. I've got to explain this to Swami, and I can, because I understand just how Vernon feels. I've been through it myself. On top of this, he's upset because of a visit to his friends in Santa Monica, who told him that mysticism and painting won't mix. This makes me furious. What the hell do they know about it? We'll have enough trouble without outside interference. . . .

(Here I want to insert a document which is practically my last word on the "should-I-have-gone-back-to-England?" question. It's a letter addressed but (for some reason) not sent to Cyril Connolly. I'm not sure when it was written—some time in 1944. Obviously before August 26.

But first I must explain that there had previously been some correspondence in Cyril's magazine, *Horizon*, about Swami, Ivar Avenue and myself. In one of the 1943 issues (I think) Tony Bower had written an article about America which poked a little fun at us and our way of life, stupidly but not aggressively, and without any real malice. It was exactly the kind of thing I'd have expected from Tony, with his confused Anglo-American background and complicated attitude towards Vedanta. It hardly annoyed me at all.

However, it hugely annoyed Bill Roerick, who was in England at the time. He wrote a reply to Tony's article, without letting me know that he was doing so. The reply, unfortunately, wasn't much better than the article, because Bill was angrily loyal and therefore a bit sweeping in his statements. It merely proved him to be a very decent, generous, impulsive person, and raised him in everybody's estimation.[1]

And now a book appeared which was called *Talking to India*. The Beesleys lent it to me. It was a collection of English broadcasts to India, mostly on cultural subjects, by Indians in England and English writers, such as Forster, Orwell, etc.[2] One of the talks was by Connolly, on "Literature in the Nineteen Thirties." It dealt, among other things, with the careers of Auden and myself, very fairly and intelligently. The only passage I need quote, in order to explain my letter, is as follows: "So much has been said about

[1] Bower's article appeared in January 1944 under the pseudonym Anthony Bourne, and Roerick's reply in March; see Glossary under Bower and Roerick.
[2] Orwell edited the book, published in 1943.

Auden and Isherwood that I would only remark that as artists they were perfectly free to go and live where they liked when they emigrated, though as leaders of a literary-political movement they have done untold harm to their cause by remaining there. I think also that they are missing a great deal, and will miss more if we who stay can make the new Europe we hope for."

This is what I wrote:

I have just been reading what you wrote in *Talking to India*, as well as Tony Bower's article in *Horizon*, and I think maybe I owe you a letter. It struck me today that my "silence" must begin to seem somewhat snooty, since I can't pretend not to know what is being written about Wystan and myself, and I can't strike the pose of being superior to criticism. I am not now objecting in any way to Tony's extremely inaccurate article. He was plainly enjoying himself, and I think it wasn't unkindly meant. As for your broadcast, I would like to thank you for it, because it put several points extremely well, and was fair. I have heard that Bill Roerick has written some sort of "answer" to Tony, and this is another reason for my writing to you. Needless to say, I didn't ask him to do this; didn't even know of Tony's article until after I heard Bill was replying to it. I am touched by Bill's gesture, as an act of friendship. But the situation is becoming slightly farcical if I go on remaining silent.

One reason I didn't write before was that I felt so confused. You see, our coming to America (or maybe I had better not speak for Wystan; this shall be purely personal) was an altogether irresponsible act, prompted by circumstances—like our trip to China, and my wanderings about Europe after 1933. When the war broke out in 1939, it was a fifty-fifty chance what I'd do. I was a bit bewildered, a bit guilty, pulled by personal relationships to stay here, and pulled by other relationships to return. I delayed, because that is always easiest. Then came the press attacks, and cowardice and defiance hardened. Yes, I quite admit that there was cowardice—not of the Blitz (which I think, from my limited experience of air raids, would have bothered me no more and no less than it did all of you) but chiefly because I knew that, if I returned to England, I would have to take the pacifist position and strike out my own line—not yours. That decision was made some while before the war started, and I have never changed it. I needn't go into the whys and wherefores of that now. I think I have always been a pacifist, and that the whole Hitler episode confused me into thinking that I wasn't, because it affected me personally. I had never properly thought the whole thing through.

But, ever since my first coming to Hollywood, I had begun meeting the Swami—Gerald Heard introduced me—and that set another influence going which has become increasingly powerful. Again, I don't want to go into the Hindu philosophy, blended with Quakerism and Heardism, except to say that it offers me personally a solution and a way of life which I desperately needed, and which seems to work, and within which I can imagine living the rest of my life with a feeling of purpose and a lack of despair. Of course, I might equally have found all this in England—there is even a swami of the same order in London—but it has so happened that I didn't. This is where I struck oil, and here for the present I must stay and develop it.

Tony says, and you report, that I may not write again. I think if I hadn't found something like this I never would have written again: now I think I shall, I'm pretty sure I shall. As for the "literary-political movement" to which you say I have done "untold harm," thank God if I have. I think your analysis of our group is pretty sound. No doubt we did advertise ourselves, though not as consciously as you seem to imply. But a certain childishness in myself—maybe in some of the others too— enjoyed the fuss and helped it develop. But now that boat is sunk and we are all separately in the water. Splendid. We shall learn to swim. You know how I was burdened with all sorts of ties in the old days. Isn't it better if I ditch them? Sure, I am missing something, but I am getting something else. And I cannot honestly say that I would exchange.

I'll be forty next birthday, which is over the present U.S. military age. If it is raised, I shall go into the Army Medical Corps—a permitted form of conscientious objection here. If not, I shall stay put for some years, unless other circumstances arise. Even if you wanted me in the New Europe (which I sincerely hope you'll get) I couldn't share it with you the way I am at present, and I couldn't contribute anything until I know more. I am trying to hatch out into something different, and if you object that I have chosen the darndest time to do it, I can only answer that chickens can't choose. This is not in any way to defend my conduct in leaving England in the first place—that, I repeat, was irresponsible. Whatever good or bad motives are found for it, I can't honestly accept them. I can't think of myself either as a traitor or as a disgusted prophet. From my personal point of view, it has all turned out for the best—through no merit or foresight of mine. And I suppose, if the result of what I am doing has literary fruit, people will one day say it was for the best all round. . . .)

September 11. A grey, busy, not unsatisfactory day, although I've smoked far too much and let down on my japam. But I did two pages of *Prater Violet* and helped mail the magazines, and cleaned out my room, and wrote some letters.

A talk with Roger Spencer last night. He's hurt because Swami disapproves of his fancy diets and fasting—prescribed by some quack in Hollywood. A friend of Roger's, a C.O. named Ed Tremblay, comes tonight, to live with us for a while. Ed wants to go on a diet, too. The girls protest. More problems.

Sudhira brought me hot milk in my room last night, and was sweet about Vernon. She said he seems like one of the family already. I'm worried, of course, about how he's making out at Ananda Bhavan. Swami called this afternoon and told us Amiya has hurt her leg and has to lie up. Vernon and Webster are digging a hole for the garbage.

September 13. Grey fog. Went down yesterday to Santa Monica. All the way down on the bus, and fairly continuously throughout the day, I made japam and this had two very apparent effects. First I didn't get in the least rattled by Denny's bad temper (he was in one of his worst moods) and secondly I was in a state of great awareness and kept noticing things which I could "use" in my writing. I think it was the best day of japam I have ever had in my life.

As I was waiting for the Palisades bus, I stretched myself and involuntarily smiled. An old man caught my eye and asked, in a thick foreign accent, "Feel vell?"

Sudhira, at breakfast this morning, talked about Swami Yatiswarananda (the one who's now in Philadelphia and who used to be in Switzerland). When he was ordered to go to Europe—much against his will—he decided to try to see God in everybody. But Brahmananda appeared to him in a dream and said, "No—that's wrong: try to see everybody in God."

While Yatiswarananda was staying here, he was a very strict disciplinarian. Swami was away, and he took over for a while. He ridiculed the girls because, as Sudhira put it, "We'd become terribly itsy-bitsy about Holy Mother"; they spent their time cooing over holy pictures and flower arrangements for the shrine. Yatiswarananda preached discrimination. He told them to walk every day to some place where they could see an extensive view. And to listen to music.

Woke this morning murmuring to myself, "God's Weasel out of the West." I think this title was intended for poor Ed Tremblay, who has a long, pale rodent face. He arrived looking terribly sick. His colon keeps getting irritated and he has to run for the bathroom. Sometimes, he doesn't make it. The girls find him woefully unglamorous, but Sarada has hopefully decided that he looks "spiritual." Actually, he's very obliging and anxious to help. When he's better I think he'll make an excellent secretary for the magazine.

Lunch at the Farmer's Market with the Huxleys and Kiskaddens. Afterwards, I found myself telling Aldous that I don't want to go to Trabuco because, "I hate talking about God." Maria was delighted.

Vernon called, this evening. He told me that, earlier today, he'd been feeling rather desperate and had planned to ask me to come up to Montecito at once. But that now he'd had a good talk with Amiya and felt better.

September 18. For a long time, now, a fight has been brewing between Swami and the draft board, over Asit. Selective Service wants to put him in the army. Swami says no, they shan't—because Asit is not only a visitor in this country but a member of a subject race, which isn't eligible for U.S. citizenship (though, of course, Asit *could* become a citizen if he chose to, as a U.S. soldier). Furthermore, the British themselves don't conscript Indians. Swami has taken the matter up with the American Civil Liberties people, and there will be a court case; but meanwhile Swami is advised not to resist the induction. And today Asit was actually inducted. Before he left, with Sudhira and myself, to the center, a wonderful little Hindu ceremony took place on the temple steps. Asit, the hundred-percent westernized future movie director, suddenly prostrated before Swami and made the traditional gesture of taking the dust from his feet and scattering it on his own head (this is only pantomime, and anyway Swami's shoes were flashing with polish) and Swami blessed him. It was startlingly beautiful. I felt a sudden affection for Asit, and hugged him when we said goodbye. On the way home, I remarked to Sudhira how foggy the streets were: we found that clouds of oil fumes were pouring out of the old family car.

September 20. Swami and I visited a Mr. Williams downtown who is responsible for deciding cases of religious objection. We were trying to get a 4-D classification for Webster, as a future monk. Mr. Williams received us in a very bare office: Swami and I had to sit on piles of fishing-tackle. Taking it in turns, contradicting and correcting each other, we delivered an extremely garbled lecture on the aims of

Vedanta philosophy. Mr.Williams sat silent, apparently not under-standing a word. But when we'd finished, he said smiling, "What you've just told me isn't as unfamiliar to me as you may think, gentlemen—" and he produced from his desk drawer a small volume of Ramakrishna's sayings. (Webster finally got his classification, just as the war ended.)

Now that my movie story with Aldous has come to nothing, I plan to go up to Ananda Bhavan with Swami, next Sunday or Monday. I want to get on with the second draft of *Prater Violet* and finish it, if possible, while it's warm. Also I must read through the back issues of the magazine and make a book of selected articles. Later on, there will be difficulties about money—but they must be let solve themselves, as such difficulties always have. What matters to me now is my writing, and Vernon. For his sake, the effort to live this life always seems worthwhile now, even on a dull dormouse day like this, when I can find no personal desire at all, except to sleep.

Stephen writes from England—obviously feeling that Wystan and I have "missed everything." I don't feel that. I hardly know what he means, even. In life, I feel it's less and less possible for me to regret having taken one road rather than another. Could any other have been as interesting, as extraordinary as the one I chose? Yes, any other. Life isn't "about" air raids, swamis, love affairs, places, deeds done or undone—those are only the shapes of the letters in which the message is written. To read the message, that's all that matters. But how? By being very alert, very still. By holding your breath and listening, always, everywhere, in the midst of this earsplitting uproar.

September 22. Today is scarcely bearable, it's so hot. Asit has shown up already, delighted with Fort MacArthur and his uniform and the boys he has met there. The girls pamper their little warrior and goggle at his stories. He won't be sent any place else until after the court hearing; and the lawyer is sure he'll win it and be let out.

> (Asit did win his case, and was let out. In fact, he left the army quite unwillingly, he enjoyed it so. His officers, not to mention his buddies, seem to have been entirely on his side and taken a sporting interest in the whole affair. The judge was Irish and pretty openly anti-British. And, while he was in camp, Asit was actually asked to lecture to several hundred men on the Indian situation. He delivered a rousing anti-British speech which was received with great enthusiasm.)

Vernon came up this morning. We sat around, at a loose end. He was bored, after having had so much to do at Ananda Bhavan. I realize that, when I'm with him, I must keep busy.

Lunch with Chris Wood. Paul Sorel is about to leave for New York, and, according to Chris, he's on the verge of insanity. He plans to be the most famous American who ever lived; and he wants a sapphire. He has two daemons—a good one and a bad one. He has never, he says, met anybody whose daemon didn't bow down before his daemon. All this nonsense is to protect himself from having to admit how badly he's treated Chris. Actually, the relationship with Paul has done Chris infinitely more good than harm, and is yet another illustration of the truth that one is *never* the loser, spiritually, by behaving well and generously to anyone. But Chris is very sad, now Paul has gone.

Now remember—I'll repeat it again—if you're going to make a success of your life with Vernon, there's only one way to do it: you've got to be strong. Follow along your own line, make japam, keep busy. Always be ready when he needs you. Don't run after him. Don't ever be possessive. Sentimentality won't help. Be a tree, not a vine.

Can I do this, all day, every day? Only if I draw help perpetually from the inner source. Then it'll be easy, natural. Well now, let's see you try.

September 24. A party last night at Denny's, for Stefan Brecht, who is leaving for the army. Denny asked me to preside, because I don't drink too much on these occasions, as he does, and pass out. "You can't possibly have a good party," says Denny, "without at least one monk." Sure enough, there were tears before bedtime. Some of Johnny Goodwin's records were smashed, and he left in a huff. Stef Brecht told a rather dreary movie director, "I think you are a most unpleasant person." Finally, there was a terrible scene with a Jewish refugee who had been in the siege of Warsaw and was in love with Stef's girlfriend and jealous of Stef. He broke a lot of glasses and seemed about to slash the Picasso. Much later in the night, when everybody was asleep, he crept back into the apartment and tidied everything up; a gesture which merely earned him Denny's increased contempt. Denny said he would put a notice on the door in our favorite kind of dog German, "Warschauerbelagerungsopfer nicht erwünscht."[1]

Stef himself was extremely sympathetic throughout the evening. When he was already fairly drunk, he told me, "I hope I have not caused you any pain. I don't refer to criticism. I should never apologize for criticism. But I should not like to cause you pain

[1] "Warsaw siege victims not wanted." See Glossary under Warsaw.

because I respect you very much." So I assured him that he had never caused me pain, and we shook hands solemnly, and bowed.

September 25. Swami, George, Sarada and I drove to Ananda Bhavan this morning. At present, there is really nothing to report. It's just another move. I have a dear little room, with a light nicely fixed over the desk, and a shower, and now all I have to do is finish *Prater Violet* and get the Vedanta book prepared, and pray and pray and pray. Meanwhile, something will develop between Vernon and myself, for good or bad. No use worrying. Amiya is girlishly happy. She plans a little family within a family—herself, Vernon and myself. She's prepared to make us comfortable, like an affectionate aunt. This is her home now. It is not my home. Perhaps no place ever will be again. There's nothing tragic in that. To learn to be alone and at home inside myself—that's what I'm here for. What more can I possibly ask than I already have? Conditions are perfect, if I know how to get the best out of them.

September 26. This morning, Swami and George went for a walk in the grounds after breakfast. They got talking about the seventeen acres which lie above our property, higher up the hill. George asked, "How much would they cost?" and Swami answered, "About seven thousand." George said, "They're ours." At first, Swami didn't understand. "And then," (he was telling me the story), "George bowed down in the bushes and gave me a check. I said to him, 'George, how can you afford this?' And he answered me, 'It's the money I use to gamble with.'"

In other words, George staged this whole little drama, and wrote out the check in advance. He really is the strangest character.

Bekins arrived with Vernon's things. He still has an immense accumulation of books, pictures, etc., which he drags around with him. All part of his frustrated instinct for homemaking.

A class in the afternoon. Vernon was depressed. He complains that Amiya fusses around him too much, and that nobody here speaks his language. He doesn't know if he'll be able to stick it out. Some friends have offered him a dog, but Swami doesn't want him to have it, because then Sister wouldn't be able to bring Dhruva, who fights everything on four legs. "If I had a dog," said Vernon, "I'd feel less lonely." This hurt me, of course. I can't give him as much as he gives me. Or maybe I can, but he isn't prepared to admit it. I asked him if he wanted to leave and he said coldly that he felt an "obligation" towards me. That word stung me more than anything. I feel as if all our troubles are starting, just as they started before.

However, tonight, Swami said he could have the dog; and Vernon brightened.

September 27. A fairly good day. Did four pages of my story, a reasonable amount of japam, and worked in the garden most of the afternoon. Swami, George and Sarada left this morning, and now we three are on our own.

There is somehow a cloud between me and Vernon—so faint that I can't define it. He isn't exactly sulking, but he avoids talking to me, and we aren't gay. Today, I heard him working in the toolshed, so I looked in to see what he was doing. As I opened the door, he turned quickly and said in a cold, angry voice, "What do you want?" I was simply staggered by his hostility—all the more so because it was obviously involuntary. He recovered himself almost at once, and I pretended not to notice, and left, after asking him some question about the gardening. But it was a shock. Part of him actually hates me, I believe. Because I'm identified with the Vedanta Society, and the minority in him is already rebelling against it. Well, I ought to be able to understand his reactions, if anyone does. No good feeling sorry for myself. Be clinical.

October 1. Yesterday morning, Vernon summoned me into his studio after breakfast and reproved me because, at breakfast, in Amiya's presence, I'd talked about the kittens we used to have at the Harratt Street house. Any reference to our previous life together embarrasses and annoys him—I suppose because it makes him feel guilty. I must be patient. He hasn't much humor, and he's a prig; but that's largely his age. I'm slowly learning how to treat him, good-humored but tough.

October 6. Vernon is away in Los Angeles, seeing the dentist, and I'm alone here with Amiya. I hadn't realized how fond of her I am. Old Mr. Kellog, with his shock of white hair, fussy and spry, keeps descending on us, and puttering around the place, suggesting this and that. Amiya is always sparring with him. Like all former owners, he still feels that the place partly belongs to him, and reserves the right to arrive without warning. He likes to meditate in the little shrine he built in the garden: it is really in charming taste, except for some dreadful stained glass. His sulky, youngish wife disapproves of these excursions, saying that they're a strain on his health; he has a bad heart. Actually, she disapproves of the Vedanta Society and Kellog's financial interest in it. She grudges the gift of Ananda Bhavan, although they've a huge house down in Montecito and an enormous income. She's an unhappy, discontented woman. Amiya says she married the old man for his money, thinking he'd die soon; but he has lived ten years since then, and even run after other women (once they were nearly divorced) and she has to look after him and study his whims. You can't help feeling sorry for her; it's such a mess. And they're both nice people, taken separately.

It's so beautiful here. So calm and still. The grounds are three quarters wild, with thick jungly undergrowth, and a creek, and huge rocks which you can climb on to and look out over the valley. At night we hear the howling of the coyotes, and the quick, uncanny trotting of the deer; the deer come right down through the garden, nibbling everything which isn't fenced in. It is cold, and we build huge log fires on the open hearth, and sit talking about England, and Vedanta, and the members of the family. It is very snug.

The other evening, toward sunset, a great white floe of cloud far out on the water made a false horizon, above which the ridges of the islands rose, as if surrounded by pack ice in an Arctic sea.

October 10. Swami is up here again, with Yogi and Yogini. Today he gave a class, and Krishnamurti came, with Iris Tree. He and Swami had never met before. (Swami has always been a bit prejudiced against him, on account of Mrs. Besant's activities in India. He was terribly shocked when Mrs. Besant declared that he [Krishnamurti] was an avatar. Also, Mrs. Besant used to annoy Brahmananda and try to involve him in the Theosophical movement, and Swami had standing orders not to admit her to the monastery when Brahmananda was there.) However, the meeting today was a huge success. Krishnamurti sat quietly and modestly at the back of the class; and when Swami was through he came over and they greeted each other with the deepest respect, bowing again and again with folded palms. And then they had a long chat, becoming very gay and Indian, and laughing like schoolboys. Some of Krishnamurti's followers, who had sneaked in knowing he was coming (we didn't), stood eyeing us a bit suspiciously. But within fifteen minutes we had begun to fraternize. So one more little bridge was built.

Vernon is back here, with his dog, a very sweet-natured Airedale bitch. We are all fond of her, and Vernon's mood is better, in consequence.

October 12. Down to the beach to swim, with Yogi and Yogini. Afterward, I got into the car to put on my clothes. Just as I'd taken off my trunks and was stark naked, an old lady popped her head in through the window and asked when the next bus left for Ventura.

I was embarrassed, but she wasn't in the least; she seemed in no hurry to go away, and we had quite a long conversation, about the weather and the war, at the end of which she thanked me very politely.

October 19. Well, there's good and bad to report. A swollen gland in my throat, due to the poison from my bad teeth, which will have to come out next week. And a general failure in discipline, a relapse into pessimism, due to the Vernon situation, which gets no better. He continues to sulk and snap at me, and generally make it clear that he'd rather not have me around. I really think he is a little mad. It's like banging up against a brick wall. The other, charming, intelligent, cooperative personality which he showed me when he first arrived here in August has vanished without a trace. He is just like he was when things were at their worst in 1940.

But blaming him won't help. With or without him, I have to go on trying to live this life. The problem is to win over the minority opposition inside this yelling parliament of myself. The minority—or at least the greater part of it, because there will always be a few die-hards—has to be made to understand that this life is in their best interests. Violence is no use. No use trying to dissolve parliament altogether and rule by dictatorship. The mere brutal will is useless, because it is never strong enough for the job. In the long run, there has to be control through discrimination, there has to be assent. The minority always tries to avoid debate. It uses shock tactics, snap votes, demonstrations, filibusters.

The good thing is that, last Sunday the 15th, I finished the revised draft of *Prater Violet*. Also I've written ten pages of an introduction to our book of selections from the magazine, *Vedanta for the Western World*.

November 7. I returned to Ananda Bhavan yesterday, after a week in Los Angeles, staying with Peggy. The visit wasn't a success. I had a tooth pulled, and ran one of my fevers afterward, and retired to bed at Alto Cedro, stupidly not realizing that the old days are over and that Peggy, under Bill's influence, has become as spartan as he is. One day, while I was still feeling lousy, she made a remark which showed me only too plainly that I wasn't welcome. She was horrified, later; but there wasn't any way we could unsay what had been said, and we were both embarrassed as we said goodbye. Henceforward, their house will be a place to which I am careful not to come too often, a place where I mustn't presume on my status as a guest. That's all right, if it's the way Peggy wants it. After all, she's married now, properly married, and her family is all that matters to her. She's got Bill. Artificial uncles are no longer needed.

November 11. Heavy rain. Have just been down to the mailbox. Nothing. Have tried to get on with the Vedanta introduction. Can't.

Next week, I plan to visit Chris Wood. I want to get away from here. The Vernon experiment has failed. Never mind whose fault that is—to be perfectly honest, I think it's nearly one hundred percent his—that isn't the point. The point is that I must stop expecting the very least help or support from him in the future, and probably I'd better see as little of him as possible. He's in the hell of a mess, but I'm not the one to help him. My motives aren't sufficiently disinterested.

Needless to say, I'm not feeling too bright. Props are being kicked away from under me, right and left. I can't live here, because of Vernon. I don't want to live at Ivar Avenue because of Sudhira, who is beginning to suffocate me as I seem to suffocate him. I feel that I never want to stay at Peggy's again. Denny nowadays is so distracted that I couldn't have any sort of relationship with him. Chris I am very fond of, but certainly not to lean on. The same with the Huxleys. The same with the Beesleys.

Well, it's no good groaning. Let me try a new approach. Not so much on the negative side. Never mind the don'ts. Think of the Reality. Make japam. Try to get on with your work. Rely on nobody.

November 16. The sun is just going down into a sheeted calm of peacock blue and gold, with the islands all outlined in blue-black contours against a pure sky like a Japanese print. Tomorrow I leave for Laguna. Sad, because of the failure with Vernon. The bitterest part of it is that, if I'm not allowed to love him as a little brother, I find that, as an acquaintance, a casual house-companion, I rather dislike him. And yet I feel sorry and protective and hate to see him making things so hard for himself. I'm sure it's good for him to be here. He's painting quite a lot, and meditating (which is more than I am) and this place with its quietness and beauty is what he needs. The sun has touched the horizon. The land has grown suddenly very dark and densely wooded and still. Great winding trails of golden light on the water. Goodbye. Nothing now but the red horizon-glow. It's turning chilly. I must go in.

November 25. Am writing this in the downstair bedroom at Rockledge Road, waiting for Chris to come down and say it's time to go swimming. The weather has been glorious all this week.

Gerald was here when I arrived, on the 17th. He went back to Trabuco three days later. He seemed depressed. Peggy had already told me that Felix Greene has announced that he's getting married, to a girl who lives up there; and that Gerald is terribly upset about it. But this wasn't referred to. Also, there's a coolness with the Hunters, because Gerald's Gamaliel novel is so anti-Christian, from their point of view. Also, there's the situation here: Gerald's attitude to Chris doesn't seem to have changed in the least. He is still possessively affectionate, still dreadfully jealous of Paul. And Chris, rather naively, still says why can't they all three live together, the way they used to? There is a great deal of obstinacy on both sides.

I expect to go back to Ivar Avenue next Monday or Tuesday, to stay for some while. I've got to try and get a movie job. I need money badly. Yesterday I finished the final polishing of *Prater Violet*.

There is no sense in running away from Ivar Avenue at present. I've got to make up my mind to that. I've got to learn to live with the family without becoming involved in it. Avoid gossip. Avoid participation in their feuds. Concentrate on what is essential—contact with the Swami and prayer. The time will come for me to leave. Wait for it. Keep on working. Associate with people you can really help in some way, and not with those whose curiosity is always offering you a basin for your tears. Best leave Vernon alone altogether. You don't really understand him. You are terribly resentful towards him, underneath. You still want to make him submit to your will, and confess that he has wronged you. Maybe you *are* "in the right." So what?

Now that Paul is in New York, Chris leads an entirely solitary life, with Tiny, the dachshund. He goes for walks, plays Chopin, listens to his favorite radio programs—"Gang Busters," "Suspense," "Henry Aldrich." It's really a marvel that he hasn't become more set in his ways, more eccentric than he is. But then, Chris *is* a marvel. In many respects, he's extraordinarily wise.

From Vivekananda's letters: "I am glad I was born, glad I suffered so, glad I did make big blunders, glad to enter peace. . . . Behind my work was ambition, behind my love was personality, behind my purity was fear, behind my guidance the thirst of power. Now they are vanishing and I drift. . . ."[1]

November 30. Back at Ivar Avenue since Tuesday. The possible job with Wolfgang Reinhardt at Warner's has fallen through, and though I hated the story I'd have liked to work with Wolfgang, and I need money badly. Meanwhile, Edna Schley has had a cerebral

---

[1] *Letters of Swami Vivekananda*, April 18, 1900.

hemorrhage. I talked to her on the phone before I knew this, and thought she must be drunk: she spoke fairly logically but kept wandering and changing the subject. Later, Dan called me and told me about it. He is terribly upset. After the attack, she was quite blind for a while, and completely crazy. Now she's better and the doctor is hopeful. Dan said he hoped she'd "pass on" if she didn't get better. It was terribly painful, talking to him, because he kept bursting into tears. He adores her, and she's all he has in the world to care for.

(Edna never did get better, and now it's obvious that she never will. For two years, she has been in hospital, blind, half-crazy, full of horrible nightmares and fears. And Dan has spent everything, every cent he can borrow or scrape together, to keep her alive. His misery is so dreadful that Johnny [van Druten] and I avoid it, as people avoided Oedipus. There is nothing to be done, except to give him about fifty thousand dollars, which we can't afford: and even this would only be a palliative. In the old days, a simple country doctor would have had the courage and charity to give Edna an overdose of morphia. But that's "murder." So modern medical science, with fiendish ingenuity, continues to keep her a quarter alive, and pockets seven hundred dollars a week for doing it.)

Swami asked me how I was feeling, and I told him a little, not much, about Vernon. This evening, in the shrine, I saw the various alternatives so clearly that it frightened me. Can I possibly face continuing to live here indefinitely? Can I grow old messily, like poor Uncle Henry? The X. situation is beginning again. An awful lot of my guilt about this is simply fear of appearances. Suppose somebody found out? I know quite well that I shouldn't feel guilty if I were not living at Ivar Avenue. That being true, my guilt is worthless. . . . Swami says what I've written so often in this diary—that the only refuge is in God. What a terrible thought that is! Shall I ever get it properly through my head, before it's too late?

December 3. Down to Santa Monica to see Denny. He was very sweet and sympathetic. He suggested, as so often before, that I should come and live with him here, or that we should go East together and he'd study at Columbia. But I can't. I can't walk out on Swami right now. And something warns me against living with Denny, at present: he's so unsettled himself.

Swami was still up, sitting by the fire, when I got home. "You will live long," he told me—and explained that he had been thinking about me just as I came in. Suddenly, I felt such peace. There he sits, while I roam around. After all, there is really no problem, no difficulty. Why do I tie myself into all these knots?

December 10. On December 5, I had supper with Clifford Odets[1] and his wife. The Chaplins were there. Charlie is getting to be a regular opinionated elderly club-bore Englishman. He talked about the war, bullfighting, politics, and everything he said was silly—until he began to act it out: his gestures are so much more intelligent than his conversation. He was very funny, describing his new Bluebeard picture, and taking off his jacket to show us how to make passes at a bull. His wife Oona, who looks about sixteen, scarcely spoke, but I had the impression that she has the marriage well in hand. "Eat your soup," she told Charlie, in the midst of one of his performances. Odets is rather a bore, I'm afraid. He made an extraordinarily stupid, Hollywoodish speech about Shakespeare's "virility." But he was very friendly and pleasant.

Vernon is here this weekend, very polite and agreeable, like an acquaintance. When I think of our first weeks together, last summer, I want to pinch myself. Can this really be the same person? In a way, I no longer care. And yet I do, because I feel so damned sorry for him. Something is fatally wrong, somewhere. He's fed up with Santa Barbara, particularly Amiya's ill-natured gossip, and talks of leaving. But don't we all?

December 16. Just back from the beach. Denny found a seagull with a broken wing, and amputated it, which was quite a sensible thing to do and made the bird more comfortable, but didn't solve its problem. I followed it up the beach and saw how it couldn't fly or swim and would almost certainly starve: so I killed it. This made me feel horrible all day. I asked Swami, did I do right? And he said no: one shouldn't interfere in the karma of any creature. This doesn't convince me, however. What else could I have done? Taken the seagull home, I suppose, and made a pet of it. But this wasn't practical; especially with Dhruva around.

December 20. Sister is sick—not dangerously—but Kolisch has put the girls on a twenty-four-hour nursing shift, chiefly, I think, to punish them for not taking better care of Ed Tremblay (who's nearly well, now, and going home). Mr. Kellog died this morning. Swami's going to the funeral on Friday. Roughie, Vernon's Airedale, has been taken to the vet to be destroyed; she had a bad sore on her back.

Willie Maugham's friend, Gerald Haxton, is dead. I heard this from

---

[1] American playwright and screenwriter (1903–1963).

Gerald Heard, when the Beesleys drove me down to Laguna Beach yesterday, to look at a house they may rent. We had lunch with Chris. Gerald went into a number for Dodie's benefit—but it was the wrong one, and he realized it too late, and started to overact and ham it up until I wanted to sink through the patio floor. "He fills me with a kind of horror," Dodie said later.

December 31. Something has happened. Or rather, nothing has happened but I accept that nothing. Suddenly, I feel quite calm. Sure, the situation is impossible. Sure, I ought to stop seeing X., or leave Ivar Avenue, or both. I ought either to get a movie job or start a new story. But the whole problem—just because it seems insoluble at present—has to be accepted for what it is, and simply offered up. I'll let it develop and try to stop worrying. Sooner or later—probably much sooner—X. will go away. Sooner or later, I shall write another story, or get work, or money, or go East or to England. Nothing that is happening or may happen really prevents me from doing the one thing which ultimately matters. Make japam, watch and wait. Put all your emphasis upon that. Everything else—even your scruples about your conduct—is vanity, in the last analysis. Never mind what other people think of you. Never mind what you think of yourself. Go ahead with the only valid activity, the one which never fails. Stop trying to tidy up your life. Stop making vows—you'll only break them. Less fussing and more faith. You've been an awful nuisance lately, but I forgive you. No, don't thank me. No more tears, I beg. Blow your nose, and pull up your socks, and shut up. You don't have to be a grim old stoic, either. Your life could be such fun. Now run along and enjoy yourself. And let's try to make this a *happy* new year.

The Postwar Years
1945–1956

January 1, 1945–December 26, 1949

[From the start of 1945 until late 1947, Isherwood made no entries at all in his diary. The affair with "X." (Bill Harris) lasted only until February 1945, when Harris left for New York. A few days earlier, Isherwood had become jealous when a soldier arrived for a tryst at Harris's apartment while Isherwood was there. Harris fled wearing only his bathrobe and, in the street, told Isherwood that he couldn't stand "all this love." Later Isherwood and the soldier left together and had drinks at the soldier's apartment. There were other brief relationships, including one with a boy called Steve Conway. Then in June 1945, Isherwood met William Caskey, who was to prove far more important in his life. Over the course of the summer, Isherwood and Caskey, just turned twenty-four, began a serious affair, and this, perhaps more than anything else, finally precipitated Isherwood's long meditated departure from the monastery in August 1945—nine days after the war ended. Caskey came to stay as soon as Isherwood had his own apartment (the chauffeur's bedroom and bathroom at the Beesleys' current rented house), and a few months later they moved into Denny Fouts's empty apartment while Fouts was away in the East. For the next six years, Isherwood and Caskey lived mostly together, and their relationship involved Isherwood with many other new friends in Santa Monica.

During 1945, Isherwood worked off and on at Warner Brothers. He devoted some time in February to a screenplay of Wilkie Collins's 1860 novel, *The Woman in White* (later finished by another writer, Stephen Moorehouse Avery, and released in 1948). Then from June to September, he worked for Wolfgang Reinhardt, scripting Somerset Maugham's *Up at the Villa* (1941). Isherwood polished this script during an extra week at the studio in late September 1945, but the film was never made. He also tried to advise Maugham on filming *The Razor's Edge,* and arranged meetings for Maugham and George Cukor with Swami Prabhavananda, but in the end the script for *The Razor's Edge* was written by Lamarr Trotti, the film was directed not by Cukor but by Edmund Goulding, and Isherwood and Prabhavananda's advice about the teachings of the fictionalized Indian holy man "Sri Ganesha" were largely ignored. *Prater Violet* was published that November (the U.K. edition appeared the following year), and also during the autumn Isherwood travelled a little with Caskey.

At the start of 1946, Isherwood had to undergo an operation: a Dr. A. D. Gorfain removed a median bar from the top of Isherwood's urethra, inside the bladder. To guard against infection during the operation, Gorfain tied off Isherwood's sperm tubes, making him sterile and unable to ejaculate more than a few drops of semen. Isherwood did not understand the consequences of the operation until after it was completed. In later years he came to believe it might have been unnecessary, but he insisted he had suffered no adverse effects in his sex life—perhaps the reverse. And yet from the end of the 1940s onward, he occasionally refers in his diary to being partially (and inexplicably) impotent.

In the spring of 1946, when Denny Fouts returned from New York, Fouts and Caskey quarrelled so fiercely that Isherwood and Caskey left Fouts's apartment and went to live over Salka Viertel's garage. This all but ended Isherwood's friendship with Fouts. That same year, Isherwood revised his 1939–1944 journals and worked with Swami Prabhavananda on a translation of Shankara's *The Crest Jewel of Discrimination*. Caskey had decided to become a professional photographer soon after moving in with Isherwood, and during this period he was studying in preparation, probably at Santa Monica City College. Towards the end of 1946, Isherwood became an American citizen, and he began helping Lesser Samuels with a film treatment which was to bring them both a large sum of money. They called the story *Judgement Day in Pittsburgh* and sold it to RKO for $50,000. The treatment was Samuels's idea, and Isherwood collaborated out of friendship, but contributed little professionally. (RKO released the film in 1949 as *Adventure in Baltimore*, written by Lionel Houser and starring Shirley Temple, Robert Young and John Agar.)

Once the treatment was finished, Isherwood made his first postwar journey back to England, at the beginning of 1947. He saw many of his London friends, was introduced to new ones, and twice he went north to visit his mother and his brother Richard who, during the war, had moved together back to Wyberslegh Hall, Isherwood's birthplace in Cheshire. He also stayed with Olive Mangeot in Cheltenham, where he saw Jean Ross (the original of "Sally Bowles" in *Goodbye to Berlin*), now the mother of a daughter, Sarah, by Claude Cockburn. Olive Mangeot's housekeeper and cook, Hilda Hauser, whom Isherwood had known since the 1920s (she appears as "Rose" in *Lions and Shadows*), was with them, looking after a young granddaughter, Amber, so-called because she was half black, half white: Hilda's daughter, Phyllis, had been raped by a black G.I. during the war and left the baby with Hilda. While Isherwood was in Cheltenham, Rosamond Lehmann's former husband, the communist painter Wogan Philipps, asked him to serve as interpreter at a hearing conducted in German in a nearby prisoner of war camp. Philipps and his second wife, Cristina, employed German and Italian prisoners of war as farmhands, a common practice at the time. One of their German laborers was accused of having participated, as an S.S. member, in a massacre of civilians in Russia. The Philippses could not believe the charge, but the laborer was found guilty and prevented from returning to farm work. Then, at the end of March, during Isherwood's second stay in Cheshire, he and his mother visited the family solicitor, and Isherwood signed the papers which formally made over the Marple and Wyberslegh estates to his brother Richard, an intention Isherwood had indicated when he first inherited the property on his Uncle Henry's death in 1940.

Despite his relatively steady relationship with Caskey, Isherwood expressed a lively interest in various other men that he met. While in London, he stayed a night with his old boyfriend, Jacky Hewit, and he also renewed other once romantic friendships. He lunched with a young man that he found attractive, Neville King-Page, after meeting him at a party at John Lehmann's in April, but nothing came of it. Then on board the *Queen Elizabeth* on the way back to New York, Isherwood became friendly with John Holmes, who had worked for the Canadian government during the war.

Caskey was waiting for Isherwood in New York, and they soon sublet an apartment belonging to Isherwood's friends, James and Tania Stern, who were away in Europe. During that spring and summer in New York there were numerous parties and outings. E. M. Forster was visiting from England, and Isherwood saw him several times. In mid-May, Caskey and Isherwood went to stay with a wealthy acquaintance, Ollie Jennings, in his summer house at Sneden's Landing, an artists' colony on the Hudson River just north of the Palisades. Jennings was accompanied by his Mexican boyfriend Ben Baz, a commercial artist, and also by another man with whom Baz was then friendly, Bill Bailey. While they were at Sneden's Landing, Isherwood and Caskey visited the Chilean-born surrealist painter, Roberto Sebastián Matta Echaurren and his wife. Matta Echaurren mentioned some homosexual experiences he had had, and Caskey responded angrily, causing a fierce argument.

July and August 1947 were a continual progress from one summer community to another: visits to W. H. Auden and Chester Kallman on Fire Island; to Truman Capote and his companion Newton Arvin on Nantucket; to Paul Cadmus in Provincetown with a group of New York friends (including George Tooker, Cadmus's boyfriend of the period; the painter Jared French whom Cadmus had lived with before French married in 1937; Sandy Campbell, also a former lover of Cadmus; and Donald Windham). At the beginning of August, Caskey and Isherwood attended a celebrity-studded party in New York (Garbo and Noël Coward were among the guests), hosted by "Horst," the German-born fashion photographer who was the protégé of George Hoyningen-Huene. And they went on several expeditions with Lincoln Kirstein. Kirstein was then trying to revive the reputation of the sculptor Elie Nadelman and was a force behind the Nadelman retrospective at the Museum of Modern Art in 1948, for which he wrote the catalogue essay. He took them to see some sculptures by Nadelman, and he also took them to Washington D.C. to see a collection of art works confiscated in Germany by the U.S. government and brought to America in secret. Kirstein had special access to the 22,000-odd cultural treasures which had been hidden in a salt mine for safety during the war. Eventually they were exhibited around the country, and then returned to Germany. Stephen Spender was teaching at Sarah Lawrence, in Bronxville, New York, and Isherwood and Caskey also visited him in Fairfield, Connecticut, not far from the college.

In September 1947, Isherwood and Caskey left for South America together. On the way, Isherwood once again began to record his life in detail, and his diary of their South American trip was published as a travel book, *The Condor and the Cows* (1949), with photographs by Caskey. The journey began by ship, from New York to La Guaira, Venezuela, at the northern end of the continent; then they voyaged west to Cartagena, Colombia. From Cartagena they went overland via Bogotá and with many other stopovers to Quito in Ecuador, then continued down near the western coast to Lima, Machu Picchu, and Lake Titicaca in Peru, across the southwest corner of Bolivia by way of La Paz and south again through Argentina to Buenos Aires.

The Condor and the Cows concludes in March 1948, and the diary printed here picks up soon after that, in April 1948, when Isherwood and Caskey were travelling onward by ship, from Argentina, by way of Montevideo, Rio, and Dakar to Le Havre in France. In Paris, Isherwood saw Denny Fouts for what proved to be the last time and met Gore Vidal for the first time. He also saw Auden there, before taking Caskey to London, where he introduced him to many friends. From London, Isherwood and Caskey went on to Wyberslegh, and in June they attended the first-ever Aldeburgh Festival, organized by Benjamin Britten and Peter Pears, on the Suffolk coast. Caskey wanted to photograph the English painter Graham Sutherland, so in the beginning of July he and Isherwood went to Sutherland's house, probably with an introduction from a friend of Isherwood's. The two of them sailed for New York together in mid-July, and Isherwood went on alone to Los Angeles to begin work on *The Great Sinner*. This was an adaptation of Dostoevsky's *The Gambler* and incorporated aspects of Dostoevsky's own life and elements from his other works. The script had already been written by the emigré Hungarian playwright, Ladislaus Fodor, and Isherwood was hired—by Gottfried Reinhardt—to refine it. (The 1949 film starred Gregory Peck and Ava Gardner and was directed by Robert Siodmak.)

By mid-August Isherwood had begun to spend time with Jim Charlton, with whom he found he could be exceedingly happy, but when Caskey returned in late September, Isherwood and Caskey moved into a little house together on East Rustic Road while Isherwood finished his MGM job for Gottfried Reinhardt. That autumn, Isherwood's original American boyfriend, Vernon Old, got married, and Denny Fouts died in Rome of a heart attack evidently precipitated by his drug habit. These events suggest a closing cadence to Isherwood's first decade in America. And the next few years with Caskey—1948 to 1951—were to be increasingly confused and unhappy.

The year 1949 began with Isherwood's discovery that his books had been damaged by a flood in the cellar of James and Tania Stern's building on East Fifty-second Street in Manhattan; he had stored them there after living in the apartment with Caskey. Meanwhile, he continued working for Gottfried Reinhardt at MGM and finished writing *The Condor and the Cows* during the spring. He also took up again what was to prove a long and painful struggle to write his next novel, partly based on his wartime experiences in America; his working title was *The School of Tragedy*, but eventually he published the book as *The World in the Evening*.

In early August he attended a party at Sam and Isadore From's house where he met, among others, Evelyn Caldwell, who was researching the Los Angeles homosexual community, and a young man called Alvin Novak whom he brought home with him. Around the same time, he drafted another script with Lesser Samuels, *The Easiest Thing in the World*, and one day at lunch with Aldous and Maria Huxley, he met Igor and Vera Stravinsky and Stravinsky's colleague—who lived with them and accompanied them everywhere—Robert Craft. Also in August, George Bradshaw, a screenwriter, involved Isherwood in a project to encourage paraplegic and quadriplegic veterans to write stories and articles with advice from professional writers. This took place at Birmingham Hospital, in the San Fernando Valley, then an armed services hospital for veterans.

Isherwood's diary entries are intermittent at best from April 1948 until the early 1950s. His life with Caskey was unsettled, sometimes turbulent, and Caskey's coming and goings are not all accounted for in the record Isherwood kept during their years together. Through 1949, other young men appear in Isherwood's life with increasing frequency. He became interested in Russ Zeininger in August, and when Caskey left town in mid-November, Isherwood again spent time with Jim Charlton. Caskey went east to Florida and was away five months, returning in April 1950 by way of Kentucky. Meanwhile, in December 1949, Isherwood and Charlton were caught together in a raid on the Variety, a gay bar on the Pacific Coast Highway. About a week later, another new friend, an English professor, Don Coombs, spent the night, and before the end of the year, a slightly more serious romance had begun with a very young man, Michael Leopold. As his relationship with Caskey grew more strained, Isherwood's diary keeping became more regular.

Caskey returned to Rustic Road in April 1950, and that December the pair moved together to South Laguna, on the coast below Los Angeles. But their lives were increasingly in conflict, with Isherwood professing that he wanted a settled domestic routine which would permit him to work steadily in the daytime, and Caskey preferring to drink and have spontaneous parties, friends, and loud music on the record player. Several of Isherwood's friends—Gerald Heard, Aldous Huxley, and the Swami—admonished Isherwood about his way of life; the drinking and promiscuity could not be blamed entirely on Caskey's influence. In May 1951, Isherwood left Caskey and went to stay at the Huntington Hartford Foundation, north of Los Angeles, where he felt he could work. By August, he was back in Laguna, but only briefly; he left Caskey for good in late summer, going back to the Huntington Hartford Foundation and then east in November for the opening of *I Am a Camera*, which was to make him famous well beyond his literary audience. The play was adapted by John van Druten from *Goodbye to Berlin* at the suggestion of Dodie Smith and her husband Alec Beesley, and it effected a kind of preliminary rescue for Isherwood from one of the most desperately undirected periods of his life. That December, Isherwood sailed for England for the third time since the war, and Caskey joined the merchant marine. Isherwood had a semi-serious affair with Sam Costidy in the spring of 1952, but the next time he returned to California, in mid-April 1952, he lived briefly at Trabuco, southeast of Los Angeles, then in an apartment in Santa Monica, and finally settled down alone in Evelyn Caldwell Hooker's garden house, which his architect friend, Jim Charlton, remodelled for him.

He drove to Mexico with Caskey in November, but in January 1953, Caskey shipped out again in the merchant marine and a month later, Isherwood became involved with Don Bachardy, not yet nineteen, who was to become his companion for the rest of his life. Isherwood and Bachardy rapidly established the home life and routine which Isherwood had long craved, and while their relationship was to produce its own drama, Isherwood wrote with increasing regularity in his diary and he never again abandoned the practice altogether until 1983, just a few years before his death.

During the late 1940s, when Isherwood was not writing much in his diary, he did maintain his lifelong habit of recording appointments and some important events in a pocket date book. Around 1955 or soon after, he used his pocket date books to make an outline of what had happened in his life during what he considered to be the missing years: 1945 through 1949. The outline, written inside the front cover and front free endpapers of Isherwood's 1945–1956 diary, is included here as a preamble to the 1945–1956 diary entries. Parts of the outline are cryptic, but many events that occurred in 1948 and 1949 are expanded upon and illuminated in Isherwood's few diary entries for the same years. Other important or obscure episodes I have tried to elucidate in the paragraphs above. A few more details are explained or reiterated in footnotes, and a glance at the chronology of Isherwood's life included at the back of this volume should clarify any uncertainties about the sequence of events. As in other sections of this book, more information about many of the people and events referred to can be found in the glossary.]

An outline—made from my pocket diaries—of events between January 1, 1945 (when my first set of U.S. journals end) and February 1955[1] (when the entries in this journal get more or less continuous).

1945. January 2. Asit released from army.   *8.* Sudhira enlisted in navy.   *19.* The kite accident with Bill Harris.[2]   *22.* Harris and I tried to hitchhike north.   *28.* Met Katharine Hepburn at Beesleys'.   *31.* Scene with the soldier at Harris's.   *February 3.* Saw

[1] In fact the outline stops in 1949.
[2] See Glossary under Harris.

Robeson–Ferrer *Othello*[1] with Denny and Harris.   *4*. Last lunch with Harris at Beesleys'.   *5*. Harris left for New York. Visited AJC Ranch and Idyllwild cabin, returning 12th.   *17*. Lunch with Beesleys at their new house, 19130 Pacific Coast Highway.   *21*. Started at Warner's on *Woman in White*.   *March 12*. Studio strike began.[2]   *April 8*. Albert Brush took us to see the Arensbergs.[3]   *May 25*. First supper with Stevie [Conway].   *28*. Left Warner job.   *June 2*. Caskey's birthday—party at Jay [de Laval]'s.   *3*. With Stevie to Lake Sherwood.   *4*. Back to Warner's on *Up at the Villa*.   *6*. Shots from Dr. Zeiler.[4]   *7*. Party at Rex Evans's[5]: Maugham, Ethel Barrymore, Ronald Colman, Edna Best,[6] Cukor etc.   *18*. Supper with Swami and Maugham at Players. *July 6*. Party at Cukor's—Swami, Maugham, Ethel Barrymore, Hepburn.   *8*. Denny started work at Bel Air Bay Club.   *21*. Slept on beach with Caskey.   *29*. Roland Culver[7] at Beesleys'. *August 6*. Corrected proofs of *Prater Violet*.   *14*. Peace declared. *23*. Moved into Beesleys' chauffeur's apartment. Caskey visited. *September 21*. Finished script of *Up at the Villa* at Warner's. Bought Lincoln–Mercury.[8]   *29*. Finished at Warner's. Denny left for New York. Caskey and I moved into his apartment (137 Entrada). *October 1*. Caskey and I left by car for Santa Barbara. Thru to San Francisco, Fresno, Yosemite, Sequoia, Bakersfield, Las Vegas, Phoenix, El Centro, John Goodwin's ranch, Palm Springs, Laguna Beach, returning to Santa Monica 19th. Hayden Lewis stayed with us.   *27*. Glen Lewis[9] to stay.   *November 11*. Caskey and I helped Beesleys move to Malibu house.   *17*. Tommy Tittle[10] to stay.   *22–25*. Caskey, Hayden, Tittle and I visited Goodwin's ranch.   *December 21*. We gave a party: Boks, Huxleys, Beesleys,

---

[1] Paul Robeson, José Ferrer and Uta Hagen at the Biltmore.
[2] Members of the Writers' Guild were allowed to cross the picket line to work.
[3] Brush, a friend of Jay de Laval, took Isherwood and Denny Fouts to meet Walter Arensberg, an art collector and a devotee of the Renaissance philosopher Francis Bacon.
[4] Penicillin, for the gonorrhea Isherwood had caught from Steve Conway.
[5] British actor and art gallery owner.
[6] British actress, in Hollywood from 1939 onward.
[7] British actor, of both stage and film.
[8] A Lincoln-Mercury Zephyr convertible; he gave the Packard he already owned to Hayden Lewis.
[9] Possibly Hayden Lewis's brother.
[10] A blond naval officer who had fought in the Battle of the Pacific.

Peter Viertel, Pitoeffs.[1]   *25*. With Caskey to Beesleys' for Christmas.

1946. This pocket diary has been lost. Sometime early in the year, I was operated on at Santa Monica Hospital for a median bar. Moved from Denny's apartment to stay in apartment over Salka Viertel's garage (165 Mabery Road). We remained there the rest of the year. During the summer and fall I revised my 1939–44 journals. Caskey studied photography. On November 8, I became a U.S. citizen. From Christmas to New Year's, we made a trip by air to Mexico City.

1947. *January 1*. Returned from Mexico—hold up at Mazatlán because of engine trouble. *4*. Worked with Lesser Samuels on *Judgement Day in Pittsburgh*. *5*. Supper at Salka's with Cyril Connolly and the Chaplins. *11*. Finished *Judgement Day in Pittsburgh*. *13*. Made my will. *17*. Got visa for England. Goodbye party at Salka's—Huxleys, Kiskaddens, van Druten, Garbo. *19*. Left by air for New York. Grounded at Buffalo. Took train. Stayed night of 20th with Wystan. Left 21st by air for England. Arrived Bovingdon[2] 5:00 p.m. 22nd. To stay with John Lehmann—saw Forster, Buckingham, Doone, Medley, MacNeice, Peter Viertels, Henry Green, Plomer, Alan Ross, Keith Vaughan, Ackerley, Robson-Scott. *25*. To Wyberslegh, where the blizzards started. *February 1*. Tea at Monkhouses'—Mrs. Monkhouse, Paddy, Mitty. *27*. Heard *Judgement Day in Pittsburgh* was sold. *28*. To London, stayed with Spenders, saw *The Alchemist*.[3] *March 1*. Lunch with Jack Hewit, supper with Britten and Pears. To stay with Forster in Chiswick. *4*. Moved to Lehmann's. Lunch with Brian Howard and Sam [Langford]. Supper with Connollys.[4] *6*. Lunch with Gerald Hamilton. *7*. Stayed with Jack Hewit. *8*. To stay at Oddenino's Hotel. Supper with Guy Burgess and Peter Pollock.[5] *9*. Day with the Upwards. *10*. Saw *The Winslow Boy*.[6] *11*. Moved to John Lehmann's. Bought Keith Vaughan painting. Saw Ian Scott-Kilvert. *13*. To Cheltenham to stay with Olive Mangeot. *14*. Saw Hilda [Hauser], Amber, Jean Ross, Sarah. With Wogan and Cristina Philipps to POW camp. *16*. Big wind.

[1] The actress Ludmilla Pitoeff and her daughter, Anita, then having an affair with Vernon Old.
[2] Military airfield near London.
[3] Ben Jonson's play.
[4] Cyril Connolly and Lys Lubbock; see Glossary under Connolly.
[5] Burgess's lover since 1938.
[6] Terence Rattigan's play.

With Olive and Jean to movies.   *17.* Back to Wyberslegh.
28. Signed deed of gift of Marple.   *30.* Walk with Mitty
Monkhouse on Whaley Moor.   *April 14.* Left for London. Stayed
with Lehmann.   *15.* Saw *Now Barabbas*—[1]   *16.* Saw tapestry
exhibit and *The White Devil*.[2]   *17.* Saw Neville King-Page.
18. Embarked on *Queen Elizabeth*, met John Holmes.   *19.* Sailed.
25. Docked at New York. With Caskey to stay at the Park Central
Hotel.   *26.* Moved into [James and Tania] Stern's apartment (207
East 52nd Street).   *May 5.* Started at Pilates' gym.[3] Forster and Bill
Roerick to supper.   *17.* To stay with Ollie Jennings, Ben Baz and
Bill Bailey. We had supper and a quarrel with the Mattas.
27. Borrowed two-sided Edward Burra painting from gallery.[4]
29. Drove to Montauk Point on Long Island.   *June 1.* To Fire
Island, stayed with Wystan.   *12.* Books arrived from England.
13. With Forster.   *15.* To Quaker Meeting; met Caroline
Norment again.   *July 11.* Drove to New London.   *12.* To New
Bedford.   *13.* Steamer to Nantucket, where we stayed with
Capote and Arvin at Siasconset.   *20.* We left Nantucket.
21. Arrived, via New Bedford, at Provincetown, to see Cadmus,
George Tooker, the Jared Frenches, Sandy Campbell, Don
Windham.   *26.* Back to New York.   *August 3.* Party at Horst's:
Garbo, Noël Coward.   *4.* Lunch with Andrew Lyndon.[5]
5. Kirstein took us to see Nadelman sculpture.   *6.* Kirstein took us to
Washington to see the German pictures found stored in the salt
mine.   *15.* Drove with Kirstein to visit Mina Curtiss near
Williamsburg[, Massachusetts].   *17.* Back to New York.   *18.* Saw
Berthold Szczesny.   *26.* Drove to Fire Island to see Wystan and
Chester.   *27.* Back to New York.   *31.* We went to Fairfield
[, Connecticut] to see Spender, who was teaching at Sarah
Lawrence.   *September 1.* Back to New York.   *10.* Peggy and Bill
Kiskadden, Chris Wood, John Gielgud for drinks.   *13.* With
Berthold Szczesny, Chris Wood, Kirstein, Spender to spend day
on Fire Island with Wystan and Chester.   *September 19.* We sailed
at midday on the *Santa Paula* for South America.   *23.* Curaçao.

[1] Another play, by William Douglas-Home.
[2] The tapestry exhibit was at the Victoria and Albert Museum; *The White Devil* is
John Webster's play.
[3] On the West Side of Manhattan, run by the German, Joseph Pilates (b. 1880),
who emigrated to the U.S. by way of England. The exercises he invented, called
the Pilates Method, are still widely used.
[4] Isherwood borrowed but decided not to buy two paintings, framed back to
back, by the English painter Edward Burra (1905–1976), who visited New York
in the 1930s and 1940s chiefly to paint subjects in black Harlem.
[5] A young naval officer from Macon, Georgia, met while visiting Capote on
Nantucket.

24. La Guaira.   *27*. Landed at Cartagena.

See *The Condor and the Cows* for diary of trip.

1948.   March 27. Sailed from Buenos Aires on the *Groix*.
28. Montevideo.   *April 1*. Rio: saw René Berger and Jorge de
Castro.   *8*. Crossed the equator.   *12*. Dakar.   *22*. Le Havre—Paris,
Hotel d'Isly. Saw Denny Fouts. Bill's traveler's checks stolen.
25. Met Gore Vidal.   *28*. Day with Wystan, Chester and Denny.
29. Breakfast with Gore.   *30*. We left for London.   *May 1*. Moved
to 31 Egerton Crescent to stay with Alexis Rassine.   *6*. Saw *Peter
Grimes.*[1]   *7*. Moved to Tudor Court Hotel. Party at *Horizon*
office.   *8*. Saw *The Rake's Progress* ballet.[2]   *13*. To Wyberslegh.
18. Caskey joined me.   *22*. Returned to London.   *23*. Back to
Wyberslegh.   *June 6*. Back to London.   *7*. We went to Aldeburgh
for festival. Saw *Albert Herring*.[3]   *10*. Left Aldeburgh. Stayed with
Cuthbert Worsley.   *18*. Party at Lehmann's: Gore Vidal, Tennessee
Williams.   *17*. Lunch with Cliff Gordon.[4]   *July 2*. To Wyberslegh.
6. Visit to Graham Sutherland.   *9*. Sailed for U.S. in the *Queen
Elizabeth*.   *14*. Landed New York.   *15*. Left for Los Angeles by
train.   *18*. Arrived Los Angeles. Stayed at El Kanan Hotel, Santa
Monica.   *19*. Started work at MGM on *The Great Sinner*.   *August
14*. Supper with Jim Charlton.   *September 4*. With Charlton to
Laguna Beach.   *5*. To Mount Palomar and Warner Hot Springs.
6. Back to Los Angeles.   *11–14*. With Charlton to Laguna Beach,
Ensenada, Coronado.   *20*. Caskey arrived.   *28*. We moved into
333 East Rustic Road.   *October 6*. Started filming *The Great Sinner*.
9. Finished work at MGM.   *16*. Spender stayed the night.
November 5. Vernon Old and Patty O'Neill[5] married.   *December
16*. Denny Fouts died in Rome.   *20*. Our furniture arrived from
New York.   *22*. Ben Bok and Coral got married.   *28*. Party for the
end of *The Great Sinner*, at MGM, Stage 15.

1949.   January 4. My books arrived from New York damaged by
flood.   *6–13*. Worked with Gottfried Reinhardt at MGM.
February 21. Watched Bill Kiskadden operate at Good Samaritan
Hospital.   *March 12*. Glenway Wescott arrived to stay in the
Canyon.   *18*. Glenway left.   *22*. Sneak preview of *Great Sinner*,
Criterion, Santa Monica.   *April 2*. Finished *The Condor and the
Cows*.   *19*. Visited Dodie and Alec Beesley, just settled into Cove

---

[1] Britten's opera.
[2] Choreographed by Ninette de Valois to Gavin Gordon's music.
[3] Britten's new opera, previously performed at Covent Garden.
[4] Radio and nightclub entertainer.
[5] Not her real name.

Way house. *May 29*. Mrs. Caskey arrived. *June 11*. Supper at Charpentier's, Redondo, with Caskey, Mrs. Caskey, Jay Laval, Aileen Pringle,[1] the Masselinks. *14–16*. Spender, Bill Goyen and Walter Berns visited. *July 20*. Drove to Santa Barbara, to see Sister who was dying. *26*. Sister's funeral. *August 6–7*. All-night party at Sam From's—Evelyn Caldwell, Paul Goodman,[2] Charles Aufderheide, Alvin Novak. *9*. Finished draft of *The Easiest Thing in the World*, with Lesser Samuels. *10*. Lunch with the Huxleys, Robert Craft and Stravinskys. *14*. Mrs. Caskey left. *19*. Visited Birmingham Hospital for first time with George Bradshaw, to see the paraplegic patients. *27*. Met Russ Zeininger. *September 7*. To dedication of Trabuco as Ramakrishna Monastery. *November 11*. Caskey left for Florida. *November 26–28*. Charlton, Ben Britten, Peter Pears and I drove to Palm Springs, Palomar, Oceanside, stayed night with Chris Wood at Laguna Beach, and home. *December 1*. Wrote article on Klaus Mann. *4*. With Charlton in police raid at the Variety. *9*. Don Coombs stayed. *20*. Posed for drawing by Fechin.[3] *26*. Michael Leopold stayed, until 29th.

April 11, 1948–April 13, 1956

1948

On board the *Groix*
April 11. Tomorrow, we are scheduled to land at Dakar. Maybe we'll stay there overnight. From there to Le Havre should take ten to twelve days. The weather has turned much colder since we crossed the equator. The old gentleman in our cabin is much worried by the prospect of an extra passenger joining us—and so am I; the old gentleman, with his bad leg, takes up enough psychological room for two, already. He always seems to be washing when you want to use the bowl. At night he groans—*Ah, Madre!*—and gradually fills a

[1] Silent film star (1895–1989).
[2] American novelist, poet, and social critic (1911–1972).
[3] Nicolai Fechin (1881–1955), the Russian artist, lived in Santa Monica Canyon and was friendly with Ben and Jo Masselink; Isherwood sat for a charcoal portrait on December 20 and 23. Its whereabouts are unknown.

chamber pot. Caskey fears he will put his foot into it one morning, getting out of the upper bunk.

But our second-class cabin (*troisième supérieure*) is luxury compared to the third class. They sleep six or eight in a room—either without a porthole or with one which won't open. Our cabin has formed a cabin cabinet: president, vice-president, minister of the fine arts, minister of supply, foreign minister, etc. They are a very sympathetic group: much the nicest and liveliest people on board. Mike, who reads the Gita, Fatty the ballet dancer, the bearded painter who imitates a singing Cossack, the negroid boy from Tahiti, the Belgian, the Breton whose French nobody can understand, the Russian boy who rolls up his shorts. Less sympathetic are Steve, the fussy Argentine journalist, and the tall dark Parisian who doesn't like the English. More about all of them in due course.

But I'm not unhappy here and neither is Caskey. I'm working on the travel book—still don't know what to call it. Today I finished chapter two. Caskey is writing a novel based on the life of Bill Harris. The rest of the time we sunbathe, read (*Nostromo*, which was published the year I was born, is still a marvellous picture of Ecuador, Peru or Bolivia), or drink. The Pernod has run out, so we have to make do with cognac. One jigger of crème de menthe and one of cognac, on ice, does for a predinner cocktail. There is no place to drink except the *fumoir*, which is usually crowded—third-class passengers and crew use it too. They play cards or dice or checkers, try to read amidst the din, teach each other languages. Caskey is learning French from a tall sad Pole, in exchange for lessons in Kentucky.

In our class, a group has been formed by the hunchback lady, the old professor and the big man who is, I believe, a German and a poet. They hold a nonstop talkfest throughout the day. The professor is a Jules Verne character. He can tell you the exact number of plums, apples, grapes, etc. he has eaten during his life. Indeed, he remembers everything; he has total recall. The others listen to him with great respect but kid him along. They encouraged him to take a photograph of the equator. The big man played Neptune when we had the ceremony of crossing the line.[1] I got nearly all the flour and water in my hair. It isn't really clean yet.

There are a lot of nuns on the boat, and some extremely gloomy and drab Dutch missionary priests. They read crime stories and smoke small cigars. The nuns are much more devout. They tell their beads all day long.

---

[1] Travelers crossing the equator for the first time are tried at a mock "Court of Neptune" and subjected to ritual practical jokes such as ducking or being lathered and roughly shaved.

How the French chatter! Especially at meals. They start the second they sit down to breakfast. "How did you sleep?" the hunchback asks the professor. "I slept perfectly, madame. I always sleep perfectly. I can sleep perfectly anywhere. I can sleep in the rain, in the sunshine, in the mud, in the snow, in the forest, in the great city." And then he goes into anecdotes of how he did, and where, and when. If one of them utters a word which is going to be the keynote of a discussion, they all take it up, repeating it with different modulations, singing it, shouting it in chorus. They discuss everything—politics, art, food, South America, love, the war ("J'ai fait la guerre"[1] is said repeatedly, to back up and authorize some opinion)—and all from the French angle. They are incredibly provincial. Is a little personal resentment entering here? Well—yes. They know I am a writer, but they don't show the faintest curiosity about my work. I'm English—or worse, American—so I can't possibly be any good. I resent this—but I'm only too thankful not to be involved in their discussions. And I couldn't follow them, anyway. I have almost lost whatever ear I had for French. Caskey says he is preparing a great impersonation of the French at meals, to amuse the Canyon on our return.

It is very easy to get into a state of Francophobia which stops you working or even thinking about anything important. Must guard against this, reminding myself that after all nobody forced me to sail in one of their ships or go to their country at all. Also, on a long voyage like this, I dare say I'd get almost equally exasperated by a shipload of Germans, Swedes or Finns.

April 12. Dakar—the town is much less "African" than I'd expected. Instead of dazzling white buildings, palms, grass huts, there were shabby streets of nondescript yellow houses—few sidewalk cafés or planted boulevards; little of the charm of, say, Saigon. But the Senegalese make up for everything. They have a kind of nonhuman, birdlike beauty. Mostly very tall, with the long legs of herons, and very dark, almost blue-black. They wear long flapping robes, and sometimes turbans of dark heavy material. Some have long horizontal nostrils like Donald Duck; they hold their heads back and look at you along their noses with eyes three quarters closed. The salesmen (and nearly everyone has something for sale; crocodile bags and billfolds, chiefly) seem more sleepy than sly. Wearily they ask huge prices and accept half almost without argument. Toward evening, they grow somewhat impatient: "Give me five hundred francs. Come on. I have to go home." The women are amazing. Even taller than the men, wonderfully elegant, in loose white garments with many bangles and

[1] "I was in the war."

all kinds of gaudy bows and scarves, they look like female impersonators who have put on everything they could find in their mothers' bedrooms, including the sheets and the curtains. They billow slowly along, veiling and unveiling their faces, tying and untying the scarves around their solid cakes of black hair, with coy graceful movements. They are very shy of being photographed. Caskey could get no decent pictures.

Meanwhile, of course, there are the French. Some are muscular and handsome, but all—fat or thin, old or young—wear very short shorts. Among these tall swaying dreamy bird-people, they seem almost indecently physical, hairy and solid.

April 13. The boat is now very crowded. The *fumoir* is crammed with people. We are no longer allowed to use our little dining room to work in. There are two services for meals. Quite a lot of French soldiers on board. The weather is already much colder.

Caskey and I got drunk and threw the chamber pot out of the porthole. Later we felt very ashamed of ourselves; especially as he had to use one of the water glasses. The smell of urine gets worse and worse.

April 14. One is never alone, not for an instant. Our only protection is our language. We have very private conversations in the midst of the crowd in the *fumoir*. This morning, we saw a whale. Its spouts looked like small bombs bursting on the sea, and the thin cloud of spray afterward is like smoke blowing away in the wind. As it came nearer, you could see its black shining body heaving out of the water.

Four Senegalese stowaways were caught this morning. A freighter on its way to Dakar was radioed, we stopped, and the boys were transferred in one of the lifeboats. Everybody took photographs. It was unpleasant: not because we gloated but because the general smugness of our lives seemed exposed by this incident. The boys will go to prison. Nearly every voyage some stowaways are discovered. I longed to be a millionaire and pay their passage, first class.

Our consciences have been relieved in another direction, however. The old man has managed to get another chamber pot. He has never referred to the loss of the first.

April 17. The couple who have the dog are the only people in the second class who have a cabin to themselves—God only knows what they did to get it. He is the type of baby husband, somewhat peevish. She peels his fruit for him at table. Yesterday I saw the two of them going in to take a bath together; she probably scrubs him.

Early yesterday morning, we passed the Canaries. I was still asleep; a disappointment. I'd looked forward to seeing Tenerife again. Since Dakar there has been a fairly heavy swell, but it's calmer right at the moment.

Last night and the night before, Mike, Fatty, the bearded painter, the son of Bernanos[1] and the boy from Tahiti fooled about on the deck, ballet dancing, imitating animals, talking mock Russian. There were complaints. We pulled a rope down, acting the Volga Boatmen.[2]

The homely girl with the glasses whom they call La Marquise has gotten herself a beau. He is a very small and somewhat villainous-looking soldier. He sits all day long on deck with his arm around her, occasionally whispering in her ear or feeling her breasts. She is a bit embarrassed, because she keeps catching the eye of one of her former gang: the boys are a bit reproachful and a bit hurt in their masculine vanity—they talk about Love from morning till night, Love with a capital L, Love in poetry, Love in philosophy etc.—and here comes this coarse little character and just grabs her. They pretend much concern that she will lose her honor. She now wears lipstick.

Never, never again—unless I am escaping from a plague-stricken (and/or a blazing) town—will I travel like this. My privacy has been raped. It will take days for me to be able to think again. I only hope I will get through this voyage without doing something childish. Yesterday I was suddenly furious because the steward always brings fruit to the couple with the dog to compensate them for not liking cheese, and he always omits to bring me any until I ask. So I said very loud: "Does one have to be French?" This produced a painful impression, as it does in anti–Semitic circles when a Jew calls attention to the discrimination against him. I am really deadly bored with myself at present. I'm so spiteful, so touchy, so resentful—and hence so stupid, such dull company. I really must try to pull myself together. Had better retire to my bunk and sleep or read a book.

This business of the revolt in Colombia is still, as far as I'm concerned, wrapped in mystery. The day we were in Dakar, the local paper carried a report of it which for vagueness might as well have come out of a Kafka novel. Firing had almost ceased, after four days. Most of the center of Bogotá was in ruins. All the documents relative to the Bogotá conference had been destroyed. General Marshall was safe, outside the city, under the protection of the army. The new

[1] The French Catholic novelist Georges Bernanos had lived with his family on a buffalo farm in Brazil during the war.
[2] As in Konrad Bercovici's 1926 novel *The Volga Boatmen*, filmed by Cecil B. DeMille the year it was published.

coalition government had restored order. The conference would be resumed either in Lima or Mexico City. Not one word of real explanation: who had revolted? why? Now our radio bulletin tells us quite blandly that conditions in Bogotá are practically normal and that the conference has been reopened. This radio bulletin, issued by a French news agency, couldn't be stupider. We are treated to such thrilling items as: "Yesterday M. Vincent Auriol received the Argentine Ambassador." "The government has made an important pronouncement on the international situation."[1]

This evening, Franco-American relations further deteriorated. Caskey was ordered out of the lobby in front of the purser's office because he wasn't a first-class passenger. (Everybody always uses the lobby and anyhow it was empty—this being 11:30 p.m.) When he didn't understand, the officer who had spoken to him sent for a waiter. Caskey was furious—especially as it later appeared that the officer spoke quite adequate English and could easily have asked him to leave in a polite manner. Caskey yelled insults: "America grand, France très petit . . . Piss."[2] (Luckily this is the worst word he knows. I shall be careful not to teach him any more till we are safely out of the country.)

April 19. Yesterday was really quite rough. We skidded sideways over big rollers. The boat rolled like a barrel but didn't pitch. We neither of us felt sick but the constant physical adjustment makes you tired and sleepy. Lay in my bunk and read *Capricornia*[3] and Boswell. *Capricornia* disappointed me; it's very superficial and amateurish, and the author really doesn't like the natives as much as he pretends, in spite of all his raving against race prejudice.

Now we are somewhere off the coast of Portugal. Late yesterday, it got much calmer, but now we're beginning to roll again and Biscay will probably be bad.

April 20. Biscay; only medium swell so far. The Pole keeps telling us that this is part of France—"We are in France," he exclaims delightedly. The professor has changed his shirt, for the first time since he came on board. Last night, as always, we got drunk, sitting facing each other like a row of convicts and prison visitors across the two

---

[1] The liberal leader, Jorge Eliécer Gaitán, was assassinated in Bogotá April 9, sparking major riots and disrupting the Ninth International Conference of American States; General George C. Marshall, as secretary of state, was leading the U.S. delegation.

[2] "America big, France very little . . . Piss." (Isherwood's spelling evidently reflects Caskey's poor pronunciation.)

[3] Xavier Herbert's 1938 novel about the Australian outback.

tables in the jammed *fumoir*. Oh, I am weary of them all—even the nice ones. Mike rambling on about mysticism, the Breton painter Ray Borel talking incessantly about his book, the son of Bernanos making his literary jokes, Fatty getting dressed up to dance in the first class. Steve popping in and out with his face of an unhealthy moon. The Russian touching everyone for small loans.

Mike's story of Brazilian touchiness: In the midst of a passionate affair, a man brought flowers to his mistress. She shot him dead—she thought he was trying to pay her. According to Mike, it is absolutely fatal to get the least bit involved with any girl in Rio. In a second, you belong to her—and to her family. If you leave her she'll stab you. He makes the whole place sound like utter hell. The jealousy, the violence, the fatal inertia. The code of honor and appearances, and the dishonesty underneath, rotting away the foundations of life.

April 24. We disembarked at Le Havre on Thursday, two days ago, and came straight here, to Paris. This was our last sight of our fellow passengers—I trust; although, actually, they started to seem much more sympathetic as soon as we were off that damned boat. Old Rognoni, his wife and Fatty rejoiced to be in France again. As we passed Rouen Cathedral, everyone stood up to look. "Hideous," said Caskey, who has already decided he doesn't like Gothic. There were many traces of the war—small military graveyards, smashed houses, provisional half-rebuilt bridges over which the train moved cautiously. The countryside was very green—with that light uncanny greenness of northern spring—and thick with fruit blossom. Caskey said he had expected it to be quainter. I suppose he expected sabots and peasant costume.

From the Gare Saint Lazare we drove straight to the Hotel Voltaire—nostalgic for me because of so many visits, with Wystan, Heinz, Johnny Andrews—but it was being redecorated. After several tries, we landed up in the Hotel d'Isly on the rue Jacob, which is clean, quiet and cheap.

Round to see Denny that same evening, at his apartment on the rue du Bac. It is a huge shabby place, with traces of the splendor of his pre-1939 period, in which he leads a nocturnal Proustian life with the tattered curtains always drawn. He lies most of the day in bed, with Trotsky[1] and the pipe at his side, reading and dozing, often eating nothing but a plate of cooked cereal. When he can't afford opium, he drinks a kind of tea made of the dross, which gives him stomach cramps. He is as pale as a corpse, but quite unchanged, slim as ever, and with a sort of waxen beauty. He did not seem at all vague or

---

[1] His dog.

stupefied, as Harris had told us—and he welcomed us both warmly. He is liable to be thrown out of the apartment before long, and doesn't know where he'll go.

Caskey and I went on to the place Pigalle, where I left him, as he had decided that he wanted to talk to some very old Toulouse-Lautrec whores. He found them all right, and didn't return till midday yesterday, much battered, having woken that morning to find himself in a police station with all his traveler's checks stolen and owing a taxi driver one hundred francs for the fare.

Paris seems hardly to have changed at all. It is wonderfully beautiful in its outward aspect—the chestnut trees all in blossom, the buildings elegantly shabby. The food in the restaurants is as good as ever, but very expensive. The Louvre has been thoroughly tidied up, the junk hidden away and the good pictures spaced out and properly hung, so that the place no longer looks like the residence of a megalomaniac millionaire collector who bought everything he could lay hands on. But Caskey doesn't really like it. He finds it lacking in character. I know what he means—there is a displeasing overall slickness in the effect, rather like the fashion photographs in *Vogue* and *Harper's Bazaar*. Maybe the whole place has just been overpublicized.

April 27. Two days ago, while Caskey and I were sitting in the Deux Magots, up came a young man and introduced himself as Gore Vidal. Since then, we've seen a good deal of him—two evenings at dinner and today an expedition to Versailles. He's a big husky boy with fair wavy hair and a funny, rather attractive face—sometimes he reminds me of a teddy bear, sometimes of a duck. Caskey says he's typical American prep school. His conversation is all about Love, which he doesn't believe in—or rather, he believes it's Tragic. He talks about "peeing machines" and "mice," and says things like, "We looked at each other and our tails started to wag." He asks questions like, "What did Frederick the Great do in bed?" But he's also a pretty shrewd operator—or would like to be. He wanted advice on "how to manage my career." He is very jealous of Truman [Capote], but determined not to quarrel with him because he feels that when a group of writers sticks together it's better business for all of them. (He drew this moral from the Auden-Spender-Day Lewis-MacNeice-Isherwood gang, he says.) He has written enough books already to see him through to 1952. What I respect about him is his courage. I do think he has that—though it is mingled, as in many much greater heroes, with a desire for self-advertisement.

Last night, while we were all three having dinner, a man at the next table sent a note over to us, saying that he'd heard our conversation and might he come and talk—he had something of interest to tell us. He turned out to be a slightly crazy Englishman who announced that he'd been "hunting communists up and down the Limpopo."

Denny treats Gore with the slightly sarcastic tolerance of an elder uncle. He let us all take puffs at the pipe, scolding us for our awkwardness and saying we should never make real smokers. It tasted like incense and had no apparent effect whatsoever.

Versailles was rather a disappointment—too big and barracklike, despite the decorations and statues. But the woods were wonderful. Marie Antoinette's sham cottages were the first film sets. After all this time they still look fakey and new.

April 28. Yesterday evening, while we were sitting at the Flore, we saw Chester [Kallman]. We didn't even know he and Wystan were in Paris, and this was really a piece of luck, because they were only stopping the night and leaving today for Florence. Later, they are going down to Naples. They plan to see all available operas during the summer. Chester and Wystan have already finished the libretto of *The Rake's Progress* and now Stravinsky is writing the music. Wystan insists that Chester did a good half of the work, and that you can't possibly tell where the joins come.

I get to like Chester much more as he grows older. He must be around thirty now, and he looks all of that, with stooped shoulders and big pouches under his eyes. Indeed, he is getting to look more and more like Wystan. He is very funny, and so anxious to be friendly that it is quite touching. We all got a bit high; and Chester said to me: "I feel at last that you really don't disapprove of me."

As for Wystan, he's quite middle-aged, with a thick waist and such a sad anxiously lined face. We sat together this morning on the boulevard in the sunshine, and suddenly it was like a scene from Chekhov. I thought: "Here we are, just two old bags—and only a moment ago, it seems, we were boys, talking about our careers. Like Truman and Gore. How sad." Wystan still fusses and rags anxiously at Chester, and screws up his eyebrows when he fears that Chester will say or do something tiresome or upsetting to his plans. Chester teases him, of course. But, watching them, you feel: "They're together, now, till the end."

Denny joined us for cocktails at the Ritz—like Dorian Gray emerging from the tomb—death-pale and very slim in his dark elegant suit, with black hat and umbrella. He looks like the Necropolitan ambassador.

May 1. Yesterday, we crossed to England on the *Golden Arrow*. It was a bad arrival: France in sunshine, Dover cliffs veiled in rain, no reservation at the Regent Palace, so we had to spend the night in an unsavory annex of the Grosvenor Hotel. We went to see Eric [Falk] in his rooms in the Temple. He is really one of the most human, decent people I know: there is real goodness in his face. I love the way he talks, getting terrifically excited about some play or movie: "You haven't seen it? Oh, but my dear man . . . Well . . . It's absolutely stupendous . . . If ever you see it's on anywhere, just drop everything and make a beeline for it. . . ."

Today we have moved to Egerton Crescent (John [Lehmann]'s still away in the states) at Alexis [Rassine]'s invitation. The crescent has been repainted since I was here last year; in fact all this part of Kensington has been spruced up a lot. Alexis is as gracious as ever, wearing his honors with perfect dignity. I don't think he cares for anything except the ballet, and working in the back garden, which he has already made much prettier than any of the neighbors'. He *is* an odd character, so very self-contained, so adult in a way which is curiously feminine without being in the least effeminate. He looks forward to coming to New York next year and buying "everything in the shops."

May 8. Yesterday, as John is coming home today from the U.S., we moved to the Tudor Court Hotel—a stuffy expensive place originally inhabited by old ladies, where the staff is cruelly overworked and the service is very bad in consequence. We have seen all sorts of people— Jacky [Hewit], fatter than ever, who has been in Pakistan, Cyril [Connolly], Peter Watson, Edward [Upward], Brian [Howard], Sam [Langford], Morgan [Forster], Keith Vaughan, John Minton, and Benjy [Britten], looking mortally weary and beset with financial troubles for his opera company. Caskey has decided that London is far more interesting than Paris, and that it is full of lesbians. (We certainly *have* noticed a very large number of them in the streets.)

Last night, there was a big party at the new offices of *Horizon* in Bedford Square. Nothing but champagne was served—about one hundred bottles—of which Caskey and I got our full share. Met Desmond MacCarthy[1] and Arthur Waley.[2] MacCarthy was interested in the Gita. Waley told me that the Chinese translator of *Prater Violet*, Mr. Pien Chihlin, is in England and wants to meet me. William Plomer was imperturbable and funny, as always. The man I would most like to be with in an air raid. Lucian Freud[3] arrived with a

---

[1] Literature and drama critic, then writing weekly for *The Sunday Times*.
[2] Poet and translator from Chinese and Japanese.
[3] German-born English painter, grandson of Sigmund Freud.

famous Evelyn Waugh character named Scotty Wilson,[1] and adroitly left him on our hands—he hadn't been invited, but, "Dear Lucian is so vague." Peter Watson helped us cart him around north London in a taxi, maudlin drunk and occasionally vomiting, but refusing to give us his address. We searched his coat and found an identity card with several addresses, all of which were out of date. Finally we took him to a police station, where the sergeant sympathetically but firmly insisted on the truth. I think Scotty had been ashamed because it was in a very poor street. He is a touching character, a drunken painter, who has been victimized, I suspect, by heartless snobs who exploit him for laughs. Later, Brian joined us and we ate supper. Brian and I made a drunken nuisance of ourselves trying to remember the A. E. Housman poem which begins: "Crossing alone the nighted ferry."[2] After about two hours, we succeeded.

May 10. Saturday evening, two nights ago, we went to the ballet. Alexis danced in *Les Patineurs* and *The Rake's Progress*. Technically, he is excellent, but one doesn't feel much theatrical presence. He is satirically elfin. Probably he needs a larger part—I'd like to see him in *Giselle*. *The Rake's Progress* is really first-class: I never saw the horror of the eighteenth century so well captured and conveyed on the stage. Again and again, Hogarth's line seemed actually to have been animated, translated into movement. Robert Helpmann is perfect, especially in the whorehouse and the madhouse scenes. His death, with that last convulsion, was one of those effects which succeed so brilliantly because they are on the extreme verge of being funny.[3]

Supper last night with Henry Yorke ("Henry Green") and his wife. I met him at the *Horizon* party. He came up to me and said: "Don't suppose you remember me. My name's Green. I write." He is really very nice and so much fun; and so is she. They were very pleased because Caskey told them their American nightclub records were valuable. Yorke is really an extraordinary character. He is the typical businessman, with a dash of the Old Etonian. He loves football matches and blondes. He poses as an amateur—a "Sunday writer." He does a lot of business with the Russians and has many stories of their cagey mentality. (At a dinner, he met a Mr. Z., member of a Soviet trade delegation. Yorke told funny stories, which an interpreter translated into Russian. Mr. Z., as soon as the jokes had been translated, laughed until he coughed and shed tears holding his sides. Some days later, Yorke met another Russian and complimented him

---

[1] Naif painter funded by Peter Watson; Waugh mentions "Scottie" Wilson in the opening chapter of *The Loved One* (1948).
[2] *More Poems*, XXIII.
[3] Rassine was the dancing master, Helpmann the Rake.

on his English. "Ah," said the Russian, "that is nothing. We all wish we could speak as perfectly as Mr. Z.")

Talk about Evelyn Waugh, with whom Yorke was at Oxford. The other day, Yorke met Waugh in deep mourning and asked the cause. "It's for the King of Denmark," Waugh explained: "You see, I feel I have to—I was in the Household Cavalry during the war." Yorke has great arguments with Waugh about Catholicism, and kids him because the Pope holds shares in the Casino at Monte Carlo. Waugh explains that gambling isn't a sin unless you lose more than you can afford.

Yorke also told some good stories of the Blitz and the Fire Service. He says he got the characters of the Irish servants in *Loving* from Irishmen he met in the service. One of them told him that life's greatest pleasure is to lie in bed in the morning "eating hot buttered toast with cunty fingers."

May 11. Lunch with Connollys, Rose Macaulay,[1] Raymond Mortimer. Talk about the Sitwells—their despotism. Everybody is scared of them. They never forgive an attack—or, at any rate, as Cyril said, not for seven years. Edith has just forced Oscar Williams and the publishers of a modern verse anthology to print the following apology: "We deeply regret that by an oversight two poems by Miss Edith Sitwell have been included in this anthology without her permission. We appreciate that the inclusion of two poems only is entirely inadequate to represent her."

May 17. Have been up here at Wyberslegh since the 13th. Caskey is supposed to arrive tomorrow—he has been staying on in London and then with Morgan at Cambridge. Glorious weather. The landscape, which I last saw under deep snow, summery and vivid green. Streams of cyclists in shorts along the Buxton Road. M. looking even younger than last year—at seventy-nine! Richard is at Marple. I haven't seen him yet. M. says he has worked himself into a fit of jealousy about me as the Favored Son. It is pitiful. I suppose he has to hate someone. I keep wondering what Caskey will make of all this.

May 29. From *The Daily Mail*:

Scotland Yard ... received a letter purporting to have been written by John Edward Allen, the "mad parson" who escaped from Broadmoor last July. It said: "You might tell the police that I have hidden the new notes in Heath's sports coat in Madame

[1] Novelist, essayist and travel writer (1881–1958).

Tussaud's." The two detectives each took a section of the chamber of horrors. Mr. Reginald Edds, an official of Madame Tussaud's, took a third group of waxworks. Nothing whatever was found in the pockets of Neville George Clevely Heath, no. 63. He was not in fact wearing a sports coat, but a replica of the neat grey pin-striped suit in which he was sentenced to death in September 1946.[1]

It was the "mad parson's" boast that he had stolen £300 from a brass foundry.

The Cheshire police were last night investigating a report that a man answering the description of the "mad parson" had been seen "cycling furiously in the Sandbach area."

From *The Daily Telegraph*:

Mr. R. T. Paget K.C.,[2] commentating on the 69% vote in favour of retaining capital punishment in the *Telegraph*'s Mass-Observation survey, said: "If we are to hang people because the crowd wants it, then we follow a precedent set by Pontius Pilate." (He's Socialist member[3] for Northampton.)

(It's too bad I let this diary lapse, and didn't describe the rest of our visit—the Aldeburgh Festival, the time at Cuthbert Worsley's, the parties, the arrival of Gore Vidal and Tennessee Williams, Morgan's doings and sayings, and the sudden call from Gottfried Reinhardt to come back to Hollywood and work on *The Great Sinner* for MGM. Too late for that now, and too late even for the period which followed—my drunken, restless life at the Hotel Kanan, the meeting with Jim Charlton, the trip to Ensenada and the wonderful drive around Mount Palomar, which was one of the happiest days of my life.

Never mind, we'll start here, established with Caskey in the little house with the broken bridge over the creek—333 Rustic Road.)

November 6. Another beautiful day. Caskey and I lay on the beach. Later, we more or less deliberately let the canaries (which Hayden [Lewis] and Rod [Owens] brought as a present to our party two nights ago) fly away into the trees. We now both have a bad conscience about this. They'll probably die tonight, when it gets cold. There's also a gull on the beach with a broken wing. Should we have brought it home? We didn't. Oh dear—I am getting like dear Dodie.

---

[1] Heath was executed for the savage sexual murders of two women.
[2] King's Counsel, i.e., a barrister who serves as counsel to the Crown, taking precedence over other barristers.
[3] I.e., Member of Parliament.

As for the party, it was a massacre. I had a terrible hangover—very unusual for me—yesterday, and had to drag myself to Vernon's wedding with Patty O'Neill. Allan Hunter married them, in his living room. He made the threadbare words of the ceremony sound friendly and sincere. I think Vernon cried. Afterwards, we had a "reception" down here—consisting of Peggy Kiskadden, a huge cake she had bought, and three bottles of champagne. Peggy was very bright, and kept the atmosphere at the right temperature. She still disapproves of Vernon, though, and the way she kissed Patty suggested the deepest sympathy. Later, we went to see Salka, who held forth about the elections. One thing we all agree on—we are delighted that those infuriating pollsters and experts were dead wrong about Dewey. It restores one's faith in the American capacity to disregard the newspapers.[1]

Am plugging along at the South American book. Ah—how boring! The truth is, I am bored by the very mention of the place, and feel ashamed that I'm bored. I *must* finish it, however.

Caskey is endlessly busy, home building. It is really a deep instinct of his nature. He never ceases to carpenter, sew, paint, cook. Sometimes I ask myself uneasily, what will happen when the home *is* built? But I don't think I really need worry. It's just that I'm being confronted, at last, with the problems of the Householder—and who ever dares to say they are less than the problems of the Monk? Which reminds me, I'm reading Thomas Merton's *The Seven Storey Mountain*.[2] Merton is now a Trappist. It is very interesting, and even inspiring, but I keep being repelled by his Catholic arrogance. They're so very sure that they, and nobody else, have all the answers.

No doubt the life in Santa Monica Canyon is empty, vain, trivial, tragic, indigent of God. But that's no reason not to live here and try to do the best you can. I always think of William Plomer, who makes existence less odious wherever he goes.

Lincoln writes that Wystan is going to settle in Italy.

Master, be with me specially at this time. Help me to remember you constantly and let me feel your presence. You aren't shocked by the camping of the publicans and the screaming of the sinners. You too got into drag, and you didn't condemn—you danced with the drunkards.[3] If I could be clear and happy and funny—that at least

---

[1] A Dewey victory in the November 2 presidential election was so confidently predicted that newspapers announced the outcome wrongly with banner headlines; Truman was the winner.

[2] *The Seven Storey Mountain: Autobiographical Reminiscences* (1948).

[3] See Glossary under Ramakrishna.

would be something. What would you like me to do now? Tell my beads, and then wash the dishes? Okay—I'm off.

November 7. Yesterday we saw Steinbeck's film *The Pearl.* Wasn't much impressed. The photography is good—if you aren't tired of filter shots of cirrus clouds. But the grouping of the figures was much too consciously artistic—it smelled of ballet—and the mildly pinkish story contains all kinds of quite arbitrary tragic twists. It's just what I wrote about Steinbeck when I reviewed *The Grapes of Wrath*: he kills off characters right and left, and then blames the economic setup. All—or nearly all—the players were Mexican and they were handicapped by having to talk English: this made the dialogue sound ridiculously clumsy. I've heard that Armendariz[1] speaks fluent English. If so, he deliberately faked a thick Mexican accent to fit in with the others.

On the beach with Caskey, Bill Bailey, Jim Charlton. I told how a boy on Franny's[2] island in Greece had killed a chicken by screwing it. Bill wouldn't believe this. "I wouldn't die if I were screwed," he said. "Ah, Bill," Caskey instantly replied: "But you're no chicken."

Still grinding out the Bogotá chapter. I feel, if once I can get through that, I have a clear run ahead—at least till after Quito.

1949

February 20. Another lapse. Let's start with an attempt at a new deal. It is absolutely useless and self-destructive to get mad at Caskey about his all-night record playing. Never mind why he does it, either. I must simply take precautions and try to stay away whenever a party of this kind seems to be forming. The great problem is—where to go?

Oh dear—it's Asit with his radio, all over again. Not to mention the days at Entrada Drive just after the war.

March 1. Ramakrishna's birthday puja at Ivar Avenue. Almost all the old faces, including Webster. At first, he was a little awkward and on the defensive with me. Then we settled down into the mood of old alumni, and joked about the new building schemes—the temple is to have enlarged wings, and already the boy named Henry [Denison], who has money of his own, is paying to have a big carpentry shed put in the garden. The old place certainly has changed—with the girls all up at Santa Barbara, and the new monks—Ben, John [Schenkel],

---

[1] Pedro Armendariz (1912–1963), Mexican film star.
[2] Francis Turville-Petre; see Glossary.

Kenny [Critchfield] and Henry. George has become more of a privileged eccentric than ever. He now takes flashbulb photos throughout the puja, whenever he feels so inclined. The other worshippers hate it, but they can't do anything, because Swami permits it, so as not to hurt George's feelings. George now goes in for monster enlargements. He has found some commercial studio which will blow pictures up to billboard size. Swami still keeps a room in the other house—the one behind 1946—which he says is for me. It rather scares me—the way he waits. Shall I ever find myself back there? It seems impossible—and yet—

While he was in Arizona the other day, staying with Mrs. Maury, Swami was taken to Taliesin West, and met Frank Lloyd Wright. Swami, who had never heard of Wright—and whose ideas of architecture were previously limited to domes and lots of gold—was greatly impressed. "Mr. Wright," he said, "you are not an architect— you are a philosopher." And he added that, at Taliesin, you felt yourself "not in a house, but protected by nature." Needless to say, Wright was enchanted. And I've no doubt that he will end up doing something at Santa Barbara.

Web wants to become a probation officer. I said I thought he'd make a very good one.

A party at the Manns'. A Franco-Russian named Sasha[1] sang songs with a guitar. The French songs were treated with the greatest respect. But Erika urged him on to sing "Ein kleiner Gardeoffizier," just to sneer at it. It was very ugly and tasteless—this silly hate against their own old world. And, actually, these songs—which admittedly are trash—were written mostly by Jewish refugees. As for myself—I don't give a damn—they moved me to tears. Because of what they brought back with them—the *dielen*[2] and the boys I used to know, and the Berlin streets. When we arrived at the party, Erika took me aside and told me: "Christopher—I want you to know—I *love* the Germans." I don't know what she meant by this. She doesn't.

Later, Caskey and I took Peter Watson to the Gala, because it was such a haunt of Denny's. It was almost empty, and very sad.

From the local paper: "In Santa Monica Canyon" by Nell Jones.

> One stands a long while looking
> At the curve of the canyon rim,
> The exquisite contour of the canyon
> With a growing awareness of Him.

---

[1] Possibly Sasha Pitoeff, a member of the theatrical family.
[2] Evidently slang for music halls or dance floors.

Our Creator was careful of hand.
Take freely of the miracle set,
The varied trees, green clad slopes,
Chaparral and the wild violet.

Oh live here with your eternal self,
Emerge not from the wonder of it,
Walk these roads that you know and love
Gathering beauty bit by bit!

March 2. Trying to get started with chapter ten—there'll be this one and another on the Argentine, and then some sort of epilogue; and it all has to be finished by April 15. Also, I have to get on with the translation of Patanjali. Swami's way ahead of me.

Caskey painted the bathroom floor, and finished *Light in August.* I'm reading Elizabeth Bowen's *The Heat of the Day.* Quite exciting—and some good characters. But I hate her little bits of fancy writing, such as: ". . . away on the mound each ilex stained with a little night of its own the after-death shining of the day."

Went shopping with Jimmy [Charlton], who is away from work with a bad cold. We got a ticket for jaywalking. I think Jimmy is beginning to feel the strain of sharing an apartment with his mother.

I'm apparently under a strain too, because I keep bleeding from the rectum. Probably nothing serious—but I worry a little, as I always do. Kolisch is going to look at it if his salve doesn't work.

March 3. Paid my fine at the City Hall—two dollars. The other people who had fines to pay were all automobile drivers, and each one of them argued with the stenographer—as though she were the judge. She was very patient, but with a playful air of reproach, like the nurse in the office of a doctor who handles V.D. patients. "Well, perhaps you'll be a good boy now."

Tim Brooke and Nicky Nadeau to supper. Despite his charm, I don't really like Tim. He has a tiresome masochistic air of complaint. He is always hard up, always being badly treated. He smiles bravely under it—but Society, you are given to understand, owes him an unpayable debt. Whatever it may offer him, it can never really console him, never quite make up for the years of neglect. He showed me a newspaper clipping from an Oxford paper, dated 1933, reviewing *The Memorial* and his own book *Man Made Angry.* Tim's novel was much more favorably reviewed than mine. And the moral of course was: look how the second-rate always wins out in the end and patient merit is forgotten.

Nicky is dancing for television now. He is in coarse good health. He is a vulgar boy and I find his pose of indifference very tiresome.

And yet he's nice to have around, simply because he *doesn't* complain—although he has certainly been through some hard times.

Tim says Vernon isn't getting along at all well with Patty.

Lunch today with Eugene Exman. He hasn't changed. Cautious and prim, but shrewd. I could see he was thinking that I've coarsened. I suppose I have. To all these people, I'm a sad backslider.

Caskey went out late, and we had another mild scene about the record playing in the middle of the night. It is a most curious deadlock—arising, apparently, out of an emotional blind spot in Caskey. He absolutely cannot understand why I mind being kept awake. And I absolutely cannot understand how he can keep me awake, even if he doesn't understand why. However, I freely admit that I am kept awake by a kind of obstinacy—just as it is obstinacy which makes him play the records.

Oh, if only he could find something he really wanted to do! Yet no one could complain he is idle. Today he painted the front porch.

Tim and Nicky warmly praised his pictures and photographs. This pleased him.

May 22. I turn to this book after another too-long lapse. Perhaps it will help.

I'm in a strange condition—highly toxic, I feel—and really verging on some kind of a nervous breakdown. Only I probably won't break down as long as I keep hold of some threads of reason. The depressing thing about my state of mind is that it so closely resembles the mood of 1940, in which I was bubbling with resentment against Vernon. Now Caskey is the victim. And, of course, I have built up a *rational* case against him as well-documented as the prosecution's case in the Nuremberg Trials. He is lazy. He won't earn money. He won't even try to draw his pension. He stays out late. He is cold, bitchy, selfish, etc. etc. I rehearse bits of this great accusation as I lie in bed in the morning, until it seems as if my thoughts would wake him up, they are so loud. Sometimes, I actually tell him what I am thinking—but I never do this in the right way: either I'm cold and spiteful, or I shout and thump my fist. I don't think it makes much impression.

Now, it is absolutely essential that this state of affairs shall *stop*. And the only question is: how?

Well—there are two alternatives: either I leave Caskey, or I don't.

Leaving Caskey—quite aside from being terribly painful—wouldn't really solve anything. Unless there were someone else to go to—which there isn't. Or unless I were prepared to return to Ivar Avenue—which I'm not.

Therefore we have to stay together.

Now, this much is clear: staying together means accepting Caskey *exactly as he is.* I *must* remember this. I must renounce *all* attempts to change Caskey's attitude, behavior or habits. I must accept him, and thereby renounce my whole possessive attitude towards him.

This does *not* mean that I shouldn't give my honest opinion and advice—if asked.

And it doesn't mean that I shouldn't insist on a few simple rules— like the business of making a noise at night. That's all right, because it's no more than anybody would ask, even in the most casually polite relationship.

I *must* stop trying to subdue Caskey, to shame him, to make him feel guilty.

Oh dear—is this possible?

It is not possible if it's done as an act. It is not possible if you are all the time watching to see the effect of your new technique on Caskey. It *is* possible if you build up your inner life of prayer, meditation, artistic creation, physical exercise and routine, and simply let Caskey do as he pleases—always welcoming any advance on his part.

Well—go ahead. You have plenty of work: your novel,[1] the story with Samuels.[2] Take it easy. Don't get tense.

July 26. Today I went to Ivar Avenue, to attend Sister's funeral—or rather, the part of it, the little ceremony, which took place up at the temple.

Sister died last week—Saturday [the] 23rd, I think it was. In Santa Barbara.

I was up to see her there on the 20th. I drove up for lunch. She had had pneumonia then, and an attack of uremia, but she seemed better that day. The dark plum-colored rash which had broken out in several places on her body was clearing. She apologized for it, with her usual courtesy. She didn't want me to touch her hand, which was smeared with salve. She knew me as soon as I came into the room. "It's so nice to see old friends," she said. But she drowsed off again. Amiya and Swami told me that, much of the time, she thought she was in Honolulu. However, she really seemed better, and I somehow felt she'd recover. (Swami told me that she was able to urinate after he gave her a drop of Ganges water.) We were all quite cheerful; and I sang those silly songs I wrote while I was living at Ivar Avenue— about Ramakrishna, and Jesus and the turkey, and "Never smoke before the Swami"—and George (who's now called Krishna, since

---

[1] *The School of Tragedy,* later *The World in the Evening.*
[2] *The Easiest Thing in the World.*

he took the brahmacharya vow) made me record them on his machine.

Then, as I say, on Saturday, Kenny (whom I've become fond of—I hardly know why) called to say that Sister had died, quite painlessly, in her sleep.

Today was a hot morning and I arrived at the temple in a bad mood. I'd been horrible and unkind to Caskey before I left the house, because I'm worried about our money and I keep feeling he ought to help us earn some more. (Which is true, in a way, but no reason for being unpleasant.) There was the usual atmosphere of pre-puja fuss. All kinds of people arriving with flowers, and women in various degrees of elegant mourning. Swami sat on the sofa. You couldn't exactly say his face looked tragic. But the brightness had left it, and today it was almost frighteningly austere. The eyebrows drawn down at the corners. He seemed impersonal and forbidding, like a thundercloud. He took my arm and led me into his room, where he told me about Sister's death. Just before it happened, Swami found himself "in a high spiritual mood," and then they called him in, and at that moment the breath left her body with a faint puff, through the lips.

"She was a saint," Swami said. He believes she passed into samadhi. He told us how, latterly, she had told him that she never left the shrine room until she had seen "a light." She thought this quite normal. She supposed everybody saw it.

Sudhira came to the ceremony—grey haired now, but still with her pale sad slap-happy beauty. An almost legendary figure, whom we embraced like a visitor from the dead. She is living in Long Beach with her husband, and has been doing surgical nursing. And then there was Web, fat and thirtyish looking, with his homely wife. And Tito [Renaldo] in his neat blue jacket with gold buttons and his clean slacks, and Bill Forthman—neither of them emotionally involved; they had scarcely known Sister at all. And Aldous, whom I had lunch with, later.

August 17. Something stopped me from continuing my account of Sister's funeral, and now I have forgotten the details, but the point is that I came away from it in a calm, happy "open" mood which lasted for several days—and I felt a real horror of my unkindness to Caskey—or of any unkindness to anyone.

And so things were better for a while; but then came another bad patch, which we have just passed through. Catherine, Caskey's mother, left three days ago, and Caskey says that his drinking and neurotic laziness were largely due to her being here. She is a bright, chattery little lady, genuinely kind and helpful, but terribly wrong for Caskey because she is determined to regard him as the model son, no matter what he does. I think—in taking this attitude—she is somehow trying to spite her ex-husband, whom she has never forgiven, and is probably still in love with. Her obviously excessive (and insincere) praises make poor Caskey quite frantic with guilt. He says that he has never had enough discipline in his life. He wants to be loved and yet criticized. Oh—it's very difficult; but obviously we are in this together and I must keep trying. All that stuff I wrote about leaving him is beside the point. I can't. I must not. At least not now. The day may come when I ought to. I don't know. I certainly don't want to.

Lesser [Samuels] and I have practically finished the movie story. Shall we sell it? How shall I manage if we don't? Will Mrs. Strasberg[1] let us have the house for another year? All these questions will be decided in September—the month of decisions.

The great thing, at the moment, is to restart my novel. "Stephen Monkhouse" has got to be me—not some synthetic Anglo-American. The few circumstances can so easily be imagined—his ex-wife, his Quaker background, etc. But it must be written out of the middle of *my* consciousness.

Prayer, meditation, thought, creation, are the *only* refuge and stronghold. Without them, I am nothing. Without them, life is really an agony. And I say this with absolute authority, because, at the moment, my life is, by all external standards, extraordinarily fortunate and pleasant. I'm blessed with great graces—independence, constant occupation in work I have chosen, a home, a companion, wonderful friends, a teacher who is a saint. Who has more—or as much? Oh, for shame! How dare I fail, or complain, or waste a single instant of these beautiful days? I must try to keep this diary. It is an act of sanity.

August 18. Visit last night to the Down-Beat Café on Central Avenue, with Bernie Hamilton[2] and his girl friend Maxine. The sax player, a colored boy of about eighteen, sweating, with eyes closed and an expression of great suffering—the agony of self-explanation by means of blasts and toots. He was blowing his whole personality out through the instrument. It was a language—and sometimes you felt his triumph at having stated something *exactly* as he wished to state it. He was obviously full of marijuana. The two handsome white boys did not presume to interrupt with their clarinets—they regarded him with respect, and the audience with a certain scorn. The bass player

[1] The owner of 333 East Rustic Road.
[2] A black acquaintance.

peeped at us round his great engine like a squirrel. The drummer never tired. The piano player flickered his thin stiff fingers over the keys, without paying the least attention to anybody. When the sax player wasn't playing, he kept opening and shutting his mouth like a fish gasping for air—as though he could only breathe music.

Extraordinary difficulty in restarting my novel. The problem of the opening sentence.

November 8. Initiation Day—the day Swami gave me my mantram, in 1940, the day I became an American citizen, in 1946. (Today I did my duty in the latter capacity, by voting on our twelve state propositions.)

I *must*, I *will* keep up this diary—no matter what shames and failures I have to report. This summer has been really disgraceful. I don't think I can ever remember having been so idle, dull, resentful and unhappy. The novel is barely at page eighteen, creeping along against frightful resistance. My life with Bill has reached such a point of emotional bankruptcy that he is leaving, by mutual consent, in a day or two, to hitchhike to Florida to see his sister. Will this solve anything? It didn't with Vernon. Well, anyhow, we have to try it.

I feel sick, stupid, middle-aged, impotent. I have just got to make an effort, and not wail and weep. I bore myself beyond tears. Work, work—what else means anything? But work is all emptiness if I can't get back the sense of direction.

It is an untellable boredom, even writing this down; but I must do it. I must take my boredom and impotence and cram myself full of them until I gag and vomit up all this poison.

Jobs—to write something about Klaus Mann, for the memorial volume;[1] to write an article for Gerald, about Vedanta and Christianity;[2] to write an article about Santa Monica Canyon, for John Lehmann.[3]

And get on with Patanjali.

And my novel.

And see if any kind of a job, preferably short, can be obtained.

Now then, let's see you make the effort.

November 15. Bill left on Friday last, the 11th, and thank God for that. It certainly is a relief having him away—but I'm still messing— accomplishing very little. This amazing hot spell has something to do with it. And my throat is very bad, sometimes I can hardly swallow.

---

[1] Mann had committed suicide in May; see Glossary.

[2] Probably for the Vedanta Society magazine, but never written.

[3] "California Story" (1951), given not to Lehmann but to *Harper's Bazaar* and later reprinted in *Exhumations* as "The Shore."

I'm already tired of wasting money in restaurants, making infinitely cautious overtures to prospective affairs, etc.

Well—that's all there is to confess, but I can only repeat that I have got to snap out of it. Let's try again.

November 18. No smokes at all since the night before yesterday. Somewhat dumb and dazed. I only want to sleep—although I slept nearly ten hours at Jimmy [Charlton]'s, last night: it was so wonderfully peaceful, we just dozed off after supper and only woke long enough at 3:00 a.m. to get into bed. This morning, the noise of the dredger, which had been going all night—lighted up like a cocktail party—reminded me of how it is on board ship, when you wake and hear the engines and know that no time has been wasted; they've been working for you while you were unconscious.

Thoughts about Bill still resentful—with a kind of wondering horror: how did I ever stand it? The great thing, now, is to relax. Sure, I have endless chores awaiting me—but don't worry too much. See how they work out, but your health comes first. You've got to get that battered old engine running again. Last night, my throat was closed, it seemed, to an aperture the size of a pinhole.

Woke, a few mornings ago, murmuring: "Into each drain some wife must fall."

Jim—his foxy nose, his pale washed-out stiffly ironed army pants, his skivvy shirts, his bright pretty socks, his old blue sneakers, his lonely air when he is opening a can, like a prospector out in the desert. He is one of the Dog People. Sometimes he smells very strongly of Airedale terrier. His large smooth body, clumsy, boyish, with very small buttocks and big rather weary shoulders. He has the weary face of a young officer—a boy prematurely saddled with responsibility. When women are around, he puts on a knitted wool tie and laughs with his front teeth. He grunts in the morning—surly. But likes it when I say, "You old cow" or, "Okay, Miss Nosey." The Dog People share this quality with real dogs—you mustn't kid yourself that their devotion is personal. If you go away and someone else feeds them for a month—well—that's all the same. And, after all, why not? The vanity of loving a Dog Person is expressed by Cocteau's remark about Radiguet—"Le ciel de mes mains te protège."[1] That's sheer megalomania, and deserves the punishment it will receive. I know so *exactly* how it would feel to be a father.

[1] "The heaven of my hands protects you." The French novelist and poet Raymond Radiguet, Cocteau's lover, died at twenty.

November 22. Getting ready for this party.[1] I've invited far too many people and God knows how they'll all fit into the house. Well—Leif [Argo] and David [Robertson] will help out. Sixth day of disintoxication. It is nearly impossible to write anything—that's the hardest part—but otherwise I feel wonderful. I'm only scared because I have to meet a deadline for the magazine[2] and for the piece on Klaus. Oh dear—

It's shameful and petty to have to confess it—but I despise Jim just the least bit for his behavior the other evening. Anyhow, I despise his self-pity over it. Also, he looks so silly, all banged up.[3] But that's unkind, and I must be very careful not to show it.

Sometimes I feel I've gotten myself into a position vis-à-vis the younger generation, where they are always saying, "You show *me*"—well, I'm tired of showing them.

He was guilty of conduct befitting an old auntie.

Names—Waldo Angelo, Hank Burczinsky, Hanns Hagenbuehler, Nicky Nadeau, Victor Rueda, Leif Argo, Russ Zeininger, Ted Baccardi,[4] Amos Shepherd. American names.

Question of the hour: how to stop sex murders. Suggestions: arrest everybody and keep them in jail for life. Isolate all children on islands until the age of eighteen.

December 6. 8:20 a.m., and a fine morning. What are we going to do with it?

I feel a bit stale, because I woke and got up at 5:00, not being able to sleep after drinking last night with Tito. Now that he has left Trabuco, Tito feels sad and lost between two worlds. He sits in his horrid *moderne* little apartment, waiting for the call to work at the studio, and drinking [. . .]. Soon he'll start having sex again, then asthma. Poor kid. He clings to me, as the only person who can understand the particular kind of mess he's in. But I can't really help him.

When I got up it was dark, of course, with the peculiar dead darkness of the late night. I came down into the kitchen and there were more ants: I doggedly destroyed them with the Flit gun, and then made myself a too-large plate of scrambled eggs, thinking how

[1] For Britten and Pears, on tour in America.
[2] Of the Vedanta Society.
[3] On November 18 or 19, Charlton brought three or four men to Isherwood's house for a drink and got into a fight with one of them. Charlton deliberately allowed the man to bloody his face because, as he later told Isherwood, the fight might have attracted the police if he had tried to defend himself.
[4] Don Bachardy's older brother; Isherwood did not yet know the correct spelling.

that nursery jingle, "Poached eggs on toast are very nice / If you try them once you'll want them twice," makes me feel horribly sad. Because it is such a terribly limited objective. You hear a cheery little voice saying it—a voice which takes no account of the atom bomb, the Sermon on the Mount or Beethoven's C-sharp minor Quartet. The false snugness of the tiny nursery pleasures; and all around, the howling wilderness of life. The utter brutality of those cops, the night before last, and my guilt that I didn't handle them properly—wasn't wonderful and poised and mature. I ought to have called their bluff, insisted on being locked up, hired a lawyer, taken the case to the Supreme Court, started a nationwide stink.[1] Why didn't I? Because I'm cowardly, slack, weak, compromised. My life at present is such a mess.

Well—that's not too important.

But my novel—that's sitting in front of me again, undented, unformed—like some rubbery bit of material which pops back into shapelessness the minute you take your hands from it. The approach I've been trying is no good. I simply cannot believe in Stephen Monkhouse, or any other fictitious character, as the narrator. I can't narrate this myself. And so I'm driven to the conclusion—I discussed it with Dodie on Sunday—that the novel must be written in the style of *The Memorial*: third person, and viewing the action from inside one or other of the characters—Stephen, Sarah, Gerda and the doctor, probably.

This method would have certain great advantages. Stephen's complicated past could be told by him to Gerda. The way I have it now, with Stephen as narrator, there is a certain false unpleasant coquetry about his withholding this information from the reader as long as he does. Also, the doctor's point of view could be expressed so much better from inside the doctor. And Gerda's and Sarah's too, for that matter. Also, Stephen has to be much more violent, more unhappy, more confused, in the beginning. As long as he was the narrator, you got that emotion-recollected-in-tranquillity tone, which took the sting out of everything.

The only *loss*, as I see it, is that we can't have an epilogue or bridge passage connecting the whole narrative with the present day.

December 13. Stuck. I can't get the right technique for writing this book. Stephen can't narrate, and yet, if he doesn't, I can't say half the things I want to. I don't know—

---

[1] During the raid at the Variety on December 4, Isherwood and Charlton were questioned at the Santa Monica police station. Both denied being homosexual, and they were released.

Helen [Kennedy]'s story of the rattlesnake that got into the boat. The fishermen dove into the water, lost all their equipment. The rattler rode to the shore, driven by the outboard engine, disembarked and disappeared into the woods.

December 14. I think there is no doubt about it, I'm going through the "change of life." Gerald Heard put that idea into my head the other day, and I take it on as a sort of reassurance—for I'm really alarmed at the state I'm in. (This despite what I told Gerald: that one of the chief benefits that remain to me from the Ivar Avenue days is that I have learned *not* to be alarmed by any mental symptoms, however violent and odd.)

Certainly, my mind is softening, weakening. I have so little coordination that I putter around like a dotard. I'll go upstairs to find a book, forget all about it, pick up something else, start to bring it downstairs, leave it in the kitchen and then hunt for it for hours.

Then there is this constant sexual itch, which never seems to be satisfied—or very seldom—because it is accompanied by a certain degree of impotence. And there is a hyper-tension, worse, I think, than I have ever experienced.

And so I fail to write. I put it off and put it off, and I do nothing about getting a job, and I drift toward complete pauperism, with nothing in sight. I am lazy and dreamy and lecherous. I hate being alone. I don't exactly want Billy back—at least, I certainly don't want him the way he was when he left. And I am fundamentally unserious in my approach to other people. I don't believe in myself or my future, and all my "reputation" is just a delayed-action mechanism which only impresses the very young.

Well—there is only one answer to all this. I've repeated it a thousand times already, and I'll repeat it till I die: just keep right on trying and struggling. The situation is very bad but not hopeless. After all, you *did* get that thing about Klaus Mann written. That was something. Don't be scared.

1950

January 2. Some ideas for stories:

A dope addict is nursed devotedly by a younger man, a character of great warmth, innocence, sweetness. The dope addict dies. A third person, who is in love with the young man and hates the dope addict as an evil influence, is delighted, thinks, "Now he won't be able to do any more harm to anyone." But the young man, going through the dope addict's belongings, finds a small packet of heroin. This starts him off. He becomes an addict.[1]

Relationship between a middle-aged, "established" writer and a very young writer, still unpublished. The middle-aged writer is going through a period of complete impotence, but the young one doesn't know this. He is tremendously impressed by the older man and quite overwhelmed when the latter asks him to stay. Every morning, the young man sits down joyfully in the living room, thinking, "We are working under the same roof," and writes as never before, in a fever of inspiration. Meanwhile, the older man goes up to his study and stays there all day, pretending to work. Does the young man unconsciously "cure" him? Perhaps.[2]

The Strongheart story—the very mean dog who is trained, given a wonderful disposition, so that it turns into a canine saint and finally dies trying to understand and mutate.[3]

January 3. Now, after months of pushing and pulling, this way and that, I must try to discover just what *is* wrong with my novel and why I can't write it.

What elements do I have?

There is Stephen, with his past marriages, his terrible resentment against Jane. The "plot" of his development is simply that he comes to accept the failure of his marriage with Jane and to see that this was largely his own fault.

Why was it his fault?

Because he is a split personality. He's torn between his Quaker background and the urge toward "bohemianism"; the misery of dilettantism keeps him in a perpetual state of guilt. He is chronically guilty. That's his innermost meaning as a character: he is the embodiment of guilt, impotent guilt.

How does he get over this?

By understanding the lives of those who aren't guilty—Sarah, Gerda, Dr. Kennedy and the best of the refugees.

His story ends with a decision—to do something. Something antidramatic. I'm not sure what this is, but I can explain, in general, what I mean. For instance, if it's pacifism, the temptation would be to refuse to register for the draft and to go to prison. The antidramatic decision would be to go to a CPS camp.

---

[1] Based on the relationship between Denny Fouts and Tony Watson-Gandy.
[2] Based on Isherwood's friendship with Michael Leopold.
[3] Based on Strongheart (the film dog) and Gerald Heard's theories of psychological evolution.

Well now—that's a perfectly good progression for a novel. Why am I stuck in it?

Because I can't make up my mind how the story should be told.

Should it be told by Stephen in the first person?

Perhaps yes. But there are difficulties.

If in the first person, what is the viewpoint in time? Is Stephen telling us all this from the viewpoint of 1950, looking back to 1941? If so, I fear the necessarily indulgent tone, the wise smile over the mistakes of the past.

Is Stephen telling us this from day to day—i.e. in a diary? This seems too contrived. Why should he be taking all this trouble to present his experiences, to make them into an aesthetic performance, if he is really suffering?

But suppose Stephen is in the third person? What do we lose? Some sense of immediacy. Yes. But we gain advantages.

What matters so supremely is the *style* of the narration. Somehow, I see, or hear, a very simple tone of voice. Something inside me keeps saying *Candide*. I hardly know what I mean by this. Maybe just that it has to be straightforward. When we look inside Stephen's head, the thoughts we overhear must be very direct, immediate and, in a sense, naive. When I want him to be articulate, analytical, he must express himself in conversation. Ditto when he tells anything about the past. But when we're listening to his mind, we should really only get his *feelings*. Very important, this.

January 5. [Wallace] Bobo took Howard [Kelley] a sweater to wear in jail.[1] Howard spent a whole afternoon, with another prisoner, cleaning it by picking off hairs from the three cats. Howard was able to identify each separate hair. They put them into three separate piles and put each into a separate matchbox.

January 23. Aldous says: "Cynicism is contrition without repentance."

A lady in the stationer's this morning, buying a box of pale blue notepaper with a white border: "I know I've enjoyed mine, and it makes such a nice little present."

Salka's story of E. von M.[2] When E. was married to the actor R.F.,[3] she started taking a lot of heroin. R.F. in despair, called Salka—

---

[1] Kelley was arrested for indecent exposure in a round-up of gay nude swimmers on the Riviera Beach near Point Dume.

[2] Eleonora von Mendelssohn, a German actress in Max Reinhart's ensemble; her brother, Francesco von Mendelssohn, was a Viertel family friend.

[3] Rudolf Forster.

wouldn't she come around to the Garden of Allah, where they were staying, and persuade E. to enter a nursing home to be cured? When Salka arrived, E. was in the kitchen, doped up to the eyes, preparing borscht soup. She was putting everything into it—including whole steaks. She wore a wonderful lace dress, enormously valuable. Salka set the table, and E. swept in, carrying the soup in a tureen. Just before she reached the table, she stumbled, spilled all of the soup on to the floor, swept the train of her dress through it, and set down the empty tureen, quite unconscious that anything was wrong. To humor her, Salka and R.F. pretended to ladle out and eat the soup. Then E. fell under the table. But before they could call an ambulance, she had revived again, taken another shot, and was as lively as a monkey. She refused absolutely to leave.

Bill Harris had two great-uncles named Reservéd and Resolvéd. They made garden furniture. Never married.

A neighbor of Iris Tree brought her the manuscript of his novel, very big.

"What is it about, Mr. Jones?" Iris asked.

"Germany."

"But—have you ever been to Germany?"

"Oh no. Germany has always interested me, though."

Irish never read it. Months later, Mr. Jones appeared: "How did you like my novel?"

"Well," said Iris, desperately, eyeing the bulky manuscript. "I think—yes—I think it needs condensing."

Mr. Jones went off, apparently satisfied. Some time after this, Iris met him in the street. Guilt prompted her to ask: "How's your novel, Mr. Jones?"

"Oh," said Mr. Jones, very casually, "I sold that one to the movies. Now I'm working on another."

April 24. Three or four weeks ago, I hit upon what I believe is the correct method of narration for *The School of Tragedy*. It is a kind of unwritten or mental diary—that is, a diary without dates, and without asides such as, "I am writing this in the garden before breakfast," etc. Instantaneous reportage of thought is allowed—I mean, I can say just what I am feeling, thinking, observing at that very moment, *provided* I *could*, conceivably, have a pen in my hand. So, for example, I can report what I'm thinking on a plane or in bed, but *not* what I'm thinking on a motorcycle or during a sex act.

Time lapses will be marked by new sections, but not dated.

I am allowed to say: "Yesterday morning, I went to see J. . . . ." *or* "I walk into the house without knocking. J. is sitting as usual before the fire . . ." *or* "Tomorrow, as usual, I shall go down to J.'s house . . ." *or* "At J.'s house last night. Talk, as usual, about K. and L. . . ."

John Huston's story of Hemingway out in a boat off the coast of Cuba. They saw an iguana on the rocks by the shore. Hemingway fired and hit it. It was wounded. When they got on shore, they found a trail of blood, but no iguana. Hemingway, although tired and sick, spent four hours hunting for it, among the rocks, in the blazing sun, because he said it was unsportsmanlike to leave wounded game to die. Finally, he found it.

Hemingway is proud of his son's marksmanship. He wouldn't let his son take part in a shooting match in Sun Valley, because there were two contestants who were very good, and he feared his son might lose.

James Joyce, says Aldous, hated flowers, liked only white wine, cared only for operas which had tenor parts with very high notes (being himself a singer). He delighted in fantastically far-fetched medieval etymology. For example, he explained to Aldous that Odysseus is derived from οὐδείς and Zeus—God and nothing.[1]

May 13. Thirteenth anniversary of Heinz's arrest—or rather, of our parting, in Luxembourg.[2]

Overheard on beach: "Do you know the sequel to *My Foolish Heart? My Silly Liver.*"[3]

June 29. "From now on, I'll try to write every day. It will be a discipline—and these messages from the doomed ship may even be of some value, to somebody, later."

It's nearly twelve years since I wrote those words, on August 20, 1938. And again I find myself having to declare my own private State of Emergency in order to be able to adjust to this Korean crisis.[4]

The Los Angeles Times this morning carries an obviously press-agented account of how the veteran diva, General MacArthur, flew to the South Korean war front in an unarmed transport. "The general summoned the newsmen to his office and told them his plans secretly last night. He said he did not know the war situation clearly and wanted a personal glimpse. Talking seriously and eagerly, he said the trip might be risky. 'It will be an unarmed plane and we are not sure of

---

[1] In fact, οὐδείς means no one.

[2] In *Christopher and His Kind*, Isherwood explains they parted May 12 and Heinz was arrested May 13.

[3] The film *My Foolish Heart*, adapted from J. D. Salinger's story "Uncle Wiggily in Connecticut," premiered in 1949 and launched a popular song of the same title.

[4] North Korea invaded South Korea on June 25, the start of the Korean War.

getting fighter cover, not sure where we will land.' He added: 'If you are not at the airport I will know you have other commitments.' One correspondent said, 'There's no doubt we'll be there.' MacArthur grinned and replied, 'I have no doubt of your courage. I just wanted to give your judgment a chance to work.' "

The great effort I must make is to realize that this fighting is actually taking place, that people are being killed, that the fighting may spread into a general war, that many people I know, including Bill [Caskey], may be drafted,[1] even that Los Angeles and other cities may be bombed—perhaps with atom bombs. It is very hard to realize the horror of all this—precisely because I have already spent most of one war right here in this city and so the prospect seems deceptively familiar and scarcely more than depressing. The danger of taking the war unseriously is a truly hideous spiritual danger. If I give way to it, I shall relapse into the smugness of the middle aged, who have nothing much to fear because they won't be drafted, or the animal imbecility of queens who look forward to an increase in the number of sailors around town.

To see Jo and Ben Masselink this morning. Both are worried, because now it seems that Washington will have to send troops to Korea as well as guns and planes, and they rightly see this as an added risk. Told Ben how much I liked his travel-book manuscript, which delighted Jo; she embraced me several times. In this time of anxiety, one sees how motherly she is. Her baby may be taken away from her. And this is really heartbreaking, because they so deserve to be happy. They have built up such a charming yet modest life together. Jo is so industrious, and clever, making swimming suits for her customers. Ben works so hard at his writing. They are gay and bright eyed and grateful for every instant of pleasure, and yet they demand so little in order to enjoy it.

With their example, I ought to be unfailingly kind and thoughtful in my dealings with Billy. How can I ever be otherwise? Especially at a time like this.

Talked to John van Druten on the phone. He's enthusiastic about the writings of Vivekananda.

A copy of Gandhi's letters arrived this morning from the publisher. Smog early, but it's sunny now.

Another day is going to be wasted. I have to review Lowell Naeve's *A Field of Broken Stones*. And get on with my novel.

Evelyn Caldwell came by for a drink. Both Jim [Charlton] and Bill liked her; in fact everybody liked everybody. Later we had supper

---

[1] Caskey had returned to California in April; his "blue discharge" from the navy (neither honorable nor dishonorable) made it unlikely he would be drafted.

with Bill Kennedy at Holiday House—Neutra-by-the-sea.[1] Both got drunk—Kennedy isn't allowed to—and Bill [Caskey] denounced Kennedy for belonging to the entrepreneur class, staying at the Miramar, etc. We parted late.

June 30. Troops have been sent to Korea.

Failure to finish the Naeve review. Acute spinal headache and angst-gut ache. Drove to Malibu pier with Kennedy in the afternoon. Long talk about Billy's accusations. Kennedy had been much hurt, had even considered leaving this morning. He is full of guilt and self-depreciation and takes us all far too seriously. Billy doesn't like him. I don't feel much either way. But his proposals for me to work on the magazine *Tomorrow* may open a way out of this whole movie mess into a more serious literary life.

Party at Salka's for two Peruvian dancers and a guitarist—Yma Sumac, her husband and a cousin. Their bird cries and slight, arresting, mock serious gestures. As a group, they were incredibly beautiful. The slant-eyed Yma and her cousin, balancing so lightly on their little feet, and uttering sudden wails of mimic despair. And the boy behind them, very close, and thrusting forward with his guitar; so that they seemed to be continually advancing upon us with the compactness and drive of a little military formation. The boy had a soft waxy skin and wet-black eyes that had the quality of introversion; they didn't bulge or roll. The dances had an airy uncanny birdlike authority: you got the feeling of the uncanny jungle and the discontinuous, abrupt movements of the birds. And also the sense of tradition. They appeared to listen for it, pick it up like a wavelength and then relay it, quite impersonally, without comment.

Chaplin, Oona, Iris Tree in a converted sari, Friedrich Ledebur with a bored, tennis-playing maharajah, Hedy Lamarr very pretty and ungrand, John Huston, Ivan Moffat serious, or rather poker-faced, appalled by all the imitations he would have to give, Natasha[2] verging on insanity, very beautiful, John Houseman, Ella Winter[3] etc. etc. etc.

I have written all this and said nothing, really. But I must go on writing this record. Things will emerge.

July 7. Missed some days. Never mind. All that has happened so far is still preliminary—the Yanks falling back, and more and more North

---

[1] Influenced by the work of Austrian emigré architect Richard Neutra.

[2] Natasha Sorokin, Moffat's wife; see Glossary under Moffat.

[3] Author and translator, widow of journalist Lincoln Steffens (1866–1936) and afterwards wife of playwright and screenwriter Donald Ogden Stewart.

Korean troops (which may include lots of Chinese and some Russians) being poured into the battle.

What matters is that I should work, constantly, every instant. There is so endlessly much to do. For instance:

The novel. Get on with it—never mind how, as long as I make a draft.

This reviewing for *Tomorrow*. Choose a book. Start thinking what you'll say about it.

Patanjali. More aphorisms for the next number of the magazine.

And then there's the question of working with Frank Taylor and/ or [Howard] Griffin on either *The Journeying Boy* or *The Vacant Room*.

Come on, now. Let's see what you're made of.

July 9. Yesterday, Billy and I drove to Sequoia with Igor and Vera Stravinsky and Bob Craft. Igor doesn't think there'll be World War III, but an indefinitely prolonged border struggle between the two empires. Bob is worried because he's still draft age—but he's a vet, so won't be called right now.

On the way across the San Fernando Valley I had some valuable ideas for my novel—probably because Igor was in deep meditation on his opera.[1]

I described how, when you approach Sequoia, everything seems out of proportion, because surrounded by little trees, you look up and see huge trees on the skyline, thousands of feet above. Igor said: "Just like Shostakovich in the Hollywood Bowl." When he saw the General Sherman tree, he said, "That's very serious."

We ate on the side of the path leading to Moro Rock. Plodding climbers covered us with dust. Igor said that Derain had told him that a mountain is the most difficult object, technically, to paint.

Bob felt wonderful, because the air was so dry, and drove all the way home.

Igor has a huge appetite and suffers if meals are late. He has a very trim well-knit figure, due to exercising.

Moro Rock was terrific, and the view was clear. Unlike that time, five years ago, when Bill danced about all over it in the fog and refused to believe there was a precipice below. Before leaving, we drove down into King's Canyon which I've never seen before. It's one of the best I've seen, anywhere.

Home at 2:00 a.m.—quite silly with exhaustion.

This kind of naked mountain scenery makes you see the earth in relation to other planets, as a planet. There is no disguise. No cozy illusion that this particular planet is "the world." This is the naked

[1] *The Rake's Progress.*

geological, astronomical fact. The very *old* sunlight on the upper limbs of the forest. Life is seen in its unimaginable slowness.

August 5. Woke, saying: "It was a dark *wormy* morning."

August 13. Two days ago, on August 11th, Peggy Kiskadden, her little three-year-old Bull [Kiskadden] and I started at 5:00 a.m. from Los Angeles, drove via Blyth, Prescott, to Oak Creek Canyon, stayed the night with Jimmy Charlton and his friends the Kittredges, then drove on yesterday via Flagstaff, Gallup, Albuquerque and Santa Fe to stay with Georgia O'Keeffe at her house at Abiquiu. We got there late last night, and we plan to be here most of this week.

I found Jim going through a sort of monastic phase—a secular monastic phase, of course. He works every day with Bob Kittredge on the house he has designed. They are building it with their own hands—plumbing, carpentering and all. Jim lost no time in telling me that he misses nothing and nobody in Santa Monica, is perfectly happy here, and looks forward to staying through the winter. (Just the same, he was obviously very pleased to see me, and had even bought a special bottle of rum for us to drink after we went to bed at night in the house where he sleeps. The Kittredges have several houses on their property, and plan to rent them for an income.) I think the actual situation is that Jim is afraid of being upset in his new life by outside criticism. He particularly feared mine; and I believe and hope I relieved this fear to some extent by approving (quite sincerely) of his life, the Kittredges, their house, kids, animals, etc. etc. Jim is now drinking very little, having no sex, making no trips to Flagstaff, even. In the most practical and manual way he is exercising his art, leading a healthy outdoor life and gratifying his need for affection as an adopted member of the Kittredge family. This is excellent—ten million times better, certainly, than loneliness at the apartment on Santa Monica beach, evenings at bars, and no work. I have no right to feel hurt or slighted, and I really don't. I shall keep his friendship if I endorse this venture, wherever it may lead him.

Peggy was pained by the untidiness in which the Kittredges live. To get to their house you actually have to ford the stream which runs down through the canyon. There is only one bathroom, and meals are vague. Mary Kittredge, Peggy pointed out, is a typical slovenly Southerner, and, said Peggy, there is a far wider gap between New Englanders and Southerners than between New Englanders and British. As for the Kittredges, I think they liked Peggy very much. Bob Kittredge, especially, because he found that he and Peggy are distant cousins. I had told Bob how much I long to see Monument

Valley, and immediately this created a situation, because Bob wanted to close the house and leave next morning on a three-day trip. Peggy was greatly alarmed. She wanted to get on to Georgia's, she dislikes haphazard camping, she was somehow jealous of the Kittredges' Arizona as against Georgia's New Mexico. So of course I backed down. Jim wants me to go there on the way back and make the trip then. Maybe I will.

Actually, I found the Kittredges charming. They are sort of nature saints. They make long pack trips up on to the plateau above the canyon, where few white men have ever been, and there are huge mountain lions and moose and deer. (They gave us venison for dinner. Peggy heroically ate some.) They have two sons, one of them adopted, who seem unusually sweet, simple and natural, and who were extremely kind to Bull. They have the only good-natured collie and Siamese cat I have ever met. It seems that their house is really full of peace. It was built twenty years ago, by Bob Kittredge—and all the woodwork is most attractively warped and weathered; it is as easy as an old shoe. I don't care much for the location, because I hate being in a hole, and this is right at the bottom of the creek, amidst Douglas firs and yellow pines. But you can see the great ramparts of the canyon above you, golden in the evening light when the bottom of the canyon is already dark. Further down, the canyon has wonderfully architectured blood-crimson towers and organ pipes and spires.

Peggy says Bob Kittredge is the type of Easterner who was born one hundred years too late. He should have been an Indian guide; and now, though he comes out to the West and learns all about camping and hunting and wild life, he is really lost and isolated in the middle of the twentieth century.

Peggy's guilt at having been allowed to get her own way (and I see she will get nothing else throughout this trip) occupied us with the most elaborate self-justifications and generalizations during most of yesterday's drive. But I didn't really care. I was—and still am—in a fairly well-balanced mood of happiness-unhappiness. I keep thinking of the misery of the mess at Rustic Road—what in the world is to happen when I return—and of the slowly maturing war situation; and at the same time, I was happy to be out on the endless blue levels of the plateau, with the strange flat-topped truncated mesa shapes which are like ominous, primitive forts. (How ominous they must have seemed to covered wagon parties watching always for the smoke puffs which signalled the encircling Indians!)

August 15. Georgia O'Keeffe's house. The massive adobe walls—big round pine beams with cross rafters of aspen or cedar. In some rooms, old cedar has been used; it looks like bundles of firewood. The pastel colors of New Mexico—pinkish brown or grey of adobe, pale green of sage. The black modernistic chair sitting like a spider in a corner of the hot patio.

Up in the rock-littered hills—covered with piñon and weeping cedar—there are parklike clearings, great outcroppings of lichen-green rock, rolling uplands swept by a cold wind. The country is so empty that it makes you uneasy—it refuses all associations.

August 19. Reading F[ord] M[adox] Ford's *Parade's End*[1] has somehow shown me, once again, that I must not make any conditions, any plans as to my relations with Billy. Billy is a human being in trouble, and so am I. We are not Truman and Stalin, or a pair of businessmen. We cannot settle anything by bargaining. We have to live this through, with great patience, but without any of that "neither-do-I-condemn-thee" stuff. Oh, I shall never, never get out of this rut until I do that, once. The funny thing is—it's exactly the subject of my novel (which looks promising, at present).

That's enough about myself. And the war? I'll attend to the war when I get back to Santa Monica—Tuesday night is scheduled for our arrival; we leave Monday morning.

The day before yesterday, Georgia drove us up to Taos. (The cottonwoods get a disease called chlorosis which makes them turn the most breathtaking, flaming yellow.) We saw Carl van Vechten again, and his friend Saul [Mauriber] at the awful vulgar over-planted estate of his niece Duane. We saw the wonderful church at the Rancho de Taos. We saw the pueblo. We saw [Dorothy] Brett, and shrill blonde-white witchlike Frieda [Lawrence], who is very sympathetic, and Angelino [Ravagli], who is rather too sleek and suave. Also, his Latin sex act bores me. He picked Peggy up in his arms, and this excited little Bull so much that he bit her in the buttock—"the haunch," Peggy calls it.

We went up and spent the night sleeping out of doors at the Lawrence ranch. It is exactly as Lawrence described it in *St. Mawr*. Brett came up with us. I really love her, with her hearing aid and her enormous ass and absurd bandit's jacket. I said how good I always feel in the mornings, and she said, "Yes—but by the afternoon one has worried oneself into a fit." She slept in the house—the new one Angelino built, blocking out the view from the old Lawrence house behind it, from jealousy, probably. It has a very squalid atmosphere, whereas the older house seems strangely joyful. The dead bees on

[1] Isherwood was reviewing it for *Tomorrow*.

Lawrence's bed, and the yellow *santo*,[1] and the string mat Lawrence made to sit on by the fireplace. A reproduction or small copy of the awful Lawrence painting Frieda has down in her house—the great tortured German frau dragging a factory after her by a harness of ropes, and straining up towards a bearded Lawrence figure, who is rolling his eyes with horror and apparently fighting off another frau with a sword, maybe, or a radioactive rolling pin. All of these Lawrence paintings are surprisingly dirty. Brett says she and Lawrence did all the work, while Frieda lay on the bed smoking cigarettes. But you can't believe a word these women disciples say of each other.

(I like some of Brett's Indian paintings, though. The portraits of Stokowski are absurd—rather like Van Meegeren.[2]) She had a very beautiful Union Jack, faded to rose pink, on the wall; and on the garage doors the arms of her family.

The night began cloudy, with wide lightning flashes and approaching thunder. Some drops of rain fell, nearly driving us indoors. Then the sky cleared and swarmed with stars. Peggy identified Vega and Cygnus. I recited Shakespeare to make her and Georgia go to sleep, but could think only of unsuitable murder and ghost scenes. Brett's dog began to bark and we pretended to fear the spooks had got her. Little Bull was delighted, because he was going to bed the same time as the grown-ups.

Lawrence's tomb is very amateur-dauby. Peggy was shocked because I signed the guest book. Didn't tell her that I also took two red flowers from the hillside in front of it and pressed them in my billfold for relics. Georgia went striding off through the morning woods, "walking the ditch," to keep it clear of undergrowth. Some animal had died in the tank, and the water stank badly.

Yesterday we visited Mabel Dodge Luhan—a great disappointment, after all the stories about her witchlike fiendishness, jealousy and ruthless egotism. Such a dowdy little old woman—as Peggy said, "She's reverted to Buffalo."[3] She looks like a landlady. And her house is full of the stupidest junk. It was very sad; the feeling of the old days gone—John Reed gone—Lawrence gone—and this old frump stuck with her fat Indian man, building houses and drinking whiskey in the morning. And yet the stories persist. The woman who lent Mabel a jacket. Mabel wore it all summer, then returned it. One night, the woman was out riding in the jacket, and a bullet whizzed past her. She dismounted, ran to the nearest bush, where a young Mexican, whom

[1] Saint's image, probably made of wood and painted or carved.
[2] The Dutch forger; see Glossary.
[3] Her birthplace; see Glossary.

she knew, was crouching with a gun. "Forgive me," he gasped, "I thought you were Mrs. Luhan."

When we got home again, there was a young Jewish girl, Doris Bry, just arrived from New York. She is Georgia's secretary. Pale, tall, thin, exhausted; just a trifle murderee, but nice, I think. An argument between Peggy and Georgia about the Woman's Party—Peggy being antilegislation and in favor of women getting their way *through* men. Georgia and Doris on the other side, and telling me later that of course Peggy didn't understand. She had always been so attractive and had never had to earn her living.

Peggy is much concerned with the change of life and anxious not to try to be attractive anymore. (She will, though.) She is transferring her sexual vanity to her children, as bankers transfer money from a city which may be bombed. (This is happening in New York, also with the pictures at the Met—evacuation plans are being made. And yet rents in Manhattan are actually rising, Doris tells us.) Peggy goes on and on about her children until one could scream. She oversells everything she admires. So does Georgia—that sturdy old beautiful weather-beaten cedar root. (Georgia gave me a cedar root she found at the Lawrence ranch.)

Remember how Georgia had a cat which used to catch rats and eat only the heads, leaving the other half for the kittens. So Georgia kept the half rats in the icebox till they were needed. (A good scene: two drunken people raiding the icebox. One of them nearly eats the rat.)

Georgia's feminist approach to art. She had a very handsome, much spoiled elder brother—so got the feeling, "Anything you can do, I can do as well, or better." She keeps apologizing, half humorously, for being "cruel."

Abiquiu is less than thirty miles from Los Alamos, so it might well go up in the air at any minute. Los Alamos now employs thousands of people, making Española into a boomtown. Los Alamos is referred to as "the mountain."

Stieglitz[1] was fond of insisting that the artist only needs a minimum of material for his work. A great number of his best pictures were taken within a radius of a few yards at his house on Lake George—the interior, the exterior, the view from the porch, the poplars, the clouds.

November 30. Speed Lamkin took Bill and me to dinner with Marion Davies. (Bill, actually, arrived late because he had to go down with

---

[1] The photographer Alfred Stieglitz (1864–1946) had been Georgia O'Keeffe's husband.

Lennie [Newman] to the court at Manhattan Beach, where Lennie got fined for drunk driving.)

The Hearst house is guarded by several cops. Only the servants' entrance, on Shadow Hill Drive, is open. You go in by the little office from which, Speed says, the whole Hearst empire is controlled. He adores this smell of power, in a sort of Balzacian way. With his vulgarity, snobbery and naive appetite for display, he might well become a minor Balzac of Hollywood. There is something about him I rather like, or at any rate find touching. He is so crude and vulnerable, and not malicious, I think. He reminds me of Paul Sorel, but he is much more intelligent; and he has energy and talent.

The inside of the house is heavily ornate baroque Spanish. The full-length portraits of Marion in her most famous roles. The murals in the dining room: an Eskimo woman seeing a vision at a totem pole, a Renaissance painter at work, an Asiatic prince out hunting. Gold plate on the sideboard. Six armchairs facing each other, three to three, each with ashtrays and cigarettes, as if for a game.

[Two editors from] the New York office of some Hearst publication. [The wife of one], much younger, a Catholic, an orphan raised by [wealthy benefactors in California]. She was given everything she wanted. The two men were called upstairs to see Hearst and stayed a long while. They are almost unbelievably paranoiac. Everybody is accused of being either a Jew (President Truman, Roosevelt, etc.) or a Red (Dorothy Parker, the CBS news analysts, the Hollywood producers). General MacArthur is the Galahad of their mythology. His portrait hangs in the office. [The woman], though a Catholic, approves of the Ku Klux Klan.

Marion Davies, thin, pink, raddled, with luxuriant dead-looking fair hair, very innocent blue eyes, came in drunk. One wanted to say, like a Shakespearean character: "Alack, poor lady. . . ." She stumbled a little and had to be helped to her chair; but she made a lot of sense, and talked seriously to the two men about business. Between whiles, she spoke of the stage; with Speed drinking in every word. Later, in the office, very drunk, she danced with Speed and Billy, and did the splits to "Baby, It's Cold Outside," until her nurse (who sits reading in the toilet) came to take her to bed around 3:30 a.m.

December 11. We came down here—31152 Monterey Street, South Laguna—last night. And now I'm writing this on the porch outside; partly because Bill has driven down to the lumber company to get wood for bookshelves, and I have to stay home waiting for a man to come and put in the telephone and there isn't anything else for me to do; partly because I want to signalize our move from Santa Monica and our settling here by an "act of composition," no matter how slight.

I like this house, despite its knotty pine walls, because it fits into a picture I have of the atmosphere of "Old Laguna"—the original colony of third-rate watercolorists, mild eccentrics, British expatriate ladies who ran "Scottish" tea shops, astrologers, breeders of poodles, all kinds of refugees from American city life. Also, this whole area of small houses, gardens of flowering shrubs and sheltered winter sunshine, sandy lanes winding up and down the steep hillside, takes me back to early memories of Penmaenmawr[1] and Ventnor.[2] I have an agreeable feeling of having come to the very last western edge of America, looking out over the pale bright Pacific—much cleaner than at Santa Monica—with nothing between me and Catalina but mist and a huge telephone pole.

Like all our other moves, this one takes place at a most alarming moment, under the shadow of total war, regimentation, hysteria and panic. On top of that, we have very little money and not much prospect of making any. And I'm worried, of course, about the prospects of Bill's getting drafted. Yet I have often been far more depressed with less reason. The weather is perfect. And Bill, working like a beaver on all the details of fixing this place up, is at his best—cheerful, funny and energetic. I know that he *means* to make this "a new start," though we don't discuss it much, and I'm eager to meet him three quarters of the way. Sometimes I begin to venture to say to myself that maybe we *have* passed some kind of danger point and are now on our way to better times. But that's still wishful thinking. I do know that *if* it were true, and *if* the political situation improves, and *if* we can get enough money to live on, this this might be the start of one of the happiest periods of my life.

And, let me repeat it, that so largely depends on myself. Calm, meditation, work, regular habits, study, discipline, proper exercise; the absolutely necessary regime for middle age. The past two years have been so incredibly wasteful. I've been like an engine with the belt slipping. And yet I know quite well how to employ the proper technique. (I certainly *ought* to, after impressing everybody with the clarity of my comments on Patanjali! What an old hypocrite, if I don't follow them!) The whole art of intentional living is in variety. You don't want to write your novel? Very well, do some other work, answer letters, get on with translating, read something instructive, take exercise, fix something in the garden, and fill every crack, every odd moment, with japam. Never loll and smoke and go into tense

[1] In Wales.
[2] In the Isle of Wight.

rigid daymares. Don't waste an instant on hate or anxiety. Practice Benoit's exercise of disconnecting the imagination.[1] Never bear down with your will on Billy—willing *him* to do something, to be active, just because that excuses you from guilt at your own idleness.

Anybody who can sit on this porch as you're doing right now, and work in the sunshine (hurrah, here comes the telephone man!) is luckier than ninety-nine percent of the population of the world today.

1951

March 6. This afternoon is chilly but brilliant—the ocean glittering and lazy, the big clouds piled along Catalina, Clemente and Palos Verdes visible. Bill has gone shopping in the Anglia.[2] I'm dull and wretched, so weary of my stupid aging slothful self in its alienation from God. It comes to me, again and again, how I have deteriorated into a dull-witted selfish useless creature—the most shameful failure, since I asked the way to God, was shown it, and then didn't take it. Even now (but for how much longer?) Swami stands ready to help me if I'll even raise one finger. But I won't. I won't go to live at Trabuco.

Billy drinks a lot at weekends, comes back in the middle of the night, and keeps me awake playing records. I hate him for this, hate him for refusing to take a job. But I won't help him. I'm probably bad for him, but I don't leave him.

Self-accusation is useless. There is absolutely no sense in writing all this down, and I'm really only doodling, trying somehow to induce a more lucid mood. I know exactly what I ought to be doing. I ought to make japam, go for a walk, write letters, get on with my novel. I ought. I ought. I ought. How sick I am of that word!

Good. Now do something.

April 27. Thy will be done—how often must I say it?

Every day, every hour, every moment.

What I really am trying to run away from is myself.

What I am trying to impose—under the disguise of "reasonableness"—is my own will. "Nothing burns in hell except the self,"[3] and I am miserable because the self is burning.

In the simplest, most terrible manner I am being taught that no other kind of life is possible for me. The monastery is *here*, is wherever

---

[1] A technique derived from Zen; see Glossary under Benoit.

[2] Their new car, a Ford Anglia.

[3] A slight misquotation from the *Theologia Germanica*; see Glossary under Eckhart.

I am. When Swami said: "Ramaskrishna will hound you," he wasn't kidding.

And yet, how merciful life has been to me; and how happy my life could be, if I would just give it to him! I have my duty, my *dharma*, so clearly set before me. Write, work, meditate, offer everything to him.

Leave Billy, and what'll you get? Another Billy.

I should be glad of all this agony, which only shows me that I'm at grips with my problem. Let go—can't you? Are you crazy, to torture yourself like this?

Oh Master; let me know the peace of doing your will. Help me to stop judging, criticizing, hating. Help me to know and live within your love.

Never mind how far I've fallen back from what I once seemed to know so clearly. As long as I struggle, I'll never be lost. I can start every instant. This very instant.

May 6. It is so terrible, so criminal to be unhappy, the way I'm unhappy now. Just tamas. Oh Master, deliver me from it. I just wrote and burnt a letter to Jim. It was a cry for help, and I mustn't cry for help to anyone except you.

After the last entry in this book, all sorts of people came down for the weekend, and I was cheerful and it "went" very well. But afterwards I felt—well, sort of disturbed in my inmost nest. It was hard to settle down on the eggs again. (The eggs, this week, were a rather stupid review I did of a book on Katherine Mansfield.[1])

The kind of life Billy wants to make me lead isn't hellishly wicked or degraded—it would even allow for a certain amount of work—but it isn't my kind of life.

Well, what *is* my kind of life?

I must confess, I want to be looked after. I want the background of a home. I see now how well the arrangement at Pembroke Gardens[2] suited me, during the last year or so in England (much as I complained about it). I could go out as much as I wanted to, but I had the snugness of a bedroom and breakfast. Now, I suppose I must admit that this arrangement is really almost impossible to set up again. One needs an undemanding aunt. A wife would be no good, because she'd demand all kinds of things.

What I really want is solitude in the midst of snugness.

Well, you won't get it, Mac.

Why do I dislike it here?

[1] Sylvia Berkman's *Katherine Mansfield: A Critical Study*; the review, for *Tomorrow*, was reprinted in *Exhumations*.
[2] Kathleen Isherwood's London house.

Partly because I feel no security. Maybe Bill will stay home, maybe he won't. Maybe I'll get a night's sleep, maybe Bill will come back late and play the phonograph. Maybe I can work. Maybe I can't.

I suppose I ought to accept the idea of being alone. It doesn't really terrify me as much as all that. And, of course, if Vedanta means *anything* to me at all, it should not.

But when I see myself in my daydreams of freedom, I am always traveling—alone at the rail of a boat, with my coat collar turned up. Or traveling *toward* New York, London, etc. And, of course, there's someone I meet, en route.

There is absolutely no doubt, I really *ought* to leave Bill. I am only plaguing him. And yet, somehow, to leave—just like that—as the result of a "sensible" decision—or in a towering rage; both seem wrong.

Oh Master—give me a sign. Help me. Please help me. You won't desert me. Help me now.

Two stories Eddie James told about Tallulah Bankhead.

1. Tallulah was at a party at which Peggy Kiskadden was also a guest. Tallulah and Anita Loos were wisecracking, and Peggy, feeling somewhat left out of things, turned to the man she was with and said: "Aren't they amusing?" Her tone must have sounded patronizing, for it annoyed Tallulah who turned on her and retorted: "My good woman, *we* are no more 'they' than you are!"

2. Tallulah met a young man at a party who wanted to go to bed with her. Unwilling to turn him down but feeling that maybe she'd find something better later, she gave him her latch key and said: "I have to go on to another party, darling; but you go back to my place, and if I'm not home by two o'clock, just start without me."

Eddie has what I call "a treasure-hunt complex." He contrives to leave pairs of shoes, valuable books, etc., lying around half-hidden in unlikely corners of your house—always wrapped in tissue paper. If you don't find them in time and return them, he later accuses you of stealing them. He is constantly being stolen from.

May 28. A week ago, on the 21st, I left Laguna and came here to the foundation.[1] I moved because life with Billy had become unbearable. It doesn't matter just how, or why; and it is certainly no use passing moral judgments.

I am very unhappy, of course. And the danger is that I'll waste my time flapping around in a state of feverish disturbance. Part of me is still living with Billy—and all Speed's plans for me, for my "success," are no consolation; though he's a good boy and really generous and

[1] The Huntington Hartford Foundation; see Glossary.

affectionate. It's wonderful, of course, that Johnnie [van Druten] is doing *Sally Bowles*, and that there are prospects of selling *The Vacant Room*; but I am nevertheless worried and scared. It seems as if I'm completely cold on my novel. I feel an utter lack of interest in it. But it seems quite clear that I must go on with it and try to find some solution. I will never get any place by despairing and wringing my hands. Stop flapping, old hen. Sit down on the nest and lay your eggs.

July 3. I am writing this from—of all unlikely places—room 839 of the Beverly Wilshire Hotel. Johnnie asked me to stay the night here as his guest, so we could make an early start down to Trabuco this morning. He, Starcke and I are going there for the puja and dedication of Vivekananda's statue (done by Malvina Hoffman) tomorrow.

It's just on 7:00 a.m.—grey and cold. There's a big view from my window, way out over the south part of the city to the hills. It is surprising, how many trees you can see—almost as if the town were in a wood.

Am writing this—just putting down any old thing—to test myself. Ten days ago, I gave up smoking; and now, with my actual nicotine disintoxication well advanced, I'm up against the same old problem: can I write—I mean create—without getting the jitters? I'm scared of this—because last time I quit I ran into what seemed a hopeless block—I had to get the article on Klaus Mann finished, and I just couldn't. So I restarted smoking, and it came like magic. Now I have the "What Vedanta Means to Me"[1] and the Patanjali to do—and I'm way behind the schedule, and this bothers me.

Increasing worry about Billy. Where is he? Why hasn't he written? What is going to become of the house? Well—we shall have to wait and see.

I'm really *very* grateful about the smoking—this includes release from "making faces" and other nervous tricks—and I do hope I'll be able to go through with it.

Saw Cocteau's *Orpheus*, last night. (Also his *Beauty and the Beast* last week.)[2] Much moved and impressed by both.

August 22. Still off smoking and other manifestations of tension. That's something. The novel goes very slowly, but I do see my way through it. No news yet from Johnnie about casting *Sally Bowles*. He gets back with Starcke from England, France and Germany, today.

[1] For the Vedanta Society magazine, later reprinted in John Yale's book *What Vedanta Means to Me* (1960).
[2] The films, made in 1949 and 1946 respectively.

Catherine [Caskey], Bill's mother, is staying with us.[1] This isn't easy to take. I hope she leaves before I'm rude or unkind to her. She and Bill are spending the day in Los Angeles.

Today I had lunch at Trabuco. Swami urged me, more strongly than ever before, to go up and live there. He said: "It *must* happen. I've wanted it and prayed for it so much." I answered evasively, as usual.

Gerald Heard and Chris [Wood] came up later; and I returned with them to Laguna and had tea. Asked Gerald what he thought I should do about Trabuco. He said without hesitation that I should obey Swami and go to live there. He said that he knew Swami was "deeply disturbed" about me; and that he was disturbed himself. If I didn't do as Swami told me, something terrible might happen to me. I asked—what? And Gerald said that I might lose my faith entirely and cease to believe that Vedanta was true. He also told me that he thought I was being followed by something that was trying to possess me. I answered that I felt Ramakrishna would surely protect me from anything of that kind. He agreed.

I must admit that I'm suddenly much disturbed and concerned. It is so terribly hard to know what's best to do. On the one hand, it is evident to me that I've passed through an acute phase of alienation from the grace of God—the last three years have been pretty bad, with occasional *very* bad spots, like that dreadful party on May 20, when I decided to go to the foundation.[2] I can't find any answer to the proposition that man's aim here is to know the Atman. I have to admit that I'm not meditating properly—hardly at all—in this house, and that I would do far more at Trabuco. But, on the other hand, Trabuco is what I shrink from. I dread the boredom of the place and the isolation. I shouldn't be a good companion for the "boys." I remember all the difficulties of my life at Ivar Avenue. Could I possibly go through with it?

Suppose I don't go to Trabuco? What are the alternatives?

(i) Continued life with Bill.

Possible, provided I can see Bill sub specie aeternitatis, cease to feel possessive toward him, develop a positive spiritual life and cut out this drinking, sex, bar lounging, etc. etc. A very very big *if*. In the event of my failure, there is nothing to look forward to but more frustration, guilt and fairly frequent outbursts of hate and mutual opposition of wills.

[1] Isherwood and Caskey were both now back in South Laguna.
[2] Isherwood and Caskey gave the party. The guests included two men besides Caskey in whom Isherwood was interested; Isherwood later recalled that he probably argued with Caskey afterwards.

(ii) Life with Jim (now back from Arizona).

A better idea in some ways. But he doesn't really want it. He fears being tied down. There would be other people in his life, and scenes about them. The very real and strong affection between us is better left as it is and fed on frequent meetings.

(iii) Life with Speed.

Not to be considered seriously—though he's a sweet, intelligent boy, and he understands me pretty well and likes me, I believe.

(iv) Life with some old friend or group of friends—Peggy? Beesleys? Chris Wood? Jo and Ben? Evelyn Caldwell and Ed Hooker, her new husband? The Froms?[1] Wystan? Lincoln? All these suggestions have grave objections; and, in general, I'm afraid life with any of them would lead to loneliness, isolation, etc.

Well, I must think about it all very seriously and pray for a sign. I do still firmly believe in the power and grace of the guru. I know that he can give me strength if I truly want it. And I don't believe that he ever will, or can, desert me.

Gerald is still much excited about the flying saucers.[2] He now allows that there may be man-sized creatures in them, because he thinks they move within their own magnetic field and therefore aren't subject to the pull of gravity which would tear apart the bodies of airmen making such turns in ordinary planes. He says, "Liberation is my vocation. The saucers are my avocation."

9:30 p.m. Dodie just called. She heard from Johnnie in New York. He is still determined to go ahead with *Sally Bowles*.

August 23. This morning, on a sudden impulse, I drove to Trabuco and saw Swami and talked to him about the possibility of coming to live up there, or at Ivar Avenue. I was careful not to commit myself, but of course Swami takes it for granted I'm coming. He told me that both Gerald and Aldous had come to him and told him things about the way I was living and asked him to remonstrate with me. So Swami had answered: "Why don't you pray for him?"

August 29. Catherine left this morning, for Kentucky

I got back yesterday from a weekend in Los Angeles, during which Jim definitely offered to live with me. I said no—and I'm glad I did; and he later said I was right.

What I now dimly begin to see is that there must be no more categorical relationships. I believe that's what went wrong with Bill

[1] Sam and Isadore.
[2] See Glossary under UFOs.

and me, and Ivar Avenue and me. Trying to fix a situation and ensure security by involving yourself, is no good. No good saying: "Now I'm married" or "Now I'm a monk"—and *therefore* I'm committed. It is simply weakness to talk that way.

Memories of the weekend:

Speed saying, "My screams will bring the Jews."

Aldous saying, "Peggy thinks she's St. Jeanne de Chantal."[1]

Frank [Taylor] and Van [Varner]'s great farewell scene.

August 30. When I woke this morning, I simply couldn't figure out how old I was—I thought, about nineteen or twenty. It was a shock, and yet rather farcical to realize that I'm forty-seven. I'm afraid I think too much about my age, right now. It is disconcerting to see this body getting so ugly.

An appalling confession: during the past six years, I've very very very seldom prayed for Bill.

Without some awareness of God or some movement of the will toward him, everything is madness and nonsense. It's far better to feel alienated from God than to feel nothing. I shrink from "the spiritual life" because I immediately visualize the circumstances which usually surround it—the "seeking" women coming round to ask questions after lectures, the pujas, the dreadfully harmless table humor. All this is aesthetic snobbery—*and* unnecessary. If you don't like gymnasiums don't go to them: you can exercise anywhere. Yes—but mind you *do* exercise.

September 14. On the eve of great changes—I hope.

No word yet about the play. If *that* falls in the water, I won't quite know where to turn; but, in a sense, it doesn't terribly matter because *something* will happen.

Aldous, much better, and playing happily as a child with his book about nymphomaniac nuns,[2] advises me never to travel without Terramycin tablets, and maybe some Chloromycetin as well—just in case the Terramycin leaves some bugs alive. Iris Tree recommends Pangamityn, which is made of rice polish. Jo Lathwood, who has just been very sick, says they're *all* junk. Nowadays, no one has any known disease: you simply pick up the fashionable bug (a different

---

[1] Baroness de Chantal (1572–1641), widowed at twenty-eight with four children, took a vow of chastity and found a spiritual advisor in St. François de Sales. He called her "the perfect woman": of noble family, a faithful wife, devoted mother, and good housekeeper. She founded the Order of the Visitation to enable ladies of delicate health to lead the religious life by emphasizing humility and meekness rather than corporal austerity.

[2] *The Devils of Loudun*; Huxley was recovering from a severe attack of iritis.

one each year) and attack it with a miracle drug. You run high fever, have dysentery, wish you were dead, don't die.

Projects before leaving for New York.

Finish part one (first three chapters) of novel.

Finish book three of Patanjali, and translate a Sanskrit prayer Swami gave me.

Review *The House of Breath* and *The Dog Star*[1] for *The Observer*.

That's an awful lot of work. I *just* might be able to do it.

September 22. Sad as mud, stuck out here at the foundation while Bill entertains the U.S. Marine Corps, plus Jim [Charlton] and Don Pfeiffer, the fat boy who looks like Bill Harris. No news from New York about the play.

But, though sad, I'm sort of elated because at last I have been forced to a decision. I cannot possibly go on living with Bill. As long as I do so, *he* is forced to behave in the way he does: there is a head-on clash of wills. We have to separate—certainly for six months or a year; almost certainly for always.

So now it's up to me to get on with my life.

Jim said, the other evening, "I want to be lucky and carefree and gay." This statement depressed me profoundly, because it is the kind of thing that is only said by the weak, the hopelessly hopelessly weak.

November 8. Anniversary of my initiation by Prabhavananda in 1940 and my getting my citizenship in 1946 is also, it seems, to have a third kind of memorableness in my life—tonight, here in Hartford, Connecticut, we open *I Am a Camera.* I'm not particularly excited by the event itself. This isn't my own child.[2] But it certainly is a milestone. Here I am, in this gloomy New England town; and there are Billy and Jim out there on the Coast. Bill is getting ready to leave for San Francisco and ship out with Harold [Fairbanks]. Jim may be going to Japan. I seem headed for England.

Mannish Gert Macy[3] with her poodle, Scottish Monica McCall,[4] Johnnie the spoiled but hard working and sometimes wonderful pussycat, Starcke oh so bossy and religious—yes, I'm on good terms with them all—quite good. But they are not my people, and this dishonest overstrained theater world is not my world. I'll be glad to get back to New York and see Wystan, who is very great, glad to see Lincoln tomorrow night, glad even to see Steve Jackson and Pablo

---

[1] By William Goyen and Donald Windham respectively.

[2] John van Druten adapted Isherwood's Berlin stories for the stage.

[3] Co-producer with Starcke of *I Am a Camera.*

[4] Van Druten's agent.

Rocha of Bogotá, who are coming this evening. I must be very careful to behave well, and not let any of this throw me, however it turns out.

Remember what it is that matters. There is nothing else.

1952

March 4. On the *Queen Elizabeth.*

This evening, we're due to dock in New York.

Another woeful failure to record all that's happened.[1]

And another opportunity to make a fresh start (how many hundreds have I thrown away?). My plans are quite fluid, and my objectives very definite: to get on with the novel, to finish the Prabhavananda translation, to do the text to accompany Sandford Roth's pictures of Los Angeles.[2] No more journalism till all that is finished.

What'll happen about Bill? What about Jimmy? Never mind. All that will arrange itself.

I should spend a good deal of this summer with Swami; that's certain.

My two deadly weaknesses: dullness and the jitters. My greatest vice: an increasing, really horrible vanity. I'm eaten up with it.

And yet, there is no reason to despair, no cause not to rejoice. I am still one of the luckiest people I know. And there is still some love and joy somewhere in this old pincushion of a heart. And something I still want to say in my writing—oh, I haven't even started. Fear not. Cling to what you know is real.

The great joy of the past months has been the discovery that my real friends are still as wonderful as ever. Wystan, Lincoln, Morgan, Stephen, Edward, Eric [Falk]—these are people anybody should be proud to have as friends. And there are at least a dozen others. Surely I shouldn't feel discouraged as long as such people believe in me and love me? I have no right to.

Okay—now you've had your customary spiritual douche. But now, listen to me. We have come back here to work, and to learn

---

[1] At the end of November 1951, *I Am a Camera* transferred to New York where it became a hit and Julie Harris a star as "Sally Bowles"; Isherwood spent Christmas with his mother and brother in London, and in February 1952 he visited Berlin—for the first time since 1933—where he saw Heinz Neddermeyer with his wife and son and visited his former landlady, Fräulein Thurau, now famous as Fräulein Schroeder (Schneider in Van Druten's version). Caskey had joined the merchant marine.

[2] "California Story" for *Harper's Bazaar.*

self-discipline, and to regain what we lost in those messy years of unhappiness since 1948. This place is a jungle, a wilderness—it isn't venerable and traditional and mentally cozy, like King's College.[1] One can only live here by being strong and standing alone. And how does one get to be strong and stand alone? By opening the heart to the source of all strength and all love and not-aloneness. Stop posturing and idling and thinking of yourself. Don't strain. Don't plan. There is always something to be done, at any given moment. Do it. Go among others as the vehicle of joy. If you're tired, lie down and rest.

I shall expect you to keep this journal regularly—to revive the faculty of observation. And to remind you of your job. And I *mean* observation. Not personal moanings. Don't flatter yourself: you are neither as good nor as bad as you think.

Tell me about somebody on this boat—just for exercise.

Mr. Kinsley (don't know his first name). Around twenty-seven. Dark eyes, dark brown hair, tallish, skinny. A nice looking weakish face. An engineer. Works as chief on a tanker. Is bringing home a French wife to his folks' home in Germantown, Pennsylvania. She was sick at first till I gave her my Dramamine pills. She was born in the Saar, is vehemently French, loathes the Germans. When the U.S. consul told her she was technically a German, she sat down and cried.

Kinsley has a little of the usual American virility fetish. He told me he had lost weight making love so often to his wife (Yvette). He wears the tiniest moustache, which is slightly crooked. He likes to drink with me at the bar. Perhaps he feels socially a little out of his depth among all these nonprofessional passengers. He describes the voyage as a busman's holiday.

There is something about him that's truly nice and gentle—chiefly because he's in love. But he is a dog person, anyway; ready to attach himself.

March 20. Bermuda, where Sam Costidy and I arrived last night.[2]

Today we cycled about eighteen miles and swam from a cove. What shall I say about it? There is nothing to say—directly. Except to state that this has certainly been the happiest day of my life since 1948, when I went to Ensenada with Jim.

The great mystery of happiness. What is it? As far as I can tell, just absence of pain. The moment the bandages are relaxed, joy spurts out of the heart.

And then, how wonderful, after this corrupt city-winter, to feel the ocean sunshine and see the blue of the Gulf Stream and the clouds

[1] Cambridge, where Forster was a Fellow.
[2] They had just met in New York; see Glossary under Costidy.

puffing over the still innocent (or relatively innocent) island! What joy to sweat up the hills and drink Coke and swim in clear water!

As for Sam, I will really truly and sincerely try to give him an experience of happiness—however he wants it—without intrusion of my dreary old show-off ego. Surely, for five days, that's possible?

I'm beginning to respect and like him so much. And I feel a certain identification with his problems, which helps. But I find it impossible to write more about this when he's sitting on his bed beside me in our hotel room, writing *his* journal—which he has just started. Also a letter to [James] Thurber, whom we may see before we leave—if he'll see us.

About Sam—he would do very well, in many ways, as a partial model for Bob Wood in my novel. He's about the right age, twenty-four. He is a tall skinny boy with short untidy dark hair, wide shoulders and a stoop. His face is pale and scarred with old acne marks, and he has large uneven rabbit teeth. And yet, quite often, he looks touchingly and innocently beautiful, with his small sensitive rabbit nose and clear brilliant blue eyes. His voice is rather deep, and the general impression he makes is extremely masculine, though boyish. I think he has a tremendous capacity for affection. He thinks he has a disgustingly weak will. We both agree that, just because of his shyness, he is all too apt, when drunk, to switch on an indiscriminate Irish charm which is dangerously facile. He pulls his mouth sideways at moments—when he is making self-conscious, deprecating remarks—into an ugly, disfiguring grimace. Standing alone—and in this, particularly, he resembles Bob Wood—he looks like the last lone Irish immigrant, utterly utterly abandoned by life, the predestined victim of all the wickedness of the world. Yesterday, we were out in the pouring rain in New York; and Sam wore my elegant raglan. By the time he was through with it, it looked like a garment which might be worn by a modern Oliver Twist.

Impressions of Bermuda: The number of churches. The beauty of old weather-stained red walls. The unbecoming length of the shorts. The accent—neither quite British nor American. The bicycles with engines on the front wheel. The absence of U.S. advertising. The friendliness and good looks of the Negroes. The large number of houses one would love to live in, overlooking the sea. The sense of the past is much stronger than I had expected; and yet, perhaps, there is an ultimate smugness, a boring, insipid atmosphere of a "model colony" which would become tiresome—if one stayed long, or wasn't with someone one was fond of. As I am not, and am—I'm not really conscious of this however.

March 22. It still warbles on, this daydream experience, like the very best of Mozart. *La*-de-*da*-da-da, *la*-de-*da*. After all, it is possible, under optimum conditions, and within a time limit, for human beings to behave like angels.

The roofs of the houses here are covered with lime, to purify the rainwater as it runs off them into the tanks.

The Guinness house, with his[1] collection of music boxes. Kate Sadler, the girl who played in Burgess Meredith's production of *The Playboy of the Western World*, thought they were babies' coffins. (Later we found out that some of them *were*: Guinness had had them converted.)

March 24. Thurber, whom we met last night. Very tall, handsome, white haired, with a single black streak, due, he thinks, to shots of vitamin B_1, after a nervous breakdown. He is so nearly blind that he sees only the flame of a match or a cigarette lighter; but he gives none of the impression of blindness. He talks, drinks, eagerly—and is full of anecdotes.

Well, we're off this afternoon. I'll have more to say about this trip later, perhaps. Right now, I don't know what I feel. I move blindly into the future. This island—including the cove where we swam, with its blighted cedar woods and dried Portuguese man-of-war—is only a token, or symbol of experience. What I need, I suppose, more than anything, are long long periods of meditation. Slowly, I have to calm myself.

Even if Sam were a toad-headed, hateful fiend; even if it had rained; even if I had been bored to death—I should still owe him one huge debt of gratitude, because I have restarted my novel here. Work, calm, self-purification. A new try—and always with humility and gratitude. Stop defining your relationships. That's for Art, not Life.

Oh Lord, help me to wake from this extraordinary dream. For it *is* a dream. That much I know. That's all I know.

May 12. From the *Inferno*:

> "Tristi fummo
> nell' aer dolce che dal sol s'allegra,
> portando dentro accidioso fummo;
>
> or ci attristiam nella belletta negra." (vii. 121–24)

---

[1] Murtogh David Guinness (b. 1913), younger brother of the second Baron Moyne.

and:

> chè non è impresa da pigliare a gabbo
> descriver fondo a tutto l'universo,
> nè da lingua che chiami mamma e babbo. (xxxii. 7–9)[1]

At Trabuco. I've been here since the 4th and plan to stay till the 21st. The Patanjali aphorisms are practically finished. Now I'm trying to finish part one of my novel before I leave here.

I feel very calm and in a way unwilling to leave this place. But I don't consider seriously for a moment the idea of becoming a monk again. I don't consider anything except getting my novel done. My only worries are connected with money—how much must I set aside for income tax?—and what is to be done with Sam Costidy. But I must just wait for these problems to solve themselves.

"Six individualists," is how John [Schenkel] describes this group, "all going different ways." Yet they're wonderfully harmonious on the whole, and all likable. I'm fond of Mike and am becoming increasingly fond of John, who feels about Swami ("the old man" they call him, in distinction to "Swami A."[2]) much as I do. Everything centering on him. John says that, "Too many people around here are scared of the old man, or they've got him figured all wrong." John says of him that, "He's the only person I ever met in my life I like everything about."

Ken [Critchfield] is grouchy and Phil [Griggs?] is a fussbudget, but I feel a deep sympathy for them. And Dell is a really good boy, I'm sure, though he's so solitary—after eight years in the air force—that you only get glimpses of him. And no one could help liking Rich; he's such a good-natured eager beaver.

I try to fit in unobtrusively, and not get in the way of their routine. Am not getting much—or indeed anything—consciously—out of the meditation periods. But I often feel very happy. Hardly any

---

[1] Isherwood had a 1929 dual language text with John Carlyle's translation (edited by H. Oelsner):

> . . . "Sullen were we
> in the sweet air, that is gladdened by the sun,
> Carrying lazy smoke within our hearts;
>
> Now lie we sullen here in the black mire."

and:

> for to describe the bottom of all the Universe is
> not an enterprise for being taken up in sport,
> nor for a tongue that cries mamma and pappa.

[2] Swami Asheshananda.

trouble with sex, yet. I think that's mostly middle age. Anyhow, I certainly needed the rest!

May 13. Drove Dell into Santa Ana, to catch a train to Los Angeles, where he has to stay overnight, in order to sell his car. We passed El Toro Marine Air Base, where he was stationed for some time, quite unaware of Trabuco or Vedanta. He went to Ashokananda's lectures while stationed up at San Francisco, and visited the Olima Monastery, but didn't like the life there—only one period of meditation a day, in the morning, and they all sleep together in one room. Dell hates this, after his life in the service. He needs privacy.

On the way home, in Tustin, I went to the barber's and, on an impulse, got my hair cropped short. I look very strange—like a rather crazy old man.

Still no sensible satisfaction from the meditations. In fact, I *can't* meditate, even for a moment. I just make japam and my thoughts race around. I think about my novel (which I've started again). About Sam Costidy, Tom Wright. Money (the "take" on *Camera* is down again). Where I'll live when I leave here. I feel sympathy and liking for these boys—but their problems aren't very real to me. Because this situation is so utterly different from mine. I'm only like a war correspondent visiting the front for one day. I can't know how it feels to be stuck in this place.

The pleasure of working in the blazing sun, pulling weeds out of the vines or raking the kitchen garden. The somehow *secret* stillness of the hot courtyard, with the dark-leaved fruit trees. At night, we look through the telescope, at Saturn and the ranger station on the top of the mountain. Nothing seems disturbing here. I actually like to hear Mike playing his organ even when I'm writing.

May 14. A little stirring of sex today. Not much. It occurs to me that, of all the sensual pleasures, sex is the only one which depends partly on reciprocation. That's its power. Imagine if an orange said: "Darling, I was just longing for *you* to eat me. I was so afraid that horrible old man would. He's not at *all* my type."

Fog coming down—threatening poor Dell's much-looked-forward-to party on the beach tomorrow. But it's beautiful here; with the rays of light shining through the archway into it.

Felt, in the shrine tonight, that I'd just as soon stay here all summer. Would I, *really*? Probably not. But the immediate prospect of going back into "the world" isn't particularly attractive.

Today I finished chapter three of my novel, and hence part one.

May 19. Brutally stuffed and fat after a big lunch I gave the Swamis and boys and Chris Wood at The Happy Ranch. Squab and birthday cake for Dell and ice cream.

Jim Charlton has been down in Laguna for the weekend. Chris says he thinks Jim is seriously gone in drinking and won't be able to stop. Jim went to hear Gerald lecture at Ivar Avenue. Don't know what he thought of it.

The day after tomorrow, back to Santa Monica. Back to the problem of finding a place to live. And the problem of Sam Costidy. I don't know how he'll react to the news that Gerry Lansing has a job and isn't coming out here. I'm deeply fond of him, and find him often companionable and always touching and sometimes acutely exasperating. But every instinct tells me to live alone, and work quietly and regularly at the book. It is really rolling along now and I'm excited. I mustn't miss the tide. If I can get part two drafted, even roughly, then I *know* I'll finish the whole thing.

I've done wonders of work since I arrived here, on the 4th. Finished Patanjali, finished part one of the novel and made a promising start on part two, worked over some Vedic prayers Swami wanted, written lots of letters, *and* pulled lots of weeds out of vines. In the shrine, I've been quite dry and emotionless, but with a certain sense of contact reestablished. I *must* keep up japam and try to meditate at least once a day, when I leave here.

When I typed out the title page of the Patanjali this morning, I put "by Swami Prabhavananda and Christopher Isherwood," and Swami said, "Why put *and*, Chris? It separates us." It's impossible to convey the sweetness and meaning with which he said this. All day long, he fairly shines with love. It was the same when he was here at the beginning of my stay, and told us: "If you have a friend and do good things for him for years and years—and then do *one* bad thing; he'll never forgive you. But if you do bad things to God for years and years, and only one good thing—*that* He never forgets." It's his complete assurance, and his smiling, almost sly air of having a private source of information.

May 25. Well, I left Trabuco and came to Santa Monica and got settled three days ago into this tacky but clean apartment house called the Mermira, on 2nd Street, behind the Miramar Hotel. Lots of noise, above and all around. A plaintive neighbor woman next door was heard saying: "Well, what do you *want* me to do?" And her much more plaintive companion answered: "I don't know, but you could do it differently, somehow."

I am committed to the Hookers' garden house. Jim is going to redecorate it. It'll cost me most of my savings, I fear.

Sam Costidy is sometimes so sweet he moves me to tears. And then again I feel he's an expensive nuisance and a burden. When he finally stops bothering me to live with him and settles on someone else, I shall be terribly miserable and relieved.

The novel must go on. That's what matters.

A woman called to a neighbor: "Sorry to interrupt you in the middle of your hair."

June 8. Just two months since I arrived back here from Reno. What is there to report?

Well, the novel is coming along. Not as quickly as I could wish, but definitely coming. I've practically finished a fairly adequate rough draft of chapter one, part two, and arrived at page sixty-one. I could go much faster, if it weren't for psychic sloth-blocks. Must devise techniques to remove these.

Am still in this noisy little apartment, and have gotten so used to it that I hardly care to move until the Hooker garden house is finished. That certainly won't be till well into July. Jim has sloth blocks, too. I get irritated with him sometimes. But the way to overcome this, *and* to speed him up, is to improve our personal relationship. This, goodness knows, I'm more than happy to do. I have neglected him— and for what? He is really one of my dearest friends. And I'd do better to concentrate on my friends and take the time off from acquaintances.

Sam Costidy is only an acquaintance, and let's recognize that fact. I spoke to him unkindly, brutally, yesterday morning—which I shouldn't have—about his cadging, gimme attitude; but it's true. He never comes here without a motive, even if it's only to borrow the car. And he has to realize this about himself, or he'll become very unpopular. He is pleasant to be with, and potentially a decent, intelligent person: but he has to face this.

I feel very good about Caskey. He visited here for his birthday, and everything went perfectly, and I feel that our relationship is permanently established—though there'll be many more fights, I don't doubt. You've got Caskey. You could have Jim. What more do you want? Everything else is just vanity.

I find I like being alone, much of the time, and I must cultivate that feeling. I must bring my life "in the world" closer to the Ivar Avenue part of it. That's the only happiness.

I feel as though I were being given a second chance—only it isn't the second, it's about the two hundredth. Come on, now. Work hard. Organize your time. Give up vanity, window shopping, yearning for those greener pastures. You're much older than you think.

I'm wonderfully indifferent to alcohol, thank goodness. Even at Ivan [Moffat]'s farewell party for Boon and Henrietta Ledebur, last night, I drank only two glasses of wine with soda water. I didn't even want whiskey or martinis. I smoke too much, though.

How nice Gottfried Reinhardt is! He forced himself to climb ladders to a catwalk in the studio, because he has to direct a picture about acrobats. Silvia [Reinhardt] is much concerned about the Lillian Ross articles in *The New Yorker*.[1] Harry Brown sitting apart, staring at a plant—isolated in our midst by his love for Marguerite Lamkin, Speed's sister, whom he'll marry in the fall. Iris imitating a woman who'd had her husband "fixed"; then annoyed with me because I wouldn't go on, at 1:00 a.m., to Jim Agee's.[2] (But I *must* stop doing things I don't want to, out of mere weakness. There's no virtue in that; and it breeds resentment later.)

I don't know why I'm reminded of this, suddenly. But the other day I asked Swami how it is that he can always end a meditation period so punctually. He said it's like being able to sleep and wake up at a certain time, no matter how deeply you become absorbed. The notion that meditation periods should be of varying length, according to mood, is "romantic," he said.

I've smoked eight cigarettes this morning, so far. That's up to midday. Tomorrow, I'll try cutting each cigarette in half, and see if that automatically makes a difference.

June 30. This evening, Sam Costidy and Tom Wright left together in Tom Wright's car for Wright's home, Monroe, Louisiana. I was glad to see them go, I'm afraid. Costidy, certainly. He has been an increasing nuisance. But now he has gone I shall be able to remember the good parts of our relationship—the time on Bermuda. I must always be grateful to him for that.

I've been bad about my novel—slothful and slow. I *must* get on, and lick this second chapter of part two. Then I'll be really deep in the wood. I only wish I knew a technique for cheating my own sloth.

Have been drinking again. This is fatal. Well—I must stop it.

Bad relations with Jim. I blame him for his selfishness—but the truth is, I must demand less, I must demand nothing at all. I must be stronger than ever. This is no time for props.

---

[1] Ross covered the filming of *The Red Badge of Courage* for *The New Yorker*; Gottfried Reinhardt was the producer.

[2] James Agee (1909–1955), American novelist, poet, critic, screenwriter.

Ben and Jo are being helpful, simply by existing. A peaceful evening with them tonight, talking about the old days.

July 12. Bad things that have happened:
The play is about to close on Broadway.
The garden house is taking longer and is to cost more than I'd expected.
I've been drinking, oversmoking, and hence am practically stuck in the novel.
Am mad at Jim, very mad at myself.
Well—do you want to hear my comments? No—I thought you didn't.

September 13. A dream:
My father, in uniform, at a table. I'm sitting beside him.
"Are you lonely here, Daddy?" I ask.
"Yes."
"So am I. But never mind. You get used to it."
I pat him on the shoulder, rather deliberately, never having done this before but feeling that it's right. A very strong feeling of rapport, between us.
Woke happy. This was a good dream.

November 30. The Day of the Dead.[1] Late, after a supper at Salka's, with John Collier soon to leave permanently to go and live in Mexico, and Gottfried Reinhardt, complaining that Hemingway lives in an unreal world of his own. "He goes to Venice—Venice of all places—and what does he do? He hunts *duck*! *Duck*! Can you imagine! *I* never heard of any duck in Venice. It's *fantastic*!" Gottfried's voice keeps rising into squeaks of protest. He loves talking like this.

Finished chapter three, part two a few days ago. This must be the all-time slowness record. Usual resolutions. Push ahead *fast*, somehow, anyhow. You know you never regret when you do. No one *ever* had less excuse to idle than you have.

Sadness about Billy. Our relations are all right—since that awful scene driving back from Nogales[2] on the 21st, and the weepy aftermath, when he told me that my moving into the garden house was "ruthless." But I'm sad it's not better between us, since he's going away so soon. I feel sad and lonely. He's up at Hayden and Rod's.

---

[1] In fact, the Latin-American festival welcoming back the souls of the dead is generally celebrated on November 1, All Saints Day.
[2] Straddling the border of Arizona and Mexico.

When he leaves for San Francisco, I'll go to Trabuco for a while. It's best for me there right now. I feel tense and restless and dissatisfied here.

December 1. Got started, today, on chapter four. I'm making another effort to bust this "writer's block" by just going ahead. I wrote a page and a half, very rough, but with some quite promising ideas.

Heavy rain, on and off. A regular stream is running through the garden. Jack Mershon brought a Canadian named Lucas, a lawyer, to talk or rather be talked to about Vedanta. We lunched at Ted's.[1] What can I say to anybody about Vedanta that's the least impressive, as long as I'm what I am? Never mind that, though. Get on with your job.

Up at Hayden and Rod's, Bill Caskey told the story (told him by Bill Harris) of how a huge Negro rode all the way from São Paulo to Rio for the Carnival on the train dressed as a swan.

A wonderful letter from Morgan, saying how he'd been rereading my old letters to him—"Dear Christopher oh you have been a good friend."

Actual physical vertigo induced by rereading Whymper's account of the Matterhorn disaster.[2] I felt quite sick.

1953

January 6. This is one of those real low-ebb days, when the whole day is like 3:00 a.m. of a sleepless night. After several days of perfect, brilliant weather, it has drizzled since dawn. Bill Caskey spent the night here and left in his car for San Francisco, saying, "Pray for me sometimes." He has never been gentler or sweeter, ever since our trip to Ensenada at Christmas. Kindness is the most heartbreaking thing in the world. I think he must have come to some decision within himself.

My nerves are all shot—this is the thirteenth, and so far worst, day without smoking—and I can't write. I'm in such a mess. Salka's old mother is dead, and I was down to see Salka. And Collier has just had a bad operation for a polyp—not malignant. And Maria Huxley may have to have one, for a recurrence of the breast cancer.

I'm going to Trabuco as soon as possible. I *must* relax and work.

The other night I was struck by the beauty of the phrase "Flos Campi" (it's actually the title of a work by Vaughan Williams).[3]

---

[1] Ted's Grill.
[2] Edward Whymper, *Scrambles Amongst the Alps in the Years 1860–1869* (1900).
[3] Composed in 1924 for viola and small chorus; inspired by the Song of Songs.

"Flower of the Field"—I think of the Bible, and then, perhaps because of the association with *campagna*, with Rome, about Piranesi; and it seems wonderfully romantic. Such things are inexplicable. Notes that make the whole being vibrate—but only for a limited time. Flos Campi—already it has lost its power.

January 27. Have been up at Trabuco since January 9. (Caskey left for San Francisco on the 6th and I haven't heard from him yet, which worries me. I don't know if he has a ship or is in prison, or what.)

Very fine weather, hot, utterly unlike this time of year.

Today I finished the rough draft of my novel—all the way from the beginning of chapter five, part two, till the end of part three. About eighty-eight pages in eighteen days.

This has been one of the strangest of all my literary experiences. A sheer frontal attack on a laziness block so gross and solid and almost sentient and malevolent that it might be the devil as an incarnation of tamas—or Goethe's fault-and-obstacle-finding, all-denying Mephistopheles. What with having given up smoking, having no drink (except an occasional sherry with Swami before lunch) and no sex, I was nearly crazy with tension. I actually said to Ramakrishna in the shrine: "If it's your will that I finish this thing, then help me." And so we began to move. But it was a hard push all the way through; and what I've written is the crudest nonsense. It is only slowly taking shape as a novel. Much, I now see, is completely irrelevant. . . . However, this isn't the place or the time to go into all that.

What matters is a genuine victory; and I am very grateful for it. I feel as if my whole future as a writer—and my sanity, almost—had been at stake. And yet I daresay I seemed quite cheerful, relaxed and level headed to the boys. These struggles go on deep underground.

It's a hard life they have here, in spite of all outward advantages, and I feel great respect and sympathy for them. Tito seems to be wearing himself down, overstraining and fighting every inch—but that may be only temporary. There are strange sudden unexpected let ups. I feel fond of all the boys—John [Schenkel], Ken, Phil [Griggs], Mike, Lee (whom I feel I know least); and they all seem as if they had a chance of staying the course—but it's nearly impossible to know. This worship of Ramakrishna—its Indianness—still bothers me often; and yet I find the actual dualistic-devotional relationship quite natural in itself. I'm pretty sure I couldn't live here permanently at present, though—much as I like coming here on visits.

March 6. Why, oh why, can't I keep this journal regularly?

After January's industry, February has been a truly wasteful, manic month. Despite my rough draft, I've only done twenty-six pages of the revised chapter four, part two. Terrible arrears of letters.

Oh yes, I have alibis. Jim's [enthusiastic socializing] with Earl [McGrath], which meant a lot of drinking, the garage fire on February 5, and Ted Bachardy's breakdown, which lasted from about the 20th until he was committed on the 26th. But all that is no real excuse.

I woke, around 2:30 a.m., from a nightmare that I was being chased by Nazis who'd seen me watching them bury the corpses of murdered children. There was a strange unpleasant smell which I didn't immediately identify as burning, but when I went to the door—hearing roaring, crackling sounds in the high wind—the garage was full of fire. Half asleep still, I ran to warn the Hookers, and banged on the wrong door, the one I know is always locked, until I realized what I was doing. I never once thought of my novel, or of taking anything with me. I don't know what this proves. I'm sure I wasn't that scared.

But, looking out of the Hookers' window and seeing the blaze and thinking that for sure everything I owned was burned, I felt a very curious exhilaration. It was almost as if I understood, for the first time, the meaning of the homa fire. "Okay—a real fresh start, then, if that's your will. What do you want now? Tell me. I'm ready."

But when the firemen arrived, and I knew my little house was safe, *then* I was frantic, lest water might have come in through the ceiling and spoiled something! But it hadn't. This is as near as I've ever been to a miracle: I honestly feel I was "protected."

The Ted Bachardy case was very ugly and horribly tragic. The way his gentle charming face became thin and wolflike and crafty. I found I could only handle him by relaxing toward his madness, making myself become quite passive and silly and weak—seeking *his* protection, almost. I understood how deep the relationship is between Lear and the Fool. "You're like me, Chris. We both get pushed around. But I'm not going to stand for it. I know how to play my cards. I can handle anyone."

The parents sent for the police, and Ted was dragged away, screaming and fighting, in handcuffs. And his little brother Don cried in my car afterwards: "Chris, he's really *insane*."

I feel a special kind of love for Don. I suppose I'm just another frustrated father. But this feeling exists at a very deep level, beneath names for things or their appearances. We're just back from a trip to Palm Springs together, which was one of those rare experiences of nearly pure joy. There's a brilliant wide-openness about his mouse face, with its brown eyes and tooth gap and bristling crew cut, which affects everybody who sees him. If one could still be like that at forty, one would be a saint.

March 7. Supper at the Huxleys', with Gerald, Chris Wood, Eileen Garrett and a young man named Rolf who's a friend of Eileen's. She had wanted this meeting, and it was certainly a feat, getting Chris to come clear up from Laguna Beach for it. But, now it's over, I don't really know just why Eileen wanted to see us all. She's an odd creature, with many purposes and lots of blarney. She keeps going on about how she sees a light all around me. Her sittings in the Faraday Box produced shingles which turned into cysts. She saw Stalin dead in a dream and predicted it for this year, four years ago—she says.[1]

Gerald is quite transformed. His health has become wonderful. He is very lively and greatly interested in the problem of what he calls the "intergrade."[2] He'll drink sherry, and eat meat sometimes. He seems to have so much more warmth and charity, and less malice. Eileen told us that Gerald and Chris must never let themselves be separated.

I told Gerald how I believe that Ted could have been cured, or at least temporarily brought to himself if someone could have (a) provoked him to a friendly fight, a wrestling match, and (b) gotten him to perform an active sexual role. That's the only way I could imagine his aggression and his pathic fear being gradually dispelled. Ted could only fight in anger and when he was in this manic phase, but all he really wanted was to assert himself as a man. He could only approach sex passively, but he really longed to be the aggressor.

April 20. Coming back at 10:45 from supper at Jo and Ben's, with talk about the war, *This Is My Beloved*,[3] and Jay [de Laval] and the old Canyon—the nice smell of redwood as I lifted the garage door. And the feeling of impotence—or, what it really amounts to, lack of inclination to cope with a constructed, invented plot—the feeling, why not write what one experiences, from day to day? And then, as I slid my door back, this sinking-sick feeling of love for Don— somehow connected with the torn shorts—and the reality of that—so far more than all this tiresome fiction. Why invent—when Life is so prodigious?

---

[1] Stalin's death in 1953 was announced March 6. For the Faraday Box, see Glossary under Garrett.
[2] Heard's term for the homosexual and for the homosexual's desirable role in social evolution.
[3] Walter Benton's 1943 book of love poetry; the Masselinks liked it, but Isherwood did not.

Perhaps I'll never write another novel, or anything invented—except, of course, for money.

Write, live what happens: Life is too sacred for invention—though we may lie about it sometimes, to heighten it.

Oh, if I could have the wisdom to spend these last twenty years in some better way—not messing with this crap.

Let me try.

April 21. I was more than somewhat drunk when I wrote the above, but that doesn't signify. It's how I feel.

I'm really very dissatisfied with the novel—it's so lifeless. None of the characters are unique, like the best in my other books. And I don't feel I have put anything of importance into the book itself: no deep thought or sincere feeling.

What a strange time this is for me! Perhaps a sort of change of life doldrums. My head feels so dull. (Just looked at the small knob on the second hand of my wristwatch and thought it was an insect—wondered how it ever got inside the watch glass!) I feel impotent—though I'm not, physically. But there's a kind of gone feeling.

The situation with Billy is so strange. I mind, and yet I don't. My only nostalgia seems to be for the pain he caused me. Am I really such a masochist? Have I ever had any relationships of this kind that weren't painful—and is that because I feel guilty about them anyway; feel that they alienate me from God? Am I still a monk at heart? Ramakrishna will hound you, Swami said.

[On a separate sheet dropped into his diary notebook, Isherwood recorded a car trip with Don Bachardy to Arizona, New Mexico, Colorado, and Nevada during Bachardy's spring vacation in early May, as follows.]

May 4. Picked up Don at City College and we left, at 1:30 p.m., for Blythe, arriving 6:55, 223 miles. Stayed at Monterey Motel. Supper at Chicken House.

May 5. Left Blythe 6:55, via Prescott, Jerome, Oak Creek Canyon, Flagstaff, to Gallup, arriving 7:45. Stayed at Log Cabin Lodge. Supper at Luigi's. 434 miles. Lost spectacles.

May 6. Left Gallup 8:12, via Ganado, Canyon de Chelly, Rough Rock, Chilchonbeta, Kayenta, arriving Monument Valley 7:00. Stayed at Harry Goulding's Lodge, 217 miles.

May 7. Toured Monument Valley in jeep stationwagon, 8:35 a.m. to 3:00 p.m. Left Monument Lodge 3:15, via Kayenta, Tuba City, to Cameron, arriving 7:00, 121 miles. Ate supper at Cameron

Trading Post. Stayed at Cameron Court Hotel. Gale with sandstorms.

May 8. Left Cameron 9:33, for Grand Canyon Village, arriving 12:07. Left Grand Canyon 2:25, via Williams, Kingman, to Boulder City arriving 8:25, 330 miles. Ate at Bob's. Stayed at Black Canyon Motel.

May 9. 9:20. Left Boulder City to visit Boulder Dam, Lake Meade. Then to Las Vegas, arriving 12:25, 40 miles. Stayed at Gateway Motel. Supper at Last Frontier. Saw Marge and Gower Champion[1] at the Flamingo.

May 10. Left Las Vegas 9:30 a.m., via Barstow, Victorville, San Fernando Valley for home, arriving 5:00 p.m.—294 miles. Total trip 1,704. Supper at El Coyote. Saw *The Glass Wall* and part of *The Four Poster.*

June 23. Supper with John van Druten, after a day at Santa Barbara, with Swami and John Yale.

Johnnie (van Druten) and I ate at Musso Frank's. Johnnie sententious—how *he* felt about Syngman Rhee[2] and Korea, how—when he and Starcke were waiting for a decision on *Camera* as a movie, *he* thought, "What have I ever suffered in comparison with what the Rosenbergs are feeling, waiting for execution?"[3] I guess, when he talks like this, one is supposed to fall on one's ass with amazement at such charity and cosmic sensibility.

He announced, with great dramatic pathos, that he no longer felt Dodie was a great friend. But actually what he never realizes is that Dodie felt this years ago. He says he told Charlie Brackett, and Charlie said that it was Henry James's fault.[4]

After supper, he was drunk in the Pickwick bookshop and announced that he had written an essay on Arnold Bennett.

He is very proud because he meditated four times a day in Honolulu with Joel Goldsmith. He and Starcke. Another guy they met there only meditated twice. And then the other guy was seen dining with Johnnie and Starcke at Chasen's, and the people who saw them thought it must be business—something to do with *Camera*, and this proved to Johnnie that his least action is news.

Good. I got that bitchiness off my chest. I feel better. I understand

[1] The dancers.
[2] President of South Korea, 1948–1960.
[3] For passing atomic secrets to the Soviets.
[4] Dodie Beesley was a great admirer of James (her 1949 play *Letter from Paris* is based on "The Reverberator").

Johnnie and am fond of him, up to a point. At least he goes out on a limb and is human. But oh my God what a stuffed shirt!

August 25. Three or four nights ago, I dreamt that I was sharing a bed with Swami in a hotel which I knew to be a male whorehouse. Except that we were sharing a bed, our relations were as they always are. I was full of respect and consideration for him; asking him—we were just getting up—if he wouldn't care to use the bathroom first.

But then Swami said, "I've got a new mantram for you, Chris. It is: 'Always dance.' " "What a strange mantram!" I said. Swami laughed: "Yes. It surprised me too. But I found it in the scriptures."

The *feeling* of this dream was very good. The highest kind of camp.

September 22. Bad: Don damaged the car in an accident with a trolley car yesterday evening, and so I will have to pay about forty-five dollars. Ivan Moffat still owes me two thousand, and Caskey, Jim and others another thousand or more between them. And Bob Linscott of Random House wants changes in the novel, and Alan White of Methuen hasn't even written me yet, which looks sinister.

I'm very happy in my father relationship with Don, except that he makes me feel so terribly responsible. It's nearly as bad as Heinz all over again. Nearly, but not quite, because Don is a lot brighter, and really much more able to look out for himself.

Good: I still have over six thousand dollars clear of income tax, even if none of the above-mentioned debts are repaid. Also, I have plenty of time to write something else or get a job before the money runs out. (It's unlikely I will earn anything from the U.S. edition of my novel for quite some while, because I owe Random House three thousand dollars.)

As usual, of course, all this material bookkeeping is utterly beside the point. The point is that I'm going through another period of alienation from God, and that's why I'm worried, anxious, unhappy, pessimistic. I could do a lot with this time, while Don's at school and I can come down here to work. Why don't I? Fear-sloth. Come on, now. You got that book finished, even if it *does* have to be revised. One spell is broken. Why weave another?

November 19. Maria Huxley, describing how she'd reacted to Audrey Hepburn, who came to dinner with them the other night and was a great success: "When she put her head on one side and looked through those eyes, it was very natural and quite first-rate."

December 8. I think I will write down my memories of Dylan Thomas now. After he died, Stephen asked me to write something about him, and I replied that I couldn't, because my memories were unsuitable for an obituary notice, too much involved with other people, who would be offended. But I'd better record them here, before they get too vague.

I think I really only had two meetings with Dylan. The first was on Monday, April 10, 1950, while I was living down in Santa Monica Canyon, at 333 East Rustic Road. Bill Caskey was away at the time, in Kentucky—it was after his father had died.

Fairly early that morning, the telephone rang. It was Dylan, whom I'd never met. Someone had given him my number. He sounded terribly lost and remote. "I'm down here," he said in his beautiful deep little voice—"down here" might have been purgatory, the way he sounded, but it turned out to be the Biltmore. I then learnt that he was to give a reading at UCLA that afternoon, and that the English department had provided no transportation, simply telling him that there was a bus. I was suitably indignant—partly because I really thought this an outrageous rudeness, partly because I knew I had to go down and get him myself.

I found him alone, in the morning desolation of the long bar. He was a touching, but not in the least pathetic, little figure in a blue serge suit which looked as though he often fought and slept in it. (He often did.) The front of the jacket was sprinkled and smeared with cigarette ash. The impression he made on me was, primarily, of struggle: he seemed to be right in the midst of his life—not off on one side looking at it—and he grappled with it as though it were a policeman.

He told me that he'd arrived in Los Angeles the night before—called me several times in vain—as a matter of fact, I was out with Speed Lamkin, our first meeting, too—and then gone on the town. A taxi driver had taken him to some after-hours place, in the Negro section, and they had become such friends that he had given Dylan a ring. It was a very cheap one, but Dylan showed it [to] me with pride, and it was plain how greatly he valued friendship, no matter who offered it, if the offer was sincere. He adopted me as a friend immediately, on the strength of my having come to fetch him, and very soon he gave *me* a present—a small crab inlaid in a half ovoid of plastic, with a key ring attached. This I treasured until I lost it last year, drunk, at Long Beach. Now I have only his signature in two of his own books.

As we drove out to Santa Monica, Dylan gradually heightened the steam pressure of his indignation against the English department of UCLA. He also kept pressing me to stop for a drink. This I evaded, because I was afraid he was going to get so high that he wouldn't be able to give his reading.

Dylan also talked about his wife and children, and again I felt his great warmth. He seemed eager to enter into the lives of his friends and understand *their* relationships, too. When I showed him my workroom he at once noticed Denny's photograph on the wall and said respectfully, "He's very beautiful." I felt quite sorry that I had to explain the mistake. Dylan then told me how, in San Francisco, a party of queens had taken him around the bars—and how, being grateful for their kindness, he had tried to enjoy himself but had longed for a woman. At last, in one bar, he saw a most lovely girl, alone amongst all the men. He had run to her eagerly and seized her in his arms—only to find that this was a boy in drag. He seemed very gentle, now, and trustful. There was also, in him, a kind of apologetic Colonel Blimpishness. "Of course, the Russians *are* rather awful," he said, "but one can't very well say so nowadays, when all these swine are attacking them."

Then it was time to go to lunch with some of the English department before Dylan's reading, which was set for the early afternoon. I already knew and disliked the head of the department, a bogus, oily, sanctimonious creature named Majal Ewing, who had married money. But, oddly enough, I can't be sure if he was at this lunch, which was eaten at a restaurant on Wilshire Boulevard, called the Fox and Hounds—or some such Olde Englishe title.

Lunch was tense. Dylan had had some drinks at my house, and now accepted more—unwillingly as they were offered. The nice clean youngish-oldish blank-faced anxious English teachers sat around, waiting for the volcano to erupt. Actually, it never quite did; but there were some powerful rumblings. Somebody remarked that Los Angeles was a big city. "*Very* big," said Dylan ominously. "Especially if you have no friends." He was asked his opinion on various literary matters; I forget what his answers were, but they were peppered with four-letter words which made the academics wince. They were pretty contemptible, altogether; and yet I could see the farcical side of their prissiness. They had conjured up this dangerous little creature, excited by the dangerousness in his poems, and now that they had him there in the flesh, he terrified and shocked them by those very qualities which are so admirable as long as they remain merely literary. How many times the same thing must have happened with Rimbaud! But the dilemma really exists in childhood. It's the attitude of the small boy who would love (he thinks) to have live roaring tigers leap into the room out of his picture books, but who doesn't want to be afraid of them if they appear.

I was nervous too, of course. I felt sure that Dylan would disgrace himself at the reading. But I was entirely wrong. When Dylan got on the platform, no one could have told that he wasn't sober. He gave a masterly performance, not only of his own work, but of Hardy and many others. (I wish I had the program.) The marvellous beauty of his voice in the more serious poems can be heard on records, but I do wish I also had records of his comic reading. He was a brilliant comedian and mimic. The audience loved him—the students, that is. I got an impression of sourness among most of the faculty members who were present.

The moment Dylan was through, he was eager to get away—as eager as I was. We hurried across the campus to my car, laughing gleefully with a conspiratorial feeling of escape. I congratulated him on his performance and we talked about Hardy. He knew most of Hardy's work, far more than I did, but it so happened that I quoted a poem he didn't remember. "Whenever you meet someone who likes Hardy," he said, "he always quotes something you haven't heard before."

Dylan was now in the best of spirits—all ready for the fun which he trusted me to provide. As it happened, I was lucky. I had gotten hold of Ivan Moffat, and (I think) Frank Taylor. Dylan had told me he wanted to meet Chaplin, and a movie actress. Chaplin was willing—I guess Frank arranged this—and Ivan provided Shelley Winters. We ate at The Players Restaurant, on Sunset.

Shelley was a good choice, because she is a naturally easygoing girl and the situation intrigued her. When Dylan started to stare at her breasts, and asked, "Are they real?" she laughed and told him, "Sure." "Let me feel them," said Dylan. "All right," said Shelley, "but only with two fingers." This wasn't enough for Dylan, however. He pawed her and reached across to grab her—he was like a very rough baby with its mother—and finally they both fell off the[ir] chair[s] onto the ground. A waiter arrived and fussed somewhat, but Shelley laughed it off, and we weren't asked to leave.

Of course by this time I was very drunk too, so I don't remember much of our visit to Chaplin. Ivan says that Dylan was rude to him, and that Chaplin (who was a bit of a Blimp himself, especially in his own home and Oona's presence) was offended. But the visit went off quite well, and I'm sure that Dylan didn't mean to offend Chaplin. He admired him enormously.

The last phase of our evening was at the Café de Paris restaurant on Sunset. By then, everything was very muddled. I don't think Shelley was with us anymore. Some man came in—maybe a movie writer or director. Anyhow, he was a reader of my work, and he told me, quite courteously, that he hadn't liked my last book as much as the others he'd read. Whereupon Dylan—bored, maybe, because there were no girls and no action—yelled, "Don't you insult my friend, you fucking etc. etc. etc." and threw himself on the man, who was big; nearly twice his own size. The man pushed him off, good-naturedly. So Dylan walked over to the wall, took a run of several yards, and attacked again. This time we all helped repel him. And he turned and ran out of the bar into the street. We thought he'd come back, but he didn't.

Next day, there was a crisis, because it seemed that Dylan had left some of the books he read from at my house. Majal Ewing's secretary rang up to tell me this. It was apparently expected that I should take them over to UCLA to be given to Dylan before his next reading, in Santa Barbara. I was busy and this enraged me. I told the secretary that Professor Ewing certainly must have some student who could come and pick them up. Nothing was done about this, however. I believe Dylan gave his reading as best he could, without the books, and that he came by for them very briefly, before leaving for the East. Anyhow, this started some bitchy gossip to the effect that I'd tried to steal some of Dylan's manuscripts. I retorted in kind, and no doubt my remarks about Ewing and the English department got right back to them.

My other meeting with Dylan was on March 6, 1952 in New York, at the Chelsea Hotel. I'd arrived there the day before, on my return from a visit to England, and discovered that Dylan and his wife were also staying there. At this time, New York was full of talk about the violent behavior of the Thomases, their drunken fights at parties and the valuable objects they had smashed in the drawing rooms of rich hostesses. The Chelsea is a huge old gloomy place, and its charm is a quality of apartness. The dark passages are almost always empty, however crowded the building may be, and few sounds reach you from other guests. Each room is a separate world and not, as in most modern hotels, a place which you seem to be partly sharing with your next-door neighbors. And this gives you the exciting sense of possibility—the neighbors seem all the more exciting; they might be absolutely anybody.

I saw Dylan very briefly, because I myself was in a rush of engagements, and he was soon leaving New York. I met and got little impression of his wife—she seemed shy and rather homely. Dylan and I (and I think Bob MacGregor of New Directions) went downstairs to the bar for a drink, and Dylan said, "This is the hottest bar in New York," which may have been literally true; because the steam heating seemed to be built right into the bar itself. Alas, that's all I remember that he *did* say. He looked paler and fatter; otherwise as before. I never saw him again.

December 17. I'm writing this at Saltair Avenue, on the morning of our departure—Don's and mine—to spend Christmas and New Year's in New York. As always before flying, I'm in a state of acute nervous apprehension. I really do loathe it. And at the same time I'm aware that this is only a mental symptom of the pyloric spasms I had last month. I'll try not to let Don see how I feel. He is just radiant with joy and excitement—letting out little cries like a bird.

This place is really all the home I have anywhere—despite the behavior of the Hookers, and I always leave it with regret. There is a good smell of work here, despite much lazing and mooning around.

A couple of days ago, Gerald Heard read the novel and seemed to like it enormously. I don't know why I write "seemed"—I'm sure he did. He raised all kinds of points, had obviously studied it most carefully—and yet he kept referring to Elizabeth as "Margaret"! I'm so very happy that he likes it, and so happy that we are friends, now; real friends, like we used to be.

Gerald urged me to write about Don and myself—"for the record." I probably will, if we go on together. And, barring accidents, I think we may, for quite a long time.

Chris Wood had dinner with me alone last night, much depressed. He feels that his life will end soon, and that it has been wasted. He blames himself for overindulging Paul [Sorel] and giving him so much money. He feels certain of reincarnation and dreads it, because of the way he has lived. Of course there is some masochism in all this, but, just the same, Chris's sincerity impressed me, as it always does. He is a very frank person, and he doesn't whine. He is far far better than he thinks himself.

Chris is saddened because, he says, his relations with Gerald are so superficial nowadays. They never talk intimately about anything. Chris thinks that the rift caused by Paul still remains between them, and that that is the reason.

Last night, I dreamed that I was helping Swami get undressed and ready for bed, in some large house or hotel. This was a sort of "companion piece" to my other dream about him. I felt eager to attend to all his wants and was very respectful. As I helped him into his dressing gown, we found that it was entangled in mine—the sleeves of my gown were pulled down into his. Swami said, "Oh, so you have a dressing gown? I was going to give you mine." And I said, "But I can throw mine away." This was a good dream.

Well, so long now. Wish me luck. And if my presentiments *are* right for once, and we get killed, well, it isn't at the worst possible moment. At least, this book is solidly finished. And, as for what happens next, I believe in mercy and the guru's grace. And Ramakrishna will be sure to love Don.

Now I must go.

1954

January 12. I ought to write all about New York, of course. But I shan't. I just don't want to. It happened, according to schedule, and for me—apart from the strain and anxiety of making it happen—it was a huge success: that is to say, Donny really loved it.

Oh, yes, and I did too. But there's more real solid happiness in sitting here in the garden house with the rain raining outside, and thinking about it, and being full of plans for the New Year, new work, and I hope a more intentional life.

I've started going to the Physical Services gym at Westwood and Santa Monica, and already the exercise makes me feel good. I needed it so badly. That's a good habit started. I must keep it up.

Now this anthology.[1] I have to ask myself a lot of questions—why do I like the things I've put in it?

It seems to me that I love some writers, and therefore the examples of their work are really examples of what I love in them. And other writers give me a world, and that's what I love. And others have a kind of tone or note they strike, and that stirs and excites me.

For example, I love Chekhov, and Hans Andersen and D. H. Lawrence. I love the worlds of Sherlock Holmes and Conrad. I love the tone of Tolstoy and Proust, and Kipling.

But perhaps I'd better not generalize. Best to get down to writing about each piece individually.

I have a tremendous lot of work ahead of me, if I can only get around to it—this anthology, the Ramakrishna book, the Los Angeles letter for John Lehmann, the story about the refugee hostel (the other part of the material for *The World in the Evening*), the stories about Basil Fry and Francis Turville-Petre, and the rewrite of my 1939–44 journal in the form of a book.

---

[1] *Great English Short Stories* (1960).

July 20. Well—that last entry reads oddly—because none of the things I mentioned got done.[1] I started working for MGM January 25[2] and am still here.

Just about four weeks ago, I quit smoking. Still a lot of nervous tension.

The novel is sort of a flop,[3] both here and in England, but with some good notices, much discussion and fair sales.

Don and I are still living at 364 Mesa, very happily—and we have no idea what will happen after September 1.

Now you're up to date—

As you get older, it's as if a sort of film covers your perceptions of the outer world, most of the time. But there are faces which have a sharpness, a vital sharpness, like that of an instrument, which cuts through this film—so that they seem more real than anything else.

August 27. Made it! Fifty—the unimaginable age. And now comes what might be the most interesting part of life—the twenty years till seventy. What shall I do with them? I want to talk to Gerald, and others, about this.

Am still not smoking.

Yesterday was bad, like most birthdays. Don and I squabbled most of the day. But then we went out and bought a movie projector and had fun running it with Jo and Ben. Rod Owens and his friend Jimmy the Texan showed up later, drunk.

Today I'm back in the studio. The script was finished on the 25th, but already Eddie [Knopf] and I are taking it apart, fussing with it. Jane MacIntyre's[4] off on her vacation. I may get Gottfried's Toppy.[5] Gave Jane a blue sweater embellished with Caskey's beads.[6]

Worries. Don and the draft. The Curtis Harrington case. (His lawyer now demands $600.)[7] What to do about England.[8]

---

[1] *Ramakrishna and His Disciples* eventually appeared in 1965, and the stories about Basil Fry and Francis Turville-Petre became "Mr. Lancaster" and "Ambrose" in *Down There on a Visit* (1962).
[2] On *Diane.*
[3] *The World in the Evening* had appeared in June.
[4] Isherwood's secretary.
[5] Reinhardt's secretary.
[6] Caskey had begun a business beading sweaters.
[7] Isherwood had punched Harrington; see Glossary under Harrington.
[8] Henry Cornelius, the director of the movie *I Am a Camera*, had suggested that Isherwood come to London for the filming starting in October, and Isherwood wanted to see the London stage production (John van Druten had liked Dorothy Tutin as "Sally Bowles"). But Bachardy could not get a passport without permission from his draftboard, and this depended upon the outcome of his physical, also scheduled for October. In addition, Isherwood was uneasy that Bachardy was not yet twenty-one.

But I'm truly thankful that I'm not smoking and that I'm living in less of a daze. Perhaps I can gradually calm down and get my life more into order.

Needless to say, one of my resolutions is to keep this book up again. Shall try.

September 5. Up at Ladera Lane[1]—came yesterday, leave today. Last night, watching the sun go down among the islands, with their long smears of fog, and hearing the whirring of the quail, and seeing the big motionless flowers, the roses still full of the draining light—I remembered so clearly the mood of 1944, up here in the fall, looking at this same view and feeling the aloneness and the sadness. I'm not particularly sad, now. Anyhow, not for myself which is good. I was sad for Billy, who behaved so badly to Connie[2] and John Mace[3] at the party, and then called Ed Tauch[4] and found he was just dead of a heart attack: Billy in tears, drunk and lonely—and pitiful in the way that a woman of sixty-five is pitiful—her life over. But Billy's life is by no means over. It may even be really beginning. It's just what one glimpses. Ed Tauch believed that the millennium had started. Don said I'd talked to Billy about *On the Waterfront* in a way in which I never talked to *him*. All these impressions we get of each other—so partial and wrong. In view of the whole nature of life, one can *never* be sufficiently kind and thoughtful. The utmost is too little. We are all wretchedly exposed to pain. Skinless.

Swami is Swami. No need to say more about him. The girls wanted to know all about Marlon Brando. He talked to Swami at Merle Oberon's.

September 8. I keep meaning to write here—every day I've meant to—but time slips past. Tonight we're going to a sneak of Richard Brooks's film based on Fitzgerald's *Babylon Revisited*. Going with Salka, who's still around, but apt to be leaving soon. Peter [Viertel]'s Bettina [Graziani] has already gone to New York to take a job as a model. Gerald Heard left yesterday, to lecture. Jo and Ben are with Kady Wells[5] in New Mexico.

Worries—the Formosa situation,[6] and Don's draft. Otherwise I'm well, and have plenty of dough—over $16,000—with more coming

---

[1] The Vedanta Center in Montecito (Ananda Bhavan).
[2] Conrad Salinger, an orchestral arranger at MGM.
[3] Isherwood's lawyer in the Harrington case.
[4] A New York architect Isherwood and Caskey knew during the 1940s.
[5] American painter.
[6] On September 3, China launched an artillery bombardment on Quemoy, the largest offshore island held by Chiang Kai-shek.

in. The script drags on, but I quite enjoy working on it. And I get on well with Knopf.

September 9. The chief trouble is acute nervous tension—so acute that sometimes I feel as if I'd just stopped smoking. Maybe this endocrinologist, Larry Weingarten's wife,[1] will be able to do something about it.

The parody of me in *Punch* hurt my vanity, of course.[2] I suppose that I do seem a completely bogus figure to people who dislike me—a preacher of sloppy uplift, a self-obsessed, weak-kneed, whining bore. And yet I know, quite solidly and finally, that the uplift is neither bogus nor sloppy—however unconvincingly I may preach it. And I don't honestly think that I'm given to self-pity. Inside, I'm really not in the least sorry for myself.

My besetting fault is the same as it always was—a vanity which is hypersensitive to criticism. I just can't bear to see one member of the audience yawning—even if it's someone I'd ordinarily despise as a dolt.

(I was interrupted in the midst of all this by the whine on the gears of the garbage collectors' truck. Grabbed the garbage can and ran down to the street, but too late. Now I've lost my glasses, and have had to fetch the spare pair from the car.)

Actually, when I think of almost everybody I know, I find them heroic in one respect at least—the way they face loneliness. Salka in her tiny smelly apartment on Wilshire, Peter taking Lauren Bacall to that awful preview last night. And, I suppose, Lauren Bacall going with Peter. . . . It's not just a matter of being alone, physically—no, far worse, it's the being exiled among people who never, in a million years, could understand anything you said or did.

The problem: what to do with the next twenty years—H-bomb permitting—remains unsolved. I haven't even found any hints, yet. Everything is conveniently shelved until the film is finished. The one real responsibility I have is Don. Everything revolves around him, at the moment.

September 20. Last night, Don and I had supper with Shelley Winters. Doris Dowling and Ivan Moffat were there. Ivan is full of alarm: he

---

[1] Jessie Marmorston.

[2] J. McLaren-Ross's playlet, "I Am a Chimera," spoofed *The World in the Evening* and van Druten's play of the Berlin stories, making deadly fun of Isherwood's new life and work in America (*Punch*, August 25, 1954, pp. 260–61).

has heard that the atom scientists are pressing for a preventive war at once, because, even by next year, Russia will be too strong. So he is sure we shall take the first opportunity to strike—and if we lose 20,000 of our own civilians in the bombing—well, that's tough.

I can't altogether believe this, but I'm nevertheless depressed and alarmed. And my pylorus is busy manufacturing anxiety in case it's needed suddenly in gigantic quantities. I wake, most nights, around 3 a.m., fairly shaking with terror. I convince myself that spies or thugs are coming up the stairs from the street.

Ivan, who rather revels in these warnings of doom, has a plan—half fanciful, half serious—to go to Brazil and found a "family"—not a real one, but a group of people—all talented or beautiful or charming or efficient—who will stick together under all circumstances, act in complete obedience to the will of their leader, and pool all earnings. Within five years, says Ivan, the family would run Brazil. He's probably right. The head of this family is to be—Ricki Huston![1]

Shelley had been grand marshal at a rodeo, and had also made a speech at the ball of the makeup artists' union. The speaker before her had dwelt enthusiastically on the advances the union had made in the past years. "The days are gone forever," he said, "when each actor had to carry his own makeup box." When it was Shelley's turn to speak, she was already rather high. She said, "I'm so glad I don't have to carry my own box." The audience laughed and applauded for five minutes. But Shelley was worried, because she'd been so indiscreet. For example, when she was asked what she thought of Grace Kelly, she replied, "Oh, she'll crumble."

On the set of *The Prodigal*. Thorpe[2] hunched up in a chair, utterly exhausted, like a man who has been drilling for oil in the jungle—and hasn't found any. Watched two actors practicing a sword fight. One of them was smoking a cigar which he never removed from his mouth.

Pains in the penis, bladder and rectum. Enlarged prostate? Felt awful. We had to go to a concert by Bob Craft—in memory of Dylan Thomas. But the music had nothing to do with Dylan. And Igor's setting of "Do Not Go Gentle into That Good Night" seemed almost insultingly feeble—coming right after the magnificent voice of Dylan himself, on a record. How I loathe concerts! That's a prejudice I've never lost. The audience was large and contained several people I dislike meeting—Peggy Kiskadden, Mrs. Herbold, Curtis Harrington, Bernardine Fritch.[3]

[1] John Huston's third wife, Ricki Soma, the dancer (Anjelica's mother).
[2] Richard Thorpe, the director.
[3] Bernadine Fritz-Szold; see Glossary.

Knopf and I saw [Dore] Schary this afternoon. He thinks the script is "brilliant." Tomorrow we're supposed to get it all finished.

October 23. Got back from San Francisco yesterday. We went on the train—the *Lark*. Perfect weather. The trip a real success.

Now I'm free of MGM and really have to get down to work. Jessie Marmorston's vitamins and hormone shots have made me feel wonderful—though Bill Kiskadden maintains that the hormones *may* induce cancer of the prostate—and there's no doubt that the vitamins make you fat.

While in San Francisco we saw Wystan a good deal. According to him, what I have to do is go on writing and solving the "I" problem in narration. Gerald, on the other hand, is more interested in my relationship with Don, which he regards as a most significant biological (or should I say evolutionary?) experiment.

More of all that later.

November 1. An elderly couple are staying at the Hookers'. The lady is iron-silver haired, sour-sweet faced. I was telling Evelyn about our projected trip to Key West, to visit Tennessee Williams and watch the filming of *Rose Tattoo*. Evelyn asked if we were going by plane. "Oh yes," I answered, "if you go by train it takes for ever." "It took the pioneers for ever," the elderly lady put in, with her sour-sweet smile, "to cross this country." A typical puritan rebuke.

An old page in my notebook—probably written quite early this year:

Simple questions like, "Fill it up with ethyl?"—why are they so depressing? Almost the last straw.

A young Negro driving a truck piled high with auto junk—fenders, parts of the chassis, etc. As he peered up from under the sun visor on the windshield, it looked as if he were being crushed by the weight of metal above him.

Ladislaus Fodor says: "In my young days I edited the most highbrow magazine in Hungary. The least thing we were talking about was God. God came into my plays like a butler."

An old actress—one of the public's discarded toys.

November 2. Slowly, slowly. Make no plans for writing. Don't say: I *ought* to write. Just wait until inspiration orders. Be content with daily jottings. Put down anything that occurs to you, however seemingly silly. *All* that matters is to cultivate the habit of recording. I've been saying that for the last thirty years—and yet I don't do it.

December 1. Worried about the Caskey problem. I feel there will have to be a showdown with him, now that Tennessee's here.[1] Bill tries to maintain the fiction that this house is a place he can drop into, any old time—and my life ditto. It is pathetic, of course, like Gus Field's indiscretions[2]—but both are intolerable. Bill doesn't really like Don—why should he? So I have no right to put Don in this false position, just because that's easier than quarrelling with Bill.

Now we'll see if Don gets through this next physical, and how the trip to Mexico goes off, and how I'll spend next year—will it really mean going to India and writing the Buddha picture?[3] It all sounds like fun and I am lucky. But I mustn't lose touch with Swami—I've seen hardly anything of him—and with Gerald. That is *more* important than anything else, including my writing.

Tennessee's letter to Kazan, about his play.[4] It seemed to indicate such appalling desperation that my first instinct was not to take it seriously. Must talk to Tennessee and try to find out more.

It seems chilly, almost northern, here after Key West.

We went to see Gerald this morning and he told us about his experiences while taking mescaline. These are points he made.

The drug took about forty-five minutes to begin working. Its effects lasted more than twenty-four hours.

In Gerald's case, the phase in which objects are seen with heightened intensity soon gave way to a merging of all objects into brilliant light, and an experience of what Gerald called "the second level"—the consciousness or power which projects the objects. Gerald claims that he was also aware of upper levels above this. He was also aware of power—the tremendous power of which this universe is an expression. He felt no terror, or even awe. He felt that this power was far too great to concern itself with punishment. There was no question of forgiveness, even. In the presence of this power, the little faults and failures of the personal ego seemed too small for mention. "The idea of a Last Judgement," said Gerald, "is utterly ridiculous—because one sees that there's no Last and no Judgement."

The really bad things seemed to him to be malice, and mockery of others. Also, he felt very strongly that one shouldn't be reserved, shouldn't have secrets. Nothing really mattered except letting

---

[1] Isherwood and Bachardy went to Key West, November 3–21, to watch the filming of *The Rose Tattoo*; Williams returned with the crew to finish filming at Paramount.
[2] Field gossiped about Isherwood's relationship with Bachardy; see Glossary under Field.
[3] *The Wayfarer.*
[4] Kazan was to direct Williams's new play, *Cat on a Hot Tin Roof*, and was demanding drastic changes; see Glossary under Williams.

yourself go with the cycle—birth, life, death—and not resisting it. Not holding on to possessions or power.

Gerald experienced no sensations of touch, taste or smell.

He developed psychic powers for a while, and saw "between people's eyes." He saw why Aldous had to be blind and Maria have cancer, but he didn't see her dying of it soon. He saw an immense will and ambition in Willy Forthman. It alarmed him.

He only had one hallucination—that a tree outside turned into an X-ray tube and the ferns around it became Javanese dancers.

Unlike George Huene, who wandered all around the garden, Gerald had no wish to go out. Everything was "here." George also ended up feeling this, however. He squatted down and plunged his hands into the soil in order to "get in touch"—and he said, "This is all you need."

I believed what Gerald told us. It was, indeed, very moving and at once applicable to myself—so that I saw how I should have to behave more charitably toward Caskey than I'd intended. I can't simply reject him—or Gus Field. Just the same (Don noticed this too) there was a good deal of vanity in Gerald's narrative. It was all built up to prove that he went much further than Aldous, not to mention George. Of course, I can quite believe that too, because meditation is the ideal preparation for mescaline, and Gerald really has done plenty. Gerald more or less admitted that he had advised Dr. Osmond not to give me mescaline, because I'd "been through so much." This annoyed me. But I blame myself for not having insisted on it more.

One other thing—Gerald was particularly shocked by the way people moved and walked. He described it as "spastic." He said that their movements, as seen under the influence of the drug, betrayed such terrible tensions and inhibitions.

December 11. Sitting on the second floor verandah of the Miramar Hotel on the beach at Guaymas.[1] The sun is about to set. Jo and Don are sketching it. Ben is in his room, writing up notes for an article.

We drove down here today from Hermosillo; the night before that, we slept at Gila Bend, having left Los Angeles early that morning (December 9). We're on our way down the west coast to Mexico City, where Jay Laval and Christmas parties await us.

I'll be glad when we leave Guaymas, the day after tomorrow. This place keeps reminding me of my unhappy visit here with Caskey, just over two years ago. Well, what am I to say about all of that? The vacillations of my attitude toward him are merely depressing, now. The sad thing to realize is that a relationship can eat itself away and

---

[1] In Mexico.

slowly be destroyed. I had a talk with Caskey before I left, and what it really amounted to was that I had to prevent myself turning it into a quarrel, as an easy lazy way of washing my hands of him.

Well, I think this trip is going well, anyhow. And if I learn nothing else from the memory of the other one, let me at least realize that I can never never be kind enough or considerate enough of Don's feelings and problems. He has been through a horrible experience.[1]

It's so restful being with Jo and Ben. Jo really bosses everything, decides everything—and that's what I need, right now. I sleep like a dog, in consequence, and have a terrific appetite. Mexico is one of my very favorite countries, anyhow—but I'd die rather than live here. I don't understand Latins.

Don's joy, when he is happy, is so wonderful. So is Ben's utter satisfaction when we get the right brand of Tequila (I'm sipping it now) or the dinner is good. Jo is much tenser. She has constant pain in her back, and there's the eternal strain of "keeping up." She gave her age to the customs at Nogales as forty-two. Don thinks this is ten, if not fifteen, years out.

Driving out of Gila Bend very early, we saw that much-advertised sight—the planet Venus fading slowly into the dawn. At night, in Hermosillo, the shops and vacant lots containing tractors for sale were all brilliantly lighted up, like movie theaters. As we left Gila Bend, a line came into my head: "The Department of Death announces the departure of His Holiness the Pope, now loading at Gate Number One." Would "now unloading" be better? Actually, the Pope seems to be recovering.[2]

This afternoon we strolled on the beach, and Ben lay down on the sand and said that whenever he did this in a foreign country he dreamed of being a beachcomber. This is a true revelation of his character. At lunch he started talking to me enthusiastically about three-day drunks. Jo discouraged this conversation as subversive. If she thought I was a real drinker I believe she'd never see me again—for his sake.

It's funny. If one said this about almost any other woman, it would mean she was a bitch. But Jo isn't one, and I'm really very very fond of her.

[1] Bachardy had decided to make clear to the draft board that he was homosexual. Evelyn Hooker gave him a Rorschach test and wrote a letter giving her professional view of his sexual orientation; he presented the letter to the draft board at his physical examination on October 5 after indicating his homosexuality on the written questionnaire. His psychiatric examiner was condescending and disapproving, and Bachardy had to endure a second exam on December 7, the day before leaving for Mexico. He was classified 4-F.
[2] Pius XII was ill from late November until mid-December.

December 12. This morning we went fishing. This was a great occasion for Jo and Ben, because it represented the chief ceremony of our initiation into the ritual of their holiday life. If we failed, we would be excluded—not because of their wish but because we would have failed to share in the most important of their experiences.

We didn't fail. That much is certain. Because the weather was perfect, and we both sincerely enjoyed most of the outing. The trip out of the harbor, amidst the islands and under the shadow of the fretted red rocks, streaked white with guano where the sea birds sat like saints in cathedral niches. There were pelicans, cormorants, loons, hawks and great black frigate birds sailing above. Also porpoises breaking the water, and one baby seal. Don and I were the first to catch fish—a mackerel and a sea trout respectively. Then we got into a school of mackerel and all caught lots. And then Jo caught a real big fish, a sixty-pound grouper, and made such a fuss that it was exactly like a woman having a baby in the street. Later, the mate of the boat we'd rented cooked some of the mackerel on board. They were delicious with beer. Ben kept exclaiming, "This is the life!" and gloating over the unfortunates who were driving up and down the Hollywood Freeway. Jo let out cries of utter anguish: "I'm so *happy!*"

When we got home, Don somewhat surprised me by saying exactly what I'd been feeling—that he'd enjoyed himself up to a point, but that he found the catching of the mackerel boring and inhumane—it was so ridiculously easy and we got nearly forty between us, and, of course, gave them away when we returned. (It must be said, however, that an old man got them and either ate or sold them—they weren't wasted.) And then Don added that Ben's remarks about city life made him want to rush into a bar and drink cocktails and race up and down the freeway forever.

I record all this for the sake of recording, not from bitchery. Because, actually, a foursome holiday is only healthy if it includes some criticism. I can't imagine coming down here with two more suitable people than Jo and Ben, and I feel confident the trip will be a success.

December 14. Yesterday we drove down here (Álamos) via Empalme, Obregón and Navojoa. Most of the way, the country was flat, dusty, rather uninteresting. The road in from Navojoa to Álamos is full of chuckholes but not too bad.

There is a hotel here, the Casa de los Tesoros, which is run on a kind of luxury-amateur lines. That is to say, the hot water is hot, there are fires in the rooms, everything is clean—but, you have to "mingle" with Mr. and Mrs. Gordon and their guests. The Gordons are writers, documentary moviemakers, puppeteers, professional bohemians, owners of Mexico's beauties—you've got to see them through their eyes. Well, anyhow, whatever their faults or virtues, it's most useful to find such people at a place like this. Mr. Gordon cooks—well, but not as well as he thinks.

Our fellow guests were a Mr. and Mrs. Martin. He a retired Greyhound bus driver, with white hair and (we think) a mechanical leg. She a fair-haired eager little creature, who has worked in offices and as a waitress. She read about puppets in a book and made some— beautifully—Mr. and Mrs. Santa Claus. She took a class in school on how to tell stories to children. Mr. Martin looks severe, but doesn't want to be. I think he is a member of Unity. They are going to settle in Mexico, at Lake Chapala, probably. It's their first trip outside of the States. I think they are only recently married.

Hard to describe her sweetness and her quality of pathos. Perhaps she is almost a saint, because, unlike the merely good, she doesn't seem provincial or stupid. She is so alive that she could talk to anybody—Aldous, Einstein, Eisenhower—and not lose any dignity.

This city is a sort of ghost town—formerly founded on great riches of silver. Now the tumbledown houses are being restored by Americans. But the place isn't quite beautiful enough. Only average.

The sort of American who comes here is violently possessive, and refers to people stateside as suckers. The only question is: what does one *do*, here?

Last night, a fiesta. Professional gamblers (illegal but winked at) ran two kinds of roulette games. One with a toy train running round a track and stopping opposite numbers. The other with a wheel into which you shot a dart through a blowpipe. The dart often missed and the croupier had to take another shot.

Am writing this in hot sunlight on the plaza, while Jo and Don do water colors, watched by children. On the church tower sit buzzards with outstretched wings, sunning themselves. Don said they were drying out the Mum.[1] In an hour we'll leave for Culiacán, our objective for tonight.

December 15. Culiacán is a dusty dirty town, and the Hotel Maya— without being horrifying—had almost all the features of the classic Dirty Hotel. There were chickens and roosters outside. A bad smell from some kind of filth in the stagnant water of a cistern. Strident radio from a billiard saloon and barber's, below. This recommended

---

[1] Mum underarm deodorant, then available only as moistened pads or cream which dried slowly.

at 7:00 a.m. this morning. Jo, talking to me on the house phone, said, "Shall we dance?"

Also there was the classic fanlight over the door which let in a shaft of electric light—right into Don's eyes as he lay in bed.

The old man from San Diego with a Cadillac and a Mexican driver, who'd made it down from Hermosillo since that morning and planned to reach Mazatlán the same night. Hearing we'd been six days on the road he exclaimed, almost with indignation, "What have you been doing? *Walking?*"

Now we've arrived in Mazatlán and have moved into the Siesta, in time for lunch.

December 16. Yesterday afternoon we drove out along the beach to an unfinished luxury hotel they're building. An American had gotten his car stuck in a sand road. Ben tried to help, without success. Then a man came along with a jeep. He was an American merchant seaman, out driving with a lively and gaudy Negress named Gaby Tondelayo, who told us she came from Haiti, but that Paris was her second home. She claimed to be an entertainer and invited us to come and see her at the Café O'Brien. We did, yesterday evening, but she wasn't there.

I don't know if the merchant seaman's jeep car did pull the other car out of the sand, or not.

I'm not writing down these details for any reason at all except that I want to get back into the journal habit and overcome the sloth of not writing. Very faintly, since yesterday or the day before—yes, it was at Álamos—I glimpsed an idea for a novel. Something quite unlike me—Kafkaesque—about a journey. A journey which is meticulously described and yet unreal: the reality being the relationships between the characters. Maybe they are all dead—as, in a sense, the characters are in Hemingway's *The Sun Also Rises*.[1] Also, I see elements in it of *The Day's Journey*, my projected film.[2]

We spent the day on the beach, and Ben speared a rooster fish. Again, Don and I reacted against his and Jo's excitement. The killing of the fish seemed merely senseless, and Don said that Ben suddenly seemed "oafish."

December 17. Drove to San Blas. This is an almost perfect South Sea island landscape, with straw huts, naked children, palms, overpowering ingly green shiny vegetation. The hotel out on the Playa Hermosa

[1] Published in Britain in 1927 as *Fiesta*.
[2] The Kafkaesque novel was to become *Down There on a Visit*. *The Day's Journey*—a film in which all the events were to occur in one day (as a metaphor for one life)—evolved into *A Single Man*.

had quite nice rooms reeking of antimosquito spray, and horrible food. The boredom of the immense flat sea and beach, with the water so shallow that you could wade into it until you were exhausted or got stuck by a stingray. One sensed the desperation of a tropical exile. Yet the place is so beautiful, especially where the river flows into the sea.

December 20. Here at the Hotel Frances in Guadalajara, after a night at Lake Chapala. The great lake is majestic and sad, even though it has shrunk so much, and [Witter] Bynner's house is one of the most attractive places I've ever seen.

Why is it so hard to write this diary? Because the mood of the diarist is objective and solitary. One needs to be alone, while writing—and on a trip like this one never is. Well, I shall keep making marks on the paper.

[1955]

January 13. Back at Mesa Road. Nothing from MGM yet. The problem of Don's future—shall he continue with college?

Am fussed, though for no real reason. What I miss is the contemplative side of my life. I want time alone—time just to stare out the window and take stock.

The novel still seems attractive, though still very vague.

The weather is cool but beautiful.

The inner life has to be recultivated—ruthlessly.

We all got sick in Mexico City, except Ben, and this colors my memories of it. Much was beautiful—but underneath was a feeling of harsh unease and tension. I don't think I could ever settle down to live at that altitude. And the settlers like Allen Walker were so busy proving how sensible it was to live there, because steaks were cheaper, etc. Tito [Renaldo], a rather tragic figure, uncertain if he had made the right choice.

February 25. Yesterday was Ramakrishna's birthday. I was up at Vendanta Place for vespers, and I open this to record a resolve made then—that I'll write in this book *at least* twice every week until the birthday comes round again next year. That is, barring genuinely grave obstacles.

All the details of my present situation and of the lives of my friends are duly recorded in my pocket diary. Such as Maria's death[1] and funeral, the departure of Jo's sister Jerry for Oregon with Bryson her

---

[1] On February 12.

husband, Don's switch to Theater Arts at UCLA, the return of his father to live with his mother, etc. So I'll start square with the present moment.

Met Lesser Samuels in Marian Hunter's bookshop today—after, I think, a year and a half of not seeing him. He seemed absolutely unchanged. Told me a typical Samuels story, about a man who found the number 5 recurring so often in his life that he took it as an omen—looked up the fifth race on the sports page—found a horse called 5-5-5—backed it, and—it came in fifth. On hearing I was working on Buddha's life, he said: "In other words, it's a bread-and-buddha assignment." But, alas, I didn't hear him correctly, so he had to repeat the pun.

March 1. Yesterday we decided to buy a Ford convertible, and had supper with the Stravinskys. Igor told me he's worried about Aldous, who is being too brave. He hasn't yet mentioned Maria's death to Igor. Igor has a fear that he'll suddenly break down.

They are all three going away shortly on one of their complex trips, darting around Portugal and Spain, mingling concerts and sightseeing, then to Rome, where Vera will show her pictures, then somehow or other—or did I get this mixed up?—over Greenland by air to or from California.

Marguerite [Lamkin] called up in the middle of the night, excited because we were coming to the opening of Ten's play.[1] Actually, I no longer want to go, one little bit. There has been too much fuss over the whole project.

Nerves bad. Feelings of strain and rush. Why? No reason. Nothing could be easier than the life I'm living now.

Writing this sitting in my office at MGM, waiting for Knopf to arrive and show me the test of Marisa Pavan which they shot last week. Betsy Cox, my secretary, sits in the room, as good as gold, reading books about Buddha. She's a nice girl, but I often wish she'd go away and leave me alone. I guess she has no place to go, except the script department.

I feel very dissatisfied with myself, right now. Fattish (I weigh nearly 150) and pouchy faced, I look much older than I did two to three years ago. That wouldn't matter, except that the change seems entirely for the worse. I look like a toad, or a man who is being slowly poisoned to death. My mind is dull, and my spirit is blunted. This, of course, makes me bad for Don—whose hair-trigger nerves need constant soothing.

[1] The Philadelphia opening, before New York, of Williams's *Cat on a Hot Tin Roof*; she was working on the production.

After Maria's funeral, I cried all the way to the studio, and I was really crying for myself.

March 3. Am writing this rather drunk on vodka and tonic in the evening after work, having faithfully started the barbecue fire for fish, brought lots of books from Saltair in the brand-new Ford convertible, purchased this morning, and done all my studio chores. To be domestically busy is for me *le bonheur*, happiness as the French see it—and that's not such a bad way to see it either.

Marisa Pavan was in the studio today—she has been given the part of Catherine de Medici,[1] definitely. She told us about her sister Pier [Angeli]'s accident: how she broke her pelvis in the ladies' room on a plane flying to Palm Springs. But she was smilingly firm in refusing to go to classes with MGM's dramatic coach. Knopf was rather provoked. He said: "I'm not a European, I'm an American, and I believe in saying exactly what I think." In other words, he was going to tell the dramatic coach that Marisa didn't want to go to her. Later he said: "She's going to make some man very unhappy."

Last night I had supper with Swami. After supper, he had a class in the living room and was asked what it was like to live with an illumined soul—i.e. Brahmananda and Premananda. He said: "What attracted me was their wonderful common sense." Then he talked about how few people really bothered to come and see Ramakrishna while he was alive, though most of them became ardent devotees after Ramakrishna was dead. I couldn't help applying this to Swami and myself. But at least, I told myself, I do see him *sometimes.* When we were alone in his room, he talked about Ujjvala—how terribly afraid she was of dying. "And then, when it happened, she didn't feel anything. How very merciful they were to her!"

March 4. An argument with the Breen office[2] about *Diane.* They claim that the picture condones adultery. Diane has broken "God's law." Although the office representatives kept protesting that they were only explaining the workings of the code, you could fairly smell their black pornographic Catholic spite. If they had their way, adultery would be punished by stoning, and homosexuality by being burned alive. It was interesting to watch how this pained and disgusted Knopf's liberal Jewish soul. "It's a great love," he said. And they kept replying, "It's adultery." "Stop using that word!" Eddie exclaimed.

---

[1] In *Diane.*
[2] Joseph Breen administered the film industry's Production Code.

March 8. We're in Philadelphia, at the St. James Hotel. We arrived here yesterday—plane to Washington, train on—to see Ten's *Cat on a Hot Tin Roof*, which opened at the Forrest Theater last night.

I still think it's a very good play, but the performance was awful. An awful arty expressionistic set by Jo Mielziner. This play absolutely demands realistic staging. It is not symbolic. It means exactly what it says. Ben Gazzara was all wrong as Brick. Actually he was playing someone like Golden Boy[1]—an intense Jewish-Italian character from New York, without a vestige of charm, laziness or humor. Mildred Dunnock was all wrong too. She ought to have been fat. Burl Ives is just a gifted amateur. And Kazan (who's chiefly at fault for all of this) had made him address the audience as if he were M.C. at a stag party. A lot of lines came out dirty which were perfectly all right when Tennessee read the play to us in Key West.

People who were there: Carson McCullers, Mikey Leopold and Henry Guerriero, Jay Laughlin,[2] Gore Vidal, Maria Britneva,[3] Paul Bigelow.[4] Maria's hair was dyed blonde for playing Blanche in *Streetcar*. I liked Carson—who kissed me when we were introduced. But she displays the most alarming kind of masochism. She lost all her money when she came down here. She wears a quite unnecessarily repulsive brace on her paralyzed arm. And she really ought to powder her nose. She belongs to the same psycho-physical type as Marguerite and Mikey Leopold. Mikey looked older, but was quite sweet. Marguerite kept giggling inaudible secrets to us—chiefly about Kazan having pinched her leg and William Faulkner being drunk somewhere in town. We haven't seen him yet.

March 10. Got back here yesterday evening—one of the longest plane rides I've ever endured—twelve and a half hours. Marguerite came back with us. She slept throughout the flight, or just lay collapsed in a hangover daze. I read Marguerite Yourcenar's novel about Hadrian,[5] which bored me at the time, but which I now feel has penetrated quite deeply into my consciousness at some other level. There are books like that—they give you radium burns, as it were.

What I chiefly got from the book was a sense of the quality of

---

[1] The sensitive young Italian violinist who becomes a prizefighter in Clifford Odets's 1937 play *Golden Boy*.
[2] James Laughlin, founder of New Directions; Tennessee Williams's publisher and friend.
[3] Russian-born aspiring actress, educated in England, better known for her obsessive friendship towards Williams than for her few acting roles.
[4] A former reporter and one of Williams's closest friends; he helped Williams with his plays, typing and advising.
[5] *Memoirs of Hadrian.*

growing old—something that's very real to me now. For aren't I too a sort of tacky aging emperor, with an Antinous perhaps not so unlike the original? On the flight out to Washington, I thought a great deal about my future as a writer—the fact that I'm so much out of touch with "average American life." Does this matter? When one sees Carson, or even Tennessee, one wonders, "How far out of touch can you be?" And yet they function triumphantly. No. Everybody has *something* to write about. The problem is: find it.

March 15. Knopf is away, so my life at the studio centers around David Miller, who's a nice guy, though a little too glad-handed and anxious to keep us all happy. He spent *hours* on Saturday trying to get Lana Turner to accept the line: "I know your majesty has a heart, and I fear it. But your heart is ruled by your head . . . etc." Finally we found a solution: Diane now says: "I know your majesty has a heart, and I *should* fear it . . ."[1]

Don is much worried. What shall he do? He hates school. Doesn't want to be a student. Doesn't seem to have any specific ambition, yet is guilt ridden—as I am—at the thought of idleness. Like me, he suffers from neurotic laziness.

What am I to tell him? I can't advise—only say: I'm here, as long as you need me.

And it seems Ted is going to have another attack. He is exhibiting the usual unnatural excitement, hyperenthusiasm. He has given up his job at Ohrbach's[2] and wants to get an agent and try his luck at acting again. Neither of the parents can do anything. And this of course upsets Don horribly—especially as he fears Ted will vent his jealousy and resentment against him, as he did last time—hitting him in the face as they were walking down the street.

The Hoerners are now almost reunited. Mrs. Hoerner[3] has her husband and her younger son Griff with her for the rest of this week—all three packed into the tiny garage apartment. She cooks for them on a hot plate which she keeps inside a closet, lest the Lights[4] shall denounce her for breaking the building code.

Marguerite is going back East, for the New York opening. It seems she has already talked Harry [Brown][5] into this. We still don't know her real motive. Ben Gazzara?

---

[1] David Miller was directing *Diane* in which Lana Turner had the lead.
[2] As a clerk in the department store.
[3] Isherwood and Bachardy's landlady and neighbor.
[4] Also neighbors.
[5] Now her husband.

March 18. Angst. Partly to be rationalized by the fact that Ted is having another of his attacks. He left home last night, after pulling his father's hair, and is to be expected down in the beach area today. His nice friend, Don Eliot (?), has obviously behaved very decently about all of this, but he won't be able to restrain him.

But, aside from the Ted situation, I feel a formless unease and dissatisfaction. Yesterday night we fixed dinner for Aldous, Gerald, Chris Wood and Michael Barrie—and somehow it didn't go well. Aldous, particularly, was tired after an excursion to Pasadena to see Mrs. Hubble, the astronomer's widow. He yawned and kept closing his eyes, and his face was thin and grey. Also, they arrived early and had to wait an hour till the fish was cooked. And there was no real relaxation. Aldous refers without hesitation to Maria and the times they were together, but he is utterly lacking in any other kind of intimacy. He just voices negative opinions—how Bernard Shaw hasn't lasted, or how much he and Maria were disappointed in Marguerite Yourcenar's *Hadrian* after the first sixty pages. He described her French as "elegant"—which sounded somehow strange in his mouth.

Gerald, far more sociable, told us that the collision of two galaxies—so far away as to be invisible to any telescope—is nevertheless the strongest vibration that listening devices can pick up in the universe. You can hear the planets grinding together.

Aldous referred several times to the Buddha film. He objects to our telling Siddhartha's story at all. "It's completely uninteresting. Before the enlightenment, he was simply a young millionaire."

Later. Ted was picked up on Hollywood Boulevard this morning. Apparently, he started to undress on the street. He has been taken to General Hospital.

March 21. First day of spring. Yesterday was to have been a great event. Bette Davis was coming to lunch with us. But she sent a telegram at the last moment to say she had a cold. So we had John van Druten and Gerald. It went very well. Gerald talked about mescaline—saying it was the greatest experience he had ever had; and about Maria's death, which greatly upset Don. Johnnie went on excitedly about *Edwin Drood*, which he had just read.

In the evening we went to Luchita Paalens's.[1] The highbrow group from the school of cinematography at UCLA. Bearded men and flowsy women. And no food served till eleven! We both woke up with stomachaches.

---

[1] A Latin beauty then trying to become an actress; she lived next door.

March 23. Well, I've done all my homework—a chunk of *The Wayfarer* (Buddha) which I dislike, and a rewrite of a scene for *Diane*—and am now waiting for Knopf's call.

Have just been up to see Lennie Spigelgass, to ask him if he thought there was any chance of Speed getting a job in the studio. Lennie said it was impossible. Speed got here two days ago and has decided to settle, and take care of all our lives.

Donny started Monday night scene shifting for a production at UCLA. This is a compulsory chore for Theater Arts students. He'll be at it about twenty nights.

This is the ominous spring period—a feeling of impending war in the Pacific, cancer danger from atomic fallout, etc. etc. At the same time, prosperity as never before. For the first time in my life, I've bought some savings bonds—$15,000 worth of government E.[1]

Now I must pull myself together in every way. There is plenty of time to exercise, study Spanish, sort my files and, above all, start thinking about my novel. I ought to welcome these evenings at home, alone or while Don is studying. Instead, I drink to relax into dullness.

Remember what Gerald told us—how Maria said to him: "I'm *perfectly* happy, except that I've got a little cancer."

Monday evening, I ate with Don at Ted's Grill. He had brought two bottles of Dietonic quinine water which he'd mixed half and half with vodka. These we drank, under the waitress's nose.

Ted is being sent to Camarillo again. Mrs. Bachardy insists on this. Her husband wants him put into the care of the psychiatrist he went to—or rather, didn't go to—last time.

Speed gave me a teddy bear called Bunchbaby which belonged to an Englishman who lived in Cyprus and Istanbul, and who recently committed suicide. The bear moves its head if you move its tail.

March 24. Don is at UCLA, scene shifting. I've just eaten at Ted's Grill. Am drinking too much too regularly. Tonight—two vodka and tonics and a bottle of Schlitz, my minimum nowadays. I find myself missing smoking after eight, nearly nine months, quite acutely. The jitters set in every evening and my face twitches.

What a curious phase of my life this is! A coarse, American-way-of-living kind of happiness which nevertheless *is* happiness—not because of the new Ford or my accumulated books and other possessions, or my savings in the bank—but because of Don. The possessions represent "security," which—however reassuring it may

[1] U.S. Savings Bonds were issued in alphabetical groups; series "E" first appeared in 1954.

be—makes me, in the last analysis, feel guilty and insecure. But Don, who is the soul of insecurity, makes me feel unguilty because he stops me thinking about myself.

Perhaps the real trouble is simply that I never heard or knew of anyone whose life was like mine. Therefore I'm naturally uneasy and feel: "There *must* be *something* wrong, surely?"

I wish, I wish I had the leisure and occasion to sit down quietly and figure all this out!

Jo and Ben Masselink are off, this weekend, to observe the uranium rush in Kern County. They have no Geiger counter—only an ultraviolet lamp which makes rocks glow with marvellous jewel-lights which are quite invisible ordinarily. Jo has terrible pains in her back and leg. And these are all the worse for her because of her obvious fear of not being able to keep up with Ben. She looks older and more wrinkled as he grows younger and sleeker.

(At this point I'm taking a shot of brandy—making a definite step in my *untergang*,[1] as I scarcely ever drink when absolutely alone. In bars or restaurants is psychologically different.)

Am rereading—after about thirty years—Hope Mirrlees's novel *The Counterplot*, which I got here, after long advertisement. I find I know whole passages of it nearly by heart. It must have been one of the truly "formative" books in my life. And yet it represents so much that I used to imagine I hated and was fighting to the death— Cambridge cleverness and the whole *Waste Land* technique of describing moods by quotations from the classics—in fact, indulging in moods that were nothing else but the quotations themselves. It's a second-rate book, but I still feel some of the charm it used to have for me. And just because its "sophistication" is transparently naive, I find it warmer and more sympathetic than that of the early Aldous Huxley.

There! I've dropped some brandy on the opposite page. Yet I can't leave the ground, as I'd hoped to, and go into a mood of utterance rather than notation. Well—that'll come some other time. I'm at least happy that I'm keeping my resolve to write in this book fairly regularly. Everything develops out of exercise.

Have just looked up "fescennine" in the dictionary—I found the word in *The Mint*,[2] which arrived the other day. Haven't started it yet.

March 25. Don came home last night depressed because another student had told him his voice was too high. Also, he broke half of the

---

[1] Decline.
[2] By T. E. Lawrence; Isherwood bought the expurgated version published by Jonathan Cape in 1955 but had read a friend's unpublished copy in Buenos Aires in 1948.

glass steam-saucepan. Also, he'd told the captain of his scene-shifting crew that he had to work in a movie theater over the weekends and he didn't like it when I told him that this lie was silly and unwise. (The whole study of Don's minor dishonesties—lies like this one, and sneakings into loge seats with general admission tickets—would reveal, I suppose, a mixture of insecurity and wilful exclusion of the outside world, denial of involvement with it. And I suppose the denial of involvement has something to do with his curiously sheltered teenage years, when he and Ted and his mother went to movies together, every available moment.)

Good notices of *Cat* this morning in *Variety* and the *Hollywood Reporter*. It opened last night.

Later. Floods of tears from Don this evening—why, I don't yet exactly know. The given reason was that he'd been to lunch with Speed and met Eddie James at the entrance to the restaurant, and Speed had asked Eddie to join them, and then he had talked to Eddie all through the meal about people in England, completely ignoring Don. And, on top of that, John van Druten had written thanking me but not Don for lunch last Sunday. So Don feels left out of everything, ignored, overlooked, slighted. And what am I to say? It's true. That's how the world treats young people, and it hasn't changed since I was twenty.

Personally I suspect that Don is suffering on a much deeper level the backwash of Ted's breakdown. The terrific undermining shock to his security such a disloyalty—for Ted's breakdowns *are* a kind of disloyalty, or refusal to cooperate—must be. I can only be glad that Don is able to cry about it, because I believe that's a safety valve.

"How vise it is to hafe much money!" the Baron de Nucingen says.[1] How wise it is to have much love!

(Am drinking brandy again—the second glass—as I write this.)

March 27. Yesterday night, Don got almost hysterical because he couldn't get the movie projector working to show the four films we have just had developed—of our visit to New York, our sightseeing in Washington on the way to Philadelphia, etc. Later he told me he'd decided to "give up feeling insecure." That's what's so lovable and truly admirable about Don. He never takes refuge in self-pitying sulks for more than a few hours—always he comes out of them and accepts responsibility for his life.

Today was dull and cloudy. Don had to read *Six Characters in Search of an Author*. I cleaned house, shopped. Then Harry, Speed and Marguerite came, and we showed them the films. Harry was in a bad

---

[1] Balzac's character (a German) in *La Comédie humaine*.

mood—partly dysentery, partly jealousy of the fun Marguerite had had in New York, where she went for the triumphant opening of *Cat*. Truman took her to a lesbian bar which is guarded by gangsters, where he claims to have escorted Garbo and Jennifer Jones. But, this time, he wasn't let in, and neither was Marguerite.

After supper, I saw Jo and Ben, back from their tour of the uranium-rush country. They had slept out in bags, under Mount Whitney, and talked to lots of prospectors. Jo was triumphant—despite her bad back, they had had fun, and her way of life was vindicated.

A fortune teller in New York has told Marguerite that she made a bad mistake in her marriage, but not to worry, because in June a big change is coming. Her husband, who has been doing work he doesn't like, will start doing something congenial and be very happy.

March 29. This morning I've decided not to go to the studio—"to work at home" as it's called—unless I'm called in to see some film of Pedro Armendariz in *Lucretia Borgia*. David Niven can't play Francis in our picture—he's sick—so there's a desperate search for someone else. Or we'll end up with John Williams, who has to be paid anyhow.

Have just vacuumed part of the straw matting. It looks no better for it. Don is still in school.

Last night I had supper with Peggy and Bill Kiskadden. Chris Wood was there too. Both Peggy and Bill looked well. Peggy in a Chinese gown almost indecently sexy, showing glimpses of leg up the thigh, through the side slits. Bill thinner and tanned from his Oriental trip. He went right round the world, via India, Hong Kong and Japan. Peggy turned back with little Bull at Beirut, because she realized from Maria Huxley's letters that she was getting worse. Sentences stopped in the middle. And it seems that Maria would sometimes say very strange things in conversation, too. Over the phone, she told Grace Hubble, who was coming to lunch: "Always wear lipstick." (Peggy thinks that this expressed her own preoccupation with keeping up appearances—trying to look well and pretty so as not to alarm Aldous.) Bill says this wandering of the mind was probably due to Maria's toxic condition.

Peggy says that Maria wasn't scared at the end, but that she was terribly scared in Paris, while they were on their trip. (I suppose Maria told her this.) Once, while Aldous was away in England, Maria went into a restaurant and ordered coffee, and then suddenly had this sense of utter isolation—knowing she must die soon—and rushed out into the street.

Peggy's old mother, who has had both breasts removed for cancer, is still alive and perfectly well at eighty. She had written to Peggy "touchingly" about Maria's death—saying that it seemed so strange that Maria should have been taken first, and that this was no doubt because Maria had done all she was appointed to do in this life, and because, "I, apparently, haven't." One saw that Peggy hasn't forgiven her mother yet, however.

She snorted at me a little—first when I told her jokingly how scared I'd been when the doctor made such a mystery out of what proved to be the amoebic dysentery—and Peggy retorted: "Knowing *you*, dear, I can imagine!" And then when I described our various trips, she said: "Somehow, I can't imagine doing that sort of thing after twenty. It seems Peter Pannish, sort of." She *is* such a bitch. And yet I'm fond of her.

Then we saw a picture of Derek [Bok]'s fiancée—the daughter of two famous Swedish political economists, the Myrdals.[1] A very pretty blonde, except her chin looks too pointed. Peggy exultantly reported how strict her principles were and how uncompromising she is. She takes it for granted that Derek will give up his inherited money as soon as he's through college. And she'll keep him from being a corruptly successful young lawyer. In any case, it would seem that Derek can't possibly work for the State Department at present, because the girl's brother is a communist.[2] [Derek went] to Spain for a week or two and [presumably thought] over whether he wanted to make a marriage which [might] be so bad for his career. Well, Derek decided he did. [. . .] As for Peggy, I'm sure she'll end up fighting this new daughter-in-law. All this praise of her now has a masochistic note.

We also looked at dozens of photos—three-dimensional transparencies—of the trip. A marvellous rose-colored tower somewhere in India. Little Bull looking out over Istanbul from a hotel balcony on which half a dozen doves were perched. Little Bull standing proudly in front of airplanes; wearing short pants—I suppose Peggy thought them suitable as European "native costume."

April 3. The day before yesterday, I spent the evening at Gerald's, and tried, for the second time, inhaling a mixture of oxygen and carbon dioxide (70% oxygen, 30% carbon dioxide). The first time I tried this was on February 8. Then, after a couple of breaths, I got a most unpleasant feeling—that the oxygen cylinder was breathing *me*, forcing me to inhale and inhale, and preventing exhalation, until I

[1] Sissela Myrdal, daughter of Gunnar and Alva Myrdal; see Glossary.
[2] Jan Myrdal; see Glossary.

thought I would choke and had to take off the mask. Gerald ascribes this to a fear of death—that is, a fear of losing one's sense of identity. Naturally this explanation irritates me, and, in all honesty, I must say that I don't believe I have the least fear of such an experience, though I may well have a fear of this particular apparatus—the rubber mask. Anyhow, this time it went better and I did partially go under. The effect was that the ceiling above me seemed to open and the black dome of the sky appeared, full of stars. Not realistic stars, but stars arranged in a formal pattern. Other than this, I can't say that the experience was particularly exciting or interesting. There is a terrific sense of "lift," that's all.

Gerald talked about the two satellites and "MOUSE," the one we are making to go up and investigate them.[1] Also about the group of imprisoned homosexuals near San Luis Obispo who meet for discussions.[2] Also about the latest flying saucer sightings. Also about Marguerite Yourcenar's *Hadrian*, which he, also, admires. Also about Salinger's stories.[3]

Windy today and yesterday. On the shore the sea glittered and the light was bright and hard. The red storm flag on the pier flapping against the blue sky. The crowds of sandpipers. And always the thought: after I'm dead, all this will still be going on.

Don felt very badly yesterday. Today he was sorry. If only everybody could be as frank and self-critical and unresentful as he is! But I mustn't forget Knopf, who completely changed his attitude toward Pedro Armendariz after seeing him in *Lucretia Borgia*. Now he wants Armendariz to play Francis I in *Diane*.

April 4. Just back from supper at the Weingartens'—mostly great doctors, research scientists and their wives. One of them told me how a woman once sued the City of London for rape, because she had swum in a public pool after men had used it and had become pregnant. The doctor had had to give medical evidence that you can't become pregnant by swimming in water even if it is full of semen.

He also said he thought he'd rather die of cancer than arterial sclerosis—because the latter produces personality changes, and makes you ga-ga and a nuisance to your relatives.

[1] In his 1950 UFO book, Heard speculates that Deimos and Phobos, the moons of Mars, might be Martian-made satellites used as launching stations to investigate Earth. MOUSE (Minimal Orbiting Unmanned Satellite, Earth), proposed by Professor S. Fred Singer, was much-discussed in the early 1950s, but no manmade satellites were launched before the Soviet *Sputnik* in October 1957.
[2] Probably at Atascadero.
[3] "Franny" had just appeared in *The New Yorker* in January 1955. Earlier work was collected in *Nine Stories* (1953).

Jessie embarrassed me by talking about me to her woman guests, just out of earshot.

Speed came to lunch with me at the studio. He is writing an original, with Lennie Spigelgass's encouragement, which he hopes to sell. He expressed concern over Don. Don, he said, must have friends of his own and not rely on me. He went over and talked to Tony Duquette about the possibility of Don getting into interior designing. I was very embarrassed, but Tony was nice about it and said he'd be glad to talk to Don.

The worst of Speed is that his motives are so mixed. I have a lot of faith in his intuitions about people, but there is always a little bit of him that wants to stir the mud up to the surface and make a mess, just for the hell of it.

Another of the guests at the Weingartens', a very nice doctor, had just started reading nonscientific books. He had only started two years ago, and his favorite so far was *South Wind*.[1]

April 6. Marvellous warm weather. We're getting steadily into the preproduction rush. The picture starts filming in three weeks.

Am trying to get Tony Duquette to do something for Don, to help him get into the theatrical designing profession.

A boy who runs the sports department at Magnin's was at Jo and Ben's last night. Whenever he heard an anecdote he liked, he said, "Good enough!"

Oscar Levant, at lunch yesterday, wanted to know about classical Greek homosexuality. He usually seems dopey from sleeping tablets. But I'm never sure if acting dopey isn't part of his particular kind of humor. "I like you," he said—in the tone drunks use—"I always enjoy our meetings." But perhaps he meant this, and was merely too shy to say it in any other way.

April 9. Don will be out late this evening. It's his last night of scene shifting at UCLA, and he will have to stay on after the performance and help strike the set and maybe go to a party for the cast as well.

Now, in thirty-five minutes, it will be Easter. I feel sad and apprehensive and unsure of myself—without any particular reason. It's just that I don't want things to change, and yet I know that they must and will—quickly.

If only I could help Don more! All my sympathy and understanding, all my quite genuine knowledge—through my own past experience—of what he is feeling—no, they just don't help. I'm not him. Thirty years are between us, and so much else. Our lives are like

[1] By Norman Douglas.

two quite different diseases from which we are suffering. We enquire sympathetically about each other's symptoms from time to time, but for the most part we keep quiet—because one can't keep on and on saying, "Oh, my head!" or, "Oh, my poor back!"

Have just finished Colette's *The Vagabond*—the best thing of hers I've read. But—no, it doesn't "speak to my condition." I guess it's some sort of romanticism in me that makes me despise people who "refuse to suffer." Even when the refusal is so beautifully prepared as it is in this book.

How I wish this Easter could be a complete renewal for me! This is the turning point, if there's to be one. Or my middle age is going to be just a waning of powers, a narrowing, an increase in squalor— messy—better brought to a quick close.

Well—come on. Nobody's stopping you from trying.

I remember how, on Easter Sunday lunches, darling Dodie used to greet me at the door with, "He is risen!" And that takes me back to that Russian Easter service I went to with Wystan in Hankow— seventeen years ago! I was telling Don about it at breakfast, this morning.

Thick fog all day on the beach. We went shopping in Beverly Hills. At William Riley's[1] we met a boy who had known Derek Bok. He raised his eyebrows meaningly when we talked of the marriage.

April 12. Yesterday morning, Catherine Caskey called me and told me tearfully that she thinks Billy is "sick" and that he wants to give up the business.[2] Today I talked to Jim Charlton on the phone. He says he thinks Billy is crazy. He's running some kind of beach wear shop down near the Tropical Village[3] and living in squalor with Lou Strong. Jim (who always manages to introduce the note of silent reproach) also said that Billy was drunk for a week because I walked out of Henrietta Ledebur's party (on March 19) as soon as he came in. Now I know quite well that I'm behaving badly, even cruelly, to Billy. And I know that, in a way, he respects and appreciates this. That's the awful complexity of dealing with someone who's a masochist and self-destroyer. If I were on my own, perhaps I could do something. But I doubt it. And, anyhow, I'm not on my own. There's Don to be considered and he can't be expected to put up with Billy—especially with his big-brother act, which is nothing but sheer bitchery.

[1] A shop.
[2] Beading sweaters; Caskey consigned them to various Los Angeles shops.
[3] A bar on the boardwalk in southern Santa Monica.

April 16. This in great haste and just in order not to break my two-entries-a-week record. Marisa Pavan, her boyfriend Arthur Loew Jr.,[1] Salka and Virginia [Viertel] are coming to supper.

Last night I went to dinner with the Knopfs, where Walter Pidgeon told how his mother kept a tin of "blue-mold bread" and used to moisten bits of it and bandage it on to family cuts, long before the days of penicillin. Pidgeon himself had had his hand possibly saved by this treatment.

Meanwhile Don went with Speed and Marguerite and Harry to dinner with Marion Davies. She did her usual performance, it seems. Speed, said Don, was vulgar—that's to say, he acted as ringmaster to the show and encouraged Marion to act up.

April 17. The supper party last night was quite a success—except that Arthur Loew didn't eat more than a few morsels—but it made both Don and me feel that Marisa is [bitchy]. Her venom is astonishing and dismaying. Not only against Magnani, but almost anyone you mention. As for Loew—didn't like him. He's one of the ones who "continually deny." Always sneering at himself and his work—and therefore at everybody else. But Salka was wonderful as usual, and Virginia seemed very lively.

Today there's a high wind. The sea is bright and covered with whitecaps. We were down on the beach. I read extracts from my commonplace book at the temple, this morning.

April 18. Jim came to lunch and we looked at the sets of *Forbidden Planet*, saw an attractive robot getting into his rubber suit and Pidgeon's home on the planet, which looked like a home in the San Fernando Valley, furnished out of the "Home" supplement in *The Los Angeles Sunday Times*.

Supper with Peter Viertel. He told me that a lawyer, quizzing him on his "loyalty," actually suggested that he should say he'd divorced Virginia because she was a communist! A glimpse of the Lower Depths.

We went to see Aldous—who's leaving in two days to spend the summer with Matthew [Huxley] and his wife on the New England coast. He looked so thin and wan. Almost a death mask. The Kiskaddens were there. And Father McLane.[2] And his wife.

Billy told Jim that his happiest times were at Laguna Beach. To me, these were the most awful. Mine, I told Jim, were at Rustic Road

---

[1] The movie producer.
[2] Episcopalian priest, a close friend of the Huxleys, he conducted Maria's funeral.

while Billy was away in Kentucky. But, I said, those times were like the great pauses in the middle of Beethoven's sonatas. They wouldn't have been possible if Beethoven hadn't provided the sonatas—awful as they were.

This morning, in *Georgian Poetry 1911–12*, I read a poem by James Stephens about the garden of Eden that I don't believe I have ever read before—though I have owned the book at least thirty-five years.[1] How strange that seems!

Aldous remarked this evening how some new kind of radiation had produced an entirely new kind of cancer in mice. Peggy winced, as if this were in very poor taste. Aldous no longer has the right to mention cancer at all!

April 19. Worried. Not seriously but chronically, because of Don's restlessness. It's very natural, no doubt, that he should want parties, excitement. But underneath this demand, I seem to detect a certain hysteria—something unhealthy, like the peevishness of a sick, spoiled child. Also—as is always the way in such situations—he is inclined to show a resentment—only partly conscious—against me, as the personification of whatever it is that keeps him bored and quiet.

Well, I only hope something comes up for him with Tony Duquette.

Costume tests, this morning. [Lana] Turner looking svelte but quite definitely fortyish in a wonderful cherry-red velvet and silk gown with long sleeves of fur. [Roger] Moore is fine in his beard and magnificently embroidered doublets, but I do wish he could borrow another pair of legs!

Lunch with Arnold [Dobrin], who would like me to write something about the underworld of the studio—all its little holes and corners, odd jobs, minor people—which he would illustrate. It would be fascinating—for this is really a small town—but I don't see how I could do it except by working all over the lot and spending my nights at meetings of the studio club, etc. etc.

April 20. After writing what I wrote yesterday about Don, I should record that when I came home last night I found him quite relaxed and not in the least peevish, having washed about thirty pairs of socks, done all kinds of other chores and some homework. We spent a quiet pleasant evening together—as so often. As so often—that's what I *must* remember about this period. It is *not* like living with Caskey, or with anybody else I've known. There really is a quality of "home life" in it, and there'd be much more, if my temperament weren't so

---

[1] "The Lonely God," a 240-line poem from Stephens's *The Hill of Vision* (1912).

mistrustful of any happiness in the present tense. (How I lie to myself about the past and fool myself about the future!)

Am writing this at the studio. Spent the afternoon at work on our Buddha treatment—Knopf shows signs of impatience, as yet disguised in a bantering tone and a kidding smile. Betsy Cox just fixed coffee on the electric coffeepot and we each ate one of the Huntley & Palmer imported oatmeal biscuits. Outside the studio, a bunch of teenage girls in those hideously unbecoming knee breeches are waiting to hold up stars for their autographs. One has red stockings and a cap with a coonskin tail attached to it. She's fat and bespectacled and very brash.

April 21. Rain—the first in months, or so it seems to me. Don has gone to see his mother tonight. He suggested bringing me along but she didn't want me to come because, she said, she was too fat!

Worked on Buddha, talked to Dorothy McGuire on the set of *Trial,* listened to Richard Brooks,[1] at lunch, dogmatically describing the function of the ideal screenwriter. A day I have failed to make memorable. But now I'm going out to supper with Jo and Ben, which will at any rate be cozy and cheerful.

April 25. Got back from a weekend at the AJC Ranch last night. Johnnie, Starcke, Carter and Dick [Foote] were all there. Johnnie had just finished a play, which I don't care for much:[2] it demonstrates the utter bankruptcy of ideas in the sort of theater he's trying to write, and he really knows nothing about young people. And his girl is horribly sentimentalized—nearly as bad as Sally in *Voice of the Turtle.*

Starcke was being very possessive about the play—affecting utter exhaustion because "we" had just finished it. Carter and Dick think that Starcke has ruined it by insisting on all sorts of changes. Certainly Starcke's air of a ringmaster, cracking the whip to make Johnnie do tricks, is repulsive and grotesque. But Johnnie wants it that way. Even harder to take is Starcke's "spirituality." He and Johnnie are careful to announce each time they are going to withdraw for a meditation—although these meditations only last ten minutes, as far as Johnnie is concerned.

Meanwhile, Johnnie affects great concern for Dick Foote—"Poor Dick—it's so tragic—what's to become of him?" etc. This seems to me utterly insincere, and indeed the whole atmosphere of the place, when all four of them are around, reeks with falseness and under-the-surface feuds. It makes me almost hate them—although taken

---

[1] Writer and director.
[2] *Dancing in the Checkered Shade.*

separately, I feel considerable warmth toward all of them—even Dick, even Starcke. I suppose it is something deeply false in their relationship which creates this evil stink.

And yet—what a beautiful place—and what a beautifully simple-luxurious life might be lived in it! The big pool with the cotton trees, and the flatness of the fields of corn, and the blue silhouette of the mountains through late afternoon dust-light and blinding sun-haze. The shed where they pack the two-months-old tomato plants in peat moss and ship them off to the north of the state and into Oregon in refrigerator trucks. The Mexicans working at the conveyor belt which carries the peat moss, and Carter counting the plants all day long—the total runs into millions.

Although *Diane* is theoretically only a week from shooting, we still haven't gotten down to cutting the picture or doing any of the other final things that have to be done to the script.

April 28. "The absolute determination of people to be inferior—and all the rest is flying saucers." These words I wrote down in a notebook, last evening, after two vodka and tonics. Don said them and they seemed marvellous, and I went into the bathroom so he shouldn't see me noting them. Now I'm not sure exactly what he meant. But most probably he was referring to his parents' attitude toward everybody and everything not usual. People like that *want* to be underdogs, are glad they're inferior, and they hate the guts of what they don't understand, in fact they affect almost to disbelieve in its existence.

Don, after nearly turning into an angel and flying away during the weekend, was in a hair-trigger mood of resentful presulks. I think part of him is terribly afraid he'll get involved in working for Tony Duquette. They spent yesterday together doing chores in connection with Tony's work on *Kismet*,[1] and they're working together again this afternoon. Personally, I like Tony and I quite understand and sympathize with his motives for helping Don—he wants to get to know me better because he sees me as representing the opposite of the chichi life he has to lead as a decorator. This isn't true, but that makes no difference.

Well, then comes the question—*should* Don go into this kind of work? I think Speed, as so often, was very wise about this. He points out that my danger for younger people is, I'm apt to make them despise all kinds of occupations, without giving them any positive interest. So that Caskey, for example, finding he couldn't be a serious creative artist, first became a seaman (one of the uncondemned,

[1] The movie of the Broadway musical.

"epic" professions) and then took up bead millinery, which was just about at the top of my black list.

May 2. This morning they started shooting *Diane.* Work has been slow all day, and Lana is getting her soft pink piggy pout, and Torin Thatcher is annoying everybody with his big-star grandeur. His attitude toward the script is that of disgusted condescension.

We had quite a rugged weekend.

Friday night I went to the Knopfs', and Mildred said: "Tonight we all intend to get drunk." The reasons for this were (a) *The King's Thief* preview was a disaster, with seven wrong laughs. (b) The "treasure" of a secretary-handyman-chauffeur, who was discovered by the Knopfs and passed on by them to Jessie Marmorston, has absconded, having robbed Jessie of over $6,000—part of which was research fund money—by means of forged checks, etc. Jessie refuses to prosecute and is paying the money back into the fund herself. And Mildred went around and helped the man's deserted and pregnant wife straighten up her apartment.

Jessie was with the Knopfs for dinner—just us four—and we *did* get very drunk and I felt I liked them all much better. *Liked* them, in fact. Drove Jessie home, and she started giving me such a buildup that I had to tell her a bit about myself. She claimed she'd known from the beginning. Nevertheless, it'll probably damp her down.

Saturday night we had a birthday party for Harry Brown. Michael Barrie helped us get ready for it. We decorated the living room with paper balls and fans and Japanese paper flowers. The best were the white balls that looked like chrysanthemums. Don hung them from the ceiling, using scotch tape to hold the strings. When it got warm, the balls fell to the ground, and then they were just like fallen blossoms. Michael was a tower of strength. He cooked meat loaf and served everything. The Larmores and Speed and Marguerite held arms and kicked. As always, with Speed, it was loud and niggery and somehow aggressive. James Larmore was very sympathetic. He used to be a chorus boy, and it showed: he was much more professional. I gave Harry the manuscript of Auden's "Spain," in one of those cellophane-page albums with embossed leather covers which are designed to hold the pictures of Beverly Hills moppets. Harry cried.

It wasn't really a very enjoyable party. There was an air of strain about it. And afterwards Don (drunk) said, "I wish I was dead," and, "I hate them all," and, "I want them to like me for what I really am, but I don't know what I am."

Sunday lunch we went to the Bracketts'—why, God knows. Ilka

Chase[1] was there, and Bette Davis, who is quite an arrogant and not overly talented parrot-faced bitch. Muff [Brackett] is sweet, though—making us all put a white flower in our left shoe, to be beautiful throughout the year. A lily of the valley.

Later we lay on the beach. Wonderful swan-white clouds against the retreating black masses of Saturday's rain storm. Then Tom Hatcher and Riley his employer came, and Bill Roerick and Tom Coley for supper.

I do *not* like parties, especially when I have to give them. And I hate drinking so much.

May 6. Nevertheless we had another party last night and we have another one tonight! Last night were Salka, Peter Viertel, the Parrishes[2] and Lauren Bacall, who later took us to her house where we watched *To Have and Have Not*. Judy Garland came in, very fat, with her husband.[3] I liked Betty Bogart,[4] who's a very lively do-it-yourself kind of girl. Don just loved every minute.

Today Jo has been in to see me after seeing the studio doctor about her back. She is very unhappy. She fears it's incurable and may get worse, till she loses the use of her legs. Betsy Cox is away, which is heaven. I've done little chores and idled all day. Watched a rehearsal of a scene from *Forbidden Planet* and saw the gigantic pig they're using for a wild boar in *Diane*. He's so tough, the first thing he did was to chew up his property tusks.

I also talked to Tony Duquette at lunch. I think he's prepared to take Don on at once full-time, if he leaves school right now. This might be a good thing.

May 8. A beautiful day with hot sun, wind, blowing clouds. Have been lying in the garden, reading a play called *Chindee* about an Indian reservation, by a man named Guy Barrows, who works in the reading department at MGM.

And now—a couple of hours later—I've read the other one he gave me, called *Bivouac at Lucca*. What's wrong with both of them is that old theatrical fault of overly pat philosophical explanations—everything solved so neatly, and someone seeing the light at the end.

The party on Friday was quite a fair success,[5] because Gerald talked

[1] Columnist and actress.
[2] The director Robert Parrish and his wife Kathy.
[3] Sid Luft.
[4] Lauren Bacall.
[5] The third party at Isherwood and Bachardy's house, this one all men.

so well and held all the boys fascinated. Dick Keate[1] was specially impressed and wanted to read his books.

Yesterday I drove with John Yale to Trabuco—we stayed there about three hours and returned after supper. John thinks there is a very good atmosphere there now, and I agree. What I particularly like about it is the absence of religiosity. The boys are more like soldiers, in the G.I. work clothes, with their touching air of masculine fatigue, simple and humble and dirty, a bit hollow eyed from lack of sleep. (They are cleaning the sand out of the well in the pasture, and this means watching the compressor day and night, in shifts—sheltering in the car or under a tarpaulin.) They sing beautifully—led by Jimmy [Barnes], the saxophone player whose wife is up at Santa Barbara. Graham [Johnson], the Negro dancer, sings baritone with Frank, Webster Milam's cousin. Then there's David [Allais], the engineer. And, of course, the old gang. Of these, Phil [Griggs] is the most lovable, bustling around the kitchen.

Talked over the usual problems with John Yale, during our drive. His pale ravaged face. He had recently told Swami how desperately bored he was; and so Swami told him to drop all work here and go up to Santa Barbara to supervise the building of the temple and make japam. John says he never ceases to be tormented by thoughts of lust. And he is distressed because so many of the swamis over here turn out failures. It seems that Asheshananda is beginning already to make a mess of things at the Portland Center.

That's why Trabuco is so important. Because there it *may* be possible to make the transfer just in time, and start a line of native U.S. swamis before the movement loses Prabhavananda's guidance. Otherwise, the whole thing will come to an end—temporarily at any rate.

May 9. Last night we went down to Jim's for a drink. Afterward, Don made one of his scenes. He has no real friends—all of mine disregard or despise him, etc. etc. He declared he didn't want to see Jo and Ben tonight. But this morning he has changed his mind. Also, he is in a terribly disturbed state about his birthday party. He wants it to be full of stars, and yet he doesn't want them. All this is terribly tiresome, exhausting and exasperating, and sometimes I could shake him. But I can't say it really alarms me. It's just that Don feels perfectly free to make an exhibition of himself in front of me and that's to the good. He still behaves far better than I did at his age. I wish he'd grow up, but maybe I shan't like it when he does.

---

[1] A young friend decorated for bravery in WWII and widely admired for his blond good looks.

Absent mindedly, I went to the toilet yesterday afternoon, and thus invalidated my urine test. Jessie Marmorston tells me that every such test involves the life of 150 mice. And so, as there have to be two for each person, I shall kill 300 mice, just in order to know if I have enough hormones.

May 10. Oh, the wonder of deep deep sleep! The blessing of it. It is a very great blessing, especially at my age. Last night I slept from about 10:30 to 8:00 this morning, and woke so calm. It's only now wearing off at 10:15 in the office at MGM, with all the petty annoyances buzzing around my head.

Don is still in his resentment phase. He has quite forgiven Jo and Ben—they couldn't come last night, anyway, because Jo's back hurts so much. But now he feels that Marguerite doesn't really want to give this party, and he's going to ask her to let us do it. He may well be right.

The good thing is that Don has started work for the Duquettes. Yesterday, significantly enough, he cut his wrist while working—only just a nick—but he had to be taken to emergency hospital.

Speed, Paul [Millard] and Peter Kortner to lunch. Also Jack Kelly and his father and mother. I can't ever quite figure why Speed does these things. I was supposed to be selling him to Kortner, who works for NBC, but in fact we just chattered away and got no place in particular.

Today I had the feeling that maybe if I were to sit down and simply start, I might get some valuable material for my new novel. Perhaps I'll try.

May 14. If I knew how much longer I have to live, perhaps I would be able to realize properly the criminal insanity of my behavior this morning. I've wasted nearly four hours fiddling and idling, when there's so endlessly much to do.

Don has gone to work with Beagle (how *does* she spell it, and how did she get the name?)[1] on a mural. He gladly works Saturdays and Sundays, because, as he says, "It's so wonderful to feel you're useful and needed." This is fine, as long as Tony and Beagle [sic] are so busy, but I don't want them exploiting his enthusiasm, or the honeymoon will come to an abrupt end.

Great excitement about the birthday party and endless telephonings with Marguerite. *If* all the invitees were to come, we'd have Lana

---

[1] Later Isherwood learned the correct spelling of Elizabeth Duquette's nickname, Beegle.

Turner, Crawford, Judy Garland, Dorothy McGuire, Lauren Bacall, Bogart, Burt Lancaster, Shelley Winters, etc. etc.

Later: Marguerite just called (around 3:00 p.m.) to say that Harry is off on one of his binges and she's scared—he always threatens to shoot himself and her. Gore Vidal is coming to them for drinks and she doesn't want to be present, because it's worse if she's there and Harry starts bawling her out in front of Gore. "If it wasn't for the party on Wednesday," she said, "I'd leave him today—right now this minute." And then she laughed, as she always does—a kind of silly little hopeless laugh which is very endearing.

May 15. Last night, while Jo and Ben were here for dinner, Marguerite arrived with Joan Elan. Later she and Joan went to a motel, where she registered as Mrs. Don Bachardy. This morning she went back home, found Harry drunk and so left again. But she plans to return tonight.

It's a glorious day. I went in swimming early. Don has gone to the Duquettes'. I lay in the sun up here in the garden for a while. I've been tape-recording the plays I wrote for Chris [Wood]'s recorder in Laguna Beach in 1942[1]—as a gala performance for Don's birthday.

May 17. Waiting to go out on lot two with Eddie Knopf to watch them shoot the going-away-to-war scene. Hoping Brando will consent to come to the party. I'll certainly sigh with relief when it's over. Joan Crawford can't come. Lana'll probably say she's too tired. Garland will probably be too drunk. Also, I have to go downtown this afternoon with Tony Duquette to get an emerald for Don. And who knows if Harry won't blow up before the party?

But let's not get gloomy. At least the international situation looks almost cheerful. And at least Don is working on this mural with Beegle Duquette, which he really seems to enjoy. And at least we have enough money. That's saying a huge mouthful.

May 18. This morning, I gave Don the two emeralds to choose from for his birthday-present ring. Also, during breakfast, played him the tape-recorded plays. He was delighted, and delighted also by the weather, which is the best in two weeks.

But the prospects for his party aren't bright. Apparently, Marguerite has already told Harry that she's going to leave him, in a couple of days—which won't exactly promote *stimmung*.[2] Then Crawford,

---

[1] One-minute monologues, described in Isherwood's diary entry for September 23, 1942.
[2] Atmosphere.

Judy Garland and Brando, the Bogarts and Shelley Winters definitely aren't coming. This will be an awful disappointment for Don, and I hate them for it, even though some of them have alibis.

Knopf has just reproved me (not offensively) for telling David Miller that I disliked both Turner and Armendariz in the packing-up scene. I'm afraid Armendariz just isn't much good. No fun.

Today they're shooting out on the back lot in sweltering heat, and I fear Turner will say she's too tired to come.

May 20. That's exactly what Turner *did* say. And as for Burt Lancaster, he just didn't show. I was so angry that I actually shed tears of rage, but that was when we got home after the party and I was good and drunk. What really upset me was that Don's mother had to be sent away—Don went out and met her and told her not to come—because there wasn't a single star present, and because everybody had sat down, so Mrs. Bachardy wouldn't have been able to mingle inconspicuously with the crowd.

However, the party certainly wasn't dull, or unmemorable. Everybody who *did* come was lively. We danced and kicked. And Don really enjoyed himself. Also there was a big dramatic climax: Marguerite left Harry—walked out of the house with Joan Elan, after Harry had [been extremely unpleasant to her].

Then, yesterday, when Marguerite went back to the house to pack her clothes, Harry pulled a gun on her, said he was going to kill her and himself, and [seemed to mean it]. Marguerite called me and told me this later—she was in hysterics. She thinks Harry would have killed her, and maybe also the colored maid, if Speed hadn't arrived. Then they all settled down to get ready for dinner, and Marguerite said she must go out and buy some chops, and so she escaped.

Harry (whom we visited later, yesterday evening) takes the attitude that this escape was an immoral trick. He had really trusted Marguerite to return with the chops. This, after he'd been waving a gun at her for an hour and a half!

In fact, it's one of those situations which—though it might quite possibly have ended in three or four deaths—simply can't be taken seriously. Harry is perfectly confident that he'll get Marguerite back. And Marguerite won't do the one really decisive thing—go off to Louisiana and make a public break. They are both becoming deadly nuisances, and I certainly don't want a repetition of last night—the yakking at the Masselinks', and the late dinner at Marino's, and then having to go into town, dog tired, to see baby Harry, sitting up sulking like a spoiled kid but loving the attention, just the same. This business gives me some idea how tiresome my fights with Caskey must have been to the onlookers.

Charlie Lederer,[1] the day before yesterday, was telling Knopf and me about his trip into the desert with Richard Haydn.[2] They had read a book about a gold mine that was protected by a yellow cloud that hurt your eyes, blinded you—and also burnt your hands—so that you couldn't stay on the spot. So they went, with a jeep, and they found the spot—a volcanic chimney—and there was a cloud of alkali dust, which burned them. But they found no gold. Apparently it had just occurred in relatively small quantities among the other volcanic debris. The original prospectors must have picked up most of it—and the rest must have gotten covered over with sand.

May 22. The day before yesterday, I'm happy to say, Marguerite *did* go off to Louisiana and so this nonsense is coming to an end, let's hope. But she still hasn't told Harry, which means we have to lie to him, and Harry still thinks she's in Tijuana or someplace, and will return. Harry is coming to supper tonight, which I dread; but it was I who invited him because I felt I had to.

It's a grey cheerless Sunday. Don has gone to work with Tony and Beegle. Charlie Brackett just called. He is getting into the act tomorrow, as Harry's producer, in loco parentis.

My interest in my novel is stirring again; but I'm recording that in the other diary.

As for Don—all that part of my life couldn't be happier and more harmonious. I've started reading aloud to him before we go to sleep—from *The Snow Queen.*[3]

Speed has become a disciple of Gerald Heard!

May 23. No special news from the Brown front. Harry spent all of yesterday drinking and whining and threatening suicide. I called Marguerite in Monroe and got her to authorize me to tell Harry where she is. So I did; and he was worse than ever. But it's better than having him kid himself that she'll return.

Lunched with Tony Duquette today. He says he's eager to talk to Gerald and find some kind of religion for himself.

I want to get on with the Buddha treatment—finish it before June 1 and then begin the screenplay.

I'm all right, really—but I get unnecessarily rattled by all this fussing that's going on around me. And why? the old old reason—

---

[1] Screenwriter
[2] British actor.
[3] By Hans Andersen.

failure to perform acts of recollection. They ought to be constant. There's no reason why they shouldn't be—for, honestly, right now, I don't feel I'm engaged in any particularly God-alienating activity. My home life and my work life—at least they represent an effort toward something worthwhile. Well, I just have to keep trying.

May 25. Yesterday was a gloomy day and Don was depressed in the evening. As he himself said, it was a delayed reaction to the birthday party. He had been running around all day trying to buy a kitten for Beegle Duquette's birthday—today. We ate at the Lobster and walked on the pier. It was wonderful. So cold and empty. Just a few diners, hushed, dispirited, waiting listlessly for bedtime. An exhibition of inexcusably bad abstract art in the merry-go-round building was put to shame by the nobility and beauty of the wooden horses. The fun park pier at Ocean Park was lighted up, nearly empty probably, but going through the motions of fun. And then there was the cold, foaming sea—the other world. No possible pretense, that evening, that there could be any dealings between it and us. The differences are irreconcilable.

Don showed the snapshots he and Ted used to take with a flash, of stars signing their autograph albums at premieres. Don and Ted took it in turns to pose and snap the pictures. They have come out wonderfully well. But I don't like looking at them because they show something in Don's face which is a faint reflection of Ted's—an awful staring vacuous emptiness, with eyes bright and hard as those of a stuffed bird. I hope that look has disappeared forever now. It's the brightness of madness.

It seems that Harry has gone back to work at Fox. Marguerite called him personally and told him that she wasn't coming back to him. But he still believes she is, and this isn't so surprising, because Marguerite is returning to Los Angeles in two weeks to take this job at Fox. I still wouldn't be surprised if they get together.

May 26. A party at the Weingartens', last night, in honor of a British doctor and his wife—[George] Pickering—he perfected a treatment of hypertension, using a drug called Serpasol, known in India for centuries.

They were really very sweet people, especially the wife, and they had both been up at Cambridge at the same time I was. The evening, otherwise, could hardly have been worse. Nothing but doctors—the Knopfs and I were the only "civilians"—unspiced hamburgers, beer, and, after dinner, a showing of *The Glass Slipper*. Jessie's almost sadistic expressions of admiration for me continue. I can't figure out if she just wants to see how much I'll stand, or how long I can bear being embarrassed in public. Or maybe this is just Russian Jewish behavior. The worst of it is, the daughters are expected to get in the act.

Came back to find Don terribly gloomy. And he's just as bad this morning. Says he's appalled to find how much he depends on me. Also, I see a beginning of turning against the Duquettes. Yesterday he dropped a bed and broke some valuable carving. I asked if Beegle was cross. "No," said Don bitterly. "She said accidents must happen, but I know she meant they mustn't happen too often—even with unpaid workers." Of course, the truth is that Don is on the verge of a whole fugue of accidents, designed to test the Duquettes and find out if they really love him.

Masochism is always infuriating. It *tries*, in fact, to provoke one's sadism. But if I am to understand Don I must write down everything about him here, the good and the bad. I still think I can help him— but it will be very difficult and I'll have to keep my head.

Fan note: whenever Lana Turner gets tired, her left eye begins to close. Her tiredness is a weapon with which she keeps everybody under control. And if you try to buck it, she can make herself look startlingly ugly.

May 27. Don cheered up a lot last night. At supper he was very funny, telling me how much he'd hoped I'd come back from the Marmorstons' drunk, so he could bawl me out. But I didn't, and that made him mad.

Today I finish the rough draft of the treatment of *The Wayfarer*. And tonight supper with Jo and Ben—and then *three* days' holiday, because of Memorial Day. Why not start that novel? Well—why not?

May 28. Yes, why not?

This is a solemn moment, because I'm just about to start.

I went in swimming this morning, as I did yesterday. The water isn't cold. They have torn down the old beach club—the building immediately south of State Beach—and they'll probably destroy the wall which makes it possible to undress on the beach without being seen from the houses along the highway.

Yesterday I went on the set with Don and suddenly realized that Catherine and indeed the whole court ought to be wearing mourning—the day after the dauphin's death! Nobody had noticed this. Consternation. Then Knopf was telephoned, and he ruled that it didn't matter.

Yesterday evening, we went to supper with Jo and Ben. Don and

Jo drew sketches later. Don's were very good—full of life. He really does have a talent. But they make Jo look so old!

I find it so touching to think of Don's childhood—being taken downtown on Saturdays by his mother with Ted, to see movies. How they loved Alice Faye! The pathos of that childhood snugness—false security, so soon to be destroyed.

10:29 a.m. A grey morning with sun behind the fog. No more excuses for delay. Okay, boys—this is a TAKE!

May 29. Well, I actually did write something—a page of utter nonsense. And I've just finished another page today. (Thick fog out. Don clipping pictures from movie magazines for his collection. The Siamese kitten (Kabuki) he gave Beegle Duquette is frisking around the room—it's spending the weekend with us because the Duquettes have gone to Palm Springs. A kind of wet-day-in-the-nursery atmosphere.)

Yesterday morning, I talked to Mrs. Hoerner to find out if we can have the house for another year from next September. This isn't certain, because her husband may be stationed out here instead of at Norfolk. Otherwise, he'll go to Washington. Mrs. Hoerner seems placidly indifferent. She's staying here in any case. If he comes, she'll move up into this house and live with him. She won't go to Washington.

She tells me she is looking for a Buddha. She wants to put it in a shrine and light incense sticks in front of it. The Buddha she has now is unsatisfactory, but she burns the incense, just the same; and if she's out, her son Griff does it—although he squirms if ever she talks about religion. Griff is nearly seventeen, and the other day she found he'd started taking flying lessons without her permission. Eleven dollars a lesson—he makes the money by washing cars.

A party last night given by Jesse Lasky Jr.[1] and Olive Deering. Couldn't have been more bored. We went because Don hoped Anne Baxter would be there. A director (middle European—Brahm?) got me in a corner and told me Conrad was psychopathic. He feared and hated the sea but forced himself to be a sailor because he was ashamed of not being a Polish revolutionary, like his parents. The director also said that the man in *Heart of Darkness* is a prophetic portrait of Hitler. (He himself had directed "The Secret Sharer" for Hartford.)[2] For some reason, he made me very angry.

---

[1] Screenwriter.

[2] John Brahm (1893–1982), a German, directed Conrad's short story "The Secret Sharer" as the first part of a two-story movie, *Face to Face*. The producer was Huntington Hartford.

May 31. Last night, we went to Peter and Alice Gowland's. Their children danced—Mary Lee, six, dressed up in her mother's black lace slip, winking and leering and gesturing with a cigarette holder: it was frighteningly obscene. Ann, doing rock and roll with her girlfriend Sue, wasn't frightening but overpowering. Ann is twelve, and already she has a steady—the son of Johnny Weissmuller, who's six foot at fourteen and carries a spring knife with which he occasionally "nicks" her. Peter and Alice are utterly helpless and childlike as parents. Mary Lee treats them as her victims. She has to be bribed to be quiet with "six presents" (apparently a kind of inflation has set in). She gets out of going to school by saying she's sick, and sits watching TV all day long.

The object of our visit—with Jo and Ben—was to see *The Petrified Forest* on TV.[1] A truly poor play—how did it ever get such a reputation? I remember seeing it as a film, in London, with Stephen [Spender]. Even then we disliked it, but Bogart was much better then, I'm sure.

Wrote some of my book—page four—today. Every voice of reason tells me this is idiotic—without a plan I'll get nowhere. But the whole point of this method is not to care *where* I get. It corresponds to making acts of spiritual recollection, with the faith that *no* act is wasted. No act of artistic recollection is wasted.

Lunch with Tony Duquette. He wants to open the theater in his studio with a masque, something part play, part ballet. We discussed the possibility of adapting something from the animal books illustrated by Grandville.[2] Talked also about all four going abroad together this fall.

June 1. Today I'm depressed, partly because of a hangover, chiefly because of a letter from Glenway Wescott yesterday, telling that George Platt Lynes has an inoperable tumor on the lung and can't live more than a few weeks. How glad I am we gave him that lunch at the Pavillon![3]

Last night we had Gerald and the Bracketts to dinner, with Michael [Barrie] helping as cook. The party itself was a huge success—Gerald highly elated by news of a saucer crash in England and the capture of its midget crew. But later Michael came back and talked religion—he still feels guilty, underneath, about having left Trabuco. And this talk caused Don to feel excluded; which was all the more bitter because

---

[1] Robert Sherwood's play, filmed in 1936 and remade for TV in the 1950s; Humphrey Bogart starred in both versions (as well as on Broadway).
[2] *Scènes de la vie privée et publique des animaux*; see Glossary under Grandville.
[3] In January 1955, during a brief trip to New York.

he'd just been saying how much he liked Michael and Gerald. "As soon as they get drunk," he said, "they all show how little they care about me or what I think. They all treat me the same way."

This new technique of novel writing is fascinating. Because I seem to have put the subconscious on the spot. Now it's trying to bribe me to stop by offering me suggestions on how to write it properly. I must listen carefully to the suggestions—and go right ahead with this version.

Latest Brown news: Harry has been drunk for two days—says he refuses to go back to work, will starve Marguerite out by going bankrupt. Charlie Brackett is all set to deliver a severe reprimand. Marguerite is due to return here shortly. Speed is so tired he says he aches all over.

June 3. Talked to Henry Daniell on the set yesterday. He told me he suspects the communists are "getting at" the younger generation of Americans. Because his daughter, teenaged, said the other day, "The Russians wouldn't hurt us if we let them alone."[1] He says acting is an impossible career. He wishes he'd gone into the law.

Am worried about pains in the top of my head, darting like neuralgia and sometimes quite sharp. Can I be starting a brain tumor?

Marguerite is scheduled to return from Louisiana today. She'll start divorce proceedings at once.

June 7. Yesterday we went to a party at the Archers'[2]—a big affair with a tent and 150 guests. Both Harry and Marguerite came, separately. Harry says he has given up drinking for keeps. They didn't reconcile, and Harry is still saying she shan't have any money.

Afterwards Don and I and some of the others went up to the Duquettes' house, which is extraordinarily sinister—sort of ghoul-baroque—and did kicks to the ubiquitous glad-rag-doll record.[3] It was quite a lot of fun.

I still have these head pains, *and* a hangover.

June 9. Two nights ago, I went to the Knopfs', and Allen Rivkin[4] described in detail how he'd had a brain tumor scare, and how he saw

---

[1] Daniell was British, but acted in Hollywood from the start of the 1930s (he was in *Diane*).

[2] Actor John Archer and his wife.

[3] Speed Lamkin then carried a recording of "The Glad Rag Doll" everywhere he went and encouraged friends to dance (as at Harry Brown's birthday party where there was a similar kick line, mentioned in Isherwood's diary entry for May 2).

[4] Screenwriter, mostly of B-movies.

double in one eye, etc. And Eddie told me how [George] Gershwin came to the house only a couple of weeks before he died, and how he kept dropping things. So I feel less worried about my headache, though it persists.

Yesterday Thom Gunn came to lunch with me, en route for Texas. Liked him so much I asked him to come on with us to Michael [Barrie]'s for supper. He has pockmarks and a vertically lined face like a convict's, and his nose and chin are both too big—yet he's quite attractive, with his bright brown eyes. He likes America, especially California. I warm to all Britishers who do that. And he's intelligent, and warm.

Loathsome sad grey dreary weather. No news of how Schary likes *The Wayfarer*. Marguerite is living at the Duquettes', getting a divorce. Caskey is reported raging drunk. I keep on with my novel. I'm reading *The Inferno*.

June 11. The day before yesterday, we went to supper at the Parrishes'. Don got drunk—we all did—and felt he was being neglected and left abruptly, without saying anything to anybody. I came home later and kidded him, and he was so furious he ran out and slept in the Ford downstairs. So yesterday I had a fearful hangover and stayed home. And Don and I had a long talk, which added up to this: that Don undoubtedly *is* rejected by people some of the time, but that it's nevertheless neurotic to mind about it so much. On the whole, this blowup reassured me rather than otherwise, because Don managed to be fairly objective about it and didn't get furious when I said maybe we should try a psychiatrist. Needless to say, I don't want that any more than he does.

Sunshine today and beach weather, after days and days of grey cloudiness. I still have this headache—no worse but no better.

June 13. Back at the studio. A grey day. The *Diane* company went out to the Adams Boulevard location, but I'm sure they'll have to give up. It's hopeless.

Marguerite saw Harry last night—but no reconciliation, according to Speed. Harry was expecting one, when I talked to him at the Bracketts' lunch—where Monty Woolley[1] retired in a state of collapse, and Dick Cromwell got drunk. Harry looked awful—his face covered with blotches, his eyes dull and dead. He drinks only soda water.

Speed says Caskey is going to Italy in August—having let his business slide and sold his lot. Hayden and Rod's business is slipping

---

[1] American character actor.

too. And Jim is "pitiful." But this is all part of Speed's view of the "sick people"—the Canyon folk. I don't take it too seriously.

June 14. I feel really lousy today—tired and shaky, and this pain in my head steadily continues. I wish I could get over it without going through all the fuss of having it examined. Maybe it *is* something—but yet I've had far more alarming symptoms so often before this.

June 20. A big gap. Must be careful.

Well, I went to see Sellars on the 16th and Irvine on the 17th, and both seem agreed that it isn't anything very serious. Irvine thinks it may be eyes and is giving me some bifocals. Sellars, however, thinks it's my back and could be adjusted by Dr. Mitchell here. But he doesn't want me to be treated without X raying because—as he cheerfully tells me—he had another patient who had something wrong with his back—didn't have X rays—went to a bone setter, and then found he had a tumor of the spine!

Right now, due to my relief, the pain has nearly disappeared. That began yesterday, although I went into the ocean twice—the first time in weeks and weeks; because at last the weather has improved.

Today, Knopf tells me he's terribly upset by night terrors. He wakes in the small hours, trembling, from terrible nightmares—that Leland Hayward[1] upset some sauce. He says he can understand, now, about nervous breakdowns. Sellars tells him: Either take phenobarbital or spend $10,000 on an analyst.

From a shooting schedule: "Outer space. Exterior."

I stop and talk to a writer. He's working for Joe Pasternak.[2] "What's the picture?" "*Four Girls.*" "What's it about?" "We don't know yet. But Joe said to me—You know all those marvellous terrific gals that keep coming over from Italy? Lollobrigida, Mangano—sensational! Well, how'd it be if we took four of them?"

Madame Grenier, our technical advisor on the *Diane* set, tells me how, when she had to become a U.S. citizen (because of her husband), Queen Mary said to her consolingly: "The women of my family *always* have to change their nationality when they marry." And she took from a drawer a brooch made of diamonds and rubies representing the U.S. flag, and gave it to Madame Grenier, who wears it still.

How in the world did Queen Mary get such a thing?

This isn't correct, but an effort to remember John van Druten's latest "poor little" verse:

[1] The agent and Broadway producer.
[2] Hungarian producer, long in Hollywood.

Poor Mrs. Lodovic Vroom
Is going to redo her womb,
For her suitors have all of them started to shout
That they feel claustrophobic and want to get out.
Poor Mr. Lodovic Vroom
Puts up signboards: "This way to the tomb."
Now they're letting in windows, which serves as a clue
Why the place is described as a womb with a view.

We saw him and Starcke on the 15th. They're off to New York for the play.[1]

Other news—*Diane* may be called *Cage of Gold* after all. Schary has gotten around to the idea.

Marguerite has settled into an apartment, on Harratt Street below the strip, where I used to live with Vernon in 1940. And she has started work on *The View from Pompey's Head* as a technical advisor. And Harry has started drinking again.

On father's day I gave Swami a bottle of sherry, which had to be hidden from a party of visiting Hindus. Swami gave me a shaving brush he'd just received, but didn't want because he has an electric razor.

Five minutes of eight. Just finished the first page of a new draft of my novel, having stayed late at the studio. How wonderful! Now supper with Don at El Coyote, and then a movie. And my conscience shining like a new nickel.

June 21. It's after five in the afternoon and I'm lingering on here because I don't quite know where else to go. Don's out with his mother. Also, I want to write another page of my novel.

Knopf is radiant today, because Dr. Sellars examined him thoroughly, and there's nothing whatever wrong with him. His heart is one and a half centimeters smaller than last year. Eddie now confesses that he was terrified of having a stroke. He'd been brooding over the death of Walter Hampden, who had been just about to start playing Ruggieri in our picture when he died.

Lunch with Tony Duquette, who has decided to go ahead with his schemes for a theater in his studio, despite being hard up. He's very hostile to Speed, because of Speed's indiscretion.

Don seems happy and lively again. But he's very anxious to be reassured that Beegle and Tony like him.

Rehearsals with Lana and Marisa, of the last scene but one. They'll be good, I think. Lana gives one a terrible impression of nerves and

[1] Van Druten's new play, *Dancing in the Checkered Shade*, which flopped and closed immediately.

weariness—the faded lachrymose blonde, all too apt to sob into her cocktail.

June 23. Last night we went to a preview of *I Am a Camera*—a truly shocking and disgraceful mess. I must admit that John Collier is largely to blame—for a sloppy, confused script. But everything is awful—except for Julie, who was misdirected.

Today, Roger Moore had a slight accident on the set. Fell off his horse and bruised himself. He was taken to hospital, X rayed and put in ice.

Don went to see Ted yesterday. He says Ted showed hardly any interest in outside news—only wanted to talk about a television play he'd seen.

June 25. Depressed. Dull grey weather. Don has to work for the Duquettes. Also, he has started to complain again, because we don't get invited out enough. He doesn't mean to be tiresome about this. He blames himself. He is ashamed. But he slips back into it.

I'm tired to the bone. And bored. I don't want to go to this party at the Froms' tonight. I don't know what I want. I don't want to write in this journal—that's for sure.

June 29. Four days since I wrote that—and such ups and downs. Actually, the Froms' party was quite a success, because, before going to it, Don and I visited the Luau and had an excellent dinner and lots of rum drinks. And the next day (Sunday) there was fine weather and we went on the beach and were happy, and then saw *Land of the Pharaohs* and enjoyed that too. But the night before last I got impatient because Don took such ages undressing and I snapped at him and he sulked, and we are only just now getting over it.

Last night I saw Gerald, and we had a long talk alone. I can see that he really disapproves of—or, at any rate, feels superior to the life I'm living: the studio, prosperity, domesticity. As opposed to his life (as he sees it) of comfortable poverty, shabby, lonely. (But he forgets Margaret [Gage] and Willie [Forthman] and everything they do— with Michael—to surround him with security.) He feels that only those who live such a life as his—far from tycoons and producers (but he forgets he just told me of meetings with the heads of Chrysler and General Electric)—can hope to find out what is really worth knowing. No, no—the truth is that Gerald is a vain old bird. And if he doesn't want to go to the Bracketts' lunch or meet the Cottens, it's only because they refuse to break down and repent and let him lecture them.

Nevertheless, he is right in some respects. It *is* easier to follow up the latest information on flying saucers, mescaline, psychical research, etc. if you are a free agent.

I'm truly fond of Gerald nowadays, and I do value greatly the privilege of being able to talk to him. I think his generalizations are most untrustworthy, but they are extremely stimulating. The "breakthroughs" he says, are becoming more frequent on all levels. Homosexuals are increasing in numbers. More and more people are having mystical experiences and sighting "unidentified aerial objects." Newer and even stronger drugs are being discovered to shift the focal length of consciousness. A great new age is dawning with the realization that there will be no war, after all. "I knew it, as soon I saw all those red cars rushing about the streets. . . . A terrible outburst of relief." But Gerald also thinks it will lead to more nervous breakdowns and even insanity—because people will feel so utterly lost under the changed conditions.

July 1. This is just another of those entries made so as not to break the record. I feel lazy and sticky after a hot afternoon spent rewriting a scene for *Diane.* Eddie From to lunch, with his rather annoying air of wisdom and silent judgement. None of these pure souls can ever, *ever* forgive me for being a "success." But still, I like seeing him. Like Swami, he disapproves of mescaline—feeling, approximately, that one should do the work oneself.

Got a traffic ticket—and declined an invitation to go to supper and meet the president of Burma.

The weekend doesn't look very promising. Grey mornings till two. And, on Monday, the horror of Trabuco.

July 3. Yesterday afternoon, Jo and Ben took us round to visit Lola Lane[1] and her husband Bob, who live in the old Thelma Todd restaurant building. It's certainly one of the most glamorous places in town—quite aside from having been a whorehouse and the scene of a murder.[2] Real Californian-Twenties style. Lola's sitting room at the top of the house—which is on a level with the upper garden—used to be the gambling room, so the doors are all of iron, with a speaking window in one of them. Lola has her bed on a curtained platform which used to be the bandstand. There are still banquettes which used to stand around the dance floor, and they still have the round table which reverses so you can play poker or dice on it. The woodwork has simulated chisel marks on it, and it's painted with a cream varnish.

[1] Eldest of the five Lane Sisters, all actresses (only three had significant careers).
[2] Actress Thelma Todd was murdered there; see Glossary under Todd.

There are panels of rainbow glass in the closet doors. The room looks rather like the cabin of a luxury yacht in a novel by Elinor Glyn.

The peculiar acrid smell of old houses along this coast. It reminds you of seaweed, wet bathing suits, stinky rubber shoes.

We spent this morning visiting the *Kearsarge*—the flattop[1] which is visiting here for the Fourth. It's rather frightening, below decks—such a warren of narrow passages, vertical ladders. When you see someone appear, framed in one of the many doorways, it's like your own reflection. A horrible chaplain was conducting a Protestant service on the flight deck, in a voice so much amplified by the mike that it could be heard all over the bay.

July 5. Yesterday I drove to Trabuco for the annual doings.[2] It was even worse than usual, because there were so few people I knew. Gave one of my "don't know what to say but Swami insists" speeches. Boshi Sen[3] was there. He patted my cheeks, hugged me and made me promise to visit him in India.

News heard on the car radio as I drove. The pilot of an American airliner killed a rattlesnake in the baggage compartment just before landing in London. None of the passengers knew. Bulganin and Khrushchev dropped in on a Fourth of July celebration at the U.S. Embassy in Moscow.

Gore Vidal tells me he hears that Gerald Hamilton posed for the body of a portrait of Churchill. Gore may take a job at MGM.

Ted is out on leave from the hospital. He came to lunch here with Don today. He seems absolutely normal. Looks healthy and tanned and a little plump.

There's something strange about Speed. We saw him last night at Marguerite's, and he's obviously sulking and cross. Maybe he's having a struggle to keep his influence over Marguerite. Harry comes around quite often, but no scenes.

July 7. Gore is definitely taking the job. Don had lunch with Speed yesterday but Speed got Don to talk about himself, and revealed nothing. He advised Don not to lose his temper because it becomes a habit, and told Don to cultivate friends of his own age with whom he can be a star. Also to save money.

We had supper with Salka alone in her new apartment. She was so

[1] Aircraft carrier.
[2] An open house is customarily held at Trabuco on July 4, American Independence Day and the day of Vivekananda's death.
[3] Botanist and head of a laboratory in Almore, India; he was a boyhood friend of Swami Prabhavananda and long associated with the Ramakrishna movement.

charming and amusing, talking about the old times—how she came to be an actress, and how she and Berthold came to Hollywood.

Jo tells me this morning that her back was so bad last night she's in utter despair.

July 8. One of those late evenings at the office—the only time there's real quiet. And it's a Friday, with all the promise of liberty and relaxation ahead.

We're coming to the end of the picture—finish, more or less, this next week. David Miller told how he wanted to make Lana really weep in the last scene. So he said: "By sending you the ring, the queen acknowledges that you were really Henri's wife—not a mistress, not a kept woman." And at this Lana wept and wept. David could only shoot the scene once. And Lana went on weeping for fifteen minutes after it was over.

Compare this with the story of Kazan directing Jo Van Fleet.[1] He told James Dean—in order to get a sudden reaction of fury—to go up to her and whisper: "You fucking cunt!" Dean did, and Jo Van Fleet was furious, but only with Kazan. She told him: "That's not the way to make me act."

Money worries—not serious—chiefly sheer stinginess—like grudging two hundred dollars for Salka's bookshelves, because I'd expected to pay around eighty. Actually, I'm richer than ever before.

Arthur Freed[2] has had one of his periodic fits of raving about *Prater Violet*. But he doesn't buy it.

Don seems happier, getting along well. The Duquettes may start paying him soon.

I don't think I'll take this job in Italy, doing a screenplay on Mario Soldati's *The Capri Letters*. They just don't interest me much.

This is such a curious phase in my life: grossly materialistic, very comfortable, and, I guess, happy—in the sense *Life* magazine means happy. But I could make it so much more than that if I exercised a little recollection. Why not make japam? Why not get on with my novel?

July 11. I think our neighbor Mr. Light is really nuts, poor creature. Yesterday he painted, carefully and beautifully, on his garage wall in bold black letters: No Parking on Walk. Vehicle Code 586 F.

Diane ends officially tomorrow.

I'm full of ideas for my novel, which looks like being a catchall for all kinds of earlier stories and projects.

[1] In *East of Eden*.
[2] Lyricist and MGM producer.

July 15. I'm depressed and worried about Don. He had another outburst two nights ago, telling me with tears that he is "so terribly unhappy," and giving the reason that he has no friends of his own. Well, that's true of course. But at the same time, as I've told him before, it is also a rationalization of neurotic melancholia. I can understand this when I think it over, but when we're actually in the midst of the scene, I feel awful, and quite helpless. And, of course, it *is* true that I'm often neglectful and insensitive to his feelings, because I want a quiet home life so I can think about my work undisturbed.

Now I feel completely insecure. What in the world is the point of all this work at Metro, these efforts to get another house—if Don suddenly leaves me?

On the 12th we had a party on the set for the end of *Diane*. I got paralytically drunk and had to be driven to Eddie Knopf's for dinner. I'm told that I actually licked someone's face—whose, or why, I don't know. Next day I felt ashamed—but on the whole I think most people found it rather sympathetic.

It's very hot. Thank God for a weekend coming up!

July 18. The weekend was a success—glorious hot beach weather and Don happy—all except for Friday night, when Harry brought Marguerite to dinner and sulked clear through the evening. Maybe because we'd also invited Salka and Joan Elan and gotten stuck with Brendan Toomey[1]—such a silly little boy.

Ivan, just back from Europe, looked into my office today—sleek with pleasure and success. He has a new girl whom he took to Greece, and he threatened to throw a glass of wine in Philip Toynbee's[2] face when Philip got drunk and talked dirty to Iris (told her he'd fuck her stiff) and later apologized. Iris has written two chapters of a novel about her childhood and early life, which has been accepted by a publisher.[3] Cyril Connolly's wife[4] has left him, taking their cottage with her. Stephen [Spender] is seen at parties with Princess Margaret and Lucian Freud. Ivan's overall impression was that the British aristocracy is flourishing, the intelligentsia brilliant and amusing but almost exclusively critical not creative, the middle and working classes very pleased with themselves but inefficient, second rate, full of alibis, the Labor leaders at a loss.

Lunch with wisecracking Gore and a silent Tony [Duquette]—an

[1] Young friend of Leonard Spigelgass, the MGM screenwriter (see Glossary).
[2] English novelist and critic (1916–1981).
[3] Never finished.
[4] Barbara Skelton, his second wife.

uneasy combination—the two of them unhappy in different ways. Tony is depressed because he feels they've ruined *Kismet*. Gore, because he finds himself unable to care for anyone seriously.

July 22. Ups and downs. Two days ago, one of Don's biggest explosions, out of a clear sky, after supper at the Red Snapper. Since then, cleared air. What am I to say? Nothing. They distress me, and I even get mad; but I'm not alarmed. I feel we shall get through this phase and learn to understand it.

It's very warm. I feel tense and don't sleep as well as usually.

Lunch with Harry. He has been making drastic scenes with Marguerite—the divorce is next week—and yet they see each other in between. I taxed Harry with the things he allegedly said about Don and me—that we were against him and pro-Marguerite. But he evaded the issue, assured me he didn't believe anything like that. I think he's very near schizophrenia. His blotched unhappy face, with ill-matched eyes. He sees Marguerite all the time—"as friends," and then gets drunk and tries to kick her door in!

Talked to Ivan about it last night. He was having supper with us. (So were the Stravinskys.) Ivan says he warned Marguerite that if she was going to marry Harry she must make up her mind never to divorce him. He thinks Harry is potentially very violent.

Meanwhile Speed and Paul [Millard] have decided to stop sharing their apartment. Speed, I think, pretends to mind this more than he does. But it has one good aspect—Harry is genuinely impressed by Speed's self-control. He talked a lot about it at lunch today.

Igor and Vera were so sweet, as always. Igor got quite drunk, which was nice, because he likes to. But it was a pity in another way because I missed one more opportunity—and how many more will there be—of talking to him quietly.

July 25. A quiet weekend. Grey weather, with a chilly wind that spoilt the chances of swimming. Wrote letters and hunted houses. It's fun seeing them, but I suspect we'll end up moving into Mr. Light's next door because it's so much less trouble.

Don's mood is good again and all is happiness, despite the irritations of having Kabuki[1] over the weekend. This is the last time the Duquettes are going to park him on us. Life is pleasant, but I would like to get my novel started. And the answer is: start it.

This week, Marguerite and Harry go into court and whatever nastiness there is going to be will come to the surface. I'm worried about this, but hope for the best.

[1] The kitten.

July 26. Aldous's birthday, and only a month from mine. I must pull myself together. I'd planned to have accomplished *something* by fifty-one—and I shan't have.

Waiting for Knopf to see me, and meanwhile stalled on *The Wayfarer*—and well I know that when I do see him it'll only be to receive some snap judgement. So I'm in a bad mood.

And then I was cross with Don this morning because he dawdled so. And last night *he* was upset because he feels the Duquette job is getting him nowhere. And also depressed because of a lunch with Marguerite and Speed at which they bitched Tony.

That's it—life is a bit smelly right now—like something that has been too long in the closet. I need a change.

Last night we had supper up at Gerald's, with Will Forthman. Margaret Gage was away. They have a colored cook who served roast chicken, and Will had the air of doing something sinful—having such a meal. He is quite a bit of an old maid. And his presence inhibits Gerald curiously, so that we talked tea-table talk about religious sects which was superficial and coy. I saw Don being bored and felt mad at them for not explaining to him what the long words meant that they used.

Don told me last night that he only collects these movie pictures because they remind him of the time when he felt secure.

My job is very simple—i.e. provide a background of security for Don and at the same time leave the door open for him to issue forth from it at any time he wants to. Is that impossible? No. Can I do it? I don't know. Isn't it the same problem as with Caskey? No—I really *don't* think so—because Don isn't self-destructive. Anyhow, I've taken on this project and I obviously have to do my best. And I do *want* to do my best. I'm not being noble about that. It is a genuine vocation. Don is by far the most interesting person I've ever lived with. Why? Because he *minds* the most about things.

July 27. This morning I talked to Arthur Freed about the possibility of making a film out of *Prater Violet*. He has such a strange mixture of pictures in his office—a Gauguin (and a good one), Rouaults, Tamayos—mixed with junk. I like him—there's something touching and cozy about him—like visiting a badger in his lair.

Lunch with Speed. He's full of the return of Paul after their quarrel and of a talk with Bill Caskey, who wants to see me and has apparently instructed Speed to arrange it. But how can I be friends with Caskey (or Jim Charlton either) as long as I feel they are hating and bitching Don and treating me as a corrupt old fool who has sold out to the movies and to whom one therefore doesn't have to repay one's debts?

There can be no friendship with Caskey until we've had it out about the will—and all those pictures of ours he's selling.[1] And as for Jim, I can't forget what the Hookers told me about his overcharging on the house. I hate being vindictive—but I can't make myself be generous beyond a certain point. I'm trembling with rage as I write this.

August 1. Well, now I really have to get to work and do something about the Siddhartha script—because Tony and Beegle are eager to leave in October, and it has to be finished first. I still have an awful lot to do.

No word from Caskey; but Don saw him at Julian Morton's.

Tonight, I'm going to meet the new Swami—Vandanananda.

A charming evening with the Stravinskys last night. Igor is really one of the most uninhibitedly sweet people I know. He threw his arms around me and told me how fond he was of me. A conversation with slimy Lukas Voss[2] under the impression that he was Michael Mann.[3] Luckily I only asked: "How's your father?"

August 3. Swami Vandanananda turns out to be youngish, hook nosed, bright eyed, shock haired—rather like a comic kind of bird. He talked very little while I was there, which wasn't surprising—as our meeting was the usual jam session with half a dozen girls, and Krishna taking notes on the floor in the corner.

John Yale and Phil [Griggs] are taking their brahmachari vows today.

Yesterday I stayed home from the studio, partly because I wanted to see Johnny Goodwin, partly because my office was being painted. John and I went on the beach. He's very little changed—the thin pinch-faced, handsome yet shrivelled boy, whose life, as he says, is, "A Greek tragedy produced by Mack Sennett."[4] Quite objectively and with a straight face and no apologies, he related the extraordinary details of his European trip with a protégé—an Italian–American boy who had been a boxer and reform school inmate and knew all the correct scientific words, because he'd gone through analysis. "The trouble with me is, I'm looking for security"—that might be the slogan of the 1950s.

They went to Barcelona together, where the boy—for the sake of

---

[1] Caskey's sisters tried to take his share of their inheritance from their father, and Isherwood objected to Caskey's passivity. Caskey was trying to sell paintings bought together with Isherwood; Isherwood never received any money for them—some were valuable Haitian primitives.

[2] The conductor.

[3] One of Thomas Mann's sons; he introduced Isherwood to Voss.

[4] Producer of slapstick comedies.

"security"—decided to marry a whore. Unfortunately, she was already married to an older man, who didn't want to give her up because he made money by pimping with her. So the boy had the brilliant notion of giving a valuable ring (a present from Johnny) to her sister, on condition that the sisters should exchange identity papers. When Johnny pointed out that this would prevent the sister from ever marrying—since *she'd* then be officially married to the pimp—the boy replied: "Aw, them foreigners will do anything for money! She won't care." However, he later abandoned the scheme and decided instead to go to a priest. But the pimp (or maybe it was some other pimp) persuaded him to go to "a saint" instead. "A saint's better than a priest, ain't he, John?" John agreed that this was indeed true, if you could find a saint. But, unfortunately, by this time it was Easter and the saint's stigmata had started to bleed. So there was nothing to be done—he couldn't be visited. So the boy left Barcelona with John for northern Europe—where they later parted.

John has taken mescaline several times, with various friends. He says it's extraordinary how much basic agreement there is about the nature of the perceptions and intuitions you get from it. He didn't have any "mystical" experiences (but this may be a purely semantic distinction) but he agreed with Gerald in saying how horribly people walked. He found the falseness, avarice, self-will, etc. in people's faces so embarrassing that he didn't want to see it. He said, however, that he had no sense of moral judgment in experiencing this. In general, he felt that man has lost touch with nature. That almost everything man-made was evil and horrible.

He got the mescaline by simply going into a drugstore and asking for it.

Today there was a luncheon in the executive dining room for the people who sell the studio's pictures. Stills from the newest, including *Diane*, were exhibited round the walls. But the whole thing was fantastically mismanaged, because though the producers and writers were invited they weren't seated next to the salesmen—so we couldn't "sell the product," and our presence was quite useless. Actually I sat with Lennie Spigelgass, Walter Reilly and Adolph Green[1] and spent lunch talking to Adolph about mescaline!

Gore Vidal brought in his father,[2] who's assistant to the Defense Department and has a whole staff of military aides. Gore says they're

---

[1] Lyricist and musical book writer.
[2] Eugene L. Vidal (1895–1969), former army pilot, pioneer of commercial aviation and Roosevelt's head of air commerce during the 1930s, afterwards a liaison between the army and the new air force and head of a Pentagon committee on secret weapons.

all appalled by the capacities of the new nuclear weapons. They don't think the Russians have nearly as many.

August 5. One of the suggested titles (in the usual studio contest) for our film: *The King and Di.*

Last night, the Bracketts showed *The Virgin Queen* at Fox, and then gave a party at Romanoff's. Don was very penitent because—having been put between a boy and a college-age girl (considered by Muff as suitable company for him)—and having had them talk across him for a long time, he got up in a rage and changed places. Mistook Edna Ferber for Cobina Wright.[1] She didn't remember me, anyway.

Lunch yesterday with Gore and Paddy Chayevsky.[2] Liked him. He described how he is haunted by a feeling of horror and unreality which he can only reduce by constantly smoking, and by eating chocolate layer cake. He was amusing about American "virility." He thinks the U.S. is a nation of repressed and terrified homosexuals. Women hunters who loathe women. Men who can only lay girls if their best buddy is watching.

August 6. Glorious weather. We're just back from the beach with John Goodwin.

Yesterday afternoon I saw Jessie Marmorston, returned from Europe. Told her to get some mescaline for us to take.

Then went around to Harry's. Speed and Paul have just moved in there. Speed has brightened the place with more pictures and there is nonstop record playing and nonstop rhumba dancing by Speed. A young man was engaged in putting a lock on Speed and Paul's bedroom door—just in case Harry gets wild. Harry himself, sweaty and sloppy-drunk on beer but quite amiable, was flirting with Henrietta Ledebur, also drunk. When she'd gone, Harry announced that he could lay her anytime he wanted. Later Joan Elan arrived, and they all started to fix lamb chops, no one quite knowing how.

Don spent the night at home, because he had to see his mother off to Cleveland early today on a bus. I had supper at Salka's, with Virginia and a nice couple—the Fred Greens—who are friends of Montgomery Clift—now reportedly drinking himself out of his career in the elderly arms of Libby Holman.[3] Salka greatly shocked me by telling me that Maria Huxley said they had decided never to let

---

[1] Cobina Wright was a society columnist (her daughter, with the same name, was an actress).
[2] Screenwriter and playwright.
[3] Known as a nightclub singer in the 1930s and later for the alleged murder of her husband, a Reynolds Tobacco heir.

me have mescaline, as it would undoubtedly prove fatally habit-forming—since I'm so weak willed! The puritanism back of this decision is what's so shocking—quite aside from its injustice. And of course Gerald is mixed up in it too. So I'm determined to get mescaline elsewhere and tell him nothing till I've tried it.

August 8. My weight's up to 150, which is almost unheard of. So I'm starting a campaign, to practice the posture exercises which are given in Davan's *Exercise without Exercises*. I can't remember exactly when I did them before, but I know I got good results.

Don and I went to Tony Duquette's last night, and Tony held forth at great length about his plans. He wants to establish a workshop-school—a kind of team which will produce artwork of whatever kind his employers require. He wants me to get in on this team, and of course I'm prepared to do so, up to a certain point, as long as it helps Don.

We also talked more about the proposed trip to Europe. I must say, I'm really rather worried about that—not at all sure what the Duquettes will be like to travel with.

And yesterday we talked to the Lights, and looked over their house again. We both now feel very doubtful if this is the right place for us: it's so tacky and the rooms really are too small.

In the night, quite often now, I wake—not with the horrors, but calmly and lucidly. Then I know certain things clearly—it's almost as if they belonged to another order of reality: that I shall die one day—that much of my life has been wasted—that the life of the spirit is the only valid occupation—that I really care for Don and that I have, as it were, adopted him, much as I adopted Heinz, but more completely. In the daytime, these facts are obscured, by studio noise and as-if behavior, and insane resentments and mental and physical slumping. Also I know that all occupations, even Art, are symbolic, and all are valid, so long as they represent right-livelihood.

Tony's amazing treasures—Venetian paintings, marvellous photos. And the fat old lady, Alice Toulmin, with one whole leg in the tomb, nevertheless can't bear to give him a lacquer box she has, because she "clings to it." Claire Michell—her attractive yet somehow faintly sinister British niece, who has been a waitress at Lyons' Corner House[1] and sails on the Norfolk Broads.

The Duquettes served their usual stodgy Mexican dinner. The night-blooming cereus bloomed on their patio. They gave Don the blossom.

---

[1] Chain of British tea shops run by the Lyons tea company.

August 10. Johnny Goodwin came to supper with us last night. He has taken a violent dislike to Speed, whom he met the day before yesterday. He even thinks that Speed has encouraged the divorce—and he was shocked by Harry's condition.

Yesterday, Don went to a fortune-teller with Joan Elan. She told Don that a relative put $5,000 aside for him on his twenty-first birthday. He'll inherit it in a few years. She said Don will get work in connection with the theater when he's twenty-seven, but not acting. He'll go abroad in September and visit two countries principally—France only for a short time—and in one of them he'll make many friends.

August 11. John Goodwin, after inviting us to a party tonight, has suddenly decided to leave town. A typical caprice of his. He hasn't changed.

A charming letter from Stephen, inviting us to stay with him in England.

Don is beginning to talk of a showdown with the Duquettes: either they treat him like a proper apprentice and teach him things, or he doesn't want to stay with them. I'm careful not to interfere in this.

Gore, at lunch today, told me I was cold. We were discussing George Cukor and why he doesn't invite me to his house.

August 14. Thomas Mann died last Friday—tidily, as he did everything. There was a greatness in his dry neatness, and I must say—in spite of the gap in time since I saw him and the slightness of our friendship—I think of him with real love. He was somehow very supporting—not because of his great gestures, his "open letters" to world leaders, his public self-questionings. No, he was lovable in a tiny, cozy way—he was kind, he was genuinely interested in other people, he kept cheerful, he was gossipy, he was quite brave—he had the virtues of a truly admirable nursery governess.

Thinking of him, and communing with him as I dipped into *Disorder and Early Sorrow*,[1] I said to myself: "At least I'll write two more books—the Inferno novel, and the 1939–44 autobiography, based on my diary." I feel real eagerness, an appetite for these projects.

Incidentally, I heard a few days ago that Billy Caskey has had another drunk-driving ticket and has skipped bail and left the state with a boy who builds cyclone cellars in Oklahoma and came out West, only to find that we don't have cyclones!

---

[1] Mann's 1926 story.

August 15. For hours I've been wading through the tournament scenes of *The Wayfarer*, as if through thick tropical swamp. What a weary bore! I lie down, pace the floor, pick my nose, belch, go to the men's room, glance through books and magazines—and all the while Betsy Cox sits there, like a watermelon, waiting for the next sentence to be dictated. Has she no temperament at all? Is she a saint? Or does she smolder inwardly, curse me and my British accent and affectations, and imagine herself—to while away the hours of her imprisonment with me—naked in the arms of her lover? I suppose she has one.

Lunch with Gore. I guess he's still wondering what I think of *Messiah*, his novel. Well, I don't. I'm bored and stuck fast. He asks quite often about my journal and talks apprehensively about the famous one Anaïs Nin is keeping—seventy volumes already!—in which he believes he figures most unfavorably. I believe he really thinks about "posterity" and its "verdict"—just like a nineteenth-century writer! And I don't know whether to admire this, or feel touched by it, or just regard him as a conceited idiot.

Tinker[1] has arrived and told him he must work out because he's getting fat. So Gore is looking for a gym. Actually, he says, it's natural for him to be fat. All the family are—except his father, who exercises frantically.

Yesterday we had lunch with the Bracketts—a very quiet and unglamorous affair, for the benefit of Charlie's other daughter,[2] her husband and her kids. Charlie, pulling a long face, took me out into the garden to confide that *The Virgin Queen* is a flop at the box office, and Zanuck is beginning to say: No more costume pictures for the present. I can't really see why Charlie is so upset—he has so many irons in the fire. I urged him to write his autobiography and he insinuated that he couldn't because he had to earn money—which seems a ludicrous excuse. He also told me that he's very worried about Muff, because she looks so tired (which she does). All the while he kept gobbling caviar canapés like an addict.

One of the reasons Muff looks tired may be Xan.[3] She was stiff drunk even before lunch, and Don says James Larmore slapped her for it as they left the table. Later, she and Muff disappeared.

Marguerite and Harry were there too—she unostentatiously avoiding him as usual, and he ostentatiously being avoided. And there was Ivan with his Chessy-cat smile, recommending life in a beach house at Malibu. (I think we'll store the furniture in September and

[1] Howard Austen.
[2] Elizabeth, known as "Beau."
[3] Charles Brackett's elder daughter, Alexandra, married to James Larmore; see Glossary.

take a place on the beach until it's time for us to go to Europe.) And Speed—who for some reason is concerned about the fate of the Inez Johnson[1] painting belonging to Caskey. And Peter Hartshorne, who manages to give the most unpleasant impression of corrupt double-facedness while saying only the most harmless things. He reminds me of what Caesar said about thin people.[2]

We had supper with Dick Foote, out at a motel up the coast called Malibu Lodge. Carter wasn't there, because he had to attend a business meeting: he may become head of a company making glass swimming pools: a new process—much cheaper, and this kind of glass comes in different colors, is very light, and as hard as iron. Dick talked a lot about Carter's financial genius—how much money he has made for himself and John—and how we ought to let him advise us—which Don wants me to do. Also, of course, Dick held forth against Starcke, saying how [. . .] mercenary [he is] and what bad business judgement he has, and how he makes a show of his religion. But Dick himself quite naively revealed his own fortune-hunting exploits—affairs with older women who had "millions"—and one old flame that nearly got relighted the other day, if Carter hadn't objected. He has had his nose put straight by plastic surgery, so he can play heavies. Over it all was the weird empty fata morgana shine of the "as-if" life—in which all the values are really advertisements which interrupt the "life" itself like commercials interrupting the action of a TV drama. Even views, sunsets, ocean breezes have price tags on them. This weekend at Malibu was costing them $45.50.

I hope Don gets through the next month without unnecessary friction with the Duquettes—but I doubt it. He's mad at them right now because they went away for a long weekend leaving him and Jimmy Daugherty, the colored boy, to paint screens and fix abalone shells on to them—a loathsomely chichi effect. He wants to take tomorrow off but he can't if they don't come back. He thinks (and so do I) that they ought to teach him more things as long as they're paying him so little—actually, they're teaching him almost nothing. He doesn't want to go with them to Europe—and neither do I, really. I'd much rather see Venice alone with Don. Well, time will tell. Our plans are straightening out, and I don't think this move will be too difficult, after all.

The new hurricane, "Dianne," ought to be used, I think, to advertise our picture. "She raised the roof when she blew into court

---

[1] A California painter of some reputation.
[2] That thin men are dangerous, in Shakespeare's *Julius Caesar* I : ii. Peter Hartshorne was skinny.

to shoot the breeze with the King." "When she hit Paris at 120 miles an hour, the pressure was plenty low."

August 16. When I look back on this period, how·will it seem to me, I wonder? Quite possibly idyllic. The circumstances of *le bonheur* are all present—money, occupation, domesticity, pleasant surroundings etc.—yet most of the time I'm strained and worried. Don came back yesterday evening depressed again, and uncertain whether to talk to Tony himself or to get me to talk to him. The difficulty is really this: if I talk to Tony and explain to him how he unconsciously neglects Don, treats him as a mere odd-job boy, fails to teach him anything or show him any techniques—if, in a word, I make Tony see what a monstrously selfish creature he is—then, ten to one, he'll repent (temporarily) being anyhow in a "repenting" mood and wanting to see Gerald Heard—and we shall be "better friends than ever" and it will be inevitable that we go to Europe together. Now the truth is, I feel nothing special toward Tony. As soon as I imagine myself moving toward intimacy with him, I'm blocked by embarrassment at his marriage—[. . .]. Not that I believe he and Beegle aren't fond of each other, but, no—I don't know exactly *what* it is—she's somehow a slave, a Trilby,[1] a zombie—I sense something quite uncanny there. And I sense, in Tony, the uncanny cold-blooded cruelty of the fish. He's a fish person, with his big round eyes and round quick-snapping acquisitive mouth.

Well, anyhow, we keep running into patches of Don's melancholy and discussing it and getting nowhere, because all I can say is: it will pass. I would find all of this very tiresome if Don weren't so sincerely disgusted with it himself. He never sulks, like Vernon. Also, I remember that I acted just the same at his age, only worse. Also, as I keep reminding myself, it's much preferable to have someone with problems to worry over, than to have no one at all.

A strange pair we make! I'm getting to be such a crazy old thing—frittering away the last of my life—uneasily dozing, or drunk, or going around in a daze. I seem to myself much more like an old-fashioned, creaky machine than a sentient human being. I make a great show of functioning. I know many people regard me as well able to be allowed out by myself. Yet I'm actually next door to madness, with my frantic resentments, my fears, my refusal to believe I shall die. I have the cunning of a miser when I think of the time remaining to me. Instead of laying it out prudently and deciding how to spend it, I just clutch it like a bag of coins—in which there's a hole I can't mend.

[1] The artist's model mesmerized by Svengali in George du Maurier's 1894 novel *Trilby*.

Oh shit! This talk is all insincere. I'm just playing around the subject—it's the madman himself who's writing this. But one day I'll catch him off guard, maybe, and get some message through.

August 20. Sad today—first because it was grey and I couldn't go on the beach, then because the sun came out and it was too late to go on the beach—and anyhow I didn't want to, because Don wasn't home. He has to work today. The Duquettes have some rush job on. They're certainly exploiting him—giving him nothing interesting to do and no proper training at all—and now I feel just as mad at them as he is.

Then we're in this rush to find a place to live and get out of here. And I can't make up my mind what to do—buy a house now or later. And there's a fuss brewing about my birthday: Marguerite wants to give a party, but I don't want anybody at it except the Stravinskys, Salka, and Jo and Ben. I'm so full of resentment, just now. I feel I hate nearly everybody—Gerald, for advising the Huxleys not to let me have mescaline (I'm certain he did)—Marguerite and Harry and Speed for their dreary divorce which drags in everybody else—Peggy for snooting Don (she just sent me a birthday present—essays by Trilling—should I send it back?[1])—John van Druten for being such a pompous sanctimonius asshole—Jim Charlton for being such a sponger—and, oh God, when one starts listing spongers!

The pains in my head have started again.

August 23. New eruptions of the Brown volcano. Speed called this morning, reporting that Harry threatened *him* with a gun yesterday and also said he'd shoot Gore (just why, I don't know). So Speed and Paul are leaving the house. The divorce suit comes up on Thursday. Speed claims that Harry is also very hostile to Don, which worries me. I never quite feel sure that Harry won't finally *do* something.

This morning, Don showed me the ring that Tony designed for him and that the jeweller finally got around to fixing. It's just awful—looks like the interior decoration of a movie theater. We will have to get another. Tony (Don told me today on the phone) is much upset that we don't like it. But luckily Beegle agrees with us.

Appropriately enough, I spent yesterday evening at Sawtelle,[2] in the neuropsychiatric division, talking to a small group of the patients about writing. They run their own magazine. I was invited to do this

---

[1] Probably Lionel Trilling's collection *The Opposing Self* (1955); apparently Isherwood returned or gave away the book as it was not in his library at his death.
[2] The veterans hospital on Sawtelle Boulevard.

by a young man named Edward Lyons, who is a friend of Ernest Jones[1] and works there at occupational therapy.

The patients—there were only about ten of them—were rather sympathetic. I don't think any single one of them attended all of the time to what I was saying—and they didn't pretend to. One read a newspaper for a while. Another kept turning his head aside to giggle to himself. When one of them read a poem aloud, the other poets would drum with their fingers and act bored. Lyons says they are terribly jealous.

I talked about writing chiefly from an autotherapeutic angle— stressing the insight and relaxation and solution of problems I had found in keeping a diary—even forcing myself to keep one—and how valuable and reassuring it was to reread it later. I quoted D. H. Lawrence's remark about "Art for *my* sake." They liked that. On the whole, I was dissatisfied with myself, but Lyons assured me the talk was a success—neither of the two catatonics had blacked out; and the husky rather nice looking young man with curly hair hadn't become violent—before being committed, he had beaten up both his parents and broken his brother-in-law's arm with judo. Lyons had to take one of the patients back to his ward—he was sometimes suicidal. Meanwhile I remained with three of the others. "Who's he?" one of them asked, looking at Lyons. "I think he's a janitor," one of the others answered. And they snickered. This was probably a joke.

August 24. Yesterday afternoon, Speed called again to say that Harry has been hospitalized—has apparently committed himself voluntarily to some kind of mental home for treatment. Harry's agent is the only person who knows where he is, and he won't tell. He just passes on the message that Harry doesn't wish to see either Marguerite *or* Speed. He is supposed to be going away for a week only—but of course he can't really know that. What's wonderful is that at least he admits he's sick.

Speed also says that Caskey has been heard from. He's in Montana—working in a coal mine with this friend of his who builds the storm cellars—the Oklahoman.

Last night I had supper at the Knopfs' and Alfred Knopf was there, visiting them. I rather liked him—he is a chipmunk person with a round belly, a curving snout and bright eyes. His manner, as I once said of G. B. Smith,[2] is cold and friendly. Eddie pointed to the way he sits in a chair and said, "He's the most relaxed person I know." As

---

[1] Colleague and biographer of Freud.
[2] Isherwood's history master at Repton; he appears as "Mr. Holmes" in *Lions and Shadows*.

Eddie had let his wine cellar get empty because they're about to move, Alfred went out in search of a good liquor store and came back with a bottle of Montrachet, 1953. 1952 and 3 are good years for white wine, he says. Nevertheless, the chicken was undercooked, as usual.

Alfred talked about the national parks (he's on some commission or other) and particularly Dinosaur, where he has twice frustrated the attempts of a power company to put in a dam and thus ruin one of the most beautiful canyons.

Jessie Marmorston, who was also there, told me that she got a chemist's report on mescaline, and that it's definitely harmful. It can injure the eyes, even after a long interval of time.

Today I had lunch with Jim Maloney, the soulful young agent who is with MCA[1] and believes in Buddhism. He told me how he had picked up a cat injured by an automobile, and how it hadn't scratched him and he had communicated with it. Also how, when he was twenty-three: "I decided that I was going to run Me." Such a handsome Irish face, ascetically lean-cheekboned like a young priest's, with the well-formed nose slightly arched, the grey eyes, the dark wavy hair low peaked on the forehead, the small full-lipped mouth—the face of a perfectly humorless natural bore.

Gore has started working out at the gym. He wanted to go and see Harry and make it up with him. So I had to tell him that Harry's in hospital. Meanwhile, I talked on the phone to Harry's agent, who seemed not nearly such a skunk as Marguerite has been making out. He'd been to the hospital, today. Harry is not to see anyone till next week.

I also talked to Marguerite, who plans to leave for Reno very soon and get a divorce.

August 25. Don is working late at the Duquettes', and I'm home, getting steadily drunk on vodka and tonics, and enjoying it.

All sorts of good resolutions, on the eve of my birthday—to avoid tension, "making faces," useless resentments—to try to make myself more useful. I really do feel the bitterest regret for all the years I've wasted. Life is such an amazing experience. Every instant lost—is lost.

I called Swami this morning, and asked for his blessing. He said: "Live many years—and I'll watch you from heaven." He also said

[1] Music Corporation of America—originally founded to book bands—was a powerful Hollywood talent agency until 1961 and later became the global entertainment giant.

that he was so pleased with Swami Vandanananda, and that he would look after the society efficiently after he (Prabhavananda) was gone.

I feel such a gratitude for Don. And yet, of course, I must be prepared to see him pass on to other experiences. But it has been a great happiness, watching him grow up.

Altogether—I must say—I feel gratitude. My life, to this point, has been truly fortunate. I blame myself for nearly all of the glooms. It has been extraordinary, how I've been spared real suffering. "God tempers the wind to the shorn lamb." And yet—*should* one be glad of that? Perhaps the greatest disaster is not to have suffered?

Looking at my hands. Such bold lines—but broken.

August 26. 3:50 p.m. and still drunk—due to a breakfast of bouillon and champagne—Don's idea. We drank two bottles—the good Roger, and the very inferior U.S. kind. And Don gave me an Olivetti typewriter. And everything was as wonderful as mescaline could have made it.

Lunch with Gore, who told me (a) that he's thinking of getting married (which is amazing, because I dreamed the other night that Gore came in and said: "I'm married") and (b) that Tinker is Jewish. We went on the set of *The Last Hunt* and met John O'Hara,[1] who actually remembered meeting me that time in the bar of the old Romanoff's. I don't know if he remembered how badly he behaved. He has just finished a novel.

I've napped all afternoon but can't seem to get sober. And I really dread the party tonight, when I'll have to get drunk again—though the second night is usually easier.

August 31. One of the hottest, stickiest days I've ever known out here. There's so much to write in this book and I have so little time or energy to do it.

First of all, that sensational party on my birthday. Thinking I was going to the Duquettes' for a drink—and Don throwing open the door and there they were—everybody—including the Stravinskys who Don had pretended were out of town—all with champagne classes raised—in the utterly transformed main room of the studio, now turned into a theater and looking absolutely beautiful—thanks to the day and night toiling of Don, Jimmy Daugherty and the Duquettes.

Then frantic house hunting and the final decision to take the place

[1] Best-selling American novelist and screenwriter.

out at Trancas,[1] though God knows how we'll ever commute. And how I'll get the script written in time to go away. It's really tough. There are still at least fifty pages of it to do.

September 1. Still this boiling heat.

Last night, we took Marguerite to the Luau—because she leaves today for Las Vagas, to establish residence for a divorce. Harry, who came out of hospital for my birthday party, appears to think he has had sufficient treatment. Anyhow, he's around again.

Perhaps I was cross because Don had suggested Marguerite's coming and, after all, I didn't particularly want to see her, and she was an hour late and the bill was thirty dollars. Anyhow, I was cross. And later I said [. . .] I never wanted to see her or Speed again, because they run around with the Hartfords—which is disingenuous, to say the least. Later, we went swimming in the ocean, still full of people at 10:30, and I felt tired and went to bed while Don packed. In the night I woke and was ashamed of myself because I'm so resentful and mean and full of hate toward all. And now I'm going to try and be better.

The funny thing is—despite this heat—I did a huge amount of work.

September 5. Saying goodbye to the sun—from 29938 Pacific Coast Highway—is one of my favorite outdoor sports. The sun turned into a red-hot jar with a lid. The gulls were raiding the yellow garbage cans. On our gate is written: Prenez garde le chien[2]—why?

I just record that we arrived, on Friday [the] 2nd and that Jo and Ben were here the first day; and that Salka is staying till tomorrow with her granddaughter, Christine. Salka says that Garbo could never have made a talkie without her. Salka always coached her.

September 6. I started the foregoing in the hope of writing something interesting, intuitive or frank while half-drunk. Christine interrupted me. But the reason I was half-drunk was that I was, and am, extremely worried about Don. After being his ordinary charming self almost unbrokenly since my birthday, he suddenly gave way to sulks because Richie—a boy we met at Johnny Darrow's the day we heard of this house from Ray Ohge—suggested bringing a friend here to meet me yesterday. These sulks of Don's verge on hysteria—and the worst of it is, they make me angry, so I want to see him whipped out of them—

---

[1] On the Pacific Coast Highway north of Malibu; Ray Ohge rented them the house.
[2] Correct French would be, Prenez garde du chien (Beware of the dog).

which means that I'm worse than useless around him. I really don't see how this situation can possibly be corrected unless he makes a big effort—quite aside from the effort *I* must make.

It's a shame, because we might be happy in this house in quite a special kind of way. It's a strange place, full of the atmosphere of childhood and the beach, and there are all kinds of touches of imagination (Ray Ohge's, I suppose) which make it strange and different—the classical statue on the lamp pedestal so rightly-wrongly clashing with the un-chichi cozy stuffiness of the bedrooms—the port and starboard lights on the front gate with the inscription in incorrect French—the two armchairs in the big window overlooking the beach which face each other, like seats in a train.

I race on with *The Wayfarer*. Today I got Siddhartha out of the palace and on the way to the river of renunciation. Don is with his folks and still out (10:55 p.m.). He probably won't get back till very late—it's a long, long drive—twenty-five minutes from Santa Monica Canyon. I like the distance—out here you are in another country—you might as well be in Santa Barbara or Laguna Beach. It feels very lonely, although the lifeguard station is only a hundred yards away and occupied all the time. I've been having supper with the Masselinks—talking of the old days and how the landlord has raised their rent five dollars—$38 to $43—and how odd it is that Peggy and I have drifted apart.

September 8. It's 7:10 a.m. I got up at dawn and went swimming—the ocean, to my surprise, was warm. Now I'm sitting on one of the "train" armchairs by the big window. There are tiny fruit flies on the grapes on the table beside me.

A headache from the drinking we did last night. Ted [Bachardy] and Bob Hoover came out to visit us, and they're still here, asleep. Bob is quite a nice boy, but he doesn't understand the first thing about Ted. He expects Ted to be capable of love—when the whole point is that Ted is sick *because* he isn't capable of love—or his incapacity for love is a symptom of his sickness, however you want to put it.

September 10. Listening to Marlene Dietrich singing the German version of "Miss Otis Regrets," on the portable. Jimmy Daugherty, the colored boy who works for the Duquettes, is staying with us. Tony and Beegle Duquette stayed last night. Tony made me for a birthday present a dried baby alligator painted up to represent Diane, with a pole with a fish on it and a fish skeleton tied to its head. It's a real "rats" joke—such as would have delighted Edward and me in 1923.[1] I want to get an engraved metal plaque for it, reading: "Miss Lana Turner attempting to interpret the role of Diane."

The cleaning lady is very elegant in her ideas. She arranged Don's passport, an envelope with government bonds, and a copy of Conrad's *Youth* on top of each other, like magazines in a dentist's office.

September 11. A new symptom to worry about—a small lump in my mouth which prevents me from putting in my lower bridgework. I'll try to see Dr. Dickinson early tomorrow.

Jo and Ben were here last night—chiefly because Jo wanted to talk to Michael Barrie, who was having supper with us and Jimmy Daugherty, about the terrible shock she has just received—the manufacturers turned her new "line" down flat. I've long had the idea that Michael should be her manager, and she certainly needs someone. Michael was also telling us how we should see an investment firm and get more for our money. Perhaps I'll try this, if all goes well.

September 14. Well, the symptoms didn't prove to be anything much. The lump had been there all the time—it was just that the bridgework had "settled."

Yesterday I went downtown to apply for a new passport. It does seem as if we really shall leave in October sometime. The cruel little Chinese named Mr. Ralph Thling who bullies all applicants was almost kind to me—thanks to the sponsorship of Metro's Mary Clark in the contract department. As ill luck would have it, yesterday was Los Angeles's all-time smog record day. My eyes burned so much I thought I would have to stop driving. I was still crying as I drove past the dingy little church on Washington where they had the funeral service for Maria Huxley. (Aldous is in town—I heard this at Metro from Rita Allen, the woman who's going to produce Aldous's play of *The Genius and the Goddess* this winter. They wanted to have Ingrid Bergman in it, but she refused because she's doing films in France—all this is in parenthesis to say that Aldous has never called, which hurts my feelings a little.)

Am writing this at 10:20 p.m., while waiting for Don to return from seeing his mother. He has been in a bad state, lately—half kidding but half meaning it, he keeps expressing his jealousy because he hasn't got people like Gore, Jim Maloney, Quentin Kelly etc. to

[1] As Isherwood tells in *Lions and Shadows*, he and Edward Upward called their fantasy world "the rat's hostel" before they invented the name "Mortmere." "The rat's hostel" suggested to them an atmosphere of medieval surrealism.

have lunch with. It's hard for me to take this kind of jealousy (or perhaps it's more envy) seriously—but I always end by having to. I only hope that our trip to Europe will make things better. At least, Don'll be taken much more seriously in England, and will get a lot more notice.

This evening, I was up at Vedanta Place. Both the swamis were there. Prabhavananda looked very well and happy. He said: "I get so *bored* with philosophy nowadays—even Shankara." Then he told how, this morning in the shrine, he had been so intensely aware of the presence of Swamiji and Maharaj. "If there hadn't been anyone else there, I'd have bawled." John Yale (now renamed Prema) also looked well and much more attractive—with a sunburn from being up at Santa Barbara and a short haircut, after taking his brahmachari vows.

Ben and Jo have decided to take a short trip to Hawaii—as a relief from their present spell of bad luck, and in order to look around for any business prospects in Jo's line. They'll only be gone about three weeks, but we may just miss their return.

Gore Vidal has been asked to write a movie about the Dreyfus case. Speed has jobs at NBC and at Columbia. The watchword is—success is not to be sneered at. It's okay to earn show-business money.

More about Swami. He says his favorite chapter in the Gita is the chapter on devotion.[1] He says: "I used to want visions and ecstasies—now I don't care. I only pray to love God." He says: "I don't care to lecture now. But when I start talking, I enjoy myself. I enjoy talking about God." (I thought to myself—he's like a young man in love.)

Swami said: "Webster Milam came to me the other day. He said to me, 'Swami, it's your fault that I went away. You should have used your power to stop me.' I asked him if he was meditating and making japam. He said, 'No. You must make me do it.' I was very touched. Such devotion!"

September 19. Last Friday, the 16th, I finished the first draft of my screenplay on *The Wayfarer*. At least I can say this—it's just exactly the way I wanted to make it. Nobody interfered. Knopf hasn't read it yet.

I love this house so much—better than any place I've lived in. And this weekend has been a specially happy one. We've had lots of guests—Michael Barrie, Chris Wood, Gerald, John Darrow, [. . .] Don Burnett, Jim Charlton, Arthur Laurents, Tom Hatcher. Don has been at his sweetest—all fears, resentments and sulks forgotten—and he is full of resolutions that they shan't return.

And now we plan to sail on October 19 for Italy—just one month from now.

---

[1] Chapter twelve.

September 21. Yesterday I went to the Beverly Hilton which is the ugliest hotel I've ever seen, and had drinks with Frank Taylor, and Nan, and her brother Joe, who's an intern at UCLA, where they have a marvellously equipped hospital, with remote-control cobalt radiation for cancer and a reactor—the only one of its kind in the West. Frank was very funny about his efforts to leave the hotel in shorts— since wearing them is forbidden in the lobby. Joe Scallon seemed a very sweet-natured, dedicated person. He has switched from surgery (chiefly brain) to radiology because he thinks it's so neglected in this country and just as important.

After this cancer talk, it was a rather ghastly coincidence that I went round to Gore Vidal's apartment at the Chateau Marmont and found that Tinker (Howard Austen) had just been told he has a cancer on his ear. Tinker was quite carefree about this. Gore is very worried. I recommended Dr. Sellars.

A very drunken supper at Romanoff's with David Miller and his wife—what *is* her name?—ostensibly to discuss his doing *The Vacant Room.*

September 22. Supper, last night, with Jo and Ben turned into a sort of love feast. Quite spontaneously, we found ourselves saying how much we liked each other. "What we always say about you, Chris," said Ben, "is you're so damn *honest.*"

Ricky, the seventeen-year-old blond lifeguard, was there for a few minutes, shivering cold, in nothing but his trunks. A few weeks ago, he won a paddleboard race from Catalina to the mainland, in thick fog, thirty-some miles—which took him most of the day. Then he went out with his girl, took her home, stopped in to see some friends, played a game of basketball, got back in the small hours, and got up early next morning—a Monday—to go to school!

September 23. Tinker's cancer scare seems over. I don't yet know about his ear, but Dr. Sellars says his lungs are definitely all right. And the other wouldn't be at all serious, even if it *is* cancer.

Had supper with Michael Barrie last night. Gerald and Chris were there. Gerald very gay and playful. He told me that he had felt—and that "someone" (he couldn't remember who) had confirmed it—our new house is haunted. After this I went back there and slept alone— Don's mother was sick and he stayed the night with her—somewhat nervously. It *is* very creaky, and certainly thick with "atmosphere"— but I don't feel anything evil.

Today Knopf and I have been revising *The Wayfarer* script. I also told him I hate the ending of *Gaby,* and now it may be changed. On the set[1] to watch Leslie Caron and John Kerr act. I must say, they are adorable together—although I know what a cold little bitch she is.[2]

Betsy Cox is leaving for her vacation, so I doubt if I'll see her again. I'm giving her a bottle of Tabac Blanc perfume. Jo and Ben leave tonight by plane for Hawaii. We're taking them to the Trader's Restaurant at the Beverly Hilton. My passport has arrived. Violent departure jitters.

September 29. It's bad that I haven't kept this record day by day lately—because there have been quite a lot of minor developments, and changes of mood now lost.

Two days ago, for example, I was quite blue, with acute travel jitters—the feeling that life is really too much trouble. I walked around some movie sets with Gore, who looked at the books to see if any of them were by him. Being with Gore depresses me, unless I'm feeling absolutely up to the mark, because Gore really exudes despair and cynical misery and a grudge against society which is really based on his own lack of talent and creative joy.

Another reason for feeling blue was that on the evening of the 26th I broke off my capped tooth (and swallowed it) as the result of biting violently into a piece of saltwater taffy—due to my indignation at having to watch *The Farmer's Daughter* and reflect that Loretta Young got an Oscar for it. (We had to sit through the film in order to see *Notorious*, in which [Ingrid] Bergman, after all these years, seemed better than ever.)

But now I have a good recap job, and today the doctor (one of Jessie's sidekicks) examined me and declared that my heart, lungs and blood pressure were better than his own. And yesterday I stayed home with Don and we had one of the best days we've had in this house—walking on the beach in the marvellous afternoon light and watching a dog chase the gulls. Again it was there—*le bonheur.*

Today the whole studio has been buzzing over the victory of the Yankees over the Dodgers. And I've been fidgeting because of the time slipping by and the endless delays caused by Bob Andrews's[3] scruples and warnings about the possible reactions of the Buddhists.[4] I'm scared they may possibly foul up our going away on the 12th. But they won't if I can help it.

September 30. Don has been with his parents, so I spent last night in the house alone. It was rather enjoyable for a change, waking up and

[1] Of *Gaby*.
[2] Isherwood later changed his mind and they became close friends.
[3] Robert Hardy Andrews, the screenwriter.
[4] To *The Wayfarer*.

reading *The Books of Charles Fort*[1] in bed. This is a grey–blue morning, probably clearing later. Iron lights in the sea and a big rough dangerous surf. The useless yellow machine is noisily raking a perfectly clean beach, untrodden for days except by the gulls.

Last night I had a nice supper with Ivan Moffat at Frascati's on Wilshire. He is always so pretty and bright eyed and clean—he has to be, for I imagine his evenings usually end, if they don't begin, visiting some girl. He has the slightly guilty grin of the accepted lover. I ate excellent roast chicken and we drank Löwenbräu beer and talked easily and intimately—pleasant relaxed heterosexual conversation, with no strings. Ivan said Harry was terribly drunk at the Bracketts', after leaving us last Sunday—and Kenneth MacKenna was there: Harry will gradually build up a reputation that will make every studio hesitate to hire him. Then Ivan talked about Joan [Elan] and what a marvellous girl she is—but how he could never marry her because she'd become too clinging. He talked about the girl he *is* probably going to marry. She is clinging too, it seems—but not in the same way: "wifely" was the word he used, I believe. When she was married to an astronomer, she used to polish his lenses for him.[2] We talked also about life, and I said if I had mine to live over again I would try to live without fear. And Ivan said that was just exactly how he felt too. Then he told me that he's dissatisfied with his studio work at present—because he is pouring out the "dearest secrets" of his feelings about the last war into a trashy film story. He feels all of this is waste. Talking of that evening we spent with Dylan Thomas at Charlie Chaplin's (see page 461 of this diary). Ivan says that Dylan was describing how he'd met an English professor here who had described himself as "a refugee from the Labor government." "And so," said Dylan, "I gave him the only possible answer. I said: 'Go and fuck your bloody eyeballs.' " This greatly displeased the Chaplins— especially Oona, who is prudish. This was also the evening on which I allegedly urinated on one of their sofas while I was asleep. But I shall never believe I did this, because I've never done such a thing before or since.

October 1. In view of our many complaints, it's worth recording that Don said this morning: "Here we are, having breakfast out of doors on this marvellous beach, with the sun shining and that terrific white surf, and the lifeguards playing ball to amuse us—really, I ought to be flogged when I forget things like that and make a fuss—" We both agreed that we somewhat dread leaving.

[1] A 1941 compilation of Fort's various books of inexplicable phenomena.
[2] Moffat did not marry her.

October 5. All dressed up in my suit and the Speed Lamkin Club tie, I'm waiting to go off to the preview of *Diane*, in Burbank. I saw it yesterday in the projection room—the beginning was slow, and neither Lana nor Marisa are really much more than amateurs—but it takes hold toward the end.

A shameful weekend of drinking with Don, Jim [Charlton], Michael [Barrie], Tom Wright, his friend Scott Poland, and Jimmy Daugherty. We sank right to the depths of Rustic Road, and I was mean to Don. Next day I had an almost paralytic hangover—the kind which makes you fear you'll lose your nerve in the middle of the street and have to park the car and scream for help. In the midst of this I had lunch with Aldous—thin and pale but lively and full of talk. He urged me to get him some mescaline in New York, spoke of his play, and discussed money—practically asking me outright how much I have. I told him at once, of course. He has $80,000.

October 8. The preview was only so-so. General opinion—it's too long, Lana's a bore, Marisa is great. Marisa isn't great, though. She looks wonderful but she's still an amateur. Well, I did my best, and they ruined my dialogue and drowned it in Hungarian music—at the cost of $2,300,000. Nunc dimittis.

Predeparture misery. Chris Wood leaves for New York tomorrow by plane—his first in about twenty-five years. He is terrified. Gerald has become dressy again. He sports a tailor-made waistcoat.

MGM has also ruined *Kismet*, by photographing it so poorly.

A story of Vera Stravinsky's—a very dumb wife is warned by her husband not to say anything during a dinner party. At length the hostess says: "Shall we have coffee in the library?" The wife inquires innocently: "Is it still open?"

October 9. Woke up in the middle of the night and thought: "God is a Being whom my whole life insults." But this was largely a phrase. I don't really feel so alienated.

Ted and his friend Bob Hoover are here, and Don is fixing banana waffles, and there is the usual fuss with our very inefficient wiring. The telephone is out of order since yesterday, because some of the party-liners have taken it off the hook. This afternoon, Michael will come, and Jim, and Brad Saunders, and this evening we go out to supper with Marisa Pavan. Lots of fuss-fuss-fussing about last-minute arrangements.

October 11. Brad Saunders told us how a whole squadron of bombers had to be grounded because they became infested with rats. The rats chewed through wiring, and in one instance, very nearly caused a crash.

Brad used to room with James Dean in the days when he worked on a car lot. He always wanted to be an actor. At parties he sat in corners. Brad would introduce him as "Hamlet."

Sandy Roth was following Dean in his car at the time of the accident, because he was going to cover the auto races that Dean was to take part in. We met Sandy at Marisa's party, which was a bore, despite the excellent food and the elegance of Marisa's lively young mother. I quarrelled hotly with Salka about the French.

Yesterday we buzzed hither and thither. The cap came off my tooth again, so Dr. Dickinson stuck it on and gave me a do-it-yourself kit, including spatula, dental mirror and cement, in case it comes off while we're away in Europe. We bought $4,000 worth of traveler's checks. I suddenly feel poor. All our money is leaking away.

Last night we had supper at the Stravinskys'. Igor seemed old and pale and shrunken. He was doing a jigsaw puzzle—Newlyn Harbor.[1]

Don and I both wish Michael wouldn't talk so glibly about God—he's coy, as if it were a slightly daring secret. At supper, he asked us all to define Love. The Stravinskys were embarrassed.

After dinner, I smoked one of Igor's cigarettes—the first in fifteen months—because it smelled so nice. It's a truly strange thing—I noticed it before when I wasn't smoking—I could always smoke when drunk without restarting the addiction.

October 12. 1:00 p.m. The living room is still full of cartons with books, clothes, etc. We have far, far too much of everything and it's almost incredible to think that most of our possessions are already in storage. Don, who has a bad cold, is packing diligently but I know we'll be late. We always are. At 9:00 this evening we take off for New York. I don't feel any sense, yet, of the journey ahead—and I won't, until we're on that boat.

Saw Speed yesterday, who advised me to write a play. And [Hans] Rameau, who showed me photographs—bringing them out of carefully tied envelopes in a suitcase like a connoisseur showing rare wines to a guest. While in Europe, he fulfilled a great ambition—to have sex in Hitler's bedroom at Berchtesgaden.

October 15. Well, we're safely here, and staying with Julie Harris and Manning Gurian at their nice little house on East Fiftieth, nearly over to the river. It's not such a little house, either. Four floors and very

---

[1] The Cornish fishing port whose artists' colony has given its name to an open air school of painting.

steep stairs. The baby, Peter, is teething; but he's away up at the top and you don't hear him at night, you hear everything else, though. What a brutally noisy city! People seem to spend the night shovelling gravel, collecting tin cans, or just beating the sidewalk with spades. The weather is muggy and dirty. You keep busting out into a sweat, and the sweat has grime in it. Yesterday it poured and we both got wet through.

Julie seems happy. She adores the baby, Manning obviously protects and encourages her at every turn, and she's hard at work on rehearsals of *The Lark*.[1] She doesn't seem as lively, quite, as in the old days. But then she isn't as tense, and she probably no longer has her moods of despair.

We've seen Chris Wood and Hugh Wheeler, Wystan, Lincoln. Wystan looks awful—so ravaged and weary. He's lecturing on the sonnets—they were written, he has decided, to several different boys. Chris begged me to be forgiving toward Peggy. But I can't sincerely say that I am until she makes a gesture toward Don. It's not enough to invite him to the house in a big party. She has to understand that she's a common middle-class bitch pretending to be a lady, a shrew who has driven her husband and her children away from the house. She despises Don because she thinks he's cheap and unpresentable, and she isn't fit to lick his boots. But I mustn't give way to the rage I feel against her. I'd like to see her humiliated and thrashed.

October 20. Yesterday, at noon, when the great ship thundered goodbye to the echoing towers of Manhattan, I could hardly told back my tears—it was so beautiful—the Hudson full of fussing tugboats and brimming with silver light—the thought that it was Don's first voyage, never never to be quite duplicated for him—and then there was the brandy we'd drunk with Frank Merlo, who saw us off, bringing with him an inscribed copy of Ten's *Kingdom of Earth*[2] and a big bottle of champagne.

The evening before, John Goodwin gave us a party in his art nouveau house. He has procured me seven tablets of mescaline—six at the price of twelve dollars each, the seventh a gift. Tennessee and Frank came, and Paul Cadmus and Bill Miller looking fat but not older, and Bill Harris looking older, but not fatter. Also a lot of young men, including some cute twins called Barth. Someone offered me a cigar. I bit the end off, and broke my capped tooth again. Julie and

---

[1] Jean Anouilh's play, adapted by Lillian Hellman.
[2] *The Kingdom of Earth with Hard Candy*, a collection of nine Tennessee Williams short stories published by New Directions in 1954.

Manning's nice dentist, Dr. Theodore Cohn, put on another, quickly and cheaply. I only pray that it holds.

This visit to Manhattan has been more than usually gruelling—what with dashing to Philadelphia to see *A Hatful of Rain*[1] with Frank and Ten and not getting back till 5:00 a.m.—and then a party at Harold Clurman's,[2] at which Michael Redgrave mistook Oscar Hammerstein for John Steinbeck—at which Hammerstein countered by saying, "Hello, Mr. Olivier."

Sometime yesterday, or maybe it was the evening before, I started to form the project of making a play out of *The World in the Evening*. (Once more, following Speed's advice!) I see it essentially as a dialogue between Stephen and Elizabeth—though using other characters, of course. Don and I discussed this excitedly during supper last night, drinking a wine called Barolo.

This boat, the *Saturnia*, has an old-fashioned grandeur—somewhat art nouveau. It was launched in 1927. There are very few people in the first class, and most of them seem uninteresting. We have a cabin with a veranda, and it is so snug.

October 21. Two whole days at sea completed—this is the third evening. But it won't be till the 26th that we arrive in Lisbon, and that only for a couple of hours.

Today the sun shone and the swimming pool was filled and we went in. The swell was strong but smoothed away to nothing. I finished Norman Mailer's awful book[3]—such trash—and am now in the doldrums of John Lehmann's autobiography—*The Whispering Gallery*. All accounts of childhood are boring, except the very greatest, and his is not the very greatest or the greatest or even the very.

It's dull on this boat but pleasantly so. We know no one—have barely talked to a soul, except for a boy going to join a seminary in Rome, and a fat lady from Florida—and the captain's cocktail party and the get-together dinner left us isolated. I have a nasty cold and cough and have taken Tabcin. Don is reading Stephen [Spender]'s *The Burning Cactus*.

October 23. The tense spuffle of the steam and the tearing noise of the foam. Today the sea is black, the sky overcast, a strongish wind from the southeast but very little rolling. Yesterday and the day before were sunny and warm. This morning we slept very late—till after

---

[1] The play by Michael Gazzo.
[2] Theater director and critic.
[3] *The Deer Park*.

11:00 a.m.—after getting quite drunk. We met a boring young man from Chicago, who explained that he was with his mother who had had a nervous breakdown and went to bed early. We had decided he was a fortune hunter with an elderly wife, so this was a disappointment. He bored us so much that Don pretended, very convincingly, to be seasick.

This is perhaps the dullest boat trip I've ever taken, but it's quite enjoyable as a rest cure and I think Don feels the same way. But I wish I could get rid of this tickling cough.

October 25. Last day at sea before Lisbon. Yesterday there was strong wind and rain and quite a nasty roll. But neither of us felt worse than slightly queasy.

Today we've come to a decision—to leave this boat at Gilbraltar, the day after tomorrow, go over to Tangier, where we hope to see Paul and Jane Bowles, return to Gibraltar after two days and pick up the *Andrea Doria* to take us on to Naples, which we'll explore first. Then on to Rome. Then to Venice later. This seems a much better plan.

I do wish I didn't feel so fat—but that can be remedied. I do hope my capped tooth won't fall out before I'm within reach of a dentist. I lost a bit of bridgework down the washbasin last night, but the steward unscrewed the trap and recovered it. My fingers are all blue from fixing the ribbon on the Olivetti.

October 27. Yesterday, at 8:15 in the evening, we docked at Lisbon. (We made the landfall about four hours earlier, when the hills around Sintra appeared over the horizon, while we were drinking tea to the accompaniment of "Claire de Lune.") It was too dark to see much, but we went into the town and walked around, through crowds of dark homely runty but charmingly polite Portuguese. Chief impression: a beautiful tower with an elevator in it, leading to a covered passage high above the street, by which, apparently, you could reach an upper level. Immense numbers of taxis, nearly all empty, darting back and forth. Cafés occupied almost entirely by men. The beautiful old houses with tiled facades and the narrow lanes.

We sailed again shortly after midnight, which means we'll be late getting into Gibraltar, maybe we won't arrive till after dark. Now we're going through the fuss and nuisance of tipping—who shall get how much? No land in sight, but quite a lot of tankers and fishing boats.

October 28. Here we are, on board a boat called the *Monte Calpe*, crossing the straits from Gilbraltar to Tangier. We only left the *Saturnia* last night at 7:00, but already we seem completely transplanted from a first-class to a second- or third-class world.

Leaving the *Saturnia* was, of course, interminable. We packed, stood around, were told to wait upstairs, downstairs, upstairs again. Don was angelic—as he has been throughout this voyage—and did all the tipping himself.

We found we couldn't get a room in the good hotel "The Rock," nor in the middling hotel "The Bristol," so we had to be content with "The Grand," which isn't. But the manager was one of the most charming and helpful hotelkeepers I have ever met. And the food wasn't bad.

We went into a bar called the Café Universal which was crowded with sailors, British and Australian, as well as a few Latin-looking civilians, some of whom may have been pimps. As we drank our warm whiskey, a man beside me crashed over on to the floor and lay there. He seemed drunk, but Don noticed that the mouths of his two friends were twitching as if from dope. Many of the sailors were staggering drunk. A few camped, hugged each other, mouthed kisses and executed hula dances. All this in spite of shore patrol and M.P.s outside. A bunch of sturdy, horse- or pig-faced little whores executed Spanish dances with great goodwill and were deafeningly applauded. Huge photographs of [Queen] Elizabeth and [Prince] Philip looked down on the scene. They were both facing toward the left—which made it look as if Philip had made an off-color remark and Elizabeth had turned away from him in disgust.

Our bedroom was of the interior Spanish kind, with windows opening on to a staircase. Every sound made by anybody in any of the rooms was clearly aubible. The man and woman going to bed next door might just as well have been going to bed with us. On top of this, my cough came back, together with grave suspicions that I have crabs—God knows how. However, we got to sleep somehow, and I dreamed, quite sympathetically, of Peggy.

The breakfast tea and the mealy sausages were as British as the uniformed father of three giggling transparent-skinned charming skinny little children at the next table. And yet the Grand Hotel is pure Moorish, and Spanish seems to be spoken far more frequently than English in this town. It would be fascinating to stay here for several weeks and study the cultural tangle—the dark Spanish faces under the helmets of London bobbies—one of them wished us "all the best" as we were leaving.

Amazing to think that I visited this place with Heinz—twenty-one years ago?

October 30. I can't hope to record more than the tiniest fraction of what has happened to us since we got here. So I'll take for granted Tangier itself—the Casbah; the veiled women and baggy-pant men, the Minzah hotel where we're staying—although this alone is absorbing and quite as good or better than I remembered from our visit to Ceuta and Tetuán: the mélange here is richer and more exciting.

We met Herbert List by accident outside the British post office, where we'd gone to contact Paul Bowles. Herbert is traveling with a German boy named Robert Furst[1], a pretty, fluffy-haired blond with spots and a tendency to sulk. More of this later. The point is that we did meet Paul, and he invited us to his apartment—a very grand penthouse at the top of a big building—and there we ate *majoon* and smoked *kif.* That was the night before last, and already the full sharpness of the experience is fading. I'll note down as much as I can.

The drug was prepared by Ahmed [Yacoubi], Paul's Arab friend, who is a painter. He is a curiously powerful person—his father and grandfather were healers and Paul says that Ahmed is one of the best doctors he has ever met. Whether his power is used entirely for good—that's the question.

Also present with Paul, Ahmed, Don and myself were two Americans, who have both taken this stuff fairly often. A special room is dedicated to the smoking—with black mattresses and pillows (very hard ones) on the floor, and brightly colored Arab hangings around the lower part of the walls—purple, orange and green.

Ahmed showed us a wonderful *kif* pipe, hung with all sorts of charms and amulets of gold, silver and cowrie shell. Ahmed had long coveted this pipe, which belonged to an old Negro who wouldn't sell it. Then, a few days ago, the Negro suddenly let him have it, quite cheap. And the next morning he died, while saying his prayers in the mosque.

Majoon looks and tastes rather like Christmas pudding.[2] *Kif* smells like cut grass in the catcher of a lawn mower. (I notice that, as I now begin the description of the intoxication, I feel an extreme unwillingness to continue—a slight fear, even.) The *majoon* is eaten from a tiny coffee spoon. The *kif* is smoked. I ate only two spoonfuls of *majoon* and took a few puffs from the pipe—being careful to inhale very little.

Symptoms began for me about an hour later—around 10:00 p.m. From the first, they were unpleasant. Dizziness. Claustrophobia. Acute nervous tension. I had to get up, leave the little room, go

[1] Not his real name.
[2] *Majoon* is a narcotic confection made from hemp leaves, henbane, datum seeds, poppy seeds, honey, and ghee.

outside on the balcony. I was aware that part of me was fighting the action of the drug, but I couldn't let myself go with it. Paul played music on the phonograph, and this I hated. I hated also the gossip of the two Americans, who were bitching everybody in Tangier. I wanted silence, or some talk about God. And, at the same time, I was critical of myself—thinking that I was playing the part of a "pure soul" who feels defilement from contact with the impure.

Now the room became distorted—sometimes it opened out one way, sometimes another. The wall behind my head seemed immensely tall or perhaps nonexistent. All kinds of objects and thoughts were experienced discontinuously, like pieces in a kaleidoscope. However, there was no change in color perception, the patterns on the wall did not increase in significance, and I had no special perceptions about the people I was with—as described by the mescaline takers.

Only—and this brings me to the most important feature—a sense of the relative intensities of relationships was very strong. Don seemed very much more present—even more distinct and larger—than anyone else in the room. I didn't mind Paul's being there—though he seemed a bit futile. But I really resented the other two, with their trivial chatter. Ahmed came in and out, like a male nurse, bringing soup and other food. He was indefatigable. He had changed into Moorish clothes, bag-trousers and an open sleeveless jacket, which showed his brown, beautifully made body. He smiled with rather mocking amusement at my intoxication. I don't think he took much himself.

I'm fairly certain that, if I had taken this stuff among real friends, the effect would have been quite different. As it was, I saw myself now as a pretty wretched creature, scared, claustrophobic, utterly insecure. I was afraid they would leave me alone. I was afraid of what lay outside our circle. I was aware that I was terrified of being on my own. Yet I was able to speak of this to Paul—in the intervals when I could talk lucidly. The rest of the time, the words wouldn't come out, or were hindered by a huge disinclination to say anything.

Ahmed played an Arab flute—beautifully. So, later, did Paul. But none of that was really to the point, for me. And when Paul made dopey aesthetic remarks to the others, I was merely irritated. (I should remark that the two Americans appeared to be placidly enjoying themselves. They even drank gin while they smoked.) Then Paul and one of the Americans talked Arabic. This bothered me because I kept trying to understand it—to relate it to some language I knew: oddly enough, it often sounded like Yiddish. Throughout this experience, it was peculiarly unpleasant to feel my mind racing so fast. It made me horribly tired. And now it became more and more noticeable how slowly time was moving. I kept looking at my watch and checking this.

I told Paul and Ahmed I was scared—though Don says I seemed quite calm and even relaxed. Ahmed offered to get me out of the intoxication—which you can do, he says, by drinking a mixture of lemon, sugar, hot water and salt. But I refused, several times. I'm very glad, now that I did.

All this while, Don had said that he felt absolutely no reactions. So they gave him more *majoon*—four spoons in all—and several puffs of *kif*, both in the pipe and in cigarettes where it was mixed with tobacco. My feeling toward Don became my one reassurance; but it was selfish of me to tell him I was scared, because naturally he began to dread the moment when the drug would take effect on *him*.

Then, shortly before midnight, it did.

He began to be very disturbed, almost at once. And soon he told me we must go home—immediately. He was scared. They were plotting against us. Ahmed was a witch. At the same time, he was horrified because he was aware that these feelings might be entirely subjective—which would mean that he was going insane, like Ted.

I now realized what I should have known from the start—that I ought never to have let Don take the stuff. Because the whole Ted problem now came up to the surface. And yet, in another way, it was good that he *did* take it, because he passed through the experience and to some degree overcame it.

Well, Don said we must go and that Paul mustn't come down with us in the elevator—"I want to be alone with Chris." So Paul had to wait until we'd reached the ground floor and then get the elevator up and come down with it. While we were waiting for him was one of the very worst moments, because I thought Don would begin screaming if he couldn't get outside. And I knew that if he began screaming I would probably scream too. That was what was so awful about the next two hours—I had to reassure Don while I myself was at the height of my intoxication.

We walked quite some distance and then saw a cop in the distance. Don was talking very loud about the conspiracy, but when I warned him to talk more quietly he did so immediately—one isn't irresponsible the same way as when drunk on alcohol. Then a taxi came and we took it to the hotel. I had a moment of terrified suspicion (these suspicions are said to be symptomatic) that maybe the taxi driver was an agent of Paul's and would take us back to his apartment. I know if I'd told Don this he would have jumped out of the taxi.

The final phase, in our hotel room, was the worst and yet the most reassuring—because I saw that the relationship between two people can be a rock to which they cling in the midst of chaos. Don kept getting the horrors—and I kept telling him, and he kept repeating: "We went to Paul Bowles's and got high on hashish—that's all—we're high on hashish." Don was terrified, however, that this, like all the rest of his experiences, was illusory. He hadn't taken hashish, wasn't in Tangier, was in fact still back in California, and insane. And I, while trying to keep him calm—several times I thought he'd rush screaming and crying into the passage and maybe out into the street—was having the most alarming time illusions. Once, after a long conversation, I looked at my watch and found it hadn't moved *at all*. Then I thought, I really *am* insane, and I began sweating and trembling. But I couldn't tell Don this. I still can't imagine how the time illusion works, because I'm certain the conversation really did take place.

We got back to the hotel around midnight, and the intoxication continued until 2:30 approximately. Toward the end of this time, I was fairly continuously conscious that I had taken hashish and that my experiences were subjective, but I was afraid, almost to the end, of putting out the electric light. We slept about eight hours and woke without a hangover of any kind. But I felt tired all yesterday and a little dizzy. I feel that a new and very strong bond exists between Don and myself. This is a tremendous experience we've shared. And I must say that Don showed willpower of really heroic proportions. He fought the horrors all the way. No doubt this isn't the best way to deal with them—but it was still very courageous and touching.

November 1. On board the *Andrea Doria*. We embarked from Gilbraltar last night. Tomorrow afternoon, we're scheduled to disembark in Naples.

At present, our reactions to this ship—or at least the first class—are extremely negative. It is far grander and even stuffier than the *Saturnia*. Being relatively modern, its decor is inspired by Picasso, Miro and [Eugene] Berman, rather than art nouveau. The swimming pool is surrounded by abstract shapes. Perhaps the best thing that can be said for this ship is that the second and third classes seem quite grand too, in their degrees—both have swimming pools. Also, the library includes a copy of *Prater Violet*! Oh yes—and Ramon Novarro[1] is among the passengers. Don spotted him at once.

Oddly enough, the boat, in these supposedly sheltered waters, is rolling quite heavily.

But I must try to set down a few more impressions of Tangier.

---

[1] Mexican star of Hollywood films.

Saturday the 29th, we spent mostly in resting up from the hashish experience. In the afternoon, Herbert List and Robert drove us out in their Volkswagen to the Caves of Hercules. It's a magnificent wild spot facing out to the Atlantic. Down in one of the caves there is a great hole full of foam suds from the waves that kept bursting in through the entrance. Arabs crouch in the darkness with home made lamps to guide you, and clamor for pesetas. Herbert thinks the caves were once sacred to a cult of Hercules.

During this, and our other outings, Herbert and Robert bickered spasmodically. Robert is pretty pleased with himself and plays the spoilt darling. Herbert consistently strikes the wrong note. He is indulgent when he should be quite brutal or indifferent.

We had supper that night with a Frenchman who told us about wonderful places in the Sahara—an oasis where there's a camel market, and you see white camels, driven in from all quarters of the desert.

On Sunday, we had lunch with Jane and Paul Bowles, and Ahmed, who no longer seemed the least sinister. Jane took us to her house in the Casbah—formerly occupied by Paul. As in many of them (I imagine) the staircase was so narrow that you could barely squeeze up it, and most of the rooms would barely hold three people. But when you got up on to the tiny rooftop, it was wonderful—you looked all over the harbor and the hills, and down into the maze of alleys, beautified, with wonderful haphazard beauty, by touches of blue standing out amidst the prevailing orange-yellow. I think if you got the horrors in that house you'd really go crazy.

Jane Bowles is such a strange little person, full of fears and yet somehow sly and even a little mocking. There was much discussion as to whether she could spend a night alone in the house. Her servant was away, but still she couldn't leave her Siamese cat. Paul was very patient and concerned about all of this, and we felt that he really is fond of her.

One of the things Jane was afraid about was the Arabs. This was the celebration of the Prophet's birthday, but their excitement is due to the return of the sultan who defied the French.[1] All through the weekend, there were demonstrations in his favor—mostly by quite young people, who were being quite visibly urged on by agitators amongst the crowd. In each procession, the sultan's picture was

---

[1] Muhammad Ibn Yusuf aligned himself with the Moroccan nationalist movement in the late 1940s and was deported in 1953; after two years of accelerating riots and organized killing, the French agreed to restore Moroccan sovereignty. Muhammad returned in November 1955 and later became Muhammad V.

carried by a girl, riding on a boy's shoulders. Don got a good movie picture of some of them as they passed our hotel window. A little boy threatened to throw a stone at him, but didn't. Finally, on the Sunday evening, the police got alarmed and exploded two tear-gas bombs on the square. They made a terrific detonation, and one of them blew open a window of the hotel bar where we were sitting, listening to a man named George Grieves telling us how Gerald Hamilton had been run out of Tangier for passing bad checks. Up on the square, the police had fire carts with hoses, to disperse the crowd—a rather meaningless threat, since most people must have been wet through from the constant heavy showers that fell throughout the weekend. Actually, I don't believe that the demonstrations were at all dangerous, anyway.

One of our greatest experiences in Tangier was a visit to the Thousand and One restaurant. This is an old Arab house, beautifully decorated by a painter named Brion Gysin.[1] They serve genuine Arab food—couscous and so forth. We went there on Sunday night with Herbert and Robert. There is an orchestra and they have two dancing boys—they are trained to perform at weddings. The boys were very interesting to watch—their negligent grace, their vague yet exact gestures, their delicately mocking salutes when you gave them money, which they placed in their turbans. Their hip movements and flirtatious play with their scarves is exquisitely campy and yet essentially masculine: this is in no sense a drag show. In the most beautiful of the dances, the boy carries a whole tray of glasses and lights on his head. Later the boys sang with one of the musicians, and I felt they were really enjoying themselves. There were also two tumblers, a man and a boy.

Later we met Jamie Caffery,[2] who is living here with David Herbert.[3] Jamie looks shockingly older. He was very friendly, and saw us off on the boat yesterday, back to Gibraltar.

All of the people we met in Tangier had taken hashish at one time or another—and I was surprised, when I described our unpleasant symptoms—to find that they had had them too. Only Jane said she wouldn't take it again. I seemed to detect, in the attitude of the others, a certain disapproval of my weakness and cowardice in being ready to give up. Herbert actually wanted us to smoke *kif* on Sunday night,

[1] Gysin, also a novelist, poet, and collaborator of William Burroughs, owned the Thousand and One Nights.
[2] Southern nephew of a former U.S. ambassador to Paris, once a researcher for *Fortune*; he moved with Herbert from London to Tangier in 1950 and became garden columnist for the *Tangier Gazette*.
[3] Second son of the Earl of Pembroke, raised at Wilton, a close friend of Cecil Beaton and Jane Bowles; he reputedly ran the expatriate social life in Tangier.

and Paul half-seriously offered to give us some *majoon* to take with us.

I think there is a definite association in my mind, now, of the *majoon* experience with Arab culture. Because I find myself now regarding the Arab culture as sinister and rather frightening. Its rigidity and extreme formalism scare me, and I can imagine myself mentally trapped within the patterns of its arabesques. Like the drug, it makes me feel claustrophobic.

November 6. Now we're well and truly in the midst of our travels—at the moment on board a steamer, going to Capri. And, as usual, when one is doing the sights, there's hardly anything to write.

We disembarked at Naples on the 2nd, in pouring rain, and felt miserable. But since then the weather has been fine, though misty. The next day we went over to Ischia and saw Chester [Kallman]. Wystan's new house is even more squalid and unattractive than I'd expected.[1] Chester was very nice—over anxious, perhaps, to be pleasant—since, as he confessed, he still feels I'm critical of him after all these years.

We met all the local worthies and unworthies and there was much drinking and the usual expatriate bitchery and the stuffiness of a tiny colony. The island is beautiful—particularly the mountain—but I'd rather live in Porto than Forio.[2]

We spent the night on Ischia and returned to Naples next afternoon. Then yesterday drove to Pompeii and Vesuvius. After much hunting around, we found the pornographic pictures—Cadmus is far better—all hidden under wooden shutters. The strangely delicate chichi of the painting—a sad little culture, I felt, over which there's no need to get sentimental. It was like excavating Tony Duquette. Most of Pompeii is just plain ruins, with the usual amount of shit and empty bottles in odd corners.

Then on to Vesuvius, which I didn't reach the top of because I couldn't face the chair lift. (My vertigo works chiefly upward.) Now I'm sorry. However, Don went up. He has been in very good spirits lately—except on Ischia, where he went through his usual reactions to large groups of strangers. But today his tongue is suddenly and mysteriously stained black. At least, we hope it's stain. He's worried

---

[1] Auden's landlord was involved in a family property squabble so Auden had to change houses in September 1955 just before leaving Ischia for New York; Kallman stayed behind to work on the new house.
[2] Auden lived in Forio d'Ischia; Porto d'Ischia is on the other side of the island, perhaps six miles away by road.

about this, naturally. My current ailment is a disgusting taste of decay when I suck on my capped tooth, which worries *me*, of course.

November 7. Just got back from doing the Amalfi drive in a hired car—not quite all of it, but we went beyond Amalfi as far as Ravello, where we had lunch at a good but expensive restaurant, the Caruso, on a terrace overlooking the bay, and saw the wonderful church with pulpit supported by lions. We also went in swimming at Positano. It was a beautiful day, though a little hazy. The first view of Positano is one of the most sensational things I've ever seen in my life. You expect the whole town to spill down into the sea, and the cliffs to crash over and fall on top of it.

Yesterday was not such a success. I refused to go on the chair lift at Anacapri—more on principle than because it scared me—and Don did go and was late and we had to plunge vertically down to the harbor to catch the boat in a taxi, which made me sick to my stomach. But there was an annoyance before this—a typical piece of Italian trickery. We got in a motorboat to go to the Blue Grotto, and were only then told we'd have to pay extra for a rowboat to go inside, and there was a long long wait, while other boats jostled each other and passengers screamed as they lay down to pass through the uterine entrance. The grotto's blue all right, but less impressive than I'd hoped. I think I might like Capri to live in, though. It has some of the suntrap snugness of Ventnor.

We have quite a nice hotel here in Sorrento—the Eden—with views of the sea and the mountains. Don has succeeded in scrubbing the black off his tongue. But my tooth still tastes foul.

November 11. Bad days. We got to Rome on the 8th, and are now staying in a room in a very untidy apartment belonging to Stanley Moss, an American poet who works on *Botteghe Oscura*,[1] and his beautiful Spanish wife. On the 9th I had to go to the dentist to see about my tooth. He pulled off the cap and a torrent of rotting food matter came out. He hopes he can save it.

Yesterday, Don had an outburst about the rudeness of a young writer named Bill Weaver, and today I cancelled all the dates Iris [Tree] had made for us. Her feelings were hurt, but it was all to the good. I get so furious when I feel I'm being socially exploited, and why *should* I be, on holiday?

Torrents of rain yesterday—but we saw St. Peter's, and today we went to the Forum and the Colosseum, and it was warm and lovely. Chief impression of Rome: dampness, mottled walls, dim green

---

[1] The international literary magazine published in Rome from 1949 to 1960.

gloom, the smell of the past. The cats of Rome, everywhere—defying Iris's muzzled dog. And the awful insane traffic tearing everywhere—especially the auto-scooters.

Iris is very sweet and quite pathetic—very low on money—trying to get on with her novel, which is charming.

With her usual genius for house finding she has discovered an apartment on the roof, overlooking the Spanish Steps. It has a fountain in the wall of the bed-sitting room, and you reach it by a circular iron outside ladder (against which I bumped my head agonizingly this evening). The first time we went up there, Iris wasn't home, so we waited on the roof outside her door. And so it came about that we saw that amazing sight—the thousands of starlings (or swifts) circling and swooping in clouds, thickening to dark blobs, diving with an uncanny, frightening speed down over the rooftops out of the yellow sunset sky.

November 12. I just wish to record that I'm unhappy, tense, and worried. But that will pass. The weather is beautiful again this morning and it's still early. I've just written cards to M., Stephen, John Lehmann and Willie Maugham about our impending approach. Now I must get up and go to the dentist. We have gotten off on the wrong foot here—spent too much money already and isolated ourselves by refusing Iris's plans for getting us invited. And yet I suppose, in retrospect, sightseeing memories will loom bigger than the discomfort of this apartment and the constant worry about Don—he's in a difficult, neurotic state, and seems about to start a cold.

This morning, waking up, I thought how we kept saying, that night in Tangier, "I have taken hashish"—and how, throughout one's life, one ought to keep reminding oneself, "I have taken maya. This is just an intoxication. It isn't the reality."

Iris talked very interestingly about Krishnamurti last night. I think he has been her really big experience as a teacher, and she made him sound very convincing. But I know that his way isn't mine, and he could never have helped me as Swami has.

November 14. It's hard to imagine just how this period will appear in retrospect. At present, I'm not really happy here. We've found nothing to do with our evenings—no movies or plays we can understand (except some uninteresting U.S. films) and few people we can see, and apparently almost no amusing café or bar life. Yet Rome imposes itself solidly. The unexpected glimpses—the sudden coming upon a fountain or a pillar or a cypress seen through an archway—those are the most memorable.

With Iris again yesterday—long rambling talks about the people she knows. And she read us poetry—sympathetically but not well. I see her somewhat marooned here, in spite of talk that it's so much better than California. But is it? Milton Gendel, her nice friend who works for Olivetti, confesses he finds the place provincial and only half-alive, though he loves the city. And if it's so wonderful, why does every Italian (allegedly) want to emigrate to the U.S.? It can't be just the lure of TV and automobiles. Or can it?

Bill Weaver, with whom we had lunch yesterday, says Clare Luce[1] is despised and hated here, and Spellman is known as Cardinal Dollars.[2]

Rain threatens again this morning. It's a real nuisance and menace. We are going to a place where you can get a bath—then hunting old movie magazines, shoes and shirts. Don is restless, but was better yesterday. In some way, this travelling makes him feel more than ever insecure. He acts badly and then, as he admits, hates me for making him feel guilty. As for me, I'm depressed by my growing fatness, brought on by all this fried food. But yesterday evening, at Don's suggestion, we went to bed without supper. Am reading John Symonds's life of Aleister Crowley, *The Great Beast*. What a dreary mess!

Am disinclined to take mescaline at present. The circumstances are all wrong. No calm.

The truly awful thing about Crowley is that one suspects he didn't really believe in anything. Even his wickedness. Perhaps the only thing that wasn't fake was his addiction to heroin and cocaine.

November 15. Milton Gendel drove us and Iris out to Tivoli today. But it got very cold and rained and we did not get to see the Villa d'Este or Hadrian's Villa. Yesterday we went to Denny [Fouts]'s grave in the Protestant Cemetery, and I cried. It all seemed such a wretched tangle—his life, and mine too. I'm depressed here, and I guess I depress Don too. Europe, in its autumn, reminds me of my own. And I seem to myself to look older every day. And I feel no ripening, no resignation. I don't want to get old or die. "Instead of ripening like an apple, I'm getting older like a worn-out boot."

November 19. It has turned much colder, and this unheated room is pretty wretched—not to mention the misery of washing and shaving

---

[1] Then U.S. Ambassador to Italy.
[2] Pius XII depended on Spellman, the powerful New York cardinal, for financial and diplomatic advice; Spellman was a fierce anti-communist, and poured Catholic relief money into areas threatened by communism.

in cold water. Also, Don is sick. His tongue keeps turning black—despite his drastic scrapings of it. This afternoon we're going to see a doctor. I'm more worried about this than I admit to him.

Otherwise, however, things are much more cheerful. Four nights ago, we ran into Chuck Turner[1] at a party, and he has been very sweet and helpful, driving us around in his car. We're planning to drive with him to Milan, the week after next. In the interim, we juggle plans around—either to go to Venice first. Or to pay a flying visit to Athens and Istanbul.

Yesterday we went to the Vatican museums. The Sistine chapel is certainly terrific, but I don't like its shape or all the surplus decoration—the non-Michelangelo pictures. And I hate the forest of white new plaster fig leaves on all the statues. What I really liked best was the Angelico chapel, which no one ever told me about.

Chuck drove us out to lunch in Ostia, with an Italian friend of his, Enrico Medioli. Enrico told us how, during the war, his family used to play a joke on friends, serving an "economy lunch" consisting of salted hot water, boiled bones, and a "Swedish dessert," snow with a drop of wine on it and an apple skin. The guests were, of course, too polite to protest. Later they were given a proper meal.

Last night, at a party at Bill Weaver's, I met [Alberto] Moravia, a worried, aggressive, unhappy man with a limp. He spoke of his play about the Cenci and told me [Frederic] Prokosch's novel wasn't much good.[2] Fritz [Prokosch] was there too, and he too seemed restless and unhappy. He has quite lost his wonderful good looks.

The city is all yellows and browns—the buildings and the autumn leaves. It seems relatively very small and exceedingly provincial. The only "important" play is Visconti's production of Arthur Miller's *The Crucible*. Everybody knows everybody. The scandal mongering is of the usual snickering-snobbish Latin kind.

November 20. Don's tongue was due to a harmless fungus, possibly caused by taking penicillin. This was the diagnosis of a nice Dr. Hirschfeld (a distant relative of Magnus) who knows Tennessee and Truman Capote and had read *Goodbye to Berlin*.

Another bad evening. We went out with Bill Weaver and Don got cross because Bill ignored him in conversation; he wanted to go home, and then *I* got cross. It's hardly worth recording, but it's well to remember the downs with the ups. And I have to watch myself all of the time.

[1] Charles Turner, American composer.
[2] Italian novelist Moravia's play is *Beatrice Cenci* (1955); Prokosch's *A Tale for Midnight* (1955) is also about the Cenci.

This morning we more or less decided to cut out Athens and Istanbul and go instead to Venice during the interval before leaving Rome for good. The other project is just too expensive, especially as we know nobody in either city.

So cold here. The Mosses lent us their stove and it smoked. Got a hot bath, however.

November 22. Yesterday we started into a phase of fine and warmer weather—long may it continue! We have now definitely decided to leave for Venice tomorrow. Athens and Istanbul are to be skipped, or visited later, on the way back to the States.

On Sunday (20th) we went out to Hugh Chisholm's villa, on the Old Appian Way. Hugh and Brad Fuller are leaving very soon for the States. Hugh, now grey haired and silvery voiced and a little sad and infinitely gracious, is suffering from ulcers—so he must not be worried about anything. He has to keep very very quiet. He has the air of lowering his voice in the presence of his own sickness. His hands shake a little. When he leaves the room, Brad takes his arm.

Among other guests, we met a youngish dark man with a stoop, named Filippo Sanjust, who is a painter.[1] He turned out to be a highly informed fan of mine, and also a mine of information about Rome. Yesterday he drove us out to see Hadrian's Villa and the Villa d'Este, which is almost the most wonderful thing I've seen so far—a cathedral of water. The sun was setting and the gardens can never have been more romantic. What makes them so marvellous is that the place is so small and enclosed. You feel the power of the water. It seems to be all around you—spurting up at you, bursting out over you, shooting out horizontally from every angle. And the dank alleys of cypress and the mottled stone stairs—

Meanwhile Filippo held forth, without ever stopping, being both brilliant and boring simultaneously. He talked as if he hadn't talked for a week. He claimed that no great artist has ever been a Roman—that Rome is an imaginary city which has existence only as an artistic ideal.

Later. We just saw Iris who told us, quite casually, that Friedrich has divorced (or is divorcing) her to marry "one of his followers" who is going to have a baby. She added: "I think he rather hates the whole thing." She seemed sad and nervous, and I was really distressed to hear this about Friedrich, because, in some way, they belong together although they spend so much time apart.

Speaking of Filippo Sanjust, I was struck by the casual, proprietary

[1] Also known as an opera designer and book illustrator.

way he struck matches and climbed up on the altar of the church on the Piazza del Popolo, in order to show us the Caravaggios.

November 24. It's incredible, but we are really and truly in Venice—and outside our hotel window is the end of the Grand Canal and Santa Maria della Salute and the tower of San Giorgio away to the left across the water, just as in all the watercolors and oils and photographs I've known since childhood.

We arrived last night, after a long long train ride from Rome, and came up from the station on a motor launch in a thick fog. Nothing but a few blurred lights visible. And the utter dank canal cold in our bones. Today has been only misty, with beautiful faint golden sunshine—Venice by Turner, not Canaletto. Tonight it's quite clear—the lights sharp, and canals full of lamp glitter. We're off to a Thanksgiving party at Peggy Guggenheim's.

November 28. Peggy Guggenheim turned out to be a bottle-nosed, potbellied woman with dyed black hair—"good-natured," I guess, in the rough and tough manner of rich American women. She tried to sell me a picture by an artist she'd discovered. But the chief advantage of our visit was that we met Martyn Coleman and his friend Bill Ames. I used to know Martyn Coleman in the days when he was in Los Angeles at the beginning of the war. We've seen them both several times since then and they've shown us around. Martyn reminds me so much of Chris [Wood]—his battered slimness, his anti-American grumbling and his general determination to retire into a shell. They are fitting up an apartment overlooking the Grand Canal—taking the kind of trouble over it which never fails to depress me and make me feel guilty. Building the house upon the sand. Incidentally—and this is also very Chris Wood—Martyn has let his British citizenship lapse and now he's stateless, unless he's ready to settle for seven years in England. He says he wouldn't live anywhere but in Italy.

Tonight we leave by train for Rome. Two days there, then off again with Chuck Turner in his car to Milan.

Impressions of Venice: The gondolas, black against the glitter of the water, with upcurving bow and stern, and the rowers bent forward at such an angle that their movement seems to have an extreme urgency. The dark cold of black canal water between sunless walls. The terrifying pigeons of St. Mark, whizzing past your ears like jets. The tidy, leafy streets of the Lido, like a German town. The Tintoretto crucifixion.[1] The incredible heavy gold ceilings of the

---

[1] In the Scuola di San Rocco.

Ducal Palace. The soapsuds flooding the canal from hotel washing machines. The snugness of lighted restaurants in the narrow streets. The strange sinister silence of the winter afternoon on Torcello, with its deserted gardens and fields, and the mud flats all around. The gold of the Fenice Theater—but what's the use of writing all this down? There is nothing left to say about Venice. There's just the incredulity of finding oneself there—like having stepped into a picture.

December 3. This is being written merely in order not to break my record. So much has happened so fast that I can't go into details. Also, I have to go out to supper with the others in a few minutes.

We are in Florence.

On Tuesday last, 29th, we got back to Rome. Left on December 1st by car, with Chuck Turner. Spent that night in San Gimignano. Spent last night here.

Mixed impressions. The towers of San Gimignano, which I've known all my life from M.'s pictures, very Gordon Craig,[1] especially at night: the light tower against two dark ones. The nervousness of Viterbo, on a dark day, very depressing and not even sinister: one saw how awful the Middle Ages must have been when it rained. Florence doesn't so far impress me greatly as a city—but the statues! and the paintings! Favorites: Michelangelo's David (oddly enough) and the Duke of Urbino in meditation and *Night*[2] and the Victory.[3] The bronze doors of the Baptistery facing the Duomo—particularly the deceit upon Esau.[4] The satyrs around the fountain of the Piazza della Signoria. The staircase of the Laurenziana Library. At the Uffizi— Cimabue's crucifix, Uccello's *Battle of San Romano*, van der Goes' *Adoration [of the Shepherds]*, Dürer's *Adoration [of the Kings]*, Altdorfer's *Martyrdom of St. Florian*, Bellini's *Sacred Allegory*, all the Caravaggios,[5] the two Guardis,[6] the Magnasco,[7] Rubens's *Isabella Brandt*. But my head is whirling—and tomorrow we have to see the Pitti, and leave for the next place!

Don's tongue is still black, despite treatment.

We left Iris with a mescaline tablet and begged her to lay in stores of sugar for the experiment.

---

[1] English artist and stage designer.
[2] Both in the Medici funerary chapel.
[3] *The Genius of Victory* in the Palazzo Vecchio.
[4] As in Genesis 27.
[5] Probably *Bacchus*, *Medusa*, *Sacrifice of Abraham*, and *Youthful Bacchus*.
[6] *Capriccio* and *Village with Canal* by Francesco Guardi.
[7] *Gypsies' Meal*.

December 7. At the Manin Hotel in Milan, with a cold coming on and a general fit of the blues. It's grey and wintry up here in the north. Am just finishing *Villette*, which is one of the worst books I've ever read. Don is delighted with *Wuthering Heights*.[1] I've made up my mind to cut down on food to a minimum and lose some weight. Never have I been more toadlike.

Chuck Turner left us yesterday evening, on the train for Paris. Tomorrow he sails for the States. He's a strange cagey boy, underneath his surface charm—intensely ambitious and on his guard against everybody. Once again I see that bottomless American insecurity.

Talking over impressions, I find that Don and I agree that the sight of the Leaning Tower, together with the Baptistery and Duomo, was one of the very strangest we've had on our trip. We stayed at Pisa the night before last. The night before that was at Lucca, which I remember principally for its town walls. You can drive along the top—all the way around the city.

Talked to Mario Soldati this evening, in Alessandria. He and King Vidor are shooting there till Saturday on *War and Peace*,[2] then they go up into the mountains in search of snow. We'll probably go to see them in Alessandria the day after tomorrow.

This evening is the opening of the Scala—[Maria] Callas in *Norma*. Chuck promised heaven-high he'd get us in, but needless to say the two rich bitches on whom he relied—Signora [Something-or-Other] and her daughter—weren't about to help us.

Milan seems a big gloomy un-Italian sort of town—more like I imagine Switzerland. The cathedral is very impressive, until your eyes get used to the dark.

Don and I have given up wine—to see if that's what makes his tongue black. Already it seems better.

December 8. A bad night with a full nose and aching sinuses. I feel better up than in bed. Don's tongue gets cleaner and cleaner. He is greatly occupied with *Wuthering Heights*.

Waking at night, particularly when I'm sick, I terribly fear old age and death. I hope I'll get through the experience somehow, by losing consciousness—whatever *that* means! When Don is very desperate and dependent, I see us as a tragi-comic couple—Lear and his Fool in the storm.

This is miserable cold grey weather—the kind I hate most. The faces in the streets look furrowed with worry and defeat.

[1] *Villette* is by Charlotte Brontë, *Wuthering Heights* by Emily.
[2] Vidor was directing the film with stars brought from Hollywood; Soldati directed all the battle scenes.

And how I hate "grand" restaurants! We went to one yesterday, Savini's, in the Gallery (which utterly lacks the glamor of Naples). The hushed, poker-faced air of the far too many majordomos—the mixed atmosphere of a church and a hospital.

December 10. I sincerely hope that December 8 may have been the most—and one of the very few—boring days of this trip. Today was not boring. We are in Alessandria—got here yesterday and will leave tomorrow. This morning early we drove out with Soldati over the flat ice-foggy country to the banks of the Po, which was being used for the Berezina in the film. The Italian army is supplying the extras. Today there were 3,000 of them—about a third in Napoleonic uniforms, others in blue aprons over their uniforms to give a background effect, others in their ordinary modern equipment. But the scene was very moving. Napoleon (Herbert Lom) orders the burning of the standards, and, in the background you see the huddled line crossing the pontoon bridge (which the army built), Russian guns firing from the heights along the river, bright orange flames bursting out in the fog, the sad grove of naked poplars, the stream flowing very swiftly and darkly.

Soldati and King Vidor make an almost absurd contrast—Soldati flapping like a Groucho Marx scarecrow, Vidor very relaxed, careful of his health, no doubt, for he often looks quite old. He never seems rattled or unkind.

We had lunch in a small-town restaurant on the way home, with a lot of news cameramen—including Max Scheler (a friend of Herbert List) and a man who was the (half-Italian?) son of Gordon Craig.

The soldiers looked quite natural in their Napoleonic uniforms—for, after all, they *were* soldiers. They didn't smell good, and they laughed a lot. In fact, it was nearly impossible to stop them laughing. One of them rolled over in ecstasies of amusement when he was supposed to be blown up by a shell.

(Incidental information—I forget who we got it from: the Hotel Europa we stayed in, in Venice, was the one where Henry James always stayed.)

This visit has made me feel very dubious that I want to work with Soldati, at any future time. (He wants me to read a short story of his with a view to making a picture out of it.) I see too much of Berthold Viertel in him, and I'm too old for the embrace of such a father, with his total demand, his terrible poignant reproachfulness, his subconscious determination to make me somehow betray him.

Don says he has decided to cut down sharply on drinking—not that he drinks much anyway—but he hates the scenes he makes when drunk. He couldn't be sweeter-natured than he is at present—most like his best self.

Went out into the town to try to buy an English book. The only one they had was Fielding's *Joseph Andrews*.

December 12. Yesterday we came back from Alessandria on the train and returned to the Hotel Manin. This time they gave us a room on the front—a really nice one with a balcony, and it's a shame we can't enjoy the view because of miserable thick fog. My cold is letting up. Don is starting one.

Last night we saw Callas in *Norma* at the Scala. And she really is terrific—one of the most immediately effective theatrical personalities I've ever seen. She manages the tiger slink without being ridiculous. Or rather, she includes the element of camp in her performance. The sets were far better than I'd expected.

Today we're expecting to leave, and I think it'll be France.

December 14. We didn't leave till yesterday, because the train times didn't fit. As it was, we had a nice trip, leaving foggy old gloomy Milan at 9:10, getting down to Genoa, where the sun almost shone, by lunchtime, arriving in Nice at half past five. Our hotel, the Scribe, has its own charms—a rather 1900ish honeymoon air—with brass bedsteads. We have seen nothing of Nice yet, except the Avenue de la Victoire after dark. I have an idea that we should use the days until we go up to visit Maugham by making a side trip to Avignon or someplace. But I also want to take mescaline soon.

It was worth staying on in Milan to have visited the Poldi Pezzoli Museum. And it was worth visiting the Poldi Pezzoli for the painting by Ghislandi of the Young Gentleman—the most terrifying evocation of an eighteenth-century beau, with his great black three-cornered hat, his powder grey wig (suggesting premature age) his heavy-lidded, pouched, rather glassy eyes, his huge mulberry-colored lips, the weak sloping shoulders. With almost imbecile sensuality dressed up in lace. And the cruel plump white hand. A character right out of Browning's "A Toccata of Galuppi's." I notice from the postcard of it I bought that Ghislandi is also known as Fra Galzario. Did he become a monk? Was this perhaps a self-portrait—or his view of the world after leaving it? I must read up and find out.[1]

Great problems last night because of my snoring—the last remnant of my cold. Don got very provoked.

---

[1] In fact, the painting was generally called *Gentleman with a Tricorn*, though after 1954 it was also known as *Portrait of a Cavaliere of the Order of Constantine*.

December 18. The day before yesterday, we rented a car and drove to Avignon. Yesterday we returned by way of Marseille and all along the corniche, through the little seaside towns that are shrines to the great names of the twenties—Picasso painting, Kathy[1] writing her journal and looking out of the window at the cruel mistral vexing the sea, [D. H.] Lawrence dying. St. Tropez seemed almost unchanged since I was there in 1928, but different perhaps from the town I described in my novels. What I forgot was the redness of the earth—all red.

We have both had bad colds, are better. Don is reading Maugham with passion—and today we're going up to the Villa Mauresque[2] to stay. Am nervous about this. More later.

Later. We are at the Villa Mauresque!

I want to say ssh!—as if we were in Mecca in disguise, and might give ourselves away and be instantly strangled.

This place is truly a palace. Ice water, Vichy and cookies in glass caskets by the beds. Your clothes unpacked by the faultless menservants—I think there are only two, but there seem to be about twenty. And they unpacked *everything*—including Don's movie magazines, our powder to kill crab lice and our K.Y.[3]

Willie seems extraordinarily intact and scarcely older at all. And Alan Searle hasn't changed much. But I'll write about them at length tomorrow.

December 19. Feeling somewhat stifled by much food and drink and little exercise—though I did walk down with the others to the rocks below Jean Cocteau's villa. Don thought he'd swim but was dissuaded by Willie and Alan.

I'll just put down at random some things Willie, or Willie and Alan, told us.

Willie remarked that after his death he wants Alan to go and live in London. "If he stays here, he'll go to pieces."

Willie said that a dramatist doesn't need brains—only a knack of writing. He doesn't believe Aldous has that knack—but admittedly he hadn't seen *The Giaconda Smile*. He said: "Graham Greene said that *The Sacred Flame*[4] was the worst play ever written. I replied that he made that remark before writing *The Living Room*." He said that he hadn't known many really evil men. The only two he could think of offhand were Aleister Crowley and Norman Douglas—but that it was extraordinary how Douglas commanded devotion even from the

[1] Katherine Mansfield.
[2] Maugham's house.
[3] K.Y. Jelly, used as a sexual lubricant.
[4] By Maugham.

little boys to whom he often behaved so meanly. He remembered an occasion when Douglas had been so sick and weak that he couldn't walk up to his villa unaided. Two little boys had appeared, kissed his hands and then supported him home.[1] Willie remarked about the Villa Mauresque: "During the war, it was occupied first by the Italians and then by the Germans, who did it no damage. But then the British came and shelled it—trying to hit the semaphore on the hilltop. And finally the French looted it from top to bottom." Both Willie and Alan declare they were shocked, during their recent visit, by the envy and spitefulness of the English. They feel that the English have changed very greatly since the war.

Willie has a painting of a naked man which is the most untypical Toulouse-Lautrec one could imagine. Only two people have ever recognized its authorship—Sir Kenneth Clark, and a young American tourist—who got lunch and two signed copies of Maugham books as a reward.

December 20. Today the weather was much better. We drove with Alan Searle up to the village of Eze—a natural fortress which was never captured throughout the Middle Ages. Yesterday night we went over to Monte Carlo and gambled. Alan won five thousand francs, we won two thousand. The place was rather empty and disappointingly unglamorous.

In a short private talk, Alan told me how the Maugham family hates him, and how he feels he has acquired so many enemies by being with Willie that he dreads going to live in London after Willie's death. Paunchy, jowly and spotty, Alan is a rather sad figure but not really a pitiful one, because he obviously cares for Willie and considers those years spent with him well worth while.

Willie himself shows immense energy—today he walked up to the abandoned chapel at the top of the hill and all along the ridge, over a trail of broken stones. He talked about Glenway Wescott, saying that his journals could be of no real interest because he was a mass of insincerity and had no real talent as a writer. Passing a mimosa tree in blossom, he turned to Don and said: "You must remember, Don—anything that's very beautiful only lasts a very short time." Don didn't quite know whether to take this as a compliment or merely an admonition.

Willie remarked that he takes far more trouble over his work than he did. Nowadays he rewrites several times.

Alan assures us that Willie is greatly enjoying our visit.

[1] The novelist Norman Douglas (1868–1952) lived in Capri, where Maugham often visited.

December 22. Willie once knocked Alan down, for throwing a stone at a frog. Yesterday, a copy of an address on Colette arrived from Cocteau, with an inscription to "his dear neighbor." (Cocteau has a house very near this one.) Willie dislikes Cocteau rather (says Alan) and he commented on Cocteau's long-winded insincerity. He thought this applied to nearly all French writers.

Willie couldn't have been sweeter, yesterday. We went for a walk and he posed for movie shots whenever asked to, and signed a copy of *The Casuarina Tree* for Don, who is now his devoted fan.

I'm shocked to learn from Alan that Willie is no longer on good terms with any of his family, including his nephew Robin. Both Robin and also Maugham's daughter sent for Alan while he was in London and asked him why this is. They blame Alan, which distresses him very much.

Tonight we have a most disagreeable journey ahead of us—about twenty-two hours—train to Geneva, sitting upright, then by air to Munich via Zurich.

December 25. The journey was indeed disagreeable—the only pleasant part of it being our parting from Alan and Willie, who said, "You've been model guests." It was delightful to feel so sad at leaving and to know that our visit had been such a success. Otherwise, we had recourse to the box supper Willie's staff had packed, including a bottle of wine, and to a bottle of whiskey we bought in the station. The compartment got steadily hotter—in fact, the actual seats got hotter—until midnight; then quickly colder and colder. We wandered around Geneva in a drizzle. Was chiefly struck by the immense number of swans on the lake.

Then by plane to Zurich, where we spent an hour in the beautiful white watch-and-toy shop of an airport and saw a plane from India disgorge men in crumpled suits and pink turbans.

Then we flew on to Munich, arriving in a drizzle which hasn't let up since, and this evening is turning to heavy rain. Munich is a stark, empty-looking city of huge plain buildings and very wide streets. The bomb damage is still enormous but severely tidy. The city is like a mouth with many gaps but all the remaining teeth strong. There's a certain German smugness, despite this grim exterior. The local accent is almost farcically *gemütlich.*[1] And there's the eternal smell of Turkish cigarettes.

It was a hideous and costly mistake coming here. How can we possibly have imagined we wanted to see Herbert List? He is such a

[1] Good-natured.

bore—a sadist too, perhaps. (His face, when he let his giant poodle loose on us as we climbed the stairs to his apartment, had that wooden look of sub-cruelty which must have been common on the faces of medieval torturers.) And his friend Max Scheler is a bore too, and [also a bit of] a sulker. I feel, in these young Germans, the rude weary superiority of the European. They know better what it's like to suffer. Okay, agreed. But must suffering make people merely more unpleasant?

All this is, of course, unfair to Herbert—who fixed us a Christmas Eve dinner, complete with goose—which Don was then too sick to eat. He vomited and shat all night long. Today I went to a doctor and got him some pills and he seems slowly recovering. But he still hasn't eaten anything. He thinks his sickness is partly due to the train journey, and partly to some vile sausage with sauerkraut we ate for lunch yesterday.

This hotel, the Carlton, is small and family and very respectable. Our bedroom, with its *federbetten*,[1] is still somehow more like a sitting room. (Just as many European restaurants are like drawing rooms.) There are brass lamp hangings and there's a big oil painting of an Alpine scene. A shower but no toilet, unfortunately—so poor Don has to shit in the shower, as the toilet is down at the far end of the passage.

December 28. A depressing morning for departure, with rain coming down hard—but at least thank goodness we *are* departing. Yesterday was quite enough of Munich. We went to the Haus der Kunst and saw the two marvellous Altdorfers—*Susannah at the Bath* and the *Alexanderschlacht*.[2] Also discovered that one of the statues on the Luitpoldbrücke[3] is exactly like Burt Lancaster. Also went to see a film called *Der Himmel ist nie ausverkauft*,[4] in which Frank Diernhammer (calling himself Frank Holms) appeared. That's as much as you can say—he appeared. We left in the middle.

We had supper with Herbert, Max Scheler and Robert Furst. It was as depressing as usual. Max and Robert have the sulky mouths of spoiled children. Max wants to go to the U.S. His editor doesn't want him to go—says he's not interested in the U.S.—would only accept articles showing the U.S. to be militaristic. At the same time, he *is* interested in Russia!

[1] Featherbeds.
[2] *The Battle of Alexander* (his victory over Darius at Issus).
[3] The bridge over the Isar named after the Prince Regent, Luitpolde (1888–1912).
[4] *Heaven Is Never Sold Out.*

Herbert, Robert and Max had taken *majoon* yesterday evening— [Herbert had] smuggled some out of Tangier. That was probably why they were so listless.

One very big good mark I must give to Munich—the service. The people in the hotel have been admirable, and when I went into a restaurant with the loop of my topcoat broken the woman at the hat-check desk mended it for me without saying anything. I didn't notice what she'd done till much later.

December 30. Paris—we got here by train near midnight the day before yesterday. A tiresome journey, with a quick change at Strasbourg into a very crowded train. A charmingly polite man gave up his seat so Don and I could sit in the same compartment. He only found another with great difficulty. Big mark for the oft-accused French.

So far, our visit hasn't gone well. We successfully got a room at the Hotel Voltaire (this must be at least my fifth visit—I was here four times in the thirties that I can definitely remember—with Heinz, Johnny Andrews, Ian Scott-Kilvert, and Wystan, on his way to the Spanish war) but it seems horribly noisy and no longer so glamorous. Then it has rained, on and off, since our arrival. And Don is disappointed because Audrey Hepburn obviously doesn't want to see us, and because he could only ascend to the second platform of the Eiffel Tower. And I'm depressed because two lousy notices of *Diane* have just arrived from *Variety* and *The Hollywood Reporter*, both blaming the script—calling it wordy and slow.

Well, shit. All this isn't very important and indeed mostly subjective—and anyhow one nice thing has happened: we met John Gielgud yesterday on the street quite by accident, and we're seeing him tomorrow.

Also, I must say that Paris—even in the rain—appears wonderfully lively, bright and interesting at every turn. This afternoon we walked along the Boulevard Raspail as far as the Balzac statue, had a coffee in the Dôme and returned through the streets alongside the Luxembourg Gardens.

[1956]

January 5. Second day of black depression, assisted by a thin sad fog that hangs over the city and makes the morning delay its start until around 10:00. The truth is, I dread going to England. I dread seeing M. and Richard and reopening the whole dismal tragedy. And even the lesser effort of brightly smiling every time I'm asked how I like living in the States—well, I have to go and that's that.

Actually, we've had some quite amusing times while here in Paris. With John Gielgud and his friend Paul Anstee, mostly. I think I really like John—at any rate, I find his weaknesses extremely sympathetic. He is terribly superstitious. At the little restaurant in the market, there were gypsies, and one of them took him aside and asked him in a threatening tone: "Do you want to be happy?" and he was so scared he gave her 5,000 francs. Meanwhile, a strange little American named Gladys Solomon made us draw horses on the backs of the menus. She uses them for character analysis, and, as a matter of fact, she's very good at it. Nearly all her subjects draw their horses facing left—unless, of course, they're left-handed. I drew only a head, and was told that I concentrate on essential details. Don drew a careful neat little horse, and was told that he's a perfectionist.

On New Year's Eve, we went to a bar called the Fiacre and met Ray Ohge, jammed into a crowd so dense you could only sway with it like seaweed in water. He has been in Copenhagen and was travelling with what he described as a Danish princess. We also saw Audrey Hepburn and Mel Ferrer—we went with them to the movies on New Year's Day. And Mel took us out to the St. Maurice Studio in Joinville, where he is making a film with Ingrid Bergman and Jean Marais.[1]

Bergman didn't recognize me—I've aged so much since 1940, when we did *Rage in Heaven*. *She* still looks wonderful, and she has a warmth and naturalness which are quite unactressy. She enjoyed herself enormously at lunch, telling the old story of the man who had the robot wife.

Jean Marais, foxy and bedroom eyed and much more intelligent than I'd expected, told me about his first meeting with Denny [Fouts]. Denny came into his dressing room in pajamas, explaining quite casually that he had been sick and his friends had taken his clothes away to prevent him from going out, but that he'd made up his mind to come, anyway. Last year, Marais came to Hollywood, to visit some friends who were in *The Glass Slipper* with the Roland Petit Ballet. He saw no agents, gave no interviews and spent his time at a little apartment near Culver City, marketing and cooking while his hosts were working at the studio.

Mel talked a lot about U.S. gangsters, particularly those in the gambling racket, and pointed out that they are still just as ruthless, though not so spectacularly—instancing the murder of Bugsy Siegel. Siegel's daughter now lives in Klosters and Irwin Shaw knows her

---

[1] *Eléna et les hommes (Paris Does Strange Things)*, directed by Jean Renoir.

well. But [. . .] she never talks about the murder. [Also, she never travels back to] the [United] States.

Talking of Irwin Shaw reminds me that we hear that Bettina Graziani, Peter's ex-girl, is about to marry Ali Khan.[1]

The studio was astonishingly tacky—holes in the sound proofing of the ceiling. And Renoir always refuses to say which scene is coming next, so the actors have to stick around all day.

January 6. Today we went to Versailles in a thick fog. The chateau seemed utterly dead, deserted even by its ghosts. And the park was bitterly cold with loudly dripping trees, although it wasn't raining.

Another day of deep gloom. We shall be glad to get out of here.

One of the greatest disappointments of this visit has been the food. Restaurant after restaurant failed us. And all so expensive.

January 10. Fred Ditis remarked on this very point while he was driving us to the Gare du Nord (on the morning of the 7th) to catch the Golden Arrow to England. He said that it's a myth that all Parisian restaurants are good. There are many good (and even cheap ones) but one may spend a long time in Paris without finding them.

Fred is a Swiss, a publisher of crime fiction, rather attractive looking and really quite intelligent. We met him through Gielgud. He has been very kind.

Throughout the journey to England I was in an absurd state of jitters lest anything should go wrong at the passport office and customs. Actually, it couldn't have been easier, but I never can forget that traumatic experience with Heinz.[2]

And maybe it wouldn't have been so *very* unfortunate if we had been turned away from the white cliffs. For our stay here has opened disastrously. After two days at John Lehmann's, Don announced that he just couldn't take it any more—he even thought we'd have to stop living together—because my friends all treated him like dirt, or worse.

I'm bound to admit that this is true. John Lehmann couldn't have been stuffier if he'd been John van Druten. Alexis [Rassine] was pissy and grand. Stephen, even, was very off-handed in his manner. Even William Plomer, the affable, took very little trouble to make Don feel at home.

On the other hand, however, Don will have to realize that being

---

[1] Irwin Shaw, the novelist and screenwriter, was a close friend of Peter Viertel.
[2] See Glossary under Neddermeyer.

accepted by my friends would be no solution of his difficulties. He has to find his own world.

Now we have moved to the Cavendish Hotel—got here this morning—and the strain is eased. I'm sick—a cold and the shivers—and have gone to bed. Don went out to see *Peter Pan*.[1] He has piles, but they are yielding to treatment.

It's snug here, like an Edwardian country house. Such a nice old housekeeper brought me mulligatawny soup. It's snug being in the large back bedroom, with awkward furniture, mirrors in the wrong places, electric lights ditto—so quiet, yet right in the center of the city.

John and Stephen both look terribly fat in the face—round swollen red bladders. I'm still sorry for John—perhaps it would be friendlier not to be—but oh God he is such a square! So stupid. And their little world is so tiny. And his life in that house with Alexis seems really suffocating.

London looks much smarter, these days. Lots more restaurants. Lots of travel agencies. Everything pretty expensive. The people extraordinarily friendly and polite. I notice that, whenever I go into a shop, I'm taken for granted as an American—though my accent seems British to anyone in the States.

Getting back to John Lehmann—I suppose his stupidity really consists in this: he has no curiosity. He dismisses Vedanta, Gerald Heard, California, the United States. He isn't prepared to listen to anything I tell him about the life I lead in Los Angeles. He thinks I'm quite simply "in movies"—and therefore temporarily lost. He hasn't enlarged his ideas one little bit since the thirties. He still talks like the silliest kind of publisher about someone's book "showing an advance." But why am I getting so heated? I knew all this twenty years ago.

January 14. In a bad mood this morning. It's raining. The hotel people have deserted the switchboard. Don is in his most tiresome helpless mood—furious because the old-fashioned bath plug won't work, and blaming me for it. And yet, by and large, we're having a good time here in London. Don has met a young American with whom he'll be able to go around. We have seen several interesting films and plays, and I really enjoy being at this absurd hotel.

Don had a very nasty attack of stomach cramps the night before last, and maybe that accounts for his behavior—although he seems quite recovered now. There has been a situation today because he refuses to have lunch with Stephen, Natasha and Peter Watson.

[1] J.M. Barrie's play, with Peggy Cummins as Peter.

I can't blame him, and yet I resent this because ultimately I'm burdened with all the explaining that has to be done.

January 16. Well, now I'm really mad at Don. He walked out of a party at John Gielgud's which I only went to to amuse him—Martita Hunt and Edith Evans were there.[1] He is too tiresome with his neurosis, and I'm weary of being tied to all this fuss, when there is so much fun to be had.

Had lunch with Stephen and Natasha, the other day. Stephen said: "The trouble with the Lehmanns is, they think they're the Brontës, when actually they're the Marx Brothers."

Stephen said how tired he is of England: "There's nothing here but personal relationships and maneuvers—and I'm tired of both."

The thing is this. Does Don want to be regarded as crazy? If so, I'll be patient with him. If not, he's just being insufferable.

January 19. It's no use getting mad, and I wouldn't have written as I did above if I hadn't been drunk. This is a tough time for Don—especially so because we'd both hoped he'd have a lot of social success here—and we shall both have to be patient.

Amiya arrived at the hotel yesterday for two nights, with old George[2] in tow. We had supper alone together and got very drunk, and she told me hair-raising tales of his lechery and miserliness. She also told me that Franz Dispeker is dead, which made me cry in the restaurant. In spite of all Amiya's complaints, I feel she has a pretty good time. Shouting at George and bullying him takes up most of her surplus energy. She is full of asides at every remark he makes, like a comedian in a patsy act. If George says: "I got a surprise this afternoon," Amiya comments behind his back: "You'll get another one when you see the fur coat I bought."

Yesterday morning, their butler got on to the train to help them with their luggage. The train left before he could get off it again—and, as it was nonstop, he had to come with them to London.

George doesn't look at all like dying. He has a wiry strength, resembling the old ravens we saw, yesterday morning, on Tower Green.[3]

Later. To lunch as Stephen's guest at a lunch club which meets at Bertorelli's, on Charlotte Street. The twenty or so members mostly seemed shrivelled, lopsided, thin haired or otherwise stricken by

---

[1] The actresses.
[2] George Montagu, her husband.
[3] Traditionally kept at the Tower of London with clipped wings because superstition says the British monarchy will fall if they fly away.

middle age. Kenneth Tynan, one of the few who looked youngish, had been in Russia and seemed greatly excited. Questions were asked. "Russia has done away with nostalgia," he told us—meaning that Russians think only of the future. (Nevertheless, they produce Shakespeare and Wilde.) He quoted a Russian as saying, "*King Lear* couldn't happen here—we look after our old people." Edward Crankshaw, the puckered Russian expert, was less enthusiastic. When I asked if there weren't some people who were against the government just for the sake of being against the government, he said that in Russia the feeling against the government is so basic that people take it as a matter of course. Nevertheless, Tynan's enthusiasm was rather touching. He was making the point that, in the West, modern movements are only carried on by individuals in revolt against the mass. In Russia, modern movements are carried on *by* the mass. To me, this sounds exceedingly phoney.

Alas, under the influence of the lunch wine, I spoke very incautiously to Stephen about John, saying what an idiot I think he is.

January 20. This is just to record that the Don crisis has broken out again and hit a new peak. I'm alarmed, because I see, in back of it all, an ugly dangerous psychotic will-to-unhappiness. He is in a bad state, and probably in need of treatment. Oh, how I wish, wish, wish we were safely out of England. I dread going up to Wyberslegh and leaving him alone to his hysteria and self-pity.

The devilish thing is—his complaints are partially justified. There is no question: many people treat him (and indeed all young people) as if he were a small mess made by the cat. What is sickly is his determination to take all these insults to himself exclusively.

Oh—it's really a problem. And the only way through it, as far as I'm concerned, is to offer the whole thing up continually in prayer. Try to get my ego completely out of the picture.

Have just realized that I'm writing this with just the faintest suspicion that Don *might* read it.

January 25. It's late and I feel disinclined to write anything, especially as Don is waltzing around the room. But at least he *is* waltzing. His mood has been ever so much better since our visit to Dodie and Alec [Beesley] last weekend. Indeed, it was truly touching how he responded to their kindness—which, actually, wasn't so kind after all, because why in hell shouldn't they like him—he is (and was particularly on this occasion) charming.

Dodie and Alec made altogether a very good and reassuring impression. Dodie didn't seem at all crazy—as John Gielgud and

Emlyn Williams had hinted. She even said that she and Alec wouldn't have any more dogs for a long time. (Folly is dead, Buzz dying of old age, and Dandy already stiff in the joints.)

She also remarked that she had found no friends in England to be compared with John van Druten, Charlie Brackett and me. And yet she seems perfectly happy in the cottage, and so does Alec, though he talks a lot about California. Their cottage is thatched, like most of those in this part of Essex[1]—thatch with TV aerials on it, and the contrails of U.S. planes overhead. The cottage seems half-submerged, like a boat, in the heave of the land. Saffron streaks of sky over leafless trees and rough brown ploughed fields. The roof of the barn sags between its oak beams like the canvas of a tent. There are fires everywhere and conveniently placed oil lamps and candles. As always, I felt Alec's amazing flair for organization and comfort.

Much talk about John van Druten. Indeed, the reading aloud of a letter from him spoiled our last hour together. "As usual," said Dodie, "John has monopolized the conversation." John is still fooling around with Joel Goldsmith, and Starcke is actually going out to Hawaii to see Joel. And yet I feel Johnnie knows that Joel is a fake. Joel had had the gall to write and tell Johnnie that he should never have published his novel[2]—it was utterly unspiritual. It's really clever of him, the way he takes the offensive with Johnnie and anticipates attacks. But Johnnie will never be able to resist trying to use religion to win with—and the flops he has never seem to teach him. As if Starcke wasn't bad enough, Carter is at his other elbow, telling him the stars are against him.[3]

Today I had a drink with John Lehmann, Graham Greene and Henry Yorke. They told me about Evelyn Waugh's nervous breakdown. He went into a bar in Cairo, and the bartender said, "Good afternoon, Sir," and Waugh just grunted. And a voice said to Waugh: "You'd have spoken to him if he'd been a Lord." Graham looked quite sleek and handsome—much younger than his photographs. He said that this was because he is always photographed when he has a hangover.

Much talk about Cyril Connolly's famous marital troubles, which he broadcasts all over Europe.

January 28. A grey morning. Sitting up in bed waiting for breakfast, I feel utterly depressed. I'm old and fat. I overeat. I have something wrong with my leg—might be varicose veins. Don is frankly

[1] The cottage was The Barretts, at Finchingfield, Essex.
[2] *The Vicarious Years* (1956).
[3] Carter Lodge was avidly interested in astrology.

miserable and helpless because I'm going away and leaving him alone—and this makes me mad at him, and mad at M. for dragging me up there. I have to leave on Monday.

Diane is in town, at the Empire, Leicester Square. And I actually mind because it is having bad notices and is a flop.

What *I* want is to get back to California and get my things around me and work. I'm sick with guilt at all this idling.

An amusing lunch, two days ago, with Emlyn and Molly Williams, Dorothy Tutin and Michael Gwynn. Laurence Harvey appeared suddenly sitting at another table in the restaurant. It was like the banquet scene in *Macbeth*.[1]

Also saw Rupert Doone and Robert Medley. Rupert seemed very old and very fat—almost Falstaffian, but tragic.

Morgan Forster, on the other hand, is full of life and good humor, though he has lumbago.

Later. Just been out in the rain to see Frank Auerbach's show at the Beaux Arts Gallery on Bruton Place. He creates a sort of bas-relief effect by building layer upon layer of paint. There are some big pumpkin-shaped heads which are "effective" in the sense that they would make you scream if you saw one of them looking at you through a window at night. But the total impression was one of cruddy gloom. Meanwhile, Auerbach himself was up in a gallery with a woman, listening to our remarks—and this created an atmosphere of churchlike tension, with corresponding feelings of revolt. Don in a very bad mood—but he has let off some steam by now, I hope, as he has been writing his diary.

Worry about money—ridiculous, really, since I have, for the first time in my life 15,000 dollars saved and a further 10,000 in the bank. But the more you have, the more you want.

January 29. Raining stolidly this morning. And now I hear from Bob [Buckingham] on the telephone that Morgan has lumbago and a swollen toe and won't be able to have lunch with us. Only barrier against total depression—the vitamin pills given me yesterday by Patrick Woodcock, who thinks a vitamin deficiency is all that's wrong with my leg.

Yesterday afternoon we rode out in the drizzly fog to Dalston, to see *San Francisco*.[2] It was nostalgic, because it brought back all my pilgrimages of thirty years ago to the outlying suburbs to see and resee

[1] Dorothy Tutin and Michael Gwynn played "Sally Bowles" and "Christopher Isherwood" in the original London production of *I Am a Camera*. Laurence Harvey was the male lead in the movie version.
[2] The 1936 MGM film.

American films—and all the nostalgic blurring of U.S. urban ugliness (known to me only from these films) with the ugliness of the London setting. The U.S. ugliness was infinitely romantic, for it symbolized escape from Home. The English ugliness was the ugliness of my prison.

There was nothing nostalgic about the Franco-Irish ugliness and stupidity of *Waiting for Godot*,[1] which we saw last night.

February 1. The day before yesterday, I came up here, to Wyberslegh, by train from London. I'm planning to stay until next Monday, the 6th. Don is in London.

I'm worried about him, of course. And yet this was obviously the only possible thing to do. I had to come here alone. And maybe this week will make Don feel more independent and freer and perhaps he will find out some useful things about himself, and us.

Richard met me at Stockport station. At first, his appearance gave me a shock. Stooped over, with head bowed, he came toward me, looking down and away. Then he threw his head back, and his eyes closed as if he were blind as he turned his face to the sky. His cheeks are rough red and his nose quite purple—probably because of bad circulation. Several of his front teeth are missing. His thick curling dark hair shows no sign of grey. His hands are nicotine stained, chapped and usually covered with coal dust, since he is constantly building fires. There were marks of coal dust on the sheets of my bed, where he had put the hot-water bottle. His blue eyes are still innocent and charming, and he is constantly eager to serve my wishes. He apologizes for the cold, begs me to accept extra blankets and overcoats. During the day, he wears a sport jacket so dark and stiff with grease that it might belong to a garage mechanic. But only a real hobo would accept his shirt. He laughs loudly and explosively, startling and annoying M., as always.

M., at eighty-six-eighty-seven, seems hardly any older. Her hair is still plentiful. Her cheeks are pink, not yellowish. She sees well, hears perfectly, remembers not only the distant but the immediate past and seems keenly aware of the present. Amiya is quite right in describing her as "pretty and feminine." Her knees are a little stiff and she sometimes has to be helped out of her chair. But she still cooks the meals, counts the laundry and attends to all kinds of chores.

I arrived in mild damp weather, and this little old stone house, standing amidst its sodden fields, was sponge wet. The books in the shelves smelled of corpse, the bedclothes were like shrouds, you smelt stale smells everywhere of old fat in unscoured skillets. The two

---

[1] The first London production of Samuel Beckett's play.

white, black–patched cats eat food all over the kitchen floor. The rugs
are dark with grime. In buckets you [find] very old, frighteningly foul
black rags, reminiscent of the labor conditions of the nineteenth
century and *Oliver Twist*. But last night the snow fell. It is very cold.
Even standing in front of the fire you can see your breath—but the
smell of damp and the stink of dirt are less noxious. The countryside is
beautiful under the snow. Cobden Edge crisscrossed by black stone
walls; Kinder Scout pure unbroken white. And then, this morning,
the snow had a strange orange light on it from the weak sunshine.
Only a few scattered handfuls have fallen during the day, but it looks
as if there'll be more tonight. I walked with Richard up to the
mailbox on the corner to post a letter to Don—he might as well be
back in the States, he seems so utterly remote.

February 2. This morning I heard from Don. He is writing a play, and
seems, altogether, quite cheerful. His letter made me feel so happy
that I don't feel too depressed by the frost, which was the worst in
years last night and is to be worse tonight. The washbasin in M.'s
room is frozen, and the gas pipes are partially frozen, so that our fires
will only burn very low. So far the bath is all right, but the kitchen
range doesn't seem to heat the water properly. Three more whole
days to go, before I can leave for London!

There have been several events today. A young woman who was
born on St. Helena and was perhaps a quarter Negro came to apply
for the job of maid here. M. says she liked her. But the fact remains
that M.'s manner with her was very grand and quite definitely
patronizing—and I quite see how she may have discouraged many
promising applicants. Also, because she looks about twenty years
younger than she really is, she fails to enlist any sympathy as a "dear
old lady" who needs support. I told M. this—also Richard—but of
course wasn't believed. (This evening, the girl called and told us she
has another job.)

M. is still amazingly obstinate and, like so many Englishwomen,
full of a kind of puritanical glee when things are bad. She is really glad
that the weather is so lousy, and she very nearly made me really angry
this morning by suggesting that it would do Don good to experience
the cold here. She hates getting anything new for the house, and
affects, for example, to believe that paper towels are some weird
newfangled and somehow degenerate U.S. invention. (I had the
satisfaction of proving to her that the High Lane chemist knew all
about them.) She nurses an obstinate grudge against the present and
cultivates a nostalgia for the "peaceful" Victorian times.

We had lunch at a fish and chip shop in High Lane, where

Richard's strange appearance aroused a good deal of amused curiosity. (He has just now mysteriously taken a taxi, saying he won't be gone long. M. says he has gone to get beer. Good luck to him. I wish he'd give me some.) The sun shone all day long and the landscape couldn't have been lovelier. If only they'd invent warm snow!

Now, a stroke of luck. One of M.'s day helpers, a Mrs. Barber— very Cheshire, buxom and loud, has unexpectedly arrived and is fixing us our supper—curry.

Rereading recent parts of this journal, I find far too much pessimism. And why? Neglect of japam. Relying on what is by its very nature unreliable.

February 3. Last night, Mrs. Barber cooked a niceish meal of curried steak (except that it was the wrong sort of curry powder—practically tasteless—the local shops seem, according to M., to delight in stocking the inferior brands of everything). Luckily, we had had supper before Richard appeared, very drunk (on four whole bottles of beer, it seems) and threw the table over, exclaiming: "This is the end! I'm at the end of my tether! I haven't a friend in the world! You're all prigs—all of you!" He turned on me, raised his arm, seemed about to hit me: "I hate you! You come up here so smug and tell me my Mother's overworked. I hate you! I hate you!"

After the first moment of being startled, I felt more amused than anything. I ought to have felt sorry for Richard, I know, and I do, theoretically—but the fact is, there have been too many such scenes in my life during the past few years—Billy [Caskey], Harry Brown, Don, etc. etc.— Well, anyhow, I tried to get him to talk but I couldn't, properly, because the women were there. M. left the room when I asked her to, but Mrs. Barber—as she mopped up the mess— everything on the table had been smashed—kept reproving Richard like a nanny; telling him he'd be ashamed in the morning, that he knew we were all his friends, that he loved his kind brother, etc. Worse, Richard fell in with this mood and clasped my hand and told me he loved me very much, which only embarrassed me, because I don't love *him*—most certainly not as a brother. I have had a hundred brothers already and a thousand sons—and all this talk about blood relationships just nauseates me. It's the evil old sentimental lie I've been fighting for the past thirty-five years. Later Richard was sick, and Mrs. Barber cleaned him off as though he were a dog, and coaxed him to go to his room. A rather disgusting complicity now appeared between the two women. They were fairly used to these attacks, it seemed. The only special feature of this one was that more crockery had been broken. I went to bed reflecting that it is silly to compare this house to Wuthering Heights. Emily Brontë would have left it within a week, for Cannes. The gas fire in my room was down to a blue line, and the water faucet was frozen. (But today a man came and fixed the gas. It seems that gas makes water in the pipes; the cold weather had merely hurried up the precipitation. And the faucets unfroze of their own accord.)

When Richard brought me tea this morning, I noticed the smell of beer and vomit still on his filthy clothes. We had a fairly constructive talk at breakfast—on my side, I kept reminding him that he has enough money, and that, if he wants to move to London, it's entirely possible for him to do so. He agreed—but will he ever do anything as long as M. is alive? The truth is, she's a miser—with *his* money. They live like pigs for no earthly reason, because she thinks, deep down, that it's wicked to be really comfortable or to eat nicely. I'm not being cruel to her in her old age when I write this, because she has always been the same. Indeed, I feel a kind of hard-hearted benevolence toward both of them. From that point of view, this visit is, so far, going better than the others.

Another day of bright blue weather, hard frost. This afternoon I walked to Ridge End, where some townspeople have converted the old inn into a modish roadhouse (would-be) called The Romper. The farm where the Nazi airman landed with a parachute. ("Would you believe it, the police wanted to take the poor boy away before he'd 'ad 'is breakfast?!") The curving hill (called "Hill Haze") where my father had the accident on his bike. The haunted wood. The chimneys that let the train smoke out of the long tunnel: they seem like some volcanic phenomena. The view at the Ridge End corner: a wall of dark-mottled piled stones, a corn-golden pony in a field scattered sparsely with snow, and beyond, New Mills smoke stack rising so august and beautiful between the snowy hills. I felt deeply moved. This is my native country. Thank God for it—and thank God, *on my knees*, that I got out of it!

Later. M. and I went to supper with Mrs. Barber this evening—in a little brick box on Disley Brow, overlooking the church and the chain of lights climbing the opposite hill, up the Old Buxton Road. "*With* Mrs. Barber" is hardly accurate, because she left us alone most of the time in the sitting room and served us our supper there, while she ate with her husband and youngest son in the kitchen. How to define the essential lower-middle-class quality of the room? It was skirted by a strip of board about four feet above the ground which had cross pieces running diagonally to the floor suggesting the timbering of a "black and white" farmhouse, except that this was brown and

coffee. No—that's utterly undescriptive. More symptomatic, perhaps, was the *smallness* of the pictures—no more than postcard size,
but framed: flower pieces, etc. And the ornaments were all small—a
miniature warming pan, china foals—very cute, plates painted with
classical scenes. One word to describe it all—dainty.

Toward the end of our visit, Mr. and Mrs. Barber came in for a
while and sat with us. But presently Mr. Barber said, "I'll goa in
t'other rume n' taake a stoomach-taablet." This was delivered
without the least suggestion of humor, apology or embarrassment. A
line that would bring down the house if it came at the end of act one
of a Noël Coward play.

Returned to find Richard's friend Alan Bradley just about to leave.
He had shaved Richard (for the first time since my arrival) and
combed his hair. He often does this. He used to be a farm worker on
Wyberslegh Farm, now he's in the building trade. He has a wife and
child and lives in Disley. A rather nice looking man, thin, hawk
nosed, in his early thirties, who suffers from stomach troubles and is
obviously intelligent above the average.

February 4. It's snowing hard, this morning. I watch the snow
anxiously, wondering if it will interfere with my return to London on
Monday. It has already prevented us from visiting Marple Hall today,
as we'd planned.

In the night, the smudge-eyed cat gave birth to three kittens.

Just finished Elizabeth Montagu's *The Small Corner*, which seems to
me much above the average in readability. Is this because it is written
like a detective story? Yes, largely. What I miss here—and almost
everywhere—are characters and a world: characters described with
the gusto of scandalous but affectionate gossip, and a world you can
enter and inhabit as you read about it.

Am also reading James Agate's *A Shorter Ego* (1932–38).[1] This at
least succeeds on both the above counts—as far as it goes. Agate
comes to life in the most embarrassing way. He reminds me often of
John van Druten, especially when being sententious. He is coarser
and less pompous, and I think I would have liked him better. But, oh
dear, what a fool! And how hopelessly subjective and imprecise he
makes dramatic criticism seem. I suppose it is, especially because of
the conditions under which the critic sees the play and writes the
notice.

Many thoughts about my own projected novel. The Dante idea
continues to please me, but somehow I can't transpose it into the right
key—that is to say, the same key as the characters and incidents I want

---

[1] A volume of the abridged version of the drama critic's autobiography.

to put into the story. If Dante is in C, the "Damned" are in C-sharp minor. I await a sort of musical inspiration which will show me how to integrate them with each other.

Many thoughts, also, about Don. I've dwelt nearly always upon his weaknesses in this record—inevitably, because it is the weaknesses that create the problems that "make news." But I find that, when I look at him from a distance, as now, I don't at all see him as a weak person. Caskey is fundamentally (whatever that means) weak, I believe. But Don has—or seems at present to have—two immensely strong positive qualities: his capacity for affection and his moral courage (as for instance shown in his dealings with the draft board). I think, however, that he could be cruel, in a way Caskey couldn't. His laziness is probably just the guilt paralysis of a naturally overenergetic person.

But how futile it is to write about live characters! As futile as dramatic criticism—no, more so. Hence one turns to making one's own characters. Fiction, as far as I'm concerned, is an attempt to control life—none the less fascinating because it's hopeless.

Health note: the vitamin B and calcium pills given me by Patrick Woodcock have not only cured my right leg but greatly increased my physical energy. I noticed this while out walking yesterday, but no doubt the cold helped.

11:30 a.m. It has stopped snowing, thank God.

Later. (3:45) The snow has turned to rain and the snow is melting from the soggy fields. Oh the sheer brute miserableness of mid-England! A natural thought, on returning to one's birthplace: why not die here, as well?

M. disapproves of Princess Margaret, thinks her a show-off. This is very important—for M. always seems to me to embody British upper-middle-class opinion.

We had lunch at the café in High Lane, whose walls are lined with scoops and smears of a custard-colored substance called (M. thinks) "lincrusta"—anyhow, that's an excellent name for it. The only possible way to decorate such a place would be with murals. Why not a Last Judgment on the ceiling, featuring all the local notables? Then I went to get my hair cut at the only barber's. He has no shop—just the front parlor of his house. You turn left into it, after running up against a velvet curtain marked "private." The sort of place one (romantically) imagines people going to get abortions. But the barber was adequately efficient, and he heated the clippers against the oil stove before using them, which I found very thoughtful.

I notice how my appetite for journal writing increases here, day by day. Journals thrive on loneliness.

February 5. The frost has broken and all of the snow has disappeared from the fields in front of the house. A landscape of faintest grey silhouettes under a yellowish overcast. The utter sadness of wet slate roofs. They remind me of the grey sea.

The last day of my confinement.

Yesterday evening, after drinking one glass of sweetish sherry and one of stout, I was sufficiently loosened up to make a declaration which could easily have been avoided. M. had been needling me by talking family—did I remember this or that cousin's cousin? I didn't go so far as to say—as I have often said before—that I hate the whole idea of being "related" to anyone. But I did launch into a speech about "living out in the woods," being "a Protestant," and having nothing to do with "the people who live in zoos." As I spoke, I heard in my voice a faint echo of Richard's hysteria the other evening, when he pushed the table over. And I was conscious of the desire to hurt M., to stab through the hard fat of her wilful, obstinate stupidity. I wanted to denounce her, and the society she represents, and its sanction of motherhood and the marriage bed. It is shocking to realize how insane and immature I must still be—that I can harbor such feelings against a poor old woman. And yet—to be sincere—I must say that I believe this insecurity and immaturity is perhaps also my only protection against smugness and spiritual death. All around me, I see people of my own age cooling and setting hard, like dripping. Ah, the hateful cold fat of the elderly!

I said last night, and this I wouldn't unsay—I'm glad that my life is what it is—wandering, insecure, imprudent. I'm glad that I have no idea what I'll be doing ten years from now, glad that I'm still thrilled by Carmen's words about "la chose enivrante."[1] There's only one thing I really fear and that's dependence. That's why I was and am worried by my reactions under hashish—the fear I felt, then, of being on my own. But that fear passed later as I started to make japam. And I dare to believe that it will always pass.

Finished Agate's *Ego* this morning. Poor silly old thing, one can't help rather liking him for writing it—though he certainly didn't dream how stupid it was.

Later. This afternoon Richard and I took a taxi and drove over to Marple Hall. Last time I saw it was in the summer of 1948, with Bill Caskey. Then it was dilapidated. Now it is a ruin—indeed, it has an almost gutted look, as though it had been bombed and burned. Several people were wandering around, taking photographs. We went up the back stairs—the front staircase looks unsafe and there is a

---

[1] "The intoxicating thing," freedom; see Isherwood's diary entry for September 15, 1943 and note.

great hole in the roof above it where the chimney-stack fell through—and had to climb over the bathtub which had been dragged halfway down the steps and left stuck between the banisters. The only intact thing left in the house is the pink marble fireplace which Uncle Henry brought back from Venice and had fixed up in the drawing room.

A double row of red brick villas runs along the edge of the park bordering the main road. Before long, the council is going to force Richard to sell land opposite the house in order to put up a school and lay out sport fields. But before this happens, a good deal more of the Hall will most probably collapse. It is a perfect death trap for children. Richard and I left like two ghosts—the kind that other people see and never suspect of being ghosts until much later, when someone exclaims in horror: "You say you saw Mr. Richard and Mr. Christopher? But, man, *they've* been dead for *years!*"

On the way home, we stopped to visit the two spinsters who live in the cottage opposite Wyberslegh Farm—Miss Laura and Miss Sadie Storer. Two faintly twittering, thin-legged birds who live on tiny crumbs of gossip—they need so little, you feel, to keep them going. So I was exhibited to them, but there was nothing I could tell them: they knew it all already from M. and Richard. Miss Laura—or is it Miss Sadie—has the tiniest mouth you ever saw. It got even tinier, in prim slyness, as they spoke of some people named Cotton who have a Maltese lodger. Mrs. Cotton is younger than her husband, and "*lively.*" And—well, you know the Maltese!

Got home and urged M. to have the Venetian fireplace removed. She probably won't, till it's too late. I realize now that all kinds of things in the house could have been rescued from theft and vandalism if M. and Richard hadn't absolutely refused to admit to themselves months ago that it was a doomed ruin. Even now, M. doesn't admit it. She kept asking if certain parts were still standing, as if it matters.

Well, my vigil is nearly over, now. Roll on, tomorrow. Needless to say, I'm quite worried and anxious, wondering how Don has gotten through his week; but at least I can be glad that I've done my part—written only one letter, not fussed, not bothered him with phone calls, not come running back before I said I would. Well, I shall soon see—

February 7. Incredible to relate, I actually caught the train, yesterday, that I planned to catch and actually got back safe and sound to Euston, barely two minutes late! I never thought fate would permit it.

Richard came with me to Stockport station. There had been an increasingly intimate atmosphere between us during the last twenty-four hours—he evidently set some special, symbolic significance on our visit to Marple Hall. During breakfast, he told me how he was arrested seven years ago in London for being drunk on the street. M., typically, hadn't told me this. (No—perhaps that's unfair—I suppose it really wasn't her place to tell me.)

M. talked of coming to London, but I don't know if she really meant it—don't know if she really wants to, in a strange way. Maybe, at that age, what's most important is simply not to be disturbed. But I saw her eyes fill with tears as I drove away.

The journey down to London was most enjoyable—chiefly because of its direction, but also because I was reading Kingsley Amis's *That Uncertain Feeling*. I roared with laughter all the way through.

Mortmere note: an antiquated guard's van on a siding. On it was printed NOT IN COMMON USE—*in quotes*.

Don was at the station to meet me. He cried. But he hadn't merely been lonely. I think this week was a valuable experience for him—as it was for me.

Yesterday evening we saw *Henry V* at the Old Vic. Most of it was dull and hateful, as always—Miss Shakespeare being the National Bard until one wants to hide one's head. But Richard Burton was fine, and often very moving. Best were the scene before Agincourt and the wooing of the French princess. The line I most remember was when he said, of the enemy: "We are in God's hand brother, not theirs." Burton spoke this exactly right, curtly, almost impatiently, without the slightest pathos.

The production was pretty tacky. When the Chorus swirled his cloak, a cloud of dust flew out of it. Don loathed the play but ended by being glad we'd stayed, because of Burton. I am amazed to find him so good—almost in Gielgud's class—his movies don't show him to any advantage at all.

February 9. This, from yesterday's *Daily Express*, is so good that I almost think it may be deliberate: "And in Germany the French run into heavy resentment because they are stationing North African troops in the Black Forest." Presumably the Germans are saying: "It was quite black enough already without all these Niggers."

This morning, yesterday and the day before, I've been out shopping and seeing people while Don has stayed in the hotel room, working. (Since my return our relations have been as harmonious as it is possible to imagine.) He says he is really making progress with his play. Now he has stopped planning and actually begun to write dialogue.

The day before yesterday, we went to *Cavalleria Rusticana* and *Pagliacci* at Sadler's Wells. Opera at its most ridiculous. Both the men in *Cavalleria* were pear bellied—and apparently very proud of it. Both were hideous, and one had a tic. The chorus all sang with their eyes fixed on the conductor.

Yesterday evening we had supper at John Gielgud's. He described the hideous boredom of a stag dinner party at the Russian embassy. Some visiting Soviet official was doing a lightning cultural tour of Britain. He didn't know who John was. He asked John, "What is your country?" and John, out of mischief, said, "Poland," (his ancestors being Polish). "And what is your theater?" the Soviet official asked. "I haven't got one," John answered modestly—whereat the Soviet official decided that he must be a person of no importance.

Esmé Percy[1] was there—rather a forlorn little figure with his glass eye. After dinner, John played records of himself and Edith Evans, in scenes from plays and also reading poems. They both read the poems poorly. Dylan Thomas would have made them sound like amateurs.

Saw John Baker of Phoenix House this morning—chiefly in order to interest him in John Yale's book.[2] He isn't a very nice man. "These young writers who come from the red brick universities—well, I don't mean to be snobbish, but frankly—they're the scum of the earth!" He holds that the welfare state has spoilt working-class literature by abolishing poverty.

February 10. It came to me in a flash—while Don and I were sitting at Simpson's yesterday, awaiting the special steak and kidney pudding advertised for Thursdays, only to find that it was all gone. "Imagine," I told Don, "that John van Druten gets a call, long distance, from the editor of the London *Times*. He comes from the phone into the living room, sits down dramatically: 'Well—! They want me to leave for hell on Thursday. I'm to do a series of ten articles—' Shall he accept? He phones Dodie in England, Joel Goldsmith in Honolulu. He studies Dante, tries an article to see if he can do it, decides that he can. Carter and Starcke encourage him. He says yes. Then hasty reading up on Virgil, who is to come by to fetch him and will lunch at the ranch first. Virgil arrives. Johnny is terribly thrilled. Virgil reminisces about the Roman theater. Johnny is enchanted. Finally they drive away together—"

This could be truly hilarious. But isn't it quite another sort of

[1] Actor.
[2] *What Vedanta Means to Me*, containing a chapter by Isherwood.

book—a hard-boiled modern version of the *Inferno*, which, incidentally, would soon get boring beyond belief? No—not necessarily. It might be a dream—a dream which gives my principal character the idea of *pretending* he is visiting hell, as a sort of sophisticated game. He goes to Mexico, keeping up the pretense. Then, right at the end, during the hashish experience in Mexico City, he gets a horrible scare: maybe he really *is* in hell?

This isn't right, but it's the nearest I've come to a workable scheme. Here's another idea that seems significant: all the flames and horrors that Dante sees in hell are actually subjective. "He had a very unpleasant mind," Virgil says. So what *is* hell? "Ah," says Virgil, "*you* tell *me* that! I only work here."

Peter Watson had lunch with us. He's such a strangely charming wry-smiling creature, with an almost coquettish air of despair about him. He described how crazy his brother and his nephew are getting. "They always treated me as the abnormal one, and now I'm beginning to see that I'm far saner than they are!" We went to look at some Francis Bacon paintings at the Hanover Gallery. I remember Francis saying to me that he always tries to "get down to the nerve." He certainly has genius of a sort. Those businessmen, apparently in cages; their blurred faces and wide-open mouths as if they were bellowing with pain. And the blurred grey dog tearing along the edge of the gutter, perhaps in flight from some ghastly monster. A Bacon costs £300. A Canaletto at Tooth's—the Piazza San Marco, with the base of the Campanile—£20,000!

Talking of money, we find we face a financial crisis. We must economize. Don says we mustn't spend more than six pounds a day. This is actually harder than it sounds.

February 12. Yesterday, in Moscow, Burgess and Maclean reappeared unto a privileged group of journalists. A quasi-religious event.[1]

Yesterday we came down here, to stay with the Beesleys—catching a later train because I had to rush early to the dentist, to get the cap stuck back on my tooth—it has held ever since Rome. The dentist held out little hope of my being able to keep it on. He recommends more elaborate bridgework.

Plenty of snow down here. It thawed today but it's freezing and snowing again tonight.

Talk with Dodie about the novel—from now on, I'll call it *The Lost*. The idea seems workable, but the question remains: who and what are Dante and Virgil? Dodie rather dismisses the idea of the

[1] Guy Burgess and Donald Maclean had defected to the USSR in May 1951; see Glossary under Burgess.

play—saying that one shouldn't rework old material. But I still feel an urge to do it.

Since we were here last, Buzz has had to be "put to sleep." A vet came down specially from London to do it, arriving at midnight. Dodie still talks with mystical passion about dogs—as much on the defensive as ever. "What people won't realize is that if you're separated from your dog for more than five hours, you become absolutely miserable. Five hours is the absolute maximum." Of course, this *is* neurotic, however you look at it. It's perfectly true, for example, that I dislike being separated from Don for very long; but just for this reason, I see how necessary it is that we *should* be separated. Otherwise, Don would become a mere chattel, an annex of my ego. And that's what pets are. Annexes that one imposes, in the most brutal manner, on one's friends.

A very happy evening. Don drew sketches of Dodie and Alec. How he expands and warms, as soon as he dares to believe that he's amongst friends!

A suggested ending for *The Lost*: "Am writing this on the plane, on the way back to the States. Am perfectly sane and sober, now. But what is most important is that I mustn't, in my sobriety, forget the lesson I've learnt. Let me never deceive myself into thinking of it as an hallucination. I doubt if I shall ever venture across the border again."

February 15. Just returned from Cambridge. The Beesleys drove us over there two days ago, because Dodie wanted to do some shopping. We arrived in time for lunch. We ate all our meals with Morgan Forster, either in King's hall or in his rooms—except for breakfast, which we had at the Garden House Hotel, where we stayed. A very nice visit, but hellishly cold. Yesterday morning, after brilliant early sunshine, the snow fell very thickly. It didn't lie, however. Back here in London, it's much warmer.

Morgan seemed very lively and much enjoying his partial immersion in college affairs. I say "partial" because he seems able to regard them with humor as well as heat. But the heat is certainly present. For example, there has been a fine row about where to hang a piece of the Flemish tapestry which was presented to the college— Morgan's party wanted it behind the high table, the opposition wanted it up in the minstrels' gallery, more or less out of sight from the floor of the hall. The opposition has won.

At a succession of wine parties (red and white wine or sherry seem the usual drinks) we met all kinds of young men—a pudgy gay indiscreet don named Norman Routledge,[1] who understands

---

[1] A mathematician (b. 1928); later Assistant Master at Eton.

mechanical brains; a skinny don named Francis Haskell[1] who lectures on baroque art; an undergraduate who, with Emlyn Williams's elder son, rescued from Red Poland an enormous athlete by stowing him away in the baggage rack behind an even more enormous English girl from Cambridge; a cute but perhaps rather sly boy of seventeen from Utah who is an exchange student from Clifton; an Indian undergraduate who is Nehru's nephew; and an undergraduate named Nick(?) who is one of the university's perennial types: casually handsome, with careless wavy hair, bohemian tie and corduroys, and an Irish smile, who is nevertheless quite shrewd and not at all effete. This type usually ends up on the stage and sometimes gets itself knighted.

Don was somewhat horrified, at first, by the whole place—perhaps because he saw it through my eyes. But toward the end he began to enjoy himself. He received a good deal of attention. As for me—well, I never dislike these visits, but whiffs of the past give me occasional shudders. We went into Corpus[2] and I showed Don Edward [Upward]'s rooms, and Philip Gilchrist's,[3] and mine. We watched the half-frozen boys rowing on the river below the town. I failed to solve a puzzle that was being passed round at high table: "$A_{BCD}E_{FG}$—complete the alphabet in accordance with this pattern." I helped the ex-Provost on with his overcoat, enjoyed the chatter of Dadie Rylands,[4] and listened respectfully to the Vice-Provost on skating; learning therefrom that the Fenmen always skate with their hands behind their backs, but are usually beaten by townees who practice unfairly throughout the summer in rinks.[5]

Cambridge has its sinister side now, as always, for me. Don and I went into King's chapel during the evening service and listened to the choirboys' voices soaring up into the shadows of the fan tracery, high above the rumbling organ with its two seraph trumpeters. As Don said, they sounded like angels—not in the pretty sense, but spooky, disembodied.

King's chapel also has the extra sinister distinction of a recent suicide. Not so long ago, the Dean climbed up to the roof, at 3:00 a.m., and jumped.[6] His body was found a few hours later. Norman Routledge and Francis Haskell discussed the motive, and decided that

[1] The art historian (b. 1928); author on baroque and neo-classical art, later Professor of Art History at Oxford.
[2] Corpus Christi College.
[3] Another Cambridge contemporary; he matriculated with Isherwood in 1923 and took a degree in Geography in 1926.
[4] George Rylands, the Shakespeare scholar.
[5] Fenmen are inhabitants of the low-lying, marshy countryside surrounding Cambridge; townees are town-dwellers but not members of the university.
[6] Ivor Ramsay killed himself January 21.

it was simply because he was neglected: people omitted to ask him to parties because they thought him dull. He was a mother's boy, unmarried. He had felt out of place at King's and had wanted to return to Scotland, but his mother had insisted that he should stay because *she* preferred Cambridge life. Before jumping, he had removed his clerical collar. Une vie.[1]

Morgan himself hardly seems at all changed, except that he's stiffer in the joints. He is still just as eagerly interested in everybody. He has taken to watching boxing matches. He has an undergraduate friend named Southwell[2]—a charming rather large-nosed boy who rows—who is planning to go to Cyprus this summer as a reserve officer of the ROTC. Morgan is much concerned as to the ethics of this and has decided to speak to Southwell about it.[3] Don says that Morgan reminds him so much of Tennessee Williams.

February 16. Went last night to supper with Stephen. Don refused to come with me, feeling that Stephen doesn't take the least interest in him. I was quite prepared for embarrassing enquiries, and was greatly surprised when Stephen didn't mention Don or ask about him at all. But maybe this was tact.... Just the same, I can't help blaming Stephen. I find it very thick-skinned of him not to be aware that there's something wrong. No—I just cannot believe that he isn't aware.

Well, it was a stag party but curiously formal and unbohemian. Everyone except Joe Ackerley and I wore suits, and really you might have taken us for a bunch of publishers. Angus Wilson,[4] prissy and high voiced like a silver-haired little lady; but nevertheless sympathetic because of an obvious sincerity in his reactions. Angus's friend Tony [Garrett], who's a juvenile delinquent officer and doesn't talk: maybe he's really interesting and nice. A skinny art critic named Robin Ironside who seemed dry and sterile and bitter and a bore. Joe who is always a real person, despite his dog addiction and Chris Wood-like bachelor selfishness. And dear William Plomer—who, as I once said, and meant, makes life less odious for all who know him. William was funny as usual. He described how George Gissing used to say to his wife at parties: "Nine-thirty already! Now, Clara; time you were on the streets!"

---

[1] A life.
[2] Not his real name.
[3] The British suppressed the movement among the Greek-speaking majority in Cyprus for union with Greece, and between 1955 and 1959 the pro-union terrorist organization persistently attacked the British presence. (ROTC is the Reserve Officers Training Corps.)
[4] Novelist and critic (1913–1991).

A long discussion about Burgess and Maclean. It was generally agreed that if they were to return and a party was to be given for them, everyone would go to it. In other words, they have somehow become an institution and been forgiven, even though they haven't repented.

Stephen played the host with a great deal of style. He has developed a very shiny surface manner. Oh God, I thought to myself, imagine being shut up on this island and having to ring the changes on this handful of personalities and talents! No wonder Stephen is as he is. A great wonder that he's no worse. I must never cease to thank heaven for my escape.

February 18. Vows for Ramakrishna's birthday. One round of japam *at least*, every day for a year. No more mugging and mooning. Touch my toes every day.

Still a bit drunk after lunch with the Tynans plus a wedding reception for Louie Ramsay and Ronan O'Casey. She's in a musical at the Hippodrome, *Meet Me on the Corner;* he's a Canadian actor of whom the best man said: "I've been to six of his first nights—in one week."

The Tynans bicker a lot but are quite sympathetic. They put up the bail for Peter Wildeblood when he was arrested. Ken Tynan is impressed by the Soviet Union because it discourages drinking. I told them firmly that, as an ex-monk, I believe in people being allowed to be ascetic on their own, without dragging in the rest of the community. We had a high-class lunch at Pruniers, with the Tynans getting less and less coherent.

Seen written on a van the other day: "Diploma Bagwash." The perfect name for a Shaw heroine.

Another explosion by Don two nights ago, after meeting Peter Watson and Francis Bacon. I'm seriously worried about this, because it was so neurotic. He is getting an obsession about being rejected, and I don't seem to be able to help him. But more of this another time.

I forgot to mention tea at Dorothy Tutin's, yesterday—on her little houseboat anchored off Cheyne Walk. Michael Gwynn was there and the two actresses who respectively played the landlady and Sally's mother in *Camera.* The tide was just turning on the river and the water was astonishingly rough—especially when, three or four times, a biggish ship passed. Once the houseboat pitched so hard that a lamp fell down.

Dorothy was very bright and tense—so eager to make the party a success.

February 20. The misery of this cold! Snow falls almost everyday, melts, falls. You have to be very young to appreciate the winter. Even Don is tired of it.

But things are better. Yesterday we saw Patrick Woodcock. He drove us around the East End and then gave us lunch. And Don definitely likes him.

A horrible pilgrimage to Brixton to see *The Great Sinner.* It is far, far worse—coyer, more overwritten—than I'd remembered.

A story about the Tynans I forgot to write down. They were in the Gargoyle the other night and Ken (who fancies himself as an aficionado) got into an argument about a certain bullfighter: had he retired or not? Ken said not and bet twenty pounds, which was accepted. So they called Spain to find out. The first person they tried was Ava Gardner; but they were told—this was around 3:00 a.m.— that she had gone out pigeon shooting! So they called elsewhere, and finally discovered that Ken was right. I find this anecdote rather distasteful. The creation of such "legendary behavior" should be left to professional hams, like John Huston.

February 25. So much to report that I scarcely know where to start. Will take the odds and ends first.

On the 21st, we went to a party at the Tynans'—actually a wedding party—for a bridal pair we never got to meet. If the Tynans paid for this do, they must have plenty of money: it was very stylish. Ken explained his theory that the theater exists only in order to produce situations of intolerable crisis; and Henry Yorke complained of the difficulties of play writing, an occupation which he regards as a typical disease of middle-aged novelists. Later, they had flamenco dancers, but we'd left before that.

On the 22nd, and again on the 23rd, I posed for Michael Ayrton, whom Methuen's have commissioned to draw me. But he had great difficulties, and still hasn't done anything he'll show me. We sat in what I believe was Rosa Lewis's[1] old bedroom. It was hideously cold.

The cold has been getting Don down, and this led to another outburst. So we arranged to fly back a week earlier than originally intended—on March 11th. I'm not really at all sorry about this. The only reason I mind is that it creates new tensions and the need for all sorts of rearrangements. As for Don's own problem, well, we've settled that he shall see Evelyn Hooker and maybe some other psychiatrist when he gets back home.

[1] Former proprietress of the Cavendish Hotel (where Isherwood and Bachardy were staying); portrayed as "Lottie Crump" in Evelyn Waugh's *Vile Bodies* (1930).

On the 23rd, there was an account in the *Daily Telegraph* of the suffocation of 180 Sudanese cotton farmers who were being held in "detention rooms" (whatever they are) at Kosti, south of Khartoum. Here is the prize sentence: "When the gates of the rooms were opened this morning, it was found with deep regret that no small numbers of them were dead, and some others in a very bad condition."

In the evening we saw *Diane*. It is a hideous mess—so badly cut and directed and (for the most part) acted. But now I quite clearly know that I'm not in the least ashamed of the script. Many of the scenes are still excellent. But of course no one else has noticed or will ever notice this.

Have just finished Kingsley Amis's *Lucky Jim*, which I don't like nearly as much as his *That Uncertain Feeling*. But there's one phrase I like very much: (The hero has just landed a dream job, quite unexpectedly.) "What noise could he make to express his frenzy of hilarious awe?"

Finally, I'm happy to record that it's just a year since I made my vow to write in this book more regularly, and I'm proud that I've done much better than my minimum target. The same resolution is hereby made for another year—acts of God and man permitting.

And now—I can get down to my big news. Yesterday, I finally took mescaline.

I'd been intending this for some days and had already set aside Friday [the] 24th as M.E. Day;[1] but I didn't mention that here out of superstition—I was afraid an obstacle might arise at the last moment.

I swallowed the capsule at a few minutes before 10:00 a.m. I was a bit scared, of course, and the reason I didn't wait till exactly 10:00 was that I was beginning to get jittery and wanted to have it over with. Then I got back into bed. I had eaten a light breakfast around 9:00—a cup of tea, unsweetened; a boiled egg and some dry toast.

After about half an hour, I began to shiver and feel chills. This is a known symptom. (Pat Trevor-Roper couldn't get warm even with hot-water bottles, and his temperature went up above 104—I should have taken mine but didn't.) However, it must be noted that the room was cold anyway, the weather outside was freezing, *and* I may well have been shaking with nervous excitement. Presently, I began to feel nausea. This wasn't acute and I never seriously expected to vomit. Otherwise, my mood throughout the entire experience was cheerful. Not the least trace of fear—although I was expecting it, after the reaction to the hashish.

Around 11:00, the first heightening of color perception was

[1] Mescaline Experience Day.

noticeable. Very delicate. I admired the shadows on the ceiling—seeing greens and blues in them—and felt that the black inner frame of the gilt mirror somehow perfectly completed the effect of the reflected wall: it seemed to express the entire mood I would describe as "Regency." But these were not very remarkable sensations. I might easily have had them at any ordinary meditative moment.

Between 11:00 and about 12:30 I got up. The intoxication was now definite. I was a bit unsteady—especially when managing the hot and cold water faucets. But I felt exhilarated. Indeed, I was strongly tempted to take another capsule—just as one is naturally tempted to take more drink when drunk, in order to be drunker. I didn't take another capsule, though; deciding I'd better go easy, this first time. I knew I ought to record my sensations, but I didn't want to—I even felt that writing might bring back the nausea. (The few notes I did make are legible but the handwriting shows effort—like the drunk's extra effort to speak distinctly.)

Don had to have his lunch. I had decided to eat nothing, for fear of weakening the effect of the drug. (I thought Gerald had told me that food would do this.) So I gave him time to go out and start his meal—at Andrew's Restaurant around the corner. Then I followed him. This was between 1:00 and 1:15. I walked carefully, without swaying or stumbling. I don't think I behaved with noticeable strangeness.

It was bitterly cold outside, and this heightened the shock of coming into the warm restaurant—but it would have been a shock at any temperature, because the place was wildly gaudy with color. The drug was now working at full power. I was chiefly conscious of everything red—a poster on the window, women's sweaters, the leather-bound menu: all challenged the eye like flags—scarlet, vermilion, rose, crimson, and a pink that was literally shocking. Also, I remember the outrageous prettiness of a little boy's dark blue jersey seen against the light blue of a parked car in the street outside.

It was too exciting in the restaurant. I was afraid I'd attract attention by my excited comments to Don, especially as a stranger was sitting opposite us. So I went out and walked around St. James's Square. I would have enjoyed this hugely if it hadn't been so cold. Indeed, I felt an almost equal interest in anything or anybody—provided they were alive. I could have loitered there for hours, if I hadn't been shivering so. Now I began to notice the faces of the people. It is hard to describe what had happened to them. Their features had been, as it were, "Breughelized." Not caricatured, but more deeply engraved; treated with a sort of Flemish realism which brought out all their funny tricks of expression—making them unromantic but far more interesting. I saw them now very much as "folk"—rather animal—each one going about his business intently, like winter creatures who must hunt for food. Each had his secret problem—which, I was pretty sure, I could find out if I paused to look closely. But I knew I mustn't do this. I had no right to pry. And I was rather absurdly afraid of attracting attention. I had caught sight of my eyes in a shop mirror and seen how much the irises were enlarged. Surely, anyone who looked directly at them would notice? The oddity of these people's faces didn't repel me in the least. Indeed, I felt for them a good-humored, amused friendliness. That, but no more. I was a detached, though benevolent observer. Absolutely no cosmic feelings of oneness or universal brotherhood. Indeed, the whole mescaline experience was, for me, quite unspiritual—just aesthetically and physically pleasing. I was, as I say, detached. And, in trying to describe my state of mind, I thought of Priestley's title *An Inspector Calls*. Returning to the restaurant, I wrote in my notebook: "The inspector examined all the arrangements that had been made to cope with the situation, and reported that they seemed admirable." When I showed this to Don, he commented: "But they were only temporary arrangements, weren't they?" This was very apt. Because, certainly, "the arrangements" weren't eternal. I had had no glimpses of nature's law or God's will.

I did, at this point (about 1:30), however, think of God. I felt a sudden desire to go to Westminster Cathedral. (Instinctively, I felt that a Protestant church would be useless: they aren't really sacred buildings, at all.)[1] But when we got to the Cathedral, God definitely wasn't at home, as far as I was concerned. So we walked along the street to the Abbey, for want of any better place to go. Don hadn't been there before. The Abbey was very funny—a charmingly absurd little antique shop, full of ridiculous statues. (Sir Cloudesley Shovel was specially pleasing.) Its little old black rock-ribbed carcass seemed shrunken; I felt I was inside a dead and dried-up animal. Maybe a whale. No God there. No life at all—even the poppies around the Unknown Soldier were artificial. So we walked out into the icy afternoon again. Having been told by John Goodwin and others that I must be sure to get close to nature, I could think of no place to go except a flower shop. When we found one, I immediately seemed to see a great difference between the cut flowers and the ones growing in pots. "This one," I told Don, "is just as alive as a snake." And looking at a pot of azaleas, I could see the petals moving all the time, the stamens making constant tiny phototropic adjustments toward the light coming through the shop window. But did I really see this? I would have had to buy the flowers and bring them home and set them

---

[1] Westminster Cathedral is the Roman Catholic cathedral near Westminster Abbey (which is Anglican).

down on a table and study them closely—to be sure. We returned to Piccadilly Circus by underground. I got a lot of amusement and pleasure from the other passengers. Two or three of them moved so quaintly that I had to hide my laughter. And there was one little Negress in a red coat who was as natural as a small dog. (Most of the time, I merely found my own reflected face funny, like other people's. But there was a moment when the ears drooped and stuck out horizontally, while my nose became very long and thin and sour. That was repulsive to me.)

We were back at the hotel by 3:30, and already the effects of the drug were noticeably wearing off. But I spent some time studying Don's face. Amazing, how it changed from minute to minute! There was the bright-eyed, sharp-nosed bobcat or fox at one end of the scale, and at the other a hollow-cheeked, wearily composed mask that might have been taken after death. Also, I glimpsed a handsome Latin gentleman in his late thirties, with a moustache. And, aside from this, there were increases and decreases of flesh on the bony substructure, tightenings of muscles around the nose and the mouth. (For an instant, I saw a trick of Dick Foote's!) And yet—it was always a mask. I couldn't penetrate it. I felt that the person inside was playing a game with me, mockingly smiling.

Then we looked at some reproductions of Ingres. These were wonderful—better for me than ordinarily—but I felt, impatiently, that this was predigested experience. I didn't need a great artist to show me how to look at people. I wanted to choose my own subjects and look at them myself.

By this time, the color perception had returned to dim normality—my last flash of it had been the black telephone on the pink directory—and my integral view of people (or whatever you call it) was only very occasional and momentary. So, at 5:00 we had tea with fruitcake. I ate greedily, feeling sharp pleasure in my appetite. (Later, at Pat Trevor-Roper's, I drank three scotch and waters with equally keen enjoyment.) Indeed, all my faculties for sense enjoyment seemed stimulated, including the sexual. Throughout the whole experience, my mood was extra cheerful and relaxed and I felt ready for almost anything anyone might propose—from going to a party to going to sleep. This morning, I have no hangover whatever.

Of course, in many ways, this first experiment was disappointing. I had no drastic adventures, gained no spiritual insights, went neither to heaven nor to hell. I think next time, I should take a double dose. But not in this town, in this weather. I'd like to experiment in the country or on a beach—to listen to music—to try to meditate—oh, well—at least it was a start.

February 27. Yesterday I saw Edward and told him about *The Lost.* He is definitely impressed, I think, by the idea of it. He says it excites him much more than *The World in the Evening* did. (But then I didn't tell him about that until it was a quarter written, so he could hardly have been expected to be frank with me. What could he say except, Go ahead?)

Am I being frank with him about *his* novel?[1] Well—ninety per-cent. I think and hope it'll work out—what I fear is a suburban thin wanness and dullness, a grey Dulwich lighting. But I know I have really succeeded in encouraging him. And that, surely, is good.

Talked to Stephen, this morning in his office. He repeats that he would like to get out of England because it's so dead and everybody wants to avoid doing any extra work. Fears the competitiveness of the States, hates the political situation in South Africa, says Australia is like Lyons' Corner House—the people are so obstinately British that they make all their houses face south although they live south of the equator. On the whole, Stephen favors Canada. Or Brazil.

Hans Viertel and his wife, with whom I had lunch, also say that England (and indeed all Western Europe) is bad for writers. They think things must be much better in Asia. But they admit that England is still an important meeting place of ideas; an East-West exchange, much more tolerant than the U.S.

Salka is in Munich, writing a film called *The Volga Boatmen*!

I forgot to mention that Edward said *World in the Evening* reminded him most of my first unpublished novel, *Lions and Shadows*. He said the dialogue was too ordinary and flat. He read out some samples, to prove this—comparing them unfavorably with passages from *Prater Violet*.

February 28. Yesterday I saw two invalids—John Hayward and a boy named Paul Taylor—a stranger who wrote me a fan letter last year, and then wrote again to tell me he had TB, so amusingly and charmingly and unsentimentally that I long ago made up my mind to go and see him in hospital when I got to London.

John told me how young I still looked and went on to deplore his own fatness and baldness. It's positively uncanny to hear him, as he sits grotesquely twisted up in his wheelchair, making remarks like: "You know, after bronchitis a morning always comes—though one *never* can believe that it will—when one wakes up and suddenly one's legs belong to one again and one leaps out of bed like a two year old." (Does he say these things from bravado, or to make his hearer uncomfortable, or does he will himself to think like a normally active

[1] Upward was struggling with *In the Thirties* (1962); see Glossary.

person?) Actually, he was referring to [T. S.] Eliot, who has been very sick and still doesn't care to see anyone. John says Eliot ought really to go away to the West Indies every winter, but there's no one he can go with. He has no close friends but John, who can't travel.

Paul Taylor had just had a bitter disappointment. His doctor (in the Brompton Hospital) has told him he must spend another three months lying on his right side with his feet higher than his head—to drain the cavity in his lung. (He got it as the result of breathing in coal dust while he was a miner during the war.) Yet he was most cheerful and even flirtatious. He told me how he'd gained weight in hospital and was no longer "a skinny thing," and how he hated having to lie there instead of showing himself off on Brighton Beach! I promised to write to him sometimes.

In the evening, we saw *The Rivals*,[1] which Don really enjoyed—a bit to my surprise. I was fearing he'd find it boring. It *was* well done, certainly, especially John Clements as Sir Anthony Absolute.

Today it's really mild at last, with the temperature up in the forties.

March 3. Yesterday we saw Dodie and Alec and had a longer talk about *The Lost*. Some further ideas emerged.

"Virgil" is Denny Fouts, I think. I see him as a Mr. Hyde to my Dr. Jekyll, and this is excellent, because, in Denny's half-kidding, half-seriously-reproving attitude toward me, I can mirror my faults without the pomposity of serious confession. If Dante has been taking himself too reverently, if he has been addressing meetings of businessmen on the Perennial Philosophy—well, Denny can puncture him. Denny, I think, is confined to The Shades—i.e. he can't enter the United States because of some offense—probably something with little girls.

What is the symbolic nature of the United States and what is the symbolic nature of Mexico? The U.S. is the real, everyday world. And "Dante" is someone who believes in it, who swims in its success, who has the philosophy of a successful person: that it's God's will he should succeed. Therefore, he is wrong about the real world—because he thinks it exists for his pleasure, instead of for his spiritual exercise.

Mexico is The Shades—the place of retreat for those who have made the denial of the real world. Therefore, the inhabitants of The Shades (the expatriates—not the Mexicans, who are perfectly at home in their land) are all lost—temporarily, until they decide to return to the States and face the implications of the real world (which include the spiritual implications—the true ones, as opposed to the

[1] Sheridan's play.

false, Christian-Scientist rationalizations of "Dante"). Denny is lost. He came to The Shades because of his search for the mystical concept of 'Pleasure'. Naturally he wants "Dante" to like The Shades and stay there. So we have the paradox—that The Shades are *seemingly* pleasant. Denny should kid about the original Dante, saying that he only saw torments and flames because he was such a dreary old paranoiac.

During the hashish episode, it should become clear that Dante and Denny are two halves of the same person. They are said to resemble each other. There's something spooky about Denny. He looks far too young. Dante is never quite sure how old he is.

A great question still remains—what relation exists between Dante and the three set pieces—the refugees, the consul, the archaeologist? I'm tempted by the idea that Dante might be different ages when he goes to see these different people. For instance, a young man when he sees the consul. Or could it be that the consul treats him like a young man? I don't know this yet.

During the past two to three days, Don has been very much upset; but in a new and, I feel, much more constructive way. Instead of moaning over the neglect and indifference toward him of the people we meet, he is sincerely disgusted by his own laziness and alarmed because of the way he has been wasting his time, failing to educate himself, etc. He is also very contrite because he feels he has behaved badly to me.

It's difficult for me to know quite how to handle this problem; because much of what Don feels seems to me to be quite healthy. As he puts it, it's as if he's at last breaking out of an egg. And yet, on the other hand, Don's *manner* of feeling—this too easy yielding to depression—is certainly neurotic and shouldn't be encouraged. Today, after a talk this morning, he's much better—despite the weather which is rainy and gloomy.

On the 28th, we went to the Old Vic and saw Burton as Iago. He was quite a revelation to me; I'd never imagined the character like that. He was like a tough, attractive, dishonest American G.I. The kind who did black-market deals in Europe at the end of the war. Not the least sinister, but perhaps a little crazy. Obsessed by his me-first philosophy.

Later we had supper with Terence Rattigan, to whom Cuthbert Worsley introduced us. He seemed very pleasant. Quite reckless about money—and probably living well beyond his huge means. The flat was full of pictures he'd bought.

March 5. On the evening of the 3rd, we had supper with Morgan—

probably the last time we'll see him this trip. And maybe—the thought is unavoidable—the last time ever. . . . Though, indeed, he seems very well and hardly changed since our earliest meetings. Sweetly affectionate, as always. He said how he felt lost, now that his latest book is finished and he can't think what else to write about. "I hope I shan't get depressed," he said thoughtfully, looking into the future. Then, reassuring himself: "I expect not. I've been cheerful so long, I've got into the habit."

Well, now we begin our last week. We're due to fly to New York on the 11th, where Julie awaits us. And then Jo and Ben, and Michael Barrie, and Gerald, in California. I'd like very much to start my novel before I leave.

March 7. A horrible week of pretravel jitters. Awful insoluble problems about excess baggage and airfreight, which will nevertheless somehow be solved. And this afternoon, M. and Richard arrive, to stay at one of those ghastly Kensington residential hotels, until we leave.

Yesterday I started the novel, but only as a token. It will perhaps be weeks before I get on with it.

March 9. Every morning, the sense of the flight ahead makes me chill with foreboding, like the prospect of a surgical operation.

M. and Richard arrived the day before yesterday—Richard rather drunk, M. worried because she has a prolapsed womb and the doctor wants to operate. "I'm sitting on it at this moment," she says. "It's like a rubber ball." Don has met them both and was a success.

Also saw Salka, who tells me that Charlie Chaplin absolutely refuses to see me. It must be because someone has made mischief between us—but I can't imagine what kind. The humiliating thing is that *I* didn't particularly want to see him at all—only to amuse Don.

Last night we went with John Gielgud to see some films—a TV of [Edward] Murrow's interview with [Robert] Oppenheimer,[1] a couple of documentaries and a very badly edited story about two deaf-mutes called *Together*. The Oppenheimer film was extremely interesting, because it exposed every facet of the great man's famous charm—its genuineness (about ninety percent) and its falseness. What a tricky, strange, vain, humble-proud, crafty-simple man! What an utterly Jewish Jew! I was much reminded of Hans Viertel, but that was the genuine part.

[1] The American physicist who headed the atomic bomb project and afterwards was accused of communist sympathies.

John and Peter Brook[1] exchanged some rather irritating dialogue about the Americans having no sense of humor and the British having one. Peter Brook had made a travelogue about his visit to Russia with the Paul Scofield *Hamlet* production, and he was very scornful about some CBS executives who had seen it and been scared to exhibit it in the States. They had wanted him to make changes. For example, Peter in his commentary had said: "We were received by a fat smiling Russian," and the CBS people had objected that Russians don't smile. He had said: "We were sad to leave Russia," and this had shocked them. All this annoyed me, because of the facile equation of fat slimy and probably European Jewish television executives with average Americans—by Peter Brook, himself a Russian Jew (with a changed name, probably) taking it upon himself to speak for the English and John Gielgud, a Pole, agreeing with him. Am I being chauvinistic? Yes. But so were they. My annoyance splashed over on to poor little Mrs. Brook, another Russian, who was doing no one any harm and just recovering from TB. For some reason, I found her irritating.

Later. We have just returned from a day with William Plomer and his friend Charles at Angmering[2]—"bungalow land" William calls it, and "the bungalow belt." *Why* does he live there? and *why* does he live with Charles, who seems no longer quite "all there," though certainly amiable enough? William is harder to understand than anyone else I know. His easy bantering manner hides some kind of austere devotion to a code of duty which is so utterly mysterious as to seem perverse. We walked in the keen wind and winter sunshine on the beach, which is still spiky with the rusted remains of wartime tank traps.

March 11. In two hours we're due to start on our flight to New York. As always, I'm scared and miserable. Also I have a deadly hangover from an evening with M., Richard, Amiya, Peter Watson, Norman Fowler, Stephen and Natasha.

This morning we went on Dorothy Tutin's barge and took pictures of her. She is really very sweet. I feel we could become great friends—indeed, I feel for her in rather the same way as I feel for Julie. It seemed so strange to be talking to her about Julie and to know that, all being well, we should be talking to Julie about *her* tomorrow!

Don has been very sick, too. He and Stephen had some kind of a showdown at the end of the evening, but it wasn't an unpleasant

[1] British stage and film director.
[2] In West Sussex.

one. Indeed, we all came away better friends. I fear, however, that I mortally offended John Lehmann by not going to see *him*.

A very mysterious scar on my lips, caused by some fall or blow that neither Don nor I can remember.

Amiya is delighted with Don. She finds him so "mature."

March 12. I'm still under the spell of the journey—it happened so smoothly. Amiya took us out to the airport in a hired car and filled us with whisky. I could hardly stay awake to eat my supper. Then there was Gander, where Don lost his gloves. Then New York and Julie and Manning and the baby. The shaving lotion leaked out of its bottle, because it had been put in a briefcase in the baggage compartment, which isn't pressurized.

Lunch today with Wystan and Chester. Chester very tactlessly forced us into buying a deluxe copy of his poems[1] (twenty-five dollars). This probably embarrassed Wystan but he didn't show it.

Later. Wet snow, this evening.

Don and I went to see Jimmy and Tania Stern—with what success, it's hard to tell. Don went off in a sulk to a movie. I went into a delicatessen and ate a liverwurst sandwich. At 11:30 this evening—it's now barely 9:00—there is to be a party for us. I shall be glad when it's over. This has been a long, long day.

March 13. New York at its starkest, this morning. In the raw spring light, the city looks dilapidated, almost ruined. All along Third Avenue, now that the El[2] has disappeared, they're tearing up the roadway.

Last night, Julie and Manning gave a party. It was vaguely supposed to be for us, but it wasn't. And the guests somehow got off on the wrong note. Marian Winters[3] was far too noisy in her delight to see us. Joan Elan underplayed it so that she seemed like an iceberg. Maureen Stapleton[4] began crying toward the end, and this led me into a curious conversation with Julie. Julie said Maureen was unhappy because, in spite of all her talents, she couldn't succeed. "That's something you and I can never understand," I said kiddingly, "we who know what it is to have the crowd at our feet." But Julie didn't laugh. She said very seriously: "I used to think I had guts. Now I know I haven't. I get so terribly scared. Sometimes, in the middle of the play, I think I'll never make it. I just want to give up and walk off."

---

[1] *Storm at Castelfranco.*
[2] Elevated railroad.
[3] "Natalia Landauer" in the original stage production of *I Am a Camera*.
[4] American stage and film actress.

I don't know how much of this was said alcoholically: she seemed to mean it. I asked her if she was happy in her home life and she said yes, with great conviction. I think she is, too. I'm sure the chief trouble is in her relations to her father and mother. But, anyhow, she is certainly much more neurotic than I'd suspected.

March 19. We're in the midst of a blizzard. It's lying so thick that there's hardly any traffic in this part of town. The parked cars are disappearing into deep drifts along the sidewalk. How I loathe weather extremes! And heaven only knows if we can possibly leave New York on Thursday. I only wish we were safely back in California.

Manning has fixed up a microphone in the baby Peter's room, so Julie and he can hear him all night.

Julie often gets letters asking her what it was like to be kissed by James Dean.

I've been neglectful about writing of the people we've met: Lincoln, who seems not quite himself, maybe getting ready for another breakdown—Wystan, somehow a bit alienated from us this time; he's never the same when Chester's around—Jimmy and Tania Stern, very sweet and quite their old selves, though both are plumper, now—Glenway [Wescott], on the contrary, looking thinner and handsomer; much occupied with sorting and identifying George Lynes's nude photographs and seeing himself as a great social historian of his times—Marian [Winters] and Jay Smolin,[1] very hospitable, but suffering under a big black mark from us because Marian failed to pass on an invitation to an exciting party given by Siobhan McKenna,[2] where we should have met Shelley Winters, Michael Redgrave, Shirley Booth, etc. The reason for this: Marian didn't want us to leave *her* party, at which we were being bored by drunken James Farrell.[3] Farrell talked about his virility and his greatness as a writer. I can't say I disliked him—I didn't. One can be an egomaniac and still make a relatively pleasant impression, in short spells.

March 22. We are leaving this morning by plane for the Coast. Don is packing. Going through the chest of drawers to find if he'd missed anything, I came upon a homemade doll, of black chiffon, I think, with a sort of pincushion head. I've seen it before—Don usually kept it stuffed into an overcoat pocket, during this trip—but he doesn't know I've examined it. When I seemed about to discover it, he got

---

[1] Her husband, a lawyer.
[2] Actress.
[3] American novelist (1904–1979).

excited and cross. I suppose it is some very private kind of magic, and I mustn't ask him about it for several years at least.[1]

The sun is shining brightly this morning and the snow is more or less cleared away, after the big fall. It has made an astonishing mess and the city seems short of shovellers to deal with it.

Last night we were round at the Kirsteins' again. Lincoln got up in the middle of supper and walked out. Fido didn't seem much surprised. She discussed with Paul Cadmus the question of Lincoln's sleeplessness and overtiredness. "Or was it just that I got on his nerves by talking too much?" she asked, very objectively: "No—I don't think so." Fido *does* ramble on, in an inconsequential way that sometimes seems silly. She has a sort of compulsion to cross the t's and dot the i's. But on the whole I think she's much saner. Probably Lincoln's breakdowns have compelled her to be.

March 25. Well, this is quite a solemn moment. A new start.

I'm sitting cross-legged on cushions at the low teak table, because we have no proper table or desk, yet, to write at. And here we are, installed amidst cartons of books, in the front part of the little house Michael Barrie has bought on East Rustic Road—number 322, almost directly across from 333, where Bill Caskey and I lived in 1948. So, after six years and maybe 30,000 miles of travel, I've shifted my base about one hundred yards!

It's a grey Pacific morning, and my sinus is giving me perpetual sniffles. But I feel well and quite energetic. There is nothing to stop me from getting on with the novel except my own neurotic laziness and anxieties. The same applies to Don and *his* future work. He thinks, at present, that he'll join an art school.

Our flight was uneventful, but I hated it as much as ever. When I look down on beautiful snow-mountains from a plane, my attitude is that of a child who's nervous with animals: "Nice doggie! Doggie's my friend, isn't he? Doggie won't bite me, will he?" Jo and Ben met us at the airport, with a bottle of champagne which we drank in the car. It was so wonderful to see them again and be enfolded into their snugness. We had supper with them, and later Michael and his friend Bill [Stroud] (of whom more later) and Gerald Heard and Chris Wood came in. This was a mistake, because we only wanted to be snug and drunken—and Gerald made me self-conscious, but I don't

---

[1] Bachardy made himself a number of dolls, which he did not want Isherwood to discover. The one Isherwood found was a stocking doll with a black silk dress made from a scarf. Bachardy's mother embroidered the dolls' faces, and he made different colored hair for each doll, from embroidery thread, which could be combed.

think it mattered. That night (the 22nd) we stayed at the motel on Entrada Drive. It was five dollars for two—although the sign said six dollars. The landlady explained, in the most matter-of-fact tones, that she was quoting the higher price, "In case there's another war. I don't want to get stuck under one of those price ceilings."

The next morning we drove into town to see Geller and collect our mail. (Quite a lot of my books, and Don's movie magazines, haven't shown up yet and we're beginning to be anxious.) But it was a lovely morning and we were both in a daze of joy to find ourselves back here in this lovely place—this hideous dump of a city with its beautiful gardens and balmy air, and foul smog.

After Easter, we tell ourselves, we will start in earnest. But much has to be done first. And we shall begin right away looking around for a place to buy, since this is anyway much too small.

Later. Have talked on the phone this morning to Edward Hooker, Aldous, Swami, Speed. We are going over to the Hookers' this afternoon to pick up the frame of the bed I used to have in Saltair Avenue, to use for a living-room couch. Aldous married (last Monday) an Italian named Laura Archera who used to be a concert violinist. She is an old friend of his and of Maria's. They were married at a wedding chapel drive-in at Yuma, with "a broken-down cowboy" as witness. Aldous was quite his old self describing this, and the leakage to the press that followed. Nevertheless, he seemed deeply happy and in a most benign state of mind. "Really," he exclaimed, "there are so many delightful and intelligent and unusual people in the world!" Then he added: "And so many unspeakably awful ones!"

Swami is going to New York on Wednesday, to say goodbye to the visiting swamis from India. Speed we shall see this evening.

March 28. Last night I drove home fairly drunk, enough drunk, apparently, to be weaving a bit. This enraged another driver so much that he followed me all the way home, bawled me out, threatened to hit me and/or call a cop. I said mildly that I'd much rather he hit me, which was the psychologically correct answer, because it made him get into his car and drive away. Don thinks the man was psychopathic and says he was actually foaming at the mouth. (The man told me he was a doctor—and of course I now regret I wasn't sober enough to think of answering with mock-earnestness: "Well, if you're a doctor you should be sorry for me and try to cure me.") But all the same, it was a well-timed warning, because I always need to be brought sharply to my senses at the beginning of each new driving season.

I was drunk because I wanted to relax (at the Duquettes') after a big crying scene made by Don—not directed against me—because he felt Marguerite had been cold and unfriendly. She had asked him to what looked like a cozy tête-à-tête, and then produced her lover, Emmett Blow—a fat rich man with whom she has been in Las Vegas. Furthermore, she had spent the short time before Emmett's appearance in bitching Joan Elan, whom she and Speed now accuse of being a tramp and sleeping with Harry, Blow, the producer of *The Lark* etc. etc. Don felt excluded and therefore unhappy, because he counts on Marguerite as a friend.

However, today all has been happiness. Lovely weather, and we shopped for a lamp, a bureau and various other things. Speed thinks Don should get a job in television. The Duquettes were using all their charm to get him to come back and work for them, but he doesn't intend to.

Swami, with his usual persistence, has brought up the question of the Ramakrishna book again. So now I really shall have to start work on it. Also, there are Frank Taylor's two projects—the anthology of English short stories, and the Maugham anthology. *Also* there is my novel. I really ought to stick to these and not fuss about any movie jobs for the present. We can certainly afford to.

March 31. Another hangover, because I was at Jim's last night and got drunk waiting for supper. Betty Andrews was there, and Oliver [Andrews], grown squarely fat from the chill of skin diving, and Jack Hillmer, Jim's colleague, who is said by Jim to be the best architect in the country, and sleepy sly Tom Wright who acts so amiable but is really quite a bitch. He and Jim are catty about Michael Barrie. They accuse him of having urged the landlady to raise the rent when he left. "Christ would have got her to raise the rent when he moved *in*," Jim commented. Jim has decided to give up architecture and try writing.

Yesterday I had lunch with Speed, who is glowing with triumph over his play.[1] He strongly hinted that he wants to dramatize *The World in the Evening*—which, he says, "is still the best novel written since I've been around." He is also much preoccupied by the scandalous history of the Charlie Brackett family. I think he must be planning to write about it.

We are very seriously considering buying Hal Greene's house on Sycamore Road, number 434. It's the most attractive place I've seen around here, a real snug nest, and just the right size for us.

April 1. Easter morning. We got up early and went on the beach. But, around ten o'clock, clouds gathered and it got very windy. Now, just

---

[1] *Out by the Country Club*, never produced.

after 12:00, it's still windy but the sun's shining. We have to go to lunch at the Bracketts'.

This morning I restarted *The Lost*, also made a token start on Saradananda's life of Ramakrishna.[1] My resolve is to do something on the novel at least twice a week, and some reading on Ramakrishna at least four times a week. That's a good minimum.

Later. Easter lunch at the Bracketts'. The almost incredible bad taste of James Larmore, who told Speed—for an April Fool's joke—that Harry was drunk outside with a gun, wanting to kill him. Marguerite in a big hat, and Ivan slyly grinning. The terrible service—the food took hours and there wasn't enough of it. Don much upset because he felt Marguerite had treated him bitchily again—and in front of "Ivin" Moffat, as she calls him.

April 3. Yesterday I worked some more on *The Lost*. The dream at the beginning hasn't come right, yet, but it will. Don went to see about art classes at the Chouinard,[2] and returned terribly depressed, and suffering from psychosomatic stomachache—because the Chouinard had depressed him or scared him, and because he'd seen his mother and she was in such a mess. Don's father won't give her any money, so she sits home and mopes.

I intended to write something about Michael's friend Bill Stroud—but he still remains mysterious. Very broad shouldered, almost rectangular, he digs his thumbs into his side pockets, tenses his back and says nothing. There is something very sweet and sad in his face. Chris Wood has heard that he's an epileptic.

April 7. Last night, we had supper at the Stravinskys'—Michael Barrie, Bill Stroud, Chris Wood, [Gerald Heard,] Aldous and Laura Huxley were also there.

On first meeting (actually I met her first the day before yesterday, when I went around to the house to talk to Aldous and Bill Froug, the writer who is adapting *Jacob's Hands* for a radio performance) I find I don't altogether like Laura. She's good-looking, smart and stylish in a "sensible" way and adequately intelligent; but she has a curious tactlessness—[. . .]. She tries, I think, to be friendly and man-to-man, and only succeeds in being rather rude. However, Aldous seems very happy with her. He was wearing a twenty-year-old tie (from Paris?) which he described as looking like an early Rouault.

Talk about dreams. Igor had once dreamed a passage of music

[1] Swami Saradananda, *Sri Ramakrishna The Great Master*.
[2] Chouinard Art Institute.

which he was able to use. Also a whole lot of pastiche Beethoven—a sort of Tenth Symphony, as Aldous said.

I detect a slight snootiness toward my mescaline experience on the part of both Aldous and Gerald. I suppose they regard it as hopelessly unscientific. I don't really resent this—indeed, it's quite true. Both Aldous and Gerald agree that you get more out of the mescaline each time you take it; that is to say, you go in deeper.

Both Igor and Vera were adorable, as usual; and Bob [Craft] was in a friendly mood. They served magnums of champagne, which Gerald managed to drink and disapprove of, simultaneously. They're planning to go to Greece in June. Igor looked very well, but complained of all kinds of ailments. Michael kept Bill Stroud off in a corner, as if he weren't big enough to listen to grown-up conversation.

The night before last, I saw Harry Brown. We got drunk together and played pool at the Try Later bar. Harry, though obviously drinking heavily, was quite cheerful and looked sunburnt and much slimmer. He blames Speed for the breakup of his marriage, says he's still in love with Marguerite ("I only pulled a gun on her once, to keep her at home") but is anxious to marry again as soon as he can afford it.

As for our buying the Sycamore Road house, we're still waiting to hear from Hal Greene. I think he is passing through a phase of final jitters about parting with it.

Since our return, Don's morale has been fairly good—despite the depressive behavior of his mother, who seems determined to shed as much gloom around her as she possibly can. She refused to come and look at our movies the other night, on the ground that she didn't want me to see her so fat! All this upsets Don, of course; and his problem of what to do with himself remains unsolved. All *I* can do is to try to stop him getting panicky and remind him constantly that there's plenty of time.

April 8. Grey all day yesterday. Grey again this morning. Dangerous idling weather.

Last night we had supper with Jo and Ben, and they showed their slides of our Mexican trip. I wanted to see them, to recapture some of the Mexican atmosphere, for my novel. What chiefly struck me: the dark blueness of the sky, the extraordinarily strong light of the setting or rising sun striking upward at the undersides of the palm trees and making their fronds flash with a metallic sheen, like swords. The bandstands—some of them imported from France, perhaps: fancy lace ironwork, supported by naked girls. The disproportionate size of the great twin-towered baroque churches. The utter absence of any sort of landscape gardening: buildings arise and stand up unapologetically in the midst of dumps and barren lots.

I absolutely, absolutely must get on with the novel. Just add page to page, without too much considering, until I have a first draft—no matter how short, how crude.

Quoted by Gerald at the Stravinskys' party: "Talent does what it can, genius does what it must." I don't really understand what this means.

April 9. Grey again today, but there was a bright spell around lunchtime which I could have taken advantage of but didn't, because Don had gone into town and I didn't feel like going on the beach alone. Instead, I'm grateful to say, I've worked on the novel. Another page. *All* that matters right now is to go quietly, almost stealthily ahead—to sneak up on the pony in the field and catch it while it's grazing.

Otherwise, everything seems either negative or neutral. The war situation gets to look worse and worse in Israel.[1] We saw Jo and Ben off to Portland and Seattle this morning, and they'll return next week only to leave again for Florida till June 1st. Hal Greene has given us no word about the house. No signs of a job or a sale of material to TV, radio or film—other than the tiny windfall from *Jacob's Hands*.

Last night we had supper with Marguerite. She's now staying at one of the Duquettes' apartments—$150 a month with only a shared bathroom and no kitchen.

Marguerite herself didn't make a very pleasing impression. She talked indiscreetly of Kazan's efforts to seduce her—yet admitted that when he called her in the middle of the night she changed into morning clothes ("because I knew he'd keep me a long time") and drove clear into town to his hotel. Furthermore, when he opened the door to her with no clothes on, she went into his room "as if there was nothing the matter" and lay down on his other bed. Nevertheless, she told him that he was completely unattractive to her!

Don was much depressed after this and began to slip back into one of his black, self-hating moods. He has been almost entirely free of them since we got back here. I hope he finds an art school or something regular to do, soon. At least, he has started at Harvey Easton's gym, and Easton has told him to eat more, which is good because I often think his tenseness is due to undernourishment.

[1] Israeli troops had raided the Gaza Strip in 1955, killing thirty-six Egyptians in a professed attempt to control Arab terrorism; President Nasser responded by blockading Eilat, effectively closing the Gulf of Aqaba.

April 10. Supper at the Weingartens', last night. Jessie looked much slimmer and younger, after her serious heart attacks—but later in the evening her face was very tired. Two daughters were there, with husbands, a British doctor and his wife, a man who was something to do with smog control. The British doctor is a member of Jessie's team which is researching the causes of coronary disease. They think it has something to do with an excess of male hormone in men, of female in women.

Dinner was dull, as it always is at their house. Not enough wine, and the beef was tough. The British doctor was covertly aggressive—wanting to pick a quarrel with someone over Cyprus.

Larry, unusually friendly, talked about the old days in Hollywood and how beautiful the city used to be. (The smog expert thought that the problem was practically hopeless, as long as automobiles are automobiles and rubbish is incinerated.) Larry was Jackie Coogan's press agent. He told stories of fortunes made and lost in real estate.

April 13. Rain the last two days, and it still hasn't cleared properly. Tomorrow I'm to go up to Santa Barbara with Swami, see the new temple and spend the night.

The novel is started (seven pages) which is some encouragement; but I'm really still pushing ahead through the darkness, hoping some light will break.

We've just been to see Scott Poland in the UCLA hospital. He really is a very sweet boy, and I wish Don would make friends with him. Don made another big scene last night, and cried. It was the usual thing: his terror of the future and his guilt because nothing has been started yet. Also he was terribly depressed by *Madame Bovary*, which he has just finished. Last night, he said he wanted to have a talk with Evelyn Hooker about his problems—but today her number didn't answer, and I have the feeling he'll back out of it.

Meanwhile, it begins to look as if Hal Greene had found a house for himself, which would mean that we could move into 434 Sycamore without much delay. But he wants us to put up more money—nearly 20,000 in all, plus 3,000 odd for the furniture. This will save us interest later, but it will mean that we shall be down to our last couple of thousand dollars, until I can make some more. Don immediately volunteered to add his one thousand dollars he has saved up, remarking: "After all, if I expect to be treated as an adult, I ought to share expenses." This is typical of the quality in him that makes all his character problems not only bearable but endearing. I never for one moment regret our having settled down together—and it is much more often for better than for worse.

Yesterday I had supper with Tom Wright. Speed and Paul [Millard] were there. Speed whispered to me that they had been having "a big fuss" and I got the impression that Speed wants out. He seems to be regretting his old freedom.

In the afternoon, we had drinks with Kazan. He isn't a very pleasant character, I think. He talked quite bitchily of Tennessee. Tennessee's new play is opening in Miami on Monday,[1] being done by some local theater group. How I wish we could be there! Since making *Baby Doll*,[2] Kazan has really fallen in love with the South, which he describes as "grotesque and tragic." He says he never understood Faulkner till he went there and saw it for himself. At first he was threatened and the set was actually fired on. A Negro who was being hunted by the marshal took refuge with his company. But later, everybody got along fine.

Well, here's the end of this volume at last. I'm so glad that I've gotten back the diary habit and I hope I won't ever lose it again. Will try to start the new volume tomorrow.

---

[1] *Sweet Bird of Youth.*
[2] The film of Williams's story.

The Late Fifties
1956–1960

April 14, 1956–May 25, 1958

April 14. Though tired, I want to make an entry today so as to keep continuity with the volume I finished yesterday. I'm up at Santa Barbara with Swami, staying at the house of one of his devotees, Mrs. Wright (a lady with only one leg) because the convent is full.

The convent is full because Tarini (Mrs. Nixon) has been moved up here to die of stomach cancer. It is supposed to be painless, but she did have pain today and Dr. Austin was called. She looks skinny and tired and a bit older, but is not shockingly changed—in appearance, that is. John Yale (whom I have to remember to call Prema) and Swami tell me that she is startlingly changed in character. She used to be a shrew and a bitch, now she is all sweetness, and consideration for others. "When I saw how she was turning into a saint," said Swami, with his giggle, "I just knew there was something seriously wrong with her."

Swami seems tired, and was noticeably quiet throughout the evening, while the girls questioned me eagerly about Amiya. Sarada and Barada were very lively. I thought I detected a good deal of friction between them and Prema. He is quietly bossy. More than ever an eminence, but no longer a grey one; working on the landscaping around the new temple has made him look tanned and healthy.

The temple has a lovely smell of Douglas fir. The pillars and arches are all natural, unsmoothed, unpainted wood, full of cracks and axe marks. It is really much the nicest of the Vedanta temples; just the right mixture of rugged simplicity and oriental camp—the curly-carved gold shrine is under a palanquin quite like the one Tony Duquette used in *Kismet*.

And then the location is magnificent, with the long downhill view to the sea and the islands. The landscape around here is, to all intents and purposes, unchanged since I lived here twelve years ago.

Before we left Hollywood to drive up here, we had to go to a meeting at a women's club near Vermont and Wilshire, where Swami had to speak for twenty minutes to open a prayer-discussion group. Swami in a grey suit with a pearl-grey tie. He always seems, at first sight, so much less "religious" than the sort of people who introduce him on these occasions. More like a doctor or even a bank manager than a minister.

The stage hung with blue velvet curtains. On one side, the flag. On either side, unsteadily arranged branches of rhododendron, somewhat wilted. In the center, a flower piece, featuring daffodils. The audience is chiefly composed of women in very small hats, many of them with folded-back veils in which tiny spangles sparkle.

April 15. A few notes, half an hour before lecture time.

I forgot to mention yesterday that I sent a pot of caladiums to Peggy (it being her birthday) with a note, more or less as follows: "Several mutual friends tell me you say I have 'dropped' you. Needless to say, I'm convinced it's the other way around. But my birthday wishes are absolutely sincere because I know that, if we both have enough 'happy returns' we're certain, in the course of nature, to come together again." This is a little bitchy, I admit, but it's as forgiving as I can manage under the circumstances.

The clouds are low on the hills, this morning, but it's palely bright out on the water. The garden is heavy with after-rain colors. I took the manuscript of the new pamphlet on the Vedanta Society up to the temple, and read it in the office at the back. Also I told my beads in front of the shrine. Krishna ran back and forth, muttering some unintelligible holy sounds into the microphone at the pulpit, then playing them back on the recording machine by the entrance. But this didn't bother me. The family feeling here is so strong that it absorbs such disturbances and even makes them seem charming and sympathetic. And the temple itself grows on me, more and more. Partly, I think, because it's made of wood. It seems so much more alive, so much more an organism, than a stone or plaster or brick building would.

April 18. This afternoon, I went with Hal Greene to put the two houses, 434 Sycamore Road and the one he's going to buy, into escrow. A solemn moment. The first time I ever bought a house. The thought of the tying up of all my savings scares me. It seems strange that I won't any longer be able to be extravagant. But Don is pleased and excited—and eager to contribute his thousand dollars to our fund.

Yesterday we went to the airport and brought Jo and Ben home. They had been with Jo's family at Yakima, Washington, and enjoyed it, apparently, though the visit sounded just ghastly—people putting on funny masks and roaring with laughter. Ben, however, provided a clue to the *stimmung* by telling me (so Jo shouldn't hear) that personally he'd been either drunk or hung over from beginning to end. All the men, he said, were sneaking drinks behind their wives' backs. One time, Jo had very nearly caught him fixing himself a shot of whiskey in the kitchen; he had had to gulp it down so fast that he had somehow strained his throat and could still feel the effects.

Jo's father, who is seventy-five, has two photographs of naked women in his bedroom.

April 19. Don had his first shot of polio vaccine yesterday. It came to me very strongly that he ought to do this, and so I urged him to. The strange thing is, I've seen so many references to polio in the newspapers, etc., during the last few days, could it also have been a subconscious suggestion from *Jacob's Hands*? We've heard nothing more, so far, of [Ernest] Borgnine's alleged interest in it, and I'm beginning to lose hope again.

Don also went to see Evelyn Hooker about his state of mind and problems. Evelyn seems to have reassured him, insofar as the state of mind was concerned. She didn't think it neurotic of him to be upset, under the circumstances. In other words, she thinks that our life together constitutes a genuinely big problem. Now of course I quite see this. And yet I can't, in my weakness, help feeling hurt when I'm treated as a sort of classic monster—a standard monster, almost—out of a textbook, like a dragon in a fairy tale. Don, on his side, cannot understand that I mind. I ought to accept my monsterhood humbly, he thinks.

But isn't all this the purest justice of karma? Go back twenty years. For Don, substitute Richard. For Evelyn, John Layard. For me, my mother.

Glorious weather, this morning, after days of dull greyness. Jo and Ben leave on their trip to Florida next Sunday. I'm in pretty good spirits, because I've been working steadily—reading for the Rama-krishna book, getting on with my novel, keeping my letter writing up to date.

The lack of a desk here has forced me to sit on cushions on the floor, with no back support, and write at the low teak table. I have gotten to like doing this, because it's so good to have to keep a straight back again, after all this while. Maybe I'll go on working like this at our new house.

April 22. A baddish, dull patch. We're suspended in midair, waiting for the house, waiting for money to pay for it, waiting for Don to find out what he's going to do. He was depressed yesterday, because of all this; and then we went to see *The Prisoner*[1] (in which Alec Guinness gives the worst performance of a cardinal I've ever seen) and that made him feel worse. And then, in the middle of the night, Bob Hoover rang up blubbering-drunk because Ted had gone off on a date without him.

Apparently they made it up, because Ted and Bob showed up this morning. And Bob actually referred to the scene he'd made—in front of Ted. He's quite shameless—quite utterly selfish in the snugness of his self-pity.

It was foggy and grey down on the beach, so we drove out to the Simi Valley, where it was blazing hot. Jim Charlton came with us. He showed up uninvited and unannounced, and there was nothing to do but ask him. The crowd of cars—herds of hot ironmongery—made the valley hideous. But when we got out into the backcountry, it was so beautiful, with the hills still yellowish and bluish green—not yet baked golden by the summer.

April 24. Right after the drive mentioned above, Jim called and asked me to come over. He wanted to know why I'd bought a house instead of having him design one. Replied that we needed a house in a hurry, and cheap. This is 99.99% true, but of course I was also glad to avoid the inevitable personal clash with Jim. I can never forget his basic dishonesty about money.

However, that wasn't the point. Jim wanted to know did I believe in his talent as an architect—and to that I can unhesitatingly answer yes, anytime. Jim is very depressed, because, he says, he has failed over and over again, at the last moment, to secure apparently certain assignments. And the reason for this I cannot explain to him. I don't know what it is—unless simply that most everybody loathes and fears anything original. But, on the other hand, Jim isn't all that original. Plenty of architects are quite successful who build in his general style.

I, myself, was quite badly depressed this morning and still am, a bit. I'm worried about Don. He isn't well, and he's frankly disinclined to do anything except read (which would be perfectly okay except that he feels guilty about it). And I'm worried about money. When we've paid everything off, we'll only have about $3,000 or $4,000 if I let Don contribute. Of course, I've been lower far than this before, but it worries me now because I see expenses ahead and no great hopes of a job. Also, I don't really *want* a job. I want to get on with my novel—

[1] 1954 film of Bridget Boland's play.

which is utterly crazy but still somehow alive. And I must not stop it. Have reached page fourteen.

Yesterday afternoon was grey, and we walked on the beach and clambered on the rocks by the lighthouse café and then came home to a muffin tea. The feeling between us is very good, right now. Very gentle, as if we were both invalids—of different kinds—and didn't want to hurt each other. A sort of nursery-sickroom atmosphere, which reminds me of the last scene in O'Neill's *All God's Chillun*. Kittycat and old Dobbin.

Yesterday night we showed our travel film up at Margaret Gage's. Don was infuriated, because she used the occasion to invite all sorts of guests and we also had to see George Huene's two films—about Toledo and the Bosch in the Escorial,[1] with Hugh Chisholm's shamingly bogus commentaries.

This morning was grey, and I spent hours at Peschelt's, to get my front tooth recapped. But this afternoon the sun is shining. So cheer up, old horse.

Contemporary joke, heard last night: "There's to be a Bridey Murphy TV program—from nine to eight."[2]

Before 8.00 a.m. this morning I got a wrong-number call. The voice of a seemingly very old, very hoarse woman said, "I feel as grey as the weather."

April 26. Yesterday morning Don still felt bad, so I told him to see Dr. Sellars, who said he had hepatitis and must be hospitalized at once. This meant the Cedars of Lebanon, because Sellars is on the staff. So I drove him there. He has quite a nice private room, and I hope and think that his isn't a very bad attack. He's being fed glucose intravenously.

It seems that Michael's Bill Stroud had left for the East—I don't know how many days ago—but this afternoon Michael remarked quite casually that he was going to meet him—so he must have changed his mind and returned.

Yesterday evening I had supper at the Knopfs'. Joshua Logan was there, and greatly raised my morale by saying how much he had admired the script of *Diane* and how tragic it was that Lana Turner had ruined it. He also asked me if I'd like to do a picture with him

---

[1] Juan Bautista de Toledo, first architect of the Escorial, the royal monastery northwest of Madrid; the Hieronymus Bosch painting there is *Christ Mocked*.
[2] Bridey Murphy, while under hypnosis, claimed to recollect a former life; she became the subject of a book by Morey Bernstein, *The Search for Bridey Murphy*, released as a film in 1956.

and said he'd send me a copy of *Mistress Masham's Repose* by E. H. White(?)[1] to see if I could see a script in it.

Mrs. Logan, meanwhile, raved about Marilyn Monroe, whom Logan is directing in *Bus Stop*. Monroe, she says, is so misunderstood, so fundamentally simple, so starved for affection. When she [Monroe] was hospitalized the other day, she was asked was she a Catholic? A Protestant? "No—I just believe in God." She came in one morning with cold cream on her face. Asked did she always put it on at night, she said: "No—only when I sleep alone." She may marry Arthur Miller, the dramatist. She is now studying the last section of Joyce's *Ulysses*.

I just report all this. No comment.

I miss Don terribly, already. But my job now is not to feel sorry for myself. I have to get us moved into 434 Sycamore. I have to avoid getting hepatitis myself (it's infectious). I have to earn some money, quick. (Don's hospital bill will be at least $350.)

Later. I spent the evening with Gerald—just got home. Not a very interesting evening, because Margaret Gage was present and there were only four of us (with Will Forthman) altogether—so Gerald was inhibited from cozy gossip and deprived of an audience worth dazzling. Yet it was pleasant—the feeling of our being together was good. Topics: the cowardice of Napoleon, the government's decision to release the flying saucer films, the uses of various sedatives such as Seconal, the character of Peggy Kiskadden compared with that of Amiya.

Have started reading Arnold Bennett's *Journals* again. He says, "I constantly gloat over the number of words I have written in a given period." And well he might! He wrote over 100,000 words in the first quarter of 1908! And I? My absurdly modest schedule calls for writing a minimum of two pages on my novel and reading forty pages of the Ramakrisna book—*a week*! And yet—such has been my former sloth—I can legitimately congratulate myself that I have at least kept to this and bettered it a little—*four* pages a week, so far, on my novel. And that I've answered all my letters to date. And that I've kept up with this journal.

Talking of Peggy Kiskadden, she answered my note as follows: "It was good to hear from you—and it gives me an opportunity to assure you that I'm always 'right there'—as little Bill used to say—and sending good wishes to you as ever—lovingly Peggy."

No—this isn't the answer I wanted. It says, in effect, "No, I don't yield an inch. You have to come to me and surrender. I'm the holy one—the one in the right."

[1] T. H. White.

May 2. To the Cedars today. Found Don in a fuss about the huge hospital bill—he wanted to leave at once. We talked to Sellars and he agreed (rather unwillingly) that Don could leave tomorrow. But he'll have to stay in bed for several days.

Yesterday and the day before I moved everything into 434 Sycamore Road, and have already slept two nights there. What with that, and seeing Don and keeping up my novel and work on the Ramakrishna book, I've seldom been under greater pressure. But I think I shall manage now.

Yesterday night I saw Jim Costigan, the plump young actor-writer who is Julie Harris's friend. He says the young actors all complained that John van Druten is a bad director and that he didn't understand his characters in the *Checkered Shade*. I think the truth is that John is wonderful at controlling old bitch prima donnas like Gertrude Lawrence and Margaret Sullavan—but he quite probably doesn't understand boys and girls from the Actors' Lab.[1]

Of all the people who helped me move—Jim [Charlton], Michael, Bill Stroud and Tom [Wright]—the best and most hardworking was Tom. He really seems to enjoy it. He plodded back and forth, always sweet tempered, never lazy or temperamental.

May 4. What a week of work! Today I've been running around since I got up, cooking, shopping, unpacking, doing whatever came to hand. And I've managed so far to keep up with my chores, and indeed quite enjoyed it all. Don has been home since yesterday, and we have never been happier together. My only worries are that he'll have some kind of relapse, and/or that we won't get any more money. But still this is a happy time, oddly enough—and I shall remember it as such.

Madge MacDonald and her sister Renée Rubin were in to see us. Madge has given Don his B_1 shot. She is aggressive toward Dr. Sellars and is secretly taking the hypodermic needles with her to UCLA Hospital, to have them sterilized *her* fashion; boiling, she says, is worse than useless against hepatitis infection.

Don's eyes are no longer noticeably yellow, and his urine is light again. But Hayden Lewis, whom I met yesterday, told me that Rod has had this disease, on and off, for nearly three years! All because he got up too soon.

May 7. Well, we plod along. Sellars came today and told Don he could get up. Actually he's been wandering around the house for

---

[1] Alluding to The Actors Studio, fount of naturalistic, psychologically revealing Method acting.

several days already. In a week, he may be allowed outdoors. But he mustn't drink any alcohol for a year!

Actually, I have been very happy cooking for the two of us, and I haven't in the least missed seeing other people. It's so nice here, and the weather has been windy, but so beautiful—quite smogless even downtown.

News from Santa Barbara, via John Yale, that Tarini is sinking.

If only I could get some money without having to go back to work in the studios! I'd like to spend the entire summer writing this first draft of my novel. At present it's flowing with such magic smoothness, I hate to think of interrupting it.

The days are far too short—cooking, shopping, watering the garden. I've unpacked all my books now, and my workroom is really snug.

Such happiness, this past week.

May 11. Worried about Don, who felt tired this morning. He didn't sleep well. He was upset yesterday because, as he confessed, he'd read two letters I wrote to Caskey while I was in England in 1947—the letters were in one of the boxes of Caskey's photographs which we've been sorting—and it hurt him to find that they were exactly like the letter I wrote Don from Wyberslegh this trip. I didn't know what to say to this: there is nothing I *can* say. It's probably true, and I know exactly how Don feels, and how can I prove to him that he's wrong to feel that way? He is—and yet it's so natural.

Also, quite abruptly, he yesterday announced that he is going to UCLA this summer. And we went there, and he registered.

But work goes excellently. Two and one-third pages today. John Lehmann has cabled, wanting the article I'm to write on returning to London in 1947.[1] And there is the short story anthology for Frank Taylor. But I rather like being rushed like this. I feel equal to the demand.

Today I went to MGM and saw Knopf. But he's going away to France to make this picture and obviously there's no prospect of any job for him before the late fall, at the earliest. Well, we shall manage somehow.

A symbolic incident I forgot to record. After all this while—during the time Don was in hospital and I was moving into this house—Jim Charlton brought round Lefty—the paper "Judas" baseball player Jo and Ben sent us from Mexico. We left it with Jim while we were in Europe—telling him to explode it on the beach. But he hadn't. So

---

[1] "Coming to London," published in Lehmann's book of the same title in 1957 and reprinted in *Exhumations*.

now we opened it. And there were no firecrackers in him, after all; only a heavy fragment of earthenware crockery—I suppose what they call a posada.[1] Another menace proved to be harmless!

Eddie Knopf is taking French lessons. He looked very sick, I thought. His eyes are grey.

Heinz has written, suggesting that I sponsor the immigration of Gerda, Christian and himself to the States, and that we shall then all live together in a house that I'm to buy. He offers, of course, to pay all this money back by degrees. And now I must answer his letter—explaining tactfully that this scheme is impossible; that is to say, I'd rather die than agree to it.

May 16. It's overpoweringly hot—has been for the past three days. I feel such exhaustion that I can hardly make myself write this—yet it's the very last of my chores. I've done all the required Ramakrishna reading, more than my minimum stint at the novel, and the accursed Lehmann article which was sheer loveless grind, and done for no reason on earth except to appease the maddening neuroticism of Lehmann, and, incidentally, to pay for Don's refusal to see more of him. I will *not* suffer for any more such causes. From now on, I'm going to avoid this kind of work like the plague.

Otherwise, all is happiness. Tomorrow we plan to drive down to Ensenada to celebrate Don's birthday.

Brad Saunders was here—full of incredible tales of air force crackups. A pilot who put a dixie cup over the light signal which told him to put his wheels down—because the light annoyed him—and *then* forgot to lower his wheels!

Marguerite is going to New York on vacation, until Clift has sufficiently recovered from his accident for them to go on making *Raintree County*.[2]

Ben and Jo saw Tennessee's new play in Miami, *Sweet Bird of Youth*.

May 17. Woke up running a slight fever (sunstroke? beginning of hepatitis?). So am not sure if we'll go down to Mexico or not. In any case, I must go and pick up my social security check first.

John van Druten came to supper with us last night. He suddenly decided that he might possibly dramatize *Mr. Norris*—this because I told him Terry Rattigan had considered doing it. He was as pompous as ever, but most gracious.

Marguerite Lamkin looked in with Paul Millard on her way to the

---

[1] Isherwood evidently meant piñata.
[2] The actor, Montgomery Clift, crashed his car after a drunken party and damaged his face and jaw.

airport for New York. She really has changed—she is so amazingly
indiscreet, vulgar and tactless; much more like Speed, but without
Speed's wisdom.

John is really as spoiled as a baby. The minute he set eyes on
Marguerite, he pouted and sulked till she left. On his way home, he
went into a drugstore and saw some German pastilles, of which the
title had been translated as "violate pastilles." He called to tell me this.
Obviously it had never ever occurred to him that we might have
gone to bed.

The great heat has completely broken. It's grey and cold.

May 19. In bed all yesterday and part of the day before, with some
kind of flu bug. I'm up today, but slightly shaky. So poor Don was
disappointed of his Mexican trip. We may go next week.

I think I was just awfully tired. I lay there in bed not stirring a
muscle. It's so good to do that.

Johnnie wrote this morning to say he had decided not to adapt *Mr.
Norris.* A small blow, but maybe he wouldn't be right for it, anyhow.
As he says himself, he would echo *Sally Bowles.*

May 23. Dull weather, dull times. I've been sick on and off. Got up
yesterday to have lunch with Jim Geller and David Brown of Fox. No
immediate reaction. Brown talked about the poorness of the movie
industry, the disappearance of theaters, TV bigger and better, with a
slot-machine charge of twenty-five cents a night, no commercials,
color, a three by three foot screen. Felt exhausted and returned to
bed, where I finished *Our Mutual Friend*—very enjoyable but actually
such a bunch of nonsense. And the happy ending starts halfway
through volume two.

Good things to report: I've kept up steadily with my quota of the
Ramakrishna book. And with my novel, which is now at page thirty-
eight.

Relations with Don are pretty good, though he's inevitably
approaching a new crisis, as he has to decide about the future: shall he
return to UCLA, go to an art school, or what?

I can count on *some* money from the pocketbook edition of *World*
and from the Frank Taylor short story anthology. Let's say $3,500.
That would bring us to about $6,000 altogether.

Bad things: We actually have very poor prospects of making any
more money than this, for the present.

As far as I can learn from John Lehmann, Peter Watson is dead. But
he gives no details. And to think Peter was one of the last people we
saw in England! This isn't very real to me yet. In fact, I don't

altogether believe it. Maybe melodramatic old John just means he has gone to prison or something.

I keep this journal up with an effort, knowing that it's good to do so. On the whole, this is a quiet but satisfactory time. At least I'm working—and, as far as the novel is concerned, with enjoyment and curiosity.

May 24. Another grey morning. Woke with sinus headache and didn't lose it until I took three aspirins after lunch and napped. The whole morning was wasted at social security, explaining to them that I earned some royalties this week from *Camera* in England, and therefore wasn't eligible for a payment. A nice Dutchman named Cyfer handled my case.

Geller called to say that CBS doesn't want *The Vacant Room* for radio. Another hope dashed. The volume of *Mistress Masham's Repose* has arrived. I can't believe I shall want to do it. And yet I am loath to talk myself out of a job with Joshua Logan.

Don worked all day sorting my photographs. Another slothful failure to get started on the pieces I must write for the short story anthology.

May 28. It seems as if I cannot shake off this tiredness. It comes on in midafternoon, and I have to lie down and doze; I'm fit for nothing. And it's particularly annoying right now, because there's so much I want to do.

We are snug in this house. It's a nice nest, and a good place to work. I can't say more than that. It doesn't lift up my heart. I don't feel that kind of wild romantic childhood joy that I used to feel on fine mornings in the house we rented out at Trancas.

Otherwise, Don and I live harmoniously, quite disinclined to go out, even to the movies. Don is reading through the stories I want to use for the Frank Taylor anthology. I find his reactions very valuable. He has already made me decide to throw out Stevenson's "Suicide Club."

Am also reading *Mistress Masham's Repose* by T. H. White, which Joshua Logan wanted me to consider turning into a movie. I fear I shall have to say no. It is hideously coy. And yet I hate to turn down the money. And the worst of it is, Logan probably thinks this is a masterpiece and we shall clash seriously.

May 30. Felt sick again last night and weary this morning, but always just able to do my stint for the day, which is something. So far, I have kept up with all my chores.

Last night, Marguerite came to supper with Ivan Moffat. Marguerite was on her way to the airport for another trip to New York. Clift, it now seems, won't be well till July. Everybody is on half-pay. The picture will cost fortunes. Marguerite, meanwhile, has a Long Island millionaire interested in her.

Ivan tells us that *Giant* is a masterpiece, and he feels that this is all due to George Stevens[1]—no one else. James Dean's selfishness as an actor; he did nothing whatever to help the girl.[2] Meanwhile, old Edna Ferber is writing a novel about the Esquimos in Alaska.[3]

What an interesting figure Ivan is! I feel I would like to know much more about him—what he really wants, what he hopes for. Is it to be a good writer? A good director? He seems to be avoiding marriage, and he repeatedly says that one of the great advantages of his house up on Adelaide is that you couldn't possibly share it with anyone else.

I think he is a prey to great terrors. Last night he talked about his horror of planes. Whenever he's in them, he expects to be burned alive.

The Duquettes' birthday party and dance for Beegle on the 27th was a sensation. Marion Davies' husband[4] threatened to shoot down the chandelier while Agnes Moorhead was reciting. "It'll be like Booth and Lincoln," he said. Later at Pickfair,[5] he somehow or other fired two shots, one of which grazed Mary Pickford's forehead.

Heard from Gerald Hamilton yesterday, confirming the news that Peter Watson is dead. But still no details.

June 4. Cedars of Lebanon Hospital. I came here last Friday, the 1st, after Dr. Sellars suddenly informed me that I had hepatitis—from Don, I suppose. The time of incubation was just right. Actually, I've been feeling lousy ever since May 17, when I started what Sellars thought was flu. Now that the jaundice is visibly "out," I'm better.

The unpleasant part of this illness is the feeling of utter fatigue. Also a tendency to grey thoughts of old age, weakness, death. These somewhat stimulated by reading Arnold Bennett's *Journals*—a very sympathetic man, but such a pitiful blind workhorse, self-driven until he dropped. At the end of it all, he could say: "I made a plan and stuck to it." Well, that's something, certainly. But the note of obstinacy is tragic, too. It's the obstinacy of an insect.

Being in this hospital is really quite absorbing. I see so many people

---

[1] The director; Moffat co-wrote the screenplay.
[2] Elizabeth Taylor.
[3] *Ice Palace* (1958); the film *Giant* was based on Ferber's 1952 novel.
[4] Captain Horace Brown.
[5] The house *Pick*ford and Douglas *Fair*banks, her second husband, had shared.

every day and it is possible to observe their reactions to a known and constant object, the Patient. I hope to write more about this when I have more energy.

My more immediate concerns are: how much is all this going to cost? And also the question of quarantine: Jo (who's just back with Ben from Florida) asked her doctor (Kirby) and was told on no account to visit me and on no account to see me or Don until five to six weeks after the end of the jaundice. This would mean, in my case, not until about August 1! Dr. Surrey, who is looking after me while Sellars is out of town, says all these precautions are quite unnecessary. They are far in excess, even, of what's demanded by the health department.

The bad part of it is that Jo and Ben would have been company for Don while I'm in here.

June 6. This being in the hospital gets quite tiresome, especially now that my symptoms are gradually disappearing. And yet I can't hope to get out for another three days at least.

What makes the place bearable is its good-humored inefficiency. We are awakened much too early, far too many people do tiny services for us—often the same service. Two different people cleaned my room this morning, and at the end of it I found a large piece of wood, which I'd dropped the night before, lying right in the middle of the floor. Most of the nurses seem to be colored. Colored people are of two kinds in the nursing profession; angels of cuteness or motherly sweetness—and real zombies, so dumb that they are rude, and so clumsy that they kick the bed every time they pass it. Thank God, there seem to be very few white nurses of the prim, we-know-best type. There's one very tiresome Russian male nurse, who thinks he has carte blanche to breeze in at all hours and talk—about himself and the parts he has acted in Russian colony dramatic shows here. He is studying to be a doctor. His name is Nicolas Tolotshko.

June 7. I'm slightly less mad at him today—for the quite usual reason that I have just done him a favor. I typed out for him an application in German to the University of Bonn, where he wants to study medicine.

View from my window. There really are cedars in front of this hospital. They are planted too close to the building. Beyond them, you see telegraph poles with lots and lots of wires. Four palms—about sixty to seventy feet tall, with small heads on them—the kind which seem typical of the older sections of Los Angeles. Dead fronds form a thick dry brownish muffler on two of the palms, reaching about three quarters of their length and coming to a point near the ground, so that they look like furled umbrellas. The other two palms have been clipped right up, nearly to their heads, so that they only wear throat mufflers. The principal building in sight is a block of apartments, red (brick?) with the windows outlined in white and a battlement design around the top of the facade. Could it be a tiny bit Venetian? A tiny bit Gothic? God knows. The houses in the foreground are white stucco boxes with tiled roofs, or cream-painted wood with green shingled roofs. There would be quite a lot more houses, palms, telegraph poles and TV aerials visible in the background, if it wasn't for a warm bright white haze which is only slightly smoggy.

June 8. Didn't sleep well last night, because of recurring backache; I have to keep taking aspirin to stop it. Now I'm waiting for my IV—dextrose and water—and waiting for the reappearance of Dr. Sellars, who has been in Chicago, I believe. I want to get him to let me go.

Being sick this time hasn't seemed at all inspiring or enlightening—only confusing. No revelations about life. Only the hint that one might quite well die asking: is *that* all? The end of life, a dark chaos and muddle for most people, no doubt. With the church and the journalists and all kinds of other agencies glibly explaining what is happening—and nobody believing one single word of his own explanation. Nevertheless, against all this, I *have* had some very strange glimpses and insights from reading Saradananda's Ramakrishna book. At least, he contrives to take you by the ear and drag you right up to face the unimaginable. At least, he gives you some slight idea of the infinite gap between Ramakrishna's world and yours. How utterly futile the conventional church religion seems, by comparison! No—not just futile. Quite, quite irrelevant. It has as much relation to what Ramakrishna meant by religion as running a dime store.

June 11. Back home, since Saturday the 9th.

And being back home has never been better. Don is looking after me with the utmost sweetness and consideration, and I feel, more strongly than ever before, that we are "kin"—related to each other in the deepest sense.

As for my symptoms—the backache has let up a little, but I still have to take aspirin for it. I get tired very easily—took two naps today.

June 15. Yesterday, they sent a doctor and a technician to do blood tests on me, and later Sellars came and told me the tests showed that the jaundice had absolutely disappeared. So I can get up and walk around, but mustn't leave the house for another week.

Jo and Ben cooked us a wonderful supper last night—chicken and vegetables—all wrapped in tinfoil. Don called for it and brought it home in a carton, and it was still hot.

First night without any pain.

All this week we've had glorious beach weather, and Don has been in swimming. He's going through a phase of Katherine Mansfield.

Speed came in, full of advice. I'm to write to Joshua Logan and keep him interested in the Mistress Masham project. This is quite sensible, and, God knows, we need the money. It's just that I *hate* the book—it's rotten slush. And, I have reservations about working with Logan, who seems to be a neurotic slave driver.

Still and all, we've got to get some money soon, somehow.

Miscellaneous news: Tarini died, about two weeks ago—without severe pain, I'm happy to say. Harry Brown has a new girlfriend, introduced to him by Speed, of course. Don has signed on for the summer term at the Chouinard art school. Speed may get a job at MGM.

June 17. I've worked very hard today—maybe a little too hard. I feel tired. Got to page forty-seven of my novel—still shooting for page sixty by July 1. Did my stint on the Ramakrishna book. Tried to start the article for Gerald Hamilton's book;[1] this was very difficult and I'm not sure I can do it. Also, Jo and Ben were in this afternoon and their visit was complicated by Madge MacDonald arriving to give me a shot and then wanting her little dog photographed immediately, so his picture could go in next Sunday's newspaper. So Ben took my camera, which luckily was supplied with film, and did it. The dog had to be placed on a table, with a plate of fruit beside him to show how small he is, and a screen behind him—for background. And oh, the yapping!

Seen from my window this morning—two of our next-door neighbors' (Heinz? Hines?) sons and another little boy, armed with spades, wooden guns, German-style tin helmets, advancing across the vacant lot opposite, on some military project.[2] The biggest boy had a pack on his back; he kept giving orders to halt, turn, etc.—which the smallest of the three did his best to obey. But whenever he halted his helmet would slip down over his eyes, and whenever he started turning he couldn't stop doing it until he fell down on his ass. All three kids wore long pants—blue jeans, one of them with cowboy boots—although they're so tiny. The sight of the smallest one desperately trying to imitate the others was touching, and at the same

[1] The Prologue to *Mr. Norris and I....*
[2] Isherwood later added in the margin: "(Used this in *A Single Man*)."

time horribly depressing, because you always feel: yes, and that's what he'll go on doing for the rest of his life.

Friday—day before yesterday—Swami came to tea, along with Krishna and John Yale. Don was pleased, because I told him that serving a meal to a Swami would probably save him five hundred rebirths. He also drank the remains of Swami's tea as prasad. I think that reading my 1939–44 diaries, which he has been doing, has made him much more interested in everything to do with Vedanta Place.

June 22. Yesterday I saw Sellars at his office in Beverly Hills. He said that I'm probably cured. His partner simply cannot believe that I could have recovered so quickly. However—no exertion for another month, and no fats. And no alcohol for at least six months. (Last time, he said a year.)

Also in Sellars's office (by appointment) I met a ghost from the past—Otto Guttchen. He called me a few days ago and asked if I would write him a letter to the German Consulate, recommending that he should receive his citizenship back—the Nazis took it away. It seems that he could have regained his citizenship quite easily, a few years ago. But 1952 was the deadline for such cases. Guttchen looked very well. He told me they removed one of his damaged kidneys about a year ago, and that since then he'd been feeling much better.

Chris Wood came to supper. Don cooked bouillabaisse, and we solemnly served him a whole bottle of white wine, which he couldn't finish. After supper, he became engrossed in a book of pictures of silent movies, and didn't leave until after eleven. Chris revels in nostalgia—a somewhat masochistic kind, for he gets kicks out of the pain of wishing he were back in the teens and the twenties.

Chris says that Gerald and Aldous and their circle are having frequent mescaline and lysergic acid sessions. I'm slightly mad at them both—rather childishly, I admit—because they snoot *my* experiences and tell people that my mescaline is of an inferior make. I do wish I could get hold of one of their doctors, though, and find out from him if it will be possible for me to take mescaline again, after this illness. The worst of it is, I can't trust Gerald not to persuade the doctor to tell me no. I'm sure the Huxleys persuaded Osmond not to give me any two years ago.

Michael Barrie and Bill Stroud are also on my blacklist because they haven't been in to see us. Michael is scared of infection, Chris thinks—but if he is, why can't he be man enough to say so? Harry Brown did.

A grey morning—quite quiet so far. The children on this street are being a sore trial. I used to blame everything on the boys next door, but the little girls opposite are really much more irritating. They come and play right under this window. And they slam the swing door of their house all day long, and the boys chase them around, and play miniature billiards on their porch. Besides—they are girls.

Yesterday, I sent off a little article—barely three pages—to Gerald Hamilton for his book. Thank God that's done with!

Utter silence from England. Still no news of Peter Watson's death. Nothing from M., Amiya, Dodie and Alec, Stephen, John Lehmann.

June 24. Don and I went to tea at Vedanta Place on Friday (the 22nd) with Swami, Aldous and Laura. It was rather a success. Swami seems to have accepted Don's relation to me as a matter of course. He said to Don, as we were leaving: "Come again—every time Chris comes." Aldous looked very handsome and was quite smartly dressed. Laura, no doubt, has spruced him up. She has also, probably, been the one who decided they should move from King's Road—up to a house on a road which is on the hillside above Hollywood—just below the "Hollywoodland" sign. They are going there soon, and selling the other house. I'm still not sure if I like Laura—but at least she tries to be friendly. They are to come and visit us soon.

Yesterday we saw *Anastasia*. Viveca Lindfors was excellent—[Eugenie] Leontovich very good toward the end, but wildly theatrical and affected—far more like a great actress in retirement than an ex-empress.[1]

Supper with Speed and Paul Millard, at the Sunset Frascati's. Douglas Dick[2] was there. Speed asked me to ask him to our table, and then snooted him. So typical. Speed's behavior is nearly always intolerable, unless you get him alone. A boring evening.

June 27. The Canyon is choked up by one of its local fogs. Don has gone off to the gym. I gave the kids next door our old weighing machine. The smallest one immediately began smashing it with a hammer, uttering, as he did so, cries of pain—he was making believe that the machine was crying out. Charming creatures! Why are we so sentimental about them and so horrified at the sight of a brood of baby snakes?[3]

A talk with Jo on the phone. She has a lot of trouble with nausea, sleeplessness, feelings of heaviness under the ribs. She thinks it's gallbladder.

---

[1] Isherwood and Bachardy saw a performance of Marcelle Maurette's play, later filmed with Ingrid Bergman and Helen Hayes.
[2] The actor.
[3] Beside this paragraph Isherwood later wrote: "(Used in *A Single Man*)."

Last night, John van Druten and Starcke came to dinner. John had been "terribly shocked" because Swami said that Christ's teaching was only for monks. He was very solemn about this. He always has the air of a judge very unwillingly pronouncing sentence. It hurts him more than it hurts the criminal, but he just *has* to do it. He can't conscientiously refrain.

John has written a fantastic play, which he may put on at some just-off-Broadway theater. He has also written an autobiographical book of opinions, called *Here We Go Looby-Loo* (or some such). I have provisionally entitled it: *Here We Go to the Loo.*[1]

As usual, John spread depressing waves around him. I think Starcke has something to do with it. He made me worry about the difficulty of finding a movie job. He says the film market is dead.

Again with the air of a judge—but this time awarding the Nobel prizes—he chose to borrow Mansfield's *Journal*, Plomer's *Child of Queen Victoria* and Pember's *The Needle's Eye*.

This morning I'm a bit depressed. Stomachache and money worries. But really I should never be seriously depressed as long as all goes well with Don. That's what chiefly matters to me.

June 30. John Yale came to tea yesterday to discuss a book of selections from Vivekananda they want to do.[2] He was in a very malicious mood, and eager to discuss John van Druten and Starcke. He said, "They use Swami for a rabbit's foot." He also commented on how nice Swami had been to Don when we went to tea there—and managed to insinuate that this was just tactics. But he was forced to admit that Don had made a very good impression on everybody at Vedanta Place.

Bob Hoover came in with Ted afterwards to say goodbye. Bob is leaving—has already left—this morning for New York to conduct a party around Europe for his travel agency.

Am trying to compose a note to Charlie Brackett about his film of *The King and I* which we saw at the premiere, the night before last. I *hate* Anna, that sweetly smiling, gently snooty apostle of democracy and "our" way of doing things. Hammerstein has written some of his vilest lyrics for this play—particularly the one about "whistling a little tune" and "Getting to Know You."

Have just talked to Johnnie on the phone about this. He says he

---

[1] The memoir was published as *The Widening Circle* (1957); the play was never produced.
[2] *What Religion Is: In the Words of Swami Vivekananda*, with an introduction by Isherwood and edited by John Yale (1962).

would never have agreed to do *Anna* if they hadn't got Gertrude Lawrence.[1]

A sore appeared in my mouth yesterday. I showed it to Dr. Peschelt who says it's caused by lingering results of the jaundice—excess uric acid. It's nasty to think of oneself as being full of bitterness but it's literally true. I only hope I can get rid of it.

Yesterday was the first day I did no work since I left hospital. Never mind, I'm quite well up in all my chores. Reached page sixty of my novel, kept to my schedule of Saradananda, and have done rough drafts of all the commentaries for the anthology. But still no word from Frank Taylor about this. I begin to suspect that the project is off.

July 1. Yesterday was a fine beach day (today is cloudy, so far) and Don and I were down there from 1:00 to 3:30 and again for a picnic supper with Jo and Ben. Went in swimming for the second time since I got sick. The water is fairly warm.

A record number of people I knew were around: Jim Charlton, who is hitting a new low of gloom because all his architectural projects have failed, and who wanted to know if this bad luck were his fault; I told him yes, partly. Ted, who had with him a boy named Mike Pederson whom I used to know in the 333 East Rustic Road days, when he was a friend of Harold Fairbanks. Also Wayne Parkes, whom Speed used to know in the Hartford Foundation days. And Ed Cornell, outraged because his friend wouldn't do the kitchen floor, and had called him "stupid." Also Paul Millard, who *is* stupid, I fear—maybe almost as stupid as Ed. Also Speed, who appeared briefly with Eva Wolas,[2] and was rude to Starcke. Starcke himself was as bouncy as ever. He took us over to where Johnnie was sitting, absurdly out of place amidst the holiday crowd, and somewhat sulky. Starcke held forth brightly about Johnnie's book, which Heinemann likes but wants called *The Widening Circle*. Also the usual urgings that I should write a play.

A picnic supper with Jo and Ben on the beach. Cold albacore. It was windy, turning cold, and we went back to their apartment for coffee; and talked about Jim and how his unfortunate surly manner gets him into so many difficulties. Jo wondered if she should speak to him about it, but despaired of making him understand.

Michael Barrie and Bill Stroud have got the flu again. It seems to be their chief indoor sport.

---

[1] Van Druten directed the Broadway musical version of *The King and I* which was based on the 1946 film *Anna and the King of Siam* (based in turn on the book about Anna Leonowens by Margaret Landon).

[2] His writing partner on stage and film projects.

This morning, Johnnie phoned after seeing *The King and I.* He liked it much better than we did, but not Deborah Kerr, whom he called "Mrs. Miniver at the Court of Siam."

Don hurt his back at the gym and again yesterday while swimming.

Our neighbor, Mr. Hines,[1] whom Speed called "The Buck," is shaming us again this morning by cutting the grass strip in front of our house. But he is also doing it across the road as well. Maybe, however, this is just a project for the oldest son's scouting; because the other week he fixed up a neighbor's garden, with the help of the rest of the family.

July 3. Yesterday, Don started work at the Chouinard art school. The first day seems to have been a great success. Don was able to follow the instruction and certainly his first attempts at figure drawing are really quite amazingly good. He came home in good spirits. He had been dreading this start for weeks.

Yesterday afternoon I went to see Eddie From, who is spending the summer with Hans Hokanson at one of those shacky houses out among the oil derricks, beyond Venice. Each of the little cross streets is called an "avenue" or a "place" alternately. Each contains maybe six houses and ends on the beach. They have yards which are simply sand lots. The creaking of the oil pumps is louder than the surf.

Eddie looked sick—sallow and red eyed. He had his usual air of quietly amused patronage—the children (all of us) make him smile, just a little wearily. His adventures with a Catholic millionaire in Columbus, Ohio. He says he doesn't like to go up to the Palazzo,[2] it reminds him of Sam. And the life there is no longer campy, but merely comfortable.

Am making a drive to do forty pages this month on my novel, which will get me to 100 pages by August 1st. Am having great difficulties with the anthology—the introduction to Conan Doyle. It seems that I can't hit the right note.

Let me never forget that this is really a very happy time for me. Steady work which interests me. Don busy and happy—I think. And a nice comfortable home.

July 5. I'm glad the Fourth is over. It always makes a big gap in the continuity of things. Also, yesterday was dull. Don, just getting into the swing of art school, felt at a loss. He has just been reading the

[1] Here Isherwood added two notes in the margin: "Or maybe Hind—we have a lot of trouble with this man's name." And later, "No—it's apparently Hine!"
[2] The house he had shared with his brother, Sam, recently dead, and others; see Glossary under From.

passages in my 1944 journal about X., and this put him into a suspicious, questioning mood. He finds my attitude toward X. cynical—which I suppose it is, in a sense. The point is, I am attacking the X. sensations quite subjectively as if they were symptoms of a disease I longed to get rid of. And, at the same time, I'm dwelling morbidly on these symptoms—gloating over them, indeed. It's the same attitude that's so distasteful in Proust. He talks constantly of love, yet it's clear that he really loathes Albertine.

Don returns again and again to the examination of my character—with the furious impatience, indignation and fascination of one who studies a book which is full of matters vitally interesting to him, but which is very badly and ambiguously written. What *does* the goddam author mean?

Don is going through a phase which is very important in his development and much more positive than his moods of last winter. I think that the art school may really be an answer to his vocational problem. But now he has to get to feel independent in himself, and thus turn his dependence on me into a free association. This will be a great test for both of us, of course.

The day before yesterday, a man named Bob Vogel came to see me. He is the secretary(?) of the Friends Service Committee out here. He wants me to participate in their work in some way, and I probably will. Also, he tells me that the Friends have a center in Berlin which deals with the emigration of Germans to the States. This would be a possible way for Heinz and his family to get here. And now the question arises—do I want them to come? And the answer is NO. But have I the right to withhold help for them to come? No, of course not. Don warns me against getting into this mess. I warn myself. But what else am I to do?

Chief topic of talk: the double air crash near the Grand Canyon.[1] I have two ideas for bad-taste imaginary advertisements: "Fly American Airlines and see the Grand Canyon—from above." "Fly United Airlines and meet people—from TWA."

July 8. A grey day, which is disappointing, because the last two have been wonderful on the beach, with big surf. Ted is staying the night with us, and now he and Don are working on the project which was set them by one of their instructors at the Chouinard—Ted goes there two evenings a week, and they are both studying composition.

My various chores keep me steadily going. Am up to page seventy-two of the novel. It couldn't seem sillier or more inept, but

---

[1] On June 30, a TWA flight bound for Kansas City collided with a United Airlines DC-7 headed for Chicago and Newark; 128 were killed.

nevertheless great chunks of subconscious intention are gradually separating themselves off and fitting into the scheme of the book.

Don has started well at the Chouinard, I hope and think—although he is worried about oil painting. He is still full of tensions and problems, and so am I, of course; but all this will straighten itself out if only we keep our wigs on and give it time.

Joshua Logan has gone away to Japan, Fred Zinnemann hasn't called me, MGM is said to be cutting salaries. Well, we shall see. I'm worried, but somehow not seriously. Not yet.

Gerrit Lansing, Sam Costidy's friend, is here on a short visit. He has grown quite sloppy-fat, but is very amiable and quite intelligent. I like him very much.

This is a great period for rejection neurosis. Some of the people who have rejected me, or Don, or both: Peggy, Michael Barrie, Gerald, Aldous, Gottfried Reinhardt, Joan Elan, the Bracketts, Marguerite, Jessie Marmorston. But, on inspection, this list gets considerably shorter. Peggy, I needn't speak of—I could go back to her at any time—on her terms. Michael *did* react, after I'd let him know we were offended, through Chris Wood, that invaluable ambassador; he came around with Bill Stroud and a portable radio which he didn't want—but unfortunately Swami was having tea with me (to talk about obscure passages in Saradananda's Ramakrishna book) so Michael left again immediately in a sharp frost. Gerald is probably just busy; Aldous ditto. Gottfried, I hear from Speed, is in town and working at Columbia—*he* might have called, but since when have I expected any attention from film people? Joan is a more solid rejection candidate; she has been here quite a while and we have heard nothing from her. The Bracketts *did* send a couple of tickets to *The King and I* which I hated, and Muff is away; so that's nothing.

Marguerite is in New York and never writes—but why should she? Jessie hasn't called, and that's *really* mysterious, after all the fuss she used to make.

But how many people have *I* rejected (neglected)?: Harry Brown, Rodney Owens, Paul Sorel, Carter Lodge and Dick Foote, everybody up at the Palazzo From, etc. etc. And what's the reason? Just simple apathy. Why, right in this Canyon are at least half a dozen people I should see occasionally, and don't—Mrs. Hoerner, Don Litebaum, Jack Dominguez, Bob Gallagher, Lee Mullican,[1] Renée Rubin. Oh, yes, and then there's Virginia Viertel—but at least we did call her once, and she never called back.

---

[1] Mullican, a painter, lived next door to Isherwood and Bachardy's Mesa Road house; Litebaum, Gallagher, and Dominguez were friends of Caskey, and Isherwood knew them during the 1940s.

Fred Zinnemann just called. As always very cordial and stalling desperately. Why doesn't he call me next Thursday? Fine, I say; do that. But he won't.

July 9. An idea I had yesterday—to turn the living room gradually into a big studio-sitting room, put in the north skylight that Jim recommended, get rid of the piss-elegant furniture we bought from Hal Greene, make the place human. This is a long-term objective.

If only every day could be like today—I worked on my novel, the Ramakrishna book *and* the anthology (about Chesterton), did errands in town, spent nearly two hours on the beach, wrote to M. (from whom I've just heard, worried because Amiya told her I'd had jaundice) *and* am about to water the garden!

Glorious weather. Another swimming day.

Resolves—to read *Piers Plowman* (or at least the extracts in Wystan's anthology[1]), more Chaucer, *Don Quixote* and all of the *Divine Comedy*. Also do something about Spanish.

Reached page seventy-six of rough draft of *The Forgotten.* Am reading O'Flaherty, O'Faolain, etc. to see if I can find extra Irish stories, as Frank Taylor requests. Tomorrow I am seeing Jerry Wald about a possible job. I want one and yet I don't, because this working at home is really my ideal of happiness, right now.

In the morning, after the men (including Don) have left for work, the women and children take over on this street. Mrs. Hine is heard in her corncrake voice, admonishing her youngest: "Stay out of the road now, won't you? Put that bottle back! Back in the can! Back! Put it back, now! Atta Boy!" Two little girls sit on a porch fanning a small dog. They giggle when they see I've seen what they are doing. Greg, Mrs. Hine's youngest, will *never* forgive me for running him off our steps. He calls me "that man."[2]

Today, two people on the rejector list were heard from—Marguerite wrote, Joan Elan phoned.

July 13. Eight twenty-four in the morning—our breakfast made, eaten, cleared away. Don's lunch—turkey sandwiches with lettuce—prepared and packed. Don seen off to school with his half-finished oil painting of the lantern on the chair, his colors, his notes, his palette, etc. Late for a rendezvous with a girl student named [Jeanne] Le Gon, whom he's to drive in to school every morning.

---

[1] *Poets of the English Language* (1952), edited by Auden and Norman Holmes Pearson.

[2] Beside this paragraph Isherwood added: "(Used in *A Single Man.*)"

The satisfaction in this for me—as in so much of life—is just the sense of having fulfilled a schedule, beaten the clock.

Yesterday afternoon I was so exhausted that I slept for three and a half hours. This pleased Don very much. And today I feel plenty of energy again. Waking this morning, I was aware, as often before, how dulled the mind and senses become, as you get older. Or is it just the senses that are dulled? Is the mind even maybe clearer for a while and better able to grasp things?

What I really find wrong with the way I spend my life is this—and I've been commenting on it on and off for the past twenty-five years at least—I'm so apt to lead the life of symbolic action. I'm so apt to carry out the *forms* of action, merely writing forty pages a month, no matter what. Even in my relationships, even in my religion (such as it is) I'm so apt to step aside and call the attention of a third party (*who* is he?) to what I am making or being—like a guide taking tourists around a city and showing the quaint natives at work. To so many (not all—yet!) of the pleasures of my life, you could tie the label: "as advertised." Even now, I'm writing a "sincere" entry in this journal—"self-revealing"—"as advertised."

That's what Edward and I meant by "The Watcher in Spanish" at Cambridge: the Devil of self-consciousness.[1] And yet—it's something to be aware of this falseness and emptiness. *Nothing* is safe from it. There is no top shelf on which I can put my superior experiences. No—all I can say is: amidst the grey mud there are occasional sparkles of genuineness. Alas, they are *mostly* the product of pain, anxiety, a bad scare; then something comes through. Because the advertisements don't include pains and scares, your reactions are your own.

(Even now, I feel satisfaction at having written nearly a whole page of *pensées*!)

July 16. Another Monday morning. Glorious weather. The garden too dry. I feel guilty about this, but never seem to get it properly watered. Chores, chores, chores. And yet I'm happy. It's so good to see Don go off to school really pleased with his work and eager to learn more. We're worried about Ted, though. It seems possible he may be getting up steam for another attack. Right now, he's all alone except for us—Bob Hoover away in Europe for another month or more. Even Mr. and Mrs. Bachardy away on a trip to Las Vegas, Yellowstone, etc. (This is truly a remarkable decision, because Mr. Bachardy is so stingy.)

Harry Brown visited us yesterday with his girlfriend, June [de Baum]. He seems in good spirits and doesn't look drink-sodden. She

---

[1] Described in *Lions and Shadows*, chapter 2.

seems nice, but playing it careful, as well she may! Rather a piss-English accent; actually she's from Rhode Island.

Everybody remarks on Don's physique. Two months at the gym have really built him up extraordinarily, especially the arms and pectoral muscles.

Meeting our neighbor Roy Parry—the MGM scene painter—on the street the other day: he said to me, "When I was young, I never knew when Christmas was until I saw the pantomime posters." *What* is one supposed to answer to such a remark?

On the beach yesterday. Jo and Ben with hangovers after a luau. (It's interesting what an intense aversion they both now express toward teenagers; as if they really feared them.) Jim Charlton cheerful again because he has a house to do and a remodelling job promised by Fred Zinnemann on a ranch house near Nogales. It's noticeable how good Jim looks now. His figure is still like a boy's, and he must be going on forty. Also Speed (whose figure is, on the contrary, a bit bulgy!) lamenting because I told him van Druten is going to write *First Love*[1] as a movie for Hecht-Lancaster.[2] That rather unpleasant person, Ted Schultz, reports that Bill Stroud showed up at his apartment yesterday and asked if he might stay. This is *very* mysterious because Michael Barrie assured us—on Saturday—that Bill was in the East visiting relatives and wouldn't be back till September 1! Our rapprochement with Michael followed a tea with Gerald, on Saturday afternoon. (Gerald and Michael have now left for a week's seminar in the redwoods near Santa Cruz.) Michael proved to be rather dull, however. He got drunk very easily and became snail tongued and sententious. It's amusing to see what puritans Don and I have become, since we stopped drinking. We serve drinks, but scowl at the drinkers.

Swami called yesterday, much worried because Willie Maugham had sent him an article on the Maharshi, and *all* the philosophy in it was wrong![3] Now we have to concoct a tactful reply.

No novel yesterday or Saturday. But I still have several days in hand. I only need eight days to reach page 100. The anthology is dragging, though.

July 18. Fred Zinnemann has just been here, to talk about the possibility of our doing *The Narrow Corner*[4] together. I rather doubt if

[1] Turgenev's novella.
[2] The production company; see Glossary.
[3] "The Saint"; see Glossary under Maugham.
[4] Maugham's 1932 novel.

anything will come of this—we shall see. At any rate, I'd far rather work on that and with him than go for any of the other possible offers.

Every day is a scramble—to get my stint of the Ramakrishna reading and of my novel done—to water some of the garden—to buy what's required from the market. It's a very happy time, though.

The day before yesterday, we met Perle Mesta at the Duquettes'. Speed had brought her there. He seemed to be turning quickly into a television impresario.[1] But Mesta herself wasn't nearly as vulgar or silly as I'd expected—indeed, she seemed shrewd and competent. She talked about the extraordinary behavior of the Russians—now hot, now cold—when they invited her to come to visit the country. She still doesn't know exactly why they asked her.

Today I rewrote a page of my novel—the poetry parodies. This is a dangerous practice. I must drive blindly forward.

Zinnemann's face, as he grows older, is becoming severe and eccentric looking. There is something aristocratically birdlike about it. He looks like an autocratic old lady of good family, or her grimly beaked parrot. Yet he is kind, helpful. You feel he is the servant of everybody—darting hither and yon, like a waiter, in obedience to the commands of his own conscience.

He says Montgomery Clift has the same urge to self-destruction as James Dean had.

July 21. A bad evening. After quite a long period of the happiest relations, Don flew into a rage with me as we were going to the beach this morning, because I wanted to cross the road by the underpass—if you dodge through the traffic you're liable to get a ticket. He sulked on and off all afternoon. Now he has gone out to spend the evening on his own—as why in the world shouldn't he? The bad thing is that he has to make all this fuss to lead up to doing what he might do so easily and pleasantly. He said: "I'm getting so much older and nothing is happening." I take this to mean that he wants some kind of sex adventures—since quite a lot has certainly happened to him in other ways. Well, that's only natural. And my part of the deal is somehow to get it through his head that all this can take place without ugliness. Oh dear, it's so fatal to be spiteful and sulky! It destroys everything.

So now I'm sad and depressed, and facing a lonely evening of dull work. Just the same, I shall be glad to have gotten the work over with—*if* I do it. It's the corrections Swami wants me to write Willie Maugham on his Maharshi article.

What's so disconcerting, when something like this situation with

---

[1] Lamkin was writing a TV show about Mesta; see Glossary under Lamkin, Speed and under Mesta.

Don takes place, is that I realize how insecure my "home life" is. Of course, my "home life" isn't the whole of my life, thank God—but I feel the insecurity, just the same. It's inside myself. At the least setback I feel wearily, Oh, what's the use, why did I buy this house, why do I make any effort at all?

July 22. What actually happened was that Don came back, after seeing *Juarez* at the Coronet, and we had supper together at Ted's [Grill]—and now all is peace. Armistice, rather. This isn't settled, perhaps won't ever be, except by time. Don says he gets this terrible sense of loneliness—the inability to communicate with anyone, even me.

Met Speed and Paul Millard on the street after supper last night, and had a drink at the Friendship. It has quite lost its atmosphere. Instead of the long narrow crowded room, you have a big empty space behind your back as you sit at the bar—the wall has been taken out, and this is what used to be Doc Law's drug store, completely empty now—except for the old photographs of Santa Monica bathing beauties, and a pool table and the shuffle board.

Speed talked about Hedda Hopper[1]—how amusing she is. I'm afraid corruptness is going to prevent Speed from ever becoming the sort of American Balzac he could possibly be. This tolerance of what is rotten and evil is very dangerous for a novelist. Or I should say "tolerance" period. Because the actual moral standards the novelist has are quite unimportant, as long as he does have *some* standards. No standards, no indignation. No indignation, no steam pressure. No steam pressure, no drama. You can't be Balzac on a wry ironic smile.

July 24. I have the yawns. Just slept an hour but still tired. Am slightly worried that this may be a relapse. Yesterday I had a high stomachache all day. I eat and eat and eat. Soon I shall be really fat again.

But today I got to page 100, by dint of doing four pages, so I'm well on schedule, or rather, well ahead of it. Getting on with the introduction to the anthology, as well.

Grey all day long at the beach. Terribly hot in town, they say. Yesterday, Don was praised by his figure-drawing instructor, and his drawing was held up for the admiration of the whole class.

July 26. Have just finished *Basilissa* by John Masefield. There are about half a dozen of his later books in the Santa Monica library. I want to read all of them. I sometimes think I'm the only person in the world who admires him. What is his charm, for me?

[1] Actress and columnist.

"Theodora, the cast mistress of Hekebolos…"

"She was dressed in black, and wept as she went."

"…a Syrian woman, with a pale, ugly, clever face…"

"Most theaters are flower shows," he said, "displaying youth in flower."[1]

I can't explain why I like this kind of thing so much. Perhaps it is just a sense of personal contact with Masefield himself that I get—and he is such a lovable man.

Other books I have to read or finish off:

Dante, *Don Quixote, John Inglesant,*[2] *The Lion and the Fox,*[3] *The Sorrows of Young Werther,*[4] *The Bachelor's House,*[5] *The Devil,*[6] *The Quest for Corvo,*[7] *An Outcast of the Islands,*[8] *Practical Criticism*[9]—to name a few!

Zinnemann just called. *The Narrow Corner* deal is definitely off. But there's still the possibility of David Brown's Japanese picture.[10] And I suppose Joshua Logan will return from Japan *some* day.

Don is skirting along the edge of a bad mood. I do wish something nice would come up for the weekend, to make him feel better.

Now I have to rewrite the Maugham corrections, which were not correct. Swami has just been on the phone about this.

Later. 8:05 p.m. The papers full of the sinking of the *Andrea Doria.*[11]

Don is out with Ted, and I'm here alone. For no reason except that I want to be. Rod Owens, whom I drove up to see this afternoon, warmly invited me to supper. He really is nice. I do wish Don didn't feel so resentful against him, but I guess this will all be cleared up, sooner or later.

Have just discovered a parking ticket issued against the Sunbeam by the Beverly Hills police. Should I pay it and say nothing? If I do, then Don will feel I'm treating him like a child. If I mention it, however, he will feel guilty and rebuked. Perhaps I'll lead up to it by

---

[1] All four quotations are from the first chapter of Masefield's *Basilissa: A Tale of the Empress Theodora* (1940).

[2] *John Inglesant: A Romance* (1881), by J. H. Shorthouse.

[3] Probably Wyndham Lewis's *The Lion and the Fox: The Role of the Hero in Shakespeare's Plays* (1927), republished in 1955.

[4] By Goethe.

[5] A 1956 translation by Frances Frenaye of Balzac's *La Rabouilleuse, ou Un Ménage de garçon.*

[6] By Tolstoy.

[7] A. J. A. Symons's biography of Frederick William Rolfe ("Baron Corvo").

[8] By Conrad.

[9] By I. A. Richards.

[10] *The Barbarian and the Geisha.*

[11] Accidentally struck sideways on by the *Stockholm,* July 25, off Nantucket; all but forty-six of 1,706 aboard were saved. Isherwood and Bachardy travelled on the *Andrea Doria* from Gibraltar to Naples in November 1955.

telling him that *I* was stopped for speeding today. The cop asked me how fast I thought I was going. "About fifty," I said. "Exactly," said the cop, "in a thirty-five mile zone. But you're the first honest man I've met today. I'm letting you off."

I worry so much about Don. Can he gradually ease himself out of his insecurity without deciding that I'm to blame for it and revolting against me? Things *do* seem better, but he's often unhappy and dissatisfied. What he needs are friends of his own. But he won't make them. Presumably there must be plenty of potential friends at the Chouinard and the gym.

July 27. But Don came home happy, because the professor had praised his design above every other in the class. "Why do I want so terribly to be liked?" he asked me.

I should have said yesterday that Rod Owens made a very good impression on me. And I didn't think he looked so fat, at all. (Speed had viciously described him as "a spayed cat.") Their place is really beautiful, now. All the trees are growing up. Two beautiful rice-paper trees, on either side of the front door, give a real jungly effect. Rod says Caskey still owns the lot on the hilltop. He has paid off all the installments on it, and it's cost him $10,000! No more news of him, it seems.

This morning, I drove into Beverly Hills and paid the ticket, because in one place on the ticket it said you had only five days' grace. On the envelope, it said ten. The woman clerk told me that actually it's two weeks! I'm always scrupulously careful where the law is concerned. I think of myself as a serious criminal who can't afford to get caught out on trifles. (Caskey, Rod says, has let all kinds of payments slide, with the result that they might easily find out about his property and attach it.)

July 29. The night before last, we had supper with Jo and Ben. They fixed Japanese food. Afterwards we had a potentially interesting discussion: Why, said Jo, don't we get around more—have more contacts with other people? It was only potentially interesting, because nobody quite spoke his mind. What did Jo mean by "getting around?" Apparently just a very quick peek at other people's lives and then a hasty retreat, lest one should get seriously involved. What did Ben mean? He quoted a remark of Peter Gowland's (made, it seems, in the presence of his wife and therefore, somewhat sadistically) that he didn't care to go to parties because he couldn't make passes at girls and lay them—and that was all that parties were for. Ben expressed, perhaps, a tacit agreement; but he didn't dare say so. As for Don, he's still in the midst of the great problem: Why won't people be interested in me? And yet he already half knows his own answer: Because I'm not sufficiently interested in *them*.

Last night, supper with Johnnie and Starcke. Starcke talked about the Joel Goldsmith reading room he has set up, and about his own healing work. He was trying to find out, through me, why Swami disapproves of the healing. And of course I know why. Because, whatever you may say, it's *wrong* for Starcke: whenever he talks like this, you see "salesman" written all over him. His metaphysical talk may be perfect sense, but one hardly bothers to listen to it, because *he* is false, false. By this, I do not mean repulsive. As a matter of fact, I rather like Starcke; and in a curious way, he makes a very sympathetic fake.

As for Johnnie, we think he's bored by Starcke's spiritual flights but also intimidated. He doesn't dare utter a word; but maybe he *longs* to exclaim: "Get you, Mary!"

August 1. Last night, Johnnie and Starcke came to have dinner with *us*. The Bracketts had been invited and called it off at the last moment, because (they *said*) Charlie had to preview his new picture with Zanuck. Whether this was true or not, Johnnie and Starcke were relieved, and so were we, and it was really a nice evening, despite the behavior of our movie projector, which mysteriously speeded up in the midst of showing our Europe trip film, and couldn't be made to slow down.

The truth is, we get along with Johnnie and Starcke and feel comfortable with them and like them, despite all the bitchy things I say about them in this journal. Johnnie described Charlie coming down to lunch absolutely exhausted, to meet a guest he didn't want to see, and then, at the last turn of the staircase, pulling himself together and exclaiming: "Where's my favorite woman?"

Yesterday I got a letter from a professor at the University of Mississippi (wanting to quote from the Gita). On the envelope was stamped—with a rubber stamp, in red ink: "With a tradition of Quality, Integrity and Progress"—as though this were a meat-packing firm.

Have bought a new pen—a Shaeffer Snorkel. The old Parker covers my fingers with ink even after it has been immersed in water and washed out. Almost miraculous—like one of those sacred pictures that bleed.

August 6. Oh dear, Don is depressed again! After working all yesterday evening on a design problem and failing to solve it, he became terribly gloomy, said nothing was fun, he wasn't really enjoying art school, he'd been desperately scared that his youth was slipping away from him and that there would be no future, etc. If *only* I knew how to handle him! But I don't. Deep down, I'm selfishly resentful because I want to get on with my own work and this mood of his weakens me and makes me unhappy, but this is mere selfishness, and I wish I knew the answer. If only Don would make friends of his own and go out more. He says he wants what Speed calls "glitter." Well, why not?

Me, I only know that I must go on working. And making much more japam.

We saw Evelyn Hooker on Saturday—just about to leave for the High Sierras with Edward. Then she's going to read a startling paper to a congress in Chicago which will state (1) that there are exactly as many well-adjusted homosexuals (percentually) as heterosexuals (2) that homosexuality may, in certain cases, be regarded as psychologically as well as biologically "normal." All this was arrived at by getting a great expert to examine a large batch of ink-blot tests.[1] The expert arrived at these conclusions very unwillingly and against his own theories. Maybe this will be celebrated one day as a great historic event—Hooker reading the Declaration of Adjustment.

August 9. Rush, rush! I'm always in a hurry, it seems.

Right now, I've just managed to catch up on my novel, haven't done my anthology work, haven't worked on Ramakrishna, haven't read *The Lost Girl*,[2] haven't answered letters, haven't shaved. Haven't had enough sleep, because we keep staying up late. And all this rushing is in order to have time to rush down to San Diego—well, anyway La Jolla—the weekend after next, and then maybe rush up to San Francisco the weekend after *that*! What do I *really* want to do? Lie flat on my back and relax. Then why don't I—it only takes fifteen minutes. Because the rushing bee is in my bonnet.

August 14. Another entry just made in order not to break my record. This is definitely not a good diary-keeping time for me. I really *am* busy, no kidding about that. This morning we woke late—7:50—so I had ten minutes to get breakfast, make Don his sandwiches. Don left shortly after 8:00 for school, as usual. Then I listened to the news (Suez seems "better" at the moment, but is still dangerously "sick"[3])

---

[1] Isherwood added "Rorschach" in the margin. The expert was Bruno Klopfer; see Glossary under Hooker, Evelyn.

[2] By D. H. Lawrence.

[3] Egypt had nationalized the Suez Canal July 26; see Glossary under Suez crisis.

while I washed up the breakfast things, read what Wystan has to say about heroic couplets[1] while I was shitting, worked on the Ramakrishna book (a double portion, to get it over with) till 10:00. Since then I've written four pages of my novel (because I'm rushing to finish the 150 pages this week), watered most of the front garden, talked to Jo and a travel service (about motel reservations at La Jolla) on the phone and read mail from Tito (verging on suicidal despair in Mexico) and a lady from New Zealand (wanting to know what happened to Sally Bowles). I now have to do at least one of the prefaces to an author for my anthology; two would be desirable. *And*, if possible, write some letters. *And*, if possible, get my driver's license renewed.

Since Saturday afternoon, a *great* improvement in Don's morale. On Sunday we cycled up the coast to the beach house Shelley Winters has rented. A typical Jewish chaos of elderly female relatives and young kids. Not enough to eat. A very ineffective barbecue. Don and I had to cook the hamburgers by lighting bits of paper under them. The water was good for swimming, though, and I felt nostalgic because the house where Dodie and Alec used to live was only a few doors away.

Ivan Moffat said Patrick Kinross[2] looked like the summer number of *Punch*—his baldness and his potbelly.

The girl who stayed on the telephone all afternoon.

William Marchant, who wrote *The Desk Set*,[3] taking pictures with his Polaroid camera—one of me coming out of the ocean decked in seaweed—and being cured of a headache with Miltown.[4]

Jim Charlton has at last passed his architect's exam.

August 15. This rush of work is becoming quite compulsionistic, but it's good, I guess. My three objectives, before we leave for our trip north on the 24th or 25th—get to page 150 of novel, finish the anthology, finish the Saradananda book. That'll really be a big chunk of stuff accomplished.

Heavy, misty heat, smog in town. The radio full of the Democratic convention. Am still stalling on the two jobs at Fox—the Townsend Harris story and Lawrence's *The Lost Girl*. But I'd prefer working on the Lawrence and with Wald—or rather *not* with Frenke.[5]

---

[1] In the introduction to *Poets of the English Language*, volume 3.
[2] Third Baron Kinross (1904–1976), journalist and travel writer.
[3] 1955 Broadway play (later a film).
[4] A tranquilizer; see Glossary.
[5] Eugene Frenke produced *The Barbarian and the Geisha*, about Townsend Harris, an 18th-century American ambassador to Japan.

Don is absorbed in his design for the week. This'll be a late night. He's looking tired—so late to bed, getting up early and dashing out half asleep, and then slaving at the gym in this heat; but he's in a very good sweet mood. I hope the blues are leaving him for a while.

Vernon Old called me today. He wanted me to put a girlfriend of his, an actress named Joanna Merlin, in touch with Starcke and Johnnie. She's going to New York shortly, looking for a job. So is Michael Hall. Vernon is very, very grown-up nowadays, not to say elderly. I noticed that he has an excellent accent when he pronounces French words. His son Chris is six. Patty his wife remarried.

August 20. Got off to a good start today in finishing my pre-birthday chores. Wrote forewords to three stories for the anthology—Forster, Katherine Mansfield, Graves.

Don got an A at school for life drawing, with a special commendation.

Ben's book of stories[1] has been definitely accepted by Methuen.

John van Druten is greatly upset because Hecht-Lancaster doesn't like his screenplay on *First Love*.

This evening we had supper at The Cock 'n Bull, as guests of William Marchant. Barbara Baxley, who played Sally Bowles on Broadway while Julie was filming *Member of the Wedding* was there. I doubt if Baxley can have been right for Sally—she looks too much like Bette Davis. But I like her, and I really quite like Marchant. He reminds me greatly of Tony Duquette, but is much nicer. "Light" but amusing dinner talk about Forest Lawn posters, books, plays, etc.

This last weekend, we drove down to Coronado, stayed at the wonderful wooden seventy-year-old hotel, then up to La Jolla to see Viveca Lindfors in *Miss Julie*—not very good, chiefly because Stephen Bekassy[2] was so stupid. But we had some nice swimming at Coronado, La Jolla and San Onofre Beach—on the way home. Don in very good spirits, and so was I, except for a background anxiety about the Suez crisis.

August 22. Another late night for Don. I open this chiefly to report progress.

I now have an almost all right draft of the foreword to Ethel Mayne.[3] Which means I can get that fixed tomorrow. Then there's only Dylan Thomas.

Still about thirty pages of the Saradananda book to read.

---

[1] *Partly Submerged.*
[2] Hungarian actor.
[3] For *Great English Short Stories.*

Still three and three-quarter pages of my novel to write—or a bit more, if necessary, to get through to the end of part three, which will be a good place to stop.

Possible obstacles: an interview at Fox with Brown on the Harris story and/or with Wald on the Lawrence novel.

This evening I finished Johnnie's manuscript, *The Widening Circle*. So dreadfully sententious.

Got my driver's license renewed, with four mistakes. The chief one: I didn't know or remember that a car coming out of a cross street from your right has the right of way. But that's easy: if he's *from* the right he *is* right!

A man from Jehovah's Witnesses came to the door and argued with me for nearly half an hour. He seemed to think it very important to find out from the Bible what God had foretold would happen to the world. I said I didn't see it mattered if the Kingdom of Heaven came here on earth or somewhere else. Then, of course, he started in about the destruction of the wicked. Told him I don't believe in it.

To the public library to find out what I could about Ethel Mayne. Apparently there was an article about her death by Rebecca West in the May 3, 1941 issue of *The New York Herald Tribune*. Must get this. Got two issues of *The Yellow Book* with her pitiful fluttery little stories. She improved almost incredibly, later.

August 25. Thursday I finished Saradananda's Ramakrishna book and the third part of my novel, to page 151. Yesterday I finished the anthology with a piece on Dylan Thomas, and sent it off to Frank Taylor.

This morning, Kinsey[1] died, of a heart attack. I found that some kind of dark mold had started in the remaining mescaline capsules, so I flushed them down the toilet.

Preparations for leaving on our trip, tomorrow morning. We're going up to see Brad Saunders first, at Fairfield.

Who should turn up on the beach but Dick LaPan. He lives down in Guadalajara now and teaches English. He says he much prefers Mexico to the States; people are kinder. He even tolerates the Catholic Church.

After a week of marvellous weather, we had a light fog most of today, but the water was warm and the surf quite big.

August 26. Twenty of eleven, and we haven't even begun to pack—so no time for philosophical birthday statements. Am too fat but in good health.

[1] Alfred Kinsey, the sex researcher.

Johnnie van Druten called me in the middle of the night to tell me how wonderful he thought *War and Peace* was as a film. He and Starcke were leaving later for Honolulu to consult Joel Goldsmith—partly, I guess, because of Johnnie's disappointment at Hecht-Lancaster.

August 27. Hasty notes before starting—7:25 a.m.—from a motel in King City. We drove up here yesterday, along a back road which was marvellously uncrowded considering this was a Sunday—via Ojai, Maricopa, Coalinga. The pale lion-furred landscape, with soft looking hills—actually they're prickly with dried grasses—soft and rather indecent, with hollows like buttocks have or dimples in shoulders. The oil country around Maricopa, almost absurdly ugly, especially as billboards congratulate you on travelling this "fabulous" route. Maricopa was very hot. The two skinny old women in the Texaco station. They came from Oklahoma. One of them spat. And the derricks all around.

Keefer's restaurant, where we ate in King City—would do as a setting for the first chapter of my novel; his last night in the States. Oz-land furnishings. The beaten copper bar. The nursery mural of rooftops, rather German. The crazy up and down shelf with bits of china on it. Oh, I can't describe it, but I shall remember.

August 28. At the Solano Motel outside Fairfield. We drove up here yesterday, via Salinas, San Jose, Oakland, Berkeley, arriving around 2:00 p.m. We called Bradley Saunders and he came over for us right away and drove us out to the Travis airfield. Brad is attached to MATS, Military Air Transportation Service; but the base is also used by the Strategic Air Command, which has B-36 bombers ready to deliver "thermo-nukes" anywhere, anytime.

Brad took us over his plane, a C-124. It is enormous. In the air it looks like a dirigible, its body is so thick and heavy. It can carry a tank, or 200 men or 17,000,000 ping-pong balls. The shabby looking pilot's cabin, reached by a ladder, about thirty feet above the ground; dozens and dozens of dials. The sanitary toilets behind a curtain, with sanitary towels for women. Brad said: "You don't pilot a B-36; you command it." Later we saw a jet landing (only the latest models have to be stopped by parachute), and another taking off, and a B-36 landing, and part of an A-bomb being wheeled past, like the Blessed Sacrament, under a tarpaulin.

Last March, Brad's roommate Jim was about to take off in a C-124. But they had put the elevator flaps on backwards, so it went straight up into the air and turned upside down and burst into flames. Three were killed, three, including Jim, were saved but badly burned. The civilian employee responsible for this was censured but not fired.

Jim is still going to hospital every day for treatment but he has returned to share Brad's apartment. He is badly scarred but not actually disfigured. Now Brad is making up his mind if he shall set up housekeeping with his Aunt Lavinia and her daughter. Jim is going to get married.

The life on the base sounds acutely depressing. They all drink gallons and watch television and Brad rates as *the* intellectual. Almost everyone is married and the wives are mostly waddling-pregnant and jokes are made about this; and you can't go into the officers' club without uniform. And the Catholic chapel broadcasts its services all over the base by loudspeaker. And there is a strong prevailing wind from the ocean.

But still, I can see that Brad loves being a big, or at least a medium-sized wheel in this great machine. And he loves flying. He talked about Ultima Thule, the base in Greenland which is mostly underground, except for one huge hangar, which has to have a refrigerating system under it, lest the heat of the interior should melt the ice on which it stands. He may leave shortly on a twenty-five-day journey—Alaska, Japan, Hawaii and home.

7:30 p.m. We've just installed ourselves at the Sempervirens Motel on the northern outskirts of Eureka—after a long drive through the redwoods. Don went swimming in Russian River. The weather was fine and hot. This would have been delightful if the highway hadn't been so narrow and so terribly crowded.

The view from this motel isn't inspiring: a pool with ducks, a huge vacant lot scattered with tin cans and bricks, the highway crossing a bridge nearby with much whining and rattling of trucks. But hills in the background with bare redwoods on them; the tree tops mere sticks after some vast fire.

September 1. In a rush again. Why is one always in a rush on holidays? The only time to write this seems to be while Don is getting shaved.

On the 29th, we drove further north, as far as Klamath, which has a bridge with stone bears on it, over the river. All along the way through the woods, there was the smell of sawdust from the mills, and we kept passing the mills themselves, with their nub-shaped furnaces. The beaches are scattered with huge logs, very grey and dead, like cadavers. We looked into one of those miserable menageries—a baby bear circling a tiny cage and uttering cries of distress, a very bored looking cobra, a stinky gila monster underneath the desk at which the teenage girl in charge of the place was sitting.

Back down through Eureka and out of the redwoods at Leggett over the pass that leads to the coast. We wanted to stay at Mendocino but there seemed to be no accommodations. So we went back to Fort Bragg.

Next day, a winding drive to San Francisco. The fog rolls over the sea and up the face of the shore—but the beaches in the distance are a pale line of light shining under the overcast. The water is scattered with great rocks and streaked with long scribbles of foam. Woods of laurel, cedar, cypress, manzanita. The faces of the hills are bare, but between them, filling the many creeks and lagoons, you see the redwoods, coming nearly down to the shore. The thick, brambly hedgerows, reminding me of an English lane.

We're rather at a loose end here, and may leave tomorrow. The truth is, we know nobody here we really want to see, and there isn't much to do except go to movies. We've seen most of the sights.

September 4. As a matter of fact, we stayed through Sunday—having suddenly contacted Vincent Porcaro, who seemed very nice—nicer than before—and had a pleasant but short visit with Jim Graham—and flown over the city in another little seaplane, as on the previous visit—and seen Jack Dempsey—and Brad Saunders again.

Yesterday we drove down to Santa Maria, via Big Sur—not much fun because the weather was gloomy with fog along the coast.

Today we drove down here, arriving shortly after midday, to find the house in one piece and the garden not quite dead.

There now seems a possibility that I will work on [Romain] Rolland's *Jean-Christophe* for Jerry Wald.

Geller is going into hospital to be operated [on] for cataract next Friday. Lennie Newman has had some kind of an attack—heart or otherwise—caused by fatigue. Ben Masselink is going over to Catalina on Thursday in a civilian submarine.

Spent the afternoon watering the garden and tearing out the morning glories that were strangling the loquat tree.

Frank Taylor wires: "We are most enthusiastic. It is a superb job." But meanwhile Don read the manuscript of the anthology prefaces while we were on our trip, and made several criticisms which I shall have to consider. I want to get these attended to before I start working at Fox—*and* I want to begin on part four of my novel. I thought a lot about this while we were away. I see—more than ever—that this first draft is like a shot fired blindfold, in the vague general direction the book must take. But I'm very much excited. I see it opening out in all directions.

One key phrase: "Hell, nowadays, is a hospital."

September 7. I must train myself to live always in the presence of my death. The waste of time in my life is simply criminal—and by waste of time I don't mean that I should attempt a sort of executive efficiency. No. Only that I must try to be more aware of the day-to-day experience and keep seeing it in the perspective of the inevitable end. It's just terrible, the way I let time slither by.

I missed an opportunity to gain Don's confidence more completely and give him a greater reassurance of freedom. We were in San Francisco, and he went "on the town" as they say, with Brad Saunders. I sulked about this a bit, which led to an explosion as we drove home through Big Sur. But it'll be all right now, I think. I'll just have to be more on my toes the next time it happens. Right now, Don couldn't possibly be in a sweeter mood.

Yesterday I had a sore throat and today I felt exhausted, which alarms me a bit as I fear it may be a relapse due to the hepatitis. Don has gone to the movies with Ted.

September 10. Second day of a heatwave. I have to confess to criminal laziness. While Don went to art school, to begin the fall semester, and everybody else worked or at least swam, I went to bed and slept all afternoon. Now I am scribbling this before Max Scheler and Marcel Fischer[1], the eager beaver camera boys we met in Munich, come around for supper.

No novel done, but I made a restart on Saturday and wrote a page yesterday. No restart, as yet, on the Ramakrishna work.

I have a bad sniffle and sinus infection. Geller has had his cataract operation but complains of a throat infection caused by the anaesthetic. I'm supposed to hear definitely from Jerry Wald tomorrow, about *Jean-Christophe*.

Ivan Moffat has suddenly left for Greece to do a movie rewrite.

The Suez situation continues serious but is played down in the papers here.

I don't think Don has ever been more angelic than he was over the weekend. (It seems stupid to record this, but if I don't it simply means that I only mention the comparatively rare times when he *isn't*.) He is certainly in a much happier mood nowadays. He said repeatedly that he was looking forward to going back to school. He is at present delighting in *Pride and Prejudice*, which surprises me a little. Before that he read *Lady Windermere's Fan*, which I knew he would like. Mrs. Erlynne is absolutely "his kind of person."

---

[1] Not his real name.

Nearly seven in the evening and it's still breathless. How I hate heat—*and* cold!

September 11. Still struggling against this heat and my weakness. I really begin to fear that the hepatitis has exhausted me more permanently than I'd realized but it's hard to be sure—laziness has so many masks.

Yesterday evening Max and Marcel came. Max I rather liked, though he's a bit of a snob. Marcel hardly spoke. They had been in Monument Valley and had met [Adlai] Stevenson. Max says he's for the Democrats. We went up to Jim Charlton's. Speed was there. Never has he been ruder. He passed around a clipping about himself and the Perle Mesta film. He played the phonograph so loud that we couldn't hear ourselves talk. One day he will get himself very painfully kicked.

September 14. All this week we've had cold nights and fine days—since the end of the heat wave, that is. Don has gone to school in the Ford, because the Sunbeam suddenly refuses to reverse. The Suez situation looks bad, but I'm not seriously alarmed because I don't think our dear government will get into a war just before the elections; and I hope it will manage to restrain that enraged rabbit Eden.

I'm plugging ahead with the novel. Bored but dogged. Have reached page 164. Nothing matters except to get on and on and on. This may all be wrong, every word. Never mind.

Had supper with Johnnie last night. He confessed that he doesn't like Joel Goldsmith but nevertheless feels that he is capable of getting "on the beam spiritually." In other words, Johnnie sees him as a rather unpleasant person who frequently sheds his personality and becomes possessed by the spirit. Starcke, however, objects to this distinction between the ordinary and the extraordinary Joel. He tells Johnnie that the two are one.

Johnnie is going to Santa Barbara for the weekend with Carter. He is looking forward to this because he feels they have lost touch. Carter has been very unhappy about Dick Foote and very near a nervous breakdown, but Johnnie thinks he is better now.

All this Johnnie told me quite sincerely; and, in a way, his character is most transparent, innocent and guileless; but that doesn't prevent him from playacting and hamming it up outrageously. He is full of little arts—side glances, coy gestures, flickers of the eyelashes. This is the feminine side of him.

The almost incredible dishonesty of Hecht-Lancaster. They are now trying to get out of their watertight contract with Johnnie—brazenly asking his agent if he'll sue them unless they give way.

I also saw Gerald last night. He talked mostly mescaline, as usual. He has just finished a book about it.[1]

Geller calls this morning to tell me that the delays on the deal with Wald are merely due to legal formalities—the Fox lawyers must assure themselves that Wald really does have the rights of *Jean-Christophe*, since Fox now has to assume responsibility for making it. I wonder? I trust nobody in this business. They offered me five thousand for the treatment. I've asked for six.

Gerald showed me Mars last night, blazing white it seemed, not reddish, and bigger than Jupiter. It has been passing relatively close to the earth. Astronomers have observed the spread of its vegetation.

September 16. Yesterday we went on the beach, and there was Eddie James, just returned from Mexico to deal with his income tax. He looked fatter and had shaved the beard from his cheeks so that it was just a fringe along the jaw. Noticed how yellow his teeth are.

Speed—temporarily released from the surveillance of Paul Millard (who has gone to Ohio)—was in his most excitable niggery state. He kept urging us to come with him to the Ebb Tide, promising vague but tremendous thrills. Don knows Speed well enough by this time to be able to discount such talk—and yet it upsets him. He feels that it's hard, somehow wrong, to spend a Saturday evening at home. I can't blame him, either. My stay-at-home urges are mostly due to laziness and middle age. However, we did stay home, and Don started urging that we should at least go ahead with redecorating this place—as of course we should. The living room is still half in darkness for want of lamps, and our dining alcove could be altogether transformed by cozier lighting. And then there are the really big projects—the windows to be put in, the walls to be painted, etc. etc. I only try to put the brake on these schemes because I want to try to save some money for a trip to New York next Christmas and the eventual trip to Tahiti next year. Don got a little bit impatient with me, saying I was throwing cold water. But he quickly recovered his temper. He really is making tremendous efforts to be more self-controlled. It's a long time since we had a bad explosion.

I write this, as I have so often written in this book about Don, making it sound as though the problem were all *his*. But, of course, it's mine—much more mine—entirely mine, as far as I'm concerned. Japam. Japam. The only possible answer to every question. And I ought to be stressing it more and more—instead of neglecting it

---

[1] Reading, not writing; none of Heard's own books is about mescaline.

altogether, as I have lately—because I'm sadly aware of becoming increasingly resentful. The list of people who have "rejected" and "wronged" me grows and grows. I *must* make a fresh start. I must shake my back hard and let all this shit of resentment slide off it. It's nothing but a meaningless burden.

September 20. Johnnie has taken to calling me, right after breakfast, for a daily gossip. The day before yesterday he was bursting with the information that he didn't enjoy reading *Madame Bovary*—she wasn't a real character; yesterday, he called to tell me that there was a piece in *The Los Angeles Times* by Edwin Schallert, headlined, "Isherwood Will Script *Jean-Christophe*." And in fact the deal is now settled. I went to Fox yesterday and talked to Jerry Wald—mostly about Scott Fitzgerald. He seems to be very pleasant, though a great name dropper and time waster. All right—I'm to be paid $2,000 down and $4,000 on delivery of the treatment; and now it merely remains to deliver the treatment! So far, I haven't the least clue as to how I'm going to handle this gush of French wah-wah. I've promised to finish reading the book by next Monday the 24th. That means 1,300 pages in four days!

Having seen Wald yesterday, I returned home, went on the beach and into the ocean and lost the gold ring I bought in New Orleans on November 19, 1954. I'm always a bit superstitious about the 19th— particularly January and September—and I have the feeling that the sea, which has taken nearly all my rings, took this one in payment for the job. A big price for not so very much, because this was the prettiest ring I have ever owned. The last one, given me by Caskey, was lost in the dark on the beach at Fire Island in 1947. The one before that, given me by Chris Wood, I lost while swimming in 1945—I think it was on VJ Day, and that *did* seem a price worth paying.

The evening before last, I got Max Scheler together again with Jim Charlton and the others. Max's friend, Marcel Fischer, wasn't present because he's having an affair with a colored policewoman!

Saw Swami yesterday. He looked very well and happy. He has been up in the Sierras, at one of the Mammoth lakes. He spent most of the time there in meditation. He said that he felt the presence of Thakur, Swamiji and Maharaj very strongly. "I felt there was only a very thin screen between me and them. *Very* thin. I felt that nearly all of the time."

Don and I had supper with Marguerite Lamkin last night. Horrific tales of her adventures with the *Raintree County* company. Clift's drinking and the love life of Elizabeth Taylor. Marguerite adores all of this and recounts it with niggery glee. She really longs to be involved with [anything melodramatic and exciting]. Now she's "mothering" Monty Clift. She wants to bring him to supper on Saturday night—promising that he will probably smash everything and have to stay the night. The prospect doesn't charm me. I am wondering whether to call it off.

A precipice of work ahead: keep the novel going—I missed yesterday. Keep working on the Ramakrishna project—I missed yesterday. Do the Brecht translation for Lincoln Kirstein.[1] Read *Jean-Christophe*. Anything else?!

September 24. Clift behaved neither worse nor better than I'd expected. He arrived drunk, crumpled somewhat during supper but didn't spill anything and left soon after. I was really shocked by the change in his appearance since I saw him last. Nearly all of his good looks have gone. He has a ghastly, shattered expression.

Both Don and I felt we could have handled Monty better without Marguerite. It is obvious that she arouses his sadism. She fusses at him the whole time, subconsciously provoking violence. Monty is touching, and very anxious to be friendly—but, oh dear, how sorry he is for himself!

Yesterday, Marguerite met Johnnie at the Bracketts' lunch and invited *him* to come out on the MGM set today and talk to Monty! Johnnie is kind of thrilled at the prospect of a *voyage au bout de la nuit*.[2]

Also on Saturday we bought two new table lamps and a hanging lamp for the dining alcove, and talked with Bill Reid about various possible reconstructions and improvements on the house. This way we can easily spend $2,500.

Today I did my first full day's work at Fox. I have what seems to be a dream secretary, Eleanor Breese. But more of all this later.

September 28. Very warm again today. Smoggy in town. But I didn't have to go to the studio because I finished a rough first treatment yesterday and it has to be typed up and read by Jerry Wald.

So far, the honeymoon atmosphere prevails, as far as I am concerned. (But, admittedly, I haven't seen Jerry since I began.) I work in an absurd haunted house type structure called the Old Writers' Building. It has a clock tower arch and a clock, beneath which is written: "A play ought to be an image of human nature for

---

[1] Possibly *The Seven Deadly Sins*. Isherwood never translated Brecht for Kirstein, though he translated the verses in Desmond Vesey's 1937 version of *Dreigroschenro-man, A Penny for the Poor*, later republished as *Three Penny Novel* (1958).
[2] A journey to the end of the night (echoing Céline's title).

the delight and instruction of mankind." Also there are holes for pigeons—but the pigeons themselves were removed long ago, because they distracted the writers by their cooing.

My secretary, Eleanor Breese, has written a novel about being married to a test pilot (it was her second husband) and another novel called *The Valley of Power*. Her writing name is Eleanor Buckles.

Got my contract signed this morning, and received my first check. So far, I've only earned $5,626.44 this year.

Johnnie came to lunch with me at the studio three days ago. He says he asks himself what he shall write about next—it must be something he knows really well. He decided it must be half-Jews, and Jews who "pass." He, himself, is half Jewish. I never realized this—always thought it was only a quarter, at most. He is *far* less Jewish than Stephen or John Lehmann, not to mention the Reinhardts. Has he anything Jewish about him? Yes—a certain *gemütlichkeit* and a certain furtiveness.

Today he's having lunch with Swami, who's trying to persuade him to write a popular book about Vedanta. He says he won't, because it's opposed to what Joel Goldsmith believes.

Marguerite tells us that when Clift is very drunk on the set the crew have passwords—bad is "Georgia," very bad is "Florida," worst of all is "Zanzibar."

Have done almost nothing on my novel. *Must* keep it going.

September 30. Well, I *did* work on the novel, both Friday and yesterday; and I must try to again today. But it's not enough just to keep doing a page a day. I want to hurry up and finish this draft. I should be able to find time at Fox, easily.

On Friday night, the Bracketts came in and we showed them our Europe film. Don had previously cut out a piece of footage which seemed to linger unduly on the weird fishy-shaped cocks of the statues in the fountain in Florence.

This steamy smoggy heatwave continues. Today, Julie and Manning are due to arrive in town.

Yesterday we went with Marguerite Lamkin to a party given for the cast of *Raintree County* at Nigel Patrick's[1] Malibu beach house. Nigel Balchin[2] was there. He is now working at Fox on *Lucy Crown*.[3] He has written a script of Melville's *Typee* for John Huston. He says Tahiti is marvellous, and that they're going to film the picture there

---

[1] British actor, filming in *Raintree County*.
[2] British novelist and screenwriter (he scripted *The Barbarian and the Geisha*, among others).
[3] The film of Irwin Shaw's novel.

from next June on. This seemed like a sign. Decided that we'll make arrangements to go there then—the worst that can happen is that we'll have to cancel them.

October 1. Went to the studio this morning but Jerry Wald didn't get around to seeing me, and I left in the afternoon. Geller says, however, that he talked to Jerry and that Jerry is very pleased with my outline. I felt so tired that I slept all afternoon. Am hoping to get more hormone shots soon.

Talked to Julie Harris this morning. They arrived last night, to open for two weeks in *The Lark.*

Speed came to lunch at the studio, very manic. He talks about people who "have the rock inside of them"—i.e. an obsessive drive to write. He wants me to do a play. He says of *World in the Evening,* "It's your *Tender Is the Night*"—whatever that means. He believes he has "saved" Jim Charlton from the "sick people." He advises me to borrow scenes from Balzac for *Jean-Christophe.* I told him I see *Jean-Christophe* essentially as a farce. Speed said I mustn't tell Jerry that. He wouldn't understand what I meant.

October 2. So tired again. It's quite alarming. I certainly hope I don't have a relapse, after all this time.

Saw Jerry Wald this morning, I fear he'll be a nuisance, giving advice. Already this afternoon, he sent me notes. Lunch with Ellis St. Joseph, who is working on Townsend Harris and assures me that Frenke and David Brown had no right to offer the screenplay to anyone else—it was nothing but brain picking. Ellis suspects, as I do, that Harris must really have been queer.

This afternoon we started the *Jean-Christophe* treatment. I think it's quite promising.

John van Druten to supper last night. He is thinking of writing a play about a character like Laurette Taylor.[1] He is really quite sweet and cozy and pleasant to have around—but, in the last analysis, he just doesn't speak my language. I don't feel he's a companion of my own age; and that's what I need here.

I find myself relying more and more entirely on Don. He is my whole family. I hate to think how utterly lost I'd be without him. That isn't good.

No work on novel today. That isn't good, either.

Later. I've just been in to see Gerald. He'll be sixty-seven next Saturday (the 6th); it seems incredible, for he doesn't look more than

---

[1] American stage star (1884–1946); long after her retirement, she originated the role of Amanda Wakefield in *The Glass Menagerie* (1945) on Broadway.

forty-seven—even though he is obviously tired from working at the big book he's doing.[1] And how alive he is! How truly forward-looking. We were talking about this book of Colin Wilson's, *The Outsider*. All the literary preoccupations of this young man seem so elderly in comparison with Gerald's youthful enthusiasm for unidentified aerial objects, mescaline and lysergic acid, the new psychology, the new discoveries which may lead to control of extrasensory perception, the new sources of sugar and vitamins which may solve the food problem! And yet, at the same time, Gerald—who, you'd think, would want to live another hundred years just to satisfy his scientific curiosity—still maintains that he'd gladly die any time if he could do it painlessly! He talked about suicide—San Diego has the highest rate in the U.S. About the success of Evelyn Hooker's paper at Chicago. About Margaret Mead's book on the Stone Age tribe (in New Guinea?) which has become "civilized" within twenty-five years and has already rejected Catholicism.[2] About a new kind of therapy based on getting the different kinds of lunatics to talk to each other—since each, being opposite numbers, can see exactly what makes *the other* crazy.

October 8. This evening, for some inscrutable reason, I felt a desire to read Corvo—not so much for his sake as to get a whiff of Venice. Dipped into *The Quest for Corvo*, then read all of the fragment *Amico di Sandro*,[3] then looked at *The Desire and Pursuit of the Whole*.[4] Well, and—? I don't know. The feeling was somewhat muddled.

John van Druten called to say that he is pleased with the way his hearing went—his case against Hecht-Lancaster before the Screen Writers' Guild. He is now asking for all of the money. They're trying to prove that he didn't take trouble. He thinks he'll win.

Yesterday Julie Harris came, and Manning and Peter. They had lunch at our place and we all went on the beach, and then we drove them home again. Manning said this was the only really relaxing day Julie had had in weeks. I hope it was, because it made me as tense as a fiddle string. When your friends get children it's exactly as if they'd taken to drink—you can't talk to them any more. They can't concentrate.

On the 3rd we went to see *The Lark*. Julie seemed better this time,

[1] Probably *The Five Ages of Man: The Psychology of Human History* (1963).
[2] *New Lives for Old: Cultural Transformation—Manus 1928–1953* (1956); Manus, named for its tribal inhabitants, is the largest of the Admiralty Islands, northwest of New Guinea.
[3] An unfinished novel by "Corvo."
[4] An autobiographical novel, written mostly in 1909 after Corvo moved to Venice (subtitled *A Romance of Modern Venice*).

the play even less good. She certainly does everything that can possibly be done with it.

Tomorrow, or at latest on Wednesday, I hope to finish my treatment on *Jean-Christophe*. Very awkward moments lie ahead because Curtis Harrington is still Jerry Wald's personal assistant, and we shall have to meet and get along somehow.

Then I *must* get on with my novel. This is really serious.

October 10. Have just returned from seeing Marguerite Lamkin to the airport. She's leaving for New York tonight. Johnnie is also leaving by air tonight for Chicago. Last night he took me to dinner at Chasen's and thanked me for my "kindness to" him and for "the time" I had given him during his stay in Hollywood. I was quite embarrassed and touched. Johnnie has won his case against Hecht-Lancaster before the Screen Writers' tribunal. The only question now is will they pay up or refuse and force him to sue them?

This morning, before noon, I finished my treatment on *Jean-Christophe*. Now we'll see if Jerry Wald likes it.

This afternoon I had some free time, so could work on my novel as well as clip the ivy, sweep up, and water the front garden. I wrote two pages. This must now be my daily minimum, if I'm to finish the rough draft by Thanksgiving, as I would like. Unless it's to have a stunted last part, I have still seventy pages to write. Thanksgiving will fall on November 22 this year.

Don's life has been greatly affected by the release of old movie films to TV. Last night he saw *Mr.*———, how interesting! My resentment against the damned thing has made me "forget" its name![1] Tonight, he sees *The Letter*. They are only shown at 11 p.m. and run till 1 a.m., and he has to go to a friend of Ted's to see them. So he's exhausted and will get in very late, and miss school tomorrow—and disturb me by coming in in the middle of the night. (Last night he slept at his mother's.) And yet, how dismal of me to disapprove! Why shouldn't he have this fun?

October 12. The Outsider by Colin Wilson. I looked into it a short while ago. It didn't interest me much as a book. But as a theme it is of prime significance. I believe the English like it so much because they think of themselves collectively as The Outsider. And, as far as I'm concerned, I not only take it for granted that I'm an Outsider but I really am only interested in modern books if they are written from an Outsider's point of view. An Outsider but not a No Sider. I'm not interested in tales of fey folk who live in trees. The Outsider stands

[1] Later, in the margin, Isherwood added: "*Mr. Skeffington*, I now remember."

outside the modern conformist world, looking in—but with passion, with sincere involvement, with heartfelt hostility.

Last night Jo and Ben and Don and I had supper with Julie and Manning at a beautiful Japanese restaurant, the Imperial Gardens, near their hotel. Julie looked wonderfully elegant, as she sometimes can look, in black with earrings. She told us of a (fictitious) theme song plugging the movie of *War and Peace*: "Oh, *War and Peace*, I love you!"

This morning, I saw Jerry Wald about my treatment on *Jean-Christophe*. He had prepared a whole typed criticism of it, written in the vaguest language, but he didn't say one word about liking any of it. My resentment grew and grew—I know damn well that I've done a good job—and, good or bad, no kind of a job deserves to be treated in that way. So I called Geller, and Geller called Wald and asked him did he really dislike the treatment, because if so, we'd call it quits. Wald professed amazement. So now I hope that he'll be suitably apologetic on Monday morning. If I handle this right, I can turn the whole thing to the benefit of our future relations.

The novel is going again, but I must keep at it.

October 16. Reached page 200 of the novel tonight.

Lunch with Jerry Wald and Yul Brynner at Romanoff's. Jerry thinks he's right for Christophe. I'm sure he isn't. He is suave and tomcat voiced, purry masculine, with flirty brown eyes like Bill Harris. He kissed his wife's hand when they parted.

Listening to my neighbors talking—their loud masculine banter, like boys talking to each other while exploring a dark cave—talking very loud, just for reassurance. Are they consciously scared? No. But they are *plenty* scared.[1]

Over the weekend, a flare-up of infection above my capped tooth—all the symptoms of an abscess—then it dies away and I can bite on the tooth again: three days ago, it was agony. Very strange. Maybe due to rejection feelings regarding Wald's behavior. Teeth are said to be psychological indicators. But now, after our talk yesterday, all is sweetness again.

Curtis Harrington lurks in the background. We still haven't spoken to each other, though I'm quite prepared to.

Have spent this evening at home, working. Don is away at evening class, followed by a Bette Davis movie on TV. I miss him so much when he's away evenings, and yet I like being alone, too.

---

[1] Beside this paragraph Isherwood wrote: "Used in *A Single Man*." The neighbors were Mr. Hine, next door, and Mr Hine's good friend Mr. Stickel, across the street.

*October 20.*The day before yesterday, Thursday, was quite eventful. I saw Jessie Marmorston again after this long, long time. She told me how her heart attacks had changed her completely—not that it had made her more afraid of death—she still felt prepared for that—but it had shaken her confidence. She no longer feels now that she can cope with any emergency and remain serene. She told me that she would like to talk to Swami. I felt very warmly toward her—there's something about her that's wonderful.

Started my new series of hormone shots, hoping they'll pep me up. I've been feeling low; and today I have that wretched sickish sensation in the stomach which has come from time to time through the last ten years—ever since the operation.

Then on Thursday evening, we went in to see Jo and Ben, and they were just in the process of hearing from Irma, the woman who runs the cleaning business downstairs, that the house has been sold behind their backs by Andy, their landlord, whom they'd trusted as a faithful friend. Now the question is—will they be allowed to stay on there? Even if they are, their rent is sure to be raised.

This weekend, I have the unpleasant prospect of having to write the epilogue to my treatment for *Jean-Christophe*. I've stuck and stuck in it, despite the quite genuine interest I feel in the story, and despite the fact that I know I'm wasting my own money—I'll have been working on it five weeks—which comes to $1,200 a week—fifty dollars a week less than my usual salary!

Met Curtis Harrington in a corridor yesterday, face to face. Said hello. So the spell is broken.

Saw *Giant* yesterday. There are beautiful things in it. But it doesn't add up to a great deal. What is memorable is a certain horror—the rawness, the tawdriness, the self-satisfied vulgarity, the folksiness of oil millionaires. Loud children amazed and indignant when they grow tired of their toys. Oh yes, they are touching, too. But ultimately you feel tired of being sorry for them—you leave them to their games, deciding to save what little compassion you have and use it on something worthwhile.

Two most important observations I've read lately (I forget where). (i) This is the age of respectability. The boys who, in the twenties, would have been members of the Lost Generation, are today married men with three or four children, owing money on everything they possess and voting for Ike because "we never had it so good." (ii) Successful films and novels nowadays are about money, rather than sex.

*October 22.*Talking of successful novels, Jerry Wald has bought a book called *No Down Payment* to make into a movie. It's by John McPartland, and it's about people who live on a big new building development, where everything's standardized. Of course, the book itself may be satirical, for all I know. It isn't published yet, and all I've read is a synopsis prepared for the studio by a (probably) hostile writer. This fascinated me—it seemed positively a parody of the modern best-seller. (I should explain that David is the intellectual in the story—i.e. the not-perfectly-adjusted man. Leola Noon has a husband named Troy Noon—would a satirical writer *dare* to call him that? no, I think it *must* be serious—who rapes Jean, and she loves it because she isn't satisfied. Later, David gets wised up and treats her brutally in bed, and everything's all right.) Here's an excerpt from the synopsis: "The act was completed" (i.e. they'd been screwing), "but David knew that tonight it was not complete for Jean, and David felt a hidden inadequacy. Why, he asks himself, in unconscious searching, why had he asked about Leola Noon before he made love to the woman he loved?"

There you have the very essence of our time—this half-baked pseudopsychiatric groping around for "adjustment," which means getting a good fucking and becoming pregnant.

Don came home depressed. He has mountains of homework to do—and his teacher always sets the problems in the most cryptic art jargon, so that poor Don often finds he has completely misunderstood. Today for example: "To create shapes by the fabrication of elements. Start out with patterns that end up in shapes."

Some momentous steps today. We made reservations for our trip to New York at Christmas—exactly two months ahead. We put down our names on waiting lists for freighters to go to Tahiti, any time after next June 15. I finished the revised treatment for *Jean-Christophe* and handed it in to Jerry Wald. Began taking hormone pills.

Tomorrow, Bill Reid is starting alterations on the house.

I did no novel over the weekend—was busy with the treatment. But I worked on it at the office today, while Eleanor typed. Her ex-husband, Vance Breese, has offered to take me flying around the northwest in his Beechcraft plane. Don can come too.

Jo and Ben now have reason to hope that their house was merely bought (by a lady who's a partner in the Golden Bull[1]) in order to prevent the hateful Louis[2] from buying it. Otherwise he'd have closed half their parking lot and frozen them out of business.

---

[1] A restaurant and bar next to Jo Masselink's apartment.
[2] Louis (his first name) owned a motel and gas station (later just a parking lot) next door to Jo Masselink's building and an apartment building across the street.

October 24. Today Eleanor and I had lunch with her husband, Vance Breese, who is one of the greatest of the former test-pilot engineers. I was quite astonished by him. He is a massive, heavy, nearly bald man of my own age, with the most vulnerable eyes one can imagine, and a mouth that reminds me of Bob Buckingham. He is terribly anxious to please. He kept calling me Sir. We ate at the Luau. He brought maps with him—suggesting that we fly on Sunday over the Mono Lake country behind Yosemite. On the whole, he makes a very reassuring impression as a prospective pilot—but Eleanor says that her doctor friend, Spud Taylor, thinks he may have a heart attack at any time! She says also that he's subject to frightful rages and might have a stroke.

Jo has just heard another rumor—from the Filipino who works at the Golden Bull—that their house is going to be torn down to make room for a new Golden Bull: the old one having been condemned.

Don is wondering if he should go to the Chouinard ball on Saturday. He may get a costume from Beegle.

October 27. The morning of the day before yesterday, I went up to see Swami. He was in his most loving mood. He seemed entirely relaxed in love, or by it, as people are relaxed by a few drinks. He wasn't authoritative. He didn't shine or project: he just beamed. I noticed that the whites of his eyes are very yellow, but this added, in a way, to their beauty, making an effect as if the gold was spreading from the iris over the whole eyeball.

We were talking about the possible number of inhabited worlds. Swami said: "And, only think, the God who made those thousands of worlds comes to earth as a man!" Something about the way he said this—his wonder and his absolute belief, I suppose—made my skin go into goose pimples. I said, "How terrifying!" and that was how I felt. (It is quite impossible to convey in words the effect made on you by things like this said by someone like Swami—because, of course, it is the man himself, present and speaking to you, and conveying in some otherwise banal sentence, a glimpse of *what he is*, that makes all the difference.)

He told me that one of his ambitions is to found a boarding school, one half for boys, the other for girls, where "they would be given the ideal"—first on the high-school level, later as a university. He repeated what he has so often told me, that he feels in all his work responsible to Brahmananda. When he initiates new disciples, he hands them over to Brahmananda or Holy Mother. He would like to stop giving lectures, but if he tries to shirk any duty he finds that he loses touch with Brahmananda—"I can't find him. Then I know he is displeased."

Talking about Santa Barbara and Trabuco, he remarked that boys always seem more restless than girls. The boys always feel that they ought to *do* something or *get* something. Swami tells them they have to *be* something.

Phil (Buddha) is at Vedanta Place, recovering from his delusion that Trabuco would collapse without him. Ken grumbled, "I've spent ten years of my life here." "That oak," said Swami, "has spent five hundred years. Go and bow down to it." David is "having trouble with lust" and wants to leave.

Prema (John Yale) tells me that when he was very sick the other day with kidney trouble and thought he was dying, he saw all his rage and other sins so objectively that he called Swami in and told all about them. Then he felt much better, and, he says, "I saw how a sudden conversion would be possible."

Going to see Swami is like opening a window into my life. I have to keep doing this or my life gets stuffy. It doesn't matter what we talk about. He said: "Come again soon. I like seeing you, Chris," and I told him I think about him all the time and have conversations with him in my mind. I was moved, as we parted, and felt shy.

This evening I'm depressed. Gerald Heard and George Huene looked in unexpectedly for tea, which was nice in itself but threw Don's plans completely askew. He exclaimed that he couldn't come flying tomorrow because of homework, and rushed off to look for Nicky Nadeau, who suggested going with him to the Chouinard ball. He has a pair of antlers and a goatskin from Beegle.

No sign of Bill Reid to start work on the house. The *Christophe* treatment still isn't okayed by Buddy Adler,[1] so I can't start work on Monday. And of course, I'm scared at the prospect of flying over Yosemite and Mono Lake tomorrow. Especially if Don doesn't come. Because I'd far rather stay home and work on my novel—I'm two pages behind schedule, as it is.

Harry [Brown] just called. He's back from New York—possibly about to marry a girl named June [de Baum]. He sounded rather less drunk, but worried about money.

October 29. Well, wonders will never cease. I really enjoyed our flying trip yesterday—and although I was slightly scared several times I really felt a great increase of confidence—in Vance Breese as a pilot, but also in light-airplane flying in general.

---

[1] Producer; head of studio at Fox from 1956.

We took off from Cloverfield[1] about 10:30 and flew around until 4:30, only landing at Bakersfield for lunch. It wasn't very good weather—piles of clouds over the Sierras, so we couldn't get into Yosemite or Mono, or even Bass Lake. And when we left Bakersfield to come home, we couldn't even cross the coastal range. So we flew back to Palmdale through a heavy rainstorm and then it was fine and bright out to Santa Monica. What I got for the first time and what was so thrilling was the sense of the airplane in the element of air, like a boat on the sea. The feeling of the tiny but entirely adequate contraption meeting the forces of nature and riding them— sometimes by outclimbing and outspeeding them, sometimes by skillfully giving way. Vance is obviously a supremely competent pilot, quite relaxed and yet instantly ready to meet every situation.

Impressions of flying: The spooky blurred white cloud-wing erect over the ridge and seeming to extend, pointing higher and higher, menacing you like the dramatically outspread wing of a theatrical angel from which you are supposed to shrink back, covering your eyes. The shabby velvet hills, green or beige, worn threadbare in their folds. The bicycle lightness of the taut bright yellow aircraft with its rosy profile, bouncing and jarring on the elastic surge of the air. Angled headlong views of Three Rivers Airport, down, down in a seemingly narrow cleft, the runways newly tarred and therefore unsuitable to land on, lest they should mess up the immaculate plane. Tearing head-on through a horizontal rainstorm, only a few hundred feet above a highway where the cars had switched on their headlights; and far ahead of us but growing broader, the pale bright strip of sunshine on the desert around Palmdale. An altercation with the man in the control tower at Bakersfield because he let so many planes "touch and go" ahead of us, as we stood waiting to start. Thus we got a glimpse of Vance's famous temper.

Don came back from the Chouinard ball saying he "felt like Dante"—because the drunken drag show had seemed so revolting to him, sober. Later, he admitted he'd been rude to his hosts.

We just heard that Johnnie has had a heart attack in New York. Talked to Dick Foote, who obviously blames Starcke for running Johnnie's life and creating tension, so that [something] was bound to [happen].

Bad news from the east. Israel has attacked Egypt. No hint yet of repercussions.

It's now decided that we start on the screenplay tomorrow. But I can't get a raise on $1,250 a week.

Later. Got home to find that Ben had been taken to hospital and

[1] The Santa Monica airport.

operated on. Don and I went around to the Santa Monica Hospital and saw Jo, who was waiting with the Gowlands for Ben to come out of the operating theater. Then the surgeon came and said it wasn't appendicitis but an infection of the cecum. However, they'd taken out the appendix while they were at it.

Bill Reid finally made a start on the house today. He has opened a big slot in the roof for the coming skylight, and the furniture is covered with plaster dust.

Harry Brown called this morning to put off our lunch, on the grounds that he still felt drowsy after the change of atmosphere from New York!

Vance Breese, according to Eleanor, is most enthusiastic about our flight yesterday—saying that we were such good sports not to mind going up to 15,000 feet (which usually isn't necessary) and not to be upset by the turbulence, which was quite considerable while we were over the hills. As a matter of fact, Don got sick—probably because of his late night—although we both of us took Bonamine!

October 31. Am slipping steadily behind on my novel. Thirty-seven pages remain to be written in twenty-two days—*if* I do the full fifty pages on part five. Tired this evening, but today I made a good start on the script.

Harry Brown to lunch, looking pouchy eyed but seeming sober and alert. He plans to marry June shortly.

Dick Foote on the phone again, says Starcke says Johnnie is worse. Carter may go to New York. Dick continued to rage against Starcke and against Joel Goldsmith. "That's carrying religion *too* far!" he exclaimed.

Eleanor Breese tells me that children at the schools around here actually have professionals to make them up for Halloween!

She is still teetering back and forth. She figures she must be married, for the sake of the children. Shall she go back to Vance? Or to the doctor—if he asks her? In any case, she says, she'll stay in this job until we've finished, because she's learning such a lot.

Don has just finished a still life which really shows talent.

This evening, for some strange reason, things seem quieter, although the British have been bombing Egyptian airports—an act which seems, from here, quite unintelligibly vile, and unprovoked. Yet Eisenhower's assurance that we won't be involved isn't any more reassuring, really, than Wilson's was, or Roosevelt's.

Terrific gusts of wind tonight, threatening to tear off the temporary cover Bill Reid has made on the hole in our roof for the skylight. A dry dusty demon of a wind. How I hate it!

Jo is practically living up at the hospital with Ben. Her possessiveness is almost horrible, and yet he seems genuinely to want and encourage it. One gets a new angle on Ben, now he's sick. He seems a bit babyish. He has a babyish amazement that he is running a fever or has pain. It's extraordinarily naive. And yet I guess it is simply that he has hardly ever been sick before.

Harry says Stephen Spender is, or has been, in New York. But no word from him.

November 4. This house is utterly cheerless at the moment, because the heater doesn't work—it nearly started a fire by steadily charring the woodwork around it—and there are the half-made apertures in the walls of my workroom and the dining alcove, awaiting their windows.

I'm depressed because of this psychological difficulty[1] with Don— due perhaps, on my side, to aftereffects of the hepatitis. It makes me feel so insecure, although at present he's taking it very well.

Right thumb mysteriously painful for many weeks now, and getting worse. Also worried about soreness in anus—but largely because Eleanor's telling me her doctor friend specializes in rectal cancer has given me a new cancer scare.

Good progress on the novel. If I write two pages Monday through Friday, I shall have twenty-eight pages finished by Thanksgiving, and that's my target—to end the book on page 250.

Talked to Dick Foote again today. Johnnie is still very bad with dropsy and hardening of the arteries as added complications. Carter is now with him in New York.

Chris Wood took LSD yesterday. He got the same color perceptions as I did with mescaline. The doctor (from Sawtelle) told him that I could certainly take it. A bad liver would simply mean that the drug takes longer to wear off.

Swami, whom I saw yesterday, told me he believes these drugs have had a bad effect on Aldous—taking away his faith in God.

November 8. Dick Foote called this afternoon, to tell me Johnnie has taken a turn for the worse. He has had a heart attack *and* a stroke. The doctors say he has lost the will to live. Dick and Carter blame Starcke, particularly for involving Johnnie with Joel Goldsmith—but of course, Johnnie knew Joel before he knew Starcke. Dick says Starcke was always reminding Johnnie how old he was. Dick has practically thought himself into accusing Starcke of murdering John by worrying

---

[1] Isherwood later added in the margin: "My impotence."

him into a heart attack—in order to get the money John has willed him.

How strange—utterly unbelievable it is that Johnnie maybe is dying as I write this! Do I care? Not at the moment, because I can't grasp it. I shall care if he dies, though—and more and more as time goes on. Dick Foote doesn't care much, of course; he is thinking of his concert and how Johnnie has ruined it by taking Carter away. As for Charlie Brackett, he made a lot of noise but he didn't care much. He resigned himself to it almost instantly.

Bill Caskey is here—in bed with a cold at Hayden and Rod's. He has come to raise a mortgage on his land.

Just heard from Heinz, who left East Berlin in a hurry, for fear of arrest after a political argument in his factory. He's now in Hamburg. Sent him a little money.

Lunched with Vernon Old yesterday. He sent messages to Don— urging him to study and get a degree. He feels he missed a lot by not doing this.

Went to see Swami, today being the sixteenth anniversary of my initiation and the tenth of my becoming a U.S. citizen. Swami said that drugs could never change your life or give you the feeling of love and peace that you get from spiritual visions. Drugs only made you marvel—and then later you lost your faith.

This evening Swami called in great distress, because [one of the boys] has been arrested on a morals charge outside Hollywood High School. His trial is tomorrow.

We are in the midst of a fierce heat wave. My novel is lagging again. Nine working days in which to write twenty-two pages. But I suspect it won't run nearly that long—so I have time.

Charlie Brackett phoned Dodie in England today to ask if she'd let him have the screen rights to *I Capture the Castle*. But he doubts if the front office will let him do it.

Have just had a call from Prema about the [Hollywood High] situation. He obviously resents my mixing in. "Thank you for your interest," he said. I merely offered to help get Prema a psychiatrist,[1] if that were necessary. Swami says that Prema suffers terribly from frustrated ambition. He also showed me a most shaming letter from Starcke, in which Starcke claimed that he longed only for God. Swami was about to write back telling him not to be so romantic. Now, of course, he'll wait.

My right thumb is very painful tonight.

---

[1] I.e., for the monk who had been arrested.

November 11. The phonograph is playing because Ted is here after the beach, and we're waiting until it's time to go and see a juvenile delinquent movie made in Sweden.

Today on the beach has been incredibly warm, but not nearly so much as yesterday. The heat wave is tapering off.

The house is a ruin of plaster, but at least the windows are in. By the time everything is fixed and painted, we'll have spent at least 5,000 dollars.

The day before yesterday, I sent in my first twenty pages of the screenplay to Jerry Wald.

Yesterday, we went flying again with Vance Breese, starting early, shortly after seven, and getting back on the beach by twelve-thirty. We flew over the Yosemite gorge, circling Half Dome Rock, and then landed at Bass Lake. I am getting almost at ease, flying with Vance. Only a little nervous when we dipped steeply sideways into the gorge. But Vance afterwards reassured me by saying that he had been figuring all the time where we could have landed if the engine failed. He is reassuring just *because* he is anxious.

A bee stung me in the arm yesterday, while I was dozing on the beach. Today it's quite swollen.

Johnnie, according to Dick Foote, is now definitely out of danger. Now the struggle between Carter and Starcke begins: shall Johnnie go to the ranch to convalesce, or shall Starcke take him to a rented house in Key West?

November 13. Last night, Don and I went to Vance Breese's house, taking Jo and Ben with us. The idea was for us to see color TV and for Jo and Ben to get acquainted with Vance—swapping their knowledge of the West Indies for possible airplane rides while they were down there. But much of this project went askew. It turned out that Vance is going only for two weeks, because he is anxious to get back home and restart life with Eleanor. Also, Ben and Jo couldn't very well talk to him because there were so many other people around—an architect named Parsons and his Peruvian wife; a woman named Kirk, who is a flier and an international lawyer; and her daughter who works in TV and is a fan of mine. Also there was Eleanor, wearing a sort of underskirt dress—it almost seemed to be a slip—like the one [Anna] Magnani wore in *The Rose Tattoo.* Jo and Ben and Don all like Eleanor, but Don says she is no lady. Vance, who proved himself a very great gentleman by walking Don out to his car (the first time any host anywhere has ever done this), was clownishly rude in other respects. He pushed the hi-fi cabinet right into the room and played dirty songs at full blast, because Mrs. Kirk's laugh irritated him. This treatment was absurdly inept—it deterred Mrs. Kirk about as little as the entry of a full orchestra would deter an opera star: she simply made more noise. In fact, it was a noisy, vulgar, rather tragic evening, with Vance restlessly wandering back and forth, demonstrating the tricks of his various possessions. I felt that, after all, Eleanor would be mistaken if she went back to him, but, of course, I can't and shan't say this.

The color TV of "Jack and the Beanstalk" was beneath all criticism—produced by and for those who are constitutionally unable to believe in any kind of magic. It was the ultimate in the non-magical.

November 16. The plastering is done now. Next week, they start painting the house. Johnnie is said to be entirely convalescent. Lincoln writes that Igor has had a stroke and is in hospital at Munich.

I have done very little of the script this week. The novel is within a few pages of the end, however.

Was worried about burning sensations in my rectum. Went to Sellars this afternoon. He says it's all right.

We had supper with Speed this evening. He plans to suggest to David Brown that he write a film of *The World in the Evening*.

Saw Swami yesterday. He said of [the morals case]: "If only he hadn't got caught! Why didn't he go to some bar!" Also talked to [the monk] himself. There is really no case against him—only the word[1] of a deaf-mute boy who claims that [our boy] beckoned to him; that's all. But unfortunately [our boy] has to explain *why* he was in the can at the Hollywood High!

A big lunch given at the Miramar Hotel yesterday by the doctors at UCLA who are experimenting with mescaline to Dr. Humphry Osmond from Canada. Osmond told me I could certainly take mescaline six months after my hepatitis.

Ivan Moffat, just back from Europe, says Iris had a terrible time after taking the mescaline capsule I gave her. She thought she was going mad.

November 18. Rereading what I just wrote, I should amplify about Swami's attitude to [the monk in trouble]. He feels, of course, that the act itself was supremely unimportant—just a venial slip. "If he had come and confessed it to me, I'd have told him, 'Forget it.' " Swami's kind of rueful worldliness—the state of mind that makes him say, "Why didn't he go to some bar!"—is just exactly what's so unworldly about him. A really worldly person would have been either shocked or cynically indifferent—saying the whole thing was unimportant

---

[1] Later Isherwood underlined *word* and put an exclamation mark in the margin.

(the act *and* its relation to [this monk]'s vocation and attempted self-discipline) which of course it isn't; and thereby throwing out the baby with the bathwater.

Am at page 244 of the novel.

We slept till 11:30 today, because Don worked so late.

I doubt if we have ever been so happy together as we are now—and I *very* much doubt if I have ever approached such happiness with anyone else. And yet—there's no security here. Old age coming soon, and death, which I sometimes greatly fear, sometimes think I can fairly easily accept. We walked on the beach. It was so calm and beautiful, with the sea shallow at ebb. I thought with regret of my body as it used to be when I first came here in 1939—still so lithe and young by comparison, and still throbbing with sex. Since the hepatitis, I feel myself becoming more and more impotent. But maybe this is a phase. Gerald used to say that, "The train stops—and you can get off if you want to—otherwise, it will start and take you on again."

Last night, an eclipse of the moon in a clear sky. The strange transparent blood-brown shadow, lasting a long time.

Tonight the eclipse of Dick Foote, I fear, after this dreadful concert which we all have to go to.

Speed woke me up at 8:00 a.m. this morning to say that Joshua Logan is definitely going to do the play very soon.[1]

November 22. My Thanksgiving thanks are basically: that I know Swami and Don. That I finished the rough draft of *The Forgotten* this afternoon. That I have a job and am earning money to pay for this house—which is going to be really nice, when finished.

Have just returned from seeing Swami. He talked about Grace. How Maharaj had told them that there are some people who just get it. "God can't be bought." Even if you do all the japam and spiritual disciplines, you still can't command enlightenment. It's always by Grace. Swami's youngest brother got samadhi while being initiated by Swami Saradananda. Then he became an extremely avaricious lawyer. But, no matter what he does, he is liberated. On his deathbed he will "remember."

The scandal [at Hollywood High] has had various developments. [The poor monk] has been let out of the Vedanta Society. But his brother, a doctor in Pasadena, will look out for him. However, [the boy] doesn't want to live with the brother. He's going to take a room in Hollywood and get a job.

---

[1] Logan was to direct a play by Lamkin, *Out by the Country Club*, but the production never came about.

Prema, meanwhile, is upset because Swami has taken this occasion to say that he doesn't want any more boys "of that kind" coming to Trabuco, and that he thinks it difficult if not impossible for such a boy to make good in the spiritual life. Prema feels condemned, and yet he doesn't have the nerve to talk to Swami and bring the whole problem out into the open.

I, myself, wish Swami wouldn't talk this way. I'm quite accustomed, by now, to love and look up to him without expecting him to be a pillar of wisdom and consistency on all occasions. It's rather that, *because* I love him so much, I want him at least to impress others in this respect. For myself, I don't mind. I know that Swami makes exceptions in my case. I'm privileged. He tells Prema—so Prema says—that I'm a model of devotion—(this seems incredible, but I doubt if Prema would lie about such a thing)—that he wishes *he* had my devotion, etc. etc. So I'm forgiven, and allowed to get away with murder.

Swami even said that now he didn't want to take Tito back— because of [the incident at the high school]. But, I'm glad to say, he feels himself obligated. It would have been too shameful to turn him away now. Tito, it seems, has now made the necessary money arrangements to come.

Last night, we saw *The Ten Commandments*, with Speed and Paul. A dismal bore of a film. It makes you loathe the Jews and their god. Only one line I liked. When the old pharaoh dies, his son announces: "The royal falcon has flown into the sun." That's the sort of melodrama I enjoy.

Still this extraordinary dry hot weather.

November 26. The heat wave continues. Today, the humidity was zero! No smog.

We have stayed home tonight. I cooked pork chops. Don did homework. The house is now bleak with fresh white paint. We have become so accustomed to living in this mess, with workmen coming in every weekday morning before eight, that we almost take it for granted.

Have just finished rereading the manuscript of my novel. It really is *nothing* yet—except a provocation to make *something* out of that nothing—which is a sort of achievement, I suppose. My present plan is to write the second draft in the same mood as that in which I wrote the first—good-humored patient fumbling—to "get down to the nerve."[1]

Its feeling should be somewhat like that of *An Adventure*, the book

---

[1] Francis Bacon told Isherwood this was his intention in his paintings; see diary entry for February 10, 1956.

about the psychic experience in Versailles.[1] We have to get quietly deeper and deeper into the weirdness.

Jim Charlton, Betty Andrews and a young man named Ted Holcomb came to lunch at the studio today. Holcomb seemed unusual and charming, a wartime flier born in San Bernardino, who has spent ten years in Europe (much of it in Venice) and is now a private tutor up at Santa Barbara. Jim says Caskey is living at Pasadena, Texas, with a man from Bohemia. He must have a certain amount of money. He doesn't work, doesn't drink much.

November 30. Yesterday I had a letter from Johnnie, written in pencil from the hospital. He writes fairly cheerfully but I get the underlying impression that he has been terribly shaken. (Carter, with whom I lunched on Tuesday, says Johnnie doesn't realize how sick he is; but I doubt this. Some part of you *knows*.) What I found particularly touching was Johnnie's saying that, when we had supper together at Chasen's on October 9, and I told him to go into the men's room and look at the pornographic pictures, he hadn't felt sure he could walk that far. And I never noticed anything! Because, I suppose, I didn't want to. It would have been emotionally disturbing and tiresome to admit that Johnnie was sick. So I didn't. Just like the Duchesse de Guermantes in that famous last scene with Swann![2] Which reminds me, Johnnie says he is reading it. The pathos of this letter is that it reads almost as a farewell. And now I see the significance of Johnnie's little speech of thanks to me at Chasen's.

The news is very bad this morning—Turkey getting steam up for war with Syria and everybody else taking sides. I'm still optimistic, but chiefly because the *U.S. News and World Report* is.[3] They'd better be right.

Discovery that I have no income tax to pay, this year, encourages more spending on the house. Now that the place is painted and the woodwork "pickled," we are thinking of a tile floor, new furniture, a reorganized garden.

Went up to Vedanta Place two nights ago, and had a talk to Prema. He had already gone to bed when I knocked on his door, after seeing

[1] By Charlotte Anne Elizabeth Moberly and Eleanor Frances Jourdain, first published in 1911 under the pseudonyms "Elisabeth Morison" and "Frances Lamont."

[2] In Proust's *Le Côté de Guermantes (The Guermantes Way)*, when Swann reveals he is dying and the Duchess does not pause to react because the Duke says they will be late for supper—but then sends her upstairs to change her shoes which do not match her dress.

[3] Longstanding differences between neighboring Turkey and Syria were heightened by the Suez war; see Glossary under Suez crisis.

Swami, and—lying in bed—he appeared very much *in his own predicament*: having made the bed of his life, so to speak, he was obstinately but dubiously lying on it. He longs to go and have a frank talk with Swami, but he can't, he is afraid of him. (Afraid of Swami! That only shows me how many different Swamis there must be, for different people.) Prema keeps wondering how he can possibly stay there, when Swami dies. But where else can he go? How else could he earn his living? He wants to take a holiday and think things over.

Don is making steady progress, both in drawing and painting. Our life continues to be marvellously harmonious. I hardly dare breathe on it or even glance at it, though. It's like an organ of the body whose operation must never be interfered with by the conscious will.

Perfect fall weather all this week.

December 2. On Friday the painters finished the inside of the house. Today we put the furniture back in place and vacuumed and cleaned the windows, although a new mess is due to begin shortly when our tiled floor is put in. Also, we shot the subtitles for the bit of film about the Gurians' visit here, which we plan to give Julie and Manning as a Christmas present. This included a scene on the beach, where I wrote "The End" in the sand.

Ted, Don's brother, was arrested yesterday for shoplifting. A detective at Sears caught him stealing phonograph records. The lawyer says he'll be let off with a fine.

On Friday I had [the boy who was arrested] to lunch at the studio and we talked about *his* difficulties. He says he only does these things for excitement, not out of lust. Now that his career as a monk is wrecked, he doubts if he will ever want to repeat them. He was pleasant and almost cheerful, yet I felt the completeness of his loss. Now he really doesn't know *where* to turn—and yet I can't help feeling that maybe, in some mysterious way, it'll be for the best. I suppose the truth is that I really believe in change, both as a stimulant and a cure—even though it always terrifies me when I have to face it myself.

This evening, I restarted the novel, beginning the second draft. I'm still working blind and I still am not *quite* sure that this is a possible theme for a novel, at all. All I do know is, how to rewrite most of the first chapter. So I'll begin with that and trust to receive further guidance.

December 4. We have been reading Dodie's *Hundred and One Dalmatians* in bed. Not that I greatly enjoy it so far, but it seems very snug to be reading Dodie's book *together*; it brings us into relation with her.

Lots of bother with my teeth, and no prospect of Peschelt's fixing them for three more days. Also vague threat hanging over me of something Jessie Marmorston found in my urine tests. But she's too busy to see me and tell me about it because her old mother-in-law has had a stroke.

The radio says it's going to rain, tonight or tomorrow.

Ted has been let out on bail till his trial.

Prema, who came to lunch yesterday, was much shocked because Swami Vandanananda had asked Buddha (Phil) for exact details of his sex life. If he is really pure, says Prema, why the curiosity?

Jo and Ben left by car yesterday for Florida en route to the West Indies.

Today I bought a big lolly-eared stuffed dog for Peter Gurian. One of those loveless symbolic presents—but what else can one do? At least Julie and Manning will probably like the film we're giving them.

Prema brought me part of a vast manuscript by Swami Gambhirananda of Calcutta—a history of the Ramakrishna Math and Mission—to have its English corrected.[1] This is my newest piece of homework, interrupting Ramakrishna's life. It will probably take years. But first I want to finish the Rolland book on Ramakrishna.[2]

December 8. We've had some rain, this week. Now it's windy, brilliant but a lot cooler. The house is all painted and looks good. We are waiting for a man to appear from the auctioneer's and tell us if they'll sell the furniture. Last night, Bill Reid came in while Tony and Beegle Duquette were there, to talk about the floor. Tony decided for us that the kind of tiling we'd admired in Jimmy Pendleton's shop window—four big white squares with a little black diamond in the middle—is too elegant for the kind of living room we want to have. Bill Reid was opposed to it anyway, because it would mean a lot of work, cutting up the tile. So he tried to intimidate us by estimates of the extra expense and then psychosomatically cut his own finger, right through the nail, while cutting a specimen piece of tile to show us. Tony seemed very exhausted and kept blinking with his mouth open in his fishlike way. He has just read *Lions and Shadows* and is very enthusiastic about Mortmere.

Don and I had a talk, after they'd left. We agreed that neither of us want a house we have to live up to—that, in fact, we only want to be snug. We are, to some extent, being intimidated into making this place "grand." We have to find a happy medium. Tony said: "You

[1] *History of the Ramakrishna Math and Mission* (1957).
[2] Romain Rolland, *The Life of Ramakrishna* (1929).

might have the chest painted black, to hide what it is." Don told me, "I didn't dare ask him what it was."

Supper with Evelyn Hooker the night before last, to discuss her Chicago paper, which is now to be published, and her future investigations into the social life of homosexuals, which will oblige her to go to parties, dance and get drunk. Could she use a tape recorder, she wondered. I suggested that the only way to reassure her hosts about this would be to say awful things into it herself—so compromising that it could never be used except for scientific purposes. Evelyn had asked Edward if he would mind her going to these parties and getting into possible scandals. He replied: "No, if it doesn't take up all of your time." There is really something very noble and admirable about Evelyn. I love to think of her getting drunk and living it up in the interests of science—the good thing about her is that she'll really enjoy doing this.

Evelyn told me how [Bruno] Klopfer, the great Rorschach expert, can actually tell from Rorschachs which patients have slow-growing cancers and which fast-growing ones—because patients who have made a good adjustment to life are able to put up a much greater resistance to them. *And yet*, Klopfer wasn't able from Rorschachs to tell a homosexual from a heterosexual.

Had lunch with Speed, who told me that he compensates for his hates by positive feelings for something or someone else. So he doesn't waste energy.

Eleanor Breese just called me to say that she has talked long distance to Vance in Miami and he's hurrying home—so all her suspicions that he was planning to meet the other Eleanor in New York were ill founded.

Walked with Don on the beach. A feeling of great mutual happiness in being together. I think we're both lucky. How many people can say that?

December 11. Vance Breese got back yesterday from the Caribbean, having broken his record for hurry in his impatience to get back. Now Eleanor feels she may leave right after my return *or* may wait until the first draft of the screenplay is finished—all depending on how far she finds it possible to live with Vance and come to work here with me. At present she's doubtful, because Vance is so demanding, despite all his resolutions to be more considerate.

The Japanese gardeners have gleefully stripped all the ivy from the terraces of the back garden. Don says it looks like the foundations of the pyramids.

Am sticking in the rewrite of my novel. Now that I have to take more trouble, I'm suddenly meticulous.

Hugh Chisholm and Brad Fuller to lunch today. Hugh has aged a lot, but is still boyish, flirtatious, almost elfin when he talks about real estate and the furniture business. For the second time, he has solemnly left Italy—regretfully abandoning it to its fate.

December 15. Depressed. I don't want to go to New York. I dread the trip, the cold, the discomfort of Julie's house, the strain of parties, the uncertainty of Don's mood. He is very upset today. Everything he says is well founded. I do not find his behavior neurotic. And yet, of course, I resent his unhappiness. It makes me insecure and miserable.

Also, those horrible attacks of rage I get. Against Eleanor, for being late back from lunch yesterday. Against the trustees of the Conan Doyle estate, for attacking my foreword in the anthology.[1]

December 16. Still depressed—though things are all right with Don again. He is amazingly good considering his age and his problems and I have no right to expect more of him. When I compare him with Caskey—! I am amazingly bad, considering my age and my problems. I'm horrified at myself—at my fits of rage, during which I want my enemies throttled black and their faces stamped in. My attitude seems to get more and more negative as I grow older, fatter, feebler. And yet I know that this self-condemnation is even worse than what it condemns.

We saw Speed yesterday and he took us to meet Ralph Meeker[2] at the Garden of Allah.[3] Speed was even more shockingly vulgar than usual. He told Meeker, "He wants to look you over," indicating me. And then he went on about how Fonda wasn't right for his play because he's had an operation on his cock and his wife killed herself,[4] and he couldn't play "studsy" roles! Really it is no wonder that many people refuse to see Speed at all—or at any rate are very unwilling to be seen with him in public.

December 18. Don has been at school this evening, and I've worked on a foreword to "The Secret Sharer" in case Dell decides to have that in

---

[1] Isherwood's introduction to "The Speckled Band" characterized Holmes as essentially comic; he dropped Conan Doyle from the anthology, but later printed the introduction in *Exhumations*.
[2] American actor.
[3] Hotel on Sunset Boulevard, torn down in the 1960s.
[4] Henry Fonda's second wife, Frances, mother of Peter and Jane, cut her own throat over a proposed divorce in 1950.

my anthology in place of the Dylan Thomas (which was too expensive) and the Conan Doyle (which Frank Taylor is ready to join me in rejecting).[1]

Tennessee isn't in New York—but Truman Capote is, and Marguerite, and of course Julie and Lincoln, and Hugh Wheeler will be coming down. So we can look forward to some sociability.

Great agitation on the part of Eleanor Breese, choosing me a secretary to succeed her. The one she wanted, Christina Pettigrew, can't come because she's earning much more in the job she has.

Am dissatisfied with the few pages I've rewritten of my novel. It should be in diary form, as I originally intended—terse, abrupt, sometimes inconsequent. Not a smooth narrative.

December 22. Just about to leave. The usual misery and jitters.

Saw Swami yesterday, who told me that he'd been making japam for me. Nevertheless, I was sulky in the evening because we saw a bad film, *The Rainmaker,* and I got no supper till 10:00 and was rude to Glade [Bachardy] and Ted. Such behavior is inexcusable.

December 26. Well, here we are in New York. Arrived on the afternoon of the 23rd, very late, after delays due to fog.

As usual, when on a holiday of this kind, I feel very disinclined to write anything in this book. Just can't be bothered.

But so far the trip is being a success. I enjoyed going to the El Morocco on Christmas Eve and hearing the Salvation Army sing carols. Also, Gottfried [Reinhardt] was there—along with Silvia [Reinhardt], Marguerite, that masochistic bore, Emmett Blow, and an Englishman named Keating. Gottfried was drunk and insisted that the musicians in the Champagne Room play something *echt Wienerisch,*[2] not operetta. Silvia was frantically impatient with him because they were leaving the next day for Europe.

Then yesterday we had Christmas dinner by candlelight in the tall dining room at the Plaza, looking out over the twilit park. It was stuffy and plushy and comfortably sad and we felt like characters in a Henry James novel. I caught a whiff of New York in the 1900s.

Johnnie, up in a suite at the Dorset, seems much better but you feel how he has been shaken. Shaken to the very depths. He now has to be careful. You feel his care in everything he says. Starcke, I could feel, is pushing him already—talking about his career, etc.

[1] Conrad's "The Secret Sharer" was included.
[2] Authentically Viennese.

Julie and Manning are more completely absorbed than ever in the business and game of being parents. They are nice to stay with, because we're so free. But their Christmas presents were worse than nothing—two ugly identical faggoty belts from Carlos McClendon's shop.

Yesterday we walked miles and miles, looking at the Christmas shop windows. It was very enjoyable and I didn't feel a bit tired. New York really wakes you up.

December 28. Still rushing, and it's really cheating to make this entry—just that I don't want to break my record, and am in such a desperate hurry that I can't think. Hurry to do what? Go to Frank Taylor's office and fix up my forewords to the anthology items. To lunch with Glenway [Wescott]. Drinks with Paul Cadmus. But now I must go—

1957

January 1. Happy New Year! It's snowing, and Don is depressed, after the party at Bernie Perlin's[1] last night, because he felt he had no identity. So I'm a bit miserable—how easily I turn to hating "pleasure" as soon as the least thing goes wrong.

Sybil Thorndike, whom we met yesterday at Johnnie's, was even more wonderful than I'd expected. She *is* a sort of saint—if only because, as an actress, she still doesn't seem to give a damn what sort of an impression she creates.

Johnnie himself looked grey and shaken and sad. We felt some strain between him and Starcke.

But no—I *can't* write any more. Everything is against it, including the discomfort of this desk. New Yorkers live in the most utter squalor—all of them. The dirt and the old broken-down slum houses.

I decided yesterday to try writing *The Forgotten* in the third person with "William Bradshaw" as its chief character.

At seventy-some, Sybil Thorndike is learning Greek!

January 5. We got back home the night before yesterday—around one, because a seventy-mile-an-hour headwind held us back while we were flying over the mountains. Don had a stomach upset and felt awful throughout the flight—and he spent yesterday in bed. But now he seems much better. And we agree that, despite some bad moods and moments, this was really the nicest of all our visits to New York.

[1] American painter.

The best things—the meeting with Sybil Thorndike, the performances of *Major Barbara*[1] and *Long Day's Journey Into Night*,[2] Christmas Day dinner at the Plaza, the hilarious morning and lunch with Truman, the Balthus paintings.[3]

Now Natasha Spender is staying with the Hookers. We had supper with them this evening. Natasha is really very sweet and not at all crazy as I feared.

She says an old Russian she knew prophesied many years ago that before the end of 1957 New York wouldn't have one stone standing on another. And all his other prophecies have already come true!

I drove Natasha up to see the Huxleys in their new home in the hills, under the Hollywoodland sign. Laura very elegant. Aldous looked pinched and tired. The house is enchanting. Aldous's study has the true snugness—something about it partly suggests a nursery.

Natasha, on the way home, spoke of Evelyn Hooker's hopeless pessimism about her appearance. Evelyn can't believe that anything she could wear would be becoming.

Two college boys just called me to settle an argument—is Konrad Bercovici[4] "more important" than Alan Paton[5] or Joyce Cary![6]

January 6. This evening I have at last finished tidying up my desk—more or less—and now we are going out to see the Hookers and Natasha and Raymond Chandler, who describes himself as Natasha's "nanny." She isn't quite sure that she likes the idea of him following her around; it was all right as long as they were driving about Arizona, but now she is settling in Palm Springs for a couple of weeks and wants to be quiet and play Beethoven sonatas.

Natasha says that Chandler is a Walter Mitty. Certainly one doesn't see any resemblance between him and the he-detective in his books—quite aside from his being nearly seventy. He told some funny stories—of how Harry Tugend[7] said of Betty Hutton,[8] "She'd be a nymphomaniac, if they could slow her down." His favorite

[1] Shaw's play starred Glynis Johns, Charles Laughton, Burgess Meredith, and Cornelia Otis Skinner.
[2] José Quintero's original posthumous production of O'Neill's masterpiece, with Fredric March, Florence Eldridge, Jason Robards Jr., and Bradford Dillman.
[3] A retrospective of the Swiss painter at the Museum of Modern Art.
[4] Eastern European novelist and folklorist, best-known for his gypsy stories and for *The Volga Boatmen* (1926).
[5] South African novelist.
[6] British novelist.
[7] Screenwriter (often for Shirley Temple and Alice Faye) and producer.
[8] Film star.

Hollywood expressions: "It's terrific—but we can fix it," "Do you want it good, or do you want it Friday?"

I felt, when the three of us had lunch together (Don didn't come with us because he is still keeping to liquids and also wanted to finish a homework portrait of himself as the boy in El Greco's *El Entierro del Conde de Orgaz*[1]), that Chandler was jealous of my presence. He wants to monopolize Natasha.

He rather reminds me of Faulkner.

I have a feeling that this year is going to rush by like a jet. I must be quick. So much to do. Make a definite new start on my novel. Get started revising the history of the Vedanta Society.[2] *And* finish the foreword to Conrad for the anthology.

Talked to Ray Ohge on the phone. The Trancas restaurant escaped but the garbage cans were burned. His house escaped too, but the lot next to it burned. Beegle also had a narrow escape out at Anne's[3] ranch.

January 7. It has been raining on and off all day and will rain more. My first day at the studio, and without a secretary. The new one I'm promised, Joan Waugh, claims she worked for me in another studio—MGM, I guess, but I can't place her and I don't like to offend her by asking.

So today I've done next to no work, and it's really impossible for me to do any until this girl has familiarized herself with the script.

In the morning I talked to a writer named Pat Frank who is doing an air force picture, and tells me that at present we are ahead in the race with Russia, but within ten years both sides will be even. Then what? Buddhism or bust?

Eleanor Breese came to lunch, already [wondering whether] she [should have gone] back to Vance. He is so possessive. She wants to go on working with me, on the side—but I'm not encouraging this. Eleanor is now thinking tenderly of her doctor.

Talked to Rod Owens. He and Hayden nearly lost their house in the fire. Rod feels awful, thinks he's going to have a breakdown. Called Evelyn Hooker to try to find him a psychiatrist.

January 13. Heard from Evelyn Hooker this morning that Edward died two days ago, of a heart attack. The funeral is on Tuesday. Natasha is coming up for it, from the desert. At present, I feel nothing

[1] *The Burial of the Count of Orgaz.*
[2] Swami Gambhirananda's *History of the Ramakrishna Math and Mission.*
[3] Anne Cramer, a wealthy client and friend of the Duquettes; fires are frequent in the Topanga, Malibu, and Trancas area.

particular about this; the news is too surprising. My only clear resolution is that I ought to remake my will. I can't expose Don to the danger of being left homeless just because of a personal scruple about my promise to Billy [Caskey] never to alter my will—an unsolicited promise, at that.

Heavy rain yesterday, and depression, which I conquered in the only possible way, by doing lots of work—letter writing and other hated chores. My physical problem[1] loomed large yesterday because we discussed it, and assumed the air of a tragedy. Today, because nothing was said about it, it solved itself absolutely—for the time being. But whether it is going to disappear slowly or reassert itself in the worst way, I can't possibly tell.

As I suspected, this year is tearing by. Have failed to restart my novel, done very little about revising the Vedanta history. I barely keep up with my work at Fox—in fact, this week has been disgracefully slack.

January 14. Bogart died, which was somehow quite shockingly sad. I minded far more than I did about Edward Hooker, although I never knew him and scarcely knew Bacall. Such is the power of glamor?

Frank Taylor and one of his publishing colleagues, Walter Mitchell, took me out to lunch at Romanoff's. The atmosphere of businessmen on a spree. Frank told me how cultured Mike Romanoff is. He had read a government white paper on China.

Don's homework is to analyze the composition of Velasquez's *Las Meninas.*[2]

Have reached an all time high of over 150 pounds. Started to diet.

Don couldn't possibly be nicer to live with or more sweet natured than he is at present. It seems to me—touch wood!—that his lows of depression and negative emotion are getting much shallower than they used to be. His future and his development is the great absorbing interest of my life, now. I couldn't possibly feel this more strongly if he were my own son.

January 15. This morning I had a Salk vaccine shot, saw Harry Brown (who may be coming to work at Fox) and ate with Fred Zinnemann on the set of *A Hatful of Rain*—one sandwich apiece in paper bags. Fred appealed to me to invite Renée [Zinnemann] while he was away. He says she feels people only want to see her because he's

---

[1] Isherwood later added in the margin: "(Impotence—why was I so mealy mouthed about this?)"

[2] *The Maids of Honor.*

around. I told this to Don and left him to see the reflection of himself—which he instantly did.

Edward Hooker's funeral in the afternoon. A dreary but quick business. Allan Hunter delivered a rambling, almost senile address, but seemed quite his old self when I met him outside. Evelyn had the appearance of being half-doped—she had been given a Miltown before the ceremony.

There was a full moon, and the sea was breaking to show an underlining of silver flashing from beneath the fold of its black cape. We ate at the Holiday House, with Natasha Spender, who talked about Lolly Spender's death—how slow it was, and how hideously emaciated Lolly became, and how hard she fought.[1] The blind man who used to visit her and make her temporarily better. Natasha's very understandable resentment against Bill Goyen. She calls him a man-eating orchid.

We have now reached a low of denudation—the table, the chest and the couch have all been taken away to be fixed up. Don is drawing on the small kitchen table.

When I met Allan Hunter at the funeral, I said, "How nice to see you!" and immediately felt I'd been tactless. Allan, on his side, asked me, "What are you working on at Fox?" and then obviously felt *he'd* been tactless and added hastily, "It doesn't matter!"

January 22. Vivekananda's birthday puja. Read the Katha Upanishad in the shrine before breakfast. Swami gave me a new raw silk wrapper—my old one seems to have been lost at the Trancas beach house.

Pains right up my arm from the injury I did my thumb by playing with the modelling wax.[2]

Many thoughts about death. How will I face it? And/or old age? Will Don be around? What will I do if he isn't? I'm really disconcerted by my weakness.

Weekend at Palm Springs with Natasha Spender, Evelyn Hooker, Raymond Chandler. Ray undoubtedly in love with Natasha. How does she feel? [. . .] Natasha told Evelyn that Stephen is asexual[3]—I suppose she means, fundamentally.

[1] Margaret Spender, wife of Stephen Spender's brother Humphrey, died of Hodgkin's disease on Christmas Day 1945.
[2] Isherwood added in the margin: "(This became permanent, in *both* thumbs.)"
[3] Natasha Spender explains that she was in fact repeating a remark made by Auden, that as an undergraduate in Oxford during the 1920s, Spender had been asexual.

Evelyn assured us that she isn't having to brace herself. This amazes her. But I fear she may have a terrible relapse later.

January 23. Just talked to Evelyn on the phone this morning. She's back at Saltair Avenue. She says she feels able to start to work again. She is worried about Natasha and Chandler, because apparently Chandler has restarted drinking heavily.

Yesterday evening I signed my will, up at Mrs. Herbold's. So now Don is protected.

Then Swami took me (and Tito) to the little house in Pasadena where Vivekananda stayed for a few weeks in 1900.[1] His bedroom is now made into a shrine. We went up there with Swami and sat for a while, while the other guests downstairs chattered loudly. I tried to concentrate on Swami's meditation. What an amazing privilege—to be with him, in Vivekananda's presence. Felt a keen elation—I was so safe with him. I tried to hold this. I want some of it for when I die. Can I be afraid while he's with me? We shall see. I do hope not.

Another note from poor crazy Bill Stroud: "As an Adult Friend of Mr. Gerald Heard, would you plead with him to use his mobile consciousness a little more intelligently. He [may] disregard Vedanta because of repression, but his own provisional immorality stinks stinks raised to the n'th power of infinity…"

January 29. Torrents of cold dreary rain. How I hate it! They say there's snow in Topanga Canyon and down to the foothills around Malibu. Natasha went off yesterday night on the plane to Washington, after two dreary strained days spent entertaining her. If I'd been alone with her, I wouldn't have minded, but Ivan and Caroline Freud made me embarrassed and Evelyn (with a virus infection, poor thing) was dull, and Don was being neglected. I must say that—though he *is* sometimes hypersensitive—I'm often quite infuriated at the way people take him for granted as the dear little kitten. This morning, tiresome old Chandler called from La Jolla, drunk, to tell me he liked me—am I supposed to fall on my ass with joy?—and that we were invited to stay with him. He graciously included Don but added that he was "overdefensive and that makes him a bit chichi, but I don't mind." I told Don the first bit of this sentence—not fortunately the rest of it—but he was depressed, just the same, saying how hard he had tried and how it never worked, and how he didn't want to see any more of my friends, and how he didn't know what he really did want, etc. However, the *mood* of all this talk was much better than it used to be.

[1] 309 Monterey Road.

I decided not to go to work in all this rain. And I won't go tomorrow, either, if it doesn't clear.

January 31. It did clear, but I didn't go. Today, however, I've spent at the studio, racing to finish off the Paris sequence of *Jean-Christophe*. Am still not sure if I can do it.

Magnificent after-rain weather with the snow-covered mountains in their splendor. I feel happy, yet I so miss the keenness of appetite and response to this kind of beauty I used to have—even up to a few years ago. Has the hepatitis permanently dulled me?

A weird thing happened. The lady who has lived at 333 East Rustic Road since Bill and I left, fell into the channel last weekend in broad daylight (and sober), cracked her skull and died. I would love to know if they had had any unpleasant experiences previous to this, in that horrible spooky little place. It ought to be torn down. It's full of bad luck.

February 1. Last night we had supper with Renée Zinnemann and took her to see *Tiger at the Gates*.[1] This was a great success—partly because *Tiger* was, or seemed, much better than in New York— Robert Ryan superior to Redgrave, and perhaps in New York we were drunk?—partly because Renée was lively and such fun.

She told us that Peggy and Bill Kiskadden embarrassed her the other evening by quarrelling savagely in her presence. Peggy said she was going east to see her mother. Bill retorted that he was only being told this for the first time in the presence of a guest. Peggy said well, it would be nice for him to come home early and be with little Bill. Bill said it wouldn't always be convenient for him to come home early. Peggy said he didn't love his son, etc. etc.

I can't help being pleased to hear this—and yet I know it's evil to be pleased and that the evil will rebound on me. It is truly appalling, how resentful I've become. Do I use up all my affection on Don and Swami? Swami is the only person against whom I *never* feel resentful.

A strange mood of nostalgia this morning for England—a kind of Mortmere country village with a churchyard, dark overgrown tombs, a study where you could read the classics in mouldy leather volumes. It would be easier to die in such a place, I thought.

February 4. I'm getting to the point where I *must* get restarted on my novel.

[1] Christopher Fry's translation of Jean Giraudoux's play *La Guerre de Troie n'aura pas lieu*.

I have such a desire to do this, and yet I cannot hit the right note. I must absolutely start soon.

Rod Owens to lunch with me at the studio. His nerves are terrible. He dulls them with Miltown. He feels horrible even if he has to drive a short distance. He only feels safe at home. He has cheered himself up a little, lately, by having a love affair. But he worries because his life is going by. He looks big and gross and sleepy.

I feel a curiously strong affection for him. Is it partly for mysterious astrological reasons? We were born on the same day.

Rod and Hayden think that Caskey is going crazy. He has left his friend in Texas and now no one knows where he is. Rod described how, after a big argument they had with him up at the house, he took all of his pictures out of it and stacked them in the garden in the rain. It is really heartbreaking. How sad that all that part of my life had to end in unkindness and sulks, miserable though it certainly was!

February 6. I have been getting letters from Bill Stroud, abusing Gerald. One of these arrived yesterday with a Santa Monica postmark. So I alerted Gerald and Michael Barrie, and we all half expected to be visited by a madman with an axe. Now examining the envelope very closely, I realize that I sent out a false alarm. The Santa Monica post office must have stamped the letter merely because the St. Louis post office had done it so badly—nearly missing the letter altogether.

This morning I drove downtown and bought a cabochon star ruby for Don for the fourth anniversary, on the 14th.[1]

A tiresome tight headache around the temples—the kind Peschelt says is due to atomic fallout affecting the liver.

Finished a big swatch of script in the rough today. Now I can take it easy, rewriting.

But I still long to get on with my novel!

February 7. This morning I had my eyes tested, and at noon I had an electrocardiograph, both normal. That is, my eyes are little if any worse.

Valentine cards are in the shops. I wanted one to give Don with his ruby, and found another, of Beethoven scowling with red glass eyes captioned: "What the hell are you so mad about?" I put this up on the bulletin board in my office to remind me. My resentments are becoming chronic. I detect a growing rejection–hate against women which is truly disconcerting in its proportions.

---

[1] Isherwood and Bachardy first spent the night together on Valentine's Day 1953.

As much as anybody has a right and a reason to be happy in our present world, I have a right and a reason. And a duty—even if it were only for Don's sake. Very well, I'll make a big try.

February 11. Struggles, yesterday, to restart my novel. I now believe I know what's wrong. It oughtn't to begin with the dream telegram. Too tricky.

Don and I walked on the beach. Wonderful pale blue Japanese silhouette-mountains—not a house visible along the Topanga-Malibu shore. In the evening Don did some homework on a process called (I think) monoprinting. He made a mess over the floor and had to clean the tiles. Our life together is a whole world in miniature—despair, reassurance, snugness, triumph—all under the microscope. Such a tiny world—and yet—what else does life offer? I don't think two people could possibly be happier together.

On Saturday, we had supper with Speed. He lectured Don on the necessity of associating with your superiors. He was at his best. He seemed honest, decent, humble, compassionate, vitally curious and very strong. Yes—there's a wonderful person inside Speed. I only hope it will one day permanently dominate the other personae—the skipping spiteful niggery indiscreet gossip mongers.

How dull the *Satyricon*[1] is! Am rereading it by sheer determination.

February 12. I'm badly scared. This morning, while shaving, I noticed a bump on the side of my belly. I showed it to Dr. Lewis when I went for my shot, and he thinks I should have it cut out at once. True, he says it's probably nothing—and the operation should be very slight. But all the same, the possibility of cancer exists.

I shall go through all manner of attitudes toward this emergency, no doubt. Right now, I'm shaking. Perhaps—even if the news is bad—I'll feel better when I know something for certain. The great fear of death at present is its approach. And the agony of leaving Don. That's too painful to think about, even.

At five I'm going to see the surgeon, Dr. Lichtenstein.

I've finished another batch of pages. Marian is typing them. So I've been lying on the sofa, thinking about myself (which is the worst thing I could do) and sweating in this sudden incredible heat wave.

February 13. Last night, I saw the surgeon, Dr. Lichtenstein, who says yes it's a tumor and must come out but he doesn't think it's serious. This morning I saw Sellars, and he was almost positive that it isn't

[1] By Petronius.

cancer. Still—the whole thing is scary and horrid and I do wish it was over.

Last night, I gave the ruby to Don because I couldn't wait until just before going into hospital. He was delighted, and that made me cry. At a time like this, it is horribly painful to have someone you love and who loves you. The terrible vulnerability you feel—for both of you.

February 14. Talked to Swami, last night. He says he isn't afraid of dying now at all—though of course he would prefer to avoid pain. This life seems to him "all shadows." He was very convincing, and I believed in his belief—but there is one problem he doesn't have and I can't explain to him—the pain of separation from those who aren't in "the gang." What if Don were excluded from the Ramakrishna loka? But, of course, such questions can't be asked except in terms of our present life and its appearances.

This morning I tried to explain to Don why I prefer to face the possible worst now (or try to; one can't, properly, till one is certain) rather than "refusing to dwell on the negative side," as many advise. But he doesn't see this; it shocks him. I guess it is a profound difference in temperament.

Am writing this in the office at Twentieth Century, waiting until it's time to go and see Jessie Marmorston. Yes, I *am* anxious and tense—I won't pretend I'm not—but I must say I would still rather have gone through this anxiety than dulled it with happy drugs. Whatever there is to be learned from this experience, you aren't going to learn it in the midst of a Miltown daze.

February 15. Well, here I am—just about seventy-two hours since Dr. Lewis found the tumor, and it's out and I'm sitting dressed in my room, waiting to go home as soon as Don calls to pick me up.

The tumor was between the size of a dime and a nickel, but rounded like an eggplant. White—pinkish with blood. I had a local anesthetic, something like Novocain. When they'd cut it out, the pathologist came in and looked at it, to be sure it wasn't malignant. My only discomfort is that my belt presses against the dressing.

But now, let this be a lesson. Let me not forget what I felt—and let it make a difference. Let me think of myself as a reprieved person— with the obligations of the reprieved.

The man in the other bed in my room, Mr. Graw. He had an operation on his ear, and it was pretty successful—but he couldn't help blasting with the TV set, because he didn't hear well. Amazing how you can relax toward these things, if you don't immediately stiffen with resentment. Mr. Graw is an accountant at Las Vegas. He wants to have a plastic valve made for his heart. He really seems to like operations. He read in the newspaper about a woman who has a ping-pong ball in her heart, and it makes a noise like an alarm clock. Of such are the servants of science.

February 17. Am really quite shaken up because I got mad at the kids next door for jumping in our geraniums while playing hide-and-seek. This is the first time I lost my temper or got at all excited since the sedation I got for the operation. How nasty this kind of anger is! Old maidish.

But I'm full of resolves—to let this be a lesson, as I said.

I will try to make more sense of my life—that's the only way I can put it.

How strange—I discovered the tumor on the second anniversary of Maria Huxley's death.

It is silly to say that my present relations with Don are too good to last—because everything is too something or other to last—but they really do mark a new high record of happiness for me. And yet—isn't this happiness organically part of what I've just been through? Is it possible at all without poignancy?

It now begins to look as if maybe we won't go to Tahiti in June, but postpone that trip and wait and go to India in the fall. Reasons—I must go to India now, because of the Ramakrishna book; Don could then get another continuing term at art school; I could perhaps finish another draft of my novel, earn more movie money, make a more complete recovery from the hepatitis—on which Jessie Marmorston blames my tumor.

The lady at the flower shop, when I was buying daffodils: "Don't give them too much water. They're little drunkards. They drink themselves to death."

February 21. Lunch today with Jessie Marmorston, who told me that Ken MacKenna of MGM has a cancer which is probably incurable. She asked me all about my early life.

I really must now get into a recovery frame of mind. As it is, I'm worried about my right hand which is shooting pains right up the arm.

This is a very strange passage in my life—a kind of knife-edge. On the one hand, these negative fears and clouds of sickness; on the other, the truly idyllic life I'm leading with Don, the keen interest I feel in my novel and even, to a far greater degree than usual, in my movie work. Also—and this is most important of all—I feel a new or renewed relationship to Swami. This has been growing for months.

It's as if he were exposing me to stronger and stronger vibrations of his love—yet, all the while, making almost no personal demand. I saw him last night—still, as he said "floating" a little after an operation he had on a cyst. He was like a small adorable animal with ruffled fur as he sat on his bed telling us about the early days at the monastery. I don't feel he is altogether a person, any longer. This light seems to flood through him more and more continuously.

February 24. The night before last, rain fell in torrents, making our bedroom roof leak and even driving some water in through the skylight. Some streets—such as La Cienega—were flooded and cars were afloat and crashing into each other. We are told to expect more tonight.

Today the muscles of my stomach around the wound are sore, which worries me, rather. I'm so disgustingly fat—really fleshy—round the waist. And I feel weak. I know that I must fight my way out of this condition step by step, or else I'll get sick again in one way or another.

I keep on at my novel, revising a page a day, going slow until I've built up about thirty to forty pages and thus regained interest and confidence.

Yesterday Ted was again arrested for shoplifting and I had to guarantee the bail bond. We went to see a lawyer in Beverly Hills, Sheldon Andelson, to arrange this.

Despite my good resolutions after the operation, I still find myself fussing about the absurdest trifles. I keep looking out the window to be sure the children aren't jumping on our geranium bed, as they have been.

February 26. Dick Foote called yesterday to tell me jubilantly that Johnnie and Starcke have split up. It seems that Starcke demanded Johnnie should quit the ranch (and, I suppose, Carter's influence) for good and put himself unreservedly under Goldsmith's and Starcke's metaphysical guidance. Really, it seems that Starcke must be a little bit insane! So Johnnie has legally dissolved the "partnership" between them. Starcke, according to Dick, gets about $100,000! He was splitting Johnnie's earnings fifty-fifty.

Johnnie is reported to have said that he feels a great load off his mind, as when Auriol Lee died.

But it's sad. I do like Starcke, crazy though he is, and a rogue—so long as he keeps off God. The prospect for poor Johnnie now is pretty dreary, especially as he does not like Dick, I think. He is actually in a worse position than if he'd been left completely alone.

Saw Dr. Lichtenstein today. He says everything is going well. I was most agreeably surprised by his fee—only $160!

Speed has read my *Jean-Christophe* script, all but the ending, and plainly isn't much impressed by it. He would like a punchy drama in three acts. He recommends my asking for a collaborator, so as to have an ally. I guess he thinks I couldn't manage to rewrite it alone. I don't quite know what to do about this.

March 4. Yesterday I drove up to the Sarada Math with Evelyn Hooker and gave a talk on "Who is Ramakrishna?" I thought I was rather dull and flat, but people seemed pleased. The girls, as usual, seemed so sweet and naturally intimate like the right kind of relatives—the kind you forget when you're not with them but who are always there and whose love you rediscover each time you meet. Sarada was wonderful as always; and I was greatly impressed by Barada, who seemed to have acquired great maturity all of a sudden. She complimented me on my talk, saying that it was "so bold"—and I heard the tone of Sister—a great lady's courtesy.

I'm very glad I invited Evelyn to come with me. Not only did the experience interest her, and maybe help her (because I think she got a lot out of talking to Sarada), but also we were able to talk in a relaxed way about Edward.

She says she is determined not to be an "amputated" person. She is going to make a complete new life for herself. She feels that the homosexual research project will help her do this. She has decided to buy a TV set and put it in the living room, where Edward had always declared he wouldn't have it. "I hope the shade of Edward won't rise up and smite me," she added. (It was a very good sign, I thought, that she could talk like this.)

There's a boy who comes to the lectures at Santa Barbara. About ten years old. I think his name's Jonathan. He has something extraordinary in his smile. Maybe he's a junior saint. Evelyn noticed it too. And already everybody is kidding him about becoming a monk.

When I mentioned him to Don, Don exclaimed impatiently: "I hate child prodigies!" I know so exactly why he said this—it's his horror of competition. And nowadays we have this disgusting cult of the young who are "going places."

Nonetheless, a genuine prodigy *is* fascinating!

Yesterday evening, after getting back from Santa Barbara, we drove up to Vedanta Place in time to catch the end of vespers and be touched by Swami with the tray of relics. It was Don's own idea that he should come with me, and I was very happy that he suggested it. (When we went to vespers at the Brahmananda puja on February 1, he wouldn't be touched by the relics.) Now I feel he has joined the Ramakrishna family.

Speed and Paul have left for a Perle Mesta party in Philadelphia and the opening of Tennessee's *Orpheus Descending*.

On Saturday night I talked to Johnnie on the phone. He told me, with the air of a president declaring a state of war, that he and Starcke *have* split up. Dick and Carter were present at the other end; and it was sadder than hell, this feeling of divorce and the triumph of the maiden aunts.

My operation scar is still sore, but I guess it will be for a long while.

Don fears that Ted may be getting ready to have another attack. He has been laid off from his job and is now in a lively irresponsible mood—the kind which usually means trouble.

March 9. At the AJC ranch. Don and I drove down here last night.

A very strong wind this afternoon. Clouds of sunlit dust blowing over the fields. The cotton woods make a noise like rushing water.

The inevitable private conferences with Carter and Johnnie. Carter told us that the doctor doesn't expect Johnnie to live more than three to five years—not so much because of his heart as his liver. But I get the impression that Johnnie does *want* to live, and so he probably will. As for Johnnie he says that he feels only relief at having gotten rid of Starcke. But of course he is suffering; and the saddest thing is that he is basically alone, with Carter and Dick offering him their kindness as a married pair offers shelter to a widower. Carter is insensitive in this respect. He is a good nurse to John—does everything possible for him, rations his cigarettes, arranges his meals, puts him to bed, protects him from disturbance—but he was about to show Johnnie a letter from Dick which arrived today—a letter bubbling with naive good-hearted tactless protectiveness: how *we* are going to take care of poor Johnnie, etc. Just the very thing to make Johnnie feel completely out in the cold. As far as I am concerned, I feel I would rather be quite alone than in such a threesome, especially remembering what Carter used to be to Johnnie.

This afternoon, Johnnie showed us old theatrical magazines, with pictures of *The Speckled Band, Dr. Jekyll and Mr. Hyde*, etc. etc.

Joel Goldsmith wrote Johnnie a revolting letter today—which Carter *is* going to show him—all about God consciousness and material consciousness. D. H. Lawrence used to exclaim against people who had "sex in the head." Goldsmith has religion in the head. Every word he utters is *false*.

March 11. Speed came to lunch with me at the studio today—just back from Philadelphia. Perle Mesta's party had more gate crashers than guests. He didn't like Tennessee's play. Tennessee had been very drunk, he said, and screamed at him because he couldn't think of anything to praise in it. Speed also says he is seriously thinking of getting rid of Joshua Logan[1] as director of his play and switching to Kazan, if it can be arranged. He was very manic and violent. "I'd cut my own mother's throat if she got in the way of my work. When it comes to my work, I'm *absolutely* cold. It's the only way to be."

Driving back from the ranch last night, Don said he had never before understood how nice it would be to bury oneself in the country. We also discussed the impossibility of dealing with liars—with reference to Speed. I told Don about the Swiss scientist who had snipped off a bit of ectoplasm and kept it alive—and about the clairvoyant experience in which two women relived the Dieppe Raid. He said this made him feel frightened. I reminded him that he is now protected by Ramakrishna. Ramakrishna has touched him.

The almost terrifying mystery of happiness with another human being! It scares me, and so I keep fearing its end, and dwelling on the danger of its ending. I would do much better to try to understand it and learn something from it. *Why* are Don and I so happy right now? *Why* isn't everybody?

March 15. Not feeling good. My operation scar is sensitive, and my belly is swollen up, apparently with gas which I can't get rid of. I'm full of dull anxieties.

Today Swamis Prabhavananda and Vandanananda, and Krishna and Don came to lunch. Swami Vandanananda is really movie struck, but ashamed to admit it in front of Prabhavananda.

Have just told Jack Goodman of Simon and Schuster that I want to switch to them.

Ploughing along through *Jean-Christophe* with difficulty. It's hard to rewrite. Also my novel—but there I feel I really have made a good start.

Yesterday, Vance Breese called and told me a friend of his was leaving for Tahiti tomorrow to deliver a flying boat to the governor. He would gladly have taken Don and me along! I went into quite a tailspin—but of course it was impossible at such short notice.

Gloomy thoughts of old age and/or death. Answer: japam. Again and again today I've remembered this and then lapsed back into tamasic anxiety—and forgotten the japam.

---

[1] Isherwood added in the margin, "As Speed put it: 'I'm going to jerk him.'"

Gave a ride to a Chilean who is studying at UCLA. He had the beautiful name of Duilio Ottonini.

They've been shooting this building for *The Three Faces of Eve* disguised as "The Dixie Motel." At lunch today, they filled my office with huge lights. Afterwards, the walls were quite hot.

March 18. Still feeling lousy and worried about myself. I have a dull headache. My scar is sore. I feel sleepy and rotten. I do wish I could snap out of this state.

Yesterday we saw Terence Rattigan and a boy named Kenley Saville whom I used to know slightly in 1948. Terry is really very nice. But it does seem amazing to me that he, who seems in every way such a darling of success, should have settled for such a squalid, miserable and fundamentally boring private life. Drinking is so *awful*! It is a bog which holds you and everybody you know, so that relationships become just that much harder to get out of.

I'm quite interested in my novel—so I'll get on with that.

March 21. Saw Dr. Lichtenstein again yesterday evening. He assures me that my scar is healing normally. Many small nerves are cut through when the flesh is cut, and these are bound to hurt for a while. So I should just ignore the whole thing—and I will try to.

Last night we went to a goodbye party for Terence Rattigan, given by Hecht-Hill-Lancaster—more specifically by Hill, who is having an affair with Rita Hayworth. Because of this affair, apparently, Hayworth has been forced on to poor Terry as one of the stars in the movie version of his *Separate Tables*. She is somewhat spectral, now, but still, in a grim way, beautiful. Judy Garland looked like a cook, in a small white glittering round pie-shaped hat and a black dress that didn't fasten behind, because she's so fat, and that looked as if it might have come from the Goodwill. Lenore Cotten talked and talked and the two coons from Trinidad sang, while one of them scraped a gourd with a nail until all but the strongest nerves were ready to snap. Cedric Hardwicke's young wife insisted on sharing my chair, as she told me that Hardwicke was the kindest of husbands but that she has more fun when he's away.

The only positive result of the party for us was that Lenore Cotten invited us to lunch, and promises to get us together with Jennifer Jones.[1] We are considering "training" Lenore as "our" hostess and rewarding her by bringing her an occasional celebrity from "our" world.

[1] A favorite actress of Bachardy.

Reread the first eight pages of my revised novel this morning. Not bad.

March 25. Black depression. Have just lost my wig with Mr. Coates, the upholsterer, because without one word of apology he coolly announced that the material for our cushions has been found defective and so we would have to wait.

But I'm also deeply upset and disturbed about the situation with Don.[1] He couldn't possibly be sweeter and gentler in the way he takes this; but it is a terrible obstacle, nevertheless, and many—most—relationships don't survive it, or at least only outwardly. I realize that we can only work through it by the greatest patience and love, and I know myself well enough to know that this will be *almost* too much for me to manage. Perhaps too much. I simply do not know. I dread what's coming.

March 28. Have just talked to Carter on the phone. He still thinks—and the doctor thinks—that Johnnie won't really ever get better. He is greatly concerned because Johnnie's jealous resentment against Dick Foote is coming up to the surface. Here the three of them are—bound together as long as Johnnie lives—and there's this friction. Carter said, "I have to be a little selfish," and, "Johnnie's attitude could very easily turn into tyranny." All this has the makings of a truly hideous tragedy.

As for *our* problem—Don's and mine—it isn't solved and yet it seems temporarily much less acute, because we had a long talk about it at the beginning of the week. Don is really incredible, especially when you consider his age: he has so much understanding. What I must learn is to be absolutely frank with him always, and to be certain that I have made my own feelings quite clear.

Ivan Moffat is in a sad state because Caroline prefers to stay in New York. If she really loved him, he says, she'd stay here with him no matter how much she hated the place. He's right, I fear.

April 2. Much to report, but nothing of any great importance.

On Friday we started our program of giving one-a-week suppers. Miss Burns who gives me my hormone shots has a cook who has a sister, Dorothy Miller, an enormous Negress, frowning faced but quite good-natured, who is cooking them for us. The Huxleys came, and the Adrians,[2] as well as Thom Gunn and his friend, Mike Kitay,

---

[1] Isherwood added in the margin: "(Impotence again, I guess)."
[2] The actress, Janet Gaynor, and her husband, Gilbert Adrian, celebrated costume and fashion designer (known as "Adrian").

who were down for the week from San Francisco—or rather Stanford, where Thom teaches and Mike studies. The party was quite a success. Aldous looked tired and seemed sleepy but Janet and Laura were bright as queen bees. Adrian giggled and made bad puns. And Thom and Mike were thrilled to meet Aldous, and Dorothy was thrilled to cook for Janet.

Then on Saturday a fantastically boring party at Ray Ohge's—we were invited for 7:00. There weren't even any hors d'oeuvres till 9:45. Supper was to have been at midnight, but we left. It seems incredible that Ray could have persuaded all these well-to-do people to stick around through all those hours. And oh, how messy drinking is!

High winds the last two days—as violent as I've ever known them here.

April 3. Dissatisfied with myself. The novel is at a standstill—and why? Because I have gotten into this hair-splitting perfectionistic mood in which I piddle for weeks over a few pages. I must realize that this is just another draft, and get the hell on with it.

I don't bring my weight down because I'm greedy. I buy bags of marshmallows and guzzle them in the evenings when Don isn't home.

I'm getting bored with *Jean-Christophe.* It crawls along. I lack invention, feel lazy and sleepy.

I'm also making heavy weather with the foreword to *All the Conspirators.*[1] After this I must absolutely decline all journalistic jobs. They cost me too much trouble.

A boy named Jim Sherwood came to see me today. He is twenty, fair haired, blue eyed, with the humorless handsome intelligence of a Vernon. He is working at Paramount. Claims he has written seventeen (or seven?) novels, all unpublished, has a rich father he has quarrelled with, has worked as a clown in a circus, been a newspaper man. His latest novel is called *The Charliquinade.* He is so impressive that you wonder if he'll become president.[2]

Impressive in another way is Charles O. Locke—a chunky white-haired man who has the office next to mine. He has written a really beautiful book, *The Hell-Bent Kid.* He is terribly worried that he won't be able to master the technique of movie writing. I have told

[1] About to be republished by Jonathan Cape (for the second time, in 1957) and by New Directions (in 1958); Isherwood wrote a new foreword for each edition and eventually reprinted the later American one, which he preferred, in *Exhumations.*

[2] Sherwood later published at least one novel, *Stradella* (1966), set in Hollywood.

him that there isn't any. Today he sends me a charming note of gratitude.

Saw Swami tonight. He's better. He told me the Swami in Paris died a few days ago, and he doesn't trust the Swami's assistant; thinks he's lustful.

April 6. Yesterday, Harry Brown brought Robert ("Cal") Lowell, the poet, to lunch. Harry doesn't drink at all. He looked well but a trifle shrunk, as people do who have lost a whiskey bloat. He left for New York last night to see this girl, June de Baum, whom he hopes to make change her mind and marry him. Probably she hinted she'd do so if he gave up drink. Then, with or without June, he plans to go down to Haiti.

After lunch, at the Luau, we went on the set of *Will Success Spoil Rock Hunter?* Jayne Mansfield was playing a scene in which she lies on a table and is massaged. As she lay down, she opened her robe and showed her breasts completely—not quickly and coquettishly, but quite slowly, while she was waiting for a scarf to bind around them. This is in the presence of at least forty people, including male and female visitors! Cal Lowell fairly drooled; and Harry, who was fussing about time, had to drag him away from the set.

It was our Dorothy cooking night. We invited Gerald, the Stravinskys and Bob Craft. Gerald arrived on time and at once began talking mescaline which is becoming more and more irritating as he refuses to give us any. The Stravinskys were nearly three quarters of an hour late—they hadn't been able to find the way—and Bob Craft was sick with a terrible headache in the car, with the shakes, and believing himself sickening for polio or starting a nervous break-down. Igor and Vera were both greatly upset over this—he more than she—one sees how deeply they love him. Vera wanted to know didn't we have some Miltown or anything similar? So Don went down to the Masselinks and got some Equanil from Jo. Quite soon, Bob had apparently recovered and was with us at the table, laughing and eating stuffed chicken.

Igor, in his seventy-fifth year, looks good but complains of insomnia. He asked Gerald how to meditate, saying that he might as well do this while he was lying awake. Igor said, "I am not sure I am creative, only inventive." He said, "All the time I am saying to myself—yes, I am thinking, but am I thinking well?" He was so sweet and touching.

Dorothy had never heard of the Stravinskys. She thought she recognized Igor as a Jewish comic on the Molly Goldberg show![1]

---

[1] "The Goldbergs," on TV.

Don thoroughly enjoyed the evening, he says—much more so than last week. So did I, except that I have an upset stomach.

A grey chilly day. Am still stuck in my foreword to *All the Conspirators*. I must learn to avoid these short chores. They're always the worst.

April 10. Stomach symptoms continue, after a letup yesterday. They are like ones I've had before—in the pyloric region; discomfort and an acute sense of anxiety. I'm worried about myself. I feel very much bogged down in sickness, unable to get my vitality back. And yet I don't want to go through all the fuss of X rays again. It's too tedious.

Work rises in mountains before me. At present, I'm eager to see if I can't altogether avoid writing a travel book and travel articles, and just do the Ramakrishna book. Random House can then be gotten rid of, without involving myself in all manner of other work.

Now I must make a stand—stop worrying—get organized.

Later. I've just been up to Vedanta Place. Swami told me that he dreamt he was handing out copies of my book on Ramakrishna to crowds of people. And he was saying, "Chris's book!" I was present too.

This dream makes me feel very happy—as if all would be well, after all. Swami said, "It will be a turning point in the growth of the society."

And now for the first time I dimly get a new conception of the book. I want to work Ramakrishna's life in with some autobiographical material—telling something about the way in which I, myself, got to know of Ramakrishna but without too many personal details and without indiscretion. I mentioned this to Swami this evening. He said, "However you write it will be all right."

I felt his love very strongly. And I felt also a great warmth from Vandanananda, which is good.

Great love also between me and Jessie Marmorston, whom I saw this evening, briefly. She gave me some pills which she hopes will fix my stomach. If not, she'll examine it on Friday.

Her electric chair for going up and downstairs, to save her heart.

April 12. Terrible persecutions, yesterday and today, by men who are painting the writers' building. They sing, shout to each other. And if one complains one feels somehow bad, out of touch with the big simple life of the big simple masses.

Am getting seriously worried about my stomach. It doesn't let up. Not really painful but menacing, full of dread. And oh, how sick I am of medical examinations! I dread more X rays and barium meals.

Jessie has started giving me something in my shots which is supposed to increase my libido! Got the first yesterday. All quiet down there so far!

April 14. Just a year since I started this volume of my journal. Not a bad year; at least I have gotten something accomplished. In many ways a very happy year with Don. The chief snag has been my poor health.

That continues. Today my stomach is vaguely wretched, despite the temporary relief I get from taking Gelusil. I'm worried about myself. Is something organically wrong? Cancer? An ulcer? More liver trouble? I have a sharp pain in my right side, now—that's something brand-new since yesterday.

The wisteria vine is beginning to spill its blossom. It's swarming with fat black-brown bees. The yellow roses are starting to come out on the wall. In fact, the house is at its showiest—the way we first saw it before buying it last year.

I'm at present absolutely stuck fast in *Jean-Christophe*. I cannot see how to lick the problem of handling Olivier's death.

I have resolved to restart the novel, rewriting it as quickly as possible, without hesitations.

I think I might be able to begin the Ramakrishna book, before I leave for India.

Don and I rather decided yesterday not to go to the Orient by way of Australia. Don doesn't relish the long uneventful boat trip. We will go by boat or plane direct to Hong Kong, say, and then on, via Siam, etc.

Don said something very good yesterday—I wish I could remember it verbatim. It was an expression of dismay at the way in which "all the little years suddenly add up, and that's what a person's life means." He has his holiday now from Chouinard, and is repainting the lamps in the alcove and revarnishing our sundeck.

On Friday night we had Anne Baxter and Perle Mesta to supper with Speed and Paul. Baxter was lively and most anxious to be pleasant—but quite embarrassingly artificial. She chattered without ceasing. Whenever something unflattering was said about another actress, she looked pained. I said how someone had remarked you could never recognize Eleanor Parker from one day to another, and Baxter agreed eagerly, wincing with pain as she did so: "*Yes*—why *is* that?" As for Mesta, she ate heartily of the pot roast, and spent most of the evening watching Don's face—the way old people watch the faces of the young—to get vitality out of them. They watch without the least attempt to participate in the conversation, like viewers of TV. One feels a kind of grim good nature in her, however.

April 19. My indigestion bothers me again, after a respite.

Don said this morning, "Drive carefully—the life you are living may be your own."

While he had his holiday this week, he has beautifully repainted the lamps and painted the drawers of the bedroom bureau in various colors.

He says: "I don't care to be alone for long, because I don't like myself very much."

He says: "I'm two cats, really. One of them is a little flighty white one that likes to lie on a cushion and have a lot of toms around. The other is a big mean black one with very sharp claws. The black one keeps the white one in order. It's very strict."

Swami, whom we saw last night, liked *Heaven Knows, Mr. Allison* (!)[1]

Don writes in his journal, almost every night, in bed.

I have nearly finished Aldous's *Texts and Pretexts*. I read it only on the toilet, here at the studio.

April 21. On Easter Sunday last year, I began the first draft of my novel.

Today I started working on the rewrite more intensively, and I now want to try to finish this rewrite before we leave for the Orient.

Woke this morning, as so often nowadays, feeling that I'm old and sick—definitely much older and sicker than a year ago. But a good long walk with Don and Jo, along the beach as far as the Norma Shearer house and then back up the cliff stairs and through the Palisades Park has made me feel so much better that I suspect I merely needed exercise.

The pigeon lady in the park and her enemy, the man who feeds the pigeons hard uncooked rice, which will kill them. She wants to become a game warden. Right now, she has no money at all and has to sleep on a friend's porch. She has poison-oak poisoning, carried by the pigeons.

April 22. Charley Locke has written a poem to his wife Virginia. Here is the second stanza:

> I do not love enough in all this time
> Though I have learned of love in every phase

---

[1] Huston's film about a nun and a marine stranded on a desert island in WWII (starring Deborah Kerr and Robert Mitchum).

With diligence and thrift have gathered love
Heaping my treasure over many days
Toiling to love you more, with deeper love
Like hopeless love that does not count the cost
Guiding my love through many devious ways
Knowing that those becalmed in love are lost—
Patience! My own dear love whom I adore
Each day I learn to love you more and more.

He is very sweet. I feel terribly embarrassed because he is reading through *The World in the Evening*, very slowly—even rereading it, he says—I feel with a rather horrified fascination. He calls it "clever."

I have done some work on the novel today and on the Vedanta history, but nothing for Wald, because he's been too busy to see me about the problem of the rioting. I find it nearly impossible to push on with the script until this is cleared up.

My health is good again. The stomach twinges are gone. What I need now is lots of money for the trip.

Don restarted school today, after a week's holiday which he described as "some of the unhappiest days of my life."

April 24. Decided to call my novel simply *Forgotten*.

Don was greatly depressed yesterday—so this morning I gave him a pep talk, reminding him that nothing learned is ever a dead loss, that he may as well stay in school until some other line of action presents itself—as it surely will, etc. He seemed much reassured by this talk.

A bad day at the studio. Drove and drove at the scene between Jean-Christophe and Olivier just before the riots. Couldn't get it.

Lunch with Charley Locke at the Swiss restaurant on Westwood. He is sweet and innocent and I like being with him, but he demands so much time. He unwinds so slowly.

Gore Vidal came by. He is suffering from rectal bleeding. I felt very sympathetically toward him. Jerry Wald has asked him to do the Proust film.

April 30. Am feeling worried because of this indigestion. I mean, I'm worried that it may not be indigestion. And yet I have to smile at myself, even as I write this, thinking how differently we appear to ourselves and others! Here am I, a bundle of worries about myself— and yet this very day Charley Locke told me that I ought to have been a minister of the Gospel because I had so much inner strength—his secretary had said the same thing—and that this inner strength was undoubtedly due to my British ancestry! Poor Charley is in a terrible state of mind, because his producer casually told him yesterday that he will be off the picture by next Tuesday—just when he was having his wife come out to visit him! I comforted him as best I could.

As for the indigestion—well, it must wait till next week. I have to give Jessie's pills a tryout.

Feelings of general dullness and elderly weakness are no doubt due to reading Balzac's *Curé de Tours*, and falling asleep this noon, on the office couch.

Finished the Paris part of the script—up to Jean-Christophe's departure for Switzerland—and sent it in.

Getting on slowly with the novel.

May 1. Indigestion continues. Stomach swollen up big. Wretchedness.

But I want to finish the screenplay before there's any serious trouble.

Gore Vidal, with whom I had lunch on Monday, thinks that Tennessee is pathologically obsessed by the pursuit of success and the fear of losing it.

I make arrangements for our trip to the Orient, and yet a voice whispers to me that I won't go—that I may be seriously sick—may die soon. I'm weary, weary, weary. I keep on with my novel, however; and keep working through the Vedanta history. If only I could stop feeling so rushed! In fact, *no one* is rushing me, except myself.

Don just finished painting the downstair bedroom. He's nervous-sick too, strained and rushed. But we seldom lose contact with each other now, and if we do it's soon regained.

May 3. This stomach thing continues. I'm now resigned to the fact that I will have to tell Jessie Marmorston about it on Monday. Ironically enough, my sex feelings have meanwhile returned to quite an extent!

Saw Swami, the night before last. He held forth against mescaline—or rather, against the cult of mescaline. He doesn't feel that the experiences it provides are valid. *I* think there is a semantic block here. Swami is not unnaturally annoyed when he hears it talked of as a substitute for meditation.

I'm deeply depressed, right now. Because I'm sick? Or is it just a guna? Who knows? I keep on working and functioning, but without joy.

And how much japam have I made? None!

May 6. This morning, I went to see the famous Charles Taylor, who told me that my rectal bleeding was only due to an unimportant pile—not to the other trouble I'm having. Taylor complimented me on being able to relax to such an extent when he put in his sigmoidoscope! So now both Eleanor's men, pilot and proctologist, have awarded me good marks for sangfroid—me who am literally dying of tension! Taylor is very dapper and charming—compared to Vance, he seems almost courtly! And he certainly handles his instrument with the same quality of reassurance as Vance his airplane!

But, all kidding aside, this choked-up sensation in my stomach persists; and the day after tomorrow it's to be X-rayed. I've been having the most horrible sensations of depression. Yesterday I kept wanting to weep. Yes, underneath, as I discovered under hashish, I'm a sorry creature—terrified of being deserted by all, and particularly by Don. Terrified of getting old and sick and dying of cancer.

Don has said he wants to go to New York alone—because he feels incapable of having any relationship to anyone while I'm around. So he is going as soon as school ends—June 15—and already I'm miserable about it—*for no reason*—for actually, as the sane half of me knows, it's good and healthy and desirable. He has to feel free to do such things.

Misery, dread, weariness, weakness. And what's the answer? Japam.

Supper with Ken Wasson, whom Caskey and I met in Bolivia.[1] His talk brought back the black manic-depressive nostalgia for the *altiplano*. He told me about a tribe which reckons everything by twos. One is a half. When they drink, they use two cups simultaneously.

May 8. To Dr. Danelius for X rays. He gave me *1066 and All That*[2] to read while waiting, and talked excitedly about the Jungian analytical interpretation of *Moby Dick*. I don't have a tumor, it seems. But still this feeling of discomfort persists, and they don't know what causes it.

Some tension with Don. He says he is bored by my affectation of strength and would like me to lean on him more. But when I do lean on him, he gets rattled. Or am I being a bit unjust? Yesterday he said he hadn't realized I was worried about the result of the X-ray tests, until I told him I was.

I'm a leaky, creaky but still quite powerful old ship. Some of my passengers are sincerely shocked, however, to discover that the captain carries a private life belt.

---

[1] Wasson and his wife lived in La Paz; he made documentary films.
[2] By W. C. Sellar and R. J. Yeatman.

May 9. The day my father was killed.

What a long long siege of melancholic tamas I'm undergoing! Miserable slothful sadness and aimless worry. Defeatism without cause. Already I dread Don's departure for New York. In my present state, I really don't want to travel anywhere myself. The India trip looms as a dreary menace. I don't want to go. I want to lie down and moan.

It's *most* instructive to go through this kind of thing at a time when there is no question of its being rationally justified. Just shows you!

"Though we know not always whither we are going, we know well what the journey costs us." Balzac—*Le Curé de Tours.*[1]

May 10. Last night, we had supper with Jo and Ben, and Eddie James came too. He seemed more balanced, more relaxed, more genial, less crazy than I'd remembered. But how he remembers, and how he can hate. The extraordinary intensity of his resentment is best expressed in his imitations. He told an annihilating story of how Tchelitchev[2] had tried to double the prices of his pictures—"For you, as a friend." He still remembers every slight he has suffered, as a rich man in the hands of bohemians.

But he was also charming and interesting about Xilitla, his Mexican home. How he has learned to be observant because if you aren't the tarantulas may fall on you from the trees, or you may tread on a coral snake or a deadly lizard—so deadly that a man was killed by spreading his blanket on the ground, lying down and inadvertently squashing one. And the parrots that sleep lying on their backs on your pillow, like men. And the rats and the goats. And the casual murders committed by the Indians and never or lightly punished. He made the whole place come alive.

Afterward, when we got home, Don said: "I feel I'm stifling here!" He talked a lot about my qualities as a monster—how I force people to leave me, etc. But the end result of the talk was a letting off of steam, and somehow the atmosphere cleared. I only wish he could go to New York at once and then perhaps we'd be able to see things clearer.

He *is* right about one thing—and I write this knowing that one day he'll read this, most probably. There *are* times when I think bitterly: *I* support us both—and what's *his* contribution—making neurotic fusses!

But that's only half of the truth. I'm still happier with Don than I've

---

[1] Isherwood had Katharine Prescott Wormeley's translation of *The Vicar of Tours.*
[2] Pavel Tchelitchev, the Russian-born painter.

ever been with anybody. And I don't really in the least mind earning the money—at any rate, not when I'm well.

Jessie Marmorston tells me this morning that the rugae (wrinkles) of my stomach are slightly inflamed. I'm to go on a diet. No raw vegetables or fruit. Eat only chicken and hamburgers.

May 12. Stomach a bit better. Or anyhow my mood is better. Don seems happier. The sun has been shining. But more rain seems to threaten. The huge inscription which the high-school boys painted on the wall down at State Beach—"This wall is for queers, homosexuals and perverts only"—has been removed, somehow, by the authorities.

Don went to Mother's Day dinner with his mother. I've been pondering over my novel and reading *Fires on the Plain* by Shohei Ooka. I'm about to start a course of Jap novel reading, so I'll be hep for our trip.

Yesterday night, we had supper with the Stravinskys. A journalist once asked him; "When you wrote *Orpheus*, did you think about classical Greece?" And he replied, "I thought about strings." Bob Craft took this as a text for a diatribe against critics. I felt very warmly toward him, and Vera and Igor—they are all lovable. Igor complained of headaches. He works even after supper. Eddie James was there, with a silver non-rep statuette made by Oliver Andrews—obviously an ideal object to "lose" in friends' houses. Eddie, I noticed, has a technique of carrying two tissue-paper parcels—one a real one, one just paper. At the end of the evening, he leaves the real one behind him while he ostentatiously pockets the paper one.

Igor showed us the back garden, remarking that it was always overrun by the neighbors' children and that he didn't at all mind this, but that they were not always "prudent" with the water hose—left it flowing and thus caused landslides. Imagine the fits *we'd* have thrown if anything like that had happened!

Jim Charlton actually left the Masselinks' in a hurry yesterday, because he thought I was coming up there! I don't know why he is putting on this act—but I must confess I'm beginning to get really mad at *him*. This is very silly—and, on top of that, it's just exactly what he wants!

May 16. It has turned a lot warmer. A piercing headache last night and this morning. But the gastritis—that's what Jessie says it is—has yielded amazingly to the treatment she prescribed—no raw fruit, milk drinking, and giving up coffee altogether.

All is cheerful at home. "We have such fun together, don't we?" said Don this morning at breakfast.

Vera Stravinsky and he came to lunch with me. We took her on the set of *Kiss Them for Me*. She told us how she once played Elena in a Russian film of *War and Peace*.

May 17. Amazing, the headaches and bodyaches I suffered last night! And yet I'm sort of optimistic. I know I'm quite sick, but I don't care. You get used to it so easily. Sickness only becomes depressing if things are going badly—then it's the last straw.

Ivan told me yesterday on the phone how Caroline had said gaily—after he'd sat up all night writing her long introspective fault-finding letters—"Let's draw a veil over those, shall we?" She's coming out this weekend.

Charley Locke has received notice that he's through, here. He is leaving with no regrets—sincerely shocked by the life that is led in movie circles: he finds it hectic and decadent. He met Harry Brown the other day, and thought him: "self-confident." He told me that I'm one of the few people he isn't afraid of!

May 20. We drove to the AJC Ranch and spent the weekend. John [van Druten] seems definitely better, although he has lost a great deal of weight—thirty pounds—and continues to do so. Saturday, Don's birthday, was beautiful. We swam in the pool and I started to feel a good bit better inside. Don loves the peacefulness of the ranch. Later we drove to the rather grim stony valley end where the Crippens (the murderer's son and his wife) live. John has a great curiosity to meet them.[1] The houses stand in little carpets of garden, always with bushes of oleanders and sometimes some palms, with the grey volcanic rubble all around. Later in the evening, a roaring wind got up, thrashing the cottonwoods, and blew all night.

Yesterday, after a tedious drive in fast but thick traffic, we got home and went to supper with the Masselinks, celebrating Don's birthday by having our first drinks.[2] The drinks went down well and warmly and the evening was pleasant, without aftereffects.

Today I learn that I'm to finish here at the end of the week. MGM offers a polish job on *Ben Hur*. Geller irritates me by staying on in New York because his wife is sick.

May 21. I forgot to mention a conversation I had with Johnnie. He said again that he doesn't feel the least bit upset about Starcke. "If he hadn't left," Johnnie said, "I should have killed him, just as I killed

---

[1] Van Druten based a play on the Crippen murder; see Glossary under Crippen.
[2] Since contracting hepatitis.

Auriol." I said, "Are you planning to kill Dick Foote?" "Oh, *no!*" he replied.

This idea of Johnnie's, that he can "kill" people—force them to die—is quite crazy, of course. But not the least bit crazier than the ideas *I* get.

Don is promoting this trip to San Francisco. He longs for the rush and excitement of it. I hate the idea. I just want to stay home and relax and sleep. But I'll probably enjoy it when I get there.

To lunch with Gore at MGM and see Zimbalist[1] about *Ben Hur.* He keeps opening his eyes at you, like a revolving lighthouse.

Stomach better but back aches.

Another thing Johnnie told me: that if Carter should die, he'd go back to England and settle in Folkestone or Eastbourne.

May 31. Pete Martinez and his friend, David MacFadden, brought Jen Yow,[2] who's staying with them, over from Long Beach to see us. Jen is here because he is in charge of a traveling exhibit from the Pierpont Morgan [Library]. I haven't seen Pete since the winter of 1951–52, when I was in New York for the opening of *Camera.* He was fat then; now he looks good. His thick furry black hair just touched with grey. The visit was a great success. Don got along well with both Pete and Jen. Only David turned tiresome when he had drunk a bit—we felt a submerged spite against Pete. Also he was academically sententious about Thoreau, on whom he's writing a thesis for a master's degree.

My stomach is slowly getting better, I think. I stick to wine on Stravinsky's advice. But my fat disgusts me, 152 pounds.

Mr. Jalal Ahmed, deputy director of films and publications for the Pakistan government, came to lunch with me today. He says that Pakistan has no culture yet—it's a melting pot. He has the tiniest moustache I have ever seen. We are to meet in India—of course.

June 1. A date to be recorded with dismay. Only four months till we start and so much to accomplish.

Today has flown by. We got up at nearly 11:00, decided to have only juice for breakfast, Don worked on his design, hating it—an oriental dancer. At 2:00 he came out with me to lunch at Ted's Grill. Now it's after 5:00 and we're supposed to have supper at 7:00 with Michael and Gerald Heard, and Don says he has to go to the gym first.

---

[1] Sam Zimbalist (he died in 1958 while producing *Ben Hur*).
[2] Jensen Yow, an artist and curator, was a friend of Lincoln Kirstein and had a room in Kirstein's house.

He is very cross, as so often, because an hour consists of sixty minutes—not five or six hundred, as he'd like.

Jerry [Wald] now says that we will be through by the end of the week. And then I shall be free to get on. But I'd like to make token beginnings today.

June 2. The supper at Michael Barrie's with Gerald last night was definitely not a success. The two of them got on to their eternal subject, LSD, and served up the usual line of talk. Michael was very holy. He spoke with holy, smug satisfaction about people who get the horrors when they take it. "People who haven't meditated just can't stand it," he announced. Then turned to Don with what seemed the most bogus solicitude: "Do you meditate, Don?" "*No.*" "Ah—"

We had had champagne for supper, which made Don a bit high, and he was in a towering fury all the way to Dick Hopper's, where we calmed down, watching *Humoresque* on TV. Don says he never wants to see either Michael or Gerald again.

Yesterday I restarted my novel and tried to begin the Ramakrishna book. But it isn't easy to do so. *Some* kind of personal approach seems desirable, but what?

This morning, Vernon Old showed up, and stayed talking for nearly an hour and a half, although we obviously wanted to get rid of him and start work. He was very self-contained, gracious, good humored, thick skinned. He told us to go and see a mural he has painted in the cocktail lounge of the Normandie Hotel, also a painting he has had accepted by the county museum. He has been interesting himself in falconry as a hobby. Now that he is nearly bald, his big smooth face seems even bigger and the scars on it more noticeable.

A foggy day here on the beach; sunny inland.

June 5. This is to record that today I broke all records for criminal laziness. Stayed home from the studio and did nothing. If I had *decided* to do nothing, this would have been okay and even quite sensible—I need a rest. But to wander about, too lazy to read—mugging, puttering, fiddling with things—shameful. I must relearn the art of being alone, or I shall be miserable when Don goes.

Grey lifeless fog all morning. Then it cleared and I went on the beach and swam.

Later. A warmish night with a misty moon. The frogs in the channel making a noise that reminds me of the clatter of a funicular railway. Why do they sometimes suddenly stop?

Supper with Jo and Ben, alone—Don is in school. They have just returned from Jo's home, Yakima, Washington, where there was a family conference on what to do about Jo's alcoholic brother. He became alcoholic because he was the smaller of two twins, and because all his sisters were so strong. Ben, telling about this, said, "They all married weak guys."

Jim Charlton had been in to see them. He is still nursing this grudge against me, because I didn't give him the remodelling job on the house. Ben thinks all this is nothing but jealousy, and that it goes way back—back to the fuss about my going to Bermuda with Sam Costidy in March 1952!

We hear Tennessee has had an operation but is better.

June 9. Two days ago, I finished work at Fox—at least for the time being. That is to say, the script of *Jean-Christophe* is now to be mimeographed and read by the front office, and offered to stars and directors.

Now I'm at home hoping I can make good use of my time.

Rather against my inclination, we are going to San Francisco on Thursday for three to four days. I'm unwilling to do this, because it makes a rather meaningless break, and because it'll cost money—of which we do not have much, considering the expense of the trip before us. However, the tickets are paid for already.

Don leaves the following week—the 18th—for New York.

Today was grey but with some sun. We lay on the beach. Don and I went in the water—the first time we had a good long swim this year. Jo gave me some trunks which had been a present to Ben but were too small for him—and horrors!—they fit rather snugly, thirty-fours. I am getting loathsomely fat. I have just taken the tape measure and looked to see how big four inches is. That's what I've gained.

June 10. Last night it rained. Today was sunny and hot and I went in the ocean; it was quite warm.

I have quite lost the art of being alone. My mind is dull. I get no bite out of sensations. I'm merely restless. Then tired out. Got my "upside-down" board from upstairs, and lay on it.

However—my stomach seems better and I feel a certain return of sex vitality.

Today in Campbell's book store (where I went to buy a Greek dictionary as a birthday present for Igor) I read an article in a book edited by John Lehmann, which said I was through—my good work all finished in the thirties, and thereafter nothing but the inconsiderable *Prater Violet* and the "unsatisfactory and uncharacteristic"

World in the Evening.[1] This depressed me. And yet I don't know why it should, because I don't really care what they think. But then I ask myself: What am I fit for, nowadays? What am I accomplishing? What does my life mean? And the answer seems to be I have to write that Ramakrishna book. *That* will sum up what my life has been about since the thirties. As for the novel, I don't know what to think about it. But I do know I want to write it.

June 12. Today we heard that Thom Gunn isn't going to be in Palo Alto this weekend, because he leaves for England tomorrow. So Don said he didn't want to go to San Francisco at all. This relieved me. We have decided that he'll leave earlier on his trip—as soon as he can get reservations. I welcome this, too, because it may mean that he comes back earlier. I want to get his absence over with. I shall miss him horribly. Today we drove up to the Observatory in Griffith Park— which we haven't done since February 20, 1953, when we talked about Ted's breakdown and Don's decision to leave home. I said that I'd never guessed, then, that here we'd be, four years later. Don said that it wouldn't have surprised him. "That's what I mean by being obstinate."

When I went up to see Swami, and put out my hand to shake his, he first made me bend down and gave me his blessing. He seldom does this. He told me again how very near Maharaj is to him, all the time. "Whenever you think of God, He thinks of you."

June 15. Don left two days ago, at 11:00 p.m. on Thursday. I'm sort of taking this easy for the present, breathing deeply, swimming slowly along—lest I get rattled and start wondering if anything is happening that I wouldn't like to happen. So I try to be very calm.

Yesterday night I had supper with Hayden and Rod. It was really very nice—though Don's right, they are both bitch[y] and would hurt anyone to the quick, just for the sake of a wisecrack.

Today I had lunch at Vedanta Place—a "Father's Day" celebration, arranged by the congregation for the Swamis and the monks and nuns. We were all garlanded with flowers. Afterwards, some of the congregation performed a very amusing play based on the story of the twenty-four teachers of Avadhuta, from the Bhagavatam.[2] When I congratulated the author, Mr. Sharp (?) he said, "Oh, it was all a mad camp!" It *was* campy, in just the right way.

---

[1] "Twenty-Five Years of the Novel" by Francis Wyndham, in Lehmann's *The Craft of Letters in England* (1956).
[2] The Bhagavatam Purana; see Glossary under Avadhuta.

June 17. 6:45 a.m. Have already said my beads and am now ready to begin the day. It's going to be beautiful. The chill of early morning. The white half shell of the moon in the sky—looking like a place you could really get to, if you took the trouble. Stomach symptoms persist, faintly, in the background and no wonder: last night with Evelyn Hooker I drank two martinis and some wine. Evelyn looks mortally tired, but she is full of plans for "entering the jungle" on her search for the social customs of the intergrades. We had supper at Sinbad's and talked to [Lennie] Newman who told me, drunk, that he can't get any intellectual companionship.

Mr. Hine, Mr. Stickel and his daughters have just come back in the car from swimming. The sunshine is nearly down to the bottom of the hill opposite. The vacant lot strewn with papers. The sycamore tree opposite, with the four mail boxes on it and the sign warning you that children are at play. Pink roses are blooming in front of my study window and the rice-paper plant (a native of Formosa) is getting big. I find the tree in front of the house is not a palm but a green dracaena.

I wonder where Don is.

June 18. Yesterday was scorching hot; today looks like being hotter. Jo, Ben and I took gluttonously to the beach. We went in the water half a dozen times at least.

To the Stravinsky concert in the evening—for Igor's seventy-fifth birthday. Bob Craft, pale as a lily and quite beautiful in his exhaustion. He looked, as it were, purged through hard work and so curiously innocent and good. He hadn't had enough rehearsals with his orchestra of the *Canticum Sacrum* and the *Agon*. Then Igor came on, limp with sweat but wonderfully svelte, although he had hurt his back against the corner of a couch. He conducts with the most graceful, campy gestures, like a ballerina. Bob is stiff, sudden, birdlike. He jabs at the musicians with his fingers, and you feel an almost vengeful birdlike harshness, a pecking and a dry ruthless demandingness.

Of course I didn't enjoy the music. I didn't expect to. It seems chiefly to consist of nervous stabbing sounds, the creakings and squeaks of a door swinging in the wind. Little fizzes of energy from the violins. Short desert twisters of revolving noise, which soon pass.

Yet I believed it when Aldous—looking more beautifully slim and distinguished than I have ever seen him—called Igor "a great genius," a "saint of music" and the maker of "the Stravinsky revolution." What struck me so, thinking it over this morning, is the token quality of any kind of a life—viewed as a story of achievement, every life is a little ridiculous: what a to-do about nothing! So Igor has made a revolution—! So you were president of the USA—how absurd! But it seems more absurd to be president. Eisenhower sent an asinine telegram, obviously composed by one of his aides and carefully worded so Igor shouldn't be praised *too* highly—after all, he is only a naturalized citizen.

All these lives—they're absolutely convincing "on paper"—one accepts "the idea" of them without question. But—what a strange masquerade!

Vera's sweetly lovable dazed innocent fatness. The bohemian mixture of languages they all speak—which somehow creates Paris in the twenties. Igor always scolds her in Russian.

Have just heard from Geller that they like the script at Fox. They want to put me on something else, soon.

June 20. Don called from New York this morning, early. He is having a great time, seeing everybody, and he doesn't plan to return until the last moment before school—in ten days. I can't say I'm altogether pleased. Selfishly, I'm worried. I imagine him forming all sorts of new relationships outside of my sphere, and maybe one in particular which will keep pulling his thoughts eastward after his return. And yet I am glad he went, and glad that the visit *has* been a success.

The trouble with me is that I give up so easily. I just cannot face the prospect of losing Don, and so I prepare to lose him at the first hint that he isn't yearning to return. Partly, too, this pessimism is due to my stomach, which keeps acting up.

It isn't so hot, today.

Oh, I must conquer tamas, sad sloth.

Last night I visited Jack Larson in Salka's old apartment. He had a young actor friend with him, named Jimmy Bridges, who said to me, "You must have had a marvellous life." I agreed with him, but it's surprising how little this thought consoles you for sadness in the present. Jack has a rubber monkey wrench used by Chaplin in *Modern Times* and an original poster of *The Kid*. We watched an awful TV film of him trapped with three others in a burning flattop. They played cards until the ship blew up. Jack photographs very badly, all chin.

Later: Melancholy. Stomachache. Loneliness—terrible sad unromantic loneliness. Lay on beach with Speed who is wild with excitement because he has finished two acts of *Comes A Day*. He started on his favorite theme—that there was soon going to be an explosion between me and Don, and between him and Paul. "I don't know why," he said, "I just know it." He "knows" it because he wants it to happen, partly because of his love of explosions, partly because he thinks it would be good if we two lived together. Our living together he imagines in terms of continuous excitement, sparks jumping back and forth. But my battery is dead. I couldn't work after I left him. I lay down on my upside-down board and slept like an old dog.

June 21. Every day I feel worse. Miserable loneliness. And stomach blues, which no kind of dieting seems to dispel. Time has begun to crawl. I can hardly imagine how I'll get through it till Don comes back.

Had lunch with Charlie Brackett at Romanoff's, to meet a French journalist, Michel Clerc, who is doing a lightning book about the USA. He was obviously impressed by my energy and youthful appearance!

"On my tongue the taste is sour/Of all I ever did"[1] —how well that describes my mood!

Tonight the Lockes and the Anhalts are coming to dinner. *Why?*

June 22. God, I was so bored last night! The only relief, in a way, was that I didn't have to talk. Charley Locke and Eddie Anhalt yakked away at each other—chiefly about Eddie's dealings with the army in relation to his work on *The Young Lions*. Eddie speaks of the army with terrific love-hate, admiration-contempt. Obviously, being in it was the only thing in his life that actually mattered a damn. I quite like bossy Mrs. Locke, who has a hugely fat, piggy daughter—a nice hard-boiled jolly girl who drinks a lot. Eddie's Jackie George [was] a bit of a bitch.

Woke up feeling so blue. I can't figure out where the pain in my stomach ends and my mood begins. Grovelling loneliness and longing for Don to come back—and yet the feeling: what have I to offer him but gloom and misery? He should stay away and make his own life.

June 23. I have to record ten days almost utterly wasted in sloth and self-pity. True, I have felt sick and lonely, but that's nothing new.

Now, let's have a couple of resolutions:
Before Don returns, I'll—
    finish revising the Vedanta history
    write their foreword for them
    and solve the problem which prevents me from finishing
        chapter one.

June 25. Another incredibly sluggish day—slept one and a half hours on the couch this afternoon! I say to myself: Well, why not be sluggish?

[1] A. E. Housman, "Additional Poems," IX, in *Collected Poems*.

Cultivate a noble idleness, like Augustus John, whose memoirs I'm reading.[1] But—with me, sluggishness is sluggishness.

However, I have done *some* work.

Roll on the weekend and Don's return!

I torment myself, imagining that he has become deeply involved with someone else, or simply discovered that he prefers to be on his own.

Stomach better, after Jessie Marmorston told me yesterday that she is taking me to a specialist! She declares she'll fix it up, no matter what, and that she'll restore my virility by bigger and better shots.

Today I went swimming. The water was warm though the weather was grey with drops of rain. The atmosphere of "bathing" in England but about twenty degrees warmer! A portable radio carried by a teenage girl was hoarsely raving.

Later. Rereading this diary at 11:50 p.m., after supper with Harry and June de Bon (?)—I *never* will get her name straight[2]—I'm disturbed to detect an underlying note of resentment against Don. It keeps appearing throughout the past few months. Do we basically hate what makes us suffer? If so, we must hate everything we love—including God. If God doesn't make us suffer, it means that we don't love him. But—since the aim of journal writing is to be frank—I must be very careful not to gloss over any feelings of resentment I have against Don. Don is in this respect much more honest than I am, I'm bound to admit. He says he has to focus all his aggression on me because I'm the only person he cares about. Well—maybe after this trip he'll feel differently. Would I prefer that? No.

June is a nice girl, but she suffers from a fatal lack of what, for want of a better word, must be called sophistication. She says things which must make Harry squirm, I should think. For example, I was saying how much I'd like to do the screenplay of *The Day Christ Died*, and I outlined a notion—obviously out of the question as a practical possibility—of having a centurion running through the picture who is terribly worried about an inspection by the general which is to take place the day *after* the crucifixion. So at the end of the picture, he remarks: "Got to hit the sack. Big day tomorrow!" When I'd told this, June exclaimed: "Oh, what a grim ironic tag!"

June 27. A wonderful letter, full of love, arrived from Don yesterday. So now I'm happily awaiting his return and should doubtless have forgotten already about my fears if they weren't recorded in this book.

[1] *Chiaroscuro: Fragments of Autobiography*, First Series (1952).
[2] June de Baum.

Even my stomach is better, despite the fact that I drank too much last night with Vance and Eleanor Breese. I drank because I was hating the evening; it was full of unease. Vance is so nervous and so possessive. If you don't like the oysters, if the singer in the nightclub is not amusing, it is his fault, he takes the responsibility—like a martyr. And you feel like his executioner.

Eleanor says she is happy, but [maybe] she [. . .] only means that she feels she has made the best of a bad bargain.

I spent most of today reading Gavin Lambert's *Slide Area* manuscript. It's not bad, and I envied him for having seized the opportunity to write about Los Angeles—but it's mostly just journalism.

June 30. Don has telegraphed that he's coming in on a TWA flight at 6:10 p.m. today. If he arrives safe and sound, and the trip turns out to have been not only a success but a valuable experience for him and a step forward in our own relationship, I still can't flatter myself that I've had anything to do with it. For me, this separation has simply been a failure. I failed to make any constructive use of it. I'm shocked to find how much worse I am at being alone than I used to be. I had looked forward to pleasures of meditation, survey, reevaluation of the past—and what have I done? Mugged and idled around. The only positive achievement was writing a foreword to the Ramakrishna movement history—and that's not so hot.

July 2. Don arrived safely, and all was happiness and joy. That's all I can report, as of now. I haven't any idea how school is going to work out for him, or how long the glamor of the holiday will carry him, or what changes, if any, have taken place in him.

I still don't see how things are going to work out with this trip. Can we afford it?

Went to a party at Jessie Marmorston's last night, at which I got drunk on wine and today have a hangover. Also, I smoked a cigarette.

My body is putting on fat like a woman's, 155 pounds!

Today Gavin Lambert agreed to do the TV story with me for Hermione Gingold.

July 5. Yesterday we went to Trabuco. Gruelling heat and a lot of traffic on the way down—better coming back. We were late for lunch and had to sit right in the middle of the table, as it were. Swami Akhilananda and Dr. Chakravaty gave dull talks in dead voices. The play was fun, however. Don liked that.

Later we saw the fireworks. Don had another of his attacks of depression. What was he to do? Should he stay in school? He hates it because he gets no encouragement.

After we talk, he feels better. All the usual things have to be said, but the fact remains that it seems best for Don to stay in school right now. What else would be better?

John van Druten is installed at the rented house on the Pacific Coast Highway. He seems shaky, but is eagerly planning a new play.

Today I have talked three times to John Kulberg, about his "Mad Poet." Got on with the novel. I'm utterly bored by it but want to finish part one and show it to Don.

July 10. This disease or neurosis of aggressive resentment is getting more and more serious. I find myself chewing on it, like a lemon. I hate everybody—lady drivers, children, cops, Jews, journalists, etc. etc. Never mind about the moral side of this. The point is, if I don't stop I shall make myself seriously ill.

Needless to say, it affects Don, whose nerves are bad anyway after a long hot day downtown at school. He snapped at me yesterday because I hadn't called Lena Horne,[1] and because I'd sent off letters to Lincoln and Johnnie Goodwin without showing them to him.

We saw *The Matchmaker* again,[2] and Aldous was there. It seemed so strange to see his bowed, distinguished head in such an audience. I suppose Laura had dragged him. I do not like her. There is something shameful in Aldous's subjection to this mannish well-tailored bitch.

July 11. "All things can tempt me from this craft of verse"—how distinguished Yeats makes his laziness sound! This morning I'm trying to start chapter two of my novel—dashing it off in a rough draft again, because it is so completely wrong in its present form—and I have been tempted already—it's only 10:35—as follows:

Took the Sunbeam down to be washed and have its wheel straightened. Got into a talk with Ben, who's expecting a copy of his short stories from Methuen. Met Michael Barrie—getting fatter, like me—on the way home and talked about a young English actor he knows who wants to get into Ben Bard's school at Fox.[3] So I called Pam in David Brown's office and she gave me some advice, which I phoned back to Michael. Then Johnnie called to say Dick Foote had caught a fish which gave birth to young, so I phoned Ben who told

---

[1] Isherwood and Bachardy saw her show at the Coconut Grove on July 3, and Bachardy wanted to visit Horne at home, which they did on July 13.
[2] They had seen the same production of Thornton Wilder's play, starring Ruth Gordon, in New York.
[3] An acting school.

me that all the surf perch of the Pacific Coast do this. So I phoned Dick. Meanwhile, I also kept phoning to tell Kent Chapman how much I like his story, "The End of Everything," in the Santa Barbara College magazine, *Spectrum*, which he gave me last night. No answer.

The boy from the Sammets' and Ollie, the one-eyed German boy, are at baseball practice. I don't mind how much noise they make, because they are cute and sweet. But an uncute boy with glasses from across the road is firing a toy carbide cannon at irregular intervals. Of this I do not approve. The Hines are suffering from flu, so are quiet.

The Sammet boy has just told the boy with the cannon to stop firing it—and I shouted "Hear! Hear!" out the window. But the boy goes on shooting.

July 16. Worry, depression, fat, anxiety—this trip hanging over us and no money available for it. No job or prospect of one—other than a possible rewrite on *Jean-Christophe* for Wald. My stomach still acting up. Shall have to see a specialist. And somehow or other, I don't lose weight, although I seem to be eating almost nothing—because I keep sneaking in tiny snacks.

And my novel doesn't get on. Why? I think because the character of Paul is wrong.

What's good about anything, then?

Don. He's an angel.

Nice Yukio Mishima, whom I met yesterday and took out to see John van Druten. But oh, the hopelessness of communication! Here's this guy, with all of his qualities, his ear for words, etc.—and nothing of it came across.

Nice Don Murray, for calling and saying he enjoyed our dinner party on Friday.

Nice Paulette Goddard, for ditto reason.

Yes, and we slept on the beach at John's.

It all sounds fun, doesn't it—and so it should be—but underneath I feel only gnawing anxiety, despair, the deadness of everything. I turn to making japam, but that doesn't seem to improve my mood.

Oh, Jesus—a huge carload of kids just arrived, to visit the Hines! There'll be noise all morning.

July 17. Ollie, the little German boy, is playing ball with the Sammet boy. Ollie keeps touching his glass eye, as if it were loose and might fall out. Yesterday I went around to see Mrs. Hine, to ask her if she would say something to the lady opposite her about her grandson's carbide cannon. She said she would, but obviously she doesn't think it is very important. Mrs. Hine says that [a boy in the neighborhood (whose parents are divorced)] is a juvenile delinquent. He steals cars. His mother beats him and screams, and the Hines call the police. (This shocks me.)

Last night Don read the first chapter of my novel. We had a valuable talk and now I see the way to certain improvements.

John van Druten called to say that Dodie has a tame thrush. She wants it to eat well—but *must* it eat worms?

Still no news about money for the trip. And my stomach symptoms persist. This morning I asked Don if he'd mind very much if we had to postpone it. He said no—there was always school. This made me very happy.

Ollie lost his eye in a bicycle accident—riding behind his big brother. They ran into a car. In Germany, an attempt was made to graft on a living eye. But it failed.

July 18. For once, I'm in an optimistic mood!

Jessie Marmorston and I went down to see a Dr. Griffith this morning—he's *so* grand, so entirely the medical doyen, it seems, of Jessie's circle—that he isn't even Jewish! He says I'm in fine shape, all except for my vagus nerve, which is causing this upset in the pyloric region. So I'm to take belladonna to stop the spasms. And if that doesn't help—well—they'll cut part of the vagus nerve!

Jessie also went after me about my financial mismanagement. She says she has made a million for Larry[1] since she has known him. She was horrified to hear that I only have ten thousand in the bank. She says she is going to see about this.

But, senselessly, I feel cheered up. I resolve to write the first two chapters of my novel before we leave. Jack Goodman called me this morning saying he would produce the 11,200 dollars I need for the trip. Now I almost believe in our going.

But tomorrow we're off to Santa Fe for the weekend.

I was quite amazed to discover that Jessie is so businesslike. She talked about amortization as though it were some process connected with the ductless glands. She says Larry has always been so scared. He didn't dare ask MGM to pay him his salary in a different way, so as to avoid supertax. He feared he'd be fired.

This afternoon, full of my new energy, I went swimming in the bright windy sea. A boy and girl on the beach, evidently newly married. He was really handsome and sexy and conscious of it. She, merely pug-face cute, and anxious already. With a teasing grin, he went and lay down several yards away from her. She called, "Come back to your wife. You're embarrassing me." Finally he crossed to the

---

[1] Weingarten, her husband.

other side of her, eyeing some teenage girls. She buried him in the sand and passionately kissed him on the mouth. He let her, grinning at the teenagers. They snickered. I saw their whole marriage—probably not a long one.

July 24. Yesterday I began another draft of my novel, in the third person. I have no idea how this will turn out.

We spent the weekend in Santa Fe, staying with the Winfield Scotts, an arrangement made by Mirandi [Masocco], the all-powerful proprietress of the Thunderbird shop. We saw *The Rake's Progress* twice and also the worst imaginable performance of *I Am a Camera*, by a Taos theater group.

Mrs. Scott is very rich and liberal, apple cheeked and haystack haired, with glasses. She goes around in shorts and travels barefoot to New York on the Super Chief. To kid her, a bunch of her friends once saw her off at Lamy junction, all wearing hillbilly clothes and accompanied by a mob of borrowed children.

Winfield Townley Scott is a poet and critic. He has a pipe and a seventeen-year-old son by a former marriage—very handsome and quite a junior thug—who unfortunately is only about the height of a twelve-year-old boy. He is allowed to drink and smoke and stay up late. He lolls around sexily, demands to be shown nudes of girls, keeps rolling up one of his sleeves to the armpit, calls his father Daddy-O and his step-mother El.

The hot dry air. The plain with the bright, bright, vivid cottonwoods, ringed around by far blue mountains, and the piled thunderheads, so firmly rounded and white.

Taos is unspeakable now. The drugstore people have utterly ruined it. But the landscape around [Dorothy] Brett's cottage hasn't changed. It is open and beautiful. She wasn't home. We peeked in and saw her brass bed, and books and paintings. Such an innocent interior—like the home of a saint.

The Rake grew on me. There is something heartlessly brisk in the music which suggests the eighteenth-century equivalent of the Bandwagon.[1] All aboard for London, sex, success. Oops—you fell off? Too bad! Goodbye—we won't be seeing you!

One afternoon we swam in a natural pool fed by a spring—the property of the Finnish consul. He has built a Finnish-style rock-steam bathhouse, with grass planted on the roof.

The Spanish-American boys in Santa Fe hate the "Anglos." The

[1] Possibly referring to the Broadway musical *The Bandwagon*; Isherwood visited the set of the film, released in 1953.

other day they severely beat up the clerk at one of the biggest hotels because he told them not to make a noise in the street outside.

Vronsky and Babin, the pianists—a pair of squirrels who have hoarded Picassos and Chagalls.

Don and I agree that Vera Stravinsky is one of the un-nastiest people we know. There seems absolutely nothing bad about her. She is sweet tempered, funny, silly, kind, intelligent and very industrious. She had a show on in Santa Fe of her paintings. We bought one called *Reflections.*

Witter Bynner has already gone to Greece with Bob Hunt. We were shown over his house, however. It is really rather dreadful—so dark with old teaky chinoiserie. Such a great burden of stuff to carry to your grave. And there is something sinister about having youthful portraits of yourself hanging in your study.

Bynner's witchlike housekeeper Rita—a white witch—said, about Bob Hunt, "It's good to have a friend."

Last night we had dinner with Alex Quiroga and his Texan friend at Sinbad's, and went up to Lennie [Newman]'s apartment later. He seemed in a very bad state—maybe a sort of softening of the brain. He declared that he'd given up after four piano lessons because he was a perfectionist and knew he could never be great—as great, he implied, as he is at cooking. It was sad and embarrassing. I had never seen this megalomaniac side of him before.

July 26. Frank Taylor called this morning from New York to tell me that Jack Goodman of Simon and Schuster died suddenly a couple of days ago. However, he thinks Simon and Schuster is ready to go through with the advance.

Gavin Lambert with incredible industry has written the whole of the script for the first TV play of our series for Gingold. We're to start peddling this next week.

In a month, my birthday. In two months we'll be nearly ready to leave. My novel crawls. I'm slothful and fat, as never before. I seem to have lost the knack of work. I waste time on anything and everything that comes handy.

July 30. Two days ago we spent the evening with Paulette Goddard, Remarque, and Florence Homolka. We ate at the Traders[1] and got very, very drunk on rum—including those fatal communal bowls you drink out of from straws. And I was sick. So was Don, later. And we had to spend most of yesterday in bed. Awful guilt today, as a result.

[1] I.e., Trader Vic's.

I do like Paulette; she is tough and good humored. She calls Remarque "Death." She says he looks like Death when he's asleep in the morning. What she means is that he wears a smiling mask. He smiles everything away. He's like a Conrad Veidt[1] character. You can imagine him shooting himself, with a smile. Paulette also said that the only three possible roles for a woman were to be a wife, a secretary or a movie star.

As for Florence, she kept announcing that she is going to lose twenty pounds. But she won't. And she won't lose her twenty millions, either. She's a great big cry-baby millionairess.

Don's mother didn't want to go to Mexico as her husband suggested so now she insinuates that she somehow sensed that there would be this big earthquake in Mexico City. She called to announce the news of the earthquake to us, *weeping*. With delight, I suppose. Because God killed all these people so she could have her own way!

Supper alone with Johnnie last night. He says he has no idea how his life will develop, now. He doesn't know if he'll ever be able to direct again, or even travel. He is quite calm about this.

August 2. Another heat wave, though a bit cooler today. We are now sliding into the smoothly accelerating slipstream of time before we leave. About nine complete weeks, starting Monday next, the 5th.

I have now decided not to promise *any* books to Simon and Schuster—if possible—and hope to get by on our savings and what I can earn on our return.

Yesterday it looked as if I could get a TV job with CBS—Robert Graves's *They Hanged My Saintly Billy*; but now I see that this is impossible because of our deadline.

I am doing a strange new experiment with the novel—writing it as a simple dialogue between Paul and William.

August 5. Beginning of the nine weeks—the solemn period of our journey preparation.

A glorious day on the beach, with wind and sun. Mishima's modern *No* plays[2] arrived, and I read them. The bathers, advancing into the water in one long straggling line, remind you of naked African hunters heading off a lion. They advance upon the immense uncatchable water beast.

Don said the other day: "I'm afraid we came in during act three, scene three of Mr. Hine. Now there's only a short epilogue in which

[1] German character actor (1893–1943).
[2] *Five Modern No Plays.*

he turns into a toad." The *tone* of this remark would be right for a novel in a modern Jane Austen manner.

There is something quite fascinating in the lack of consideration shown by Mr. Hine, who, after all, must be fairly regarded as a well-educated, good-natured man, far above the average in intelligence and even sensibility. Yesterday—Sunday morning of all mornings—he began work on his television aerial shortly before 7:00 with some kind of small electric circular saw which could be heard all over the Canyon! And yet this same Mr. Hine called the police when the German woman next door fought with her husband one night and disturbed *him*!

I'm going ahead with this dialogue idea for my novel. It may be bad, but it's really an original technique, I feel. To write the fundamental, underlying, unspoken dialogue between two people. The dialogue of their relationship, as it were. As I was saying to Don yesterday, it is really much more satisfying to feel that your work is genuinely experimental than to feel that it is merely good—safely good within the easy compass of your powers.

Ollie and the Sammet boy are playing ball as I write this and making a hell of a noise. But I don't mind, because they're so lovable together. All right—now why not try some love on the Stickel girls? Any offers? No? No saints around here.

August 11. To my dismay I find that I've broken the record—only one entry last week. It's silly to mind about such things—and yet I find that the alternative to keeping schedules is doing nothing whatever.

Never have I known time to go as fast as it's going now.

Tito has just left Vedanta Place, with no warning but a note which said that he is going to look for work.

Mike Kitay has a growth in his rectum but it isn't malignant. My nice Dr. Lichtenstein is going to operate on him.

I'm still trying to write the dialogue version of my novel.

August 15. I've just heard from Geller that *Jean-Christophe* has been shelved. So that's that. It looks like I shall earn no more money before we leave. There *is* a vague idea of collaborating with Gavin Lambert—but who knows when? I smell a period of unsuccess.

Marisa Pavan has just had a baby boy.

Johnnie has just had a letter from Starcke, who is in Honolulu with Joel Goldsmith, asking for Johnnie's forgiveness and prayers. Johnnie says that this has "shaken" him. Carter finds the letter false and nauseating.

Talking of nausea, poor Don gets sick to his stomach nearly every day. He wants to see Jessie Marmorston about this, but she has been up north all this week, apparently consulting with someone about L. B. Mayer's health.

August 17. Yesterday was a day of good deeds and bad movies. Don and I got our yellow fever shots downtown, bought a painting by a Mary Vitz at the County Art Institute, saw Mike Kitay at the Good Samaritan where he is recovering from his operation and Marisa Pavan at St. John's, where she has just had a son. The bad movies were *Jeanne Eagles* and *Silk Stockings.*

The baby room at the hospital. Here all the babies are alone together, except for the attending nurse. All waiting, behind glass, for the take-off into life. Their footprints and the mother's fingerprints are stamped on the same card for identification. You can only look at them through the glass pane. Jean Pierre Aumont was very proud. Marisa smiles and smiles, and is "sweet," but somehow I feel no warmth.

August 19. Listening to the radio this morning, I heard a man named Ed Hart(?) lecturing on the Indian religious beliefs and rituals involving the use of peyote. The lecture was quite daring, in that it didn't condemn the Indians and even drew a parallel between their ritual and that of the Catholic Mass: when the supply of peyote runs out, the congregation, instead of taking the drug, will pay homage, ritualistically, to a single peyote bud. As in the elevation of the Host.

The insurance agent, Walter Burke, who called about insuring this house, told me that business is definitely counting on at least another ten years of slowly increasing inflation, during which costs will rise as much as $4\frac{1}{2}$%. Women will drop out of the labor market as automation increases. But the men will be better and better paid for less and less machine minding. They will be able to support the family alone.

Yesterday I had earache and felt lazy, possibly because of the yellow fever shots. Stayed home and read all of *Les Liaisons Dangereuses.*[1] Today, I have the strange gradual realization of having been in the presence of a masterpiece. In this case, the sensation is spooky, because of the sense of cold evil in the Marquise de Merteuil. That woman —Jesus—she wasn't kidding! It makes me shiver to think of her.

August 23. Yesterday, I saw Tito, who is staying with a friend, Stanley Musgrove. He is so handsome, neat and well preserved, yet with the premature elderly anxious dried-upness of the neurotic. There is a

[1] Laclos' 1782 novel.

permanent furrow between his eyebrows. He says he left Vedanta Place because he was being overworked, and because Prema and Paul [Hamilton] watched him all the time. They were particularly suspicious whenever he talked to Phil (Buddha). And once, when Tito went for a walk along the boulevard, he found that Paul was tailing him.

Tito said: "I have to realize that I'm quite an ordinary guy with quite ordinary problems—nothing special."

I went on to Vedanta Place. Swami told me that [the boy who was arrested at Hollywood High] is very unhappy. He asked to be taken back into Trabuco. Swami said this was impossible, suggested that he should go to India and live at the Belur Math. [The boy] agreed, so the arrangements are to be made.

We talked about Vandanananda. Swami feels that Vandanananda is still resentful because Swami rebuked him for going out so much in the evenings. Vandanananda is so cold, underneath his surface amiability. Swami says that none of the girls at Santa Barbara feel at ease with him. Those that got the habit in India of "taking the dust of the feet" always do this when Swami, and any visiting Swami, comes. But they never do it to Vandanananda. The other day, however, Daya did it—just to see what would happen. And Vandanananda said, "Thank you!" This, in India, would be unheard of behavior—a Swami taking such homage *personally*.

So I agreed, and said it was true: I never wanted to talk to Vandanananda except on quite superficial matters. Whereas Swami Satprakashananda, whom I'd never met before, seemed immediately lovable. And that got us on to the subject of Krishna (George)—how, from being a sort of hunchback of Holy Mother, an abject, comic, pitiful, almost animal figure, he has developed, during the past fifteen years, into this very strange individual; cantankerous, obstinate, certainly—even still malicious—but so radioactive with love that he's the only person around (excepting maybe Sarada) whom one could dream of calling a saint.

So Swami said that Krishna is going to India toward the start of this spring, to take the vows of sannyas. Then he'll come back here.

After supper I talked for a long time with Prema, on the temple steps. How strange and dry and yet sympathetic he is! I felt as if I were talking to Judas Iscariot. He loves and hates Swami. He is full of bitter resentment and intrigue. He can feel no warmth and yet suspects and dislikes all who can. In a way, he wants me to come back and live there, and yet he'd soon get to hating me if I did. He longs for freedom, and yet he feels that leaving Vedanta Place would be a confession of failure. He said bitter-humorously: "When Swami told

me I would get brahmacharya, I thought I must go to India first and
see the source of all this, and then make up my mind if it was really the
thing that mattered. I went to India, and found everything horrible
and completely disillusioning—so I came right on back here and took
the brahmachari vows."

I like Prema very much when he talks like that. But oh, he is in a
mess! And Ramakrishna help the society when Swami dies! Tito says
Prema will run it, along with Daya.

Don and Ted have had one of their big quarrels. Ted is in a bossy,
infuriating, manic state which is usually the prelude to a breakdown.
Don says he [Don] won't go to Bart [Lord]'s house any more to watch
TV.

Don has done a portrait of a Negress which is really good. His best
painting, so far.

I'm reading up on the Dead Sea Scrolls for a possible movie job.

August 25. Yesterday Dr. Lewis gave us our typhoid, typhus and
cholera shots. We both had very sore arms and felt terrible. Today is a
little better. I've never had such a violent reaction before. Dr. Lewis
says, however, that Don's sickness is merely due to his failure to eat in
the middle of the day.

Johnnie called this morning to ask the derivation of the word
"blighty." It is Hindustani. The word means "foreign" (*bilayati*).

We had supper last night with Harry Brown and June. Harry has
rented a little house perched on the side of the "Appian Way,"[1] high
up in the hills. A thick black ceiling divides the valley haze, which is
yellowish, from the dark blue upper air. And yet you can see lights
through it. The cut-out black toy silhouettes of three fir trees on the
ridge. The houses and gardens up here seem curiously snug, tucked
away out of reach of the city. Harry quite sober, drinking nothing at
all, and doing all the cooking: he even makes cakes. A slightly boring
but pleasant evening.

The result of Ted and Don's quarrel is that Ted sneaked into the
house while we were asleep and left an unwanted present, a record of
The Pajama Game. Instead of gradually seeing less of them, which is
what Don would like, we shall now have to make it up!

Don wrote a letter to Ted which was really quite masterly. And he
says he did this with very little trouble—the words ran off his pen. All
our grievances are so neatly and convincingly arranged in our minds,
ready for presentation at any moment. If only a novel could write
itself like that—or even a thank-you letter!

An unexpected rain shower this afternoon. This place is becoming

---

[1] A road off Mulholland Drive.

more and more like the tropics. Jo and Ben came around. We had tea and the remains of the cake we fed to the Swamis and Paulette Goddard. Jo was enthusing over Erica Steele (who now calls herself Gayle) the madam who was involved in the Jelke scandal.[1] Jo admires her clothes, her dancing, her skill at cookery, and her capacity for enjoying herself. Jo and Ben had told her she should buy a rubber raft and fins, so she went and bought them right away. ("You know why you aren't catching those waves just right, Gayle? It's because you need fins. You can't do a thing without them!")

Jo gets more and more fervent about all things aquatic. Her agonized wail: "Oh, the water was so *warm*! We had so much *fun*!"

Down the street, the children are screaming—for the sake of screaming. That acutely high note, to which no grown-up can listen for long without discomfort, actually gives them some sort of nervous release, I'm sure. And here am I, nearly fifty-three, and hating them worse than ever—wasting the few remaining years of my life in homicidal fantasies too silly to be written down. I *must* stop. Not for ethical reasons. Not because little children are of the Kingdom of Heaven, not because *tet twam asi*[2] is eternal truth. No—simply for my own sake. I'm making myself miserable.

August 30. This frantic rat race continues. Another week gone by. Nothing settled. Far too little work done. I had all sorts of comments to make about my birthday, but now they're forgotten. I'm behind with the section of novel I wanted to write. The Dead Sea Scroll project has flopped, at least until next week.

Patrick Woodcock is here. He's nice, but he has to be entertained.

My arm aches like hell. The inflammation flared up again, after going down following last week's shot.

Frankly, as of now, I'd be enchanted if I could find a way of putting off this trip *altogether*. It is just too fucking much of an exertion.

September 1. Last week, by and large, was one of the worst in a long while.

My birthday was a bore. Jo and Ben gave me a "joke present," an ink ball to tell fortunes with, like theirs. I asked it, "Will next year be happy?" It answered, "No." So I threw it out with the trash.

Then we had a ghastly boring party at Gavin Lambert's, and a

---

[1] Erica Steele was the professional name of Gay Vaughan (later Gayle), a red-headed, tough-talking New York madam who supplied women for the friends of oleomargarine heir Minot Jelke; she was one of the photographer Peter Gowland's first nude models in 1938 and became a friend.

[2] A Hindu saying, "Thou art that."

much dreadfuller party at the Hacketts' to welcome Patrick Wood-
cock from England, and a mismatched emergency dinner at home for
Dick Hopper and his friend John, to which we were compelled to ask
Gavin Lambert so he and I could discuss the new script idea for
Gingold, and a disaster dinner for the Cottens, Gore Vidal and
Howard Austen, at which Gore insulted the Cottens' darling friend
Bouverie, the widower of *his* friend Alice Bouverie—calling him a
crook, a fortune hunter[1] and a cocksucker. And this led to a row later
between me and Don, who accused me of letting him use me by
inviting to the house people who bored me. I could easily have
shown him the ridiculousness of this accusation if I hadn't been
drunk, exhausted and in great pain from my arm which was swollen
up after a cholera shot. As it was, we are only just getting over the
unpleasantness, and relations have been set back quite a long way.

I'm still in a great fuss about money. And sure that both the Dead
Sea and the Gingold projects are going to fold.

I think we may fly to Japan. That boat trip threatens to be a bore.

As for the novel, it *is* interesting; and I must absolutely get on with
it—do a big chunk before I leave.

September 3. Somehow a better day today—though both cars failed
us: the Ford wouldn't start for about ten minutes, and the battery is
dead on the Sunbeam. But the weather is brilliant, cooler, breezier
and more invigorating. I seem to have lost a little weight, and my arm,
after a second flare up yesterday, is much better, nearly okay. And
Don and I had a good talk which revealed, as so often, his terrible,
almost pathological feelings of insecurity about our life together—
which you'd think would be passing off by *this* time! As I see it, Don
feels compelled to test the relationship in all sorts of ways. Is there
anything that'll make me break it up?

We spent yesterday with Patrick Woodcock. He says he finds great
security in the knowledge that, twenty years hence, he'll be leading
just the same life as he's leading now—attending the children's clinic,
looking after a convent full of nuns, soothing loonies, getting up in
the middle of the night to see patients. There is no uncertainty in his
future, no hope of exciting change, no scope for the ordinary kind of
ambition. A vocation.

At Gore Vidal's yesterday, the gross blond baby-bully actor, Albert
Salmi. (I told Johnnie on the phone this morning that he was rude,
and Johnnie said, "Yes, and he's rude when he acts.") Gore much
outraged because *Time* and *The New Yorker* have acclaimed [James
Gould] Cozzens's *By Love Possessed* as a masterpiece. Personally, I

---

[1] She was an Astor, and wealthy.

only read a couple of dozen pages and stuck. It is quite well and solidly put together, but so prim and prissy and patty paws. So utterly, utterly not what I care about in art.

Got on with the novel today. It isn't right, but now it begins to excite me.

September 4. Waiting for Don to get back from the gym so I can eat lunch with him and then hurry off to try to sell our story to the Burns brothers.[1] It still seems to me like a forlorn hope. In fact, I hardly know just what the story *is*. And then hierarchies of sponsor-fools will have to approve it. Surely it will terrify and bewilder them?

My novel is very interesting to me and I feel really sad that I must leave it, and think such other thoughts and break the good routine of work. Something is alive. I'm down near the nerve—as I *never* was in *World in the Evening.*

September 9. I'm convalescent again, after a real setback—first a drunken evening last Friday at Gore's rented Malibu house, with Howard, Paul Newman, Joanne Woodward, Claire Bloom; then more shots from Dr. Lewis, which made me feel lousy again.

The Gore-Newman-Woodward household is curious. These people who perhaps don't like each other too well but are closely involved. Paul isn't a bad boy, but he's so hard at work every instant proving that he is an anti-intellectual nature boy. Joanne has decided, as she puts it, that she is not "the mother of us all." In other words, she finds it a bore to sort the linen and keep the place clean. Claire is demure, but probably quite a bit of a bitch. Her imitations of Queen Elizabeth II are extraordinarily funny. She is hopelessly in love with Richard Burton. Gore is such a resentful unhappy creature. He makes embarrassing references to his books—sort of challenging me to say I don't like them; and keeps bracketing himself with me as a pair of "literary men." Howard, I think, is unhappy because he can't have a complete domestic life with Gore, whom he adores.

Have just finished a day's work with Gavin Lambert on the TV story. Since we are pretty sure that that old bitch Gingold will wriggle her way out of the deal, it's a thankless labor, and also an irritating shame, because she could have been so marvellous in it.

The young-old daughter next door just stopped me to tell me she is getting married to an Austrian, "about your age," who is in "international commerce," has written several books on mathematics, and who speaks Japanese. He sounds really sinister.

[1] The TV series with Gavin Lambert for Hermione Gingold; see Glossary for the Burns brothers.

Jo has her stomach pains again. She is taking Equanil and belladonna, which reminds me that I must take mine. I've been letting it slide—not because I have had *no* pain but because the alarm has been lifted. Also, my cholera-sore arm has helped. As Jo says: "There's nothing like a pain for getting rid of another pain."

Today we had our passport photos taken for visas. We've ordered twenty each to allow for unexpected demands. The photographer told us that another customer who was going to the Orient had taken one hundred. But that was for two years.

One of the little girls opposite has tied a tin can to her pedal car— just so it will drag along the sidewalk and make more noise, apparently!

September 10. Geller called this morning to tell me that Gingold's agent has announced her decision not to have anything to do with TV work for the present. So we're just shown the door. All our work is rejected, unseen. And that's that.

Of course she's an old bitch. And it would be wonderful to get revenge on her by selling the idea of the story to Beatrice Lillie,[1] as Geller suggests. Nevertheless, I feel a certain relief, which isn't altogether laziness. Now I *can* get a good big swatch of the new draft of my novel—I like the title *Down There on a Visit* better and better— finished before we leave.

Talked to Swami on the phone this morning. He says his vacation in the High Sierras was wonderful. But when he got back to Hollywood he felt such a letdown that, "I wanted to cry." "And then," he concluded, "this morning I went to the dentist and I thought of calling you."

One of the nice features of a setback of this sort is that it draws people who love each other closer together. This was Don's immediate reaction. I have been worried about him—particularly worried about the upsetting effect this trip may have on his development. But, after all, why worry? And what's the ultimate harm in being upset, anyway? Isn't it something one should pray for?

6:40 p.m. The latest news is that Geller talked to Gingold and she denied what *her* agent had said. She claims she merely said she couldn't make a pilot film during work on *Gigi* at MGM—which nobody has ever asked her to do, anyway. I'm so disgusted and bored that I'd just as soon drop the whole deal now; because it's a cinch that if we write out this treatment and show it to her she'll merely turn it down anyway. But Gavin is inclined to give her one more chance, so I suppose we shall.

[1] The British revue star.

A fine windy day on the beach with a crumpled tinfoil sea, not too cold, however. Read *Tom Jones*. I don't like it nearly as much as Smollett.

Last night I looked through Whymper's *Scrambles*,[1] after seeing a terrible film called *The Mountain*, with Spencer Tracy and Robert Wagner: like so many bad dramas it would have made an excellent farce.

September 13. Friday 13th—hope this is lucky because we finished the treatment of the TV story for Gingold today; Gavin and I dictating, Don typing. Don has typed the whole thing, as well as taking down the rough draft in pencil. Gavin and I gave it to Gingold this evening. She *says* she likes it, but you can't tell. She is so foxy, and tonight she had as her excuse her exhaustion after five twelve-hour days of work at MGM on *Gigi*.

Not to be sly—this was the essence of a revelation Prema feels he's had, after cooking for the Swamis up in the Sierras. He says he used to be ashamed of Swami Prabhavananda for sounding off and yelling at people and banging the table—but now he sees that it is wonderful not to be afraid to show one's feelings. This really impresses me, coming from Prema.

He says Prabhavananda spent most of his time shut up in his cabin, and that his mood seemed continuously indrawn.

Only three weeks from Sunday! But I still promise myself a big swatch of work on the novel.

September 14. A resolve: to struggle hard, between now and our departure, to overcome this terrible cultivation of resentment inside myself. It is *deadly* dangerous.

Much reassured by my talk with Prema last night. If he becomes changed, all will be well. It will make an immense difference to me personally and I think to the Vedanta Society. It was so strange to hear Prema say: "We must be bold. We mustn't be conservative."

Oh, I have slipped back so far. And for no reason. There is nothing that I can find morally wrong with my way of life at present. Oh, yes—there is: the giving way to tamas. Perhaps even the glorification of tamas as snug catlike laziness. That's very bad. I must struggle and struggle against it.

Resolves: to write the draft of my novel at least to page thirty— forty, if possible.

---

[1] *Scrambles Amongst the Alps in the Years 1860–1869*; see diary entry for December 1, 1952.

To finish Dante's *Inferno*, the Caitlin Thomas book[1] and odds and ends. To finish this diary—if possible, without cheating too much.

My arm still aches, and I feel heavy and log headed and dazed. The atmosphere is like flat soda water. Never mind, old horse—scramble to your feet and let's get going.

September 16. Sad, sad, sad. The sun shines, and yet I'm sad. I feel defeated, self-defeated, inviting defeat and desertion. What a stupid scene on Saturday, a squalid mess. The only consolation: I didn't behave badly to Thom Gunn, or in front of Cecil Beaton.[2]

Is melancholy catching? Yes, very.

Nevertheless, I have gotten ahead with my novel.

Gingold, after being all smiles to the Burns brothers yesterday, says today through her agent that she doesn't want the deal. Gavin thinks the agent's to blame. But she is certainly a pathological hesitant.

September 18. Apparent disappearance of all hopes of Gingold. She wants to go back to the theater and stage her own dreary dull dead-serious (so we are told) play, and act in it.

We had supper last night with the Don Murrays. They are almost becoming serious friends—perhaps they will. Don [Murray] was full of the fact that he has discovered how to fire a rifle with one hand (for his part in *The Hell-Bent Kid*[3]). He is getting an extra thrill out of handling firearms, he says, because he's a pacifist. We also laughed a lot over the Cadillac they have just bought—it doesn't sound too good for the director of a refugee relief project to be riding around in one!

They are quite a sweet pair, who seem a little sweeter than life because of their physical beauty. But Don is capable of being unkind to Hope—or at any rate of embarrassing her. We were all rather drunk and he told stories about the wedding. A friend of Don's was staying with him—a somewhat enigmatic German? Italian? who has helped Don with the relief project and with a TV play about refugees in which Don is soon to appear.

Don also signed a photograph of them both with a drunken-embarrassing inscription which I'm sure he regrets this morning.

[1] *Leftover Life to Kill* (1957).
[2] On Saturday, September 14 Isherwood went with Bachardy and Thom Gunn to visit Jerry Lawrence; Cecil Beaton joined them for supper at Sinbad's on the Santa Monica Pier. The scene evidently occurred afterwards, possibly over Bachardy's frustration in trying to befriend Gunn. Isherwood may have been drunk.
[3] The 1958 film of Charles Locke's novel was actually called *From Hell to Texas*; Murray starred with Diane Varsi and Dennis Hopper.

Their house is still as bare as a prison. We ate on straight-backed chairs in the Californian–Spanish dining room which is still their only furnished room.

September 19. I went to see Swami yesterday, for the first time since he got back from the Sierras. I remarked that Prema had told me how Swami had spent most of his time in his cabin, and Swami said: "Yes—I was having such a wonderful time with the Lord." It is a measure of the doubleness of my life that I can both accept this statement as literally true and also marvel that such a statement, made by anybody, could *ever* be literally true. I realize more and more that Swami is my only real link with spiritual life. But this is rather like saying that the Golden Gate Bridge is one's only link with Marin County. What more could I ask for? I was very much moved, last night, as we sat together and he told me how he wants to have this joy not only occasionally but always. "Then I can pass it on to you all."

"It's all Maharaj," he said, "everything he told me is coming true. I didn't understand him at the time. Now I begin to know what he was talking about." Swami keeps repeating that Maharaj matters most to him—more than Thakur—because Swami actually knew Maharaj. "And that's how I feel about you," I said. "Ah but Chris," Swami said, "I am like a little pebble against the Himalayas." "I have absolute confidence in you, Swami," I said, with tears of love in my eyes, but still aware of how funny it sounded.

As a contrast, Don and I had supper with Cecil Beaton at La Rue. But that was a very happy evening in its different way. We both like Cecil a great deal. He is lonely and his talent gets him into feuds. He is having one now with Sidney Guilaroff,[1] because he (Cecil) fixed Leslie Caron's hair, without thinking that he shouldn't. Cecil's charm is in his frankness. He makes no bones about his resentments and dislikes—for example, of Stephen Spender and of Speed. ("I don't feel guilty about not liking Speed, whereas I *do* feel guilty about not liking Stephen.") His feeling against Stephen is, I think, quite largely due to jealousy in relation to Peter Watson, whom Cecil unhappily adored. He says Stephen is vulgar and ambitious—and one agrees, remembering however that many people must have said the same thing about Cecil. Nevertheless, he *is* nice. Don used a very good phrase about him: "I like the warmth of Cecil's indiscretion."

Hopes for Gingold fade fast. But now it seems that we may be commissioned to write the teleplay anyhow, maybe for Elsa Lanchester or Lillie or who knows.

---

[1] MGM's star hairdresser.

September 23. Aching depression. An awful sick sadness which is partly sulks. I am furious because Don has bullied me into letting Marguerite [Lamkin] stay here while we're away. She's a sl[ob] and she'll mess up everything and have her messy friends around, poking and prying. And we shall end being let in for all kinds of expenses— I know it.

But also I'm utterly off this trip. I long for it *not* to take place—with such intensity that I may quite easily make myself sick. And now I'm tired of this house, too. Tired of the noise of the kids outside. Why can't we live on the beach?

In the midst of this, Don remains Don. I mean, although I blame him for some of the fuss, I never for one moment lose sight of the fact that he matters most. (I only blame him for appealing to the Supreme Court, as it were, of our feeling for each other in order to put over this inviting of Marguerite, which is an unworthy cause and really only done for the sake of asserting his own will.)

Yesterday evening we took Norman Routledge[1] to dinner. He's a very young wriggly gay young-maidish don from King's, whose specialties are electronic brains and earthquakes. This is an absolutely alien type of creature—a real institution dweller, as happy in King's as a monk in his monastery—and just palpitating with gossip and academic politics. His idea of a real big thrill is to find some double entendre in a serious document or inscription—or, on another level, to get rather drunk on the train to Cambridge from the same bottle with a couple of G.I.s. He is really quite touching and likeable. But, as Don says, he gives you a genuine horror-glimpse into that life. "I kept thinking," said Don to me later, "what a ghastly narrow escape you had, and how amazingly daring of you to have left Cambridge when you did."

Yesterday noon we had a very successful picnic with Don [Murray] and Hope Murray and Cecil Beaton. By the grace of the sun, which emerged, at the very last moment, from the fog. We went in the water, which was fairly cold, and then ate sandwiches and drank wine and slept. Don Murray and Hope looked like the Babes in the Wood.

September 24. Such a glorious morning. Don said: "You're much sadder than you used to be, aren't you?" Later we got into a quarrel, because he says I groan under responsibilities and blame him for them, which is true. I find myself sinking more and more into the nihilistic mood I was in during my first year and a half in this country— 1939–40. But then I had the war as an excuse; *and*, there's no doubt of

[1] See diary entry for February 15, 1956.

it, I was trying to shake Vernon, as a horse tries to shake a rider. I do not want to shake Don. That's sincerely true. Yes, he may sometimes be a nuisance; but I *never* say to myself that I wish he wasn't here.

He has just gone off—the quarrel made up—to take Marguerite's red Dior dress to the cleaner's because Monty Clift vomited over it or made her vomit, and to get us some typing paper because Gavin and I are going to start the teleplay this morning because Gingold has unexpectedly said yes.

At least, the Burns brothers believe she has. Her agent has agreed and says she'll sign. Me, I'll believe it when I see it, and when the pilot film has been shot, and when the whole series has run its course. I believe her (and him) capable of infinite bitcheries.

I like the Burns brothers. But there's something just a little sinister about the domesticity of TV. George and Willy and Gracie and Ronnie and the rest of them are becoming (one imagines) more and more what they appear to be on the screen. The medium is ruthlessly *sincere*.

September 28. Gavin and I finished the rough draft of the teleplay yesterday. Gingold still hasn't signed and Cecil Beaton, who sees a lot of her on the *Gigi* set, thinks she won't. Meanwhile Gavin and I are getting seriously concerned—should we really commit ourselves to the responsibility of producing thirty-nine teleplays the first year, not to mention more the second year and more the third?

Leonard Gershe,[1] whom we met at Roger Edens's house the night before last, put this idea into my head. He described the horrors of trying to supervise the work of other writers—how you always end up doing all the work yourself.

The almost spooky tropical beauty of Roger's garden, on its narrow shelf, with a safe-seeming overgrown wall hiding the sheer drop of the cliff, and beyond, the magic of the moonpath on a misty overcast sea. The house is well proportioned, but like a very grand gift-shop.

Roger's imitation of Tallulah Bankhead, clutching Judy Garland's knees in insincere, drunken adoration.

Cecil sat through all this quizzically. He is very patient and cheerful and polite.

Yesterday night we bored him again, I fear—though at his own suggestion—by inviting Romain Gary and Lesley Blanch. Gary could be sympathetic in the very bogusness of his virility and old-tomcat girl chasing, and he makes shrewd intuitive remarks about China and the

---

[1] Screenwriter, playwright, and lyricist; longtime collaborator and friend of Roger Edens.

Andes. Her I find a little depressing. She is in a permanent sulk because of Gary and his amours. And it was bitchy of her to have corrected one of the few bad mistakes he made in English—"box fight."

Blanch is pale, with blue rings under her eyes. She has slightly puffy cheeks. She could be a sister of John van Druten.

September 29. On the telephone this morning, Cecil Beaton said he thought that he would give Lesley Blanch "a pi-jaw,"[1] telling her that her sulks would cause her to lose her husband. "She's a born spinster," he said. It interests me very much that Cecil is prepared to do this—it shows that he has a kind of disinterested goodwill which is quite rare. And yet many people regard him as a rather heartless bitchy man-about-town. No bitch would stick his neck out in this way.

As I have said already, Don and I are getting to like Cecil more and more.

Jo and Ben returned from their San Francisco trip. They had seen J. B. Blunk and his wife who are living up in the woods north of the city. J. B. is building his own house, grinding his own corn, making his own pots;[2] and his son is allowed to crawl around the woods, where he recently ate poison ivy and got bitten in the lip by a lizard. Jo was a little strident in her screams of praise for J. B.'s way of life—she and Ben both have the tendency to play up any back-to-nature stuff with religious fervor.

After they'd gone, Don and I had another quarrel about Marguerite's coming. Don says I let Jo and Ben see that I don't want Marguerite in the house; which is probably true. Anyhow, after a lot more shouting and arguing, I think things have definitely calmed down; and today I feel quite resigned to the whole affair. It will probably seem microscopically unimportant in retrospect.

I should be, and am, distressed and disgusted by the deterioration of my character, this last year or two. And yet, somehow, I know that this isn't ultimately important. Even if my "faith" wavers—and it does from time to time, of course—even this isn't important. Even if I cease to "believe in" Swami—I mean, believe in the reality of his religious experience—the fact remains that he is there and his experience is a reality. I know this, somehow. As one just knows that a certain artist is great, even during periods when one feels no contact with his work.

Let me write this down clearly and definitely: I believe that there is something called (for convenience) God, and that this something can

---

[1] A serious talk.
[2] He was a potter by profession.

be experienced (don't ask me how), and that a man I know (Swami) has had this experience, partially, at any rate. All this I believe because my instinct, as a novelist and connoisseur of people, assures me, after long, long observation, that it is true in Swami's case.

All right then—believing this is also my guarantee that somehow in the end everything will come out all right for me and everyone. Because if God *is* there, then we needn't be afraid.

I write this in a time of dryness, degradation, dullness and general alienation—sincerely believing it to be *no shit*. This is what Swami has done for me. And it's certainly enough.

Goodness, though, some of his stories about Maharaj are disconcerting. When I saw him last Wednesday, he told me that Swami Sankarananda, the present head of the Math, used to be Maharaj's secretary and that Maharaj got mad at him and wouldn't see him for years—wouldn't have him in the same monastery, even. Swami Sankarananda's offense was that he had been setting himself up as a judge of Maharaj's visitors, saying who might see him and who might not. So Maharaj turned him away and only forgave him on his deathbed!

Swami Prabhavananda seems to find this all quite as it should be. He even remarked admiringly that it gave Swami Shankarananda the opportunity to show his greatness; because he never left the order or bore Maharaj any ill will. He stuck around and was there at Maharaj's death bed, to be forgiven. Swami Prabhavananda added that Maharaj gave people the power and strength to endure his displeasure. At the same time, however, he, Prabhavananda, had the nerve to protest to Maharaj against this treatment of Sankarananda. So maybe this is just one of the things which Swami has only come to understand lately— as he, himself, said.

A marvellous day on the beach. The sea cold with quite big surf. The sun bitingly hot. Visibility so good that you could even see the peak of Catalina which makes it look a little like Tahiti.

Read a weak worthless novel by a nice old lady, about the Dutch East Indies, *The Ten Thousand Things*.[1] Simon and Schuster sent it me—they are publishing it. I feel tempted to say something really crushing about it, because Peter Schwed[2] just wrote me that Ben's book is "slick."

Apropos of nothing in particular, I'm happy to record that my "virility" (the word is so silly it ought always to be in quotes) seems to be definitely reestablished. In spite of the fact that I haven't had any hormone shots for at least a month.

---

[1] By Maria Dermoût, translated from the Dutch by Hans Koningsberger.
[2] Isherwood's new editor at Simon and Schuster; see Glossary.

Later. We're just back from supper with Evelyn Hooker. She fixed us a deliciously stuffed roast duck. The house is very clean, very neat, very dead. Evelyn has absolutely no taste. She has all sorts of pieces of furniture and pictures, objects, etc., which just don't go with each other. Worst of all, the rosebud wallpaper in her bedroom—a suggestion made by Natasha Spender!

Evelyn has now started her "field work" on her new project—the investigation of social patterns of homosexuality. As she says herself, the only way she can do this is to follow up every clue and see and talk to anybody who is willing. For instance, she was told of the existence of a queer science-fiction club, which turned out to be merely a science-fiction club containing some queers. She visited an after-hours bar, run by a white boy and a colored boy, both Korean veterans. The colored boy had started it because he wanted his friend to meet "a better class of people"; however, shortly after Evelyn's visit, the club was raided and the colored boy lost his job—which was some kind of white collar work for the city police! Then in New York, Evelyn met the men who have opened a new branch of the Mattachine Society[1]—and found that they were being so cagey with each other that they didn't even know each other's professions. A commander in the navy was much bolder, however. He took his boyfriend to visit the family. The boyfriend rather dismayed the family by sewing, but reassured them by watching football games on TV as he did so!

Such scraps Evelyn is collecting. It all seems slightly futile, and yet I don't see any other way she could go about the job, and maybe a pattern will emerge.

We got almost no glimpse of Evelyn's own life. There she is, sleeping in the marriage bed. And there's her dog Star, who barks at everything but makes her feel protected. And there's her work. I suppose she seems lonelier than she actually is, because the house is too large.

October 1. Yesterday Don and I went to MGM to have lunch with Cecil Beaton and go on the sets of *Gigi*. I seem to see more and more how much of Cecil's art is nostalgia for this period—the nineties and the nineteen hundreds. Perhaps a nostalgic whiff of the glamor of royalty as it exuded from the figure of Edward VII. Happy is the artist who digests his nostalgia in this way. I felt Cecil's joy in thus swimming in the element of his favorite world. And it seems that Minnelli[2] feels the same.

---

[1] One of the earliest homosexual organizations.
[2] Vincente Minnelli was the director of *Gigi*.

Gingold, looking younger but not better in a curly black wig, was table hopping during lunch in the commissary—quite beside herself with archness and glee. She is a sort of sublimated nymphomaniac, you feel. Maybe not so sublimated, either. I agree with Cecil—it seems doubtful that she will ever sign this TV contract.

In the afternoon, Gavin and I went to see the Burns brothers about our teleplay. They suggested quite a few alterations, but nothing very radical. We are to get a secretary tomorrow and do them right in the studio.

George Burns was most interesting about comedy. Speaking of a character who is to wear a false beard, he describes it as "sweaty." In other words, it is promising something—going out on a limb. It had better be good. The false beard is a promise of comedy, which the audience reacts to with a "you show me." Whereas, if the character *doesn't* wear a false beard, there is no promise. If he's funny it's not expected, and so it seems funnier. George and Gracie Allen were the first team to abandon "funny" costumes because they realized this.

George carries a cane, like Chaplin's but longer and solider. He also wears a kind of beret. Their assistant is a monkeylike, rather girly young man named Tommy, who reads the teleplays aloud to them—well. He is a friend of Tom Wright.

Despite the niceness of the Burns brothers, I felt a horror coming over me. I *cannot* go on with this project. Certainly not tie myself down for a year. I talked to Gavin, who I think may be willing to take over the responsibility. We'll see. I have decided to offer the Burnses to do six shows for their first year; but this is far less than they will agree to, I know.

Supper this evening with John van Druten at the Imperial Gardens. A nasty shock when we found that Carter and Dick were waiting for us there. Dick is such a fat old hypocrite. Having spent all the money on redecorating his house Faggot Chinese, he announces that he cannot possibly spend Christmas away from dear Johnnie, so they'll all go to Death Valley, instead of Carter and Dick going to Samoa.

Johnnie seemed tired—but no wonder. He had done one third of the adaptation of *Anatomy of a Murder*[1] in two days! He was also upset because he has had a quarrel with Pamela Frankau.[2] She asked him to pay her fare out here and put her up. When he refused, at short notice, because he is busy working, she got furious and reminded him he owed her thirteen pounds.

---

[1] From the novel by Robert Travers; the script was finished by Wendell Mayes.
[2] English novelist with whom van Druten corresponded and swapped limericks; she lived on the East Coast.

Am racing ahead with my novel. Only eight more pages to reach forty before I leave. *But* there's the teleplay.

October 7. I have just been roaring like a cross old bear at Mrs. Hine's and Mrs. Stickel's youngest children, and then at Geller, because he hinted I was to blame for not letting the Burnses know sooner that I wouldn't agree to their terms. Now all is confusion. And the Burnses are starting to say they won't make the series at all.

I'm too depressed to write any more just now.

Well, yes, I *must* write, because it's disgraceful to give way to tamasic blues and travel jitters. At least I have finished the first chapter of the new draft of my novel—thirty-nine pages. Not nearly right, but amounting to something. As for this journal, I can't finish it before we leave, but never mind.

Don and I are both on edge at the prospect of starting—or rather, at the delay before starting. Yesterday, we went to a movie theater to see *An Affair to Remember*—God knows why; we left almost at once. But aside from that, the place was almost uninhabitable because of the mob of children. One little girl kept running up and down the aisle. Finally Don tripped her, and she fell screaming. After this he said he felt much better.

October 8. Yesterday, we took Hope Murray out to dinner. She really is an enchantingly attractive girl. One of the few people you could describe as "fun." Got quite drunk; then went on to see *No Down Payment* at Fox. The part they got wrong was the ending. In suburbia every misbehavior is absorbed. Within two to three weeks they'd have been inviting the rapist to their barbecues again.[1]

Saw Jessie Marmorston, who wrote me a prescription for Miltown to relieve the tension of the journey. I took some last night and have taken two today. Can't say I feel that much less tense, but I suppose it's something that I'm not climbing up the walls.

Although quite well aware—as always when starting on a journey of this kind—that I may never return, that the next hand which opens this book may not be mine—I still feel unable to write any memorable last words. Perhaps the Miltown really *is* dulling my wits? I wish it gave more euphoria, at the same time.

[On October 8, Isherwood and Bachardy flew to Japan; they went on to Hong Kong, Singapore, Bali, Bangkok, Angkor, and then Calcutta where, as background for Isherwood's biography of Ramakrishna, they visited places associated with Ramakrishna and stayed at the

---

[1] The rapist is beaten up by his victim's husband and leaves town.

Belur Math. On the way home they stopped for nearly a month in London, where they received the news of John van Druten's death, on December 19, 1957. Afterwards they spent roughly another month in New York, returning to Los Angeles at the end of January.]

1958

February 2. Well, hi.

Yes I'm back. We got here three days ago, early in the morning of the 30th. A very thick white fog around the airport. The pilot *said* the ceiling was 500 feet, but it seemed to me that we had almost touched down on the runway before we saw it. Some cute paratroopers across the aisle of the plane were visibly worried.

It is pouring down rain. I've been working all day, getting my desk tidied and my accounts and papers sorted and straightened out. I still have rather a bad cold on my chest, with a cough. The day after our arrival I spent mostly in bed.

The idea is to start work tomorrow morning on *both* the Ramakrishna book and the novel. We have $5,162 in our account here. That won't last long. I had hoped there would be some money coming to me from Johnnie's will, but Carter blandly informed me that I'm no longer the literary executor. Johnnie made three different wills last year. I wonder who was responsible for that?

I went to supper with them the night we arrived. Dick seemed as much of an ass as ever, only now he's a rich ass. As usual, he was planning to advance his "career," with a couple of agents.

Don goes back to school tomorrow. He couldn't possibly be sweeter than he has been since we arrived home.

February 3. Don went to school. It rained heavily in the night and our bedroom leaked. This morning it cleared. More rain is expected tonight.

Today has been a day of doing dozens of evasive chores to escape working on my two books. I suppose this was inevitable. One can't expect to snap smartly back into work after nearly four months of doing nothing about it.

Talked to Gerald on the phone. He described, with a certain relish, the truly horrible last phase of poor Bill Kiskadden—he leaks at the sphincter, has a nylon aorta and is going blind.[1] On top of that, he has been forced by ill health to return to live here with Peggy, which he'd previously refused to do.

---

[1] In fact, Kiskadden recovered; see Glossary.

Talked to Tom Wright, who tells me (a) that Jim Charlton has just gotten married to a rich Swiss woman of his own age, with three children (b) that [a friend] ran off to Portland with Tom's car and Jim's camera. Jim never got the camera back, but Tom went up to Portland and recovered the car.

February 11. Yesterday and the day before were bad. I had bellyache and fever. Then felt absolutely exhausted and lay down resting on the couch. Don was away all day yesterday at school and phoned to say he was spending the night downtown. Maybe at his mother's. I don't know.

Today I got a page of the novel and a page of the Ramakrishna book done. Never mind if it takes an eternity. I must keep at it.

To see Kent Chapman yesterday evening. He lives down in Venice, which I still think the most glamorous slum in the world. I do like him. He is intelligent and innocent. He has a candid eye. He told me about the Venice West school of poets and painters. They have a special jargon: they talk about "wailing," meaning riding high in any sense. You can "wail" by writing or painting or simply smoking marijuana. The aim of their art is to make you sick to your stomach. One painting is of a figure with a death's head. One arm ends in a great spike. The other arm has a bleeding wound in it.

February 14. This diary keeping goes hard, but I must keep after it. I've been rereading the earlier pages of this volume with quite a lot of enjoyment. Meanwhile I've *got* to get some notes written down on our trip.

Ben and Jo return on Sunday. In lifemanship terms, they are one up. *They* have "made contact with the environment" (I only write this in quotes because it sounds so pompous). We failed.

Today is the fifth anniversary of my meeting with Don. I gave him a star ruby last night to replace the one that got lost or stolen last year.

There isn't even any statement to be made about this anniversary: we are so much in the midst of getting on with our lives. I do pray that Don is going to find more happiness in his work. I can't help hoping that this idea of his going to a class with Vernon Old might work out well. Because Vernon can surely understand many of his problems.

We had Vernon to supper, three nights ago. He really seemed very nice; much less pompous and patronizing. I took him up to see Swami the day before yesterday. Not sure how much of a success that was. Not a smash—but maybe all right. Vernon is still very critical of things up at Vedanta Place.

Prema whispered to me an amazing story: Phil (Buddha) has seen

Tito fairly recently. He thinks Tito is crazy. Tito has a terrible hate on against Ramakrishna and Swami. Phil and/or Prema suspect that it may have been Tito who disfigured the picture in the Santa Barbara shrine. A symbolic murder. What makes this idea even more alarming is of course the possibility that Tito *might* attempt to hurt Swami. I very much doubt this, though. And the whole theory has big holes in it. I can't picture the circumstances in which Tito would get clear up to Santa Barabara, hide, presumably in the bushes, and sneak into the temple.

Don and I had supper with the Stravinskys and Bob Craft last night. Chris Wood was also there. A wonderful evening of joy and love, in which I felt we were all included. I never can remember what is said on these occasions—oh yes, we were looking through a book of very inadequate illustrations by de Staël to poems by René Char.[1] But it was all joyful. We had fish soup. Igor seemed much better and looked younger.

Today I've been bad. I ought to have gotten on with my novel and the Ramakrishna book. Instead, I slept; after working outside putting some of the garden debris into cartons. But at least my social security application is all set up. I start it in a couple of weeks.

February 17. The day before yesterday, Saturday, at 10 a.m., I took the half bottle of mescaline (dissolved, I suppose, in water) which Pat Trevor-Roper gave me when we saw him in London last month.

(Pat fished the bottle out from behind a row of antique leather books. I think he had had it with him for some time, and this may possibly explain some of the disagreeable symptoms I got from taking it—symptoms quite different from those of my first mescaline experience on February 24, 1956.)

The solution tasted bitter, but not sufficiently so to make me want to get rid of the taste by eating something sweet. (A puritan reaction here: I had a feeling that maybe it was good that the stuff should be bitter—that this meant it was still potent!) After taking the mescaline, I went ahead and ate breakfast—orange juice and a boiled egg. No coffee, but I'd had some just before taking it.

Symptoms, as before, of sickness and nervous excitement. I thought of myself as a rocket, tearing upward through the atmosphere layers. In an hour, I should begin to orbit.

Sure enough, the first visual phenomena began to appear just round 11:00 a.m. By 11:30 they were quite vivid. Above all, I was aware most strongly of the rich texture of the "pickled" woodwork of

---

[1] The Russian-born painter, Nicholas de Staël, made woodcuts to illustrate Char's volume *Poèmes* (1952).

our ceiling. Also of the many tints of light in our whitewashed walls. The yellows and reds and blues of books on the shelves stood out very sharply. Also I became aware of every particle of dirt and dust on our living room floor. The folds of the window curtains were deeply sculptured.

The sun was shining outside, though somewhat hazily. I was aware of the prettiness of the plants, which became full of blue shadows. But when I went outside to examine them, I was rather disappointed. I felt no sense of their being alive (as in the previous mescaline experience). Indeed the potted plants on either side of the front door seemed quite definitely dead (which they are not) and very dry. Only some small flowers held out their blossoms toward the sun like begging hands—that is to say, in a gesture which seemed human.

Don asked me: how do I look with the moustache? I replied that it seemed natural to his face, and that it was perhaps the lack of it which had bothered me when I examined his face under mescaline before. But I was also, not agreeably, aware of his terrible restlessness—of his anxiety about his appearance and of what people might think of it. I saw him positively tormented by his ego—his ego perpetually stepping between him and the possibility of real enjoyment and satisfaction and knowledge. Yet, at the same time, how gallantly and touchingly he struggles! Such a quick nervous beautiful restless creature, sometimes momentarily so ugly with cruelty and misery. One of the smaller cats, an ocelot, maybe. He brought me two or three of his pictures to look at. They didn't fail the test by any means—there was evident power in them. (But I'm anyhow *very* sceptical of John Goodwin's theory that mescaline endows you with an absolute criterion of aesthetic judgment.)

The unpleasantness of this dose now began to become more evident. I mean, when I took mescaline before, I seem to remember that the nausea quickly passed off. This time it continued throughout. Also I became increasingly aware of acute nervous tension which expressed itself as a feeling of pressure at the back of the skull and at the base of the spine. I was terribly restless.

I called Ivan Moffat. I wanted to see him because he is to be the chief character in my novel. He said he would come around as quickly as possible.

At 12:15 I noted "a very intense secret kind of nervous trembling." By this time I had showered and gotten dressed. I was clumsy (as before) and dropped the soap a couple of times.

I closed my eyes, expecting to see patterns. But the only patterns I saw were stupid, sharp cut, dull colored, metallic. "My thoughts are all tin," I wrote.

By this time, the wall boards seemed semitransparent. Whenever I fixed my eyes on them, the white in them began to run down like milk. I said to myself, "Isn't all this just an artistic kind of nausea?" I was *very* far from any sense of genuine insight or vision. *Most* unspiritual. I also felt the reticence of one who is nauseated. I could say literally, pointing to anything: "All that makes me sick."

When Ivan arrived—I think around 1:00 p.m.—I was sitting on the step of the front door. "Like an old Provençal peasant," he said. My first impression of *him* was almost that of a George Grosz drawing: the high white bulging forehead of an unhealthy child, and below it the wrinkled eyes and the sagging purplish fruit-heavy cheeks of senility. His legs seemed disproportionately short.

Later, I saw that he too is a cat—one of the big ones: a heavy old panther sitting patiently in a tree, waiting for his prey. He has a heavy-jowled face, grave with patience. He is cruel in a sense, but not fierce. He even waits with humor. "I've had everything I wanted," he said, "even the most unlikely things." I asked him if he was afraid of impotence. He said yes—he was afraid of any loss of potentiality.

He drove me up to the house he wants to buy. He only has about $4,000 saved, because of all the people he has had to support, and because he eats at Chasen's three or four times a week. The house will keep him slaving at movies for years. It is high up the hillside above the mouth of Sunset Boulevard—not far from the Cottens. Quite a big place, about twenty to thirty years old, Spanish style. Ivan wants to take it to make a home for his daughter, Lorna. If Caroline Freud can get her divorce, he'll marry her. "If not," I told him, "you'll find yourself with a sixteen-year-old bride, one of your daughter's friends." He admitted to lecherous daydreams along these lines.

I had to ask him to drive home, because I was feeling sick.

After we got back, he borrowed an issue of the *U.S. News and World Report* which contained an alarmist article on Russia's military intentions. Ivan is haunted by war fears.

Shortly after he'd left, I phoned him to ask if he is ever bothered by resentment against his dependents. He says almost never. I believe him. But this is flatly opposed to the character in my novel.

The visual effects continued till between 4:00 and 5:00 p.m. Toward the end, I noticed a lot of caricature faces in the woodwork. I said to myself that, if this picture-making faculty were to persist after dark, it might become annoying and ultimately frightening. Otherwise, I felt absolutely no fear.

But I was getting very tired of the visual effects. Also of feeling so sick and tense. All this while I'd felt absolutely no hunger. But now

I forced myself to take several spoonfuls of honey—hoping to stop the action of the drug.

Don—who'd been doing homework upstairs all this while—hadn't eaten; so we went out to Ted's [Grill]. Either because of the honey or because the drug was anyhow losing its power, I now ceased to see things abnormally. But the feeling of tension increased and increased, until it became quite agonizing. I felt almost unable to sit still. I wanted out. It was like suffocating, although you could breathe. "I'm not sure I can bear this," I thought; and then: "What will happen if I *can't* bear it? Nothing." And I felt ready to scream. Gradually the worst of the distress passed off, as we walked home. But I never felt hungry, and never really relaxed—even in sleep—until next day.

To sum up: a disappointing, acutely unpleasant, uninstructive experience. My immediate reaction would be never to take the stuff again. But I have these five capsules I got from the drugstore in New York. So I think I have to try. I'll wait awhile.

Yesterday night, Jo and Ben returned from their Tahitian tour, flying back from Honolulu. They arrived in a thick fog, and had to land at Burbank. Most of the rest of the country is being swept by blizzards.

February 20. Ramakrishna's birthday—but I'm not going up to Vedanta Place because Swami is sick with a cold and won't be taking out the relics at vespers.

A lovely cool sunshiny day, after yesterday's rain—which dripped into the downstair bedroom closet and over the record player and over my books, ruining, among others, Marjorie Bowen's *Black Magic* which I've loved for more than thirty years.

A very nice evening, the day before yesterday, with Jo and Ben. They say that Tahiti has almost no native life left. But they loved visiting the smaller islands. Jo is much worried because her White Stag[1] job has come to an end.

My own prospects, none of them very dazzling are:

The possibility Jerry Wald will succeed in casting *Jean-Christophe* (as he says he's trying to)—that Elsa Lanchester will like the Gingold teleplay (which goes to her today)—that I'll be hired to write *Tender Is the Night* for Selznick and [Jennifer] Jones (which is being considered)—that I'll be taken on to do a movie about the Dead Sea Scrolls (in which a producer at Fox is interested). Of these choices, I guess I'd most rather do rewriting on *Jean-Christophe*.

If I had money, I'd just keep going on the novel and the

---

[1] The sports wear manufacturer.

Ramakrishna biography. Both grow very slowly—a page a day—but I know I shall become increasingly absorbed in them.

February 25. We're as busy as bees right now. Don has supplemented his classes at the Chouinard by taking lessons with Vernon Old. That is, he took the first today and it seems to be a great success. Oddly enough, the still life he painted for Vernon was in quite a different manner—much more relaxed. I am so delighted, but hardly dare breathe lest it shouldn't last.

Heavy rain last night, and the leak reopened over my bookcase, which is most tiresome. The roof will have to be fixed—and where is all the money to come from? Still waiting to hear if maybe Selznick wants me for *Tender Is the Night*—but of course I don't really want to work with Selznick or with anybody. I want to get the hell on with my books.

Met Betty Andrews in the Canyon, with her little boy Christopher. He had a plastic toy doctor's outfit. He said: "Show me your braces." I said: "I'll only show you, because you're a doctor, not your mother," and I took my lower bridge out and showed it to him.

Prema drove me up to Santa Barbara on Sunday. I had to pinch-hit for Swami, who still has a cold. On the way, Prema told me Maughamlike stories about the congregation.

For example: J., a building contractor, seemed the archetype of husky virile American male. *But* he began saying that his wife, K., really ought to be a nun. So finally K. joined the convent. Prema found this so odd that he decided J. must be impotent—especially as J. sometimes spoke of a serious accident he'd had. Finally, K. fell in love with or was at any rate fallen in love with by D., one of the nuns. The two of them finally had to leave the convent. But now, J., the supposedly impotent mate, springs a surprise. He comes to Swami and says there's a beautiful young millionairess wants to marry him; and he's going to marry her. And one supposes that millionairesses do *not* marry impotent men. Or do they?

February 28. I seem to have no particular desire to keep this diary going, but I shall try to do so—at least to the two entry a week minimum. It has been thundering this afternoon. Now it's raining. Don has worked steadily at art school. I've kept the Ramakrishna book and my novel going—without much enthusiasm. The novel seems such a bore, and the Ramakrishna book is weary work. But I know from experience that some good always comes of steady progress. Pages always pile up into something.

The latest scandal is that one of Marguerite's beaux now thinks he may be in love with Speed. Actually, [. . .] the whole pentagon—Marguerite, Marguerite's number one beau, Marguerite's number two beau, Speed, Paul—[is a bore. T]he whole thing's an utter bore. Marguerite's chief preoccupation is lest she should be publicly humiliated, because Muff Brackett has already announced a big Sunday Lunch "to meet Marguerite's beau."

There's a kind of gleeful masochistic indiscretion in all this which I find repulsive, and which makes me rather hate both Marguerite and Speed. Rather, not altogether. Well, it's not important—except that Don minds. Says I don't like his friends.

March 5. We had quite a big party last Sunday night. Dorothy Miller fixed a turkey and Ivan Moffat, Joan Elan, Paul Millard, Harry Brown, June de Baum, Ellis St. Joseph and Gavin Lambert came and ate it. Ivan was bored by Paul, who has been told by Marguerite all about Speed's behavior and couldn't stop talking about it and protesting he didn't care. Joan Elan has been warned by a fortune teller not to travel at the end of this month—it would be disastrous; *but* she has been offered an excellent job in New York television. Shall she disregard the warning? Harry has a job at Fox, and seemingly he still has June. Ellis has bought a house down our street, which doesn't charm me at all. Hope he won't be a nuisance. Gavin had been in a fire that afternoon. A gas explosion in the house he's renting. All his books and a lot of clothes burned. And he burned his hand, not badly. He was very good-humored and stoical about this.

The Selznicks are back in town, and no word—so I fear *Tender Is the Night* is off.

Glorious weather. Today I was on the beach, but the ocean is too cold for swimming. Don is working very hard and the lessons with Vernon are still a success. He now plans to take two a week. I'm really impressed by the painting he is doing now.

March 7. This shameful laziness. It's partly the result of drinking too much last night at the Duquettes'—too much, for me, being now almost any amount of hard liquor whatsoever. Taina Elg[1] was there. We kicked. I was silly.

But I must pull myself together. Look at it like this—the effective part of one's life, barring sickness, falls into three thirds—twenty-five to forty, forty to fifty-five, fifty-five to seventy. My impression is that I packed a terrific amount into the first third, and that I've wasted a

---

[1] Finnish actress; she had a small part in *Diane*, and Isherwood got to know and like her.

great deal of the second. (In the first third, I produced twelve works—including two translations and three collaborations: the plays. In the second third, I have so far produced four works—including two translations. Maybe I can pack in the novel and the Ramakrishna book before the August 1959 deadline—but I doubt it.)

March 12. Strange weather—sunshine, rainstorms, wind, cold, sunshine. I made a terrific scene on Sunday with Marguerite because she'd been telling Curtis Harrington that I did not like Wald's picture—*The Long Hot Summer*. At least, I'm not sure exactly what she *did* tell, but I seized the opportunity of bawling her out. The truth is, I *don't* like her and thus it was actually a great mistake, because now there will have to be a reconciliation.

Meanwhile great excitement because Don Murray has got the rights to *Jean-Christophe*—an option for six months. He'll ask Joshua Logan to direct it. I have to be careful not to get involved, until a workable agreement has been reached with Fox—who, of course, own the screenplay which I wrote. Otherwise, I'll be in the doghouse with Fox *and* not get to work on the script for Don's production.

Despite the utter uncertainty of business, I must say that I'm very happy right now. Partly because I'm working steadily without letup on the Ramakrishna book and the novel—chiefly because of good relations with Don, who is happy (I think and hope) in *his* work and couldn't be sweeter.

March 13. Today I suddenly got the call to see Selznick next Monday—on *Mary Magdalene*. Don't know if this is a novel they've bought or an original story, or what. Very dubious about working for Selznick, anyway. He sounds so horrible.

Showers continue.

The Hine kids are digging a big hole in the waste lot opposite. Greg peels off his shirt—in imitation of his father?—and tosses it nonchalantly to the girls before digging. Roy Parry is painting the platform of his monster TV antenna. The pretty Sammet boy, now grown enormous, still comes to play with the kids.

To see Swami last night. He seems listless, complains of headaches. Prema thinks it's nothing serious. Swami was saying that the people at the Belur Math had written saying that Krishna had been utterly transformed by sannyas, in a single day—but they didn't say *how*! Swami was much intrigued. Krishna had written: "Three days ago, I became a Brahmin. Two days ago I became a ghost[1]—one always

---

[1] For sannyas, the aspirant must renounce caste and life itself; thus Krishna first had to join a caste, the Brahmins, and then "die." See Glossary under sannyas.

becomes what one fears! Yesterday I became Krishnananda." There is a majestic note of impersonality in this last sentence. Like when you say in the ritual: "I am He."

Don Murray is sending the screenplay to Logan.

March 18. The day before yesterday was perhaps the highest high point in my relations with Don. I don't mean that anything happened—actually we went to a stag party at Jerry Lawrence's, followed by a very bad TV show (Jeanette MacDonald in *The Girl of the Golden West*[1]). But we had a talk—that sounds so dry; it was really a kind of verbal duet—in which we both quite spontaneously declared how completely we belong to each other. This is my whole happiness, now.

But altogether it is a very happy time, with work and thought calmly flowing. I'm even very sorry that it seems as if it would shortly end in a job. I talked to Selznick this morning and he was quite charming; and I like his plans for *Mary Magdalene*. She will be rather like Brett in *The Sun Also Rises*.

Jim [Charlton] and his wife are going to have a baby. Today I wrote him a note asking him to pay the rest of the money he owes me. This was a kind of psychological victory, and might even end in my forgiving him. (If he pays, of course!)

March 21. This morning, we had a runaround with Selznick. After the most cordial talk last night—at which you'd have thought we were just a pair of buddy-buddy artists whom the word money would make wince—Selznick suddenly comes up with the most impudent proposition: $1,000 a week, and the balance up to $1,250 retro-actively *if* I get my name on the picture. This we refused. So now Selznick has gone to $1,250 and the balance retroactively up to $1,500. This at least saves my face. But it makes me wonder how long we'll last together.

Selznick's attitude may have had something to do with the depression. At the social security office yesterday, a brown-eyed, long-nosed young man (rather like Gore Vidal) with a knot of anxiety between his eyes, was holding forth about how tough everything was. "I tried to get into the police. They told me I didn't have enough teeth. Hell—I had enough for the marines. Hell, there were guys with us no bigger'n I am, could have taken any of those cops and turned them inside out." He expressed hatred of the Bank of America, and huge satisfaction because a little old lady went into one of its branches a few days ago, stuck them up and got $2,000. (The

---

[1] The 1939 film, shown on TV.

Bank of America is where we cash our social security checks.) A little later, at my bank, I heard two other boys speaking of her, also with approval—a typical folk heroine of the depression.

My thumb is so painful I can hardly write. I'm going with Jessie Marmorston tomorrow to have it X-rayed.

Don had a terrific scene with his mother on the phone this morning. She feels unwanted, she says. Don reduced to fury by her sadistic masochism. Later I phoned and persuaded her to come to supper, tomorrow.

March 28. I haven't written, because my thumb has been bad. They found traces of arthritis in it when they X-rayed it. I'm supposed to have some treatment, but that's hardly possible, now that I'm working with Selznick. I started last Monday. Am greatly worried about it. I don't feel it's going well.

A huge slide on the Pacific Highway. One car was carried right to the edge of the waves. Others may be buried. They're still digging.

Jim has invited us to a party at his house. I doubt if Don'll go.

Swami told me that he has only recently discovered that God's grace is actually *in* the mantram. Maharaj had told him that this was so.

I have *never* been so fat.

March 29. Sunshine again, after so much rain. But they say more is coming. I have just had a visit from George Koniaris, a young Greek student at UCLA who is to be our technical advisor.[1] He knows Greek and Latin, archaeology, philosophy, history—*and* he longs to be connected with the theater! In other words, he is slightly too good to be true.

Still worried about the *Magdalene* project. I don't feel at all sure that I have anything.

My thumb is still bad.

April 3. Terrific winds, more landslides; they say the Coast Highway can never be used again. It must be rebuilt out on the beach, or inland, or something.

A bad time with Don, at the beginning of the week. A visit from the personality I call "Black Tom."

Oh God, how easily I get sad and discouraged!

Work with Selznick is going better, but I fail to get on with the Ramakrishna book and my novel. Why?

[1] On *Mary Magdalene*.

Saw Aldous, looking very old, at an absurd lunch for Radha-krishnan[1], at the Ambassador. He is quite belligerent about his drugs and their power to provide labor-saving spiritual insights. He knows Swami won't approve.

April 4. A really bad cold starting—the worst in a long time. My throat is raw. The pills and vitamins don't help.

Yesterday evening we went to a weird dinner at the Duquettes'. Tony wanted to railroad me into doing "an English pantomime" for them to play at the studio. Their brazen arrogance—and the amazing tactlessness of asking all these rich half-witted women to be present. Jimmy Pendleton's pathetic old henna-haired bag of a wife said, "We've been together twenty-five years—and I've been *so* happy—*so* happy." It was heartbreaking, like *Long Day's Journey into Night*.

Today Krishnananda returned from India.

April 6. Well, Happy Easter!

A lousy day. Another of those big rainstorms has hit the coast. Causing more slides, probably.

We had a third strange meal last week—supper with Jim Charlton and his wife. She's a dowdy little thing, brown eyed with glasses. Very snug in her new pregnancy. I quite liked her; Don and Jo don't. Jim seemed a bit pathetic; I think he's beginning to realize the jam he's gotten himself into. He seemed to be appealing for help—in vain, of course. Who can help him? He was very grateful that we came.

Henrietta [Ledebur] was also there, with a tacky little [admirer], a bit piss-elegant, saying that San Francisco isn't a real city. And awful old Mrs. Lautner.[2] And square, square Oliver Andrews, being aesthetic about skin diving and the kelp.

Looking back over the last two years, to Easter 1956, I'm really most agreeably surprised to find how much activity we've packed into them—

A whole draft of the new novel. A whole screenplay (*Christophe*). A good start on the Ramakrishna book.

A journey round the world.

Hepatitis, had and recovered from. My first operation for tumor.

Don's definite embarkation on art study, which really seems to be getting him somewhere, largely thanks to Vernon.

[1] Sarvepalli Radhakrishnan (1888–1975), scholar of Hindu religion and philosophy, Vice President of India throughout the 1950s and President from 1962 until 1967.
[2] The wife of Los Angeles architect John Lautner, who was a Frank Lloyd Wright disciple and a mentor to Charlton.

All-round development and growth of Don, outwardly demons-trated by muscles and moustache.

Acquisition of the first house I have ever bought, and the development of a happy life in it, despite obstacles.

Against this, I must own that I am fatter, a bit blinder, and much tenser than ever. Much of my physical breakdown could be checked and even reversed, if I wasn't so lazy.

Again, I must say, as so often before, I have no excuse whatever to be unhappy. My relationship with Don is by far the happiest I have known. I have quite good health, lots of work in prospect. I even have a job, in these hard times. *And* I have Swami, and all he stands for.

What have I to complain of, as of this moment? Arthritis in my thumb! And even that could be cured if I wasn't too lazy to see Jessie and take shots.

Much talk about the stabbing of Lana Turner's boyfriend by her daughter.[1] Some say Lana did it and the daughter covered up. On the corpse was found a bracelet—"I'll always be yours: Lanita."

April 8. Woke this morning feeling very good. Partly just because the weather was really beautiful, without the least threat of rain—for the first time in days.

But also I had the feeling, "My devil has left me." This black mood has gotten off my back. It has been sitting there a long while. If it weren't for Don, I'd be far more conscious of its presence than I usually am.

Resolves to work more, quit stalling, fidgeting, mugging. Maybe to join the gym—American Health—that Howard Kelley goes to. I saw him and Bobo last night. Howard looks good. Bo is like a shrunken old man, a bit foolish, very gentle. I went by to have dinner with them after seeing Selznick. The interview was quite friendly— he was dead tired after Easter—but I got the feeling our work together was about to end. Today, however, I saw him again and it was much better—partly because our meeting was up at his house; not in his tacky Culver City office. His daughter Mary Jennifer's dog was eating the shrubs. Selznick said to the nurse: "Your dog's eating the shrubs." "It's not *my* dog," she snapped. One sensed a feud.

For the first time, we called each other "Chris" and "David."

April 12. Don went off this morning in a black state, exclaiming, "I feel awful!" This was apparently because of a conflict: should he stay

[1] The boyfriend was a smalltime gangster, Johnny Stompanato; the daughter was Cheryl Crane.

home and enjoy the marvelous weather on the beach, or go and paint at Vernon's? I really dread his return. I dread these moods. I feel utterly unable to cope with them. I feel like M. with Richard.

And there is the question of selfishness. Isn't it selfish of me to demand that Don shall be perpetually cheerful?

Arnold Dobrin just called to tell me he is the father of a boy. What shall he call it? He favors Andrew, or possibly Lincoln.

On good terms with Selznick right now. We have decided that the screenplay is to be a Shavian comedy with a background of violence; not a "Jewish Western."

To visit Gerald Heard this afternoon, to ask him some questions—how much does he meditate nowadays? how does he feel about the mantram? how does he feel toward the Vedanta Society?

Gerald, of course, replied indirectly, in a fascinating rigmarole. I learned that he thinks Soviet Russia is approaching the caste system and the psychological revolution. (Only one person in ten is capable of inductive reasoning.) Mescaline may be bad for the eyes—both Gerald and Michael find themselves losing focus constantly—Gerald thinks he'll give it up. Gerald got nothing out of his formal meditations except distractions and the willpower to force himself to meditate. So now he meditates "when the tide is flowing," chiefly at night. He uses his "short mantram." (Swami gave him two.) He has never thought much about the mantram as a chain of power between the guru and the disciple, leading back to Ramakrishna. As for the Vedanta Society—but here we were interrupted by Michael, come to take photographs of Gerald, Margaret Gage and Mary Wigman.[1]

Talking of the mantram reminds me that, about six or eight months ago, I suggested that Don should try repeating "Om" to himself. The other day he told me that he had given it up, because it scared him; he felt he might be getting too deep into something he didn't want or, at any rate, couldn't control.

My thumb is very painful. Luckily I don't have to write much by hand.

April 17. Two encounters this week with professional crazyman, Oscar Levant. On Monday last I went to supper with him, visiting the psychiatric ward at Mt. Sinai Hospital (where he has lately been shut up), an Italian restaurant in Beverly Hills (where he nearly had a fist fight with a fan), the house of Ira Gershwin (where he played the piano). Then I was on television with him the next day.

A bad thumb and the impending arrival of Stephen Spender makes me unwilling to write more.

[1] German modernist dancer.

April 19. Stephen leaves tonight—more about his visit tomorrow. It has been truly enjoyable, though, of course, it has unsettled our working schedule and utterly retarded my own work.

All I want to record today is Swami's strange, rather ominous concern about Aldous. Aldous has been constantly in his thoughts, he says, and he has been praying for him. Swami telephoned Aldous to find out if he is all right, but Aldous has been away—in New York, presumably.

April 22. Stephen left as scheduled. We felt in him [at least then,] quite a considerable [sense of difficulty in his marriage]. He seems [perhaps to be a little bit restless]. Otherwise he was charming, and I think he enjoyed his visit, if only because it gave him lots of time to sleep and rest up.

A wind today. It makes my bad thumb kick up.

But I have written a page of Ramakrishna and a page of novel— this despite a session with Selznick, during which he fell asleep and snored. We are fairly badly stuck, but on marvellously good terms. His constant anxiety about the builders on the opposite hill. Will he be overlooked? Shouldn't he have bought more adjacent lots? All this while I'm reading him from the Gospels, about how Jesus said the rich man couldn't enter the Kingdom of God.

April 24. At Swami's last night. He said that visions don't matter— only devotion matters. He told me "to remember the Lord."

Yesterday and this morning, they're working on our roof, giving us a new one. An unpleasant feeling, every moment, that they're about to bang a hole in it.

A nice young man named Bill Brame drove me up to Vedanta Place, because he wanted to talk to me, and because I had no car. He is directing a production of *I Am a Camera* here. Interested in mental hospitals and psychotherapy.

The prospect of Rosamond Lehmann coming to stay with us next weekend, does not please. I only hope we can get rid of her soon. She asked herself. We're far too busy to be able to entertain guests at this time.

Tomorrow will be one of the test days for Selznick. He may quite possibly call off our project.

April 25. Last night I dreamed about John van Druten—for the second time.

In the first dream, several weeks ago, Johnnie came to me and suggested we have lunch. So I answered: "But, Johnnie, you're dead." Johnnie seemed slightly amused, slightly embarrassed: "Oh, yes, so I am—aren't I!" He said this *exactly* as Johnnie would have said it.

In the second dream, Johnnie was very sick and yellow faced, lying in bed. He explained that he was already dead, and soon he'd disappear altogether. His bed was out of doors. He said death had been "most unpleasant." As happens in dreams, I went away, then remembered I wanted to ask him all sorts of questions: What about God? Did Johnnie still believe in Joel Goldsmith's teachings? etc. I hurried back. Johnnie was now terribly cold. He complained of the inefficiency of an old Dutch nurse, who wore velvet. I called her and ordered more blankets, for which she went into the house which was nearby. I came to the bed and held Johnnie in my arms. He said: "Chris, I want to tell you something—" I waited. He was very weak. I woke up, before he could summon the strength to speak.

April 28. Rosamond Lehmann left today—at least, I hope she didn't miss her train (Don started late to drive her down to the depot)—because, quite as I like her, her presence here was much more of an intrusion than Stephen's.

I think her stay was a success, though. On Saturday, we had the Stravinskys, Bob [Craft] and the Huxleys to supper. Igor became wonderfully oracular, said, "Music is the art of time." Aldous talked mescaline, recommended *The Relic* by [José Maria de] Eça de Queiroz, and said that he had met Father Bruckberger recently and that he was going to France to make his own Mary Magdalene film and would probably sue Selznick.[1] (In all Aldous's remarks I seemed to detect a certain venom and aggression: he looked much better, though very thin.) Rosamond did her best to keep up with the highbrow talk. She used phrases like "an organic whole." She wore a most elaborate grey dress and was covered with makeup. Laura seemed less rude and more feminine than usual. Bob, as always, was lovable. Vera told me that, the day before, when I'd phoned her, she had been napping in her studio, and she had actually been dreaming of me and Auden. Auden was present in the dream—very elegant, wearing long white gloves. I had told Vera that I was about to give up writing and sell pictures. I had a Cézanne for sale. Vera dissuaded me.

[1] Raymond Leopold Bruckberger, a French Dominican friar who was a twice-captured hero of the Resistance and an intellectual figure in post-war France, had published a biography of Mary Magdalene, *Marie-Madeleine* (1952; English translation, 1954) and, during the war, had made a prize-winning film, set in a Dominican convent *Les Anges du péché (Angels of Sin)*. See also Glossary under Selznick, David O.

She said that it was a terrible profession, you never knew which pictures were fakes, etc. etc. I told her I thought this a very friendly dream.

Just before our guests arrived, Ted showed up and said he had broken with Bart and wasn't going to see him again. He was greatly upset, and both Don and I were a bit jittery because we'd just been to see *Three Faces of Eve*. So Don misunderstood and thought Ted had said, "I just left Bart dead"—meaning he'd killed him. Later, Ted seemed to calm down. He went off quite cheerful.

Last night we went to a glamor party at the Selznicks', for Rosamond's benefit. Don was enchanted because he was going to meet Joan Fontaine. He did meet her indeed—she talked his ear off about cooking until he was utterly exhausted! I felt rather disgusted by both Sam and Frances Goldwyn. There is something vile about them. I feel ashamed to have shaken hands with them. Of the guests, Louis Jourdan was the handsomest, Rock Hudson the dumbest, Janet Gaynor the coyest, Lauren Bacall one of the nicest—though maybe a little bit too much of a regular guy. I do like Selznick and Jennifer—particularly Selznick. Today, Jennifer leaves for India, on a solo trip.

Marjorie Ramsey, my secretary, had a dream a few weeks ago. She was going to die at a certain time—I think it was 2:00 a.m.—and she realized with horror that she had no religious belief. She thought: I should try what Mr. Isherwood believes in—the—she couldn't think of its proper name—but it was the Gita.

Swami thought this dream was very significant.

Lately, I have arrived at this formulation: religion—as I understand it—means a relationship. Either directly with God, or with someone who has a relationship with God: belief in another's belief—as I have with Swami.

April 30. Yesterday I got this cable from Richard: "Deeply regret to tell you Mum seriously ill following stroke writing fondest love."

I just feel dully wretched about this. No more news so far. I cabled back that I would come if I could be really useful. I don't want to go, of course.

Decided not to tell anyone except Don, and I didn't tell him until after we'd had supper with Jo and Ben at the Brown Derby and taken them to the Oscar Levant show where I was appearing. I had to take part in singing "Huxley wants to dedicate a book to me,"[1] and I blew up on one of my solo lines.

Don was very sweet about it. But I made him spend the night in town. I don't want to make the usual kind of tragedy out of this—the

---

[1] A line from the stripper's song, "Zip," in Rodgers and Hart's *Pal Joey*.

kind which consists in imposing funeral faces on your friends and embarrassing everybody for a month.

May 1. Another cable from Richard this morning: "Mum slightly better and is going to nursing home tomorrow for treatment Amiya is with us."

A dull bad day. No work accomplished, either on the movie story or on anything else.

May 4. Today we have been on the beach and now are getting ready to spend the evening at Selznick's. Jennifer is in India.

Don just said he'd like to go to New York for his birthday present. I guess that will be in June when his school semester is over.

The wisteria is quite over now. But there are spilling yellow roses along the patio wall.

I get the feeling, so often lately, of how fragmentary life is. "Es hat wohl einen Anfang, hat ein Ende, / Allein ein Ganzes ist es nicht."[1] This realization comes whenever I think how I might die right now, leaving everything "out on the floor." And yet—is there any way to tidy it up—and—far more important—is tidying up really desirable? More of this another time.

May 9. Grey. A sad dull day. No more news from England.

Saw Swami the day before yesterday. He said that enlightenment is not loss of individuality but enlargement of individuality, because you realize that you're everything. When he says things like this they seem like revelations, because it is he who says them. A very sattvic mood all the time I was with him.

This treatment writing for Selznick drags on and on. We are now on the eighth draft. I still can't really believe that the movie will ever be made. I like getting the money, but I would love to stop and get on with my other work. No novel for a long time. Very little on the Ramakrishna book.

May 11. The evening of the 9th I got really quite sick and spent the night vomiting. My shit is very light colored and I still feel shaky. Hope it's not the liver acting up again.

A cable from Richard yesterday—which I spent mostly in bed— says that M. is "wonderfully better and has recovered her speech"; but I doubt if this will be more than a temporary relief.

Well—I thought I wanted to write something here but I find

---

[1] "It has a beginning, has an end, but it is not a whole." From "Abkündigung" ("Curtain Speech"), a posthumously published epigram which Goethe wrote for but did not use in *Faust*.

I don't. Except that I just finished a novel I really like: *The Relic* by Eça de Queiroz. It takes a real artist to write a bitchy novel which is not too bitchy. This is almost perfect tightrope walking.

Had the great satisfaction of writing the following to the Hartford Foundation:[1] "Because of the situation which led to my resignation from the board, six years ago, I have made it a rule to have no dealings whatsoever with the foundation. I must therefore regretfully ask you to tell Mr. Themistocles Hoetis that he must find another sponsor."

May 13. Supper last night with George Koniaris and his wife, Angela, a rather beautiful Greek girl with a big ass, hairy arms and a light moustache. Koniaris, drinking resinated wine and eating the very good dinner Angela had fixed, declared fiercely that everything he saw in the world around him was rotten, he was so alone but an atheist, and unable to accept the consolations of religion, that no real tragedy could be written around a woman, etc. He is quite a ferocious little thing. He finds that tragedy in America is on too small a scale, everything is ordinary. In Greece people feel more passionately and don't care about money. The best ancient Greek dramatist, in his opinion, is Aeschylus. It surprised me a good deal that he likes Cavafy.

Extract from his credentials—he wanted me to show them to Selznick, "After his graduation from the high school, this Prince of Thought had overrun the highest academic studies..." etc. The funny thing is, despite all this nonsense and because of the egomania, I guess he will "succeed."

Oh, this goddam success, which nearly everyone has to have, it seems, before he can become even halfway sane! And by then he's old and awful.

Miss Ramsey smells of dog. She keeps them. I wish she didn't get on my nerves so.

May 15. Don and I are going through a not-so-good phase. He is under strain; too much rushing back and forth in the car to school and back. Vernon is a most valuable calming influence, but not quite strong enough. I really rather hope he'll go to San Francisco alone, the weekend after next—and to New York later. Yet I know I shall miss him horribly. And as for the thought of his leaving me—it would be the end of everything. It's true, I depend on him too much.

And I criticize his selfishness, instead of restraining my own.

May 21. After a day with Selznick, it really looks like we are running into a bog with *Mary Magdalene*. He is the soul of indecision, and today he took the story all apart. Well—this will be the ninth week,

[1] The Huntington Hartford Foundation; see Glossary under Huntington.

anyhow. Harry Brown didn't last nearly that long on *Tender Is the Night*.

Don had a nice birthday supper last Sunday at La Rue, given by Marguerite [Lamkin] and Paul Millard. Don and Hope Murray came, and Bob Craft, and we got very drunk.

Don has done a good portrait of Marguerite and some truly brilliant and funny sketches for his fashion class. He does seem to be making marvellous progress now.

A long talk on Sunday cleared the air a whole lot, I think. I must learn to be much franker with him, always.

May 23. Time rushing by. Nothing done. It's all very well to fool with this Magdalene story but I ought at least to be inching ahead with my novel and the Ramakrishna book.

Nature note: a snail ate the words "Dear Chris" from a note Don had left for me on the chest in the living room.

Glorious weather. War talk.[1] Uneasiness. The recession doesn't seem to recede. My thumb is as bad as ever; maybe worse.

May 25. A marvellous day, but we couldn't go to the beach because Don has to do a design project for school. He loathes this design class; it's the only thing he does in school now which he's bad at and has no pleasure in. But he has to do it to get a credit toward his degree. Only a few more weeks, however. Then he gets off, and goes to New York. He wants to stay with Marguerite in Monroe first.

Today I made a feeble first move toward writing a travel article (which I must do to substantiate my income tax claim for travel expenses). So I read through Don's diary of the trip. It was quite a big surprise, both disagreeable and agreeable. The disagreeable things he writes about me are no more than he has often said. And of course the claustrophobia of a relationship is much more strongly felt while travelling. He is obsessively selfish in his reactions; but then I probably am too. On the other side, his talent for describing people—although too negatively—is astonishing. His description of Dodie Smith, written on January 1st of this year, while we were staying at the Beesleys' cottage:

> There were a few moments last night after the New Year, when Chris had gone to the bathroom upstairs to brush his teeth, when I was left alone with Dodie. Almost unaware of me and visibly hardly able to bear any longer the strain of the long day, she began

[1] Vice-President Richard Nixon made a goodwill tour of South America from April 27 to May 15; hostile demonstrations in Peru and especially Venezuela prompted Eisenhower to order U.S. forces into the Caribbean as a precaution.

pacing the floor, fidgeting, passing from the living room to Alec's study and back again, eking out a note or two of half-hearted conversation to keep me occupied while her mind was all but absorbed in something else. I watched her face: it was ugly with tension and pain and anxiety. The corners of her mouth drew down in grotesque expressions of tragedy, her thin nervous eyebrows met and parted in spasms, her whole face changed quickly and horribly in a succession of almost ridiculous stage masks, happy, sad, fearful, resigned, hopeful, determined, grim, like waves of emotion splashing flooding disappearing and forming again over her face. At one point, after a short silence in which she was incapable of disguising her distraction, and even, I think, completely forgetting I was in the room, so difficult was her struggle with herself, she sighed rather than spoke, "Johnny." Not John, but Johnny, only just audible, as though she were speaking to him personally, intimately, alone. I'm sure she didn't realize she'd said anything.

There is a touch of Proust in this.

I'll finish up this volume on an "up-beat," by describing a dream I had just at that time—to be exact, on the early morning of December 31, just before going from the Cavendish Hotel, where we were staying in London, down into Essex for the above-mentioned visit to the Beesleys:

I dreamed that I had a talk with Brahmananda. He remarked that he didn't know why Ramakrishna moved around at all, since he could see God everywhere. I went away, thought this over, and decided to ask Brahmananda why *he* moved around so much—actually far more than Ramakrishna. So I went back to see him. He was seated on a high platform in a wood (the scenery was vaguely Japanese and may have been "borrowed" from Nara[1]); this platform was about six feet high. As Brahmananda saw me approaching, he prostrated. I understood immediately why he did this. (It was a bit like Zossima prostrating before Dmitri Karamazov.[2]) I prostrated also, with tears, thinking of my many impurities but feeling at the same time great joy. Although the platform was so high, I felt Brahmananda's hands touching the back of my head in blessing—which would have been physically impossible. No questions were asked or answered: there was no need. As I walked away, there were other people around. One of them said: "Did Maharaj tell you anything you may tell *us*?" This

[1] The city in Japan; Isherwood and Bachardy visited Nara in October 1957.
[2] In Dostoevsky's *The Brothers Karamazov*.

was asked most respectfully. I shook my head, still crying, but now beginning to feel vain and take credit to myself for the great honor of this experience—and I woke.

I knew at once that this wasn't merely a dream but a vision—far more memorable than anything I saw or felt while in India—or for many years. Swami—when I told him on my return here—agreed. "It was a great grace," he said, solemnly. "Perhaps you'll come to——" (I can't remember the word he used: it wasn't as strong as "illumination") "——in this life."

I think perhaps what was so particularly convincing about this vision was that it was my first intimation of contact with Brahmananda—to whose personality I've never been particularly drawn. I really felt that tremendous love radiating from him, of which Swami so often speaks.

[The entry for May 25, 1958, brought Isherwood to the last page of his notebook and he began a new notebook here.]

May 26, 1958–August 26, 1960

May 26. Had lunch with Carter Lodge and Dick Foote today. As a memento of Johnnie, Carter gave me a pair of gold cuff links which he had given Johnnie at the opening of *I Am a Camera*. They are made of gold, in the shape of cameras, each with a tiny ruby in it. In one camera is engraved: "I am a camera"; and in the other: "What are you?" Not very nice, and quite useless to me. But a logical present, I suppose; and it must have been very hard for Carter, picking out gifts for all Johnie's friends.

Lesley Blanch (Mrs. Gary) called this morning and asked me what were the latest bulletins from France in the crisis[1]—a funny question for the wife of the French consul to ask! Their radio had broken down.

Very warm, brilliantly clear weather after a cold night. All of Catalina sharply visible as I left Selznick's. David is bad to work with in the afternoons. His attention strays, he yawns, lies down on the

---

[1] The Fourth French Republic collapsed in May 1958 over the Algerian war; de Gaulle returned from retirement and took over on June 1.

sofa, apologizes, snores. The grim nanny of Mary Jennifer came up to report that, "We and Frank have reached the parting of the ways." Frank is the tall arrogant chauffeur. He is to leave at once.

My hand very painful as I write this.

Don is spending the night in town and not with his folks; they are motoring through Mexico. I hope I hit the right tone of voice on the phone when he told me he was going to do this. "Oh, good." Not "Oh, *good*!" Or "*Oh,*—good."

May 28. As a matter of fact, Don showed up later, saying that he'd been unable to find anywhere to sleep—whatever that meant. But tonight, again, he's called to say he'll stay away. Not that I mind that, particularly. I'd just as soon not have him around when I feel sad as I do now—and yet his not being here makes me sadder.

Why are you sad, you stupid creature? Because I'm old, old, old— and getting older, older, older. A dying animal. And even though my health is relatively good right now, I have no sparkle left, no joy in me, as I had even a few years ago.

I dread loneliness. I dread losing Don.

Worked all day on the *Mary Magdalene* script, which I've just started. It reads like inch-deep shallow Shaw.

Yesterday we went to see the Stravinskys, and Igor talked with nervous anxiety about the severe bleeding he has had from a broken vein in the intestine, and that was so sad. And I got drunk and was nasty to Don for not taking more interest in our money problems. And that was so ugly.

Oh, I'm *sick* of myself.

June 2. My hand got so bad the day before yesterday that I had to go to Dr. Sellars, who wrapped it in an elastic bandage and told me to take aspirin. Igor is now in hospital—Cedars of Lebanon—with two bleeding ulcers. Jo has a mysterious pain in her kidneys.

Saddened by Don's approaching departure for New York. He has done two really amazing flower paintings.

Selznick continues to hound me on. On Friday last we had him to dinner—with the absurd Garys, the enigmatic Alan Pakula[1] and the bright-eyed glassy-girlish bitch, Anita Colby.[2] Afterwards, he went into the downstair bedroom and slept. Jennifer, just back from India, and her battle with the Italian police chief at the airport, woke him up and apologized to us. These power figures are actually intolerable except in their own homes.

[1] Then a film producer, now a director.
[2] Fashion model, and briefly an actress.

Waiting to get the Sunbeam-Talbot fixed the other day, I was accosted by a round-faced little Jewboy of about twenty. "Gee, Mr. Isherwood," he said. "I hope when I'm your age I'll be as famous as you are. Why, even my sister has heard of you!" He was a great reader of Dostoevsky.[1]

June 5. Changes are on foot.

Selznick leaves for New York on Monday, instructing me to forget all about the treatment and the screenplay and write a synopsis, "As you would for one of your own novels." How very surprised he'd be if I did just that!

Every so often during the day I feel sad, remembering that Don is soon leaving for New York. He stayed away last night, again. I don't ask where. I suppose I should, in a way, just to make it more natural.

I feel a great urge to pull myself together, stop being fat and sedentary, get on with the Ramakrishna book and my novel. "One instant's toil to Thee denied"[2] does *not* apply to Selznick.

Ernie Brossard's tale of his paranoia-train journey in Florida, shortly before his breakdown. Detectives watched him at the station. He was put into an old-fashioned car with no lights, after being the only passenger who was asked for his ticket. His bag was dusted. Men banged chains against his seat. He decided that the FBI thought he had a bomb in his bag. And yet all these were real incidents. Paranoia is a kind of heightened awareness which makes one see how extraordinarily sinister ordinary life is—or can seem, if one wishes. What else but this were Edward and I cultivating at Cambridge, when we invented Mortmere?

Sellars has more or less told me to bear my thumb, and wait and see if my wrist gets worse. It may be gout.

Who are you—who writes all this? Why do you write? Is it compulsion? Or an alibi—to disprove the charge of what crime? What am I, I wonder? God seems real but very remote. Daily life seems remote but very near. Don is real, but I take him for granted. I ought to be far, far more interested in him. I don't mean—for his sake; for mine. Through him I could understand a lot.

Oh Lord, help me to understand where I am going. Take me up high and show me my life.

June 9. Heavenly weather, clear, bright, a breeze, no smog, not too hot. I went on the beach, frittered the day away—but who cares? Selznick has left for New York.

---

[1] Later Isherwood added the boy's name, Marshall Ephron.
[2] "One instant's toil to Thee denied/Stands all Eternity's offence." Rudyard Kipling, "My New-Cut Ashlar."

Last night we went up to supper there. Betty Bacall said that she'd never known what a woman's life was *for* until she felt a baby kick inside her—this for the benefit of a hugely pregnant Frenchwoman who'd come along with the Louis Jourdans. (Jourdan took off his shirt to play ping-pong rather too readily—though he certainly looked good without it—and beat Romain Gary, but was defeated by Greg Bautzer[1]—and Gary exclaimed: "The French are beaten—good! I loathe the French!") Later, Gary proclaimed that he doesn't give a damn what people think of him, and this he proved by telling how he goes track running at UCLA and how a press photographer got pictures of him doing it and published them. Betty Bacall was gleeful because of the mess Peter Viertel is in with Deborah Kerr. She ruled that this was more serious than Peter's involvement with Joan Fontaine, because Joan is older than he is. After supper, Lenore Cotten was telling, also with zest, how Lesley Gary had been snubbed by David Selznick when she asked him about his career.

A good—because psychologically true—Hollywood story. A maid boasts to her friend—also a maid—about the house she works at: wonderful people—they entertain every night—and always big celebrities, top stars. The friend is thrilled: "And what do they talk about?" The maid: "Us."

June 13. Finished my work for Selznick yesterday. Today I'm at a loose end, rather. Don leaves Sunday night. I shall have all of next week free.

The tragedy of Tom Wright. His father phoned to say his mother was sick in hospital, then died himself that same night. And the mother is found to have advanced cancer and is a hopeless case. She had been one of the foremost workers in the local cancer society, putting around the leaflets which tell you of cancer's danger signals. But she had disregarded her own symptoms, having decided that they were of something else quite minor. What a parable!

June 17. At 1:05 a.m. yesterday morning Don took off for Louisiana, to stay with Marguerite and her family at Monroe and maybe go on to New York later.

Have bought Chris Wood's Simca and sold the Ford—mainly because Don had a mysterious grudge against it. But the Simca is quite nice, although I was against it at first and sulked.

On Monday I found I weighed 155 lbs, an all-time high. So I have

---

[1] Hollywood agent.

gone on a proper scientific calorie-counting diet, plus giving up all alcohol. I am to get back down below 145.

Am also trying to produce a version of the first forty pages of my novel I can send to Edward, soon.

Salka Viertel is back here. She and I had supper together last night on the pier. She was tired and shaky with nerves, because she hasn't got a job, and Virginia is making difficulties about divorcing Peter and is herself near-alcoholic and therefore most unsuited to looking after Christine.

Salka says she loves Christine as much as she ever loved anyone.

I gave her several Miltown tablets and a strong suggestion that they would make her sleep. This morning she told me that they had.

June 21. Am just below 150 lbs—maybe 148. The diet works all right and one doesn't even feel particularly hungry.

A gruelling session with Gerald Heard and Michael Barrie at Vera Stravinsky's opening of her show of paintings. I still only like the earlier ones. The strangest people were there: "Father" McLane's son, firing off champagne corks in the backyard like rockets, the boy who runs the Canyon laundromat, Mr. Lee the builder, a Russian lady of eighty who could stand on her head, another who was about three feet high and couldn't, and of course lots of musicians. Many people greeted me with respect because of my appearance on the Oscar Levant show—it is my *only* claim to fame.

Paul Millard called to tell me that Marguerite's father shot himself. Don must have been there. No direct word from them yet. Paul says Don is going to New York at once.

Lunched with Clifton Webb[1] and Ray Stricklyn.[2] Clifton asserting, a little peevishly, his rights as a major star. While he was away from the studio—two and a half years—because of pictures abroad, he is careful to add—they took the record player out of his dressing room.

Michael Barrie had a papilloma removed by a Russian Jewish surgeon named Max Cutler who described (he came with us to Vera's show) how he had won a seal for his daughter at the Beaumont cherry festival by bouncing ping-pong balls into a bowl. He says that even malignant skin cancers are always curable if taken in time.

Jennifer Jones came with me to see Swami yesterday. The family watched her from behind the blinds. The meeting was apparently a

---

[1] American actor; former Broadway star in musicals and revues.
[2] Lesser-known American actor, also with stage background.

success, but who knows? What are the chances of poor Jones entering through the needle's eye?

And this morning Swami tells me "one bad news"—Jimmy [Barnes] is leaving, "because of sex." "We are all very sad—and now who is to cook for me in Laguna?" When I told him that Jennifer had asked me about Tantra, he said: "What for does she want Tantra? She has her husband!"

I record all this mess of facts to try, somehow, to convey the *strangeness*. Is it all, all a dream? My life seems always bearable, often pleasant, sometimes delightful—but it is just a few inches *apart* from me. Swami, I suppose, is the reallest person in it. But do I want to spend all my time with him? Even three nights a week? Even stay with him in Laguna? No. Why not? Because of the Vedanta Place group (whom individually I like) and the strained social atmosphere around him. I *would* like to be with him often—quietly, without speaking, like his dog.

And Don? He fills a deep need in me. Could anyone else fill it? Theoretically yes, I guess so. But there never has been anyone who filled it as he has—and why change, when the chances of finding anyone better are astronomically tiny? And anyhow, this could also be said of Swami.

Besides, there is love. When I think "love," the idea of getting a new Swami or a new Don seems insane. It *is* insane. But still, on another level, love is bound up with the concept of myself. And who is myself? Not the consciousness which watches me writing down these thoughts.

June 23. This is a sort of turning point, because today I found that Selznick isn't going on with *Mary Magdalene*—at least, not at present—or not with me. So now I have no excuse—I must get on with the rewriting of the first part of my novel—and with the Ramakrishna book.

Don's account of the attempted suicide of Mr. Lamkin is really a marvellous document. Particularly when Marguerite says, of the blood on the carpet, "We'll never get it out again!"

Supper with Jack Larson yesterday evening was simply and solely a bore. I was bored. He probably was, too. But he's a nice boy.

Today a visit with Jo and Ben to the Thurlows, who make hooked rugs in Venice. Mr. Thurlow is eighty-two and has received an illuminated address from the City of Los Angeles, congratulating him on being one of Venice's oldest inhabitants. His house used to stand on the edge of a canal. It was filled with fresh seawater every day.

Now the canals are drained—Mr. Thurlow voted for this but now feels he made a mistake. The house smells of age and cat piss. Both cats are fourteen—one is crippled, the other has extra toes.

The daughter is turning grey but still is plump and virginal. One feels a tragedy. She never married. The mother works only till 2:00, but the daughter keeps going till 4 a.m. and rises early to start work again. The rugs are huge—they are shaped to cover whole floors of houses and also form stair carpets; and there are appropriate designs. Signs of the zodiac, animals, locomotives. Big stars buy them.

To make them, dozens of old coats are torn up, into long strips.

June 24. The day began badly because I flew out and shouted at the kids, who were spraying water from the Hines' hose over the Simca. Not much water—that didn't matter—but the noise! It not only disturbs me when I'm working, it threatens me with not being able to work if I want to. I heard Mrs. Hine reproving the kids later. Of course she thinks I'm an old prissy ill-natured queen, and let her, with all my heart, if it makes her keep her children away!

Also—after a mild debauch yesterday: a glass of sugary lemonade (no, two!) and a tiny rock cake at the Thurlows', a glass of wine at Jo and Ben's and a cookie and a large helping of fish—I was back to 150. All that self-denial wasted!

But, courage! The children left me fairly alone all day. I rearranged the whole sequence of the restaurant scene in my novel, reopened my unemployment insurance claim, and kept the calories low.

Bart Lord called up with a long tale of woe. He must break with Ted, who continues to shoplift and who isn't interested in Bart's new house—which he's going to buy in the Valley, to get "security." Of course, Bart is shallow [. . .] from one viewpoint. But the fact remains that only a St. Francis of Assisi could handle Ted. You'd have to sacrifice everything—maybe get yourself arrested for shoplifting. Whereas Bart doesn't even want to give up listening to classical records, which Ted hates. And am I any different?

June 25. Today (8:30 a.m.) is grey and muted—with the children muted also as if in obedience to the mood of the weather—after the hot bright mornings of the last few weeks. This is the kind of weather in which I love the Canyon best. I am working cross-legged on cushions, typewriting at the low teak table, which keeps the back erect and is far less tiring. Why don't I always do this?

I feel a great appetite for, and joy in work. I have the money now to go ahead for months without worrying. Clouds on the horizon—the

Lebanon crisis,[1] my weight refusing to drop (only 149 lbs this morning, in spite of my efforts yesterday!).

Had supper with Kent Chapman and his girl, Nancy Dvorak. Kent talked a lot about the Beat Generation and Venice West. What most interests me is Laurence Lipton's attempt to go along with them, which has seemingly failed: the older man learning the younger generation's jargon, "Man, the scene is here!"[2] Kent is sort of between the camps. He got sick the only time he smoked "pot."[3] But according to these Venice West boys you're a square if you don't. Kent wants me to come and see them, but I know they would reject me utterly, on the charge of being rich. They are all poor and they help each other. They'll see that you have a "pad," and they'll steal milk for you, from doorsteps. It's a kind of Assisi-like ideal, plus marijuana. They reject the commercial arms-and-business race. They are pacifists. They also mingle with the motorbike gangs—"The Venice Rats"—with the result that some of the rats now write poetry.

June 26. Talk with Swami last night. He told me that he feels the presence of the Lord almost continuously; he no longer has to make much of an effort. When he wakes up in the night—which he has to do, two or three times, to go to the toilet because of his prostate—he feels the presence. Sometimes it is Ramakrishna, sometimes Holy Mother, Maharaj or Swamiji. I asked if it made any difference that he had known Maharaj and seen Holy Mother in life, but not the others. No, he said: they were all equally real.

Swami says he never prays directly for problems to be solved. He only asks for more devotion to the Lord.

Later I went on to see Salka, who was alone. We talked about Garbo. Berthold had said: "She lives by rejection." When young, she was eager to learn—watched Salka for hours playing out her old roles. Garbo was so inadequate in the last scene of *Camille* that Salka had them give all the lines to Robert Taylor. Garbo had only to say "Yes" and "No," and it came out great.

Salka is sick of movie writing. She would like to become a story editor.

She doesn't mind being alone, I think. But she is very worried about Christine.

---

[1] Official Lebanese support for Britain and France during the Suez crisis nearly brought down President Chamoun, whose regime was preserved only by the intervention of U.S. Marines.

[2] Lipton was, or wanted to be, the guru of the Venice West Beat Generation; he had a bookshop in Venice and wrote about the Beats.

[3] In the margin Isherwood added, "I think this should be 'pod.'" And later still, "*No. Pot.*"

July 3. Don got back last Sunday morning, the 29th.

Life closed over us immediately—hardly making a splash. I'm so much in the midst of it that my diary-keeping mood is nil. But—

I'm getting ahead with my novel and the Ramakrishna book: That alone is *le bonheur*.

The back bumper of the Simca has been dented by an old Jewess in a Cadillac.

I've met Phil Burns again. Not only is he very cute looking but he has become amazingly self-sufficient. He designs country clubs, stores, bars, and lives alone but not alone. He rather impresses me. It's as if he'd discovered just the right mixture of selfishness and concern for others. But of course I don't seriously believe this. It must be some kind of bluff.

July 5. Fatigue! I guess I'm undernourished, although I seem to eat plenty. But I cannot get the weight down below 148. Working hard—getting on with novel, Ramakrishna book and today I finished a new foreword for *All the Conspirators*.

A big party yesterday at the Selznicks'. Louis Jourdan so worried because his little boy wouldn't *mix*. Mel Ferrer's son worried because he let his dad down at tennis. Selznick worried because he couldn't get everyone to play games all at once. Jennifer's younger Walker son[1] is a really artistic drummer. Collier Young annoyed Joan Fontaine by harping on anti-British jokes.[2]

July 9. Keeping steadily—but too slowly—along with Ramakrishna and the rewrite of my novel. Ramakrishna is at page sixty-three, with maybe two to three more pages to go till the end of chapter three. This will be the end of the introductory part. Chapter four will lead into my visit to India and so the beginning of Ramakrishna's life. That should make a proportion of three chapters of introduction to twelve chapters of Ramakrishna's life.

The novel is on page twenty. I have no idea how long the whole of this draft will be. My first whole draft is 251 pages. I can scarcely believe that I shall ever get through it. And yet this new draft does, so far, seem far superior to the old.

My weight has gotten down to around 146. I need to make one last big push to get it below the 145 mark, where I want to keep it.

A girl named Liz Murphy and a rather older but much more attractive woman whose name I forget—she was Chinese—came by

---

[1] From her first marriage; see Glossary.
[2] Fontaine was the first wife of American writer and producer Collier Young; her parents were British.

this afternoon to interview me about the Beat Generation. So I repeated more or less what I have just written in my new foreword to *All the Conspirators*. Also I suggested that the Beat Generation is rejecting the pairs of opposites, as in Zen, and going out for satori. Both of the women were delighted when I attacked *Time*, and *Newsweek*—for which they were interviewing me. They seemed to be repressed leftists.

July 11. Foggy along the coast, hot and smoggy inland. Tristeza y soledad.[1] Because Don apologetically announced this morning that he'd quite forgotten but he had a dinner date tonight. Well—so what? It really is better, I guess, since his "freedom" has been officially recognized. Anyhow I know it's the right thing and I'm in favor of it unshakably—in principle.

No, I'm merely sad because I'm in a rut, low vitality, rather bored by my novel. Under these circumstances there is nothing on earth to be done but go *on*.

Read Disraeli's *Endymion* today. I like his high camp irony: "I think now we have got rid of Liberalism forever." Maybe it is his oriental quality—I don't know—but he somehow succeeds in making London seem a bit like a city of Asia Minor, mysterious, with inner sanctums within sanctums, and weirdly magnificent female powers behind the scenes—like Zenobia.[2]

July 14. All day I've been useless for work, because I got drunk last night. So I slept a lot and took Miltown and went in the ocean with Don—and it was pretty nice. All except for the beginning of this crisis in Iraq, which looks *really* ugly.[3]

We were drunk because we had the Stravinskys to dinner; in a week they will be leaving on one of their long European tours, and of course the thought always occurs: shall we ever see Igor again? Actually he seemed in fine form last night. He and Vera both drink far too much though, and it seems as if Bob were getting shaky too; something with his liver.

A great sense of love and rapport between us and them. Vera and Igor talked about Diaghilev. He used to tell Vera all about his boyfriends. Vera thinks he killed himself by excessive dieting. Igor said that Diaghilev surrounded himself with people who were

[1] Sadness and loneliness.
[2] Disraeli's Tory hostess and lady of fashion.
[3] The Iraqi revolution; King Faisal II and many of his family and supporters were murdered in a military coup and the Republic of Iraq was proclaimed.

inventive. "And inventions," Igor added, "are the only things worth stealing."

Laura Huxley told me on the phone that during the thunderstorm in her production of *The Giaconda Smile*,[1] she had the word "passion" in big letters across the window. The word couldn't be consciously read because the flashes of "lightning" were so brief: but a subliminal mood is supposed to have been created.

Gerald Heard yesterday at Michael Barrie's cocktail party wore grass-green slacks, so thin he says he can't stand against the light.

July 16. Crisis blues. Yesterday I was sleepy and miserable, because of the Miltown I'd taken. Today, I prefer not to be sleepy. The kids are being particularly noisy. I ground out a page of the Ramakrishna book, remembering all the other times like this, when writing seemed a futility. Yes, but one must write. Don is worried and edgy, but he has made himself paint this morning. So it goes. I hardly even want to listen to the radio and get more bad news.

July 20. Today we haven't heard any news at all—which is symptomatic of our modern delusion that there can't be news on Sunday because the newspapers wouldn't allow it.

Last night to the Huxleys'. An Irish lady slaughtered the government for getting us into danger for the sake of oil. Aldous pointed out that the Arabs must ultimately sell their oil to the West— Russia doesn't need it. It was a very fourth-rate party, badly managed. Laura and Aldous both sat at the same table, and Laura served sherry as a dinner wine.

I am utterly disgusted by my own laziness. Only one page of my novel today. And now I'm starting to negotiate with Roger Edens about doing another film.

July 24. The crisis is passing, unless we have a flare-up.

Oh, why do I write in the diary, when there seems nothing to report but deadened vitality, slowed-down reactions? All my energy goes into resentment nowadays, mostly against the noisy kids on this street and hence their parents. Today I walked home from the unemployment bureau through the park, and it was so beautiful but somehow I was dead to it. And my novel isn't right, and the Ramakrishna book is wordy and pompous. Don is very sweet most of the time—but as he said himself the other day, why does living together have to be so terribly painful.

[1] A play based on Huxley's story, staged at a small theater in Los Angeles.

Which reminds me, my thumb is giving me hell—trying to stop me from writing this as usual. I'll soon have to keep a typescript diary.

August 1. I meant to start typing this, but I haven't—so I'll write something here to keep the record going.

By and large, all goes well here. Don and I are getting along very well on our design for living, even though it *is* a design. Time will show.

I have been bad and lazy about my two books. The novel crawls and the Ramakrishna book sticks because I now have to make the transition to the actual biography.

The Roger Edens deal looks like it was falling through. No word from him.

Down to Laguna with Prema last Saturday, to see Swami who has been staying there with Swami Vandanananda and Krishna. Prema told me how he hates Usha—called her a bitch—because she is attempting to sabotage an article he has been writing about the bramachari vows. Usha thinks they should never be made known to anyone who isn't a brahmachari. Prema says that after all any Catholic novice is encouraged to read the vows over and over—every day for a year, before he takes them. Usha's method is to organize support among the girls and then go to Swami and make a fuss.

Prema feels that there is a perpetual struggle going on between the women and the men. Also that the boys at Trabuco are all so selfish and this explains the bad atmosphere there is there. Prema thinks that I'm "idealistic" about spiritual devotees and therefore have to be disillusioned!

Swami himself, as if at Prema's suggestion, also displayed the weaker side of his character. He forbids the sale of Marie Louise Burke's book on Vivekananda[1] because he says it's so inaccurate. But Prema is sure that Swami's real motive is that she is a disciple of Ashokananda and Swami is always jealous of Ashokananda.

Now what do I feel about this? It is certainly true to some degree. And it seems almost inexplicable, because why in the world should Prabhavananda find anything in Ashokananda's setup to be jealous of? And yet—just because it's Swami—this absurdity seems to me largely lovable. I almost like him to be weak in this way.

The boys came down from Trabuco and we had a picnic after dark on the beach.

August 2. Selznick, Jennifer, Adrian and Janet [Gaynor Adrian] to dinner last night.

[1] *Swami Vivekananda in America: New Discoveries* (1958).

Selznick seemed very likeable but revealed his megalomania. He sends telegrams of advice to Dulles[1] and receives "evasive" answers. Specifically, he advised Dulles to get a Russian Jew to advise him in dealing with the Russians. He feels that Dulles's midwestern moralistic attitude is hopeless. He believes Nixon has some statesmanship. He thinks Kennedy a "reactionary in the wrong party." He speaks of himself as a Tory Republican.

Adrian went in for Vedanta too strenuously, couldn't breathe for hours after being touched by the relics. So now they (he and Janet) have turned against renunciation and toward the teachings of a Dr. Holmes, whom Janet appealed to by telegram when Adrian was terribly sick in Brazil and about to have a lung removed. Holmes (whom they didn't know) cabled back "work in progress." And then their Californian doctor called and told them to bring Adrian home at once. This they judged a miracle due to Holmes's influence; because their doctor made the decision without even consulting the Brazilian doctors.

Selznick stands out against all this woolly womanly faith. He says that if anybody had really developed any powers beyond the five senses, the whole world would know of them and profit by them. I can't help sympathizing with his agnosticism. There is something about it which is curiously decent, and Jewish in a good sense. Religious faith doesn't really suit Jews, any more than homosexuality.

Fashion note of the period: Jennifer wore a black chemise dress, with a big bow on the back of it way down below the ass, against her knees.

August 7. Roger Edens has been unable to get Columbia to back his project, so *The Living Lotus* is off.

Which would be perfectly okay if only I can make a big drive to get on with my work. Nothing done today because of a hangover: Jerry Lawrence came over yesterday evening with a young actor named Chuck van Haren, who said—looking at our empty fireplace—that when a fireplace isn't used it withers and dies. He also dropped ash in it from his cigarette. He also boasted that Vasari's *Lives of the Painters* was his constant companion, not to mention Graves's *[The] Greek Myths* and Will Durant's historical volumes.[2] Still, he was quite charming and even rather bright.

A *very* happy time this, with Don. I feel we've reached an

---

[1] John Foster Dulles (1888–1959), then secretary of state.
[2] *The Story of Civilization*; six of ten volumes by the historian and philosopher had appeared by 1958 (some co-authored with his wife, Ariel Durant).

understanding—temporarily at any rate. It's not just an armistice, either, or a deadlock. It is literally an understanding.

He has just painted another very good picture.

August 9. Gerald Heard, Michael Barrie and George Huene to supper last night.

Gerald was delighted because the sighting of a giant saucer over Alamogordo[, New Mexico] has been officially admitted to, after being suppressed. Gerald believes that this loosening up is due to Jung's statement that he has been interested in saucer sightings for many years.

Also discussion of the voyage of the *Nautilus* under the Polar ice cap.[1] And a remarkable case, known personally to Gerald and Michael, in which a cancer of the pancreas was reduced by building up the patient's vitality and will to resist, both by psychological methods and drugs.

George Huene held forth on the decay of taste in the middle of the nineteenth century, when the bourgeoisie got control. I guess he thinks of himself as an aristocrat, being an ex-baron. His generalizations rattled Don who became altogether much upset, though he didn't really admit this till this morning.

Oh, it's so hot! And I feel tired and lousy and sick to my stomach— the vagus nerve is acting up again. No work today. And more guests tonight—Shelley Winters, James Costigan, Caroline Freud, Collier Young. I couldn't want to see any of them less.

August 10. Well, they came. And Shelley got drunk and was very rude to Jim Costigan and I more or less threw her out of the house, but just the same she was in many ways the most sympathetic person at the party—and I really got her out because it was nearly 3:00 a.m. and I was exhausted beyond words. This afternoon I slept heavily. It is still mercilessly hot.

Shelley attacked Costigan because he didn't understand Joan of Arc (she said) and because he said Lillian Hellman wasn't a great dramatist. He was quite courteous to her and made the mistake of arguing seriously. So she descended to the lowest depths and asked who was he but a corrupt little TV writer, a servant of the sponsors? The truth is that Costigan obviously *isn't* corrupt, painfully noncorrupt even— though fairly dull.

Shelley is a blundering Jewish leftwing ass, who "accepts Christ as a

[1] The first nuclear powered submarine and the first journey under the Polar ice cap, in August 1958.

man" and quotes the unspeakable arch-ass Lee Strasberg,[1] who will never tell you to enter right but insists that you wait until you *feel* the approach. Yet Shelley manages to be a good and moving actress by playing everything from bits of her own personal experience.

Collier Young told amusingly of how he was elected, when seventeen, the Most Representative American Boy, and met Calvin Coolidge. His election was engineered by Miss Virginia. But Miss Florida became Miss America. Collier is a dapper little man, very proud of being married to Joan Fontaine, who couldn't come because of mononucleosis. He might be partly queer.

Caroline was round eyed as usual, either dumb or scared.

Today on the beach, a man and a girl were making love, without the least regard for anyone but each other. Suddenly the man called over to Don: "Where did you buy that hat?"

August 11. Very hot again this morning. We are in the midst of a big heatwave—earthquake weather, says Dorothy with relish; she loves all disasters and incurable diseases. I feel soggy and toxic and weak— so does Don—but determined nevertheless to do energetically our long and heavy task. Mr. Oshinomi the gardener arrives just as I am fishing out of the garden trash box a recipe for mulligatawny soup, which Don had thrown out with the Sunday newspaper. I want to fix this soup for nostalgic reasons; it's one of the few items of British food I cherish. To make conversation to Mr. Oshinomi, I ask him if he thinks the potted plant is alive which we moved outdoors and replanted under the magnolia tree. He replies in his Jap-English jargon: "Back for grow for dis dinium, see? All right—they grow!"[2]

Mrs. Stickel with her wobbly thighs in shorts is wearily putting out the last of the family garbage—licked by the heat already, but somehow game to go on till she drops.

I call up to Don, to know if I shall throw out some boxes of old cereal. He calls down, "What?" in his semihostile, we-do-not-wish-to-be-disturbed voice. But later, more friendly, *he* calls down to ask how to spell Churchill. I know he must be writing to Truman Capote about my row with Levant, over Churchill. This was one more instance of my usual tactics. I didn't want to go on the Levant show any more—so I worked myself into a rage in order to quarrel with him in order not to go on.

For some wonderful reason, there are no children playing outside on the street today.

---

[1] Director of the Actors Studio and leading exponent of Method acting.
[2] Evidently referring to a geranium, of which Isherwood and Bachardy had many.

Don has just been down to get the exact facts about the Levant quarrel. I suppose I may as well record them, myself.

Levant: What do you think of Churchill?

Me: I respect him as a man. I don't like his politics.

Levant: But don't you admire him as a writer?

Me: Not particularly.

Levant: But they gave him the Nobel Prize.

Me: Yes, and I think it was disgraceful. They only gave it him because he's such a celebrity.

Levant: You hurt me.

Now, on a later broadcast, when I wasn't there, Levant said: "In 1941, when Churchill was making his great speech, Isherwood was in Hollywood writing *I Am a Camera*."

So, when Levant's manager called, last week, to know if I'd be on the show again, I said: "Never. There is no free speech on Mr. Levant's show. Because I disagreed with him about Churchill's writing, Mr. Levant first deliberately misrepresented what I said— claiming that I had attacked Churchill as a man. He followed this up by making a vicious attack on me, for which I expect him to apologize."

Incidentally, Levant did apologize.

The Ramakrishna book is stalled because I decided I wanted to get the first sixty-some pages typed up in a revised form and shown to Swami. This meant getting a good shorthand typist. Marg Ramsey, who worked for me on *Mary Magdalene*, got me one, but she belonged to the Fellowship of Self-Realization, and Prema thought she might prove to be dangerously interested in our book, and therefore indiscreet.

Miss Ramsey said she'd find another girl but she hasn't yet.

August 12. Up to see Gerald last night. He says he wants to buy one of Don's paintings, the portrait of Vernon's girlfriend, for Michael's birthday. Then he plans to "make" Don by introducing him to Florence Vidor![1]

Gerald says he thinks Aldous will never write anything more of importance. One can see he blames Laura, although he is careful to say she's a kind woman. She leaves him alone, up at their house on Deronda, with nobody to drive him.

Gerald was much disappointed in the latest mushroom drug.[2] It just takes away your power to think—and there you sit.

[1] Silent film star; she was married first to film director King Vidor and afterwards to violinist Jascha Heifetz.

[2] Probably psilocybin, first written up in 1958 (by A. Hofmann et al).

He described satirically a visit from Father d'Arcy[1]—whose face in youth used to be tortured, but is now a "small dainty man" who looks like a woman dressed as a priest. Gerald found no serenity in him.

He made me read aloud (to him and Margaret Gage) the article Forster wrote on the imagined later lives of his characters in *A Room with a View*. His pacifist George becomes a combatant in World War II, distinguishing between the Germanys of 1914 and 1939.[2]

August 13. Depressed after reading a [Georges] Simenon sex-murder book, *Belle*. Dreary stuff by a dreary little mind.

Also I feel bad because Rita Cowan[3] came in to borrow $200 to pay her mother's hospital bills, and I refused. Why? Because I wouldn't have given the money willingly; I'd have regretted it if I had given it; Rita has never done anything for me and indeed has made use of me in a mild way a couple of times. Yet I feel guilty—wish I'd loaned her the money. I can't help thinking that after all one should be ready to answer any call on one's charity that's within one's power—considering that there really aren't very many calls.

Last night, Don and I spent what we agreed was one of our most desperate evenings of boredom. Gavin Lambert invited us to supper with Nicholas Ray,[4] a dancer named Betty Uti—said by Ray to be the greatest in the world; she works at MGM as assistant to Hermes Pan[5]—and Mike Steen, who has just done a bit in a picture Ray is directing—as a stuntman, falling downstairs. The boredom was because Ray arrived eloquent drunk, and held forth and forth and forth. His attitude toward me was based on that type of aggression which consists in accusing you of having betrayed your own talents and sold out. Why didn't I write poetry any more, he wanted to know—I who had belonged to that group of poets he, Ray, had regarded as the gods of his youth—Auden, Spender, MacNeice, Day Lewis? Nobly refraining from saying what I think of Day Lewis's work, I pointed out that I had never been a poet anyway. But he continued to reproach me—pretending not to believe me—and also to reproach Day Lewis for having stopped writing poetry—and then

[1] Martin Cyril D'Arcy (1888–1976), English Jesuit, Roman Catholic apologist, scholar, author, collector of sacred art; liturgically and theologically conservative, he received Evelyn Waugh, among others, into the Roman Catholic church.

[2] "A View Without a Room: Old Friends Fifty Years Later," appeared in *The New York Times Book Review*, July 27, 1958 and, on the same day, in the London *Observer*.

[3] Sister of John Cowan, a friend through Bill Caskey.

[4] American director (1911–1979) of *Rebel Without a Cause* and many others.

[5] Choreographer and dance director; often worked on films with Fred Astaire.

me again for not having written a first-class movie with a first-class director. I finally replied with some heat. But we parted friends—as they say.

A strange heavy rainshower this morning, but not again later, and I went in swimming. Today—as also yesterday and Monday—I did a decent swatch of my novel rewrite; four pages. Am eager to get back up to Los Olvidados[1] before my birthday.

August 22. I have come to a disturbing conclusion—at least I think I have. I believe that the whole section of *Approach to Ramakrishna* that I have nearly completed—seventy pages—is irrelevant. Not badly done, most of it, but really not part of this book. It belongs to some future autobiography.[2]

Well then, I must start fresh when I get back from San Francisco, where we're going the day after tomorrow.

As for *Down There on a Visit*, I have done quite well and am practically up to Los Olvidados, as I hoped. But the contents of the Olvidados section is still vague. What I now see as the basic theme is the deliberate masochistic servitude of Mary, Wes[3] and their Quaker helpers to the whims and antics of the horrible aggressive lazy inmates.

August 23. Slight depression—because Don is staying away tonight, because I don't *really* want to go to San Francisco tomorrow, because we shall be seeing Thom Gunn there, and I'm jealous of him. All this is foolishness, of course. And it only represents one aspect of how I'm feeling. But as I can't tell anyone about it, I may as well write it down.

I *can* tell Don how I feel about him, so I needn't write that.

Also worry about our money, which is dwindling again. And no clear prospects of a job in sight.

And a new crisis starting on Quemoy.[4]

August 24. Just off to San Francisco on the train. Shall not take this book—so as to make it a real holiday.

---

[1] The Forgotten, the imaginary town south of the border where Isherwood set much of the first draft of *Down There on a Visit*; the name alludes to Buñuel's 1950 film *Los Olvidados* (*The Young and the Damned*)—about juvenile delinquents in the slums of Mexico city—which uses surrealist dream sequences. Isherwood later abandoned this setting.
[2] Later published as *An Approach to Vedanta* (1963).
[3] Later called Mary and Clem Griffiths.
[4] The renewed threat of invasion from mainland China was again stemmed by a U.S. naval presence.

Don just did three paintings of me from sketches. We had a picnic on the beach, drank Pouilly Fuissé.

Mr. Hine "taught" Diane Varsi's[1] dog not to snap at cyclists, by kicking it and chasing it. Then he put a new brake on Don's bike—just to amuse himself.

August 30. Just arrived back, to find the house still in one piece and everything apparently all right.

On the train coming down here, I dreamed of a tremendous earthquake. We met Dore Schary in the dining car, returning from doing some final takes for *Lonelyhearts*. A deposed monarch with his little court of faithful followers.[2] He was very affable. Liked him, as always. He says he'll invite us to the preview.

On opening the shade of the sleeping berth this morning, I saw first an empty misty beach with small grey sandy waves breaking. Then a tanker, lying off shore, out in the fog. Then a family, apparently just aroused from uncomfortable outdoor sleep, standing helplessly beside their station wagon and looking at the train. Then oil-storage tanks and a palm tree. Then a fishing pier, a few people. Then oil wells, oil tanks, tank cars, wooden homes of oilmen, and all the debris caused by the extraction of oil. If Hercules lived today, they'd tell him to tidy up America.

Oh God, those fucking children are yelling. I hate it more than all the police sirens, tram clanging and road drilling of San Francisco.

Our trip was pleasant. We ate and drank too much. On Thursday, when we went to see Thom Gunn and Mike Kitay at Palo Alto, we drank continuously for twelve hours. It was warm in San Francisco and we sweated hugely—hill climbing in ties and suits. Our feet ached. My left thumb started yesterday to hurt as much as my right does.

Much thought about the Ramakrishna book. I think I shall do an introductory chapter in dialogue. There has to be some kind of an introduction, if I'm really going to scrap what I've so far written.

Beginning of a new interest in Goethe because of the Goethe paperback which Stephen has edited.[3] He is far livelier than I'd expected.

As the result of this visit we have vowed not to go to San Francisco again without getting introductions to a new set of people. The ones we know there are all egotistical drab bores—that goes for Jan Gay,

---

[1] Actress, briefly a neighbor on Sycamore Road.
[2] Schary had been head of MGM until 1956; see Glossary.
[3] *Great Writings of Goethe* (1958), edited by Spender and translated by Spender and others.

Vincent Porcaro, Jack Dempsey, Grady Norris, Jerry Ogle, Andrew Biggi—

Just as I wrote this, the telephone rang. It was Don, calling me from the barber's shop in Beverly Hills, where he had just overheard people talking about a major earthquake which is supposed to have taken place in San Francisco today!

August 31. The earthquake turned out to be nothing very much—but still there *was* one, and one in Japan as well!

Swami told me on the phone that Jennifer [Jones] came to him and asked if she should go to India again. Swami said: "Why? You won't get anything out of India unless you have reached something inside yourself." He then asked her if she had meditated according to his instructions. When she told him, "No," he got "all excited" and told her not to come back until she had done so for a month. So then Jennifer got out of her chair and sat on the floor at Swami's feet and said: "Teach me once again." So he did, and she went away—on probation!

Don spent the night in town. So I ate at Ted's [Grill], and ran into [an acquaintance], one of those once good-looking vague eye-rolling easygoing faintly bitchy but not-nearly-so-stupid-as-you-might-think boys one has known for years on the beach. His gland trouble. His little apartment, for which he collects things with the patience of a Darwin, buying himself two cocktail glasses a year each Christmas until he has a set. He has studied art, and juggles quite easily with terms like expressionism and abstraction, but misuses quite ordinary words and admits without the least shame that he is semi-illiterate. He talked about himself and the lieutenant in the Army of Occupation in Tokyo, and himself and the professor from Texas, and himself and his ideas about gracious living, and himself and himself and himself until eleven o'clock. I was bored, and regretted I had wasted an evening.

Which brings me to the subject of WORK!

How can I ever do enough before I die?

Right now, the novel, Ramakrishna and my diary of the Asian trip are the priorities. The Ramakrishna book has to be restructured, and a whole lot of preliminary research done.

Well, what's stopping you, you lazy old Dobbin?

September 1. Today, which was to have seen the opening of my attack on sloth and the beginning of speeded-up production is spoiled because I got drunk last night. We'd had a pleasant and relatively sober supper at Jo and Ben's—their cooking is now marvellous; quite equal to the best restaurants. But on the way home along Rustic Road we were accosted by Zena (don't know her other name)[1] the Czech lady with orange hair who knows Michael Barrie. She was livelier even than usual—truly a Czech that bounced—and invited us in for a drink. What followed was quite horrible. She had a number of very drunk guests, whom she tried to impress with my importance—"This is such an honor," she kept saying, as she fixed us drinks that were nearly straight whiskey. One of the men was glowering and mean. His wife was afraid to drive home with him. "My husband knows judo," she said, ruefully. One of the women was repeatedly told by her husband to keep her skirt down. She protested that she had sexy legs. She also kept asking aggressively: "Are you really Christopher Isherwood?" And another woman decided that she disapproved of Don. She called him [. . .][2]

Nevertheless, despite this hangover, I mean to work.

September 2. Today I collected my unemployment check, bought a book by Dr. Lester Morrison called *The Low-Fat Way to Health and Longer Life*, and under its directions got lecithin tablets, soy lecithin spread (instead of butter), brewer's yeast and powdered liver extract: all this to increase my energy, calm my nerves. I also started the Ramakrishna book over again, did a page of my novel and started a diary of our Asian trip. So I can say I haven't been too lazy!

This morning Don told me he is going away this weekend to Yosemite with a friend, who has a friend who rents a lodge there and is giving a party. Do I mind? Yes, of course. But not really very much. Don makes me feel that this is another part of his life, which doesn't concern ours. At least, I want to feel it.

September 3. Black depression, partly hangover from an evening at Ivan Moffat's. It's twenty of two and I haven't even begun to work, and the kids outside are screaming, and Don leaves tomorrow—altogether he'll be away six days. And then there's the Quemoy situation getting steadily worse and worse.

But now two bits of *good* news. The lady next door calls through the hedge to tell me she is getting married at last. She leaves for New York the day after tomorrow to join him.

And Carter calls to say he's read in *The New York Times* that Dodie Smith is getting a play produced in England; it's about a publishing firm and is to be called *These People* (?).[3]

---

[1] Zena Parkes.
[2] Isherwood left the sentence unfinished.
[3] *These People, Those Books*; see Glossary under Beesley.

September 7. On Thursday night (the 4th) after Don had left, Gavin Lambert came. I had asked him on the phone, "Do you feel in the mood for some very sophisticated entertainment?" and he replied at once, "Do you mean you want to see *How to Make a Monster* and *Teen-Age Caveman*?" He was right, and we had supper and went. *Monster* had something. *Caveman* was just nothing; the boy was a nervous worried white-collar lad with his shirt off.

When we had gotten back here again and had had another drink and it was around midnight, I impulsively suggested taking mescaline. (I still had the five tablets I bought in New York.) Gavin agreed.

Symptoms began at 1:00 a.m. and lasted till around 9:00 a.m. We stayed awake the whole time, in the living room. Our symptoms were more or less the same. Shivers and some nausea but not too bad. Absolutely no fear of the darkness and the night—as I had half expected. Color perception just as good by artificial light. Don's big portrait of me stood the test very well. But the blue bathrobe one I put upstairs, fearing it might depress me. The best of the experience was the coming of daylight among the plants in the garden—subtly, down there; radiantly and gloriously above, over the walls around the skylight.

But we both agreed that it was a disappointment, and that we didn't want to take any more. It was tiresome being kept awake for so long, and one wearied of the translucence of the ceiling beams. Personally I was disappointed because I felt the barrier between Gavin and me unremoved. He is cagey or hostile or just plain blocked up: don't know which. As for me, I talked too much, boasted, bored myself. Maybe he'll take notes of it and write a snide story. Then I'll know more of what he's like.

Of course, our dullness may have been partly due to the alcohol we'd drunk. Not much, but enough to be felt.

Perhaps thanks to the lecithin, brewer's yeast and liver extract, I came through this self-abuse pretty well, and had energy enough for Bill Robinson, who came and spent the next day with me. We went in swimming, and later fixed supper and he stayed the night. His great enthusiasm and preoccupation is his analyst. Their relationship has the fascination, for Bill, of an aesthetic experience: they are collaborating, as it were, on a novel of which he is the hero. And also of an exceedingly complicated card game: Bill is continually trying to maneuver the analyst into showing his hand—i.e. revealing something about *him*self and his feelings for Bill. But I think Bill is really quite a nice boy, whom I might get to like.

Yesterday I had lunch at Vedanta Place, because Swami is back from his holiday at Laguna and Pavitrananda had just arrived by air from India, en route for New York. He is the only other swami I actually love. He is adorable, with his buckteeth, as skinny as a monkey.

He was saying that he had had no trouble readjusting to Indian ways. He loved the Ganges more than ever. Only the heat had troubled him. In Japan, he had rebuked a lady who had claimed to have had samadhi: "Do not *dare* to utter that word!" He was very pleased with this rebuke and repeated it twice. Vanity still exists in people like Swami and Pavitrananda, but it becomes more and more childlike.

Yesterday evening, I had a visit from Vernon: we had supper together. He has grown a beard. He talked nicely and sensibly about Don's painting and the problems of being an artist and the question of getting married and settling down. He keeps wondering if he should give up sex, but then he always meets a new girl. He still meditates. He is very talkative and very serious, yet not altogether without humor, though I think he mistrusts it.

The past two days, the heat has been overpowering. Thunderstorms in the mountains. But this morning there's a breeze.

Marguerite Lamkin just called. She arrived at the Chateau Marmont this morning from New York to start work on *The Sound and the Fury*. She says she and Speed are good friends again.

September 8. This morning I woke early and suddenly decided to meditate—something I haven't done in weeks. I decided to stay with it at least until the light came; I began at about ten minutes of five. To my surprise and satisfaction, when I finally got up and looked at the clock, it was six twenty.

I'm not using any of the old instructions; just thinking of Swami in meditation, and of the shrine in the Vedanta Place temple, as it feels when you sit in front of it. That, and making japam.

September 10. The night before last, I had supper with Jo and Ben. Jim Charlton came by. He looked good. I felt a great wall between us which I knew I mustn't climb over. However, after supper, when I'd had a few drinks and had left the Masselinks', I felt tempted to try. And I actually phoned Jim, who was up at his apartment in the Canyon. When he didn't answer the phone at once, I hung up. But I think he was there.

Last night Don returned. I was full of good resolutions, but we had a couple of drinks and so I made a small scene. Not one that I'm altogether ashamed of, because at least it was honest. I was and am quite simply jealous because Don saw a thunderstorm from Glacier

Point and visited San Simeon without me. My possessiveness hates to face the fact that he can have important experiences with other people. Well, I have got to face it. The trick is to stop minding without ceasing to care for him. Always, before this, the injured ego has simply ducked out from under. Will it do it again? I don't know. He should go slow.

Big anxieties about the Quemoy crisis, minor but growing ones about money. I really am at grips with my novel, but oh it is hard! Now I'm about to start another rough draft of the Los Olvidados section.

September 11. Saw Gore Vidal last night. He is in town to get a director and a star for his new (Civil War) play.[1] I do like him. He is handsome, sad, sardonic, plump—quite Byronic, in a way. His amazing stamina: he is writing half-hour TV shows at the rate of one every two days while he is here. He gets paid $2,500 a show, and he needs the money badly. He finds he can't live on less than $2,000 a month. Howard [Austen] is in New York studying singing.

Gore's favorite quotation "I am Duchess of Malfi still."[2] He sees himself as the ex-champ, out of condition and punchy, who still has a fight in him.

And all the time this rather disconcerting literary ambition: he thinks of himself as a writer of quality—a neglected writer, because readers are turning from his kind of quality to the meanderings of Jack Kerouac. (Whom, incidentally—being halfway through *The Subterraneans*—I'm beginning to admire!) Gore regards me, also, as a neglected writer of quality, so he feels a bond between us.

September 14. On Thursday night, Marguerite brought John Foster[3] to supper. He is terribly square and doesn't drink and he ate slice after slice of roast beef, declining vegetables. I suppose he's bright in his own way. He told a funny story about a friend of his in Russia, who frankly told a Russian that the execution of Nagy[4] was shameful. "You see," the Russian blandly replied, "we don't believe in keeping innocent men in prison."

As usual, when Marguerite brings one of her beaux, there was a

[1] Probably *On the March to the Sea*; see Glossary under Vidal.
[2] In Webster's play (act 4, scene 2).
[3] English barrister and Conservative M.P. for Northwich, Cheshire; held government and international posts and was later knighted; eventually introduced Marguerite Lamkin to her third husband.
[4] Imre Nagy, Hungarian Prime Minister, seized by the Soviets at the end of the 1956 revolution, then handed over to the new regime which had him shot, June 18, 1958.

strained atmosphere. You felt that the whole thing was an exhibitionistic provocation. Marguerite wore a wig to show us how it looked. Then took it off, scattering hairpins I'm still picking up. I find her really too tiresome.

On Friday, I drove Don and Vernon Old to see the exhibition of fruit and flower painting at the Santa Barbara Museum.

The extraordinary lemons of Willem Kalf—the cut-open fruit looking as if it were made of glass and gold wire; the lemon peel massive like an embossed bracelet. The *sobriety* of Cézanne's dark cold blue; his apples are like facts of life. Also a wonderfully deep Monet pool of water lilies. Some roses of Delacroix as wild as lions. Derain's strangely Chardin-like table with a pumpkin.

Vernon liked the Cézanne best. Don loved the Monet and a vase of flowers by Redon. He thought the Kalf was like a landscape on Mars.

There is also a perfectly wonderful doll exhibition there. The French nineteenth-century dolls are really scary: the women have the heavy relentlessly evil faces of poisoners from the novels of Zola.

After the museum we had tea at the Sarada convent. Such a delightful atmosphere there, as always. And I always feel that Sarada and Prabha particularly are my sisters. I love Sarada. I can quite imagine going to her in real trouble. She could understand anything. She gives forth light.

As for me, I'm in a worse state than ever, I think—and with less reason. Because Don, most of the time, is absolutely adorable; and even when he isn't I can understand exactly how he feels, or should be able to. And there is Swami. And there is my work. True, the money is running away and I'm anxious, but not really anxious yet. There are plenty of prospects.

Yet I glower and grind with resentment—against the neighbors' children, and most women, and anyone who seems about to intrude in any way upon my privacy. How I keep peering from the window to see if the children are jumping on our rock garden!

And now there are only a little over thirteen weeks to Christmas. I have got to do better. Stop idling. Get ahead with rough drafts of my novel and the Ramakrishna book. Or I shall *never* make my own deadline of my fifty-fifth birthday.

Throughout these days of the Chinese crisis, the headlines have been all about Debbie and Eddie splitting up on account of Liz![1]

September 16. Last night we were supposed to have supper with Marguerite at the Chateau Marmont and see this Russian boy who is

---

[1] Debbie Reynolds, Eddie Fisher, and Elizabeth Taylor.

supposed to be madly in love with her and has followed her out here and cooks for her, although he's quite rich. Don saw the boy, whom he described as a huge dope who appeared to be a pathological liar. But we ate in Caroline's apartment with Ivan and a Negro authoress who is working at Columbia [Pictures]. And it was dull, dull, dull. And we both got drunk. And today I have scarcely worked at all, because of my hangover. And we are both indignant at having had these bores wished on us.

September 20. Yesterday, September 19, is usually a day of the year on which I expect happenings;[1] but nothing happened. It was very hot and Don didn't go into town because of the smog, and I did almost nothing; though I did read quite a bit of material for the Ramakrishna book. Geller called to tell me that Selznick had told [David] Brown at Fox that he "got more than his money's worth" from me; and Brown had told Geller he wouldn't be surprised if Selznick wanted to hire me again soon.

Talked to Jim Charlton, who has just had a son. They'll call him Tim.

Krishna gave me a sealed brass pot of Ganges water from Benares. Prema gave me a tiny silver image of Ganesha, also from India. With this equipment, I ought to be able to make japam more. I realize that I must. That that's all I have to do, really, and let the rest just happen.

Don will be out tonight. He still tells me he is going to do this with an air of apology, which is bad. But at least he does it. As for me, I don't really mind; I just feel sad when he's not around but not painfully sad.

September 25. Just to record that it was hot again, and today I did nothing, and read Mary Renault's *The King Must Die*. Also I decided that my novel won't work, the way it is. Depression—but Don did his best to cheer me up, was so sweet, we went in swimming when he got home from school. Then saw a dreadful film, *Damn Yankees*.

September 26. More optimistic. A careful analysis of the novel material shows that there *is* something here.

Don talked to me as we drank our morning coffee. Shouldn't he give up art and work with me, be my secretary and collaborator? He

---

[1] In a datebook of significant events, Isherwood recorded for September 19 leaving for South America with Caskey in 1947 and Peron's expulsion from power in 1955. The 19th was also numinous in other months: on January 19 he had departed for China in 1938, for America in 1939, and for England in 1947.

said, "Am I intelligent enough?" "Do you like me, as well as love me?" and "I'm only really happy when I know I'm giving someone pleasure."

I, of course, said what I had to say: don't put your eggs in one basket. Besides, I sincerely believe in Don's painting now, even if *he* doesn't. I think he would regret giving it up, terribly.

But, of course, no decision has to be final. We could try it.

Meanwhile, we've *got* to earn money! My new tooth from Peschelt costs $125!

Hot again.

Such a wonderful poem by Whitman I never read through before: "Out of the cradle..." How one takes anthology pieces for granted!

September 27. Last night I dreamt that a fortune-teller said to me: "I see nothing for you in October," meaning I was going to die then.

Yesterday evening we went to a reading of *The Glass Menagerie*, spoilt because the actors weren't much good; but anyhow I like it the least of Ten's plays.

The play was given in aid of The Little Village Nursery School on Westwood. Here's a sample of academic wa-wa talk from their statement of their "Principles":

> The aims of our school are based upon the insights provided by modern dynamic psychological, psychiatric and educational knowledge. By this we understand provisions for the satisfaction of the child's needs as well as measures to help the child to learn the delay and the control of satisfactions.... We seek out and employ a staff trained and experienced in nursery school work with a creative attitude towards children and a capacity to assist parents. We also draw on the professional knowledge of experts in the various areas contingent upon the work of the school.

September 30. Slept till 10:30 after being out late with Bill Robinson. Was bored, really. I'm getting weary of playing poker with the young—they are so suspicious and so rightly so! The truth is, I would far rather spend an evening with that yakkety little freak Marshall Ephron, who calls me sometimes to talk about books, plays, etc. Last time it was Swift, and Addison!

Middle-aged, impotent, dull headed, but somehow not dull. I have quite a good time with myself. And perhaps my behavior is a shade less compulsive than it used to be. I think about God, and Swami and Zen—having been much interested in Alan Watts's article and the bit of Kerouac's new novel[1]—and Byron, about whom I'm reading in the second volume of Marchand's life[2]—he has never seemed as adorable and funny and truly sweet as he does during the separation from Annabella—and about Caskey, oddly enough—I thought I saw him in the street as I drove home late last night; I must never forget what we did have together in the early days—not allow that to be cheapened by the malice of people like Speed.

As for Don—he's a complete family, and I wouldn't exchange this relationship for any other kind; unless—yes—the perfect twin brother—is that what my novel is really all about?

Up at Carter and Dick Foote's last night. Carter seemed so weary. Oh, the despair of not *having* to work any more! Won't he die? And yet I sure as hell would like some of that money!

I feel a sudden "concern" to go see him while Dick Foote is away on this tour.

An unspoken (as yet) conversation:

"Why do you keep asking me about my affairs? You ask me, was I in love with X., did I live with Y.?"

"All right, let's talk about *me*. You came to the house with J. What did you think? What were your plans? Did you want to go to bed with me? Why? What did you think *I* wanted? What do you think I want *now*? Surely not just to prove I can get someone to sleep with, if I have to? Or do I? Or what?"

"Well—what *do* you want?"

"Oh, my dear child—something hopeless … I just want to clear out the furniture, so we can dance."

When Dorothy Miller talks about her diet, she always puts on a special falsetto voice to imitate the tones of the scoffers and doubters, her enemies.

October 1. Hangover today. Nevertheless I went in swimming early—the first time in don't know how long—but Mr. Hine and Mr. Stickle make it nearly impossible by their friendly splashing and barking; they are *such* dog people. Also started a rough draft of my novel along the new lines I just planned. And got on with the Ramakrishna book, which now seems well and truly started. And continued the travel diary of last winter's journey.

The hangover is because I got very drunk last night because Marguerite was coming. I was nice to her but horrid to Don later

[1] Watts's "Beat Zen, Square Zen, and Zen" and an excerpt entitled "Meditation in the Woods" from Kerouac's *Dharma Bums*, appeared in the summer number of the *Chicago Review*; see Glossary under Watts.

[2] L. A. Marchand, *Byron: A Biography* (1958), three volumes.

(apparently) blaming him for having her around. *Why*? Is it jealousy? I *know* I don't dislike Marguerite nearly as much as I pretend. I merely don't *like* her very much.

Tom Wright has been told his mother won't live.

Oh, I'm sick at the thought of my cruelty to Don, who is truly and absolutely on my side and could not be sweeter. I really frightened him, I think. He said he felt I didn't care for anything except my own thoughts, and being alone and getting on with my novel. That's not true. In a way it might be good if it were. I need him *too* much.

Then of course in my drunkeness, I had to blab that I'd had this death premonition. So this morning I had to tell him about my dream. It *does* scare me, a little. And why not turn that to good account? Why don't I live *as if* I were going to die this month? That's quite an idea.

October 3. Fantastic heat. The sun, through a cloud of smog or smoke—there's a big fire over in Monrovia—is bright orange. The air stinks. It is breathlessly hot.

Don has decided to stop going to Vernon for a while, and consider his future as a painter. He'll still go three days a week to school.

Right now, he's helping me a lot with my novel, which I've restarted. It *does* seem a lot better this way.

October 9. Good progress in planning my novel and getting the Ramakrishna book started. Oh, if only someone would *give* me money, so I would not have to work on anything else! Besides, "anything else" is not so easy to find.

Amiya was drunk, egocentric and raucous last night at Vedanta Place. Swami didn't seem to mind. She says M. has only a little numbness as the after effect of the stroke; but she can't use her hand. Amiya believes that if she could have Richard all to herself for six months, she could "rehabilitate" him.

The pope's dead.[1]

Now they tell us that the U.S. is militarily stronger than Russia after all; and all this yelling scared was a mistake. *Somebody* is guilty of high treason.

Don is going to Ensenada this weekend. I wish I didn't hate this so. It's not that I *really* care—not the better part of me—only the possessive grim old dreary sex miser.

Japam. Actually I make lots. Well, make more.

October 11. Yesterday was one of the really bad days. Geller phoned in the morning to say that Eddie Anhalt had gone to Switzerland to

---

[1] Pius XII.

work with Selznick on *Magdalene*. Well, it wasn't that I wanted to go to Switzerland, but somehow it put the lid on things. And then Don went off for a long weekend at Ensenada, and I couldn't help feeling that he was deserting me when I most needed him; though as a matter of fact he is far better out of the way when I'm like this.

So I did no work, and read Edward's novel,[1] which is marvellous, but depressing as hell.

How the devil are we going to manage if I can't get more work?

Amiya came with us to the premiere of *Bell, Book and Candle* the night before last, with Elsa Lanchester.[2] Amiya was so drunk and awful; she and Elsa hated each other. Don wrote about this in his diary yesterday morning with giggles.

Einsamkeit.[3] I went yesterday night to see *Andy Hardy Comes Home* and *Tarzan's Fight for Life*.

Have I really any mental resources at all? My despair yesterday was really *ugly*.

October 13. The day before yesterday Phil Burns came down, stayed the night and only left to go back into town after supper yesterday. I do like him and respect him; and I'm happy with him. We had such a wonderful time together on Saturday afternoon, and then went to Pacific Ocean Park, which was just the right thing to do.

Yet he couldn't make me feel better about Don's going to Ensenada. I *mind* that. It burns deep. I sort of hate him for it.

Yes, and I know one *should* mind. It is inhuman to be reasonable about these things. And yet, in the last resort, one must be fair, must show understanding, must admit that being twenty-four and fifty-four are two worlds.

Dorothy Miller, talking about the color question as I drove her home from working here, told me a landlord of hers had objected to Negroes because "they hang out of windows." Dorothy is in favor of legalizing whorehouses and gambling in California.

Ben told me of a man whom he met at work whose tools were constantly being stolen from his car. So he put a small rattlesnake in the toolbox.

Don still isn't home (5:45 p.m.) and I kind of instinctively know he won't show up until late. And I'm *mad* because of that. And I know I shall show it.

---

[1] Upward's *In the Thirties*, still unpublished.
[2] The film version of van Druten's play, starring James Stewart and Kim Novak; Lanchester had a supporting role.
[3] Loneliness.

As I reread Edward's novel, it seems better and better. It is so solid—and the main character, Alan, who at first seems thin blooded and unemotional, is later shown to be impulsive in the best sense of the word. He follows the motions of his heart, calmly but recklessly. I could never write about anybody in that way, I fear. The "Peter"[1] in my novel is just the opposite—all *outward* emotion, fireworks, sound and postures. He is not a real man, like Alan; I mean a self-directed human being, open to reason, swept by passion, willing to change his course or be driven right off it by temporary emotion, but never to throw up his hands and stop steering. I like the solid argumentation, doggedly followed through. And I have the feeling that, when Edward's trilogy is complete, relations between the characters will become apparent which Edward didn't even intend. In other words, they are what's called "alive."

Alan is a moralist. I suppose that's rare in literature nowadays.

I can easily believe they won't publish this book as it stands.[2] It makes no concession to popular taste. It is utterly unshowy.

October 16. Yesterday evening, my brakes failed on the Simca. I was lucky to get it into a garage without accident; but now I'm stuck without a car.

As for the situation arising out of last weekend, I can only remember Eckhart's line: "Nothing burns in hell except the self."[3]

The weather is oven-hot.

After I finish this novel, maybe I'll stop altogether writing about myself.

In a strange irrelevant way, I am happy. Perhaps merely because the ego, after its recent display, is tired and has let go. But, oh goodness, how aware I am that this is only temporary!

Because of the breakdown, Krishna drove me home last night. Such acute embarrassment and good will between us, especially on my side. Swami is cagey about Amiya. Last night she was drunk again, at a little party given at her house by the DePrys.[4] She kept showing us the hats she'd bought. When she got on to the subject of mescaline—Aldous has just published an article about this in *The Saturday Evening Post*—he very nearly snapped at her.

---

[1] "Peter" does not appear in later versions of *Down There on a Visit*.

[2] *In the Thirties* was rejected by eight or nine publishers and appeared only in 1962; see Glossary.

[3] Like Isherwood's diary entry for April 27, 1950, this slightly misquotes the *Theologia Germanica*; see Glossary under Eckhart.

[4] Bert and Bess DePry were Vedanta devotees; he was president of the Vedanta Society of Southern California. The house was no longer Amiya's.

October 23. Suddenly cold and grey. A bad morning—which should have been a good one; I went early and sober to bed—I began rereading *The Heart in Exile*[1] and *The Gay Year!*[2] A throbbing in my ear when first awake—heart?

Endless telephone talk with a silly boy trying to sell me *The Encyclopedia Americana.*

October 24. Stormy weather! We are just about to give a party for Amiya and I smell trouble. Don is nervous, and blew his top because I'm writing to tell Don Parks he can't have the option to do his *Sally Bowles* musical. Don blames me for deferring to Carter, whom he hates.[3] I'm sure we'll quarrel tonight. What a bore! I feel tired and out of sorts and resentful and fat.

We like Paul Bowles, though. He came last evening to dinner. He was so funny about John Goodwin taking mescaline. The whole solemn cult of it.

Mrs. Stickel came in to ask me if I minded her playing the piano. She told me she'd had a nervous breakdown a few years ago, and Mr. Sammet cured her by telling her she was just bored. Mr. Sammet used to be a doctor in England, but he doesn't practice here, except among the neighbors, unofficially. He cures falling hair. Timmy is adopted. They have never punished him; although he once threatened Mrs. Stickel with a garden fork.

October 25. The party last night was one of the worst we've had. Amiya was real loud, and she stuck around with Prema long after the others had gone, talking about the sacrifice she'd made when she married George and other such self-pitying crap. As for Prema he got quite fascinatingly sentimental. He told me he'd once attacked me to Swami and Swami had replied: "Always love Chris. He's a great devotee."

Don and I sat up talking till 4:00 a.m., after they'd eaten with us at Zucky's and left. And this morning Don decided not to look at his movie magazines or clip any more pictures till our play is finished.[4]

Good effect of Dexedrine: no hangover, and today I have written a

[1] By Rodney Garland, who also used the pseudonym Adam Hegediis (1953).
[2] By M. J. De Forrest (1949).
[3] Parks sent Isherwood a tape of songs he had written, possibly with a collaborator, for the proposed musical. Bachardy liked the music, but Roger Edens told Isherwood it was not first rate; Carter Lodge represented John van Druten's interest as the author of the play.
[4] Isherwood and Bachardy had begun writing a play, eventually titled *The Monsters.*

page of the Ramakrishna book, my novel, the travel diary, *and* a bit of the play; and rewritten the letter to Don Parks.

October 28. Last night we attended the fourth of four truly ghastly parties in a row—our party for Amiya, supper with Jo and Ben at the Harvey Eastons', supper at the Hacketts', supper with Tom and Emily Wright.

We are getting ahead with the plan for our play.

Don is in town, for the night. He left a fountain pen on the desk and it made a big ink mark. I scrubbed the mark out but have scrubbed off the varnish.

Listening to Johnnie's voice on his record, telling how to write a play.[1]

About those parties—the Eastons' was the squarest, the Hacketts' the most meaningless, the Wrights' the southernmost. I think the Wrights win for sheer desperate horror; and I believe Mrs. Wright *is* dying—though Rabwin holds out hopes.

Ben Masselink's marines novel[2] was accepted by Little Brown. He heard yesterday.

October 31. Two days ago, Mrs. Pearson, who runs the liquor store, won a huge prize in the Irish Sweepstake. Who will the third fortunate person be?

I'm on page forty-six of my novel. During November I should be able to write enough to make it certain that the problem is solved. I now believe that the whole thing will be fairly short—say 150–60 pages. In two parts, one of them—the first—a good bit longer than the other.

Last night we went to Elsa Lanchester's, to listen to a recording of two operettas she'd made. One—the better—was by Ray Bradbury.[3] The composer of both of them was there, a strange fat boy name Ray Henderson, very drunk. Smiling, campy, maybe a bit sinister. Elsa fixed chicken curry.

November 3. It's just six o'clock in the evening and Don is going to spend the night in town but he hasn't left yet; he is doing a design of a spider and its egg sack against a dark background—school home-work. However he's rather off art at the moment, working eagerly on our play. I seriously believe it is a good idea, well constructed;

---

[1] *John van Druten, Distinguished Playwright Series* (Westminster Spoken Arts, 1956).
[2] *The Crackerjack Marines.*
[3] The science fiction writer.

and goodness knows I could *never* finish it without Don. He is doing all the spadework.

Glorious weather, though cooler at last; I went in swimming today.

Finances sinking steadily, but we still have about $6,500, all told. Oh, how I wish I could somehow get an advance! I think I have more work on my hands than at any other time in my life.

1. The novel. This, it now seems, will be quite short—about 40–50,000 words. Right now I have written maybe 16,000. All the big problems are ahead. I shall be lucky if I finish this by Christmas 1959.

2. The Ramakrishna book. I have so far only written fourteen pages of the new version. Admittedly, this work should go ahead faster now I am past the introductory section, because it is really a rehash of Saradananda. Nevertheless, I'd say Christmas 1959 for that, too. I can hardly believe I could possibly get both books finished by then, even if I did no other work—as I must, to live.

3. The play. This is a very difficult project to assess time for—especially as Don is helping. I *would* like to get a draft out before this Christmas.

4. The travel diary I'm retrospectively writing, based on Don's diary, some notes and some letters of mine, of our trip to Asia last winter. This isn't even for publication, except in snippets.

Now, none of this stuff is very promising financially. The novel will be a critical success at best; it has no adaptation value for stage or screen. The Ramakrishna book doesn't bring me a cent—everything goes to the Vedanta Society. The play *might* be a goldmine—but when? Not for ages.

Thumb very painful again.

November 7. I have just been hunting high and low for my tie clip—only to find it in the tray where it belongs!

Fog, quite thick for the daytime. Smog in town.

Amiya really is an egomaniac. She cannot stop talking about herself. She says she said to Swami: "Haven't you anything to tell me before I go?" and he said, "No—I don't think so." Then he said: "You have made a success of your life." What did he mean?

Tension. Strain. Great weariness. But never mind—

Last night was so nice. Don drew me, while I listened to Gerald Heard's record.[1] Very snug. We ate salmon loaf at home.

---

[1] Probably *Explorations with Gerald Heard* (Pacific Records, 1957), still in Isherwood's collection.

November 12. Don has been making some big scenes—crying because he feels such terrible anxiety, about losing his hair, growing old, never amounting to anything, etc. Then disgusted with himself for making the scenes. He is so nervous and miserable, and yet we really have never been happier together and the dips are followed not merely by highs—that would be run-of-the-mill neurosis—but by real periods of happiness and calm.

Maybe Don is a person who ought never to live in this country.

Amazingly enough our play—I call it provisionally *The Monsters*—goes steadily ahead. We have a rough draft of act one, and of the first half of act two, scene one. Target: a complete rough draft by Thanksgiving. Part of Don's scene was because he found he couldn't write the dialogue, but now I dictate to him, and he makes plenty of suggestions and really is most helpful.

Really agonizing pain in my *left* thumb. Also a tiresome canker sore in my mouth. But my morale is good. *Lots* of work to be done!

November 14. Yesterday I realized that my novel just doesn't amount to anything. More about that in my work notebook. I'm not particularly depressed because, of course, there *is* something in all the stuff I've written. Just a matter of disentanglement. Why do I always give birth to these Siamese twins? Same with *The Lost*. Same with *The School of Tragedy*.

There is still a tremendous lot to be done before Christmas—a rough draft of the play, get *The Vacant Room* started with Gavin,[1] get some travel stuff written for a magazine. And always the Ramakrishna book.

Spent yesterday afternoon with Gerald. He is still as sharp as a pin and I felt pricked by his aliveness. His wonderful poetic-scientific generalizations. Example: every living organism can be said to be a tune or pattern. If we could learn our own human tune we should know how to live our lives, instead of resisting the changes in them—trying to play the largo passages allegretto, etc.

November 18. Still have this sore on my lip. Peschelt wasn't alarmed by it last week but he'll see it again Thursday.

Don and I are now hard at work on the play—*The Monsters*. He is so happy to be doing this; he feels he has found something worthwhile. Of course I'm worried. I fear his abandonment of painting, his lapse into dilettantism, and I remember the (apparently)

[1] Lambert was to help revise the screenplay written with Lesser Samuels (it was never produced).

bad effects I had on Heinz and Caskey. And yet I don't for one moment seriously think Don is like either of them.

These are happy days of work—walks on the beach in brilliant weather and yet my natural melancholy is so easily aroused. And then I pray—but not nearly often enough.

There is so much to do, and one should just be thankful for that.

November 19. Today we finished act two. Heaven only knows what it's *really* all about. It *seems* to be making sense.

Ben brought round his contract for the marines novel, and Jo complained how sore her arms are still. My lip ditto. Also thumbs.

Tony Perkins[1] to supper last night. We gave him such good steaks. Don fixed them. The almost unimaginable loneliness of Perkins's life. One sees him as completely solitary. But he is going to an analyst four times a week (at 6:30 a.m.!)—apparently to get over the effects of splitting up with a roommate. He didn't say who. And we couldn't *quite* ask him.

Tonight I went up to Vedanta Place. Suddenly I was so glad to be sitting on the floor beside Swami—without a word, like his dog. After supper, I read them the first chapter of the Ramakrishna book.

November 27. What I chiefly have to give thanks for, this Thanksgiving, is that I'm still alive. The night before yesterday, bored after a long long evening with a not very nice friend of Wystan's named Robin Hope, and somewhat though not really drunk, I fell asleep at the wheel driving home and ran smash into a parked car. I guess I was knocked out. I remember nothing—until there was this very furious man, the owner of the parked car, yelling at me that he'd like to bash me to pulp—"And I'd do it too," he said, "if you hadn't got blood on your face already." I had, as a matter of fact, hit the steering wheel, which was twisted up, cut myself between the eyes, bruised both eyes, maybe broken my nose, cut one knee and maybe hurt some ribs. The furious man, Mr. Raasch, was eagerly expecting my arrest on a drunk driving charge. But the police were very nice and sent me home in a taxi after I'd been fixed up at an emergency dressing station.

The other thing to be thankful for is that Don and I have finished the rough draft of our play *The Monsters*, also the day before yesterday. We are cautiously starting the rewrite.

Don has hit a new high of sweetness. He is very happy about the play.

November 28. Feeling lousy. My cold still very bad, knee hurts and pain in the ribs when I cough. Yesterday I got furious with kids

---

[1] Anthony Perkins, American actor.

playing ball outside and made such a fuss that they have been told to move down the road, but only a short way. The only thing which makes all this bearable is Don's behavior. Oh, I do hope I don't have to become an invalid later! The misery of minor ailments.

Swami sent Krishna down with some turkey. Jo and Ben were there when he arrived. Jo was off to some Thanksgiving parties, dressed as a "lobster" in a scarlet jumper and tights, with a bullfighter's tie. I guess Krishna must have thought she was supposed to be the goddess Kali.

December 2. We have decided not to go to New York for Christmas.

Of course I never really wanted to go. As always, I loathe travel. And I hate the cold. *Or* the hot. Only this part of California is really habitable for me. But I'd never have said any of this. We came to it quite naturally and logically, realizing what an interruption this trip would be to our work on the play. The play is really our baby. Needless to say, I have misgivings; but still I do continue to feel that, fundamentally, it makes sense. It adds up to something. Probably it is too small beer for New York audiences—but that's neither here nor there. We're about halfway through act one, in our second draft.

My car injuries are clearing up. My knee's still stiff but today I borrowed Bill Hawes's car, which he so kindly loaned, and was able to drive it.

Don and I have a curiously snug relationship right now, thanks to the play. We're like winter animals, snugly storing nuts.

December 6. John Gielgud is really a very lovable person. We saw him last night and the night before, and on Tuesday. He's here giving readings from Shakespeare. What is interesting is his obsession with the poetry itself; you really do feel that he has a need to proclaim it. When he recites, he actually cries. Dame Edith Evans said to him: "If you would cry less, John, the audience would cry more."

He is also obsessed by the fear of another scandal,[1] and here also he is sympathetic, because he has the keenest concern for everyone else who gets into trouble with the police. What I find less admirable is his acquiescence, to some extent, in the theory that the royal family has been "hurt" by his behavior. But I suppose, if you didn't feel like that, you couldn't go on living in England.

The awful youthful squareness of Jack Larson, who told John his performance was "deeply beautiful."

[1] Gielgud had been arrested in a men's room for importuning; see Glossary.

December 11. Such a beautiful blue morning. Yesterday was so hot that you could easily have gone in the ocean.

Don and I finished the rewrite of act one three days ago. Now it looks as if we might get act two by Christmas and maybe act three by New Year's. But act three is tricky. Too much exposition, at present.

Yesterday evening, driving up to Vedanta Place for supper, I suddenly felt so exhausted that I had to lie down in Prema's room. Prema talked about his loneliness. He longs for a friend—he longs for affection—he even wishes he could go up to San Francisco and cut loose for a week; but he won't, I don't think. He says all the boys really hate each other. There's no love in the place. [There is a] new monk, [who] is apparently about to have a breakdown, because [one of the old monks] is so horrid to him.

All this, and then I went in to see Swami, who told me he'd had "a terrible time" that morning "in the shrine—I mean a good terrible time." He had been overpowered by the knowledge that, "There is abundant Grace." He had cried so much that he had to leave the shrine room. He said what was the use of reasoning and philosophy— when all that mattered was knowledge of God? I told him he was an existentialist.

I asked him when he had started to feel that God really existed. He said, "As soon as I met Maharaj. Then I knew at once. He made it seem so easy."

Jack Lewis thinks I'm healing up all right. But my nose is broken and I have a tear in the pleura, which hurts when I cough.

December 13. We're approaching the end of act two, scene one. I still don't in the least know just what we have or haven't caught in our net.

Don sulked last night because the bathroom light dropped on his head and he thought my attitude was callous. As a matter of fact, I often am less demonstrative when something bad like that happens, because I begin thinking in terms of what's to be done.

Since I so often praise Don in this journal, let's have a few words about his shortcomings.

He is still terribly silly about his appearance—wastes so much time curling or combing his eyebrows and fooling with his hair.

He is obstinately stupid at not seeing the connections of things, in our work on the play. Often I feel he simply isn't trying—just idling and thinking about Lana Turner and waiting for me to get on with the work.

Then he is a sulker. And blindly obstinate about trifles, out of mere weakness.

Well, all right. At least he knows all this. And at least he is trying. I know similar things about myself, and I hardly try at all.

December 15. Ivan Moffat, back from Zurich, Selznick and *Tender Is the Night* for a few days, gave a party the night before last. Gia Scala,[1] very drunk, philosophic about life and death, and about to drive to Topanga, seemed in danger of remaking *The Green Hat*[2] in a wonderful red cloak. Ivan had ordered four trays of hors d'oeuvres from Romanoff's for the party. For this, he had received a bill for $360! I must say, he showed an altogether classic self-control about this. He never even mentioned it till we were talking on the telephone next morning.

Yesterday we finished act two, scene one—half the play. Great reconstructions are now necessary, however, because the first draft has far too much exposition in the last act.

A huge fire somewhere near San Juan Capistrano. Smoke all over the sea, greenish grey, blowing up from the south. The sun turned bright pink.

Don now tells me he went to a fortune-teller around August, who said 1959 was to be a marvellous year for him. Also that I had been through a bad period which was just about to end. He told Don we would do no more travelling this year, although Don assured him that we would—because, at that time, of course, our New York trip still seemed definite. The fortune-teller said Don would make money with his commercial drawing, but didn't see a future for him in portrait painting.

December 19. A ghastly party at Doris Dowling's last night. She told us she has a Christ complex. The house is full of pictures of Christ, including a reproduction of Dali's.

And today comes a letter from Mina Curtiss, saying that it would be very difficult to give me a Chapelbrook grant because I live in Hollywood which "is synonymous with money," because I haven't saved enough money to take a couple of years off which is highly suspicious, because I am "able to earn money outside my art" and because I am not "in quite desperate need."

Well, I'm writing to tell her I withdraw my application.

December 24. Don has gone to Christmas Eve dinner with his mother. Tonight we go to a party at Stanley Kubrick's.

---

[1] Italian actress.
[2] Michael Arlen's novel, adapted as a play and a film, which ends with the heroine crashing her car, only her hat landing safely.

What is to be said about this Christmas? Our first at home since I've known Don—1953 New York, 1954 Mexico City, 1955 Munich, 1956 New York, 1957 London. All rather miserable: 1953—a party of rather unpleasant people at Wystan's. 1954—me sick. 1955—Don sick. 1956—we ate Christmas dinner all alone (but that was the best year). 1957—a miserable scramble through London to find *any* place open to eat at.

This year at home we at least have the comforts of our own house; and two nice "Englishmen" (one Canadian) whom Phil Burns introduced me to—John Durst and Jonathan Preston—are coming to us for Christmas dinner.

This year is also our first with a Christmas tree. Don was eager for it but now rather hates it—has most carefully put on and taken off again the Spanish-moss-like tinsel. Some of the lights on it have gone out and won't be repaired.

We are hoping to have the second draft of our play by New Year's or soon after.

I now await the Hines and the Stickels for Christmas drinks. Also Bill Hawes, who lent me the Ford. The Simca returned yesterday—but its brakes are *not* guaranteed!

Hal Greene (who came in for drinks yesterday) is "working" with a teacher called Lillian de Waters.[1]

Don is mad because Ray Henderson—Elsa Lanchester's accompanist—sends me a Christmas card inscribed, "To the most charming man in the Western Hemisphere"!

December 27. The Hine-Stickel visit was quite a success, due to Bill Hawes's presence. He played it real butch, talked to them about Tahiti, and War and Wife. How very surprised they'd have been to hear he makes hats! After Bill had left, there was an amusing revelation about Mr. Hine's (alleged by Hal Greene) FBI activities. I remarked, as we parted, that I would have to be careful because of the police roadblocks against drunk drivers, and Mr. Stickel put in, innocently, to Mr. Hine: "*You* should know all about that, Frank." Mr. Hine did not react.

That evening we had supper with Stanley Kubrick and Christiane Harlan. Her daughter had been given a copy of *Shock-headed Peter* in German for Christmas.[2] Kubrick seems to be going astray on all kinds of screwy projects—*Lolita*, a film about the end of the war in Berlin, a love story called *Sick, Sick, Sick*. A young writer with inflamed eyes named Dick Adams is working for him.

[1] A psychotherapist.
[2] Harlan is German.

Christmas day was beautiful, and altogether pleasant. We had John Durst and Jonathan Preston as our guests. They went in swimming before lunch and brought with them a magnum of Mumm. John is not very thrilling but I like him. Jonathan is cute and lively. He described how Bullock's Department stores take down *all* their decorations on Christmas Eve. Right after Christmas come the sales. We went to Pacific Ocean Park later. Don and Jonathan rode in the revolving tub which holds you to its sides by centrifugal power after its bottom sinks.

Yesterday we had Russian vodka with Bill Hoover,[1] who told us that the Russians (in Moscow) are squatty, homely, rather dull and lifeless.

Then we went on to a very dull though not lifeless party at Paul Millard's—a collection of (perhaps) the most boring people I've ever known: the Bracketts, the Jimmy Pendletons, the Larmores, Joan Elan, Gene Nash,[2] Paul himself, etc. etc.

On the way home, Don and I had a terrific quarrel—I forget what about. He slapped my face, for the first time. We haven't gone into the whole thing yet—and now we have guests coming here, including Joan Elan and Paul Millard—so must stop.

December 28. Don has a very badly inflamed throat. His bad mood has turned septic but not altogether left him; he still gives me glances of deep hostility. It's beautiful but sharply windy weather. We worked on the play again today. We work, some, every day. But it definitely will not be finished before the New Year. Am quite cold on it at present. It seems entirely uninteresting. There is only one thing to do: finish it as quickly as possible.

Doris Dowling is a lysergic acid bore. She has been through the mystic experience, she says. I have a wild notion that she may be planning to marry Gavin.

Our party was a disaster. Dowling shocked Harvey and June Easton—and Paul Millard and Joan Elan were as boring as ever. Salka, who could have partially saved the evening, didn't come and didn't call us.

December 31. A tremendous fire is sending up an orange cloud from behind Topanga. On the beach it was very hot. Don and I got on with the play, right into the final scene between Elizabeth and Stephen, but it will take at least a week more to finish.

[1] Hoover's brother Lamar was also there; they were not related to Ted Bachardy's friend, Bob Hoover.
[2] Elan's lover at the time.

And now we have to go off to this party tonight in our ridiculous rented tuxedos. The idea bores me to death, but never mind—no sulks!

1959

January 1. No sulks—and the party really wasn't bad at all. Lots to drink, truly delicious sandwiches, and a parade of elderly stars—ranging from Marion Davies to Laurence Olivier. Bing Crosby, poker-faced with the middle-aged misery of being up too late, dancing with his flirty-eyed young wife; he wore a cardboard crown. So did Edward G. Robinson. Lance Reventlow[1] was among the very few attractive young males; but he is so humorlessly blond and bull-faced as to seem quite sinister. At midnight I lost Don in the crowd. I hope this wasn't a bad omen for the year.

At the end of the street—up in the hills of Benedict Canyon—you could see the shockingly naked flames licking up the brush. They looked very near, and there were rumors that many houses had been burned. This made the party a bit like the voyage of the *Titanic*. People who lived in the area were exchanging tips for "getting through." "Drive to the police block on Beverly Glen and ask for a cop named Fritz."

Despite hangover, Don and I went ahead with our work on the play today.

Saw Kent Chapman and a girlfriend of his in the afternoon. He is less skinny since being drafted into the army. Is leaving soon for Korea or Germany. He always annoys me by his helplessness when he calls; and then I always warm to him when we talk—he is very endearing. We all three went out on the boardwalk and watched the sun set.

This evening Don and I burned all the branches of the Christmas tree, leaving only the trunk to be cut up and burned tomorrow, when Gerald comes to supper.

Pessimistic New Year's thoughts about money. It suddenly seems so hard to get.

January 6. The first rain of the season is pouring down tonight. We'll see if the new roof leaks. Don is in town for the night. I've just returned from an Oscar Levant show, or rather, the process of taping it. I rather stank—loused up nearly all of my quotations. But I guess they liked it.

The night before last, Don and Hope Murray came to dinner, just

---

[1] Barbara Hutton's son and Jill St. John's boyfriend (later briefly her husband).

back from making a baby and a film (*Shake Hands with the Devil*) in Ireland. Don enthusiastically praised Don's painting of me and his drawings, remarking rather sweetly how nice it is to be able to praise a friend's work sincerely.

At supper we got talking of George Stevens's Christ picture,[1] and I said that Pat Boone would never be able to play Judas, because he refuses to kiss anyone on the screen. Don Murray roared at this, but then most unkindly exposed Hope, who'd also laughed, for not knowing what I was talking about. She was raised a Christian Scientist.

At the Serbia restaurant on Montana, Don overheard the lady of the house say to the headwaiter: "I dreamed about you last night. You brought in the menu, and it was covered in blood."

On the 3rd, we finished act two of the play. Now we're well into act three. What we're doing is certainly a vast improvement over the first draft. But oh what a long way to go yet!

January 8. Last night I had supper at Vedanta Place and Swami urged me to come and live in one of the apartments of the new apartment house they are going to build. Of course this is quite out of the question at present because of Don, and anyhow I do *not* want to become part of the "congregation." That's unthinkable, anyway. And I shan't even mention this offer to Don because I know it would upset him and make him feel insecure. (Just when he's feeling reassured, because his teacher and fellow students praised his work very highly at school.)

I only regret Swami's offer because I fear it means the start of another come-back-to-Vedanta offensive, such as Swami waged while I was with Caskey.

The Levant show was a great hit, it seems. And I must say I was agreeably surprised how relaxed I looked on the show and how my voice has lost its tightness.

Two disasters: a drunk ran into the Sunbeam, and my workroom roof suddenly gushed water yesterday during a rainstorm and wetted a lot of my books. They are all out on the living room floor to dry.

Ill-wind department—as a result of the rain, the phone shorted, and so it was finally possible to get it moved across the room to a point by the door, from which it'll reach right down the passage into the bedroom.

January 10. Aldous invited me and Don to lunch today, and to our surprise we found ourselves alone with him. I then suspected that

---

[1] *The Greatest Story Ever Told* (1965).

maybe he was going to propose some literary collaboration project—but no. I guess he was just lonely. Laura was away for the weekend.

He looked tired and older—he was sick after his return. He talked about the trip—Lima, Machu Pichu, Brasília and Rio. Everywhere the growing overpopulation, the inflation, the mad building of government offices on money produced by the printing press. In London, Tom Eliot has become a bore, Morgan looks just the same, John Lehmann seems to be "made of wood" and Rosamond [Lehmann] has taken up spiritualism since her daughter's death and believes they are in communication. Why is it always so shocking to hear this? I suppose because people always seem to be convinced at the wrong time and for the wrong reason—when and because they desperately desire to be convinced.

Evelyn Hooker, with clean new front teeth—Don says she used to foam at the side of the mouth—came to supper last night and bored us. Don doesn't think she really likes me or vice versa. Maybe not. She says she thinks Kinsey was queer. She told us about the Heavenly Twins, fifty-eight and thirty-two, who dress identically down to their underclothes. And about clubs young married couples belong to for the exchange of bed partners. I seem to see a most curious streak of puritanism in her—for example when she said that sadism was *bad* even when both parties enjoyed it.

Every day, Don and I keep on at the play, and soon we should have the second draft complete. We are in the middle of the third act. But what it adds up to—still no idea.

January 14. Right now, Don is doing over the final scene between Elizabeth and Stephen in our play. (When we rewrite, we shall change the names; probably as follows—Catherine Derwent, Michael Grant, Joan Watson, Nancy Lord.) We have already done this scene twice and reached the end, but it's still a muddle—like landing by plane in a thick fog—you *know* you're nearly there, but not one glimpse of the airport.

We saw Julie's play *The Warm Peninsula*[1] last night. On the stage it seemed fully as bad as it did when we read it. Julie has an insignificant, rather unsympathetic part which she keeps alive by technical tricks, not by genuine feeling. And Manning [Gurian]'s attitude to the whole enterprise seemed just about as wrong as possible. He gloats over the pictures of himself in the brochure, bills himself and Julie as a "theatrical team," and is frankly out for the buck and nothing else. If he can make it by cheap movies without quality, well, he'll make it. We feel he is playing on Julie's timidity and insecurity. This play *must*

---

[1] By Joe Masteroff; Harris was starring in it.

be a flop when it hits Broadway. Yet Manning remarked, in the most relaxed manner, "Of course, Julie has nothing to do in the second act," as if this were a slight defect which could quite easily be fixed.

January 17. Today we finished the second draft of the play.

Marguerite called from New York to say she is getting married to Rory Harrity, a young actor who was in Gore's *Visit to a Small Planet.*

Ivan is back from Switzerland. *Mary Magdalene* is again shelved. Gavin has a job, starting Monday, on *Sons and Lovers,* for Jerry Wald.

Marguerite will marry in Monroe, on March 15. She wants us to come. We can combine that with the opening of Tennessee's play.[1] Marguerite had taken the mescaline tablet I gave her. She got the horrors and thought the ceiling was coming down.

Ivan's hors d'oeuvres from Romanoff's were reduced from $360 to $200, with profuse apologies.

A drunken evening with Jim Charlton yesterday. He seems happy with Hilda, says the sex is a success still, and anyhow he can't be bothered to have outside affairs.

We had supper at the Red Snapper with a friend of Jim's named Bill Claxton,[2] with whom he hopes to make documentary films—because a fortune-teller whom he brought to their Thanksgiving (or Halloween) party told him he would succeed in a job not his own.

An amazing thing happened today. We had decided to get the play typed in a rush for Dodie and Alec to read; so we planned to hire another typewriter and split the work. We were talking of this at Ted's counter and a grey-haired woman next to us introduced herself as Mrs. Pierce and offered *her* portable typewriter. And it turned out to be a Royal, with exactly the same type as mine! A sign from heaven?

January 20. After frantic typing the night before last, and all yesterday up to 4:30, we finished three copies of the play in time to take one of them up to the post office and airmail it to Dodie and Alec. Later I found one glaring typographical—by me. In the midst of the big emotional scene in act two, scene two, Michael suddenly addresses Catherine as Elizabeth! This because we were copying from a script which had the old names.

Today is glorious, but I feel let down and depressed, wondering how we can get money. Talked to Ivan on the phone. He says business is very bad.

And I have to admit that my novel, in its present form, has folded.

---

[1] *Sweet Bird of Youth.*
[2] Photographer, known for his pictures of musicians and actors.

Still and all, I think I see a new line on this, which I'll sketch out in my big notebook.

And I *must* get on with the Ramakrishna book.

January 23. This beautiful weather continues.

Am increasingly worried about money. It now looks as if Bob Gottschalk of Panavision isn't really interested. So we are left to the mercies of Hal Roach.[1] All other work in prospect seems highly dubious.

To Vedanta Place last night. I was amused by Swami's plotting to go behind the back of the Math council if necessary and get Swami Sankarananda to okay his project of bringing the girls to India for sannyas.

Gerald, who came to tea yesterday, bitched Aldous a little. He refuses to be associated with Aldous's claim that mescaline gives you spiritual experiences.

Great unwillingness to restart the Ramakrishna book—but I *must.*

Don is sad. Let down after finishing the play. And sad because we can't afford to fly over to New York and see Gielgud again. I would like to, too. What I resent about Don's sadness is that it demands that we somehow *shall* do this, despite the lack of money. Which is childishly selfish, and leaves me in the position of an unkind parent, refusing.

January 27. Needless to say, we *are* going to New York! The excuse is that the money pig was found to contain far more than we had expected—470-odd dollars! It's still crazy of us to go, and Don believes we can stay there two weeks and only spend $300, which is just an example of his obstinate self-deception. Still, he's an angel— even if an obstinate one. And maybe I'll somehow scratch up some money while we're there. And of course it *will* be fun. If only it's not too hatefully cold!

A wonderful reunion with the Stravinskys yesterday. Igor said how he loves to get drunk. He only drinks whiskey now. Vera said, "I am fat," and was.

Not one word from Dodie and Alec! Where are they?

Today it was said that we'd be approached by an Italian producer, who wants to make Melville's *Benito Cereno.* Ken MacKenna recommended me to him. But no word as yet.

[1] Producer, especially of gag comedies; a possible buyer of Isherwood and Lambert's TV idea, *Emily Ermingarde.*

January 28. One of those dog-sad evenings before a journey. Oh, if only I didn't have to go! How I loathe the whole idea!

Now Don has come in late and is sulking because I said he was. We shall get no sleep and dash out late for the plane. God, what hell.

Phil Taber is leaving Vedanta. They ribbed him at supper about it.

February 7. This utter hell of so-called pleasure. We are in New York, "amusing" ourselves.

We never get up till 11:00 or 12:00, which I find deadly wicked. I can never write this journal because there is no time. Having gotten up we go out and trot around all day long until late. Usually we eat and drink enormously.

Don is getting sick. He had a bad stomach all last night.

Nothing from Geller about *The Vacant Room*.

Lincoln never referred to the affair of Mina [Curtiss] and the application for a grant which I made.[1] Just avoided the whole subject. I don't think I shall ever really like him again. After all, the rich are the rich.

We gave the play to Cecil Beaton and I gave the first three chapters of my novel to Frank Taylor. We now await their verdicts.

God, I am in a pessimistic, paranoiac mood! And yet Don was never sweeter.

February 8. Snow has started. Not much yet. That would be the last straw. We are leaving for Philadelphia to see *Sweet Bird*, this afternoon.

Cecil Beaton doesn't like our play *at all*. He couldn't find one good word to say about it.

A truly terrific performance of *The Crucible*, in the round, at a little hall in the Martinique Hotel. That and *Epitaph for George Dillon*[2] make this trip worthwhile.

And Don makes everything worthwhile. Last night we looked back on the last six years and agreed how really wonderful they have been. Only, we have to stop bickering. That's childish and unworthy.

February 10. This season in New York is the season of Baroness Blixen. She is dying, weighs sixty pounds, wears a hat with black ostrich plumes, can eat only oysters, grapes and champagne, looks like a withered monkey, enchants everybody. They say she will get the Nobel Prize. Our song: "We've been mixin' with Baroness Blixen."

At Zachary and Ruth Scott's party for her, a copy of her *Gothic*

---

[1] At Kirstein's suggestion; see Glossary under Curtiss.
[2] An early play by John Osborne and Anthony Creighton.

Tales[1] had been carefully placed at the end of the shelf and put in back to front, so you couldn't help reading the title.

The horror of the first night of *Sweet Bird of Youth* at Philadelphia. The heat of the auditorium, the blinding cigarette smoke, the rudeness of the club audience which talked throughout the show. Geraldine Page was excellent. But Paul Newman is just not a Lost Boy.[2] Oh, the terrible theatrical rat race! And the maddening difficulty of thinking a play through to a clear-cut conclusion, and then bringing it to pass without banality.

Tennessee dazed, irritable, jittery. Paul Bowles seemed nicer than ever.

February 16. Here we are, back home, after a most hateful twenty minutes this morning while the plane bumped down down down through rainy clouds. Torrents of rain today.

Geller reports that negotiations for *The Vacant Room* have all broken down. But in a way I don't despair any more. I won't be pessimistic. We'll go on trying everything. The travel article shall be next.

I do rather wish Stephen and Natasha weren't coming this weekend. It makes another interruption, and so soon.

Cheered up by finding Ben Jonson's poem: "Where dost thou careless lie?"[3]

Cecil Beaton and Truman Capote, at a goodbye dinner, told us we were so cagey, too nice.

An old-fashioned penthouse on Central Park South—the windows toward the park were mere slits, while a huge stained glass window looked out on a blank wall.

People who came out well on our visit: Tom Hatcher, Arthur Laurents, Truman, Cecil, Mrs. Ira Gershwin, Lesser and Helene Samuels, Howard Austen (E for effort), Paul Bowles, John Goodwin, John Gielgud, Hugh Wheeler, and that angel Pavitrananda. I think I liked my call on him best of anything.

February 19. A beautiful fresh sunshiny morning, after rain. But I feel so dissatisfied with myself. Is our play any good at all? Can I really split up the novel into pieces, and do I want to write them anyway? Can I write this travel article? The first draft rings false.

---

[1] *Seven Gothic Tales* (1934).

[2] Newman played Chance Wayne to whom the Princess says, "Chance, you're a lost little boy that I really would like to help find himself," (act 1, scene 2). Isherwood is also alluding to *Peter Pan*.

[3] "An Ode to Himself."

I weigh 154 lbs. I mean to do something about this, at once.

Stephen and Natasha are coming this weekend, with that rather loathsome pale Matthew who is always being told how marvellous he is. I want to see Stephen—always. But Natasha is just a big wistful nuisance. Why can't she stay with Evelyn Hooker, who wants her and who is anyhow being saddled with Matthew?

Don is getting over a cold he caught in New York. I'm rather concerned about him, he looks so tense and desperate, and is constantly attacked by doubt and despair. But I can do nothing, except make japam and maintain my own self-discipline.

I found Swami (last night) still much concerned by the problem of getting the people at Belur Math to give the girls sannyas. But then he became very gay, remembering how poor mad Medora had told him he was Ramakrishna. Swami expected her to go on to say that *she* was Holy Mother and therefore his consort, and was greatly relieved when she merely announced that she was Vivekananda!

The evening before yesterday, Don spent the night in town. Jim Charlton called and asked me to have dinner with him. He says Caskey is expected back on a visit. Jim said of his marriage: "I got what I needed, not what I wanted." We had drinks at the Friendship, now sadly stripped of most of Doc Law's trophies.[1] Then down to the Carousel, where "Exotica," who looks exactly like Callas, did the dance with two bowls of fire. As we said goodnight, Jim said, "I still love you, you know." And he urged me to come up and visit Hilde.

February 26. Missed some important days, because of arthritis in my thumb.

We had heavy rain at the end of last week. The roof didn't leak, thank goodness. Stephen, Natasha and Matthew Spender came for the weekend. Matthew (who is really intelligent and nice and seemingly a very talented artist) stayed at Evelyn Hooker's and provoked in her such feelings of mother love that she is seriously considering adopting someone! Evelyn hastened to assure me that she didn't believe in the maternal instinct, however. "On the human level, it's nothing but possessiveness." She was really quite touching. When Matthew left, she gave him the duplicating machine which had belonged to Edward.

It was rather embarrassing, having both Natasha and Stephen in the

---

[1] In *A Single Man*, Isherwood describes the disappearance of the "dusty marine trophies and yellow group photographs"; the photographs were mostly of Doc Law's close friend, Will Rogers, and the two of them together and with other friends—Ken Maynard, Ian Hunter (an actor), and Bide Dudley (a journalist).

house. Because Stephen obviously longed to talk about forbidden subjects. He says he is horrified by respectability, and that, when he is alone with [. . .] his square colleagues at Berkeley, he is bored.

I am amazed by Stephen's energy. He is always getting on with the job of supporting his family, and with no hint of complaint or anxiety; and he makes it look so easy. By contrast, I *horrify* myself. That's no exaggeration. I am weak and lazy and obsessed by fears. I just fear life altogether. It seems quite beyond me. Too strenuous. Too demanding. Even the sight of two planes drawing their contrails across the evening sky depresses me: all that thrust!

Our insurance policies have been cancelled. And today I got a flat tire. I begin to think I'm accident-prone, hexed, neurotically unlucky. In fact, I get so depressed I think it must be hepatitis recurring. And then I fear I infect Don.

February 28. Good news this morning. Wystan and Chester are ready to do the lyrics for our Berlin musical, if it can be arranged.

Last night we went with Caroline Blackwood (Freud) to a couple of beatnik bars, because Caroline is writing an article about them for *Encounter*, which Don may illustrate. The Venice West is tacky, the Renaissance (on the Strip) is quite grand. Both are enormously depressing. "Cool" seems to be an extra dull degree of being "square." And the only external resemblance to Zen is that you can't see what is going on inside these people.

Caroline was dull, too; because she is only capable of thinking negatively. Confronted by a phenomenon, she asks herself: what is wrong with it?

She tells us that "beat" is short for "beatific," which I didn't know. Specimen conversation: "Pad me." "I'm frigid." "I'll make you wail." If you agree with a statement, you say, "Dig"—*not*, "I dig you"; that'd be crude.

Don has started taking great interest in G[erard] M[anley] Hopkins.

March 4. Frantic long distance calls from Mrs. Degener of Curtis Brown and from Frank Taylor, who are both phone-happy. Net result: Wystan and I are to do lots of work, and *then* we'll see. No money yet. Fine words butter no parsnips.

Sinister soreness on left side of belly. But I had this before, in London last visit.

Reading John van Druten's diaries. Piqued because there is very little about me. The salutary truth: he was far less interested in me than I was in him!

Am pulling through a phase of inky black depression. *Must* work. Have at last got the Ramakrishna book restarted.

Hot. No rain in sight.

The Berlin crisis looming up black.[1]

March 5. Last night, up at Vedanta Place—a typical example of Prema's malicious joking. He took a stick of Basu's Kashidarbar incense, which is the usual kind burned in the shrine, lit it and stuck it into the living room wall up near the ceiling, a little while before I was due to start reading from the gospel. Whereupon—just as he'd hoped—several of the girls started complaining: "Who's been burning that horrible *Christian* incense here?" It took them quite some while to locate the incense stick.

On April Fool's Day—which is Prema's tenth anniversary of becoming a monk—Prema plans to buy a children's elephant rug—a toy replica of a big game hunter's trophy skin—and put it in the shrine in place of Swami's deerskin. He's a little scared about doing this, however.

March 11. Ramakrishna's Birthday. I'm to go up to Vedanta Place and read the second chapter of the biography after vespers—this is Swami's idea, and it'll probably seem like the last straw to puja-burdened camels.

Jack Lewis couldn't find anything wrong with me yesterday; so next week he goes to work with sigmoidoscope and X rays. I do feel there's *something*.

Very low finances. And now we have to pay huge assigned-risk insurance as a punishment for our accidents.

The Maurice Evans[2] deal and the Hecht-Lancaster deal and all the other deals are simmering, but only just.

Don is going through a negative mood.

BUT—let's count the good things:

He sold a drawing (of me) to the Stravinskys for twenty-five dollars.

We are invited to a party by Olivier for Emlyn Williams.

I *may* get $4,500 back from the government in overpaid taxes.

Stephen likes the fragment of my novel I showed him.

It's marvellous weather.

Courage!

---

[1] Diplomatic tension over the status of Berlin began to build in November 1958; see Glossary under Berlin crisis.

[2] Welsh actor and Broadway star.

March 12. Desperate worry about money—the Hecht–Hill–Lancaster job seems stalled. I feel as if I'm really hexed. Also bothered about my health. The pain continues in my intestine.

Mrs. Degener of Curtis Brown drove me nuts this morning on the phone. And then Frank Taylor called. Why wouldn't I come to New York and confer about the musical? Said I must have lots of money first—which pained them.

March 16. Don spent the night in town. I woke early, around 6:00, after big jitters last night because I have to have a sigmoidoscopic examination by Dr. Lewis this morning.

But I woke knowing that, if I am to go on living, I must make a much better job of it or I really shall get sicker and sicker. I must work sanely and not idle through my days. I must constantly pray for strength against this shameful useless melancholy. I must not infect Don with it.

The way I have been carrying on, I'm unworthy of health or any happiness. I mean that.

Don was pressing me yesterday to do something about my novel. So I'll try. How shall I describe my difficulty? It's as if I can no longer see things wholly. I can only see slices of them. I can't see all around this book in one glance, and that I must be able to do.

March 20. A change in climate—at last!

My examination by Dr. Lewis was negative. I signed on for teaching at L.A. State College. I believe, since the 17th, that I really see a way of doing this book! Have written nine pages.

Tomorrow, we leave with Jo and Ben for Frank Lloyd Wright and Taliesin.[1]

At Olivier's party for Emlyn Williams last night, Richard Burton got drunk and told Don he was as beautiful as Vivien Leigh! He also made a clowning pass at Judith Anderson,[2] who got furious and delighted. Emlyn called her, to her face, "the Madonna of the Sleeping Cars." Burton recited Dylan Thomas, said Emlyn couldn't. (Emlyn's been giving a Dylan Thomas recital.) A man with a fat face said that Huxley was getting gaga and that his lectures at Santa Barbara were awful, and when Don protested, the man said, "Quiet, child!" Later he got quite a wigging for this, both from Burton and from Don, and ended up making a pass at Don. Emlyn said to Clifford Odets, "You're a B–O–R–E." Odets left soon after.

[1] In fact, they were headed for Taliesin West in Scottsdale, Arizona; see Glossary under Wright.
[2] Australian actress.

A talk with Evelyn Hooker on the phone. She believes that Natasha is very seriously worried about Stephen—that's the real reason she insists on coming down here with him, despite the inconvenience. She told Evelyn that Stephen has now [been], for the first time, [. . .] unpleasant to her. Also [she feels anxious about] the Osamu[1] business in Japan [which she thought was] more serious than anything in Stephen's life previously.

My intestinal symptoms have almost entirely cleared up, thanks to these pills Jack Lewis gave me: Combid Spansules. It says on the container: "They reduce gastric secretion and motility, relieve anxiety and tension—without troublesome drowsiness—and control nausea and vomiting." Quite a trick!

A hangover after last night's party. So I went in swimming. It was so warm and beautiful on the beach, even at 9:30 a.m.

March 24. Despite the fact that I'm trying to push on with my novel, and the Ramakrishna book, I must try to write down a few notes about our trip to Taliesin—by car with Jo and Ben. We went there on the 21st, got back yesterday night—and it was truly memorable.

One of the great events for me, privately, was that I had a really vivid glimpse of how my novel should be; but no more of that here.

Eugene Masselink says that Wright (who'll be ninety next June) hasn't made any arrangements for the future of the foundation because he refuses to think about any event after his own death.

(Which reminds me that, this morning, I discovered Hugo's marvellous sonnet which ends: "Nous sommes tous les deux voisins du ciel, madame, / Puisque vous êtes belle et puisque je suis vieux."[2])

Wright is terribly jealous if anybody spends even a few moments alone with Mrs. Wright (Olgivanna). When she wanted to have a talk with me yesterday morning, we had to hide out in her daughter's cottage. Wright is always saying that the boys should show more initiative. Actually, he is so jealous that Eugene has to hide the fact that he has done a lot of murals for different clients. When Wright saw one of his designs accidentally, Gene pretended it was five years old—something he'd done and then forgotten all about.

Is Mrs. Wright a phoney? She talks with Russian mystic intensity about the difference between destiny and providence. Nevertheless,

---

[1] Possibly the young man called "Masao" in Spender's account of his 1957 and 1958 trips to Japan in his *Journals 1939–1983*.

[2] "We are both neighbors of the heavens, madame,/Because you are beautiful and because I am old." Written for Judith Mendés, Théophile Gautier's daughter, a few months before Hugo died, and entitled "Ave, Dea; Moriturus Te Salutat" (Hail Goddess, He Who Must Die Salutes You," after the Roman gladiators' salute to the emperor).

says Eugene (who worships her), she keeps Wright alive—largely by getting him into arguments which rouse his aggressive instincts.

One disconcerting feature of Taliesin is its non-allergy to millionaires. There were a pair of hogs there the night we arrived, Mr. and Mrs. Price. They have a fortune from pipelines. They were carrying on because the Duke and Duchess of Windsor have been in Phoenix. So I said: "I'm afraid I'm a terrible snob. I only admire talent." Then there was a Mrs. Sharpe, of whom Don said: "I'm sure she's had an operation so she can't fart."

During the nights—the cries of coyotes and babies.

The Tonto Park where we picknicked: the ocotillo, the vicious cholla like a snake, the greasebush, the paloverde, the great columns which are sometimes more than ten feet high. The mottled desert plains, with streaks of dark green which looks from a distance like turf, and of pale gold sand. The cacti look as if they're trying to catch your attention.

Wright's architecture suffers from all the imitations of it one has seen. Very satisfactory is the fruitcake effect of burying blocks of rock in concrete. But a lot of the carving in the woodwork seems disconcertingly trivial. And if you put almost anything on the shelves, you are in great danger of making the whole place look like a gift shop. The Biltmore Hotel in Scottsdale really does give an effect of splendor and luxury, which you seldom get nowadays.

Mrs. Wright adored Tantine.[1] Says she didn't like Prabhavananda.

Gene defends the Wright protocol: the dressing for dinner and for Sunday breakfast. He says that without it the whole institution goes to pieces. The boys grow beards, pitch their tents way back in the hills, etc.

The Wrights say: let there be dancing, or singing or whatever— and somehow or other there is, although nobody had been trained previously to do any of these things.

The problem of the wives—and of children who have grown up on the place. One boy, of seventeen, doesn't know what he's going to do. His mother left his father, married another man, and the two of them are coming back to Taliesin; where the father still is.

March 28. Well, I'm really getting along with my novel—the first episode that is; "Mr. Lancaster." Expect I will finish it in rough by the end of the month. I do believe, this time, I'm genuinely on to the track of something. For that, I can't be thankful enough.

---

[1] Josephine MacLeod, an American friend of Vivekananda who devoted her life to promoting his teachings; she died in Hollywood in 1949, well past ninety years old.

All the movie projects have temporarily fallen through. I'm considering trying to scare up an advance from Random House, and thereby bury the hatchet with them. Have written Truman Capote for his advice on this.

Now meanwhile Don got into another mess—his fifth traffic ticket (for shooting a red light, this time) this year. He had a hysterical outburst, exclaimed he couldn't drive anymore. So we are seriously considering moving into town, to Hollywood. Am getting the people at Vedanta Place to help us find a house near them. This just *may* be a great idea. I'm excited about it.

Don's fortune-teller said my bad period would end the end of March. So let's see. I've turned down the Berlin TV story offer for CBS. Now I seem embarked on trying to earn my living outside the movies. We have $3,000 still left, my job at Los Angeles State College in the fall, and a possible $4,000 refund from the income tax in June. We won't starve!

Unless I get sick. My intestine *still* bothers me, and I don't feel really good—but I haven't told Don that. Everything is suspended till I finish "Mr. Lancaster."

And, quite aside from this novel, I see another novel—or at least a publishable beginning and end—contained in my material. New Directions might do it, or *Botthege Oscure*.

It's 1:10 and we haven't yet heard from Emlyn Williams, who is supposed to be coming to lunch. He asked to bring loathsome slimy Tim Brooke. So we had to say yes. And now they're late—up drinking at Cukor's, apparently.

We went to Emlyn's Dylan Thomas recital last night. Emlyn is too tricky—or tricky in the wrong way; his camp is quite other than Dylan's. And his attempt at pathos at the end is downright embarrassing.

March 29. Just to wish myself a happy Easter.

We're off to the Bracketts' for lunch—god my arthritis is bad—if I get through this volume I'll type the rest of my journal till I die. I have fulfilled my ritual by doing one page of the Ramakrishna book—thirty-eight to thirty-nine—and one page of my novel—thirty-seven. I'm fairly sure I'll finish the rough draft of "Mr. Lancaster" on Tuesday. I'm wild to get ahead, and only hope my health won't hold me up.

Just written to Dodie and Alec.

Well, at least, I'm thankful to be working and so full of plans, this Easter morning. And thankful above all for Don, who makes everything worthwhile.

The Williams-Brooke lunch yesterday wasn't so bad. Because they arrived drunk and we got drunker, and slept on the beach. Emlyn told me Olivier had said my blue eyes were frightening, and Molly Williams said I had the sweetest, kindest face! Emlyn very pussy-sly, and pleased with himself, in a nice way. He says Olivier told him he wished he had been queer—it would have been so much easier—but that he had been frightened off it by the advances of another boy, when very young. Emlyn believes in asking everybody the most personal questions. He says they nearly always answer.

March 31. This morning, I finished the rough draft of "Mr. Lancaster." God knows if it's about anything.

The Bracketts' Easter party was for some reason more enjoyable than most. And we went on to see the Laughtons, who were most friendly. He demonstrated how he's going to play *Lear* at Stratford. The high note of the storm—which he heard while crossing on the *Champlain*. His idea is that Lear starts power-crazy and becomes sane in the storm sequence.

April 10. Depressed tonight.

I have rewritten about forty-four pages of "Mr. Lancaster" and roughly fudged the rest, so Don can read it. He's doing that now. I feel he's in a bad mood about something—maybe that I didn't recognize one of his self-portraits. The children this evening have made more noise than ever before. We *must* get out of here.

And [Frank Lloyd] Wright is dead.

And I have broken a tooth, which'll cost $200 to replace.

And I have got to go to New York, to see Auden and Frank Taylor about the musical.

And—and what? I don't want to.

Stephen visited us last weekend. He says he doesn't really like [living as a] bourgeois. He feels trapped [. . .]. Jim Charlton says he likes Hilde but wishes she were more fun.

April 11. I wish I could describe the ice cold toxic despair I feel. I feel as if I were chewing on ashes.

Don read the manuscript last night. Didn't like it. Then he had an outburst. He feels terrible. And there is a problem he can't tell me about because I would mind too much. Etc.

Oh the *boredom* of being unhappy!

The awful awful kids outside, screaming like demons.

And yet, if I were incurably sick or sentenced to die, I should be terrified.

April 12. Things are a little better. I'm convinced that I must keep taking sedatives to quiet the vagus nerve. That kicks up and causes my depression.

To see Charles Laughton today and we went through a lot of *Lear* together. Don lay by the pool and was bored.

I can't understand why Charles keeps saying he wants to hear *my* opinion. He has studied the play for thirty years and believes he is the only man who has understood it in the past two hundred. Maybe he is!

He thinks that Cordelia's offense from Lear's point of view was making a fool of herself *in public*. Lear's vulgarity is in staging this land-distribution scene in public, as a Hollywood tycoon would. His story of Cecil B. DeMille making the whores scramble for gifts. The same ugly megalomania. Lear begins to recover from it in act three, scene two, when he realizes that the Fool is a suffering human being: "How dost, my boy? Art cold?"

More work on the end of "Mr. Lancaster." Don likes it better now.

April 14. Yesterday I showed "Mr. Lancaster" to Gavin Lambert. This morning early he phoned to say he thinks it one of the best things I've written! Triumph! I did a few last things to it this morning and mailed it off to Curtis Brown. Triumph for Don, too. He has *eleven* of his drawings in the Chouinard art show!

April 18. Usual pre-trip misery. Particularly because this time I'm leaving Don behind.

To Vedanta Place to get Swami's blessing; then to see Laughton. I do like him. He is worried about *Lear*—feels the audience won't understand his rendering of it. They'll label it "a comic *Lear*." But of course he is right—*Lear is* partly farce; that's just what makes it so terrific. Laughton says of Lear that he is "antic."

His story of how Frank Lloyd Wright said to him quite seriously: "You are the Frank Lloyd Wright of the theater."

I asked Laughton how he would make his first entrance. He said: "You know these old men in England who walk straight at a grand piano as if they were certain someone would move it out of their way at the last moment?"

April 24. Got back yesterday afternoon.

Have spent today working on an outline of what Wystan and I discussed. Until he has it, Frank Taylor won't say if he wants an option or not. Why—since I've already told him all of it? Because the sonofabitch has no opinion of his own. He'll take it to Arthur Miller probably, and God knows who else. Just as he went all around town asking people if Wystan can really write poetry.

Between you and Don and me, I *am* worried a little about Wystan. If maybe he won't be too cerebral about these lyrics. The latest poems he showed me disconcerted me, rather. They seemed juiceless. But Frank Taylor isn't to know that. As Don says, Chester will most likely save the situation.

Being with Wystan alone was marvellous, as it always is.

And coming back to Don was ditto, ditto. He really is, at times like these, a most improbable kind of angel.

April 25. Rain. *The New Yorker* has refused "Mr. Lancaster." Gloom, which I allayed by working on, and finishing the outline of the musical, and by writing to Chester Kallman.

Reading through one of my diaries of the thirties, I'm struck by the note of utter despair. Maybe I will do a fourth section of my novel—it would come third in order—about the Munich crisis.[1]

Great harmony with Don.

Jo and Ben came and he drew them, brilliantly.

May 1. Have finished (yesterday) chapter three of the Ramakrishna book. It's *such* a bore, but I have to keep after it.

No news about "Mr. Lancaster" or Random House and the option.

The day before yesterday, Don took his drawings to the May Company[2] and was immediately offered a job, three days a week, to learn the ropes. This is really a triumph.

So now *I* must get busy and start "Ambrose."[3]

Time has a not-hostile review of *All the Conspirators*. Is their attitude to me changing?

Swami, last Wednesday, told how he believes that he, in his last incarnation, as an old man, met Brahmananda who was then a young man, on the banks of the river Narmada, where they were both practicing austerities.

May 2. Talked to Elsa Lanchester last night. She says that she hardly speaks while Charles is in the house—he's so domineering. Sometimes she is useful to him, but they have very little conversation. She

---

[1] "Waldemar," set during August–October 1938.
[2] A department store.
[3] The second section of the novel.

thinks it sad that he has no equals as friends, only inferiors, pupils and assistants. She wishes that he and I could be friends.

She thinks that the study of *Lear* has opened Charles's eyes to his own character.

May 7. Not one word from New York—about the musical, or "Mr. Lancaster" or the Random House advance.

I'm driving doggedly ahead with "Ambrose," which, so far, means absolutely nothing.

May 8. I must *not* weaken, however meaningless "Ambrose" seems. I must go ahead, at all costs.

Bad arthritis, as usual, in right thumb, tongue burns—from the few cigarettes I sometimes now smoke when I drink in the evening. But no bother with intestines. Left knee bad.

Good news today and bad. Random House *may* be going to give me my advance. Frank Taylor doesn't want me to start the script with Auden. I'm to collaborate with a professional musical comedy writer then Auden can come in later and write the lyrics. I think I shall tell him to go fuck himself, but perhaps had better wait and see what Frank writes me. How can Wystan do lyrics for a script he doesn't approve of?

Played records today—Gerald Heard on prayer,[1] Beethoven's *Les Adieux*, Franck's String Quartet—a thing I very seldom do.

An idea: to use Waldemar as Iris Wright's[2] lover in the Munich sequence.

May 11. This is sort of a Black Monday.

Stephen has been staying the weekend. And while it is wonderful, as always, seeing him, this definitely wasn't the right moment for a visitor, because Don is terribly nervous, feeling insecure in his job and even afraid that they may either throw him out for not being able to draw their way, or else they may succeed in teaching him to draw their way—and ruin his style.

Then, like an idiot, I took Stephen up to see Hayden and Rod and Bill Caskey—and I asked Bill for the $400 he owes me, and he flew into a tantrum and said he never expected I'd dun him for the money. And he called up in the middle of the night, drunk and called Don a praying mantis—"snap, snap"—and said that was what Speed had called Don. So then neither Don nor I could sleep, for rage, and Don has gone off to work utterly exhausted.

---

[1] *Gerald Heard, Reflections* (Pacific Records, 1959).
[2] Later changed to "Dorothy."

All this is absurd but nevertheless unpleasant.

Don was so upset about the falsity of Mother's Day, Ted's tiresomeness in calling just as he was starting to work, etc., that he hurled a paperful of coffee into the sink, scattering coffee in all directions. This upset him even more, after he'd done it.

Later. Terrible depression. Stephen was around all day, so I couldn't work. He played *Carmen* on the phonograph. I feel absolutely sick with nerves.

May 14. Ups and downs. Don did much better at the May Company, and so felt better. But was mad at me for trying to get him a gold wristwatch through Rod Owens. Well, I might have known he would be—

Yesterday evening, I met Swami Nikhilananda[1] for the last first time. (A Freudian, or a prophetic error?) He seemed intelligent and was charming. But I felt a certain destructive cynicism in him. And I felt Swami feeling it.

To Evelyn Hooker's later. She had Stephen staying with her. And she'd been up to her usual trick, involving him with some of her colleagues—in this instance, a professor of literature from Cal Tech. A terrible square, with a dazed, sleepy wife, who was maybe more fun when drunk. However, he and Stephen and Evelyn had a quite interesting conversation about the young and the state of America. For example—

Politics nowadays are a matter of accommodation rather than debate. If they weren't, the country would fall apart, like France did. It's more important to find ways of agreeing than to disagree.

We are all "fat cats."

Socialized medicine is being achieved through insurance.

The young read *Mad* magazine, because it attacks the values of the advertising business.

The country is ceasing to be agrarian.

The great issues are: overpopulation, natural resources, the growth of China, the H-bomb.

Evelyn said she wished the young would get excited about issues— the way they did in the thirties.

May 18. Saturday was such a happy day. Don and I lunched at Frascati's and then shopped. Got him a gold Rolex watch and a suit and a book of Miro engravings and an *American College Dictionary*.

[1] Head of the Ramakrishna-Vivekananda Center in New York; he wrote many books on Vedanta and supervised the English translation of *The Gospel of Sri Ramakrishna*.

Yesterday we went in swimming—the first time for him this year. And Olivier, the Burtons,[1] Emlyn Williams, Ivan Moffat and Caroline came to dinner. Caroline was a frost, as usual. Olivier, Richard Burton and Emlyn very lively and drunk. They took Emlyn to the airport later to go back to England.

Don to work today, although it's his birthday. He's still unsure if he can hold down the job.

Frank Taylor is coming out here—a bore.

Nothing from *Esquire*.

Am breaking with Random House.

Swishing heartbeat in my ears as I woke.

May 21. Heartbeat merely due to water in ears.

Talked to Frank Taylor last night. He was very understanding about my relations with and obligation to Wystan—that I couldn't go back on this—but he won't put up any money till Wystan and I can work and be together. And this means—well, not till next February. I think Frank wants to back out.

Have restarted "Ambrose," after realizing that the other draft was just a tangle.

This morning, after leaving the Simca to have its brakes fixed, I walked home through the park. And suddenly I felt exhausted, and lay down on the grass and slept with the sun on my face. It was so good. I felt a stirring of those feelings of compassion which I seem to have had quite often with me in the old days. That is to say, I didn't see everything and everybody, as I usually do, through a dull red murk of resentment.

Business gifts. Frank Taylor had had sent him, as a welcome gift, a bottle of twenty-one-year-old whiskey from a man at Warner Brothers he'd never heard of. As he said, it tasted of "sick piss."

May 24. The other evening, Don told me that I don't like Americans, though I love some of them. This may be true.

I do not love the Hine boys. They and their friends have been playing ball more often and more screechingly than ever. Again, we feel resolved to leave.

On Thursday, I restarted "Ambrose." I believe I'm on a better track now.

"Mr. Lancaster" turned down by *Esquire*. On Don's advice I'm not sending it to any more U.S. magazines. I'll have Edward read it first.

Don's job seems to be going well. Thank God for that, and for him. Having this job has done wonders for his morale.

---

[1] Burton's wife at the time was Sybil Burton, also Welsh, and a former actress.

Met the whole TV Nelson family[1] at a party at Jerry Lawrence's. David is much more attractive than Ricky.

June 2. Missed a day last week and broke my record.

With Virginia Viertel and Berel Firestone to see the lawyer yesterday, to be coached as a witness in her divorce case. Virginia is shockingly changed. All through lunch she was coaxing Berel for more drinks. Her confession to the lawyer that Peter got disgusted when she became pregnant and couldn't bear the sight of her.

We're considering buying a house on the beach near Jerry.

Chris Wood called today to say he finds "Mr. Lancaster" *ghostly*.

June 6. He called again today to say that he likes it a lot better on rereading. And Simon and Schuster like it well enough to offer a contract. So things look brighter, and now I must really get on with "Ambrose."

We have fallen out of love with the beach house and now may buy a house on Adelaide Drive.

Don in a bad state, yesterday and today. Well—that's something I think I'm learning to accept. I was really delighted when he decided at the last minute to spend the night in town. He decides at the last minute so I shan't be able to make any plans. Is he aware of this?

June 9. Don got fired from his job yesterday. They told him they were laying off all the "voucher holders" (I think they're called; anyhow, the temporary employees) for the summer. Don is terribly hurt, shaken in his confidence. So, after all, he thinks, he hasn't made the grade. Untrue as this may be, it's a serious setback—Don being what Don is.

Stravinskys came on Sunday. We had a very happy time together. Talk about Wystan—the sadistic antitheater side of him which occasionally appears in the plays. The covering of Baba's head with the tea cozy in *The Rake's Progress*, for instance. Igor is fascinated by fire. He comes out with me when I barbecue the steaks, and keeps up a commentary: "Etwas umdrehen. Wasser.[2] Here also. Oh, bravo!"

Yesterday saw an exhibition of neurotic laziness such as I haven't known since the worst days of *World in the Evening*. Today I have got to do at least six pages.

---

[1] Bandleader Ozzie Nelson, his wife Harriet, and their sons, Ricky (also a singer) and David, stars of the long-running family comedy, *Ozzie and Harriet*.
[2] "Something to turn. Water. . . ." as Isherwood cooked over the open flame.

David Abell is repairing the closet, repainting roof of shower, etc.

Marinette Andrews keeps bringing in prospective buyers for the house.

June 13. Here I am, having to squeeze in under the gate again. And in a rush because the Spenders are at Evelyn Hooker's, waiting for me to join them.

Don went through a very bad mood yesterday about losing his job. He's better today. On Tuesday last, on a sudden impulse, started writing a queer story. It is to be absolutely frank. I just want to see how near I could get to the nerve.

June 16. Triumph today, because Don took his drawings down to the office of the *California Stylist* magazine, and they were delighted with them and he is to do some work for them.

I wish we could sell our house. We go into escrow tomorrow, and we run a risk of being stuck with a huge debt if we can't. How I hate business! And how Marinette Andrews loves it! She waltzes in and out of this house as if she owned it, and there is much loud bold laughter with the lady clients—somewhat dikey.

This strange story of mine is writing itself—almost against my will. I've called it "Afterwards."

A card from George Manitzas, saying that Fräulein Thurau is dead. She died two years ago.

Bob Craft, says Vera Stravinsky, is so fat he couldn't get into his evening shirts[1] for the Rossignol concert, last night. That's a warning to me. I think I'm fatter than I have ever been.

June 17. Edward Upward writes that he likes "Mr. Lancaster" very much. His only criticisms are of the way I handle the Christopher of 1928—and those I agree with. But now I absolutely must go ahead with "Ambrose." I've been idling. Having so much material to work on is actually a handicap. And I still don't have an anecdote.

Doris Dowling at the Carousel, where we went after dinner with Gavin last night, was like a tourist visiting the Taos pueblo. She fraternized with the dancers. One of them had a lei and a derby hat. Doris put on the hat. And Salka (who always makes a bore of herself when other women are around, because she wants to show off) complained that the bars in Berlin were better. I pointed out that these people get pushed around by the police. She acted surprised. But just let anyone touch her Jews—!

---

[1] Craft always put on a fresh shirt during intermission when conducting.

June 18. When I saw Swami last night, as usual, he told me that [one of the monks] is seriously thinking of leaving Trabuco. While visiting his folks in Mexico City, he fell in love with the wife of [an] Indian [diplomat]. So that's why he was asking me about earning one's living as a writer. Swami says sadly that it's Mahamaya,[1] and he only hopes it'll pass.

Marvellous weather. In swimming yesterday and today. A big shark scare is on. Helicopters patrol the beach.

The escrow papers for 145 Adelaide Drive have arrived. But no sale for our house yet.

June 24. Well, we went into escrow yesterday. Still no buyer for this place.

Glorious weather, the sea filthy with weed and tar.

Last night I was drunk with Jim [Charlton] and we more or less got back to our old relationship, which was very nice. Don spent the night in town.

Lincoln Kirstein comes tomorrow. We're going to ask him to stay with us.

My left knee very painful.

The novel crawls.

June 30. Lincoln only left this morning because he couldn't get a plane.

His visit was nearly a disaster, because I was furious with him for refusing at the last moment to come with us to the Stravinskys', so I got mad and said exactly what I thought of the Gagaku[2]—in fact, said more than I thought. Because, deadly dull as it is, it still makes a sort of grave ritualistic impression which would be quite satisfactory if only it didn't go on so long.

However, the nasty taste of all this was removed yesterday by an amusing visit by Lincoln and me to Forest Lawn and the Brooks baths.

But no work done. And I feel guilty about that.

And how tiresome, people coming in to look around the house.

Lincoln seemed much less crazy, indeed quite relaxed, though he showed his usual violent resentments from time to time. He says that nearly all of his thinking is based on Auden's and that it is terribly hard for him to disagree with Auden about anything.

He quite coldly refused to give or attend a farewell party for the Gagaku.

Do I still like him? Oh yes. I rather love him.

[1] The mother of the universe; see Glossary.
[2] The dancers and musicians of the Japanese imperial household; Kirstein and Dag Hammarskjöld arranged for them to tour the U.S. in 1959.

July 1. A bad lazy day, because I haven't yet recovered from Lincoln. And I *must not* get up late!

Swami told me more, this evening, about [the monk who wants to leave]. He has actually had sex with this woman—the wife of the Indian [diplomat] in Mexico. She is older than he is, has grown-up [children]. She is from Malabar, where inheritance is matrilineal, and the women are immoral (says Swami). She and [he] can't possibly live in India together, so he would have to support her here. Swami hopes she won't be able to get a divorce from her husband, who already knows. Swami says no one at Trabuco knows. He will not tell them, in case the whole thing blows over, and [the monk] stays on there.

I said: "Swami, you aren't nearly as upset about this as you were about Sarada[1]—why? Don't you feel [this boy] has a real vocation?"

Swami: "I couldn't pray for him. I don't know why. I only said that the Lord must do his will. I prayed three whole nights for Sarada."

I said: "What about the other boys? Don't you feel that any of them has a real vocation?"

Swami: "No. Not yet. [This one] is a good boy. He loves me. But he is selfish. And he lets his parents influence him. They want to stop him from being a monk.

"Prema is good, but he isn't straight. If he doesn't like someone he tries in an underhanded way to get him out of the society."

Dr. Peschelt told me today that he wants to do $3,000 worth of work on my teeth!

Marinette Andrews talking to other real estate brokers: "Every house has its buyer…But I never sell an easy house. There are no easy houses."

July 5. A drunken and somewhat violent Fourth.

Coming back from a morning swim—without breakfast, which may account for my nervousness—I saw that Marinette had brought Madge MacDonald to the house. Madge was sitting up there with her dog. How I immediately saw it was: How dare Marinette pretend that Madge is a bona fide buyer, and how dare Madge pretend she is? So I ran up the stairs to the sundeck shouting: "Get that woman out of the house!"

This morning, Marinette explains that Madge was only there to describe the house to a doctor at UCLA hospital, and that Madge has helped her sell other houses to doctors, already. BUT Don heard Madge say: "Marinette has been persuading me to sell my house and buy this one." No—Marinette is not quite straight.

[1] Who also left Vedanta suddenly; see Glossary.

After a drunken red white and blue party at the Cottens', I went in swimming again and cut my elbow and hand.

Today we went to the Eames's studio in Venice, to see the film they will show in Moscow.[1] As Don said, you feel you are really in the presence of somebody—a dedicated person. What fun they have! Their lives seem so dedicated, inventive and innocent.

The marvellous contraption in which a falling marble plays a xylophone by the force of gravity.

The gravely smiling sly faces of grown-up play-children. They are actually grandparents!

July 8. Last two days, I've been sick—a wretched cold with fever and back pains. Struggled out last night to see the opening of Vernon Old's exhibition—quite a triumph for him. He is certainly far better than his colleagues, Shifrin and Totter. He looked very handsome and mature, talking to admiring girls.

Gerald (with whom we had supper first) seemed tired too. So it was dull. Don is depressed because the *California Stylist* is giving him the runaround. It is glorious but too hot, this weather. Septic for invalids. Read about Benedict Arnold this morning.

July 16. The weather is still very hot and the sea full of rocks. Not much fun swimming from dirty crowded State Beach. We keep hoping to sell the house, but don't. Now I'm scared, because Paul Millard has told Don it's greatly overpriced and we should hasten to settle for anything near thirty we can get.

Gerald Heard in great style at lunch yesterday, declaring that we don't understand the Red Chinese (Felix Greene says they're sweet, humane and witty) and that we grossly overestimate the evil effects of heroin, cocaine and opium. He also said that Aldous Huxley is probably dying of cancer. He is terribly thin, wasted and yellow. He just had a bad fall.

Yesterday morning, I went as witness to the court when Virginia Viertel applied for a divorce. Virginia had a nasty bump on the temple—I suppose from falling down when drunk. But the photographers shot quite a flattering picture of her. Peter is now free to marry Deborah Kerr as soon as the divorces become absolute.[2]

In the water on the beach above Trancas with Peter and Deborah

---

[1] The designer Charles Eames and his wife and collaborator, Ray Eames, made a multi-screen film about the history of man to show at the 1959 U.S. Exhibition in Moscow.

[2] Deborah Kerr was also obtaining a divorce.

last Sunday, we saw what seemed to be a shark. I was surprised what a lot of Lorca Peter knows.

I keep the novel and the Ramakrishna book going—also this strange story "Afterwards." I just go from step to step like a climber, not quite knowing where I'll arrive.

Don is away most of most days, at his studio,[1] drawing. On the whole, we get along very happily. I hope he is happy. At least he is fairly free—about as free as you can be and live with another person. I think of him with constant anxiety and love.

Just talked to Salka, who feels that Virginia made a terrible mistake in testifying that Peter told her he loved another woman. Because all the papers today assume that the other woman was Deborah, though as a matter of fact Peter didn't even know Deborah in 1952 when he left Virginia.

July 18. Yesterday, after two days' work with Gavin Lambert, I completed a really much superior version of *The Vacant Room.* Gavin is quite helpful, and good psychologically as a collaborator, though I can't say I feel he gets many ideas. He waits for me. Or is it that I insist on being the active partner? John van Druten always dried me up by doing that.

Am trying hard to lose weight.

Oh, how slowly I work! It's terrible—it crawls. Like wading in mud. The Ramakrishna book bores me to death, but that doesn't faze me so much; after all, it's an austerity. The Greek episode of my novel bores me—why? I'm not cutting deep enough into anything. As for my story, I'm somewhat stuck in that, too.

Still the house is not sold! Panic beginning, but Marinette continues to promise.

July 24. It appears that Aldous is recovering from his fall. This morning, on the telephone, he said how terribly obscurantist the professors at Santa Barbara were. When they talked about D. H. Lawrence, they used so much academic jargon, he couldn't understand them. "They feel they have to justify their existence by pretending that literature is a branch of science."

Igor, last night, seemed very depressed. He played solitaire in silence. Poor Bob can't straighten his arm, after *his* fall. Vera very fat.

I'm trying to kid myself that the electric typewriter Carter Lodge has given me makes me actually able to write more. I *have* managed to finish chapter five of the Ramakrishna book in record time. Now for the novel.

[1] Loaned by Paul Millard; see Glossary under Millard.

Dick Foote keeps saying of himself: "I'm very outgoing." They were here to talk to Jo and Ben about Tahiti.

July 26. Failed again to keep up my diary minimum.

The hot weather continues. I can scarcely remember any other kind. But I *am* getting on with work. A couple of days ago, I finished chapter five of the Ramakrishna book. Now I'm hurrying ahead to finish my queer story.

A hot foggy day on the beach. We went to the beach house Doris Dowling has borrowed. A dreary traffic jam both ways. The utter squalor of beach life—angling fathers, cooking mothers, children, dogs.

No sale on house.

July 30. After fury at Marinette's evasions, and other violent but unimportant emotions, we went into escrow with Mrs. Perls this morning. So the house is sold, barring accidents.

Yesterday I went down to Laguna, to see Swamis Prabhavananda and Vandanananda and drove home with [the monk who wants to marry]. He told me the whole story of his love affair with this Indian woman, and his resolve to leave Trabuco.

The chief thing which struck me is [his] basic indifference. His attitude is: "If the Lord doesn't want me to do this, He'll stop it." And I really feel this is sincere. Yet, at the same time, it appears as a kind of emotional lameness in him. It makes you wonder—does he *really* care for the woman *or* for being a swami?

He keeps repeating: "I know this life is nothing. I'm ready to die any time."

He claims this has nothing to do with mere sex urge. This is a relationship with a particular person.

He says Swami said: "I'd like to poison her!"

He's quite aware that his leaving will be an awful blow to the boys. But he has something of the cynical selfishness of an old soldier. He's sorry for the green recruits, but they must stand their chances.

He's often seen how Swami couldn't sleep all night, and prayed and shed tears because somebody was leaving. Now he feels that Swami should do the same for *him*.

There's also a lot of arrogance in him. He says in effect: whatever kind of life I have to lead, I can take it.

August 1. Peter Viertel was in, the day before yesterday, bringing me part of his novel.[1] He talked of the rivalry between Domínguín and

---

[1] Probably *Love Lies Bleeding* (1964), about an aging torero.

Ordóñez. He said, "One of them's going to end in hospital." And that very same day the news came that Dominguín has been gored.[1]

Yesterday I finished this queer story "Afterwards." Is it sheer pornographic sentimentalism? It seems to me to have some emotion. It was certainly a strange experience, writing it.

Don Murray clowning last night at his surprise birthday party. He put on the tennis shorts he'd been given, over his pants. "The revolution is about to break out!" The guests eyed him coldly.

August 7. Since last Monday, the 3rd, we have been involved in a mad scheme to go to Europe, see Maugham and M. and Laughton's *Lear* and Olivier's *Coriolanus*, and come back via a visit to Truman Capote on Clark's Island, Massachusetts. Of course, I don't really *want* to go—the rat race will be fantastic—but it seems like we're going.

Talk at Claude Short's[2] with Bob Schubert, the dancer–cashier who had a nervous breakdown when he didn't get a contract at Fox.

I have done a huge amount of work lately. The "fantasy" version of *Down There On a Visit* is now ready revised for Stephen, and I've nearly written the rough draft of chapter six.

Don is delighted with "Afterwards."

August 14. Well, the trip seems pretty much set. I wish it were over, but I'll enjoy it, I guess.

[The monk who fell in love with the wife of the Indian diplomat] is now ready to leave.

Joan Elan is said to be pregnant, by Ivan Moffat.

In one objective—in some ways, the most important one, I've failed. Haven't finished even a rough draft of "Ambrose." Don't know why I have such a block.

Gavin Lambert is enthusiastic over "Afterwards."

September 2. How often I've meant to write in this book before today! Now a lot is forgotten. Some of it no doubt just as well. But at least this is being a memorable trip.

We flew to New York the night of August 18–19 by jet. Very calm flight, with none of the expected horrifying noise on landing. But New York was just awful—a heat like Singapore. I must never again unnecessarily expose myself to great heat. It turns me into a miserable

[1] Luis Miguel Dominguín and Antonio Ordóñez (married to Dominguín's sister) were each gored twice that summer and recovered; Hemingway—who had modelled "Pedro Romero" in *The Sun Also Rises* on Ordóñez's father Cayetano, "Niño de la Palma," and who was close to Antonio—described the rivalry in "The Dangerous Summer" (*Life*, September 1960).
[2] A car dealer.

petulant invalid. Don and I clashed bitterly and sulked and hated each other. One thing I must say about him—because I would have said it at the time if I had written in this book—he has an absolutely female obstinacy coupled with an inertia about making decisions. Having let me agree to go to see Lincoln in the country—and be bored pissless by a terrible performance of *All's Well That Ends Well* at Stratford, Connecticut—he tried every which way to get me to call it off, with an idiotic lie we would certainly have been caught out in. Yesterday he went ahead and bought all the theater tickets against our return to London, although this made us too late to see about our return flight from Nice. (Annoyingly enough, we didn't miss our bus to the airport because it was later than we'd been told; and Alan Searle was able to fix our reservations over the phone in a couple of minutes. So I was made to seem like a fusspot, and Don's confidence that he will always muddle through was triumphantly vindicated!) We had another quarrel at Stratford,[1] during and after which Don declared that we both hate each other a little bit and are in constant competition. But right now all is love, and I don't mean that ironically. It really is. Nothing has been really damaged between us. It's just that we're both intensely selfish, and bad travellers.

We crossed to London on August 23–24, spent one night with John Lehmann, then up to Wyberslegh.

John, more bloated, red faced and silver haired than ever, is in a good mood. He really likes "Mr. Lancaster." (Rereading the proofs, I like it much less than I thought I did.) And he has decided that I'm in the process of making a comeback.

The visit to Wyberslegh was truly shocking. Not on M.'s account. She really does seem to have recovered largely from the stroke. The worst that has happened is that she has lost the sight of one eye, but the other is perfectly all right. She has a remarkably strong grip in her hand, even though the arm is still slightly paralyzed. And her speech is sometimes a bit indistinct; that's all. But Richard looks terrible—he has a wild look of dismayed despair which I have never seen before, also he has lost more teeth and is dirtier than ever, and unshaved, with greyish stubble. Both he and M. smell bad—M.'s urine leaks out of her.

And the house! Black sooty cobwebs everywhere. The walls cracked. The wallpaper hanging in tatters. The carpets stiff with greasy grime. The kitchen and scullery so dirty that you didn't dare look at them. We had one meal—supper on the first night—fixed by Richard. There were sickeningly fatty chops warmed up, and I could smell them on the sheets when we went to bed. As for the larder—

[1] Stratford-upon-Avon, England.

well, it is also the coal cellar; and its two functions are becoming less and less distinguishable.

Saying goodbye to M.—probably for the last time—didn't bother me much, because of course I won't admit it's the last time. I know I shall mind when she dies—more than I can now imagine.

One very good thing about this horrible and distressing visit was that we took a marvellous drive through the Peak District—Glossop, the Snake [Pass], Castleton, Miller's Dale, Buxton; and the weather was perfect. It was like that sinister summer passage in *Wuthering Heights*, when they go up to Penistone Crag and it is so lovely, but the shadow of the oncoming winter and death is over everything.

On the 28th, we went to Stratford and stayed with Laughton. His *Lear* wasn't so good as the performances he gave in Hollywood, but still I cried twice; it was wonderful on the heath, with the Fool clinging to his enormous skirts, and wonderful at the "Never, never, never, never" end. Olivier as Coriolanus was witty and somehow Jewish, but I do like him. Charles is a megalomaniac. He quite seriously believes that he is more of a success than Larry. He has fantastic dreams of masseurs. He imagines he is too famous to go into bars—even in Hamburg. I am fond of him, though. I do like monsters. Charles says he is a monster. And that I am one, too.

Stephen was very sweet to us in London, as always—though Don still suspects him. A ghastly cocktail party at which Sonia (ex-Orwell) Pitt-Rivers[1] debated logical positivism with Colin Wilson—who is a doll, but a dumb doll. The Australian boyfriend of Sandy Wilson[2] struck Sonia's hand and said, "What does that prove?" And Sonia said, "It proves I've been struck by a drunken little queer." So fuck her—though I must admit he was hard to take.

William Plomer like the Rock of Gilbraltar, as always—if the Rock of Gilbraltar were also adorable.

Stephen, poor dear, reading aloud the letter from Pasternak, in an effort to stop the discussion. It was absolutely incomprehensible; and everyone said, "How marvellous."[3]

Since yesterday, we are here, at the Villa Mauresque, with darling Willie [Maugham] and Alan [Searle]. More of that tomorrow.

September 3. What a bad bogus painter Marie Laurencin is! Two of her pictures are in this bedroom. It is luxurious, almost more so because the luxury is rather old-fashioned; the toilet seat is quite

---

[1] The widow of George Orwell, remarried to Michael Pitt-Rivers.

[2] British composer and lyricist.

[3] Evidently sent to Spender in his role as literary editor of the essentially anti-communist magazine *Encounter*; see Glossary under Pasternak.

crudely made and hurts your ass. I have shooting nerve pains in my shin, knee, thigh and groin. They have been bad for several days, now.

Last night we sat up drinking and talking to Alan. He is worried because Willie's memory is going. But Willie seems well. He can still walk. We went through the rue Obscure down in Villefranche harbor. Alan says he [Willie] is writing autobiography—about his marriage, etc.

Willie is rather deaf, and shouting at him is an effort. He reads a great deal, and is full of interest in new writers.

He says of the drawing-room carpet: "It's the only thing in the house which I actually know to be stolen."

Typical Willie remark: "Don, if you can persuade Christopher to come down, you'll be offered a cocktail."

The journalist, Cruzeman, who came to tea today buttering up Willie: "If I may say so, Sir," "If this doesn't sound like the most terrible flattery"... etc. Willie deliberately glanced at his watch, so Cruzeman should see him doing it and leave. He had come to find out if the rumor was true that Willie was writing a novel set in Venice. Willie said: "It's the most utter balls."

September 11. Back home since the day before yesterday.

I have this ache in my left testicle, not bad, a kind of bruised feeling. Dr. Lewis thinks it may be a kidney stone. I don't know. I can't help remembering that man Donald Ritchie[1] told us about, in Japan, who got sensitive testicles and then it was cancer.

The escrow postponed, thank God. So we have a breathing spell.

Don and I were both so scared on the jet flight home that we resolved never to fly again.

Very hot weather, but cool in comparison to New York.

What I liked on the trip:

Stratford, Villa Mauresque, *Roots*,[2] our visit to Gore's house on the Hudson, last evening in New York with Tom Hatcher. Yes—and that wonderful drive around the Peak [District].

September 13. Still the pain, neither more nor less. And still the heat—rather less. But on the beach it looks steamy with tropical clouds. Big thunderheads over the mountains.

Today I restarted "Ambrose." In my blindness, because I don't really know what I'm going to do with it. But the opening, about

---

[1] American writer on film and on Japan; Isherwood and Bachardy saw him in Tokyo in 1957.
[2] Arnold Wesker's 1959 play, seen at the Royal Court in London.

leaving Berlin with Waldemar, seems good and gives me a running start.

Even if there is no serious outcome of these ailments, I have a mountain of work ahead of me. The move. College. "Ambrose." Ramakrishna. And now maybe this Suzanne Valadon[1] film with Salka. *No!* From that I revolt. Yet I've promised to go with her and see the director tomorrow.

September 15. Frank Taylor is a compulsive idiot. Gavin and I had supper with him yesterday. His droolings over Marilyn Monroe, and some wonder-hack who for $3,500 rewrote for him the whole of *Peyton Place Revisited.* The Monroe–Miller film[2] sounds too corny for words. These men want to rape her in the desert and she looks up at the moon and says, "Help!" Gavin couldn't get any promise out of him for his *Vanity Fair* musical project. Meanwhile, Frank is dead set on taking Monroe up to the Positano Coffee House next Saturday night.

No word from the escrow about our house; or from Douglas Sirk[3] about the Valadon film.

Good progress in planning "Ambrose." I must get ahead with that now as the top priority.

Jack Lewis doesn't seem alarmed about my pains, so I won't be for a while—though they're just as bad today. But yesterday the hot weather let up and we have the proper glorious fall sunshine. In the water with Don today; it was quite warm.

Relations with Don very good since our return.

September 17. A cool beautiful day of sane autumn weather. We went in swimming. The ocean still warm.

I still have the pain on and off.

At work on "Ambrose."

No word from Sirk.

The money for Mrs. Perls's escrow is *said* to be coming tomorrow. We can't possibly move till next week now.

Swami leaves for India next Tuesday. *Thank God* I'm not going anyplace. All I ask is my health, for working. And some money—preferably *not* at the cost of writing a movie. But how else?

Don busy at school.

[1] French painter; see Glossary under Valadon.
[2] *The Misfits* (1960).
[3] Danish-born film and stage director.

September 18. This morning, Mr. Cabral[1] called me to say that if the escrow goes through on Tuesday or Wednesday next—as it now almost certainly will—then he's prepared to let us move into Adelaide Drive on Wednesday, September 30. Mrs. Perls is fit to be tied, but there's nothing she can do. It's her fault anyhow, for causing the delay.

Geller called to say that Douglas Sirk had told him Lana Turner doesn't want me for the Suzanne Valadon film, because of *Diane*. Maybe this is a big fat blessing in disguise. But I do want some money.

The pains quite bad today. I just have to wait and see how they develop.

A wonderful clear day of sunshine, but with black storm clouds all around the horizon, even out to sea. The water still warm. We went in swimming again.

Elsa Lanchester to supper last night. Not a success. Don had fixed shrimp jambalaya and Elsa immediately said she couldn't eat garlic and implied a reproof because I hadn't remembered this. She ignored Don, who got mad and washed the dishes while she was still here. She is an underdog herself, a slave—and, as I pointed out to Don—slaves are never very nice. Her venom against John Hayward, because he was jealous of T. S. Eliot's new wife.

To top it off, Don got mad at me for snoring and went upstairs. But today peace is restored. Now he's been rereading our play *The Monsters*. Says it's awful and an utter bore. I've only read one act. On that I agree with him. Whatever possessed us to write this crap?

September 25. I started at L.A. State last Tuesday. Two classes that day, and another yesterday. It's fun, but I feel dissatisfied with myself. I feel the courses lack direction. In my evening class there is a nun, who sat prune faced while another student asked what I thought of *Lolita*. I said: "I don't like it because I don't feel the hero really likes little girls. I feel it's all an affectation. In my opinion, lust should be taken seriously."

The pains have been much less, these last few days.

Wonderful weather. The beach deserted. We were in swimming again yesterday. We both have suntans, and my weight has dropped to about 147. Steady work on "Ambrose" and on the revision and typing of "Afterwards."

Perfect harmony and happiness with Don.

Now at last it seems settled that we're to move on September 30, next Wednesday. Escrow is closed. We only got $1,235 out of the deal. This means we have only about $4,600 altogether. But there will

[1] The previous owner of 145 Adelaide Drive.

be my earning from State College. And there is the Simon and Schuster money to fall back on.

Marilyn Monroe said to Khrushchev: "I hope we can be friends." She told me this at a party Frank Taylor gave for her, on the 19th. The next day, Jo and Ben Masselink flew to Chicago and New York. And Swami and the five sannyas girls took off for Tokyo on the 22nd, en route for India.

Last night, Don and I had supper with Gerald Heard and Michael. Gerald looked marvellously well. He held forth on the usual themes—mostly to Don. "You are an iceberg, of which Don Bachardy is only the part above the surface. This submerged part— that never dies. You are its experiment. Its novel written in protoplasm. For some reason of its own, it has chosen to project you, like an instrument, into space-time. When the experiment has been completed, it will withdraw you." His usual bitching of me: "One can always tell the people who are afraid of death—they react badly to nitrous oxide." I think he was annoyed because I had referred to lysergic acid as "a drug"; he describes it as a sacrament. If you partake of a sacrament with the right attitude, in the right frame of mind, you get something out of it.

September 26. [The monk who wanted to marry] *is* going to Mexico, but he quite frankly admits that he is considering ditching this woman. He talks about it with curious cold-bloodedness. Swami's view is, why not have an affair with her, leave her and go to India and be a monk again. [The boy's] place is open for him, as long as he doesn't get married. But if he returns, he'll go to India, not back to Trabuco.

Doris Dowling, Len Kaufman and Gavin to supper last night. I like Len. He's already as good as married to Doris and he accepts us as family friends. He even tried to get Don a job, and has a scheme for getting me a TV program. But when I suggested that Russia's treatment of homosexuals was a valid reason for not being a communist, he was sincerely amazed. So I pointed out that Russia is also anti–Semitic. *Then* he got the point.

September 28. Pains bad yesterday and again today—brought on maybe by heavy drinking at the Richard Burtons'. I do like them. There was a stolid bucolic brother and his wife.[1] You felt the relationship between the brothers was very good; no condescension and no criticism.

Gladys Cooper[2] had never heard of either Edward Thomas or

---

[1] Ivor and Gwen Burton.
[2] English actress.

Edmund Blunden. The subject came up because I am about to discuss them with my class, and Richard said he had read selections from Thomas, and I asked him which he had chosen and he said he'd be glad to read for the class—but this proved impossible because he is filming all day.

Last night I went to Elsa Lanchester's. Oh the horror of TV! It is so utterly utterly *inferior*, yet just enough to keep you enslaved, entrapped, on the lower levels of consciousness—for a whole lifetime, if necessary. It is a bondage like that of Tennyson's Lady of Shallot.

October 2. The day before yesterday we moved here—to 145 Adelaide Drive. We are both still in the first delight of being here. Principally, it's the view—being able to see the sky and the hills and the ocean. We can see the hills from our bed. Don is so delighted, it warms my heart. But this is a real house, a long in-and-out place of many rooms and half-rooms, passageways and alcoves. And, in spite of the power pole and power lines and TV aerials, there really is a hillside privacy and snugness—something that suggests a run-down villa above Positano.

Pains bad on moving day. I think I must cut out drinking. I worry about the pain, and then don't. But it's always there.

Usual moving-day shocks. The bill was $142, when we'd had an estimate of $81. (But there will be some refund.) Don's traveler's checks got lost; but I found them this morning in his wastebasket with the rope lion Marguerite gave us.

October 4. Pains bad yesterday, perhaps a little better today. It is hard to tell if anything specific brings them on. I vaguely resolve to tell Jack Lewis if they don't stop soon.

Tonight Don has gone into town to spend the night.

Today (as yesterday) we went in swimming. While we were in the water, I asked him if he foresaw any big change in our future relations. "Oh no," he said. "At least, I feel that it's up to me now to do the adjusting to Dobbin. I think I've become much more mature about all that. I see now that I was wrong, a lot of the time, when I blamed Dobbin for things. He's really quite first-rate."

That miserable Coleman from the van company never came back to put the bookcases together. Or even called. So this evening I've had nothing to do but read. (I *could* have restarted "Afterwards.")

11 p.m. Carter Lodge and Dick Foote have finished supper on Tahiti. Tennessee and Lincoln are having five o'clock tea tomorrow

afternoon. Swami is getting ready for lunch tomorrow in Calcutta. Stephen is probably still asleep but getting ready to wake up, for tomorrow's breakfast.

October 9. Pains off and on. I minimized them to Jack Lewis when asking him if I could conscientiously say I was in perfect health for the new screen writers' insurance application. "You *are*, you know," Jack said firmly; and I realized he thinks me a hypochondriac. Well, let him.

The heartrending squalor of Fred Shroyer's home, where he took me yesterday. And yet he has made this marvellously snug womblike library in the garage, with stacks to the ceiling. I do like him. And I respect him greatly for collecting science fiction. But oh, the horror of those sad brown dusty hills covered with "homes" and telephone poles!

As for this house, it continues to be a joy. How marvellous it is to see the sky. And the silver light on the water. Don seems very happy—all is well between us.

Restarted "Ambrose" today. Now I have to pull myself together and get ahead with all the projects.

October 14. Don has been having what I cannot help thinking of as a relapse. I mean—I know I hurt his feelings because (in my irritation because he was nagging at me to agree to spend hundreds of dollars immediately on the house) I said, "In that case you'll have to get a job." But the fact is that his reaction was still utterly hysterical. But god how cunningly it camouflages itself! Next day, yesterday, he makes me a speech about how I am taking away his identity. And— concealed threat—he doesn't feel resentful when he's with *any of his other friends*.

Well, I know I *am* far from guiltless. It is perfectly true that I want him to be sweet and pleasant so I can get on with my work unworried.

Is that so sinister? Doesn't he demand the same?

Most of the time, I'm ready to go three quarters of the way to meet him. Tonight I'm a bit worried about my pains again.

But today was so beautiful. I cycled down to the beach and swam, and met Marguerite and Rory [Harrity].

Tonight I've been revising "Afterwards"—nearly finished; and reading up about the Spanish Civil War for my class tomorrow.

Today Shroyer called to ask me officially if I would like to teach again next semester. I'm not sure. But I'm pleased to be asked.

October 20. New worries: did I send "Afterwards" off properly this morning? Won't they open it, and prosecute me?

Are the income tax people going to charge me for overestimating my expenses? (As a matter of fact, that was Freedman's fault.)

John Lehmann writes from England that people are "in raptures" over "Mr. Lancaster."

Dick Foote has had notepaper printed: "Dick Foote. Tahiti." Jo and Ben showed me some.

Don made another scene, Sunday night. All well now.

The house is horrible, stripped bare, with the staring uncovered windows at night, and the stink of paint.

I am so tired. The pain just sits there. Oh I am weary. All I want is to be made snug, and to sleep, sleep, sleep.

October 21. Today I restarted "Ambrose." I now have a fairly clear story line to the end. Don, who is in school all day, called for news and was mad at me because I'd let them bring the sofa (which has just been recovered) back. It *was* stupid, admittedly; but I rather hate him when he screams.

Pains today. Coffee brings them on.

Got the car washed, badly.

Don wants to have the beams taken out of the living room ceiling. I don't. But I feel that this must be his decision.

Still worried about income tax, and the safety of the copy of "Afterwards" I sent to John Lehmann.

No idea what I'll talk about tomorrow in class.

October 24. Foggy, but it cleared a little and I went on the beach. Marguerite and Rory were there. He still makes love to her a lot. He expects his screen test at Columbia the end of next week. They had seen me on TV last night. I was good, I guess; but I have to stop this ingenue–oldboyish act which is inseparable from appearances with Levant.

Pains very bad yesterday. Middling bad today.

Reading *Goodbye to All That*[1] for class.

Bad sloth. I must force myself to do a little of "Ambrose." I just took a hot bath to settle the pain. But I can feel it.

Must pay at least $250 income tax penalty, Freedman says.

October 30. A terrific wind. Big sandstorm on the beach. We feel the wind strongly, up here; but it's enjoyable and exciting.

[1] By Robert Graves.

The pains have let up a lot, the past two days. It's only provoked by coffee drinking.

But now there are money worries. We're rushing into big expense on the house. Taking out the beams in the roof. Tom Calhoun and Red Tully are doing that right now. It's so exciting that I can't settle to work on "Ambrose."

I just called Fred Shroyer and told him I'll teach for another semester. So at least we'll have *some* money.

This afternoon I'll devote to letters, accounts, etc.

4:20. Red and the others have gone. Two beams are out, without too much mess.

October 31. The rest of the beams are out. Tonight, Tom, Red and Joe borrowed twenty dollars from me. They are hard up and scared, because Tom Calhoun's wife is divorcing him and he's afraid she may seize all the money in his account.

Meanwhile, the beams are out—all of them.

Prema came by and looked at everything with an air of faint disapproval. It is all worldly. But he accepted a gin and tonic.

Walked in the park with Gavin, planning a foreword to *The Vacant Room*, for the benefit of producers who don't know what possession is. Gavin thinks there are prospects for it. And Peter Kortner at CBS is interested in Elsa Lanchester as Emily Ermingarde.

Don has a small job, drawing hats for Charles LeMaire.[1]

Am working on Cyril Connolly's *Enemies of Promise* for my class. I feel a sincere dissatisfaction with my teaching. So much of it is treading water. I don't communicate anything solid. But I hope to be better next time.

November 4. Cold, grey weather; but beautiful. The tiles are reset in the living room floor. Soon we can start to paint.

The poignant happiness of being with Don—all the greater because he's out so much. He talks of making a studio downstairs. He is getting bored with Paul Millard's frequent interruptions.

David Hatmaker, one of my students, is quite a talented poet. He [tells of going to some wild parties].

My pains have almost entirely stopped for nearly a week, now. Am very happy about this.

November 7. Burning hot weather. So dry that the leaves of the calendar curl and the corner of my blotter turns up on my desk. This

---

[1] Costume designer.

morning, the sea like a Dufy painting was blue and flat and dotted with toy boats.

Don having a crisis because he hates the hackwork of faking heads to wear LeMaire's cap designs. And yet he longs to make money, to help out with our expenses. He says he's getting old, etc. I tell him to rejoice that he has talent and a vocation—how many young men have either? Now he feels better and resolves—after a talk with Marguerite and Rory on the beach—to get together a portfolio of drawings of famous people. Something which could be sold to *Vogue*.

The sorrows of Prema. Should he have spoken crossly to one of the girls because she hadn't done the household accounts? She wept, and he knew this was just a bitch trick, and yet he felt guilty. And mad John [Schenkel] left the monastery and then begged to be taken back. Mark[1] is afraid of him—because Mark once sat down in John's chair, and John trembled all over and hissed: "Don't you *ever* do that again!"

November 9. Still very hot. I lay on the beach reading Lionel Trilling's book on Forster,[2] for my next class. Amazing what these critics see! I realize, once again, how superficial, lazy and altogether fifth-rate that part of my intelligence is.

Just finished Lehmann's *I Am My Brother*, which is worthy and well documented and liberal and almost noble and a big fat bore. John is a bore because he's so fucking grand. Rather like van Druten, he watches himself with the greatest respect, to see what he'll do next—but alas no humor.

Jimmy Daugherty came to breakfast yesterday and told us that we look so much alike, now. Jimmy is really quite sweet and lovable—the nicest kind of colored girl. I can see him absolutely enveloping some[one] in domestic bliss. So many people one sees—going around absolutely loaded with potential love.

I am very lucky. So I must *remember* to be very happy. So often it's a question of remembering.

Funny old thing, glimpsed today in the barber's mirror—with a neck turning scraggy unless pulled tight, and eye bags. But still potentially useful and capable of being used, if only the old silly doesn't waste its few precious years in resentments, tantrums, cantankerousness. I really *must* try to keep it in better order. And not let it drink too much.

Have restarted japam as of yesterday—the anniversary of my initiation—the nineteenth.

---

[1] John Markovitz, a monk at Trabuco and later a swami.
[2] *E. M. Forster* (1943).

November 11. A bad day—depressed and upset. I have stuck in "Ambrose." And we have spent far more than we can afford. And I have toothache.

I feel that "Ambrose" just isn't right. The anecdote isn't quite interesting enough, perhaps. Or is it too slight? Or what *is* the matter? And I *am* worried about money. When we get through, we shall be down to about a thousand dollars, which makes me really nervous. We haven't sunk that low in a long while. I can't help worrying and feeling insecure.

Reading *After Many a Summer*[1] for class. It is *so* dry and prissy. I know how my students' stomachs will be turned by it.

November 16. Lunch with Aldous up at his house, alone. He is very thin with a kind of benevolent falcon face; but he seems well.

Says he's far along with his utopia book; about an island between Ceylon and Sumatra, where life is sane.[2] He will get it finished after he stops teaching at Santa Barbara.

He does definitely believe that mescaline produces spiritual experiences.

His dream about Denny Fouts. He saw Denny naked, on a horse. Riding along a precipice road, bounded by a cliff. There was a door in the cliff, into a cave. The horse threw Denny and he banged through the door and fell into the cave. He was very badly hurt. One of his legs twitched uncontrollably. He crawled back out of the cave on to the road and collapsed. Aldous was bending over him with extreme concern and compassion; then Aldous woke.

Aldous still uses the Bates method.[3]

Says the Kiskaddens are both miserable. Bill has insisted on sending little Bull away to school in the East. Spite against Peggy?

November 21. Two heroes—Edward Chappel, the polio-crippled vaudeville star I went to see two days ago. His bland determination to become a writer—a commercial one, however; mainly for TV. He is quite stupid but nevertheless admirable. And Francesca Macklem (Jill) who is Fred Shroyer's secretary, a dynamo of energy and enthusiasm, married and a would be novelist, who carries nitro-glycerine tablets around with her because she has already had several bad heart attacks and expects a fatal one.

Today I sketched an outline of a Sleeping Beauty film for Lincoln

---

[1] By Aldous Huxley.
[2] *Island* (1962).
[3] Exercises to relieve strain, re-educate the eye and improve defective sight; developed by the New York oculist W. H. Bates early this century.

Kirstein. He won't take it, though. He's committed to Balanchine and the New York City Ballet.

I really have been quite creative, lately. There's "Afterwards." And in these past two weeks, the Sleeping Beauty idea. And an idea I gave Edward Chappel for a serial—he didn't understand it, though. An idea I gave a man named Stoloff for a TV serial for Rory Harrity. And a completely new idea for Emily Ermingarde I had yesterday—to turn her into a detective.

Why can't I make money?

Also, today, Don read the draft of "Ambrose" and was most encouraging about it. So my enthusiasm's renewed. I must get ahead with that, now.

November 25. How bad it is to putter! All day and evening long I have been home alone—and what have I done?

Restarted "Ambrose." Good—but only five pages.

Clipped the pages of the magazine, in preparation for making a "book" out of the printed Ramakrishna chapters.

Read some of *The Sun Also Rises* for our TV program.[1]

Puttered around the market.

Made a list of the fuses and the lights they control.

Gossiped on the phone.

And now my thumb hurts—to stop me writing more.

November 26. A dream last night:

Don and I were leaving on a journey. Our hosts (presumably) were seeing us off. I said to them, "One of my mottoes in life is: Always visit the outlying islands. It's amazing, the people you find living there. And the others always try to discourage you from going. They say: There's nothing on it but sheep."

The feel of this dream wasn't good. I was too pleased with myself. I was showing off. Because the truth was, I knew that I *hadn't* visited the outlying islands. Or only very seldom.

Again and again I find this about dreams: one can analyze them psychologically right along, as they unroll. In the action of real life you can seldom do that.

You watch yourself, in dreams, much more consciously.

December 4. Must scold myself again.

Not nearly enough progress with "Ambrose"—though I feel much more confident I'll finish it now.

---

[1] Isherwood was to appear December 3 with Fred Shroyer on a half-hour show about Hemingway's novel.

Yesterday I started to get drunk at the Duquettes' studio—converted into a super fairy palace for Christmas. There was a party for Pat Delpesh, Leonard Stanley's sister, over from the [Hawaiian] Islands. Pat looked frumpish and ill humored. I talked to a man named Charles de Finis[1], who was about to settle on a ranch near Taos with a boyfriend and a girl. He asked me if I believed in luck. No, I said, because I'm a Hindu. We must have a long talk, he said; come and stay with us. Then Rory began talking about Jo and Ben, and how *he* would slap a woman's face if she ordered him around the way Jo does Ben. This annoyed Don, who told Rory he was quite wrong—Ben really runs things.

Don had to go to school, so I went to supper with Marguerite and Rory. Ivan Moffat was there, and homely Nicola Lubitsch.[2] Ivan seemed dull—dulled by his dull trade. He did the usual imitations—including one of me, which I pretended to find brilliantly amusing but didn't. Got very very drunk. Came home. Passed out. Snored. How I drove is a mystery. Yet I even remembered to bring down the groceries and put them in the icebox.

This kind of behavior is boring and unfunny.

A peach-colored fog-sunset, with a silver contrail above it. Don is waxing the tiled floor for the second time. It looks marvellous.

Dissatisfied with myself on the TV show, but that was partly Fred Shroyer's fault. He is such a bore, so soft-spoken and prudent. He strikes no sparks from you.

December 5. Strong dry wind. Swept up the leaves on the terrace, watered, vacuumed. But all this really to avoid getting on with "Ambrose"—of which today I did only a page. WHY? I reread it today, and really it isn't bad and only the end needs serious fixing. So why shouldn't I hurry ahead?

As the result of putting my name on the letter to the court in favor of Caryl Chessman, I received today one letter praising me from an importer of Italian wood carvings named Max Hart, and one anonymous postcard sent from Val Yermo, California, as follows: "I bet you would hum a different tune if your friend Chessman were to attach (sic) your sister, daughter, wife or mother. Why should he get this consideration, the beast."[3]

---

[1] Not his real name.
[2] Daughter of the film director Ernst Lubitsch.
[3] Isherwood, Huxley and others requested clemency for the alleged child molester and murderer whose conviction was surrounded by doubt, but Chessman went to the gas chamber in May 1960.

December 11. Well, the holiday season is sort of starting. Today we got invited to the preview of *On the Beach*,[1] with supper at the Escoffier Room of the Beverly Hilton first. And Charles and Elsa Laughton came by to see the house, which is still inside out, because Don is painting the dining room floor. Elsa is like a detective; she putters around, tapping walls and discovering apparently useless ventilators and wanting to know *why*.

December 12. Christmas crowds in Santa Monica. The big bright-colored bogus tinny decorations slung across the streets in the hot sunshine. The ocean marvellous. But I am dull. There is a real danger that I shall sink into a drab ugly interior life of sex fantasies and absurd grotesque resentments—and this *in spite* of all I have and know and am. My underside is increasingly sordid. That's why this journal gets duller and duller. I force myself to write it, because it somehow keeps a door open between myself and me. The moment this wretched book is full up, I shall switch to typewriting and stop torturing my poor old thumb.

How I waste time!

I suppose, if I could see myself objectively, I should *marvel* that anyone could maintain a relationship like the one between myself and Don and yet be, much of the time, a drab self-regarding character like a miser in Dickens.

My life, even now, could be so marvellous. My health isn't bad. I have my work, my interests, my books. I am capable of being quite useful to a lot of other people. I have the immeasurable blessings of Swami and Don—not to mention all the others. I live in one of the most beautiful houses in Los Angeles.

Well—it's the old story. I have made less use of my life than any one I know—considering what opportunities I've had. No—that's going too far. But I *have* been shockingly lazy, dull, depressive.

Come on—a new effort.

December 18. I can't forget last night's preview of *On the Beach*—chiefly because the picture was so unsatisfactory it set me wanting to rewrite it entirely.

Marlon Brando in the limousine on the way to the preview telling Tennessee and me we were whores because we'd appeared on TV. He refused his autograph to Ted Bachardy, saying he only gave it to children.

At the Fishers' bungalow with Ten today. The moppets just arrived by plane from New York. Eddie furious because the little

[1] The nuclear holocaust film based on Nevil Shute's novel; Tennessee Williams invited them.

Todd girl[1] called him "Mr. Fisher." (So Jewish, she looks like a tiny Assyrian bull.) The dealer coming in with a coat of Russian sable. $11,000. He would do anything for Elizabeth Taylor, he said; it was just a matter of her pleasure. But when she suggested paying in two years, he at once refused. She may rent it to the studio for her new picture, *Butterfield 8*, and get it that way.

Tennessee in the pool, swimming back and forth very slowly, like a channel swimmer. His firm powerful little potbelly.

December 21. The winter solstice—or is it tomorrow? Anyhow, the season for serious resolves. As always not to worry so much. We are very low on money, according to our standards. But in fact we have about $3,000 left. And there will be the L.A. State College check coming in until the end of August—that's about $5,500 right there, after tax deductions. Meanwhile, I'll just have to hustle and earn more. There is still the Simon and Schuster money intact, to be dipped into.

Rain last night. Jo and Ben came in with lobsters Tom Calhoun had caught and given them. We ate them barbecued. The fire worked all right, despite the rain. The lobsters kept twitching on the grill—a nasty sight.

Today the Sunbeam's brakes gave out on the garage ramp and the car rushed down, smashed into the Simca, broke one of its back lights and banged it into one of the bicycles, breaking the front wheel. Don jumped out of the car screaming with rage—completely out of control. He does his best, but his nerves are very bad. He's so upset because he can't get a job or sell his work or get any recognition. He is afraid of getting a job, of course. He just wants the money to fall into his mouth. So do I.

An omen for the solstice? The log, which we tried unsuccessfully to kindle all yesterday evening, has begun to smoke and is now slowly burning itself away.

[A] neighbor [. . .] came and introduced himself as I was collecting beer cans from our upper lot. He is married, has kids, is queer I think.

The humane (why) police department came and collected the dead possum in a carton which somebody left on us, wrapped in papers.

---

[1] Elizabeth Taylor's daughter with her third husband, Broadway impresario Michael Todd.

December 23. Yesterday I went with Steve Black[1] to visit [one of my students], who is in Brentwood Hospital after a breakdown. [He] was no longer wearing his hairpiece—he'd always worn it at college and I'd never noticed. We walked about the grounds, watched a man with several lines of writing tattooed on his arm, playing golf with a nurse. "He's our only murderer," [my student] told us. He likes being in the hospital. He has a friend who thinks he is a devil and can put out stars, seven at a time. The police have a Mo-machine (opposite of Om), which catches devils and liquidates them. "So the police are angels?" I asked. A man went by muttering: "Fakes, fakes—all of them!"

Steve Black is pretty humorless, but I like him. He is sternly critical of Fred Shroyer—says Fred takes no trouble preparing his lectures, makes jokes about the weather, evades awkward questions. But I liked his description of how he argued all evening about Joyce with his friend Gene; then challenged him to a chinning contest. Gene won, thirteen to eleven.

Saw Gerald in the evening, full of a lecture by Maxwell Jones.[1] Jones is in favor of out-patient treatment for many mental cases. "The one weapon you have is talk. So long as they talk they don't act."

Don seems very nervous and low. Christmas rattles him terribly.

December 27. Am upset tonight because Bill Caskey called a few hours ago and wanted the two of us to have supper alone together. And I said no—it was no good our meeting any more, because we only fight when we do. Caskey acted very hurt, and I felt like a heel; and yet I know I am right and it is just silly for us to kid ourselves we'll behave. We won't. Or not for another ten years at least. Caskey simply does not realize how jealous he is of Don.

Relations with Don are quite good and he feels better now, I think. But I don't feel like writing about that, just now. Too depressed.

December 31. A cold staring-bright day with high wind. A rush day, as they all are nowadays—for which I ought to be thankful. Today I've:

Taken Tom Wright's car back to him.

Walked home—my only exercise.

Done two pages of the Ramakrishna book.

Put a new calendar in the container.

Had a three-quarter hour conversation with Fred Shroyer (speaking on the State of California's money from college) about [John] O'Hara, Van Vechten, etc. He says, "One of the happiest events of the year was getting to know you." What was *I* to say?

[1] A student at L.A. State College.
[2] Psychiatrist, pioneered the open ward system in English mental hospitals.

Now I'm hastily cooking—heating up the last of the stew for lunch—at 3:05!

I still have to shave and wash, write three pages of "Ambrose" and a letter to Tennessee Williams, thanking for the fern he gave us. Don is at the studio, painting. He restarted painting this week.

At six, Hal Greene and Dick Lee for drinks. Gavin to supper. An evening at Jerry Lawrence's.

No time for any New Year's resolution except GET ON WITH IT—FASTER!

Here are some of the chief events of 1959:

January 19.	We finished our play *The Monsters* and sent it to Dodie and Alec.
January 29.	We went to New York.
February 16.	Returned home.
February 19.	Got the offer to teach at L.A. State.
February 21–24.	Spenders stayed with us.
March 10.	Rory and Marguerite got married.
March 17.	Started writing "Mr. Lancaster."
March 19.	The party at Olivier's.
March 21–23.	We went to Taliesin West with Jo and Ben.
April 5–7.	Stephen visited.
April 13.	Finished "Mr. Lancaster."
April 18–23.	Trip to New York alone to see Auden about *Sally Bowles.*
May 1.	Started "Ambrose."
May 4.	Don started work at May Co.
May 9.	Stephen to stay.
May 11.	Stephen left.
June 9.	Don laid off at May Co. Started "Afterwards."
June 16.	Don got work on *California Stylist.*
June 25–30.	Lincoln to stay.
July 4.	Cottens' party.
July 7.	Don started in his studio.
July 15.	Virginia Viertel's divorce.
July 31.	Finished "Afterwards."
August 18.	We left for New York, England, South of France.
Sept 9.	Returned.
Sept 22.	Started teaching at L.A. State.
September 30.	We moved to 145 Adelaide Drive.
October 16.	Don to work at Broadway.[1]
October 25.	Don drew hats for LeMaire.
December 13.	The living room in working order.

[1] The Broadway Department Store.

December 17.   *On the Beach* premiere.
December 26.   *Life* magazine lunch at the Huxleys'.[1]

1960

January 3. Two days spent in getting drunk, recovering, getting drunk again, recovering. I won't write "wasted" because I'm going to try to give up puritanism for the sixties. I enjoyed quite a lot of it, so why not? It is probably inevitable that such enjoyment becomes increasingly compulsive. You want to prove you can still do it. Well, why not? Why not be silly once in a while, if you must. Only what matters is to get back to work.

I have mountains of work ahead of me. I should be delighted and thankful that this is so—because it's all work I believe in and want to do. (Or at least want to get done.)

I'm in good health. (Worried, however, about a lump in the pad of my left thumb.)

Relations with Don are perfect. (Admittedly, this varies from day to day. But at least I can say this: I sincerely believe that I am good for him, or at worst much more good than bad. I do not feel that either of us is the prisoner of the other.)

So—forward! Attack the job, anywhere. I'll begin by paying bills. That's the chief worry at the moment—our lack of money.

January 13. Yesterday—my last day but one of the semester at L.A. State—my voice went right out during the evening class. Today I can only whisper.

Have had the whole day alone. Terrible sloth. A bright beautiful windy day after the heavy rain. I had to walk to the store on 7th and Montana to buy stuff and phone the company that our phone was out. My throat is swollen up big.

A dream, the night before last: Auden and I were talking—apparently after a lecture. (Don was present, too; but played no part.) Wystan and I were in great spirits, laughing. I said, "When you talked about the future, I thought you'd give the whole show away." "No—" said Wystan, "they didn't notice anything. I knew they wouldn't—" (Obviously he was referring to the audience.) Then I laughed some more, and kicked at a long electric light cord that lay on

---

[1] The "brains" of Southern California were collected for a group photograph: Heard, Huxley, Isherwood, Buckminster Fuller, Richard Neutra, Linus Pauling, and Julian Huxley who was visiting.

the floor. (In my workroom, here?) "My god," I said, "Why don't we drop this whole farce?"

Now the amazing thing about the dream is this: I am sure that in the dream, Wystan and I were dead—but no one knew it. (Except Don. Was he dead too? Somehow, I think not. I feel he shared in the joke but was to a certain degree excluded.)

January 14. Jo and Ben hurried back from Florida because their agent told them he'd sold *The Crackerjack Marines.* Now they find that the whole thing seems to be a trick—Warner's will only buy it if Ben will work on it now, during the writers' strike. Ivan Moffat strongly urges Ben not to do this, lest he gets himself forever blacklisted by the Screen Writers Guild, which he is sure to want to join, sooner or later.

A talk with a young man on the phone who was sure I was his girlfriend disguising my voice. (I can't speak above a whisper.)

Jack Lewis has given me expensive medicine, but my voice is as bad as ever.

January 15. A tremendous sunset, between rainstorms.

My voice is still bad but has begun to come back in blurts, like a radio working badly.

Ben decided not to accept Warner's offer. He has decided that he owes everything to me. He said on the phone that he felt "cleansed" and "like Christ." He didn't use these expressions ironically, but obviously he didn't mean them quite as they sounded. Is this just lack of feeling for words? Or was he drunk?

Jill Macklem has been told by her doctor that she may live on "indefinitely," but that she had better do everything she wants to do. So she is telling me how fond she is of me. Do I accept this at its face value? I can't—not quite. I can't help remembering what Jill herself told me—that she used to be violently neurotic and tried to kill herself. Is this the story of Sudhira's cancer all over again? Is she just trying to make herself interesting?

(Jo just called to tell me Warner's are buying the book anyhow. Ben can work on it after the strike is over. Jo says, "This is what comes of doing the *right* thing.")

January 21. Voice quite all right now. I read the Katha Upanishad in the shrine this morning at the Vivekananda puja. Then I went to Peschelt and had the root of my tooth pulled out, plus an abscess. It hurt so when he injected the Novocaine that I yelled. Came home and took a pain pill, which hit the spot.

Then Hal Greene came in to tell us he has an offer for his house and land. Do we want to buy the balance of the lot next to us for $7,500? Don is in favor of this. It would mean taking all of the Simon and Schuster money and then some. And this just for the negative sake of privacy.

It would be utterly out of the question if I hadn't just had this offer from Don Murray, to work for a week on his Sardinian film. It still seems crazy, but I guess we'll do it.

January 28. Things are rather better.

I did the work for Don Murray—the Sardinia treatment—in four days, Friday, Saturday, Monday, Tuesday—fifty pages; and got my $1,250 for them. And Don and Walter Wood[1] were delighted.

Today I have just finished the rough draft of chapter seven of the Ramakrishna book.

Hal Greene says that this woman's offer has fallen through—so we are in the clear for the moment.

Much ado about the Huxleys—

A few days ago, Aldous called and asked me to read his novel—the first two-thirds of it—in typescript. Yesterday, Jerry Wald writes me he's interested in doing *Point Counter Point*—have I any suggestions? The night before last I dreamed (1) that Aldous was dead, (2) that Maria came to see me. (This was a visitation, I feel—not a dream. Maria looked younger, around thirty, and plumper than when I saw her last. She seemed very happy and smiling. I knew quite well that she was dead, and she knew that I knew. This seemed perfectly natural. I asked, "Have you been up to see them at Deronda Drive?" And Maria answered, "Oh, *no!*" Not bitchily, but with a certain amusement—exactly the way she would have said it.)

I told Aldous my dream about Maria (omitting my question and the "Oh, no!") when I went up to see him yesterday to get the manuscript. I felt that he was very glad. Later I saw some tears running down his cheeks.

January 29. Ted seems like he is getting ready to have another of his breakdowns after all this time. We are worried about this, and about a new breakdown of the Sunbeam, last night: the gears are all grinding together and it just won't go at all. So we seem condemned to another week on the one-car plan, which is such a nuisance. Don began carrying on at breakfast about how he ought not to be living in Santa Monica—*his* studio, *his* school, *his* gym are all in town. I try to let this go over me, but the whine of neurotic selfishness is irritating. Oh

[1] The producer.

well—moods. What *does* it matter? What does this house matter? Why not move, or not move, or do anything the Lord wills? Don may be maddening at times, but he is far, far, oh infinitely better than the others. I mean, I would far rather be with him than the others. And I'm terrible, I know—a real old bastard, obstinate, spiteful, jealous, sly. No use blaming him. Try to be better. Make japam. Offer it all up. Get on with my work.

The wonderful weather—wasted on me. I don't go out. I should be on the beach, every day. I should exercise. Don complains that I stand around, watching him and not helping. And he's right.

A young man with a shovel, quite attractive, sitting on the hillside looking down on the cars coming up the hill below. He told me he'd just seen a woman in a convertible with her skirts up to her knees and no pants on—jeez!

February 1. Jigee Viertel died yesterday morning in hospital.[1] If she had lived, she would have been horribly scarred. Salka thinks she would have ended by killing herself anyway. She had no breasts left.

Yesterday was a bad bad day. Don was increasingly furious because Thom Gunn didn't take any notice of him. He got drunk, and after Thom and his friend Bill Webster and Bill Inge and Mike Steen and Gavin Lambert had left, he blew up and screamed at me. It's as if Ted's craziness is affecting him. Ted is skirting a nervous breakdown. It is pouring down rain. Again, the Sunbeam is out of action, so I'm stuck here. I do hope Don isn't going to sulk tonight. Well, shit anyway.

February 3. I was unfair to Don. This breakdown of Ted's—which threatens but doesn't quite explode—is hell for him. Altogether, he is having a rough time. Of course it is partly his fault. He rushes compulsionistically around, from art school to gym to studio, nearly knocking himself out. But he is so poignantly eager to do his best, to fulfill his dharma!

Drizzly today. Have worked on the Ramakrishna book. Strange how even that becomes easier and more fun if only I will make the effort! I *must* finish this chapter and get "Ambrose" finished.

February 8. Phyllis Kirk[2] called this morning, saying that they definitely want Aldous, Steve Allen[3] and me to fly to Sacramento and see Governor Brown about Chessman, next week—just before his

---

[1] Of burns; see Glossary.
[2] American actress with political interests, a friend of Gore Vidal.
[3] TV talk show host.

scheduled day of execution. It seems crazy, and I cannot believe it will do any good; but it might be amusing.

It has rained all day, and I feel rather depressed. But have been pushing doggedly ahead with "Ambrose," and thank god chapter seven of the Ramakrishna book is finished!

Igor and Vera and Bob Craft to supper last night. Igor seems a bit shaky. He limps—presumably as the result of his stroke. He seemed sweeter and tinier than ever.

Ted Bachardy is now in a sanatorium; he agreed to commit himself. Don is furious with him, for the things he said to their parents about Don and me. So we have a blockade: we don't answer any calls, leave them to the answering service. Ted has called several times. Now he has given up.

February 10. Ted just called; he ran away from the sanatorium. It seems there was trouble later with his family, Bart Lord and the police. Could he stay here? No, I said, very firmly. He's going to Vince [Davis]'s.

Yesterday, I restarted at L.A. State. One class—the evening one— is nearly eighty! I have this character Kahn, Chester Kallman's [. . .] crazy cousin, in it.[1] Already he held up the class for about five minutes, saying how he is going to send home for a photograph of people being executed by Franco troops: he'll blow it up, he says, and show it to us.

The flight to Sacramento is off. Brown won't see us.

On Monday, Don said he'd like to have an apartment near school and spend about four nights there a week. I think this was largely a sort of test of my reactions. Anyhow, it ended well; because I managed to convince Don that I really care for him. And that still seems to be what really matters to him.

February 14. 6:30 p.m. We are coming to the end of what has been a really happy day—our seventh anniversary. Don has been painting the insides of the windows in my study and I have been writing away at "Ambrose." I'm now about a dozen pages from the end. But many problems are still to be solved.

What shall I write about Don, after seven years? Only this—and I've written it often before—he has mattered and does matter more than any of the others. Because he imposes himself more, demands more, cares more—about everything he does and encounters. He is so desperately alive.

---

[1] Probably David Kahn, Kallman's second cousin, whom Kallman intensely disliked.

Shall I call this novel *The Others*? Thought of it just now. Not bad.

Ted is still crazy and at large—staying with Vince, who it seems will put up with absolutely anything. He [Ted] called me yesterday. "This is Eve Black,"[1] he said; and he announced that he's going to change his hair to platinum. He has been fired from his job. He plans to paint and act.

Started to read Don the introduction by [T. E.] Lawrence to *Memoirs of the Foreign Legion*. The Stravinskys lent it to us.

February 17. Ted finally caught Don at home, on the phone, this morning. Don told him off, and said he didn't want to talk to him again for a long time. But Don hated doing this. He is deeply upset and will remain so until Ted recovers. I know that.

Am at last approaching the end of "Ambrose"—about ten more pages.

The people at the L.A. State College library, without saying a word to me in advance, have made an exhibit: "Christopher Isherwood—Man of Letters," with the foreign translations of my books which I gave them, plus newspaper articles, etc. etc. I was really touched and pleased and surprised.

February 26. When I was up at Vedanta Place on Wednesday, Swami said, "I saw Maharaj the other night, at Santa Barbara," but he wouldn't tell me any more—maybe because Krishna was there and might have taken it down.

Tonight our car broke down for lack of water and had to be pushed.

I got all the books back on the shelves.

The Screen Writers Guild are indignant, because they caught Don Murray offering our story to Columbia. He doesn't seem the least bit worried about this.

March 3. At the beginning of the week, Don was sick and in bed. On Monday, I fixed food for him. This situation—of waiting on him when he is sick—I found strangely saddening, because the strength of the love between us and our dependence upon each other makes us seem an isolated pair, threatened by all the ills and evils of the world. How poignant love is! What a tiny island! And yet one wouldn't wish it any different. Do I feel this simply because I have a spasm in my vagus nerve, and can therefore only experience everything—even what is called happiness—in terms of dread and guilt? Would I be

---

[1] "Eve Black" is a "bad" personality of the schizophrenic woman played by Joanne Woodward in *The Three Faces of Eve* (1957).

[2] By M[aurice] M[agnus]

"happier" if I could legalize the guilt by making it theological—by believing, for instance, that my relationship with Don is a mortal sin? I don't know. In any case, I should then be a different person. And I should also be a different person, I guess, if I had my vagus nerve cut.

Don interests me more and more. How he ventures further and further, deeper and deeper, into the jungle of his life! It is terribly moving, and exciting, to watch him.

Right now, he is just finishing Alan Watts's *The Wisdom of Insecurity*. He says he'll never be quite the same again, after reading it.

I cannot say that I find it either moving or exciting to watch myself. Aside from my life with Don, I am a rather dreary aging creature, much given to paranoia and self-pity; always groaning about how hard my daily task is.

But at least this afternoon—after getting back from State College—I've got my work restarted. If only I could finish "Ambrose" this weekend—in draft at least! This slowness is unhealthy, and shows there is something wrong.

March 11. Today I finished the draft of "Ambrose." Went for a walk on the cliffs at sunset, quite elated. I still don't know what, if anything, it adds up to. But it is another job done.

Now I await Don's reading it.

The Stravinskys came to my lecture yesterday, on Kipling. Igor very shaky. He complains of constriction and cramps, following his stroke. We ate an expensive lunch at Lucy's. I felt his sadness, and need to rally and be gay. It's really heartbreaking.

A list of projects which *might* come off, if—

Don Murray's projected play.

Laughton's projected Socrates play.

Shelley Winters and Tony Franciosa's projected TV or film documentary on Gandhi.

Peter Viertel's film of *Cakes and Ale*.[1]

Lincoln Kirstein's Sleeping Beauty film.

Jerry Lawrence's TV series.

The Vacant Room, which Gavin is seeing about, in New York.

The projected TV show with Aldous.

Bob Craft's idea that I should narrate something for a Stravinsky composition—in 1962!

If even *one* of these goes through, I'll be amazed.

March 19. Well—since writing the above—what has happened?

---

[1] Maugham's 1930 novel.

It seems Hope and Don Murray are trying a trial separation; so no prospects of the play for the present.

This girl, Phyllis English, is deciding whether she wants to do the Socrates play for us or not. If not, I must find another translator.

No word from Shelley Winters, Peter Viertel, Lincoln Kirstein, Jerry Lawrence.

Aldous has gone off to lecture at the Menninger Foundation,[1] so that's all postponed.

Today, Jed Harris[2] brought a play about William Herschel,[3] on which he wants me to work, so they can make a movie.

Crowds on the beach, which has more rocks washed up on it than I've ever seen. Don is drawing Marguerite, trying to get a better likeness for *The Paris Review*. All his other pictures are done; really excellent.[4] I'm so proud.

And last night, when they came to dinner, Bob Craft suggested Don should draw him and Stravinsky together as a jacket for their third conversation book.

I still have this problem with "Ambrose." Am trying hard to finish it off this weekend. But it's not easy.

March 20. Thick sea fog in the Canyon all day; very hot in town. I worked on "Ambrose"—I think I *may* finish tomorrow. Alas, this play that Jed Harris wants me turn into a movie—*The Miles of Heaven* by David Hertz—won't do. It's just another cute little triangle.

Don was here all day, drawing with Marcia King, who leaves tomorrow for New York.

Laughton came by, blowing and wheezing and puffing. He's an old fusspot, but at least *his* project is something worthwhile.

Every morning I have bad anxiety dreams before waking—because of my vagus nerve trouble. And I wake with a sense of depression which has to be promptly analyzed away.

March 21. Well, today I finished my revisions of "Ambrose." Don approves. Shall show the manuscript to Gavin—who is starting *his* new novel today.

Have practically decided not to take on the play *The Miles of Heaven*

---

[1] Center for psychiatric training founded by Dr. Karl Menninger and associated with his clinic and with other hospitals in Topeka, Kansas.
[2] Theatrical impresario of the 1930s and 1940s.
[3] German-born English astronomer (1738–1822).
[4] Bachardy drew a set of Hollywood portraits including producers Jerry Wald and Joe Pasternak, writers Gavin Lambert and Ivan Moffat, director Richard Brooks, and Marguerite Lamkin (who planned the piece).

for Jed Harris. But I didn't call him. Why should *I* pay for a long toll call? Why not be the Jew for once?

Jewish behavior, deliberately practiced, is a cure for anti-Semitism.

We ate home tonight—a delicious "peasant" supper, made of bits and leftovers: Ala[1], mushrooms, squash, eggs, baloney, etc.

Last night, Don said, "Why are the animals so happy, nowadays?" Fog again.

I have quite a project, watering plants—the pulla, the anthericum, the ruffled Boston fern, the philodendron, the two palms in the living room. The air roots of the anthericum have to be dowsed in a cup of water every Monday.

Homework for the class—Forster.

Laughton called. He is hot after the Plato project. Going away for a few days. Who with? "None of your damned business!" But he loved being asked. I think his chief reason for wanting to work with me is so he can talk freely about his private life. And why not?

March 23. Today I mailed a copy of "Ambrose" to Stephen Spender.

Gavin has read it. I think he likes it very much.

Don had a terrific row with his mother on the phone, because she said he had offended his uncle by only staying there two hours.

Yesterday, Marvin Laser said I might be invited to stay on at L.A. State. What would I feel about this? Said I'd consider it very seriously.

Walked with Jill Macklem in the park. Last weekend, she had the worst of all her heart attacks. She thinks the doctor is experimenting with her.

March 25. Read Balzac's play *Vautrin* this morning, because Gide in his *Journal* says that it is there that Vautrin "confesses himself most significantly."[2] Maybe he does, but I didn't find it very thrilling.

A grey day, clouds down on the hills.

Jim Charlton called. He's leaving soon for San Francisco.

I reread my diaries of 1935–38, to see if there is material for a Munich crisis episode for my novel. God, I was unhappy, then. Or does it only seem so?

Last night, at the Stravinskys', Don did excellent drawings of Igor and Bob. Bob has hepatitis. He feels awful. He assures us that he dreads the South American trip (Mirandi [Masocco] claims that he is the one who's determined it shall go through!) and that Vera dreads it, and that only Igor wants it.

[1] A brand of bulgar wheat.
[2] Gide's entry for April 26, 1918; Isherwood had Justin O'Brien's four-volume English translation.

Igor had taken something to stop the pain in his arm. He was quite lively, and showed Don the Russian-character typewriter given him by Diaghilev. But later he complained of his headache. I rubbed the back of his neck. He exclaimed affectionately "Ah, you are so gentle! You know just where to touch the nerves." Bob showed me the rest of the proofs of their new book of conversations. He's afraid Chester will resent the way they make it clear that Wystan was alone responsible (with Igor) for the outline of *The Rake's Progress* libretto. Altogether one of our pleasantest and most "family" evenings together.

I'm becoming what Caskey used to call a "plant queen." I feel, when I water the anthericum and douse its air roots, as if I am feeding a live pet.

March 27. Cloudy and rainy—the Canyon full of dripping mist. I called Gavin (who has just started his new novel) and said "novelists' weather." He answered "*English* novelists' weather, and I'm sick of it!"

Read Raymond Chandler's *The Little Sister* yesterday evening and this morning. Also *Where Angels Fear to Tread*.[1]

Tried to have supper with Jim Charlton, who's leaving for San Francisco very soon. But he couldn't. So stayed home. I wish I were better at staying home. I get jittery. Maybe I bore myself. Don in town.

March 28. Just got a cable from Stephen: "Thank you for your story which is marvellous. Will be writing this week." But of course he may still be going to beg off publishing it[2]—or at best may want to cut it.

Last night we went with Gavin to see Agnes Moorehead.[3] She has a real palazzo of a house—overgrown doorway, cloudy mirrors, draped beams, chandeliers, colored sanctuary lights, a toilet set in an old chair. She leaves tonight for a film festival in Cartagena. She described Ginger Rogers's incompetence in *The Pink Jungle*: "Whatever she does, it's as if it were for the first time. You give her a glass of champagne: she squeals, 'Ooh, champagne! For *me*!'" Agnes calls Mrs. Rogers Senior "Mother Barracuda."

Ken and Elaine Tynan came and we went on with them to Chasen's. Larry Harvey was giving a party there. He got up and embraced me in front of everybody. That's the kind of thing which

[1] By E. M. Forster.
[2] In *Encounter*.
[3] American actress.

sets him apart from most actors. Olivier would do it. Almost no American.

Ken and Elaine are very strange. One feels an absolutely desperate insecurity. And yet, they don't merely run around with the famous. Ken had been making an apparently quite serious investigation of communists and beatniks in San Francisco. And he visited San Quentin *without* asking to see Chessman.

April 1. Dorothy Miller is here to clean. As usual she abounded in gleefully pessimistic information: there is a shop in Los Angeles where you can buy bombs to throw at people; a nurse she knows, driving near La Brea, was hit by a bit of radioactive fallout and received a burn which gets bigger and bigger. Dorothy's landlady has said she won't let the census takers inside her house.

The last three days I've been feeling rather lousy. A repressed attack of flu.

Charles Laughton called to say he'd almost decided to do a Billy Wilder film ("a Laughton film") rather than Falstaff at Stratford. ("Because one wants, as one gets older, to belong to one's own day.")

Jed Harris is still wooing me to do the Herschel film. He really is very intelligent and charming, even if a monster. He may buy Hal Greene's house next door.

April 7. This morning, Guyer and Laser, with many compliments and apologies, broke the news to me that I couldn't be employed next semester—though probably they can take me back in the spring, if I like.[1]

Still haven't started on the next episode of my novel; partly because Stephen has never written to say if he really is going to publish it as it stands—only cabled that it's "marvellous."

Still haven't signed any contract with Laughton.

When I told him and Elsa about Vedanta Place and how we spend the evenings I go there, Charles said: "I rather envy you." This hurt Elsa's feelings. She is terribly touchy, just now.

April 8. I realized again today how terribly I fool around and waste time. I could *easily* do three times what I do do.

However, I got along with the Ramakrishna chapter. And I read the adaptation of Plato's account of Socrates's death. At present, it's hopeless. As Laughton says, Socrates simply isn't made alive enough to be worth killing. But I think Charles has really made up his mind to go ahead with the project.

[1] At L.A. State College.

April 9. Gavin and the Masselinks to supper last night. It was rather a bore. They didn't quite get along. Don says he thinks most people dislike Gavin, because he is ugly and unchic and not quite talented enough. But that he will nevertheless (or because of this) become powerful, and perhaps feared [. . .].

We slept *eleven hours* last night! It is almost alarming, this indulgence. I had some very subtle dreams—dreams which made me feel how gross my mind ordinarily is, nowadays. Can't remember them, except for one, of two ugly middle-aged women fighting, because of a man. (During the fight I was shitting, in what I had believed to be a toilet and which turned out to be a projection room or small theater which had several extra doors I had neglected to lock. So lots of people came in. What was subtle about this dream was a sense of universalized horror-compassion at the ugliness of the fight. But I can't really explain. Tried to, to Don. His half serious pique because he hadn't been in my dream. Read him Whitman at breakfast. He shed tears over "As I Lay with My Head in Your Lap, Camerado" and "Vigil Strange…"

April 15. Yesterday, I performed a real feat of rush work. Got chapter eight of the Ramakrishna book finished in a tremendous burst.

This morning, I went on the beach for the first time. The sea too cold to swim in. Felt a great surge of energy.

April 16. What's this—a glass of Scotch on the desk! And you told Prema and Arup yesterday, quite gratuitously, that you never drink alone.

Well, I'm depressed—so much so that I really wonder if maybe the hepatitis is coming back. Because all that's happened is that I got a letter from Stephen saying that "Ambrose" is unsatisfactory in its present form. One of the things that upset me about the letter was that it seemed chiefly concerned with what other people think of the story. It seemed written (or rather, dictated—another sore point!) in haste and carelessly, and I don't feel he is saying what he really thinks.

Well, to hell with all that. I mustn't lose heart. I must push ahead. Am writing to ask Stephen to send the manuscript to Edward Upward.

Don has gone into town tonight. He didn't want to go, seeing me so upset, but I wouldn't ask him not to. He really could not be sweeter, and I have never felt closer to him. We went on the beach today for the first time in a long long while.

Carter Lodge came to supper last night with Jo and Ben, and they talked Tahiti. All about people who were awful or "good"—Ben's favorite word. We felt that Carter is very much disillusioned about Dick Foote, who went wild about the island social whirl.

April 18. Yesterday, after the amazingly violent dip on Saturday, I manic-depressively zoomed up again, started the next episode of my novel *The Others*, and also another chapter (nine) of the Ramakrishna book. True, this was partly due to a Dexamyl tablet.

I believe that Don probably loves me more than anybody else ever has. But that's not surprising; he needs me more. And sometimes I think I need him more. Our life together right now is really a joy. But it will have its ups and downs, as always.

A lovely, snug Easter lunch at the Stravinskys'—with wonderful Russian dishes. Igor, Don and I drank up a whole bottle of some special old Scotch—General Grant—without ice or mix. Igor was adorable, as usual.

About "Ambrose": I just know that I must leave it until I have the whole book finished and can relate the parts to each other.

April 25. Don was away this weekend—the first time in a long long while. It was rather funny, how I got to know about it. I'd just been laying down the law, pompously, about how one should never never break any engagements—and so Don had a most marvellous cue. He said, "I'd been meaning to tell someone who asked me to go away with him for this weekend that I'd changed my mind. But you're right, I guess I shouldn't."

Actually the going away was a success. Because I had a nice evening with Jim [Charlton], and another with Dean Campbell[1] and Jerry Lawrence and Jack Larson and Jimmy Bridges. Also, Don came back full of warmth and we were delighted to be together again. And now we have a nice evening ahead of us—going with Jo and Ben to see *Sons and Lovers* at Fox.

April 29. The evening was nice—though *Sons and Lovers* wasn't so hot; actually it should end (as the book doesn't) with meeting Frieda.

Paul Kennedy went off to New York yesterday. This certainly didn't break my heart—in fact, I am a bit relieved. But I felt sad for him because the prospect of his ever getting anywhere with anything, or ever being anything but mildly frustrated, mildly unhappy—seems slight. Oh, the sadness of these half-lives!

[1] American musical comedy actor, singer, dancer and singing coach.

Don painted the front bedroom, a kind of blood orange. It's beautiful.

Phyllis Kirk called this morning—will I fly with her and Brando to Sacramento on Sunday, to see Governor Brown? Said yes.

Party for Doris Dowling and Len [Kaufman] tonight.

May 2. Phyllis called our flight to see Brown off, because it seemed to be useless.

And now, incredibly, this morning, Chessman was executed. We listened to the bulletin in the front bathroom, because the radio wouldn't work from the other plug. And then Dorothy [Miller] called to tell us, in case we didn't know.

May 4. Jill Macklem told me yesterday that, at ten o'clock on Monday morning, a lot of students cheered because Chessman was executed. I hope they were police students. We have a whole bunch of them on campus, studying narcotics, homicide, etc.

May 11. Carter Lodge, whom we had supper with last night, seems so lonely. He talks with eager fatherliness of Dick, who is cutting up in Australia, Singapore, Bali—but there is a streak of resentment in it all; maybe now, he says, Dick will learn to look after himself while travelling and not leave everything to Carter. A sad aftermath somehow it all seems—as if the little cozy fire of fun which Johnny kindled has now died down to nearly nothing. How desperately the many depend on the few to amuse them!

One sees Carter, rich and alone, growing old in a good second-class hotel where he knows the manager and gets a special price.

Edward Upward wrote last week to say Ambrose "moved me to the core" and that the novel "promises to be the best, the most moving, you have done yet." So my morale is almost restored.

Also, Santa Barbara seems about to make an offer; and L.A. State is making terrific efforts to underwrite me for the fall semester. So I feel "wanted."

Lovely weather, but smoggy in town.

May 13. Friday! May it bring luck!

One can never be sufficiently grateful for the great mercy of sleep. Don was away last night in town, and I slept on the old hard Saltair Avenue bed in the back room—the bed on which so many of the best things happened—and woke, beside the open window, so refreshed and happy.

Yesterday evening, there was a symposium at State College, in which Jack Rathbun,[1] Wirt Williams,[2] Wright Morris[3] and I took part. Wright Morris did nearly all the talking; one of those little men with a tight-clipped white moustache and wavy artist-hair. He made a lot of sense, though. But how dull it somehow all was!

Got home to find a letter from Dr. Stuurman, apologizing to the earth, because the chancellor has turned down my appointment for next fall.[4] Well, my heart isn't broken. It would have been fun, in a way, but an awful rat race, commuting.

Dorothy, who has come this morning to clean, feels that she was "protected" from coming to cook for us last week, when we asked her. Because, that night, her toilet overflowed and if she hadn't been at home it would have flooded the whole place.

Dorothy was very pleased because, at the corner of Adelaide and 4th, she saw a gentleman in one of the houses being served his breakfast by a real butler!

She was conned into buying a beige telephone, believing there was no extra charge for a colored one.

Wednesday night, Swami told me Vandanananda is having trouble with lust—specifically, lust for the woman who owns the Camel Point Drive house at Laguna.[5] However, she didn't encourage him. Swami wants Ritajananda to take over the French center. He says Prema admitted to him that he, Prema, was going through "a bad time." I've noticed for some weeks when I go up there that he acts strangely—very cagey.

May 18. Don's birthday—not much of one for him, I fear. The day before yesterday, he had this bad accident which wasn't his fault, wrecked the car and hurt his knee. Today he has to fuss with insurance forms. However, we had a nice breakfast at the Monica Hotel. Now he's writing letters of introduction for Paul Millard to take to England. Paul has earned these by lending Don his car until the Sunbeam is repaired or we get another.

On Saturday (May 14) we went up to supper with Gerald Heard and Michael—with the Stravinskys and Bob Craft. Gerald looks wonderfully trim and youthful these days. He bitched the Stravinskys and monopolized the conversation all evening.

For example: Gerald had a postcard of a volcanic eruption on Hawaii. "It looks just like one of your paintings," he told Vera.

---

[1] Professor of American literature at L.A. State.
[2] Novelist.
[3] Novelist, he later taught briefly at L.A. State.
[4] To teach at Santa Barbara.
[5] Ruth Conrad.

"Won't you sign it?" So Vera signed it, "From Vera to Gerald." But Gerald insisted she should add: "To my good friend Gerald, from Vera."

Gerald kept saying, "Vera has that sad, distant look," and "Maestro is aloof."

As for poor Igor, all he wanted to talk about was his health. One felt they were ill at ease with Gerald—quite different from when they come to our house.

On Sunday, we went to the Selznicks' and I got drunk and hugged Marilyn Monroe a lot, and then banged with my fist on the piano, saying, "That's how I feel." In the morning, my wrist was so sore I had to stop typing. Otherwise, I'd have finished a rough draft of "The Others."[1]

Dr. Stuurman phoned to tell me that, after all, the chancellor has agreed to have me, so the Santa Barbara offer is definite.

When I told my evening class, yesterday, that I would let them off next week, they all loudly protested. Which made me feel good. So I told them funny stories.

Jill Macklem had one of our picnic lunches in the park. She tells me that she and her husband "live together like brother and sister" now. They have two children. In between the children, they got divorced and she married a man who was a painter and really romantic. He used to go into the fields in the early morning and pick daisies for her. But he was so possessive she left him and remarried Les, the first husband.

The big stink made by Mr. Khrushchev continues to spread.[2] At a party we went to last night, Selznick and Ivan agreed that he certainly does not want war. But there are dangerous times ahead.

The party was at the beach home of Tim Durant's[3] daughter, a big blonde brute who has married a footballer. Football photographs over the bar, and, behind it, Jeff Richards—a former MGM hope, now going to fat. Durant's daughter accused Ivan Moffat of being a pansy and said approvingly that Jeff Richards was cruel to "the poor little fags." Jeff had mimicked Don's voice girlishly.

Ivan was rather grim, what with the summit breakdown and the decision of the screenwriters *not* to settle the strike.

David Selznick walked with me on the beach and talked about

---

[1] Isherwood's title since February 14 for *Down There on a Visit* is now temporarily the title for the episode on which he is working, eventually published as "Waldemar."

[2] The 1960 Paris summit broke up in confusion on May 17 after Khrushchev, referring to the American U-2 spy plane shot down on May 1 over the USSR, denounced U.S. espionage, and Eisenhower refused to apologize.

[3] Former tennis star.

Wendell Willkie. David supported him for a while, then realized he was a lush and a girl chaser.

May 19. Yesterday I was approached through Geller by MGM— would I work for them? No doubt there's a lot of scabbing already.

Don has just called to say he's staying the night in town, which annoys me, because I'm stuck with spending the evening seeing that boring Brecht's play.[1] He is always telling me these things at the last moment—and of course it's partly a subconscious wish to prevent *me* from making any dates.

However, his birthday yesterday was very harmonious. We spent the evening watching Laughton hamming it up on TV, as a rabbi.[2]

May 30. One of my longest lapses in months. I don't really know why. I have certainly been no busier than usual.

On the 19th, I finished a rough draft of "The Others"—the Munich crisis episode of my novel. It is *very* rough—the Waldemar-Karin[3] relationship hardly integrated at all, as yet, with my diary material. Nevertheless, I still feel that it's greatly needed. Since then, I haven't done anything to it. Hope to start the revision tomorrow.

On the 21st, Eddie James came to supper, with an exceedingly square British secretary named Michael Bryan. Eddie was fascinating, as usual, telling of the attempt to murder him by a boy at his Mexican ranch. The boy fixed a booby trap, a dead tree log, with a trip line attached to a rare orchid floating in Eddie's swimming pool.

But since then, Eddie has been a damned bore, fussing about the safety of his pictures in Paul Millard's apartment, now that Paul is away and his friend Dick Dobyns is giving drunken parties there.

That day, both Don and I stopped drinking and we have agreed to keep off it for a month, at any rate. What chiefly upsets me about drinking is the smoking that goes with it. I feel so awful in the morning. I'd hoped that giving up drinking would make me lose weight—but I don't seem to be—or only very slowly.

Charles Laughton is at the Cedars of Lebanon with gallbladder trouble. He'll have to have an operation later. He talks of buying Hal Greene's house next door, so as to have a place to get away from Elsa. Meanwhile, he's inviting his friend Terry [Jenkins] to come over from England.

Charles and I are much better friends now than before. I lent him

[1] *The Good Woman of Szechwan*; he went with Gavin Lambert.
[2] In "In the Presence of My Enemies."
[3] Karin later became Dorothy.

"Afterwards," which he liked, and *Maurice*.[1] Don has been drawing him.

In addition to the Plato project, Charles wants me to do a modern version of *The School for Scandal*,[2] set in Hollywood. Am very dubious about this.

Jed Harris wants me to do a revised version of *Hedda Gabler* for Bette Davis at the Pasadena Playhouse.

On the 24th, they had a "reception" for me at State College, fruit punch and cookies, in the afternoon. The president shook my hand and told me, "You're the kind of person we want here." How often I have been told the opposite! He gave me a printed testimonial and we were photographed as it changed hands.

But a much better testimonial was from the cute blonde girl (Nancy Bernard? Gay Robertson?[3]) in my morning class, who said, "Don't ever change, Mr. Isherwood!"

On the 25th, I drove up to Goleta and got the job at UCSB[4] for next fall. They agreed to all my requests and I think I shall like it there.

May 26 was Rory Harrity's birthday. Don and I had the worst scene we've had in six months or more, because I'd forgotten to have the steaks cut up for barbecuing. Don became quite hysterical and screamed at me like a mistress at a servant. Then he was ashamed and furious with me. He's still sulking about this, but things are better. When shall I learn how to handle this kind of thing? Maybe never.

The worst of not getting drunk is that most people bore me pissless—at least, parties bore me pissless. Hideously bored by Marguerite, Rory and Gavin. Bored last night at the Selznicks' till I could have screamed.

Two of Don's friends came in to draw today, and then announced they were going on the beach. So Don's working day is ruined. He'll probably be in a bad mood about this later. Also, the girl announces with a certain glee that she and her husband are going to emigrate to Brazil, because there's certain to be an atomic war. This too has probably upset Don.

He is at present tremendously fascinated by astrology. Carter Lodge gave him *From Pioneer to Poet* by Isabelle M. Pagan.

June 5. Another shorter lapse, because this week has been so busy.

Gore Vidal arrived at the beginning of it; we had supper with him last Monday the 31st. Gore is running for Congress and full of politics,

---

[1] Forster's then unpublished novel.
[2] Sheridan's eighteenth-century comedy.
[3] Isherwood added in the margin: "Gay Robertson."
[4] University of California at Santa Barbara.

which, he rather hints, is his alternative to writing. (As a matter of fact, his play *The Best Man* is probably the best thing he has done, and it is the vilest spite of bad luck that the strike should have cut it short.) He thoroughly enjoys the rat race, even including huge shindigs at his home for his backers and their wives, and the danger that the Republicans may smear his private life. He seems to view without alarm the prospect of Washington, and hole-and-corner sex. He has made some deal with a bank which guarantees him $50,000 a year for the next ten years; this he did by selling all rights to *The Best Man*. He is sure Jack Kennedy will win, and he expresses enormous admiration for Kennedy, as the happy-go-lucky kid who turned tough and ambitious. "Russell" in his play is obviously part Kennedy, part Gore.

What one feels and rather loves in Gore is his courage. He's most definitely not a crybaby. He has a great good-humored brazen air of playing the game—constantly using the latest fashionable expressions, such as "grimsville" and "closetwise." Last night, he nearly got into a fight on a parking lot, because the man in front of him wouldn't move on. He jumped out of the car, ready for battle. Later he told us with self-satisfaction, that he finds a fistfight so relaxing; and that no young delinquent has ever attacked him, because they all sense immediately that Gore would fight back.

Then, on June 2, Tennessee came down to the house for drinks— bringing his mother (who is right out of *The Glass Menagerie*, and boasts of it), his younger brother Dakin and his sister-in-law Joyce. Also the ubiquitous Mike Steen. Dakin and Joyce look so like the relatives in *Cat on a Hot Tin Roof* that I wanted to roar with laughter when they came in. But actually Dakin is rather charming and quite bright, and so is she—relatively. Tennessee was utterly doped. He says the only way he can face being with the family is to put a Seconal in his drink every evening.

A minor miracle. On the very day Tennessee came here, the fern he gave us last year—which has been withered all this time—began to uncurl its new fronds.

On June 2, Jill Macklem came and went through the term papers and graded them.

On June 3, Jed Harris came and talked some more to me about the *Hedda Gabler* project, which really seems interesting.

Yesterday, there was a big party for Tennessee at the Duquettes'. Mary Pickford was there, stoned, and Edwina, Tennessee's mother, said to her: "Do you remember your long yellow curls?" Gore said, "She's the last of the great room-emptiers." Buddy Rogers,[1] also stoned, was there in evening tails, a really shall-we-dance? figure out

[1] The actor and Pickford's husband.

of a twenties musical: his mottled red face and elegant figure. And Rory [Harrity] has gone off the wagon again. He looks marvellous still, however; about nineteen. But he is certainly the most boring of all drunks.

Today, Gore has left for New York again, flying. He was quite scared, last night, and kept saying, "See you in July, if I'm not killed."

Last night, after we left them, Ten, Mike, Jim Charlton, Gavin all went up to Ivan Moffat's and swam. Iris jumped into the pool with her clothes on. Today she is driving up to San Francisco for a round of parties. She really is turning into a dancing grandmother.

Don and I are still holding to our nondrinking resolution, despite tremendous pressure. The boredom is excruciating—but it's good in the mornings. Our relations are much much better again, now. Don's state of mind is always precarious, of course. He is buffetted by storms of anxiety, resentment and melancholia. Against these, he takes Dexamyl, which worries me a bit, but Dr. Lewis doesn't seem bothered by it. He did a good drawing of Jan Clayton[1] this week, a poor one of Gore, and two goodish ones of Tennessee. Jan and Ten bought theirs. So that wasn't bad. And all the time, underneath all of this, I have the feeling that things are all right. I can never be thankful enough for our life here, in this beautiful house. I only wish Don could have a proper studio. Then it would be really home for both of us.

June 8. Yesterday, Swami phoned to tell me that Amiya had written to him to "prepare me" for the news of M.'s death; she is failing rapidly, and Amiya will go up to Wyberslegh just as soon as she's well enough, after an operation she's had. But, as yet, no cable has come from Richard—although, when M. had the stroke, he let me know at once.

Jo and Ben left this morning for Mexico, where Ben is to write some travel pieces. Jo had a stomach upset, and our parting—we drove them to the airport—lacked the usual effusiveness.

They went through a big fuss with Marguerite and Rory last Sunday. Rory came down to the Canyon, told them that Marguerite was impossible [. . .] — [that she was even] calling him a fat drunken faggot and accusing him of going to bed with Ben! Rory got very drunk, telling his woes, and had to stay the night. Next morning, Marguerite called—where was Rory? Jo, instructed by Rory, said they didn't know. Half an hour later, Marguerite burst in, found Rory still there and one of Jo's girl customers in the back room, with her pants off because Jo was fixing them. Tableau! On top of that,

---

[1] Singer and actress.

Rory had left his billfold at the house of some girl [. . .] in the Canyon, with whom he'd been screwing. The girl (mother of several children, who picked Rory up at the art show at the Canyon school, where he'd gone with Jo and Ben because Jo had watercolors exhibited there) brought the billfold to Jo and Ben, not knowing how to reach Rory. So now *we* have to return it to him!

And, on Saturday night, after the drunken evening, Jim Charlton stayed at the Beverly Hills Hotel, with Tennessee. So there was a stink with Hilde. Jim took his clothes and autographed books and left the house, for his Canyon apartment, saying, "There must be someone somewhere who'll accept me as I am." Then he got drunk. No doubt all is peace by this time.

June 9. No word from Wyberslegh, yet.

Swami told me last night that he's decided to let Tito come back to Trabuco—this is for the fifth time! A record.

Don read "The Others" yesterday and liked it. So now I'm going to go right ahead with "Paul" and rewrite both of them later.

Two nights ago, we saw *Ivan the Terrible*—the second part[1] for the first time. I think it's one of the greatest things I've ever seen. The furred Tsar and his courtiers, like great heavy animals in their winter coats, suddenly whisking around and disappearing through the small rounded doorways of the palace, which are like rat holes. The flaming dance, the curly-haired jealous boy in the woman's mask, the crowning of the drunken pretender. God!

A theory—maybe all crap: if you confine drama in a room and want to keep it truly cinematic, you must stylize it, slow it down (in this instance) into a kind of slow symbolic dance, and heighten the mood until it approaches the mood of opera. Otherwise—if it's confined—if there are no great surges of movement—all you are left with is a dull canned realistic play, which belongs in the theater.

Today, for the first time, after days and days of greyness, we have the bright sun and sparkling sea. Don and I on the beach together. Very happy.

But work *must* start tomorrow on the two projects: "Paul," and the introduction to the Vivekananda selections.[2]

Laughton, meanwhile, begins to fuss about the proposed adaptation of *School for Scandal.* He'll be a nuisance, now he's better. And Terry has agreed to come and visit him here; so he's eager to buy Hal Greene's house.

[1] Sergei Eisenstein's film; the second part was made in 1946 but suppressed by Stalin and released only in 1958, long after his death.
[2] *What Religion Is: In the Words of Swami Vivekananda,* edited by John Yale.

Swami spoke, last night, of the fear that precedes a vision. A fear of going into nothingness, like death. But then, bliss.

June 12. On the 10th, I'm happy to say, I started both my introduction to Prema's book of selections from Vivekananda, *and* "Paul," the last of the four sections of my novel. It'll be impossible to know, for some time yet, what the difficulties of "Paul" are going to be.

Right now, I rather incline to calling the whole book *The Lost*.

Don, on a boy named Chuck van Haren, whom he has been drawing: "He doesn't want to be a hairdresser more than he wants to be an actor."

Tennessee returned from La Jolla and then left again yesterday. He wants us to visit him in Key West, this summer. I felt a warmth toward and from him yesterday which I hadn't otherwise felt during this visit. Most of the time, he's been so bothered by his mother, and so dazed with drink and sleeping pills. Yet he seems as keen witted and creative as ever, underneath this. He is very pleased with Don's drawings of him.

We are going through a good period now, in many ways. Don of course is always poised on the knife-edge of melancholia, but he has formed an image of himself as "being brave," which is very helpful. I've started using the record player to raise our spirits in the mornings—ballet music seems best. We both take lots of Dexamyl— Don does, nearly every day.

I don't think I have ever, in my entire life, felt so involved with another human being as I am with Don. But this is a relatively good kind of involvement. Rereading the Vedanta Society part of my 1944 journal (which I've just gotten back from the Stravinskys) I note that I rejoiced, at that time, in having ceased to feel any desire for personal relationships. But the kind of personal relationships I meant then were obsessive and fundamentally degrading. This time, it really is different.

Yesterday, we went to a party held by Paul Sorel in his newly acquired room at the Sunset Towers West—another gem of modernistic expensive squalor. A miserable little hole, hot and viewless and claustrophobic. What a relief to go on to the (in every sense) spacious Stravinskys for supper! They have built a huge new living room onto the house. Igor was quite reproachful because we're still not drinking. But we certainly do feel better for it—and I'm very slowly losing weight: 147 pounds to date.

June 14. Yesterday, I got a letter from Richard. M. is very weak and dying slowly, without pain. Richard says she's drowsy most of the time but quite clear headed. I feel sad about this, and vaguely guilty that I'm not with them, but I can't possibly afford to go to England now.

Don could not be sweeter. And I'm so deeply happy that his work is going so well. Donna O'Neill and Ivan were in yesterday evening very enthusiastic about Don's drawings of Donna. Ivan has bought two, and Donna has ordered two more. And the Selznicks are going to pay for theirs of Mary Jennifer. And Tennessee bought his.

Have told Laughton I won't do *School for Scandal*, but we're more or less committed to Socrates. Today he came, with his friend Bill Phipps, to see Hal Greene's house, and loved it—thus completely reversing Elsa's judgement. He at once got the point—that Elsa had panned the house out of jealousy—of what Charles plans to do with it. He determined to tax her with this at once, but then got so bothered that he couldn't make up his mind to go home, and instead, oiled the fronds of the palms in our living room. (He knew how to do this, he explained, because of his early hotel experience.)

Marguerite on the phone, drooling on and on about her difficulties with Rory, who is drunk and out with this woman in the Canyon. At length, an emergency call cut us short.

Am stuck with "Paul." It needs more thought.

June 16. Yesterday at noon, I got a cable from Richard to say that M. is dead. She died yesterday afternoon, and the cable was sent so promptly that it reached me before California had caught up with English time.

There is nothing to be said about this at present. I am sad, yes, but I don't really feel M.'s loss. Perhaps I never shall; perhaps I've been through it already. My feelings aren't important, anyway.

Everything seems suspended, until I know if I shall have to go to England. I do hope not, and we can't afford it.

Don was sweet, and put off a date to spend the night in town, so as not to leave me alone, and we went to two films—a terrible version of Tennessee's *Orpheus Descending*, almost a parody of Tennessee, and a rather inept low-budget picture about juvenile delinquents trying to make a married woman (*Private Property*).

Kent Diegaard, Jerry Siegel and a girl[1]—I think a girlfriend of Kent's—came around to see me this afternoon. Kent (I think it was) said of the girl—when I asked if she wrote—"No, but she has insights into people." This sounded like a joke when the girl told me she was an X-ray technician.

[1] Probably either students or fans.

The usual kind of talk, ranging from Hemingway to Trocchi.[1] The two boys were showing off (a little) how at ease they felt with me. The girl watched. It is part of my function to be available for this kind of darshan. I guess it sometimes stimulates people to get on with their own work—which makes it important that I shall tell them how well I'm getting on with *mine*. And anyhow, I don't pretend it doesn't flatter me.

Both Don and I are taking Dexamyl nearly every day. Don probably every day. In my case, I fear it is losing its potency. I was very bad tempered this morning—first flaring up because the cablegram company in London had wired Santa Monica there was no such place as High Lane. Then because two boys came over our bridge and climbed down over the gate. I yelled at them like I used to on Sycamore Road.

Charles Laughton seems to have come to an understanding with Elsa about the Hal Greene house—I saw him yesterday—so now I suppose they will probably take it.

Not one word more from Jed Harris about *Hedda Gabler*.

The first day of glorious weather, after this long period of greyness and fog. Lay in the sun and read two of Leslie Fiedler's articles in *Encounter*, because he's coming here tonight; his wife called this morning and suggested it. Fiedler is going to be at the State College writers' conference.

Marguerite called this morning to say that all's well between her and Rory. But they are having trouble with this woman in the Canyon he's slept with. She threatens that if she gets pregnant she'll tell the columnists. Rory is said to be penitent and to have sworn off drinking.

Which reminds me—Don and I have stayed on the wagon for almost a month, but must get off it tomorrow, at least temporarily, in honor of Igor's birthday.

June 17. Leslie and Margaret Fiedler came by to see me last night. He's a funny vain plump little man, pink cheeked, slightly bearded and somehow girlish. She's dark haired, still young looking and almost pretty, the typical Russian Jewish student. They have this regular job and home at Missoula, Montana, the State University—and six children. "I thought everyone knew we had six!" said Mrs. Fiedler, rather the way a famous queer expects to be known. Anxious to flatter me, I guess, and therefore tactless, she said "...back in the thirties, when we all read you"! Fiedler didn't bother to make any

---

[1] Alexander Trocchi (1923–1984), British underground poet—writer, performer, protester.

compliments. He was too entirely concerned with himself. He had come to see me, I gathered, largely because he hoped to get some advice on how to break into movie writing. He has an idea for doing Hawthorne's *The Marble Faun* (I must read it). So this morning I called Jerry Wald to tell him about this. (Jerry had just bought Fiedler's new book, but referred to it as *The Life and Death of the American Novel!*[1])

Beautiful weather again. With Don on the beach. He did a really perceptive and beautiful drawing of Jan Clayton yesterday, showing her sadness and advancing age. (Needless to say, she didn't like it much!) Also some nudes of Chuck van Haren.

We lay on the beach. Don was in his teasing-provocative mood, and said I loved him "not well but too wisely" and we laughed a lot. But there's always a faint reproach somewhere, when he's like this. He says he wants to be really good, great—"because what I'm doing is so tiny." I must honestly say—though he never believes this when I tell him so—that I do now firmly believe in the *psychological* possibility of his becoming a really good artist. I mean, he has the right attitude toward the object. He is genuinely, passionately interested. By degrees, he has to learn to care more and more and more. That's all. But he really and truly cares—and you couldn't have said that three years ago.

Don feels his problem is to become able to take more trouble over each individual drawing. It's as if he were compelled to hurry; and this hurry imposes a superficial technique on him. Of course, on the surface of things, it would seem that he *is* compelled to hurry—either his sitters don't want to stick around indefinitely, or else he's drawing with a group and has to suit his speed to theirs. But the fact is, Don is always in a rush, and this rush is part of the pattern of his life, and he will just have to slow down all along the line and relax, if he's to draw differently. I really think this is the truth. However, meanwhile, I've told him I'll sit and sit and sit for him, by the hour if necessary, while he tries to work this out for himself.

Laughton called this afternoon. It seems we really are going to start on the Socrates project. And that he is seriously considering buying Hal Greene's house. But probably he'll stand out for a lower price, which may cause Hal to call the deal off.

The Fiedlers say Wystan is dieting, and that he's had his moles removed surgically! (The latter may, of course, be on the advice of a doctor for fear of cancer—not because of vanity!)

Nothing from Wyberslegh yet. I hope and pray Amiya is up there by this time and has taken charge.

Just got a partial transcript of my talk at USC. The person who sent

---

[1] *Love and Death in the American Novel* (1960).

it to me claims, with a slight air of reproach, that it took a student *seven hours* to type it out—less than eleven pages. It is full of grotesque misprints: "sub-specia ternitartous" (for sub specie aeternitatis), "Battow Bresh" (Bertolt Brecht) and "plutonic" for Platonic!

Don got back from marketing for the Stravinskys' dinner and I told him what I've written above. He says he draws quickly because he feels the impermanence of things, and because he fears that if he doesn't drive himself he'll get nowhere.

But we agree to try another approach.

Just phoned Hugh Gray[1] to check on my spelling of sub specie aeternitatis—correct!

June 18. Last night we had the Stravinskys and Bob Craft to dinner, because of Igor's birthday, which, according to the mysterious arrangements of the Russian church, is either on the 17th (in the nineteenth century) or the 18th (in this century) or the 20th (in the next century). Vera bought our presents to him for us—a British handbook on South America, and a book of synonyms. She also brought two silk scarves for us. Also a bottle of Haig and Haig. Also a bottle of champagne.

I had one Scotch and a little champagne, and don't feel the tiniest bit affected by it this morning. Don had an extra Scotch and says he feels it a little.

While we were barbecuing, a plane came in from the ocean—from Hawaii, maybe. It was a blue–dark night, very calm, not long after sunset. The plane was a big one, but it made very little noise. As it flew overhead, it switched on its ground lights and turned, beginning its approach pattern to the airport. Igor watched it and said softly, "Welcome!"

After supper he seemed drowsy and spoke very little. Vera assured Don once more that it isn't she or Bob who are set on this South American trip, it's Igor himself. He is so accustomed to being a great celebrity that he feels he has to keep making public appearances, she says.

Later: To a Father's Day lunch for Swami—one day early. The garden had been fixed up with lanterns by a member of the congregation who decorates for Disneyland. The swamis and I sat under a tent, which protected us from the hot sun, and ate turkey and cake. We were all decorated with flower wreaths. Afterwards, there was a performance in the temple. Barada sang songs which were favorites of Ramakrishna; they were of the wailing variety which merely make me nervous. The young girl—Vigli(?)—played on two

[1] Literature professor at UCLA.

drums, with fingers and heel of hand, most skillfully. And another girl plucked the tanpura belonging to Swami Ritajananda—she did this in a self-consciously profiled pose, turned toward Barada and away from the instrument, as if disclaiming all responsibility for the sounds it made. Then two of the men performed a scene from M.'s[1] gospel— M. talking to Vivekananda about his first meeting with Ramakrishna. The actor who played Vivekananda couldn't have been hammier, but his abrasiveness was effective. Which shows that the old tricks work, provided you play them with conviction and without a hint of apology.

Calling in for messages, I learned that Eddie James had said he was coming by on his way back from the beach, around 6:00. So I hurried home, closed the shutters and locked the back door, having left my car parked up on the street, so he should think I was out. Unfortunately I neglected to unlock the door again, and Don, coming back early, found it shut and flew into a tantrum—he was in a bad mood because he'd had a Father's Day dinner with his father.

When he storms like this, I don't know what to say. I just *wish* he'd grow up. But then, lots of people never do.

Depressed this evening, because the latest Gallup poll says that fifty percent of the population now thinks there'll be war with Russia sooner or later.

Also depressed because I've done no work for the past two days.

June 20. A beautiful day—without any morning fog. We had breakfast at the coffee shack at the entrance to Entrada and went on the beach early.

Nothing in the mail from Wyberslegh.

Edward James called to say Aldous has had a growth removed from his tongue and looks terribly sick. Just now Laura called to ask me urgently to speak at their symposium at Tecate, because Aldous is in hospital "with acute laryngitis, and has to be fed intravenously to build him up." (Am not sure if this is true or not.) Anyhow, I resist Laura's bulldozing methods, her taking it for granted that, because *she* has gone to all this trouble to arrange the symposium, *I* have to help them out. This kind of thick-skinned pushfulness is so [insensitive]. I got obstinate and said no—impossible—I am too busy. She's mad at me, now. Can't help it. I never really liked her.

Yesterday I did quite a bit of work on "Paul." I feel it's slowly opening up.

We had Mary Ure, Tony Richardson and his friend Wyatt Cooper to supper. The house and the evening were at their best, and they

[1] Mahendranath Gupta's gospel; see Glossary under "M."

were all entranced by a vision of domestic snugness which is, after all, quite largely genuine. Barbecued steaks, and peaches with Cointreau.

Don raved about Mary Ure's beauty, finding her much superior to Marilyn Monroe. I agree. You feel she's really a sweet nice girl and not at all dumb, either. Tony is interesting—quite sly and subterranean, and with a wild manic side to him (after brandy) which promises great talent. Don thinks him very attractive. Wyatt is a well-meaning but unthrilling young actor.

Tony likes all kinds of pets. He wants to buy lizards and birds. For a time he had a slender loris (described by the dictionary as "a small nocturnal slow-moving lemur"). It would bite you unless you picked it up by the back feet.

Yes, there is something really stimulating in Tony—a wildness. He is all for visiting dangerous night spots and doesn't care if they're raided. They had taken Mary (whose attitude to all this seems just right—neither shocked nor too insistently "one of the boys") to the Carousel the other night and been refused entrance on the ground that she was a minor—but they suspect she was actually mistaken for a boy in drag! Don says there's a resemblance between Tony and Gavin. There is; but it's just this wildness which Gavin seems to lack. They are both terribly shy. Tony has the explosive quality of a very shy person who occasionally uncorks himself. Gavin is cagier.

I forgot to mention that I recommended both Leslie Fiedler and Ray Bradbury to Laura Huxley as speakers for her symposium. She was very contemptuous, because she hadn't heard of them. The ass.

Talking to Don on the beach about Doris Dowling, for whom he painted a floor yesterday. He said that she has resigned herself to Len and her marriage and not being a success. I asked, "You mean, she's stopped putting on her act?" "Oh no," said Don, "she still puts on her act, only the curtain's gone down."

June 21. Wolfgang Reinhardt has just left. He wants me to do a screenplay based on a German historical novel called *Ein Kampf um Rom*,[1] by Felix Dahn; it's about seventy years old and is set in Rome in the sixth century A.D. And I have to do it with Guy Endore[2] and share the money with him—which is $24,000 altogether. It doesn't sound very promising, especially as I'm supposed to do three-quarters of the work—Endore being busy on a book.

Wolfgang hasn't changed much, to look at. He has the same yellow teeth, vague charm, and slyness underneath.

Yesterday we went to Vera Stravinsky's picture show. This new

---

[1] *A Struggle for Rome.*
[2] American screenwriter and novelist.

batch of them is far more decorative than the earlier ones—if anything, too pretty, and they have somewhat the air of having been improvised out of blots. Then we went on to see some paintings by a Mary Vecht—all of them were of owls—cuteness without competence. They maneuvered me into being photographed with her, shaking hands as if to congratulate her on this mess. So I rather bitchily changed the significance of the photo by roaring with laughter, as if the whole thing were too silly for serious comment.

While there, we heard that Patterson had knocked out Johansson, which shocked and quite saddened me. Don't know why. For some obscure reason, I wanted a European champion this time. And Patterson takes boxing much too seriously. He's an earnest bore.

Today it has become very hot. Tonight, though cool enough out here at the beach, is quite windless. For the first time since we've been in the house, we have front and back doors and the front bedroom window all open, without any draft or door slamming. The surf is loud.

Nothing from Wyberslegh.

No news of Aldous. And nothing all this time from Jill Macklem. I begin to fear she's had a serious heart attack.

Finished a kind of straggly rough draft of the Vivekananda introduction today. Also got on with "Paul."

June 23. Yesterday evening Don, who'd been drawing Mary Ure, and I had supper with her and Tony Richardson. And, like idiots, we proceeded to get utterly plastered. And I fell down some steps into their garage and hurt my back—quite badly, I fear. Today I can hardly walk and have stabs of pain which make me yell. Otherwise, the evening seems to have been pleasant, though I remember very little about it. Tony is taking driving lessons. They asked us a lot about our hashish experience.

Today, I've read right through [Plato's] *Gorgias*, as the Laughton job seems quite definitely on. We are to start our meetings on Sunday, and I'll get $5,000 this year.

Yesterday I went through the form of picking up the German treatment of *Ein Kampf um Rom* from Guy Endore. This morning I told Wolfgang I don't want to do it—though I haven't even read it. Didn't like the smell of the job; it seemed I would be left to do all the donkeywork. And I didn't at all like Endore, who kept closing his eyes wearily and grandly and talking about how he had to get back to his book. He never even asked me what I was writing.

In a great surge of Dexamyl energy yesterday, I got seven pages of the final draft of the Vivekananda introduction finished. Very soon, the decks will be cleared for me to get ahead with "Paul."

After all the hot sunshine, today has been cloudy all day.

June 24. My back is perhaps a trifle better this morning, after a good night's sleep. But I'll see Dr. Lewis this afternoon.

Heard from Amiya yesterday. She describes how Richard drank most of a bottle of whiskey while she was out getting roses for the coffin, and passed out cold. She was writing the letter as she sat waiting for him to come round.

Dorothy tells us that the remains of the birthday cake we gave her—the one we got for Rory—provided a feast. She was waiting for her bus and felt hungry and opened the box, and the cake looked so beautiful that two other cleaning ladies, who were sitting beside her on the bench, exclaimed in wonder. So then the three of them ate up every bit of it.

June 26. It really isn't amusing, being a semicripple. Not that I so much mind the twinges of pain—which were getting less severe anyway, or are dulled by some pills called Soma which Dr. Lewis gave me. But I am confined. I can't drive the car. I can't walk more than a few paces. Lewis told me, the day before yesterday, that I have a slipped disk in my spine and that it'll take weeks, and be expensive. Don hates my being sick. It irritates him. But he tries to be good about it. It's one of the functional disadvantages of our relationship: he just isn't the nurse type: I am. This hasn't anything to do with age. M., all her life, really hated sickness in others and always contrived to insinuate that I was shamming if I took to my bed.

Evelyn Hooker came to supper last night. She talked so much that we hardly had to say anything. But she was quite interesting and she was sincerely impressed by Don's drawings. She says that someone (C. S. Lewis?) says that the fault of this age is that it stresses *genitality* rather than *communion*, and mistakes contact for communion. In other words, all the emphasis is on getting into bed and screwing, rather than on establishing a truly intimate relationship. This is no doubt very true. But what a jargon these psychologists use!

Evelyn told how a perfectly serious psychologist asked her: "Is there anything in homosexuality which corresponds to falling in love?"!!

She is triumphant because one of the annual conventions of churches has decided, next year, to learn about sex. She is to address them on homosexuality, and one of her colleagues is to speak on masturbation.

The crazy artist who, during her visit to the sex offenders' institution at Atascadero drew a picture of her in crayons brandishing a huge penis! Evelyn complains that the patients there are too much encouraged to think of themselves under the label of their offense. One of them will introduce himself saying, "I'm an exhibitionist."

One always feels drawn to Evelyn, because she is indeed doing so much good in the world. And how lonely she must be! One sees her all alone in that garden house, surrounded by her tapes of statements—by the gay bar owner, the wealthy male prostitute, etc. etc.

Am getting along steadily with the Vivekananda introduction. Then I can take at least a solid month and a half for "Paul." Except, of course, that there's the Plato project. Charles is just about to arrive now, for our first serious conference.

The drunk (?) woman friend of Jerry Lawrence who called up in the middle of last night and wanted me to take in a sick cat, immediately, as she was leaving for Tijuana in the morning. I was so mad, I hung up on her, which was rude and wrong.

Later: 6:00 p.m. Charles has been here and we've read through chapter eight of the *Republic.* Some of it is really startlingly contemporary. Charles is now very hopeful about the whole project. "Let's shake hands, Christopher," he said: "We can do this thing." His idea, which is really very sensible, is that we shall keep picking out bits we like and then see how they all fit together. But, roughly, the plan is: act one—political ideas, why Socrates was the only serious political philosopher of his time, why his ideas were so obnoxious and therefore why he was so apt to get himself condemned to death. Act two—love, and what Socrates thought it ought to mean. Act three— trial, imprisonment, death.

We're to meet again on Friday, having read the *Republic,* books four and seven, the *Symposium,* the *Phaedrus.*

In some ways, Charles reminds me so much of van Druten: his eagerness to be the bright boy in class who puts his hand up, and his underlying inferiority. He tells me he feared that I should make him feel inferior—i.e., be smarter than him. And now, he implies, he *knows* I'm not.

Dieting hasn't exactly made him look slimmer but his face has much more expression.

It seems that Hal Greene has suddenly demanded $49,000 for the house and adjoining lot, *not* including the four-fifths of a lot next to our land. In fact, *if* this is true, he has quite brutally upped the price by $9,000, and made a liar out of me to Charles. However, this isn't quite certain yet.

I have the impression that Charles may well buy it anyway.

Lay on my upside-down board and did the pelvis exercise as Dr. Lewis prescribed. Is it my imagination, or is my back just a shade better? Certainly this squatting instead of bending down must be good for me; and the sitting upright.

June 28. Well, today I finished the Vivekananda introduction—thank Vivekananda! It is such a bore, but serviceable, I guess.

My optimism about my back was premature. On Sunday evening, we went to see Tony Richardson and Mary Ure again and got rather drunk, and in the morning, yesterday, I felt bad. Then, yesterday evening, we went with the Stravinskys to the Kabuki, and that was too much for it, too. Today has been better, because I kept quiet and lay in the sun and on my board.

Tony Richardson says he identifies with the boy in Alan Sillitoe's "The Loneliness of the Long Distance Runner," because he's tall and skinny and because fundamentally he rebels against everyone.

Olivier fell—also on two steps—while working in Tony's film of *The Entertainer,* and slipped a disk in *his* back; he's better now.

The Kabuki last night was a terrible disappointment—so inferior to the time we saw them in Tokyo. I suppose what one missed was the outrageous and somewhat Elizabethan melodrama: the ghost of the murdered hero, the man struck by lightning, the fight with the witch. These two plays—we left before the third—were so tame; the loyal servant who—unthinkably according to the classic Japanese code—strikes his disguised young master, so as to deceive the guards on the road who have been posted to prevent his escape. And the blind man who thinks his wife's unfaithful so he throws himself into a ravine, and she throws herself faithfully after him, and then they're both restored to life and his eyesight is restored by the goddess of mercy. (True, there was an interesting idea in the first one: namely that the chief of the road guards *isn't* really deceived, but that he's so impressed by the devotion of the servant in striking his master—and thus suffering agonies of guilt and shame—that he lets them through anyway, and even provides the saki for a drinking party at which the young master pardons and thanks the loyal servant—who then dances. But this idea, which is fun now I write it out, is not theatrically effective. It's too esoteric.)

Poor Igor was suffering from diarrhea. (He had to go to the men's room during the first play and asked me to come with him, but then he whispered, "Don't hold my arm!" And at the entrance I ran into Bill Robinson, who was managing a cushion concession and told me that he [is] still very happy [. . .].) Bob and Vera are increasingly worried about Igor's health, and it seems as if the trip to South America might still be cancelled. I have a sad presentiment that I may not see him again if he goes.

(And this makes me remember hurrying back into M.'s bedroom at Wyberslegh last summer to give her what I guessed might be a goodbye kiss—an extra one after we'd already said goodbye. Richard wrote such a moving letter—I got it yesterday—describing how: "The morning of the day she died, she kept on saying, 'Oh for peace, for peace,' which wrung one's heart. I was alone with her when she passed away, holding her hand, but she had fallen asleep and did not wake up again. Just before this, I told her how much you and I loved her, and she pressed my hand with hers and I knew she understood, although she had got beyond articulating." And later he tells how M.'s ashes were buried in the right-hand mound in front of the house, "Close to the remains of her two dear pussies." That makes me cry as I write it, but I know that's because pussies are part of the great sensitive area in my feelings surrounding Don.)

Hal Greene called this morning to tell me that the man Laughton's lawyer had had come out from the loan company had made an offer for the house *for himself*. "For how much?" I asked. "Why, my price," Hal said, "$47,500 for the house, the next lot, and the piece next to you." So I called Charles, who came rushing out here and now has practically bought the place. The mystery deepens. Who was lying? Why this business about $49,000? It is too mysterious—and not quite interesting enough—to worry about.

July 1. This fucking back doesn't get any better. I'm weary of it, and ill-tempered because of a hangover; I went up to Ivan's last night and drank too much. George Stevens Jr[1] was there with Hope Lange— maybe romancing her in his little boy way. He described how shocked he and his father had been, getting material for *The Greatest Story* [*Ever Told*] in Israel. As the makers of *Anne Frank* they had taken it almost as a personal affront when they found that Jews in Israel are unpleasant, nationalistic, imperialistic, chauvinistic and contemptuous of the Jewish faith. Oliver and Betty Andrews were there too, and Donna [O'Neill], of course. Oliver very stuffy and opinionated, but I quite like him. He said that portraiture was "impossible at this time." Luckily Don didn't hear this; he arrived later to pick me up to go to the airport to meet Jo and Ben. But their plane back from Mexico was hours late, so we left again. Talking to Jo this morning, I hear that they didn't get home till 4:00 a.m.

Yesterday noon, I talked to the Pacific Coast Writers' Conference

---

[1] The producer (son of the director).

at State College on "How I Wrote My Berlin Stories." I think I was quite a bore. The room was hot, and the pills I'd taken for my back made me drowsy. Leon Surmelian[1] drove me out and back. I'd been dreading this but ended by liking him rather—but oh, he's so *deadly* serious. It was amazing to hear him holding forth about the national destiny of Armenia; how one cannot be an Armenian without being a "Christian warrior." He thinks, however, that the USA ought to be kept predominantly Anglo-Saxon. [. . .] He gave me a copy of his book *I Ask You, Ladies and Gentlemen.*[2] He has decided that he "respects" me and that I'm a "good man." The friendship of a person like Surmelian makes one groan, and I have visions of evenings of serious talk with shish kebab—and yet he is obviously decent, quite intelligent, and even, to a large extent, on my side. He thinks capitalistic society is necessarily rotten, and he says that, among Armenians who come to America, it is always the third-rate who succeed. Armenians are either businessmen or "dreamers."

Betty Andrews had borrowed from Eugenie Leontovich[3] a book of photos of the pre-1914 productions of the Moscow Art Theater, with pictures of the first productions of Chekhov's plays. The unbelievable hamminess of the character actors, and the fatness and homeliness of the leading ladies. It isn't until the very last pictures—1916—that you see what one would now call a pretty girl. Noticed how strangely deep the sets were. A dinner-table alcove (in *The Seagull?*) was set so far back that you couldn't—you'd think—have seen the actors properly. Wonderful "outdoor" backdrops—"realistically" painted and yet so hopelessly unrealistic that they have an impressionist charm which would delight audiences today.

July 2. Last night we had supper with Lydia Minevitch[4] and her boyfriend, a young lawyer named Bert Fields. I drove the car for the first time since I hurt my back, and it seems all right today—I mean, it seems no worse. Dinner was a bore, and I boringly held forth on the history of the Nazi movement, which seemed to interest the boyfriend but was simply stirring the muddy waters of boredom into more mud. Drank again, but fortunately not too much.

Today has been very hot. Slowly, with all my usual pathological

[1] Armenian novelist and popular historian.
[2] His 1946 autobiographical account of the deportation and murder by the Turks of the Armenians in his childhood village, and of his own eventual escape to America.
[3] Russian stage actress in a few Hollywood films.
[4] Fashion model and daughter of the Russian-American harmonica player, Borrah Minevitch.

delays, I've restarted "Paul," and now I must plough ahead. I think it's apt to be very long.

Presently I'm going out to supper with Mary Ure and Tony Richardson. Don has been there all afternoon, drawing Tony and then taking him to his first lesson at Harvey Easton's gym.

July 3. Don did some really excellent drawings of Tony Richardson yesterday. He is in a wonderfully creative period; he succeeds nearly every day in producing at least some first rate work. I joined them and we all drove down to supper in Chinatown. Tony drove, very cautiously; he is learning. He was in a rather wild mood, otherwise, and eager to get drunk. He has the wild eye of a horse in a Delacroix battle painting. He and Wyatt Cooper leave next week to visit the South—Mississippi—and look for locations, for *Requiem*.[1] Wyatt seemed nicer, because he admitted to his fear of water, even in swimming pools. Told stories of times he'd been seduced. "Let's cut out all this talk. I'm interested in what's between your legs." The mystery of the attraction exercised by fat men on certain people. At the Chinese restaurant, we played the game of "Who would you choose to sleep with?" choosing mostly the most undesirable people thinkable. Mary Ure entered enthusiastically into the game and gave her answers with decision; though she seems exclusively heterosexual, she seemed to know exactly how she'd react to various women. Don thinks she is very sexual.

Touched by a telegram of sympathy on M.'s death from Tennessee and Frank [Merlo].

July 4. Quite early—8:20—and a grey misty morning—the ocean absolutely indistinguishable from the sky, except for a few wrinkles and a border of white foam. What a bore to think of all the people and cars who'll come swarming down here later!

Don seems quite sick, with pains in his stomach. He complained of them yesterday morning too, but today seems much worse. He's had two hot water bottles, and some tea, and keeps trying to shit. So far he refuses to let me send for the doctor.

(When I went to fix the tea this morning, I found that there was nothing left but the flower-decorated pot of "celebration tea" which was given us by John Durst and Jonathan Preston on Christmas Day 1958, when we had them in for Christmas dinner. Thoughts about

---

[1] Richardson had directed the adaptation of Faulkner's novel, *Requiem for a Nun*, on stage in London, but in the end, his film drew more from Faulkner's earlier novel *Sanctuary*—including its title; see Glossary under Richardson.

Jonathan—wondering where he is, now. There was really something very sweet about him.)

Yesterday was a bad day. Charles Laughton came and we read the *Phaedrus*, and I was bored—not by it, but by the contact with Charles, with whom I can't possibly converse because he's stupid, vain *and* pretentious. Not that I mind people being just stupid, one bit, but the combination is impenetrable. He *does* so remind me of van Druten, and, as in Johnnie's case, I'm sorry for and quite fond of him. Charles is *much* stupider than Johnnie, though.

Well then, I saw a man and a woman come up to the gate and try to get through; and then the man climbed over. So I came out, trembling with rage, and said, "Will you *please* go away? Why do you think that gate is locked?" So the man said, "I used to come through here twenty-five years ago," and I said, "I don't care!" and went back into the house and they went away. After this, I was upset all evening. I am quite sick on this point. It is unreasonable, among other things, because I have never even bothered to put up notices saying the walk is private. I must do this.

Don came home and found me upset, so he got upset and put on a faggoty display of temperament, refusing to eat in three restaurants and finally landing us in a Coffee Dan's. And then he wanted to see Lana Turner in her new film—so I said all right, for peace, and there was a line; so we went home, but then Don said let's go later and there was a longer line, and he was furious. And then, just as we'd nearly made it all up, he said that Mrs. Paxton[1] knew of a cheap house painter in Burbank but he'd have to come and sleep here while he was working. So I said I couldn't stand having anyone around; and he said, "That's the way it's going to be."

I record all this because it is too often not recorded. And one ought, when things are going well, to *marvel* at the madness of human beings who claim they love each other and yet can behave like this—with death and H-bombs and every sort of real disaster just around the corner. How *dare* we act like whining ten-year-old spoilt darlings? Well, we dare. We shall go on doing it until we drop.

We're supposed to go with Tony Richardson and Mary Ure to the Selznicks' for lunch. Doubt if we shall, though.

July 5. I did—Don started to get dressed, felt bad and went back to bed.

The party at the Selznicks' was quite fun, just because Tony and Mary were so scared by it, and we laughed a lot in corners. Tony insisted on having a cardboard Uncle Sam top hat. Norma Shearer,

---

[1] Wife of screenwriter and playwright John Paxton.

looking like the mummy's bride, introduced herself and told me how honored she was because I'd used her pool doll's house for a model in *The World in the Evening*. Martin Manulis's[1] car went out of control down the hill and he knocked out four front teeth; David Selznick announced this to our table, saying, "Don't tell anyone," which was funny because, drunk and greedy, we couldn't have cared less—it was a bit like the end of *The Seagull*. Jennifer had invited the leading members of the Kabuki company, so there was much bowing and hissing. I did my best to remove the unpleasant impression made by Mike Connolly's remark in his column in *The Hollywood Reporter* that Stravinsky and Isherwood left after the first act of the Kabuki and Hitchcock after the second—by telling them all how sick Igor was.

I got on with "Paul," and started chapter ten of the Ramakrishna book in the morning.

Don was so sweet yesterday evening. He still felt shaky and we just walked as far as the park to watch the fireworks. Tremendous banging all round the Canyon for nearly two hours. It echoed so loud off our retaining wall that I felt quite uneasy lest a window should break.

It was sad to see poor old Joe Cotten plastered at the Selznicks', and remember it was only last July 4th that we were up there with Lenore.[2]

Today, Charles and I read the *Apology* and *Crito*. Don asked Charles when he could draw him and Charles got quite grand and put him off, and talked about Don's "pursuit" of him and said he was too busy "with Elsa's thing" (it's just some TV show or other) and when Don asked what that was, said, "None of your damn business," and added—as *he* thought good-naturedly—"and now get out." Don took this perfectly; he left, smiling pleasantly. But I'm not sure if I ought not to terminate all relations with Charles—he really is insufferable—an arrogant old fool. There is going to be big trouble ahead if he behaves like this. Especially if he fondly imagines that Don is going to take a hand in keeping Terry entertained when he comes here. Oh dear, how tiresome all this is! I fear a tremendous, slowly growing feud; especially after Elsa's impossible behavior to Don. He is still out, and I'm wondering what kind of a mood he'll return in. He must be just boiling with fury. And Charles left, utterly unconscious that there was anything wrong!

July 6. Well, Don was very self-controlled about the whole thing, but nevertheless, great damage has been done and I feel really bored by the prospect of having to go on associating with this old fool.

[1] Television and film producer.
[2] Lenore Cotten had recently died.

Last night we had Mary Ure, Wyatt Cooper and Tony Richardson to dinner. Tony wouldn't say until the last moment if he was coming or not, and at last he arrived late and drunk in despair. He had failed his driving test (he didn't tell us this—Mary did, though he'd told her, for some inscrutable reason, that he didn't want me to know) and Richard Zanuck, his producer, had just announced that they couldn't afford to shoot *any* of the picture on location, and his writer Jim Poe had been behaving like an ass.

(Cooking note: I must have had the salmon steaks on the barbecue for at least half an hour, owing to Tony's suddenly announced and then delayed arrival. I put them out of range of the direct fire, on the circumference of the grill, and kept drenching them in soy oil—and, wonder of wonders, they were moist, edible, in fact cooked just right!)

After dinner, we were scheduled to go to hear Bertice Reading, the colored actress who was so bad in *Requiem for a Nun* in London. So Tony insisted on driving their car. The others went with Don in the borrowed Ford. Tony drove very uncertainly and kept apologizing. When we got to their house, Wyatt insisted on everybody coming along in the Ford. Evidently, he told Tony he [Tony] couldn't drive. Tony was quite furious with Wyatt for this, and sulked, even after we got to the Crescendo. Mary tried to soothe him. (One sees her rather typically in this role.) Bertice Reading, absolutely spherical in a twenties-ish dress pulled in like a powder puff around the legs, stomped and shrieked and rolled her eyes. She was at least much more amusing than as a tragic actress. Mort Sahl was funny but nevertheless unpleasant, as usual. Mostly jokes about the convention.[1] But he got in a good dig at the Council of Churches for upholding capital punishment. "They say, 'After all, we know a few people get executed unjustly and the communists make a big thing out of it. But it doesn't happen often, and the exception proves the rule and all that jazz ...' It sounds a bit strange, doesn't it, the Council of Churches not being worried about *one* unjust execution!"

David and Helen Laird from L.A. State were there, and Hope Lange—quite drunk—with her brother and his roommate the youngest Stevenson son, John (they're all three to come to supper tomorrow) and George Stevens and George Stevens Jr, and Ivan Moffat, who seems to be circling buzzardlike over Hope's head. Hope told me she felt we were "losing contact." She was sad about this.

Tony left in the midst of all this, and only showed up when we got

[1] The Democratic convention (which nominated Kennedy) was to be held in Los Angeles starting July 11.

back to their house, where he was sulking in a car. Later, he became a little more cheerful over a nightcap and told me, "You're *so beautiful*, Christopher." Mary says he went off this morning still on bad terms with Wyatt, however.

Don just called in (10:30 p.m.) to say he's staying the night in town. The first time, I believe, since May 28! Can this have any connection with what happened this morning?[1] My instinct tells me it does have, and instinct is the only guide to Don's behavior. But, at least, all is harmonious.

My back does seem to be better.

Today I only wrote one page of "Paul." Bad. I'll get up real early and do some before I go to Charles's.

Rather cool weather—with a sense of relief that the Fourth is over.

Bought three "Private Property: Keep Out" signs and now, with my usual perversity, feel badly about putting them up. But I shall.

Incidentally, Tony Richardson, who's known Gavin for years, also feels that there's something emotionally mysterious about Gavin, says you never really know if Gavin likes you or not. "I felt more at ease with you and Don," said Tony, "the first time I met you."

July 9. Have allowed a lapse—don't know why. (I'm racing to fill up this diary because, as I've said already, I want to start typing the future ones, to save my hand.)

The only social event to record is that we had Hope Lange, her brother David and his best buddy, John, one of Adlai Stevenson's sons, to supper, the night before last. Also, Glenn Ford showed up! It was sort of embarrassing—for him at least—because Hope had evidently told him, "Oh, just come along!"—most likely when drunk. We get the impression that Hope is running a bit wild, right now; which is fine, except that blondes take to fat and bloat so easily. Is she grieving over Don Murray? One can't tell.

The evening was further complicated by the fact that Hope had suggested arriving at 6:00 with a photographer, who was to take some pictures of her for a magazine interview, including some of Don drawing her. In fact, Hope didn't arrive till 7:00, with the boys. And of course the photographer started taking *them* and Hope and me, and neglecting the drawing act, and I, knowing Hope's utter vagueness, suspected she had neglected to tell the photographer anything about the drawing, so I spoke up and reminded them of it. And Don was furious and hissed in his most basilisk manner, "Don't *ever* do that

[1] Referring either to Laughton's outrageous rudeness to Bachardy, which in fact occurred the previous day, or to Isherwood and Bachardy's discussion that morning of the incident.

again!" And I thought we were to have an evening of submerged sulks; but he snapped out of it and said he was sorry. Anyhow, the pictures got taken. I am a fusspot, I know. But there's a time to fuss.

Glenn Ford arrived, and would accept nothing but a coke. He's a nice man—lonely, I guess, after a divorce (?) and perhaps trailing after Hope a bit. He talked nicely about his debt to Bette Davis for insisting on having him for her leading man in *A Stolen Life*. Left early.

John Stevenson is quite a doll, in a piggy pudgy slit-eyed way. Temperamentally, he reminds me of Sylvain Mangeot as a young man. He is sleepy and pig-sly. He acted rather indifferent when his father was mentioned; but that's most likely a guard he keeps up. He remained quite sober, while David Lange and Hopey proceeded to get plastered. So did we, rather. But, despite hangovers, Don did some good drawings of Connie Dowling (haven't seen them) which she bought. On the 7th he did two marvellous ones of Tom Wright—who bought one of them.

Yesterday and the day before I went to Laughton's and we read the *Crito* and *Phaedo*, and now Charles wants to put part of the last act together, inserting the cave passage from book seven of the *Republic*, instead of the long dialogue on immortality which simply doesn't work. I think this is a good idea. Charles was very proud that *he* had had it—so exactly as John van Druten would have been.

Meanwhile, there's an offer from Fox, to polish the script of a film about St. Francis. It's called *The Joyful Beggar*, a sufficiently off-putting title. Quote from the first page—"We see and feel the turbulence of the twelfth century under this narration"—oh yeah? The film is to be produced by one of the young Skourases, and directed by Michael Curtiz—two more strikes against it. Don says don't touch it—we'll get by. But the money isn't to be sneezed at.

Very slowly, page by page, I grind at "Paul." No sparks yet—but I must just keep on.

July 11. The worst of this period is that I'm giving way to jitters, because I'm constantly being kept waiting for people or phone calls. So I don't get ahead with "Paul." *And nothing else matters.*

Today, Laughton and I started a scissors-and-paste job, inserting the cave speech from the *Republic* between the beginning and end of the *Phaedo*. Charles thinks there's also a place for the *Crito*—some of it. This snipping and pasting gave the work a kind of nursery atmosphere which was agreeable.

Yesterday a really funereal party at the Bracketts', for some distinguished Democrats. But all I heard was Rory's domestic misery with Marguerite (he says she hates his career), Agnes Moorehead's worry about not getting a job (Rory recommended she should switch to Hugh French) and Marguerite's bitchery (she hates Hope Lange). Don thought she was looking terribly ugly. That strange old freak, Dodo Pendleton, told the story of the keepsakes and accessories she has in her purse, all chained together with gold. A handsome airline pilot in Rome gave her his badge, saying that whenever she was scared on a plane she should think of him, because he had flown so many thousands of miles without an accident—and, within two months, he was killed!

Obscene old Polly Adler[1] was at Jerry Lawrence's. We visited him later. And a younger woman who had a voice—Russian Jewish?—which made me want to scream. She went on and on and on about what she called mysticism—which meant being successful and keeping your youth. Both she and Polly had been down to the symposium at Tecate. It sounded like the dreariest crank-fest. Aldous's speech was played on tape.

In the morning we visited Doris (Dowling) and Len Kaufman, who are spending their weekends at an apartment over the Housemans' garage in Malibu Colony. Len very Jewish and fat. Doris was seriously jealous because her miserable whining brat John-oh (or however she'd spell it) had gotten a crush on the man next door, a TV writer[2] who fascinates all the neighbor children so much that they've formed a club with him as the only adult member. Every day, he finds new ways of amazing them. The day before, he'd caught a moray eel and today he was going to barbecue it. This was thought to be a slight on Len, who had said that, this summer, he wanted "to get close to the kid." Len doesn't really mind, though—only Doris. Len is writing a TV story about the whole thing.

July 14. Something bad has happened. The night before last, very late, after the performance of *Duel of Angels*[3] and a dreary party at Scandia with Paul Kohner,[4] William Wyler,[5] Mary Ure and Tony, and lots of agents, Don said goodbye, and drove off. He explained that he had to

---

[1] A madam of the period; she told her story in a bestselling book *A House Is Not a Home*, later filmed.
[2] Isherwood added in the margin: "Mr Peckanpaugh (?)," evidently referring to the director Sam Peckinpah, who wrote television Westerns (*The Rifleman, The Westerner*) before making films.
[3] Christopher Fry's translation of Jean Giraudoux's play *Pour Lucrèce*, running in Los Angeles before the New York opening; Mary Ure had a lead.
[4] Hollywood agent.
[5] German-born film director.

spend the night and last night looking after Paul Millard's studio because Dick Dobyns[1] had gone to Claremont.

This morning, Tony Richardson calls me, saying he wants to meet Don early this afternoon, as he'll be free on account of Buddy Adler's funeral. So I call Paul Millard's apartment, and, to my stupefaction, find myself talking to Paul, who's been back from Europe two days already, he says. So then I get an inspiration and call Apple[2] because I know Don was going to draw her yesterday afternoon. And she tells me Don called her and told her he had a stomach upset—food poisoning—and a friend was looking after him; so he couldn't come.

So now here I am, sitting on the phone and feeling sick with worry. And behind the worry, all kinds of other feelings crowding in. A voice keeps reminding me that he told me a totally unnecessary, elaborate lie—or so it seems. But right now I don't give a shit about that. I only want to know he's all right. I am gradually getting very scared—and writing this is just a way of killing time.

This makes me realize how desperately insecure the whole structure of my present life really is. It depends so utterly on Don and on my belief in our relationship. That's wrong, of course. And perhaps this will teach me something. But for the moment the only question is—*where is he?*

Later. Don called about 11:30 a.m. It seems he really was sick—it wasn't just an excuse to Apple; and he did arrive at Paul's apartment the night before last and find Paul in bed asleep and leave without waking him. So he didn't tell a lie, and now it seems incredible that I should have ever thought he would. The truth is, I am sort of half prepared for anybody to do anything. That's not entirely a fault, of course. It makes for understanding.

Now I feel nothing but utter relief.

July 17. There's a lot to write but I doubt if I can do much because my hand is shaking a bit. It's shaking because (1) I have a huge hangover, (2) I have taken, for the first time, one of the all-black (highest strength) Biphetamine capsules which Carter Lodge gave me, (3) I have drunk gallons of coffee on top of it.

Never mind! The result is that I have written eight whole pages of "Paul" and am halfway into a ninth!

Thick fog in the Canyon—ideal working weather. In town it's very hot. Don spent last night sleeping at his studio because he wanted to make an early start, and we were up till I guess nearly 4:00 a.m. After the theater, we took Vivien Leigh to the Carousel with Tony

[1] Dobyns lived in and helped manage Millard's apartment building.
[2] Gertrude Appelbaum, secretary to Manning Gurian.

Richardson, his friend Jim the driving instructor, Robert Helpmann[1] and Jack Merivale. Merivale, who is an almost unbelievable young-old British prude, who belongs in the last century, sat in the car after taking one horrified look. He is in the play and is thought by many to be Vivien Leigh's lover.

Vivien loved the Carousel—where she was recognized; and it was a pity we got there so late that they were on the point of closing. It was packed. At closing time, the boys were all shouting, "Where's a party?" and then a couple were announced and the addresses given.

Vivien didn't seem at all crazy; but she is neurotically self-obsessed and aggressive in her opinions of plays, etc. You feel her devotion to Larry, however. That's tragic. She talks of him constantly. After the Carousel, Mary Ure gave us a delicious supper—cold leek soup, cold salmon, pouilly, strawberries. I really love Mary—she is an adorable girl; one of the most lovable people I have met in a long time. And Tony I like very much, too—though he's wild and difficult and might easily become resentful and quarrelsome.

Don seemed very tense and edgy on his return home, but the atmosphere got better last night. I simply must not make any kind of demand on him at this time—even for love.

All I saw of the convention was Kennedy's short speech (on TV) after his nomination. It put me off, rather. He seemed cold and stiff. But his acceptance speech is generally thought to have been promising. And Gore, still loyal to him, says he sometimes has the look "of a young Caesar"(!)

July 18. 7:25 a.m. Woke early, feeling still heartthrobby and overstimulated from the pill I took yesterday. It certainly doesn't mix with coffee or liquor. We were drunk again last night. That's three nights in the last four. And tonight I'm going out with Gore. Diana Lynn and her husband[2] gave a party for him yesterday. *Why* did we go? Well, of course, because of Gore. But we didn't see much of him. I sat next to a very pretty blonde girl who poured out the tale of how her husband was involved in the Tallman scandal where they were caught naked with marijuana and chorus girls (or boys), and how she forgave him because she loved him. I warned her not to run around telling this story to everybody—which was probably my only good deed of the evening. Don was very sweet to me, but suffering from some kind of persecution resentments against the hosts, because he'd been put at an awful table. I like Agnes Moorehead.

[1] Vivien Leigh was starring with Mary Ure in *Duel of Angels*, directed by Helpmann, the Australian ballet dancer and actor.
[2] The actress and pianist and her wealthy second husband, Mortimer Hall.

My weight is again down to 146, but, as before, I *cannot* cross that psycho-physical shadow line, 145.

Such a beautiful pale gold morning. It'll probably fog in later.

Now I'm going to do something I haven't done in months and months—work (on "Paul") before breakfast.

July 19. I had supper with Gore last night. I do like and admire him—absurd and serious simultaneously, and all the time. He is now rather playing the role of the reckless young political gambler, rushing to fame or disaster. He enjoys playing with the idea that the Republicans will launch some terrific smear campaign against his private life—but I don't think he seriously believes this will happen. He talked about "the new Athens" which will arise when Kennedy is in power; but at the same time he described, rather admiringly, instances of Bob Kennedy's ruthless methods. Gore also admires Jack Kennedy's ruthless sex life. As for himself, he claims that he now feels no sentiment whatever—nothing but lust. He can't imagine kissing anyone. The way he has to have these sex dates set up is certainly compulsive.

He talks of himself as a failed writer. But there's a questioning look in his eye as he tells me this. I protest, quite sincerely, with praise of *The Best Man.* But I think I know what he means. First, he wants to be a novelist, not a playwright. Then he wants to write fantasy, not realism. He feels he lacks imagination. And I think he does.

At the same time, he is pleased and amused by his own performance as an operator. He likes himself making speeches. (He was excellent on the Levant show; we watched it up at Chris Wood's.) He told me, in deadly confidence, that he is planning a marriage of convenience with—Phyllis Kirk!

He pleased me by speaking with real appreciation of Don and his talent. And not just the talent but the observation behind it.

July 20. I wish I could write something which would catch a sense of now-at-this-moment—it's about 4:15 p.m. I have been lying naked on my upside-down board doing the exercises Dr. Jack Lewis prescribed for my back. Put on weight again, probably because of the gnocchi I ate with Gore at the Marquis. It's funny how one thinks about one's body. Actually, I'm very stiff most of the time, with my bad knee (a little worried about the lump there) and my back. I suppose I seem like a stiff, painfully walking elderly man. And yet, again, I refuse to admit this to myself. I still think of myself as moderately active and quite capable of violent physical behavior, as I was up to the age of fifty at least.

And yet, in many respects—I can never repeat this too often—this is certainly one of the happiest periods of my life. Because of Don. Because I have work to do. Because I am living exactly where I want to live. Today I wrote some more on "Paul"—to the end of page thirty-five, and now I see quite a way ahead. I got some really exciting and important insights as I was reading Plato with Charles, yesterday.

Of course, this happiness of mine is terribly insecure. It rests on Don. On my own health, which could easily go wrong and make work impossible and run us into financial difficulty. And on the international situation, which looks terrible and promises big crises this fall in Cuba, Africa, Berlin and elsewhere. (I still believe, however, that Russia won't deliberately get us into all-out rocket war.)

All of this points to one thing—hold on to the anchor. Make japam. Nothing else can be relied on, and all other activity is, in the last analysis, merely symbolic. Do I *entirely* believe this? Very, very nearly. Ninety-five percent. Do I act as if I did? Very, very, very seldom. I rely on Swami to do the work.

I look at my body, with its wrinkles and slackness of the skin and other imperfections which can never be set right any more now. It is wearing out, tiring, getting ready, whether I like it or not, to die. *I* am getting ready to die. All very well to say I am not my body and even believe this—still, it is a parting. All very well to say that my whole life has been a dying and saying goodbye to the past; this will be different. Even if it is quite painless, it will be different.

And there is saying goodbye to Don. Nobody who has ever loved anyone as I love Don can seriously pretend that *that* won't be painful.

July 21. Terrific heat in town. Even out here, at 10:00 (sun time) it's already muggy. And I have to go in and read with Laughton. He's in a great state of excitement today because Terry arrives tomorrow. Charles and I wallow naked in the pool like a pair of old hippos.

Supper last night with Jerry Lawrence. Middle-aged bachelors leering over photos from his European trip. Jerry loved the Russians, with their spontaneous kissing and cuddling, but said they weren't as nice in Moscow as in Leningrad. They had actually tried to reassure him, had begged him not to mind about the U-2 incident (which took place while he was there). Jerry went with some men from the embassy and questioned a long line of people waiting to buy newspapers, to find if they wanted to read about the breakdown of the summit conference. They mostly didn't. They wanted to know what was playing at the movies. Politically, they seemed quite apathetic.

Hugh and Robin French came in this morning with a novel by Arthur Calder-Marshall, *Occasion of Glory*, about Mexico. They want to make a film of it with James Mason.

July 22. Charles, who is now in a state of jitters about Terry Jenkins's arrival, again hinted that Don would be able to lend a hand at amusing him. So I said Don was much too busy drawing. So Charles said there was something wrong with his drawing, something unresolved. Which was really just irritation. But then he got much more sensible, admitted Don's talent and said the unresolved thing was due to the conflict between wanting to do a picture and wanting to get a pleasing likeness. So he said Don should study Sharaku,[1] who did all of his work in 1794—all that remains of it, at least—bitching female impersonators and other actors of the period—and was, according to Charles a very great artist. So Charles wrote a note to Don, along with the book[2]—making it clear it was loaned, not a gift—"I think," he wrote, "there may be a streak of this kind of talent struggling to be noticed." Then, realizing this didn't sound right, he added "by you" after "noticed." And added, "Sharaku it is said was executed for having made these prints." When I told all this on the phone to Don, he—with that brilliant but rather infuriating perception of the masochist—knew at once that Charles had done it because of Terry!

Good progress again this morning on "Paul." I must drive and drive to the end of that. Then the summer won't have been wasted.

Disappointed by the last section of *Passage to India*. It seems "set-up," mechanical, and curiously trivial. The rest is so marvellous. I love it more than ever.

Calder-Marshall's *Occasion of Glory* very unpromising so far.

Don spent the night in town. Supper with Leo Castillo.[3] He seemed very artificial and bored me with his chatter, except about politics. We walked and looked into stores on Robertson, and I was embarrassed at having to disagree with his taste so often, so I lied. But he *did* pay his share of dinner. And all of Will Wright's[4] bill!

Still hot—but a breeze.

[1] Japanese painter and draughtsman whose portraits of Kabuki actors were produced as woodblock prints; he may have been a No actor.
[2] Several illustrated studies appeared in the 1950s; Laughton might have had *Tosushai Sharaku (Worked 1794–1795)* (1955) by Ichituro Kondo (adapted for English by Paul Blum) or Elise Grilli's *Sharaku* (1959).
[3] Assistant to Louella O. Parsons, Hollywood gossip columnist for the Hearst newspapers.
[4] Proprietor of a chain of ice cream parlors in Los Angeles.

July 23. Last night we had supper with Chris Wood at the Red Snapper and went with him to see Fred Zinnemann's *The Sundowners* at Warner's Studio. A "wholesome" picture—by no means bad and containing some real insights into Australian life—but never in any way memorable.

This morning, the painters—Mr. Gardner and his brother—arrived and went to work at great speed. The kitchen is a shambles, with displaced pots and pans everywhere. And then Charles Laughton arrived, with Terry Jenkins and Bill Phipps. Terry is handsome, unexciting, and, I really think, a very nice boy. Charles sent him and Bill out driving while we finished off the *Republic*. When they returned, it developed that Terry had read it; he has studied philosophy. He seems to be quite unvain and not dumb. I do hope Don likes him. Charles is in a dither, of course. And I'm the only one he can fully confide in. Elsa seems to be playing it cool—having Terry in the house and praising him greatly afterwards. But always on the lines of, "Why—you could take him anywhere!" Well, we shall see how it all develops.

Finished *Occasion of Glory* this morning. Oh dear, it is a dog! Magazine Hemingway. How could Calder-Marshall have written anything so trivial? I don't see how I can possibly take it on. And yet I hate to lose this contact with Hugh French, because I really would prefer working with him to most of the jobs one's offered.

July 26. Today I finished page forty-nine of "Paul." I guess *something* is emerging, though I am just scrambling from handhold to handhold, working my way up. I hardly dare hope the entire draft will be ready for my birthday.

Last night, Don spent the night in town and I, on the impulse, invited Terry Jenkins to have supper with me—Charles being busy. He really is a very unusual boy. He likes working as a model, and loves buying clothes—and yet he seems almost without physical vanity. He is very easy to talk to, and he reacted with enthusiasm to our evening—I drove him up into the hills to look at the lights of Hollywood and of the valley. He has been around a lot in London, but he never drops names. He isn't a sulker or the least superior or stupid, and yet he doesn't come forth to meet you; he is simply waiting for you, as it were, whenever you want him. One sees him as an ideal male nurse.

Now I must go and get some liquor for tonight—Gerald Heard, Michael and Chris are coming.

Much cooler today.

July 28. Gerald Heard, Michael Barrie and Chris Wood came to supper on the evening of the 26th. Gerald and Michael have been in Hawaii. They got in a car accident, a pileup of four cars, coming down from the Pali.[1] Gerald was quite badly hurt but he seemed in the highest spirits now. He described a married couple they met who seemed concerned to tell everybody that they always took their morning shit together. Furthermore, they took it sitting side by side on the edge of an extinct volcano. Furthermore, one morning while they were taking it, they looked down and saw, in the abyss below them, an unidentified aerial object. Furthermore, this object, after remaining motionless for a while, zoomed right up high into the sky above their heads, and disappeared!

Chris, with his usual obstinacy, brought Penny[2] with him. She fussed and snuffled about and irritated me a good deal and interrupted the conversation.

Mike had taken many pictures of Gerald, flirtily leggy in shorts and a great sun hat, under palms. In some of them, he looks astonishly young. No more than forty-five.

Charles Laughton and I are now getting to the point at which we've almost decided what material goes into act one of our Plato play. Yesterday he was here, after staying with Terry out at their house on Palos Verdes. Terry remains as mysterious to me as ever. He is so pleasant, so relaxed and yet not stupid or calculating. However, being with him and Charles together is less easy than being with him alone. While I made conversation about Los Angeles, Charles just sat there heavily and let me get on with it. Terry has his own (rented) car now, and delights in driving around to men's clothes shops.

Yesterday, Don drew Evelyn Hooker. She said to me on the phone this morning that it had been, "A very strange experience, like having one's own Rorschach test made." One of the drawings is brilliant.

July 31. Yesterday I got on to page sixty-two, and I hope to finish page sixty-five today. This will mean that I may aim at writing at least one hundred pages before my birthday. These compulsive writing plans sound silly, but they are very important when you are doing a first draft.

The weather here is heavenly, yet I seldom seem to get out into it, and almost never go on the beach, or in the ocean. I hope to do so this fall, when the beach crowds thin out.

But what a happy time! What joy to have one's work always asking

---

[1] A mountain on Oahu.
[2] His dachshund.

to be continued! This house has a lot to do with it, too—just because of its view and sense of space. But most of all there is Don. I do feel that he is at least more happy than not, right now. Though he did say yesterday that he wished he could "get more out of being young." What he seems to mean by this is, he wishes he could be in a group, as I was, and be violently pro and con in his opinions, and have at least some people who believed in him, and called him important. That, of course, is the lack, in this place. And, of course, it would anyway have to be done by Don's contemporaries. I can't praise him too much, or even, in a sense, root for him beyond a certain bound, because I am so absolutely concerned for his overall development. I have to be ready to "absorb" his possible failure as well as his success. The thought does occur to me that he might be better off without me—at least at some future date. But it's no use getting too noble about this. Much better to admit that I'm a monster of possessiveness but try to be a relatively benign one. I shall *never* surrender him willingly.

What *did* occur to me this morning as I sat down to write this was that it's just during "seasons of calm weather"[1] such as this that I have to remind myself of the inner resource, make japam and try to remember God. Well, I try. Not often enough.

Yesterday evening we had supper with the Stravinskys—they took us to The Oyster House. Igor is so childlike in his greed; he was gobbling down all kinds of canapés and then feeling nausea. It is not very cheering to see what a mess of minor ailments his old age is. And yet he is so wonderful still—bright and sharp and full of warmth—so considerate, for instance, of Don. And setting forth, tomorrow morning, on this new musical safari—Mexico City, Bogotá, Lima, Santiago, Buenos Aires, Rio, Brasília, Trinidad, New York, Venice! He spoke of his happiness in *The Rake's Progress*—they'd heard it again in Santa Fe with a very good, young cast. "A great opera!" Igor exclaimed delightedly, but added that he was speaking just as much of the libretto.

Dear Vera drives worse than one could think possible, especially as she does so much of it. She terrified us utterly coming to and from the restaurant. We said goodbye at the gas station where they were fixing the Simca; it developed a leak in the pipe to its radiator. I do love them both so much.

The painters are to finish the house today, we hope.

August 2. A beautiful day. Don has been putting up shades all morning, and they won't roll. Geller is back. I sicked him on to Laughton's lawyers, who *still* haven't produced our agreement or any

[1] A slight misquotation from Wordsworth, "Immortality" Ode, l. 161.

money. Meanwhile Laughton, busy learning lines for "Wagon Train," calls to say that Taft Schreiber[1] advises him to devote the rest of his life to serious projects—which means, at the moment, Plato! God, how public-spirited these characters get—with other people's time and efforts! Laughton *does* remind me of Johnnie so often; he takes himself just as grandly.

Yesterday Prema drove Don and me down to Laguna Beach to see Swami and the others, including Pavitrananda, on vacation here from the East. The sunshine, the ocean, everything seemed brighter and newer than up here. We went swimming and I lost my false front tooth—the sea just swallowed it in a single gulp. Don drew Swami, but was dissatisfied—too many people around. My knee hurts from climbing (twice) all those steps to the beach.

As of yesterday evening—supper at Tom Wright's—I have decided to cut out drinking entirely or almost. I feel so much better without it.

Now I have to make a big drive to get my last episode finished. My target is one hundred pages by my birthday.

Swami seemed radiant, yesterday; and all of them—Vandanananda, Ritajananda, Krishna and Pavitrananda—are being stuffed with food like pussycats. Only Tito, who cooks for them from morning till night, looks worried and exhausted. He is obviously on the verge of a breakdown.

A card arrived from Heinz, black edged, with "Aufrichtige Teilnahme"[2] printed on it. On the card, Heinz has written, "Deeply depressed that your mother has gone forever poor Chris."

August 4. Today I reached the end of page seventy-six. Another difficult part is approaching, and I'm not at all sure where I go from there—but it'll be all right. I'm sure I can get a first draft out—the only question is, can it be before the start of the fall semester? I still have little or no idea how long it will take.

This afternoon, Don drew Chris Wood, rather wonderfully, and then we drove down to look at the Monet exhibition,[3] which is simply terrific—the haystacks, Rouen cathedral, the poplars, the water lilies. Two of the poplar paintings—the one with the sunlight on them, the other when it has moved and they have turned purple. Don said, "That's really *shocking!*" and it *was*. A public scandal.

---

[1] His agent.
[2] "Sincere Sympathy."
[3] At the Los Angeles County Museum of Art.

August 5. Monet was an art saint, in the Japanese-Chinese tradition. I felt, before everything else, his love for the environment—particularly the north of France. The Riviera and the London paintings are, from his viewpoint, somewhat Arabian Nights—tropic magic and fog magic. I wish one could be great like that in prose, getting variations out of a theme. You could in poetry, of course. But the novel is so scattered.

Geller is engaged excitedly in trying to extract the signed contract, plus five thousand dollars from Laughton's lawyers. Charles himself I haven't seen. He is busy learning his lines for "Wagon Train." Then, when it's over, I guess he'll suddenly need me and expect me to pop to it. Never mind, I keep steadily on at "Paul." Finished page eighty-one today and saw several new handholds ahead of me, up the precipice. Just keep right on steadily climbing and I'll get to the top.

I still don't see how our Plato play is to open. The opening of the *Republic* is messy, because it arises out of this discussion of old age. The opening of the *Timaeus* is better, because it purports to take place the day after the *Republic* dialogue, and Socrates recapitulates the argument. But at present it looks as if we really *must* have some stuff of our own, to introduce Socrates in a suitably theatrical manner.

A very strange synchronicity—just as I am writing about "Ronny" in "Paul"—just the very day, yesterday, when I was thinking about the character and seeing its importance—Tony Bower[1] calls long-distance from New York! I wasn't home and he hasn't called back. What did he want? I haven't heard from him in ages.

August 6. Just back from Tony Richardson's, having drunk three Bloody Marys and listened to a frustrated love affair of Tony's. John Osborne meanwhile was interviewing an ex-girlfriend—he knew her when he was eighteen in Brighton. Since then, both of them have gotten fat.

Last night, when they came to supper and I undercooked the shish kebab, I didn't care for Osborne—thought him conceited and grand; now I like him better. Mary's relation to him is undoubtedly masochistic. He doesn't take much trouble to be nice to her, but I suppose she likes it.

August 7. Just reached the bottom of page eighty-five—all I shall do for today. But I do earnestly hope I have a good day tomorrow: even to ninety-five if possible. This sounds insanely compulsive but it's the only way to get a first draft written. And I realize more and more how *very* rough this draft will be. After all, I'm just merely scratching the surface.

[1] The model for Ronny.

I'm hoping, of course, not merely to reach page one hundred but the end of the draft itself, by my birthday. This will be an awful lot more pages—perhaps even fifty or sixty—but quite a lot of it I *know*. My hope is based on a conversation with Elsa Lanchester on the phone this morning. Poor woman, I can't dislike her, she's so desperate with bitchy fear.

She now takes the line that probably *she* will move into the house next door. Charles should never have bought it. She says Terry is helpless—she even describes him as "retarded." Charles has to cook for him down at Palos Verdes—where they are now, learning the lines of "Wagon Train." It seems that the "Wagon Train" episode won't go on until just before Charles's operation starts—so there'll be no time for our Plato work. So much the better! I can get on with "Paul."

(Meanwhile, Hal Greene's mother really is on the point of death. If she had died earlier, Hal might never have sold the house to Charles.)

Elsa talked darkly about how Charles would certainly victimize me—he can't be alone for a moment. (Elsa claims that *she* can be alone, but she admits that Charles infuriates her by suddenly leaving for the evening at around six, without having warned her or given her any time to invite someone to watch TV with her.) I replied that I am a monster and quite able to take care of myself with other monsters such as Charles. This brought us to the interesting revelation that Enid Bagnold[1] (who used to be very thick with Charles and is hurt because he has dropped her) is writing a play called *The Monsters*. So then I told Elsa that *I* had worked for a while on a play with that title—I didn't mention Don's part in it, for fear of Elsa's bitchery. "But," I added, "monsters are very loyal in their own way." So Elsa and I laughed a lot and I felt I had cheered her up.

Don and I got up very late this morning because we were very late going to bed, after supper at the Selznicks', where they showed three one-hour films of interviews with Jung. The interviews couldn't have been worse presented—just one shot held on Jung throughout. And the interviewer, a sweaty-faced humorless Jewish-American doctor, who kept cutting in, "—But, to be specific—" Nevertheless, Jung was adorable; you saw how very cute he must have been as a young man. Like all great men, he spent most of the time disentangling himself from the net of formalization which the questioner kept trying to throw over him.

His most interesting (to me) statement: as early as 1919, he began to realize, in studying the unconscious of his German patients, that

---

[1] English novelist and playwright.

something catastrophic was shortly going to happen to the psyche of the German people as a whole.

Aldous and Laura were there. Aldous very wan and shrivelled, but very animated and friendly. Laura definitely hostile to me.

And that ass David Susskind. He claims psychoanalysis is not a science and believes that he proved this in an argument with a group of analysts on his latest TV open-end show. He asked me to be on one of them. I agreed. Wish now that I hadn't. It'll be nothing but baiting and aggression.

Don has left to spend the night in town. We parted lovingly, but after mutual exasperation over the sending off of a letter to Frank Taylor with specimen photostats of Don's drawings—so Frank can make up his mind if he wants Don to come to Reno and draw the principals in *The Misfits*. (They're already filming.) Don gets absolutely hysterical over these small chores—typing the letter, choosing which photos to send, etc. etc. And this rattled *me* because I was frantic to start work, after missing yesterday because of a hangover.

August 10. Am now on page 104 of "Paul" and have come to the end of what one might call the second act. How much longer it'll be, heaven knows.

Last night we went to see *Three Sisters* at UCLA—poorly acted and directed, but how marvellous! It is all about happiness—as a reality and/or as an illusion. It is the most perfectly sub specie aeternitatis work imaginable. It is also a great classic of "tea-tabling."[1] Although firearms figure importantly in three of Chekhov's major plays, they are always "tea-tabled." In *Uncle Vanya*, the shooting is farce. Yet it is always poignant, too. It is the shooters who are really suffering—Vanya, Solyony[2] and of course Treplyov,[3] who shoots himself. Technically, it is very interesting how Chekhov blends the exterior dialogue with the interior monologue—in other words, how he introduces soliloquies into the scene, on full stage, and keeps them realistic: i.e. a character is talking to himself and to anybody else who wants to listen. But usually no one wants to. For *Three Sisters* is about the preoccupation of people with themselves and their consequent inattention to others.

Yesterday we had lunch with Tony Richardson and later went to Fox to watch him direct *Sanctuary*. Tony says that—the last evening

[1] The technique of understatement that Isherwood admired in Forster's work; see Glossary under Forster.
[2] In *Three Sisters*.
[3] In *The Seagull*.

we spent together—Mary and John Osborne were having a desperate quarrel over his mistress, and that Mary went out and rolled sobbing on the bathroom floor. I feel so ashamed of myself because I never noticed anything was wrong—partly of course, because I was drunk. There's an example of "basic inattention" for you!

On the set, Tony is quite wonderful—so perfectly calm. He told me he loves directing—would like to direct all the time, without even bothering what became of the pictures. They had a fine set, a speakeasy, with a fan dancer. Lee Remick looked as if she'll be very good in the part.

A long talk on the phone, yesterday morning, with a woman who works for David Susskind and who had called wanting me to take part in a program of "people with strong views," including Steve Allen and Shelley Winters. I said no, and explained that I don't like Susskind's attitude. He is such a little bitch and his idea of "discussion" is to keep baiting his guest with insults. Also, he's ignorant and proud of it. Of course, I said all this politely. But she got the point.

August 11. Finished page 114. This was another record spell of work—under the influence of Dexamyl I'm becoming absolutely frantic. I still am not at all sure I can finish before the 26th, however, because there really does seem to be more and more to say. Still, I'm very grateful for this impetus.

This morning I passed my test for renewal of my driver's license— only one mistake: I said 65 miles per hour was *not* the maximum speed limit in California. This was a relief because I've been afraid that I might somehow flunk it.

Walter Starcke came by, en route for Japan and round the world. He has become a little white on the temples, which suits him. Otherwise, he seemed exactly the same. But he feels he's changed. 1959 brought an end to a period of his life. "Now I belong to myself." He says he used to have dreams in which Johnnie rejected him. But the other day he dreamed that Johnnie was playing the piano and he turned and smiled and said, "Come!" and they sat down together and played a duet. "Now I live by grace," says Starcke. "I live every hour of every day to the fullest." Actually he is in Key West, dealing in real estate and having parties with Herlihy[1] and his friend which sometimes go on till morning. Lots of sex. He took a violent fancy to the kaleidoscope on our table, so I gave it him. Otherwise he seemed very little interested in my doings, or Don's—and hardly at all in this house, although he says he finds he has a great talent for interior decoration. He hurried off to have supper with some millionaire.

---

[1] James Leo Herlihy, novelist and playwright.

The other day I saw a cream car on which its owner had painted the name "Slow White."

Two boys pushing their car, which had evidently run out of gas, along Entrada Drive to the point where it would coast downhill. "Oh, Jesus!" one of the boys kept crying out, very loudly, in mock agony, "Oh dear Jesus, help me! Help me in my hour of need!" The other boy was rather embarrassed.

August 13. Yesterday, Don painted the kitchen and porch floors (black) and this morning they were still sticky so I had to breakfast off fruit and drink some disgusting instant coffee made with the bathroom hot water. Lacking coffee, I couldn't do much on "Paul." A terrific lot still remains—or so it seems.

The "monks' picnic" at Laguna yesterday was a frost—partly because the dreary but unanswerably efficient Prema had decreed it shouldn't be on the beach but up in the patio, where it was much less messy but utterly unromantic, uncozy and unjoyful. A devotee who is a patient of Dr. Bieler told me how Dr. Bieler had kept him for the past year eating practically nothing but fruit and a few vegetables—and now his shit didn't stink. Tito seemed far less worried and crazy. An Irish folksinger led us in spirituals—that was the only lively part of the evening. Drove down with the desperate devotee named Ernie, who lives opposite the temple, and talks of his automobile accidents as a torero talks of his gorings. Drove back with Prema and a new recruit—for whose benefit Prema conducted an edifying conversation with me, about the emptiness of life without God. I said nothing I didn't mean, and tried hard to forget that the new recruit was present—but still I felt rather cheap, like a "cooperative" witness testifying before the Un-American Activities Committee.

I'm fond of Prema, though. He's a dour, crazy, bitter old thing—but a kind of frosty gleam shines through.

August 15. A miserable hangover, today, after an evening with Lesley Blanch and then a visit to Tony Richardson. Mary Ure and John Osborne were there unexpectedly and on very bad terms. I hugged Joan Plowright[1] drunkenly, which was a mistake. I feel ashamed of myself but have nevertheless written to page 129 of "Paul" and see the end in sight.

All this time, I have been idiotically thinking I'll call the novel *The Enemy*, forgetting Wirt Williams's novel, which I have right before me on the shelf! Now I'm thinking of *The Presence of the Enemy*. Not bad.

[1] The English actress who married Laurence Olivier in 1961.

August 17. In the Presence of the Enemy—better!

Today I reached 140 of "Paul." This was quite an achievement because there are a whole lot of new things in it. But the hashish episode will still be very long.

A rather wonderful evening with Jim Charlton last night. We got nearer to our old relation than in a long while—largely because he didn't whine and complain so much of Hilde. But he is still in a kind of permanent misery. (He says that, when he first met me—when I assumed I was cutting rather a glamorous figure—I was forever complaining about my age and failing powers. Now he finds me much more active and less sorry for myself, and even better looking!) But his great solution is still to get away. He wants to go to Hawaii and eventually Japan.

The kitchen floor paint is nearly dry at last.

I'm in a kind of stupid state, unfit for anything but sleep. I didn't get home from Jim's till 2:00 a.m.

August 20. Yesterday morning, I finished the rough draft of "Paul." It's much longer than I anticipated—164 pages—and I still have very little idea what it's *about*. Just the same, this is a most satisfactory achievement. I promised myself I'd get there before my birthday, and I have. I shall lay off reading it for at least a couple of weeks and I hope this will recharge my interest. Not that I'm not interested now—I am; I truly believe I have something very exciting here—maybe my best book. At least, I'm not worried that it is just dryly competent like *The World in the Evening*. It does touch some sort of nerve, at moments anyhow. It is first and foremost about living people, and only secondarily a story. And that's what I value most, at present. If I *could* make a contraption which came to life—well, that would be best of all.

Talking like this reminds me of talking to Bill Jones last evening about his short story. Oh dear—the difficulties! The imagery problem: these beginners are just rotten with similes and metaphors—every goddamn thing reminds them of some goddamn other thing. Bill listened devoutly to what I had to say, and took notes—but I doubt if he really understood. I doubt if he really has talent. But how could I tell him this? It isn't a question of compassion. I have no right to tell him, and no authority. He has to find it out for himself.

Bill and "Kap" Kidd [had a big argument]. It was up to Bill to say he was sorry, and he found this very hard. [This is the sort of selfishness which] is the same as stupidity. But there's something rather sweet about them both. I arranged for Bill to meet Ben Masselink

—they had lunch together at the studio;[1] and this was a great success.

Laughton was operated on, last Thursday. He's said to be doing well, but the operation was more serious than they expected—an extra stone was found which hadn't shown up in the X ray. Terry is still around. (He's coming to us tonight—as Charles wanted us to see him while Charles is in hospital.) Elsa is doing a TV show. Hal Greene and Dick Lee are still in the house next door—although it no longer belongs to them—"caretaking" until their new house up at Malibu has come out of escrow. Hal's old mother died at last—horribly, in great pain.

Yesterday evening I drove clear out to Milan Road in South Pasadena, where Jill Macklem and her husband Les have their new home. It is a very old wooden house, maybe from the 1890s, with leaded glass in the doorways and a stone fireplace with the rocks cut and arranged in an exactly symmetrical pattern—big ones and small ones. Les says that you can't get this kind of work done any more. The old Italian stonemasons who did it are dying off. It is quite a beautiful leafy street of old houses, with some of the feeling of old America that's in Longfellow, etc. But sad, sad.

How to describe the sad boredom I feel on such occasions? Great efforts at hospitality had been made by both of them. Jill had cooked a nice dinner, only it was four times what we needed. She'd put lilies of the valley (artificial) in her hair—which suggested perhaps some kind of an understanding between us. But Les stayed around all the time, for which I was grateful. They seem on the best of terms. There was the eager meal, the eager showing of Les's paintings (which have something and yet nothing), the eagerness for talk—about politics, Florida, life in Japan—oh, anything. And I eagerly responded, to make it all right—but *why did we have to do it?* It was sheer naked ritual. No getting together in any significant way. And the notes of my lectures which Jill typed up with such loving care and in so short a time—they're useless to me. They show no grasp of anything at all.

Now, I have to turn to other tasks. I must prepare another chapter of the Ramakrishna book. And I must do something about my lectures. This includes typing up a lot of extracts from books. I have now heard definitely that I shall "open" on September 22, but that only means holding my first seminar. The first public lecture won't be till the following Thursday, September 29.

Have just read a novel sent me by Hugh French—who keeps trying to steal me away from Geller—*A Summer World* by Richard Dougherty. A new young producer at Fox wants to do it. It's quite

[1] Warner Brothers, where Masselink was working on *The Crackerjack Marines*.

nicely written, a well-behaved "sincere" little tale of an eighteen-year-old boy having "awakenings" with girls and "finding himself." I imagine it charmed this little Jew producer because it is so non-Jew, Republican, noblesse oblige rich, civilized, indeed almost would-be country house British in feeling. (Which is maybe why a young upper-class Britisher from the embassy is the only person who is savagely attacked by the author.) Not for old Dobbin.

August 21. Idling has started. I didn't get started with Ramakrishna yesterday and I doubt if I shall today because I want to go swimming at Hugh French's. And tomorrow afternoon I'm to visit Laughton in hospital. Terry Jenkins was here to supper last night. Don liked him, and agreed that he is somehow a unique, or at least very unusual person. And one feels his feeling for Charles. It is expressed in the simplest kind of loyal matter-of-factness: he spent the *whole* of Thursday at the hospital—when Charles was having the operation and was so doped up he couldn't even recognize him.

Talked to Ivan Moffat on the phone. They had [Carl] Sandburg to dinner on Friday and had asked us to come, but I couldn't because of the Macklems and Don didn't want to, alone. When Sandburg met Iris, he said, "God must have thought twice before he made you," and later he assured her he'd never said this to anyone else. Ivan also told me that the young Dutchman who is their technical adviser on *The Greatest Story* [*Ever Told*] had insisted that the Last Supper was eaten with the hands, on the floor, in a room without windows. George Stevens, exasperated, remarked, "This story's hard enough *with* windows!"

August 22. A wasted day. Now I'm off to see Laughton in hospital, and then to Fox for a preview of *Let's Make Love.*[1] But all morning we've drowsed with hangovers and Don has thrown up several times. We both got very drunk last night after a rehearsal of *A Taste of Honey*[2] which we watched. And Don had one of his most violent and apparently unmotivated "Black Tom" attacks. He got quite frantic, tried to wreck (or rather, ferociously played at wrecking) the car. Then abandoned it and ran off down the street, then came home and smashed our dear old Mexican money pig that Julie [Harris] gave us. It was very ugly, and I feel concerned, lest these attacks may become really insane like Ted's. Of course this morning he was all contrition and very sweet.

[1] Starring Marilyn Monroe and Yves Montand.
[2] Tony Richardson's production of Shelagh Delaney's play, at the Biltmore; later headed for New York.

Although, in the attack, he was full of hate against me, I really do *not* feel that he hates me in any significant way. Elsa says she feels that Charles hates her. Maybe she hates *him*.

John Osborne told us they have been staying in San Francisco at a hotel run by a man who used to be an officer in the Gurkhas. He uses military expressions still. When they arrived, John Merivale was put up on the eleventh floor, while Vivien Leigh was put on the fifth. So she protested, because it made screwing so awkward. So the manager apologized to Merivale saying, "Awfully sorry, old man—ought to have known you'd want to be near headquarters."

I asked John Osborne about *Luther.* He said he'd gotten interested in him when he made a "study of religion." They are looking for an actor to play the part. Thinking of Jason Robards (?).[1]

Meanwhile Signoret had been visiting Mary Ure, and moaning because Yves[2] is having this affair with Monroe. Arthur Miller doesn't care, it seems. Both Simone and Mary shed tears and got drunk. Mary had been rather loving this. She luxuriates in scenes.

August 23. Am just through being interviewed by a young professor from Fresno named Stanley Poss. And tonight I have to be on a panel discussion at UCLA, after seeing these four plays—*Act Without Words, The Chairs, The Sandbox, This Property Is Condemned.*[3] I'm not in a particularly bright mood; maybe I just won't say *anything*.

Talked to Don yesterday about his outburst on Sunday night. Don denies that it was unmotivated—I forget how difficult it is to live with me—I'm so dominating, etc. But he added that he has wanted everything to happen that *has* happened since we met. So that's all right.

Of course I do realize about the domination. But what I have to keep remembering is Don's insecurity. I do believe he still imagines I might willingly leave him—which is ridiculous and unthinkable. I have never never felt so involved with anybody. And *gladly* involved. (I'm aware that I am writing this so Don may one day read it when I'm dead. Well, Don, I *mean* this!)

August 25. I feel rather bad because I have just been mean to a very rich and rather [zany] woman named Geraldine Brent. She is a friend of Jerry Lawrence, and she absolutely dragged us by main force to see

---

[1] Isherwood thought Robards dreary; Albert Finney played Luther in London and New York.

[2] Simone Signoret and Yves Montand, her husband.

[3] By Samuel Beckett, Eugene Ionesco, Edward Albee, and Tennessee Williams respectively.

a 16mm film she had made of herself playing the ex-movie star in *Sweet Bird of Youth* and also Mildred Luce in *Dogskin*.[1] She *was* terrible in both of them, but when she called me this morning I told her she ought to give up acting altogether, which I should never have done if she hadn't been rich, and a nuisance, and a woman.

Last night I stayed home—Don was in town—and read all of Jerry Lawrence's new play *The Diamond Orchid* and then *The Gang's All Here*, which Jerry gave me for a birthday present. I really like *The Gang's All Here* better—maybe just because it has a real setting; this imaginary Latin American stuff never quite convinces you.

Am now trying to get ahead with Ramakrishna—to produce at least one more chapter before school starts. Tomorrow, I *may* reread the whole manuscript of *In the Face of the Enemy*.[2]

We have decided not to go to San Francisco for the weekend, but to paint the outside of the house. Mr. Gardner will do it fairly cheaply. Furthermore, the front bathroom is to be retiled. I would feel more relaxed about all of this if we could only screw that money out of Laughton's corporation.

The panel discussion at UCLA was a farce. No one really had time to get going—and Ray Bradbury and William Fadiman[3] and John Houseman (who spoke from the audience)[4] and Julius Epstein[5] were all so *rude*. I guess I was all right—no more than that. Don was very pleased because, when my name was announced, there was a murmur of excitement, quite loud, right around the hall.

Don has drawn Terry and taken him to the gym, and they're doing it again before Terry leaves.

George Koniaris called up today after all these months to say goodbye, as he is leaving California with a scholarship to Cornell University.

Later: Don called around midday and went into a rage because I said I had agreed to have supper with Jo and Ben on Saturday and go to a party at Jerry Lawrence's on Sunday. Of course it is all jealousy, because he feels that Jo isn't really interested in him, except as *my* friend—and as for Jerry Lawrence, well, of course he thinks of Jerry's house as a place where I make friends and am influenced by people— and how right he is! But this upset me terribly, nevertheless, and so I

---

[1] Auden and Isherwood's *The Dog Beneath the Skin*.
[2] Current temporary title for *Down There on a Visit*.
[3] Studio executive at Columbia; formerly a literary journalist and RKO story editor and, later, a lecturer and writer on Hollywood.
[4] Houseman was then artistic director for the Professional Theater Group of the UCLA Adult Education Extension. He later produced a film of *This Property Is Condemned* (1966).
[5] Playwright and screenwriter, often with his twin brother Philip.

couldn't get myself to do any work, and went on the beach, instead. And I'm still depressed. And of course resentful against Don for spoiling my birthday mood. Which is babyish, I know, at fifty-six. But alas, I'm like that—I must either *mind*—or I must throw all the switches, shut off the juice, and tell him to go fuck himself. If I did *that* there would be a scene lasting maybe a week. And maybe it would startle the bitch-faggot part of him, "Black Tomasina," and make it behave. But *why* should I upset myself for Black Tomasina? Isn't it better to have peace at any price?

August 26. Well, of course, everything is all right today—it *really* is, I believe. When we woke, Don said, "I heard a rustling in the night—on your side of the bed." I was slow getting the point; then reached down and found a box of new Brooks Brothers shirts and a pair of bellows for the barbecue. And there was the sweetest old-fashioned birthday card of a kitty on a typewriter. I cried.

Today we've been on the beach and in the water. Quite warm.

I'm not going into the psychology, symbology, etc. of being fifty-six. There's nothing I can do about *that*, except work harder and faster. Today I did a page of the Ramakrishna book and started drafting a "frame" for the novel—something to surround my four scenes from the Past with Now. This, I know, is absolutely essential. I feel very excited about the novel, altogether. Think I shall go right ahead with the revision.

In addition to the Ramakrishna and novel work, I've written letters, made japam with beads for the first time in God knows how long—and exercised!

I intend that this shall be my last diary written by hand. The poor old thumb gives me so much trouble. In future, I want to type.

Must fly off, now, to take part in a nice birthday evening at Hope Lange's.

So long!

Chronology

1904 August 26, Christopher William Bradshaw Isherwood, first child of Frank Bradshaw Isherwood and Kathleen Bradshaw Isherwood (*née* Machell Smith), born at Wyberslegh Hall, High Lane, Cheshire, on the estate of his grandfather, John Bradshaw Isherwood, squire of nearby Marple Hall.

1908 February 28, moves to Strensall near York following his father's regiment; November 9, moves to Frimley near Aldershot following his father's regiment.

1909 Dictates a story, "The Adventures of Mummy and Daddy."

1910 His father begins teaching him to read and write.

1911 Begins attending local school; October 1, brother Richard Graham Bradshaw Isherwood born; November 27, father leaves to join his regiment in Limerick, Ireland.

1912 January, moves with his mother and baby brother to Limerick; September 28, sees first film.

1914 May 1, arrives at his preparatory school, St. Edmund's, Hindhead, Surrey as a nine-year-old boarder; August 4, Britain declares war on Germany and Isherwood's father receives mobilization orders; August 14, Frank Isherwood's regiment leaves Limerick for England; August 24, Isherwood and his mother and brother move back to Marple; September 8, the regiment leaves for France; Isherwood returns to St. Edmund's; November 28–29, his father visits him at school while on leave.

1915 February 28, Isherwood's father visits him at school for the last time; March, Isherwood gets measles followed by pneumonia, leaves school to convalesce; May 8 or 9, Frank Isherwood evidently wounded at Ypres, probably killed; June 24, Kathleen Isherwood receives Frank's identity disk, apparently confirming his death; September 17, Isherwood returns to school, having missed more than a term.

1917 January 1, Isherwood begins keeping a diary; he records walking with W. H. Auden at school; March 18, ill with German measles, remains at school during start of holidays with Auden and a few other boys.

1918 January 1, Isherwood begins a new diary, lasting until September; December 19, leaves St. Edmund's having won numerous prizes.

1919 January 17, arrives at Repton, his public school, near Derby; October 10, Richard Isherwood starts school at Berkhamstead; November 30, Isherwood confirmed as Anglican.

1921 Winter, joins G. B. Smith's history form at Repton where he meets Edward Upward; November, Kathleen Isherwood moves with her mother to 36 St. Mary Abbot's Terrace in West Kensington, London; December, Isherwood sits scholarship exam at Cambridge with Upward and wins £40 exhibition to Corpus Christi College; Richard Isherwood leaves his school.

1922 January 18, Richard Isherwood starts school again in London, at Norland Place; June 23, Isherwood wins English Essay Prize, History Prize, and Literature Prize at Repton speech day; July, wins form prize; summer, writes two chapters of a school novel; September, begins last term at Repton; December, wins £80 scholarship to Corpus Christi College, Cambridge.

1923 Lives at home in London; writes three chapters of a school novel; April 10–July 3, studies French in Rouen; begins writing a novel called *Lions and Shadows*; October 10, goes up to Corpus Christi, renews close friendship with Edward Upward.

1924 Around this time, Isherwood and Upward start keeping diaries and begin to invent Mortmere; Isherwood writes various shorts stories; summer, achieves 2:1 in Mays exams.

1925 January, finishes his novel, now titled *Christopher Garland*; June 1, Cambridge Tripos exams begin; June 11, Isherwood returns to London; June 18, summoned to Cambridge to explain his joke Tripos answers and withdraws; August, takes job as secretary to André Mangeot's string quartet; December, meets W. H. Auden and renews prep school friendship.

1926 January, begins writing another novel, *The Summer at the House*; Easter, begins *Seascape with Figures* (first version of *All the Conspirators*), completed by autumn.

1927 January 4, moves out of his mother's house at St. Mary Abbot's Terrace into a friend's empty lodgings in Redcliffe Road; January 24, takes job as private tutor; autumn, returns to his mother's house; decides to go to medical school.

1928 Tutoring jobs; May 18, Isherwood's first novel, *All the Conspirators*, published by Jonathan Cape; May 19, sails for Bremen where he is met by Basil Fry; May 30, returns to England; June 2–9, helps his mother move to 19 Pembroke Gardens; June 22, Auden introduces Isherwood to Stephen Spender; October, Isherwood begins as medical student at King's College, London and Auden moves to Berlin; December 13, Isherwood completes first draft of *The Memorial*; Auden visits from Berlin over Christmas and tells Isherwood about his life there and about Homer Lane's theories.

1929 March, Isherwood leaves medical school at end of spring term; March 14–27, visits Auden in Berlin, meets John Layard, begins affair with Berthold Szczesny; mid-June to end of June, Isherwood returns to Germany and pursues Szczesny to Amsterdam; end of June, Isherwood returns to London, works as tutor during summer; October, Wall Street crash; November 29, Isherwood moves to Berlin; takes room at In Den Zelten 10, next door to Magnus Hirschfeld's Institute for Sexual Science, and works on third draft of *The Memorial*.

1930 February 19, Isherwood returns to London, staying mostly at home; May 8, returns to Berlin; May 11, meets Walter Wolff and by October 4 moves in with the Wolffs at Simeonstrasse 4, Hal;esches Tor; November, Isherwood moves to Admiralstrasse 38, Kottbusser Tor; December, moves to Nollendorfstrasse 17, as tenant of Fräulein Meta Thurau; also during 1930, Isherwood's translation of the *Intimate Journals of Charles Baudelaire* published.

1931 By early 1931, Isherwood meets Jean Ross and she moves into Frl. Thurau's; that winter, he also meets Gerald Hamilton; March 10–21, Isherwood visits London; summer, works on early version of *Lions and Shadows*; plans *The Lost*; May 19, goes with Auden, Spender, and Walter Wolff to Insel Reugen, Sellin; July 10, returns to Berlin, W. 62, Kleiststrasse 9; September, begins teaching English.

1932 February 17, *The Memorial* published by Isherwood's new publisher, the Hogarth Press; March 13, Isherwood meets Heinz Neddermeyer while living at Mohrin with Francis Turville-Petre; July elections, Nazis achieve majority in the Reichstag; August 4–September 30, Isherwood visits England, meets Gerald Heard and Chris Wood; September 14, meets E. M. Forster; September 30, returns to Berlin; October, works as translator for Willi Münzenberger's communist workers' organization, the IAH (Internationale Arbeiterhilfe).

1933 January 30, Hitler becomes Chancellor of Germany; February 27, fire destroys the Berlin Reichstag and the Nazis suspend civil liberties and freedom of the press; March 5, Nazis win 288 seats in the General Election, more than twice as much as the next largest party; March 7, Dollfuss suspends the Austrian parliament; March 23, Hitler achieves dictatorial powers; April 5, Isherwood arrives in London with his belongings, preparing to leave Berlin for good; April 30, returns to Berlin where he learns the police have been asking about him; May 2, trade unions suppressed in Germany; May 13, Isherwood leaves for Prague with Heinz, they travel via Vienna to Budapest, Belgrade and Athens, and arrive May 22 on Francis Turville-Petre's Greek island, St. Nicholas; September 6, they leave for Marseille and Paris; September 30, they go on to England; October, Heinz returns to Berlin and Isherwood begins work as Berthold Viertel's collaborator on film script for *The Little Friend*.

1934 January 5, Heinz attempts to enter England and is turned back at immigration; January 20, Isherwood meets Heinz in Berlin and takes him to Amsterdam, returning alone to London; February 1, Dollfuss dissolves Austrian political parties (except his own Fatherland Front); February 12, General Strike in Austria; by February 16, socialist unrest is forcibly put down by Dollfuss; February

21, filming starts on *The Little Friend*; March 26, Isherwood joins Heinz in Amsterdam; April 4, they leave Amsterdam for Gran Canaria; Isherwood works on *The Lost*; June 8, he starts *Mr. Norris Changes Trains*; Isherwood and Heinz spend the summer touring and mountain climbing; June 11, Geneva disarmament conference ends in failure; July 25, Dollfuss assassinated; July 30, Kurt Schuschnigg becomes Austrian chancellor; August 12, Isherwood finishes *Mr. Norris Changes Trains*; August 26, *The Little Friend* opens in London; September 6, Isherwood and Heinz leave for Copenhagen via Gibraltar and Amsterdam; October 1, they settle at Classensgade 65; October 21, start of Mao's Long March in China.

1935 January, Auden visits Copenhagen to work with Isherwood on *The Dog Beneath the Skin*; February 21, *Mr. Norris Changes Trains* published by Hogarth; March 1, restoration of Saar land to Germany following plebiscite; Hitler introduces conscription; April, Isherwood visits Brussels with Heinz, whom he leaves there, travelling to Paris alone and then London; May 9, *The Last of Mr. Norris* (U.S. edition of *Mr. Norris Changes Trains*) published by William Morrow; May 12, Isherwood agrees to review for *The Listener* and returns to Heinz in Brussels; May 13, Heinz receives three-month permit for Holland and they move to Amsterdam, lodging next to Klaus Mann; also in May, *The Dog Beneath the Skin, or Where Is Francis?*, written with Auden, is published by Faber and Faber; September 16, Isherwood and Heinz return to Brussels; September 19, Isherwood signs new contract with Methuen, works on "A Berlin Diary (Autumn 1930)"; October 2, Italy invades Ethiopia; mid-November, Isherwood works on "The Nowaks"; late November, he visits England; December 10, Isherwood and Heinz leave Brussels for Antwerp; December 21, they move to Sintra, Portugal, where Spender and Tony Hyndman join them; Isherwood begins work on a novel, *Paul Is Alone*.

1936 January 12, *The Dog Beneath the Skin* opens at the Westminster Theatre in London; mid-January, Isherwood completes draft of "Sally Bowles"; January 20, death of King George V, who is succeeded by Edward VIII; March 7, Germany occupies the Rhineland; March 14, Spender and Hyndman leave Sintra for Spain; March 16–April 17, Auden visits Sintra to work on *The Ascent of F6*; May 29, Isherwood abandons *Paul Is Alone*, returns to *The Lost*; July 17, Civil War breaks out in Spain; July 25, Heinz is ordered through the German consul in Lisbon to report for military service, but does not; August 21, Isherwood arrives back in London; October 1, Franco declared chief of state by Nationalists; September 11, Faber publishes Auden and Isherwood's play *The Ascent of F6*; Isherwood works on *Lions and Shadows*; November 1, Mussolini declares Rome–Berlin axis; Germany and Japan sign anti-Comintern pact; December 11, Edward VIII abdicates and is succeeded by his brother, George VI.

1937 January 12–13, Isherwood meets Auden, headed for Spanish Civil War, in Paris; February 3–March 9, Isherwood attends rehearsals for *F6* in London; February 26, *F6* premieres at The Mercury Theatre; March 17, Isherwood joins Heinz in Brussels and takes him to Paris, then spends April in London where he is ill; April 25, he joins Heinz in Luxembourg; *F6* successfully transfers to the Adelphi Little Theatre; May 12, Heinz is forced to leave Luxembourg and goes to Trier, where he is arrested the next day by the Gestapo; Isherwood returns to London; July 7, Japanese invade northeast China; they reach Beijing before the end of the month; July 16–August 4, Isherwood works for Alexander Korda on film script of a Carl Zuckmayer story; August 12–September 17, he works with Auden in Dover on their new play, *On the Frontier*; September 15, finishes *Lions and Shadows*; October, Hogarth Press publishes *Sally Bowles* (later incorporated into *Goodbye to Berlin*); November 6, Italy joins German–Japanese anti-Comintern pact; November 11, Japanese capture Shanghai and continue to advance.

1938 January 19, Isherwood and Auden leave for China to write a travel book: *Journey to a War*; during the spring "The Landauers" appears in John Lehmann's *New Writing*; March 12, German troops enter Austria and on March 13 Hitler proclaims the *Anschluss* (union) of Austria with Germany; March 17, *Lions and Shadows* published by Hogarth Press; April 24, Sudeten Germans, on Hitler's orders, demand independence from Czechoslovakia; July 1–9, Isherwood and Auden, returning around the world from China, visit Manhattan where Isherwood meets Vernon Old; July 17, Isherwood arrives back in London; August 12, Germany mobilizes armed forces; September 7, Sudeten Germans sever relations with Czechoslovak government; September 15, Hitler tells Chamberlain he will annex the Sudetenland; September 18, British and French pressure Czechs to accept Hitler's terms, Czechs refuse, then give in on September 21; September 19, Isherwood begins writing *Journey to a War*, using his own and Auden's diary entries; September 22–24, Chamberlain visits Hitler again, and returns urging Britain, France and Czechoslovakia to allow Hitler to occupy Sudetenland; Czech government resigns; September 26, *The Ascent of F6* televised; Britain and France begin to mobilize; September 29–30, at the height of the crisis, Chamberlain, Daladier, Hitler and Mussolini meet in Munich and partition Czechoslovakia, ceding Sudetenland to Germany; October 1–10, Germany occupies Sudetenland; October 1938, Faber publishes Auden and Isherwood's last play together, *On the Frontier*; November 14, *On the Frontier* opens at the Arts Theatre in Cambridge; mid-December, Isherwood works with Auden in Brussels on *Journey to a War*, completed December 17; Jacky Hewit with Isherwood in Brussels.

1939 January 8, Isherwood returns to London; January 19, Isherwood sails for America with Auden, arriving January 26 in New York where they settle; March 6–16, Hitler divides remainder of Czechoslovakia with Hungary; Poland refuses to cede Danzig and Baltic routes; March 28, Spanish Republicans surrender in Madrid, ending the Spanish Civil War; March, *Goodbye to Berlin* published by Hogarth Press and in the U.S. by Random House; *Journey to a War* published by Faber and by Random House; April 7, Italy invades Albania and Spain joins anti-Comintern pact; early May, Isherwood applies for U.S. residency; May 6, he sets off for California with Vernon Old; they live at the Rose Garden apartments at 6406 Franklin Avenue, Hollywood; June 9, Isherwood gets quota visa; June 18, Isherwood and Vernon Old move to 7136 Sycamore Trail; during the summer,

Isherwood writes "I Am Waiting" and a review of John Steinbeck's *The Grapes of Wrath*; July, he begins working with Berthold Viertel again and meets Swami Prabhavananda; early August, Isherwood begins instruction in meditation; August 23, Russia and Germany sign non-aggression pact; September 1, Germany attacks Poland; September 3, England declares war on Germany and Germany sinks *Athenia* off Ireland; September 7–10, Germany overruns western Poland; mid-September, Isherwood and Vernon Old settle in two rooms at 303 South Amalfi Drive; September 17, USSR attacks Poland from the east; September 28, Poland surrenders and is partitioned; October, "I Am Waiting" published in *The New Yorker*; November, Isherwood gets first film job writing for Samuel Goldwyn's independent studio, Goldwyn Studios; November 30, Russia invades Finland.

1940 January, Isherwood begins first writing job at MGM, on *Rage in Heaven* for Gottfried Reinhardt; March, Finns sue for peace; by April, Isherwood prepares to sign a one year contract with MGM; April 9, Germany occupies Denmark and invades Norway; June 9, King Haakon VII of Norway flees to London with his government and the Nazis establish a puppet regime under Vidkun Quisling; May 7, Churchill forms coalition government; May 10, Nazis strike at Netherlands, Belgium, Luxembourg; May 14, Dutch army surrenders, Dutch government flees to London; May 28, Leopold III of Belgium surrenders and is taken prisoner; May 26–June 4, Dunkirk evacuations; June 14, fall of Paris; June 16, eighty-year-old Marshal Pétain becomes French premier and requests armistice; France submits to occupation with autonomous regime centered in Vichy; de Gaulle and others flee; June 30, Germany occupies Channel Islands; July 3, British navy sinks French fleet at Mers-el-Kébir, near Oran, Algeria; July 9, Uncle Henry Bradshaw-Isherwood-Bagshawe dies, Isherwood inherits his estate and gives it to his brother Richard; July 10, the Battle of Britain begins; July 11, Isherwood becomes involved on script of *Forever and a Day*, a film for the British War Relief Fund; August 23, all-night bombing raid on London begins the "Blitz," which expands to other cities during the autumn; during August, Isherwood and Vernon Old move into a rented house, 8826 Harratt Street; September 16, first-ever peacetime compulsory military service established in U.S.; November 8, Swami Prabhavananda initiates Isherwood.

1941 By January 11, Isherwood finishes working on *Rage in Heaven*; he continues at MGM, mainly "polishing" *The Stars Look Down* and *Free and Easy*; February 17, he breaks with Vernon Old and moves to Hotel Stanley; mid-March, moves into 2401 Green Valley Road, next door to Gerald Heard; March 19, German air raids resume over London; April 25, Rommel's drive across Libya reaches Egypt; early May, Isherwood finishes his first year's contract at MGM and leaves the studio; May 10, chamber of the House of Commons destroyed in heavy bombing on London; by mid-June, Denny Fouts moves in with Isherwood at Green Valley Road; June 22, Germany attacks Russia along the whole of its western frontier; July 7–August 7, Isherwood and Fouts join La Verne Seminar; July 15, Kathleen Isherwood returns to live at Wyberslegh with Richard; August 22, Isherwood flies East to visit Auden, meets Caroline Norment at the Cooperative

College Workshop, a refugee hostel in Haverford, Pennsylvania; late September, he returns to Los Angeles; October 11, he moves to Haverford to work in the hostel and lodges at 605 Railroad Avenue; November 18, British forces strike back across Libya; November 27, Soviets begin first successful counterattacks against German occupying forces; December 7, Japanese bomb Pearl Harbor; December 8, U.S. and U.K. declare war on Japan; December 19, U.S. Congress extends the draft to include twenty- to forty-year-olds; also in 1941, Gerald Heard begins to build his monastic community, Trabuco.

1942 Japan concludes treaty with Thailand, invades Burma, Malay Peninsula, Indonesia, takes Hong Kong, Singapore, and Dutch East Indies by the end of February, and then Burma; May, General Wainwright surrenders Philippines; May 7, U.S. intercepts Japanese fleet in Coral Sea; June, the Battle of Midway, Japan falls back; Isherwood writes "Take It or Leave It"; June 30, has medical exam at draft board; July 6, Haverford refugee hostel closes, Isherwood returns to California and moves in at Peggy Rodakiewicz's house, 9121 Alto Cedro Drive, Beverly Hills, living alternately there and at Chris Wood's house, 1 Rockledge Road, Laguna Beach, for the rest of the year; July 13, receives his draft classification, 4-E, and applies for Los Prietos Camp; August 7, U.S. troops hold Guadalcanal against Japanese counterattacks and begin to turn tide against the Japanese; September 23, Isherwood, applies for 4-D classification; September, Nazis reach Stalingrad; by October 12, Isherwood begins translating the Bhagavad Gita with Swami Prabhavananda; October, "Take It or Leave It" published in *The New Yorker*; October 23–November 4, second battle of El Alamein, Rommel retreats westward from Egypt; November 7–8, Eisenhower lands in North Africa and negotiates with Vichy-French Vice-Premier, Admiral Darlan; November 11, Hitler orders occupation of Vichy France; November 30, Isherwood starts work at Paramount on Somerset Maugham's *The Hour Before Dawn*; December, British forces reoccupy Benghazi in Libya; December 31, Isherwood writes "The Wishing Tree" for the Vedanta Society magazine.

1943 January 2, Nazis begin retreat from Caucasus and surrender at Stalingrad on January 31; January 18, bombing resumes over London; January 23, British take Tripoli; January 29, Isherwood finishes at Paramount; February 6, he moves into Vedanta Center, Ivar Avenue, in preparation for becoming a monk; February 25, round-the-clock bombing of German targets begins; March 20–28, British forces advance across Tunisia; May, Isherwood begins writing *Prater Violet*; April 19–16, Warsaw ghetto uprising; May 13, German army in Tunisia surrenders; July 1, U.S. begins retaking selected islands in Pacific; July 10–17, Allies invade Sicily; July 19, Allies begin bombing Rome; July 25, Mussolini dismissed as prime minister; August, Denny Fouts introduces Isherwood to "X." (Bill Harris); August 17–24, Isherwood takes a vacation from the monastery at a rented room opposite the Viertels' in Maybery Road; September 3, Italy surrenders; September 10, Nazis occupy Rome; October 13, Italian government in Brindisi declares war on Germany; November, Isherwood begins revised approach to translating the Bhagavad Gita.

1944 February, Isherwood stays with Aldous and Maria Huxley in Llano; March 11, Isherwood visits Huxley again and they work out a film story, *Jacob's Hands*; mid-March, Isherwood feels he is falling in love with Bill Harris; late March, spends ten days at John van Druten's AJC Ranch; April 17, Isherwood decides he cannot become a monk; June 4, Allies take Rome; June 6, Allied D-Day landings in France; during June, Isherwood spends a few days with Bill Harris at Denny Fouts's apartment in Santa Monica; July 4, the Soviet army advances across the 1939 border between Poland and the USSR; Isherwood and Huxley complete draft of *Jacob's Hands*; July 20, assassination attempt against Hitler; July 27, rough draft of *Prater Violet* completed; Isherwood begins writing introduction to *Vedanta for the Western World*; August 12, Vernon Old returns to Los Angeles; August 15, Allies invade southern France; August 24, French underground rises in Paris, and on August 25 de Gaulle arrives to take charge of the provisional French government transferred from Algiers; August 26, Isherwood turns forty; also in August, Isherwood and Prabhavananda's translation of the Bhagavad Gita is published; September 10, Vernon Old moves to Ananda Bhavan, the new Santa Barbara Vedanta Center in Montecito; September 25, Isherwood moves to Ananda Bhavan; October 15, Isherwood completes revised draft of *Prater Violet*; October 17–25, U.S. destroys Japanese ships at Leyte Gulf in the Philippines and retakes the island of Leyte by the end of December; USSR takes Poland and advances toward Berlin; November 17, Isherwood leaves Ananda Bhavan and moves to Laguna; late November, Isherwood returns to the Hollywood Vedanta Center on Ivar Avenue; December, Nazis launch counter-offensive in the Ardennes and nearly break Allied lines at the Battle of the Bulge.

1945 January–February, U.S. continues to retake islands in the Philippines; February 5, Isherwood's affair with Bill Harris ends; February 21, Isherwood starts three months' work on Wilkie Collins's *The Woman in White* for Warner Brothers; March 7, first U.S. troops cross the Rhine; April 28, Mussolini and his mistress are shot; April 30, Hitler and Eva Braun commit suicide; May 2, Berlin surrenders to the Soviets; May 7, Germany surrenders to the Allies; June 2, Isherwood attends Bill Caskey's twenty-fourth birthday party; June 4, returns to Warner Brothers to work on Maugham's *Up at the Villa* for Wolfgang Reinhardt; during the summer, U.S. begins aerial bombardment of Japan; July 6, MacArthur announces liberation of the Philippines; *Prater Violet* appears in *Harper's Bazaar* and New Directions publishes *The Berlin Stories*, containing *The Last of Mr. Norris* and *Goodbye to Berlin*; August 6, U.S. drops atomic bomb on Hiroshima; August 9, U.S. drops atomic bomb on Nagasaki; August 14, Japan surrenders; August 23, Isherwood moves out of the Vedanta Center into the Beesleys' chauffeur's apartment at 19130 Pacific Coast Highway, between Santa Monica and Malibu; he begins translating Shankara's *Crest-Jewel of Discrimination* with Swami Prabhavananda; September 25, Isherwood and Bill Caskey move into Denny Fouts's empty apartment, 137 Entrada Drive, Santa Monica; during the autumn, they take a three week motor trip; November, *Prater Violet* published in U.S. by Random House; towards the end of the year, *Vedanta for the Western World*, edited and introduced by Isherwood, is published by Marcel Rodd.

1946 January 12, Isherwood undergoes surgery to remove a median bar inside the bladder, at the top of the urethra; April, Caskey quarrels with Denny Fouts and Isherwood and Caskey move into Salka Viertel's garage apartment, 165 Mabery Road, Santa Monica; May, *Prater Violet* published in the U.K. by Methuen; during the summer, Isherwood revises his wartime diaries, 1939–1944; November 8, he becomes U.S. citizen; towards the end of the year, Isherwood works with Lesser Samuels on a film treatment, *Judgement Day in Pittsburgh*; December, he travels to Mexico with Caskey.

1947 January 19, Isherwood sets out (via New York) on his first post-war trip to England; March 28, he signs deed of gift of Marple estate, including Wyberslegh, to his brother Richard; April 16, returns to New York; during the summer, he lives with Caskey at James and Tania Stern's apartment at 207 East 52nd Street, Manhattan, and visits friends up and down the East Coast; during August, Shankara's *Crest-Jewel of Discrimination*, translated with Swami Prabhavananda, is published; September 19, Isherwood sails with Caskey for South America, to write a travel book, *The Condor and the Cows*; September 28, they arrive in Cartagena, Colombia; October 28, Isherwood and Caskey travel south via Bogotá; November, they continue through Ecuador and reach Lima, Peru, by year end; also in 1947, the first U.S. edition of *Lions and Shadows* is published by New Directions.

1948 January, Isherwood and Caskey travel in Peru and Bolivia; February, they leave La Paz, Bolivia, for Argentina and depart from Buenos Aires by ship in late March; April 1, they stop in Rio, then continue direct from Brazil to North Africa and France, arriving in Paris on April 22; April 30, they proceed to London; late May, Isherwood visits his family at Wyberslegh; June 9, Isherwood and Caskey sail for New York; June 15, Isherwood returns alone to California; he stays at El Kanan Hotel, Santa Monica; July 19, starts work on *The Great Sinner* at MGM; mid-August, he meets Jim Charlton; they take several motor trips and spend time together in August and September; Isherwood begins translating Patanjali's yoga aphorisms; September 20, Caskey returns to California; September 28, Isherwood moves with Caskey into 333 Rustic Road; October 9, Isherwood finishes work at MGM; November 5, Vernon Old marries Patty O'Neill; November 12, Isherwood's nanny, Annie Avis, dies; December 16, Denny Fouts dies in Rome.

1949 January 6–13, Isherwood works for Gottfried Reinhardt at MGM; April 12, he completes *The Condor and the Cows*; he begins to work intermittently on his proposed novel *The School of Tragedy*; by May, he begins working with Lesser Samuels on *The Easiest Thing in the World*; August 6–7, Isherwood meets Evelyn Caldwell (later Hooker); August, he finishes draft of *The Easiest Thing in the World* with Lesser Samuels; August 10, meets Igor and Vera Stravinsky and Robert Craft; also in August, he works on *Below the Equator* with Aldous Huxley and Lesser Samuels; September 7, Trabuco is dedicated as a Ramakrishna monastery; November 11, Caskey leaves to visit his sister in Florida; November, Methuen publishes *The Condor and the Cows*; December 1, Isherwood writes memorial article on Klaus Mann; during 1949, Isherwood elected to U.S. Academy of Arts and Sciences.

1950 Isherwood works on a film script, *The Vacant Room*, with Lesser Samuels; April 10, meets Dylan Thomas; late April, after his father's death, Caskey returns via Kentucky to Rustic Road; June 25, Korean War begins; June 29, Bill Kennedy proposes that Isherwood begin reviewing regularly for *Tomorrow*; late June, last caretakers move out of Marple Hall where part of roof collapses; August 11, Isherwood and Peggy Kiskadden leave for Arizona and New Mexico by car; during the trip, Isherwood works on a review of Ford Maddox Ford's *Parade's End*; December 10, moves with Caskey to 31152 Monterey Street, Coast Royal, South Laguna.

1951 May, Isherwood reviews a book about Katherine Mansfield and also reviews Stephen Spender's *World Within World*; May 21, he leaves Caskey and moves to the Huntington Hartford Foundation, 2000 Rustic Canyon Road, Pacific Palisades; works on *The School of Tragedy*, jettisoning material about refugees; during the summer, *I Am a Camera*, John van Druten's play based on *Goodbye to Berlin*, is cast; by August 22, Isherwood is back in South Laguna with Caskey; mid-September, he decides to break finally with Caskey and returns to Huntington Hartford Foundation; October, Isherwood goes to the East Coast for rehearsals of *I Am a Camera*, directed by John van Druten; November 8, *I Am a Camera* opens in Hartford, Connecticut; November 28, *I Am a Camera* transfers successfully to the Empire Theater, Broadway; December, Isherwood sails for England where he spends Christmas with his mother and brother in a London hotel; Caskey joins the merchant marines.

1952 February 10, Isherwood returns to Berlin after eighteen years and sees Heinz Neddermayer for the first time since Heinz's arrest by the Gestapo in 1937; February 27, Isherwood sails from England for New York; March 19, leaves New York for Bermuda holiday with Sam Costidy; by April 8, he returns to California with Costidy, via Reno; May 4, settles at Trabuco where he completes Patanjali translation and part one of his novel, still called *The School of Tragedy*; May 21, he moves alone to the Mermira apartments on 2nd Street, behind the Miramar Hotel, in Santa Monica; also during May, Isherwood resigns from the board of the Huntington Hartford Foundation and the first chapter of his unfinished novel is published in *New Writing*; June 30, Costidy leaves for Louisiana with Tom Wright; Isherwood begins fixing up Evelyn Hooker's garden house at 400 South Saltair Avenue and moves there in late summer; November, car trip with Caskey to Mexico; during 1952, *Vedanta for Modern Man*, edited by Isherwood, is published in U.S. and U.K.; Isherwood completes "California Story" (later reprinted as "The Shore" in *Exhumations*) to accompany Sanford Roth's photographs in *Harper's Bazaar*.

1953 January 6, Caskey leaves for San Francisco and ships out again; January 9, Isherwood goes to Trabuco for the rest of the month; January 27, he finishes rough draft of *The World in the Evening*; February 14, he begins relationship with Don Bachardy; February 20–26, Bachardy's brother Ted has nervous breakdown and is committed; early March, Isherwood and Bachardy visit Palm Springs together; April 25, Bachardy moves out of his mother's apartment at 5416 3/4 Harold Way, Hollywood, into his own furnished room at 942 Spaulding Avenue, Hollywood; May 16, Bachardy moves into Marguerite Lamkin and Harry Brown's apartment in West Hollywood; August 5, Isherwood completes *The World in the Evening*; August 25–September 4, he travels to San Francisco with Don Bachardy; on their return Isherwood moves out of Evelyn Hooker's garden house, at her request, and into the Browns' apartment with Bachardy; September 19, Isherwood and Bachardy move together into an apartment at 1326 Olive Drive, though Isherwood still keeps his books at Saltair Avenue and uses the garden house as a study; during October, Isherwood's article on Ernst Toller appears in *Encounter*; during the autumn, he makes final revisions to *The World in the Evening*; December 17, he leaves to spend Christmas in Manhattan with Bachardy; also in 1953, *How to Know God: The Yoga Aphorisms of Patanjali* is translated with Swami Prabhavananda.

1954 January 4, Isherwood returns to Los Angeles; begins editing an anthology, *Great English Short Stories*, plans a biography of Ramakrishna and various new pieces of autobiographical fiction; January 25, begins work for Eddie Knopf at MGM on *Diane*; February, moves with Bachardy to 364 Mesa Road, Santa Monica; March 10, Auden visits him while lecturing at Occidental College and UCLA; mid-March, Isherwood gets measles; June, *The World in the Evening* published in U.S. and U.K.; August 25, Isherwood completes script for *Diane*; August 26, Isherwood turns fifty; during spring and summer, John Collier writes screenplay based on John van Druten's play, *I Am a Camera*, and Julie Harris accepts the lead; October 5, Bachardy's draft board physical; October 16–21, trip with Bachardy to San Francisco, they see Auden and James Wong Howe; November, Isherwood and Bachardy visit Tennessee Williams in Key West to watch filming of *The Rose Tattoo*, in which Isherwood plays a bit part; late November, Auden again visits Los Angeles; December 7, Bachardy's second draft board physical; December 8, they travel to Mexico with Jo and Ben Masselink; December 16, Isherwood has first glimmer, in Mexico, of an idea for a new novel which will eventually be called *Down There on a Visit*.

1955 January, Isherwood and Bachardy return to Mesa Road; January 17, Isherwood clears his papers out of the Hookers' garden house at Saltair Avenue; January 25, they begin a five-day trip to New York to see Truman Capote's Broadway musical, *House of Flowers*; Isherwood gets more work at MGM on *Diane* and writing *The Wayfarer*, a script about Buddha; February 10, Bachardy starts his junior year at UCLA; February 12, Maria Huxley dies; February 16, Bachardy changes his major from Languages to Theater Arts; March 6–9, Isherwood and Bachardy travel to Philadelphia via Washington for the opening of Tennessee Williams's *Cat on a Hot Tin Roof*; March 18, Ted Bachardy has another breakdown and is hospitalized again; May 2, *Diane* starts filming; May 18, Bachardy's twenty-first birthday party; May 27, Isherwood finishes a rough draft of *The Wayfarer*; May 28, he begins writing the new novel whose title and conception will change often before it becomes *Down There on a Visit*; June 8, meets Thom Gunn; June 22, sees preview of film, *I Am a Camera*; July 12, *Diane* finishes filming; September 2, Isherwood moves with Bachardy to Trancas, 29938 Pacific Coast Highway, near Malibu; September 23, Isherwood is still at work with Eddie Knopf on revisions to *The Wayfarer*; October 12, he leaves with Bachardy for New York City; October 20, they sail from New York for Tangier via Gibraltar; October 28, they experiment with *kif* and *majoon* at Paul Bowles's apartment; October 30, they sail for Italy, arriving in Rome (via Ischia) on November 8; November 23–28, Thanksgiving in Venice; they return to Rome, visit Florence and other northern Italian towns, and watch the filming of *War and Peace* on December 9–10 before continuing on to Somerset Maugham's house in France by mid-December; by Christmas, they are in Munich; December 28, they arrive in Paris.

1956 January, Isherwood and Bachardy arrive in London; January 30–February 6, Isherwood stays with his mother and brother at Wyberslegh and sees Marple Hall for the last time (it will be demolished in 1959); February 12, he decides to call the new novel *The Lost*; February 24, Isherwood takes mescaline; March 6, Isherwood begins writing *The Lost*; March 11, Isherwood and Bachardy leave England for New York; March 22, they fly back to California and move into 322 Rustic Road (Michael Barrie's house); April 1, Isherwood again begins work on his novel and starts reading background material for his biography of Ramakrishna; during April, they buy 434 Sycamore Road from Hal Greene; April 25, Bachardy is diagnosed with hepatitis and hospitalized; April 30–May 1, Isherwood moves them into their new house; May 10, Bachardy registers again at UCLA; June 1–9, Isherwood is hospitalized with hepatitis; July 2, Bachardy enrolls at the Chouinard Art Institute; July 26, Egyptian president Nasser nationalizes Suez Canal Company, triggering Suez crisis; August 26–September 24, Isherwood and Bachardy drive to San Francisco; September 24, Isherwood begins work on *Jean-Christophe* for Jerry Wald at Fox; October 10, Isherwood finishes treatment for *Jean-Christophe*; October 29, Israel invades Egypt; October 31, Britain and France bomb Egyptian airfields; November 22, Isherwood finishes a rough draft of the new novel, now called *The Forgotten*; he spends Christmas and New Year in New York with Bachardy.

1957 January 3, Isherwood returns to Los Angeles with Bachardy and continues work on *Jean-Christophe*; January 11, Edward Hooker dies; February 12, Isherwood discovers lump on side of his belly; February 15, the tumor is successfully removed and proves benign, but ill-health and depression persist for many months; March 15, Isherwood commits to a new U.S. publisher, Simon and Schuster; April, he prepares an introduction for a new edition of *All the Conspirators*, to be published in the U.K.; April 24, he decides to call the new novel *Forgotten*; June 7, Fox job on *Jean-Christophe* finishes; June 13, Bachardy travels to New York alone, returning June 30; early July, Isherwood and Gavin Lambert begin television project for Hermione Gingold, eventually titled *Emily Ermingarde*; July 19, Isherwood and Bachardy leave for a weekend in Santa Fe and see *The Rake's Progress* and *I Am a Camera*; August 15, *Jean-Christophe* is shelved by Fox; September, Isherwood begins to make better progress with his novel, now in its third draft; October 8, Isherwood and Bachardy begin a round–the–world trip, via Japan, Hong Kong, Singapore, Bali, Bangkok, and Angkor; November 30, they fly to Calcutta; December 9, they continue on to London; December 19, John van Druten dies.

1958 January 12, Isherwood and Bachardy fly from London to New York; January 30, they return to Los Angeles; February 2, Bachardy returns to the Chouinard Art Institute; February 11, Isherwood gets back to work on his novel and on the Ramakrishna biography; February 17, Isherwood takes mescaline again; February 25, Bachardy begins taking painting classes from Vernon Old; mid-March, Isherwood begins work on *Mary Magdalene* for David Selznick, until late June; June 17, Bachardy, leaves for Louisiana and, on June 21, New York, returning June 29; July 5, Isherwood completes another new foreword for a U.S. edition of *All the Conspirators*; August 22, he jettisons opening chapters of Ramakrishna biography; August 24–30, visits San Francisco with Bachardy; October 10, Selznick hires Eddie Anhalt on *Mary Magdalene*; October, Isherwood and Bachardy begin writing a play, *The Monsters*; during the autumn, Isherwood and Lambert begin revising *The Vacant Room*; November 25, Isherwood has car accident.

1959 Mid-January, Isherwood and Bachardy complete *The Monsters*; January 29, they travel to New York, and on February 7 to Philadelphia, returning February 16 to Los Angeles; March 7–April 13, Isherwood writes "Mr. Lancaster," the first part of the final draft of his novel; March 20, he signs on to teach at L.A. State College; April 18–23, travels to New York alone to discuss musical version of his Berlin writings with Auden; also in April, the first installment of *Ramakrishna and His Disciples* appears in the March/April issue of the Vedanta Society magazine and eleven Bachardy drawings are included in the Chouinard exhibition; May 1, Bachardy takes first job as professional artist for the May Company; Isherwood begins writing "Ambrose," the second part of his novel; May 18, Bachardy's twenty-fifth birthday; June, Isherwood begins "Afterwards," a homosexual short story; June 9, Bachardy is laid off from the May Company; mid-June, Isherwood and Bachardy undertake to buy 145 Adelaide Drive; July 7, Bachardy begins working at the studio loaned to him by Paul Millard; July 17, Isherwood and Lambert complete revision of *The Vacant Room*; July 31, Isherwood finishes "Afterwards"; August 18, Isherwood and Bachardy travel to New York and then England; August 25, Isherwood visits Wyberslegh and sees his mother for the last time; September 1, Isherwood and Bachardy go to the Villa Mauresque, Maugham's house in France; early September, they return to New York; Isherwood visits Gore Vidal on the Hudson; September 9, Isherwood and Bachardy return to Santa Monica; September 22, Isherwood begins teaching at L.A. State College; September 30, Isherwood and Bachardy move to 145 Adelaide Drive; October, "Mr. Lancaster" appears in *The London Magazine*; October 16, Bachardy begins work at the Broadway Department Store; October 25, Bachardy draws hats for Charles LeMaire.

1960 February 9, start of Isherwood's second semester at L.A. State; February 14, decides to call his novel *The Others*; L.A. State mounts exhibition on Isherwood;

March 11, Isherwood finishes rough draft of "Ambrose" and March 21, completes revision; he begins working with Charles Laughton on a play about Socrates; April 18, Isherwood starts writing part three of his novel; May 19, finishes rough draft of part three, which he is now calling, on its own, "The Others," but will soon call "Waldemar"; May 25, accepts job at University of California at Santa Barbara (UCSB) for the following autumn; June 9, finishes revisions to "Waldemar"; June 10, begins writing "Paul," the final part of his novel; June 12, plans to title the novel *The Lost*; June 15, Kathleen Isherwood dies; August 18, Laughton has gall bladder operation; August 19, Isherwood completes rough draft of "Paul"; August 26, begins drafting frame for novel, turns fifty-six, and completes his last handwritten diary; August 27, Isherwood begins typing his diary; September 22, begins teaching at UCSB; September 27–November 4, Bachardy goes to New York to supervise framing of his drawings of the cast of *A Taste of Honey*; November 29, Isherwood completes revisions on "Waldemar"; December 7, he finally chooses the title, *Down There on a Visit*; December 23, Russell McKinnon agrees to sponsor Bachardy to study art at the Slade in London; also in 1960, *Great English Short Stories* is published.

1961 January 23, Bachardy leaves for London and the Slade, travelling via New York; April 6, Isherwood joins Bachardy in London; Isherwood works with Auden on Berlin musical, but they abandon it when Auden leaves London in mid-June; Isherwood revises *Down There on a Visit* for publication; July, he sees Heinz Neddermeyer and his wife Gerda in London; July 24–26, Isherwood visits his brother Richard at Wyberslegh; September 6–16, Isherwood and Bachardy travel to France to stay with Tony Richardson and afterwards with Maugham; October 2, Bachardy's first show opens at the Redfern Gallery, preceded by publication of his drawings in *Queen*; October 11, another brief trip to Wyberslegh; October 15, Isherwood returns to Los Angeles alone; December 11–12, he travels to New York to meet Bachardy.

1962 January 2, Bachardy's first New York show opens at the Sagittarius Gallery and he sells just over half the drawings; the relationship between Isherwood and Bachardy has become strained and a crisis air enters; January 25, Isherwood returns alone to Santa Monica; January 28, he begins teaching again at L.A. State; he plans a new novel, *The English Woman*; February 17, Bachardy returns; early March, *Down There on a Visit* published by Methuen in U.K. and by Isherwood's new publisher, Simon and Schuster in U.S.; Isherwood's UCSB lectures are on the radio; Isherwood and Bachardy begin building a studio for Bachardy; Isherwood rereads *Mrs. Dalloway*; September, Bachardy has a Los Angeles show; Isherwood's novel, *The English Woman* begins to evolve into *A Single Man*; October 22–November 20, U.S. naval blockade of Cuba (Cuban missile crisis); December 18, Laughton dies.

1963 January, Bachardy has Santa Barbara show; during the winter and early spring, Bachardy decides he wants to live alone; August, Isherwood has another car accident; October, Isherwood finishes draft of *Ramakrishna and His Disciples*;

October 21, Isherwood sends final draft of *A Single Man* to both his U.S. and U.K. publishers; November 22, Aldous Huxley dies (and John F. Kennedy); December, Isherwood travels via Japan to India with Swami Prabhavananda, and thinks for the first time of writing *A Meeting by the River*.

1964 January 6, Prema and Arup take sannyas at Belur Math; afterwards, Isherwood returns from India via Rome and New York; he begins final draft of *Ramakrishna and His Disciples*; February, begins gathering material for *Exhumations*; March, begins working on *The Loved One* with Terry Southern; meets David Hockney; during the summer, Bachardy travels to North Africa, Europe, and London; July–September, Isherwood works on screenplay of *Reflections in a Golden Eye*; *A Single Man* published in the U.S. by Simon and Schuster and, on September 10, in U.K. by Methuen; September–December, Isherwood works on screenplay of *The Sailor from Gibraltar*; October 15, Bachardy leaves for New York where he has another show and returns in December.

1965 January 6, Bachardy leaves for a further long spell in New York; Isherwood finishes *The Sailor from Gibraltar* and *Exhumations*; January 26–February 7, visits Bachardy; early February, begins as Regent's Professor at UCLA; spring, begins writing *A Meeting by the River*; April 3–May 20, Bachardy returns to Santa Monica; April 8, *Ramakrishna and His Disciples* published by Methuen and appears in the U.S. during the summer; June 21, Isherwood completes rough draft of *A Meeting by the River*; July 1, Bachardy returns again from New York; July 22, David Selznick dies; October, Isherwood completes second draft of *A Meeting by the River*; November 1, he begins *Hero-Father, Demon-Mother* (*Kathleen and Frank*); December 16, Somerset Maugham dies.

1966 January, Bachardy has another L.A. show; February 15, Bachardy leaves for New York; spring, Isherwood is visiting professor at UCLA; Gerald Heard has the first of many strokes; *Exhumations* published in U.S. and U.K.; April 24, Bachardy returns; May 31, Isherwood completes third draft of *A Meeting by the River*; July, he agrees to work on *Silent Night* with Danny Mann for ABC television and travels with Mann to Austria in September for filming; October, Isherwood visits England and stays with his brother at Wyberslegh where he reads his father's letters; stays with the Spenders in London; sees Forster; November, he returns to California; also in November, *Cabaret*—Fred Ebb and John Kander's stage musical based on *I Am a Camera*—opens in New York, directed by Hal Prince and starring Joel Grey, Lotte Lenya, and Jill Haworth.

1967 January, Isherwood begins working more earnestly on the book which eventually will be called *Kathleen and Frank*; spring, he corrects proofs of *A Meeting by the River* which is published in April in the U.S. and in June in the U.K.; May, returns to England to look at family papers at Wyberslegh for *Kathleen and Frank*; June, returns to California and continues working on family diaries and letters; also in 1967, Isherwood works with James Bridges on a play of *A Meeting by the River*.

1968 Isherwood adapts Bernard Shaw's story *The Adventures of the Black Girl in Her Search for God* for the stage, and also adapts Wedekind's *Earth Spirit* and

Pandora's Box; Bachardy spends time in London and in New York; spring, Hockney begins work on a double portrait of Isherwood and Bachardy; October, Isherwood again begins writing *Kathleen and Frank*; also during 1968, Isherwood and Bachardy work together on the play of *A Meeting by the River*.

1969 *The Adventures of the Black Girl in Her Search for God* opens at the Mark Taper Forum in Los Angeles; Isherwood begins to have problems with Depuytren's Contracture; July, Isherwood and Bachardy travel to Tahiti, Bora Bora, Samoa, New Zealand and Australia and begin work on a screenplay for Tony Richardson, *I, Claudius*, based on Robert Graves's *I, Claudius* and *Claudius the God*; also in 1969, Bachardy spends time in London, and *Essentials of Vedanta* is published.

1970 Isherwood destroys some old manuscripts, chiefly drafts of *A Meeting by the River*; February–April, in London together, he and Bachardy work on stage version of *A Meeting by the River*; Isherwood sends final draft of *Kathleen and Frank* to U.S. and U.K. publishers; also in 1970, E. M. Forster dies, leaving Isherwood the rights to *Maurice*, and Gerald Hamilton dies.

1971 Isherwood completes revisions to *Kathleen and Frank*; February, Isherwood and Bachardy start work on a TV script of *Frankenstein* for Universal Studios; April 6, Stravinsky dies; August 14, Gerald Heard dies; August 26, Isherwood begins writing reconstructed diary of the "lost years," 1945–1951; October, *Kathleen and Frank* published by Methuen; also in 1971, Bachardy spends time in New York and Isherwood undergoes hand surgery for Depuytren's Contracture.

1972 January, Isherwood sees preview of film *Cabaret*, based on the musical, and starring Liza Minelli, Joel Grey, and Michael York; U.S. edition of *Kathleen and Frank* published by Simon and Schuster, Isherwood travels to New York for publicity; February, Isherwood and Bachardy undertake another TV script for Universal, *The Mummy or The Lady from the Land of the Dead*; April, Los Angeles premiere of James Bridges' production of *A Meeting by the River*; also in 1972, Isherwood receives award from Hollywood Writers' Club for a lifetime of distinguished contributions to literature.

1973 Isherwood and Bachardy travel to London for filming of *Frankenstein*; they visit Wyberslegh and afterwards go to Switzerland and Rome; summer, they work together on screenplay of *A Meeting by the River*; Bachardy has another show; Jean Ross dies; September 29, Auden dies; William Plomer dies; October, Isherwood begins a new autobiographical book (*Christopher and His Kind*); December, Isherwood and Bachardy's screenplay, *Frankenstein: The True Story* published by Avon books.

1974 Isherwood lectures in New Orleans; Bachardy has a show at the New York Cultural Center; August 26, Isherwood turns seventy; Dorothy Miller dies.

1975 Isherwood works with Bachardy on a TV script adapted from F. Scott Fitzgerald's *The Beautiful and the Damned*; Chester Kallman dies.

1976 May, Isherwood completes final draft of *Christopher and His Kind*; Isherwood and Bachardy travel to London for "Young Writers of the Thirties," an exhibition at the National Portrait Gallery; July 4, Swami Prabhavananda dies; November, Isherwood's new U.S. publisher, Farrar Straus and Giroux, publishes *Christopher and His Kind*; *Frankenstein, the True Story* wins best scenario at the International Festival of Fantastic and Science Fiction Films.

1977 March, U.K. edition of *Christopher and His Kind* published by Methuen.

1979 May 15, Richard Isherwood dies of a heart attack; Isherwood and Bachardy collaborate on *October*.

1980 *My Guru and His Disciple* published in U.S. and U.K.; July 16, Isherwood hears that Bill Caskey is dead; Bachardy shows paintings at the Robert Miller Gallery in New York; *October*, with drawings by Bachardy, published.

1981 October, Isherwood learns that he has a malignant tumor in the prostate.

1983 July, Isherwood makes his last diary entry; Bachardy's *One Hundred Drawings* published by Twelve Trees Press.

1985 Bachardy's *Drawings of the Male Nude* published by Twelve Trees Press.

1986 January 4, Isherwood dies in Santa Monica.

Glossary

Ackerley, J. R. (1896–1967). English author and editor. As well as drama and poetry, Ackerley wrote several autobiographical works, and he is well-known for his intimate relationship with his dog, described in two of them. He was literary editor of *The Listener* from 1935 to 1959, and published work by some of the best and most important writers of his period; Isherwood contributed numerous reviews during the thirties. Their friendship was sustained in later years partly by their shared intimacy with E. M. Forster.

AFSC. American Friends Service Committee, the Quaker relief organization Isherwood worked for during the early 1940s.

AJC Ranch. Carter Lodge, John van Druten, and the British actress and director Auriol Lee, who had directed several of van Druten's plays, bought the ranch together in the early 1940s. They called it "AJC" for Auriol, John, Carter. Lee died in a car accident not long afterwards. Van Druten also owned a forest cabin nearby, in the mountains above Idyllwild. Isherwood sometimes used it, and he also stayed in another cabin nearby, with Vernon Old in 1941.

Akhilananda, Swami. Hindu monk. Head of the Vedanta Center in Providence, Rhode Island, for many years.

Aldous. See Huxley, Aldous.

Alec. See Beesley, Alec.

Allais, David. A monk at Trabuco during the mid-1950s. Later he left, married, and joined an engineering firm.

Allan. See Hunter, Allan.

Allgood, Sara (1883–1950). Irish actress. At the Abbey Theatre, Allgood created the parts of "Juno Boyle" in *Juno and the Paycock* and of "Bessie Burgess" in *The Plough and the Stars*, both by Sean O'Casey. Isherwood evidently saw the first London run of *Juno and the Paycock* between November 1925 and May 1926 and was greatly impressed by its melodrama. The "Sacred Heart of Jesus" speech (in act 3, near the final curtain) laments the death of Juno's son, Johnny, swelling to its climax with these lines:

> What was the pain I suffered, Johnny, bringin' you into the world to carry you to your cradle to the pains I'll suffer carryin' you out o' the world to bring you to

your grave! Mother o' God, Mother o' God, have pity on us all! Blessed Virgin, where were you when me darlin' son was riddled with bullets? Sacred Heart o' Jesus, take away our hearts o' stone, and give us hearts o' flesh! Take away this murdherin' hate, an' give us Thine own eternal love!

Allgood repeated the role of "Juno" for Hitchock's 1930 film, and later settled in Hollywood.

Amiya. Ella Corbin was hired by Swami Prabhavananda and Sister Lalita as housekeeper at Ivar Avenue when she was newly arrived in Hollywood from England in the early 1930s. By the time Isherwood met her at the end of the decade, she had received her Sanskrit name "Amiya" from Swami and become a nun. She became a particular friend of Isherwood's when he lived at the Vedanta Center during the 1940s, partly because they both were English. Amiya's first marriage had failed before she arrived in Hollywood. In the early 1950s she met George Montagu, ninth Earl of Sandwich (then well into his sixties), when he visited the Vedanta Center, and a few weeks later Swami gave them permission to marry. So Amiya returned to England to become the Countess of Sandwich. She became close to Isherwood's mother and his brother Richard, bringing news of them when she returned to visit the Vedanta Center.

Ananta Chaitanya. See Schenkel, John.

Andrews, Betty and Oliver. American actress Betty Harford and her husband, a promising California sculptor on the art faculty at UCLA. She acted for John Houseman in numerous stage productions and made a few movies, including *Inside Daisy Clover*. Betty was a close friend of Iris Tree; Oliver knew Alan Watts well and travelled with Watts to Japan. Oliver died suddenly of a heart attack during the 1970s, while still in his forties. Their son, Christopher, born in the 1950s, was named after Isherwood.

Andrews, John. English ballet dancer. Isherwood met Johnny Andrews in February 1937 during rehearsals for *The Ascent of F6* at the Mercury Theatre in Notting Hill. The Ballet Rambert, in which Andrews served as assistant stage manager as well as being a dancer, rehearsed in the basement while the Group Theatre used the stage. The two traveled to Paris together one weekend and took a trip with W. H. Auden to Threlkeld in March 1937. Auden mentions Andrews in "Last Will and Testament" in *Letters from Iceland*, and Isherwood describes the friendship in *Christopher and His Kind*, though he does not name Andrews.

Ananda Bhavan. See Sarada Convent.

Anhalt, Edward (Eddie) (b. 1914). American screenwriter. Anhalt wrote war, crime, and spy thrillers but also adapted *Beckett* (1964), *The Madwoman of Chaillot* (1969), and many others. He began writing with his first wife, Edna Anhalt, during the 1950s and later worked successfully by himself. His second wife, whom he married later in the 1950s, was called Jackie George. In 1958, Selznick hired Anhalt to work on *Mary Magdalene*, replacing Isherwood, but the film was never made.

Archera, Laura. See Huxley, Laura Archera.

Arup, also Arup Chaitanya. See Critchfield, Kenneth.

Aseshananda, Swami. Hindu monk. Assistant minister during the early 1950s in the Vedanta Society of Southern California, helping Swami Prabhavananda both at the Hollywood center and at Trabuco; in about 1955 he became head of the Vedanta Society at Portland, Oregon.

Ashokananda, Swami. Hindu monk, from India. Head of the Vedanta Center in San Francisco, where Isherwood visited for a few days in 1943.

Asit. See Ghosh, Asit.

Atman. The divine nature within man; the immanent, indwelling God; the self or soul, which, in Vedanta, are at once the Supreme Soul and the individual soul. The Atman can be known through the self, and faith in the Atman must be achieved through direct self-knowledge, not through faith.

Auden, W. H. (Wystan) (1907–1973). English poet, playwright, librettist. Arguably the greatest English poet of the century; his technical virtuosity and formal range are unrivalled, and his output, including a large body of critical prose, is enormous and uniformly brilliant. Auden's mastery of the English and European literary and cultural traditions is evident throughout his writing, yet his work is original and contemporary, making him an ideal librettist for Stravinsky, for whom, with Chester Kallman, Auden wrote *The Rake's Progress*. The pair also produced two librettos for Hans Werner Henze, and Auden, alone, also worked with Benjamin Britten. Auden and Isherwood met as schoolboys towards the end of Isherwood's time at St. Edmund's School, Hindhead, Surrey, where Auden, two and a half years younger than Isherwood, arrived in the autumn of 1915. Auden finished his education at Gresham's School, Holt, and Christ Church, Oxford. He and Isherwood met again in 1925. They wrote three plays together—*The Dog Beneath the Skin* (1935), *The Ascent of F6* (1936), *On the Frontier* (1938)—and an unconventional travel book about their trip to China during the Sino-Japanese war—*Journey to a War* (1939). A fourth play—*The Enemies of a Bishop* (1929)—was published posthumously. As well as several stints of schoolmastering, Auden worked for John Grierson's Film Unit, funded by the General Post Office, for about six months during 1935, mostly writing poetry to be used as sound track. Auden and Isherwood went abroad separately and together during the 1930s, most famously to Berlin (where Auden arrived first, on his own, in 1928), and finally emigrated together to the United States in 1939. After only a few months, their lives and interests diverged (Auden settled in New York where he became a U.S. citizen in 1946, while Isherwood went on to California), but they remained close friends until Auden's death. Auden is caricatured as "Hugh Weston" in *Lions and Shadows* and figures centrally in *Christopher and His Kind*. Their influence upon one another during the first half of their careers is incalculable.

Aufderheide, Charles. Younger lover of Albert Grossman. The pair shared a series of rented houses with Sam and Isadore From in Los Angeles. Aufderheide worked at the Technicolor laboratories in Hollywood. After twenty years, Grossman, who was wealthy, met an even younger man and the relationship ended in the early 1970s. Aufderheide then moved to San Francisco.

Austen, Howard (Tinker). Companion to Gore Vidal from 1950 onward. Austen worked in advertising for a time, and studied singing. He has devoted much of his life to Vidal, managing Vidal's business and social life.

Avadhuta. Wandering monk. The story "Avadhuta Had Twenty-four Teachers" appears in the Indian devotional text the Bhagavatam Purana, adapted and translated into English by Swami Prabhavananda as *The Wisdom of God* (see chapter 3). Avadhuta's twenty-four teachers include the likes of earth, air, ether, water, fire, moon, sun, pigeon, python, the courtesan, the child, the maiden, the arrow-maker and many more animals; each by its nature has taught him a lesson of spiritual wisdom, described in the story, and the lessons have helped him to overcome the gunas and become free from attachments.

Ayrton, Michael (1921–1975). British artist and writer. Ayrton worked as a sculptor, painter, stage designer and book illustrator, wrote fiction and art criticism, and made films. He drew Isherwood on a commission from Methuen in 1956, but the result was not satisfactory.

Bachardy, Don (b. 1934). American painter; Isherwood's companion from 1953 onwards. Bachardy accompanied his elder brother, Ted Bachardy, on the beach in Santa Monica from the late 1940s, and Isherwood occasionally saw him there. Ted, with other friends, first introduced them in November 1952. They met again in early February 1953 and, on February 14, began an affair which quickly became serious. Bachardy was then an eighteen-year-old college student living at home with his brother and his mother. His parents were divorced. He had studied languages for one semester at UCLA, then transferred at the start of 1953 to Los Angeles City College in Hollywood, near his mother's apartment. At first he studied French and Spanish but dropped French for German as a result of Isherwood's influence. He had worked as a grocery boy at a local market, and, like Isherwood in youth, spent most of his free time at the movies. In February 1955, Bachardy went back to UCLA to begin his junior year, and almost immediately changed his major from Languages to Theater Arts. Then in July 1956, he enrolled at the Chouinard Art Institute, supplemented his instruction there by taking classes with Vernon Old, and within a few years got his first work as a professional artist, drawing fashion illustrations for a local department store. During this period he began to do portraits of Isherwood, close friends, and favorite film stars, and began to sell his own work. He drew a set of Hollywood personalities to accompany an article in the *Paris Review* in 1960, but his first major commission as a portrait artist came from Tony Richardson, who asked him to draw each of the cast members in his 1960 stage production of *A Taste of Honey*. During 1959 and 1960, Bachardy worked a few days a week in a studio in West Hollywood loaned to him by Paul Millard. In 1961 he attended the Slade School of Art in London; this led to his first individual shows, in London in 1961 and in New York in 1962. Since then he has done countless portraits, both of the famous and the little-known, shown his work in a number of cities, and published his drawings in several books including *October* (1983) with Isherwood, and *Last Drawings of Christopher Isherwood* (1990). Together, Isherwood and Bachardy wrote the script for the TV film *Frankenstein: The True Story* (1973).

Bachardy, Glade. Don Bachardy's mother; from Ohio. Childhood polio left her with a limp resulting in extreme shyness. An ardent movie-goer, she took Don Bachardy and his brother, Ted, to the movies from early childhood, thus nurturing Don's obsession. She married in 1928 in Cleveland, Ohio and travelled to Los Angeles on her honeymoon—she never left. Her father was the captain of a cargo boat on the Great Lakes, and she met her husband, Jess Bachardy, a member of the crew, on board during a summer cruise in the 1920s. They were divorced in 1952, but later reconciled; once Ted and Don had moved out of their mother's apartment their father moved back in, early in 1955.

Bachardy, Ted. Don Bachardy's older brother; Isherwood noticed Ted Bachardy on the beach in Santa Monica, probably in the autumn of 1948 or spring of 1949, and invited him to a party in November 1949 (Ted's name first appears in Isherwood's diary the same month). Isherwood was attracted to Ted, but did not pursue him seriously because Ted was becoming involved with someone else, Ed Cornell, during 1949. Around the same time, Ted also experienced a mental breakdown—the second or third one since 1945 when he was fifteen. Eventually he was diagnosed as a manic-depressive schizophrenic. He suffers recurring periods of manic, self-destructive behavior followed by nervous breakdowns and long stays in mental hospitals. Isherwood continued to see Ted Bachardy intermittently during the early weeks of his affair with Don Bachardy, but a turning point came in February 1953 with Ted's third or fourth breakdown when Isherwood sympathized with Don and intervened to try to help prevent Ted from becoming excessively violent and having to be hospitalized; nevertheless, Ted was committed on February 26. He had another breakdown, in March 1955, and was again committed to the Camarillo State Mental Hospital for a number of weeks, until April 7. When well, Ted took odd jobs: he was employed as a tour guide and in the mail room at Warner Brothers, as a sales clerk in a department store, and as an office worker in insurance companies and advertising agencies.

Bacon, Francis (1909–1992). English painter, born in Dublin. Bacon worked as an interior decorator in London during the late 1920s and lived in Berlin in 1930, around the time that he taught himself to paint. He showed some of his work in London during the 1930s, but came to prominence only after the war when his controversial *Three Studies for Figures at the Base of a Crucifixion* made him suddenly famous in 1945. His paintings present anguished, distorted figures in vague nightmare spaces, often with deliberately smudged paintwork and blurred outlines; he urged that art should expose emotions rather than simply represent, and expressed his intention to leave an evident trace of his human presence and experience upon his work. He is widely held to be one of the great painters of this century. Isherwood recorded some of Bacon's remarks on art in his diary, and evidently set store by them; he first mentions Bacon when in London in 1956, although he met Bacon earlier, probably in 1948, otherwise in 1952 and perhaps through Stephen Spender.

Barada. A senior nun at the Santa Barbara convent; after sannyas she was called Pravrajika Baradaprana. Her original name was Doris Ludwig. Barada was interested in music and composed Vedantic hymns. She still lives at the Sarada Convent.

Bardo Thodol. A set of instructions for the dead and dying in Mahayana or Northern Buddhism. The Lama whispers the instructions into the ear of the corpse, guiding the dead man during the Bardo existence which intervenes between death and rebirth. W. Y. Evans-Wentz, an Oxford scholar and a disciple of the Tibetan sage Lama Kazi Dawa-Sandup, first compiled the text in English and named it The Tibetan Book of the Dead. Evans-Wentz translated the words *Bardo Thodol* as "Liberation by Hearing on the After-Death Plane."

Barnes, Jimmy. A monk from 1955 to 1958, living most of the time at Trabuco; his wife, possibly called Ailleen, was a nun at Santa Barbara during roughly the same period. Barnes played the saxophone and was evidently a good cook.

Barrie, Michael. A former singer with financial and administrative talents; friend and secretary to Gerald Heard from the late 1940s onward. He met Heard through Swami Prabhavananda and lived at Trabuco as a monk until about 1955 when he left on bad terms. He was friendly with Isherwood and Bachardy throughout the 1950s, and they rented his house, at 322 East Rustic Road, for roughly two months in 1956. Barrie nursed Heard through his five-year-long final illness until Heard's death in 1971.

bastrika. A bellows used in a furnace; in hatha yoga, *bastrika* is a fast vigorous intake of breath followed by a fast vigorous exhalation, making a sound like air rushing through a bellows. See also hatha yoga.

Beaton, Cecil (1904–1980). English photographer, theater designer, and author. Beaton photographed the most celebrated and fashionable people of his era, beginning in the 1920s with the Sitwells, and going on to the British royal family, actors, actresses, writers, and many other public figures. He was himself a dandy and a creature of style. From 1939 to 1945 he worked successfully as a war photographer (his photograph of a child in hospital after a bombing raid made the cover of *Life*). His numerous costume and set designs for stage and screen were widely admired; in Hollywood his most celebrated achievements were *Gigi* (1958) and *My Fair Lady* (1964), for which he won two Oscars. Isherwood and Beaton were contemporaries at Cambridge, but became friendly only in the late 1940s when Beaton visited Hollywood (with a production of *Lady Windermere's Fan* which he had designed and in which he was acting) and was helpful to Bill Caskey who was then trying to establish himself as a photographer.

Beesley, Alec and Dodie Smith Beesley. She was an English playwright, novelist and former actress, known professionally as Dodie Smith. He was a conscientious objector and an unofficial legal advisor to C.O.s in Los Angeles during the war; he also managed her career. The Beesleys spent a decade in Hollywood for the sake of Alec's pacifist convictions, and Dodie wrote scripts there for Paramount and her first novel, *I Capture the Castle*. They returned to England in the early 1950s. Isherwood met the Beesleys in November 1942, through Dodie's close friend and confidant John van Druten, and often lunched with them on Sundays. In contrast to many of his friends during that period, he felt he could speak comfortably to them about all aspects of his life. When Isherwood moved out of the Vedanta Society in August 1945, his first home was the chauffeur's apartment at the Beesleys'. Dodie Beesley in particular encouraged him to keep on with his writing, and he discussed *The World in the Evening* with her extensively. He derived some of the details of the marriage between Stephen Monk and the writer Elizabeth Rydal in *The World in the Evening* from the Beesleys' professional and domestic arrangements, and Elizabeth's correspondence with her friend Cecilia de Limbour resembles the voluminous letters continually exchanged between Dodie and John van Druten. Isherwood dedicated the novel to the Beesleys. It was Dodie Beesley who challenged John van Druten to make a play from *Sally Bowles*, ultimately leading to *I Am a Camera*. In the summer of 1943, the Beesleys mated their Dalmatians, Folly and Buzzle, and Folly produced fifteen puppies—inspiring Dodie's most famous book, *The One Hundred and One*

Dalmatians (1956), later filmed by Walt Disney. Her play writing career was less successful after the war; for example, *These People, Those Books*, which Isherwood mentions, had a pre-London run but was never produced in the West End.

Belfrage, Cedric (1904–1990). British journalist and novelist. Belfrage attended Isherwood's Cambridge college, Corpus Christi, where they knew one another. He worked alternately in Hollywood and London as a newspaper correspondent and a theater and film critic; for a time he was Samuel Goldwyn's public relations man in London. During the war he served in British intelligence, then co-founded the leftist *National Guardian* in 1948. He was deported back to England in 1955 after being hounded by the McCarthyites, and reported from abroad for various left-wing journals, eventually settling in Mexico in 1963. His books include two which Isherwood mentions, a 1940 novel about the South, *Let My People Go*, and, in 1948, *Abide With Me*, about the undertaking business.

Ben, also Benjamin. See Bok, Benjamin.

Ben. See Masselink, Ben.

Benoit, Hubert. French surgeon; his career was ended by wounds sustained during World War II, and he became a psychotherapist and a student of Vedanta and Zen Buddhism. He published several works on metaphysics, psychology and Zen, and his article "Notes in Regard to a Technique of Timeless Realization" appeared in the March–April 1950 issue of *Vedanta and the West* (translated by Huxley and later reprinted in *Vedanta for Modern Man*). According to Benoit's technique, the subject could disconnect the imagination by sitting or lying relaxed in a comfortable place, alone, and watching whatever mental images the imagination produced. Benoit argued that if the imagination was left free to produce what it liked, and the subject consciously watched, the imagination would in fact produce no images at all, and the subject would then be in a state of pure, voluntary attention.

Berlin crisis. In November 1958, the German Democratic Republic in Soviet-occupied East Germany sought official recognition abroad. Khrushchev announced his intention to transfer Soviet authority in Berlin to the East German regime, aiming to force the other three powers responsible for the city—England, France, and the U.S.—to recognize the GDR. The White House declared that it would maintain the integrity of West Berlin. In December, Khrushchev demanded that troops be withdrawn and Berlin established as a free city, putting a six-month deadline on his ultimatum for the transfer of Soviet rule in Berlin to the GDR. Feared Soviet land and air blockades and possible escalation never came about, but the crisis dominated East-West diplomacy throughout the first half of 1959. Talks were finally agreed, and the ultimatum effectively withdrawn when Khrushchev visited the U.S. in September 1959.

Berthold. See Viertel, Berthold.

Besant, Annie (1847–1933). English social reformer and a leader of Madame Blavatsky's Theosophical movement. Mrs. Besant was a Fabian and a trade union organizer before going to India where she founded what was to become the Hindu University of India, was involved in the beginning of the All India Home Rule League in 1916, and served as a President of the Indian National Congress. A prolific author on Theosophy, she had a strong personal stake in Krishnamurti's role as the new "World Teacher" since, in 1911, she herself proclaimed him the "vehicle" in which the Theosophical master might reincarnate himself, and she closely supervised Krishnamurti's upbringing and education.

Bill, also Billy. See Caskey, William.

Blanch, Lesley. English journalist and author. Blanch was an editor at *Vogue* during the 1940s. Her books include *The Wilder Shores of Love*, *The Sabres of Paradise*, *The Nine-Tiger Man*, biography, travel essays, and an autobiography, *Journey Into the Mind's Eye*. She met the French novelist Romain Gary in England during the war, and they were married for a number of years before divorcing. She now lives in France. Blanch was a close friend of Gavin Lambert who introduced her and Romain Gary to Isherwood and Bachardy during the 1950s.

Bob. See Craft, Robert.

Bobo, Wallace (Bobo). Neighbour of Denny Fouts at 137 Entrada Drive, where Bobo lived with his friend Howard Kelley. Bobo and Kelley attended all Fouts's parties in the late 1940s and were often in his apartment. Bobo worked as a gardener.

Bok, Ben. Eldest son of Peggy Kiskadden and Curtis Bok. He married in 1948 and later raised wolves near Llano, California.

Bok, W. Curtis (1897–1962). American lawyer, judge, author; first husband of Peggy Kiskadden and father of Tis, Ben, and Derek Bok. Curtis Bok was the elder son of Dutch-born Edward Bok (1863–1930), editor, author, philanthropist, and pacifist, who began his career as a Western Union office boy and retired as the wealthy and powerful editor of *Ladies Home Journal*, a success story he chronicled in his 1921 Pulitzer-Prize-winning autobiography, *The Americanization of Edward Bok*. Curtis Bok's mother, Mary Louise Curtis (1876–1970), was a great Philadelphia philanthropist in her own right and the daughter of the one-time owner of *Ladies Home Journal* and the *Saturday Evening Post*. Curtis Bok attended Williams College and studied law at the University of Virginia Law School. He practiced law in Philadelphia and became a distinguished judge and public official, serving on the Pennsylvania Supreme Court for twenty-one years. He was also the author of four books including three novels. Although he served in both World Wars, Bok was a Quaker and, like his father, a peace advocate. He first met Aldous Huxley at Dartington Hall, Leonard and Dorothy Elmhirst's school in Devonshire where Huxley's son, Matthew, was at school from 1932 until 1935. After his 1933 divorce, Bok married again and had two more daughters.

Bok, Derek (Dek) (b. 1930). Second son of Peggy Kiskadden and Curtis Bok. He became a professor of law, Dean of the Harvard Law School, and later President of Harvard University. He is the author of several books on law and on higher education. His wife is the Swedish-born philosopher and writer, Sissela Myrdal Bok.

Bok, Margaret Welmoet (Tis). Daughter of Peggy Kiskadden and Curtis Bok. She married Reynout Roland Holst.

Bok, Peggy. See Kiskadden, Peggy.

Bower, Tony. American friend of Jean and Cyril Connolly; Isherwood met him in Paris in 1937. Bower was present at lunch in Hollywood the day Isherwood met Denny Fouts, and he appears as "Ronny" in *Down There on a Visit*. He was drafted into the army twice during the war, and trained on Long Island and later in San Diego; he also wrote about film for a New York paper. The January 1944 *Horizon* carried an article by Bower (using the pseudonym Anthony Bourne) which, relatively humorously, described W. H. Auden's ménage at Middagh Street in Brooklyn and "the metaphysical development of your friends Aldous Huxley, Christopher Isherwood and Gerald Heard" in Hollywood. He called Huxley, Heard and Isherwood "the mystic Axis" and regretted the disappearance from England of so talented a novelist as Isherwood ("Where Shall John Go?" III–USA, Antony Bourne, *Horizon*, January 1944, 9.49, pp. 13–23).

Bowles, Paul (b. 1910). American composer and, later, writer. Probably best known for his novel *The Sheltering Sky* (1949), filmed by Bertolucci. In addition to fiction, he wrote poetry and travel books and made translations. Isherwood first met Bowles fleetingly in Berlin in 1931 and used his name for the character "Sally Bowles" without realizing that he would later meet Bowles again and that Bowles would become famous in his own right. Bowles and his wife, the writer Jane Bowles (1917–1973), lived in George Davis's house in Brooklyn with W. H. Auden and others during the 1940s. They later moved to Tangier where they lived separately from one another, but remained close friends. She became an invalid. In 1955 Isherwood and Bachardy visited the Bowleses, who were the object of many other literary pilgrimages as well. Later Isherwood and Bachardy met Bowles again on his visits to America.

Brackett, Charles (1892–1969). American screenwriter and producer. Charlie Brackett was from a wealthy East Coast family; he began as a novelist, then became a screenwriter, and later a producer. He often worked with the Viennese writer-director Billy Wilder. He was one of the writers who worked on the script for Garbo's *Ninotchka* (1939); he won an Academy Award as writer-producer of *The Long Weekend* (1945); and he produced *The King and I* (1956), as well as working on numerous other films. When Isherwood knew him best during the 1950s, Brackett worked for Darryl F. Zanuck at Twentieth Century-Fox where he remained for about a decade until the early 1960s. His second wife, Lillian, was called Muff; she had been the spinster sister of Brackett's first wife, who died, and was already in her sixties when Brackett married her. Brackett also had two grown daughters, and one, Alexandra (Xan), was married to James Larmore, Brackett's assistant.

brahmachari or brahmacharini. In Vedanta, a spiritual aspirant who has taken the first monastic vows. In the Ramakrishna Order, the brahmacharya vows may be taken only after five or more years as a probationer monk or nun.

Brahmananda, Swami (1863–1922). Rakhal Chandra Ghosh, the son of a wealthy landowner, was a boyhood friend of Vivekananda with whom, ultimately, he was to lead the Ramakrishna Order. Later he was also called Maharaj. Married off by his father at sixteen, he became a disciple of Ramakrishna soon afterwards. Like Vivekananda, Brahmananda, was an *Ishvarakoti*, an eternally free and perfect soul born into the world for mankind's benefit and possessing some characteristics of the avatar. He was an eternal companion of Sri Krishna, and his companionship took the especially intimate form of a parent/son relationship (thus reenacting a previously existing and eternal relationship between their two souls). After the death of Ramakrishna, Brahmananda ran the Baranagore monastery (two miles north of

Calcutta), made pilgrimages to northern India, and in 1897 became President of the Belur Math and, in 1900, of the Ramakrishna Math and Mission, founding and visiting Vedanta centers in and near India.

Breese, Eleanor and Vance. She was a novelist and secretary; he was a pilot. They were divorced but remained close and made an attempt to renew their marriage in 1956. She worked for Isherwood at Twentieth Century-Fox starting in September 1956. Her novel *The Valley of Power* appeared in 1945 under her pen name, Eleanor Buckles, but a second novel, about her marriage to Vance, was evidently never published. Later she co-wrote a memoir for Wynne O'Mara, *Gangway for the Lady Surgeon: An Account of W. O'Mara's Experiences as a Ship's Surgeon* (1958). Vance Breese also became a friend of Isherwood and Bachardy. In addition, Eleanor had a boyfriend, Charles Taylor (nicknamed Spud), who was a doctor; he examined Isherwood in May 1957 during a period of continuous ill health.

Bridges, James (Jimmy) (1936–1993). American actor, screenwriter and director. Bridges was stage manager for the UCLA Professional Theater Group in the early 1960s when John Houseman recommended him as a writer for a Hitchcock suspense series on TV. He came to prominence in the 1970s when he directed *The Paper Chase* (1973), *The China Syndrome* (1979), *Urban Cowboy* (1980), and others. He lived with the actor Jack Larson from the mid-1950s onward, and through Larson became close friends with Isherwood and Bachardy. Bridges directed the first production of Isherwood and Bachardy's play *A Meeting by the River*.

Britten, Benjamin (1913–1976). British composer. W. H. Auden worked with Britten from September 1935 at the GPO Film Unit in Soho Square and introduced him to the Group Theatre; Britten composed the music for *The Ascent of F6*, and Isherwood perhaps first met him at rehearsals in February 1937. By March 1937, the two were friendly enough to spend the night together at the Jermyn Street Turkish Baths, though they never had a sexual relationship. Britten wrote the music for the next Auden-Isherwood play, *On the Frontier*. Britten and his eventual lifelong companion, Peter Pears, went to America not long after Auden and Isherwood, reaching New York in the summer of 1939, and Auden and Britten wrote *Paul Bunyan* (1941), Britten's first opera, during this period. Britten and Pears returned to England in March 1942. Both were pacifists and registered as conscientious objectors during the war. A major figure, Britten composed songs, song cycles, orchestral music, works for chorus and orchestra such as his *War Requiem* (1961), and nine operas including *Peter Grimes* (1945), *Albert Herring* (1948), *Billy Budd* (1951), *A Midsummer Night's Dream* (1960), and *Death in Venice* (1973).

Brooke, Tim. British novelist; a contemporary of Isherwood at Cambridge, he later spent time in Los Angeles. His novels, published under the name Hugh Brooke, include *The Mad Shepherdess* (1930), *Man Made Angry* (1932), *Miss Mitchell* (1934), and *Saturday Island* (1935). He was a close friend of the dancer Nicky Nadeau.

Brown, David. American film producer. Brown was a journalist before coming to Hollywood. At Twentieth Century-Fox, he became story editor and afterwards formed a production company with Richard Zanuck, called Zanuck-Brown. Isherwood met Brown through Jim Geller in 1956, but never worked on any of the Fox projects mooted between them.

Brown, Harry (1917–1986). American screenwriter and novelist. Brown was educated at Harvard, and also wrote poetry and plays; for the movies, he wrote on a variety of subjects, including a number of war films. He won an Oscar as co-writer for *A Place in the Sun* (1951). In the early 1950s, he worked at Twentieth Century-Fox and MGM, and he was married for a few years to Marguerite Lamkin. Later he married June de Baum.

Brown, H. Runham (1879–1949). Brown went to prison for refusing to serve in World War I and was later a founder and Secretary of War Resisters International; an ardent socialist, he believed that in the class struggle, war resisters ranged themselves on the side of the oppressed. He was a friend and associate of George Lansbury.

Buckingham, Bob. British policeman; the longtime friend of E. M. Forster. His wife was called May Buckingham.

Buddha Chaitanya (Buddha). A disciple of Swami Prabhavananda, originally called Philip Griggs. He lived as a monk both at the Hollywood Center and at Trabuco during the 1950s and took brahmacharya with John Yale in August 1955, becoming Buddha Chaitanya. In 1959 he left Vedanta for a time, but he later returned, took sannyas and became Swami Yogeshananda. Later he led a Vedanta group in Georgia.

bundist. Member of a pro-Nazi German-American organization.

Burgess, Guy (1910–1963). British diplomat and double agent. Burgess became a communist while at Cambridge, and he was secretly recruited by the Soviets during the 1930s. He worked for the BBC until joining the Foreign Office in the mid-1940s, and he was meanwhile also employed by MI5. In May 1951, having been recalled from his post in Washington under Kim Philby, Burgess was warned by Anthony Blunt that he was suspected of espionage. He disappeared with Donald Maclean, also a double agent, and it eventually became clear the pair had defected to Moscow (their presence there was announced in 1956). Isherwood knew Burgess in London during the 1930s, where Burgess was also friendly with W. H. Auden and Stephen Spender, and it was Burgess who introduced Isherwood to Jacky Hewit in 1938. Hewit had been Burgess's lover until Burgess met Peter Pollock in Cannes that year. After roughly a decade with Pollock, Burgess lived with Hewit again intermittently during the three years leading up to his defection.

the Burns brothers. The comedian George Burns and his youngest brother Willy (their real name was Birnbaum) had a production company, McCadden Productions (named after Willy's street, McCadden Place). In 1957, Isherwood and Gavin Lambert tried to sell them an idea for a TV series starring Hermione Gingold. Willy was also a personal manager for George and for George's wife and comedy partner, Gracie Allen, and he occasionally wrote material for their radio and, later, television shows. Gracie Allen retired in June 1958. Ronnie Burns, only son of George and Gracie, sometimes acted in "The Burns and Allen Show" on TV, but later left show business. George Burns died in 1996, aged 100.

Burns, Phil. American designer. A young man with whom Isherwood had a friendly sexual relationship before he met Don Bachardy and occasionally afterwards. Burns was probably in his thirties at the time.

Bynner, Witter (1881–1968). American poet. In 1916, Bynner and Arthur Davison Ficke successfully launched a spoof literary movement "Spectrism," intended to parody Pound's Imagism and similar movements; *Spectra: A Book of Poetic Experiments* achieved wide recognition, and Bynner went on to write more seriously under the identity he adopted for the hoax, Emmanuel Morgan. Afterwards he translated Tang poetry from the Chinese with the scholar Kiang Kang-hu. Isherwood may have met Bynner towards the end of the 1940s; Bynner lived in Santa Fe with his friend Bob Hunt, and also had a house in Mexico, at Lake Chapala. He knew D. H. Lawrence and Frieda, and Isherwood evidently read in manuscript Bynner's book on Lawrence, *Journey With Genius* (1951).

Cadmus, Paul. American painter of Basque and Dutch background; his sister, Fidelma, was married to Lincoln Kirstein. Cadmus drew Isherwood in February 1942 in New York, where Cadmus lived, and the two became friends.

Calder-Marshall, Arthur (1908–1992). English writer and editor; a contemporary of Stephen Spender at Oxford (where Calder-Marshall composed poetry and edited *The Oxford Outlook*) and a friend afterwards. He went on to write fiction, biography, and essays, and is best-known for his public school novel *Dead Centre* (1935). Auden and Isherwood included him in their 1939 contribution to *Vogue*, "Young British Writers—On the Way Up," but Isherwood was disappointed by Calder-Marshall's novel *Occasion of Glory* (1955), which he was asked to script in 1960.

Caldwell, Evelyn. See Hooker, Evelyn.

Capote, Truman (1924–1984). American novelist, born in New Orleans. Isherwood was introduced to Capote at the Random House offices on May 1, 1947, shortly before the publication of Capote's first novel, *Other Voices, Other Rooms*. They quickly became friends. Capote wrote for *The New Yorker*, where he worked for a time, and for other magazines; his books include *The Grass Harp* (1951), *Breakfast at Tiffany's* (1958), and the chilling non-fiction novel *In Cold Blood* (1966). Capote's companion for many years was Newton Arvin, a college professor, and afterwards Jack Dunphy, a dancer and, later, a novelist (*The Nightmovers*). They travelled extensively—around the Mediterranean, in the West Indies, through Russia and the Orient—and sometimes lived abroad. Drink and drugs probably accelerated the end of Capote's career.

Carlson, Evans (1896–1947). American soldier; Carlson moved from the U.S. Army to the Marine Corps in 1922 and retired as a result of his wounds in 1946, by then a heavily decorated Brigadier General. Isherwood and Auden met him in China where, in 1937–1938, he was observing the Chinese armies and had penetrated behind Japanese lines with the communist guerrillas. Carlson resigned from the marines in 1939 and produced a scholarly analysis *The Chinese Army* (1941), which examined the success of the Chinese in repelling foreign invaders despite their lack of modern weaponry; then in 1941, he reenlisted. At his recommendation, the Marine Corps adopted some of the commando tactics Carlson had learned from the Chinese guerrillas, forming its first Raider Battalions in 1942. Carlson led the 2nd Raider Battalion and took the motto for his unit from the Chinese communists: "gung-ho" (work together), the first use of the phrase in English.

Caroline. See Freud, Caroline.

Caskey, William (Bill) (1921–1981). American photographer, born and raised in Kentucky, a lapsed Catholic of Irish background, part Cherokee Indian. Isherwood met Caskey in the first half of 1945 when Caskey arrived in Santa Monica Canyon with a friend, Hayden Lewis, and joined the circle surrounding Denny Fouts and Jay de Laval; they became lovers in June that year and by August had begun a serious affair. Caskey had been briefly in the navy, though he was once in legal trouble for avoiding the draft (his wealthy, elderly lover of the time, Len Hanna, rescued him with an expensive lawyer), and he was discharged neither honorably nor dishonorably (a "blue discharge") following a homosexual scandal in which Hayden Lewis was also implicated. Caskey had worked in photo-finish at a Kentucky racecourse and in about 1945 he took up photography seriously, proving talented. He took the photographs for *The Condor and The Cows* and did portraits of some of his and Isherwood's friends. Caskey's father bred horses, and Caskey had ridden since childhood; they had their love of horses in common but otherwise father and son fought a great deal. Caskey's parents lived apart, and he remained in touch with his mother, Catherine Caskey, a pretty woman with a southern accent who talked ceaselessly and unthinkingly. She accepted Caskey's relationship with Isherwood with whom she got on well, and *The Condor and the Cows* is dedicated to her. Caskey also had two sisters, but was on bad terms with them. Caskey and Isherwood split for good in 1951 after intermittent separations and domestic troubles. Later Caskey lived in Athens and travelled frequently to Egypt. As well as taking photographs, he made art objects out of junk, and for a time had a business beading sweaters.

Cerf, Bennett (1898–1971). American publisher. Cerf was the founder of Random House, W. H. Auden's and Isherwood's first American publisher. He had persuaded Faber and Faber jointly to commission *Journey to a War*, and in early March 1939 he gave Isherwood a $500 advance on his next (unwritten) novel. Cerf's long and distinguished literary career began in the 1920s; among other achievements, he founded the Modern Library and held senior posts at Random House until his death. He is popularly known for his books of jokes and humor. Towards the end of the 1950s, Isherwood left Random House for Simon and Schuster.

Chapman, Kent. A student acquaintance of Isherwood's with whom he corresponded and occasionally met. Isherwood first mentions Chapman in his diary in July 1957, but evidently knew him before this; Chapman was interested in Vedanta. He was an aspiring fiction writer and followed artistic developments among the California poets and painters in West Venice, where he lived during the late 1950s. At the time, he had a girlfriend called Nancy Dvorak whom Isherwood also met. In 1958 Chapman was drafted into the army and sent abroad. Isherwood's friendship with Chapman lies behind the relationship between "George" and "Kenny" in *A Single Man*, though Chapman is not the main model for Kenny.

Chandler, Raymond (1888–1959). American writer; raised and educated in England from the age of seven. Chandler created the private-eye Philip Marlowe, an attractive and incorruptible cynic, who featured in *The Big Sleep* (1939), *Farewell, My Lovely* (1940), and *The Long Goodbye* (1954), among others. Many of his novels were filmed, and they also were admired as literature, especially by W. H. Auden.

Charles. See Laughton, Charles.

Charlton, Jim (b. 1919). American architect, from Reading, Pennsylvania. Charlton had been a student with Ben Masselink at Taliesin West in Arizona, and had also been trained at Frank Lloyd Wright's other center, Taliesin, in Wisconsin. He joined the air force during the war, and flew twenty-six missions over Germany, including a July 1943 daylight raid on Hamburg. Isherwood was introduced to him by the Masselinks in August 1948, and they established a friendly-romantic attachment that lasted intermittently through a number of years during which each had various other lovers. Towards the end of the 1950s Charlton married a wealthy Swiss woman called Hilde, a mother of three, and had a son with her in September 1958. The marriage ended in divorce. Afterwards he lived in Hawaii until the late 1980s, and he wrote an autobiographical novel called *St. Mick*. Charlton was a model for Bob Wood in *The World in the Evening*.

Chisholm, Hugh (1913–1972). American poet and translator. Isherwood met Hugh Chisholm in London in 1937 when Chisholm was an undergraduate at Cambridge and asked to join Isherwood and W. H. Auden on their trip to China. Chisholm later arrived in Hollywood with his wife Bridget in 1940 to organize war relief at the Goldwyn Studios with Sam Goldwyn. The Chisholms also became involved in Isherwood's Quaker relief work, and later Hugh Chisholm worked in New York on a Quaker scheme for an alternative to compulsory service for C.O.s. Bridget Chisholm had a baby son while in Hollywood. By 1955 when Isherwood and Don Bachardy visited Chisholm in Rome, he had left his wife and was living with Brad Fuller; the pair visited Hollywood a few years later.

Chris. See Wood, Chris.

C.O. Conscientious objector; see also Selective Service.

Collier, John (1901–1980). British novelist and screenwriter. He is best known for *His Monkey Wife* (1930) and also wrote other fantastic and satirical tales. Isherwood admired his short stories. Collier was poetry editor of *Time and Tide* in the 1920s and early 1930s and came to Hollywood in 1935. Isherwood met him in the 1940s, perhaps at Salka Viertel's, and they became close friends while working at the same time at Warner Brothers during 1945. In 1951 Collier moved to Mexico, though he continued to write films, including the script for the film version of *I Am a Camera*, which Isherwood deplored.

Connolly, Cyril (1903–1974). British journalist and critic, educated at Eton and Balliol College, Oxford. Connolly was a regular contributor to English newspapers and magazines. He wrote one novel, *The Rock Pool* (1936), followed by collections that combined criticism, autobiography, and aphorism—*Enemies of Promise* (1938) and *The Unquiet Grave* (1944). Further collections appeared after the war, displaying his gift for parody. In 1939, Connolly founded the magazine *Horizon* with Stephen Spender and edited it throughout its publication until 1950. He was perhaps the nearest "friend" of Isherwood and W. H. Auden who criticized publicly and from a position of relative authority their decision to remain in America despite the outbreak of war. He blamed them for abandoning a literary-political movement which he was convinced they had begun and were responsible for. Connolly was married three times: first to Jean Bakewell, who divorced him in 1945, then to Barbara Skelton from 1950 to 1956, and finally, in 1959, to Dierdre Craig with whom he had a son, Matthew, and a daughter, Cressida. From 1940 to 1950 he lived with Lys Lubbock, who worked with him at *Horizon*; they never married, but she changed her name to Connolly by deed poll.

Connolly, Jean (1910–1949). Frances Jean Bakewell, a wealthy American from Pittsburgh and Baltimore; first wife of Cyril Connolly. They met in Paris where she was an art student, and Isherwood was introduced to her there in 1936. Both of the Connollys had other relationships, and they were often apart. She accompanied Denny Fouts to America during the war. In 1943 she fell in love with the surrealist poet and short story writer Lawrence Vail, twenty years her senior, and filed for divorce in 1945 in order to marry Vail the following year. She was a heavy drinker, which perhaps contributed to her early death from a stroke in Paris. Isherwood's character "Ruthie" in *Down There on a Visit* is modelled on her.

Conway, Steve (an assumed name). A messenger boy at Warner Brothers and an aspiring actor. Isherwood met him at the studio in May 1945, and they began an affair that lasted until about August. Conway had previously worked in a casino in Las Vegas, and on a ranch, and he had also been briefly in the navy.

Coombs, Don. American professor of English at UCLA. Isherwood met him at a party at Jay de Laval's in late 1949, and they had a casual sexual relationship.

Corbin, Ella. See Amiya.

Corpus Christi College, Cambridge. Isherwood's undergraduate college.

Costidy, Sam (not his real name). Isherwood met Costidy in New York, evidently on March 9, 1952, with another friend, Gerrit Lansing. The three spent much of the next ten days together and, on March 19, Isherwood took Costidy to Bermuda. Costidy was then about twenty-four. After the Bermuda holiday, Costidy went to California where he had a brief relationship with Tom Wright. He quarrelled with Isherwood and left with Wright to see Wright's parents in Louisiana. Afterwards Costidy visited his own parents, and never returned to California. Later he married and fell out of touch with his homosexual friends.

Costigan, James. American actor and television writer. Isherwood met him in 1956 through Julie Harris, a mutual close friend.

Cotten, Joseph (1905–1994) and Lenore. American actor and his first wife. Cotten was a drama critic and a Broadway stage star before coming to Hollywood to act in Orson Welles's *Citizen Kane* (1941). Afterwards, he was in many other films. Lenore, wealthy in her own right, was a friend to Isherwood and Bachardy until her death in 1960. In the same year, Cotten married Patricia Medina, a British film actress.

CPS camp. Civilian Public Service camp, for instance San Dimas; roughly 12,000 conscientious objectors were drafted to CPS camps during the war. See also Selective Service.

Craft, Robert (Bob). American musician, conductor, critic, and author. Colleague and adopted son to Stravinsky during the last twenty-three years of Stravinsky's life. Isherwood first met Craft with the Stravinskys in August 1949 when Craft was about twenty-five years old and had been associated with the Stravinskys for about eighteen months. Craft was part of the Stravinsky household, and travelled everywhere with them except when his professional commitments forced him to do otherwise. Increasingly he conducted for Stravinsky in rehearsals and supervised his recording sessions, substituting entirely for the elder man as Stravinsky's health declined. In 1972, a year after Stravinsky's death, Craft married Stravinsky's Danish nurse, Alva, who had remained with Stravinsky until the end. The same year, Craft published excerpts from his diaries as *Stravinsky: Chronicle of a Friendship 1948–1971*; he expanded the book and republished it in 1994.

Crippen, Hawley Harvey. Dr. Crippen, a self-effacing American in the patent medicine business, poisoned his second wife, a flamboyant, greedy and domineering would-be singer on whom he had vainly lavished training, clothing, and jewelry. He buried parts of her body under their London house and brought his mistress to live there with him, but soon fled with her and was captured on board ship in the Atlantic. After a sensational trial, Crippen was executed in November 1910. John van Druten based his play *Leave Her to Heaven* on the Crippen story. Crippen's son, Otto Hawley Crippen, who lived near the AJC Ranch, was the child of Crippen's previous wife, Charlotte Bell, who had died in California in about 1890.

Critchfield, Kenneth (Kenny). A disciple of Swami Prabhavananda; he arrived at the Vedanta Center towards the end of the 1940s and lived there as well as at Trabuco. In 1954, upon taking his brahmacharya vows, he became Arup Chaitanya. In 1963 he took sannyas and became Swami Anamananda. He died in the early 1990s.

Cromwell, Richard (Dick). American actor. His real name was Roy Radebaugh. Eventually he gave up his movie career and became a sculptor. He died of cancer in 1960.

Crowley, Aleister (1875–1947). English poet and writer on mysticism. Crowley was a Satanist and insisted he was the Beast from the Book of Revelation. He joined W. B. Yeats's theosophical association, the Order of the Golden Dawn, but caused a controversy that broke up the group. William Somerset Maugham met and intensely disliked Crowley, modelling the main character in *The Magician* (1908) on him.

Cukor, George (1899–1983). American film director. Cukor began his career on Broadway in the 1920s and came to Hollywood as a dialogue director on *All Quiet on the Western Front*. In the thirties he directed at Paramount, RKO, and then MGM, moving with his friend and producer David Selznick. He directed Garbo in *Camille* (1936) among others, and Hepburn in her debut *A Bill of Divorcement* (1932) as well as in *Philadelphia Story* (1940); other well-known work includes *Dinner at Eight* (1933), *David Copperfield* (1934), *A Star is Born* (1954), and *My Fair Lady* (1964). Isherwood met Cukor at a party at the Huxleys' in December 1939. Much later they became friends and worked together.

Curtiss, Mina. American writer and Lincoln Kirstein's sister. As a young woman, Curtiss lived in London on the fringes of the Bloomsbury milieu; later she taught French literature at Smith College and published various books on French writers, including a biography of Georges Bizet and a translation of Proust's letters. In 1924, she married Harry Curtiss, much older than she, and after his death she was for many years the lover of Alexis Saint-Léger (St.-John Perse). Like her brother, she was extremely wealthy, and she inherited her husband's farm, Chapelbrook, in Ashfield, Massachusetts, near Williamsburg and not far from Smith in Northampton. She lived there most of the time and also in Manhattan. In 1958, at Lincoln Kirstein's suggestion, Isherwood applied for a "Chapelbrook" grant, but Curtiss did not think him poor enough, partly because he lived in Hollywood. She was, however, a generous backer of other artists, sometimes including those working on stage and in film. For instance, she once gave her close friend John Houseman a large sum of money on a day's notice for a theater project in crisis.

Darrow, John. American movie actor turned agent. Darrow became powerful in Hollywood. Isherwood and Bachardy were friendly with him from the mid-1950s.

darshan. In Hinduism, a blessing or sense of purification which is achieved by paying a ceremonial visit to a holy person or place; also, the ceremonial visit itself.

Daugherty, Jimmy. Don Bachardy's co-worker in his first job, for Tony and Beegle Duquette. Daugherty later moved to New York where he became a successful designer of women's clothes, married and had a family.

Davies, Marion (c. 1898–1961). The Ziegfeld Follies chorus girl taken up by William Randolph Hearst, who tried to make her into a romantic star and financed her in both successful and unsuccessful films. Her relationship with Hearst provides the basis of the story in Orson Welles's *Citizen Kane* (1941), although Welles's heroine is not a close portrait. Charlie Chaplin, with whom she had an affair, publicly said Davies' real talent was for comedy. She lived with Hearst at San Simeon and at houses in Beverly Hills and Santa Monica until he died in 1951. In October 1951, ten weeks after Hearst's death, Davies married Captain Horace Brown, whom she first met during the war and who was previously a suitor of her sister Rose. Speed Lamkin introduced Isherwood to Davies in 1950.

Davis, George. American writer and editor. Isherwood and W. H. Auden met Davis in London in 1937. He sold an article by them about China to *Harper's Bazaar* where he was literary editor, and he escorted them around Manhattan during their nine day visit in 1938, introducing them to celebrities of New York's literary bohemia and to Vernon Old. During the 1920s, Davis had lived in Paris writing his only novel, *The Opening of a Door* (1931), and he knew Klaus Mann. In New York, he rented the house at 7 Middagh Street, Brooklyn Heights, where Auden lived from October 1940 with Davis, Golo Mann, Carson McCullers, Benjamin Britten, Peter Pears, Paul and Jane Bowles, and Gypsy Rose Lee. Later Davis married the actress Lotte Lenya.

Davis, Vince. A close friend of Ted Bachardy with whom Ted lived for about four years at the end of the 1950s (after Ted had lived with Bart Lord). The arrangement broke down over Ted's mental health problems; later Davis became a born-again Christian and married.

Daya. An Englishwoman who became a nun at the Sarada Convent in Santa Barbara. She was originally called Joan Rayne, and had been involved in theater in Britain. She also lived as a devotee in India for a time. Daya had an alcohol problem; she left the Vedanta Society in the late 1950s and committed suicide.

"de Laval, Jay" (probably an assumed name). Chef; he adopted the role of the Baron de Laval. In the mid 1940s he opened a small French restaurant on the corner of Channel Road and Chautauqua in Santa Monica called Café Jay and frequented by movie stars seeking privacy. In 1949 he opened a second restaurant in the Virgin Islands, and in 1950 he was briefly in charge of the Mocambo in Los Angeles. Eventually he left California, settled in Mexico, and opened a grand restaurant in Mexico City in the early 1950s. Isherwood met de Laval through Denny Fouts. De Laval was a friend of Bill Caskey before Isherwood was, and also a friend of Ben and Jo Masselink.

de Lichtenberg, William (Bill). English painter; a London friend during the late 1920s. Isherwood met de Lichtenberg through Olive and André Mangeot. In *Lions and Shadows,* where de Lichtenberg appears as "Bill Scott," Isherwood recalls being often drunk with him and taking exciting, escapist motor trips at short notice. One such trip, to Scotland, where they spent several days and drove as far north as Cape Wrath, became legendary when W. H. Auden referred to it in his 1929 poem beginning "From scars where kestrels hover" (later titled "Missing"). De Lichtenberg was about ten years older than Isherwood. He married a cellist and later went to live in St. Tropez where he died in an accident in his studio in 1935.

Denison, Henry. A novice monk at the Vedanta Society during the late 1940s; he left Ivar Avenue in the early 1950s to get married.

Denny. See Fouts, Denny.

Derek, also Dek. See Bok, Derek.

Devatmananda, Swami. Hindu monk, from India. Devatmananda ran the Vedanta Center in Portland, Oregon and presided over the founding of a new temple there in 1943.

Dispecker, Franz. Prussian banker. Dispecker was Jewish, wealthy, and a Vedanta devotee. He emigrated to California from Switzerland with his wife, bringing with him an impressive collection of old master paintings. He contributed to the Vedanta Society magazine and translated several Vedanta works into German.

Dobbin. A pet name for Isherwood, known only to himself and Bachardy. Other names included Dubbin, Dub, and Drub.

Dobrin, Arnold. American artist. A friend of Isherwood during the early 1950s. Dobrin married and had two sons before divorcing. In 1965 he published an attractively illustrated children's story about Thailand, *Little Monk and the Tiger.*

Dodie. See Beesley, Alec and Dodie Smith Beesley.

Don. See Bachardy, Don. See also Murray, Don, a different person. The distinction is made clear where necessary in the text by the addition of a surname in square brackets.

Doone, Rupert (1903–1966). English dancer, choreographer and theatrical producer. Founder of The Group Theatre, the cooperative venture for which Isherwood and W. H. Auden wrote plays in the 1930s. Originally called Reginald Woodfield, Doone, the son of a factory worker, ran away to London to become a dancer, then went on to Paris where he was friendly with Cocteau and met Diaghilev, turning down an opportunity to dance in the corps de ballet of the Ballets Russes. He was working in variety and revues in London during 1925 when he met Robert Medley, who became his long-term companion. Doone died of multiple sclerosis after many years of increasing illness.

Dowling, Doris (b. 1921). American actress; sister of Constance Dowling (1923–1969), also an actress. Doris Dowling's most successful films were *The Lost Weekend* (1945), *The Blue Dahlia* (1946), and an Italian movie, *Bitter Rice* (1948); she did not make a great many more. Isherwood met her in the early 1950s through Shelley Winters and Ivan Moffat. Her second marriage, to the musician and bandleader Artie Shaw with whom she had a son (his only child), was then breaking up and she later married Len Kaufman. Bachardy drew Constance Dowling in 1960 and Doris on many occasions; they remained longtime friends.

draft board and draft classifications. See Selective Service.

Durga puja. Annual autumn festival of the Divine Mother, the creative aspect of the godhead and consort of Shiva (Durga's other names include Kali, Shakti, and Parvati).

Easton, Harvey and June. Easton ran what was probably the first gym in the Los Angeles area, on Beverly Boulevard in Hollywood. Easton aspired to be a lyricist and had some talent, but died in his early forties of cancer. His wife, June, ran a dress shop. Diane Easton, their daughter, was at art school with Bachardy briefly during the 1950s, then acted for TV.

Eckhart, "Meister" (c. 1260–1327). German mystic and theologian; Dominican monk; Prior of Erfurt Convent and Vicar of Bohemia. He was criticized in his lifetime for expounding heretical scholastic philosophy in the German vernacular, and after his death many of his teachings, which implied the Church was not indispensable in achieving a spiritual life, were condemned. Their essence survived in German mysticism, and Eckhart was rediscovered by German Romanticism. The Quakers took him up as a precursor of their views.

In his diary entries for April 27, 1950 and for October 16, 1958, Isherwood attributes to Eckhart a quotation that is actually from the fourteenth-century *Theologia Germanica*, "Nothing burns in Hell but self-will." (Indeed he slightly misquotes this as "Nothing burns in Hell but the self.") Isherwood evidently came across the phrase in a footnote to Eckhart's sermon "The Love of God" in Raymond Bernard Blakney's one-volume modern translation of Eckhart. Blakney points out that Eckhart was possibly referring to the *Theologia Germanica* when he said in the sermon, "They ask, what is burned in hell? Authorities usually reply: 'This is what happens to willfulness.'"

Edens, Roger (1905–1970). American film producer. During the 1950s, Edens supervised musicals at MGM, sometimes working with Arthur Freed. He won numerous Academy Awards—including for *Annie Get Your Gun* (1950)—and later produced *Funny Face* (1956), *Hello Dolly* (1969) and others. Through Edens, Isherwood also met another friend Don Van Trees.

Edward. See Upward, Edward.

Elan, Joan. British actress. She settled in Hollywood after making her first film, *The Girls of Pleasure Island* (1953), but her career soon languished. She appeared a few times on live TV, had minor parts in undistinguished films, and played a small role in the Broadway production of Jean Anouilh's *The Lark*, in which Julie Harris starred. She was a friend of Marguerite Lamkin, and in the mid-1950s she had an affair with Ivan Moffat. She frequently sat as a model for Don Bachardy in the 1950s and early 1960s. Later she married an advertising executive, Harry Nye, and lived with him in New York until she died young, of a heart attack, in the early 1970s.

Elsa. See Lanchester, Elsa.

Ephron, Marshall. A member of the bohemian, artistic set that gathered at Sam and Eddie From's "Palazzo" for parties. He was short and fat, but highly intelligent and likeable. Ephron introduced himself to Isherwood in 1958 and they conducted much of their friendship on the telephone.

Evelyn, also Evelyn Caldwell. See Hooker, Evelyn.

Exman, Eugene. Head of religious books at Harper Brothers and Gerald Heard's publisher. He attended the seminar at La Verne in 1941, and, in 1942, arranged for Vernon Old to go to the Holy Cross monastery on the Hudson River in New York State. Exman also published Joel Goldsmith and Alan Watts, among others.

Fairbanks, Harold. American merchant seaman. Fairbanks was Klaus Mann's lover at the end of Mann's life, and Isherwood met him through Mann in July 1948. Later that year, Fairbanks was sent to a prison camp for several months for having sex with a teenager. Afterwards, he became a friend of Bill Caskey, and Caskey joined the merchant marine with him at the end of 1951.

Falk, Eric. English barrister. Falk, who was Jewish, was a schoolfriend from Repton, where he was in the same house as Isherwood, The Hall. He grew up in London, and he and Isherwood saw one another during the school holidays and often went to films together. Falk introduced Isherwood to the Mangeots, whom he had met on holiday in Brittany; he appears in *Lions and Shadows* (with his own name).

Field, Gus. The screenwriter with whom Speed Lamkin tried to adapt *Sally Bowles* for the stage in 1950–1951. After the project fell through, Field gossiped about Isherwood and his friends, including Isherwood's relationship with Bachardy, about which Isherwood felt especially sensitive. Field seemed to be unaware of harming anyone with his talk, and he had occasionally done Isherwood small favors, but Isherwood decided Field was untrustworthy and eventually dropped him as an acquaintance. Isherwood worked with Field on a TV story in 1953.

fifth column. A term coined during the Spanish Civil War and used during World War II for enemy forces hidden and waiting among the civilian population. Nazi propaganda heightened widespread fears that fifth columnists were working to undermine the morale of countries the Nazis intended to conquer and that fifth columnists would rise up and fight for Hitler once he arrived. In fact, fifth columnists existed mostly in rumor.

Fitts, George. A probationer monk at the Vedanta Center in Hollywood when Isherwood went to live there in 1943. Originally from New England, Fitts was then about forty years old, had some private wealth, and spent his time obsessively tape recording and transcribing Swami Prabhavananda's lectures and classes. He took his brahmachari vows in 1947 and was afterwards called "Krishna"; in 1958, he took sannyas and became Swami Krishnananda. He lived in Hollywood, but almost always accompanied Swami on his trips to Santa Barbara and Trabuco and sometimes elsewhere.

Flaherty, Robert J. (1884–1951). American documentary filmmaker. In youth, Bob Flaherty explored the Canadian wilderness with his father and led expeditions into sub-arctic Canada—the background for his first film, *Nanook of the North* (1922). He made a *Nanook* of the south seas—*Moana* (1926)—and in the 1930s *Man of Aran*, about the Aran Islanders, and *Elephant Boy*, shot in India. In 1931 he went to England to instruct John Grierson's Empire Marketing Board Film Unit in natural observation; Grierson's group later became the GPO Film Unit, for which W. H. Auden worked. Isherwood recalls meeting Flaherty in 1934, before Auden began work for the GPO Film Unit in 1935, so the meeting may have come about through Isherwood's work with Berthold Viertel at Gaumont-British. Pare Lorentz, head of the U.S. Film Service, invited Flaherty to make *The Land* (1941), which Isherwood refers to in December 1939. Flaherty also worked with Frank Capra at the War Department Films Division for about a year.

Folling, Sarada. See Sarada.

Foote, Dick. American actor and singer. A longtime lover of Carter Lodge. Isherwood and Bill Caskey first met him in early 1949, and saw him regularly over the years with Lodge and van Druten, sometimes at the AJC Ranch.

Forster, E. M. (Morgan) (1878–1970). English novelist, essayist and biographer; best known for *Howards End* (1910) and *A Passage to India* (1924). His homosexual novel, *Maurice*, was published posthumously in 1971 under Isherwood's supervision. Forster had been an undergraduate at King's College, Cambridge, and one of the Cambridge Apostles; afterwards he became associated with Bloomsbury and later returned to King's as a Fellow until the end of his life. Forster was a literary hero for Isherwood, Edward Upward, and W. H. Auden from the 1920s onward; Isherwood regarded him as his master. In *Lions and Shadows*, he explains that around 1926 "Chalmers" (Edward Upward) coined the phrase "tea-tabling" to describe the new method of understatement which they both admired in Forster's novels: "The whole of Forster's technique is based on the tea-table: instead of trying to screw all his scenes up to the highest possible pitch, he tones them down until they sound like mother's meeting gossip. . . There's actually less emphasis laid on the big scenes than on the unimportant ones. . . It is the completely new kind of accentuation. . . ." (London, 1938, pp. 173–74). When Isherwood met Forster in 1932 through William Plomer, Forster won his devotion by praising *The Memorial*, and although his reviews of Isherwood's later work were always candid, he was a supporter when Isherwood was publicly criticized for remaining in America after the outbreak of war in 1939.

Forthman, Bill (Willie). In 1941, Bill Forthman and his brother Bob were teenage members of Allan Hunter's congregation. Bob Forthman attended one of Gerald Heard's Trabuco seminars in 1942, and Bill Forthman continued for years to turn up at events associated with Gerald Heard and with the Vedanta Center. In the 1950s he lived at Margaret Gage's house, alongside Heard who used her garden house.

Fouts, Denny. Myth surrounds Denham Fouts. According to Truman Capote, he grew up in Florida and worked as a teenager in his father's bakery until he was swept off his feet by a passing cosmetics tycoon. He supposedly left the tycoon in Capri and was companion to various other wealthy people of both sexes. Certainly he travelled extensively with Peter Watson, and helped solicit some of the earliest contributions to *Horizon*. Watson gave him a large Picasso painting, *Girl Reading* (spring 1934), which had been loaned to the Museum of Modern Art under Watson's name for the exhibition *Picasso—Forty Years of His Art*, November 1939–January 7, 1940. Fouts later sold the painting in New York (evidently to the Florence May Schoenborn and Samuel Marx Collection, whence it is promised as a gift to MOMA). During the war, Watson sent Fouts to the USA with Jean Connolly for safety. She and Tony Bower introduced Fouts to Isherwood in mid–August 1940 in Hollywood; by late October Fouts had determined to take up a new way of life as a devotee of Swami Prabhavananda, but Swami turned him away. After a spell in the East, Fouts moved in with Isherwood in the early summer of 1941 and they led a spartan life of meditation and quiet domesticity (described in *Down There on a Visit* where Fouts appears as "Paul"). In August that year, Fouts was drafted into CPS camp as a C.O.; on his release in 1943 he lived with a friend from the camp while studying for his high school diploma; afterwards he studied medicine at UCLA. During this period, many of Fouts's friends were black, and he claimed he had an affair with Lena Horne. From the autumn of 1945 through the spring of 1946, Isherwood and Bill Caskey lived in Fouts's apartment at 147 Entrada Drive while Fouts was mostly away; eventually, when Fouts returned, Caskey quarrelled with him, and Isherwood's friendship with Fouts was badly damaged. Soon afterwards, Fouts left Los Angeles for good, moving East and then to Europe. He became an opium addict in Paris, and Isherwood saw him there for the last time in 1948. Fouts died in Rome, December 16, 1948.

Fowler, Norman. American boyfriend of Peter Watson from 1949 onward, and heir to most of Watson's estate. He had been in the navy and possibly was an epileptic (he was subject to unexplained fits or seizures from which he sometimes had to be roused); he was evidently psychologically disturbed. When Watson drowned in his bath in 1956, Fowler was in the flat; the police dismissed foul play, but the death remained somewhat suspicious. After Watson's death, Fowler bought a hotel, called The Bath Hotel, on Nevis, in the British Virgin Islands, and lived there until he himself drowned in the bath in 1971, within weeks of the fifteenth anniversary of Watson's death.

Fox. See Twentieth Century-Fox.

Frank, Bruno (1887–1945) and Liesl. German poet, playwright, and novelist and his wife. Frank was best known for his historical novel *Trenck* (1926) about a Prussian staff officer guillotined as a spy during the French Revolution. He emigrated in 1933 and eventually arrived in Los Angeles where he became a friend and neighbor of Thomas Mann and worked as screenwriter. His wife, and later widow, Liesl, was the daughter of the German musical comedy star Fritzi Massary. She worked with refugees, and founded the European Film Fund with Charlotte Dieterle, wife of the film director.

Frank. See Merlo, Frank.

French, Hugh. Hollywood agent and former actor. French took over from Jim Geller as Isherwood's film agent for a few years from the early 1960s until his death. He had first approached Isherwood with project ideas in the late 1950s.

French, Robin. Agent and later film producer. Robin French worked with his father, Hugh French, and became Isherwood's Hollywood agent when his father died. He and his wife, Jessie, and their children became long-term friends of Isherwood and Bachardy.

Freud, Caroline (1931–1996). English writer, later known under her own name, Lady Caroline Blackwood. Born and brought up in Ulster, she was married for a time to the English painter Lucian Freud—who painted her—and in 1972 she became the poet Robert Lowell's third wife. Isherwood met her after the marriage to Freud broke up, when she was romantically involved with Ivan Moffat during the mid–1950s. Her novels include *The Stepdaughter* (1976), *Great Granny Webster* (1977), *The Fate of Mary Rose* (1981), and *Corrigan* (1984); she also published journalism and other shorter prose work.

Fritz-Szold, Bernadine. Socialite and longtime friend of Glenway Wescott, who dedicated an early volume of poetry to her, *Natives of Rock* (1925). She had lived in Paris and, later, Los Angeles where she attended cultural events and sought out the company of writers and celebrities. She was friendly with Jim Charlton and with Jennifer Jones and took an interest in both Swami Prabhavananda and Gerald Heard. Don Bachardy once drew her portrait.

From, Eddie and Sam. Identical twin brothers living in Santa Monica during the 1940s and 1950s. Eddie's real name was Isadore; Isherwood first met him in 1944, though he became closer friends with Sam. (In fact, the Froms did not look alike because Sam had had his nose bobbed.) Sam became wealthy as a businessman, but was a frequent drunk driver and eventually died in a car crash in the mid–1950s. Eddie became a psychiatrist. The Froms shared various Los Angeles houses with two close friends, Albert Grossman and his lover Charles Aufderheide, and sometimes others. Isherwood referred to them as the Benton Way Group when they lived in a big house of Sam's in Benton Way; the house was called The Palazzo because it looked like an Italian villa, and the name accompanied the household to other settings even after Sam's death. The Palazzo was the scene of many parties and also of serious discussions about homosexual love. Sam From was among the first to answer one of Evelyn Hooker's exhaustive questionnaires.

Fry, Elizabeth (1780–1845). English prison reformer. Fry was a Quaker heroine; she became a preacher in the Society of Friends in 1810 and, after seeing the condition of the women prisoners in Newgate, devoted her life to prison reform. Fry greatly influenced her brother, Joseph John Gurney (1788–1847), a prosperous Oxford-educated Norwich banker. He, too, became a minister in the Society of Friends, and visited prisons with her. He also became a prominent abolitionist, and Isherwood mentions Gurney's visit to the U.S., when Gurney reviewed the condition of the slaves, met the President and preached in the Senate before returning home to write a book about what he had seen.

Gage, Margaret. A rich and elderly patroness of Gerald Heard, she loaned him her garden house on Spoleto Drive, in Pacific Palisades close to Santa Monica, from the late 1940s until the early 1960s. She also provided Will Forthman with a room in her house during the same period.

Ganesha. Hindu god of wisdom; believed to remove obstacles and grant spiritual and material success. He is the son of Shiva and Parvati and is represented as an elephant's head.

Garrett, Eileen (1893–1970). Irish-born medium. During World War I, Eileen Garrett ran a tearoom in Hampstead which was frequented by D. H. Lawrence and other intellectuals; later she ran a labor hostel in Euston Square, and then a children's soup kitchen in the south of France. In 1941, with the fall of France, she went to New York, founded a publishing firm, Creative Age Press, and launched *Tomorrow*, a monthly review of literature, art, and public affairs. Assisted by Bill Kennedy, she was able to commission work from the likes of Robert Graves, Klaus Mann, Aldous Huxley, Lord Dunsany, and Isherwood, among others; she knew many of the emigré intelligentsia, and Isherwood met her in the late 1940s or early 1950s through the Huxleys. Garrett insisted that her psychic abilities were simply a refinement of the psychic abilities that everyone possesses. She was familiar to a number of scientists and participated in scientific studies of her ESP ability. The Faraday Box or Faraday Cage, which she told Isherwood about and which he mentions in his diary, was built by John Hays Hammond Jr., an inventor (and it was evidently named after Michael Faraday who first discovered electro-magnetism in 1831). The cage, made on a wooden frame, was hung with copper screening; once Garrett was inside, the door was sealed with galvanized iron, and electrical pulses transmitted at random. Several scientists tested Garrett's ESP inside the electrical field, and her scores were higher inside the cage than outside. She could divine abstruse technical detail as well as personal secrets. Some of her insights were spectacular, and she had a healing power.

Gary, Lesley. First wife of Romain Gary; see Blanch, Lesley.

Gary, Romain (Romain Kacew) (1914–1980). French novelist; a Russian Jew raised partly in Poland, Gary became a French citizen in 1935. He won the Prix Goncourt for his 1945 novel *Les Racines du ciel* (*The Roots of Heaven*), and later, under a second pseudonym, Émile Ajar (which he used for four novels), won it again for *La Vie devant soi* (*The Life Before Him*, 1970). *The Roots of Heaven* became a Hollywood film, as did Gary's 1960 autobiographical novel *La Promesse de l'aube* (*Promise at Dawn*). Gary also directed some films, notably the widely derided *Les Oiseaux vont mourir au Pérou* (*Birds in Peru*, 1968) starring his second wife, Jean Seberg. In 1957, when Isherwood and Bachardy met him, Gary was still married to the journalist and author Lesley Blanch. In addition to his writing and film career he was also the French consul in Los Angeles.

Gavin. See Lambert, Gavin.

Geller, Jim. Isherwood's Hollywood film agent. Geller was a story editor at Warner Brothers during the 1940s and expressed interest then in Isherwood's work, especially the script written with Aldous Huxley, *Jacob's Hands*. Isherwood worked for Geller briefly on *The Woman in White* in 1945. Later Geller abandoned his studio career, and he had become Isherwood's agent by the early 1950s. Isherwood moved on to Hugh French about a decade later.

George, also Krishna. See Fitts, George.

Gerald. See Heard, Henry FitzGerald. (Occasionally "Gerald" is Gerald Hamilton, but these instances are made clear in the text.)

Ghosh, Asit. Bengali nephew of Swami Prabhavananda. Ghosh was a student at the University of Southern California and hoped to become a film director. He was in his early twenties when Isherwood met him at the Vedanta Center in about 1940, and later the two lived in next door rooms when Isherwood moved into the center. Ghosh was a devout Hindu, but he was not preparing to become a monk. He found himself inducted into the army in September 1944 even though he was not a U.S. citizen; he was released the following January as a conscientious objector. Soon afterwards he returned to India.

Gielgud, John (b. 1904). British actor and director. Isherwood first met Gielgud in New York, September 10, 1947 and didn't like him; they met again in London in 1948 and became friends. Gielgud achieved fame in the 1920s acting Shakespeare's tragedies; he also performed Wilde and Chekhov before Chekhov was well known to English audiences. During the 1950s, he worked with contemporary British playwrights, but throughout his stage and film career he continuously returned to and extended his Shakespearean repertoire. In 1954, Gielgud was convicted of importuning a plainclothes policeman in a public washroom in London. At the time he was friendly with the royal family, especially the Queen Mother, and had just been knighted the year before. He felt he had disgraced the Queen. Nonetheless, he received a standing ovation when he returned to the London stage. In 1958 he toured widely, including to Los Angeles, with an acclaimed series of readings from Shakespeare, *Ages of Man*. He was involved for some years during the 1950s with Paul Anstee, an interior decorator. Eventually Martin Hensler became Gielgud's permanent companion.

Gingold, Hermione (1897–1987). British actress and comedienne. Gingold starred in theatrical revues and had leading roles in a number of films, including *Pickwick Papers* (1952), *Bell, Book and Candle* (1958), *Gigi* (1958), and *The Music Man* (1961). In 1957, Isherwood and Gavin Lambert planned a television series, *Emily Ermingarde*, especially for her, but she dropped the project after several changes of heart.

Goddard, Paulette (1911–1990). American actress. Goddard married four times; she was Charlie Chaplin's third wife, from 1933 to 1942, and became famous in his *Modern Times* (1936) and *The Great Dictator* (1940). She had the reputation of being cleverer than other Hollywood stars and was admired by intellectuals such as Aldous Huxley and H. G. Wells. Goddard virtually retired after her 1958 marriage to the German novelist and screenwriter Erich Maria Remarque (author of *All Quiet on the Western Front*). Isherwood met her soon after coming to Hollywood, and they remained in touch for many years.

Goldsmith, Joel (1892–1964). American spiritual teacher and healer. Goldsmith came from a Jewish background in New York and turned to Christianity as a teenager; he was drawn to Christian Science when his father miraculously recovered from a grave illness. He was a Freemason for most of his life, and during the 1930s he took up meditation and studied Eastern religions. As a marine during World War II, he had a vision that he must pray for the enemy, and he never saw combat. After the war, the family business collapsed and Goldsmith fell ill with tuberculosis, but like his father he made a miraculous recovery—through Christian Science. Then, after failing as a travelling salesman, he committed himself entirely to the Church of Christian Science, in the role of spiritual reader, advisor and healer, sometimes seeing as many as 135 patients a day. He taught Bible classes in California and gathered students and devotees around him, including John van Druten, whom he had met by the mid-1940s, and Walter Starcke. Van Druten wrote the introduction to Goldsmith's first book, *The Infinite Way* (1952). Goldsmith published roughly twenty more books about his spiritual convictions and mystical experiences, and he circulated a monthly newsletter to paying subscribers. In the early 1950s he resigned from the Christian Science Church, asserting that healers become so by their own authority. His movement, known as the Infinite Way, was well-funded, partly by the voluntary donations of wealthy followers. Goldsmith urged believers to do nothing to change their material circumstances, but to live by grace alone, arguing from his own experience that success would naturally flow toward those who were spiritually "centered" or "on the path." He was married three times.

Goldwyn, Samuel (1882–1974). Polish-American film producer; his real name was Samuel Goldfish. Samuel Goldfish was partner in several early film companies before forming Goldwyn Pictures with the Goldwyn brothers in 1916; from this partnership he took his new name. He was bought out of Goldwyn when it merged in 1924 with the Metro and Mayer production companies to form Metro-Goldwyn-Mayer, and by 1925 he was independent, with his own studio and stars. He remained a top Hollywood producer for thirty years, producing many celebrated and award-winning films (*Wuthering Heights*, 1939; *The Best Years of Our Lives*, 1946; *Guys and Dolls*, 1955; *Porgy and Bess*, 1959), and the Samuel Goldwyn Studios continued in business after he retired. Isherwood's first Hollywood job was as a writer at the Goldwyn Studios, beginning November 1939 for a few weeks; he found Goldwyn difficult. Goldwyn's wife was called Frances.

Goodman, Jack. American editor. In the mid-1950s, Isherwood decided to change publishers from Random House to Simon and Schuster. Goodman arranged an advance for Isherwood's next novel (*Down There on a Visit*), but then suddenly died. Simon and Schuster stood by the promise of the advance, but Isherwood decided not to accept the money. After several vacillations, he did, however, stay with Simon and Schuster for many years; they published all his books from *Down There on a Visit* (1962) to *Kathleen and Frank* (1971).

Goodwin, John. American novelist. A wealthy friend of Denny Fouts, Johnny Goodwin is first mentioned by Isherwood in July 1943, although they apparently met earlier. He owned a ranch near Escondido and a house in New York, was talented but undirected. Goodwin published *The Idols and the Prey* (1953) and *A View of Fuji* (1963). Isherwood visted Goodwin's ranch with Bill Caskey several times in 1945 as well as seeing Goodwin in Los Angeles.

gopi. Cowgirl or milkmaid; see Krishna.

Gore. See Vidal, Gore.

Gottfried. See Reinhardt, Gottfried.

Gowland, Peter and Alice. He is a photographer and camera maker; known for his photographs of celebrities and his nudes, many of which have appeared as *Playboy* centerfolds. The Gowlands were among the Masselinks' closest friends, and Isherwood met them through the Masselinks in the early 1950s.

Goyen, William (1915–1983). American novelist, playwright, and editor. He was a protégé of Stephen Spender who brought him to visit Isherwood in 1949 with Goyen's friend, Walter Berns, later an economics professor at the University of Chicago. In 1950, Isherwood wrote a blurb for Goyen's book *The House of Breath*. Goyen had an affair with Katherine Anne Porter beginning in 1951.

Grandville (1803–1847). French artist; a caricaturist and the illustrator of such classic works as *Don Quixote, Gulliver's Travels, Aesop's Fables* and others. Isherwood gave Bachardy his two volume work *Scènes de la vie privée et publique des animaux: Vignettes par Grandville: Études de moeurs contemporaines* (1842, *Scenes from the Private and Public Life of Animals: Vignettes by Grandville: A Study of Contemporary Mores*). The work is a political and social satire, with text contributed by various writers including

Balzac (whose *Scènes de la vie privée* is parodied in the title) and George Sand. The etchings depict animals dressed as people (the method of the satire); darkly witty, fantastic, and almost surrealist.

Green, Henry (1905–73). The pen name of Henry Yorke, the novelist. He came from a privileged background, was educated at Eton and Magdalen College, Oxford, worked for a time in a factory belonging to his family and made his way up through the firm to become a managing director. His novels draw on his experience of both working class and upper class life, and also on his time in the National Fire Service during World War II (best-known among them are *Living*, *Party Going*, and *Loving*). Isherwood first mentions Green during his 1947 trip to England, and they met again in London in 1948. Yorke's wife was called Dig.

Greene, Hal. Greene sold Isherwood and Bachardy their first house, 434 Sycamore Road, in 1956. He then moved to Adelaide Drive, next door to 145 Adelaide Drive where Isherwood and Bachardy lived from 1959. He was a shrewd investor in property, buying houses to live in for a year or two, then selling them at a profit. It was probably Greene who told Isherwood and Bachardy when 145 Adelaide Drive was on the market, although they bought the house through a real estate agent. He was their neighbor for a time, then sold his Adelaide Drive house to Charles Laughton. Greene was a lover of Nicky Nadeau, who introduced him to Isherwood; later he had a young boyfriend called Dick Lee.

Griggs, Philip. See Buddha Chaitanya.

Guerriero, Henry. American artist. Guerriero was a draughtsman and sculptor. He was from Louisiana and was friendly with Tom Wright and Speed Lamkin. Michael Leopold was his lover for many years. Isherwood evidently met him at the start of the 1950s.

guna. Any one of three energies—called *sattva*, *rajas*, *tamas*—which together comprise *pakriti*, or *maya*, the illusionary universe of mind and matter. When the gunas are perfectly balanced, there is no creation or manifestation; when they are disturbed, creation occurs. Sattva is the essence of form to be realized; tamas, the obstacle to its realization; rajas, the power by which the obstacle may be removed. In nature, sattva is purity, beauty; rajas is activity, reaction; and tamas is solidity, resistance, obscurity. Similarly in man, sattva is calmness and purity; rajas, passion, restlessness; tamas, laziness, inertia, stupidity. Mood and character change according to the balance among the gunas; the spiritual aspirant must transcend each guna, even sattva, in order to realize oneness with God.

Gunn, Thom (b. 1929). English poet. Thomson Gunn served in the army for two years and then went to Trinity College, Cambridge. He first met Isherwood in 1955 when, on his way from a fellowship at Stanford to a brief teaching stint in Texas, he contacted Isherwood and was invited to lunch at MGM; they immediately became friends. Gunn later returned to San Francisco and taught at Berkeley off and on from 1958 onward. His collections of poetry include *Fighting Terms* (1954), *My Sad Captains* (1961), *Moly* (1971), *Jack Straw's Castle* (1976), and *The Man with Night Sweats* (1992). Mike Kitay, an American whom Gunn met in England, was a student at Stanford in the 1950s; he was Gunn's companion for many years and afterwards continued to live in the same house in San Francisco with him and with several other friends.

Gurian, Manning. Stage manager and, later, producer. Second husband of Julie Harris, who starred for him in *The Warm Peninsula*.

Guttchen, Otto. A German refugee who did not succeed in Hollywood. Guttchen's kidneys had been ruined while he was in a Nazi concentration camp, and he was also tortured. He had left his wife and child behind in Switzerland. In Hollywood he often had insufficient money to eat. He became suicidal in late 1939–1940 and was apparently permanently embittered; Isherwood found it difficult to help him in any adequate way and felt persistently guilty about this. Many years later they met again and Guttchen appeared to have regained his hold on life.

Hackett, Albert and Frances Goodrich. American screenwriters. They were married for many years and collaborated on plays and filmscripts, including *The Thin Man* (1934), *It's a Wonderful Life* (1946), *Father of the Bride* (1950), *Seven Brides for Seven Brothers* (1955) and, perhaps their best known, *The Diary of Anne Frank* (1960) for which they wrote both the stage and film versions. She was nearly twenty years older than Isherwood, he about ten years older, and Isherwood and Bachardy normally met them only at professionally oriented parties, such as those given by Charlie Brackett.

Hall, Michael. American actor; he appeared as the son of the Fredric March character in *The Best Years of Our Lives* (1946). Later he became a successful antiques dealer and collector in New York. Isherwood met him at a party in the winter of 1945–1946, and they had sex as friends occasionally for about twenty years.

Hamilton, Gerald (1890–1970). Isherwood's Berlin friend who was the original for Mr. Norris in *Mr. Norris Changes Trains*. Hamilton's mother died almost immediately after his birth in Shanghai, and he was raised by relatives in England and educated at Rugby (though he did not finish). His father sent him back to China to work in business, and while there Hamilton took to wearing Chinese dress and converted to Roman Catholicism, for which his father, an Irish Protestant, never forgave him. He was cut off with a small allowance and eventually, because of his unsettled life, with nothing at all. So began the persistent need for money that apparently motivated some of his subsequent dubious behavior. Hamilton was obsessed to the point of high camp with his family's aristocratic connections and with social etiquette, and lovingly recorded in his memoirs all his meetings with royalty, as well as those with crooks and with theatrical and literary celebrities. He was imprisoned from 1915 to 1918 for sympathizing with Germany and associating with the enemy during World War I, and he was imprisoned in France and Italy for a jewelry swindle in the 1920s. Afterwards he took a job selling the London *Times* in Germany and became interested there in penal reform. Throughout his life he travelled on diverse private and public errands in China, Russia, Europe, and North Africa. He returned to London during World War II, where he was again imprisoned, this time for attempting to promote peace on terms favorable to the enemy; he was released after six months. After the war he posed for the body of Churchill's Guildhall Statue and later became a regular contributor to *The Spectator*.

Hamilton, Paul. A monk at Vedanta Place, first mentioned by Isherwood in 1957. He took brahmacharya vows and sannyas, eventually becoming Swami Amohananda, but later he gave up his status as a swami.

Hardt, Etta. A German refugee who had been an executive secretary in a Berlin publishing house and fled with her Jewish employer, Annie von Bucovitch, despite being offered the management of the firm by the Nazis. She became Garbo's assistant and maid as well as Salka Viertel's housekeeper and secretary.

Hardwicke, Cedric (1893–1964). British actor. Hardwicke was successful on the London stage and made films in England before going to Hollywood in the mid-1930s. Thereafter he made films on both sides of the Atlantic, including the movie versions of many British plays and novels. He was cast as Ruggieri, the astrologer, in Isherwood's *Diane*.

Harrington, Curtis (b. 1928). American director who made underground films and then moved on to features. Isherwood met him in 1949, and they were friendly until 1954 when, at a party given by Iris Tree in early July, Isherwood punched Harrington in the face after a friend of Harrington also at the party made advances to Bachardy. Harrington sued Isherwood and they eventually settled out of court for $350. After this Isherwood avoided Harrington, although he was forced to work with him on the *Jean-Christophe* script because Harrington was then Jerry Wald's personal assistant.

Harris, Bill. American younger son of an engineer, brought up partly in the USSR and Australia. Harris painted in the 1940s, and later made art-objects and retouched photographs. Isherwood met him through Denny Fouts on August 21, 1943, while still living as a celibate at the Hollywood Vedanta Center; he began to fall in love with Harris in mid-March 1944, and this greatly weakened his already waning determination to become a monk. Harris had been discharged after only a few weeks in the army and was attending college. He was a beautiful blond with a magnificent physique and Isherwood found him erotically irresistible, though the relationship was not long lasting except as a casual friendship, and Harris later moved to New York. Isherwood refers to Harris as "X." in his 1939–1944 diaries, and he calls him "Alfred" in *My Guru and His Disciple*. Isherwood's outline of events for 1945–1949 includes a reference to a kite accident which occurred on January 19, 1945. He and Harris were on the beach flying a kite that Denny Fouts had made from his Christmas decorations. The kite dove into power lines along the highway causing a small explosion. Traffic was held up, and power to the whole area was cut. They feared arrest, but in fact were in greater danger of electrocution. Isherwood used the incident in *The World in the Evening*, part 2, chapter 6.

Harris, Julie (b. 1925). American stage and film actress. Harris's career began on Broadway when she was twenty; her rise to stardom was confirmed when she originated the role of Sally Bowles on stage in *I Am a Camera* (1951). She filmed this and another early stage role, *The Member of the Wedding*, and made a number of further Hollywood movies, including *East of Eden* (1955), *The Haunting* (1963), and *Reflections in a Golden Eye* (1967). She also worked in television and continued her stage career, receiving a Tony Award for *Forty Carats* (1969) and for *The Last of Mrs. Lincoln* (1972), and touring with a one-woman show on Emily Dickinson, *The Belle of Amherst* (1976). Isherwood first met Harris in 1951 after she was cast as Sally Bowles, and they became intimate longterm friends. Harris was married to Jay Julien, a theatrical producer, and then to Manning Gurian, a stage manager and, later, producer. She starred in Gurian's unsuccessful production of Joe Masteroff's *The*

Warm Peninsula in 1958, and with him she had one child, Peter Gurian. They were divorced at the start of the 1960s.

Harrity, Rory. American actor. Second husband of Marguerite Lamkin, from March 1959 until 1963. Harrity began on the stage and had a film role in *Where the Boys Are*. He also had writing ambitions, but died young of alcoholism.

Harvey, Laurence (Larry) (1928–1973). Lithuanian-born actor, educated in South Africa. Harvey worked on the London stage and made movies in England before going to Hollywood where his films included *The Alamo* (1960) and *The Manchurian Candidate* (1962). He played the Christopher Isherwood character in the film version of *I Am a Camera*. Isherwood first met him in London in 1956.

Hatcher, Tom. Longtime younger associate of playwright, screenwriter and director Arthur Laurents. Isherwood and Bachardy met the two around the same time and possibly introduced them to each other. Hatcher devoted all of his time to Laurents.

hatha yoga. The widely familiar system of physical exercises whose object is physical health (in contrast to other yogas which aim at spiritual perfection). From his training in 1941, Isherwood mentions several *pranayamas* (bastrika, hollow tank, air swallowing, alternate breathing); these are exercises for the extension and control of breath.

Hawes, Bill. Hatmaker. Hawes was a friend of Jo and Ben Masselink, probably through Jo's work in clothing design. When Ben Masselink eventually left Jo, it was for Hawes's wife, Dee, who acted in small theater productions in Los Angeles.

Hayden. See Lewis, Hayden.

Hayward, John (1905–1965). British editor and scholar. Hayward was crippled by muscular dystrophy and was confined to a wheelchair. He shared a flat in Chelsea with T. S. Eliot from 1946 until 1957, when Eliot remarried.

Heard, Henry FitzGerald (Gerald) (188[5]-1971). Irish writer, broadcaster, philosopher, religious teacher. W. H. Auden took Isherwood to meet Heard in London in 1932 when Heard was already well-known as a science commentator for the BBC and author of several books on the evolution of human consciousness and on religion. A charismatic talker, Heard associated with some of the most celebrated intellectuals of the time. One of his closest friends was Aldous Huxley whom he met in 1929 and with whom he joined the Reverend H. R. L. (Dick) Sheppard's Peace Pledge Union in 1935 and then emigrated to Los Angeles in 1937 accompanied by Heard's friend Chris Wood and Huxley's wife and son. Both Heard and Huxley became disciples of Swami Prabhavananda, drawing on Hindu teachings to ballast their pacifism and to try to achieve contact with spiritual reality. Isherwood followed Heard to Los Angeles and through him met Prabhavananda. Then Heard became an ascetic and broke with the Swami early in 1941, straining his friendship with Isherwood. Heard set up his own monastic community, Trabuco College, the same year. The guru-disciple relationship was to be replaced there by a free collegial association of mystics, each practicing an individual approach to religion. Heard had been secretary to the Irish statesman and agrarian reformer, Horace Plunkett, from 1920 to 1927 and was reportedly the main beneficiary of Plunkett's will; he was also a

Trustee of the Horace Plunkett Foundation until 1948. Possibly this brought him some of the money to fund Trabuco.

By 1949 Trabuco had failed, and Heard gave it to the Vedanta Society of Southern California to use as a monastery. In the early 1950s, his asceticism relaxed and Heard warmed again to his old friendship with Isherwood and eventually to Don Bachardy. During this period, he shared Huxley's experiments with mescaline and LSD. Heard contributed to *Vedanta for the Western World* (1945) edited by Isherwood, and throughout most of his life he turned out prolix and eccentric books at an impressive pace; these included *The Ascent of Humanity* (1929), *The Social Substance of Religion* (1932), *The Third Morality* (1937), *Pain, Sex, and Time* (1939), *Man the Master* (1942), *A Taste for Honey* (1942) adapted as a play by John van Druten, *The Gospel According to Gamaliel* (1944), *Is God Evident?* (1948), and *Is Another World Watching?* (1950, published in England as *The Riddle of the Flying Saucers*). For a number of years Heard was obsessively interested in flying saucers (see also UFOs). There were many more books. Heard is the original of "Augustus Parr" in *Down There on a Visit* and of "Propter" in Huxley's *After Many a Summer* (1939). His crucial role in Isherwood's approach to Vedanta is described in *My Guru and His Disciple*.

Hecht–Lancaster and Hecht–Hill–Lancaster. A Hollywood production company formed by the former literary agent and dance director Harold Hecht in partnership with Burt Lancaster. Later James Hill, the American producer and Rita Hayworth's last husband, joined them.

Heinz. See Neddermeyer, Heinz.

Henderson, Ray. Musician; longtime friend and lover of Elsa Lanchester. He composed the music for some operettas she recorded privately, and accompanied her on piano when she sang at a local theater, The Turnabout, and on her television show. He was much younger than Lanchester and left her to marry another actress, then returned after a few years. Henderson also scored a musical version of *The Dog Beneath the Skin*, but it was never produced. He died young, of a heart attack.

Herbold, Mrs. A member of Allan Hunter's Congregational church. Isherwood met her in the early 1940s. She was a typist and a notary public, whose services Isherwood evidently used over a number of years. On his recommendation she typed *Time Must Have a Stop* for Huxley in 1944, and she may have typed Isherwood's work as well.

Hewit, Jacky (b. 1917). English dancer and, later, civil servant. Isherwood was introduced to Jacky Hewit by Guy Burgess and they conducted a love affair towards the end of 1938. They went to Brussels with W. H. Auden for Christmas, and Hewit is one of the subjects of Auden's mostly unpublished poem "Ode to the New Year (1939)" of which Auden originally gave him one of the typescripts. When Hewit saw off Isherwood on his departure for America in January 1939, he presented Isherwood with a champagne cork from the New Year's Eve party given by Auden in Brussels and at which Auden read the poem aloud. Hewit was lover also to Anthony Blunt, and to the diplomat Guy Burgess with whom he lived at different periods, including the three years leading up to Burgess's defection to the Soviet Union in May 1951. (This connection bedeviled him in later life, though he finally joined the Civil Service as a clerk in 1956 and left as a Higher Executive Officer in 1977.) Before emigrating, Isherwood promised to send for Hewit once he was settled in America, but never did.

Hirschfeld, Magnus. German sex researcher; founder of the Institute for Sexual Science in Berlin, where he studied sexual deviancy. Hirschfeld was the author of books on sexual-psychological themes and he and his staff dispensed both psychological counselling and medical treatment (primarily for sexually transmitted diseases). Hirschfeld was homosexual and campaigned for reform of the German criminal code in order to legalize homosexuality between men. His work was jeopardized by the Nazis and he was beaten up several times; he left Germany soon afterwards, in 1930, and died in France in 1933, around the same time that the Nazis raided his institute and publicly burned a bust of him along with his published works. Isherwood took a room next door to the Institute in 1930 and first met Hirschfeld then, through Francis Turville-Petre.

Holy Mother. See Sarada Devi.

Homolka, Oscar (1901–1978) and Florence. He was a Viennese-born actor who moved from stage to screen in Germany at the end of the 1920s and went on to Hollywood during the 1930s. Isherwood met him in 1941 during the filming of *Rage in Heaven*. Homolka was in countless other movies as well, including *The Seven Year Itch* (1955), *War and Peace* (1956) as General Kutusov, *A Farewell to Arms* (1957), and *Funeral in Berlin* (1966). Isherwood remained friendly with Homolka's wife, Florence, though the marriage eventually ended. Florence Homolka was wealthy in her own right. She was a good photographer, and photographed Isherwood and Bachardy in 1962.

Hooker, Edward. Professor of English at UCLA; a Dryden scholar. In the early 1950s, he married Evelyn Caldwell, who took his surname to become Evelyn Hooker. He died suddenly of a heart attack in January 1957.

Hooker, Evelyn Caldwell (1907–1996). American psychologist and psychotherapist, trained at the University of Colorado and Johns Hopkins; a professor of psychology at UCLA where for a time she shared an office with the Rorschach expert, Bruno Klopfer, who was impressed by her work and assisted and encouraged her. Hooker was among the first to view homosexuality as a normal psychological condition. She worked with and studied homosexuals in the Los Angeles area for many years, venturing into rough bars and orgiastic parties in order to discuss the nature of homosexual love and to examine the social structure of the homosexual subculture. At Klopfer's urging, she first presented her research publicly at a 1956 conference in Chicago, arguing that as high a percentage of homosexuals were psychologically as well-adjusted as heterosexuals; the paper, entitled "The Adjustment of the Male Overt Homosexual," was later published in a Burbank periodical, *Projective Techniques* (this was the journal of the Society for Projective Techniques and the Rorschach Institute; it later changed its title to *Journal of Projective Techniques and Personality Assessment*). Born Evelyn Gentry, she took the name Caldwell from a brief first marriage, then changed to Hooker when she married again at the start of the 1950s. Isherwood met her in about 1949, possibly at the all-night party given by Sam From in August that year. In 1952 Isherwood rented the Hookers' garden house on Saltair Avenue, refurbished it, and lived there until a misunderstanding arose over the arrival of Don Bachardy. After an uneasy period, they continued as intimate friends.

Hoover, Bob. A lover of Ted Bachardy during the mid-1950s, and afterwards a loyal friend, occasionally helping him financially. Hoover worked as a travel agent. His main interest is movie-going.

Hope, also Hope Murray. See Lange, Hope.

Hopper, Richard (Dick). American dress designer. Hopper was a classmate of Bachardy at the Chouinard Art Institute in the 1950s. Afterwards he worked with the celebrated Hollywood dress designer, Edith Head, who won numerous Academy Awards for her costuming.

Howard, also Tinker. See Austen, Howard.

Hoyningen-Huene, George (1900–1968). Russian born photographer. Hoyningen-Huene was the son of an American diplomat's daughter and a Baltic baron who had been chief equerry to Tsar Nicholas II. By the end of World War I he was an exile in Paris, where he studied art and sold drawings to a fashion magazine. Eventually he became a regular photographer for *Vogue* and *Vanity Fair*, and, after 1936, for *Harper's Bazaar*. He also published a number of books containing his photographs of Greece, Egypt, North Africa, and Mexico. After the war, Hoyningen-Huene settled in Hollywood where he taught photography and was color consultant on many films for his longtime friend George Cukor. He also made several amateur documentaries (16mm, about twenty minutes long), which Isherwood describes in his diary. Isherwood met Hoyningen-Huene in the late 1940s or early 1950s, through Gerald Heard and the Huxleys.

homa fire. Prepared according to scriptural instructions, the homa fire is considered to be a visible manifestation of the deity worshipped. Offerings to the deity are placed in the fire. The homa ritual aims at inner purification and, at the end of it, the devotee mentally offers his words, thoughts, actions and their fruits, to the deity.

Howard, Brian (1905–1958). English poet and aesthete of American parentage; an outspoken anti-fascist. Howard was educated at Eton and Christ Church, Oxford, where W. H. Auden became friends with him. He was exceedingly dissolute, a heavy drinker and a drug user, and never lived up to his promise as a writer. Evelyn Waugh's character Ambrose Silk in *Put Out More Flags* is modelled on Howard, and Anthony Blanche in *Brideshead Revisited* is also partly inspired by him. Howard lived a vagrant's life, moving from place to place in Europe, and was often in Paris. Isherwood met him in Amsterdam in 1936, during the period when each of them was trying to find a country where he could live with his German boyfriend—Howard's boyfriend was a Bavarian called Anton Altmann (Toni). Howard was an RAF aircraftman during the war. He committed suicide with a drug overdose.

Hoyt, Karl. A close friend of Chris Wood during the early 1940s. Like Wood, Hoyt was wealthy. He was drafted into the army during World War II and afterwards settled in a Bel Air mansion. He had a relationship with the dancer Nicky Nadeau during the late 1940s.

Huene, George. See Hoynigen-Huene, George.

Hunter, Allan and Elizabeth. He was a Congregational minister and a close associate of Gerald Heard with whom Heard continually met and conversed about spiritual matters. Hunter's church was the main Christian focal point of Heard's California milieu. Isherwood met Hunter at a conference organized by Heard in

1940, and the Hunters participated in the La Verne seminar in 1941, when Isherwood came to have great respect for Elizabeth Hunter. The Hunters had a son and a daughter. Allan Hunter was the author of *Secretly Armed*, in which he included the story of the pacifist Pat Lloyd, also at the La Verne seminar. In Hunter's version, the Lloyd character is called "Mike," and he is actually court-martialled and sentenced to be shot before he comes up with the proposal that he act as a soldier in every way apart from firing a loaded weapon (see the chapter "Safety First").

Huntington Hartford Foundation, The. Funded by the A&P grocery stores multi-millionaire, Huntington Hartford, the foundation was on a large plot of land in Rustic Canyon in Pacific Palisades, north of Sunset Boulevard. In addition to the existing ranch house, Hartford built several cottages on the surrounding acreage in order to offer artists, writers, and musicians a place to live and work for up to three months. The foundation began in 1949; by 1951, there were 150 people there. Frank Taylor, a trustee of the foundation, took Isherwood to see Hartford in July 1950, pressing Isherwood to become a trustee as well. Speed Lamkin was also on the board, along with Robert Penn Warren and others; their job was to give away three-month fellowships for young writers. Isherwood never respected Hartford and found the management of the foundation inefficient and too easily swayed by gossip and favoritism; he resigned in 1952 when a resident writer was ousted from his fellowship for having an unauthorized overnight guest.

Huxley, Aldous (1894–1963). English novelist and utopian. Not long after he arrived in Los Angeles, Isherwood was introduced to Huxley by Gerald Heard. Huxley was then writing screenplays for MGM for a large weekly salary, and he and Isherwood later collaborated on several film projects. Like Heard, Huxley was a disciple of Prabhavananda, but subsequently he became close to Krishnamurti, the one-time Messiah of the Theosophical movement. Huxley was educated at Eton and Oxford, a grandson of Thomas Huxley and brother of Julian Huxley, both prominent scientists. In youth he published poetry, short stories, and satirical novels such as *Crome Yellow* (1921) and *Antic Hay* (1923) about London's literary bohemia and Lady Ottoline Morrell's Garsington Manor where Huxley lived and worked during World War I. He lived abroad in Italy and France during the 1920s and 1930s, part of the time with D. H. Lawrence—who appears in his *Point Counter Point* (1928)—and Lawrence's wife, Frieda. In 1932 he published *Brave New World*, for which he is most famous, and *Texts and Pretexts: An Anthology with Commentaries*; his last novel written in England is *Eyeless in Gaza* (1936).

An ardent pacifist, Huxley joined the Peace Pledge Union in 1935, but became disillusioned as Europe moved towards war. His *Ends and Means* (1937) was regarded as a basic book for pacifists. In April 1937 he sailed for America with his first wife, Maria, and their adolescent son, accompanied by his friend Gerald Heard and by Chris Wood. After spending the summer at Frieda Lawrence's ranch in Taos, Huxley's plans to return to Europe fell through when a screenplay was accepted in Hollywood and he became ill there and convalesced for nearly a year. He was denied U.S. citizenship on grounds of his extreme pacifism. California benefitted his health and eyesight—he had been nearly blind since an adolescent illness. *After Many a Summer* (1939) is set in Los Angeles, and Huxley wrote many other books during the period that Isherwood knew him best, including *Grey Eminence* (1941), *Time Must Have a Stop* (1944), *The Devils of Loudun* (1952), and *The Genius and the Goddess* (1956).

Huxley's study of Vedanta was part of a larger interest in mysticism and parapsychology, and beginning in the early 1950s he experimented with mescaline, LSD, and psilocybin, experiences which he wrote about in *The Doors of Perception* (1954) and *Heaven and Hell* (1956). In 1961 the house he shared with his second wife, Laura, was consumed in a brush fire. Apart from the novel he was completing at the time, *Island* (1962), all his books and papers were lost. Huxley and Isherwood planned two screenplays together: *Jacob's Hands*, about an animal healer, and *Below the Equator* (later called *Below the Horizon*), which they worked on in 1949–1950. In 1960 Huxley found a malignant tumor on his tongue but refused surgery in favor of less radical treatment; eventually the cancer killed him.

Huxley, Julian Sorel (1887–1975). English zoologist, philosopher, public servant; brother of Aldous Huxley. Isherwood met him in December 1939 when he was visiting Hollywood. Like his brother, Julian was educated at Eton and Balliol College, Oxford; afterwards he worked primarily as an academic in Oxford, America, and London. Julian pioneered the field study of animal behavior and his contributions to evolution and genetics marked turning points in these fields. Later he became concerned with over-population and conservation; he was the first director-general of UNESCO in 1946 and helped to set up the World Wildlife Fund and similar organizations. He published many books and monographs, and was an influential popularizer of science.

Huxley, Laura Archera. Italian second wife of Aldous Huxley. Isherwood first met her in the spring of 1956 at the Stravinskys' after she and Huxley married secretly in March; she was then about forty years old. Daughter of a Turin stock-broker, Laura Archera had been a concert violinist since adolescence, then worked briefly in film. She became a psychotherapist, sometimes using LSD therapy on her patients, and published two highly popular books on her psychotherapeutic techniques. Her 1963 bestseller, *You Are Not the Target*, was an early self-help book. She also published a children's book and a memoir about Huxley, *This Timeless Moment*. She first befriended Aldous and Maria Huxley in 1948 and used her special method of therapy on Huxley to help him recapture lost parts of his childhood. He incorporated some of her psychotherapy results into his utopia novel, *Island*. After Huxley's death, Laura Huxley continued to live in the Hollywood Hills and eventually became a children's rights campaigner.

Huxley, Maria Nys (1898–1955). Belgian first wife of Aldous Huxley. Isherwood met her in the summer of 1939 soon after he arrived in Los Angeles. Maria Nys was the eldest daughter of a prosperous textile merchant ruined in World War I. Her mother's family included artists and intellectuals, and her childhood was pampered, multi-lingual, and devoutly Catholic. She met Huxley at Garsington Manor where she lived as a refugee during World War I; they married in Belgium in 1919 and their only child, Matthew, was born in 1920. Before her marriage, Maria showed promise as a dancer and trained briefly with Nijinsky, but her health was too frail for a professional career. She had little formal education and devoted herself to Huxley and to his career. Her premature death resulted from cancer. According to Huxley, she was a natural mystic and had "pre-mystical" experiences in the desert in California in the 1940s.

Huxley, Matthew (b. 1920). British-born son of Aldous and Maria Huxley. Matthew Huxley was brought to America in adolescence and Isherwood met him in

Santa Monica in 1939. He attended the University of Colorado with the intention of becoming a doctor, served in the U.S. Army Medical Corps during World War II, and was invalided out of the army in 1943. He worked briefly as a reader at Warner Brothers, and as a militant socialist he was involved in a strike there in 1945. During the same year he became a U.S. citizen. He took a degree from Berkeley in 1947 and later studied public health at Harvard. This became his career, and for many years he worked at the National Institute of Mental Health in Washington, D.C. He also published a book about Peru, *Farewell to Eden* (1965). He married three times, and had two children with his first wife. In *The World in the Evening*, Isherwood used the books in Matthew Huxley's room in his parents' house in Llano—recorded in Isherwood's diary February 17, 1944—together with some fictional volumes by "Elizabeth Rydal" and a few others by real authors, to make up a revealing shelf of books belonging to the doctor, Charles Kennedy (part three, chapter one).

Hyndman, Tony. Stephen Spender's companion in the early 1930s. Hyndman, from Wales, had run away from home at eighteen and joined the army. Spender hired him as secretary, and they shared Spender's Maida Vale flat and travelled together. He appears as "Jimmy Younger" in Spender's *World Within World*. Spender, Hyndman, Isherwood and Heinz Neddermeyer shared a house in Sintra, Portugal in the winter of 1935–1936; in the autumn Spender and Hyndman parted ways. Hyndman became a communist, joined the International Brigade, and went to fight in the Spanish Civil War where he was greatly disillusioned and became a pacifist. He deserted and was imprisoned, but eventually Spender, who had followed him out to Spain, obtained his release.

Igor. See Stravinsky, Igor.

Inge, William (Bill) (1913–1973). American playwright. Inge received critical acclaim for his first play, *Come Back Little Sheba* (1950), and won a Pulitzer Prize and two Drama Critics Awards for *Picnic* (1953). After *Bus Stop* (1955) and *The Dark at the Top of the Stairs* (1957), however, his work was less successful. He was depressive, turned to alcohol and eventually committed suicide. Isherwood and Bachardy first met Inge in New York in 1953 during the original run of *Picnic*; later, in the 1960s Inge moved to Los Angeles and they saw him there.

Iris. See Tree, Iris.

Isherwood, Frank Bradshaw (1869–1915). Isherwood's father. Frank was the second son of John Bradshaw Isherwood, squire of Marple Hall, Cheshire, outside Stockport, near Manchester. He was educated at Sandhurst and commissioned in his father's old regiment, the York and Lancasters, in 1892 when he was twenty-three years old. He left for the Boer War in December 1899, caught typhoid, recovered, and served a second tour. In 1902 he left his regiment and became adjutant to the Fourth Volunteer Battalion of the Cheshire Regiment, based locally, in order to be able to offer his wife a home despite his meager income. He married Kathleen Machell Smith in 1903 and they settled for a time in a fifteenth-century manor house, Wyberslegh Hall, which was part of the Bradshaw Isherwood family estate. In 1908 Frank rejoined his regiment and the family, now including Christopher, moved several times, following the regiment; in 1911 a second son, Richard, was born and they went to Limerick, Ireland, early the following year. Frank was sent from

Limerick via England to the front line almost as soon as war was declared in the summer of 1914, and he was killed probably the night of May 8, 1915 in the second battle of Ypres in Flanders, although the exact circumstances of his death are unknown. He had achieved the rank of colonel when he died. Isherwood felt that Frank had not been temperamentally suited to the life of a professional soldier, though he was dutiful and efficient. He was a gifted water-colorist, an excellent pianist, and he liked to sing and take part in amateur theatricals. He was also a reader and a story-teller. He was shy and sensitive, but good-looking in a mild way and a keen and agile sportsman. He was conservative in taste, in values, and in politics, but, unlike Kathleen, he was agnostic in religion and was attracted to theosophy and Buddhism. Isherwood wrote about his father in *Kathleen and Frank*.

Isherwood, Henry Bradshaw. Isherwood's uncle and his father's elder brother. In 1924, Uncle Henry inherited Marple Hall and the family estates on the death of Isherwood's grandfather, John Bradshaw Isherwood. Though he married late in life (changing his name to Bradshaw-Isherwood-Bagshawe in honor of his wife), Uncle Henry had no children; Isherwood was his heir, and for a time after Isherwood's twenty-first birthday he received a quarterly allowance from his uncle. The two had an honest if self-interested friendship, occasionally dining together and sharing intimate details of their personal lives. When Uncle Henry died in 1940, Isherwood at once passed on the entire inheritance to his own younger brother, Richard Isherwood.

Isherwood, Kathleen Bradshaw (1868–1960). Isherwood's mother. The only child of Frederick Machell Smith, a successful wine merchant, and Emily Greene, Kathleen was born and lived until sixteen in Bury St. Edmunds, then moved with her parents to London. She travelled abroad, mostly with her mother, and helped her mother to write a guidebook for walkers, *Our Rambles in Old London* (1895). She married Frank Isherwood in 1903 when she was thirty-five years old. They had two sons, Isherwood, and his much younger brother, Richard. Kathleen was told her husband was missing after the second battle of Ypres in May 1915, but it was many months before his death was officially confirmed, and even then she could obtain no definite information about how he died. Isherwood's portrait of her in *Kathleen and Frank* is partly based on her own letters and diaries (he regarded the latter as her masterpiece), but heavily shaped by his attitude towards her. She was also the original for the fictional character "Lily" in *The Memorial*. Like many mothers of her class and era, Kathleen consigned her sons to the care of a nanny from infancy and later sent Isherwood to boarding school. Her husband's death affected her profoundly, which Isherwood sensed and resented from an early age. Their relationship was intensely fraught yet formal, intimate by emotional intuition rather than by shared confidence. Like her husband, Kathleen was a talented amateur painter. She was intelligent, forceful, handsome, dignified, and capable of great charm. Isherwood felt she was obsessed by class distinctions and propriety. As the surviving figure of authority in his family, she epitomized everything against which he wished to rebel. Her intellectual aspirations were narrow and traditional, despite her intelligence, and she seemed to him increasingly backward looking. Nonetheless, she was utterly loyal to both of her notably unconventional sons and, as Isherwood himself recognized, she shared many qualities with him.

Isherwood, Richard Graham Bradshaw (1911–1979). Christopher Isherwood's brother and his only sibling. Younger by seven years, Richard Isherwood was also backward in life. He was reluctant to be educated, and never held a job in adulthood, although he did wartime national service as a farmworker at Wyberslegh and at another farm nearby, Dan Bank. In childhood Richard saw little of his elder brother who was sent to boarding school by the time Richard was three. Both boys were close to their nanny, Annie Avis, and spent more time with her than with their mother. Richard later felt that Nanny had made a favorite of Isherwood and made Richard himself nervous and perhaps was even cruel to him. When Richard started school as a day boy at Berkhamsted in 1919, he lodged in the town with Nanny, and his mother visited only at weekends. Isherwood by then was at Repton. The two brothers became closer during Richard's adolescence, when Isherwood was sometimes at home in London, and Isherwood took his brother's side against their mother's efforts to advance Richard's education and settle him in a career—once even calling upon his Berlin friend John Layard to intervene with Kathleen on Richard's behalf. During this period Richard met some of Isherwood's other friends as well and even helped Isherwood with his work by taking dictation. Richard was homosexual, and his brother may have been helpful to him in this respect, but he seems to have had little opportunity to develop any long-term relationships, hampered as he was by his mother's scrutiny and his own shyness. In 1941, Richard returned permanently with his mother and Nanny to Wyberslegh—signed over to him by Isherwood with the Marple Estate—where he lived with them more and more as an eccentric semi-recluse. Nanny died in 1948, and after Kathleen Isherwood's death twelve years later, Richard depended upon a local family, the Bradleys. He had become friends with Alan Bradley after the war when Bradley was working at Wyberslegh Farm, and Bradley and his wife, Edna, cared for Richard when Kathleen died. Later, Bradley's brother, Dan Bradley, took over the role with his wife, Evelyn (Richard referred to them as the Dans). Richard was by then a heavy drinker. Marple Hall fell into ruin and became dangerous, and Richard was forced to hand it over to the local council which demolished it in 1959, building houses and a school on the grounds. He lived in one of several new houses built beside Wyberslegh, with the Dans in a similar new house next door, and when Richard died he left most of the contents of his house to the Dans and the house itself to their daughter and son-in-law. Richard's will also provided for money bequests to the Dans, Alan Bradley, and other local friends. Family property and other money was left to Isherwood and to a cousin, Thomas Isherwood, but Isherwood refused the property and passed his share of money to the Dans.

Ivan. See Moffat, Ivan.

Jacky. See Hewit, Jacky.

James, Edward (Eddie) (1907–1984). Youngest child and only son of Willie James and Evelyn Forbes; heir to an American railroad fortune. His parents frequently entertained Edward VII at their home West Dean Park, both before and after Edward's accession: James was the godson and rumored to be the son of the monarch. He was an early patron of the Surrealists (especially Dali), and was married briefly in the early 1930s to Tilly Losch, the Austrian ballerina, launching his own ballet company to further her career. His poetry appeared in vanity editions, paid for by himself. He had a kind of reverse kleptomania, leaving objects in friends' houses, and then accusing his hosts of stealing them. Sometimes he would arrive unannounced with only pennies in his pockets, even from abroad, having lost articles of clothing or abandoned his car along the way. Among his close friends in Hollywood were Marguerite Lamkin, the Stravinskys, and the Baroness d'Erlanger. James had a coffee finca in Xilitla (pronounced he-*heet*-la), near Tampico, Mexico, where he spent some of his time in company with the mysterious German writer "B. Traven" (Albert Otto Max Feige). In the last decade of his life he built an uninhabited concrete city in the jungle, a surrealist art work.

japam. A method for achieving spiritual focus in Vedanta by repeating one of the names for God, usually the name that is one's own mantra; sometimes the repetitions are counted on a rosary. The rosary of the Ramakrishna Order has 108 beads plus an extra bead, representing the guru, which hangs down with a tassel on it; at the tassel bead, the devotee reverses the rosary and begins counting again. For each rosary, the devotee counts one hundred repetitions towards his own spiritual progress and eight for mankind. Isherwood always used a rosary when making japam.

Jaya Sri Ramakrishna! This Sanskrit chant can be translated as "Hail to the great Ramakrishna!" *Jaya* or *Jai* also means "Victory to" or "Glory to." *Sri* means "revered" or "holy," though it has a secular use as "Mr."

Jay. See de Laval, Jay.

Jenkins, Terry. British model and aspiring actor. Isherwood met him when Charles Laughton brought Jenkins to Hollywood in 1960. Jenkins was then in his twenties. Laughton was in love with Jenkins, coached him and got him a screen test, but Jenkins had no real talent for acting. He was heterosexual, but admired Laughton and entered into a sexual relationship with him in an untroubled manner. When Laughton was dying, Jenkins looked after him with great care and sensitivity. Later Jenkins married.

Jennifer, also Jennifer Selznick. See Jones, Jennifer.

jnana yoga. One of the four main yogas or paths of spiritual development towards transcendence. Jnana yoga is the discipline of discrimination in which the spiritual aspirant analyzes and rejects transitory phenomena, eliminating them one at a time until realizing his union with Brahman.

Jo, also Jo Lathwood. See Masselink, Jo.

John, also Johnny, also Johnnie. See van Druten, John.

John, also Prema. See Prema Chaitanya.

Johnson, Graham. A monk at Trabuco from the mid-1950s. He was black, a dancer, and later left the monastery; for a time he lived in Europe.

Jones, Bill. An amateur writer with whom Isherwood was friendly at the end of the 1950s. Isherwood tried to help Jones with his writing, but with no success. Jones lived with an actor, "Kap" Kid, for many years.

Jones, Jennifer (Phyllis Isley) (b. 1919). American actress. She began her Hollywood career in B-movies in 1939, and was discovered in 1941 by David Selznick, who changed her name, trained her, and took control of her career. She won an Academy Award for *The Song of Bernadette* in 1943. Later she was also in *Duel in the Sun* (1946), *Portrait of Jennie* (1948), *Gone to Earth* (1950), *Carrie* (1951), *Love Is a Many-Splendored Thing* (1955), *Tender Is the Night* (1962), and others. Her first marriage, to the actor Robert Walker with whom she had two sons, ended in divorce. In 1945 Selznick left his wife, Irene Mayer, for Jones, and they married in 1949. His obsession with Jones combined with her own emotional instability (including suicide attempts) made a melodrama of their careers and their private lives. In 1965, Selznick died, leaving huge debts. In May, 1971 Jones married a third time, to the wealthy art collector Norton Simon. Later her only child with Selznick, Mary Jennifer, committed suicide. Isherwood first met Jones when he worked with Selznick on *Mary Magdalene* in 1958. He and Bachardy attended many parties at the Selznicks', and Isherwood took Jones to meet Swami Prabhavananda in June 1958. They remained friends after Selznick's death.

Jim, also Jimmy. See Charlton, Jim.

Julie. See Harris, Julie.

Kagawa, Toyohiko (1888–1960). Japanese social reformer, Christian evangelist, and author. One of four illegitimate children of an imperial adviser and a geisha, Kagawa was orphaned at four and raised by his father's wife in the ancestral home. At sixteen he met an American missionary and resolved to become a Christian minister. While he was a student at Kobe Theological Seminary, he lived in the Shinkawa slums, filling his room with outcasts and sharing his student funds with them. He contracted trachoma during this period and became half-blind; he also married. Afterwards he studied theology at Princeton and began publishing works of autobiography and Christian meditation, using his royalties for medical, educational and welfare projects in the slums and reserving only a tiny portion for his wife and three children. He inaugurated Japan's first labor union in 1921, and was continuously involved in other aspects of the labor movement. He also advised the government on slum rehabilitation and social welfare. In 1940 he was briefly imprisoned for pacifist opposition to the war with China.

Kali. Hindu goddess; the Divine Mother and the Destroyer, usually depicted dancing or standing on the breast of a prostrate Shiva, her spouse, and wearing a girdle of severed arms and a necklace of skulls. Kali has four arms: the bleeding head of a demon is in her lower left hand, the upper left holds a sword; the upper right hand gestures "be without fear," the lower right confers blessings and boons on her devotees. Kali symbolizes the dynamic aspect of the godhead: she creates and destroys, gives life and death, well-being and adversity—she does all of this through the presence of Brahman, symbolized by Shiva, the transcendent aspect of the godhead. She has other names: Shakti, Parvati, Durga. Ramakrishna devoted himself especially to the worship of Kali in her temple at Dakshineswar.

Kallman, Chester (1921–1975). American poet and librettist; companion and collaborator of W. H. Auden. Auden met Kallman in New York in May 1939 and they took a honeymoon trip across the country ending in Los Angeles. He and Auden lived together intermittently in New York, Ischia, and Kirchstetten for the rest of Auden's life, though Kallman spent a great deal of his time with other friends, often in Athens as he grew older. Kallman published three volumes of poetry and he and Auden together wrote and translated a number of operas, notably *The Rake's*

Progress (for Stravinsky), *Elegy for Young Lovers* and *The Bassarids* (for Hans Werner Henze).

Kathleen. See Isherwood, Kathleen.

Katz, Rolf. German economist. Isherwood met Katz in the early 1930s in Berlin where Katz, then a dogmatic Marxist, was writing communist propaganda prophesying the coming war. Isherwood translated some articles for him, and admired Katz's intellectual honesty. Katz fled to Paris in 1933 after Hitler's putsch, later to London, and finally to Buenos Aires, Argentina, where he became director of a respected weekly bulletin, *Economic Survey*. When Isherwood visited him there in 1948, Katz's Marxism had softened to watchful criticism of the capitalist system he now accepted. Katz appears in *The Condor and the Cows* and he was the original for Dr. Fisch in *Down There on a Visit*.

Kaufman, Len. A Beverly Hills agent and publicist; second husband of the actress Doris Dowling.

Kelley, Howard. Upstairs neighbor to Denny Fouts at 137 Entrada Drive, where Isherwood and Bill Caskey first met him with his friend, Wallace Bobo, during the late 1940s.

Kelly, Thomas Raymond (1893–1941). Quaker teacher and author of *The Testament of Devotion*, a collection of devotional essays drawing on texts from Meister Eckhart and others. Kelly was briefly a graduate student of the Quaker leader Rufus Jones at Haverford College and later returned there to teach. He trained at Hartford Theological Seminary, taught at various American universities, and worked in Europe several times as a Quaker volunteer. Kelly suffered ill-health through overwork and strain—which perhaps contributed to his sudden early death—but he also experienced mystical illuminations.

Kennedy, Bill. American editor and magazine publisher. Kennedy helped the medium Eileen Garrett to relaunch the psychic magazine *Tomorrow* as a literary publication during the 1940s, and he persuaded Isherwood to write regular reviews for it. He lived in New York.

Kennedy, Helen. See Sudhira.

Kennedy, Paul. A young man with whom Isherwood had an occasional sexual relationship towards the end of the 1950s. Kennedy developed cancer suddenly and died young. Isherwood was deeply affected by visiting Kennedy in the hospital, and drew on the experience for the episode in *A Single Man* in which George visits Doris in similar circumstances.

Kenny, also Ken, also Arup, also Arup Chaitanya. See Critchfield, Kenny.

King, Marcia. American fashion illustrator and artist. She was an instructor at the Chouinard Art Institute during the 1950s, and became friends there with Bachardy. They frequently drew together in the evenings, using hired models, friends, or one another as subjects.

Kirstein, Lincoln (1907–1996). American dance impresario, author, editor, and philanthropist. Isherwood's first meeting with Kirstein in New York in 1939 was suggested by Stephen Spender who had met Kirstein in London. Kirstein was raised in Boston, the son of a wealthy self-made businessman. He was educated at

Berkshire, Exeter, and Harvard where he was founding editor of *Hound and Horn*, the quarterly magazine on dance, art and literature. He also worked toward becoming a painter and was among the founders of the Harvard Society for Contemporary Art. In 1933 Kirstein persuaded the Russian choreographer George Balanchine to come to New York, and together they founded the School of American Ballet and the New York City Ballet. Kirstein was also involved in founding the Museum of Modern Art in New York, and in other similar projects. His taste and critical judgement combined with his entrée into wealthy society enabled him both to recognize and to promote some of the greatest artistic talent of the twentieth century. His poetry was admired by W. H. Auden. In 1941 Kirstein married Fidelma Cadmus (Fido), sister of the painter Paul Cadmus. He served in the army from 1943 to 1946.

Kiskadden, Peggy. American wife of Curtis Bok, Henwar Rodakiewicz, and Bill Kiskadden. Isherwood was introduced to her by Gerald Heard soon after arriving in Los Angeles; they became intimate friends but drew apart at the end of the 1940s and finally split irrevocably in the 1950s over Isherwood's relationship with Don Bachardy. Peggy Kiskadden was born Margaret Adams Plummer and grew up in Ardmore, Pennsylvania; she was exceptionally pretty and had an attractive singing voice. Her father was a manufacturer and her first marriage, which lasted from 1924 until 1933, was to Curtis Bok, the talented eldest son of one of Philadelphia's most prominent families. As Mrs. W. Curtis Bok, she first met Heard and the Huxleys at Dartington, England where she accompanied her Quaker husband in the early 1930s. Her marriage to Henwar Rodakiewicz foundered in 1942, and she married Bill Kiskadden in July 1943. She had four children: Margaret Welmoet Bok (called Tis), Benjamin Plummer Bok, Derek Curtis Bok, and William Elliott Kiskadden, Jr. (nicknamed "Bull").

Kiskadden, William Sherrill (Bill) (1894–1969). American plastic surgeon; third husband of Peggy Kiskadden. Kiskadden was born in Denver, Colorado, the son of a businessman. He studied medicine at the University of California and in London and Vienna in the late 1920s and eventually established his practice in Los Angeles. He preferred the more difficult and unusual reconstructive procedures to cosmetic surgery, and he was outstandingly skilled. He was the first clinical professor of plastic surgery at UCLA and founded the plastic surgical service at UCLA County Medical Center in the early 1930s. He held many distinguished positions at hospitals in Los Angeles, teaching, administering, and practicing, was responsible for setting a high standard of training in the field, and wrote many articles on particular procedures and problems. He became interested in the population problem and with Julian and Aldous Huxley and others founded Population Limited in the early 1950s. He served in both world wars, the second time in the Army Medical Corps. In February 1958, he nearly died after a cardiac operation, but survived to the end of the next decade.

Knopf, Edwin H. (Eddie) (1899–1981). American producer, screenwriter, and director. Knopf worked in the editorial department of his brother Alfred Knopf's publishing house before he became an actor in 1920; he played leads on Broadway and in Europe and produced several hit plays. In 1928 he went to Hollywood as a director and screenwriter; by 1936 he was head of MGM's scenario deparment. Isherwood met Eddie Knopf in Goldwyn's story department in November 1939, but Knopf left Goldwyn immediately after this. He then hired Isherwood to work on

Crossroads back at MGM, in 1941, Isherwood's last job before the war. Later Isherwood worked with Knopf again on *Diane* in 1954 and 1955. Knopf had lost a hand in Germany just after World War I when he took a live hand grenade away from a child. For a time he was married to the actress and singer Mary Ellis; his second wife, Mildred, wrote cookbooks.

Koehler, Wolfgang (1887–1967). German psychologist and philosopher. Koehler emigrated to America in the 1930s and taught for a time at Swarthmore where he met and was friendly with W. H. Auden in the early 1940s. He wrote *Gestalt Psychology* (1930) and *The Place of Value in a World of Fact* (1938), as well as *The Mentality of Apes* (1925) which Isherwood and Edward Upward read in the 1920s and which Gerald Heard took as a seminal text for his personal theory of psychological evolution.

Kolisch, Dr. Isherwood first saw Dr. Kolisch in January 1940 on the advice of Gerald Heard. He thought he had a recurrence of gonorrhea, though Kolisch ruled he had never had it in the first place and attributed Isherwood's symptoms to his psychological makeup. He treated Isherwood effectively, evidently on this basis, although Isherwood later suspected, half-humorously, that Kolisch had privately diagnosed syphilis. Kolisch was from Vienna and was a disciple, or at least a pupil, of Swami Prabhavananda. He was influential in Hollywood in the late 1940s and early 1950s; the nuns and monks at the Vedanta Center were on his diets, and perhaps Garbo as well for a time.

Krishna and the gopis. Krishna is the Hindu god and the divine teacher of the Bhagavad Gita. A *gopi* is a cowgirl or milkmaid; the term is usually reserved for the village girls of Vrindavan, who are the constant companions of Krishna. When they heard his flute playing on moonlit nights the gopis would leave their husbands and their work to go out and dance with Krishna. He multiplied his body and made love to them all with equal passion. The dances sometimes lasted six months, yet when the gopis returned home no one knew they had been gone. Krishna's favorite mistress and consort was Radha, wife of the cowherd Ayanaghosha. She symbolized perfect, unselfish devotion despite her jealousy at Krishna's infidelities. The Radha-Krishna cult celebrates their divine and carnal love, a favorite theme for poets and artists who described their love scenes intimately. Radha lives only for Krishna and longs to be merged with him; sometimes their love is interpreted metaphorically as the soul of man yearning for union with the divine.

Krishna. See Fitts, George.

Krishnamurti (1895–198[7]). Hindu spiritual teacher. Isherwood first met Krishnamurti in 1939 through the Huxleys and later went to hear him speak in Ojai; Huxley was very close to Krishnamurti for a time. As an impoverished boy in India, Krishnamurti was discovered by Charles Leadbeater, a leader of the Theosophical movement, and taken up by Leadbeater and Annie Besant as the "vehicle" in which their Master Maitreya would reincarnate himself. Krishna and his younger brother, Nitya, were given up by their father, also a Theosophist, as foster children, and educated in England in circumstances of remarkable privilege and isolation—messiah and assistant. In 1919 they were sent to an orange ranch in Ojai, California for their health (the ranch was purchased in 1927 as a permanent base for the Theosophical movement and called The Happy Valley). There Nitya died of tuberculosis, and Krishnamurti first underwent "the process," dramatic symptoms expressing both ecstasy and suffering, perhaps analogous to samadhi, but apparently triggered by his repressed yearning for feminine love. Disillusioned by his brother's death, in 1929 Krishnamurti renounced his messianic role and rejected the guru-disciple relationship along with the devotional and ritual aspects of Hinduism; he said he no longer wanted followers and that he could not lead others to truth. In 1933, when Annie Besant died, he broke with the Theosophists, pleading amnesia about his life up until then; nevertheless, he maintained a close relationship with the Theosophical movement, and his former benefactors continued to believe in him. He went on speaking to devotees, sometimes in huge numbers, for the rest of his life all around the world. He had a verbal gift, and was able to convey brilliantly the essence of the wisdom he had been force-fed from childhood. He was also extremely handsome and charismatic, particularly to women, and his supposedly chaste existence revolved around a twenty-five-year-long sexual affair with Rosalind Williams Rajagopal who had nursed and fallen in love with Krishnamurti's younger brother Nitya on his deathbed and then married Desikacharya Rajagopalacharya, Krishnamurti's lifelong colleague and rival. There were other affairs as well. Eventually Krishnamurti grew dissatisfied in his relationship with Rosalind and especially Rajagopal, whom he tried to sue, and he spent more and more time abroad, in Switzerland and in India, where he died.

kundalini. "That which is coiled up"; the serpent power; usually symbolized by a serpent having three and a half coils and sleeping with its tail in its mouth. In Hindu physiology, *kundalini* is a reservoir of power at the base of the spine. When aroused, it moves upward along the spinal canal passing through several centers of consciousness or *chakras*. In the lower chakras, kundalini causes only material desires such as lust. In spiritual persons, kundalini rises to higher chakras causing greater degrees of enlightenment. At the seventh chakra, kundalini causes samadhi. Chastity can preserve the kundalini that is necessary for spiritual progress. The controlled awakening of kundalini is the main object of several branches of Hindu occultism, including yoga and tantrism, but kundalini must not be roused without the instruction of a guru as there are dangers attendant upon its awakening.

Laguna. Swami Prabhavananda often spent summer months in Laguna Beach, south of Los Angeles, to escape the heat and tension of Hollywood. He stayed on Camel Point Drive at the oceanfront house of a devotee named Ruth Conrad, and other Ramakrishna followers visited and stayed with him there.

Lambert, Gavin (b. 1924). British novelist and screenwriter. Lambert edited a British film magazine, *Sight and Sound*, before coming to Hollywood in 1956. He was working for Jerry Wald at Twentieth Century-Fox on *Sons and Lovers* when Ivan Moffat introduced him to Isherwood the same year; they became longterm friends. Lambert's novel *The Slide Area: Scenes of Hollywood Life* (1959), which Isherwood read in manuscript in 1957, was influenced by Isherwood's Berlin stories. The pair worked on a television comedy project for Hermione Gingold, *Emily Ermingarde*, and when Gingold decided not to do it, they rewrote it for Elsa Lanchester, but the series was never produced. Lambert also helped Isherwood to revise the film script of *The Vacant Room*, and during the 1950s he planned a musical version, never produced, of Thackeray's novel *Vanity Fair*. Lambert wrote the screenplay for his own 1963 novel *Inside Daisy Clover* (1965) and scripted *Bitter Victory* (1957), *The*

Roman Spring of Mrs. Stone (1961), *I Never Promised You a Rose Garden* (1977), and others. He took mescaline with Isherwood in 1958. During the 1960s, he settled in Tangier for a time, returning to Los Angeles in the early 1980s.

Lamkin, Marguerite. A southern beauty, born and raised in Monroe, Louisiana like her brother Speed. She followed Speed to Hollywood, and married the screenwriter Harry Brown in 1952, but the marriage broke up melodramatically in 1955. Marguerite Lamkin assisted Tennessee Williams as a dialogue coach during the production of *Cat on a Hot Tin Roof* and afterwards worked on other films and theatrical productions on both the East and West Coasts whenever southern accents were required. She was married to Rory Harrity from 1959 to 1963, then married again, successfully, in 1966 and settled in England. Bachardy had a room in the Browns' apartment during the early months of his involvement with Isherwood, and the close friendship evidently made Isherwood jealous. In later years, Marguerite also became a close friend to Isherwood.

Lamkin, Speed. American novelist; born and raised in Louisiana. Isherwood first met Speed Lamkin April 9, 1950 when Speed was twenty-two and about to publish his first novel, *Tiger in the Garden*. Lamkin had come to Los Angeles to research his second novel, *The Easter Egg Hunt* (1954)—about movie stars, in particular Marion Davies and William Randolph Hearst—and dedicated the novel to Isherwood who appears in it as the character "Sebastian Saunders." With a screenwriter, Gus Field, Lamkin tried to adapt *Sally Bowles* for the stage in 1950–1951, but the project foundered after the first draft when Dodie Beesley criticized it and encouraged John van Druten to try instead. Lamkin was attracted by power, money, and stardom, and was alert to nuances of status (he was for instance a snob about club ties, and shared a joke with Isherwood about a black and gold striped tie with thin stripes of red and white which he gave Isherwood and which Isherwood frequently wore). He was on the board at the Huntington Hartford Foundation. In the mid-1950s Lamkin wrote a play *Out by the Country Club* which was never produced, although Joshua Logan was briefly interested in it, and in 1956, he scripted an hour-long TV film about Perle Mesta, the political hostess who had been Truman's ambassador to Luxembourg. During 1957, he wrote another play, *Comes a Day*, which later had a short run on Broadway, starring Judith Anderson and introducing George C. Scott. Eventually, Lamkin returned home to Louisiana.

Lanchester, Elsa (1902–1986). British actress; wife of Charles Laughton. She settled in Hollywood in 1940 and became an American citizen. Lanchester began making films before Laughton and they acted in several together—for instance *The Private Life of Henry VIII* (1934), *Rembrandt* (1936), and *Witness for the Prosecution* (1957). Her most famous film was *The Bride of Frankenstein* (1935), but she was in many more, and she also worked in television—for many years she had her own show, *Elsa Herself*—and sang at a Los Angeles theater, The Turnabout. She met Isherwood socially in the late 1950s, was greatly attracted to him and introduced him to Laughton, afterwards vying with Laughton and Bachardy for Isherwood's attention.

Lane, Homer (1875–1925). American psychologist, healer, and juvenile reformer. Lane established a rural community in England called The Little Commonwealth where he nurtured young delinquents with love, farm work, and the responsibility of self-government. For Lane, the fundamental instinct of mankind "is the titanic craving for spiritual perfection," and he conceived of individual growth as a process of spiritual evolution in which the full satisfaction of the instinctive desires of one stage bring an end to that stage and lay the ground for the next, higher stage; he believed that instinctive desires must be satisfied rather than repressed if the individual is to achieve psychological health and fulfillment. In practice, Lane identified himself with the patient's neurosis in order to allow it to emerge from the unconscious; by personally loving the sinner *and* the sin, he freed the patient from his sense of guilt. W. H. Auden discovered the teachings of Homer Lane through his Berlin friend, John Layard, a former patient and disciple of Lane's, and in late 1928 and early 1929, Auden became obsessed with Lane, preaching his theories to his friends and in his poems.

Lange, Hope (b. 1931). American actress. She was married to Don Murray during the 1950s and her film career began, with his, in *Bus Stop* (1956). She played leads in numerous other films and later starred in a long-running TV comedy, "The Ghost and Mrs. Muir." After two children, her marriage to Murray ended in 1960. She remained a longtime friend to Isherwood and Bachardy.

Lansbury, George (1859–1940). Leader of the British Labour Party from 1931 to 1935, editor of *Lansbury's Weekly*, *Labour Weekly*, and the *Daily Herald*, and President of the Peace Pledge Union from 1937 onward. Driven from the Labour leadership, Lansbury launched a final peace crusade, urging Roosevelt and other world leaders (including Hitler and Mussolini) to attend a world economic conference where existing treaties could be revised. Lansbury supported appeasement because he blamed German aggression on the punitive Treaty of Versailles; he proposed that Britain disarm unilaterally and renounce her colonial possessions in order that she be in a position to ask similar compromises of other countries.

Lansing, Gerrit (Gerry). American poet. Isherwood met him in New York in March 1952 with Sam Costidy.

Larmore, James and Alexandra (Xan). He was assistant to the film producer Charlie Brackett, her father. They were married during the war, when he was a soldier. Previously he had been a chorus boy, and, according to rumor, Brackett's lover. Xan became an alcoholic, and their relationship was turbulent.

Larson, Jack. American actor, playwright and librettist. Larson is best known for playing Jimmy Olsen in the original Superman TV series during the 1950s; he also wrote the libretto for Virgil Thomson's opera *Lord Byron*. He lived for over thirty-five years with the film director James Bridges, and both were close friends of Isherwood and Bachardy from the 1950s onward.

Lathwood, Jo. See Masselink, Jo.

Laughton, Charles (1899–1962). British actor. Laughton played many roles on the London stage from the 1920s onward, and began making films during the 1930s— *The Private Life of Henry VIII* (1934), for which he won an Academy Award; *Les Misérables* (1935); *Mutiny on the Bounty* (1935), in which he played Captain Bligh; *The Hunchback of Notre Dame* (1939); and many others. He also acted in New York and Paris, and gave dramatic readings throughout the U.S. from Shakespeare, the Bible, and other classic literature. He became an American citizen in 1950. Isherwood met Laughton in Hollywood in 1959 through Laughton's wife, Elsa Lanchester, and later the two worked on various projects including a play about Socrates. They became neighbors on Adelaide Drive and close friends despite Laughton's domineering character.

Laura, also Laura Archera. See Huxley, Laura Archera.

Laurents, Arthur (b. 1918). American playwright and screenwriter. Laurents is probably best known as author of the books for the musicals *West Side Story* (1957) and *Gypsy* (1960); he also wrote a number of plays. He rewrote several of his musicals and plays for the movies, and his other screenplays include *Anastasia* (1956), *The Way We Were* (1973) and *The Turning Point* (1977), which was nominated for an Academy Award. Isherwood and Bachardy first became friends with Laurents and his longterm companion Tom Hatcher in the mid-1950s.

Laval, Jay. See de Laval, Jay.

Lawrence, Jerome (Jerry) (b. 1915). American playwright; Lawrence worked in partnership with Robert Lee from 1942 onward. Together they wrote many plays, of which the best known are *Inherit the Wind* (1955) about the Scopes "monkey" trial, and their adaptation of *Auntie Mame* (1956). For the latter, they also wrote the libretto of the musical version, *Mame* (1966). Isherwood often went to parties at Lawrence's house, in particular to meet goodlooking young men; many were actors whom Lawrence knew through his theater connections. Lawrence often claimed he had introduced Isherwood and Bachardy to each other because Bachardy and his brother, Ted, attended a party at his house around the time that Isherwood and Bachardy first became involved with each other. But, in fact, Isherwood and Bachardy met elsewhere.

Layard, John (1891–1975). English anthropologist and Jungian psychoanalyst. Layard read Medieval and Modern Languages at Cambridge and did field work in the New Hebrides with the anthropologist and psychologist W. H. R. Rivers. In the early 1920s, he had a severe nervous breakdown and was partially cured by the American psychologist Homer Lane, to whom he became a devoted disciple. Lane died during the treatment, leaving Layard depressed and seeking further treatment, first unsuccessfully with Wilhelm Stekel and eventually more productively with Jung. W. H. Auden met Layard in Berlin late in 1928 and introduced him to Isherwood the following spring; for a time all three were obsessed with Lane's theories which Layard told the other two about. During this period, Layard had a brief and tortured triangular affair with Auden and a German sailor, Gerhart Meyer, whereupon he tried to kill himself. Isherwood used the suicide attempt in *The Memorial*, and Layard also appears as "Barnard" in *Lions and Shadows*. In 1930, Isherwood asked Layard to speak to Kathleen Isherwood following a family row when she insisted that Richard Isherwood be tutored for Oxford. Richard lied to his mother, saying that he had found a job and did not need to attend university. Satisfying his personal wish to defy Kathleen, Isherwood sided with his brother against her. He revealed to Kathleen the details of his own homosexual life in Berlin, and Layard was equally frank. But Kathleen was unable to change her attitude toward her sons. Layard eventually recovered his psychological health so that he was able to work and write again, and he married and had a son. Like Auden, he also returned to the Anglican faith of his childhood.

Ledebur, Christian ("Boon") and Henrietta. Iris Tree's second son (by

Friedrich Ledebur) and his wife. They lived in Santa Monica intermittently, in a corner apartment in the merry-go-round building on Santa Monica Pier where, until 1954, Iris also lived. Boon studied psychology for many years, and this became his profession. The Ledeburs had a son, Marius, before divorcing, and Boon later remarried and had another family in Switzerland.

Ledebur, Count Friedrich (b. 1908). Austrian actor; second husband of Iris Tree. The marriage ended in 1955. His films include *Moby Dick* (1956), *The Blue Max* (1966) and *Slaughterhouse Five* (1972).

Lehmann, Beatrix (Peggy). English actress; an elder sister of John Lehmann. She met Isherwood when she was visiting Berlin in 1932 and they remained close friends. She had a triumph in O'Neill's *Mourning Becomes Electra* in 1938 when Isherwood was in China, and he returned in time to see her in the Group Theatre's performance of Cocteau's *La Voix Humaine* in July. During 1938 she had an affair with Berthold Viertel.

Lehmann, John (1907–1988). English author, publisher, editor, autobiographer; educated at Cambridge. Isherwood met Lehmann in 1932 at the Hogarth Press where Lehmann was assistant (later partner) to Leonard and Virginia Woolf. Lehmann persuaded the Woolfs to publish *The Memorial* after it had been rejected by Jonathan Cape, publisher of Isherwood's first novel *All the Conspirators*. Isherwood helped Lehmann with his plans to found *New Writing*, discussing the manifesto and obtaining early contributions from friends such as W. H. Auden. Isherwood later said Lehmann's demand for short, magazine-style pieces for *New Writing* helped shape the disconnected fragments collected in *Goodbye to Berlin*. When he left the Hogarth Press, Lehmann founded his own publishing firm and later edited *The London Magazine*. He wrote three revealing volumes of autobiography, beginning with *The Whispering Gallery* (1955). For many years he shared his house with the dancer Alexis Rassine.

Lehmann, Rosamond (1901–1990). English novelist; another elder sister of Isherwood's longtime friend John Lehmann. She made a reputation with the frankness of her first novel *Dusty Answer* (1927), and her later works—including *Invitation to the Waltz* (1932), *The Weather in the Streets* (1936), *The Echoing Grove* (1953)—also shocked with their candid handling of sexual and emotional themes. She was the first wife of the painter Wogan Philipps; their grown daughter, Sally (married to P. J. Kavanagh, the poet), died suddenly of polio in 1958 and Rosamond eventually described her continuing spiritual relationship with her daughter in *The Swan in the Evening: Fragments of an Inner Life* (1967).

Leonardson, Dan. Husband and business partner of Isherwood's Hollywood agent, Edna Schley; Leonardson took over when his wife suffered a brain hemorrhage.

Leopold, Michael. A Texan, he was about eighteen years old when Isherwood met him at the apartment of a friend, Doug Ebersole, in December 1949. They began a minor affair soon afterwards. Leopold was interested in literature, admired Isherwood's work, and later wrote some stories of his own. During the 1960s, Leopold lived with Henry Guerriero in Venice, California.

Levant, Oscar (1906–1972). American composer, pianist, and actor. Levant wrote the music for several popular musicals (including *The American Way*, mentioned by

Isherwood early in 1939) and had a live talk show in Hollywood, "The Oscar Levant Show," broadcast out of a shed on a minor network. He was a peristent wag, and made comedy out of insults; his show was shut down by the sponsors in the early 1960s, despite its popularity, because Levant insulted their products and encouraged his guests to do the same. Isherwood was often a guest on the show in the mid-1950s, sometimes reading poetry. This led to his occasionally being recognized in the street. In 1958, Isherwood argued with Levant about Churchill and refused to appear on the show for a time because Levant attacked him for remaining in Hollywood during the war.

Lewis, Hayden. Isherwood met Hayden Lewis in 1945 when Lewis arrived in California with Bill Caskey (Lewis and Caskey were friends, not lovers). Lewis had been employed by the navy in a civilian clerical job and had shared an apartment with Caskey during Caskey's time in the navy. He lost his job as a result of the homosexual scandal which also led to Caskey's discharge. In 1946 Hayden Lewis began a long relationship with Rod Owens. Together they started a successful ceramics business, making dinnerware and ashtrays.

Lewis, Jack. Los Angeles doctor. A colleague of the endocrinologist Jessie Marmorston; he began to treat Isherwood in about 1957 and became his main doctor for some years.

Lichtenberg, Bill. See de Lichtenberg, William.

Lincoln. See Kirstein, Lincoln.

List, Herbert. German photographer. Probably known to Isherwood through Stephen Spender who in 1929 became friends with List in Hamburg, where List was working as a coffee merchant in his family's firm. List appears as "Joachim" in Spender's *World Within World* and as "Joachim Lenz" in Spender's *The Temple*. He introduced Isherwood to two friends, Robert Furst (not his real name), and Max Scheler, also a photographer.

Liu, T.Y. Chinese bureaucrat and newspaper correspondent who served as guide and interpreter to W. H. Auden and Isherwood in China for ten days in May 1938. He appears in *Journey to a War*.

Lodge, Carter. American friend of John van Druten. Lodge was van Druten's lover in the late 1930s and early 1940s; afterwards he began a long-term relationship with Dick Foote, but remained an intimate friend of van Druten. Isherwood first met Lodge in November 1939. Lodge lived mostly in the Coachella Valley at the AJC Ranch, which he and van Druten purchased in the early 1940s with Auriol Lee, the British actress and director. Lodge managed the ranch, where they grew corn and tomatoes, and handled his own and van Druten's financial affairs very successfully.

Logan, Joshua (1908–1988). American stage and film director, producer, and playwright. Educated at Princeton, where he headed the theatrical Triangle Club, Logan afterwards organized The University Players, including Henry Fonda, James Stewart and Margaret Sullavan. In the 1930s he went to see Stanislavsky in Moscow before beginning his career as a producer in London. Usually working with others, Logan wrote, directed or produced some of the most successful ever Broadway musicals and plays, including *Annie Get Your Gun* (1946) and *South Pacific* (1949). In Hollywood he made musicals into films, and directed *Bus Stop* (1956), *Picnic* (1956), and *Sayonara* (1957), among others. In 1956 Logan asked Isherwood to write a script for him based on a children's story by T. H. White, *Mistress Masham's Repose*, but Isherwood didn't like the novel and turned Logan down.

loka. Hindu term for sphere or plane of existence.

Loos, Anita (1891–1981). American playwright, screenwriter, and novelist. Isherwood met Loos through Aldous and Maria Huxley soon after arriving in Hollywood and sometimes attended the Sunday lunches at which Loos entertained her circle of emigré friends. She created the art of silent film captions and later wrote over 200 screenplays for sound movies. An example of her profuse talent, her novel *Gentlemen Prefer Blondes* (1925)—written solely to amuse H. L. Mencken—became a play, then a movie, then a musical comedy for stage, and finally a film of the musical comedy. By the time Huxley arrived in Hollywood, Loos was the doyenne of screenwriting. He had previously introduced himself to her in New York and she launched him in studio writing. She also introduced him socially, and it was through Loos that Huxley met Salka Viertel. In addition to her many successful plays and films, she wrote several volumes of autobiography in which Isherwood is occasionally mentioned.

Lord, Bart. Amateur actor. A boyfriend of Ted Bachardy with whom Ted lived for a few years during the 1950s. Lord is an avid movie and show-business fan. He and Ted fell out of touch as a result of Ted's mental breakdowns.

Löwenstein, Prince Hubertus zu (1906–1984). German liberal-Catholic historian. Löwenstein was an early proponent (like Harold Nicolson) of a European Economic Community which would incorporate Germany into a new European order and stop Hitler's rise. Expatriated by Hitler in 1934 for writing an "anti-German" book, he worked as a journalist and academic in England and then the U.S. He was a founder of the Hollywood Anti-Nazi League and the German Academy of Arts and Sciences in Exile which included Thomas Mann, Sigmund Freud, and other prominent artists and intellectuals. By late 1939, when Isherwood refers to him, Löwenstein was trying to enlist support for a Provisional Government of the German Republic, and to raise a German legion to fight under a red, gold and black flag against the Nazis. He lectured widely on his plans for postwar reconstruction and argued against the total destruction of Germany, on the view that annihilation would prepare the ground for a third world war. This view ultimately caused some refugee Germans to break with him, for instance, Thomas and Klaus Mann.

Luhan, Mabel Dodge (1879–1962). American writer, patron, salon hostess; married four times. Her four volumes of memoirs, begun in 1924, were published during the 1930s and were greatly admired by D. H. Lawrence, who was both attracted and repelled by her. Born in Buffalo, New York, to great wealth, she was sent to Europe in 1901 to recover from a nervous breakdown. She lived in a Medici Villa in Florence, wore Renaissance dress, had lovers, befriended Gertrude Stein, and entertained lavishly. In 1912 she returned to New York where she set up her famous salon at 23 Fifth Avenue, and had an affair with the radical journalist John Reed (*Ten Days That Shook the World*). Next she moved to Taos, New Mexico where she met Tony Luhan, a Pueblo Indian whom she married in 1923. The Indian way of life became her religion, and she believed that she and her husband were Messiahs by whose leadership white civilization would be culturally and spiritually redeemed. She brought others to Taos to celebrate her new way of life, including Georgia O'Keeffe, Leopold Stokowski, the sociologist John Collier, and Lawrence. During the 1920s and 1930s she worked for land reform, self-determination, and medical benefits for the Indians.

Lynes, George Platt (1907–1955). American photographer. Lynes first photographed W. H. Auden and Isherwood during their brief visit to New York in 1938. In the spring of 1946 he photographed Isherwood again and encouraged Bill Caskey in his efforts to become a professional photographer. Later, in 1953, Lynes photographed Bachardy. Lynes made his living from advertising and fashion photography as well as portraits (his work appeared in *Town and Country*, *Harper's Bazaar*, and *Vogue*), but he is also known for his photographs of the ballet, male nudes, and surrealistic still lifes; he did many portraits of film stars and writers.

M. Isherwood's mother. He called her "Mummy" and began letters to her with "My Darling Mummy," and later, "Dearest Mummy," but he invariably wrote "M." in his diaries. See also Isherwood, Kathleen. A few times in his diaries Isherwood uses "M." for Mahendranath Gupta, the schoolmaster who became Ramakrishna's disciple and recorded Ramakrishna's conversations and sayings in his diaries, later compiling them in Sri Ramakrishna Kathamrita or The Gospel of Ramakrishna; all such uses of "M." for Mahendranath Gupta are pointed out in footnotes.

MacDonald, Madge. British nurse. MacDonald worked at UCLA Hospital during the 1950s and attended Isherwood and Bachardy at home when they had hepatitis in 1956.

MacKenna, Kenneth (Ken) (1899–1962). American actor; he occasionally directed films and became a longtime producer at MGM. He was married to the actress Mary Philips who appeared in films in the 1940s. Isherwood met him in 1941 when MacKenna was head of the story department at MGM.

Macklem, Francesca (Jill). Secretary to Fred Shroyer at Los Angeles State College. Isherwood became friendly with her in 1959 when he began teaching there. Macklem had a life-threatening heart condition. She was married three times, the third time to her first husband, Les Macklem, again; they had two children.

MacNeice, Louis (1907–1963). English poet, born in Belfast. MacNeice was an undergraduate at Oxford with W. H. Auden and Stephen Spender and collaborated with Auden on *Letters from Iceland* (1937). He worked as a university lecturer in classics and later for the BBC as a writer and producer while publishing numerous volumes of verse, verse translation, autobiography, and plays for radio and stage.

Maharaj. See Brahmananda, Swami.

Mahamaya. In Hindu belief, the Mother of the Universe. She has two oppposed impulses: she conceals Brahman from man because she makes its single reality appear as the manifold universe, and yet through her grace man can overcome his ignorance, discover Brahman, and realize his oneness with it.

Mangeot, Olive. English wife of the Belgian violinist André Mangeot; mother of Sylvain and Fowke Mangeot. Isherwood met the Mangeots in 1925 and worked for a year as part-time secretary to André Mangeot's string quartet which was organized from the family home in Chelsea. The Mangeots' warm and chaotic household offered an irresistible contrast to the cool formality of Isherwood's own, and Olive, energetic but easy-going, was an attractive rival to Kathleen in the role of mother. Isherwood brought all his friends to meet Olive when he was in London. She is the original of "Madame Cheuret" in *Lions and Shadows* and Isherwood drew on different parts of her personality for the characters "Margaret Lanwin" and "Mary Scriven" in *The Memorial*. She had an affair with Edward Upward and through his influence became a communist. Later she separated from her husband and for a time shared a house with Jean Ross and her daughter in Cheltenham.

Mangeot, Sylvain (1913–1978). Younger son of Olive and André Mangeot. Isherwood's friend, Eric Falk, initially introduced Isherwood to the Mangeot family because Sylvain, at age eleven, had a bicycle accident which confined him to a wheelchair for a time, and Isherwood had a car in which he could take Sylvain for outings. They grew to know each other well during the time that Isherwood worked for Sylvain's father, and together they made a little book, *People One Ought to Know*, for which Isherwood wrote nonsense verses to accompany Sylvain's animal paintings (the little book was eventually published in 1982, but one pair of verses appeared earlier as "The Common Cormorant" in W. H. Auden's 1938 anthology *The Poet's Tongue*). Sylvain is portrayed as "Edouard" in *Lions and Shadows*. Later he joined the Foreign Office and then became a journalist, working as a diplomatic correspondent, an editor, and an overseas radio commentator for the BBC.

Mann, Erika (1905–1969). German actress and author; eldest daughter of Thomas Mann. Isherwood first met Erika Mann in the spring of 1935 in Amsterdam through her brother Klaus; she had fled Germany in March 1933. Her touring satirical revue, "The Peppermill" (for which she wrote most of the anti-Nazi material), earned her the status of official enemy of the Reich and she asked Isherwood to marry her and provide her with a British passport. He felt he could not, but contacted W. H. Auden who instantly agreed. The two met and married in England on June 15, 1935, the very day Goebbels revoked Mann's German citizenship. In September 1936, Erika emigrated to America with Klaus and unsuccessfully tried to reopen "The Peppermill" in New York. As the war approached, she lectured widely in the USA and wrote anti-Nazi books, two with Klaus, trying to revive sympathy for the non-Nazi Germany silenced by Hitler.

Mann, Gottfried (Golo) (1909–1994). German historian, writer, publicist; Gottfried Mann was the third child of Thomas Mann and Katja Pringsheim. He trained as an academic, emigrated in 1933, and in 1940 escaped to the USA from internment in France. He taught history at several California colleges during the 1940s and 1950s, then returned to Germany as a Professor of Political Science in 1960. He is the author in German of a substantial work on nineteenth- and twentieth-century German history and has written many other historical and political works which demonstrate a continuing preoccupation with literature. He is also editor of and contributor to a German language ten-volume history of the world.

Mann, Klaus (1906–1949). German novelist and editor; Heinrich Klaus Mann was the eldest son of Thomas Mann. Isherwood became friendly with him in Berlin in the summer of 1931. By then Klaus had written and acted with his sister, Erika, in the plays which launched her acting career, and he had published several novels in German (a few appeared in English translations) and worked as a drama critic. Klaus travelled extensively and lived in various European cities even before he left

Germany for good in 1933; he emigrated to America in 1936 when his family settled in Princeton. He lived in New York, continued to travel to Europe as a journalist, and eventually settled for a time in Santa Monica. He became a U.S. citizen and served in the U.S. army during the war. He founded the magazine *Die Sammlung* (*The Collection*) in Amsterdam in 1933, and later he founded another magazine, *Decision*, which first appeared in New York in December 1940 and was forced by the war to close in January 1942. He wrote his second volume of autobiography, *The Turning Point* (1942), in English. When Virginia Woolf committed suicide in 1941, Klaus helped Isherwood to end a long dry period by persuading him to write a memorial about her for *Decision*; Klaus committed suicide eight years later in Cannes and Isherwood then wrote a reminiscence about him for a memorial volume published in Amsterdam in 1950, *Klaus Mann—zum Gedaechtnis*. Both reminiscences—of Woolf and Klaus Mann—were later reprinted in *Exhumations*.

Mann, Thomas (1875–1955). German novelist and essayist; awarded the Nobel Prize in 1929. Mann was patriarch of a large and talented literary family; he and his wife Katja Pringsheim Mann (daughter of a mathematics professor and Wagner expert) had six children. Thomas Mann's own novels and stories are among the greatest German literature of this century. They include *Buddenbrooks* (1901), *Tonio Kröger* (1903), *Death in Venice* (1912), *The Magic Mountain* (1924), *Doktor Faustus* (1947), and *The Confessions of the Confidence Trickster Felix Krull* (1954). Mann lectured in support of the Weimar Republic both in Germany and abroad during the 1920s, and he publicly dissociated himself from the Nazi regime in 1936, taking Czech citizenship (though he had already remained in Switzerland since a 1933 holiday). Isherwood first met Mann in Princeton where Mann was a visiting professor after his flight from the Nazi regime. Then in 1941, Mann moved with his family to Pacific Palisades and became part of the circle of German emigrés and artists in which Isherwood sometimes moved. Later the Manns returned to Switzerland.

mantram or mantra. A Sanskrit word or words which the guru tells his disciple when initiating him into the spiritual life, and which is the essence of the guru's teaching to this particular disciple. The mantram is a name for God and usually includes the word *Om*; the disciple must keep the mantram secret and meditate for the rest of his life on the aspect of God which the formula represents. Repeating the mantram (making japam) purifies the mind and leads to the realization of God. With the mantram, the guru often gives a rosary—as Swami Prabhavananda gave Isherwood—on which the disciple may count the number of times he repeats his mantram.

Marguerite, also Marguerite Brown, later Marguerite Harrity. See Lamkin, Marguerite.

Maria. See Huxley, Maria Nys.

Marmorston, Jessie. American endocrinologist. Her husband was Larry Weingarten, a friend of Eddie Knopf, and Isherwood met her at a dinner party in 1954, through Knopf. She gave Isherwood vitamin and hormone shots and became a permanent medical adviser to him and a close friend. She was especially important during his depressive phase in 1957.

Marple Hall. The Bradshaw Isherwood family seat; see entries for Frank Bradshaw Isherwood, Henry Bradshaw Isherwood, and Richard Bradshaw Isherwood.

Martinez, José (Pete). Mexican ballet dancer; his real name was Pete Stefan. Isherwood first met Martinez through Lincoln Kirstein in 1939. In 1942, Martinez worked with Isherwood at the AFSC refugee hostel in Haverford, Pennsylvania, while waiting to be drafted into the army. His family moved from Texas to Long Beach soon afterwards, and Isherwood saw him in Long Beach in 1943. Afterwards they met occasionally in New York and California. When the war was over, Martinez worked as a dance instructor.

Masocco, Mirandi. Proprietress of the Thunderbird, a jewelry shop in Santa Fe. Masocco was a close friend of the Stravinskys for many years. She later married the film and television director Ralph Levy.

Masselink, Ben. American writer. Probably Isherwood and Bill Caskey met Ben Masselink with his longtime companion, Jo Lathwood, in the Friendship Bar in Santa Monica; Isherwood first mentions Ben and Jo in 1949, and they became his closest heterosexual friends. During the war, Masselink was in the marines; one night on leave, he got drunk in the Friendship and Jo Lathwood took him to her apartment nearby and looked after him. When the war was over he went back to her and stayed for twenty years. Isherwood alludes to this meeting in his description of The Starboard Side in *A Single Man*. Although they never married, Jo took Ben's surname, and Isherwood usually refers to them as the Masselinks. Masselink had studied architecture, and Isherwood helped him with his writing career during the 1950s. Masselink's first book of stories, *Partly Submerged*, was published in 1957. He then published several novels: two about his war experience—*The Crackerjack Marines* (1959) and *The Deadliest Weapon* (1965), the second of which Isherwood greatly admired—and *The Danger Islands* (1964), for teenage boys. Masselink also wrote for television throughout the 1950s and in 1960 worked at Warner Brothers on the script for a film of *The Crackerjack Marines*. In 1967, when Lathwood was in her late sixties, Masselink left her for a younger woman, Dee Hawes, the wife of their friend, Bill Hawes.

Masselink, Eugene. American artist and architect. A longtime associate of Frank Lloyd Wright. He helped Wright to run Taliesin and Taliesin West. Eugene Masselink was the elder brother of Ben Masselink.

Masselink, Jo (c. 1900–1988). Women's sportswear and bathing suit designer, from Northville, South Dakota; among her clientele were movie stars such as Janet Gaynor and Anne Baxter. Previously she had worked as a dancer and was briefly married to a man called Jack Lathwood; she kept his name professionally. She had a son and daughter with a North Dakotan, Ferdinand Hinchberger. From 1938 onwards she lived in an apartment on West Channel Road, a few doors from the Friendship Bar, and by the late 1940s she knew many of Isherwood's friends who frequented the bar—including Bill Caskey, Jay de Laval, and Jim Charlton. She never married Ben Masselink, though she lived with him for twenty years and used his surname. She felt a special sympathy with Isherwood in his involvement with the much younger Bachardy, because Masselink was twenty years her junior.

Matthew. See Huxley, Matthew.

Maugham, William Somerset (Willie) (1874–1965). British playwright and novelist. Maugham married Syrie Wellcome in 1911, and they had one daughter, Liza, but Maugham's usual companion was Gerald Haxton, eighteen years younger, whom he met in 1914 working in an ambulance unit in Flanders. Maugham and Haxton travelled a great deal, and in 1926 Maugham bought the Villa Mauresque at Cap Ferrat where they entertained. Haxton died in 1944 and Maugham's subsequent companion and heir was Alan Searle. Isherwood met Maugham in London in the late 1930s and saw him whenever Maugham visited Hollywood, where many of Maugham's works were filmed. Isherwood also made several visits to Maugham's house in France. In 1945, Isherwood worked for Wolfgang Reinhardt on a screenplay for Maugham's 1941 novel *Up at the Villa* (never made), and he enlisted Swami Prabhavananda to advise Maugham on the screenplay for *The Razor's Edge* (1944). Swami and Maugham met in June 1945 at The Players Restaurant on Sunset Strip and later discussions also included George Cukor, but the film was finally directed by Edmund Goulding, and the script was not by Maugham but by Lamarr Trotti. Despite their advice, Prabhavananda and Isherwood felt that the Indian scenes had mistakes and that the teachings of Shri Ganesha (the fictional holy man in Maugham's novel) were wrongly presented. Later, in 1956, Isherwood and Swami again helped Maugham with his essay "The Saint," about Ramana Maharshi (1879–1950), the Indian holy man Maugham had met in 1936 and on whom he had modelled Shri Ganesha. "The Saint" was published in Maugham's *Points of View* (1958).

Mausi. See Steuermann, Margeret.

maya. In Vedanta, maya is the cosmic illusion, the manifold universe which the individual perceives instead of perceiving the one reality of Brahman; in this sense, maya veils Brahman. But maya is inseparable from Brahman and can also be understood as the manifestation of Brahman's power; together maya and Brahman make Ishvara, the personal God. Maya has a double aspect encompassing opposite tendencies, toward ignorance (*avidya*) and toward knowledge (*vidya*). Avidya-maya involves the individual in worldly passions; vidya-maya leads to spiritual illumination.

Medley, Robert (1905–1995). English painter. Robert Medley attended Gresham's School, Holt with W. H. Auden, and the two remained close friends after Medley left for art school at the Slade. In London, Medley became the longtime companion of the dancer Rupert Doone and was involved with him in 1932 in founding the Group Theatre, which produced *The Dog Beneath the Skin*, *The Ascent of F6*, and *On the Frontier*. Medley also worked as a theater designer and teacher, founding the Theatre Design section at the Slade in the 1950s before becoming Head of Painting and Sculpture at the Camberwell School of Arts and Crafts in 1958.

Messel, Rudolf. A wealthy and socially well-connected left-wing English journalist, pacifist, and aspiring Labour politician whom Isherwood may have met in the 1930s through Gerald Heard, a friend of both.

Mesta, Perle. Hostess and political figure. Mesta was prominently involved in the National Woman's Party, co-chaired Truman's 1949 inaugural ball, and then became his Ambassador to Luxembourg, 1949–1953. Her story inspired Irving Berlin's musical *Call Me Madam*, released as a film in 1953. Isherwood met her in 1956 through Speed Lamkin.

Metro, also Metro-Goldwyn-Mayer. See MGM.

MGM. The preeminent Hollywood studio from the mid-1920s to the mid-1940s;

Isherwood began writing for MGM at the start of 1940, his second Hollywood job. As its name suggests, Metro-Goldwyn-Mayer was formed by a three-way merger: during the 1920s, Loewe's Inc., owner of the Metro Pictures Corp., bought the Goldwyn Studios at Culver City—destined to become the Hollywood headquarters of MGM. The new company, Metro-Goldwyn, then bought the Louis B. Mayer Pictures Corp. Mayer thus became head of the most important Hollywood studio for the next thirty years, administering it with Irving Thalberg and Harry Rapf. Their stars included Garbo, Norma Shearer, Gable, Joan Crawford, the Barrymores, Elizabeth Taylor, Garland, Katharine Hepburn, Spencer Tracy, and Greer Garson. Among the directors and producers associated with MGM were George Cukor, Clarence Brown, Victor Fleming, Mervyn LeRoy, Vincente Minnelli, Busby Berkeley, David O. Selznick and Arthur Freed. MGM was favorably publicized by the Hearst papers because Mayer invited Hearst to base his Cosmopolitan Pictures Corporation at MGM. The studio reached its apogee between 1935 and 1945, despite problems after Thalberg's death in 1936. Then conflicts gradually developed between Mayer, William Schenck (who ran the New York office), and Dore Schary, head of production from the late 1940s. Mayer resigned in 1951. After that, increasingly rigorous enforcement of the Sherman anti-trust laws eventually forced Loewe's Inc. to separate production from distribution, and Schary, who remained head of the studio until 1956, lacked the power to equal past successes. Financial losses and management upheavals plagued the studio in the 1960s, and MGM stopped making films in 1974.

Mike, also Mikey. See Leopold, Michael.

Michael. See Barrie, Michael.

Milam, Webster. Webster was among the handful of men who moved into "Brahmananda Cottage" at the Vedanta Center with Isherwood in 1943; he was then a seventeen-year-old high-school student. His family lived in Avondale, Arizona, and he had a sister, Jean Milam, who was engaged to a young man in the army. By 1949, Webster had left the Vedanta Center, and he soon married. Isherwood also mentions a cousin of Webster, Franklin (Frank), who joined the monks at Trabuco around 1955; Frank later became Asima Chaitanya.

Millard, Paul. American actor. Millard lived with Speed Lamkin in West Hollywood for a few years during the 1950s. He briefly called himself Paul Marlin, then later changed to Millard; his real name was Fink. He was good looking and his acting career was relatively successful on the New York stage and on TV, but eventually he joined his mother's real estate business and invested in property. He owned an apartment building on Norma Place in West Hollywood, and during 1959 and 1960 he loaned Bachardy a little house just behind it, meant for guests, to use as a studio. Around this time, the two had an affair which Isherwood apparently did not know about.

Miller, Dorothy. Cook and cleaner to Christopher Isherwood and Don Bachardy from 1958 onwards. On their recommendation she later kept house for the Laughtons as well, both in Hollywood and in Charles Laughton's house next door to Isherwood and Bachardy in Adelaide Drive.

Milne, A. A. English playwright and author of *Winnie-the-Pooh* (1926). He created many pacifists with his 1933 book *Peace with Honour*, but Milne came to regard war as a lesser evil than Hitlerism. He argued in support of the war in October 1939 in the *Fortnightly Review*, calling it "a civil war, or war of ideas, a revolt against an intolerable form of government," and in numerous letters to the *Times*. Later, he published two pamphlets, *War Aims Unlimited* and *War with Honour*.

Miltown. A tranquilizer evidently widely used in the 1950s. Generically called meprobamate.

Minton, John (1917–1957). English painter and theater designer. His painting was admired by Wyndham Lewis, and he taught at several London art schools. Isherwood met him in London in 1948 through Minton's friend, Keith Vaughan, and Minton drew Bill Caskey. Minton took his life with a drug overdose.

Moffat, Ivan. British-American screenwriter; son of Iris Tree and her American husband Curtis Moffat. Moffat was educated at Dartington and served in the U. S. military during World War II. He returned to Los Angeles in early 1946 as an assistant to the director George Stevens, before becoming a writer. He assisted Stevens on *A Place in the Sun* (1951), was his associate producer for *Shane* (1953), and co-wrote *Giant* (1956), before going on to work for Selznick on *Tender Is the Night*. Moffat's first wife was Natasha Sorokin, a Russian, who had for a time formed a ménage à trois with Simone de Beauvoir (her former teacher) and Jean-Paul Sartre—described in de Beauvoir's *L'invitée* (1943), where Natasha appears as "Natalie." The marriage broke up at the start of the 1950s, leaving a daughter, Lorna. Moffat then had a long succession of beautiful and talented girlfriends. Eventually he married Kate Smith, an Englishwoman whose family fortune derives from the book and stationery chain, W. H. Smith. Isherwood admired Moffat's considerable wit and charm; moreover, although Moffat has always been heterosexual, Isherwood evidently identified with him, both as an expatriate and as a romantic adventurer. He based the main character in the first draft of *Down There on a Visit* on Moffat (this character later turned into Isherwood himself) and he also based "Patrick" in *A Meeting by the River* partly on Moffat.

Monkhouse, Patrick. English journalist. Patrick Monkhouse was raised in Disley, near Marple, and became an intimate friend of Isherwood by the time they were adolescents. He was at Oxford a year or two ahead of W. H. Auden, and edited *The Oxford Outlook*. Later, he achieved a senior position at the *Manchester Guardian* and married. In the early 1920s, Patrick's father, Allan Monkhouse, wrote a novel, *My Daughter Helen*, in which one of the main characters, Marmaduke, is partly modelled on the adolescent Isherwood. For years, Isherwood was fruitlessly attracted to Patrick's younger brother John, while Patrick's sister Rachel was half in love with Isherwood. At the start of the 1930s Rachel had an affair with André Mangeot; afterwards, she married and lived with her husband at Wyberslegh during the 1930s, eventually feuding over the house with Kathleen Isherwood. Isherwood first became friendly with Patrick's youngest sister Mitty (Elizabeth) when he visited Wyberslegh in 1947.

Morgan. See Forster, E. M.

Mortimer, Raymond (1895–1980). English literary and art critic; he worked for numerous magazines and newspapers as both writer and editor and wrote a number of books on painting and the decorative arts as well as a novel. From 1948 onward Mortimer worked for the *Sunday Times* and spent the last nearly thirty years of his life as their chief reviewer. He was at Balliol with Aldous Huxley and later became a close friend of Gerald Heard, introducing Heard to Huxley in 1929.

Mortmere. An imaginary English village invented by Isherwood and Edward Upward when they were at Cambridge together in the 1920s; the inhabitants were satires of generic English social types, and were all slightly mad. As part of their rebellion against public school and university, Upward and Isherwood shared an elaborate fantasy life which was described by Isherwood in *Lions and Shadows*. The fragmentary stories the two wrote for each other about Mortmere were eventually published as a collection in 1994; Upward's *The Railway Accident* appeared on its own in 1949.

Moss, Stanley (b. 1935). American poet. He was on the staff of *Botteghe Oscura* in Rome, where Isherwood met him in 1955. Later he became poetry editor of the *New American Review* before setting himself up as an art dealer in New York. He published several volumes of poems and founded a small press in the Hudson Valley.

Moulaert, Sophie. Maria Huxley's niece, daughter of Maria's sister, Jeanne, by Jeanne's first husband, René Moulaert, a theatrical designer. Sophie arrived in the U.S. at sixteen in November 1939 and lived with the Huxleys during the war. She finished her education, briefly studied acting, and then worked as a bilingual secretary at Warner Brothers. After the liberation of Paris, she joined the Free French Forces and returned to Europe. Later she worked for UNESCO and married.

mudra. Symbolic hand gesture; in Hindu ritual, the mudras connect external actions with spiritual ideas, helping to focus the mind on God.

Murray, Don (b. 1929). American actor; also occasionally writer, producer, director. Murray played the sailor in the original production of Tennessee Williams's *The Rose Tattoo* and then came to Hollywood with his wife, Hope Lange, to make *Bus Stop* (1956), for which he received an Academy Award nomination opposite Marylin Monroe. Afterwards his career was less impressive, though he acted in many films and on TV. He had two children with Hope Lange before the marriage broke down at the end of the decade. In 1960, Isherwood did a treatment for a film about Sardinia for Murray and Walter Wood, but eventually Isherwood and Bachardy lost touch with Murray. He was a pacifist and did refugee relief work for the Quakers during the 1950s.

Murray, Hope. See Lange, Hope.

Murrow, Edward (1908–1965). American journalist and broadcaster, at CBS from 1935. Murrow made radio broadcasts from England throughout the war. Later, he worked in television in the U.S., both as presenter and producer of widely watched news programs. His interviews with public figures—such as the one with Robert Oppenheimer which Isherwood mentions in 1956—were influential.

Myrdal, Gunnar, Alva, and Jan. Parents and brother of Derek Bok's fiancée and wife, the philosopher Sissela Myrdal Bok. Gunnar Myrdal, the political economist, and his wife, Alva Reimer Myrdal, the sociologist, first became famous in 1934 for their book, *Crisis in the Population Question*, which frankly discussed sexuality and family planning and proposed social reforms that became the basis for the Swedish Welfare State. He also wrote *An American Dilemma: The Negro Problem and Modern Democracy* (1944) and *Development and Underdevelopment* (1956) and was later awarded a Nobel Prize for economics. She won a Nobel for her work in nuclear disarmament. Their son, Jan Myrdal, an outspoken communist, travelled extensively and wrote on subjects as varied as Albania, Kampuchea, China after Mao, French realism in literature and the silk road; one of his books repudiates his parents for their lack of attention to him during his childhood.

Nadeau, Nicky. American dancer. Isherwood had a sexual relationship with him in the late 1940s or early 1950s. Possibly he met Nadeau through Chris Wood's wealthy Bel Air friend Karl Hoyt; Nadeau had an affair with Hoyt and later, towards the end of the 1950s, with Chris Wood.

Naeve, Lowell. American painter. Naeve went to prison as a conscientious objector during World War II, and practiced passive resistance there. He described his experiences in *A Field of Broken Stones* (1950), written with David Wieck and including Naeve's own illustrations. Naeve's book was produced by The Libertarian Press in Glen Gardner, New Jersey, and it was excerpted in another small press book, *Prison Etiquette: The Convict's Compendium of Useful Information* (Retort Press, Bearsville, New York, 1950), for which Isherwood wrote the preface (reprinted in *Exhumations*).

Neddermeyer, Heinz. German boyfriend of Isherwood; Heinz was about seventeen when they met in Berlin, March 13, 1932. Their love affair, the most serious of Isherwood's life until then, lasted about five years. Hitler's rise forced them to leave Berlin in May 1933, and afterwards they lived and travelled in Europe and North Africa. In a traumatic confrontation with immigration officials at Harwich, Heinz was refused entry on his second visit to England in January 1934, so Isherwood went abroad more and more to be with him. In 1936 Heinz was summoned for conscription in Germany and Isherwood scrambled to obtain or extend permits for Heinz to remain in the ever-diminishing number of European countries which would receive him. An expensive but shady lawyer failed to obtain a new nationality for Heinz; he was expelled from Luxembourg on May 12, 1937, and returned to Germany where he was arrested the next day by the Gestapo and later sentenced— for "reciprocal onanism" and draft evasion—to a three and a half year term combining imprisonment, forced labour, and military service. He survived, married in 1938, and with his wife, Gerda, had a son, Christian, in 1940. Isherwood did not see Heinz again until 1952 in Berlin, though he corresponded with him both before and after this visit. Heinz's conscription first turned Isherwood towards pacifism. Their shared wanderings are described in *Christopher and His Kind*, and their friendship also serves as one basis for the "Waldemar" section of *Down There on a Visit.*

Newman, Lennie. Chef; a lapsed Mormon from Utah, Lennie was a close friend of Jay de Laval in 1946 and worked in de Laval's restaurant as assistant chef, though he often did most of the cooking. He was a favorite drinking companion of Bill Caskey. After de Laval went to Mexico, Newman took other jobs. For a time he was the chef at Sinbad's, a restaurant on the Santa Monica Pier.

Nicolson, Harold. British diplomat and author; Labour MP for West Leicester from 1935 to 1945 and Parliamentary Secretary under Alfred Duff Cooper. He aligned with Eden and Churchill against Chamberlain and the Nazis. A prolific journalist with a regular column in *The Spectator*, Nicolson wrote, lectured, and broadcast widely throughout World War II. In his *Why Britain Is at War* (1939), he argued that the war was necessary to save humanity, observing that the Nazis denied the achievements of civilization over savagery—especially the Christian values of tolerance, charity and love. Though he was a close friend of Aldous Huxley and Gerald Heard and admired both W. H. Auden and Isherwood (saying of the latter "with Isherwood rests, to my mind, the future of the English novel") he disapproved of their absence, their apparent detachment, and, especially in the case of Huxley, their pacifism (Auden was not a pacifist). See "People and Things," *The Spectator*, April 19, 1940, p. 555.

Nixon, Alice (Tarini). A well-travelled, wealthy Southerner who was already a regular member of Swami's Hollywood congregation in 1943 when Isherwood first mentions her. Her daughter Phoebe, who helped with secretarial work at the Vedanta Center, eventually became a nun, known as "Prabha." During the 1950s Mrs. Nixon lived at the Santa Barbara center where she died of stomach cancer in 1956.

Norment, Caroline. Director of the Cooperative College Workshop, the refugee hostel in Haverford, Pennsylvania, where Isherwood worked as a volunteer during the war. Isherwood first met Norment in late August or early September 1941 and returned in October to begin work. Norment was a Quaker and the hostel was one of several administered by the Quaker relief organization, the American Friends Service Committee. She had previously done relief work in Russia and Germany, and she had also served as Dean of Women at Antioch College. She was in her fifties when Isherwood met her, and she had a Boston bull terrier called Pete. Norment is the original of Sarah Pennington in *The World in the Evening*; Isherwood took the character's first name from the actress Sara Allgood, whom Norment resembled.

Ohge, Ray. Ohge ran a restaurant called Trancas, on Trancas beach north of Malibu, along the Pacific Coast Highway. In September 1955, he rented Isherwood and Bachardy his beach house, near the restaurant, for about six weeks. They left from there directly to North Africa and Europe, and met Ohge in Paris on New Year's Eve.

Old, Vernon (not his real name). American painter. During Isherwood's first visit to New York in 1938, George Davis took Isherwood to meet Vernon Old at an establishment called Matty's Cell House. Blond, beautiful, and intelligent, Vernon exactly matched the description Isherwood had given Davis of the sort of American boy he'd like to meet, and Vernon featured in Isherwood's decision to return to New York in 1939. The pair lived together in New York and Los Angeles until February 17, 1941, when they split up by mutual agreement. Vernon then lived somewhat unsteadily on his own, working on his painting. He could not return to his family as his parents were divorced and he did not like his mother's second husband. He remained unsettled during the war period, trying to become a monk, first in a Catholic monastery in the Hudson Valley and later at the Hollywood Vedanta Center and at Ananda Bhavan in Montecito. Eventually Vernon married Patty O'Neill (not her real name) in November 1948, and had a son, Christopher, before divorcing. His painting career was increasingly successful, and in the late 1950s he gave private instruction to Don Bachardy. He appears (as "Vernon," without a surname) in *Christopher and His Kind* and in *My Guru and His Disciple*.

O'Neill, Donna. A companion of Ivan Moffat. She was beautiful and married to a wealthy man who objected to her involvement with Moffat. She remained with her husband, and she also spent many years in analysis.

Osborne, John (1929–1994). English playwright. Osborne worked briefly as a journalist and as an actor in provincial repertory before his third play, *Look Back in Anger* (1956), established him at the center of a new trend in British drama toward working-class realism and also popularized the epithet frequently applied to his generation, "the angry young men." During the 1950s Osborne's work was largely produced at The Royal Court by the English Stage Company, where Osborne became friends with Tony Richardson and Laurence Olivier among others. Later plays include *The Entertainer* (1957) starring Olivier, *Luther* (1961), *Inadmissible Evidence* (1964), and *A Patriot for Me* (1965); several were filmed. Osborne also wrote the screenplay for Richardson's *Tom Jones*. Isherwood met Osborne in Hollywood in 1960 when Osborne came to join Mary Ure, then his wife, and his close friend Tony Richardson, both working there. Osborne married four other times.

Osmond, Humphry. English psychiatrist. Osmond pioneered the use of mescaline in treating alcoholics. In May 1953, Aldous Huxley volunteered as a subject in Osmond's research and took four tenths of a gram of mescaline. The next year Huxley published *The Doors of Perception*, describing his experiences with the drug. Osmond also supplied mescaline to Gerald Heard and others. In a 1956 letter to Huxley, Osmond first suggested the term "psychedelic" for mescaline and the other drugs they were experimenting with; he later glossed the word as "mind-manifesting," saying it included the concepts of "enriching the mind and enlarging the vision."

Owens, Rod. Hayden Lewis's companion and business partner from 1946 onward.

Pasternak, Boris (1890–1960). Russian poet, novelist, translator and autobiographer. His work most famous in the West, *Dr. Zhivago*—an account of the Russian intelligentsia's experience of the revolution—was never published in the USSR and Pasternak's position in his own country was precarious. *Dr. Zhivago* appeared in Italy in 1957. In 1958, Pasternak was awarded the Nobel Prize for literature but was virtually forced by the Soviets to refuse it, and his companion, Olga Ivinskaya, was imprisoned. The letter from him which Stephen Spender read aloud at a London cocktail party in 1959 was evidently intended for Pasternak's western supporters. Spender tried to meet Pasternak the following February, 1960, when he visited Moscow, but was told by the British Embassy that it would be unsafe for Pasternak. Afterwards, Pasternak wrote to Spender again, saying that he would have liked to have had the meeting. Pasternak died that May.

Paul. See Millard, Paul.

Pavan, Marisa (b. 1932). Italian actress. Marisa Pavan's career began in the early 1950s. Isherwood first met her in 1954 when she was given the role of Catherine de Medici in *Diane*, and both he and Bachardy were friendly with her during the filming in Key West and Los Angeles of Tennessee Williams's *The Rose Tattoo* (1955), for which Pavan received an Academy Award nomination. She starred in a few other Hollywood films during the fifties and acted in Hollywood again in the seventies and eighties. Her real name is Marisa Pierangeli, and her twin sister was the actress Pier Angeli. Pavan was the second wife of the French actor Jean-Pierre Aumont.

Pavitrananda, Swami. Hindu monk; head of the Vedanta Society in New York and a trustee of the Ramakrishna Math and Mission. In India, Pavitrananda spent many years in the order's editorial center, Advaita Ashrama, at Mayavati in the Himalayas. He often paid a month-long visit to Swami Prabhavananda during the summers. Other than Prabhavananda, he was Isherwood's favorite swami.

Pears, Peter. English tenor; longtime companion and musical partner to Benjamin Britten. The youngest of seven children, Pears went to boarding school at six and rarely saw his family. He was sent down from Keble College, Oxford after failing his first year music exams, became a prep school master, studied briefly at the Royal College of Music and then joined the BBC singers in 1934. Pears and Britten became close friends in 1937, shared a flat from early 1938, and began performing together in 1939. They travelled to America, via Canada, in 1939 and lived outside New York at Elizabeth Mayer's house in Amityville; they also lived for a time in Brooklyn at George Davis's house in Middagh Street and made a trip to California. Pears studied singing further in New York, and his voice developed and gained in strength there. Britten and Pears returned to England in March 1942. They were pacifists during the war. Although at first they both had other relationships, their lives became increasingly fused, with Britten writing a great deal of music for Pears, and Pears singing it expressly for Britten.

Peggy, also Peggy Bok, later Peggy Rodakiewicz. See Kiskadden, Peggy.

Pendleton, James (Jimmy) and Mary Frances (Dodo). He trained as a dancer and had a stage career before starting a highly successful interior design and antiques business, first in New York and later in Los Angeles where he and Dodo moved during World War II. His Los Angeles shop was on Sunset Strip. Dodo was wealthy in her own right. The marriage was a formality as he was homosexual. She died in 1963; Jimmy died in 1995, aged ninety.

Pete. See Martinez, José.

Peter. See Viertel, Peter.

Phil, also Philip, also Philip Griggs. See Buddha Chaitanya.

Phipps, Bill. American actor. Phipps appeared in several Hollywood films in the late 1950s and early 1960s. He was a friend of Charles Laughton, who introduced him to Isherwood and Bachardy.

Plomer, William (1903–1973). British poet and novelist born and raised in South Africa. He met Isherwood in 1932 through Stephen Spender who had already shown Isherwood Plomer's poems and stories about South Africa and Japan. Plomer was a friend of E. M. Forster and soon took Isherwood to meet him. In South Africa, Plomer and Roy Campbell had founded *Voorslag* (Whiplash), a literary magazine for which they wrote most of the satirical material (Laurens van der Post also became an editor). Plomer taught for two years in Japan, then settled in Bloomsbury in 1929 where he was befriended by the Woolfs. They had published his first novel in 1926 at the Hogarth Press. In 1937 Plomer became principal reader for Jonathan Cape. In addition to his poems and novels, Plomer wrote several libretti for Benjamin Britten, notably *Gloriana*. Plomer lived with his friend, Charles Erdmann, who was born in London of a German father and Polish mother, raised in Germany from about age five, and then returned to England in 1939 where he worked as a waiter and pastrycook among other things. Isherwood included Plomer's "The Child of Queen Victoria" (from Plomer's 1953 volume of short stories with the same title) in *Great English Short Stories* (1960).

Poland, Scott. A friend of Tom Wright during the late 1950s. His real name was Jim Hambleton. In 1956 he had an operation on his penis, and when Isherwood and Bachardy visited him in the UCLA hospital he showed them the stitches, which revealed that it had been sliced in half lengthwise and sewn up again. Isherwood and Bachardy lost touch with him after Poland moved away from Los Angeles in 1958.

Prabha. Originally Phoebe Nixon, she was the daughter of Alice Nixon ("Tarini"), and after sannyas Prabha became Pravrajika Prabhaprana. The Nixons were wealthy Southerners. Isherwood first met Prabha in the early 1940s in the Hollywood Center, where she handled much of the administrative and secretarial work, and he grew to love her genuinely. By the mid-1950s, Prabha was head nun at the Sarada Convent in Santa Barbara.

Prabhavananda, Swami (1893–1976). Hindu monk of the Ramakrishna Order, founder of the Vedanta Society of Southern California based in Hollywood. Gerald Heard introduced Isherwood to Swami Prabhavananda in July 1939. On their second meeting, August 4, Prabhavananda began to instruct Isherwood in meditation; on November 8, 1940 he initiated Isherwood, giving him a mantram and a rosary. From February 1943 until August 1945 Isherwood lived monastically at the Vedanta Center, but decided he could not become a monk as Swami wished. (Isherwood invariably pronounced it *Shwami*, as he had been taught phonetically by Prabhavananda.) Isherwood continued to be closely involved with the Vedanta Society, travelled twice to its monastery in India, and remained Prabhavananda's disciple and close friend for life. Their relationship is described in *My Guru and His Disciple*.

Prabhavananda was born in a Bengali village northwest of Calcutta and was originally named Abanindra Nath Ghosh. As a teenager he read about Ramakrishna and his disciples Vivekananda and Brahmananda and felt mysteriously attracted to their names. By chance he experienced an affecting meeting with Ramakrishna's widow, Sarada Devi. At eighteen he visited the Belur Math, the chief monastery of the Ramakrishna order beside the Ganges outside Calcutta. There he had another important encounter, this time with Brahmananda, and abandoned his studies for a month to follow him. When Abanindra returned to Calcutta, he became involved in militant opposition to British rule, and joined a revolutionary organization for which he wrote and distributed propaganda. At one time he took charge of some stolen weapons and some of his friends who engaged in terrorist activities met with violent ends. Because he was studying philosophy, Abanindra attended Belur Math regularly for instruction in the teachings of Shankara, but he regarded the monastic life as escapist and set his political duties first, until he had another compelling experience with Brahmananda and suddenly decided to give up his political activities and become a monk. He took his final vows in 1921, when his name was changed to Prabhavananda.

In 1923 Prabhavananda was sent to the United States to assist the swami at the Vedanta Society in San Francisco; later he opened a new center in Portland, Oregon. He was joined there by Sister Lalita and later, in 1929, founded the Vedanta Society of Southern California in her house in Hollywood, 1946 Ivar Avenue. Several other women joined them. By the mid-1930s the society began to expand and money was donated for a temple which was built in the garden and dedicated in July 1938. Prabhavananda remained the head of the Hollywood Center until he died; he frequently visited Trabuco and the Sarada Convent in Santa Barbara and also stayed in the home of a devotee in Laguna Beach. Isherwood and Prabhavananda worked on a number of books together, notably translations of the Bhagavad Gita (1947) and of the yoga aphorisms of Patanjali (1953). Prabhavananda contributed to two collections on Vedanta edited by Isherwood, and Isherwood also worked on Prabhavananda's translation of Shankara's *Crest Jewel of Discrimination*. Prabhavananda persuaded Isherwood to write a biography of Ramakrishna, *Ramakrishna and His Disciples* (1964); this became an official project of the Ramakrishna Order and was subject to chapter-by-chapter review by a high authority at the Belur Math.

prasad. Food or any other gift that has been consecrated in a Hindu ceremony of worship by being offered to God or to a saintly person; the food is usually eaten as part of the meal following the ritual, or the gift given to the devotees.

Prema Chaitanya (Prema). Originally John Yale, a successful Chicago publisher, Prema joined the Vedanta Center in Hollywood in 1950 after his religious faith was renewed by reading Isherwood and Prabhavananda's translation of the Gita during the 1940s. In August 1955, he took his brahmachari vows at Trabuco and was renamed Prema Chaitanya (he continued to live in Hollywood, and briefly in Santa Barbara, but never at Trabuco). Prema developed the Vedanta Center's bookshop, building a successful mail-order business, and he helped to edit the Vedanta Society magazine, *Vedanta and the West*, collaborating extensively with Isherwood on the magazine's chapter-by-chapter publication of Isherwood's biography of Ramakrishna. Prema's own 1961 book, *A Yankee and the Swamis*, described his journey in 1952–1953 to numerous holy places and to the Ramakrishna monastery in India. He also edited two books: a selection from Vivekananda, *What Religion Is: In the Words of Swami Vivekananda*, for which Isherwood wrote the introduction, and *What Vedanta Means to Me* (1960), a collection of sixteen "testimonies" by Westerners (including Isherwood) which mostly appeared first in the Hollywood magazine. In January 1964, Prema took sannyas at Belur Math and became Swami Vidyatmananda; Isherwood, who was in India with Prema from December 1963 until the sannyas ceremony took place, drew on Prema's experiences during this ritual for *A Meeting by the River*, which he once intended to dedicate to his friend. Swami Vidyatmananda left California in 1966 to assist Swami Ritajananda at the Vedanta Society in Gretz, France, east of Paris.

Premananda, Swami (1861–1918). A direct monastic disciple of Ramakrishna, from a pious Bengali family; he was originally called Baburam Ghosh. As a young man, Baburam Ghosh was first taken to meet Ramakrishna at Dakshineswar by his Calcutta classmate, Rakhal Chandra Ghosh (Brahmananda). Premananda's sister was married to one of Ramakrishna's most prominent devotees, Balaram Bose, and his mother also came to Dakshineswar as a devotee. Ramakrishna regarded him as especially pure and sweet-natured and recognized him as an *Ishvarakoti* (a perfect, free soul born for mankind's benefit) like Brahmananda and Vivekananda. During the last decades of his life Premananda ran the Belur Math and was vice-president of the Ramakrishna Order.

Preston, Jonathan. A young Englishman introduced to Isherwood by Phil Burns and whom Isherwood found attractive; they became friends around Christmas 1958. Preston had recently arrived in Los Angeles from England with a Canadian companion, John Durst; later he returned to England where he became a publicist, and Isherwood occasionally met him there.

Prokosch, Frederic ("Fritz") (1906–1989). American novelist and poet. His first novel, *The Asiatics* (1930), was his most successful, though he wrote numerous others and also published several volumes of poetry during the 1930s and early 1940s. His poetry was heavily influenced by W. H. Auden. Prokosch was educated at Haverford College before going on to Yale, and was friendly with Teddy le Boutilliere, the Bryn Mawr bookshop proprietor who introduced himself to Isherwood when Isherwood lived in Haverford, Pennsylvania, in the early 1940s. Prokosch had introduced himself to Auden and to Stephen Spender by letter during the 1930s, but met Auden only in 1939 in New York. He evidently met Isherwood around the same time.

puja. Hindu ceremony of worship; usually offerings—flowers, incense, food—are made to the object of devotion, and other ritual, symbolic acts are also carried out depending upon the occasion.

Quiroga, Alex. Mexican television cameraman working in Hollywood for ABC. Bachardy and Isherwood both thought him very attractive. In 1953, during the first weeks of his life with Isherwood, Bachardy was still having a sexual relationship with Quiroga; he confided the details to Isherwood, and Isherwood briefly encouraged him in the affair.

quota visa. The U.S. Immigration Act of 1924, known as the Quota Act, dictated that the number of immigrants admitted annually from any one country could not exceed two percent of the existing U.S. population deriving from that same national origin (as determined by the 1890 census), although a minimum quota of 100 immigrants was permitted to all countries. As the vast majority of Americans at that time traced their ancestry to Great Britain, British nationals could immigrate with ease. Of all the countries in the world, only Ireland, Germany and Britain were permitted more than 10,000 immigrants a year during the twenties and thirties; most European countries were permitted between a few hundred and a few thousand, while other countries throughout the world were generally limited to 100. Quotas published in 1940 show the dramatic range, for example: Egypt, 100; Ethiopia, 100; France, 3,086; Italy, 5,802; Ireland, 17,853; Germany, 27,370; Britain and Northern Ireland, 65,721. (The figures were adjusted annually by the Department of Labor, until 1939 when the Department of Justice took control of immigration.) After the rise of Hitler, Germany's quota was increasingly oversubscribed and soon that of surrounding European countries as well, but Britain's quota was far from full (nationality was determined by country of birth, regardless of the last time visited there, so it was not possible for non-British to immigrate via Britain). Visas were given out by the consul in the country of origin, and once a visa was obtained, the immigrant had to enter the U.S. at a designated point of entry and be inspected.

(According to the Immigration Act of 1917, immigrants could be excluded on a wide range of grounds, including alcoholism, TB, anarchist or revolutionary beliefs, criminal convictions, prostitution, vagrancy, immorality, illiteracy, physical or mental handicaps, etc.) Isherwood first entered the U.S. on a nonimmigrant visa, and had to leave and re-enter once he obtained his quota visa. To apply for citizenship, five years' continuous residence in the U.S. was required, the last six months in one county.

Rabwin, Marcus (Mark) (b. 1901). Surgeon. Rabwin studied in Minnesota and Vienna and had a private practice in Los Angeles from 1930 onward. Eventually he also became Chief of Staff at the Cedars of Lebanon Hospital. In 1934 he married David Selznick's secretary, Marcella Bennett.

Radebaugh, Roy. See Cromwell, Richard.

raja yoga. Royal yoga; one of the four main yogas. A meditation technique which concentrates the mind solely upon the Ultimate Reality until samadhi is achieved.

rajas. Activity, restlessness. See guna.

Ramakrishna (1836–1886). The Hindu holy man whose life inspired the modern renaissance of Vedanta. He is widely regarded as an incarnation of God. Ramakrishna, originally named Gadadhar Chattopadhyaya, was born in a Bengali village sixty miles from Calcutta. He was a devout Hindu from boyhood, practiced spiritual disciplines such as meditation, and served as a priest. A mystic and teacher, in 1861 he was declared an avatar: a divine incarnation sent to reestablish the truths of religion and to show by his example how to ascend towards Brahman. Also, Ramakrishna was initiated into Islam, and he had a vision of Christ. His behavior was sometimes highly unconventional, in keeping with his beliefs. For instance, he sometimes dressed in women's clothing and worshipped God in the attitude of a female lover, believing the distinction between the sexes to be an illusion. He several times danced with drunkards because their reeling reminded him of his own when he was in religious ecstasy. His followers gathered around him at Dakshineswar and later at Kashipur. His closest disciples, trained by him, later formed the nucleus of the Ramakrishna Math and Mission, now the largest monastic order in India. Ramakrishna was worshipped as God in his lifetime; he was conscious of his mission, and he was able to transmit divine knowledge by a touch, look, or wish. Isherwood wrote a biography, *Ramakrishna and His Disciples* (1964), an official project of the Ramakrishna Order.

Rameau, Hans. MGM screenwriter, possibly from Germany; Isherwood met him at the studio, probably in 1940. Rameau had an affair with Marlene Dietrich that August, and Isherwood mentions him again in 1955 upon Rameau's return from a trip to Germany.

Ram, Ram, Ram, Jaya, Ram. Ram Chandra Datta was Ramakrishna's first householder disciple, and the first to proclaim Ramakrishna as an avatar. This chant repeats his name combined with the Sanskrit word for "Hail" or "Glory to."

Rassine, Alexis (b. 1919). Ballet dancer. Alexis Rays or Raysman was born in Lithuania of Russian parents and was brought up in South Africa. He studied ballet there and in Paris, joined the Ballet Rambert in 1938, and danced with several other companies before joining the Sadler's Wells Ballet in 1942, where he became a principal and a star. He shared John Lehmann's house for many years, living in his own self-contained flat.

Rattigan, Terence (1911–1977). British playwright. Rattigan wrote mostly comedy at the start of his career, including *French Without Tears* (1936). After the war he also turned to social and psychological drama, achieving repeated acclaim with *The Winslow Boy* (1946), *The Browning Version* (1948), and *Separate Tables* (1954). He also wrote many successful screenplays, most based on his plays. Isherwood and Bachardy were introduced to Rattigan in London in 1956 and saw him again when Rattigan visited Hollywood.

Reinhardt, Gottfried (1911–199[5]). Austrian-born film producer. Reinhardt emigrated to the United States with his father, Max Reinhardt, and became assistant to Walter Wanger. Afterwards he worked as a producer for MGM from 1940 to 1954 and later directed his own films in the United States and Europe; his name is attached to many well-known films, including Garbo's *Two Faced Woman* which he produced in 1941 and *The Red Badge of Courage* which he produced in 1951. He was Salka Viertel's lover for nearly a decade before his marriage to his wife, Silvia, in 1944. Through Salka and Berthold Viertel, Reinhardt gave Isherwood his second Hollywood film job in 1940, and he remained Isherwood's favorite Hollywood boss. During the war, he enlisted and wrote scenarios for films on building latrines, preventing V.D., cleaning rifles, etc. Many years later, Reinhardt and his wife returned to Germany and settled near Salzburg.

Reinhardt, Max (1873–1943). Austrian theatrical producer. Originally called Max Goldman, Reinhardt became world-famous as the director of the Deutsches Theater in Berlin with his 1905 production of *A Midsummer Night's Dream*. He is remembered for his extravagant showmanship, though his work included serious classical theater from the Greeks to Shakespeare, Molière, Ibsen, and Shaw. He directed a few films in Germany and one later in Hollywood. Reinhardt's European empire ended when Hitler annexed Austria. He eventually opened an acting and theater school on Sunset Boulevard in Hollywood—the Workshop for Stage, Screen, and Radio—with his second wife, the German actress Helene Thimig.

Reinhardt, Wolfgang. Film producer; son of Max Reinhardt, brother of Gottfried. Isherwood probably met Wolfgang Reinhardt through Gottfried soon after arriving in Hollywood. In 1944, Isherwood met with him and Aldous Huxley to discuss working on *The Miracle*—a film version of the play produced by Max Reinhardt in the 1920s—but nothing came of it. During this period, Wolfgang was employed as a producer at Warner's, and in 1945, he hired Isherwood to work on Maugham's 1941 novel, *Up at the Villa*. The film was never made. Much later, in 1960, Reinhardt approached Isherwood to write a screenplay based on Felix Dahn's four volume 1876 novel, *Ein Kampf um Rom* (*A Struggle for Rome*), about the decline and fall of the Ostrogoth empire in Italy in the sixth century, but Isherwood turned the project down. Wolfgang's wife was called Lally.

Renaldo, Tito. Mexican actor. Isherwood first met Renaldo sometime before leaving California in 1947, apparently through Bill Caskey. When Caskey first met him, Renaldo was a companion of Cole Porter. Renaldo took up Vedanta as a disciple of Swami Prabhavananda, and for a time lived at Trabuco as a monk. In the early 1950s he left Vedanta and moved to Mexico City, but he returned to Los Angeles and to Swami before the end of the decade. He suffered from severe asthma.

Richard. See Isherwood, Richard Graham Bradshaw and Thom, Richard, a different person.

Richardson, Tony (1928–1991). British stage and film director. Richardson is admired for his work in the theater, especially at the Royal Court in London during the 1950s, and he made movies from many of these productions. His films include *Look Back in Anger* (1958), *The Entertainer* (1960), *Sanctuary* (1961), *A Taste of Honey* (1961), *The Loneliness of the Long Distance Runner* (1962), and *Tom Jones* (1963), for which he won an Academy Award. He was married for a time to Vanessa Redgrave with whom he had two daughters during the early 1960s, and he had affairs with other women and men. In 1960, when Isherwood first mentions him, Richardson was involved with Wyatt Cooper, a young actor, and he was directing for screen and stage virtually simultaneously. He was filming *Sanctuary*—amalgamated from Faulkner's *Sanctuary* (1931) and its sequel, *Requiem for a Nun* (1951), which Richardson had already directed separately as a play at the Royal Court in London in 1957—and he was also staging Shelagh Delaney's *A Taste of Honey* with a mostly English cast brought over from London.

rishi. Saint or seer; one of the ancient Hindu seers to whom the knowledge of the Vedas was revealed.

Ritajananda, Swami. Hindu monk. Ritajananda was the chief assistant to Swami Prabhavananda at the Hollywood Vedanta Center from 1958 to 1961 and then went to France to run the Vedanta Center at Gretz, near Paris, until his death in 1994. As his own assistant at Gretz, he took Prema (John Yale), who was by then called Swami Vidyatmananda.

Repton, near Derby. Isherwood's public school.

Robinson, Bill. A young man with whom Isherwood became friendly during 1958. Robinson was then in analysis, and soon settled into a successful long-term relationship.

Robson-Scott, William. An Englishman who was a close friend of Isherwood in the 1930s. Robson-Scott was lecturing in English at Berlin University in 1932 when Isherwood first met him. He summered at Ruegen Island that year with Isherwood, Heinz Neddermeyer, Stephen Spender, and others. Later he stayed with Isherwood during the agonizing period leading up to Heinz's trial, and Isherwood dedicated *Lions and Shadows* to him in gratitude. By 1947 he had married, and he fell out of touch with his old friends.

Rodakiewicz, Henwar. Polish documentary filmmaker; second husband of Peggy Kiskadden. Rodakiewicz worked on Pare Lorentz's outline for an important film about urban crisis, *The City* (1939), which was directed by Ralph Steiner and Willard Van Dyke with commentary by Lewis Mumford and music by Aaron Copland. *The City*, shown at the 1939 World's Fair, was notable for its technical innovations and experiments and its satire and humor. Rodakiewicz's film unit was called Film Associates.

Rodakiewicz, Peggy. See Kiskadden, Peggy.

Rodd, Marcel. English bookseller and publisher living in Hollywood. Isherwood met Rodd through Vernon Old and, at the suggestion of Denny Fouts, introduced him to Swami Prabhavananda as a publisher for the Vedanta Society. Rodd published Prabhavananda and Isherwood's translation of the Bhagavad Gita and *Vedanta for the Western World* as well as the magazine, *The Voice of India* (later *Vedanta and the West*). Some years afterwards, he was prosecuted for dealing in pornography, and fell out with the Vedanta Society when he would neither republish nor to give up his rights to their books.

Roder, Hellmut. A Berlin friend of Isherwood and Stephen Spender during the early 1930s; originally called Hellmut Schroeder. He emigrated to America with his friend Fritz Mosel by way of France, Spain, and Mexico.

Rod. See Owens, Rod.

Roerick, Bill. American actor. Isherwood met Roerick in 1943 when John van Druten brought him to a lecture at the Vedanta Center. Roerick was in England as a G.I. during the war and became friends there with E. M. Forster, J. R. Ackerley, and others. His companion for many years was Tom Coley. In 1944, Roerick contributed a short piece to *Horizon*, defending Isherwood's new way of life in America after Tony Bower had made fun of it in a previous number; Roerick's piece, " 'Where Shall John Go?' A Reply to Antony Bourne" appeared in March 1944, 9.1, pp. 204–207, signed (in a different spelling of his name) William Roehrich, Corporal U.S. Army.

Rory. See Harrity, Rory.

Ross, Alan (b. 1922). English poet and journalist; editor of John Lehmann's *The London Magazine* from 1961 onwards. Isherwood probably first met Ross on a trip to England after the war.

Ross, Jean (d. 1973). The original of Isherwood's character Sally Bowles in *Goodbye to Berlin*. Isherwood met Jean Ross in Berlin, possibly in October 1930, but certainly by the start of 1931. She was then occasionally singing in a night club, and they shared lodgings for a time in Fräulein Thurau's flat. Ross's father was a Scottish cotton merchant, and she had been raised in Egypt in lavish circumstances. After Berlin, she returned to England where she became close friends with Olive Mangeot, staying in her house for a time. She joined the Communist Party and had a daughter, Sarah (later a crime novelist under the name Sarah Caudwell), with Claud Cockburn, though they never married.

Roth, Sanford (Sandy). American photographer; known for his pictures of actors and actresses, and especially of James Dean. Isherwood first met Roth with Julie Harris when Roth photographed Isherwood and Harris together (Harris arrived dressed as Sally Bowles). Roth and Isherwood later collaborated on a 1952 piece for *Harper's Bazaar*, "California Story" (reprinted in *Exhumations* as "The Shore").

Russell, Bertrand Arthur William, 3rd Earl Russell (1872–1970). English philosopher and mathematician, social critic, writer. Russell was educated at Trinity College, Cambridge and was a Cambridge Apostle; afterwards he worked as a diplomat and an academic. He published countless books and is one of the most widely read philosophers of the twentieth century. Chief among his awards and honors was the Nobel Prize for Literature in 1950. Throughout his life Russell expressed his convictions in social and political activism, and he frequently changed his position. When he opposed British entry into World War I and joined the No-Conscription Fellowship, he lost his first job at Trinity, and he was fined and imprisoned more than once for his role in public demonstrations as a pacifist. Partly as a result, he became a visiting professor and lecturer in America and returned to Trinity as a fellow only in 1944. Isherwood first met Russell through Aldous and Maria Huxley in late 1939 in Hollywood. At the Huxleys' Christmas party in December 1939, Isherwood records Berthold Viertel's surprise at Russell's enthusiasm for British successes in the war—Russell had renounced pacifism because of the evils of fascism. Later, in 1949 Russell began to champion nuclear disarmament.

In January 1941, Russell accepted a $6,000 a year position with the Philadelphia pharmaceutical millionaire and art collector, Dr. Alfred Barnes, lecturing at the Barnes Foundation, not far from where Isherwood was working in Haverford. The arrangement with Barnes fell apart after Barnes criticized Russell for being a snob and barred Lady Russell from the foundation. Russell sued and won most of his fees before leaving the country. Isherwood records that his own Haverford landlady, Mrs. Yarnall, thought Russell rather shocking company, especially in his attitude to marriage. Russell's relationships with women reflect his approbation, stated in his writings, of the concept of companionate marriage—first discussed by others during the 1920s—which would permit birth control and divorce by mutual consent to childless couples, holding neither partner legally responsible to the other. He was married four times; he had two children during the 1920s by his second wife, Dora Black, and one in 1937 by his third wife, Patricia Spense, known as "Peter." The latter also collaborated with Russell on *Freedom in Organization 1814–1914* (1934).

St. Edmund's School, Hindhead, Surrey. Isherwood's preparatory school, run by Cyril Morgan Brown, a cousin of Isherwood's father.

St. Joseph, Ellis. Screenwriter and playwright. Author of the play, *Passenger to Bali*. Isherwood met him soon after arriving in Hollywood. In the 1940s he worked on Vincent Sherman's *In Our Time* and in the 1950s on John Huston's *The Barbarian and the Geisha*, for which he wrote the story about the historical figure Townsend Harris on which the script was based.

Salka. See Viertel, Sara Salomé Steuermann.

sannyas. The second and final vows of renunciation taken in the Ramakrishna order, at least four or five years after the brahmacharya vows. The sannyasin undergoes a spiritual rebirth and, as part of the preparation for this, renounces all caste distinctions. Isherwood's diary for March 13, 1958, refers to the way in which Krishna (George Fitts) had first to join the Brahmin caste in order to have a caste to renounce. Then Krishna had to imagine himself as dead, and to become a ghost in preparation for being reborn. At sannyas, the spiritual aspirant becomes a swami and takes a new Sanskrit name, ending with "ananda," bliss. Thus, the new name implies "he who has the bliss of" whatever the first element in the name specifies, as in Vivekananda, "he who has the bliss of discrimination." A woman sannyasin becomes a *pravrajika* (woman ascetic), and her new name ends in "prana," meaning "whose life is in" whatever is designated by the first element of the name.

samadhi. The state of superconsciousness in which an individual can know the highest spiritual experience; absolute oneness with the ultimate reality; transcendental consciousness.

Samuels, Lesser. American screenwriter. In 1940 Isherwood was hired to polish dialogue on Samuels's script for a remake of *A Woman's Face*; not long afterwards, Samuels asked Isherwood to help him on Maugham's *The Hour Before Dawn*. Like Isherwood, Samuels had worked for Gaumont-British during the 1930s. In subsequent years they often worked together, sometimes on their own ideas, including *Judgement Day in Pittsburgh* for which they were paid $50,000 (their story was later scripted by Lionel Houser and released as *Adventure in Baltimore*, 1949); *The Easiest Thing in the World*, completed August 1949; and *The Vacant Room*, a ghost story set in Los Angeles which they had trouble selling. Samuels was married and had a daughter.

Sankarananda, Swami. A disciple of Brahmananda and his secretary for a time; later president of the Ramakrishna Math and Mission from 1951 to 1962.

Sarada. "Sarada" Folling was a young nun at the Vedanta Center when Isherwood arrived in Hollywood in 1939. (Sarada was the Sanskrit name given her by Swami Prabhavananda; Folling was her own original surname.) She was of Norwegian descent, had studied music and dance, and while at the center learned a fair amount of Sanskrit. Her father lived in New Mexico. Sarada later moved to the convent at Santa Barbara where Isherwood occasionally saw her. She was a favorite of Prabhavananda, but eventually left the convent rather suddenly after becoming interested in men. Thereafter, Prabhavananda forbade her name to be mentioned to him.

Sarada Convent, Montecito (also called Sarada Math). In 1944, Spencer Kellogg gave his house at Montecito, near Santa Barbara, to the Vedanta Society of Southern California. The house was called "Ananda Bavan," Sanskrit for Home of Peace. Kellogg, a devotee, died the same year, and the house became a Vedanta center and eventually a convent housing about a dozen nuns. During the early 1950s, a temple was also built in the grounds.

Sarada Devi (1855–1920). Bengali wife of Ramakrishna whom he married by arrangement when she was five years old. After the marriage, she returned to her family and he to his temple, and their relationship was always chaste although she later spent long periods of time living intimately with him. She became known as a saint in her own right and was worshipped as Holy Mother, the living embodiment of Mahamaya, of the Great Mother, of the Goddess Sarasvati, and of Kali herself. Isherwood was initiated on Holy Mother's birthday, November 8, 1940.

Saradananda, Swami (1865–1927). A direct disciple of Ramakrishna; originally called Sharat Chandra Chakravarti. He had a vocation for nursing, was a medical student for a time, and nursed Ramakrishna in his last illness. After Ramakrishna's death, Saradananda joined the Baranagore monastery, travelled to London and New York to lecture on Vedanta during the 1890s, edited Vivekananda's magazine, *Udbodhan* (Awakening), and built a house in Calcutta that served as the office of the magazine and also as a residence for Sarada Devi whose countless devotees Saradananda monitored while he worked. Saradananda also wrote a biography of Ramakrishna, *Sri Ramakrishna the Great Master*, which Isherwood read carefully in 1956 before beginning work on his own book.

sattva. Purity, clarity, calm. See guna.

Saunders, Brad. American air force pilot. Bradley Saunders had distinguished himself as a pilot in World War II, and afterwards became an Air Force Reserve officer. He also served in the Korean war. Isherwood met him around November 19, 1948; Saunders was then friendly with Jay de Laval, and went with de Laval to the Virgin islands to open a new restaurant before the pair parted ways. Later Saunders had a long and serious relationship with Jim Charlton. Saunders wrote poetry for fun, and he had been a roommate of James Dean before Dean came to prominence as an actor.

Saville, Victor (1897–1979). British producer and director. During the 1930s, Saville had a successful career in England with Gaumont-British, Alexander Korda's London Films, and MGM British Studios before coming to Hollywood for MGM in 1939. He directed some films for MGM in Hollywood, occasionally returning to England to produce, and also worked independently. He was a producer both before and after he directed and was perhaps more successful as a producer than as a director. Isherwood was hired by Saville several times during his first years in Hollywood; they had in common their friendship with Berthold Viertel and Salka Viertel. Saville was a model for "Chatsworth" in *Prater Violet*.

Schary, Dore (1905–1980). American writer and film producer. Schary was an actor and a journalist as well as writing plays and screenplays and directing. He worked for several studios before achieving success at MGM in the early 1940s, then he moved to RKO and later went back to MGM, ousting Louis B. Mayer in 1951. Schary was ousted in his turn just a few years later, and formed his own production company. He wrote an award winning play about Roosevelt—*Sunrise at Campobello* —which he filmed in 1960, and he adapted the screenplay for his 1958 film *Lonelyhearts* from Nathanael West's novella, *Miss Lonelyhearts*. Schary had a reputation as a staunch liberal who tried to resist Hollywood's blacklist. Isherwood met him in the early 1950s at MGM (he first mentions Schary in his diary in 1953), and in 1955 Schary read Isherwood's script on Buddha, *The Wayfarer*.

Scheler, Max. German photographer. Isherwood and Bachardy were introduced to him by Herbert List in Munich during their 1955 European trip.

Schley, Edna. Isherwood's Hollywood agent during the early 1940s, recommended to him by John van Druten. She worked with her husband Dan Leonardson. In 1944 she had a brain hemorrhage and never recovered.

Schwed, Peter. Isherwood's editor at Simon and Schuster. In 1957, Isherwood moved from Random House to Simon and Schuster in order to work with John Goodman. When Goodman unexpectedly died, Schwed became Isherwood's editor, but Isherwood never felt that Schwed liked or understood his work. After several changes of heart, Isherwood nonetheless remained at Simon and Schuster until the start of the 1970s. Simon and Schuster published *Down There on a Visit*, *A Single Man*, *A Meeting by the River*, *Kathleen and Frank*, and *Exhumations*.

Scott-Kilvert, Ian. Isherwood had been tutor to Ian Scott-Kilvert for a short period beginning in January 1927 when Scott-Kilvert was eight; they renewed their friendship in the late 1930s. Scott-Kilvert was a pacifist at the start of the war and served in a Friends Ambulance Unit in Africa, but afterwards fought behind German lines in Greece. He married an American woman called Elizabeth. He appears as "Graham" in *Lions and Shadows*.

Searle, Alan (1905–1985). Secretary and companion to Somerset Maugham from 1938 until Maugham's death, and Maugham's heir. They first met in 1928 in London when Searle was in his early twenties. Searle was the son of a Bermondsey tailor and had a Cockney accent; when he met Maugham, he had already had relationships with older men, among them Lytton Strachey. At the time he worked with convicts—visiting them in prison and helping them to resettle in the community when they were released—but told Maugham he wanted to travel. Maugham purportedly invited him to do so on the spot, but for a decade they met again only when Maugham was in London. Eventually Searle devoted his life to Maugham.

Selective Service. Under the Selective Service and Training Act signed by Roosevelt October 16, 1940, men aged twenty-one to thirty-six were required to register for the draft. The first two selective service registrations, in October 1940 and July 1941, signed up men aged twenty-one to thirty-five, and both drafts were conducted by lottery. But the draft age, at both the youngest and oldest ends of the spectrum, went up and down throughout the war, depending on the requirements of the military. On August 16, 1941, men aged twenty-eight and over were relieved from training and service, while, on August 18, the period of service for younger men was extended to eighteen months. But then on December 20, 1941, after Pearl Harbor, the liability for service was greatly enlarged to include men aged twenty to forty-four, and all men aged eighteen to sixty-four were also required to register. At roughly the same time, the duration of service was again lengthened—to six months after the end of the war, however long it lasted. The third registration occurred in February 1942, and the third and final lottery in March; afterwards registrants were called by their birth dates, the youngest and the oldest last. Forty-five to sixty-five-year-old men were registered in the fourth registration, in April 1942, but only for occupational classification. The fifth registration, for men eighteen to twenty, began in June 1942. In December 1942, drafting of men over thirty-eight was discontinued for good, while in the same month the sixth registration signed up eighteen-year-olds and those who would reach eighteen after December 31. From April 1, 1944, the military asked for men under thirty, preferably eighteen to twenty-five year olds. The draft continued after the war in order to supply men for international reconstructive and peace keeping commitments, and later for Korea.

The men who registered for the draft were divided into four main classes: class 1 designated men available for military service and training; classes 2, 3, and 4 designated men deferred for various reasons. Each class had subclasses, and the definitions of the subclasses were continuously though slightly revised throughout the war, especially since the draft age went up and down. There were several classes for conscientious objectors, and Isherwood mentions many of them in describing his own experience and the experiences of his friends and acquaintances. 1-A-O, the classification Matthew Huxley took before being drafted into the Medical Corps, designated C.O.s who were prepared to serve in noncombatant roles in the military and who were fit for general service (1-A-O was thus a subclass of 1-A, the main group of men fit and available for general military service). 4-D designated a minister of religion or a divinity student; Isherwood applied for this in September 1942 while making up his mind to try to become a monk, and others associated with the Vedanta Society also applied for it. 4-E designated a C.O. who was not prepared to serve in the military at all, even in a noncombatant role. 4-Es were fit and available for "civilian work of national importance," an employment category Roosevelt established for them in February 1941 (4-E-LS designated the same sort of C.O., but one fit only for limited service). Denny Fouts went to CPS camp as a 4-E in the summer of 1941, and Isherwood, too old for the draft at this point, tried to volunteer to a camp the same summer but was not wanted. Then after Pearl Harbor when the draft age went up, and through much of 1942, Isherwood waited to be drafted to camp as a 4-E, but the call never came. The deferment 1-A-H (later sometimes called simply 1-H) existed initially for men who had already reached their twenty-eighth birthday without being drafted; by 1942, 1-H designated men deferred generally by reason of age—at first twenty-eight to thirty-seven year olds, later thirty-seven to forty-five year olds. By analogy, 4-E-H was, initially, a C.O. opposed to a noncombatant military role and who had reached his twenty-eighth birthday without being assigned to a task of national importance. By 1942, 4-E-H (also sometimes simply called 4-H) designated men deferred from work of national importance by reason of age. In fact, these age deferments applied to George Fitts and to Isherwood through most of the war, except the period just after Pearl Harbor when age limits were greatly extended. 4-F designated men who were physically, mentally, or morally unfit for military service—in addition to ill-health, disqualifying "crimes" ranged from treason, murder, and rape to sodomy and sexual perversion. Benjamin Bok, who had a rare, progressive arthritis, and W. H. Auden, who did not conceal his homosexuality from the draft board, were both disqualified from service under this class. A decade later, in 1954, Don Bachardy was also classified 4–F after revealing he was homosexual. The classification 4-C, for aliens who had not declared their intention to become U.S. citizens, should have deferred Swami Prabhavananda's nephew Asit Ghosh from the draft, but did not. Tony Bower had completed his military service and was designated 4-A, but after Pearl Harbor, this class was closed and Bower was drafted for a second time.

Selznick, David O. (1902–1965). Legendary American producer; most famous for *Gone with the Wind* (1939). Among his many other well-known films are *Dinner at Eight* (1933), *David Copperfield* (1934), *A Star Is Born* (1937), *The Prisoner of Zenda* (1937), *Rebecca* (1940), *Spellbound* (1945), and *Duel in the Sun* (1946). Selznick worked for his father's film company from adolescence until its bankruptcy in 1923; in 1926 he went to Hollywood where he began as an assistant story editor at MGM and worked for Harry Rapf. He then joined Paramount, and in 1931 became the first studio head at RKO—where he hired George Cukor and Katharine Hepburn, among others. In 1933, he went back to MGM, but left in 1935 to form Selznick International Pictures with John Hay Whitney. Selznick's aspirations were monumental: he was obsessed with detail, and tried to control every aspect of the pictures he was involved with. Despite the success of many of his films, he went increasingly into debt, and by the end of the 1940s he had to close his companies. He was married to Louis B. Mayer's daughter Irene from 1931 to 1945, and to Jennifer Jones from 1949 onwards. He took Jones to live and work in Europe intermittently during the 1950s, and her career absorbed Selznick almost entirely at the end of his life. Selznick traded his rights in *A Star is Born* to get the lead for Jones in *A Farewell to Arms* (1957); the film failed and proved to be his last. Isherwood worked for Selznick in 1958, developing a script for a proposed film, *Mary Magdalene*, and they became friends, often meeting at Selznick's house both for work and socially. The French Dominican friar, Father Bruckberger, evidently felt Selznick was drawing inappropriately on Bruckberger's 1952 biography of Mary Magdalene, but Selznick seemingly had ideas of his own for the script as well as a melodramatic novel about Mary Magdalene, *The Scarlet Lily*, by Edward F. Murphy. Murphy's novel, though, was only published in 1960; perhaps Selznick read it before that in typescript. Selznick replaced Isherwood with another writer, Eddie Anhalt, then abandoned the project altogether when a panel of statesmen and scholars in Tel Aviv told him the script was anti-Semitic.

Selznick, Jennifer. Second wife of David Selznick; see Jones, Jennifer.

Shankara. Hindu religious philosopher and saint of roughly the sixth to eighth centuries A.D., widely recognized as an emanation of Shiva. Shankara wrote commentaries on the Brahma Sutras, the principal Upanishads and other religious texts, as well as philosophy, poems, hymns and prayers. Much of his work is not attributed with authority. He probably organized the Hindu mendicant orders.

Shenkel, John. A novice monk at the Hollywood Vedanta Center from about 1949; by 1952 he was living at Trabuco. He became Ananta Chaitanya in 1954 and then at the end of the 1950s went to live in India.

Shroyer, Fred. A faculty member in the English department at Los Angeles State College and Isherwood's colleague. He was responsible for Isherwood being hired to teach there in 1959 and became a friend. In December that year he appeared with Isherwood on a half-hour TV program about *The Sun Also Rises*, the novel that made Hemingway famous in 1926.

Sister Lalita ("Sister") (d. 1949). Carrie Mead Wykoff was an American widow who met Vivekananda on one of his trips to America and became a disciple of Swami Turiyananda (another direct disciple of Ramakrishna). Turiyananda gave her the name Sister Lalita. She met Swami Prabhavananda when he opened the Vedanta Center in Portland, Oregon, and in 1929 invited him to live in her house in Hollywood. By 1938 they had gathered a congregation around them and they built the Hollywood temple in her garden. She had a collie dog called Dhruva.

Smith, Dodie. See Beesley.

Soldati, Mario (b. 1906). Italian novelist and film director. In the summer of 1955 Soldati evidently proposed that Isherwood write a screenplay based on Soldati's *The Capri Letters*. Isherwood decided not to, and when he nevertheless visited Soldati while in Italy later that year, Isherwood decided to turn down other projects as well.

Sophie. See Moulaert, Sophie.

Sorel, Paul. American painter, of Midwestern background; his real name is Karl Dibble. Sorel was a close friend of Chris Wood, and lived with him in Laguna from the early 1940s. Sorel moved out in 1943 after disagreements about money and in 1944 went to New York for a time. He painted portraits of Isherwood and Bill Caskey in 1950. Chris Wood continued to support him for the rest of Wood's life, though they did not live together after 1953.

Speed. See Lamkin, Speed.

Spencer, Roger. A young devotee evidently living at the Vedanta Society during 1943 and afterwards. Probably this is the same Roger Spencer whom Isherwood met at Trabuco in the summer of 1942 and who served at the Los Prietos CPS camp as a C.O. later the same year.

Spender, Stephen (1909–1995). English poet, critic, autobiographer, editor. W. H. Auden introduced Isherwood to Spender in 1928; Spender was then an undergraduate at University College, Oxford, and Isherwood became a mentor.

Afterwards Spender lived in Hamburg and near Isherwood in Berlin, and the two briefly shared a house in Sintra with Heinz Neddermeyer and Tony Hyndman. Spender was the youngest of the writers who came to prominence with Auden and Isherwood in the 1930s; after Auden and Isherwood emigrated, he gradually replaced them in the London literary world, successfully cultivating the public and social roles they abjured. He worked as a propagandist for the Republicans during the Spanish Civil War and was a member of the National Fire Service during the Blitz. He was co-editor with Cyril Connolly of *Horizon* and later an editor of *Encounter*. He moved away from his early enthusiasm for communism, but remained liberal in politics and later founded and contributed to *Index on Censorship*. His 1936 marriage to Inez Pearn was over by 1939, and in 1941 he married Natasha Litvin, a concert pianist, with whom he had two children. Spender's literary and social prominence gave him enormous influence over the reputations of Isherwood and Auden in England; latterly he used this mainly to their benefit. He appears as "Stephen Savage" in *Lions and Shadows* and is further described in *Christopher and His Kind*. He published an autobiography, *World Within World*, in 1951, and his *Journals 1939–1983* appeared in 1985.

Spender, Natasha Litvin. English concert pianist; she married Stephen Spender in 1941 and had two children with him, Matthew and Lizzie.

Spigelgass, Leonard. American screenwriter and playwright. He was about Isherwood's age, and wrote two musicals at MGM during the 1950s when Isherwood was working there. Spigelgass also wrote a play, a comedy titled *A Majority of One*, which was produced on Broadway and later filmed in 1961. His most widely known screenplay was for the 1962 film version of *Gypsy*. In the mid-1950s, Spigelgass was friendly with Brendan Toomey, whom Isherwood also met.

Stanley, Leonard. Interior decorator, born and raised in Hawaii. He was a close friend of Tony Duquette. When Isherwood and Bachardy visited Hawaii in 1957, Stanley arranged for them to stay with his mother, Geneva, in the house where Stanley and his sister, Pat Stanley Delpesh, had grown up.

Starcke, Walter. American actor and theatrical producer; he altered the spelling of his last name to Starkey, but returned to his real name, Starcke, when he gave up acting. He starred in an unsuccessful play of John van Druten's in the late 1940s, then became van Druten's producer. He also became van Druten's longterm boyfriend. Van Druten's previous lover, Carter Lodge, and Lodge's new lover, Dick Foote, never liked Starcke, resulting in complicated rivalries among the four of them; van Druten and Starcke finally split up in 1957, not long before van Druten died. Isherwood first met Starcke in January 1947, and tended to enjoy his company. Starcke was a Joel Goldsmith devotee.

Steen, Mike. American stuntman with acting ambitions. Steen was from Louisiana and was friendly with Speed Lamkin, Tom Wright, and Henry Guerriero; Lamkin introduced him to Isherwood in the early 1950s. Gavin Lambert became romantically involved with Steen during 1958, and Steen also had relationships, perhaps sexual, with Nicholas Ray, William Inge, and Tennessee Williams. Steen worked as a stuntman in Ray's *Party Girl*, and he did stunts or played bit parts in other movies in the late 1950s and 1960s, including a tiny part in the 1962 film of Williams's *Sweet Bird of Youth*.

Stephen. See Spender, Stephen.

Steve, also Stevie. See Conway, Steve.

Stern, James (1904–1993). Irish writer and translator. Educated at Eton and, briefly, Sandhurst. In youth, he worked as a farmer in Southern Rhodesia and a banker in the family bank in England and Europe, then travelled until settling for a time in Paris in the 1930s, where he married. Isherwood met Stern in Sintra, Portugal in 1936 through William Robson-Scott, and for some months Isherwood and Heinz shared their house, Alecrim do Norte, with Stern and his wife. There, Isherwood introduced Stern to W. H. Auden with whom Stern became an intimate friend, later, in America. Stern eventually returned to England. His books include *The Heartless Land* (1932) and *Something Wrong* (1938)—both story collections—and *The Hidden Damage* (1947), about his trip with Auden to postwar Germany.

Stern, Tania (1906–1995). Tania Kurella, the daughter of a German psychiatrist, was a physical therapist and exercise teacher, exponent of her own technique, the Kurella method. She fled Germany in 1933 to escape persecution for the left-wing political activities of her two brothers, already refugees, and lived for a time in Paris where she met James Stern. They married in 1935. She collaborated on some of his translations and she also shared his close friendship with W. H. Auden. Isherwood found her warm, unaffected, and beautiful. In later years, the Sterns disapproved of Isherwood, believing that he exaggerated his poverty and also imagining (wrongly) that Auden might have married and become essentially heterosexual were it not for Isherwood's influence.

Steuermann, Eduard. Polish-born concert pianist; Salka Viertel's brother and briefly a member of her extended household during the war. He re-established his career in the U.S., achieving wide recognition as an interpreter in particular of Schoenberg, Berg, and Webern. Among his students was Alfred Brendel. Steuermann married twice, and had three daughters, including "Mausi," who lived with the Viertels during the war. His second marriage was to his student, Clara Silvers, thirty years his junior.

Steuermann, Frau. Salka Viertel's mother. Frau Steuermann fled Poland during the war and arrived in California via Siberia. She lived with the Viertels and died in Santa Monica in June 1953.

Steuermann, Margeret (Mausi). Salka Viertel's niece, eldest daughter of Eduard Steuermann. Mausi was part of the Viertel household during the war, studied acting and played the piano. At twelve or thirteen she was diagnosed as schizophrenic and was committed to a clinic; eventually she improved enough to lead an almost normal life.

Steuermann, Sara Salomé. See Viertel, Salka.

Stravinsky, Igor (1882–1971). Russian-born composer; he went to Paris with Diaghilev's Ballets Russes in 1910 and brought about a rhythmic revolution in western music with his *The Rite of Spring* (1911–1913), the most sensational of his many works commissioned for the company. In youth he was greatly influenced by his teacher, Rimsky-Korsakov, but Stravinsky's originality as a composer derived partly from his ability to borrow and rework an enormously wide range of musical forms and styles. He remained continuously open to new ideas, even into old age. Many of his early works evoke Russian folk music, and he was influenced by jazz. Around 1923 he began a long neo-classical period during which he drew on and responded to the compositions of his great European predecessors. After the Russian revolution, Stravinsky remained in Europe, making his home first in Switzerland and then in Paris, and turned to performing and conducting to support his family. In 1926 he rejoined the Russian Orthodox Church, and religious music became an increasing preoccupation during the later part of his career. At the outbreak of World War II, he emigrated to America where he settled in Los Angeles and eventually became a citizen in 1945. Although he was asked to, he never composed for films. His first and most important work for English words was his opera, *The Rake's Progress* (1951), for which W. H. Auden and Chester Kallman wrote the libretto. Isherwood first met Stravinsky in August 1949 at lunch in the Farmer's Market in Hollywood with Aldous and Maria Huxley and others. He was soon invited to the Stravinskys' house for supper where he fell asleep listening to a Stravinsky recording; Stravinsky later told Robert Craft that this was the start of his great affection for Isherwood. The two became warm friends and were often drunk together. During the 1950s, with the encouragement of Robert Craft, Stravinsky began to compose according to the twelve-note serial methods invented by Schoenberg and extended by Webern—he was already past seventy. Toward the end of his life, he wrote a number of sacred cantatas and musical epitaphs, including *In Memoriam Dylan Thomas* (1954), which Isherwood heard but did not like. Despite his self-professed inability to appreciate Stravinsky's music, Isherwood was clearly impressed by the seriousness and depth of purpose with which Stravinsky approached his work, and he evidently found Stravinsky's company not only comforting but also inspiring.

Stravinsky, Vera (1888–1982). Russian-born actress and painter. Second wife of Igor Stravinsky; she was previously married three times, the third time to the painter and Ballets Russes stage designer Sergei Sudeikin. In 1917, Vera Arturovna Sudeikin fled St. Petersburg and the bohemian artistic milieu in which she was both patroness and muse, travelling in the south of Russia with Sudeikin before going on to Paris where she met Stravinsky in the early 1920s; they fell in love but did not marry until 1940 after the death of Stravinsky's first wife. Isherwood met Vera Stravinsky with her husband in August 1949 and found her extremely charming and very beautiful. She became an adored longterm friend. Her paintings were in an abstract-primitive style influenced by Paul Klee, childlike and decorative. She had her first show in March 1955 at the Galleria Obelisco in Rome.

Stroud, Bill. A friend of Michael Barrie in the mid-1950s. He was somewhat unpredictable, and Barrie had trouble with the friendship when Stroud became critical of Gerald Heard. Eventually he disappeared to the East Coast.

Sudhira. A nurse of Irish descent; she was a probationer nun at the Vedanta Center when Isherwood arrived to live there in 1943. Her real name was Helen Kennedy. In youth she had been widowed on the third day of her marriage. Afterwards she worked in hospitals and for Dr. Kolisch, and first came to the Vedanta Center professionally to nurse a devotee. Her parents were members of the original cooperative colony in the desert at Llano (where the Huxleys later briefly lived) and she had spent some time there as a child. She enlisted in the navy in January 1945, and later married for a second time and returned to nursing.

Suez crisis. Isherwood followed its development throughout 1956. Egypt's President Nasser nationalized the Suez Canal Company (in which shares were held mostly by British and French investors) in late July 1956, proposing to pay for the Aswan Dam with canal tolls after international loan offers for the project were withdrawn. The Israelis invaded on October 29, claiming Egyptian provocation; they were followed by Anglo-French air attacks and, in early November, troops. But international opposition forced the British and French to halt their operation almost immediately. They withdrew in December and the Israelis left in March 1957. U.N. troops remained for a decade.

In November 1956, Isherwood also alludes to the tensions which mounted between Turkey and Syria when Turkey, which had joined the U.S. sponsored Baghdad Pact and had also recognized the state of Israel, pressured Syria to break its alliance with Egypt (Syria shared joint command with Egypt and Jordan during the Suez war). During this time, the Soviets, a traditional threat to Turkey, began to supply weapons to Syria and Egypt in response to the crisis. Eventually, on November 26, Turkey withdrew its ambassador to Israel until differences with other Arab states could be resolved.

Swami. Used as a title to mean "Lord" or "Master." A Hindu monk or religious teacher. Isherwood used it in particular to refer to his own guru and he pronounced it *Shwami*; see also Prabhavananda.

Swamiji. An especially respectful form of "Swami," but also a particular name for Vivekananda towards the end of his life.

Szczesny, Berthold. Isherwood met Szczesny in The Cosy Corner on his first brief visit to Berlin in March 1929 and returned to Germany hoping to spend the summer with him in the Harz Mountains. But Szczesny, then called "Bubi," was in trouble with the police, fled to Amsterdam, and from there shipped out to South America. Subsequently he came to London working on board a freighter and smuggling refugees into England. As Isherwood tells in *The Condor and the Cows*, Szczesny eventually returned to Argentina, became part-owner of a factory and married an Argentine woman of privileged background. He and Isherwood met again there and in New York.

Taber, Phil. A disciple of Swami Prabhavananda. He lived at Trabuco during the 1950s, but never took any vows. He left Vedanta in 1959.

tamas. Darkness, inertia, stupidity. See guna.

Tantra. A religious philosophy whose followers mainly worship Shakti, the Mother of the Universe, and who understand the universe in terms of the relationship between Shakti and Shiva. Shakti represents the energy or dynamic power of Brahman—creating, preserving, dissolving the universe; Shiva, the father aspect, represents Brahman—the transcendent Absolute which is revealed through the grace of Shakti. Tantra is preoccupied with spiritual practices and ritual forms of worship, seeking liberation and rebirth through direct knowledge that the individual soul is one with the Godhead (Shiva-Shakti). Tantra is also the name of the scriptures associated with worshipping Shakti; it was originally a type of Hindu sacred text or ritualistic book, but usually refers to texts dealing with the secret sexual and magic practices of initiates in the cult of Shakti. *Vamachara*—the use of wine and women to teach freedom from the passions through sublimation and liberation—was outlawed among followers of Ramakrishna because it degenerated into sensualism. Vaishnava Vedanta and Buddhism also have Tantras.

Tarini. See Nixon, Alice.

Taylor, Charles ("Spud"). Los Angeles doctor; boyfriend of Isherwood's secretary Eleanor Breese. Taylor's speciality was proctology; he examined Isherwood in May 1957 when Isherwood was suffering persistent ill health, anxiety and depression.

Taylor, Frank. American movie producer (*The Misfits*) and publisher. Taylor worked at MGM in Los Angeles and was also an editor at Dell Publishers in New York. His double life extended to his personal circumstances as well; he had a number of children with his wife, Nan, and a series of male lovers. Taylor introduced Isherwood to various acquaintances, including in the 1950s John Keating (a young actor) and Van Varner. Over the years, Isherwood worked with Taylor on a number of film projects: these included *The Journeying Boy* or *The Vacant Room* and a movie written with Klaus Mann—which came to nothing—about Han Van Meegeren, the forger, and his dealings with the Nazis. Isherwood also prepared the 1960 anthology *Great English Short Stories* for Taylor at Dell. Taylor was on the Board of Trustees at the Huntington Hartford Foundation and introduced Isherwood as a new trustee. The Taylors entertained frequently, and Isherwood often attended parties at their house.

Ted. See Bachardy, Ted.

Ten, also Tennessee. See Williams, Tennessee.

Terry. See Jenkins, Terry.

Thakur. Hindu term for Master or Lord; a familiar name for Ramakrishna among his devotees.

Thom, Richard. Thom's parents had been devotees of Swami Prabhavananda in Portland, Oregon, and Thom began preparing to be a monk while still in high school. He lived at the Vedanta Center with Isherwood and the other probationer monks briefly in 1943, until he got into trouble and was expelled from school. After various jobs, he joined the marines in the autumn of 1943.

Thurau, Fräulein Meta. Isherwood's landlady in Berlin from December 1930 when he took a room in her flat in Nollendorfstrasse 17. She is the original of "Fräulein Lina Schroeder" in *Goodbye to Berlin* ("Fräulein Schneider" in John van Druten's stage version, *I Am a Camera*).

Tinker. See Austen, Howard.

Tis. See Bok, Margaret Welmoet.

Tito. See Renaldo, Tito.

Todd, Thelma (1905–1935). American movie actress. She owned a Hollywood establishment incorporating a restaurant, a gambling casino and a whorehouse, and she was murdered there. Afterwards the restaurant, Chez Roland (named after Gilbert Roland with whom Todd was supposed to be in love), continued for many years.

Toller, Christiane Grautoff (1917–1974). German actress; daughter of a prominent art historian and wife of Ernst Toller. They met when she was only sixteen, in 1932, and married in exile in London in 1935. She worked in Hollywood and New York after their emigration, but the marriage failed, adding to Toller's depression. Isherwood probably first met her in Sintra in 1936.

Toller, Ernst (1893–1939). German poet and playwright. Toller fought in World War I and afterwards became a pacifist and a left-wing revolutionary. In 1919 he went to prison for five years for his participation in the communist government of Bavaria, but continued writing. A Jew, Toller fled the Nazis, worked in London, New York, and Hollywood, wrote several more poems and plays, then hanged himself in May 1939 in New York, several weeks after Hitler invaded Czechoslovakia. Toller stayed with Isherwood in Sintra in the spring of 1936, possibly because either Isherwood or Stephen Spender invited him, and W. H. Auden was there at the time working with Isherwood on *The Ascent of F6*. Auden translated the lyrics for Toller's satirical musical play *Nie Wieder Frieden!* (*No More Peace!*) which was produced at the Gate Theatre in Notting Hill that June, 1936, and published in 1937. The title mocks the popular German slogan of the 1920s, "Nie Wieder Krieg" (No More War). After Toller's suicide, Auden wrote a poem for him, "In Memoriam Ernst Toller."

Tom. See Wright, Tom.

Trabuco. The monastic community sixty miles south of Los Angeles and about twenty miles inland which was founded by Gerald Heard in 1942. An anonymous benefactor provided $100,000 for the project, and Heard consulted at length with various friends and colleagues as well as with members of the Quaker Society of Friends about how to organize the community. In 1940 he planned only a small retreat called "Focus," then renamed the community after buying the ranch at Trabuco. Isherwood's cousin on his mother's side, Felix Greene, administered the practical side of the project, beginning with buying the property and constructing the building which could house fifty. By 1949 Heard found leading and administering the group too much of a strain and, wishing to retire, persuaded the trustees to give Trabuco to the Vedanta Society. It opened as a Vedanta monastery in September 1949.

Tree, Iris. English actress and poet; third daughter of actor Herbert Beerbohm Tree. She published three volumes of poetry (two before 1930, a third in 1966) and wrote poems and articles for magazines such as *Vogue* and *Harper's Bazaar*, as well as *Botteghe Oscura*, *Poetry Review*, and *The London Magazine*. In youth she travelled with her father to Hollywood and New York and married an American, Curtis Moffat, with whom she had her first son, Ivan Moffat, born in Havana. Until 1926 she lived mostly in London and in Paris where she acted in Max Reinhardt's *The Miracle*; she toured with the play back to America where she met her second husband, the Austrian Count Friedrich Ledebur, with whom she had another son, Christian Dion Ledebur (called Boon) in 1928. Iris Tree had known Aldous and Maria Huxley in London, and they introduced Isherwood to her in California during the war. With Allan Harkness, she brought a troupe of actors to Ojai to start a repertory theater, The High Valley Theater, concentrating on Chekhov. Many of them were pacifists like herself. She moved often—from house to house and country to country—and in July 1954 left California for good, settling in Rome where she worked on but never finished a novel about her youth. Her marriage to Ledebur ended in 1955. Isherwood modelled "Charlotte" in *A Single Man* partly on Iris Tree.

Trevor-Roper, Patrick (b. 1916). British ophthalmologist; younger brother of the historian Hugh Trevor-Roper. He had a distinguished London career in practice and research and wrote a book, *Blunted Sight: An Inquiry into the Effects of Disordered Vision on Character and Art* (1971). Isherwood first mentions him in 1956, though they may have met previously.

Truman. See Capote, Truman.

Turville-Petre, Francis. English archaeologist, from an aristocratic Catholic family. Isherwood met the eccentric Turville-Petre through W. H. Auden in Berlin in 1929, and it was at Turville-Petre's house outside Berlin that Isherwood met Heinz Neddermeyer in 1932. In 1933 when Isherwood and Heinz fled Germany, they spent nearly four months on Turville-Petre's tiny island, St. Nicholas, in Greece. Turville-Petre, known among the boys in the Berlin bars as "Der Franni," inspired the character of the lost heir in W. H. Auden's play *The Fronny* and in Auden and Isherwood's *The Dog Beneath the Skin* (1935); he is also the model for "Ambrose" in *Down There on a Visit*.

Twentieth Century-Fox Film Corporation. One of Hollywood's five biggest studios; formed in 1935 when Joseph Schenck's Twentieth Century Pictures merged with William Fox's Fox Film Corporation. Darryl Zanuck headed production from 1935 to 1952, and then the studio was run by Spyros Skouras for a decade. Zanuck returned as president from 1962, and Richard Zanuck headed production for his father until the 1970s when he formed his own production company (Zanuck-Brown). After the Zanucks, Alan Ladd Jr. took over, and Twentieth Century-Fox has since been sold and resold, eventually to Rupert Murdoch. Its many stars have included Shirley Temple and Marilyn Monroe. Fox bought the rights to a French invention producing a new wider screen image, and in 1953 came out with the first Cinemascope film, *The Robe*; all the studios soon achieved similar widescreen techniques, but Fox made the largest number of big screen spectaculars over the following decade, including *The King and I* (1956), *Cleopatra* (1963), and *The Sound of Music* (1965). Isherwood worked at Fox scripting *Jean-Christophe* in 1956 and 1957, but the film was never made.

Tynan, Kenneth (1927–1980) and Elaine Dundy Tynan. English theater critic and his American first wife, an actress, novelist and playwright. During the 1950s and 1960s Tynan wrote regularly for the London *Evening Standard* and then for the *Observer*, as well as for *The New Yorker* and other publications. He was literary adviser to the National Theatre in London from its inception in 1963, but his anti-establishment views brought about his departure before the end of the decade. His support for realistic working class drama, by new playwrights such as Osborne, Delaney and Wesker, as well as for the works of Brecht and Beckett, was widely influential. Many of his essays and reviews are collected as books. At the end of stage censorship in 1968 he devised and produced the sex revue *Oh, Calcutta!* (1969). Elaine Dundy acted intermittently, mostly for TV, then published a best-selling novel *The Dud Avocado* (1958) and wrote a successful play, *My Place*, in 1962. The Tynans married in 1951, but the marriage became unstable and increasingly belligerent. In the early 1960s, Tynan began an affair with the newly married Kathleen Gates, a cool, ambitious Canadian journalist raised in England, and they married in 1967. Isherwood first met Kenneth and Elaine Tynan in London in 1956 and later saw them again when they visited California.

UCLA. University of California at Los Angeles.

UFOs. In June 1947 an Idaho business man, Kenneth Arnold, reported seeing through the window of his private plane near Mt. Rainier, flying objects which he described to the press as looking like "skipping saucers." So many more "sightings" followed around the country that the U.S. military officially investigated the possible threat to national security. In his 1950 book *Is Another World Watching?* (*The Riddle of the Flying Saucers* in the U.K.), Gerald Heard described many of these early UFO sightings. He believed they were either top secret, ultra-fast experimental aircraft which the government was covering up or, more exciting to him, visitors from Mars. Among the vastly numerous accounts of flying saucers analyzed by the U.S. Air Force between 1947 and the mid-1950s, about ten percent of reported sightings were never accounted for. As the Air Force terminology points out, they remain Unidentified Flying Objects. Official U.S. investigations were abandoned in 1969.

Uhse, Bodo (1904–1963). German novelist and journalist. Uhse was a Nazi for roughly a year towards the end of the 1920s; then he joined the Communist Party in the early 1930s and fought in the Spanish Civil War. From 1933, he lived abroad in France, Mexico, and the U.S. and returned in 1948 to live in East Berlin, where he worked as a literary editor. He published novels, essays, and travel stories in German from the mid-1930s onward. Isherwood and Berthold Viertel worked with him briefly in 1939; possibly Isherwood had met Uhse previously in Berlin.

Ujjvala. An elderly devotee who had known Vivekananda and other direct disciples in her youth; she died while staying at the Vedanta Center in 1955.

Uncle Henry. See Isherwood, Henry Bradshaw.

Unity. Twentieth-century American religious movement based on Protestantism, but also teaching reincarnation and regeneration of the body. Unity emphasizes health and success.

The Uplifters. A men's club founded in the early decades of the century in a ranch-like setting in Santa Monica Canyon. It offered a retreat from women and family life where the members could relax and drink as much as they liked (hence the name, for lifting up of glasses).

Upward, Edward (b. 1903). English novelist and schoolmaster. Isherwood met Upward in 1921 at their public school, Repton, and followed him to Corpus Christi College, Cambridge. They were closely united by their rebellious attitude toward family and school authority and by shared literary interests. In the 1920s they created the fantasy world, Mortmere, about which they wrote surreal, macabre, and pornographic stories and poems for each other; their excited schoolboy humor is described in *Lions and Shadows* where Upward appears as "Allen Chalmers." Upward made his reputation in the 1930s with his short fiction, especially *Journey to the Border* (1938), the intense, almost mystical, and largely autobiographical account of a young upper-middle-class tutor's conversion to communism. Shortly afterwards he gave up his writing to devote himself to schoolmastering (he needed the money) and to Communist Party work. From 1931 to 1961 he taught at Alleyn's School, Dulwich where he became Head of English and a housemaster; he lived nearby with his wife,

Hilda, and their two children, Kathy and Christopher. In 1962, following his retirement, he moved to the Isle of Wight. After World War II, Upward had become disillusioned by the British Communist Party and left it, though he never abandoned his Marxist-Leninist convictions. In the face of psychological difficulties of some magnitude, he returned to his writing towards the end of the 1950s, and eventually produced a massive autobiographical trilogy, *The Spiral Ascent* (1977)—comprised of *In the Thirties* (1962), *The Rotten Elements* (1969), and *No Home but the Struggle*. But he had almost as much difficulty in getting the work published as he had had in writing it; Leonard Woolf rejected *In The Thirties* with the suggestion that Upward should cut out most of the material about communism and alter the ending so that the main character could be clearly seen to reject communism. Roughly eight more publishers, including Faber and Faber, also rejected this first volume before James Michie of Heinemann finally accepted it. Upward remained a challenging and trusted critic of Isherwood's work throughout Isherwood's life, and a loyal friend.

Ure, Mary (1933–1975). British stage actress who acted in a few Hollywood films, including *Sons and Lovers* (1960). She was married to John Osborne, the playwright, and afterwards to Robert Shaw, the actor. Isherwood met her with Tony Richardson in 1960 when she was appearing with Vivien Leigh in the touring stage production of Jean Giraudoux's *Duel of Angels*; the play went on from Los Angeles to San Francisco and eventually to a New York opening.

USC. University of Southern California.

Usha. A nun at the Vedanta Center and later at the convent in Santa Barbara; originally called Ursula Bond and later, after sannyas, Pravrajika Anandaprana. She was a German Jew, educated in England, and came to the U.S. as a young refugee during the war. Until the war ended, she worked for the U.S. government as a censor. She had been married before taking up Vedanta.

Valadon, Suzanne (1865–1938). French painter. Injured by a fall from a circus trapeze, Valadon became a model for Puvis de Chavannes and afterwards for Renoir, and was evidently mistress to both. She also modelled for Toulouse-Lautrec who introduced her to Degas. Degas took her work seriously and encouraged her. Valadon was also the mother of the painter Maurice Utrillo (1883–1935). A biography, *The Valadon Story: The Life of Suzanne Valadon*, by John Storm, appeared in 1958, possibly sparking Salka Viertel's idea for a film.

Vandanananda, Swami. Hindu monk. He arrived at the Hollywood Vendanta Center from India in the summer of 1955 and eventually became the chief assistant there, replacing Swami Aseshananda.

van Druten, John (1901–1957). English playwright and novelist. Isherwood met van Druten in New York in 1939, and they formed a friendship on the basis of their shared pacifism. Of Dutch parentage, van Druten was born and educated in London and took a degree in Law at the University of London. He achieved his first success as a playwright in New York during the 1920s, then emigrated for good in 1938 and became a U.S. citizen in 1944. His strength was light comedy; among his numerous plays and adaptations were *Voice of the Turtle* (1943), *I Remember Mama* (1944), *Bell, Book and Candle* (1950), and *I Am a Camera* (1951) based on Isherwood's *Goodbye to Berlin*. Many of these were later filmed. Some works were less successful, for example *Leave Her to Heaven* (1940), his play about the Crippen murder. In 1951, van Druten directed *The King and I* on Broadway. He also wrote a few novels and two volumes of autobiography, including *The Widening Circle* (1957). His mature habit was to spend half the year in New York and half near Los Angeles on the AJC Ranch which he owned with Carter Lodge and—before her death—the British actress and theater director Auriol Lee. Van Druten also owned a mountain cabin above Idyllwild which Isherwood sometimes used. A fall from a horse in Mexico in 1936 left van Druten with a permanently crippled arm despite numerous operations; partly as a result of this, he became attracted to Vedanta and other religions (he was a renegade Christian Scientist), and in his second autobiography he describes a minor mystical experience which he had in a drug store in Beverly Hills. He was a contributor to Isherwood's *Vedanta for the Western World*.

Van Meegeren, Han (1889–1947). Perhaps the greatest forger ever; he painted a number of Vermeers and De Hooghs which were accepted as authentic and which hung in the Rijksmuseum in Amsterdam until 1945 when Van Meegeren was arrested as a collaborator because he was associated with the sale of a Dutch master painting to Goebbels. To clear himself of the charge of collaborating, Van Meegeren confessed that the Goebbels painting and certain others were his own work. A two year scientific study confirmed his claim, uncovering his immensely complex process and also his remarkable talent. He was sentenced to a year in prison and died there of a heart attack. *Van Meegeren's Faked Vermeers and De Hooghs* by Dr. P. B. Coremans (one of the experts who confirmed the forgeries) was published in 1949 with many photographs of Van Meegeren's work, and Isherwood may have seen it.

Van Vechten, Carl (1880–1964). American novelist and poet, critic of music and dance, and, late in life, photographer. He was a prolific writer and a figure of New York's bohemia, frequenting the Harlem clubs and greatly contributing to popular recognition of black artists during the Harlem Renaissance. He was also an early editor of Gertrude Stein. Among his seven novels are *The Tattooed Countess* (1924) and *Nigger Heaven* (1926). He was married to Fania Marinoff. Saul Mauriber, still a student when they met, assisted Van Vechten for twenty years; Mauriber also became a designer.

Varner, Van. A friend of Frank Taylor at the start of the 1950s. He was slim and pale with reddish-blond hair and worked in an office job in Los Angeles.

Vaughan, Keith (1912–1977). English painter, illustrator and diarist. He worked in advertising during the 1930s and was a conscientious objector in the war; later he taught at the Camberwell School of Art, the Central School of Arts and Crafts, and the Slade, as well as briefly in America. Isherwood met him in 1947 at John Lehmann's and bought one of his pictures, "Two Bathers," a small oil painting still in his collection. Vaughan's diaries, with his own illustrations, were published in 1966.

Vedanta. "Acme of the Vedas"; one of six orthodox systems of Hindu philosophy, Vedanta is based on the Upanishads, the later portion of the ancient Hindu scriptures known as the Vedas. More generally, Vedanta is the whole body of literature which explains and comments upon these teachings. Probably first formulated by the philosopher Badarayana (second or first century B.C.), Vedanta teaches that the object of existence is not release but realization—that we should learn to know ourselves for what we really are. This realization is not obtained through logic, but through the direct intuition of the inspired sages recorded in the Upanishads. Vedanta is uncompromisingly non-dualistic. Only Brahman has existence; Brahman is existence; Brahman is consciousness. He is the Ultimate Principle and the Final Reality and the Indivisible One. References in the sacred writings to more than one principle are regarded as merely allegorical and descriptive. The phenomenal world of nature and man has merely a phantom existence, it is the result of *maya*, illusion. Ignorance of this leads to a belief that things exist apart from the Absolute. Ignorance is responsible for *samsara*, the continuous cycle of death and rebirth and death which lasts as long as an individual remains in the toils of maya. The search for Reality is a mystical search, pursued by introspective means such as meditation and spiritual discipline. Vedanta honors all the great spiritual teachers and impersonal or personal aspects of Godhead worshipped by different religions, considering them as manifestations of one Reality. The unillumined mind is incapable of imagining Brahman, so it adores the godlike in man—in Christ, in Buddha, in Kali—the highest it can conceive, yet in Vedanta the Truth is singular.

Vera. See Stravinsky, Vera.

Vernon. See Old, Vernon.

Vidal, Gore (b. 1925). American writer. Vidal introduced himself to Isherwood in a café in Paris in early 1948, having previously written to him and sent the manuscript of his novel *The City and the Pillar*. They became lasting friends. Later, Isherwood also met Howard Austen (Tinker), Vidal's companion from 1950 onward. Vidal was in the army as a young man; afterwards he wrote essays on politics and culture as well as many novels, including *Williwaw* (1946), *Myra Breckinridge* (1968, dedicated to Isherwood), and the multi-volume American chronicle now stretching from *Burr* (1974), *Lincoln* (1984), *1876* (1976), *Empire* (1987), and *Hollywood* (1989) to *Washington, D.C.* (1967). During the 1950s Vidal wrote a series of television plays for CBS, then screenplays at Twentieth Century-Fox and MGM (including part of *Ben Hur*), and two Broadway plays, *Visit to a Small Planet* (1957) and *The Best Man* (1960). Another less successful play, *On the March to the Sea*, about the Civil War, was staged at the Hyde Park Playhouse near Vidal's Hudson Valley estate and published in *Three Plays* (1962). During 1957, when Isherwood was working at Fox, Vidal also worked for Jerry Wald on a film version of Marcel Proust's *Remembrance of Things Past*. In 1960 Vidal ran for Congress, and in 1982 for the Senate, both times unsuccessfully. He describes his friendship with Isherwood in his memoir, *Palimpsest* (1995).

Viertel, Berthold (1885–1953). Viennese poet, playwright and film and theater director. Isherwood met Viertel in London in 1933 when Jean Ross suggested to Viertel that Isherwood could replace Margaret Kennedy as a screenplay writer on Viertel's film *Little Friend*. Viertel liked the scene describing "Edward's" suicide in *The Memorial* and Gaumont-British hired Isherwood as writer and, later, dialogue director. Isherwood made this first experience in the film industry the subject of *Prater Violet*, in which Viertel appears as "Friedrich Bergmann." Viertel had settled his family in Santa Monica in 1928 and returned alone to Europe for long periods to work. His description of the life in California was a glamorous lure to Isherwood; they renewed their friendship soon after Isherwood arrived in 1939, beginning work on a film vaguely inspired by *Mr. Norris Changes Trains*. At the Viertels' house in Santa Monica Canyon Isherwood met a number of the celebrated European emigrés then in Hollywood, and the friendship with Viertel led to his second job (the first of any substance) with Gottfried Reinhardt at MGM. Viertel began his career as an actor and stage director and turned to films in the 1920s. He first made films in Germany, began directing in Hollywood from the late 1920s, and in England from 1933. Viertel's second marriage to Elizabeth Neumann took place in 1949. At the end of his life, he returned successfully to directing plays in Europe, including his own German translations of Tennessee Williams.

Viertel, Hans. Eldest son of Berthold Viertel and Salka Steuermann Viertel; born in Germany. Hans studied at the Reinhardt Workshop for Stage, Screen, and Radio, was assistant and dramaturge to Max Reinhardt in 1939, and later worked in films for William Dieterle. Eventually he became a linguistics professor at Wellesley College in Massachusetts and a children's author.

Viertel, Peter (b. 1920). German-born second son of Berthold and Salka Viertel; screenplay writer and novelist. Peter Viertel attended UCLA and Dartmouth and became a free-lance writer. He served in the U.S. Marines during World War II and was decorated four times. He wrote the award-winning screenplay for Hemingway's *The Old Man and the Sea* as well as other Hemingway adaptations, and his own novels are in the Hemingway vein, with subjects such as soldiering (*Line of Departure*, 1947), big game hunting (*White Hunter, Black Heart*, 1954), and bullfighting (*Love Lies Bleeding*, 1964). His first novel *The Canyon* (published in 1941, but completed when he was just nineteen) gives a compelling adolescent view of Santa Monica Canyon as it was around the time when Isherwood first arrived there. Viertel's first marriage was to Virginia Schulberg, and in 1960 he married the actress Deborah Kerr. Like his mother and father he eventually returned to Europe, settling in Klosters and Marbella.

Viertel, Salka (1889–1978). Polish actress and screenplay writer; first wife of Berthold Viertel with whom she had three sons, Hans, Peter, and Thomas. Sara Salomé Steuermann Viertel had a successful stage career in Vienna (including acting for Max Reinhardt's Deutsches Theater) before moving to Hollywood where she became the friend and confidante of Greta Garbo; they appeared together in the German language version of *Anna Christie*, and afterwards Salka collaborated on Garbo's screenplays for MGM in the 1930s and 1940s (*Queen Christina, Anna Karenina, Conquest*, and others). Isherwood met Salka Viertel soon after arriving in Los Angeles and was often at her house socially or to work with Berthold. In the 1930s and 1940s the house was frequented by European refugees, and Salka was able to help many of them find work—some as domestic servants, others with the studios. Among her guests were some of the most celebrated writers and movie stars of the time. In 1946 Isherwood moved into her garage apartment, at 165 Mabery Road, with Bill Caskey. By then Salka was living alone and had little money, and Isherwood became a close friend. Her husband had left her; her lover Gottfried Reinhardt had married; Garbo's career was over; and later, in the 1950s, Salka was persecuted by the McCarthyites and blacklisted by MGM for her presumed communism. In January 1947, Salka herself moved into the garage apartment and let out her house; later she sold the property and moved to an apartment off Wilshire Boulevard in the early 1950s. Eventually she returned modestly to writing for the movies, but finally moved back to Europe, although she had been a U.S. citizen since 1939 . She published a memoir, *The Kindness of Strangers*, in 1969.

Viertel, Tommy. Youngest son of Berthold and Salka Viertel; he had a bad stutter. Tommy Viertel was drafted into the U.S. Army on February 5, 1944. After the war he lived in Los Angeles where he worked for Los Angeles County. He married twice.

Viertel, Virginia (Jigee). Peter Viertel's first wife, from 1944 to 1959. Born Virginia Ray to working class Americans ruined by the depression, Jigee was a dancer in the Paramount chorus and then married the writer Budd Schulberg with whom she shared strong leftist political convictions. (Schulberg's father, Ben Schulberg, was a Paramount executive.) She and Budd Schulberg divorced after having a daughter, Vicky Schulberg. Jigee's second daughter, Christine Viertel, was born in Paris in 1952, and Jigee and Peter separated immediately afterwards. Jigee's mother, Henny Ray, died of a stroke while caring for Vicky so that Salka Viertel partly raised both Vicky and Christine. After the ruin of her second marriage, Jigee drank increasingly heavily; then in January 1960 she fell asleep with a lit cigarette and died of burns in the hospital.

Vishwananda, Swami. Hindu monk, from India. Isherwood met him in 1943 when Vishwananda visited the Hollywood Vedanta Center and other centers on the West Coast. Vishwananda ran the Vedanta Center in Chicago.

Vivekananda, Swami (1863–1902). Narendranath Datta (known as Naren or Narendra and later as Swamiji) took the monastic name Vivekananda for himself only in 1893. He was Ramakrishna's chief direct disciple. He came from a wealthy and cultured background; and was attending university in Calcutta when Ramakrishna recognized him as an incarnation of one of his "eternal companions," a free, perfect soul born into maya with the avatar and possessing some of the avatar's characteristics. Vivekananda was trained by Ramakrishna to carry his message and led the disciples after Ramakrishna's death, though he left them for long periods, first to wander through India as a monastic practicing spiritual disciplines, then to travel twice to America and Europe where his lectures and classes spawned the first western Vedanta centers. In India he devoted much of his time to founding and administering the Ramakrishna Math and Mission. He also published his teachings and sayings in various volumes; Isherwood wrote the introduction to a 1960 selection from these by John Yale (Prema).

Vividishananda, Swami. Hindu monk, from India. Vividishananda ran the Seattle Vedanta Center; Isherwood met him at the dedication of the new Portland temple in 1943 and afterwards briefly visited his Seattle center.

von Alvensleben, Werner. Austrian artist, from a Junker family, and a cousin of Prince Hubertus zu Löwenstein. He arrived in Berlin, where Isherwood met him, in the 1920s or 1930s, was involved in anti-Nazi politics and later went to Paris where he mixed with the Surrealists and became a sculptor. Around 1939 he emigrated to England, adopted the name Michael Werner, worked as a journalist and translator, and also used the pseudonym Peter Purbright. He died in 1989. Von Alvensleben was possibly a model for the art student, "Werner"—met in a communist café and later wounded by the police in street fighting—in the section of *Goodbye to Berlin* titled "A Berlin Diary (Winter 1932–3)." Like so many others with anti-Nazi sentiments, he may have been conscripted and helped to build the Siegfried line (the fortification along Germany's western frontier, facing France's Maginot line), though if this is so, he apparently found a way to leave Germany for good soon afterwards.

Wald, Jerry (1911–1962). American screenwriter and producer. Wald worked as a journalist and in radio before starting as a writer for Warner Brothers in the early 1930s; he was producing by 1942 and moved on to RKO in 1950 then afterwards to Columbia Pictures as a vice-president and executive producer. In the mid-1950s he went to Twentieth Century-Fox with a high reputation and a great deal of power. As a producer, Wald was extremely prolific: his name is associated with a long list of well-known films from the 1940s and 1950s and he was rumored to be a model for Budd Schulberg's *What Makes Sammy Run?* Isherwood was hired by him in 1956 to work on *Jean-Christophe* (never made), and several of Isherwood's friends, such as Gore Vidal and Gavin Lambert, also worked for Wald during the 1950s.

Warner Brothers. One of the major Hollywood studios, especially successful from the 1930s to the 1950s. It was founded in 1923 by the four sons of a Polish shoemaker; they pioneered talking pictures in the mid-1920s and established their position by the end of the decade. The studio was known for its realistic, often black-and-white films. As well as gangster movies and musicals, there were numerous relatively highbrow, historical and political films. Increasingly the studio was run by the youngest brother, Jack Warner. The producer Darryl F. Zanuck and, after him, Hal Wallis, contributed to Jack Warner's success, but rivalry developed, and by 1944 Warner ran it on his own. Warner Brothers was sold to Seven Arts in 1967 and later taken over by a conglomerate, eventually merging with Time Inc. in 1989.

Warsaw, siege of. For three weeks in April and May 1943, the inhabitants of the Warsaw ghetto forcibly resisted the Nazis' final attempt to liquidate them; 7,000 Jewish fighters were killed, 6,000 burned in their hiding places, and 56,000 Jews captured and transported to Treblinka. The Jewish refugee at Denny Fouts's party, September 23, 1944, was apparently one of the few who escaped. (It seems less likely, though possible, that he was a refugee from the later Warsaw Rising, which led to the destruction of the entire city by the Nazis. The Warsaw Rising began August 1, 1944, and the Poles did not surrender until October 2. The Polish Home Army evacuated the old city on September 2, at which time 1,500 survivors escaped through the sewers. Few if any Jews can have remained among them, but still, with speed and luck, he might have arrived in Santa Monica by September 23.)

Watson, Peter. The financier behind *Horizon*, of which he was art editor and co-founder. Watson was heir to a margarine fortune, intelligent, and idealistically devoted to art. He collected art and befriended many artists. He was close to Denny Fouts in the 1930s and was the officially named owner of Denny Fouts's Picasso when it was exhibited at the Museum of Modern Art in New York. Watson's other companions included a young American, Norman Fowler, whom he met in New York in 1949 and brought to London where they lived together until the apparently healthy and sober Watson mysteriously drowned in his bath in 1956. (See also Fowler, Norman.)

Watts, Alan (b. 1915). English mystic, religious philosopher, author and teacher. Watts became a Buddhist while still a schoolboy at King's School, Canterbury, Kent, and went on to study all forms of religious thought and practice. His many books include *An Outline of Zen Buddhism* (1932), *Behold the Spirit: A Study in the Necessity of Mystical Religion* (1947), *The Supreme Identity: An Essay on Oriental Metaphysic and the Christian Religion* (1950), *Nature, Man and Woman: A New Approach to Sexual Experience* (1958), and *Psychotherapy East and West* (1961). Watts emigrated to America at the start of World War II, eventually settling near San Francisco where he became Dean of the American Academy of Asian Studies. He is known as a Zen Buddhist, but was also ordained as an Anglican priest in 1945. He was a close friend of Aldous Huxley, whom he first met in 1943, and he was impressed by Krishnamurti's decision to renounce his messianic role. Krishnamurti greatly influenced Watts's *The Wisdom of Insecurity* (1951), a book which Isherwood records had a profound effect on the young Don Bachardy. Watts felt that Huxley and Gerald Heard were working toward the same synthesis of Christian and oriental mysticism as himself, and like them he experimented with LSD in the 1950s. Huxley introduced him to Swami Prabhavananda in 1950, and Isherwood met Watts on the same occasion, though at first he did not like him. Watts opposed the Hindu emphasis on asceticism: he was married three times and asserted that sex improved spiritual presence. He was a figure of the San Francisco beat scene and a model for Kerouac's *Dharma Bums*. In September 1958, Isherwood read with interest Watts's article "Beat Zen, Square Zen, and Zen" (later revised as a book), which critiques Kerouac's Zen in *Dharma Bums* as "beat Zen" rather than true Zen, arguing that Kerouac is still engaged in rebelling against the culture which spawned him and is therefore no more liberated than the practitioner of "square Zen" who makes his Buddhism into a new form of conventionality.

Web, also Webster. See Milam, Webster.

Weingarten, Lawrence (Larry). Producer at MGM and husband of Jessie Marmorston, Isherwood's doctor. Isherwood met the Weingartens through their mutual friend Eddie Knopf.

Wescott, Glenway (1901–1987). American writer. Born in Wisconsin; attended the University of Chicago; lived in France in the 1920s, partly in Paris, and travelled in Europe and England. Afterwards he lived in New York. Early in his career he wrote poetry and reviews, later turning to fiction. His best known works are *The Pilgrim Hawk* (1940) and *Apartment in Athens* (1945). Wescott was President of the American Academy of Arts and Letters from 1957–1961. His longterm companion, Monroe Wheeler (1899–1988) was on the staff of The Museum of Modern Art from the mid-1930s, developed the museum's publications, and later became a trustee. Each had other lovers, including for Wheeler, George Platt Lynes. From the late 1930s, Wescott, Wheeler, and Platt Lynes shared a country house in New Jersey. In 1949 Wescott went to Los Angeles expressly to read Isherwood's 1939–1945 diaries. While he was there, Isherwood introduced Wescott to Jim Charlton with whom Wescott had an affair.

Wheeler, Hugh. English writer. Wheeler published mystery thrillers under the name Patrick Quentin. Later he wrote plays (*Big Fish, Little Fish; Look We've Come Through*; the books for the Sondheim musicals *A Little Night Music* and *Sweeney Todd*), and screenplays (*Something for Everyone*). According to rumor, he wrote much of the screenplay for *Cabaret* though he was credited only as a technical advisor because of Writers Guild rules. He lived on a farm in Massachusetts with his black lover, John Grubbs. Wheeler was a good friend of Chris Wood, and possibly it was Wood who introduced Wheeler and Isherwood, probably in the 1940s.

Wildeblood, Peter. Diplomatic correspondent for *The Daily Mail* in London. He was arrested with Michael Pitt-Rivers (who later married Sonia Orwell) and charged with acts of indecency committed in 1952 with two RAF pilots. They were convicted in 1954 along with Pitt-Rivers's cousin Lord Montagu of Beaulieu in a trial reflecting the backlash against sensitively placed homosexuals after the Burgess and Maclean defections in 1951. Wildeblood was given eighteen months in jail. He later published a book about his experiences, *Against the Law* (1955).

Williams, Emlyn (1905–1987). Welsh playwright and actor. Williams wrote psychological thrillers for the London stage, including *Night Must Fall* (1935), and is perhaps best known for *The Corn Is Green* (1935) based on his own background in Wales and in which he played the lead; both of these were later filmed. He acted in his own work and also in many other stage roles, including Shakespeare and contemporary theater. During the 1950s he toured with one-man shows of Charles Dickens and Dylan Thomas (the Dylan Thomas show was titled *Growing Up*). Isherwood first met Williams in Hollywood in 1950 and saw him and his wife, Molly, again in London and Hollywood in subsequent years.

Williams, Tennessee (1911–1983). American playwright; Thomas Lanier Williams was born in Mississippi and raised in St. Louis. His father was a travelling salesman, his mother felt herself to be a glamorous southern belle in reduced circumstances. His essentially autobiographical *The Glass Menagerie* made him famous in 1945, and soon afterwards he wrote *A Streetcar Named Desire* (1947). Many of his subsequent plays are equally well-known—including *The Rose Tattoo* (1950), *Cat on a Hot Tin Roof* (1955), *Sweet Bird of Youth* (1959), *The Night of the Iguana* (1962)—and were made into films. Williams also wrote a novella, *The Roman Spring of Mrs. Stone* (1950). When he first came to Hollywood in 1943 to work for MGM, he bore a letter of introduction to Isherwood from Lincoln Kirstein; this began a long and close friendship, with numerous visits on both coasts, often to attend openings of Williams's plays. In the autumn of 1954, Isherwood and Bachardy visited Williams and his long-term companion, Frank Merlo, in Key West during the filming of *The Rose Tattoo*. When Williams returned to Hollywood at the end of November to complete the film, he showed Isherwood a letter to Elia Kazan about his next play, *Cat on a Hot Tin Roof*. This was part of a troubled correspondence. Williams was determined to have Elia Kazan direct the play, despite the fact the Kazan insisted on the third act being rewritten. Williams complied during the autumn, but the struggle over the play carried on until the next year and into rehearsals, with Kazan continuing to change the script and the characters and increasingly softening and stylizing the production which Williams had intended to be unremitting and realistic. (Isherwood's diary entry for March 8, 1955 makes clear that he disliked Kazan's production; like Williams he felt the play should be presented realistically.) Williams was so dismayed by the way Kazan reshaped his original conception of the play that in 1955 he published the early version, without the changes required by Kazan for the Broadway production, and accompanied by a note explaining what he felt had happened. The play was a commercial success.

Willie. See Maugham, William Somerset.

Wilson, Colin (b. 1931). English novelist and critic. Wilson has published numerous psychological thrillers and studies of literature and philosophy, criminology, the imagination, the occult and the supernatural. He became well-known with his 1956 book, *The Outsider*—which Isherwood mentions October 2 and 12 that year—about the figure of the alienated solitary in modern literature. Isherwood met Wilson in London in 1959.

Windham, Donald (b. 1920). Novelist and playwright, from Georgia. Windham was a friend of Lincoln Kirstein, of Paul Cadmus, and of Glenway Wescott; Isherwood probably met him in New York early in the 1940s, though certainly by 1942. Windham worked for Kirstein at *Dance Index*, and ran the magazine while Kirstein was away in the army during the war. He also collaborated with Tennessee Williams—a close friend—on the play *You Touched Me!* (1945). Isherwood wrote a blurb for Windham's 1950 novel *The Dog Star*.

Winters, Shelley (b. 1922). American actress, from St. Louis. She worked on stage in New York and moved to Hollywood in 1943. In her energetic and versatile career she has acted both comic and dramatic roles. She was nominated for an Academy Award for *A Place in the Sun* (1951), won Academy Awards for her supporting roles in *The Diary of Anne Frank* (1959) and *A Patch of Blue* (1965), and was nominated again for *The Poseidon Adventure* (1972). She played Natalia Landauer in the film of *I Am a Camera* in 1955. From the early 1990s, she played Roseanne's grandmother in the television comedy series *Roseanne*. Isherwood met her at the start of the 1950s, and she was a friend for a number of years. She was married to the actor Tony Franciosa from 1957 to 1960.

Wood, Christopher (Chris) (d. 1976). Isherwood met Chris Wood in September 1932 when W. H. Auden took Isherwood to meet Gerald Heard, then sharing Wood's luxurious West End flat. Wood was about ten years younger than Heard, handsome and friendly but shy about his maverick talents. He played the piano well, but never professionally, wrote short stories, but not for publication, had a pilot's license and rode a bicycle for transport. He was extremely rich (the family business made jams and other canned and bottled goods), sometimes extravagant, and always generous; he secretly funded many of Heard's projects and loaned or gave money to many other friends (including Isherwood). In 1937 Wood emigrated with Heard to Los Angeles and in 1941 moved with him to Laguna. Their domestic commitment persisted for a time despite Heard's increasing asceticism and religious activities. Ultimately, the household disbanded as their lives diverged, though they remained friends. From 1939, Wood was involved with Paul Sorel, also a member of their household for about five years.

Woodcock, Patrick. British doctor. Woodcock was doctor to many London theatrical stars—including John Gielgud and Noel Coward—and also to actors based in New York and Hollywood. Isherwood and Bachardy first met him with Gielgud and Hugh Wheeler in London in 1956, and a few days later Woodcock visited Bachardy at the Cavendish Hotel to treat him for stomach cramps. Woodcock prescribed vitamins for Isherwood and became a friend.

Worsley, Cuthbert. English writer and schoolmaster. T. C. Worsley was a friend of Stephen Spender and in 1937 accompanied him to the Spanish Civil War on an assignment for *The Daily Worker*. He returned to Spain soon afterwards to join an ambulance unit. He later wrote about this period for *The Left Review* and in *Behind the Battle* (1939), as well as in a fictionalized memoir published much later, *Fellow Travellers* (1971). Isherwood liked Worsley's public school novel, set in the 1930s, *Flannelled Fool* (1967).

Wright, Frank Lloyd (1869–1959). American architect. A preeminent figure in twentieth-century architecture, Wright originated the organic principle that the form of a building should develop naturally from its setting, from its function, and from its materials. He began as a designer in a Chicago firm and eventually opened his own practice, first expressing his genius for spacious, open-plan interiors in his low-standing "prairie" houses. His houses in particular tended to conform to the features of the natural landscape in which they were set, but also, he was trained as a civil engineer, and he was able to apply the principles of engineering to his architectural designs. Thus, he initiated new techniques in offices and other large public buildings—such as concrete blocks reinforced with steel rods, air conditioning, indirect lighting, panel heat, and new uses of glass. In 1910, Wright established Taliesin, near Spring Green, Wisconsin. It was both his home and an architectural school (named after a sixth-century Welsh bard). Later, in 1938, he founded Taliesin West, in Scottsdale, Arizona, where he spent the winter months and where apprentice architects also gathered to work with him. His foundation, the Taliesin Fellowship, supported both centers. Isherwood's friend Jim Charlton had been a student of Frank Lloyd Wright, and Ben Masselink's brother, Eugene, was a longtime colleague who helped Wright to run the centers. Isherwood and Bachardy spent a weekend at Taliesin West in 1959 not long before Wright died.

Wright, Tom. American writer, from New Orleans. Isherwood met Thomas E. Wright through Gerrit Lansing while Wright and Isherwood were fellows-in-residence at the Huntington Hartford Foundation in 1951. Wright was then about twenty-four years old and had taught at NYU. They had a casual affair lasting about eight months. Wright was also a childhood friend of Marguerite and Speed Lamkin, and knew Tennessee Williams and Howard Griffin. His other lovers during the 1950s included Sam Costidy and Scott Poland. Wright was in close touch with his parents during this period and they are mentioned by Isherwood; Wright's mother, Emily Wright, visited Wright in California before she died. Bachardy drew his first of several portraits of Wright in 1960. Wright published novels and travel books. He later moved to Guatemala.

Wyberslegh Hall. The fifteenth-century manor house where Isherwood was born and where his mother lived with his brother after the war; it was part of the Bradshaw Isherwood estate. See the entries for Frank Bradshaw Isherwood and Richard Bradshaw Isherwood.

Wystan. See Auden, W. H.

X., the "X. situation." See Harris, Bill.

Yacoubi, Ahmed. Moroccan painter. Paul Bowles met Ahmed Yacoubi in Fez in 1947 when he bought some *majoon* prepared by Yacoubi's mother. They lived and travelled together for a number of years until the late 1950s when, having been tried and acquitted on a morals charge with a fifteen-year-old German boy, Yacoubi married and had a child. Francis Bacon took an interest in Yacoubi's painting and taught him to use oils in 1955; in 1957 Bacon also helped Yacoubi to show his work in the Hanover Gallery in London. Yacoubi was a model for "Amar" in Bowles's novel *The Spider's House* (1955), and, like other Moroccan friends, he told Bowles native stories which Bowles translated and later published. Yacoubi supplied *kif* and *majoon* to Isherwood and Bachardy in Tangier in 1955.

Yale, John. See Prema.

Yorke, Henry. See Green, Henry.

Zeininger, Russ. An acquaintance of Bill Caskey; Isherwood met Zeininger through Caskey in August 1949 and they had an intermittent affair through the remainder of that year, making a trip to the AJC Ranch together in December.

Zinnemann, Fred (1907–1997). Viennese-born director. He arrived in Hollywood very young, in 1929, and worked as Berthold Viertel's secretary, also as an extra, and as a studio script clerk. He was soon directing shorts at MGM. By the early 1940s, when Isherwood met him, he was living with his English wife, Renée, on Mabery Road, near the Viertels. Zinnemann directed a great many successful films— *High Noon* (1952), *The Member of the Wedding* (1953), *From Here to Eternity* (1953), *Oklahoma* (1955), *A Man for All Seasons* (1966), *The Day of the Jackal* (1973), *Julia* (1977), and others. In 1949 he made *The Men*, written by Carl Foreman and starring Marlon Brando, about paraplegics; shortly afterwards Isherwood began visiting in the Birmingham Hospital the same group of paraplegics involved in the film and talked to them about writing.

Index